COST MANAGEMENT

THIRD CANADIAN EDITION

MEASURING, MONITORING, AND MOTIVATING PERFORMANCE

ELDENBURG • WOLCOTT • CHEN • COOK

WILEY

DEDICATION

I dedicate this book to my parents, Shei-Te and YuYuon,

my husband, Dr. Louis Florence, and to our miracle baby,

Delphine Egene, for their unconditional support and encouragement.

Liang-Hsuan Chen

Dedicated to Steve, Jaclyn, and Lindsey in recognition

of their patience and understanding, and to those

students who enjoy the challenge of learning.

Gail Lynn Cook

Questions indicated are adapted from the professional examinations of the legacy accounting professional bodies, CMA and CGA (CGA-Canada Test Bank, MA2 2009 and 2010; CGA-Canada, MA1 Exam, 2005–2010; CGA-Canada MA2 Exam, 2010–2011; CMA Entrance Exam 2005; Sample Entrance Exam 2007 and 2008). This material was adapted with permission of the Chartered Professional Accountants (CPA) of Canada, Toronto, Canada. Any changes to the original material are the sole responsibility of the author and have not been reviewed or endorsed by the Chartered Professional Accountants of Canada.

Excerpts from the British Columbia *Tobacco Damages and Health Care Costs Recovery Act* has been derived from information originally made available by the Province of British Columbia at: http://www.bclaws.ca/ and this information is being used in accordance with the Queen's Printer License - British Columbia available at: http://www.bclaws.ca/standards/2014/QP-License_1.0.html. They have not, however, been produced in affiliation with, or with the endorsement of, the Province of British Columbia and **THESE MATERIALS ARE NOT AN OFFICIAL VERSION**.

Library and Archives Canada Cataloguing in Publication

Eldenburg, Leslie, author

Cost management: measuring, monitoring, and motivating performance / Eldenburg, Wolcott, Chen, Cook.
—Third Canadian edition.

Includes bibliographical references and indexes.

Issued in print and electronic formats.

ISBN 978-1-119-18569-7(binder ready version).—

ISBN 978-1-119-25433-1 (pdf)

1. Cost accounting—Textbooks. 2. Managerial accounting—Textbooks. I. Wolcott, Susan K., author II. Chen, Liang-Hsuan, 1962–, author III. Cook, Gail Lynn, author IV. Title.

HF5686.C8E44 2016   658.15'52   C2016-900017-6

                                               C2016-900018-4

Production Credits

Vice President and Director, Market Solutions: Veronica Visentin
Executive Editor: Zoë Craig
Senior Marketing Manager: Anita Osborne
Editorial Manager: Karen Staudinger
Developmental Editor: Gail Brown
Media Editor: Luisa Begani

Assistant Editor: Ashley Patterson
Production and Media Specialist: Meaghan MacDonald
Cover and interior design: Joanna Vieira
Cover Photo: © Patricia Toth McCormick/Getty Images
Typesetting: Aptara
Printing and binding: Quad/Graphics

1 2 3 4 5 QG 20 19 18 17 16
Printed and bound in the United States of America.

90 Eglinton Avenue East, Suite 300
Toronto, Ontario, M4P 2Y3 Canada

Visit our website at: www.wiley.com.

ABOUT THE AUTHORS

Third Canadian Edition

Liang-Hsuan Chen, MSEd., MBA, Ph.D., FCPA-FCGA, is an

award-winning educator who has taught public school, high school, college, and university. Liang is an Associate Professor, Teaching Stream in Accounting who served in an administrative leadership position as the Associate Dean—Registrarial and Student Services at the University of Toronto Scarborough (UTSC) from 2010 to 2013. Prior to her current position at UTSC, Liang was a professor in Accounting at Humber College. Liang was one of two recipients of the Alice L. Beeman Research Awards in Communications and Marketing for Educational Advancement, Council for Advancement and Support of Education (CASE) based in Washington, DC, in 2007. The award was for her doctoral thesis entitled "Choosing Canadian Graduate Schools from Afar: East-Asian International Students' Perspectives." She received the Lorna Henderson Outstanding Mentor Award from CGA Ontario (2009), the Fellowship Award from CGA Canada (2010), and the Mandarin Profile Award (Outstanding Profile Award-Professional Sector 2011). Liang has dedicated much of her career to exploring and understanding the rich contributions that immigrant students make to Ontario's post-secondary institutions, the economy, and quality of life. Her research interests include issues in higher education, such as university/college choice, marketing of higher education, international education and internationalization of higher education, graduate and professional education, and student experience. Her publications related to international students' choice of Canadian graduate schools and marketing of higher education can be seen in *Higher Education*, the *Canadian Journal of Higher Education*, the *International Journal of Educational Advancement*, and the *Journal of Marketing for Higher Education*. Liang served as an elected member of the Board of Directors of the Certified General Accountants of Ontario for six years, where she chaired various education-related committees, and the National Education Committee (CGA Canada). She also served as a member on the Education Committee for the Canadian Academic Accounting Association (CAAA). Liang holds an MSEd. from the University of Pennsylvania, an MBA from the University of Toronto, and a Ph.D. in Higher Education from OISE/UT. ■

Gail Lynn Cook, Ph.D., CPA_USA (inactive), is an Associate Professor at Brock with

teaching interests in cost and managerial accounting; strategic cost management; and accounting information systems. She teaches at both the undergraduate and graduate level, and enjoys exploring innovative flexible teaching and learning approaches in her classes. With colleague, Darlene Bay, she won the Howard Teall Innovation in Accounting Education Award from the CAAA in 2007 for working with masters students in accounting to plan, develop, and implement an accounting graduate student research conference. Gail served as the Faculty Associate for Service-Learning from July 2013 to June 2015 and has benefitted from a number of on-line course development grants. Her research addresses questions about individual differences and decision making. She has published in *Issues in Accounting Education, Journal of Business Ethics, Advances in Accounting Education Teaching and Curriculum Innovations, Case Research Journal, Journal of Management Education, Advances in Accounting Information Systems, The Journal of Accounting Case Research,* and *Management Accounting.* She is a reviewer for *Strategic Finance* and *Management Accounting Quarterly.* In 1990, Gail earned her Ph.D. in Business Administration with a specialization in Accounting from the University of Utah and has held her CPA certificate in the USA since 1984. Gail has served on the executive of the Fonthill Preschool and as the Treasurer of the Niagara Speedskating Club. ■

Leslie G. Eldenburg, Ph.D.,

is Deloitte Professor of Accounting at University of Arizona. She has also taught at California State University–Fresno. She received her MBA and Ph.D. from the University of Washington. She passed the CPA exam in 1985 and has taught review courses for the CMA exam. Leslie has served as faculty advisor for an IMA student chapter and for the Multicultural Business Student Association. She has received a number of awards recognizing her activities in teaching, student support, and as faculty advisor for student organizations. She is an active member of the American Accounting Association (AAA), the Management Section of the AAA, the IMA, and the Healthcare Financial Management Association. She has served on and chaired numerous committees within these organizations and has held several leadership positions in the Management Section. Before becoming an academic, she worked in hospital finance at Virginia Mason Hospital in Seattle, Washington. Leslie's research interests include issues in healthcare and hospital accounting, and she has published in *The Accounting Review*, *The Journal of Accounting and Economics*, *The Journal of Accounting Research*, *Contemporary Accounting Research*, *Accounting, Organizations and Society*, *The Journal of Accounting, Auditing and Finance*, *The Journal of Medical Decision Making*, *The Journal of Corporate Finance*, *The International Journal of Accounting*, *Information Systems Research*, *Healthcare Financial Management*, and *Controller's Quarterly*. In addition, she currently serves on several editorial boards. Leslie has also co-authored chapters in *Health Care Administration*, *The Encyclopedia of Accounting*, *Handbook of Management Accounting Research*, and *Handbook of Cost Accounting*. ▪

Susan K. Wolcott, Ph.D., CPA, CMA,

is Thought Leader for CA School of Business, in which she generates ideas for and helps to bring about innovations in the competency-based training of CA students in western Canada. She is also an educational consultant with WolcottLynch Associates, working with faculty and programs around the world to support critical thinking development, competency assessment, and curriculum innovation. Her publications include a chapter on critical thinking assessment in *Assessment of Student Learning in Business Schools: Best Practices Each Step of the Way* published by AACSB International and Association for Institutional Research, assessment materials for the AICPA *Educational Competency Assessment* website, *Steps for Better Thinking: A College Faculty Handbook*, and various articles in journals such as *Issues in Accounting Education*, *Journal of Accounting Education*, *Assessment Update*, and *IDEA Center Papers*. Susan chaired the AICPA Core Competency Framework Curriculum Evaluation Task Force, consulted with the Canadian profession's Board of Evaluators on critical thinking assessment in the Uniform Evaluation for CA candidates, and served as associate editor of *Issues in Accounting Education*. She has served on and chaired numerous committees and has held several leadership positions as a member of AAA, IMA, Washington Society of CPAs, and Colorado Society of CPAs. Susan is a part-time professor at IE Business School in Madrid (where she a multi-time recipient of the Prize of Excellence for teaching in the International Executive MBA program) and Aalto University in Finland. She previously taught at University of Denver (where she received the MBA Core Diamond Award for teaching), University of Washington, and the J. L. Kellogg Graduate School of Management at Northwestern University. She worked in public accounting for ten years, including three years with Coopers & Lybrand (Portland, Oregon). She holds Ph.D. and MS degrees in Accounting and Information Systems from Northwestern University and a BBA in Accounting from University of Portland. ▪

Bridging the Gap

Cost Management: Measuring, Monitoring, and Motivating Performance, Third Canadian Edition, was written to help students learn to appropriately apply cost accounting methods in a variety of organizational settings. To achieve this goal, students must also develop professional competencies, such as strategic/critical thinking, risk analysis, decision making, ethical reasoning, and communication. Most textbooks focus on content knowledge and then expect students to "magically" demonstrate professional competencies. As an author team, we bring to this textbook extensive knowledge about cost accounting as well as about the best approaches for teaching and learning professional competencies. This textbook bridges the gap between typical student performance and what we would like students to be able to do by:

- ▶ Maintaining a central focus on business decision making
- ▶ Explicitly addressing risk and biases
- ▶ Adopting a writing style that is accessible and interesting to students
- ▶ Concentrating on all types of organizations
- ▶ Focusing on ethical reasoning
- ▶ Simultaneously challenging and guiding students to learn

Third Canadian Edition

- ▶ *Risk of Biased Decisions* boxes: Each chapter introduces a type of bias that interferes with high-quality decision making and applies the bias to chapter material. These boxes help students understand why and how accountants and managers sometimes use information inappropriately.

- ▶ Strategic Risk Management: *Strategic Risk Management* boxes placed after selected realistic examples give students the opportunity to explore issues beyond those presented in the example. Students are guided through the process of considering biases, business risks, or other strategic matter.

- ▶ Extensive end-of-chapter problems: Each chapter includes an extensive collection of exercises and problems, as well as two to three Mini-Cases. Like problems, Mini-Cases pose open-ended questions, and the requirements support better performance by guiding students through the steps needed. However, Mini-Cases give students an opportunity to address more complex applications of cost accounting techniques involving deeper analysis. One or two *Cumulative Problems* or *Integrating Across the Curriculum* Mini-Cases in each chapter ask students to integrate cost accounting material with the content of other accounting and business core courses, such as auditing, marketing, or finance.

- ▶ A new chapter on advanced production variances and revenue/market variances continues the discussion of variances by extending the production variances and introducing externally focused market variances. The mix and yield variances provide information for management decisions about the trade-offs between substitutable inputs. Revenue and profit variances focus on the effect of changes in selling price and shifts in sales mix. Profit variances also provide information about a business's position in the external market.

▶ A new chapter on economic order quantity concepts help managers manage inventory costs. Businesses need to strategically manage inventory to provide flexibility, to minimize inventory costs, and to avoid unnecessary costs associated with inventory. This chapter introduces students to the trade-offs between these divergent costs, the costs associated with the possibility of unexpected events, and special ordering opportunities offered by suppliers.

▶ The GPK and RCA costing systems are discussed and compared to ABC. GPK (*Grenzplankostenrechnung*, a German costing system), and RCA (resource consumption accounting) costing systems aim to improve the mapping between resource use and cost flows. Cost information under alternative costing methods is also discussed.

Explicitly Addressing Risk and Biases. Many students fail to recognize that cost accounting information is subject to risks and biases. This failure causes them to place undue reliance on computational results and inhibits their ability to evaluate the assumptions, limitations, behavioural implications, and qualitative factors that influence business decisions. These types of weaknesses inhibit student development of professional competencies. To overcome these weaknesses, *Cost Management*, Third Canadian edition, explicitly addresses uncertainties and biases in the content and homework problems in every chapter.

Adopting a Writing Style that Is Accessible and Interesting to Students. *Cost Management*, Third Canadian edition, is written in a style that students can easily understand, and it incorporates interesting scenarios designed to pique student interest. The goal is to help students learn the basic cost accounting knowledge on their own before they come to class so that through class discussions, they can further develop their accounting expertise and focus on more complex issues, such as qualitative factors that influence information and decisions, and the effects of uncertainty and bias.

Concentrating on All Types of Organizations. Manufacturing is now a small part of North American business, while service and not-for-profit organizations are increasingly important. Students need to apply cost accounting techniques in a variety of settings. Accordingly, we focus throughout this textbook on a wide range of business organizations, including large and small, public and private, Canadian and international, manufacturing, retail, service, and not-for-profit. Businesses featured in this text include CN, McAfee, Bombardier, Tim Hortons, Canada Goose, Fruit D'Or, and Sun Life Assurance. Hypothetical organizations include Melodious Notes, Creaciones Concretas, Roadrunner Publishers, Boats Afloat Yacht Company, and Mont-Tremblant Bikes. Students learn to apply cost accounting in different settings, and they also learn about the types of decisions and factors that are important to different types of organizations.

Focusing on Ethical Decision Making. The accounting profession is currently facing negative media attention and increased governmental regulation, largely because a number of accountants and managers have behaved unethically. To develop better ethical reasoning skills, students need greater exposure to realistic ethical issues. *Cost Management*, Third Canadian edition, avoids scenarios that have simplistic "correct" solutions. Instead, the ethical dilemmas contain ambiguities, conflicts of interest, and value judgements. The textbook presents a framework for ethical decision making in Chapter 1. Students will use this framework when addressing ethical dilemmas in each chapter. With continual practice, students are likely to develop their own process for ethical decision making to use in other classes and over their careers.

Simultaneously Challenging and Guiding Students to Learn. Educational research indicates that students need repeated practice with *appropriately designed* learning activities to develop professional competencies such as strategic/critical thinking. Students must be challenged to develop new skills, but at the same time they need guidance so that they do not falter and become discouraged.

Organization of Cost Accounting Content

Cost Management, Third Canadian edition, includes traditional as well as the most current practices in cost accounting. The focus is on methods that will be useful to students in their professional careers. First, we introduce students to relevant costs and their use in decision-making, including cost functions and cost behaviour. Then, when students understand cost behaviour, they are better able to understand the uses and limitations of cost allocations. Because performance measurement and evaluation rely on a thorough understanding of both decision-making and allocation information, the last section of the book considers a variety of performance measurement and evaluation techniques and issues. Following is a detailed description of each of these three sections. We view some topics, such as quality and international practices, as pervasive. Therefore, we include these topics throughout the textbook rather than as stand-alone chapters.

Initial chapters focus on identifying and using relevant information for management decisions. Chapter 1 provides an overview of the strategic management process. A model for developing higher-quality decisions (*Steps for Better Thinking*) is introduced in Appendix 1B. Chapters 2, 3, and 4 address ways to categorize costs, analyze cost behaviour, and use costs to make decisions. This approach motivates interest in course material by immediately involving students in realistic business problems. Focusing on decisions also allows students to relate cost accounting material to their own personal lives, increasing their perceptions of course relevance.

The next chapters explore the assignment of costs to products and other activities of an organization. Chapter 5 begins with the relatively simple assignment of costs to customized products and services. Chapter 6 introduces the more complex cost assignment methods used in process costing. Chapter 7 explores the development and use of activity-based costing and activity-based management. Chapters 8 and 9 present the more specialized practices for assigning costs for support departments, joint products, and by-products. These chapters help students move beyond a purely mechanical application toward a deeper understanding of the reasons behind and limitations of cost assignment techniques. We also introduce basic concepts related to standard costs and overapplied and underapplied overhead, beginning with Chapter 5. This approach more closely ties chapter content to contemporary business practice.

The latter chapters use budgets and benchmarks to plan and monitor financial and nonfinancial performance. These chapters also examine the use of incentives and compensation, combined with benchmarks, to motivate performance. Chapters 10, 11, and 12 focus on the development and use of budgets and benchmarks. Chapter 13 addresses long-term, strategic investment decisions. Chapters 14 and 15 introduce contemporary issues related to pricing and cost management. Chapter 16 provides an introduction to inventory management costs. Chapter 17 examines various ways to measure and report costs for internal and external income statements. Chapter 18 provides an overview of traditional financial performance measures and introduces the challenges that accountants and managers face when motivating performance in organizations. In Chapter 19, the balanced scorecard is presented as a method for using both financial and nonfinancial information to help achieve an organization's strategic goals. Although students are asked to consider the behavioural influences of accounting practices throughout the textbook, these chapters focus more specifically on the motivational uses of accounting information. Students are asked to recognize both intended and unintended behavioural consequences of performance metrics. Chapter 20 discusses current frameworks for considering sustainability and sustainability accounting.

Sequencing

We have written the chapters so that they can be taught in any sequence, although we recommend that the first two chapters be taught sequentially at the beginning of the course. Margin notes refer students to more detailed information about a topic that is addressed in other chapters.

Chapter Focus

Chapter 1: The Role of Accounting Information in Ethical Management Decision Making

Chapter 1 provides an overview of organizational decision making and introduces students to the use of cost accounting information in decision making. Techniques for identifying and using relevant information are reviewed. *Steps for Better Thinking*, a model for developing higher quality decisions, is introduced in Appendix 1B. Finally, this model is applied to ethical decision making. We do not introduce basic accounting terms in this chapter but instead give students a general overview of the importance of cost accounting information.

Chapter 2: Cost Concepts, Behaviour, and Estimation

In this chapter, we first introduce accounting terms that relate to cost behaviour and explain the cost function. At this point, we also discuss limitations of the information produced by cost functions and problems with uncertainties and bias in developing cost functions. This focus allows students to consider the quality of information as they learn cost accounting methods. We present and illustrate techniques that are used to describe cost behaviour (engineered estimates, analysis at the account level, two-point method, and regression analysis). Scatterplots are introduced as a way to provide additional information about cost behaviour. Linear and nonlinear (e.g., learning curves) cost functions are presented.

Chapter 3: Cost-Volume-Profit Analysis

Single and multiple product examples are used in this chapter to explore the development and use of CVP information, before and after taxes. Examples of spreadsheets with input sections and cell referencing are introduced so that students can easily perform sensitivity analysis. Because of the early focus on bias and uncertainties, students better understand the need for sensitivity analysis. Qualitative factors are explored, as are problems with uncertainty and bias. The margin of safety and operating leverage are introduced and then used to analyze risk of operations. Examples show the use of CVP information for both decision-making and monitoring purposes.

Chapter 4: Relevant Information for Decision Making

Operating decisions such as those involving special orders, make-or-buy decisions, keep-or-drop decisions, product emphasis, and maximization of constrained resources are covered in Chapter 4. This chapter is placed early in the text to allow students additional practice in developing decision-making skills by using cost function information. We find that students better understand the relevancy of their cost accounting course when they immediately use skills that are taught early in the course. In addition, relatively simple decision-making scenarios allow greater discussion of qualitative factors that potentially override quantitative results. Linear programming software is used to solve for optimal sales mixes when resources are constrained. As in all the other chapters, the effects of uncertainty and bias on decision-making are also explored.

Chapter 5: Job Costing

Chapter 5 introduces job costing and accounting for spoilage under job costing. The first part of the chapter introduces job-costing basics in a manufacturing setting; this method is then extended to the service sector. Product costs and cost flows are discussed first, followed by a comparison of actual and normal job costing methods, and then calculations for over- and underapplied overhead are explained. An example in this chapter highlights potential problems that arise if allocated costs are part of the information used to choose between two different jobs when there are capacity constraints. We also include a discussion of the costs of spoilage, rework, and scrap in job costing, describing opportunity costs that arise from poor quality. Behavioural implications of the accounting methods used to record spoilage are explored.

Chapter 6: Process Costing

Chapter 6 presents process costing methods, including the FIFO, weighted averages, and standard cost methods. We develop a single format that is used to calculate equivalent units for both the FIFO and weighted averages methods. This format helps students understand the difference between the two methods. In this chapter's examples, an accountant makes a decision about the best process costing method for her organization, comparing and contrasting information from the FIFO and weighted averages methods. In addition, accounting methods for the spoilage, rework, and scrap that arise in mass production are illustrated.

Chapter 7: Activity-Based Costing and Management

A team of employees implements an ABC system in this chapter, and information from the ABC system is compared to that from a traditional job costing system. ABM is described using a specific example for customer-related costs. In another ABM example, an accountant develops quality cost information aimed at reducing costs while improving quality. The benefits, costs, and limitations of ABC systems are discussed, as are recent academic research results. Two new costing methods, GPK (*Grenzplankostenrechnung*, a German costing system) and RCA (resource consumption accounting), aiming to improve the mapping between resource use and cost flows, are introduced and compared to the ABC system.

Chapter 8: Measuring and Assigning Support Department Costs

The direct, step-down, and reciprocal methods are described and illustrated in this chapter. Excel Solver is used to develop costs for the reciprocal method. Allocations are illustrated using a hypothetical music store. Information from single- versus dual-rate allocation methods is compared. The quality of support cost allocation information is discussed, with emphasis on its limitations, including behaviour implications.

Chapter 9: Joint Product and By-product Costing

Physical volume, sales at the split-off point, net realizable value, and constant gross margin NRV methods are compared and contrasted in this chapter. Appropriate use of relevant cost information for decisions about further processing is discussed. Main products and by-products are defined, and methods for accounting for by-products are compared and contrasted.

Chapter 10: Static and Flexible Budgets

After illustrating the development of a static budget, adjustments are made to develop a flexible budget that reflects activity levels, price changes, and elimination of costs over which managers have no control. This treatment of static and flexible budgeting reflects the actual sequence of events used by most businesses. Students better understand that forecasts are made, developed into a budget, and then adjusted to develop a benchmark as actual operations unfold. This chapter introduces participative, zero-based, rolling, ABC, and kaizen budgets. Behavioural aspects of budgeting are explored, as are the effects of uncertainties and bias in budget information.

Chapter 11: Standard Costs and Variance Analysis

The development and use of direct and overhead cost standards and variances are presented in this chapter. Behavioural effects arising from the use of this information are explored through an example in which a purchasing department buys less expensive materials that require more labour time and effort. In Appendix 11A, profit-related variances (revenue and contribution margin–related variances) are described and calculated.

Chapter 12: More Variances: Revenue, Contribution Margin and Advanced Production Variances

This chapter continues the discussion of variances by extending the production variances and introducing externally focused market variances. The mix and yield variances provide information for management decisions about the trade-offs between substitutable inputs. Revenue and profit variances focus on the effect of changes in selling price and shifts in sales mix. Profit variances also provide information about a business's position in the external market.

Chapter 13: Strategic Investment Decisions

Net present value analysis and other capital budgeting techniques are described and then compared and contrasted in this chapter. Examples with increasing complexity develop capital budgeting with income taxes. Inflation effects are considered in Appendix 12A, using both the real rate and nominal rate methods. Risks and bias in capital budget information are emphasized in this chapter. A case developed for this chapter requires that students use their own judgement to apply CCA, assess the life of a project, and determine appropriate discount rates.

Chapter 14: Pricing Decisions

Product pricing techniques (cost and market based; time and materials) are introduced, with emphasis on current pricing practices that are based on demand. An economic model is introduced to calculate a profit-maximizing price using price elasticity concepts. Transfer pricing techniques (cost and market based, negotiated, dual rate) are presented.

Chapter 15: Strategic Management of Costs

In this chapter, students learn to develop and implement target, kaizen, and life cycle costing systems. Value chain and supply chain analysis to support pricing decisions are discussed. Additionally, students are introduced to lean accounting concepts.

Chapter 16: Inventory Management

Economic order quantity concepts help managers manage inventory costs. Businesses need to strategically manage inventory to provide flexibility, to minimize inventory costs, and to avoid unnecessary costs associated with inventory. This chapter introduces students to the trade-offs between these divergent costs, the costs associated with the possibility of unexpected events, and special ordering opportunities offered by suppliers.

Chapter 17: Measuring and Assigning Costs for Income Statements

Absorption, variable, and throughput income statements are compared and contrasted. Factors that affect the choice of fixed overhead allocation rate volume measures (theoretical, practical, normal, and budgeted) are explored. The uses and limitations of information produced by these three income statements are discussed. Several examples and homework problems address the incentives under absorption costing of inventory build-up to improve a period's income.

Chapter 18: Performance Evaluation and Compensation

In this chapter, responsibility centres are introduced to explore the assignment of decision-making authority and responsibility. Performance evaluation measures (ROI, residual income, and EVA) are compared and contrasted. Transfer pricing approaches are illustrated. Incentives that give rise to suboptimal decision making are described for each type of performance measure and transfer price policy.

Chapter 19: Strategic Performance Measurement

This chapter emphasizes the strategic decision making model introduced in Chapter 1, highlighting the role of long-term strategic decision making. The balanced scorecard is then introduced as a method that can be used to combine financial and nonfinancial performance measures to gauge progress and motivate employees. The strengths and weaknesses of the balanced scorecard are discussed, including uncertainties about the best choice of measures, mistakes in implementation, and the effects of bias on performance measure choices.

Chapter 20: Sustainability Accounting

This chapter expands the role of accounting in the strategic management process to include consideration of sustainability, also known as the "triple bottom line": economic, environmental, and social value systems. Motivations and frameworks for reporting sustainability information are presented, and cost accounting techniques are introduced to develop sustainability information. The chapter provides an opportunity to revisit and expand upon topics learned earlier in the textbook, including identification of relevant costs and benefits, cost assignment, process costing, life cycle costing, capital budgeting, and balanced scorecard.

Chapter Features

Cost Management, Third Canadian edition, uses a number of pedagogical features in each chapter to enhance teaching and learning.

Learning Objectives

At the beginning of each chapter, learning objectives are listed to provide a structure for student learning. These learning objectives also appear in the margins where the material is first presented, organize the chapter summary, and identify homework material and Test Bank problems.

L01	Describe the process of strategic management and decision making
L02	Identify the types of control systems that managers use
L03	Explain the role of accounting information in strategic management
L04	Explain the information systems and information that are relevant for decision making
L05	Describe how business risk affects management decision making
L06	Appreciate how biases affect management decision making
L07	Determine how managers make higher-quality decisions
L08	Explain the importance of ethical decision making

Bombardier: Custom Manufacturing

The iconic Canadian company **L'Auto-Neige Bombardier Limitée** began manufacturing tracked vehicles for snow-covered terrain in 1942. (In English, *l'auto-neige* means "snow car.") These vehicles were early models of what later became snowmobiles. Over time, the company developed expertise in building engines and expanded into other markets, such as personal watercraft, aircraft, subway cars, buses, and jet boats.

The company, now known as **Bombardier Inc.**, continued to expand, often by acquiring existing companies such as **Canadair** (the leading Canadian aircraft manufacturer), **Pullman Railcars** in the United States, and an Irish manufacturer of civil and military aircraft and defence systems.

In 1990, Bombardier acquired **Learjet Corporation**, a U.S. manufacturer of high-performance business jets with interiors designed for personal comfort and convenience. Often referred to as the limousines of the skies, these jets are built at Bombardier's plant in Wichita, Kansas. Models include the Learjet 31A (light jet), Learjet 45 (super-light jet), and Learjet 60 (midsize jet).

Bombardier operates Learjet completion centres in Wichita and Tucson, Arizona. The completion centres provide customized services such as exterior painting and installation of cabinetry and furniture. Corporate jet customers often order specialized interiors, including unique fabric, carpet, wood, and colour; ergonomic seating; sound, video, and satellite communication systems; distinctive galleys; water systems; custom wiring; bulkhead reinforcements; and soundproofing. Different types of work are performed in different areas of the facility. The facility includes two paint booths, two sand-and-strip areas, four preparation areas, and an interior mockup room. The centre in Wichita completes approximately 120 Learjet 45 aircraft per year.

Deciding what to charge for a custom manufacturing job requires considering many quantitative and qualitative factors. Even when manufacturing to standard specifications takes place over several continents, job costing can be complicated. Bombardier is designing and building a new CSeries of jets that carry 100 to 149 passengers due to be delivered to airlines around the world in 2016. The jets were being be assembled at the company's plant in Mirabel, Quebec, but components were being built by thousands of suppliers across the globe, including the wings in Northern Ireland, the fuselage in China, the landing gear in Germany, and the wheels and brakes in Ohio.

Clement Sabourin/AFP/Getty Images

Chapter Opener and Analysis

Each chapter-opening vignette motivates students by presenting an interesting, business-related application of chapter material often based on Canadian companies.

barkley basketballs
SPECIAL ORDER

Barkley Basketballs manufactures high-quality basketballs at its plant, which has a production capacity of 50,000 basketballs per month. Current production is 35,000 per month. The manufacturing costs of $24.00 per basketball are categorized as follows:

	Variable Cost per Unit	Fixed Cost per Unit (at 35,000 per month)	Total Cost per Unit
Manufacturing Costs:			
Direct materials	$12.00	$0.00	$12.00
Direct labour	2.00	0.00	2.00
Manufacturing overhead	0.50	9.50	10.00
Total cost to manufacture	$14.50	$9.50	$24.00
Sales commission	$ 1.00	$0.00	$ 1.00

Jack Chang operates not-for-profit basketball camps for disadvantaged youths on First Nations reserves and throughout inner cities in large urban areas. Jack asks Billie Park, CFO at Barkley Basketballs, to sell him 5,000 basketballs at $23.00 per ball, or $115,000 for the entire order.

Billie speaks to the cost accountant and then goes to the production floor to speak to several supervisors to gather information for this decision. She determines that the direct labour cost is variable. Workers are paid an hourly wage and are sent home when there are no balls to manufacture. These workers have no guaranteed salary, but demand is stable, so they always work at least half-time, and often 40 hours per week.

Billie asks about the manufacturing overhead and finds that it consists of variable and fixed costs incurred to run the plant where the basketballs are manufactured. Overhead includes insurance, property taxes, amortization, utilities, and various other plant-related costs. She finds that all of the fixed costs are related to a capacity level of 50,000 and will not change if she uses part of the idle capacity of 15,000 units. The foreman warns her, however, that once production exceeds 40,000 basketballs, bottlenecks occur, and the production process will slow down and cause inventory levels to congest the plant, sometimes requiring the company to pay overtime.

Quantitative Analysis

With the 5,000 basketballs produced for Jack, total production for the month would be 40,000 basketballs. Bottlenecks and slowdowns do not occur until production exceeds 40,000. Therefore, the special order is within the relevant range of production; the fixed costs should remain fixed. The relevant revenues and costs per basketball are as follows:

Selling price	$23.00
Variable costs (materials, labour, and overhead)	$14.50

In deciding whether to accept this special order, fixed costs are irrelevant because they are unavoidable. They will be incurred whether 35,000 or 40,000 basketballs are produced, with a total fixed cost of $332,500 ($9.50 × 35,000). However, the fixed cost per unit will be $8.31 instead of $9.50 if Barkley produces 40,000 basketballs. The variable cost of $1.00 sales commission per ball is also irrelevant because no sales representatives are involved in this particular transaction. Therefore, the contribution margin for each special order basketball would be $23.00 − $14.50 = $8.50. For 5,000 basketballs, the additional total contribution margin would be $42,500.

Realistic Examples

After the presentation of a major cost accounting method, a realistic example of an organizational setting with interactions between accountants and managers demonstrates the method and introduces qualitative factors and relevant decision-making issues. The same setting is often used several different times in a chapter to introduce various aspects of each method. These examples enhance student learning by demonstrating cost accounting methods, clarifying the business context, and raising issues addressed by accountants, managers, and others.

●● ▶ FOCUS ON ETHICAL DECISION MAKING: DISCRETIONARY COSTS

In some industries, marketing expenses can be one of the largest discretionary costs. This is particularly true in the pharmaceutical industry, which tries to recoup its enormous research and development costs in the brief time in which a patent protects a drug from generic competitors. One study found that U.S. drug companies spend almost twice as much on promoting their products as on developing them. American firms in 2004 spent U.S. $57.4 billion on marketing, including direct-to-consumer advertising (DTCA), which is not allowed in Canada.

Canadian pharmaceutical companies still market their products, sidestepping the ban in other ways. For example, they are allowed to advertise directly to health care providers under strict guidelines from the non-profit Pharmaceutical Advertising Advisory Board, and they can advertise to consumers if they don't mention the benefits of their products. This regulation was behind the recent TV campaigns for erectile dysfunction drugs. Pfizer Canada's Viagra and Eli Lilly's Cialis, which humorously show or imply couples being intimate and implore viewers to contact their doctor for more information.

Canada's doctors, however, do not see direct-to-consumer advertising as a laughing matter. Their professional association, the Canadian Medical Association (CMA), has a policy opposing such advertising. The CMA says it is concerned that such advertising "is not information but marketing, and sends the message that a prescription drug is a 'consumer good' rather than a health care benefit." In addition, the CMA says DTCA may not provide enough information for consumers to make informed drug choices, "may stimulate demand by exaggerating the risks of a disease and generating unnecessary fear," may strain the relationship between health care providers and patients, and even "drives up the cost of health care."

Canadian broadcasters want the DTCA ban lifted, arguing that Canadians see TV and print ads coming from the United States anyway.

sources: Canadian Press, "Study Details Drug Company Interest in Marketing Over Research," *Marketing* magazine, January 4, 2008; Jeremy Lloyd, "Viagra Ads Face Stiff Competition from Cialis," *Marketing* magazine, May 9, 2008, Canadian Medical Association, "Direct-to-Consumer Advertising (DTCA) Policy," September 2007; Pharmaceutical Advertising Advisory Board, www.paab.ca.

PRACTISING ETHICAL DECISION MAKING

In Chapter 1, you learned about a process for making ethical decisions (Exhibit 1.14). You can address the following questions for this ethical dilemma to improve your skills for making ethical decisions. Think about your answers to these questions and discuss them with others.

Ethical Decision-Making Process	Questions to Consider About This Ethical Dilemma
Identify ethical problems as they arise.	Does direct-to-consumer advertising create an ethical problem for pharmaceutical companies? Why or why not?
Objectively consider the well-being of others and society when exploring alternatives.	Describe the different viewpoints about whether pharmaceutical companies should advertise directly to consumers. What assumptions lie behind each viewpoint? Are differences in ethical values evident?
Clarify and apply ethical values when choosing a course of action.	What is the best overall solution to this problem for society? What values did you use to arrive at the solution? What ethical values should drug companies use to address the concerns of their critics?
Work toward ongoing improvement of personal and organizational ethics.	How might drug companies continuously improve their marketing practices to benefit themselves and society?

Focus on Ethical Decision Making

Each chapter includes an ethical dilemma often related to a Canadian business example. As a follow-up, one or more homework problems address ethical issues. To provide students with guidance in addressing these problems, a framework for ethical decision making is introduced in Chapter 1. This framework calls for students to:

- ▶ Identify ethical problems as they arise.
- ▶ Objectively consider the well-being of others and society when exploring alternatives.
- ▶ Clarify and apply ethical values when choosing a course of action.
- ▶ Work toward ongoing improvement of personal and organizational ethics.

Suggested answers for each dilemma are provided on the instructor and student websites.

Strategic Risk Management

After selected realistic examples, *Strategic Risk Management* boxes give students the opportunity to explore issues beyond those presented in the example. Students are guided through the process of considering biases, business risks, or other strategic matters.

Risk of Biased Decisions

Each chapter introduces a type of bias that interferes with high-quality decision making and applies the bias to chapter material. These boxes help students understand why and how accountants and managers sometimes use information inappropriately.

Margin Notes

Several types of margin notes are used throughout this textbook to briefly present supplemental information and real-world examples. *Business Practice* and *International* notes present interesting examples of cost accounting concepts, methods, and issues for real organizations. *Alternative Terms* acquaint students with terminology they may encounter in the workplace, in other textbooks, or on professional examinations. *Chapter Reference* notes help students locate expanded discussions of topics that are presented elsewhere in the textbook. *Helpful Hints* provide students with suggestions to help apply concepts or techniques.

Review

Chapter Summary

The chapter summary, organized using the learning objective questions presented at the beginning of the chapter, provides an overview of all key cost accounting methods and concepts. Thus, unlike traditional summaries, *the summary in this text reviews both quantitative and qualitative content of the chapters*. It is a visual tool for students to use as an overview when beginning a chapter and as a review when completing it.

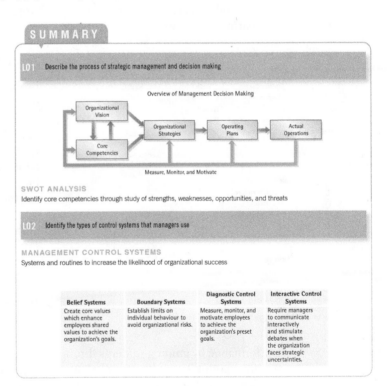

Self-Study Problems

Each chapter provides one or two self-study problems that address the most important content introduced in the chapter and are similar to end-of-chapter exercises and problems. Each self-study problem guides students through the calculations and thinking processes, and the solution is presented at the end of the chapter.

End-of-Chapter Assignment Material

The end-of-chapter material reinforces student learning of cost accounting techniques, and it helps them develop professional competencies such as analytical and decision-making skills.

Questions

Short-answer questions provide students with practice using the terminology and cost accounting techniques learned in the chapter.

Multiple-Choice Questions

Five multiple-choice questions are provided in each chapter. Some of these questions are adapted from the professional examinations of the legacy accounting professional bodies, CMA Canada and CGA Canada.

Exercises

Exercises focus primarily on ensuring that students learn to properly apply cost accounting methods. Exercises are intended to reinforce the basic concepts and techniques for each learning objective.

Problems

Problems give students additional practice using cost accounting techniques. They also present open-ended questions requiring judgment (e.g., identifying uncertainties, analyzing information, exploring incentives and biases, evaluating alternatives, recommending a course of action). More important, some problems provide students with comprehensive applications of various concepts from the chapter or previous chapters. The requirements support better performance by guiding students through the steps needed to fully address a problem, from less to more complex aspects.

11.43 Cost Variance Analysis The following information is available for ConcertWearShirts:

LO3, LO4, LO5

	Standard Quantity	Standard Cost	Total Standard Cost
Direct Materials	3 metres	$12.00/metre	$36.00
Direct Labour	2 hours	$10.00/hour	$20.00
Variable Overhead	2 machine hours	$3.00/machine hour	$6.00
Fixed Overhead	2 machine hours	$1.00/machine hour	$2.00
			$64.00

The normal production level is 300 shirts. This production period ConcertWear produced 280 shirts. ConcertWear purchased 900 metres of fabric for $9,720. The variances for the production period are:

Materials Price Variance	?
Materials Quantity Variance	$ 336 U
Labour Rate Variance	$ 532 U
Labour Efficiency Variance	$ 280 F
VOH Spending Variance	$ 98 F
VOH Efficiency Variance	$ 210 F
FOH Budget Variance	$ 110 F
FOH Volume Variance	$ 40 U

REQUIRED A. How many metres of fabric were used? (Hint: Metres used was not the same as the metres purchased.)
B. What was the materials price variance?
C. What was the actual direct labour rate?
D. What was the actual variable overhead rate?
E. How many machine hours were used?
F. What was the master budget amount for fixed overhead?

Mini-Cases

Like Problems, Mini-Cases pose open-ended questions, and the requirements support better performance by guiding students through the steps needed. However, Mini-Cases give students an opportunity to address more complex applications of cost accounting techniques involving deeper analysis. One or two Integrating Across the Curriculum or Cumulative Mini-Cases in each chapter ask students to integrate cost accounting material with the content of other accounting and business core courses, such as auditing, marketing, or finance or to reference material presented in other chapters.

Exercise and Problem Types, Codes, and Icons

A number of codes and icons are used in the end-of-chapter materials to make it easier for instructors to select homework assignments and to enhance student learning.

LO1, LO2, LO3, LO4, LO5, LO6 Learning Objectives. Each exercise and problem is keyed to one or more learning objectives.

Communication. All Canadian accounting professional organizations emphasize the importance of communication skills. Therefore, several problems in each chapter require students to prepare written memoranda or to describe communication for a given setting.

Ethics. The ethics icon indicates problems that focus on ethical dilemmas, many featuring recent business scenarios. Students explore the uncertainties and multiple perspectives before drawing conclusions. These problems are likely to generate lively class discussions because of differences among students' perceptions and values.

Professional Exams. This icon indicates that an exercise, a problem, or a multiple-choice question has been adapted from the professional examinations of the legacy accounting professional bodies, CMA Canada and CGA Canada. All these examinations currently include multiple-choice questions. Practice with prior examination problems will help students learn the cost accounting material.

Spreadsheets. Spreadsheets are introduced in various chapters, with examples of data input areas so that sensitivity analysis can be performed easily. Students replicate or expand these examples in certain homework problems, which require the use of electronic spreadsheet software. For example, students use spreadsheets to develop financial models, perform regression analysis, calculate optimal sales mixes, and perform reciprocal cost allocations (using Excel Solver for the last two activities).

Web. The Web icon indicates that a problem requires students to access information or download datasets posted on the textbook website.

www.wiley.com/
go/eldenburgcanada

Group. Certain problems are particularly useful for student group activities. These problems would be difficult for most students working alone, and student learning is enhanced through collaboration with others in the class.

Resources

The textbook's companion site located at www.wiley.com/go/eldenburgcanada provides a wealth of support materials that will help instructors more effectively teach cost management and help students develop their understanding of course concepts and increase their ability to solve problems. Resources include the following listed below. These and additional resources are available in WileyPLUS.

www.wiley.com/
go/eldenburgcanada

- ► **Instructor's Manual** Provides ways to organize course materials, suggestions for teaching each chapter, the authors' teaching philosophy and recommendations, and guidance for using the many electronic and print assessment tools available with the text.

- ► **Checklist of Key Figures** Allows students to verify the accuracy of their answers as they work through assignments.

- ► **Solutions Manual** Contains detailed solutions to end-of-chapter assignment material, and it guides students through the required computational and thinking processes. The solutions manual also includes information that maps all questions to CPA competencies.

▶ **PowerPoint Presentations** Intended as a lecture guideline, the PowerPoint slides present material in a concise bulleted format that enables easy note-taking.

▶ **Test Bank** A comprehensive testing package that allows instructors to tailor examinations according to chapter objectives, learning skills, and content. It includes traditional types of questions (e.g., true/false, multiple-choice, matching, computational, and short-answer) as well as open-ended problems that are similar to those in the textbook. All questions are cross-referenced to chapter objectives. The Test Bank is also available in computerized format.

▶ **Personal Response System (Clicker) Questions** A bank of 25 true/false and multiple choice questions is available for anyone using personal response systems technology in their classroom.

▶ **Solutions to Ethical Decision Making Questions** Analysis and solutions for the Focus on Ethical Decision Making feature in each chapter.

WileyPLUS

WileyPLUS is an innovative, research-based online environment for effective teaching and learning. *WileyPLUS* builds students' confidence because it takes the guesswork out of studying by providing students with a clear roadmap: what to do, how to do it, if they did it right. Students will take more initiative so you'll have greater impact on their achievement in the classroom and beyond.

Among its many features, this online learning interface allows students to study and practise using the digital textbook, quizzes, and algorithmic exercises. The immediate feedback helps students understand where they need to focus their study efforts.

The filtering capability in the assignment area allows instructors to customize assignments by using different filters including criteria related to CPA competencies, level of difficulty, and even learning objectives.

ACKNOWLEDGEMENTS

We would like to thank the authors, Leslie G. Eldenburg and Susan K. Wolcott, who developed the original concept for this book and who put so much thought and energy into its creation.

We would like to acknowledge the reviewers who provided the valuable feedback assessing the development of this and previous editions and provided input to the authors.

Anthony Atkinson, Wilfrid Laurier University
Vince Cappelli, Ryerson University
Heather Cornish, Northern Alberta Institute of Technology
Suresh Kalagnanam, University of Saskatchewan
Tomek Kopczynski, Concordia University
Vanessa Magness, Ryerson University
Raili Pollanen, Carleton University
George Quan Fun, University of Toronto
Gallia Singer, Concordia University
Susan Van Weelden, Redeemer University College
Kevin Veenstra, McMaster University
Annette deWeerd, Northern Alberta Institute of Technology
Karen Wight, University of Prince Edward Island
Peggy Woo, Ryerson University
Starr Zhang, Northern Alberta Institute of Technology

Thank you to the ancillary authors, contributors, and technical checkers, including:

Angela Davis, Booth University College
Sandy Kizan, Athabasca University
Howard Leaman, University of Guelph-Humber
Mary Oxner, St. Francis Xavier University
Judith Watson, Capilano University
Annette deWeerd, Northern Alberta Institute of Technology
Brad Witt, Humber College

We would like to thank all of the people at John Wiley and Sons Canada Ltd. who helped develop this edition: Veronica Visentin, Zoë Craig, Anita Osborne, Karen Staudinger, Luisa Begani, and Gail Brown. The editorial contributions of Tom Moss Gamblin are also greatly appreciated.

Liang-Hsuan Chen
Gail Lynn Cook

BRIEF CONTENTS

CONTENTS

COST
MANAGEMENT

THIRD CANADIAN EDITION

## CHAPTER 1

The Role of Accounting Information in Ethical Management Decision Making

After studying this chapter, you should be able to do the following:

LO1 Describe the process of strategic management and decision making

LO2 Identify the types of control systems that managers use

LO3 Explain the role of accounting information in strategic management

LO4 Explain the information systems and information that are relevant for decision making

LO5 Describe how business risk affects management decision making

LO6 Appreciate how biases affect management decision making

LO7 Determine how managers make higher-quality decisions

LO8 Explain the importance of ethical decision making

in brief Managers use cost accounting information to make different types of decisions, which include developing long-term strategies and creating short-term operating plans. Managers achieve higher-quality decisions by using higher-quality relevant information and decision-making practices. Accounting information systems often focus on the data needed for financial reporting rather than for management decision making, so managers need to appropriately identify the relevant information for internal decisions. Cost accounting information is also used as part of an organization's control systems, to measure and monitor organizational performance and to motivate employees to take actions consistent with organizational strategies. Some controls ensure that operations proceed according to planned strategies and others help managers determine whether strategies should be altered. Controls also include codes of conduct, values statements, and other mechanisms to ensure ethical behaviour. Although ethical behaviour can be improved through control systems, it ultimately depends on the ability of individuals to recognize ethical dilemmas and consider the well-being of others and society when making decisions. ■

Good Ethics Makes Good Business

© Pixellover RM 10/Alamy Stock Photo

Like many electronics companies, **Apple Inc.** moved its manufacturing overseas to lower its labour costs. But the cost-cutting strategy backfired by hurting Apple's reputation when stories came to light about poor working conditions at factories owned by its contract manufacturer, **Foxconn Technology Group**, in China. Allegations of Foxconn employees being forced to work long hours with low pay, in factories with poor health and safety records, caused a public backlash against Apple, one of the world's richest companies.

Apple responded by joining the Fair Labor Association (FLA) and agreeing to submit some of the Foxconn factories to an FLA audit. When the audit uncovered that the factories did not comply with the FLA's Workplace Code of Conduct and violated some Chinese labour laws, including those regarding working hours and pay, Apple and Foxconn vowed to comply. Apple now produces an annual Supplier Responsibility Progress Report to document the steps it's taken to improve working conditions at its contract factories in China and 18 other countries, including implementing programs to educate workers, stepping up the monitoring of working hours, and increasing the number of audits of working conditions.

Facing its own international scrutiny, Foxconn—China's largest private employer—raised its employees' wages. That resulted in two other of its tech giant clients—**Hewlett-Packard** and **Dell Inc.**—warning that they may need to raise the price of their consumer goods to cover increased supply chain costs. Apple didn't indicate whether it would do the same. There was speculation in the news media that Apple could absorb higher production costs due to its relatively high profit margin compared with competitors.

Apple's efforts to improve working conditions at Foxconn still met with disapproval from some observers. This included a securities analyst whose concerns over unethical business practices spurred him to write a note advising investors to sell their shares in Apple (along with shares in retail giant **Amazon.com, Inc.**, which he criticized for treating warehouse workers poorly, and cigarette maker **Philip Morris International**, which he took to task for making a dangerous product). While the analyst's recommendation didn't seem to affect those companies' share prices, it did succeed in gaining more publicity for the role of ethics in business decision making.

Growing public awareness of the need for corporate social responsibility, including the treatment of workers, means that management accountants need to consider possible effects on their employer's reputation when making cost decisions. The possibility of consumer boycotts or stock analysts' devaluation in reaction to possible unethical behaviour are just two of many factors that need to be taken into account in management decision making. Saving money by making a publicly unpopular decision might not be worth it in the long run.

SOURCES: D. Jeffries, "Is Apple Cleaning Up its Act on Labour Rights?," *The Guardian*, March 5, 2014; A. Lewis, "Analyst Shunned after Knocking Apple, Amazon for Ethics," Marketwatch.com, January 15, 2014; J. C. Hyatt, "Apple, Foxconn, Promise Improvements for Workers," Business-ethics.com, March 29, 2012; K. Eaton, "Apple and Foxconn's Ethics Hit Your Gadget Prices," *FastCompany*, February 24, 2012; Apple Inc. corporate website, www.apple.com.

Strategic Management and Decision Making

LO1   Describe the process of strategic management and decision making

People at different levels within an organization continually make many different kinds of decisions that range from the broad and long-term, such as which markets the organization will pursue, to detailed and short-term, such as how to respond to a customer on the telephone. All decisions, no matter how large or small, influence an organization's ability to achieve its overall purpose. Exhibit 1.1 presents an overview of the strategic management process. To better understand the flow of information and decision making, we consider how each part of Exhibit 1.1 relates to the strategic management of Netflix, one of the world's largest online entertainment subscription service.[1]

Organizational Vision

The most far-reaching decisions managers make identify and shape the organization's vision. The organizational vision is a core purpose or ideology that guides the organization's overall direction and its approach regarding various stakeholder groups.

In his 2008 letter to shareholders, Reed Hastings—the chief executive officer, president, and co-founder of Netflix—described the company's vision through the following statements:[2]

> ▶ We combine a superior value proposition with an outstanding customer experience, and we continually improve our product offering through investments in our website, content, distribution, and customer care.
> ▶ We remain focused on our long-term goals: To be a great Internet movie service by combining DVD-by-mail with Internet streaming . . .

Organizational Core Competencies

Organizational core competencies are the organization's strengths relative to its competitors', which creates value for stakeholders. Exhibit 1.1 presents many different areas of potential organizational strength. Managers typically identify core competencies by studying the organization's strengths, weaknesses, opportunities, and threats, an exercise called a SWOT analysis.

▷ EXHIBIT 1.1

Overview of Strategic Management Process

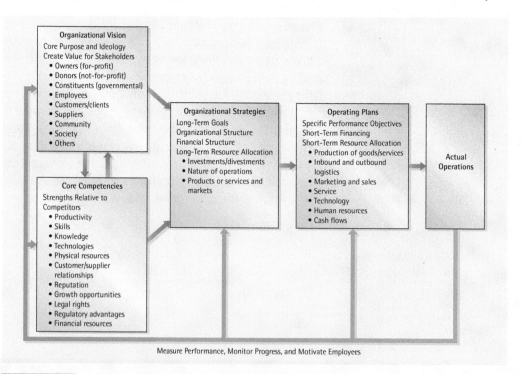

[1] Netflix Inc., 2008, Fact Sheet, downloaded from ir.netflix.com in December 2009.
[2] Excerpts from Letter to Shareholders, Netflix 2008 Annual Report, pp. 5–9.

Organizational Vision

Core Purpose and Ideology
Create Value for Stakeholders

- Owners (for profit)
- Donors (not-for-profit)
- Constituents (governmental)

- Employees
- Customers/clients
- Suppliers

- Community
- Society
- Others

▶EXHIBIT 1.2
Organizational Vision

Organizational Core Competencies

Strengths Relative to Competitors

- Productivity
- Skills
- Knowledge
- Technologies

- Physical resources
- Customer/supplier relationships
- Reputation
- Growth opportunities

- Legal rights
- Regulatory advantages
- Financial resources

▶EXHIBIT 1.3
Organizational Core Competencies

▶ BUSINESS PRACTICE

The Vision of Cara Operations Ltd.

Cara owns many of Canada's favourite restaurants, including Swiss Chalet, Harvey's, Kelsey's, Montana's Cookhouse, and Milestone's Grill & Bar, as well as Cara Airline Solutions, an airline caterer. Cara's vision is "To be Canada's leading branded restaurant and airline services company."

Its five principles are

1. Quality   **2.** Responsibility   **3.** Integrity   **4.** Efficiency   **5.** Independence

Source: Cara Operations Limited website, www.cara.com.

The organizational vision (Exhibit 1.2) and core competencies (Exhibit 1.3) are closely related, and the vision should build on existing and achievable strengths.

In its 2008 annual report, Netflix's managers identified the following competitive strengths:[3]

- ▶ Comprehensive library of titles
- ▶ Personalized merchandising
- ▶ Size of subscriber base
- ▶ Convenience, selection, and fast delivery

Organizational Strategies

Organizational strategies (Exhibit 1.4) are the tactics that managers use to take advantage of core competencies, while working toward the organizational vision. Strategies guide long-term decisions, such as the proportion of financing through debt and equity, types of goods and services offered, and investments in property, plant, and equipment. Some of these decisions are made and then rarely reconsidered (e.g., form of business organization). Other strategic decisions, such as goods and services offered, are re-evaluated periodically. Managers also establish long-term goals, such as market leadership or high-quality customer service.

Netflix's managers have announced the following strategies for long-term growth:[4]

- ▶ Provide compelling value for subscribers.
- ▶ Utilize technology to enhance subscriber experience and operate efficiently.
- ▶ Build mutually beneficial relationships with entertainment video providers.

These strategies have guided Netflix managers' long-term decisions, such as the following:

- ▶ Utilize proprietary technology to efficiently deliver DVDs and stream content over the Internet.
- ▶ Establish ties with movie and television series video providers.

---

[3] Competitive Strengths, Netflix Inc., Form 10-K, filed with the United States Securities and Exchange Commission, year ended December 31, 2008, p. 3.
[4] Excerpts from Letter to Shareholders, Netflix 2008 Annual Report, pp. 5–9.

> **EXHIBIT 1.4**
> Organizational Strategies

Organizational Strategies	
Long-Term Goals	Long-Term Resource Allocation
Organizational Structure	• Investments/divestments
Financial Structure	• Nature of operations
	• Products or services and markets

> **EXHIBIT 1.5**
> Operating Plans

Operating Plans		
Specific Performance Objectives		
Short-Term Financing		
Short-Term Resource Allocation		
• Production of goods/services	• Service	• Human resources
• Inbound and outbound logistics	• Technology	• Cash flows
• Marketing and sales		

► Create an extensive database of customer movie preference data.
► Acquire over 100,000 movie titles.
► Establish a nationwide network of shipping centres.
► Develop and maintain a website to enhance subscription signup and management and personalized customer service.
► Register and enforce intellectual property rights (e.g., patents, trademarks, copyrights, and confidentiality agreements).

Operating Plans

Operating plans (Exhibit 1.5) involve specific short-term decisions that shape an organization's day-to-day activities, such as drawing cash from a bank line of credit, hiring an employee, or ordering materials. These plans often include specific performance objectives, such as budgeted revenues and costs.

Netflix's managers make plans for numerous day-to-day and other short-term objectives; examples include the following:

► Launching advertising promotions (e.g., online, television, radio, and direct mail).
► Shipping and receiving DVDs to/from customers.
► Delivering content via the Internet.
► Monitoring third-party contracts for the collection of customers' monthly subscription fees.
► Randomly testing customer service levels.
► Maintaining the website and customer database.
► Managing inventory of over 72 million DVDs.
► Hiring and training employees.
► Producing and updating accounting records.

Actual Operations

Actual operations are the various actions taken and results achieved over a period of time. These include customer orders received, revenues earned, number of employees hired, costs incurred, units of goods or services produced, cash received and paid, and so on. Data about actual operations are collected and measured by the organization's information system and then used to monitor and motivate performance.

> **INTERNATIONAL**
> **Chrysler** launched a strategy to cut costs by sharing parts across its Mercedes, Chrysler, and Mitsubishi brands. This strategy led to quality deficiencies in Mercedes vehicles, the company's most valuable brand.[5] It's not known how much this contributed to Mercedes reverting ownership back to **Daimler-Benz** in 2007, or to Chrysler's bankruptcy proceeding in 2009 that saw it become controlled by Italian automaker **Fiat**.

---

[5] G. Edmondson and K. Kerwin, "Stalled," *BusinessWeek*, September 29, 2003, pp. 54–56.

Measuring, Monitoring, and Motivating Performance

The feedback loop in Exhibit 1.1 encompasses the systems and routines that managers use to increase the likelihood of organizational success. These systems are often called **management control systems**. For example, managers need information about costs to help decide whether to sell a particular product. They also need information to measure actual operations so that they can monitor the success of their decisions and motivate employees to work toward the organizational vision. Decisions are monitored by comparing actual operating results against plans, such as budgets, and against long-term goals. Desirable employee behaviour is often motivated by tying employee performance evaluation and pay to long-term or short-term results. An organization's information system can be designed to measure and report information used for decision making as well as for monitoring and motivating, as shown in Exhibit 1.6.

Management control systems include planning, monitoring, and motivating, as well as controlling and measuring performance. Managers use management accounting information to facilitate a management control system. Budgets help to quantify planning and accounting, and cost reports help to guide control and performance evaluation. The learning from the process provides feedback for organizations to improve planning, control, and performance. Exhibit 1.7 shows how the management control systems and management accounting interconnect to help managers implement company strategy.

> **EXHIBIT 1.6**
> Measuring Performance, Monitoring Progress, and Motivating Employees

Measuring Performance, Monitoring Progress, and Motivating Employees

Compare Actual Operating Results	Reward Employees	Report to Stakeholders	Provide Information for Evaluation of Organizational
• Specific performance objectives • Progress toward long-term goals	• Performance evaluation • Bonuses or other compensation	• Internal reporting • External reporting	• Vision • Core competencies • Strategies • Operating plans

> **EXHIBIT 1.7**
> The Role of Management Control Systems and Management Accounting in Strategy

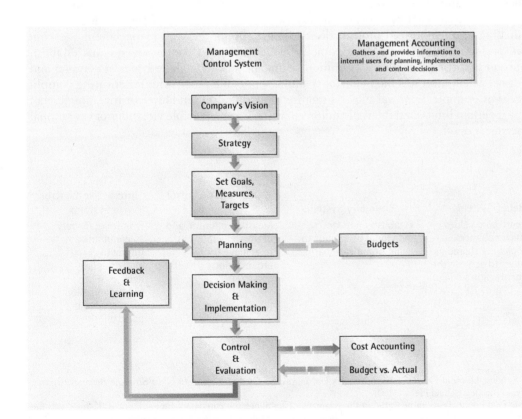

Levers of Control

LO2 Identify the types of control systems that managers use

According to Robert Simons, a professor at Harvard University and corporate consultant, managers use four levers of control to measure and monitor organizational performance and motivate employees to take actions consistent with organizational strategies.[6] Some controls ensure that operations proceed according to planned strategies, and other controls help managers determine whether strategies should be altered. Managers select and use these four systems to control business strategy, including compliance with organizational plans and guidelines, as well as for empowerment of employees in envisioning and adapting to changing economic conditions.

Belief Systems

Organizational success increases when employees understand the organization's core values and work collectively to achieve them. Belief systems inspire and direct employees to take actions that are consistent with the organizational vision. Managers may communicate belief systems using one or more formal statements, which may vary from organization to organization. In general, a vision statement is a theoretical description of what the organization should become. A mission statement is a high-level declaration of the organization's purpose. A core values statement is a summary of the beliefs that define the organization's culture. Some managers publish additional statements, such as the organization's social or environmental responsibilities.

Netflix does not appear to publish formal vision, mission, core values, or other statements. The organizational vision is, instead, communicated through various declarations made by top management, such as the excerpts quoted above from CEO Reed Hastings's 2008 Letter to Shareholders.[7]

Boundary Systems

Every organization faces risks that should be avoided. For example, unethical or illegal behaviours compromise an organization's position with investors, regulators, customers, and suppliers. Extremely risky investments expose the organization to financial disaster. The launching of unauthorized projects diverts financial resources and management attention from projects that are more likely to achieve strategic goals. Boundary systems establish limits on individual behaviour. Common boundary systems include codes of conduct and budgets, which limit specific behaviours, and also include procedures for ensuring compliance. For example, approval may be required for capital expenditures or investments that exceed certain limits, and internal auditors may investigate possible violations of operational procedures or ethical rules.

> EXHIBIT 1.8
Four Levers of Control

Belief Systems	Boundary Systems	Diagnostic Control Systems	Interactive Control Systems
Create core values which enhance employees shared values to achieve the organization's goals.	Establish limits on individual behaviour to avoid organizational risks.	Measure, monitor, and motivate employees to achieve the organization's preset goals.	Require managers to communicate interactively and stimulate debates when the organization faces strategic uncertainties.

---

[6] R. Simons, *Levers of Control: How Managers Use Innovative Control Systems to Drive Strategic Renewal* (Boston: Harvard Business School Press, 1995).
[7] Additional information can be found in the company's Fact Sheet; the company's annual Form 10-K, filed with the United States Securities and Exchange Commission; and other information available at ir.netflix.com.

Netflix publishes a code of ethics and an insider trading policy on its website. The code of ethics addresses matters of honesty, conflicts of interest, compliance with laws and regulations, internal reporting of ethical violations, and disciplinary actions.[8] The insider trading policy is designed to prevent officers, directors, employees, and others from violating securities laws by trading on nonpublic information affecting the company's stock price.[9]

Diagnostic Control Systems

Managers establish **preset goals** that must be achieved for the organization's strategy to be successful. These goals are set for variables—such as income, market share, and manufacturing output—that are critical to success. Progress toward preset goals is monitored and reported. For example, Netflix's top managers have probably established a variety of long-term and short-term goals for variables such as subscriber growth, subscriber retention, customer satisfaction ratings, DVD delivery time, and financial gross margins. **Diagnostic control systems** measure, monitor, and motivate employees to achieve preset goals.

▷ **ALTERNATIVE TERMS**
Preset goals are sometimes called *critical performance variables* or *performance targets*.

Managers throughout an organization regularly analyze reports relating to preset goals to determine whether operations are proceeding according to plan. They must decide whether actions should be taken to bring operations back under control. Common diagnostic control systems include budgets and variances (Chapters 10 and 11), performance evaluation measures and rewards (Chapter 15), and balanced scorecards (Chapter 16).

▷ **CHAPTER REFERENCE**
Chapters 17 and 18 discuss performance measures and their intended and unintended consequences.

To motivate managers and employees to achieve planned results, diagnostic control systems are often used for personnel evaluation. Bonuses or other forms of compensation are often based on achieving or exceeding budgets or other preset goals. Such rewards can, however, encourage **suboptimal decisions** and actions that benefit the employees or their business units at a cost to the organization. Suppose Netflix employees are rewarded for quickly processing returned DVDs. The employees may fail to notice that a particular DVD is damaged and should not be sent out again, as customers become dissatisfied when they receive damaged DVDs too frequently. In a manufacturing setting, poor-quality work by one group of employees can have a ripple effect through the rest of the production process.

Interactive Systems

Organizations typically operate in dynamic and uncertain business environments that threaten current strategies or cause them to become obsolete. For example, Netflix operates in an environment of continual change, such as the introduction of Blu-ray DVDs and increased use of Internet video streaming. Although Netflix managers know about the existence of these shifts, they cannot know how quickly a shift will occur, which DVD and download technologies will ultimately prevail, or how competition will change. **Interactive control systems** are recurring sets of information that demand attention from managers at many levels. The information requires them to communicate interactively and stimulates debates about what the information means, leading to new insights about strategic challenges and opportunities. For example, Netflix managers could review monthly reports about market share, customer base, and competitor's actions, and then discuss the information in meetings across employee levels as part of an interactive control system.

Controls—such as budgets, variances, and balanced scorecards—might operate as either diagnostic or interactive control systems, depending on their use. Information from interactive systems focuses manager attention on strategic risks, encourages discussions between managers and subordinates, and promotes reconsideration of the entire process shown in Exhibit 1.1—organizational vision, core competencies, strategies, and operating plans.

---

[8]Netflix Inc., Code of Ethics, ir.netflix.com/documentdisplay.cfm?DocumentID=73.
[9]Netflix Inc., Insider Trading Policy, ir.netflix.com/documentdisplay.cfm?DocumentID=74.

Cost Accounting and Decision Making

What is cost accounting, and how does it relate to the ideas of measuring, monitoring, and motivating? **Cost accounting** involves the process of tracking, recording, analyzing, and determining the cost of an organization's project, process, or activity. Cost accounting helps managers understand the costs of operating a business so that they can use the information to make sound business decisions, particularly to reduce the company's costs and to improve its profitability and productivity.

Management Accounting and Financial Accounting

Cost accounting information is used for both management and financial accounting activities. **Management accounting** is the process of gathering, summarizing, and reporting financial and nonfinancial information used internally by managers to make decisions. Because the information gathered is mainly for internal uses, management accounting is not bound by International Financial Reporting Standards (IFRS) or Canadian Accounting Standards for Private Enterprises (Canadian ASPE). Management accounting information helps managers plan, control, and measure performance. It is future oriented and concerned with reporting on a segment of an organization. An example of cost accounting information that is also management accounting information is a breakdown of customer service costs by both product line and average cost per customer service call.

Financial accounting is the process of preparing and reporting financial information that is used most frequently by decision makers outside the organization, such as shareholders and creditors. Due to the fact that the information is for external users, financial accounting must be prepared in accordance with IFRS or Canadian ASPE. The information gathered from financial accounting is historical fact and is primarily concerned with the organization as a whole. An example of cost accounting information that is also financial accounting information is the valuation of ending inventory shown on the balance sheet.

A Brief History of Cost Accounting

Cost-accounting techniques were first developed in the early 1800s. As organization size increased, the need for measuring, monitoring, and motivating performance grew. By the mid-1800s, cost accounting practices were well developed. For example, railroad accountants calculated the cost per ton-mile and operating expenses per dollar of revenue. One of the earliest detailed costing systems was developed for Andrew Carnegie's steel mills, for which material and labour cost information were produced daily. Then, in the early 1900s, organizations were required to provide external reports such as financial statements and tax returns. Because the cost of keeping two sets of books for separate information requirements was relatively high, cost accounting focused primarily on information for income tax returns and financial statements.

From the early 1900s until the mid-1970s, cost accounting practices changed very little. However, as the business environment became more global, competition increased, and, in turn, demand grew for more sophisticated cost accounting information. Recent technological innovation has enabled cost accountants to develop previously infeasible cost accounting systems. Today, cost accounting information is used for a variety of purposes, including internal decision making, measurement and monitoring of performance at all levels, and alignment of employee and stakeholder goals. Furthermore, managers now use cost accounting information to analyze the profitability of customers and to coordinate transactions with suppliers—extending traditional cost accounting beyond the walls of the organization.

Strategic Cost Management

Cost accounting is often defined narrowly as relating to the measurement of costs within an organization. However, cost accounting information is increasingly being defined more broadly to include both financial and nonfinancial information, and to include items that do not relate strictly to the measurement of costs. From this trend, a new term has been introduced: **strategic cost management** refers to simultaneous focus on both reducing costs and strengthening an organization's strategic position.[10] As strategic cost management gains in popularity, organizations are also adopting balanced scorecards. The **balanced scorecard** is a formal approach used to help organizations translate their vision into objectives that can be measured and monitored using both financial and nonfinancial performance measures.

The role of cost and managerial accountants is much broader today than it was in the past. In this text, therefore, we not only talk about techniques for generating cost accounting information but also discuss how to use that information in business decisions. You'll learn to recognize and work with information that is not perfect. Specifically, you'll learn how both uncertainties in cost accounting information and decision-maker bias can result in poor decisions.

> ► CHAPTER REFERENCE
> See Chapter 19 for a complete discussion of the balanced scorecard.

Information Systems and Relevant Information in Management Decision Making

Managers use many types of information to help make decisions. Information can be gathered formally or informally. Formal methods include point-of-service optical character readers, such as those used when customers purchase merchandise at retail stores. Such systems track inventory levels, geographic distribution of sales, trends, relationships between prices and sales, and so on. Informal methods of collecting information, from both inside and outside an organization, are also important. For example, individuals inside a company often gather product pricing information by reading industry trade journals or examining competitors' websites.

Most organizations have many databases that contain information collected formally or informally from internal or external sources. Access to database information is often restricted to specific individuals. In addition, much valuable information is not readily accessible because it is not formally captured by an information system but held in the minds of employees. This information is called *intellectual capital*. Thus, it is difficult for decision makers, even within an organization, to gain access to all the information they might wish to use. It is easy to argue that managers should obtain more and better information to help make decisions. However, the benefit must exceed the cost of generating information.

> **LO4** Explain the information systems and information that are relevant for decision making

Internal and External Reports

To facilitate decision making and meet external reporting requirements, accounting departments use software to generate a variety of internal and external reports that summarize or highlight information. An **internal report** is a document that presents information for use only inside an organization. An **external report** is a document that presents information for use outside an organization. Exhibit 1.9 summarizes common types of internal and external reports.

Internal reports are designed to provide information for the types of management decisions introduced in Exhibit 1.1 and to support the control systems shown in Exhibit 1.8. Some internal reports, such as monthly sales summaries, are issued regularly, while others, such as the analysis of a potential business acquisition, are generated for one-time use.

> ► BUSINESS PRACTICE
> U.S. hospital managers analyze reports on the percentage of receivables exceeding 90 days. This information helps them quickly learn about and correct patient billing errors, insurance claim difficulties, and other revenue problems.[11]

---

[10] See R. Cooper and R. Slagmulder, "The Scope of Strategic Cost Management," in James Edwards (ed.), *Emerging Practices in Cost Management* (Boston: Warren, Gorham & Lamont, 1999).
[11] E. Guyton and C. Lund, "Transforming the Revenue Cycle," *Healthcare Financial Management*, March 2003, pp. 72–78.

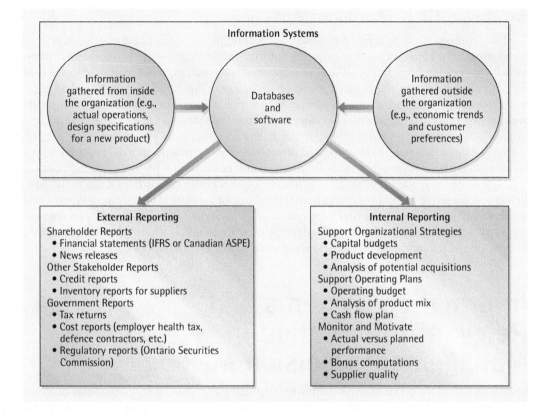

External reports can be distributed to different constituencies for many purposes. Some external reports, such as income tax returns, are required, while others, such as a news release about a joint venture agreement, are discretionary. Some reports, such as financial statements given to a supplier to obtain credit, facilitate business activities.

Although reports are developed for a specific audience, they may be used for other purposes at the same time. For example, internal reports such as quarterly sales data can be shared with people outside the organization. Similarly, external reports such as financial statements are sometimes used within the organization. In addition, organizations use reports prepared outside the organization (e.g., by consultants or vendors) for internal decision making.

Improvements in Information for Management Decision Making

The detail and quality of organizational data have improved in recent years. Historically, an organization used one accounting system that gathered data for financial statements. These data, prepared using IFRS or Canadian ASPE, were used for both external and internal reporting. This type of information was not always ideal for management decision making, and as a result, resources were often poorly allocated, leading to operating and investment inefficiencies.

Business Intelligence and Process Management Systems

Business intelligence (BI) and business process management (BPM) are software products that help managers reduce costs, improve profitability, and control operations. BI creates integrated systems across an organization or between an organization and its customers and suppliers to improve management of employee teams, customer service, and supply chains.

> BUSINESS PRACTICE

In 2008, **IBM** bought **Cognos**, a Canadian company, as part of a strategy to expand IBM's vision as the leading business intelligence (BI) and performance management provider. The acquisition of Cognos enabled IBM to provide its customers the ability to operate "multiple non-IBM technologies, solutions, and services in heterogeneous environments."[12]

---

[12] *Global Partner Community Supports IBM Acquisition Of Cognos,* www.businesswire.com/news/home/20080206005813/en/Global-Partner-Community-Supports-IBM-Acquisition-Cognos#.Vd4Oy3nbLDc.

BI systems may be used for strategic planning, budgeting, financial consolidation, decision support, and reporting to support diagnostic and interactive controls. BPM software supports the design, execution, and monitoring of repetitive, day-to-day business processes. For example, BPM systems might track the status of customer orders or monitor direct material usage and trigger purchases at the optimal time. BPM systems can also create data, such as product defect rates or customer processing time, which are used in diagnostic or interactive control systems.

▶ **BUSINESS PRACTICE**

An **International Data Corporation (IDC)** study indicates that the Canadian financial services sector is adopting business intelligence (BI) and analytics software applications to help manage risk, regulatory compliance, competition, and to understand customer behaviour.[13]

Relevant Information for Decision Making

Managers make more efficient and higher-quality decisions when they carefully identify information that is relevant to a given decision. **Relevant information** helps decision makers evaluate and choose among alternative courses of action. It concerns the future and varies with the action taken. On the other hand, **irrelevant information** does not vary with the action taken and, therefore, is not useful for decision making. Although the information may be accurate, it simply does not help the decision maker evaluate the alternatives. Whether a given type of information is relevant or irrelevant depends on the decision being made and other factors.

Relevant and Irrelevant Cash Flows

Cash flows are commonly used as information in management decisions. Thus, managers often need to distinguish between relevant and irrelevant cash flows. **Relevant cash flows** are **incremental cash flows**; that is, they occur under one course of action or decision alternative but not under another. Such cash flows are also called **avoidable cash flows** because they are avoided if the course of action or decision alternative is not taken. They are relevant because they help managers distinguish among alternatives. Suppose management is deciding between two courses of action: whether to lease or build office space. The costs of constructing the building are avoidable cash flows if management chooses the lease alternative. Therefore, the costs of constructing the building are relevant to the lease-or-build decision.

Irrelevant cash flows, also called **unavoidable cash flows**, occur regardless of which course of action or decision alternative is chosen. They are irrelevant to a specific decision because they do not help managers choose among alternatives. Whether the organization leases or builds office space, it will still incur electrical costs for lighting. Therefore, electrical costs are an unavoidable cash flow, making them irrelevant to the lease-or-build decision.

Relevance of Income Statement Information

Because financial statements are readily available, managers tend to use income statements to help them identify relevant information. However, the information in income statements may or may not be relevant for a given decision.

▶ **CHAPTER REFERENCE**

Chapter 2 provides formal definitions and more details about direct materials, direct labour, manufacturing overhead, fixed costs, and variable costs.

Costs in an income statement are categorized as product and period costs. For a manufacturer, **product costs** are the total manufacturing costs of units that are sold during the period, usually called **costs of goods sold** on the income statement. Other operating costs, such as marketing, advertising, and administration, are called **period costs**. Product costs include the costs of direct materials, direct labour, and manufacturing overhead. Following are examples of these costs for a snowboard manufacturer. Direct materials include the lumber for each board's base, metal strips for the edges, and fibreglass coatings. Direct labour is the labour required to put these materials together. Manufacturing overhead consists of all manufacturing costs other than direct materials and direct labour.[14] For a snowboard manufacturing plant, equipment costs, salaries for supervisors, and many costs related to operating the physical plant are categorized as manufacturing overhead costs and are assigned to each board or batch of boards using one of many allocation methods that we will learn in later chapters of this textbook.

---

[13]*The Role of Business Intelligence and Analytics in the Canadian Financial Services Sector: An Analysis of Trends, Challenges, and Strategies*, International Data Corporation (IDC), www.idc.com/getdoc.jsp?containerId=CA1BDA14.
[14] For more information about snowboard manufacturing, see B. Fox, *Revolution Snowboard Factory Tour*, video available at vimeo.com/3913183.

Some costs are variable—their total amounts increase or decrease in proportion with production volumes. For example, each board requires a thin strip of wood as the base and a metal strip for the edges. Therefore, the total cost of lumber and metal increases in proportion to the number of boards manufactured. Other product costs are fixed—they do not increase or decrease proportionately with changes in production volume. For example, the supervisor's salary and factory building depreciation are fixed costs.

For many business decisions, relevant information includes the incremental cost to produce additional units of a product. Managers tend to estimate this cost using the cost per unit from their income statements. However, accountants calculate cost of goods sold by combining fixed and variable manufacturing costs and calculating an average cost for each unit. Therefore, cost of goods sold includes fixed costs, which are often irrelevant for decision making. In addition, relevant costs might include some period costs, which managers may overlook. The following illustration provides an example of the problems encountered when the income statement is used to make a decision about internal operations.

example

abassaka/iStockphoto

snow-blade snowboards
IDENTIFYING RELEVANT COSTS

Snow-Blade Snowboards manufactures and sells snowboards. Recently, a representative from a sporting goods distributor in Finland contacted Kris Kransky, the general manager, about purchasing 1,000 snowboards at $100 each. The distributor does not currently sell snowboards and would like a one-time special price to avoid a large loss if snowboard sales are slow. This offer is much lower than Snow-Blade's normal selling price of $250 each. Kris would like to accept the order, but she is sure that this sale will result in a loss. The owner of Snow-Blade monitors financial performance at the end of each year and will require a full explanation for any unexpected decreases in income.

To estimate the loss on this sale, Kris examines last year's income statement.[15]

Snow-Blade Snowboards: Traditional Income Statement

Revenue	$12,500,000
Cost of goods sold	6,500,000
Gross margin	6,000,000
Selling and administration	3,750,000
Operating income	$ 2,250,000

She knows that cost of goods sold is the manufacturing cost for the units sold last year. She divides this cost by 50,000 (the number of snowboards sold) and finds that the cost is $130 per board. Therefore, she estimates that the company would lose $30 per board, or a total of $30,000 for the order. However, she wants to accept the order because the distributor promised to place a larger order at a higher price if the boards sell well.

Before Kris makes the decision, she checks with the company's accountant, Senad Mustafic, who tells her that cost of goods sold on the income statement includes both relevant and irrelevant costs for this decision. He draws the picture given in Exhibit 1.10, showing Kris the flow of costs in Snow-Blade's accounting system. The company sells all boards as they are produced, so none of the costs remained in inventory.

Senad explains that the direct materials costs include the cost of wood and laminate for each board. Direct labour cost reflects the time employees use to finish each board, and production workers are paid on an hourly basis. These costs increase proportionately with each board manufactured, so they are relevant. However, the overhead costs include the salary

---

[15] The income statements presented in this chapter assume that no beginning or ending inventories exist. In Chapter 14, the effects on income of balance sheet inventory levels are explored thoroughly.

▶EXHIBIT 1.10

Accounting for Costs at
Snow-Blade Snowboards

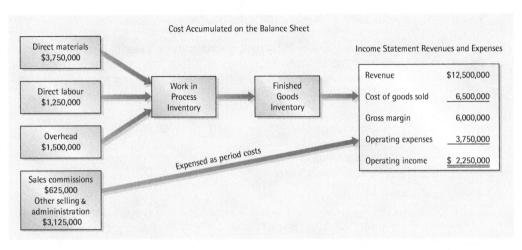

of the plant supervisor, depreciation on equipment, property taxes, and other similar costs. These costs are irrelevant because they are fixed and these costs will be incurred regardless of whether or not this special order is taken. Next, Senad checks the current capacity levels in the plant. He finds that the plant is operating at about 60% capacity; maximum operating capacity is around 80,000 boards. Therefore, accepting the order should not affect plant capacity-related costs or displace other orders. He also confirms that this year's prices for materials and wages for labour are the same as last year's.

Senad then organizes costs in a variable cost income statement format that separates variable and fixed costs. Kris can use this statement to develop information for internal decisions. She needs to be able to identify costs that increase proportionately with units produced and costs that generally do not change with volume changes. Kris and Senad discuss the following information.

Snow-Blade Snowboards: Variable Cost Income Statement	
Revenue	$12,500,000
Variable costs:	
Direct materials	3,750,000
Direct labour	1,250,000
Sales commissions	625,000
Total variable costs	$ 5,625,000
Contribution margin	6,875,000
Fixed costs:	
Manufacturing overhead	1,500,000
Selling and administration	3,125,000
Operating income	$ 2,250,000

Senad asks Kris if she will pay a sales commission for the units sold to the Finnish distributor. Because the distributor contacted her directly and no salespeople were involved, no commission will be paid. Therefore, relevant costs for the decision include only direct materials ($3,750,000) and direct labour ($1,250,000), which vary with production. Total relevant costs are $5,000,000 for last year's production volume of 50,000 snowboards, or $100 per board. Thus, the best estimate of incremental cost for units sold to the Finnish distributor is $100 per board. With a selling price of $100, Kris would expect no effect on operating income. Kris is very happy with this new information and asks Senad to provide her with both traditional income statements and variable cost income statements in the future. ▪

Importance of Identifying Relevant Information

As you can see from the Snow-Blade Snowboards example, it is important for decision makers to identify the relevant (incremental) cash flows. Failure to do so often leads to poor decisions. Identifying relevant information is a useful skill that requires practice. We will work on developing this skill throughout this textbook.

1-1 self-study problem   Relevant Costs

LO4

Micro-Fan Manufacturer produces one model of mini-fan that sells for $9 each. Direct labour workers are paid on an hourly basis and work only when needed. "Other" manufacturing overhead costs do not vary with changes in production levels. During November, 50,000 fans were produced and sold, and the company incurred the following costs.

Direct materials	$ 50,000
Direct labour	100,000
Manufacturing overhead:	
Supervisor's salary	40,000
Utilities	10,000
Depreciation	25,000
Other	5,000
Selling and administration costs	
Advertising	30,000
Sales commissions	20,000
Administration	115,000

required

A. Prepare a traditional income statement with product costs categorized as cost of goods sold.
B. Prepare a variable cost income statement with product costs separated into fixed and variable categories.
C. The accountant at Micro-Fan wants to estimate costs for next year's operations and believes that fan sales will increase to 53,000 units. This volume of production is within current capacity levels. Prepare an estimate of total costs at that level of volume. (*Hint*: Remember that fixed costs do not change with changes in volumes, but variable costs change proportionately.)

See the solution on page 28.

Business Risk

LO5 Describe how business risk affects management decision making

In a perfect world, managers would be able to perfectly foresee the future and use accounting information to make "correct" decisions. But the world is not perfect! **Business risk** is the possibility that an event could occur that interferes with an organization's ability to meet strategic goals or operating plans. Examples of business risks are shown in Exhibit 1.11. Some events, such as a hurricane or tsunami, may occur infrequently but have devastating effects. Other events, such as product returns under warranty, occur regularly but could escalate if production processes fall out of control. The degree of business risk varies across organizations, industries, geographic regions, and time periods.

Risk Management

Top managers are responsible for addressing business risks, taking calculated risks across the enterprise, and appropriately managing and mitigating the risks for the benefit of the stakeholders. Because business risks may be unknown and often interact to create even larger risks, experts advise managers to continually identify, assess, mitigate, and monitor relevant business risks in a comprehensive and integrated way, a process referred to as **enterprise risk management (ERM)**. Managers often use one or more of the four levers of control (see Exhibit 1.8) to ensure that management's risk policies are followed, and to monitor the environment for changes in business risk. Because of their knowledge of risk assessment, control, and measurement, accountants often play a key role in enterprise risk management.[16]

---

[16] Perhaps the most commonly used framework for enterprise risk management was published by the accounting profession: Committee of Sponsoring Organizations of the Treadway Commission, *Enterprise Risk Management—Integrated Framework*, 2004.

► EXHIBIT 1.11

Examples of Business Risks

Economic and Financial	Political and Social	Reputation	Weather
• Economic collapse • Changes in credit, interest, and currency markets • Strategic risks (e.g., change in customer tastes, unanticipated competition, joint venture/alliance relations, change in technology) • Change in cost/availability of labour or other resources	• Government policy or regulation change • Confinement or imprisonment of employees or families • Lawlessness and hostile demonstration • Civil war or military coup • Expropriation or forced renegotiation of royalties • Tax law changes • Foreign market protectionism	• Perceived quality • Product obsolescence • Government and/or regulatory investigation • Public boycott/condemnation • Human rights abuses • Class action lawsuits • Rumours, gossip, libel, slander • Noncompliance with laws, regulations, internal policies	• Hurricane, typhoon, tornado, waterspout • Earthquake • Flood • Wildfire • Mudslide • Extreme heat or cold • Climate change • Lightning • Sinkhole

Environmental and Man-made	Psychopathic, Criminal and Terrorist	Informational and Operational	People, Legal, Health, and Other
• Chemical, biological, radioactive, or nuclear release • Fire or explosion • Noise or dust pollution • Carbon dioxide, other hazardous gas, or liquid emission • Building, mine, facility condemnation or collapse • Damage from water, asbestos, or mould • Animal/insect infestation	• Product tampering • Terrorist acts • Arson or explosion • Sabotage, kidnapping, extortion, vandalism • Fraud, theft, embezzlement • Workplace violence • Economic espionage • Product counterfeiting	• Theft or other loss of proprietary/confidential data • Poor information quality • Technology failure • Key customer or supplier loss • Insufficient capacity • Technology obsolescence • Project management failure • Sourcing failures • Poor sales strategy/execution • Failure to innovate • Logistics disruptions • Uncompetitive cost structure	• Disease or health epidemic • Transportation accident • Loss of key personnel • Corporate governance issues • Labour slowdown or strike • Sexual harassment, workplace discrimination, wrongful dismissal, or labour law noncompliance • Executive misdeeds, bribes, or other conduct violations • Accidents, errors, omissions • Inability to attract talent

Adapted from G. S. Lynch, *At Your Own Risk: How the Risk-Conscious Culture Meets the Challenge of Business Change*, Hoboken, NJ: John Wiley and Sons, 2008, Exhibit 1.1: Risk Triggers, p. 19.

Although good risk management practices reduce the likelihood of negative consequences, it is impossible to ensure that all risks have been properly identified and mitigated. Even highly competent managers may be caught unaware. Looking south of our border, for example, between June 2006 and March 2009, homes in Phoenix, Arizona, lost an average of 53% in value.[17] In 2006, 12.8% of Phoenix jobs were in construction, compared to 8% in the rest of the country.[18] As these jobs were lost, other industries were also affected. Bankruptcy filings in Phoenix increased 91% from April 2008 to April 2009, while in the rest of the U.S. filings had increased 36%.[19] The business landscape in Phoenix changed

[17] D. Whitford, "Real Estate: What Happened in Phoenix," *Fortune Magazine*, June 12, 2009, pp. 62–68.
[18] B. Beard, "Valley Still Struggling from Recession as Other Areas Heal," *The Arizona Republic*, December 15, 2009, at www.azcentral.com/business/articles/2009/12/14/20091214biz-brookings1215.html.
[19] R. Wiles, "Phoenix-Area Bankruptcy Filings Jump 91%," *The Arizona Republic*, May 6, 2009, at www.azcentral.com/business/articles/2009/05/06/20090506biz-Bankruptcy0507.html.

> **EXHIBIT 1.12**
Management Decisions Clouded by
Business Risk

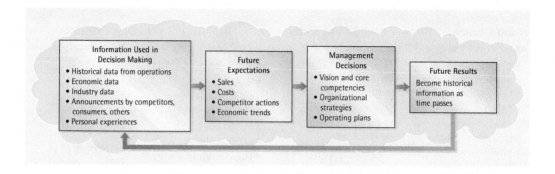

radically and quickly, forcing business owners and managers to reconsider operations and make difficult choices. These risks were magnified in Phoenix but were part of a worldwide shift in economic conditions.

Business Risk and Cost Management

Why are we learning about business risk in Chapter 1 of a cost management textbook? Management accounting information is used to help managers make business decisions, which almost always involve business risk. In the Snow-Blade Snowboards example, the general manager estimated the cost of producing and selling additional snowboards based on prior-year costs. The manager could not be certain that costs would remain unchanged, and it might not have been possible to foresee all possible costs—including the potential indirect effects of selling to a customer at a deeply discounted price. In other words, virtually all business decisions are clouded by business risk, as illustrated in Exhibit 1.12. Because the future cannot be seen, and even historical information is imperfect, decision makers cannot perfectly predict future results.

1-2 self-study problem   Business Risk

LO5

Top Flight Surveillance Company was developing a very small video camera system that would allow flight officers to monitor and record passenger behaviour from the cockpit of any airplane. The research and development costs began to increase at an alarming rate, and managers decided to stop developing the product.

required

A. Identify as many business risks as you can in evaluating the viability of this new video product.
B. Pick one of the items you identified in part (A) and explain why managers cannot completely eliminate the risk.

See the solution on page 29.

Decision-Making Biases

LO6 Appreciate how biases affect management decision making

Managers are likely to make poor decisions when they fail to recognize and correct for biases. **Biases** are systematic distortions in judgment. Three types of bias are particularly troublesome in management decision making:

▶ **Information bias:** Errors in judgment caused by data that are consistently overestimated, underestimated, or misrepresented.
▶ **Cognitive bias:** Errors in judgment caused by the way people's minds process information.
▶ **Predisposition bias:** Errors in judgment caused by preferences, attitudes, or emotions that prevent objective analysis.

Look for a "Risk of Biased Decisions" box in each chapter to learn about a range of biases that cause poor decisions. This chapter's box introduces nonrational escalation of commitment. Also, the Snow-Blade Snowboards example demonstrated a type of information bias: the average cost per unit overestimated relevant cost for the manager's decision to accept or reject a customer order.

●●● RISK OF BIASED DECISIONS : NONRATIONAL ESCALATION OF COMMITMENT

Sometimes managers make a poor decision and then commit to using more resources based on the original investment for that decision. Economists call this behaviour nonrational escalation of commitment. Behavioural researchers find that it is difficult for people to exclude irrelevant past expenditures, called *sunk costs*, when making decisions. Managers tend to inappropriately escalate commitment in situations such as the following:

1. Managers may look for evidence that confirms their belief that the first decision was appropriate and ignore disconfirming evidence. They do not recognize that further investment is likely to result in further poor performance.
2. If losses are incurred as a result of the first decision, managers tend to increase investment, hoping to recoup losses from the first decision.
3. Managers do not want others to know that a poor decision was made and may believe that further investment will hide the poor decision from others.
4. When managers are bidding against another company to buy a target firm, competitive irrationality may cause them to offer a price that is higher than the value of the target firm.

To reduce this tendency, managers should seek the opinion of a neutral third party as part of their decision-making process before investing more funds in a poor-performing project.

1-3 self-study problem   Decision Bias

LO 6

Todd Emeril's sister is deciding whether to open a small restaurant near the local university. Todd developed a spreadsheet to estimate the sales volume his sister could expect at the restaurant. Todd believes that his sister's cooking is exceptionally good and that students will flock to the restaurant, particularly for dinner when meal prices are higher. To test his assumption that students would enjoy his sister's recipes, Todd invited a number of his friends to eat dinner at his sister's home. A few of his friends were not that impressed with the food, but Todd assumes they would be in the minority when he estimates the sales volume.

required

A. In what ways does Todd appear to be biased?
B. How could Todd recognize and control for his biases?

See the solution on page 29.

Quality of Management Decision Making

Decision quality refers to the characteristics of a decision that affect the likelihood of achieving a positive outcome. Uncertainty and bias reduce decision quality. On average, higher-quality decisions have more positive outcomes resulting from better information as well as better decision processes. Organizations often use complex and sophisticated information

LO 7 Determine how managers make higher-quality decisions

systems to gather and organize information for decision making. Because of this sophistication, some decision makers are mistakenly confident that the information they use is correct, and they ignore uncertainty and risk. Other decision makers, recognizing that uncertainties and risk always cloud decisions, go to the other extreme; instead of relying on imperfect information, they believe it is sufficient to use only their intuition to make important business decisions. Neither of these approaches is optimal.

Exhibit 1.13 summarizes the path to higher-quality decisions. First, higher-quality information has fewer uncertainties, is more complete, and is directly relevant to the decision. It is timely, helping managers as they make decisions, not after the fact. In addition, it has value: the benefits exceed the cost of generating the information. An important role of accounting or other information systems is to capture higher-quality information and report it in a way that improves its usefulness for decision making. Secondly, higher-quality reports are more directly relevant to the decision. They are easily understood and readily available to decision makers. Thirdly, a higher-quality decision-making process is more thorough and unbiased. It is more clearly focused on organizational priorities and encourages strategic, creative, and visionary thinking.

Ethical Decision Making

LO 8 Explain the importance of ethical decision making

We are each responsible for our own behaviour. Furthermore, managers and accountants are responsible for the behaviour of the organizations they manage. For this reason, ethical behaviour is both an individual and an organizational obligation. A process for **ethical decision making** is presented in Exhibit 1.14.

The unethical behaviour of a few accountants and managers has greatly affected investor beliefs and the value of the stock market. When investors lose faith in information produced by organizations, they are unwilling to invest, and market downturns occur. These events happen because accountants and managers fail to practise ethical decision making.[20] Ethical behaviour is required of every employee within an organization.

>EXHIBIT 1.13

Path to Higher-Quality Management Decisions

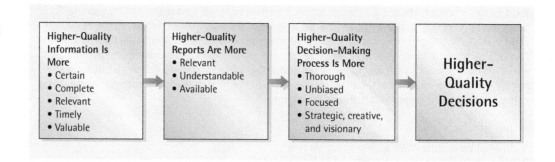

>EXHIBIT 1.14

Process for Ethical Decision Making

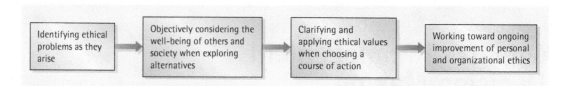

---

[20] See, for example, I. J. Dugan, "Before Enron, Greed Helped Sink the Respectability of Accounting," *The Wall Street Journal*, March 14, 2002, p. A1; and "High Profiles in Hot Water," *The Wall Street Journal*, June 28, 2002, p. B1.

ETHICAL CONSIDERATIONS IN OUTSOURCING DECISIONS

During the 2000s, Canadian companies outsourced many products and ingredients from global suppliers. When external vendors supply products and services, it becomes more difficult for the purchasing firms to detect ethical and legal problems that affect quality. Manufacturers and retailers often do not know that problems in the outsourced goods exist until customers begin to complain or the popular media exposes ethical dilemmas. In the last decade, outsourced products created problems for firms in a number of industries. As discussed more fully in Chapter 4, these problems can be characterized as follows:

Denis Kovin/Shutterstock

- Recalls and payments for injuries and deaths resulting from unsafe products and ingredients used in industries that manufacture, distribute, and sell prepackaged food, children's toys, and pet food.

- Labour controversies regarding the reduction in Canadian manufacturing and service jobs, and the low wages and poor working conditions for labour in developing countries.

- Loss of control over environmental quality and sustainability policies and practices when products are manufactured in other countries.

REPUTATION EFFECTS OF SUPPLIERS' UNETHICAL ACTIONS

To avoid potential ethical and legal problems associated with the behaviour of suppliers, management accountants need to address a variety of ethics-related questions: What are the ethical values of outsource partners? Do suppliers behave honestly and with integrity? What are their labour and environmental practices? Is their product quality reliable? What is the potential loss of reputation from suppliers' unethical actions? Should control systems be used to prevent ethical and legal problems?

Conflicting Interests

It is common in business situations for the interests of various parties to be at odds. For example, if one division's products compete successfully, another division may lose sales and then receive fewer of the organization's resources. If one person is promoted to the position of chief financial officer, someone else is not promoted, and that person may leave the firm in search of better opportunities elsewhere. If a company invests funds in an environmental protection program, less money may be available for shareholder dividends.

Motive for Ethical Behaviour

Do we expect people to resolve conflicts of interest by making choices in their own best interests? If so, this expectation raises another question: What do we mean by "best interests"? Do we necessarily mean greed, selfishness, and insensitivity? Although our society is based on capitalism, we do not believe that anything goes. More is at stake than financial gain or other supposed rewards. Integrity, reputation, self-respect, and social welfare are compelling rewards for ethical behaviour.

As discussed earlier in the chapter, organizations often use codes of ethics or other formal policies in their boundary control systems to encourage ethical behaviour. Similarly, governments establish laws, a type of boundary system, to prevent certain types of unethical behaviour. Boundary or diagnostic control systems could be used to prevent or more quickly identify the outsourcing ethics problems described in the Focus on Ethical Decision Making box.

Analyzing the Ethics of a Decision

One way to improve our ethical decision making is to apply the decision-making process in Exhibit 1.14 to a situation with ethical implications. The following discussion demonstrates analysis of ethical issues.

Identifying Ethical Problems As They Arise. Sometimes ethical problems are identified easily because they relate to clearly unacceptable behaviour. For example, most people agree that employees should not steal cash or other assets from an employer. Similarly, people agree that accountants should not falsify business records. However, some ethical problems are less obvious without careful thought or further investigation.

Sometimes biases prevent identification of an ethical problem. Although the controversy over outsourced labour has been publicized for many years, few problems with the ingredients in prepackaged human and pet food had arisen in the past. Managers probably held a predisposition bias by believing that outsource partners would hold similar values about food quality and apparently did not monitor their suppliers closely. A problem with bias and conflict of interest currently exists in the Canadian auditing profession. Although auditors generally believe they can remain objective while auditing the financial statements of managers who hire them, people increasingly perceive this as an unacceptable conflict of interest.

Even when an issue is seen as an ethical problem, the next course of action—what to do about it—may still be ambiguous. Should manufacturers discontinue outsource relationships when problems arise, or ask outsource partners to address the problem and monitor the process more closely? Similarly, disagreement exists about how auditor conflicts of interest should be resolved. When addressing an ethical problem, it helps to brainstorm about possible alternative courses of action. Sometimes decision makers close in too quickly on one solution when another alternative might be even better.

Objectively Considering the Well-Being of Others and Society. People are more likely to make ethically appropriate decisions when they objectively consider the effects of their actions on others. As discussed earlier in the chapter, biases can interfere with this aspect of ethical decision making. Decision makers should consider whether they might be biased, even if they are unaware of a bias, when evaluating the effects of their actions on others. According to Harvard Business School professor Max Bazerman, we can "recognize that honesty does not resolve the problem of conflicts of interest—even honest people are biased."[21]

Clarifying and Applying Ethical Values When Choosing a Course of Action. People often make decisions without carefully identifying the values they use. For example, managers may value cost reductions over quality implications in outsource decisions and not collect information about the effects of quality problems on overall costs.

Decision makers can improve ethical decision making by first clarifying their own ethical values and then ensuring that they consistently apply those values. Professional organizations often assist in the identification of ethical values. For example, the Chartered Professional Accountants (CPA) Canada has identified ethical conduct, fiduciary duty, integrity and due care, and objectivity as overarching principles that are essential to the ethical behaviour of management accountants (see the Business Practice box on the next page). Similarly, organizations often adopt a code of ethics to clarify acceptable ethical values for employees. To ensure ethical decision making, these types of ethical values should be prioritized as more important than other factors.

Working Toward Ongoing Improvement of Personal and Organizational Ethics. As instances of ethical wrongdoing have mounted over time, it has become increasingly clear that ethical behaviour is the responsibility of both individuals and organizations. In 2002, the U.S. Congress passed the Sarbanes-Oxley Act, which requires public company managers and boards of directors to assume greater legal responsibility. Managers are now required to self-assess internal controls and financial reporting risks. An organization's board of directors and its audit committee are required to increase their oversight of managers and auditors. The process of implementing the new requirements is an opportunity for organizations to reassess their policies and culture. The best organizations actively seek ways to learn from past behaviours and to continuously work toward becoming more ethical.[22]

---

[21] M. H. Bazerman, *Judgment in Managerial Decision Making*, 6th ed. (New York: John Wiley & Sons, 2006) p. 130.
[22] Protiviti Inc., *Insights on Today's Sarbanes-Oxley and Corporate Governance Challenges: Survey of Chief Financial Officers with 300 Publicly Held U.S. Companies* (white paper), September 2003.

Professional Conduct and Ethical Behaviour

> ⊠ BUSINESS PRACTICE
>
> The Chartered Professional Accountants of Canada (CPA Canada) represents highly qualified professionals who demonstrate an ongoing commitment to providing the highest standards of accounting, ethics, and best business practices. The organization and its affiliates have rules of professional conduct. For example, the Chartered Professional Accountants of Ontario (CPA Ontario) specifies the rules of professional conduct including an accountant's responsibilities regarding:
>
> - characteristics of a profession
> - fundamental principles governing conduct
> - ethical conflict resolution
> - fiduciary duty
> - personal character and ethical conduct
> - application of the rules
> - principles governing the responsibilities of firms, and
> - interpretation of the rules
>
> In addition, CPA Ontario's Rules of Professional Conduct outline the general rules: standards of conduct affecting the public interest, relations with fellow members and with non-members engaged in public accounting, organization and conduct of a professional practice, and rules of professional conduct applicable only to firms.
>
> For more information, refer to the CPA Ontario website, www.cpaontario.ca.
>
> *Source*: Chartered Professional Accountants of Ontario, *Rules of Professional Conduct*, February 2014. Accessed at www. cpaontario.ca/Resources/Membershandbook/1011page2635.pdf.

Steps for Better Thinking: A Decision-Making Process

Few management decisions can be made with absolute certainty. However, managers can improve the quality of decisions by using a higher-quality decision-making process. Steps for Better Thinking, presented in Exhibit 1B.1, is an example of a decision-making process that leads to higher-quality decisions.

L07 Determine how managers make higher-quality decisions

Steps for Better Thinking is a process for addressing open-ended problems—those with no single "correct" solution due to significant uncertainties, such as business risks. The decision maker's task for open-ended problems is to find the best, not the only, possible solution. Most management decisions are open ended; Steps for Better Thinking will improve your ability to address them.

Steps for Better Thinking is portrayed as a series of increasingly difficult skills that are needed for higher-quality decisions. Exhibit 1B.1 is portrayed as a set of steps, because strong performance in the lower-level skills sets the stage for strong performance in the higher-level skills. Conversely, if the lower-level skills are weak, then the entire structure will also be weak.

Knowing. The foundation of Steps for Better Thinking consists of the knowledge and basic skills needed to deal with a problem. To launch a project an organization would need to have knowledge in many areas, including the following:

- ▶ Tablet, social media, and satellite communications
- ▶ Consumer markets and distribution methods

> **EXHIBIT 1B.1**

Steps for
Better Thinking:
A Decision-Making
Process

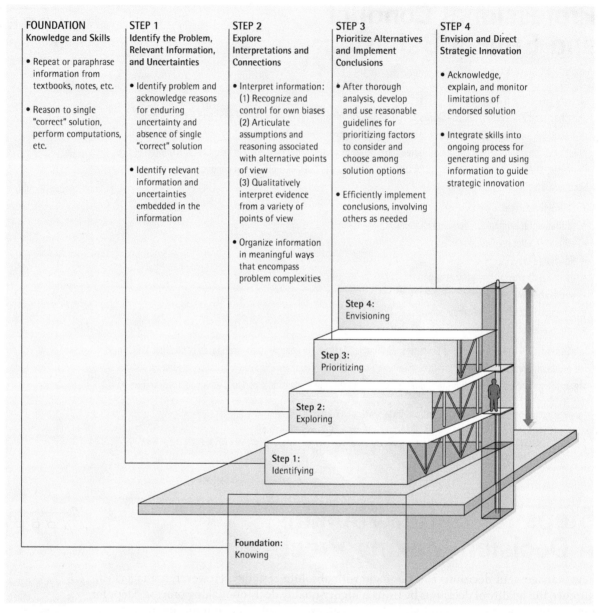

FOUNDATION Knowledge and Skills	STEP 1 Identify the Problem, Relevant Information, and Uncertainties	STEP 2 Explore Interpretations and Connections	STEP 3 Prioritize Alternatives and Implement Conclusions	STEP 4 Envision and Direct Strategic Innovation
• Repeat or paraphrase information from textbooks, notes, etc. • Reason to single "correct" solution, perform computations, etc.	• Identify problem and acknowledge reasons for enduring uncertainty and absence of single "correct" solution • Identify relevant information and uncertainties embedded in the information	• Interpret information: (1) Recognize and control for own biases (2) Articulate assumptions and reasoning associated with alternative points of view (3) Qualitatively interpret evidence from a variety of points of view • Organize information in meaningful ways that encompass problem complexities	• After thorough analysis, develop and use reasonable guidelines for prioritizing factors to consider and choose among solution options • Efficiently implement conclusions, involving others as needed	• Acknowledge, explain, and monitor limitations of endorsed solution • Integrate skills into ongoing process for generating and using information to guide strategic innovation

Step 4:
Envisioning

Step 3:
Prioritizing

Step 2:
Exploring

Step 1:
Identifying

Foundation:
Knowing

Source: © 2002, S. K. Wolcott, "Steps for Better Thinking: A Developmental Problem-Solving Process." Available at www.WolcottLynch.com.

▸ Research and development methods
▸ Technical knowledge and expertise for development of new technology
▸ Production processes and costs
▸ Sales and marketing strategies

Step 1—Identifying. This step involves identifying relevant information and uncertainties. Recognizing business risks, as highlighted in Exhibits 1.11 and 1.12, is also an extremely important part of managerial decision making. It usually requires much practice to become adept at this part of the process. There were many business risks in launching a new project, including customer preferences and the size of the customer market. Managers sometimes fail to adequately identify major risks. This failure, in turn, causes them to make decisions without adequate analysis, or to be overly confident in their decisions.

Step 2—Exploring. This step includes recognizing and controlling biases and more thoroughly considering uncertainties such as business risks, as emphasized earlier in exhibits 1.11 and 1.12, and also interpreting information from different viewpoints. For this kind of assessment, we must be adept at recognizing and evaluating assumptions, gauging the quality of information, and putting ourselves "in others' shoes." We can think of Step 2 as analyzing the strengths and weaknesses of different alternatives. Adequate performance of Step 2 is often the most time-consuming and important when addressing open-ended problems. Too often, decision makers are hasty and fail to thoroughly analyze the information related to a problem; they jump to a conclusion. Careful attention to Step 2 activities increases the probability of making the best decision. Very often, biases cause the managers to discount problematic issues.

Step 3—Prioritizing. Step 3 involves making trade-offs and choosing the best possible alternative, and then efficiently implementing it. For managers, these activities include ensuring that the organization's values, core competencies, and strategies are adequately considered. Managers must also ensure that business risks are adequately managed to achieve the organization's risk appetite. Efficient implementation includes motivating performance within the organization. Any weaknesses at Steps 1 and 2 automatically lead to weaknesses at Step 3. It is not possible to reach a high-quality decision when there are major unmitigated business risks or when managers are biased toward a course of action.

Step 4—Envisioning. This step is necessary because open-ended problems cannot be solved with absolute certainty and because the economic environment changes. Management decisions require monitoring, and possibly revision, during implementation and as new events occur over time. The most gifted decision makers act strategically to recognize change and new threats, and also to visualize new opportunities.

SUMMARY

LO1   Describe the process of strategic management and decision making

Overview of Management Decision Making

Measure, Monitor, and Motivate

SWOT ANALYSIS

Identify core competencies through study of strengths, weaknesses, opportunities, and threats

Identify the types of control systems that managers use

MANAGEMENT CONTROL SYSTEMS

Systems and routines to increase the likelihood of organizational success

Belief Systems	Boundary Systems	Diagnostic Control Systems	Interactive Control Systems
Create core values which enhance employees shared values to achieve the organization's goals.	Establish limits on individual behaviour to avoid organizational risks.	Measure, monitor, and motivate employees to achieve the organization's preset goals.	Require managers to communicate interactively and stimulate debates when the organization faces strategic uncertainties.

Explain the role of accounting information in strategic management

TERMINOLOGY

► Cost accounting
► Management accounting
► Financial accounting
► Strategic cost management
► Balanced scorecards

USES FOR WHICH ACCOUNTANTS GATHER DATA FROM INSIDE AND OUTSIDE THE ORGANIZATION

Creating external reports for

► Government
► Shareholders
► Other stakeholders

Creating internal reports for

► Evaluating and updating organizational strategies
► Communicating and monitoring operating plans
► Measuring, monitoring, and motivating performance

L04   Explain the information systems and information that are relevant for decision making

RELEVANT INFORMATION

Helps decision makers evaluate and choose among alternative courses of action by

- Being concerned about the future
- Varying with the action taken

Includes incremental (avoidable) cash flows

IRRELEVANT INFORMATION

Not useful for decision making

Includes unavoidable cash flows

FINANCIAL STATEMENT COSTS

Product costs/Cost of goods sold

Period costs

L05   Describe how business risk affects management decision making

BUSINESS RISK

Possibility that an event could occur and interfere with ability to meet strategic goals or operating plans

RISK APPETITE

Overall acceptable level of risk

EFFECTS OF BUSINESS RISK

Reduces the quality of decisions

ENTERPRISE RISK MANAGEMENT (ERM)

Continually identifying, assessing, mitigating, and monitoring relevant business risks in a comprehensive and integrated way

L06   Appreciate how biases affect management decision making

EFFECTS OF BIASES

Create barriers to high-quality of decisions

BIASES INHIBIT

- Recognition of business risks
- Thorough analyses
- Consideration of alternative viewpoints

- Critical evaluation of priorities
- Continuous improvement

BIAS CATEGORIES

- Information bias
- Cognitive bias
- Predisposition bias

L07   Determine how managers make higher-quality decisions

Path to Higher-Quality Decisionss

Higher-Quality Information Is More
- Certain
- Complete
- Relevant
- Timely
- Valuable

→

Higher-Quality Reports Are More
- Relevant
- Understandable
- Available

→

Higher-Quality Decision-Making Process Is More
- Thorough
- Unbiased
- Focused
- Strategic, creative, and visionary

→

Higher-Quality Decisions

SUMMARY

L08   Explain the importance of ethical decision making

PROCESS FOR ETHICAL DECISION MAKING

▶ Identify ethical problems as they arise
▶ Objectively consider the well-being of others and society when exploring alternatives
▶ Clarify and apply ethical values when choosing a course of action
▶ Work toward ongoing improvement of personal and organizational ethics

INDIVIDUAL AND ORGANIZATIONAL OBLIGATION

▶ Honest people may be unaware of unethical behaviour

REWARDS FOR ETHICAL BEHAVIOUR

▶ Integrity
▶ Reputation
▶ Self-respect
▶ Social welfare

APPENDIX 1A   Professional Conduct and Ethical Behaviour

CPA ONTARIO RULES OF PROFESSIONAL CONDUCT:

▶ Ethical Conduct
▶ Fiduciary duty

▶ Integrity and due care
▶ Objectivity

APPENDIX 1B   Steps for Better Thinking: A Decision-Making Process

Foundation—Knowing

Step 1—Identifying

Step 2—Exploring

Step 3—Prioritizing

Step 4—Envisioning

1-1 solution to self-study problem

A. Because the company sold all units produced, all of the product costs are included in cost of goods sold: $50,000 + $100,000 + $40,000 + $10,000 + $25,000 + $5,000 = $230,000. Period costs include all of the selling and administration costs: $30,000 + $20,000 + $115,000 = $165,000.

Micro-Fan Manufacturer: Traditional Income Statement	
Revenue	$450,000
Cost of goods sold	230,000
Gross margin	220,000
Selling and administration	165,000
Operating income	$ 55,000

B. Variable costs include direct materials, direct labour, and sales commissions. All of the manufacturing overhead costs are assumed to be fixed: $40,000 + $10,000 + $25,000 + $5,000 = $80,000. (*Note*: Utility costs might be partly variable.) Advertising and administrative costs are fixed: $30,000 + $115,000 = $145,000.

Micro-Fan Manufacturer: Variable Cost Income Statement

Revenue	$450,000
Variable costs:	
Direct materials	50,000
Direct labour	100,000
Sales commissions	20,000
Total variable costs	170,000
Contribution margin	280,000
Fixed costs:	
Manufacturing overhead	80,000
Selling and administration	145,000
Operating income	$ 55,000

C. The only costs that are expected to change with changes in production levels are the variable costs. At the original volume of 50,000 units, total variable costs were $170,000 (from part B), or $3.40 per unit. At production of 53,000 units, total variable costs are estimated to be $180,200 (53,000 × $3.40). Total fixed costs of $80,000 + $145,000 are not expected to change. Therefore, total costs for 53,000 units are expected to be $405,200 ($180,200 + $80,000 + $145,000).

1-2 solution to self-study problem

A. When answering this question, think about how circumstances might change, and review the risks listed in Exhibit 1.11. Some possible business risks for this problem include the following: Other types of security devices, such as impenetrable doors, might reduce the need for the videos. Airline companies might not want this type of product. Other possible uses for the camera might not be available. It might be difficult to estimate the additional time and money needed to develop the product. Competitors might be working on a similar product. Government regulations might prevent use of the product.

If it was difficult for you to identify more than two business risks, you should practise this skill. Look for questions at the end of each chapter that ask about business risk.

B. Knowing why managers cannot completely eliminate a risk will help you understand the difficulty of making decisions in the business world. Here is an example of an explanation for why managers cannot know whether competitors will be working on similar products. Product development is very secretive, so we do not usually know about similar new products until they are released. Product development may be happening all around the globe. If a small company were to release a similar product in a foreign country, news might not reach Top Flight Surveillance Company.

1-3 solution to self-study problem

A. Todd believes that his sister's cooking is good, and he ignores his friends' opinions that the cooking is not that good. If he does not account for this bias, the actual volume of sales at the restaurant will likely be lower than his estimate. In addition, he believes that students will buy dinners more often than lunches, so he could be overestimating cash inflows. He does not seem to know whether lunches or dinners contribute more to profits, on average. He does not explore the effects of competitors' prices and menus. He fails to consider whether students would be the best customers to attract.

B. It is usually easier to recognize someone else's biases than to recognize and control one's own biases! Todd might begin by asking himself whether he has a preference about opening the restaurant. If so, then he should carefully watch for bias as he develops the sales estimate. One way to control for bias is to use more formal methods for collecting and analyzing information. For example, Todd could ask potential customers to eat a meal and fill out a survey that has numerical ratings. When Todd tallies these ratings, he will probably be less biased in interpreting the results. Also, he could ask an independent person to interpret the survey findings. He could ask friends to compare the value of the meals his sister cooks with the value of meals from other restaurants by giving them price information with the free meals.

QUESTIONS

1.1 Explain the importance of the following types of management decisions: organizational vision, organizational core competencies, organizational strategies, and operating plans.

1.2 Why do managers need to measure, monitor, and motivate performance?

1.3 List three types of internal reports and explain how each is used. List three types of external reports and explain how each is used.

1.4 What types of information in addition to cost accounting are needed for management decisions?

1.5 Explain why avoidable (incremental) cash flows are relevant. Explain why unavoidable cash flows are irrelevant.

1.6 What are business risks, and how do they affect the quality of management decisions?

1.7 What are biases, and how do they affect the quality of management decisions?

1.8 In your own words, explain the path to higher-quality decisions (Exhibit 1.13).

1.9 Explain why it is important for both individuals and organizations to behave ethically.

1.10 In your own words, define ethical behaviour. Why do accountants have a professional responsibility to behave ethically?

1.11 In your own words, define nonrational escalation of commitment. Can you think of situations where you or people you know have inappropriately escalated their commitment to a decision or course of action?

1.12 Define belief systems and boundary systems in your own words, and describe the similarities and differences in the parts they play in the four levers of control.

1.13 Define interactive control systems in your own words, and explain the part they play in the four levers of control.

1.14 Define diagnostic control systems in your own words, and explain the part they play in the four levers of control.

1.15 Explain how the four levers of control are used together to increase an organization's strategic success.

MULTIPLE-CHOICE QUESTIONS

1.16 Which of the following statements is true?
  a. Management accounting is guided by IFRS or Canadian ASPE.
  b. Management accounting information is mainly for external users.
  c. Management accounting is future oriented.
  d. Management accounting information is mainly quantitative.

1.17 Which of the following statements is *not* true?
  a. Unavoidable cost is relevant in decision making.
  b. Avoidable cost is relevant in decision making.

  c. Additional investment is relevant in decision making.
  d. Cost saving is relevant in decision making.

1.18 Which of the following is *not* one of the components of ethical decision making?
  a. Identify ethical problems as they arise.
  b. Objectively consider the well-being of others and society when exploring alternatives.
  c. Clarify and apply ethical values, and choose a course of action that avoids the exposure of wrongdoing.
  d. Work toward ongoing improvement of personal and organizational ethics.

1.19 Which of the following statements is *not* true?
  a. Monitoring and motivating are part of an implementation function.
  b. Budgeting is a part of a control function.
  c. Performance measure is a part of a control function.
  d. Budget is a quantitative expression of a plan.

1.20 Which of the following characteristics is *not* true of high-quality information?
  a. Timely
  b. Relevant
  c. Complete
  d. Circumventing

EXERCISES

1.21 Types of Manager Decisions Suppose that each of the following is an activity conducted by Microsoft Corporation.

L01

REQUIRED Identify whether each activity is most likely part of (1) organizational strategies; (2) operating plans; (3) actual operations; or (4) measuring, monitoring, and motivating. For each item, explain why.

  A. Comparing the timeliness of the development steps of a new release of Windows® with the timeline that was laid out to guide development.
  B. Developing a timeline for release of new Windows and Microsoft Office® products over the next year.
  C. Debugging the next version of Windows.
  D. Providing technical support to customers who are having problems with Microsoft Office.
  E. Estimating cash expenditures for the next year.
  F. Comparing budgeted costs to actual costs, and discussing major differences with department managers.
  G. Deciding whether to construct a new building on the Microsoft campus.

1.22 Types of Personal Decisions Many of the ideas in this chapter relate not only to what organizations do but also to your personal life.

L01

REQUIRED For each of the following, give an example related to your personal life.

  A. Vision
  B. Core competencies
  C. Long-term strategies
  D. Short-term planning
  E. Actual results
  F. Measuring, monitoring, and motivating

1.23 Relevant Costs Avery Car Rental charges its customers $26 per day plus $0.20 per kilometre. Its competition rents cars for $35 per day and $0.08 per kilometre.

L04

REQUIRED How many kilometres would a customer need to drive on a four-day rental so that the cost of the two alternatives would be the same?

1.24 Relevant Costs Suppose the current average cost per kilometre for operating a car is $0.40. Susan is required to drive to a client's office that is 50 kilometres away (100 kilometres round-trip). She can use her own car and be reimbursed $0.30 per kilometre or use a company-owned vehicle.

L04

REQUIRED **A.** What costs would be included in the current average cost per kilometre that might be irrelevant to Susan's decision to drive 100 kilometres?
  B. Suppose Susan determined that the cost of gasoline and maintenance for her car is about $0.25 per kilometre. Which alternative is better?

1.25 Relevant Costs, Other Relevant Factors Netflix is a service that allows subscribers to rent three DVDs at a time for $21.95 per month. As soon as a customer returns one DVD, Netflix sends another. Customers can return as many movies as they want during a month, and they can keep each DVD for as long as they want.

L04

REQUIRED **A.** How many DVDs do you need to rent per month to be indifferent between the cost of renting movies from a video store at $3.95 each and subscribing to Netflix?
  B. What factors other than cost would influence your decision?

1.26 Levers of Control, Ethics Organizations sometimes suffer financially or go out of business because of fraudulent financial statements and unethical and illegal behaviour. Answer the following questions about such organizations.

LO2, LO8

REQUIRED   **A.** Some organizations may prioritize financial goals as part of their core values, and their corporate cultures may encourage managers to overlook unethical behaviour in meeting these goals. Which lever of control is most likely to address this problem? List two specific types of control used in this system that would help reduce unethical behaviour.

B. In some corporations, unethical behaviour is viewed as a risk to be avoided. Identify the lever of control that addresses such risks and describe two specific types of control used in this system.

1.27 Effects of Biases Suppose you own a small fast-food store in a large shopping mall. You hired a manager six months ago so that you could open another store in a new location. The financial performance over the last six months has not been as good as it was when you managed the outlet. The manager, who seems to be overly optimistic about the store's performance, has given you a spreadsheet forecasting large increases in sales and decreased costs over the next six months.

LO6

REQUIRED   **A.** In your own words, describe information bias, cognitive bias, and predisposition bias.

B. Are the manager's forecasts of sales and costs likely to be biased? Explain.

C. Identify ideas for checking the reliability of the revenue and cost estimates.

1.28 Master Data Management, Control Systems, Quality of Information Most organizations do not have a single, centralized system that shares data across all transaction processes. Instead, organizations tend to have different systems for different processes or different systems across business units. This practice makes it difficult to generate organization-wide reports or to share data that are needed by multiple units. To address this problem, Warren Thornthwaite of the Kimball Group recommends creating a data governance function to facilitate and maintain an enterprise-wide database. The data governance function would also ensure that common rules are used throughout the organization to enter data into the database.

LO2, LO3, LO7

Source: W. Thornthwaite, "Kimball University: Pick the Right Approach to MDM," *Intelligent Enterprise*, February 2007, available at www.intelligententerprise.com.

REQUIRED   **A.** Describe how an enterprise-wide database might be used in an organization's (1) diagnostic control systems and (2) interactive control systems.

B. Why is it useful for common rules to be used throughout an organization to enter data into an enterprise-wide database? How does this practice improve the quality of information in a diagnostic or interactive control system?

1.29 Ethics, Culture, Belief, and Boundary Systems Based on results of a 2005 national survey on ethics sponsored by Ethics Resource Center and Working Values, Amber Seligson and Laurie Choi made the following recommendation:

LO2, LO8

> *Organizations that dedicate substantial resources to the communication of ethical values may find that resources are better spent encouraging leadership to set a good example of ethical behavior, establishing organizational trustworthiness in keeping promises, and helping employees to make ethical decisions.* (p. 5)

Source: A. L. Seligson and L. Choi, "Critical Elements of an Organizational Ethical Culture," Ethics Resource Center and Working Values, 2006, available at www.ethics.org/resource/critical-elements-organizational-ethical-culture.

REQUIRED   **A.** Explain how an organization's culture can enhance or weaken employee ethical behaviour.

B. Are ethical values part of an organization's belief system, boundary system, or both? Explain.

1.30 Pace of Change, Historical Data, Control Systems In the past, organizations have often used 20 to 30 years of historical data to help develop strategic plans for the next 5 to 10 years. However, the fast pace of change in today's business world causes historical data to become irrelevant more quickly. Data Vault founder Dan Linstedt argues that managers should develop strategic plans that allow for more agile decision making in response to changing conditions.

LO1, LO2, LO3, LO4, LO5

Source: D. E. Linstedt, "Competitive Decision Time Is Shrinking," Blog, December 13, 2005, available at www.b-eye-network.com/blogs/linstedt/.

REQUIRED   **A.** Explain why rapid change causes historical data to become irrelevant more quickly.

B. When economic conditions are changing rapidly, explain why diagnostic control systems become less useful for organizational success.

C. Describe how interactive control systems can help managers adapt to changing economic conditions.

1.31 Relevant Costs, Uncertainties Toys for Boys has 10,000 toy cars painted a grey colour that are not selling well.

LO4, LO5 The selling price of the cars could be reduced from the current price of $8.00 to $5.00 each. Alternatively, the cars could be painted red at a cost of $2.00 each and sold for $8.00. Red cars sell very well.

REQUIRED **A.** Should Toys for Boys paint the cars? Show your calculations.
B. Which option seems to have less uncertainty? Discuss.

1.32 Relevant Costs, Risks, Other Relevant Factors, Bias This semester, you moved to an apartment 8 kilometres from

LO4, LO5, campus and will commute to classes three times a week. This decision will let you achieve significant savings.
LO6, LO7 However, you have not yet decided whether to use your car or ride the bus to get to campus. You estimate the following costs for each alternative:

Driving Your Car
Monthly payments on your car of $220.00
Maintenance expenses of $37.00 per month. (This cost is an average and reflects oil changes, car washes, and lubricants.)
University parking fees of $150.00 per semester (four months)
Approximately $60.00 in gasoline per month. (You estimate a total of 600 kilometres driven every month, which includes approximately 200 kilometres per month for three trips per week to campus—approximately 12 round trips per month.)

Riding the Bus
You have two alternatives regarding the purchase of bus tickets:

1. You may buy a semester ticket with unlimited rides for $225.00 per semester (Bus A).
2. You may purchase each ticket individually for $2.00 each way (Bus B).
    If you decide to buy the semester bus pass, you estimate that you will ride the bus quite often and replace approximately 200 kilometres from your car's monthly allowance of 600 kilometres.

REQUIRED **A.** Based only on cost, which alternative would you choose? Show your calculations. Assume that a semester lasts four months and that you will always ride the bus to campus if you choose one of the bus options.
B. Discuss uncertainties about your calculations for Part A.
C. List factors that could affect your decision but that cannot be valued in dollars.
D. Suppose that you had never ridden a bus. Would you be biased against the bus option? Explain.

PROBLEMS

1.33 Risks You have been admitted to the College of Business at your university. You decide to become an accounting

LO6 major and are now planning the sequence of classes that you would like to take over the next two years.

REQUIRED **A.** List several uncertainties about your class sequence. Include in your list the uncertainties at the beginning of your accounting program, as well as uncertainties that might occur as you register for courses each term.
B. Choose one of the items you identified in Part A and explain how it affects your planning.

1.34 Relevant Information, Bias Suppose you are responsible for ordering a replacement for your office photocopy

LO4, LO6, machine. Part of your job is to decide whether to buy it or lease it.
LO7

REQUIRED **A.** Describe something that could be considered relevant information in this decision and explain why it is relevant.
B. Describe something that could be considered irrelevant information in this decision and explain why it is irrelevant.
C. Explain why it was important to distinguish between relevant and irrelevant information in this problem.
D. Suppose the copy machine service person is paid a commission on all of the parts he sells. Would this ompensation method bias his recommendations about the quality and number of parts that you should purchase? Explain.

1.35 Business Risk, Degree of Risk, Risk Appetite Community Children's Hospital can invest in one of two different projects.

LO5 The first project is to purchase and operate a hotel that is located two blocks from the hospital. The CEO of the hospital has no experience operating a hotel, but the hospital does provide rooms for inpatients, and so she is familiar with cleaning requirements and managing housekeeping staff. However, the hospital does little advertising and does not have a large public relations staff. In addition, the hospital and hotel are located in a part of town that is deteriorating.

The other investment opportunity is to replace the heart monitors in the neonatal intensive care unit (critical care for newborns and infants). The new monitors would provide a range of functions, including monitoring the body temperature and blood pressure of infants, as well as monitoring heart functions. Each monitor can be used for up to four infants, with information about each infant forwarded to one computer that is monitored by a special technician. The current monitors are bedside monitors that need to be read every 10 minutes by nursing staff.

REQUIRED
A. Prepare a list of uncertainties the CEO faces if she buys the hotel.
B. Prepare a list of uncertainties the CEO faces if she replaces the heart monitors.
C. Which scenario appears to have a greater degree of uncertainty? Why?
D. Explain how the hospital's risk appetite might affect this decision.

1.36 Decision-Maker Bias Gene Horita is choosing a major in his second year. He enjoys the accounting classes
LO6, LO7 at his university but also finds the information systems classes to be interesting. Gene's father is an accountant and has been pressuring Gene to choose an accounting major. Gene has always resented the fact that his father was not home very much during income tax season and was unable to go to most sporting events in which Gene participated in high school. Gene is uncertain whether he would want that lifestyle in the future when he has a family. He is leaning toward information systems as a major because he thinks he can get a job with more regular working hours with this major.

REQUIRED
A. In what ways does Gene appear to be biased?
B. How could Gene recognize and control for his biases?

1.37 Identifying Risk We have defined business risk as the possibility that an event could occur that interferes with an
LO5 organization's ability to meet strategic goals or operating plans.

REQUIRED Identify and briefly explain business risks for each of the following decisions.

A. The managers of **Flow Systems**, an irrigation equipment manufacturer, are considering the purchase of new welding equipment that will reduce labour costs. In addition, the equipment is much safer than the equipment it would replace. The added safety is expected to reduce Flow System's insurance costs by half.
B. Amira Salazar needs to choose between two summer internship offers she recently received. If she accepts a summer internship with **IBM** in its finance department, she will be located in Canada and work in the strategic planning department. If she accepts an internship with **Hewlett-Packard**, she will be located in the United States and work on a special costing project for a new printer design.

1.38 Relevant Information, Bias, Recommendations Francisco owns a camper and loves to visit national parks with his
LO4, LO5, family. However, the family takes only two one-week trips in the camper each year. Francisco's wife would rather
LO6 stay in motels than the camper. She has presented him with the following itemization of the cost per trip, hoping that he will sell the camper and use motels instead:

	Cost per Trip
Camper:	
Cost: $20,000	
Usable for 10 seasons, 2 camping trips per season	$1,000
Transportation expense:	
1,000 kilometres @ $0.37 per kilometre	370
Includes:	
$0.15 per kilometre for gasoline, oil, tires, and maintenance	
$0.22 per kilometre for depreciation and insurance	
Groceries	250
Beverages	100
Cost per trip	$ 1,720
Cost per person ($1,720 ÷ 5 family members)	$ 344

REQUIRED
A. What are the relevant costs for deciding whether the family should go on one more camping trip this year?
B. What are the relevant costs for deciding whether Francisco should sell the camper? Assume that the family will take the same vacations but stay in motels if the camper is sold.
C. What factors other than costs might influence the decision to sell the camper? List as many as you can.

D. Consider your own preferences for this problem. Do you expect Francisco's preferences to be the same as yours? How can you control for your biases and consider this problem from Francisco's point of view?

E. Francisco asks you to help him decide what to do. Do you think he should sell the camper? Why or why not?

1.39 **Income Statement Information, Solve for Unknowns** Following is a traditional income statement for Mouse Max, a company that manufactures cordless mice for computers.

LO3, LO4, LO7

Revenue	$2,500,000
Cost of goods sold	1,220,000
Gross margin	1,280,000
Selling and administration	1,150,000
Operating income	$ 130,000

This income statement reflects sales of 100,000 mice. Direct materials cost $5.00 per mouse, direct labour was $1.00 per mouse, and sales commissions were $1.50 per mouse. Advertising costs totalled $200,000. All manufacturing overhead costs are fixed.

REQUIRED **A.** Develop a variable cost income statement.

B. Why do traditional income statements have to conform to accounting rules such as IFRS or Canadian ASPE?

C. Managers sometimes divide cost of goods sold from a traditional income statement by the quantity of units sold to calculate an average production cost per unit. They then multiply the average cost per unit by an estimated future production volume to estimate incremental future costs. Why is this method likely to produce a poor-quality cost estimate?

1.40 **Strategic Management Process** Suppose you decided to start a new fast food restaurant business to compete with McDonalds.

LO1, LO2, LO3

REQUIRED **A.** Describe your organizational vision and list two core competencies.

B. Describe your general strategy. For example, would you try to compete based on low cost? On quality of service? How does your general strategy relate to the core competencies you listed in part (A)?

C. Identify two ways in which the strategy you described in part (B) might influence your operating plans.

D. Explain why it would be useful to use accounting information to compare actual operations to the operating plans for your company.

1.41 **Strategic Decision Quality, Business Risk** In 2007, Starbucks CEO Jim Donald issued a memo criticizing some of the company's past decisions, including the installation of automatic espresso machines. He pointed out that the espresso machine decision was "probably right at the time" because it increased the speed of service and improved efficiency. However, he argued that the decision overlooked the "romance and theatre" of the customer barista experience. He emphasized that the company needed to return to its core to ensure the loyalty of Starbucks customers.

LO1, LO6, LO7

Source: J. Donald, "The Commoditization of the Starbucks Experience," memo, February 14, 2007, available as "Text of Starbucks Memo," *The Wall Street Journal Online*, February 24, 2007.

REQUIRED **A.** How does "romance and theatre" relate to Starbucks' vision and core competencies?

B. What are some of Starbucks' business risks?

C. How is it possible for a decision to be "right at the time" but incorrect in terms of a company's overall strategy?

1.42 **Steps in Decision-Making Process (Appendix 1B)** Refer to the information in Problem 1.41.

LO7

REQUIRED Using the Steps for Better Thinking model in Appendix 1B, describe Steps 1, 2, and 3 of the Starbucks' decision to install automatic espresso machines. In other words, what factors might the managers have considered as they made this decision?

1.43 **Ethical Decision Making, Relevant Information, Risks, Biases** In two of his classes, Larry's professors said that he could work homework problems with other students as long as he turned in his own answers. In another class, the professor said that students could not work with other students, and each time the professor collected homework, students were required to write a statement at the bottom of their assignment that assured the professor that the homework had been the student's own effort.

LO4, LO5, LO6

Half an hour before class, Larry's girlfriend Annie asked if he would help her finish the last three homework problems so she could hand them in on time. Larry asked her how she would feel about signing the statement if he helped her.

REQUIRED

A. What is the ethical issue here?

B. What alternatives are available to Larry?

C. If the professor discovers that Annie and Larry's answers are similar in ways that reflect the fact that they worked together, what might happen? What risks are involved?

D. What information is relevant to Larry's decision?

E. Is this an open-ended problem? Why or why not?

F. Explore this problem from different perspectives:

1. Annie's
2. Larry's
3. The professor's

G. How important is it for students to behave ethically?

H. By exploring the ethics of this situation, what could Larry and Annie learn about professional ethics?

1.44 Relevant Information, Decision-Making Biases, Quality of Decisions ProTrain is a training company that specializes in leadership and team-building programs. Recently, ProTrain hired Rico Du, a business graduate, as a general manager in hopes of expanding its business. Rico learned a lot about risk management in school and believes that managers need to have sufficient training in risk management. He gathers the financial information for the two types of existing training programs from the accounting department:

LO4, LO6, LO7

Revenue	$550,000
Cost of Delivery	357,500
Gross Margin	192,500
Marketing	82,500
Administration	44,000
Operating Income	$66,000

He estimates that the new risk management program will generate revenue of $150,000, of which 72% is the cost of delivery. Marketing expenses will be 20% of the revenue; however, he expects that administration expenses will remain the same.

REQUIRED

A. Identify the relevant information for adding the new risk management program to the existing business.

B. Will the new risk management program add value to the existing business? If so, how much operating income will this new program add to the existing operating income?

C. What are the possible biases that Rico may have when he estimates the financial information for the risk management program?

D. If you were Rico's boss, what additional information that you would like Rico gather in order to control for his biases?

1.45 Relevant Costs, Quality of Decision-Making, Ethical Decision-Making A National Accounting Case Competition is being held at a conference in Calgary, Alberta this year. You and the other two members of your team were selected to represent your school tin the competition. To obtain funding for your 4-day trip, your team is preparing a budget to submit to your school for approval. Your team has listed the following expense items for 3 people for 4 nights:

LO4, LO7, LO8

Items	Cost
Flight $500/person	$1,500
Parking on campus[1]	12
Taxi (to and from Airports)	120
Hostel $40/night per person	480
Residence[2]	300
Food on campus[3]	240
Food during conference[4]	480

---

[1] One of the team members pays $90/month for a parking pass on campus. Four days of parking cost on campus is $12.
[2] Three team members live on campus and pay rent of $750/month. Four days of residence rent for 3 members for 4 nights away is $300.
[3] Three team members pay for a campus meal plan of $600/month. No refund will be reimbursed to students who miss their meals.
[4] The team estimates the food cost will be $40/day for 3 meals.

REQUIRED **A.** Identify the relevant and irrelevant items for preparing your budget.

B. Based on (A), prepare your budget to be submitted.

C. One of your team members questions whether food on campus should be included in your budget. He argues that they should get money back from the meals not consumed during the 4 days at the conference. He suggests that instead of listing two food costs on the budget, the food costs should be combined and listed as $720. Do you agree with him? Is there any ethical issue in his suggestion? How do you resolve the issue here, if you disagree with his approach?

MINI-CASES

1.46 **Relevant Information, Risk** Janet Breton is deciding where to live during her second year in college. During her first year, she lived in the university residence. Recently, her friend Rachel asked her to share an off-campus apartment for the upcoming school year. Janet likes the idea of living in an apartment, but she is concerned about how much it will cost.

To help her decide what to do, Janet collected information about costs. She would pay $400 per month in rent. The minimum lease term on the apartment is six months. Janet estimates that her share of the utility bills will be $75 per month, and she also estimates that groceries will cost $200 per month. Janet spent $350 on a new couch over the summer, and if she lives in the residence she will put the couch in storage at a cost of $35 per month. Janet expects to spend $7,500 on tuition for the year and $450 on books each semester. Room and board at the residence would cost Janet $2,900 per semester (four months). This amount includes a food plan of 20 meals per week, and the cost is nonrefundable if the meals are not eaten.

ANALYZE INFORMATION:

Questions A to G will help you analyze the information for this problem. Do not turn in your answers to these questions unless your professor asks you to do so.

A. Use ONLY the cost information collected by Janet for the following tasks.

1. List all of the costs for each option. *Note*: Some costs may be listed under both options.

2. Review your lists and cross out the costs that are irrelevant to Janet's decision. Explain why these costs are irrelevant.

3. Calculate and compare the total *relevant* costs of each option.

4. Given the cost comparison, which living arrangement is the better choice for Janet? Explain.

B. Identify risks associated with the costs collected by Janet.

1. Determine whether each cost is likely to be (i) known for sure, (ii) estimated with little uncertainty, or (iii) estimated with moderate or high uncertainty.

2. For each cost that is known for sure, explain where Janet would obtain the information.

3. For each cost that must be estimated, explain why the cost cannot be known.

C. List additional information that might be relevant to Janet's decision (list as many items as you can).

1. Costs not identified by Janet.

2. Factors (including risks) other than costs.

D. Explain why conducting a cost comparison is useful to Janet, even if factors other than costs are important to her decision.

E. Consider your own preferences for this problem. Do you expect Janet's preferences to be the same as yours? How can you control for your biases as you give Janet advice?

F. Think about what Janet's priorities might be for choosing a housing arrangement. How might different priorities lead to different choices?

G. Describe how information that Janet gains over this next year might affect her future housing arrangements.

REQUIRED Suppose Janet asks for your advice. Turn in your answers to the following.

H. Use the information you learned from the preceding analyses to write a memo to Janet with your recommendation and a discussion of its risks. Refer in your memo to the information that would be useful to Janet.

I. How did you decide what information to include in your memo to Janet? Write one or two paragraphs explaining your thought process.

1.47 **Ethical Decision Making, Relevant Information, Risks, Biases** You are an entry-level accountant at City Hall. You work for the accounting department, but have been loaned out to the department responsible for building and maintaining roads while the managers develop their annual budget. The director of the department is in the middle of a nasty divorce. He asks you to work on a Saturday to finish up details of the budget. When you arrive, he asks you to work on a schedule for his personal financial information for the upcoming divorce court case. When you finish the task, he tells you to record your hours as overtime and bill them to the city.

REQUIRED **A.** What is the ethical issue here?

B. What are your alternatives?

C. If you do as the director asks and your boss finds out, what might happen? What risks are involved?

D. What information is relevant to your decision?

E. Is there only one correct solution to this problem? Why or why not?

F. Explore this problem from different perspectives:

    1. Your own

    2. The department director's

    3. Your boss's

    4. The taxpayers'

G. How important is it for you to behave ethically?

H. Based on your analysis of the situation, write a short "script" for how you would respond to the department director.

I. Suppose you decide not to do what the director asks. Discuss the issues you would consider as you decide whether to report this incident to your boss.

1.48 **Quality of Decisions, Risk Appetite, Bias** Maria and Tracey became good friends while working at the same company. Two years ago, they both decided to increase their savings so that they could eventually purchase homes. Each began by putting a portion of every paycheque into a savings account. At the end of the first year, they had each accumulated $4,000. Because their savings accounts paid a very small interest rate, they decided to invest the savings to earn a higher rate of return. Maria and Tracey both hoped to save enough money to buy homes within five years.

LO4, LO5, LO6, LO7

    Maria decided to take an investment course offered through the company. The course taught her about different types of investments and strategies for investing. She then purchased and read an investment book to learn more. She learned that some investments are riskier than others, and that investors must balance risk against desired return. Higher risk leads to higher returns, on average; however, higher risk could also lead to low returns or even loss. She also learned that investment advisors recommend diversifying risky investments. One way to diversify is to invest in mutual funds, which invest in many different organizations. Maria decided that she was willing to assume some risk, but was not comfortable with a high level. She decided to invest her $4,000 in a stock market mutual fund. She read *Consumer Reports* to learn about different mutual funds and selected a fund that invests conservatively in fairly stable companies. However, the stock market did not do well in the first year. The value of her mutual fund at the end of a year was $4,050.

    Tracey talked with her boyfriend and other friends about how they invest. Her boyfriend's cousin recommended investing in a start-up company that sells video games. He told her that the games were very hot with teenagers and that the company would probably be acquired, resulting in big gains for investors. This opportunity sounded good to Tracey, so she decided to invest her entire $4,000 in the company's stock. After 10 months, she was excited to learn that the company was being acquired. She received stock in the acquiring company in exchange for her original stock. At the end of the year, the market value of her stock was $8,200.

REQUIRED Evaluate the quality of the investment decisions made by Maria and Tracey. (*Hint*: Refer to Exhibit 1.13.)

A. List the information used by Maria in making her investment decision.

B. List the information used by Tracey in making her investment decision.

C. Did Maria appear to use high-quality information? Explain.

D. Did Tracey appear to use high-quality information? Explain.

E. Describe Maria's decision-making process. What did she do to explore her options? Did she appear to be biased? What were her priorities and her risk appetite? How did she reach a conclusion?

F. Describe Tracey's decision-making process. What did she do to explore her options? Did she appear to be biased? What were her priorities and her risk appetite? How did she reach a conclusion?

G. Did Maria appear to use a high-quality decision-making process? Explain.

H. Did Tracey appear to use a high-quality decision-making process? Explain.

I. Given your analyses of the information and decision-making processes used by Maria and Tracey, which investor made a higher-quality decision? Explain.

1.49 **Integrating across the Curriculum (Auditing): Information Quality, Diagnostic Controls, Relevant Information to Auditors** Aden, Inc. is a manufacturer of television sets. The company recently revised its production processes and invested in new equipment to reduce labour costs.

LO1, LO2, LO7

REQUIRED

A. Following are possible measures that Aden could use to monitor product defects. Discuss the quality of information provided by each measure. (*Hint:* See Exhibit 1.13.)
  1. Ratio of defective televisions returned to the number of televisions sold (data from customer service department records and sales department records).
  2. Monthly defective unit warranty costs incurred (data from the general ledger).
  3. Monthly number of defects discovered during routine tests of televisions at the end of the manufacturing process (data from production records).
  4. Customer survey responses to the question, "How satisfied are you with the quality of your television set?" on a scale from 1 (very satisfied) to 5 (very unsatisfied). Surveys are mailed to 1% of randomly selected repeat customers from sales records.

B. List ideas about what Aden's managers might want to learn from monitoring product defects as part of a diagnostic control system.

C. The measures used by managers to monitor operations are often used by auditors when auditing financial statements. Explain why information about product defects might be relevant to Aden's auditors when they audit the following:
  1. Warranty liabilities
  2. Lower of cost or market adjustment for inventory
  3. Allowance for doubtful accounts receivable

1.50 **Integrating across the Curriculum (Technology and Information Systems): Internal and External Information, Internal Reports, Business Risk** Managers continually seek ways to improve productivity and reduce costs. Many manufacturers and retailers incur large costs to track inventory. To reduce these costs, managers began to consider the use of radio frequency identification (RFID) tags to replace bar codes that were currently being used to track inventory receipt, movement, and sale. When embedded in individual products, RFID tags allow companies to use radio signals to track every product item. For retailers such as Walmart, RFID technology was expected not only to reduce the cost of tracking inventory, but also to reduce losses from theft.

To further investigate the use of RFID, Walmart and Procter & Gamble secretly launched a research project in a suburban Tulsa, Oklahoma, Walmart store. Researchers monitored the movement of a particular lipstick product using RFID tags in the lipstick packaging, electronic readers concealed in the store shelves, and webcams. A sign on the lipstick display informed customers about the use of closed-circuit television and electronic security at the store.

When news of the testing became publicly known, consumer advocacy groups raised alarms about the potential loss of privacy from RFID tags. They claimed that proliferation of RFID technology could eventually allow retailers to track their products after customers buy them and leave the store. These concerns prompted a California state senate subcommittee to hold public hearings on RFID. Similar actions were likely to be taken in other states.

Sources: J. Donald, "Chipping Away at Your Privacy," *Chicago Sun-Times*, November 9, 2003; H. Wolinsky, "P&G, Walmart Store Did Secret Test of RFID," *Chicago Sun-Times*, November 9, 2003; E. Shein, "Radio Flier: Walmart Presents its Vendors with an Offer They Can't Refuse," *CFO Magazine*, November 5, 2003; and J. Black, "Playing Tag with Shoppers' Anonymity," *Business Week Online*, July 21, 2003.

REQUIRED **A.** Would the information from RFID tags be considered internally or externally generated information? (See Exhibit 1.9.) Explain.

B. Information gathered by Walmart from its in-store research on the RFID technology was most likely summarized in one or more internal reports. Were these internal reports most likely used to (1) support organizational strategies, (2) support operating plans, or (3) monitor and motivate? Explain.

C. Describe the business risk associated with Walmart's decision to conduct research on its customers without explicitly informing them.

D. Provide arguments for and against Walmart's decision to conduct research on its customers without explicitly informing them.

2

Cost Concepts, Behaviour, and Estimation

in brief Managers need a basic understanding of the organization's costs if they are to react quickly to change and create successful organizational strategies and operating plans. Classifications and estimation techniques are useful to managers in understanding and anticipating future cost behaviour. As a result, they can then estimate relevant costs to help make decisions and plan future operations. ■

After studying this chapter, you should be able to do the following:

LO1 Explain cost concepts and cost terms

LO2 Describe the different types of cost behaviour

LO3 Describe cost estimation techniques

LO4 Apply cost estimation techniques to determine future costs

LO5 Utilize regression analysis in cost estimation

LO6 Appreciate the uses and limitations of cost estimates

When Cost Estimates Are Off Target

Andrew Vaughan/The Canadian Press

Estimating costs is a crucial part of business decision making. A manufacturer needs to estimate labour, land, and other costs in various locations to decide where to build a new plant. A pharmaceutical company needs to estimate research and development costs before deciding to pursue a new drug. A retailer needs to estimate the information technology, shipping, and other costs before deciding to offer online shopping.

Like any estimate, cost estimates are a best guess based on past costs to predict where an industry and the economy as a whole might be headed. Companies that don't get their cost estimates in the ballpark of reality can suffer disastrous consequences.

For example, a misstep in estimating the costs of expanding into Canada is partly to blame for the downfall of **Target Corp.'s** Canadian operations. Before deciding to open more than 100 stores across the country to great hype in 2013, Target's U.S. parent knew of some costs that were certain, such as the $1.8 billion it paid to take over the leases of a few hundred Zellers stores from HBC to use many of them as Target locations. But the company would have had to estimate the costs of such things as the renovations to those former Zellers stores. The costs of renovations, along with building distribution centres across Canada and hiring and training staff were higher than what Target had forecasted before deciding to expand north.

Target likely would have estimated the cost of its merchandise and accounted for the fact that brand manufacturers often charge more for their goods in Canada—up to 25% more—and considered the impact of possible fluctuations in the U.S.-Canadian dollar exchange rate on imported goods However, Target seems to have underestimated the reaction of Canadian shoppers to the higher-priced goods here, when they were accustomed to lower prices when shopping in Target's U.S. stores or on its U.S. website. Not meeting Canadians' price expectations is one factor that analysts point to when explaining Target's hasty retreat from Canada in 2015, closing all 133 of its stores not even two years after opening, and incurring a massive $5.4-billion writedown

Cost estimates would have been part of Target's decision to wind down its Canadian operations, too. The company forecast that it would not be profitable in Canada until at least 2021. Management wisely ignored its sunk costs—the approximately $7 billion it had already spent on its move to Canada—when deciding whether to stick it out here Target realized it was years away from profitability, and pulled the plug before costs mounted any higher. It even costs money to close up shop—Target's expected costs to wind up operations were up to $600 million. "This may be the biggest squandering of money by a retail chain," said independent retail analyst Jan Kniffen.

Because costs involve the future, we cannot perfectly predict them. The best we can do is to carefully identify and estimate how a decision will affect costs. In this chapter, we learn about identifying relevant costs and the behaviour of those costs so that cost information for decision making and planning can be estimated.

SOURCES: M. Strauss, "How Target Botched a $7-Billion Rollout," *The Globe and Mail,* January 15, 2015; G. F. Scott, "Target Announces It Will Close All 133 Canadian Stores," *Canadian Business,* January 15, 2015; Torstar News Service, "How 'Arrogance' Led to Target's Failure in Canada," *Metro News,* January 16, 2015; R. Anupindi, "Lessons from Target Canada," *Michigan News,* University of Michigan, January 20, 2015; C. Sorensen, "Off-Target: How a U.S. Retail Giant Misread the Canadian Market," *Maclean's,* January 21, 2015.

Cost Concepts and Terminology

LO 1   Explain cost concepts and cost terms

Managers need to understand cost concepts and how costs are incurred in order to analyze and manage their costs. Costs, in general, can be classified via five broad categories: (1) relevance, (2) behaviour, (3) traceability, (4) function, and (5) controllability.

Managers need relevant information on both revenues and costs to make decisions. *Relevant revenues and costs* are the revenues and costs that differentiate between alternatives that will occur in the future. *Irrelevant revenues and costs* will not make a difference to either alternative, and they therefore have no bearing on the decision. For example, opportunity cost is a relevant cost because it is the potential benefit given up by not taking one alternative over another. A *sunk cost* is an irrelevant cost because the cost has already been incurred and cannot now be avoided.

Managers need to know how costs behave in order to estimate them at a given production level. A *fixed cost* behaves such that the total cost will not change within a certain range of activity—the so-called relevant range. A *variable cost* varies in proportion to the production level. For example, the cost of leasing an airplane per month is fixed, regardless of the distance the airplane travelled during that month. On the other hand, the costs of fuel vary depending on the distance travelled.

Managers need to know whether a cost can be traced to a cost object, helping them to more accurately estimate the cost. A **cost object** is a thing or activity for which we measure costs. Cost objects include such things as individual products, product lines, projects, customers, departments, and even the entire company. They can also include activities such as putting tires on bike wheels as part of the manufacturing process for bicycles. A cost that can be directly traced to a cost object and is incurred for the benefit and the purpose of a particular cost object is called a *direct cost*. On the other hand, *indirect costs* are incurred for the benefit and the purpose of more than one cost object and, therefore, cannot be easily and economically traced to a particular cost object. For example, the salaries of the pilots for Air Canada Flight 1050 can be traced directly to the flight (the cost object), while the salaries of the ground crew are an indirect cost to Flight 1050.

In the manufacturing sector, managers need to know costs by their function, such as manufacturing (or product, or inventoriable) costs and nonmanufacturing (or period) costs. When managers understand what goes into the manufacturing costs, they can better determine the cost of goods manufactured and price products accordingly. Manufacturing costs include direct materials, direct labour, and manufacturing overhead costs. Direct materials and direct labour are called *prime costs*, and direct labour and manufacturing overhead are called *conversion costs*.

Managers may have the authority to cut costs, if the costs are controllable. On the other hand, they may not be able to change a commitment made by their senior managers and, therefore, be unable to cut uncontrollable cost. Exhibit 2.1 summarizes cost classifications, their applications, and cost terms.

Classifying Costs

To classify costs correctly, we need to identify the cost object and also understand the nature of the business. When Air Canada managers want to add a flight to their existing route from Toronto to Vancouver, the cost object is that flight. The cost of gates at the Toronto airport

> **EXHIBIT 2.1**
> Cost Classifications, Applications, and Cost Terms

Classifications	Applications	Cost Terms
Relevance	Decision making	Relevant cost vs. irrelevant cost
Behaviour	Cost estimation	Fixed cost vs. variable cost
Traceability	Cost assignment	Direct cost vs. indirect cost
Function	Cost determination	Manufacturing cost vs. nonmanufacturing cost (product vs. period)
Controllability	Performance evaluation	Controllable cost vs. uncontrollable cost

	Fixed	Variable	Direct	Indirect
Rent for manufacturing plant	X			X
Direct labour (assuming a guaranteed 40-hour week)	X		X	
Direct labour (assuming work hours fluctuate with production volume)		X	X	
Tires		X	X	
Valve caps for tires		X		X
Lubrication and other supplies for production equipment		X		X
Insurance	X			X
Product line supervisor salary	X			X

▷ EXHIBIT 2.2

Cost Classifications When a Bicycle Is the Cost Object

is fixed with respect to adding a new flight. If the managers want to add new routes, the cost of gates at new destinations varies with the number of new routes. The cost of baggage handling at each airport is a mixed cost: part of it is fixed (e.g., depreciation on equipment), and part of it is variable (e.g., labour costs).

Because variable costs are easily traceable to the units or services produced, they are often automatically considered direct costs. As a result, many people mistakenly believe that direct costs are always variable and that indirect costs are always fixed. Yet fixed and variable costs can each be either direct or indirect, depending on the cost object. In addition, some direct variable costs (e.g., valve caps for bicycle tires) are very small per unit and are pooled with a variety of indirect costs. Some direct variable costs are difficult to separate from other costs, such as lubrication and other supplies for the equipment used to assemble bikes. The cost of tracking these costs is more than the benefit, so they are classified as indirect costs. Exhibit 2.2 shows classifications of several costs for Magik Bicycles when each bicycle is the cost object and several different models are manufactured in one plant.

Relevant Range

A relevant range is a span of activity for a given cost object, where total fixed costs remain constant and variable costs per unit of activity remain constant. Suppose that Air Canada begins service to a new destination. The number of flights is estimated, gates and aircraft are leased, and employees are hired. Managers may add a few flights or drop a few flights, and the fixed costs and variable costs per flight (fuel and personnel) remain constant. However, if the new route is successful, managers may decide to add a number of new flights, in which case new gates must be leased and new employees hired. The fixed and variable costs for the original destination are no longer valid because Air Canada is now operating within a new relevant range.

Variable cost rates can also change across relevant ranges, as shown in Exhibit 2.3(b). In that graph, Magik Bicycles paid $10 per bike for 0 to 60 bikes, and $6 per bike after that. Within a particular relevant range of purchases, the variable cost per tire is constant; however, when purchase volumes move into a different relevant range, a different variable cost per bike applies. In many cases, the variable cost will be lower at a higher relevant range, but in others, especially when resources are limited, a higher variable cost might apply. For example, a utility company may charge customers one cost per kilowatt over a range of usage and then a higher amount per kilowatt for a higher level of usage. The purpose would be to encourage conservation and efficient use of utilities.

Marginal cost is the incremental cost of an activity, such as producing a unit of goods or services. Marginal cost is often relevant for decision making. Within the relevant range, variable cost approximates marginal cost, and, accordingly, accountants often use variable cost as a measure of marginal cost. Although the terms *variable cost* and *marginal cost* may be used interchangeably, they are not always the same, especially when the incremental or marginal unit moves into the next relevant range. For example, in Exhibit 2.4(b), the first $30,000 in sales has a fixed cost of $6,000 for rental of retail space. The next level of incremental sales

> **EXHIBIT 2.3**

Total Variable Cost of Tires for Bicycle Production

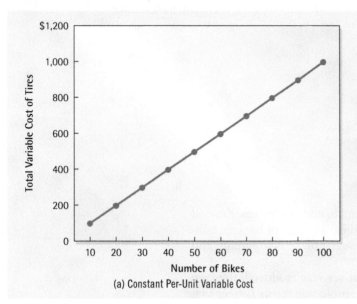

(a) Constant Per-Unit Variable Cost

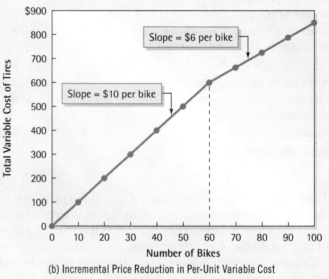

Slope = $6 per bike

Slope = $10 per bike

(b) Incremental Price Reduction in Per-Unit Variable Cost

> **EXHIBIT 2.4**

Fixed Cost of Rent

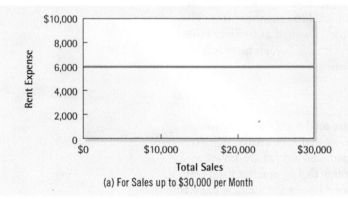

(a) For Sales up to $30,000 per Month

(b) For Sales Exceeding $30,000 When More Space Must Be Rented

(above $30,000) requires an expansion of retail space, costing an additional $2,000 in fixed costs. Thus, the marginal (first few) sales would increase fixed costs by $2,000.

Estimating Relevant Costs

Key parts of Air Canada's decision process required managers to measure the effects on cost of alternative cost-cutting scenarios. Even though this type of evaluation might sound like an obvious and simple thing to do, it is not always easy to identify or calculate relevant costs. Because relevant costs involve the future, we cannot perfectly predict them. The best we can do is to carefully identify and estimate how costs will be affected by a decision.

Relevant Costs for a Cost Object

For Air Canada's managers, a first step in evaluating relevant costs was identifying the costs that would be affected by a particular cost-cutting scenario—in other words, the relevant costs. Exhibit 2.5 provides examples of relevant costs for several alternatives that Air Canada's managers might have considered.

Managers identify one or more cost objects based on the relevant information for a particular decision, for budgeting and planning, or for valuing products or services.

▶EXHIBIT 2.5
Relevant Costs for Cost-Cutting
Alternatives

Relevant Cost	Alternative Cost-Cutting Measures			
	Cancel Food Service on a Flight	Reduce Number of Scheduled Flights	Delay Implementation of Online Booking System	Discontinue All Operations at an Airport
Food	✓	✓		✓
Fuel		✓		
Cost of new system			✓	
Wages of manager for airport operations				✓

Identifying Relevant Costs from the Accounting System

One way to identify relevant costs is to search the accounting system for costs that might be affected by a decision. However, not all relevant costs appear in the accounting system. For example, in an estimate of cost savings from layoffs, employee severance pay would not appear in the accounting system until *after* the decision is made. In addition, some costs from the accounting system are irrelevant. For example, human resources department costs would not change if only a few employees were laid off, so that cost would be irrelevant. Careful thought and judgment are required in identifying relevant costs; however, it helps to know whether costs are direct or indirect.

Direct and Indirect Costs

Direct costs are easily traced to individual cost objects because a clear cause-and-effect relationship generally exists between the cost object and the cost. Suppose managers at Magik Bicycles want to know more about their costs. The costs of parts such as tires, handlebars, and frames can be traced directly not only to the production of individual bicycles but also to an entire product line.

Indirect costs are not easily traced to individual cost objects. Often, these costs relate to more than one cost object, such as multiple products or services. For Magik Bicycles, maintenance and electricity at the manufacturing facility are indirect costs when the cost object is an individual bicycle. Although these costs are needed to produce bicycles, we cannot trace them to each unit. However, these costs are direct costs when the cost object is an entire product line. In some cases, indirect costs are potentially traceable, but gathering information is overly expensive. For example, the cost of inner tube valve caps could be traced to each bike, but the cost of each cap is very small, while the cost of tracking this would be relatively high.

All production costs except direct materials costs and direct labour costs may be combined into groups (cost pools) in the accounting system and referred to as overhead costs. These costs are often common to many different aspects of operations and cannot be easily related to individual products or services. For Magik Bicycles, it is easy to relate the cost of tires to each bike, but it is difficult to relate the salary of the production supervisor to each bike. However, the supervisor's cost is related to the production line.

Opportunity Costs

When we consider alternative courses of action, we can think of each alternative as an opportunity. When one alternative is chosen, the benefits of the other alternatives are no longer available. The benefits we forgo when we choose one alternative over the next best alternative are called opportunity costs. For example, if you attend a basketball game, you pay cash for a ticket and spend time at the game. In doing that, you forgo the opportunity to spend that money and time on something else, such as studying, going to a movie or concert, or hanging out with friends or family. The benefits forgone from the next-best alternative are the opportunity costs of attending the basketball game.

▶ HELPFUL HINT
In Chapter 1 you learned that relevant information concerns the future and varies with the action taken. Only incremental (additional or avoidable) costs are relevant.

▶ ALTERNATIVE TERMS
Some people use the term *factory burden* to refer to *overhead*.

▶ HELPFUL HINT
Cost pools are groups of costs accumulated for a particular cost object. Costs are often pooled at the department level. Costs are also sometimes pooled around activities.

▶ BUSINESS PRACTICE
When the owners of **Starbucks Coffee** opened their first coffee shops, instead of focusing on food, they adopted a strategy of offering a variety of coffee beverages that were relatively unknown to consumers at the time. Their opportunity cost was the potential profit from offering a larger food menu. See the Starbucks website, at www.starbucks.com, for more information on its history.

Opportunity costs are often difficult to measure. As individuals, we informally value opportunity costs each time we choose a particular course of action. However, managers need to formally value opportunity costs in order to make higher-quality decisions. They need to anticipate and develop estimates for future revenues and costs, regardless of whether these will later appear in the accounting system.

Sunk Costs

Sunk costs are expenditures made in the past. When deciding whether to keep already existing equipment, the original cost of the equipment is not a factor; it is a sunk cost. Because sunk costs cannot be changed by any future decisions, these costs are unavoidable and, therefore, not relevant to decision making.

Contrary to good decision-making practices, research indicates that managers tend to include sunk costs in their decisions.[1] The inclusion might occur because sunk costs are readily visible in the accounting records, or because managers become emotionally attached to prior decisions. Accountants promote improved decision making by identifying sunk costs and helping managers understand why these sunk costs should not influence the decision-making process.

BUSINESS PRACTICE

Target's expansion into Canada was its first venture outside its U.S. home market. The American retailer believed the benefits of expanding into Canada would outweigh the costs. However, Target was not able to win over Canadian customers and in January 2015 after less than two years of operations, it announced that it would be pulling out of the Canadian market. The expansion into Canada cost Target more than $7-billion.[2]

LO1

2-1 self-study problem   Opportunity Costs, Relevant Information

After a severe downturn in the economy, Frank was laid off from his position as sales director for a large resort in Banff, Alberta. While he was working at the resort, he saved enough money to start his own business. He would like to buy a franchise for a sandwich shop and open a new store, but he could also work as a salesperson in his father-in-law's hardware store and put his savings into other investments. He begins to identify all the relevant cash flows for the decision. First, he determines his opportunity costs.

required

A. If Frank decides to start a sandwich shop, what opportunities does he forgo?
B. What are the cost objects about which Frank needs to gather information?
C. List the cash flows for which Frank needs information when he evaluates the decision.
D. Frank faces the risk that the sandwich shop cash flows will not meet his needs. How does this risk affect Frank's decision?

See the solution on page 74.

Cost Behaviour

LO2 Describe the different types of cost behaviour

The next step in estimating a relevant cost is to describe how that cost would change under different decision alternatives. **Cost behaviour** is the variation in costs relative to the variation in an organization's activities. Accountants need to anticipate changes in costs as decisions are made about activities such as production, merchandise sales, and services. To understand cost behaviour, accountants analyze the effects on costs of changes in their organizations' activities.

The ability to analyze cost behaviour requires knowledge of an organization's economic environment and operations. For example, some of Air Canada's costs, such as beverage costs, vary with the number of passengers. Some costs, such as fuel costs and flight attendant wages, vary with the number of flights. Other costs, such as counter space lease and airport

---

[1] Hal Arkes and Peter Ayton, "Think Like a Dog," *Psychology Today*, January/February 2000; and Hal Arkes and Peter Ayton, "The Sunk Cost and Concorde Effects: Are Humans Less Rational Than Lower Animals?" *Psychological Bulletin*, September 1999, pp. 591–600.
[2] Marina Straus, "How Target Botched a $7-Billion Rollout," *The Globe and Mail*, January 15, 2015, accessed August 28, 2015, www.theglobeandmail.com/report-on-business/international-business/us-business/target-killing-canadian-operations/article22458161.

management salaries, vary with the number of airports that Air Canada uses. Still other costs do not vary with passenger, flight, or airport-related volumes; for example, building costs and salaries for those at corporate headquarters.

Variable, Fixed, and Mixed Costs

Total **variable costs** change proportionately with changes in activity levels. For Magik Bicycles, the cost of tires varies with the number of bicycles produced. If each tire costs $5, the variable cost per bike is $10, and total variable cost increases by $10 for each bike produced. Exhibit 2.3(a) provides a graph of the variable cost of tires. Another activity in bike production is mounting the tires onto wheels. As the number of bikes produced increases, the labour cost to mount tires onto wheels increases proportionately and is therefore a variable cost.

We assume that variable cost per unit remains constant, but sometimes this assumption is not the case. Suppose Magik's managers are able to negotiate a lower cost for tires as their purchase quantity increases. For purchases up to 120 tires, the variable cost per unit is constant, at $10 per bike. However, the variable cost per bike drops to $6 for any additional purchases after the first 120 tires, as illustrated in Exhibit 2.3(b). Therefore, the variable costs per unit remain constant at $10 within the relevant range up to 120 units, and the variable costs per unit remain constant at $6 within the next relevant range over 120 units, and so on.

Total **fixed costs** do not vary with small changes in activity levels, such as in production, sales, and services provided. Some fixed costs are easy to classify, such as rent, insurance, and property taxes. Exhibit 2.4(a) illustrates the cost of rent and sales volumes for a Magik Bicycles retail store. Within a specific range of sales ($0 to $30,000), rent cost is $6,000. However, if sales are greater than $30,000, more space will be needed, and total fixed cost will increase to $8,000, as shown in Exhibit 2.4(b). Fixed costs such as rent often increase in a stepwise manner.

Other fixed costs are more difficult to classify. For example, varying levels of bike production do not significantly change the amount of electricity used, assuming there is no change in hours of operation. Keep in mind that the dollar amount of a fixed cost is not necessarily "fixed" at one value. For Magik Bicycles, the rate for a kilowatt-hour of electricity might change, the cost for heating and cooling depends on weather conditions, and the total electric bill varies from month to month. Nevertheless, electricity is still considered a fixed cost for bike production, because the cost of electricity is not significantly affected by changes in the volumes of operating activity (i.e., number of bikes produced).

In reality, many costs are **mixed costs**—partly fixed and partly variable. Suppose that Magik Bicycles incurs a fixed cost of $10,000 to generate a television advertisement and then a variable cost of $500 each time the advertisement is aired on television. As shown in Exhibit 2.6, the total television advertising cost is a mixed cost because part is fixed and part varies with the number of times the advertisement is aired on television.

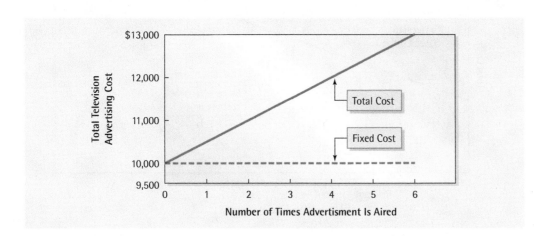

⊠**EXHIBIT 2.6**

Mixed Cost for Television Advertising

Cost Functions

It is easy to assume that costs behave linearly—in other words, that fixed costs remain fixed and the variable cost per unit remains constant. However, total costs more often resemble a large S-curve, as shown in Exhibit 2.7. Notice that within a relevant range of activity, the change in total cost as volume increases is nearly linear.

A **cost function** is an algebraic representation of the total cost of a cost object over a relevant range of activity. When we create a cost function, we assume that within a relevant range of activity, the total fixed costs remain fixed and the variable cost per unit remains constant. Notice in Exhibit 2.7 that when volume is very low or very high, the total cost function is nonlinear. However, when volume is in the relevant range, the cost function is linear or close to linear.

Given the preceding definitions of fixed and variable costs within the relevant range, we can write the cost function algebraically as

$$TC = F + VQ$$

where TC is total cost, F is total fixed cost, V is the variable cost per unit of activity, and Q is the volume of activity.

ALTERNATIVE TERMS

Some people use the term *semifixed* to describe a *stepwise linear cost*.

When the slope of a variable cost function changes at some point but remains linear after the change, it is called a **piecewise linear cost function**. The variable cost function in Exhibit 2.3(b) is piecewise linear because it involves more than one relevant range. When a fixed cost function changes at some point but remains constant after the change, it is called a **stepwise linear cost function**. The fixed cost function in Exhibit 2.4(b) is stepwise linear because it includes more than one relevant range. Exhibit 2.8 presents the algebraic expressions for the cost function in Exhibits 2.3, 2.4, and 2.6.

Cost Drivers

A **cost driver** is some input or activity that causes changes in total cost for a cost object. In cost functions, Q represents the quantity of the cost driver. For Air Canada, when the cost object is the entire organization, the number of passengers is a cost driver for in-flight beverage costs. The number of flights is a cost driver for fuel and flight attendant wages. The number of airports used by Air Canada is a cost driver for counter space lease and airport management salaries.

For retail organizations such as Banana Republic, sales are likely to be a cost driver for many costs. When the cost object is a single Banana Republic store, sales are likely to drive the cost of clothing sold, sales commissions, and shopping bags. However, sales do not

EXHIBIT 2.7

Total Costs over a Wide Range of Activity

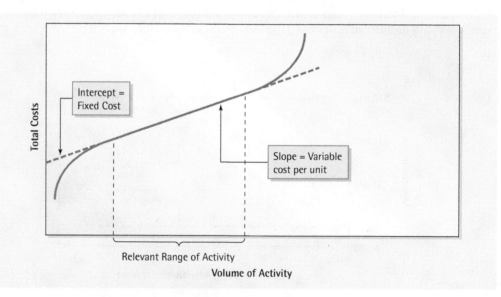

▶ EXHIBIT 2.8

Algebraic Expressions for Various Cost Functions

Type of Cost	Algebraic Function	Relevant Range	Reference
Variable	$TC = \$10 \times Q$	$Q > 0$	Exhibit 2.3(a)
	(TC = Total cost of tires)	(Q = Number of bikes produced)	
Variable (piecewise linear)	$TC = \$10 \times Q$	$Q \leq 60$	Exhibit 2.3(b)
	$TC = \$600 + \$6(Q - 60)$	$Q > 60$	
	(TC = Total cost of tires)	(Q = Number of bikes produced)	
Fixed	$TC = \$6,000$	$Q \geq 0$	Exhibit 2.4(a)
	(TC = Total cost of rent)	(Q = Sales)	
Fixed (stepwise linear)	$TC = \$6,000$	$Q \leq \$30,000$	Exhibit 2.4(b)
	$TC = \$8,000$	$Q > \$30,000$	
	(TC = Total cost of rent)	(Q = Sales)	
Mixed	$TC = \$10,000 + \$500 \times Q$	$Q \geq 0$	Exhibit 2.6
	(TC = Total cost of advertisement)	(Q = Number of times advertisement is aired)	

drive all types of costs for Banana Republic. For example, when the cost object is the entire organization, the total number of stores is likely to drive company-wide costs such as costs for store manager salaries, electricity, cash registers, and clothing racks.

The same cost object might have different cost drivers in different settings. For example, when electricity is the cost object, in a retail setting, the cost driver would be hours the store was open. In a manufacturing setting, the cost driver for electricity could be either machine hours or number of units manufactured, assuming that each unit requires the same number of machine hours.

Identifying Potential Cost Drivers. Identifying potential cost drivers is a process that is specific to the organization. When the cost object is a product or service, people closest to the manufacturing or service delivery process generally have the best information about cost drivers. By spending time in the actual manufacturing or service delivery area and asking questions about operations, we gain insight about both the activities that take place and the potential cost drivers for those activities.

An organization's information system can help identify cost drivers. Large organizations often use enterprise resource planning (ERP) to track both financial and nonfinancial information. ERP systems help identify potential cost drivers with detailed information, such as the organization's interactions with customers and suppliers.

No Apparent Cost Driver. Some costs cannot easily be associated with any type of cost driver. For example, legal costs at Magik Bicycles include any costs resulting from liability suits, costs for settling contract disputes, and costs to protect the brand name. These costs are not driven by any activity, such as the number of bicycles produced. To estimate these costs, we gather information about the type and expected costs of legal activities for the next period.

Discretionary Costs

Discretionary costs reflect periodic (usually annual) decisions about the maximum amount that will be spent on costs for activities such as advertising, executive travel, or research and development. Discretionary costs are considered managed fixed or managed variable costs, because managers decide the amount to spend on discretionary costs. These expenditures are often based on past profitability and can be altered during the period, depending on cash flow. The past behaviour of discretionary costs might not be relevant to their future behaviour.

▶ BUSINESS PRACTICE

Travel and Entertainment Expense: "Travel and entertainment is second only to payroll as the largest area of discretionary expense in a corporate budget."[3]

---

[3] Taken from the introduction to a report on travel and entertainment costs, http://www.cfo.com/guides/guide.cfm/3036066?f5search.

Economies of Scale

Accountants need to investigate possible economies of scale when estimating a cost function. For example, if we double the size of the human resources department, we may be able to handle three times as many employees. This change would cause the slope of the total cost function to flatten over large volumes of employees. Volume discounts are another example of economies of scale.

monticello/Shutterstock/Getty Images

●● > FOCUS ON ETHICAL DECISION MAKING: DISCRETIONARY COSTS

In some industries, marketing expenses can be one of the largest discretionary costs. This is particularly true in the pharmaceutical industry, which tries to recoup its enormous research and development costs in the brief time in which a patent protects a drug from generic competitors. One study found that U.S. drug companies spend almost twice as much on promoting their products as on developing them. American firms in 2004 spent U.S. $57.4 billion on marketing, including direct-to-consumer advertising (DTCA), which is not allowed in Canada.

Canadian pharmaceutical companies still market their products, sidestepping the ban in other ways. For example, they are allowed to advertise directly to health care providers under strict guidelines from the non-profit Pharmaceutical Advertising Advisory Board, and they can advertise to consumers if they don't mention the benefits of their products. This regulation was behind the recent TV campaigns for erectile dysfunction drugs, Pfizer Canada's Viagra and Eli Lilly's Cialis, which humorously show or imply couples being intimate and implore viewers to contact their doctor for more information.

Canada's doctors, however, do not see direct-to-consumer advertising as a laughing matter. Their professional association, the Canadian Medical Association (CMA), has a policy opposing such advertising. The CMA says it is concerned that such advertising "is not information but marketing, and sends the message that a prescription drug is a 'consumer good' rather than a health care benefit." In addition, the CMA says DTCA may not provide enough information for consumers to make informed drug choices, "may stimulate demand by exaggerating the risks of a disease and generating unnecessary fear," may strain the relationship between health care providers and patients, and even "drives up the cost of health care."

Canadian broadcasters want the DTCA ban lifted, arguing that Canadians see TV and print ads coming from the United States anyway.

sources: Canadian Press, "Study Details Drug Company Interest in Marketing Over Research," *Marketing* magazine, January 4, 2008; Jeromy Lloyd, "Viagra Ads Face Stiff Competition from Cialis," *Marketing* magazine, May 9, 2008; Canadian Medical Association, "Direct-to-Consumer Advertising (DTCA) Policy," September 2002; Pharmaceutical Advertising Advisory Board, www.paab.ca.

PRACTISING ETHICAL DECISION MAKING

In Chapter 1, you learned about a process for making ethical decisions (Exhibit 1.14). You can address the following questions for this ethical dilemma to improve your skills for making ethical decisions. Think about your answers to these questions and discuss them with others.

Ethical Decision-Making Process	Questions to Consider About This Ethical Dilemma
Identify ethical problems as they arise.	Does direct-to-consumer advertising create an ethical problem for pharmaceutical companies? Why or why not?
Objectively consider the well-being of others and society when exploring alternatives.	Describe the different viewpoints about whether pharmaceutical companies should advertise directly to consumers. What assumptions lie behind each viewpoint? Are differences in ethical values evident?
Clarify and apply ethical values when choosing a course of action.	What is the best overall solution to this problem for society? What values did you use to arrive at the solution? What ethical values should drug companies use to address the concerns of their critics?
Work toward ongoing improvement of personal and organizational ethics.	How might drug companies continuously improve their marketing practices to benefit themselves and society?

Cost Estimation Techniques

Although past costs are not directly relevant to decisions, they are often useful in estimating future cost behaviour. For example, past materials and labour costs might be the best estimate of future production costs. Historical costs are generally recorded and coded within the accounting system so that they can be summarized in different ways, depending on the cost object of interest. The Magik Bicycles accounting system might be used to create one or more reports of last year's production costs, material usage, and labour hours. The ease with which information can be identified for a particular cost object depends on the design of the accounting system as well as the nature of the information.

Information for some costs cannot be obtained easily from the accounting system. In estimating next year's production costs, the managers of Magik Bicycles would gather information about changes in direct materials costs from their suppliers' price lists or from other vendors' websites.

When estimating a cost function, accountants usually begin with past cost information, if it is available. Although past cost information might be accurate and useful, it may at times be unavailable, irrelevant, or outdated. Sometimes a combination of information sources is the best choice. Exhibit 2.9 presents a decision tree for deciding whether to use past costs or other information when estimating a cost function.

As we gather relevant information, we may have a general idea of the cost behaviour. However, we need to select one or more techniques for estimating the dollar amount of relevant costs. The following techniques are used to estimate a cost function:

- Engineered estimate of cost
- Analysis at the account level
- Scatter plots
- Two-point method
- High-low method
- Regression analysis

Although each of these methods may be used, the choice is open-ended; no single technique is useful in all circumstances. Although some techniques are generally better than others, the best technique often depends on the circumstances for a particular decision. As we look at each technique, pay particular attention to its assumptions. Poor management decisions can result if the quality of cost estimates is not considered.

> **EXHIBIT 2.9**

Deciding Whether to Use Past Costs for Estimating a Cost Function

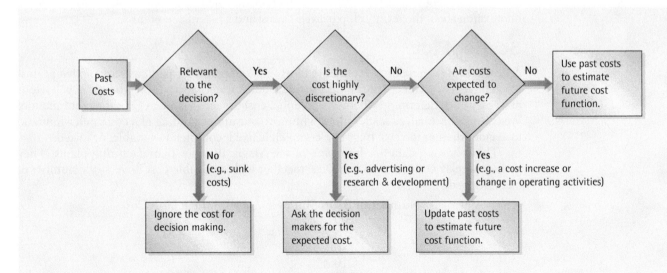

Engineered Estimates of Cost

One method used to estimate a cost function is the **engineered estimate of cost**, in which each activity is analyzed according to the amount of labour time, materials, and other resources used. Costs are assigned according to these measurements. Suppose Apple begins production of a new Apple Watch. Engineers and accountants use the new model's design specifications to estimate the cost of direct and indirect materials for a production run of Apple Watch. In addition, the proposed manufacturing process is analyzed to determine the cost effects of any changes from the existing manufacturing processes. The accountants communicate with purchasing department personnel to determine whether the prices of inputs are likely to change. From this information, a total cost function is developed for the production of Apple Watch for the next period.

Although engineers traditionally develop engineered estimates of cost, anyone who has sufficient knowledge about activities and costs can develop a cost function using this method. For example, in Appendix 2B we estimate the number of labour hours required when a learning curve is involved. We could use this approach to develop a labour cost function for new products or services.

Suppose Sunghoon, a consultant in an accounting firm, wishes to create a cost budget for a consulting job. He begins by identifying the various tasks that must be performed and incidental costs (e.g., travel, printing) that might be incurred. Sunghoon then develops a time budget by specifying the professional level (e.g., partner, manager, supervisor, staff) involved and number of hours needed to perform each task. While developing the time budget, Sunghoon refers to records from prior consulting jobs and his knowledge about the new job. He then creates a budget for professional labour cost by applying cost rates for each type of staff to the time budget. Next, Sunghoon develops budgets for each incidental cost. Finally, he combines the costs from all budgets to estimate the total cost for the job.

Analyses at the Account Level

Besides engineered estimate of cost, another way to create a cost function is to use **analysis at the account level**. Using this technique, we review the pattern of a cost over time in the accounting system and use our knowledge of operations to classify the cost as variable, fixed, or mixed. Costs such as managers' salaries are usually fixed; they are often directly associated in the general ledger with a particular department or product. Costs for variable materials used in the production process are usually available in the general ledger or in production records. Costs such as manufacturing overhead are often mixed; they tend to include fixed costs such as insurance and property taxes for the plant and variable costs such as indirect supplies used in manufacturing. For costs we identify as mixed, we must use another cost estimation technique, such as the two-point method or regression analysis, to determine the fixed and variable components. Sometimes we are uncertain about the nature of the cost function, in which case a scatter plot provides helpful information about the relationship between a cost and a potential cost driver.

Scatter Plots

A **scatter plot** is a graphical technique in which data points for past costs are plotted against a potential cost driver. Scatter plots provide a quick way to learn more about the behaviour of a cost and to determine whether a potential cost driver is viable as Q in the cost function. We can visually analyze scatter plots to improve our understanding of a cost's behaviour and to decide whether the cost might be completely fixed, completely variable, or mixed.

The following data are from one of the Magik Bicycles manufacturing plants. They include weekly costs for packing bikes, together with a possible cost driver—the number of bikes shipped:

Number of Bikes Shipped	Total Packing Cost
200	$729
270	870
250	820
210	720
300	950
175	700

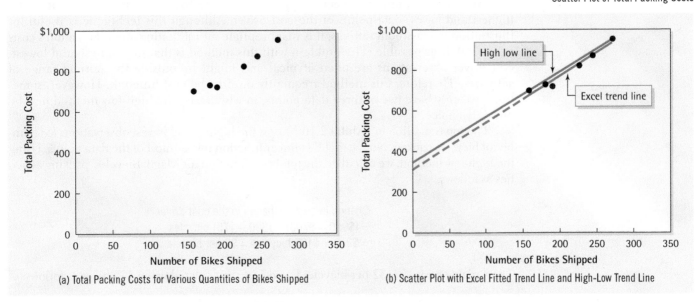

(a) Total Packing Costs for Various Quantities of Bikes Shipped

(b) Scatter Plot with Excel Fitted Trend Line and High-Low Trend Line

Exhibit 2.10(a) shows a scatter plot of these data. Notice that the data points seem to fall in a generally upward linear pattern, suggesting that total packing costs increase with the number of bikes shipped. In addition, if we draw a trend line roughly through the middle of the data points, as shown in Exhibit 2.10(b), and continue the line to the vertical axis, the intercept appears to be above zero. Thus, the scatter plot suggests that the cost of packing is a mixed cost with an apparent variable component (the slope) and a fixed component (the intercept).

▶ HELPFUL HINT
To add a trend line in Excel, create a scatter plot, right-click in the area of the data points, and then select the Add Trendline option.

Two-Point Method

The **two-point method** uses any two sets of data points for cost and a cost driver to algebraically calculate a mixed cost function. These data points can be drawn from a scatter plot. The line should resemble the general pattern of the data and be drawn using a ruler on a printed scatter plot or using a spreadsheet's line-draw feature. Spreadsheet programs such as Excel create a trend line representing the best fit for the data points.

▶ ALTERNATIVE TERMS
These terms are synonymous: *two-point method* and *scattergraph technique*.

We create the cost function by selecting and performing calculations with any two points on the line, even if they are not original data points. Variable cost (V) is calculated by computing the slope of the line—the change in cost compared to the change in the cost driver (Q) between the two points. Given V, the fixed cost is calculated by solving for F in the formula $TC = F + V \times Q$ for one of the two data points.

The lower trend line in Exhibit 2.10(b) was created using Excel. Two points on the trend line have values for Q of 240 and 190 bicycles on the horizontal axis. These same points have respective values for TC of $800 and $700 on the vertical axis. Using those two points, we calculate variable cost as follows:

Change in cost ÷ Change in the cost driver
= ($800 − $700) ÷ (240 − 190) bicycles
= ($100 ÷ 50) bicycles = $2 per bicycle

Thus, V = $2 per bicycle. We can now calculate fixed cost using 190 bikes as follows:

$700 = F + 90 bicycles × $2 per bicycle
F = $700 − $380 = $320

▶ HELPFUL HINT
We could have used the total cost for 240 units to solve for fixed costs as follows: $800 = F + 240 bicycles × $2 per bicycle, so F = $800 − $480 = $320.

The total cost function (per week) for packing bikes is estimated as

TC = $320 + $2 Q

High-Low Method

The **high-low method** is a specific application of the two-point method that uses the highest and lowest data points of the cost driver. Although this technique is useful for illustration in classroom settings, it is inappropriate for estimating an organization's costs as accurately as possible. The problem with this method is that the highest- and lowest-cost driver observations are often atypical and might lie outside the normal range of activities. Therefore, this method frequently distorts the cost function. However, sometimes we only have two or three data points, in which case the high-low method may be our only choice.

The top trend line in Exhibit 2.10(b) uses the highest and lowest observations for number of bicycles packed. Notice that this linear function misses most of the data points. Using the high-low method, we calculate the total cost function for Magik Bicycles' packing activities as follows:

$$\text{Change in cost} \div \text{Change in the cost driver}$$
$$= (\$950 - \$700) \div (300 - 175) \text{ bicycles}$$
$$= \$250 \div \$125 \text{ bicycles} = \$2 \text{ per bicycle}$$

The variable cost, V, is $2 per bicycle. Fixed cost is calculated using 175 bikes as follows:

$$\$700 = F + 175 \text{ bicycles} \times \$2 \text{ per bicycle}$$
$$F = \$700 - \$350$$
$$= \$350$$

The total cost function for packing bikes, then, is

$$TC = \$350 + \$2\ Q$$

Using this cost function, Magik Bicycles' managers can estimate the total packing costs, within the relevant range, for the following period. For example, the managers estimate a total packing cost of $910 for manufacturing 280 bicycles:

$$TC = F + V \times Q$$
$$\$910 = \$350 + \$2 \times 280$$

Estimating the Cost Function

| L04 | Apply cost estimation techniques to determine future costs |

Exhibit 2.11 summarizes the activities involved in estimating a cost function for a particular cost object. The following Small Animal Clinic example demonstrates how to create a cost function.

▷EXHIBIT 2.11

Estimating Relevant Costs
for a Cost Object

Identify relevant costs for the cost object	Estimate a Cost Function for Each Relevant Cost				Combine all relevant cost estimates for the cost object
	Obtain information needed for estimation	Categorize costs as fixed, variable, or mixed	Select and apply cost estimation techniques	Specify the cost function and then estimate the future cost	

◄───── **Continuously Evaluate Uncertainties and Quality of Information** ─────►

example

small animal clinic, part 1
CREATING A COST FUNCTION

Small Animal Clinic is a not-for-profit clinic that provides limited veterinarian services, primarily vaccinations, for the surrounding community. The clinic has been growing each year, and its manager expects this trend to continue. The recent growth has actually been driven by an economic downturn. With rising unemployment, more people are unable to pay regular veterinarian fees. Many have turned to Small Animal Clinic, which charges a lower rate for services than other clinics. A local foundation has provided Small Animal Clinic a matching grant for its services. For example, if a pet owner pays $30 for an examination and vaccines, the foundation will match the fee with an additional $30. This support has enabled the clinic to keep its rates low.

Monty Rakusen/Getty Images

Identifying Relevant Costs and Obtaining Information Needed for Estimation

As part of her operating plans, Leticia Brown, the manager of Small Animal Clinic, would like to create a budget of next year's revenues and costs. Leticia estimates that the clinic will provide services for 3,800 visits next year. The accountant, Josh Hardy, determined that the cost object is the clinic, and the cost driver for the clinic as a whole is the number of animal visits. Then, from the accounting records, he identified five relevant costs for the clinic: part-time veterinarians, technicians, treatment supplies, rent, and administration costs. He performed analysis at the account level to obtain the information needed to estimate future costs. The information for the past three years follows:

	2014	2015	2016
Animal visits	2,500	3,000	3,500
Veterinary fees	$ 72,500	$ 90,000	$105,000
Foundation matching grant	72,500	90,000	105,000
Total Revenue	145,000	180,000	210,000
Expenses:			
Part-time veterinarians	24,000	32,800	42,000
Technicians	71,000	78,000	78,049
Treatment supplies	4,000	4,600	5,200
Rent	8,000	8,500	8,750
Administration	38,000	39,600	41,200
Total expenses	145,000	163,500	175,199
Surplus	$ 0	$ 16,500	$ 34,801

Because Small Animal Clinic is a not-for-profit organization, its profit is referred to as *surplus*.

Categorizing Costs, Applying Cost Estimation Techniques, and Estimating Future Costs

To create individual cost functions, Josh categorizes each cost as fixed, variable, or mixed, and he identifies potential cost drivers for the variable and mixed costs. He then selects the appropriate cost estimation technique for the mixed costs, develops the cost function, and estimates future costs for each relevant cost.

Part-Time Veterinarians. Josh studies the payroll records and finds a lot of variation in the cost of veterinarians. Part-time veterinarians are called in as necessary and are paid on an hourly basis. Most of their time is spent with animals, so Josh determines that this is a direct cost. Therefore, he thinks that the amount of time the veterinarians spend with each animal might be a cost driver. However, the accounting system does not record the visit time per animal. Instead, records are available for the total number of animal visits. Josh considers other potential cost drivers, such as number of veterinarians on-call and the hours the clinic is open, but he eliminates them because they seem less likely than number of animal visits to have a cause-and-effect relationship with veterinarian wages. Therefore, he categorizes veterinarian fees as a variable cost and plans to use number of animal visits as the cost driver.

continued...

Josh knows that although veterinarian pay is increased periodically, no increase is planned for next year. Because last year's information is the most current, he uses only last year's data to create the cost function. In 2016, this category included no fixed costs, and the variable cost per animal visit was $12.00 ($42,000 total cost ÷ 3,500 animal visits). The cost function for veterinarians, then, is

$$TC = \$0 + \$12.00 \text{ per animal visit} \times Q \text{ animal visits}$$

Josh can now estimate 2017 costs, with $Q = 3,800$ animal visits:

$$TC = \$12.00 \text{ per animal visit} \times 3,800 \text{ animal visits} = \$45,600$$

Technicians. Josh learns from payroll records that the technician staff is permanent and paid on a salary basis. The technicians clean examination rooms, prepare supplies, fill out paperwork, handle the reception desk, and assist the veterinarians with each visit. Because they work on many different tasks, Josh concludes that this cost is indirect and fixed.

Again, Josh uses the most current information in his cost function. A 2.5% salary increase is expected for 2017. With no variable costs, and only the fixed cost of $78,049 for 2014, the updated cost function for technicians is

$$TC = (\$78,049 \times 1.025) + \$0 \, Q = \$80,000$$

Josh estimates the 2017 cost for technicians to be $80,000.

Treatment Supplies. Josh believes that treatment supplies is either a variable cost or a mixed cost. He learns from the technicians that treatment supplies include items that vary depending on the services provided, such as vaccination serum and syringes. He also learns that supplies include items, such as lab coats for clinic employees, that vary by number of employees rather than visits. He concludes that the cost of treatment supplies is a mixed cost, and he believes that number of animal visits has a cause-and-effect relationship for the variable portion.

Josh learns that few significant changes occurred in the cost or use of treatment supplies over the past three years. Therefore, he decides to use all three years' data to estimate the cost function. With only three data points, he uses the high-low method to separate the fixed and variable components of treatment supplies. He first identifies the highest and lowest data points for the cost driver, which is number of animal visits. The lowest number of animal visits was in 2014, and the highest number was in 2014. He calculates the variable cost per unit by dividing the change in cost ($5,200 – $4,000) by the change in volume (3,500 – 2,500) for these two data points:

$$(\$5,200 - \$4,000) \div (3,500 - 2,500) = \$1,200 \div 1,000 = \$1.20 \text{ per animal visit}$$

Next, Josh substitutes the variable cost rate into the cost equation for 2017 and solves for the fixed costs:

$$TC = F + V \times Q$$
$$\$5,200 = F + \$1.20 \text{ per animal visit} \times 3,500 \text{ animal visits}$$
$$\$5,200 = F + \$4,200$$
$$F = \$1,000$$

Josh's cost function for treatment supplies is

$$TC = \$1,000 + \$1.20 \text{ per animal visit} \times Q \text{ animal visits}$$

He can now estimate costs for treatment supplies in 2017, assuming 3,800 animal visits:

$$TC = \$1,000 + \$1.20 \text{ per animal visit} \times 3,800$$

Rent. Josh knows that rent can change annually when the lease is renewed. However, rent changes depend on local rates rather than on the level of operating activity at the clinic. Accordingly, he categorizes rent as a fixed cost.

Josh uses the most recent rent amount to set up his cost function:

$$TC = \$8,750 + \$0 \, Q$$
$$TC = \$8,750$$

He does not update this figure because he learns that the property manager is not planning to increase rent for 2017. Therefore, his estimate for rent is also $8,750.

Administration. Josh learns that administration includes costs to set up files for new animals and office supplies related to the paperwork for each visit. Josh reviews the general ledger entries and finds that the remainder of the administrative cost is for salaries, general office supplies, and telephone, which he concludes are fixed costs. Thus, he concludes that administration is a mixed cost, with animal visits as the cost driver for the variable portion.

Josh performs an account analysis of the administrative costs, separating out the cost of supplies such as file folders, tabs, and the forms required for each visit. From his analysis, he calculates the cost of these supplies as $8,000 in 2010, $9,600 in 2015, and $11,200 in 2016, or about $3.20 per animal visit. He bases his estimate of fixed administrative costs on the most recent year's data. During 2016, total administrative costs were $41,200. When he subtracts the variable cost of $11,200, this leaves $30,000 ($41,200 − $11,200) as his estimate of the fixed cost. Therefore, his cost function for administration is

$$TC = \$30,000 + \$3.20 \text{ per animal visit} \times Q \text{ animal visits}$$

Josh now estimates administration cost for 2017:

$$TC = \$30,000 + \$3.20 \text{ per animal visit} \times 3,800 \text{ animal visits} = \$42,160$$

Combining All Relevant Cost Estimates

Josh creates the following summary of his cost functions and estimated costs for 2017:

Cost	Category	Fixed Cost	Variable Cost per Animal Visit	2017 Estimated Cost for 3,800 Animal Visits
Part-time veterinarians	Variable	$ 0	$12.00	$ 45,600
Technicians	Fixed	80,000	0.00	80,000
Treatment supplies	Mixed	1,000	1.20	5,560
Rent	Fixed	8,750	0.00	8,750
Administration	Mixed	30,000	3.20	42,160
Total		$119,750	$16.40	$182,070

The total cost function for Small Animal Clinic is

$$TC = \$119,750 + \$16.40 \text{ per animal visit} \times Q \text{ animal visits}$$

Based on Leticia's estimate of 3,800 animal visits for next year, Josh estimates that total 2017 costs will be

$$\$119,750 + \$16.40 \text{ per animal visit} \times 3,800 \text{ animal visits} = \$182,070$$

Estimating Profit

Leticia told Josh that she did not expect any major changes from 2016 to 2017 in the types of services provided, the average fees, or the matching grant. Josh does not know the average of last year's fees, so he calculates it from last year's revenue information (which includes the matching grant):

Average revenue in 2016 = Total 2016 revenue ÷ Number of animal visits in 2016
= $210,000 ÷ 3,500 animal visits
= $60.00 per animal visit

Given average revenues of $60.00 per animal visit, budgeted revenues for 2017 (including the matching grant) are

Budgeted revenues = Estimated 2013 animal visits × Average revenue rate
= 3,800 animal visits × $60.00 per animal visit
= $228,000

Using the budgeted revenues and costs as calculated, Josh tells Leticia that he expects Small Animal Clinic to earn a surplus during 2013 of $45,930 ($228,000 − $182,070). ■

Regression Analysis

L05   Utilize regression analysis in cost estimation

In the Small Animal Clinic illustration, Josh used the high-low method to estimate the cost function for treatment supplies. This method is often not sufficiently accurate, because it uses the two most extreme data points, which could distort the cost function. An alternative estimation technique is regression analysis, a statistical technique that measures the average change in a dependent variable for every unit change in one or more independent variables. Regression analysis uses all the available data points and often improves the accuracy of a cost function.

With **simple regression analysis**, you develop a cost function by calculating values for the statistical relationship between total cost and a single cost driver. With **multiple regression analysis**, you develop a cost function by calculating values for the statistical relationship between total cost and two or more cost drivers.

Simple Regression Analysis

In Exhibit 2.10, we created a scatter plot for a cost object, packing costs, and a cost driver—the number of bikes. We used Excel to draw a trend line and developed a cost function using that data. Simple regression analysis is a statistical method used to find the trend line that minimizes the distance from every data point to the line. The slope of the line represents the variable cost per unit, and the intercept of the line with the vertical axis represents the fixed cost. The distance between each observation and the line is called the *error term*. In locating a slope that best fits all the available data, regression analysis minimizes the sum of the squared error terms.

Simple regression analysis estimates the following equation:

$$Y = \alpha + \beta X + \varepsilon$$

where Y is the dependent variable (total cost), α (alpha) is the intercept (fixed cost), β (beta) is the slope coefficient (variable cost per unit), X is the independent variable (the cost driver), and ε (epsilon) is the error term, also called the *residual*.

We usually use a computer program such as Excel or SAS to perform regression analysis. The ability of computer programs to perform regression analyses easily makes the cost of using this technique low. Thus, the cost of performing regression analysis is not likely to exceed the benefits.

Interpreting Simple Regression Results

Regression analysis provides the best estimate of the cost function in cases with a strong positive linear relationship between the cost and the cost driver. However, the data points we use in a regression rarely fit into an absolutely straight line. Deviations from linearity may occur because the true, underlying cost function is not strictly linear. They may also occur because the regression data typically come from past costs and activities that might be mismeasured or include things like unusual events, shifts in cost behaviour over time, or random fluctuations. When interpreting regression results, we need to keep in mind that we are using regression analysis *only* because we do not know the actual cost function and must estimate it. Furthermore, we might not be confident that the cost we are trying to estimate is a mixed cost. We use regression to estimate the cost function and to learn more about how the cost behaves. Exhibit 2.12 presents the questions that we address when using simple regression to estimate a cost function.

Exhibit 2.13 shows the output from regressing Magik Bicycles' packing costs on the number of bikes packed. For each coefficient (alpha and beta), the regression output includes both a *t*-statistic and a *p*-value. We examine the *t*-statistic calculated for each coefficient to evaluate whether that coefficient is significantly greater than zero. The *t*-statistic compares the coefficient with its *standard error*. If the coefficient is small relative to the standard error, we cannot be confident that the coefficient is different from zero. If the *t*-statistic is significantly

> ◢ **HELPFUL HINT**
> In this chapter, we focus only on linear regression analysis. Other nonlinear forms of regression are beyond the scope of this textbook.

> ◢ **CHAPTER REFERENCE**
> Appendix 2A presents additional regression topics, including an example of multiple regression analysis, choosing among cost drivers, assumptions for regression analysis, and other data considerations.

> ◢ **HELPFUL HINT**
> The squared error is the square of the distance from each observation to the regression trend line.

> ◢ **HELPFUL HINT**
> You can use the Help function to learn how to apply regression in Excel. The web-based option sends you directly to an Excel tutorial.

> ◢ **HELPFUL HINT**
> The standard error for each coefficient tells us the amount of variation we could expect in our estimates, using the value of the coefficient as expected cost.

Question about the Cost Function	Relevant Simple Regression Statistics
How confident can we be that the actual fixed cost is greater than zero (i.e., that there is a fixed component in the cost function)?	t-statistic and p-value for the alpha coefficient
How confident can we be that the actual variable cost per unit of the cost driver is greater than zero (i.e., that there is a variable component in the cost function)?	t-statistic and p-value for the beta coefficient
Overall, how well does the cost driver explain the behaviour (i.e., the variation) in the cost?	Adjusted R-square, as well as t-statistic and p-value for both coefficients

> **EXHIBIT 2.12**
Questions Addressed by Simple Regression Analysis

> **EXHIBIT 2.13**
Regression Analysis Results for Shipping Costs and Number of Bikes

SUMMARY OUTPUT

Regression Statistics	
Multiple R	0.98203762
R-Square	0.964397887
Adjusted R-Square	0.955497359
Standard Error	20.93063353
Observations	6

	Coefficients	Standard Error	t-Stat	P-value
Intercept	314.3742975	47.25604376	6.652573354	0.002651235
X Variable 1	2.066017235	0.198478609	10.40926901	0.000481073

large (above 2.00), we have more confidence that our estimates for fixed and variable costs are different from zero. The p-value gives the statistical significance of the t-statistic, or the probability that the coefficient is not different from zero. Acceptable p-values generally need to be less than 0.10 and preferably less than 0.05.

A low p-value for the alpha coefficient gives us confidence that the fixed cost is significantly different from zero. Similarly, a low p-value for the beta coefficient gives us confidence that the variable cost is significantly different from zero. If a p-value is too high, we conclude that the coefficient should not be used in the cost function. Sometimes, only one of the coefficients is statistically greater than zero. In such a case, we generally conclude that the cost is not mixed but instead is variable or fixed (depending on which coefficient is significant).

Interpreting the output from the Magik Bicycles example (Exhibit 2.13), the intercept (fixed cost) is $314, and the p-value for the t-statistic is 0.002. This result means that the fixed cost has a probability of being zero about 2 in 1,000 times. We are quite confident that it is different from zero. The beta coefficient ($2.07) also has a small p-value (0.0004). Using this information, our total cost function would be TC = $314 + $2.07 Q, where Q is the number of bikes.

The adjusted R-square statistic reflects an estimate of the percentage of variation in cost that is explained by the cost driver. In the Magik Bicycles example, the adjusted R-square is 0.95. This result means that the variation in number of bikes packed explains about 95% of the variation in packing cost. An advantage of regression analysis when more than one potential cost driver is involved is that we can compare the adjusted R-squares from several regressions that have different cost drivers for the same cost. The cost driver that provides the highest adjusted R-square explains the largest portion of changes in the cost.

We will next illustrate how to use simple regression analysis to estimate a cost function for Small Animal Clinic. The process we will use is summarized in Exhibit 2.14. We will also compare the results for simple regression with the two-point and high-low methods.

> **ALTERNATIVE TERMS**
The *adjusted R-square* is also called the *adjusted coefficient of determination.*

> **EXHIBIT 2.14**
Using Regression Analysis to Estimate a Cost Function

1. **Consider the behaviour of the cost.** Decide whether the cost is likely to be a good candidate for regression analysis. The best candidates for regression are costs that appear to be mixed.

2. **Generate a list of possible cost drivers.** The cost drivers must be economically plausible; changes in the cost driver could potentially affect cost.

3. **Gather data.** We need data for both the dependent variable (the cost being estimated) and one or more independent variables (the cost drivers).

4. **Plot the cost for each potential cost driver.** Scatter plots that have a positive slope or a football-shaped pattern indicate a potential linear relationship between the cost and the cost driver. Eliminate any cost drivers that do not exhibit a positive linear relationship with cost. If no cost drivers remain, the cost should not be estimated using regression analysis.

5. **Perform the regression analysis.** For each remaining potential cost driver, perform simple regression analysis, with that driver as the independent variable. If necessary, perform a series of multiple regression analyses with different combinations of cost drivers. Use a spreadsheet program such as Excel to perform the regressions.

6. **Evaluate the appropriateness of each cost driver.** Use the goodness-of-fit statistic (adjusted R-square) to select the cost drivers that explain a high proportion of variability in the cost.

7. **Evaluate the sign and significance of the cost function's components.** Verify that each coefficient is positive. Use the p-values for the t-statistics to determine whether the intercept coefficient reflecting fixed cost and slope coefficient reflecting variable cost are significantly different from zero.

8. **Write the cost function as $TC = F + V \times Q$.** If significantly different from zero, use the intercept coefficient as the estimated fixed cost and the independent variable coefficient as the estimated variable cost.

Evaluating and Choosing a Cost Driver

After obtaining the results from the regression analysis, it is important to review if the cost driver is appropriate for predicting the future cost. In evaluating a cost driver, managers need to look for three key elements. First, *economic plausibility*—the cost driver explains the change in the cost; in other words, the cost driver causes the cost. Second, *goodness of fit (R^2)*—the certainty that the regression line can predict the future cost. R-square is between 0% and 100%. The higher the percentage of R-square, the higher the certainty for predicting the future cost. Third, *slope of the regression*—the steepness of the line explains the relationship between the cost and the cost driver. A steeper line indicates a stronger relationship, as a small change in the activity will result in a significant change in the cost.

small animal clinic : part 2
TWO-POINT METHOD AND REGRESSION ANALYSIS

When Josh shows Leticia his revenue and cost estimates, she questions him about the cost of treatment supplies. Believing his estimate to be too high, she asks him to investigate this cost further.

Revised Analysis of the Treatment Supplies Cost

When Josh originally estimated the cost function for treatment supplies, he had only three data points—the cost for each of the past three years. With so few data points, he used the high-low method to estimate the cost function. Using quarterly data, however, would give him more data points, allowing him to use other estimation techniques that would generate a higher-quality cost function.

Josh is also concerned about the accuracy of the data for the number of animal visits, which are tracked manually at the reception desk, and sometimes go unrecorded. He considers using the number of bills recorded in the accounting system to count the number of animal

example

visits, but a single pet owner often brings in more than one pet during the same visit but only receives a single bill for all the pets. He considers then whether another cost driver would be more accurate.

Josh knows that the veterinarians use different supplies for each visit, because the needs of each pet are different. For example, a puppy may get a series of vaccinations at the same visit, whereas an adult dog gets only one or two vaccinations per visit. Yet when Josh uses number of animal visits as the cost driver, he assumes that the same amount of supplies is used for each visit. Josh knows that the bill for each visit includes charges for supplies, and therefore, the revenue per visit varies with the number and type of supplies used. He determines that revenue might be better correlated with treatment supplies than with number of animal visits. He also thinks that the data for revenue per visit are more accurate because they are recorded by the accounting system when bills are created.

Quarterly Data

Although Josh believes that revenue may be better correlated with treatment supplies cost than with animal visits, he decides to analyze both drivers to learn more about their behaviour. He collects the following quarterly data for his analyses:

Quarter	Treatment Animal Supplies Cost	Visits	Revenues
2014-1	$1,000	500	$18,125
2014-2	920	725	17,400
2014-3	1,120	700	20,300
2014-4	960	575	16,675
2015-1	966	750	18,900
2015-2	1,058	960	20,700
2015-3	1,288	600	24,300
2015-4	1,288	690	26,100
2016-1	1,404	700	28,350
2016-2	1,092	595	23,100
2016-3	1,404	910	29,400
2016-4	1,300	1,295	24,150

Scatter Plots

Josh creates scatter plots of the treatment supplies cost against animal visits and against revenues. When creating the scatter plots, he wants the vertical axes on the two plots to have the same scale so that he can compare them. He visually examines the plots and fits a trend line to each plot. Josh notices that most of the cost points are relatively close to the trend line in the revenue scatter plot shown in Exhibit 2.15(a), whereas many of the data points are farther away from the trend line in the animal visit scatter plot in Exhibit 2.15(b). This observation suggests that revenue is likely to provide a more accurate cost function than will number of animal visits.

▶**EXHIBIT 2.15**

Scatter Plots for Quarterly Treatment Supplies Cost

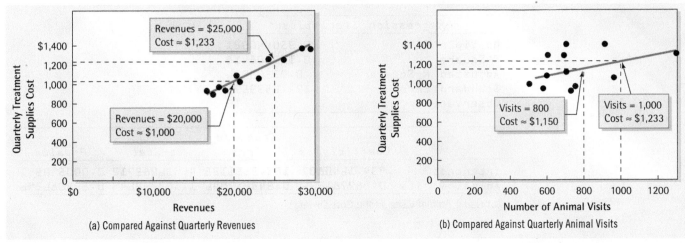

(a) Compared Against Quarterly Revenues

(b) Compared Against Quarterly Animal Visits

continued...

example

Two-Point Method

Josh decides to use the two-point method with revenue as the cost driver. He selects the points when revenues are $20,000 and $25,000, and he draws a vertical line from these points on the revenue axis to the trend line, shown in Exhibit 2.15(a). Where each vertical line intersects the trend line, Josh draws a horizontal line to the cost axis and visually estimates the cost for the two points as $1,000 and $1,233, respectively. Dividing the change in cost ($1,233 – $1,000) by the change in revenues ($25,000 – $20,000), he estimates a variable cost of $0.047 per dollar of revenue, or 4.7% of revenues. He then uses the data point for cost of $1,000 to estimate the fixed cost, using the following formula for the cost function:

$$\$1,000 = F + (4.7\% \times \$20,000)$$
$$F = \$1,000 - \$940 = \$60$$

Given these calculations, Josh estimates the cost function as

$$TC = \$60 + 4.7\% \times Revenues$$

Next, Josh uses the two-point method with animal visits as the cost driver. He uses the same procedures as previously, with revenue as the cost driver, to choose two points on the trend line, shown in Exhibit 2.15(b). Given these two points, he estimates the cost function as

$$TC = \$813 + \$0.42 \times Number\ of\ animal\ visits$$

Simple Regression Analysis

Josh is concerned that his calculations using the two-point method may not be as accurate as he would like. He decides to perform simple regression analysis. When number of animal visits is the cost driver, as in Exhibit 2.16(b), the adjusted R-square is 0.035, which is very low. But when revenue is the cost driver, as in Exhibit 2.16(a), the adjusted R-square is quite high, at 0.915, suggesting that changes in revenue explain about 91.5% of the changes in supplies cost.

▶ **EXHIBIT 2.16**

Simple Regressions for Quarterly Treatment Supplies Cost

Regression Statistics	
Multiple R	0.96078362
R-Square	0.923105164
Adjusted R-Square	0.91541568
Standard Error	51.70748707
Observations	12

	Coefficients	Standard Error	t-Stat	P-value
Intercept	258.5795187	82.71694129	3.126076891	0.010762095
Revenue	0.039988956	0.00364975	10.95663014	6.83893E-07

(a) Using Revenues as the Cost Driver

Regression Statistics	
Multiple R	0.350440321
R-Square	0.122808418
Adjusted R-Square	0.03508926
Standard Error	174.6433571
Observations	12

	Coefficients	Standard Error	t-Stat	P-value
Intercept	934.1640807	189.2521125	4.936082712	0.000590591
Animal Visits	0.287781226	0.243217946	1.183223649	0.264086296

(b) Using Animal Visits as the Cost Driver

Josh concludes that revenue is a much better cost driver than animal visits. However, he waits to reach a final conclusion until he analyzes the rest of the regression results.

Focusing on Exhibit 2.16(a), Josh observes that the coefficients for both the intercept (259) and independent variable (0.040) are positive, as required to create a cost function. He notices that the p-value for the intercept is 0.01, suggesting only a small probability that the intercept could be zero. The p-value for the coefficient on revenue is even smaller, at 0.00000068, suggesting a tiny probability that the coefficient could be zero. These results give Josh considerable confidence in the regression results. He creates a new cost function for treatment supplies, as follows:

$$TC = \$259 + 4.0\% \times Revenue$$

Revised Cost Estimate

Josh's earlier estimate of $228,000 for 2013 revenue includes the matching grant. However, the grant, which accounts for half of all revenues, is not included in the quarterly data used to estimate the new cost function. Therefore, Josh needs to divide estimated revenues in half when using the new cost function: $228,000 ÷ 2 = $114,000. His revised estimate of the treatment supply cost for 2013 is

$$TC = \$259 + (4.0\% \times \$114,000) = \$4,819$$

Next, he revises his estimate of total 2013 costs. He previously estimated total costs to be $182,070, including $5,560 in treatment supplies. His new estimate for total 2013 costs is $181,329 ($182,070 − $5,560 + $4,819). Finally, he revises his estimate of the 2013 surplus to account for changes in total costs:

$$Estimated\ surplus + \$228,000 - \$181,329 = \$46,671$$

Review of Methods, Total Cost Function

Josh reviews his results to gain a better understanding of how the various methods compare. A summary of his treatment supply cost estimates for 2013, for both cost drivers and for each estimation technique, follows:

		2013 Estimate
Number of Animal Visits (3,800 estimated for 2013):		
High-low method	TC = $1,000 + $1.20 per visit × Visits	$5,560
Two-point method	TC = $813 + $0.42 per visit × Visits	$2,409
Simple regression	TC = $934 + $0.29 per visit × Visits	$2,036
Revenues ($114,000 estimated for 2013):		
Two-point method	TC = $60 + $4.7% × Revenues	$5,700
Simple regression	TC = $259 + $4.0% × Revenues	$4,819

Josh is glad that he is no longer using his original estimate based on the high-low method and animal visits as a cost driver. He now believes that method would significantly overestimate the treatment costs. He is surprised to learn that the other two methods using animal visits as the cost driver might have significantly underestimated the cost. After comparing the two-point and regression results, he concludes that the two-point method is not very accurate. Overall, he decides that he will probably use regression analysis in the future to help with this type of estimate.

Finally, Josh revises the total cost function for the clinic. Even though revenue from pet owners is now being used as the driver for treatment supplies, other parts of the function still use the number of animal visits as the driver. He subtracts the $1.20 per animal visit that had been attributed to treatment supplies, leaving $15.20 for the other relevant variable costs. He also adjusts total fixed costs by subtracting $741 ($1,000 old fixed cost estimate − $259 new fixed cost estimate), leaving $119,009. Thus, the revised cost function is

$$TC = \$119,009 + (\$15.20 \times Number\ of\ animal\ visits) + (4.0\% \times Fee\ revenue)$$

Josh and Leticia decide to continue budgeting average revenue per animal visit at $60 ($30 in fees plus $30 in matching grant). They can now use this cost function to analyze best-case and worst-case scenarios and will be better prepared for unexpected changes that might occur next year. ■

LO2 **2-2** self-study problem   Cost Driver Choice Using Regression

Nursery Supply manufactures wooden planter tubs for small trees. Each wooden planter requires about the same level of effort in labour and machinery. The managers of Nursery Supply want to improve the quality of their budgets and are considering three alternative cost drivers for overhead: assembly time, labour hours, and machine hours. The statistics for regressions using last year's monthly data for each of the three possible cost drivers follow:

Cost driver = Assembly time
  Intercept = $55,000 ($t$-statistic = 2.44, p-value = 0.08)
  Slope = $21.00 ($t$-statistic 5 2.85, p-value = 0.05)
  Adjusted R-square = 0.31
Cost driver = Labour hours
  Intercept = $20,000 ($t$-statistic = 2.95, p-value = 0.03)
  Slope = $31.00 ($t$-statistic = 3.00, p-value = 0.01)
  Adjusted R-square = 0.46
Cost driver = Machine hours
  Intercept = $10,000 ($t$-statistic = 1.45, p-value = 0.25)
  Slope = $38.00 ($t$-statistic = 3.19, p-value = 0.005)
  Adjusted R-square = 0.70

required

A. Write the cost function for each of the cost drivers.
B. Explain the meaning of the adjusted R-square for the assembly time analysis.
C. Explain the meaning of the p-value for the intercept in the machine hours analysis.
D. Explain the meaning of the p-value for the slope in the labour hours analysis.
E. Given only the regression results, which cost driver would you choose for overhead costs? Explain.
F. Why do managers often use models such as a cost function to estimate future costs?

See the solution on page 75.

Uses and Limitations of Cost Estimates

LO6 Appreciate the uses and limitations of cost estimates

Uncertainties are a fact of life in the business world. Even the best available information and best decision-making processes may lead to poor outcomes. Nevertheless, managers make better decisions and obtain better average results when they use higher-quality information and decision-making processes. Because of uncertainties about future cost behaviour, we need to evaluate the quality of both our data and the various estimation techniques.

Information Quality

One factor that affects the quality of past cost information is whether the accounting system is able to directly trace the costs to individual cost objects. For example, if Magik Bicycles' accounting system traces the cost of handlebars to each bicycle produced, then past handlebar costs are known with high accuracy. This information, in turn, will improve the quality of future handlebar cost estimates.

If the accounting system cannot trace a relevant cost to a cost object, the cost must instead be allocated. For example, costs such as insurance costs can be traced to the production facility but cannot be traced to any one bicycle. However, a portion of these costs can be allocated to each bicycle produced. Accounting systems often accumulate indirect costs into overhead cost pools that tend to include a mixture of both fixed and variable costs. Appropriate cost drivers for these cost pools are often difficult to identify. Nevertheless, past accounting data might be the best information available for estimating indirect costs.

Recall from Chapter 1 that higher-quality information is more certain, complete, relevant, timely, and valuable. Better accounting systems improve the quantity, relevance, and timeliness of cost information. However, we may be unable to obtain higher-quality information. For example, in the Small Animal Clinic illustration, Josh initially lacked sufficient data to use regression analysis to separate mixed costs into fixed and variable components. This circumstance occurs frequently in the business world. Common reasons that past cost information might be unavailable or too unreliable to use include the following:

- ▶ The organization has operated for only a few periods.
- ▶ The organization's operations have changed substantially.
- ▶ Inflation, deflation, or other economic changes have altered the behaviour of costs.
- ▶ The organization operates in an environment where technologies and costs change rapidly.
- ▶ The organization's accounting system does not currently capture and report the needed information.

Under any of these circumstances, cost estimates based on past costs are of lower quality than cost estimates from better data. In addition, the quality of information often deteriorates over time. Accordingly, cost functions are most useful for estimating costs over short time periods, such as for the next year.

Common Errors in Estimating Relevant Costs

Because financial accounting information is readily available, accountants and managers often want to rely on it for decision making. As illustrated in Chapter 1, financial accounting measures are usually based on average costs, which are inappropriate for decision making. The **average cost (AC)** is simply computed as total costs (TC) divided by the quantity (Q) of activity or production ($AC = TC/Q$).

When average costs are used to estimate the cost function ($TC = 0 + AC \times Q$), fixed costs are assumed to be variable. Therefore, future costs are either overestimated or underestimated, unless future production is exactly the quantity used to calculate average cost per unit. Consequently, we usually avoid using financial statement costs, or any other average costs, for decision making.

Another source of error in estimating relevant costs arises from using accounting records for data. Transactions recorded in the general ledger tend to reflect purchase behaviour that does not properly match costs with the use of resources in production. For example, a production manager might purchase manufacturing supplies each time supply quantities reach a given level. Or the production manager might purchase supplies every three weeks. In either case, the timing of these purchases, and the date they are recorded in the accounting system, do not reflect when the supplies are used in production. A poorly estimated cost function results when a cost function is estimated using monthly supply purchases and volume of production as the cost driver. This type of estimation error is reduced by using accrual accounting techniques. If an inventory of production supplies is taken each month, accountants can calculate the amount of supplies used each month. Accrual-based cost data would provide a more accurate cost function.

Sometimes, managers assume that variable costs are always avoidable and are therefore relevant to decisions. Similarly, managers may assume that all fixed costs are unavoidable and irrelevant. These generalizations do not hold in all cases. From an operations perspective, costs are often categorized as fixed and variable with respect to production volumes. However, for decision making, costs are avoidable or unavoidable relative to the decision being made. For example, sales commissions are always variable, but they are not always relevant. For some decisions, such as a special order that is placed with a division manager, no sales employees are involved, so no commissions are paid. However, for sales through regular distribution channels, commissions are usually relevant. Similarly, an order for a specific customer might require a new piece of equipment. This is a fixed cost, but it is relevant to the decision to accept the order. On the other hand, if new equipment is purchased to replace old equipment that is broken, the fixed cost of the equipment is irrelevant to any decisions about customer orders.

▶ HELPFUL HINT

Cost-benefit analysis is the practice of considering the relevant costs and benefits when making decisions, such as whether to spend resources developing higher quality information.

Quality of Estimation Techniques

Exhibit 2.17 summarizes the advantages and disadvantages of each cost behaviour analysis approach introduced in this chapter. None of the methods is best in all circumstances. For example, regression analysis is a higher-quality technique than the two-point or high-low methods for separating mixed costs into fixed and variable components. However, regression cannot be used when too few observations of past costs are available. In addition, most of the methods in Exhibit 2.17 rely on past costs, which might need updating. The engineered estimate of cost method can be used when no past costs are available, and it also provides a benchmark that can be used to monitor the efficiency of costs in the future. Although we know that higher-quality techniques result in higher-quality information, we do not always use higher-quality techniques; sometimes the cost exceeds the benefit, and at other times we do not have adequate information required by a higher-quality technique.

Reliance on Cost Estimates

Concerns we have about the quality of cost information affect our reliance on the results. Managers might delay growth opportunities or alter operating decisions to avoid assuming extra risk in cases where they are less sure about their cost estimates. As managers make decisions, the quality of information affects the alternatives that they consider and the weight they place on various pieces of information.

> **EXHIBIT 2.17**

Advantages and Disadvantages of Cost Behaviour Analysis Approaches

Method and Description	Advantages	Disadvantages
Engineered Estimate of Cost • Analysis of labour time, materials, and other resources used in each activity • Cost estimates are based on resources used	• Can use when no past data are available • Provides a benchmark for what future costs should be • Most accurate for estimating costs of repetitive activities • Identifies and measures some nonlinear cost functions (e.g., economies of scale and learning curves)	• Difficult to estimate some types of costs, such as overhead
Analysis at the Account Level • A review of the pattern in past costs recorded in the accounting system • Knowledge of operations is used to classify cost as variable, fixed, or mixed	• Can be used when only one period of data is available • Best for costs that are fixed or variable • Provides information about types of costs incurred	• Difficult to identify costs that are not strictly fixed or strictly variable • Relies on past costs, which might not represent future costs • Determination of variable or fixed costs may be subjective
Scatter Plot • Plot of past data points for cost against a potential cost driver	• Provides information about cost behaviour in relation to potential cost drivers • Facilitates evaluation of whether a potential cost driver is viable	• Does not compute a cost function • Relies on past costs, which might not represent future costs
Two-Point Method • Algebraic calculation of a linear mixed cost function using any two data points of the cost and cost driver	• Can be used with as few as two data points • Computationally simple	• Difficult to identify most representative data points for estimating future costs • Ignores all but two data points (inefficient use of data) • Mismeasures the cost function if data points come from more than one relevant range • Relies on past costs, which might not represent future costs
High-Low Method • Specific application of the two-point method using the highest and lowest data points of the cost driver	• Same as two-point method • Does not require judgment for selecting data points	• Same as two-point method • Highest and lowest data points are often atypical, distorting the cost function
Regression Analysis • Statistical technique that measures the average change in a dependent variable for every unit change in one or more independent variables • Creates a linear cost function where variable cost is the slope of the regression line and fixed cost is the intercept	• Increases cost function accuracy by using all available data points • Best for a strong positive linear relationship between the cost and cost driver • Easy to perform with available software • Provides statistics for evaluating the quality of results	• Mismeasures the cost function if data points come from more than one relevant range • Inefficient for estimating a strictly fixed or strictly variable cost function • Relies on past costs, which might not represent future costs

REGRESSION ANALYSIS—ADDITIONAL TOPICS
Multiple Regression Analysis

Multiple regression is used when more than one cost driver may provide the best estimate of a cost function. Here, we use the same method to estimate the cost function as is illustrated in the chapter. The only difference is that two or more independent variables (cost drivers) are used in the regression analysis.

Choosing Cost Drivers for Multiple Regression

Sometimes several cost drivers appear to be correlated with the cost we are estimating; their scatter plots show a possible linear relationship with the cost object. In these cases, we include all the potential drivers in a multiple regression in order to determine the significance of each, and then we drop the drivers that have insignificant t-statistics. Remember, however, that each potential cost driver must have economic plausibility—a reason for us to believe that each might drive the cost we are trying to estimate.

LO5 Utilize regression analysis in cost estimation

print masters print shop
USING MULTIPLE REGRESSION TO ESTIMATE A COST FUNCTION

example

Print Masters Print Shop incurs overhead costs that are related to its printing machines (maintenance, depreciation, insurance, etc.) and to the amount of paper printed (ink, storage and handling of paper, packing materials, etc.). Exhibit 2A.1 summarizes monthly data for overhead costs, machine hours, and reams of paper used for Print Masters Print Shop.

Scatter Plots and Simple Regression Results

Exhibit 2A.2(a) shows a scatter plot for machine hours, and Exhibit 2A.2(b) shows a scatter plot for reams of paper. Each plot suggests a potential linear relationship with printing overhead costs, because it appears to have an upward slope, although the slope does not appear to be very steep in either plot. Thus, based on the scatter plots, both cost drivers appear to be viable. Simple regression analysis for each potential cost driver confirms this evidence. Following is a summary of the simple regression results:

	Machine Hours	Reams of Paper
Intercept coefficient	$58,800	$68,109
t-statistic (p-value)	11.43 (<0.0001)	11.63 (<0.0001)
Independent variable coefficient	$19.11	$0.02
t-statistic (p-value)	4.09 (0.0003)	3.08 (0.005)
Adjusted R-square	0.35	0.22

The intercepts and slope coefficients for both regressions are highly significant. However, the adjusted R-square is 0.35 for machine hours and 0.22 for reams of paper. Thus, neither driver appears to be a good overall predictor of the variation in printing overhead cost.

Multiple Regression Analysis

We can perform multiple regression analysis for printing overhead cost using both machine hours and reams of paper as independent variables. We will then see whether any improvement in overall explanatory ability occurs. The excerpts on page 69 come from the Excel printout for this regression:

continued...

> **EXHIBIT 2A.1**
> Data for Print Shop
> Overhead Costs and
> Two Potential
> Cost Drivers

example

Month	Overhead Costs	Machine Hours	Reams of Paper
1	$68,948	959	828,000
2	87,171	1,227	1,246,000
3	84,448	1,351	874,000
4	89,030	1,480	958,000
5	83,303	952	1,356,000
6	82,660	986	1,332,000
7	78,793	931	1,170,000
8	82,834	1,439	958,000
9	77,829	945	1,238,000
10	72,303	869	978,000
11	78,804	1,171	890,000
12	85,850	1,228	1,162,000
13	70,343	928	892,000
14	85,991	950	1,376,000
15	77,626	1,016	1,160,000
16	70,397	902	928,000
17	77,189	948	1,220,000
18	75,443	1,130	1,064,000
19	79,599	1,335	830,000
20	72,690	1,052	1,034,000
21	76,307	860	1,280,000
22	79,725	1,188	1,096,000
23	80,492	1,254	850,000
24	87,697	1,187	1,390,000
25	76,516	948	936,000
26	83,055	1,015	1,320,000
27	75,021	971	956,000
28	85,210	1,111	1,304,000
29	84,531	1,326	1,238,000
30	78,575	1,017	1,026,000

> **EXHIBIT 2A.2**
> Scatter Plot of Print Shop
> Overhead Costs

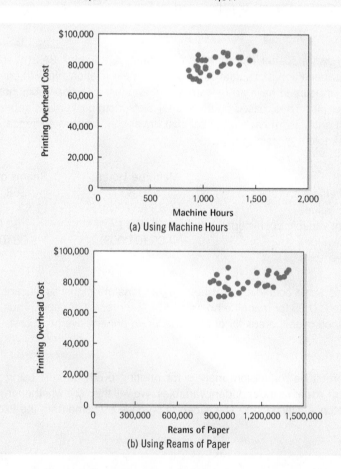

(a) Using Machine Hours

(b) Using Reams of Paper

SUMMARY OUTPUT

Regression Statistics	
Multiple R	0.909213111
R-Square	0.826668482
Adjusted R-Square	0.81382911
Standard Error	2371.304439
Observations	30

	Coefficients	Standard Error	t-Stat	P-value
Intercept	30339.41562	4371.900714	6.939639669	1.85584E-07
Machine Hours	24.37090992	2.578842323	9.450329594	4.70781E-10
Reams of Paper	0.020731337	0.00247053	8.391454669	5.29678E-09

The adjusted *R*-square of 0.81 is much higher than for either individual cost driver. Therefore, the two drivers together appear to explain much more of the variation in printing overhead cost.

The intercept term (fixed cost) is $30,339 and is statistically significant. Both potential cost drivers, machine hours and reams of paper, are positive and significant. The total cost function is

$$TC = \$30,339 + (\$24.37 \times \text{Machine hours}) + (\$0.02 \times \text{Reams of paper})$$

If we expect that next month we will use 1,000 machine hours and 1,000,000 reams, we can predict our total cost to be

$$TC = \$30,339 + (\$24.37)(1,000) + (0.02)(1,000,000)$$
$$= \$30,339 + \qquad \$24,370 + \$20,000$$
$$= \$74,709$$

Regression Analysis Assumptions

To perform regression analysis, the number of observations must be greater than the number of independent variables. In addition, a number of assumptions are used in linear regression analysis. We investigate four of them here:

1. The dependent variable can be calculated as a linear function of a set of independent variables, plus an error term. The error term is the distance from the regression trend line for each actual data point of cost versus cost driver.

2. The error terms have a normal distribution with a mean of zero. The *t*-statistics are based on the assumption that the errors are normally distributed. If this assumption is incorrect, we cannot know with any confidence whether the coefficients are different from zero.

3. The error terms have a constant variance for all the observations, and they are not correlated with each other. Constant variance can be a problem with accounting data because costs from one period could be related to costs in the next period. For example, an accrual that occurs in one period is often reversed in the next period. In addition, variance often increases at higher or lower levels of activity. If error terms are correlated, the standard errors are inaccurate, and therefore the *t*-statistics are not meaningful.

4. Relatively little correlation occurs among the independent variables. If the independent variables are highly correlated (multicollinearity), the coefficients are more likely to be inaccurate, which would create inaccuracies in our estimated cost functions. An example of correlated independent variables could be direct labour hours and machine hours, when labour is used to manage machines.

We test for the linearity assumption by examining a scatter plot to see whether the relationship between cost and the cost driver appears to have a generally linear trend. If this assumption is not met, linear regression analysis is not a useful tool. We test for normal distribution, uniform variance, and uncorrelated error terms using scatter plots or other statistics methods. We plot the error terms against the independent variables. If error terms with small (large) values are associated with independent variables of small (large) values, the error terms are correlated with each other, and the results from this model will not accurately reflect the underlying cost function. To determine whether independent variables are correlated, we use the correlation functions in a spreadsheet or statistical program. Independent variables that have a high correlation (above about 70%) may cause problems with regression analysis. The correlated variables can be entered in a regression together first and then independently to see whether the coefficient and t-statistics are affected by the correlation.

Additional Regression Analysis Considerations

LO6 Appreciate the uses and limitations of cost estimates

We can use regression analysis when we know that the majority of costs are likely to be only fixed or only variable, but in these cases other techniques may be just as accurate and require less data-gathering time. Suppose we want to estimate a cost function for handlebars, which varies with production volume at Magik Bicycles. Either we ask purchasing for the current per-unit cost and to check for price updates, or we divide the total cost of a recent purchase by the number of units purchased to develop an estimate of that variable cost. Similarly, to estimate a future fixed cost, we base our estimate on the fixed cost from one or more prior periods in the same manner shown for rent for Small Animal Clinic, Part 1.

Stepwise Linear Fixed Costs

We learned earlier that the cost function for some fixed costs is stepwise linear. For example, in Exhibit 2.4(b), the cost function for rent, which increases as more space is needed due to high sales revenues, is

$$TC = \$6,000, \quad \text{for} \quad Q \leq \$30,000 \text{ in sales}$$
$$TC = \$8,000, \quad \text{for} \quad Q > \$30,000 \text{ in sales}$$

What happens if we apply regression analysis to past cost data from this stepwise linear cost function? Consider the following three possibilities:

1. If all the data points occurred when Q was below $30,000, rent will appear to be a fixed cost at $6,000.

2. If all the data points occurred when Q was above $30,000, rent will appear to be a fixed cost at $8,000.

3. If some data points occurred when Q was below $30,000 and other data points occurred when Q was above $30,000, the regression trend line might be similar to the one shown in Exhibit 2A.3. The simple regression results would appear to have both fixed and variable components. However, the cost estimates from the regression will be accurate only at a few points along the regression trend line.

To develop the most accurate cost function, we must define the cost according to its relevant range and reflect the appropriate limits in the cost function.

Piecewise Linear Variable Costs

We learned earlier that the cost function for some variable costs is piecewise linear; the per-unit cost changes across relevant ranges of activity. For example, in Exhibit 2.3(b), the function for the total cost of bicycle tires based on a volume purchase discount is

$$TC = \$10 \, Q \quad \text{for} \quad Q \leq \text{Bikes manufactured}$$
$$TC = \$600 + \$6(Q - 60), \quad \text{for} \quad Q > 60 \text{ Bikes manufactured}$$

What happens if we apply regression analysis to past cost data from this piecewise linear cost function? Consider the following three possibilities:

1. If all the data points occurred when Q was below 60, the cost will appear to be variable at $10 per bike.

2. If all the data points occurred when Q was above 60, the cost will appear to be variable at $6 per bike.

3. If some data points occurred when Q was below 60 and other data points occurred when Q was above 60, the regression trend line might be similar to the one shown in Exhibit 2A.4. The simple regression results would underestimate per-unit variable cost when Q is reasonably close to 60 and overestimate it when Q is significantly above or below 60.

Once again, it is important to define the cost according to its relevant range and to reflect the appropriate limits in the cost function if we wish to develop the most accurate cost function.

Data Limitations

The results from regression analysis are only as accurate as the data we use. The following need to be ensured before data are used in regression analysis:

- ► The relationship between the cost and cost driver is economically plausible.
- ► Cost and cost driver data are matched and recorded in the appropriate period.
- ► Inflation and deflation have been taken into consideration.
- ► The relevant range reflects similar technologies across the range.
- ► No clerical errors occurred in the recorded data.
- ► Any data from periods with unusual events are eliminated.
- ► The activity levels for which we are predicting cost are within the relevant range; that is, we are not predicting cost for activity levels that are greater (smaller) than the largest (smallest) in our data set.
- ► We have removed any outliers—that is, observations that are much larger or much smaller and would unduly influence the regression results.

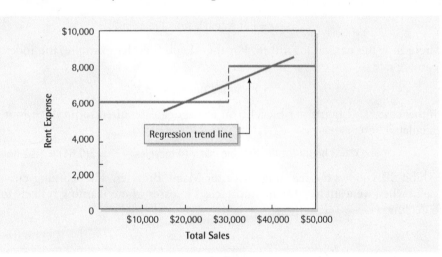

►EXHIBIT 2A.3
Regression Trend Line for a Stepwise Linear Fixed Cost

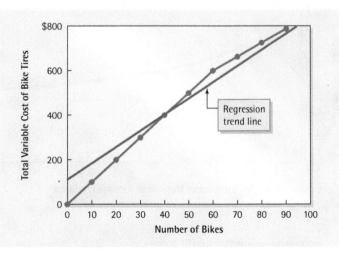

►EXHIBIT 2A.4
Regression Trend Line for a Piecewise Linear Variable Cost

APPENDIX 2B

L02   Describe the different types of cost behaviour

> **HELPFUL HINT**
>
> To use Excel to estimate a learning curve, see Charles D. Bailey, "Estimation of Production Costs and Labor Hours Using an Excel Add-in," *Management Accounting Quarterly*, Summer 2000, pp. 25–31.

> **BUSINESS PRACTICE**
>
> **Boeing** uses a learning curve calculation to allocate tooling and special equipment costs over the life of each commercial airplane.[4]

Learning Curves

When organizations start a new product line or hire new workers, the **learning curve** is the rate at which labour hours decrease as the volume of production or services increases. Over time, the learning curve results in greater productivity; goods and services are produced more quickly as workers and supervisors learn more about their jobs and develop more efficient practices. Several different ways can be used to estimate learning curves, and all of the approaches use a learning rate. This rate can be determined by analyzing historical data using statistical methods. The following example discusses the cumulative average-time learning curve approach.

Suppose that Magik Bicycles initiates a new production line, and each time the number of bicycles produced doubles, the cumulative average time to produce that number of bicycles is 80% of the time required for the previous production amount. Specifically, the average time to produce two bicycles is 80% of the time required to produce one bicycle. The average time to produce four bicycles is 80% of the average time to produce two bicycles, and so on. We would say that employees at Magik Bicycles have an 80% cumulative learning rate. If it takes 3 hours to produce the first bicycle, we estimate it will take $0.80 \times 3 = 2.4$ hours per bike, or a total of 4.8 hours to make two bicycles. To make four bicycles, it will take $0.80 \times 2.4 = 1.92$ hours per bike, or a total of 7.68 hours for the four bikes.

To simplify our calculations, we can mathematically represent the cumulative average-time learning curve for repetitive tasks using the following equation:

$$Y = \alpha X^r$$

where Y is the cumulative average labour hours used for X units of product or services produced, α is the time required for the first unit produced, and r is an index for the rate of learning calculated as follows:

$$r = \ln(\text{percent learning rate})/\ln(2)$$

where ln is the natural logarithm. For the Magik Bicycles example, the index for an 80% learning rate is

$$r = \ln(0.80)/\ln(2) = -0.322$$

In this case, 1.92 hours per bicycle, on average, are required to produce four bicycles, as calculated here:

$$Y = \alpha X^r = 3 \text{ hours for the first bicycle} \times (4 \text{ bicycles})^{-0.322} = 3(0.64) = 1.92 \text{ hours}$$

Exhibit 2B.1 shows the learning curve for Magik Bicycles. The learning curve formula is useful when we want to estimate future costs in cases where learning is likely to cause costs to decline.

> **EXHIBIT 2B.1**
>
> Learning Curve for Magik Bicycles

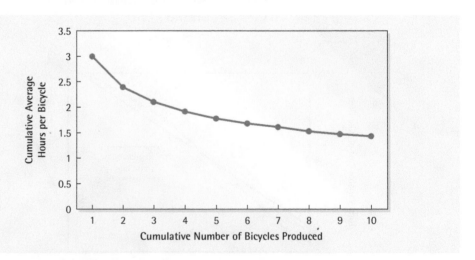

[4] Boeing, *Summary of Significant Accounting Policies, The Boeing Company 2002 Annual Report*, at www.boeing.com Investor Relations.

SUMMARY

LO1   Explain cost concepts and cost terms

COSTS

Costs can be classified into five broad categories: (1) relevance, (2) behaviour, (3) traceability, (4) function, and (5) controllability.

Classifications	Applications	Cost Terms
Relevance	Decision making	Relevant vs. irrelevant
Behaviour	Costs estimation	Fixed vs. variable
Traceability	Costs assignment	Direct vs. indirect
Function	Cost determination	Manufacturing vs. nonmanufacturing (Product vs. period)
Controllability	Performance evaluation	Controllable vs. noncontrollable

LO2   Describe the different types of cost behaviour

LINEAR COST FUNCTION

$TC = F + V \times Q$

TC = Total cost
F = Total fixed cost
V = Variable cost per unit of activity
Q = Volume of activity (cost driver)

ASSUMPTIONS

Within the relevant range, fixed costs remain fixed, and the variable cost per unit remains constant.

NONLINEAR COST FUNCTIONS

► Economies of scale: Average costs decline with volume of production.

► Learning curve (Appendix 2B): Variable costs decline with experience.
► No apparent pattern: No relationship is noted between cost and a potential cost driver.

LINEAR COST FUNCTIONS ACROSS MORE THAN ONE RELEVANT RANGE

► Stepwise linear: Fixed costs change across relevant ranges.
► Piecewise linear: Variable costs change across relevant ranges.

LO3, LO4   Describe cost estimation techniques and apply them to determine future costs

ENGINEERED ESTIMATE OF COST

Analyze amount of labour time, materials, and other resources used in each activity. Estimate costs based on resources used.

ANALYSIS AT THE ACCOUNT LEVEL

Review pattern in past costs recorded in the accounting system.

Use knowledge of operations to classify cost as variable, fixed, or mixed.

TWO-POINT METHOD

Algebraically calculate a linear mixed cost function using any two data points of the cost and a cost driver. Preferably use the most representative data points.

HIGH-LOW METHOD

Apply the two-point method, using the highest and lowest data points of the cost driver.

SCATTER PLOT

Plot past data points for cost against a potential cost driver.

Visually analyze the plot to decide whether cost might be completely fixed, completely variable, or mixed.

SUMMARY

LO5   Utilize regression analysis in cost estimation

Statistically measure the average change in a dependent variable for every unit change in one or more independent variables. Create a linear cost function where variable cost is the slope of the regression line and fixed cost is the intercept.

SIMPLE REGRESSION

One independent variable

MULTIPLE REGRESSION (APPENDIX 2A)

Two or more independent variables

LO6   Appreciate the uses and limitations of cost estimates

EXAMPLES OF REASONS TO ESTIMATE FUTURE COSTS

► Budgeting
► Planning future operations, such as setting employee work schedules or financing activities
► Making specific decisions, such as discontinuing a line of business, renting additional retail store space, or hiring new employees

WHAT DO MANAGERS NEED TO CONSIDER WHEN USING ESTIMATES OF FUTURE COSTS?

► Uncertainties:
– Actual future costs are unknown

– Reliability of cost estimates is uncertain because of uncertainties about
    Cost behaviour classification
    Cost drivers
    Changes in cost behaviour over time
► Other considerations:
– Quality of cost information
– Appropriateness of past costs for estimating future costs
– Accounting system information
– Information from outside the accounting system
    Quality of estimation techniques
    Reasonableness of cost function assumptions

2-1 solution to self-study problem

A. If Frank opens a sandwich shop, he forgoes the opportunity to work at the hardware store and use his savings for other investments. He also forgoes the opportunity for additional leisure time. Although this alternative is not specifically quantifiable, it is certainly a relevant opportunity cost.

B. The first cost object that Frank should consider is the sandwich shop franchise and the relevant cash flows to open and operate a new store. Then, he would consider the opportunity costs, which include two major cost objects: (1) his work at the hardware store and (2) potential investments.

C. Frank should be able to get estimates of cash flows from the franchise for costs such as food, labour, and incidentals. He also needs to gather information about the cost for specific locations and the costs to rent or build the store. He would collect cost information about meeting city requirements for licences and permits; insurance requirements; and local, provincial, and federal taxes. For the opportunity costs, he should know the salary and fringe benefits available from working at the hardware store. He also needs to know investment options and potential returns on his investments for the money he has in savings.

D. Frank must evaluate the likelihood that the cash flows will turn out to be as he predicts. The sandwich shop option might be riskier than either of his other options. In that case, he should consider risk in addition to estimated cost flows when evaluating his opportunities. (Note: In Chapter 13, we will discuss specific methods for incorporating risk into an investment decision.) In addition, Frank might require a minimum level of cash inflows, perhaps for supporting a family. He needs to consider the consequences of lower cash flows than predicted. If he faces a relatively high probability that the cash flows from the sandwich shop will not meet his needs, then Frank may be unwilling to consider this alternative. Frank's level of reluctance or interest in investing in the sandwich shop depends on the severity of the consequences should it fail and his degree of risk aversion.

2-2 solution to self-study problem

A. Each cost function is written using the regression intercept term as the fixed cost and the slope as the variable cost:

Cost driver = Assembly time

   TC = $55,000 + $21.00 × Assembly time

Cost driver = Labour hours

   TC = $20,000 + $31.00 × Labour hours

Cost driver = Machine hours

   TC = $10,000 + $38.00 × Machine hours

(*Note:* Because the p-value for its t-statistic is 0.25, the intercept is not statistically different from zero. Therefore, the fixed cost can be assumed to be zero.)

B. The adjusted R-square indicates that variation in assembly time explains about 31% of the variation in overhead. The remaining 69% is unexplained.

C. The p-value for the intercept in the regression of overhead cost against machine hours is 0.25. It means a 25% probability that the intercept (fixed cost) is zero instead of $10,000.

D. The p-value of the slope in the labour hours regression is 0.01, which means a 1% probability that the variable cost for overhead related to labour hours could be zero instead of $31.00 per labour hour.

E. First, we examine the adjusted R-square (see Exhibit 2.14, items 6 and 7). At 70%, machine hours appears to be the best cost driver. However, we also need to evaluate whether the coefficients are reasonable. The slope coefficient is positive and has only a small probability of being zero (p-value = 0.005), so it is likely to be a reasonable estimate. The intercept coefficient is generally reasonable, as long as it is not significantly negative. In this case, the intercept has a high p-value (0.25), so we can assume that the fixed cost is zero.

F. Managers cannot know future costs. Nevertheless, they need to estimate future costs in order to make decisions. A cost function based on past information helps managers estimate future costs; the function can also be updated to incorporate expected cost information so that predictions are as precise as possible. Using a model such as the cost function also helps managers be more methodical in their approach to cost estimation, improving the quality of cost estimates. Higher-quality estimation methods provide higher-quality information for decision making.

QUESTIONS

2.1 Describe the term *fixed cost* and give several examples of fixed costs within a car rental agency when the cost per car rental is the cost object.

2.2 Describe the term *variable* cost and give several examples of variable costs within a car rental agency when the cost per rental is the cost object.

2.3 Describe the term *mixed cost* and give several examples of mixed costs within a car rental agency when the cost per rental is the cost object.

2.4 Why are outliers a problem for any cost estimation technique?

2.5 "As volume increases, total cost increases and per-unit cost decreases." What type of linear cost function does this describe? Draw a simple graph of this type of cost function.

2.6 An automobile assembly plant closes every August to retool for the next year's model. How should August's cost data be used in estimating the overhead cost function?

2.7 Explain why it is important to consider changing circumstances when estimating a cost function.

2.8 At two levels of activity within the relevant range, average costs are $192 and $188, respectively. Assuming the cost function is linear, what can be said about the existence of fixed and variable costs?

2.9 List two opportunities you would forgo when you decide to study on a Friday night. List relevant cash flows for those two opportunities. Is it possible to assign a quantitative value to the benefits you receive from either of these two missed opportunities? Explain.

2.10 Explain how information from a scatter plot helps in categorizing a cost as fixed, variable, or mixed.

2.11 Explain the analysis at the account level approach to developing a cost function.

2.12 In your own words, define sunk costs and describe a decision for which you mistakenly included a sunk cost.

2.13 Explain why it is often difficult to identify an appropriate, relevant, and reliable measure for estimating a cost function.

2.14 The trend line developed using regression analysis provides a more accurate representation of a mixed cost function than the two-point or high-low methods. Explain why.

2.15 Explain why small sample sizes can be a problem when using historical data for estimating a cost function.

MULTIPLE-CHOICE QUESTIONS

2.16 Which of the following statements is true?

  a. A cost may be simultaneously direct and indirect to different cost objectives.
  b. Indirect costs can be identified specifically with a given cost objective in an economically feasible way.
  c. Direct costs cannot be identified specifically with a given cost objective in an economically feasible way.
  d. Managers prefer to classify costs as indirect rather than direct.

2.17 Some costs change abruptly at intervals of activity because the resources and their costs come in indivisible chunks. What is the name for these costs?
  a. Mixed costs
  b. Stepwise costs
  c. Variable costs
  d. Sunk costs

Use the following information to answer Questions 2.18 to 2.20. KEI Ltd. had the following data for the first six months of 2016:

Month	Machine Hours	Maintenance Cost
January	2,150	$21,400
February	2,100	$21,400
March	2,400	$24,850
April	2,800	$27,700
May	2,800	$27,500
June	2,500	$24,100

2.18 What is the variable cost?
  a. $8.71
  b. $9.00
  c. $9.38
  d. $9.69

2.19 What is the cost function for the maintenance cost?
  a. $Y = \$562 + 9.69X$
  b. $Y = \$1,223 + 9.38X$
  c. $Y = \$2,500 + 9.00X$
  d. $Y = \$3,100 + 8.71X$

2.20 KEI Ltd. expects to use 2,650 machine hours in July. What would be the total maintenance cost, based on the cost function derived in Question 2.19?
  a. $26,092
  b. $26,193
  c. $26,246
  d. $26,350

EXERCISES

2.21 Classification of Costs Boca manufactures LX and RX stereo systems in southern Ontario.

LO1 Boca incurs various costs both in producing these stereos and in the operations of the company.

REQUIRED Classify each of the following cost items according to the terms in the following table. A cost can be classified under more than one category. If in doubt, select the cost type based on whether the total costs will increase substantially if a large number of stereo systems are produced.

Cost	Direct Cost	Indirect Cost	Variable Cost	Fixed Cost	Product Cost	Period Cost
Speaker						
Advertising						
Design of LX stereo						
Plant janitor						
Machine depreciation						
Office rent						
Factory maintenance						
Assembly workers						

2.22 Account Analysis Method, Cost Functions Toonie Car Washing Company reports the following costs and account analysis classification for 14,400 car washings for the year ended December 31, 2016:

LO2, LO3, LO4

Account	Classification	Amount
Direct materials	100% variable	$26,000
Direct labour	100% variable	$38,000
Office support	30% variable	$12,000
Utilities	20% variable	$40,000
Rent	0% variable	$42,000
depreciation	0% variable	$32,600

REQUIRED   **A.** What is the variable cost per car wash? What is the total fixed cost for 14,400 car washings? Prepare the cost equation.

B. What will be the total costs if Toonie has 16,800 car washings in 2013 (assuming no cost increases)?

C. Assume that Toonie anticipates the following changes in the costs in 2014:
  • Direct materials to increase by 3%.
  • Direct labour to increase by 4%.
  • Rent to increase by 4%.
  • Depreciation to increase by 5%.

What is the variable cost per car wash? What is the total cost for 18,000 car washings? Prepare the cost equation.

2.23 **Cost Object, Cost Function Estimation, Opportunity Cost** A computer manufacturer is deciding whether to produce a high-definition flat screen monitor. One of the managers suggested that the incremental costs for this line of manufacturing will be primarily variable because the company currently has a lot of idle capacity.

LO2, LO4, LO5

REQUIRED   **A.** What is the cost object in this decision?

B. Is the accounting system likely to have the information needed to develop a cost function? Explain.

C. What might be an appropriate estimation technique for this cost? Explain.

D. What is the opportunity cost for using this idle capacity? Explain.

2.24 **Direct and Indirect Costs** Frida's Tax Practice has two departments: tax and audit. The tax department has two product lines: business returns and individual returns. A list of costs and three cost objects from Frida's Tax Practice follow.

LO2

REQUIRED   For each cost, identify whether it is direct or indirect for each cost object.

	Cost Object		
Cost	Tax Department	Personal Returns	Mr. Gruper's Personal Tax Return
A. Subscription to personal tax law updates publication			
B. Ink supplies for tax department photocopy machine			
C. Portion of total rent for tax department office space			
D. Wages for tax department administrative assistant			
E. Tax partner's salary			
F. Charges for long-distance call to Mr. Gruper about personal tax return questions			
G. Tax-partner lunch with Mr. Gruper (the tax partner has lunch with each client at least once per year)			

2.25 Variable and Fixed Costs Global Car Rental offers three different car rental plans.

Plan 1: $49.95 per day, unlimited mileage

Plan 2: $0.50 per kilometre

Plan 3: $24.95 per day, plus $0.25 per kilometre

REQUIRED **A.** Classify each plan as variable cost, fixed cost, or mixed cost.

B. What is the total cost under each plan if a customer rents a car for 4 days and drives 380 km? What is the average cost per kilometre under each plan?

C. A customer needs to rent a car for half of a day, and she is not sure the distance that she will drive. Which plan should she take, if she plans to drive (1) 50 km, (2) 100 km, and (3) 250 km?

2.26 Cost Behaviour, Plots, Outliers, Cost Function The assembly department of Toyco has the following costs over its relevant range of units produced in a month.

Units Produced	Direct Labour Cost	Direct Materials Cost
3,000	$95,000	$75,000
3,500	95,000	87,500
4,000	95,000	100,000
4,500	95,000	112,500
5,000	95,000	125,000

REQUIRED **A.** Analyze the costs and units produced data above. Write the algebraic expression for the direct labour cost function.

B. Direct materials costs are usually variable. Plot direct materials cost to determine whether there are any outliers that should be removed when estimating the direct materials cost function. Explain.

C. Use the high-low method or regression analysis to determine the cost function for direct materials cost.

2.27 Cost Function, Account Analysis Barney's Pizza Parlour recently opened for business. The owner wants a cost function estimate to help with future planning. The manager feels that last month's results fairly represent costs over the coming six months. Last month 600 pizzas were sold. From the following information, use account analysis to estimate the firm's cost function for pizzas sold.

Wages for part-time help	$2,340
Pizza toppings	180
Pizza dough	240
Store rent	400
Depreciation on furniture and ovens	80
Napkins, paper plates, cups, and straws	75
Liability insurance	100
Advertising	60
Cleaning supplies	15
Manager's salary	1,400
Utilities (electricity and telephone)	110
Soft drink purchases	375

REQUIRED **A.** Develop a cost function using the data from the accounting records.

B. Use the cost function to estimate the total costs if 700 pizzas are expected to be sold next month.

C. What assumptions do you make when you estimate this cost function? List two factors that could cause the assumption for variable costs to be incorrect next month.

2.28 Cost Function, Rejection Rate A department has five employees who work as a team. During productive time the team produces 20 units per hour. The employees are paid for an 8-hour day, which includes 1 hour for breaks and clean-up time. On average, 10% of the units produced are defective and must be discarded. The employees are paid as follows.

Number of Employees	Pay per Hour per Employee
1	$28
1	20
2	16
1	12

REQUIRED

A. A manager needs information for budgeting purposes. Calculate the direct labour cost of producing one good finished unit.

B. These employees are not paid for absences. However, when a regular crew member is absent, the company pays a temporary work agency $35 per hour for a worker to fill in. For accuracy in estimating future costs, such labour costs could be treated as follows:

    1. The absence is not related to the production process, so it is recorded as part of overhead cost.

    2. The cost for absences is tracked and recorded as direct labour cost.

    Recommend one of these two methods to the accountant and lists its advantages as part of your argument.

2.29 Cost Function, Account Analysis, High-Low Method, Average Cost Accuracy Following is cost data for the equipment maintenance department. This department charges other departments for the actual cost of materials and labour when making equipment repairs. The managers now want to develop a cost function that explains their overhead costs as a function of the number of service calls made each month.

	February	March	April	May
Salary—manager*	$3,000	$3,000	$3,000	$3,200
Supplies	470	578	735	650
Insurance**	200	200	250	250
Electricity	62	62	62	62
Property tax***			600	
Repair manuals	90	100	80	90
Total	$3,822	$3,940	$4,727	$4,252
Service calls	90	110	140	125

    *Salaries of all department heads are increased annually in May.
    **Insurance rates increased in April.
    ***Property taxes are paid in two equal installments in April and October.

REQUIRED

A. Estimate the department's cost function using analysis at the account level.

B. Using the cost function estimated in part (A), estimate the overhead cost for June if 135 service calls are expected.

C. Calculate the average overhead cost per unit for the four-month period. Given this average cost, what is the estimated total cost for June?

D. Which estimation method, the one in part (B) or part (C), is better? Why?

2.30 Linear, Stepwise Linear, and Piecewise Linear Cost Functions

A. Total fixed costs are $10,000 per week, and the variable cost per unit is $8.00. Write the algebraic expression for the cost function and graph it. What are the assumptions of the cost function?

REQUIRED

B. Total fixed costs are $25,000 per week up to 2,000 units per week and then jump up to $35,000 per week. The variable cost per unit is $8.00. Write the algebraic expression for the cost function and graph it.

C. The average cost to produce 10,000 units is $45.00, and the average cost to produce 12,000 units is $44.00. Estimate the average cost to produce 15,000 units.

D. The total cost function for Hot Dog Days, a hot dog cart business in Centennial Park, is TC = $5,000 + 45% × Total revenue. Estimate the total cost for a month when total revenues are $10,000.

2.31 Piecewise Linear Cost Function, Regression Measurement Error The following is the description of a cost: Total fixed costs are $5000 per month, and the variable cost per unit is $10.00 when production is under 100 units. The variable cost drops to $9.00 per unit after the first 100 units are produced.

LO4, LO5

REQUIRED   **A.** Write the algebraic expression of the cost function and graph it.
B. Assume that the cost function just described is a reasonable representation of total costs. If the accountant performed regression analysis on weekly observations of this cost and did not realize that there were two relevant ranges, what problems would arise in the cost function that was produced? In other words, how would the cost function be mismeasured?

2.32 Learning Curve, Graphing (Appendix 2B) The managers of Tax Plus hired three recent accounting graduates. When they started preparing simple tax returns, it took six hours to complete the first return. The supervisor believes an 80% learning rate is typical for this type of work.

LO2

REQUIRED   **A.** Estimate the cumulative average time per return to prepare two returns.
B. Use a spreadsheet to plot four points on the learning curve and then explain in your own words why the cumulative average time drops.

2.33 Cost Function and Assumptions Bison Sandwiches is a small restaurant that sells a variety of sandwiches and beverages. Total fixed costs are $20,000 per month. Last month, total variable costs were $8,000 when total sales were $32,000.

LO4, LO6

REQUIRED   **A.** Write out the algebraic expression for the cost function.
B. What assumptions do we make when we develop this cost function?

2.34 Direct and Indirect Costs; Fixed, Variable, and Mixed Costs Your sister turned her pottery hobby into a small business called Glazed Over. She manufactures and sells bowls that can be used for decoration or for birdbaths. She has one employee who works 40 hours per week, no matter how many bowls are made. Your sister has asked your advice in developing a cost function for the bowls so that she can estimate costs for the next period.

LO2

The following list of costs comes from your sister's general ledger. Assume that the cost object is an individual unit (i.e., bowl). Categorize each cost as direct (D) or indirect (I) and as fixed (F), variable (V), or mixed (M).

REQUIRED   **A.** Employee wages
B. Clay used to make bowls
C. Depreciation on the kilns
D. Glaze (the finish painted on the bowls)
E. Brushes for the glaze
F. Electricity
G. Business licence
H. Advertising
I. Pottery studio maintenance (cost of weekly cleaning service)
J. Packing materials for the bowls

2.35 Cost Function, Opportunity Cost, Relevant Costs Yummy Yogurt sells yogurt cones in a variety of natural flavours. Data for a recent month follow:

LO2, LO3

Revenue		$ 9,000
Cost of ingredients	$ 4,500	
Rent	1,000	
Store attendant salary	2,300	
		7,800
Profit		$ 1,200

REQUIRED   **A.** Categorize each cost as fixed or variable.
B. Create a cost function.
C. What is the opportunity cost when a new flavour of yogurt replaces an old one? (Assume that all yogurts are priced the same but the variable costs for each flavour are different because different ingredients are used.)
D. Yummy Yogurt's managers are concerned that they sometimes lose business because of long customer lines during peak times. Therefore, they are considering whether to remove one customer table and add an extra cash register in that space in order to decrease throughput time (customer wait and service time). Is the cost of store rent relevant to the decision? Why or why not?

2.36 **Relevant Costs; Fixed, Variable, and Mixed Costs** Consider the following two cost objects:

LO 2
1. Purchasing a pizza shop
2. Investing in a fishing boat

REQUIRED For each of the following costs, determine whether the cost is relevant to running a pizza shop (PS), investing in a fishing boat (FB), or both (B). Also, classify each cost as primarily fixed (F), variable (V), or mixed (M).

A. Hourly wages
B. Ingredients
C. Employee benefits
D. Fishing equipment
E. Utilities
F. Advertising
G. Insurance

2.37 **Engineered Estimate of Cost, Cost-based Price** Julie Long, the manager of the Hamburger Haven, has been told

LO 4 that to earn a reasonable profit, she should price her hamburgers at 300% of the cost of ingredients. Ms. Long has gathered the following data on the cost of ingredients used to make a hamburger:

1. Preformed frozen hamburger patties are purchased from a distributor. Each pound includes seven patties. The distributor charges $1.69 per pound.
2. Hamburger buns are purchased for $1.29 per dozen.
3. Dill pickle slices are purchased by the gallon jar. A gallon costs $8.95 and contains roughly 2,000 pickle slices. Four slices are placed on each burger.
4. Large, ripe tomatoes currently sell for $0.69 each. One tomato yields eight slices, and one slice is placed on each burger.
5. A $0.59 head of lettuce provides enough lettuce for 40 burgers.
6. Mayonnaise is purchased in 16-ounce jars for $1.49. One-quarter ounce of mayonnaise is placed on a burger.
7. A $0.79 jar of mustard provides enough mustard for 150 burgers.
8. A $0.99 jar of ketchup is sufficient for 50 burgers.
9. A pound of cheese yields 16 slices. Cheese costs $2.59 per pound, and each cheeseburger receives 1 slice.
10. Onions cost $0.15 each and yield enough chopped onions for 45 hamburgers.

REQUIRED **A.** What is the cost of ingredients for a plain burger (meat and bun only)?
B. What is the cost of materials and suggested selling price for a burger with everything except cheese?
C. People are willing to pay only $0.25 extra for cheese. What price should Ms. Long charge for a hamburger with everything except cheese if she wants the price of a cheeseburger with everything to be 300% of the cost of ingredients?
D. Should Ms. Long consider her competitors' prices in addition to her costs? Explain.

2.38 **Fixed, Variable, and Mixed Costs** Spencer and Church is a CA firm engaged in local practice. Some selected items

LO 2 from its chart of accounts are listed here.

REQUIRED For each account, indicate whether the account represents a fixed (F), variable (V), or mixed (M) cost for the operations of the local practice office. If mixed, indicate whether it is predominantly fixed or variable. Explain your answers.

A. Staff wages
B. Clerical wages
C. Rent
D. Licences
E. Insurance
F. Office supplies
G. Professional dues
H. Professional subscriptions
I. Canada Pension Plan premiums
J. Property taxes
K. Advertising

2.39 **Cost Function Using Regression, Other Potential Cost Drivers** The new cost analyst in your accounting department

LO 5 just received a computer-generated report that contains the results of a simple regression analysis. He was estimating the costs of the marketing department, using units sold as the cost driver. The summary results of the report are as follows:

Variable	Coefficient	t-statistic	p-value
Intercept	12.44	1.39	0.25
Units sold	222.35	2.48	0.001
Adjusted R-square = 0.61			

REQUIRED **A.** Write an equation for the cost function based on the regression analysis.
B. What does the adjusted R-square tell you?
C. What other cost drivers could potentially explain marketing costs? Explain.

2.40 Scatter Plot, Cost Function Using Regression, Three Potential Cost Drivers Maintenance costs covering 15 months of operation for Central Industries are available at www.wiley.com/go/eldenburgcanada. Maintenance consists of regularly scheduled tasks to keep machinery operating efficiently and occasional repairs. The regular tasks include inspecting, cleaning, oiling, and repairing worn parts. The potential cost drivers are units of output, direct labour hours, and number of machine setups. The data are presented in thousands.

LO5, LO6

REQUIRED **A.** For each potential cost driver, prepare a scatter plot versus maintenance cost and then perform a simple regression.
B. Based on the scatter plots, which cost driver appears to be the best? Explain.
www.wiley.com/
go/eldenburgcanada
C. Which cost driver appears to have the best explanatory ability for maintenance costs? Explain.
D. In the regression with the highest adjusted R-square, examine the t-statistics and p-values to determine whether both the intercept and slope coefficients are significant. Does maintenance cost appear to be primarily fixed, primarily variable, or mixed? Write out the cost function for this cost driver.
E. Explain why the future cost function might be different from a cost function based on past cost information.

PROBLEMS

2.41 Classification of Costs, Cost Function Using the High-Low Method The following table shows the manufacturing overhead costs of Denon Plastic, Inc. for the first six months of their first year of operation:

LO2, LO3, LO4

	Units	Maintenance	Material Handling	Total Manufacturing Overhead Costs
January	1,150	$37,250	$4,600	$41,850
February	1,020	35,300	4,080	39,380
March	1,250	38,750	5,000	43,750
April	1,400	41,000	5,600	46,600
May	1,350	40,250	5,400	45,650
June	1,280	39,200	5,120	44,320

REQUIRED **A.** Classify the two manufacturing overhead costs as fixed, variable, or mixed, and as direct or indirect.
B. Using the high-low method, create a cost function for (1) the maintenance cost, (2) the material handling cost, and (3) the total costs.
C. Denon Plastic plans to manufacture 1,500 units in July. At this level, what is the total fixed cost for the manufacturing overhead? What is the total variable manufacturing overhead cost? What is the total costs?

2.42 Cost Function Using High-Low and Regression, Quality of Cost Estimates Following are sales and administrative cost data for Big Jack Burgers for the past four months:

LO5, LO6

	Sales	Administrative Costs
September	$ 632,100	$43,333
October	842,500	57,770
November	1,087,900	62,800
December	1,132,100	68,333

Administrative cost is a mixed cost, and sales is a potential cost driver.

REQUIRED   **A.** Using the high-low method, create a cost function for administrative costs.
B. In your own words, explain why the high-low method might not be a good method for estimating the cost function.
C. Create a scatter plot and add a trend line. After examining the plot, use your judgment to determine whether the cost is fixed, variable, or mixed.
D. Perform regression analysis to create a cost function for administrative costs.
E. Can we know for certain that the cost function from Part D provides a good estimate for next month's administrative costs? Why or why not?
F. Discuss whether sales are an economically plausible driver for administration costs for Big Jack Burgers.

2.43 **Scatter Plot, Cost Function Using Regression** The following scatter plot and simple regression results used revenue
LO5, LO6   as a potential cost driver for research and development costs:

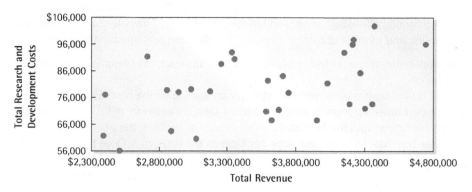

SUMMARY OUTPUT

Regression Statistics	
Multiple R	0.462332038
R-square	0.213750914
Adjusted R-square	0.185670589
Standard error	10894.44062
Observations	30

	Coefficients	Standard Error	t-Statistic	p-value
Intercept	50364.97682	10834.0628	4.648761758	7.2426E-05
Revenue	0.008179276	0.002964572	2.759007802	0.01010244

REQUIRED   **A.** Discuss whether the scatter plot suggests that revenue is a cost driver for research and development costs.
B. Using the regression results, write the cost function for research and development costs.
C. Based on the regression results, discuss whether it would be appropriate to use total revenue as a cost driver for research and development costs.
D. If you use the cost function from Part B to estimate next month's research and development costs, what assumptions are you making? Identify at least three assumptions and discuss their reasonableness.

2.44 **Cost Driver, Cost Categories, Appropriateness of Regression, Relevant Information** Susan looked at her long-distance
LO3, LO5,   telephone bill with dismay. After leaving her job last year to become a self-employed consultant, her long-distance
LO6   charges had grown considerably. She had not changed long-distance plans for years, partly because she hated
taking the time to review the range of service providers and plans. However, the size of her long-distance bill made
it clear that it was time to make a change. She had recently seen numerous telephone company ads offering
much lower rates than she was currently paying, but she was sure that at least some of those plans offered low
rates only for night and weekend calls.

Susan called her current long-distance service provider and asked how she could obtain a lower rate. She mentioned hearing that a competitor was currently offering long distance at 5¢ per minute. In responding to the service representative's questions, Susan verified that most of her long-distance calls are weekday and out-of-province calls. She also agreed that her activity over the past two months, approximately 500 minutes of long distance per month, was her best estimate for future calling activity. Given this information, the service representative suggested that Susan buy the following long-distance service plan:

1. Up to 500 minutes of long distance for a flat fee of $20 per month.
2. No refunds would be provided for usage less than 500 minutes per month.
3. Any minutes over 500 per month would be billed at 10¢ per minute.
4. No service change fee or cancellation fee would apply.

REQUIRED   **A.** What is the cost driver for Susan's long-distance telephone costs, assuming that the cost object is her consulting business?
B. In the proposed service plan, which of the costs are fixed and which are variable? Explain.
C. Would regression analysis be an appropriate tool for Susan to use in deciding whether to switch to the new service plan? Why or why not?
D. Is the cost of Susan's current long-distance service plan relevant to this decision? Why or why not?
E. Explain why Susan cannot be certain whether the new service plan will reduce her long-distance costs.
F. List additional information that might be relevant to Susan in deciding whether to switch to the new service plan.
G. Are Susan's long-distance services most likely a discretionary cost? Explain.
H. Are Susan's long-distance services most likely a direct or indirect cost, assuming that the cost object is an individual consulting job? Explain.
I. Describe the pros and cons of the new service plan.

2.45 **Learning Curve, Uncertainty, Regression Measurement Error (Appendix 2B)** The following learning curve guidelines are based on statistical analyses averaged over various industries and time periods. On average, learning rates are expected to vary depending on the proportion of work performed by workers (hand assembly) versus the proportion performed by machines:

LO3, LO5, LO6

	Learning Rate
75% hand assembly and 25% machining	80%
50% hand assembly and 50% machining	85%
25% hand assembly and 75% machining	90%

Source: Johnson Space Center, National Aeronautics and Space Administration (NASA), *Learning Curve Calculator.*

The managers of Fancy Furniture decided to start a new product line. When the production line was started, it took 10 hours to make the first batch of six chairs. The learning rate is estimated to be 90%.

REQUIRED   **A.** Estimate the cumulative average time per batch to make four batches.
B. Identify possible reasons the actual learning curve might be different from the estimate in Part A.
C. Explain how you might use the learning-rate guidelines in the chart to evaluate the reasonableness of the learning rate for Fancy Furniture.
D. What problems would arise if information for the first few weeks of production were used in a regression analysis to estimate a cost function for the new product line?

2.46 **Cost Categories, Cost Function, Opportunity Cost** The university's Wildcat Lair has been reporting losses in past months. In July, for example, the loss was $5,000:

LO2, LO3

Revenue		$70,000
Expenses		
Purchases of prepared food	$21,000	
Serving personnel	30,000	
Cashier	5,500	
Administration	10,000	
University surcharge	7,000	
Utilities	1,500	75,000
Loss		$(5,000)

The Lair purchases prepared food directly from University Food Services. The charge varies proportionately with the number and kind of meals served. Personnel who are paid by the Lair serve the food, tend the cash register, bus and clean tables, and wash dishes. The staffing levels in the Lair rarely change; the existing staff can usually handle daily fluctuations in volume. Administrative costs are primarily the salaries of the Lair manager and her office staff. The university charges the Lair a surcharge of 10% of its revenue. Utility costs are the costs of cooling, heating, and lighting the Lair during its normal operating hours.

The university's management is considering shutting down the Lair because it has been operating at a loss.

REQUIRED **A.** List the fixed expenses of the Wildcat Lair.
B. List the variable expenses of the Lair and the most likely cost driver for each expense.
C. Write out the cost function for running the Lair.
D. Estimate the profit or loss for August if the revenues of the Lair increase to $80,000.
E. Explain why the original data show a loss but Part D shows a profit. Be specific.
F. What is the university's opportunity cost if it closes the Wildcat Lair? Describe the opportunity cost and provide calculations for July and August.

2.47 **Cost Behaviour, Scatter Plot** Polar Bear Ski Wear is a shop that sells skiwear at a ski resort. Its cost accountant developed the following scatter plot for the cost of electricity for lights, heating, and cooling against retail sales revenue:

REQUIRED **A.** In a business such as retail sales, what usually causes the cost of electricity to vary?
B. During what time of year would most ski wear be sold at a ski resort?
C. In the scatter plot, the cost of electricity appears to be related to volume of retail sales. If this shop specialized in selling swimwear, would the scatter plot look different? Explain what would change.

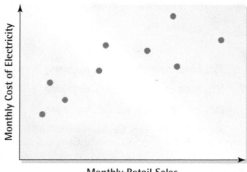

Monthly Retail Sales

D. Identify and explain another cost that is similar in nature to the cost of electricity. When you plot the cost against a cost driver, a relationship becomes apparent. However, the cost varies with something other than the cost driver. (Think of other situations where this type of relationship might occur.)

2.48 **Learning Curve, Cost-based Prices, Financial Statements (Appendix 2B)** Two competitors each began producing and selling the same product last year. In both cases, the cost of the first unit was $300. Firm A's managers were uncertain about the future of the product, so they sold each unit for actual cost plus a 50% mark-up for profit. Firm B's managers were confident that the product would be a success. They expected to sell 100 units of the product over its life. The managers set their selling price at the average cost to produce 100 units plus a 50% mark-up.

The production of this product mostly relies on labour and is subject to an 85% learning rate. Last year, Firm A sold 5 units of the product, and Firm B sold 150 units (more than initially anticipated). This year, Firm A's managers decided to match Firm B's last year's selling price. Meanwhile, Firm B's managers anticipated selling another 150 units; therefore, they calculated the average cost to produce the second group of 150 units and set their current-year price at last year's average cost plus a 50% mark-up. At the end of this year, Firm A had sold only 10 units, while Firm B had sold 150 units.

REQUIRED Calculate net income for the two firms for this year and last year. (*Hint:* The amount of time it takes to produce a unit is not specified, but you can adapt the learning curve to estimate the average cost to produce a unit by replacing cost with hours.)

2.49 **Cost Function Using Regression, Scatter Plot, Discretionary Cost** Costs for the marketing department and total sales of Belford's, a British chain of department stores located in the United Kingdom and other European countries, are available at www.wiley.com/go/eldenburgcanada. You have been asked to develop a cost function for next month's cost. The head of the marketing department believes that the department's costs are related to volume of sales (in British pounds).

LO2, LO4, LO5, LO6

www.wiley.com/ go/eldenburgcanada

REQUIRED

A. Create a scatter plot of the data.
B. From analyzing the plot, do you think sales are a potential cost driver? Explain.
C. Perform a regression analysis between marketing department costs and sales. Write the algebraic expression for total cost.
D. Explain why it is economically plausible for sales to be a cost driver for marketing costs.
E. When you present the results of the regression analysis to the head of the marketing department, she tells you that the department costs are discretionary costs. If this statement is true, why might a linear relationship appear between the cost and sales?
F. After your discussion with the head of marketing, you understand that department costs are discretionary. In this situation, explain why regression analysis would not be appropriate for estimating future marketing department costs.

2.50 **Cost Function Using Regression, Scatter Plots, Three Potential Cost Drivers** Laura Mills is the controller of Peer Jets International, a manufacturer of small corporate jets. She has undertaken a project to study the behaviour of overhead cost and has assembled factory overhead data for the past 30 months from the company's manufacturing facility. Laura has asked you to develop a model to predict the level of manufacturing overhead.

LO4, LO5

The following categories of information are available to Laura. Manufacturing overhead includes all the overhead costs associated with the manufacturing plant. Labour hours are the number of hours manufacturing employees worked. Machine hours are the total hours that machinery was used for the period. Tonnes of raw materials are all of the raw materials that were used for that particular month. Data for this problem are available at www.wiley.com/go/eldenburgcanada.

www.wiley.com/ go/eldenburgcanada

REQUIRED
A. Create a scatter plot of manufacturing overhead for each of the potential cost drivers.
B. Based on the scatter plots, would you eliminate any of the potential cost drivers? Why or why not?
C. Explain why you create a scatter plot of the data before you perform regression analysis.
D. To practise your regression analysis skills, perform a simple regression analysis of manufacturing overhead for each of the three potential cost drivers. Write the cost function from each regression.
E. Based on the simple regression results, which cost driver does the best job of explaining manufacturing overhead costs? Explain.
F. Do your regression results support your answer to Part (B)? Explain.

2.51 **Cost Function Using Multiple Regression (Appendix 2A)** Refer to the data and requirements of Problem 2.50.

REQUIRED
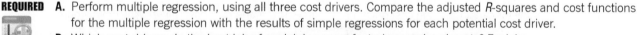

LO5

A. Perform multiple regression, using all three cost drivers. Compare the adjusted R-squares and cost functions for the multiple regression with the results of simple regressions for each potential cost driver.
B. Which cost drivers do the best job of explaining manufacturing overhead costs? Explain.
C. Select only the cost drivers that do the best job of explaining manufacturing overhead costs. Perform multiple regression analysis for those cost drivers and write the cost function.
D. Explain why more than one cost driver is plausible for manufacturing overhead costs.

2.52 **Use of Prior Year Costs, Quality of Information** Software Solutions is a family-owned business that has been in operation for more than 15 years. The board of directors is composed of mainly family members, plus a few professionals, such as an accountant and a lawyer. Regina is a staff accountant who has been working on the budget for the past several weeks. The director of finance needs to present the budget at the next board meeting and wants a preliminary copy in two days. Regina is certain that she will not be able to finish the budget within two days. Several department heads have not turned in their preliminary figures, and two departments have budgeted large increases in fixed costs for replacing computer equipment. Regina knows she should have alerted the director of finance about these budgeted increases, but she has not had time.

LO3, LO6

One of her co-workers knows that Regina is behind and suggests that she use last year's budgets for departments that have not provided information and also for the departments that increased their budgets by large amounts. The co-worker says that the budget can be straightened out later, because the board does not pay attention to the details.

REQUIRED **A.** Is this an ethical dilemma for Regina? Why or why not?

B. Why might it be important for the board of directors to have as much updated information as possible about the budget?

C. What should Regina do, given that not enough time is available to gather high-quality information? Explain your thinking.

2.53 **Scatter Plots, Cost Function Using Regression, Two Potential Cost Drivers** Suppose we need to predict the cost of maintenance for Brush Prairie High School for the upcoming school year. From the school district records, we gather weekly data about costs and volumes for two potential cost drivers: labour hours used in the maintenance department and number of enrolled students.

LO4, LO5, LO6

| | | **Potential Cost Drivers** | |
Week	Total Maintenance Cost	Number of Maintenance Hours Worked	Number of Students
1	$16,690	238	534
2	13,560	194	532
3	13,540	108	534
4	16,060	229	530
5	12,430	101	533
6	20,860	298	537
7	18,420	244	540
8	12,310	98	540
9	13,770	108	541
10	16,990	225	538
11	20,650	289	540
12	14,770	118	539

REQUIRED **A.** Identify and explain two potential cost drivers for total maintenance cost, in addition to number of students and maintenance hours worked.

B. Create a scatter plot for maintenance cost versus hours worked. Create another scatter plot for maintenance cost versus students.

C. Based on the scatter plots, would you eliminate either cost driver? Explain.

D. Perform regression analysis using each cost driver. Use your judgment to determine the most appropriate cost driver and write out the cost function for maintenance cost.

E. Can we know for certain that the cost driver chosen in Part D is the best cost driver? Why or why not?

2.54 **Personal Cost Function, Information System, Two-Point and High-Low Methods** Pick a cost from your personal budget that varies, such as entertainment, education, or automobile operating expenses. For this cost, practise using the estimation techniques you have learned in this chapter.

LO4, LO6

REQUIRED **A.** Apply engineered estimate of cost to develop a monthly budget for the cost by analyzing what you think the cost should be. Use the following steps:
- Identify the activities that drive the cost.
- Plan the monthly level for each activity.
- Determine a cost per unit for each activity.
- Combine the activity levels with the costs to create a monthly budget.

B. Apply analysis at the account level to your cost. Analyze your cheque book, credit card statements, or other spending information to gather several months' past expenditures for this cost. Study this information to gain an understanding of the types of costs you have incurred in the past. Then address the following questions:

1. Can you classify the cost as fixed, variable, or mixed? Why or why not?

2. Are you missing information for some parts of the cost (such as for cash expenditures)? In what ways could you change your record keeping to provide better information about this cost? What would be the costs and benefits of doing so?

C. Refer to the cost information you gathered for Part B. If you think that the cost is variable or mixed, select one or more potential cost drivers and collect data for them. Create a scatter plot of the cost against each cost driver. If you do not think the cost is variable or mixed, create a line chart of the cost over time. Examine your chart.

  Do you see any patterns? For example, does the cost seem to increase with a cost driver (or over time)? Does the cost seem to be fixed at a given level?

  How does the graph affect your understanding of this cost's behaviour? Explain.

D. If you think your cost is variable or mixed, refer to the data you used to create the scatter plot in Part C. Choose only one cost driver and use the two-point and high-low methods to estimate the cost function.

  1. Are the cost functions similar? Why or why not?
  2. Are the fixed and variable costs about what you would expect them to be? Why or why not?
  3. How comfortable would you be using one of these cost functions to create a budget for next month? Explain.

E. In what ways is your personal budget estimation problem the same as the cost estimation problem for a business? Explain.

2.55 **Cost Function Judgment and Methodology** Suppose you have the responsibility of creating a cost function for the costs of an Internet service provider's help line.

REQUIRED   **A.** What is the cost object? Identify where you might obtain information about past costs for the cost object.

L02, L03, L04, L06

B. Identify at least two potential cost drivers. Explain where you might obtain information about past volumes for each cost driver.

C. What other information would you like to obtain before estimating the cost function? How might you obtain that information?

D. Identify the techniques introduced in this chapter that you would be most likely to use in creating the cost function. Explain why you'd use these techniques.

MINI-CASES

2.56 **Cost Function Using Account Analysis and High-Low Method** The Little Beaver Daycare Centres, a not-for-profit

L02, L03, L04, L06

organization, provides daycare services to low-income families in 20 communities in Alberta. The manager's summary report for the past four months of operations is reproduced here:

	March	April	May	June	Total
Number of children	849	821	778	842	3,290
Daycare fees	$ 4,230	$ 4,180	$ 3,875	$ 4,260	$ 16,545
Daycare staff salaries	13,254	13,256	13,254	14,115	53,879
Daycare supplies used	3,182	3,077	2,934	3,175	12,368
Administrative salaries	3,197	3,198	3,197	3,412	13,004
Rent	1,000	1,000	1,000	1,100	4,100
Utilities	226	226	226	226	904
Other expenses	2,854	2,776	2,671	2,828	11,129
Total expenses	23,713	$23,533	$23,282	24,856	95,384
Operating surplus (loss)	$(19,483)	$(19,353)	$(19,407)	$(20,596)	$(78,839)

  The daycare receives an operating subsidy from the province, but unfortunately, the operating loss that has been incurred through June $(79,392) is larger than anticipated. Part of the problem is the salary increase that went into effect in June, which had been overlooked when the budget was submitted to the city last year. To compound the problem, the warm summer months traditionally bring with them an increase in additional summer outdoor activities. Thus, the daycare experiences additional costs during July.

  The daycare's managers are considering an increase in daycare fees to reduce losses. However, they are reluctant to raise fees because the children are from low-income families. The daycare will raise fees only if necessary.

REQUIRED INFORMATION ANALYSIS

The following questions will help you analyze the information for this problem. Do not turn in your answers to these questions unless your professor asks you to do so.

A. Use your judgment to classify costs as fixed, variable, or mixed. Explain how you classified each item.

B. Create a cost function for the Little Beaver Daycare Centres. Use the high-low method to estimate the function for any mixed costs.

C. Use the cost function to estimate July expenses based on a projection of 940 children.

D. List as many reasons as you can why management of the Little Beaver Daycare Centres cannot know with certainty what the expenses will be during July.

E. Describe the pros and cons of using your cost estimate from Part (C) to decide whether to raise daycare fees.

REQUIRED WRITTEN ASSIGNMENT

The managers need your July cost estimate to help them decide whether to raise daycare fees. Turn in your answer to the following.

F. Use the information you learned from the preceding analyses to write a memo to the director of the Little Beaver Daycare Centres, presenting your estimate of July costs. Provide the director with appropriate information for understanding your methodology and evaluating the reliability of your cost estimate.

2.57 Adjusting Data for Use with Regression, Outlier Smeyer Industries is a large firm with more than 40 departments, each employing 35 to 100 persons. Recent experience suggests that the cost function used to estimate overhead in Department IP-14 is no longer appropriate. The current function was developed three years ago. Since then, a number of changes have occurred in the facilities and processes used in Department IP-14. The changes have happened one at a time. Each time a change has been made, the cost accountant has felt that the change was not major enough to justify calculating a new overhead cost function. Now it is clear that the cumulative effect of the changes has been large.

LO3, LO5, LO6

You have been assigned the task of developing a new formula cost function for overhead in Department IP-14. Initial analysis suggests that the number of direct labour hours is an appropriate cost driver. Departmental records are available for nine months. The records reveal the following information:

Month	Actual Overhead	Direct Labour Hours
March	$68,200	8,812
April	71,250	8,538
May	68,150	8,740
June	73,500	9,176
July	38,310	2,123
August	70,790	9,218
September	80,350	8,943
October	68,750	8,821
November	68,200	8,794

An assistant has analyzed the data for March through July and made the appropriate adjustments, except for the following items (for which the assistant was unsure of the proper treatment):

1. The semi-annual property tax bill for Department IP-14 was paid on June 30. The entire amount, $3,000, was charged to overhead for June.

2. The costs to install a new piece of equipment with a life of 10 years were charged to overhead in April. The installation costs were $4,300.

3. Factory depreciation is allocated to Department IP-14 every month. The department's share, $8,000, is included in overhead.

4. A strike closed the plant for three weeks in July. Several nonunion employees were kept on payroll during the strike. Their duties were general housekeeping and "busy work." These costs were charged to overhead.

You also have the details for the overhead account for the months of August and September. They are presented in the following table. You were hired on October 1 and have been keeping the department accounts since then.

Therefore, you know that the data for October and November are correct, except for any adjustments needed for the preceding items.

Department IP-14 Overhead Control
August

Date	Explanation	Amount
Aug. 4	Miscellaneous supplies	$10,450
Aug. 5	Payroll for indirect labour	5,500
Aug. 15	Power costs: Department IP-14	12,250
Aug. 19	Payroll for indirect labour	6,000
Aug. 19	Overtime premium	890
Aug. 24	Factory depreciation	8,000
Aug. 26	Miscellaneous supplies	27,700
	Total for August	$70,790

Department IP-14 Overhead Control
September

Date	Explanation	Amount
Sept. 2	Payroll for indirect labour	$6,000
Sept. 7	Miscellaneous supplies	12,100
Sept. 15	Power costs: Department IP-14	11,100
Sept. 15	Power costs: Department IB-4	10,850
Sept. 16	Payroll for indirect labour	6,500
Sept. 16	Overtime premium	950
Sept. 21	Miscellaneous supplies	19,350
Sept. 28	Factory depreciation	8,000
Sept. 30	Payroll for indirect labour	5,500
	Total for September	$80,350

August has 31 days, and September has 30 days.

REQUIRED **A.** Using the information provided, adjust the monthly cost data to more accurately reflect the overhead costs incurred during each month.

B. Discuss whether the data for July should be included in the estimate of future costs. Create a scatter plot to help answer this question.

C. Develop a cost function by regressing overhead costs in Department IP-14 on direct labour hours. Discuss whether your cost function would be reasonable for estimating future overhead costs. Ignore any items you will discuss in Part D.

D. Identify and discuss any additional adjustments that might be needed to more accurately measure overhead costs for the regression in Part C.

E. Explain why adjustments probably need to be made to information from accounting records when estimating a cost function.

2.58 **Integrating Across the Curriculum Statistics** *Cost function using multiple regression, cost inflation, and lagged cost driver (Appendix 2A)* Red's Furniture Manufacturing produces a line of tables and chairs from specialty hardwoods. It makes three different styles of chairs, and each chair takes about the same amount of direct labour time to manufacture. Shawn Hargrove is the company's new cost accountant and is preparing a direct labour cost budget for 2017 or (next year). The previous cost accountant always estimated direct labour costs based on a regression of the cost against the number of chairs produced, using monthly data from the prior four years. This approach seemed to be economically plausible, so Shawn begins his cost estimate by following the method used in prior years. However, Shawn is not pleased with his regression results, and he thinks about ways to improve

LO5, LO6

the cost function estimate. He realizes that the past cost information did not take into account pay raises. Every January, the company gives its employees a cost-of-living pay increase. Each of the past four years, the employees have received a 2% raise. Shawn learns from management that a 2% raise is planned for 2017, too.

Shawn thinks that prior years' labour costs should be increased to 2017 pay levels to provide a more accurate prediction of 2017 costs. He plans to adjust prior-year pay using the following formula:

Labour cost at 2017 (next year's) level = Labour cost at prior pay level $\times$ $(1.02)^t$

where

$$t = 1 \text{ for } 2016$$

$$t = 2 \text{ for } 2015$$

$$t = 3 \text{ for } 2014$$

$$t = 4 \text{ for } 2013$$

Shawn is also considering the degree to which direct labour costs vary with production. The company's policy is to increase the number of workers when production volumes increase and to decrease the number of workers when production volumes decrease. However, it often takes time for the company to hire qualified new workers, and the managers often delay laying off employees when volumes decline. Thus, at least some lag is evident between the time that production volumes change and labour costs change. Shawn thinks that an additional cost driver for direct labour costs might be the prior month's volume of chairs produced.

The data provide monthly direct labour costs and number of chairs produced for the past four years. These data are available at www.wiley.com/go/eldenburgcanada.

REQUIRED

www.wiley.com/
go/eldenburgcanada

A. Estimate the cost function, using the same method as in prior years. Explain why Shawn is displeased with the results.

B. Explain why the annual pay increases cause a problem with the cost function estimated in Part A. In what way is the cost function mismeasured?

C. Use the formula Shawn developed to adjust the labour cost data for pay increases. Re-estimate the cost function. Explain whether you consider it to be a reasonable cost function for estimating 2017 direct labour costs.

D. To the analysis you performed in Part C, add a second independent variable for the number of chairs produced in the preceding month. Re-estimate the cost function. Do the statistics suggest that it is a reasonable cost function?

E. Explain what the two slope coefficients from Part D mean in terms of the cost function.

F. Do you agree that both independent variables should be used to estimate 2017 direct labour costs? Why or why not?

CHAPTER 3

Cost-Volume-Profit Analysis

in brief Managers need to estimate future revenues, costs, and profits as they plan and monitor operations. Cost-volume-profit (CVP) analysis is used to identify the levels of operating activity needed to avoid losses, achieve targeted profits, plan future operations, and monitor organizational performance. Managers also analyze operational risks as they choose an appropriate cost structure. ∎

After studying this chapter, you should be able to do the following:

LO1 Explain the concept of cost-volume-profit (CVP) analysis in decision making

LO2 Apply CVP calculations for a single product

LO3 Apply CVP calculations for multiple products

LO4 Describe the assumptions and limitations that managers consider when using CVP analysis

LO5 Assess operational risk using margin of safety and operating leverage

LO6 Analyze the difference between contribution margin and gross margin

Rising Commodity Prices
Hurt Tim Hortons

Fernando Morales/The Globe and Mail/The Canadian Press

Higher prices for commodities such as coffee, sugar, wheat, and even crude oil has been eating into the profits of **Tim Hortons Inc**. The iconic Canadian coffee and doughnut chain saw revenues increase by 10.4% in the first quarter of 2011 to $643.5 million. However, higher costs meant that earnings increased by only 2.3% to $80.7 million.

The wholesale price of coffee doubled in just seven months, prompting Tims to raise its retail price of a large coffee by about 4.5% in the spring of 2011. The cost of commodities that it uses as ingredients in its baked goods, such as wheat, corn, sugar, and vegetable oil, rose by between 50% and 100% in just 12 months.

Of further concern to the chain is the impact of higher gasoline prices on its customers' budgets and their willingness and ability to get their daily doughnut and coffee hit. "When our guests have fewer discretionary dollars, they have to make choices," said Tims CEO Don Schroeder.

To help offset the volatility of commodity prices, Tims uses purchase contracts to lock in the price it pays for things such as coffee, wheat, edible oils, and sugar over several quarters. Some of the contracts are in U.S. dollars, which should help offset some price increases if the Canadian dollar continues its strength, the company said.

The restaurant industry is constantly exposed to this price uncertainty. "Our business will continue to be subject to changes related to the underlying costs of key commodities. These cost changes can impact revenues, costs and margins, and can create volatility quarter-over-quarter and year-over-year. Increases and decreases in commodity costs are largely passed through to restaurant owners, resulting in higher or lower revenues and higher or lower costs of sales from our business. These changes may impact margins as many of these products are typically priced based on a fixed-dollar mark-up," the company said in its 2010 annual report.

Passing on higher ingredient costs to customers is always an option, but not an attractive one, the company noted. "Although we have implemented purchasing practices that mitigate our exposure to volatility to a certain degree," the report went on to say, "if costs increased to a greater degree for 2011 purchases, we and our restaurant owners have some ability to increase product pricing to offset a rise in commodity prices, but these price increases could negatively affect sales."

Achieving the optimum balance of costs to sales volume in order to maximize profit is the aim of cost-volume-profit analysis.

SOURCE: Canadian Press, "Gas and Food Costs Are Eating into Tims' Customer Budgets," *Hamilton Spectator*, May 12, 2011; Tim Hortons Inc. 2010 *Annual Report*; "Tim Hortons Inc. Announces 2011 First Quarter Results," news release, May 12, 2011.

Cost-Volume-Profit Analysis

Cost-volume-profit (CVP) analysis is a technique that examines changes in profits in response to changes in sales volumes, costs, and prices. Accountants often perform CVP analysis to plan future levels of operating activity and provide information about the following:

- ▶ Which products or services to emphasize.
- ▶ The volume of sales needed to achieve a targeted level of profit.
- ▶ The amount of revenue required to avoid losses.
- ▶ Whether to increase fixed costs.
- ▶ How much to budget for discretionary expenditures.
- ▶ Whether fixed costs expose the organization to an unacceptable level of risk.

Profit Equation and Contribution Margin

CVP analysis begins with the basic profit equation,

$$\text{Profit} = \text{Total revenue} - \text{Total costs}$$

Separating costs into variable and fixed categories, we express profit as

$$\text{Profit or earning} = \text{Total revenue} - \text{Total variable costs} - \text{Total fixed costs.}$$

The **contribution margin** is the total revenue minus the total variable costs. Similarly, the contribution margin per unit (CM_u) is the selling price per unit minus the variable cost per unit. Both contribution margin and contribution margin per unit are valuable tools when considering the effects of volume on profit. Contribution margin per unit tells us how much revenue from each unit sold can be applied toward fixed costs or contributed to cover them. Once enough units have been sold to cover all fixed costs, the contribution margin per unit from all remaining sales becomes profit.

If we assume that the selling price and variable cost per unit are constant, then total revenue is equal to price times quantity, and total variable cost is equal to variable cost per unit times quantity. We then rewrite the profit equation in terms of the contribution margin per unit:

$$EBT = S \times Q - V \times Q - F = (S - V) \times Q - F$$

where

$$EBT = \text{Earnings before taxes}$$
$$S = \text{Selling price per unit}$$
$$V = \text{Variable cost per unit}$$
$$(S - V) = \text{Contribution margin per unit } (CM_u)$$
$$Q = \text{Quantity of product sold (units of goods or services)}$$
$$F = \text{Total fixed costs}$$

We use the profit equation to plan for different volumes of operations. CVP analysis can be performed using either

- ▶ Units (quantity) of product sold
- ▶ Revenues (in dollars)

CVP Analysis in Units

We begin with the preceding profit equation. Assuming that fixed costs remain constant, we solve for the expected quantity of goods or services that must be sold to achieve a target level of profit:

$$\text{Earnings (profit) equation: } EBT = S \times Q - V \times Q - F = (S - V) \times Q - F$$

$$\text{Solving for } Q: \frac{F + EBT}{(S - V) \text{ or } CM_u} = \text{Quantity (units) required to obtain target profit}$$

Notice that the denominator in this formula, $(S - V)$, is the contribution margin per unit (CM_u).

Suppose that Magik Bicycles wants to produce a new mountain bike called Magikbike III and has forecasted the following information:

$$\text{Price per bike} = \$800$$
$$\text{Variable cost per bike} = \$300$$
$$\text{Fixed costs related to bike production} = \$5,500,000$$
$$\text{Target profit} = \$200,000$$
$$\text{Estimated sales} = 12,000 \text{ bikes}$$

We determine the quantity of bikes needed for the target profit as follows:

$$\text{Quantity} = (\$5,500,000 + \$200,000) \div (\$800 - \$300) = 11,400 \text{ bikes}$$

CVP Analysis in Revenues

The **contribution margin ratio (CMR)** is the percentage by which the selling price (or revenue) per unit exceeds the variable cost per unit; in other words, contribution margin as a percentage of revenue. For a single product, it is

$$CMR = \frac{S - V}{S}$$

To analyze CVP in terms of total revenue instead of units, we substitute the contribution margin ratio for the contribution margin per unit. We rewrite the equation to solve for the total dollar amount of revenue we need to cover fixed costs and achieve our target profit as

$$\text{Sales revenue} = \frac{F + EBT}{(S - V)/S} = \frac{F + EBT}{CMR}$$

To solve for the Magikbike III revenues needed to achieve a target profit of $200,000, we first calculate the contribution margin ratio as follows:

$$CMR = (\$800 - \$300) \div \$800 = 0.625$$

A contribution margin ratio of 0.625 means that 62.5% of the revenue from each bike sold contributes first to fixed costs and then to profit after fixed costs are covered:

$$\text{Sales revenue} = (\$5,500,000 + \$200,000) \div 0.625 = \$9,120,000$$

We check to see that the two results are identical by multiplying the number of units (11,400) by price ($800) to obtain the revenue amount ($9,120,000).

The contribution margin ratio can also be written in terms of total sales revenue (TS) and total variable costs (TVC). That is, for a single product, the CMR is the same whether we compute it using per-unit selling price and variable cost or using total revenues and total variable costs. Thus, we can create the following mathematically equivalent version of the CVP formula:

$$\text{Sales revenues} = \frac{F + EBT}{(TS - TVC)/TS}$$

For Magikbike III, we could use the forecast information about volume (12,000 bikes) to determine the contribution margin ratio:

HELPFUL HINT
Computing the CVP using total revenues and total variable costs is useful in cases where per-unit variable costs are unknown.

Contribution Income Statement

	Per Unit	Total	%
Sales revenue (12,000 bikes)	$800	$9,600,000	100.00
Less: variable cost	300	3,600,000	37.50
Contribution margin	500	6,000,000	62.50
Less: fixed costs		5,500,000	
Operating income (profit) before taxes		$ 500,000	

Performing CVP Analysis

Breakeven Point

Managers often want to know the level of activity required to break even. A CVP analysis can be used to determine the **breakeven point**, or level of operating activity at which revenues cover all fixed and variable costs, resulting in zero profit. In other words, the contribution is the same as the fixed costs, which leaves no profit. We can calculate the breakeven point from any of the preceding CVP formulas by setting profit to zero. Depending on which formula we use, we calculate the breakeven point in either number of units or in total revenues. For Magikbike III, breakeven points are

$$\text{Sales revenues} = \frac{F + EBT}{\text{CMR or } CM_u} \rightarrow \frac{CM_{Total}}{\text{CMR or } CM_u}$$

EBT is set at $0:

Breakeven quantity = ($5,500,000 + $0) ÷ ($800 – $300) = 11,000 bikes
Breakeven revenue = ($5,500,000 + $0) ÷ 0.625 = $8,800,000

Cost-Volume-Profit Graph

A **cost-volume-profit (CVP) graph** shows the relationship between total revenues and total costs; it illustrates how an organization's profits are expected to change under different volumes of activity. Exhibit 3.1 presents a CVP graph for Magikbike III. Notice that when no bikes are sold, fixed costs are $5,500,000, resulting in a loss of $5,500,000. As sales volume increases, the loss decreases by the contribution margin for each bike sold. The cost and revenue lines intersect at the breakeven point of 11,000, which means zero loss and zero profit. Then, as sales increase beyond this breakeven point, we see an increase in profit, growing by the $500 contribution margin for each bike sold. Profits achieve the target level of $200,000 when sales volume reaches 11,400.

CVP with Income Taxes

Up to this point, our CVP calculations have ignored income taxes. An organization's after-tax earnings are calculated by subtracting income tax from pretax earnings. The tax is usually calculated as a percentage of pretax earnings.

▶ **EXHIBIT 3.1**

CVP Graph for Magik Bicycles' Magikbike III

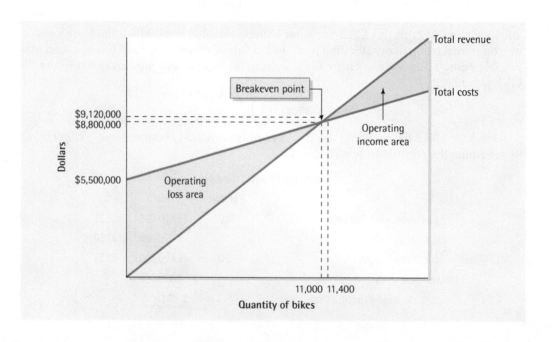

$$\text{Earnings after taxes (EAT)} = EBT - \text{Taxes}$$
$$= EBT - (\text{Tax rate} \times EBT)$$
$$= EBT \times (1 - \text{Tax rate})$$

▣ **ALTERNATIVE TERMS**

Some people use the terms *operating income (loss)* or *income (loss) before income taxes* instead of *pretax earning (loss)*. Similarly, some people use *net income (loss)* instead of *after-tax earning (loss)*.

If we want to know the pretax earnings needed to achieve a target level of after-tax earnings, we solve the following formula for pretax earnings:

$$EBT = \frac{EAT}{(1 - \text{Tax rate})}$$

$$\text{Or } EBT = EAT \div (1 - \text{Tax rate})$$

Suppose that Magik Bicycles plans for after-tax earnings of $20,000 and its tax rate is 30%. Then

$$EBT = \$20,000 \div (1 - 0.30) = \$28,571$$

The company needs earnings before tax of $28,571 to generate earnings after tax of $20,000.

The following illustration develops a cost function to calculate the volumes needed to break even and to achieve target after-tax earnings when multiple products are involved.

CVP with Variable Amount of Earning

Managers may want to set an earning amount as a variable amount of sales. This variable amount of earning should be calculated as an additional variable cost. Suppose that Magik Bicycles plans for before-tax earnings of 7.5% of sales. In this case, the CVP formula for solving the sales dollar amount is

Earnings (profit) equation: $\qquad EBT = S \times Q - V \times Q - F = x\%S$

$$S - 0.375\,S - FC = 0.075\,S$$

Solving for S: $\qquad 0.625S - 0.075\,S = \$5,500,000$

$$S = \$10,000,000$$

To incorporate the income tax in the calculation, if Magik Bicycles plans for after-tax earnings of 5.25% of sales, then the sales dollar amount is calculated as follows:

Earnings (profit) equation: $\qquad EBT = EAT \div (1 - \text{Tax})$

$$x\%S = y\%S \div (1 - 0.3)$$

$$EBT = 5.25\% \div (1 - 0.3) = 7.5\%$$

$$S - 0.375S - FC = 0.075S$$

Solving for S: $\qquad 0.625\,S - 0.075\,S = \$5,500,000$

$$S = \$10,000,000$$

$$Q = \text{Total sales/Per unit sale} = \$10,000,000/\$800 = 12,500$$

The following contribution income statement proves the above calculations:

Contribution Income Statement

	Per Unit	Total	%
Sales revenue (12,500 bikes)	$800	$10,000,000	100.00%
Less: variable cost	300	3,750,000	37.50%
Contribution margin	500	6,250,000	62.50%
Less: fixed costs		5,500,000	
Earnings (profit) before taxes		750,000	7.50%
Taxes 30%		225,000	
Earnings (profit) after taxes		$ 525,000	5.25%

> EXHIBIT 3.2
Summary of Equations for Various CVP
Analyses

$$\text{Sales} = \frac{\text{Contribution Margin}_{(\text{Total})}}{\text{Contribution Margin Ratio}} = \frac{\text{Fixed Costs} + \text{EBT}}{\text{Contribution Margin Ratio}}$$

The Breakeven Point	Fixed Amount of Earning Before & After Taxes	Variable Amount of Earning Before & After Taxes
Breakeven → CM = FC	Earning Before Tax: $$CM = FC + EBT$$ Earning After Tax: $$CM = FC + [EAT \div (1 - \text{Tax})]$$	Earning Before Tax: $$CM = FC + EBT \rightarrow EBT$$ $$= x\% \text{ of Sales}$$ Earning After Tax: $$CM = FC + [EAT \div (1 - \text{Tax})]$$ $$= FC + [y\% \div (1 - \text{Tax})]$$
Ratio Approach to Calculate Sales in $: $$CM_{(\text{Total})} = \frac{FC + 0}{CM \text{ Ratio}}$$ $$= \$$$	Ratio Approach to Calculate Sales in $: Earning Before Taxes: $$CM_{(\text{Total})} = \frac{FC + EBT}{CM \text{ Ratio}} = \$$$ Earning After Taxes: $$EBT = EAT \div (1 - \text{Tax})$$ $$CM_{(\text{Total})} = \frac{FC + [EAT \div (1 - \text{Tax})]}{CM \text{ Ratio}}$$ $$= \$$$	Earning Before Tax: $$S - x\%S - FC = y\%S$$ Where $x\%S$ = Variable Costs $y\%S$ = EBT → treated as an additional VC $$S - x\%S - y\%S = FC$$ Earning After Tax: $$EBT = EAT \div (1 - \text{Tax})$$ $$y\%S = z\%S \div (1 - \text{Tax})$$ $$S - x\%S - y\%S = FC$$ $$y\%S = EBT; z\%S = EAT$$ $$y\%S = z\% \div (1 - \text{Tax})$$
Unit Approach to Calculate Sales in Units $$CM_{(\text{Total})} = \frac{FC + 0}{CM_u}$$ $$= \text{Units}$$	Unit Approach to Calculate Sales in Units: Earning Before Taxes: $$CM_{(\text{Total})} = \frac{FC + EBT}{CM_u} = \text{Units}$$ Earning After Taxes: $$EBT = EAT \div (1 - \text{Tax})$$ $$CM_{(\text{Total})} = \frac{FC + [EAT \div (1 - \text{Tax})]}{CM \text{ Ratio}}$$ $$= \$$$	We introduce $z\%$ here to show that in this case the company wants to achieve an after-tax income, this is how we convert from after-tax income to before-tax income.

die gefleckte kuh eis (the spotted cow creamery), part 1
CVP ANALYSIS WITH INCOME TAXES

Die Gefleckte Kuh Eis (The Spotted Cow Creamery) is a popular ice cream emporium near a university in Munich, Germany. Information for the most recent month (amounts in euros) appears here:

Revenue	€40,000
Cost of food and beverages sold	20,000
Labour	15,000
Rent	1,000
Earnings before taxes	4,000
Income taxes (25%)	1,000
Earnings after taxes	€ 3,000

fotofrog/Getty Images

The store owner asked the manager, Holger Soderstrom, to estimate results for the next month. This particular outlet has not performed as well as the owner's other three outlets. Holger believes that sales volumes will increase to 48,000 next month because it has been an unusually hot and dry summer.

Estimating the Cost Function

To perform CVP analysis, Holger first estimates the cost function. Using accounting records, he classifies each cost as fixed or variable and then estimates next month's cost. Of the costs listed in the accounting records, labour (€15,000) and rent (€1,000) are most likely fixed (assuming that employees work fixed schedules). Assuming that fixed costs do not change from month to month, Holger's best estimate of next month's fixed costs is €16,000 (€15,000 + €1,000). The remaining item, cost of food and beverages sold (€20,000), is most likely a variable cost. Because The Spotted Cow Creamery's focus is retail sales of ice cream and other food items, Holger can reasonably assume that sales volume drives this variable cost. Thus, he estimates expected variable costs as a percentage of revenue:

$$€20,000 \div €40,000 = 0.50, \text{ or } 50\% \text{ of revenue}$$

Holger combines his fixed and variable cost estimates to create the following cost function for next month:

$$TC = €16,000 + (50\% \times \text{Revenues})$$

Estimating Earnings after Taxes

If next month's revenues are €48,000, Holger expects total variable costs to be (50% × €48,000) = €24,000. Therefore, his estimate of pretax earnings is

$$\text{Earnings before taxes} = €48,000 - €16,000 - €24,000 = €8,000$$

Holger estimates income taxes and after-tax earnings, assuming that income taxes remain at 25% of pretax earnings:

$$\text{Earnings after taxes} = €8,000(1 - 0.25) = €6,000$$

Calculating Revenues to Achieve Targeted Earning After Taxes

Holger presents the preceding information to the owner. However, the owner still has concerns about this outlet, because the other outlets have achieved after-tax earnings of about €8,000 each during the past few months. The owner thinks that sales volume might be the problem. To help analyze this possibility, Holger determines the sales volume necessary to earn after-tax earnings of €8,000 per month. He begins by calculating the targeted pretax earning:

$$\text{Earnings before taxes} = €8,000 \div (1 - 0.25) = €10,667$$

Next, he uses the following CVP formula to solve for targeted revenue:

$$\text{Sales revenues} = \frac{F + EBT}{CMR}$$

Substituting the preceding information, he gets

$$\text{Revenues} = (€16,000 + €10,667) \div 0.50 = €53,334$$

Notice that Holger uses the contribution margin ratio calculated with the sales revenue and variable costs from his original analysis.

continued...

example

Holger summarizes his target profit calculations in a contribution income statement format for the owner as follows:

Revenue	€53,334
Variable cost:	
Cost of food and beverages sold (50% of 53,334)	26,667
Contribution margin	26,667
Fixed costs:	
Labour	15,000
Rent	1,000
Earnings before taxes	€10,667
Income taxes (25%)	2,667
Earnings after taxes	€ 8,000

For the outlet to achieve earnings after taxes of €8,000, revenues need to increase by 33% [(€53,334 – €40,000) ÷ €40,000] over last month.

Holger presents this information to the owner and argues that sales will increase to €53,334 because the weather will be hotter next month. However, the owner thinks that Holger may be worried about being replaced, and his revenue estimates are probably biased upward. The owner decides to investigate Holger's estimates further by comparing his revenues and costs to those in the other outlets. ■

●●● ▶ RISK OF BIASED DECISIONS : OPTIMISM BIAS

OPTIMISM BIAS is a systematic tendency for people to be overly optimistic about the outcomes of their plans and projects. When accountants and managers are affected by optimism bias, they tend to underestimate costs and overestimate benefits in cost-benefit analyses. This can result in cost overruns and benefit shortfalls.

The UK government understands that optimism bias is a problem in budgeting and has developed measures to reduce this (HM Treasury, 2003). Government planners reward project promoters who present realistic costing estimates and penalize those who do not.

Professors who research the effects of bias disagree about managers' motives. Some believe that managers unconsciously exhibit optimism bias, while others maintain that managers strategically misrepresent cash flows so their projects are approved.

SOURCE: HM Treasury, *Supplementary Green Book Guidance: Optimism Bias* (London: HM Treasury, 2003).

Performing CVP Analyses with a Spreadsheet

L03   Apply CVP calculations for multiple products

Spreadsheets are often used for CVP computations, particularly when an organization has multiple products. Spreadsheets simplify the basic computations and can be designed to show how changes in volumes, selling prices, costs, or sales mix alter the results.

CVP for Multiple Products

Many organizations sell a combination of different products or services. The **sales mix** is the proportion of different products or services that an organization sells. To use CVP in the case of multiple products or services, we assume a constant sales mix in addition to the other

CVP assumptions. Assuming a constant sales mix allows CVP computations to be performed using combined unit or revenue data for an organization as a whole.

CVP Calculations for a Sales Mix

Although The Spotted Cow Creamery sells multiple products, the CVP analysis performed by the store manager did not provide computations for individual products. Instead, the analysis focused on the total amount of revenue needed to achieve a target profit. If the manager wants to use CVP results to plan future operations for individual products, the required revenue for each product needs to be determined. Such computations are performed using the sales mix. Sales mix analysis allows managers to achieve the combination of sales that will yield the greatest amount of earnings. The sales mix should be stated as a proportion of units when performing CVP computations in units, and it should be stated as a proportion of revenues when performing CVP computations in revenues.

When performing CVP computations for sales mix, we assume that the products a company sells are in a constant ratio. For example, Magik Bicycles developed three different products, a small bike for children and youth, a road bike, and a mountain bike. Whenever Magik Bicycles sells 5 youth bikes, it sells 9 road bikes and 6 mountain bikes; therefore, the ratio is expressed as 5:9:6. In other words, we should treat the sales mix as a composite unit.

To demonstrate CVP analysis for multiple products, suppose Magik Bicycles has total fixed costs of $14,700,000, and its unit sale prices and variable costs for the three types of bike are as follows:

	Youth	Road	Mountain
Price per unit	$200	$700	$800
Variable cost per unit	75	250	300
Contribution margin per unit	$125	$450	$500
Contribution margin ratio	62.50%	64.29%	62.50%

Using the 5:9:6 sales mix, the selling price, variable cost, and contribution margin of a composite unit are calculated as follows:

	Youth	Road	Mountain		
Ratio	5	9	6	Composite	Percentage
Prices	$200 × 5	$700 × 9	$800 × 6	$12,100	100.00%
Variable costs	75 × 5	250 × 9	300 × 6	4,425	36.57%
Contribution margin	$125 × 5	$450 × 9	$500 × 6	$7,675	63.43%

We can use the contribution margin $7,675 to calculate Magik Bicycles' breakeven point in composite units:

$$\text{Sales revenues}_{(composite)} = \frac{F}{CM_{u(composite)}}$$

$$\text{Sales revenues}_{(composite)} = \frac{\$14,700,000}{\$7,675} = 1,916 \text{ composite units (rounded)}$$

Magik Bicycles needs to sell 1,916 composite units of its three bikes to break even. To determine the number of units of each product that must be sold to break even, we multiply the number of units of each product in the composite by 1,916:

	Youth	Road	Mountain
Ratio	5	9	6
Units required to break even	1,916 × 5 = 9,580	1,916 × 9 = 17,244	1,916 × 6 = 11,496
Sales ($) required to break even	$1,916,000	$12,070,800	$9,196,800

Sales mix computations can become cumbersome, and a spreadsheet can assist in analysis. Exhibit 3.3 shows the spreadsheet results for the Magik Bicycles breakeven analysis.

To demonstrate CVP computations using a spreadsheet, suppose again that Magik Bicycles developed three different products, a small bike for children and youth, a road bike, and a mountain bike. Total fixed costs for the company are $14,700,000. Forecasted sales volumes are as follows. The sales mix in percentages is calculated from these volumes.

	Youth	Road	Mountain	Total
Forecasted volume (units)	10,000	18,000	12,000	40,000
Expected sales mix in units	25%	45%	30%	100%

Because of increased competition and the recent economic downturn, the managers of Magik Bicycles are uncertain about the company's ability to achieve the forecasted level

> EXHIBIT 3.3

Spreadsheet for Magik Bicycles CVP with Multiple Products

	A	B	C	D	E
1					
2	**Input section**	Youth Bikes	Road Bikes	Mtn. Bikes	
3	Expected sales volume-units	10,000	18,000	12,000	
4	Price per unit	$200	$700	$800	
5	Variable cost per unit	$75	$250	$300	
6					
7	Fixed costs	$14,700,000			
8	Desired after-tax earnings	$100,000	(enter zero for breakeven)		
9	Income tax rate	30%			
10					
11					
12	**Contribution Margin**	Youth Bikes	Road Bikes	Mtn. Bikes	Total Bikes
13	Units	10,000	18,000	12,000	40,000
14	Revenue	$2,000,000	$12,600,000	$9,600,000	$24,200,000
15	Variable costs	750,000	4,500,000	3,600,000	8,850,000
16	Contribution margin	$1,250,000	$8,100,000	$6,000,000	$15,350,000
17					
18	Contrib. margin per unit	$125.00	$450.00	$500.00	$383.75
19	Contrib. margin ratio	62.50%	64.29%	62.50%	63.43%
20					
21	Expected sales mix in units	25.00%	45.00%	30.00%	100.00%
22	Expected sales mix in revenues	8.26%	52.07%	39.67%	100.00%
23					
24	**Expected Earnings**				
25	Contribution margin (above)				$15,350,000
26	Fixed costs				14,700,000
27	Pretax earnings				650,000
28	Income taxes				195,000
29	After-tax earnings				$455,000
30					
31	**Preliminary CVP Calculations**				
32	Target pretax profit for CVP analysis				$142,857
33	Fixed costs plus target pretax profit				$14,842,857
34					
35	**CVP analysis in units**	Youth Bikes	Road Bikes	Mtn. Bikes	Total Bikes
36	CVP calculation in units	9,669.614	17,405.305	11,603.537	38,678
37	Revenue	$1,933,923	$12,183,713	$9,282,829	$23,400,465
38	Variable costs	725,221	4,351,326	3,481,061	8,557,608
39	Contribution margin	$1,208,702	$7,832,387	$5,801,768	14,842,857
40	Fixed costs				14,700,000
41	Pretax earnings				142,857
42	Income taxes				42,857
43	After-tax earnings				$100,000
44					
45	**CVP analysis in revenues**	Youth Bikes	Road Bikes	Mtn. Bikes	Total Bikes
46	CVP calculation in revenues	$1,933,923	$12,183,713	$9,282,829	$23,400,465
47	Variable costs	725,221	4,351,326	3,481,061	8,557,608
48	Contribution margin	$1,208,702	$7,832,387	$5,801,768	14,842,857
49	Fixed costs				14,700,000
50	Pretax earnings				142,857
51	Income taxes				42,857
52	After-tax earnings				$100,000

of sales. They would like to know the minimum amount of sales needed for after-tax earnings of $100,000. The company's income-tax rate is 30%.

Exhibit 3.3 showed a sample CVP spreadsheet for Magik Bicycles. Notice that in the spreadsheet all the input data are placed in an area labelled "Input section." The calculations are performed outside this area. (Formulas for this spreadsheet are shown in Appendix 3A.) Spreadsheets designed this way allow users to alter the assumptions in the input section without performing any additional programming.

The spreadsheet in Exhibit 3.3 first uses the input data to compute expected revenues, costs, and income. The revenues and variable costs for each product are computed by multiplying the expected sales volume by the selling price and variable cost per unit shown in the input area. The revenues and variable costs for the three products are then combined to determine total revenues and total variable costs for the company. After subtracting expected fixed costs and income taxes (30% of pretax income), the expected after-tax income is $455,000.

When an organization produces and sells a number of different products or services, we use the weighted average contribution margin per unit to determine the breakeven point or target profit in units. Similarly, we use the weighted average contribution margin ratio to determine the breakeven point or target profit in revenues. "Weighted average" here refers to the expected sales mix: 10,000 youth bikes, or $2,000,000 in revenues; 18,000 road bikes, or $12,600,000 in revenues; and 12,000 mountain bikes, or $9,600,000 in revenues. Given the sales mix, the weighted average contribution margin per unit is calculated as the combined contribution margin ($15,350,000) divided by the total number of units expected to be sold (40,000), or $383.75 per unit, as computed in Exhibit 3.3.[1] The weighted average contribution margin ratio is the combined contribution margin ($15,350,000) divided by combined revenue ($24,200,000), or 63.43%.[2]

The spreadsheet in Exhibit 3.3 performs CVP computations using both units and revenues. To achieve an after-tax target earning of $100,000, the company must earn pretax earnings of $142,857[$100,000 ÷ (1 − 0.30)]. To compute the total number of units (bikes) that must be sold to achieve the target profit, we divide the fixed costs plus the target profit by the weighted average contribution margin per unit:

$$\text{Units needed for target profit} = Q = \frac{F + EBT}{(S - V)} = \frac{\$14,700,000 + \$142,587}{\$383.75 \text{ per unit}} = 38,678 \text{ units}$$

Magik needs to sell 38,678 units to achieve an after-tax target earning of $100,000. To determine the number of units for each product that must be sold, we multiply the total number of units (38,678) by each product's expected sales mix in units. For example, the company must sell 38,678 units × (10,000 units ÷ 40,000 units), or 9,670 youth bikes.

To calculate the amount of revenue needed to achieve the target after-tax earnings of $100,000, we divide the fixed costs plus the target pretax earnings by the weighted average contribution margin ratio:

$$\text{Revenues} = \frac{F + EBT}{CMR} = \frac{\$14,700,000 + \$142,857}{63.43\%} = \$23,400,373$$

The difference between the spreadsheet amount and this hand-calculated amount is due to rounding, as are any differences in following amounts. To determine the revenues for each product that must be sold, we multiply the total revenues ($23,400,373) by each product's expected sales mix in revenues. For example, the company must achieve $23,400,373 × ($2,000,000 ÷ $24,200,000), or $1,933,914 in revenues from youth bikes. Notice that the required revenue for each product is equal to the required number of units times the expected selling price. For youth bikes, 9,670 units × $200 per unit = $1,934,400.

[1]Another way to compute the weighted average contribution margin per unit is to sum the contribution margins for the three products, weighted by number of units sold, as follows: (10,000 ÷ 40,000)($200 − $75) + (18,000 ÷ 40,000)($700 − $250) + (12,000 ÷ 40,000)($800 − $300) = $383.75.

[2]Another way to compute the weighted average contribution margin ratio is to sum the contribution margin ratios for the three products, weighted by revenues, as follows: ($2,000,000 ÷ $24,200,000)[($200 − $75) ÷ $200] + ($12,600,000 ÷ $24,200,000)[($700 − $250) ÷ $700] + ($9,600,000 ÷ $24,200,000)[($800 − $300) ÷ $800] = 63.43%.

The results of calculations using either units or revenues are always identical (apart from small rounding errors). Because information in the example was given in units, it would have been easiest to create the spreadsheet using only the computations for CVP in units. However, in some situations, per-unit information is not available. In those cases, it is necessary to perform CVP calculations using revenues. Later in the chapter, we'll revisit the Spotted Cow Creamery illustration to analyze the influence of sales mix on the total contribution margin.

CVP Sensitivity Analysis

One of the benefits of creating a spreadsheet with a separate input section is that additional CVP analyses can easily be performed by changing the input data. For example, suppose the managers of Magik Bicycles want to know the number of bikes they must sell to break even. We can return to the spreadsheet in Exhibit 3.3 and change the "Desired after-tax earnings" to zero. The resulting spreadsheet, showing only CVP calculations in units, is presented in Exhibit 3.4.

The managers of Magik Bicycles could use the CVP spreadsheet to perform several different types of sensitivity analyses. Suppose sales of the mountain bike are falling behind expectations. They could determine the effect that the change in sales mix will have on the results. Every assumption in the data input box can easily be changed to update information. Sensitivity analysis helps managers explore the potential impact of variations in data they consider to be particularly important or are uncertain of.

Discretionary Expenditure Decisions

Managers can use CVP analysis to make business decisions such as whether to increase or decrease discretionary expenditures. For example, suppose the managers of Magik Bicycles want to advertise one of their products more heavily. A distributor pointed out that the road bike price was less than a competitor's price for a model with fewer features. The competitor's brand name is quite well known, but the distributor thinks that he could sell at least 10% more road bikes if Magik launched a regional advertising campaign.

The managers of Magik Bicycles estimate that an additional expenditure of $100,000 in advertising will increase road bike sales by 5%, to 18,900 bikes. To estimate the effects of this proposed expenditure, we return to the spreadsheet in Exhibit 3.3 and make two changes. First, fixed costs would increase by $100,000, to $14,800,000. Second, the expected volume of road bikes sold would increase to 18,900. The resulting spreadsheet in Exhibit 3.5 indicates that after-tax earnings are expected to increase by $213,500, from $455,000 to $668,500. Notice on the spreadsheet that the change in sales mix affects the weighted average contribution margin; it changes from $383.75 to $385.21.

We could do the same calculation without the spreadsheet by subtracting the $100,000 investment in fixed costs from the additional contribution margin of $405,000 [900 bikes × ($700 − $250)]. The resulting incremental after-tax earnings are $213,500 [($405,000 − $100,000)(1 − 0.30)]. Because profits are expected to increase more than costs for this advertising campaign, the managers would be likely to make the additional investment.

▶ **EXHIBIT 3.4**

Spreadsheet Results for Magik Bicycles Breakeven Analysis

	A	B	C	D	E
31	**Preliminary CVP Calculations**				
32	Target pretax profit for CVP analysis				$0
33	Fixed costs plus target pretax profit				$14,700,000
34					
35	**CVP analysis in units**	Youth Bikes	Road Bikes	Mtn. Bikes	Total Bikes
36	CVP calculation in units	9,576.547	17,237.785	11,491.857	38,306
37	Revenue	$1,915,309	$12,066,450	$9,193,485	$23,175,244
38	Variable costs	718,241	4,309,446	3,447,557	8,475,244
39	Contribution margin	$1,197,068	$7,757,003	$5,745,928	14,700,000
40	Fixed costs				14,700,000
41	Pretax income				0
42	Income taxes				0
43	After-tax income				$0

	A	B	C	D	E
12	**Contribution Margin**	Youth Bikes	Road Bikes	Mtn. Bikes	Total Bikes
13	Units	10,000	18,900	12,000	40,900
14	Revenue	$2,000,000	$13,230,000	$9,600,000	$24,830,000
15	Variable costs	750,000	4,725,000	3,600,000	9,075,000
16	Contribution margin	$1,250,000	$8,505,000	$6,000,000	$15,755,000
17					
18	Contrib. margin per unit	$125.00	$450.00	$500.00	$385.21
19	Contrib. margin ratio	62.50%	64.29%	62.50%	63.45%
20					
21	Expected sales mix in units	24.45%	46.21%	29.34%	100.00%
22	Expected sales mix in revenues	8.05%	53.28%	38.66%	100.00%
23					
24	**Expected Income**				
25	Contribution margin (above)				$15,755,000
26	Fixed costs				14,800,000
27	Pretax income				955,000
28	Income taxes				286,500
29	After-tax income				$668,500

Planning, Monitoring, and Motivating with CVP

CVP analyses are useful for planning and monitoring operations and for motivating employee performance. If the owner of The Spotted Cow Creamery obtains similar information for all the outlets, results can be compared to identify differences in revenue levels and cost functions. For example, unusually high labour costs might suggest that the low-profit outlet is overstaffed or inefficient. When the owner analyzes the reasons for differences in profitability, emphasis can be placed on increasing revenues, reducing costs, or both. The owner can also hold managers more accountable for performance, which should motivate their work efforts toward the owner's goals.

▶ CHAPTER REFERENCE
In Chapter 4 we'll use CVP analysis for additional types of decisions. We'll also see that decisions are often influenced by qualitative information that is not valued in numerical terms.

▶ CHAPTER REFERENCE
In Chapter 10, CVP analysis is used to create flexible budgets for measuring and monitoring performance at different levels of activity.

die gefleckte kuh eis (the spotted cow creamery), part 2
THE INFLUENCE OF SALES MIX ON PROFITABILITY

example

The owner of The Spotted Cow Creamery has several profitable stores. He asked the store managers to provide information about their sales mix, specifically the amount of beverage versus ice cream products sold. Beverages provide a much larger contribution margin than ice cream. After analyzing the data, the owner found that about half of the revenues in the most profitable stores were for the sale of beverages. In addition, these stores have more stable sales throughout the winter because they sell specialty coffee beverages as well as soft drinks.

The owner shared this information with Holger, the manager of a less profitable store. Holger investigates the contribution margins from beverages and ice cream at his store. He sets up a spreadsheet to examine the influence of the sales mix on profitability, shown in Exhibit 3.6(a). He finds that beverages are about 15% of total revenue (€6,000 ÷ €40,000). The contribution margin ratio for beverages is 93% (€5,600 ÷ €6,000), whereas the contribution margin for ice cream is 42% (€14,400 ÷ €34,000). When he changes the desired sales mix in the spreadsheet from 15% to 50% beverages to match the sales mix of more profitable stores, the after-tax income increases by a sizeable amount, from €3,000 to €8,353 as indicated in Exhibit 3.6(b).

Holger realizes that several strategies would increase the percentage of beverages in his current sales mix. First, he could require the sales clerks to suggest a beverage with each sale. In addition, he could emphasize beverages in his advertising. He could also analyze his competitors' beverage prices to be certain that his prices are competitive. A small drop in the price of beverages might increase the volume sold more than enough to offset the decline in contribution margin ratio. He uses the spreadsheet to perform sensitivity analysis around these factors.

fotofrog/Getty Images

continued...

	A	B	C	D
1				
2	**Input section**			
3		Beverage	Ice Cream	Total
4	Revenue	€6,000	€34,000	€40,000
5	Variable cost	400	19,600	20,000
6	Current sales mix in revenues	15%	85%	100%
7	Fixed costs			16,000
8	Tax rate			25%
9	Desired sales mix in revenues	15%	85%	100%
10				
11				Weighted Average
12	Contribution margin ratio	93%	42%	50%
13				
14	Income statement			
15	Revenue	€6,000	€34,000	€40,000
16	Variable cost	400	19,600	20,000
17	Contribution margin	5,600	14,400	20,000
18				
19	Fixed costs			16,000
20	Pretax income			4,000
21	Taxes			1,000
22	After-tax income			€3,000

(a) Current Sales Mix

	A	B	C	D
1				
2	**Input section**			
3		Beverage	Ice Cream	Total
4	Revenue	€6,000	€34,000	€40,000
5	Variable cost	400	19,600	20,000
6	Current sales mix in revenues	15%	85%	100%
7	Fixed costs			16,000
8	Tax rate			25%
9	Desired sales mix in revenues	50%	50%	100%
10				
11				Weighted Average
12	Contribution margin ratio	93%	42%	68%
13				
14	Income statement			
15	Revenue	€20,000	€20,000	€40,000
16	Variable cost	1,333	11,529	12,863
17	Contribution margin	18,667	8,471	27,137
18				
19	Fixed costs			16,000
20	Pretax income			11,137
21	Taxes			2,784
22	After-tax income			€8,353

(b) Desired Sales Mix

●● > STRATEGIC RISK MANAGEMENT : THE SPOTTED COW CREAMERY

BUSINESS RISK AND DECISION MAKING In The Spotted Cow Creamery (Part 2), the store manager was considering several strategies for changing his store's sales mix. What business risks did the manager face, and why did he need to take these risks into account? The manager can perform sensitivity analysis using a spreadsheet to determine the effects of factors such as changes in weather and consumer preferences on sales mix and profitability. This sensitivity analysis could also help him prepare for variations in inventory levels as the sales mix changes, so that he can reduce waste and avoid stock-outs of popular products.

Assumptions and Limitations of Cost-Volume-Profit Analysis

L04

Describe the assumptions
and limitations that
managers consider when
using CVP analysis

Exhibit 3.7 summarizes the input data, assumptions, and uses of CVP analysis. CVP analysis relies on several assumptions. In Chapter 2, we assumed for the linear cost function $(F + V \times Q)$ that production volumes are within a relevant range of operations, where fixed costs remain fixed and variable costs remain constant. In addition, for CVP analysis, we assume that selling prices remain constant and that the sales mix is constant. Sensitivity analysis can be performed to determine the sensitivity of profits to these assumptions.

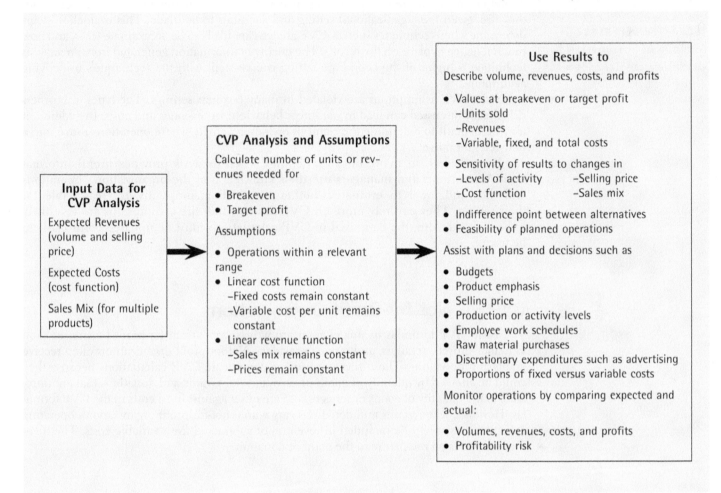

Input Data for CVP Analysis

Expected Revenues (volume and selling price)

Expected Costs (cost function)

Sales Mix (for multiple products)

CVP Analysis and Assumptions

Calculate number of units or revenues needed for

- Breakeven
- Target profit

Assumptions

- Operations within a relevant range
- Linear cost function
  - Fixed costs remain constant
  - Variable cost per unit remains constant
- Linear revenue function
  - Sales mix remains constant
  - Prices remain constant

Use Results to

Describe volume, revenues, costs, and profits

- Values at breakeven or target profit
  - Units sold
  - Revenues
  - Variable, fixed, and total costs
- Sensitivity of results to changes in
  - Levels of activity   – Selling price
  - Cost function   – Sales mix
- Indifference point between alternatives
- Feasibility of planned operations

Assist with plans and decisions such as

- Budgets
- Product emphasis
- Selling price
- Production or activity levels
- Employee work schedules
- Raw material purchases
- Discretionary expenditures such as advertising
- Proportions of fixed versus variable costs

Monitor operations by comparing expected and actual:

- Volumes, revenues, costs, and profits
- Profitability risk

Business Risk and Quality of Input Data

As indicated in Exhibit 3.7, CVP analysis relies on forecasts of expected revenues and costs. CVP assumptions rule out fluctuations in revenues or costs that might be caused by common business factors such as supplier volume discounts, learning curves, changes in production efficiency, or special customer discounts. In addition, many business risks may surround whether CVP assumptions, such as the following, will be violated:

- ▶ Can volume of operating activity be achieved?
- ▶ Will selling prices increase or decrease?
- ▶ Will sales mix remain constant?
- ▶ Will fixed or variable costs change as operations move into a new relevant range?
- ▶ Will costs change due to unforeseen causes?
- ▶ Are revenue and cost estimates biased?

All organizations are subject to uncertainties leading to risk that they will fail to meet expectations. Exhibit 3.8 summarizes major business risk for four companies in a variety of industries around the world. Even though each organization is subject to unique business risks, all face uncertainties related to the economic environment. Some organizations are subject to more risk than others; for example, business risk is greater in industries experiencing rapid technological and market change or intense competition.

▶ CHAPTER REFERENCE
Chapter 2 explains the importance of the relevant range in measuring the cost function.

Quality of CVP Technique

▶ CHAPTER REFERENCE
Chapter 10 addresses the quality of expected revenue and cost information in more detail.

To help managers make better decisions, accountants evaluate the quality of the techniques they use, given the organizational setting and decisions to be made. This evaluation helps determine when techniques such as CVP analysis are likely to be appropriate tools, and how much reliance to place on the results. The quality of information generated from an analysis technique is higher if the economic setting is consistent with the technique's underlying assumptions.

Strict CVP assumptions are violated in many business settings. The types of business risk already discussed can lead to nonlinear behaviour in revenues and costs. In addition, it may be difficult to determine the point of operating activity where operations move into a new relevant range.

Nevertheless, in many business settings, CVP analysis provides useful information. Accountants and managers use their knowledge of the organization's operations and their judgment to evaluate whether the CVP assumptions are reasonable for their setting. They can rely more on CVP results when the assumptions are less likely to be violated. Also, the data used in CVP calculations must be updated continually to be useful.

CVP for Not-for-Profit Organizations

The basic CVP formulas in this chapter are written for typical for-profit businesses such as manufacturers, retailers, and service providers. Not-for-profit organizations often receive grants and donations. These revenue sources complicate CVP calculations because they could be affected by quantity of goods or services sold. Grants and donations that are unrelated to the quantity of goods or services sold are offset against fixed costs in the CVP formulas. However, when grants and donations vary with a not-for-profit organization's operating activities, they might be included in revenues or subtracted from variable costs. The treatment depends on the nature of the grant or donation.

▶ EXHIBIT 3.8
Examples of Business Risks

Anglogold Ashanti Ltd.	Coca-Cola FEMSA, S.A de C.V.	eBay, Inc.	Sony Corporation
Ghana	Mexico	United States	Japan
Gold mining and exploration	Production and distribution of Coca-Cola products	Web-based marketplace and payment services	Electronic equipment design and manufacturing
• Changes in demand for gold • Global political or economic events • Availability of skilled labour • Environmental hazards	• Deterioration in relationships with the Coca-Cola Company • Governmental price controls • Highly competitive product environment • Water shortages	• Retaining active user base • Consumer confidence in Internet commerce • Ability to benefit from Skype purchase • Retaining key employees	• The effects of exchange rate fluctuations • Inventory control under volatile demand • Increasingly intense pricing competition • Ability to recoup R&D investments
Examples adapted from U.S. SEC Form 20-F 2005.	Examples adapted from U.S. SEC Form 20-F 2005.	Examples adapted from U.S. SEC Form 20-F 2007.	Examples adapted from U.S. SEC Form 20-F 2006.

The following illustration continues the story of Small Animal Clinic from Chapter 2. Recall that Small Animal Clinic is a not-for-profit organization that treats small animals. It received a foundation grant that matches incoming revenues; for example, if a pet owner pays $30 in fees, the foundation matches with an additional $30 to the clinic. In this case, the grant is included in revenues for CVP calculations.

small animal clinic
NOT-FOR-PROFIT ORGANIZATION CVP ANALYSIS WITH TWO RELEVANT RANGES

example

Leticia Brown, Small Animal Clinic's manager, and the accountant, Josh Hardy, are completing the operating budget for 2017. Leticia estimated that the clinic will experience 3,800 animal visits, and Josh estimated the cost function as follows:[3]

$$TC = \$119,009 + \$16.40\ Q$$

where Q is the number of animal visits. Leticia and Josh budgeted revenue per animal visit at $60 ($30 in fees plus $30 in matching grant). Thus, they estimated that the clinic should achieve a surplus of $46,671 = [($60)(3,800) − $119,009 − ($16.40)(3,800)]. The clinic is a not-for-profit organization and pays no income taxes on its surplus.

Monty Rakusen/Getty Images

To complete the planning process for next year, Leticia asks Josh to compute the clinic's breakeven point. As manager of a not-for-profit organization, she is particularly sensitive to financial risk and wants to know how much the clinic's activity levels could drop before a loss would occur.

Breakeven Compared to Budget

Josh performs the following calculations. With revenue per visit of $60, the contribution margin per animal visit is:

$$S - V = \$60.00 - \$16.40 = \$43.60$$

Josh solves for Q with profit equal to $0 to find the breakeven point in number of animal visits:

$$Q = \frac{F + \text{Profits}}{(S - V)} = \frac{(\$119,009 + \$0)}{\$43.60} = 2,730 \text{ visits}$$

Leticia is pleased to see that the budgeted number of animal visits (3,800) is significantly higher than the breakeven number. This result gives her considerable assurance that the clinic is not likely to incur a loss, even if revenues fail to achieve targeted levels or if costs exceed estimated amounts.

Potential Investment in New Equipment

During the first two months of 2017, Leticia learns that the number of animal visits at Small Animal Clinic is running approximately 10% higher than the budget, and costs seem to be under control. Leticia thinks that the clinic might be on track for a high surplus this year.

For the past two years, Leticia has been interested in purchasing equipment costing $200,000 to provide low-cost neutering services. This year PAWS, a local charity, offered to pay for half of the equipment cost, but only after the clinic raises the other half of the funds. Currently the clinic has no excess cash because surpluses from prior years were

---

[3]In the Chapter 2 illustration, Small Animal Clinic Part 2, the cost function was calculated as TC = $119,009 + ($15.20) (Number of animal visits) + (0.04)(Fee revenue). If average fee revenue is $30 per animal visit, then the last term in the cost function can be rewritten as (0.04)($30) (Number of animal visits), which can be simplified as ($1.20) (Number of animal visits). This substitution allows the cost function to be rewritten as TC = $119,009 + ($16.40) (Number of animal visits). This version of the cost function is appropriate for estimating total costs for the clinic, but it would not be appropriate for estimating total costs for a single animal visit, where the fees vary depending on the services performed.

continued…

example

invested in other projects. Thus, the clinic needs to raise $100,000 to receive the PAWS grant. Leticia asks Josh to calculate the number of animal visits needed to achieve a surplus of $100,000.

Calculating and Analyzing Targeted Activity Level

Josh calculates the expected quantity needed to achieve $100,000 surplus as follows:

$$Q = \frac{F + \text{Profits}}{S - V} = \frac{\$119,009 + \$100,000}{\$60.00 - \$16.40} = \frac{\$219,009}{\$43.60} = 5,024 \text{ animal visits}$$

He then calculates the total dollar amount of revenue needed:

$$\text{Revenues} = \frac{F + \text{Profits}}{(S - V)/S \text{ or CMR}} = \frac{\$119,009 + \$100,000}{\$43.60/\$60.00} = \$301,689$$

Josh tells Leticia that the clinic will need to earn $301,389 in revenues, or have 5,024 visits, to achieve a surplus of $100,000.

The budgeted level of activity (3,800 animal visits) is substantially higher than the level of activity needed to break even (2,730 animal visits). If animal visits continue to exceed this year's budget by 10%, Josh estimates that animal visits will reach 4,180 ($3,800 \times 1.10$) by year end. However, he thinks that it would be very difficult to achieve a targeted surplus of $100,000 (5,024 animal visits) by that time.

CVP Adjusted for Change in Relevant Range

As Josh works on his report, he realizes that the clinic's cost function might change if the number of animal visits gets very high. Leticia has told him that she will probably hire another technician and need to rent more space and purchase additional equipment if animal visits exceed 4,000 this year. Therefore, Josh's cost function for 5,024 visits is wrong. He develops a new cost function, assuming that an additional technician, space, and equipment will increase fixed costs by about $60,000 per year:

$$TC = (\$119,009 + \$60,000) + \$16.40 \, Q = \$179,009 + \$16.40 \, Q, \text{ for } Q > 4,000$$

Thus, Josh's earlier CVP analysis was incorrect when animal visits exceed 4,000. The level of activity needed for a targeted surplus of $100,000 needs to be recalculated:

$$(\$179,009 + \$100,000) \div \$43.60 = 6,400 \text{ for } Q > 4,000$$

Josh notices that an activity level of 6,400 animal visits is noticeably higher than the 5,024 visits he first calculated. He realizes how important it is to adjust for the relevant range when performing CVP analyses.

When Josh shows Leticia the new results, they agree that the clinic cannot raise the funds for new equipment by increasing the number of visits to 6,400. Leticia may need to cut costs or seek other ways to pay for the neutering equipment. The additional fixed cost would also require the clinic to have a much higher volume of operations to avoid a loss. ■

Margin of Safety and Degree of Operating Leverage

LO5   Assess operational risk using margin of safety and operating leverage

For Small Animal Clinic, the manager used CVP information to help learn how much the volume of business could decline before the clinic incurred a loss. The manager of The Spotted Cow Creamery was able to identify the specific products to emphasize for increased profitability. Managers are often interested in answers to these types of questions. In addition, information from CVP analysis can be used to help manage operational risk.

Margin of Safety

The **margin of safety** is the excess of an organization's expected future sales (in either revenue or units) above the breakeven point. The margin of safety indicates the amount by which sales could drop before profits reach the breakeven point:

Margin of safety in units = Actual or estimated units of activity – Units at breakeven point

Margin of safety in revenues = Actual or estimated revenue – Revenue at breakeven point

The margin of safety is computed using actual or estimated sales values, depending on the purpose. To evaluate future risk when planning, use estimated sales. To evaluate actual risk when monitoring operations, use actual sales. If the margin of safety is small, managers may put more emphasis on reducing costs and increasing sales to avoid potential losses. A larger margin of safety gives managers greater confidence in making plans such as incurring additional fixed costs.

The **margin of safety percentage** is the margin of safety divided by actual or estimated sales, in either units or revenues. This percentage indicates the extent to which sales can decline before profits become zero:

$$\text{Margin of safety percentage in units} = \frac{\text{Margin of safety in units}}{\text{Actual or estimated units}}$$

$$\text{Margin of safety percentage in revenues} = \frac{\text{Margin of safety in revenue}}{\text{Actual or estimated revenue}}$$

When the original budget was created for Small Animal Clinic, the breakeven point was calculated as 2,730 animal visits, or $163,800 in revenues. However, Leticia and Josh expected 3,800 animal visits, for $228,000 in revenue. Their margin of safety in units of animal visits was 1,070 (3,800 – 2,730), and in revenues it was $64,200 ($228,000 – $163,800). Their margin of safety percentage was 28.2% (1,070 ÷ 3,800, or $64,200 ÷ $228,000). In other words, their sales volume could drop 28.2% from anticipated levels before they can expect to incur a loss. Exhibit 3.9 provides a CVP graph for this information.

Degree of Operating Leverage

Managers decide how to structure the cost function for their organizations. Often, potential trade-offs are made between fixed and variable costs. For example, a company could purchase a vehicle (a fixed cost) or it could lease a vehicle under a contract that charges a rate per kilometre driven (a variable cost). Exhibit 3.10 lists some of the common advantages and disadvantages of fixed costs. One of the major disadvantages of fixed costs is that they may be difficult to reduce quickly if activity levels fail to meet expectations, thereby increasing the organization's risk of incurring losses.

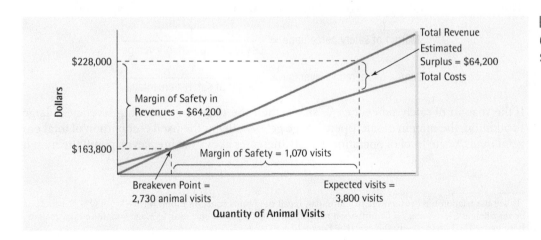

> **EXHIBIT 3.9**

CVP Graph and Margin of Safety for Small Animal Clinic

> EXHIBIT 3.10
Common Advantages and
Disadvantages of Fixed Costs

Advantages	Disadvantages
• Fixed costs might cost less in total than variable costs. • Companies might require unique assets (e.g., expert labour or specialized production facilities) that must be acquired through long-term commitments. • Fixed assets such as automation and robotics equipment can significantly improve operating efficiency. • Fixed costs are easier to plan for; they do not fluctuate with levels of activity.	• Investing in fixed resources might divert management attention away from the organization's core competencies. • Fixed costs typically require a longer financial commitment; it can be difficult to reduce them quickly. • Underinvestment or overinvestment in fixed costs could affect profits and may not easily be changed in the short term.

The **degree of operating leverage** is the extent to which the cost function is made up of fixed costs. Organizations with high operating leverage incur more risk of loss when sales decline. Conversely, when operating leverage is high, an increase in sales (after fixed costs are covered) quickly contributes to profit. The formula for operating leverage can be written in terms of either contribution margin or fixed costs, as shown here:[4]

$$\text{Degree of operating leverage in terms of contribution margin} = \frac{\text{Contribution margin}}{\text{Earnings}} = \frac{TS - TVC}{EBT} = \frac{(S-V)\times Q}{EBT}$$

$$\text{Degree of operating leverage in terms of fixed costs} = \frac{F}{EBT} + 1$$

Managers use the degree of operating leverage to gauge the risk associated with their cost function and to explicitly calculate the sensitivity of profits to changes in sales (units or revenues):

$$\text{\% change in profit} = \text{\% change in sales} \times \text{Degree of operating leverage}$$

For Small Animal Clinic, the variable cost per animal visit was $16.40, and the fixed costs were $119,009. With budgeted animal visits of 3,800, the managers expected to earn a profit of $46,671. The expected degree of operating leverage, using the contribution margin formula, is then calculated as follows:

$$\text{Degree of operating leverage} = \frac{(\$60 - \$16.40)\times 3,800 \text{ visits}}{\$46,671} = \frac{\$165,680}{\$46,671} = 3.55$$

We arrive at the same answer of 3.55 if we use the fixed cost formula:

$$\text{Degree of operating leverage} = \frac{\$119,009}{\$46,671} + 1 = 2.55 + 1 = 3.55$$

The degree of operating leverage and margin of safety percentage are reciprocals:

$$\text{Margin of safety percentage} = \frac{1}{\text{Degree of operating leverage}}$$

$$\text{Degree of operating leverage} = \frac{1}{\text{Margin of safety percentage}}$$

If the margin of safety percentage is small, then the degree of operating leverage is large. In addition, the margin of safety percentage gets smaller as the fixed cost portion of total cost gets larger. As the level of operating activity increases above the breakeven point, the margin

[4]To see the relationship between the two formulas, recall the profits equation Profits $= (S - V) \times Q - F$, which can be rewritten as $F + $ Earnings $=$ Contribution margin. In turn, Degree of operating leverage $=$ Contribution margin $\div$ Earnings $= (F + $ Earnings$) \div$ Earnings $= (F \div $ Earnings$) + 1$.

of safety increases, and the degree of operating leverage decreases. For Small Animal Clinic, the reciprocal of the margin of safety percentage is 3.55 (i.e., 1 ÷ 0.282). The reciprocal of the degree of operating leverage is 0.282 (i.e., 1 ÷ 3.55), or 28.2%.

Using the Degree of Operating Leverage to Plan and Monitor Operations

Managers need to consider the degree of operating leverage when they decide whether to incur additional fixed costs, such as purchasing new equipment or hiring new employees. They also need to consider the degree of operating leverage for potential new products and services that could increase an organization's fixed costs relative to variable costs. If additional fixed costs cause the degree of operating leverage to reach what they consider an unacceptably high level, managers often use variable costs, such as temporary labour, rather than additional fixed costs to meet their operating needs.

For example, the technicians at Small Animal Clinic are paid a salary and work 40-hour weeks. Suppose Leticia could hire part-time technicians at $20.00 per hour instead of hiring full-time technicians at the current salaries of $78,009 (for two technicians). If each visit requires about an hour of technician time, the new cost function would be TC = ($119,009 − $78,009) + ($16.40 + $20.00)Q = $41,000 + $36.40Q. The breakeven point decreases considerably, to 1,738 animal visits [i.e., $41,000 ÷ ($60.00 − $36.40) per animal visit] or $104,280. Profit at Q = 3,800 animal visits is $48,680 [i.e., $228,000 − $41,000 − (3,800 animal visits × $36.40 per animal visit)]. Operating leverage at 3,800 animal visits becomes 1.84 [i.e., ($41,000 ÷ $48,680) + 1], which is much lower than the 3.55 value when technicians are a fixed cost. Although operating leverage improved, the cost for technicians increased from $18.75 per hour [$78,009 ÷ (2 technicians × 2,080 hours per technician per year)] to $20.00 per hour.

The advantage of having technicians as hourly workers is that they can be scheduled only for hours when appointments are also scheduled. When business is slow, fewer technician hours are needed, which means less risk of incurring losses if the number of visits drops. Exhibit 3.11 provides a CVP graph of the two options. Risk decreases considerably when the breakeven point is so much lower. On the other hand, it may be more difficult to hire qualified and dependable technicians unless work hours and pay can be guaranteed.

▶ BUSINESS PRACTICE

High fixed costs, such as owning aircraft, mean high operating leverage in the airline industry. In the case of **Air Canada**, new labour contracts and a growing pension deficit added to its fixed costs in late 2011, prompting some financial analysts to downgrade the airline's share price target in light of its higher operating leverage.[5]

▶ EXHIBIT 3.11

CVP Graph for Small Animal Clinic with Different Degrees of Operating Leverage

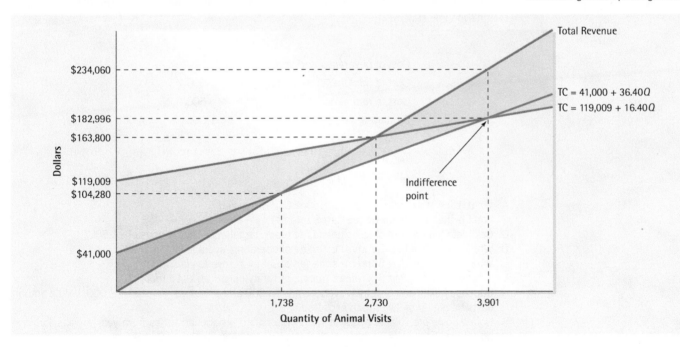

[5] Jonathan Ratner, "Air Canada Downgraded on Economic Weakness," *Financial Post*, October 21, 2011.

An **indifference point** is the level of activity at which equal cost or profit occurs across multiple alternatives. To provide Leticia with additional information as she considers changing the cost structure, Josh calculates the indifference point. Using the budgeted assumptions, Josh sets the two cost functions equal to each other and then solves for Q, as follows:

$$\$41,000 + \$36.40\ Q = \$119,009 + \$16.40\ Q$$

$$\text{so } Q = 3,901$$

When visits are fewer than 3,901, the clinic profit will be greater through using more variable cost. When visits exceed 3,901, the clinic is better off using more fixed costs, assuming that the fixed costs remain constant up to 4,000 visits. When visits exceed 4,000, we know that additional fixed costs will be incurred, and then a new indifference point will need to be calculated.

Notice that the indifference point calculation ignores operational risk. At 3,901 animal visits, the clinic is expected to earn the same profit under the two cost function alternatives. However, the clinic's operational risk is greater for the cost function having higher fixed costs. Therefore, the clinic's manager would not necessarily be indifferent between the two cost functions if 3,901 animal visits were expected.

Analysis of Income Statement Formats

LO6 Analyze the difference between contribution margin and gross margin

In this chapter, we have been discussing the concept of contribution margin, which is the difference between the sales and variable costs. Now, we will compare the contribution margin and gross margin.

$$\text{Contribution margin} = \text{Sales} - \text{Variable costs}$$

$$\text{Gross margin} = \text{Sales} - \text{Costs of goods sold}$$

LO1, LO2, LO4, LO5

3-1 self-study problem   Cost Function, Target Profit, Margin of Safety, Operating Leverage

Coffee Cart Supreme sells hot and iced coffee beverages and small snacks. The following is last month's income statement:

Revenues		$5,000
Cost of beverages and snacks	$2,000	
Cost of napkins, straws, etc.	500	
Cost to rent cart	500	
Employee wages	1,000	4,000
Pretax earnings		1,000
Taxes		250
After-tax earnings		$750

A. What is the total cost function for Coffee Cart Supreme?
B. What is the tax rate for Coffee Cart Supreme?
C. Calculate the amount of sales needed to reach target after-tax earnings of $1,500.
D. What was Coffee Cart Supreme's degree of operating leverage last month?
E. What was Coffee Cart Supreme's margin of safety in revenue last month?
F. What was Coffee Cart Supreme's margin of safety percentage last month?
G. Suppose next month's actual revenues are $8,000 and pretax earnings are $2,000. Would actual costs be higher or lower than expected?
H. Coffee costs are volatile because worldwide coffee production varies from year to year. Explain how this volatility affects the quality of the cost function for Coffee Cart Supreme.

See the solution on page 122.

> EXHIBIT 3.12
>
> The Difference Between Contribution Margin and Gross Margin for Magik Bicycles

Magik Bicycles' Contribution Margin Format (in thousands)		
Revenues		$24,200
Variable costs		
Variable manufacturing costs	$ 5,310	
Variable nonmanufacturing costs	3,540	
Total variable costs		$ 8,850
Contribution margin		$15,350
Fixed costs		
Fixed manufacturing costs	$10,290	
Fixed nonmanufacturing costs	4,410	
Total fixed costs		$14,700
Earnings before taxes		$ 650
Income taxes (30%)		$ 195
Earnings after taxes		$ 455

Magik Bicycles' Gross Margin Format (in thousands)		
Revenues		$24,200
Cost of goods sold		
Variable manufacturing costs	$ 5,310	
Fixed manufacturing costs	10,290	
Total cost of goods sold		$15,600
Gross margin		$ 8,600
Nonmanufacturing expenses		
Variable nonmanufacturing costs	$ 3,540	
Fixed nonmanufacturing costs	4,410	
Total nonmanufacturing costs		$ 7,950
Earnings before taxes		$ 650
Income taxes		$ 195
Earnings after taxes		$ 455

Variable costs include manufacturing and nonmanufacturing costs, and cost of goods sold includes only manufacturing costs. Therefore, service companies can calculate contribution margin but not gross margin. A merchandise company's cost of goods sold is made up of the purchased merchandise for resale.

Exhibit 3.12 illustrates the difference between contribution margin and gross margin for the manufacturing company Magik Bicycles.

●● > FOCUS ON ETHICAL DECISION MAKING:
TEMPORARY LABOUR

In recent years, Canadian companies have increasingly relied on temporary labour (also called contingent or contract workers) to fill positions that in the past would have been filled by regular employees. In 2014, temporary workers represented almost 10% of all Canadian workers. Managers gain many advantages from use of temporary labour, including the following:

- Reduce risk of loss by increasing the proportion of variable costs.

- Quickly increase and decrease employment levels in response to economic changes.

- Pay higher wages to skilled workers without inflating the pay scales of regular employees.

- Pay lower wages and avoid making hiring commitments to low-skilled employees.

- Fill positions while recruiting permanent workers during labour shortages.

Many economists and business analysts argue that temporary labour provides the following economic benefits:

- Reduce overall unemployment levels because employers are less reluctant to hire temporary labour than regular employees.

- Increase employment opportunities for new workforce entrants, workers laid off from jobs, and workers wanting flexible work schedules.

- Improve regular employee morale by reducing their unemployment risk.

© Lee Brown/Alamy

On the other hand, labour groups, homelessness advocacy groups, and others believe that temporary labour arrangements are socially harmful. They argue that the use of temporary labour has the following effects:

- Unfairly reduce overall pay scales for skilled and unskilled workers.

- Increase unemployment risk for the least-skilled and lowest-paid workers, contributing to poverty and homelessness.

- Reduce worker representation as well as health care and retirement benefits.

According to Statistics Canada, those working in contract jobs earn on average 14% less than those in permanent positions, while the gap is almost 34% for seasonal and casual positions.

Sources: "Study: Temporary Employment in the Downturn: 1997 to 2009," Statistics Canada, *The Daily*, November 26, 2010; J. C. Cooper and K. Madigan, "U.S.: Labor's New Flexibility Cuts Two Ways," *BusinessWeek*, December 24, 2001; and S. N. Houseman, A. L. Kalleberg, and G. A. Erickcek, "The Role of Temporary Help Employment in Tight Labor Markets," Upjohn Institute Staff Working Paper No. 01-73, July 2001.

PRACTISE ETHICAL DECISION MAKING

In Chapter 1, you learned about a process for making ethical decisions (Exhibit 1.14). You can address the following questions to improve your skills at making ethical decisions. Think about your answers to these questions and discuss them with others.

Ethical Decision-Making Process	Questions to Consider About this Ethical Dilemma
Identify ethical problems as they arise	Does the hiring of temporary labour create an ethical problem? Why or why not?
Objectively consider the well-being of others and society when exploring alternatives.	Different viewpoints for this problem were described in the preceding example. What assumptions lie behind each viewpoint?
Clarify and apply ethical values when choosing a course of action.	Is the hiring of temporary labour a business issue, a social issue, or both? Explain. Identify the values you use to answer the following questions: • Is it fair for employers to pay different wage rates and provide different benefits to temporary and permanent workers who perform the same jobs? • Is it fair for businesses to pass their business risks directly on to the employees?
Work toward ongoing improvement of personal and organizational ethics.	How can company managers determine on an ongoing basis whether their hiring practices are ethical?

LO1, LO2, LO4

3-2 self-study problem   Sensitivity Analysis

www.wiley.com/
go/eldenburgcanada

The spreadsheet developed for the Magik Bicycles examples in this chapter is available at www.wiley.com/go/eldenburgcanada. Download the template and use the spreadsheet to answer the following questions. A printout of the formulas used in the spreadsheet is available in Appendix 3A.

A. Examine the spreadsheet so that you understand how the cells in the data input section are referenced. When all the decision variables are located in one place in the spreadsheet, accountants and managers can easily perform sensitivity analysis by changing values in the data input section. Why is it important to be able to change the spreadsheet easily to reflect changes in assumptions?

B. Suppose that Magik adds a helmet to each youth bike sold. The helmets cost $25 each but incorporate new materials and an innovative design that has reduced child injuries and deaths from bike accidents. Magik's managers believe that by advertising the new helmet as part of the youth bike package, sales will increase to 13,000. However, an advertising campaign will need to be undertaken to alert parents to the benefits of the new helmet. How much can Magik afford to spend on advertising and still expect to earn the original after-tax earnings of $455,000? Assume that the selling price remains at $200 per bike package.

C. Identify CVP input factors that you believe are uncertain for this decision and use your judgment to determine a new value for each factor. Reflect these changes in the spreadsheet to see how they affect the breakeven point and profitability. Choose a best-case and worst-case scenario to present to the managers of Magik Bicycles. Make a list of the points you would include in a memo explaining your sensitivity analysis to the managers.

See the solution on page 123.

Spreadsheet Formulas for Magik Bicycles Spreadsheet

The following formulas were used for the spreadsheet shown in Exhibit 3.4:

	A	B	C	D	E
1					
2	**Input section**	Youth Bikes	Road Bikes	Mtn. Bikes	
3	Expected sales volume-units	10,000	18,000	12,000	
4	Price per unit	200	700	800	
5	Variable cost per unit	75	250	300	
6					
7	Fixed costs	14,700,000			
8	Desired after-tax profit	100,000	(enter zero for breakeven)		
9	Income tax rate	0.3			
10					
11					
12	**Contribution Margin**	Youth Bikes	Road Bikes	Mtn. Bikes	Total Bikes
13	Units	=B3	=C3	=D3	=SUM(B3:D3)
14	Revenue	=B3*B4	=C3*C4	=D3*D4	=SUM(B14:D14)
15	Variable costs	=B5*B3	=C5*C3	=D5*D3	=SUM(B15:D15)
16	Contribution margin	=B14-B15	=C14-C15	=D14-D15	=SUM(B16:D16)
17					
18	Contrib. margin per unit	=B16/B13	=C16/C13	=D16/D13	=E16/E13
19	Contrib. margin ratio	=B16/B14	=C16/C14	=D16/D14	=E16/E14
20					
21	Expected sales mix in units	=B3/$E13	=C3/$E13	=D3/$E13	=SUM(B21:D21)
22	Expected sales mix in revenues	=B14/$E14	=C14/$E14	=D14/$E14	=SUM(B22:D22)
23					
24	**Expected Income**				
25	Contribution margin (above)				=E16
26	Fixed costs				=B7
27	Pretax income				=E16-E26
28	Income taxes				=B9*E27
29	After-tax income				=E27-E28
30					
31	**Preliminary CVP Calculations**				
32	Target pretax profit for CVP analysis				=B8/(1-B9)
33	Fixed costs plus target pretax profit				=B7+E32
34					
35	**CVP analysis in units**	Youth Bikes	Road Bikes	Mtn. Bikes	Total Bikes
36	CVP calculation in units	=B21*$E$36	=C21*$E$36	=D21*$E$36	=E33/E18
37	Revenue	=B36*B4	=C36*C4	=D36*D4	=SUM(B37:D37)
38	Variable costs	=B36*B5	=C36*C5	=D36*D5	=SUM(B38:D38)
39	Contribution margin	=B37-B38	=C37-C38	=D37-D38	=E37-E38
40	Fixed costs				=B7
41	Pretax income				=E39-E40
42	Income taxes				=E41*B9
43	After-tax income				=E41-E42
44					
45	**CVP analysis in revenues**	Youth Bikes	Road Bikes	Mtn. Bikes	Total Bikes
46	CVP calculation in revenues	=$E$46*B22	=$E$46*C22	=$E$46*D22	=E33/E19
47	Variable costs	=B46*B5/B4	=C46*C5/C4	=D46*D5/D4	=SUM(B47:D47)
48	Contribution margin	=B46-B47	=C46-C47	=D46-D47	=E46-E47
49	Fixed costs				=B7
50	Pretax income				=E48-E49
51	Income taxes				=B9*E50
52	After-tax income				=E50-E51

SUMMARY

LO1 Explain the concept of cost-volume-profit (CVP) analysis in decision making

COST-VOLUME-PROFIT (CVP) ANALYSIS

A technique that examines changes in profits in response to changes in sales volumes, costs, and prices

CVP USES

Describe volume, revenues, costs, and profits

- Values at breakeven or target profit
  - Units sold
  - Revenues
  - Variable, fixed, and total costs
- Sensitivity of results to changes in
  - Levels of activity
  - Cost function
  - Selling price
  - Sales mix
- Indifference point between alternatives
- Feasibility of planned operations

CVP GRAPH

Shows the relationship between total revenues and total costs; illustrates how an organization's profits are expected to change under different volumes of activity.
   Assist with plans and decisions such as

- Budgets
- Product emphasis
- Selling price
- Production or activity levels
- Employee work schedules
- Raw material purchases
- Discretionary expenditures such as advertising
- Proportions of fixed versus variable costs

Monitor operations by comparing expected and actual

- Volumes, revenues, costs, and profits
- Profitability risk

LO2 Apply CVP calculations for a single product

CVP FORMULAS

CVP analysis in units needed to attain target earnings:

$$S \text{ or } Q = \frac{F + \text{Earnings}}{\text{Contribution margin per unit}} = \frac{F + \text{Earnings}}{S - V}$$

CVP ANALYSIS IN REVENUES NEEDED TO ATTAIN TARGET EARNINGS:

$$\text{Sales} = \frac{F + \text{Earnings}}{\text{Contribution margin ratio}} = \frac{F + \text{Earnings}}{(S - V)/P}$$
$$= \frac{F + \text{Earnings}}{(TR + TVC)/TR}$$

PRETAX EARNINGS NEEDED TO ACHIEVE A GIVEN LEVEL OF AFTER-TAX EARNINGS:

$$\text{Pretax earnings (EBT)} = \frac{\text{After-tax earnings}}{(1 - \text{Tax rate})}$$

BREAKEVEN POINT

Level of operating activity at which revenues cover all fixed and variable costs, resulting in zero profit.

BREAKEVEN POINT CALCULATION

Set target profit equal to zero in the CVP formula.

LO3 Apply CVP calculations for multiple products

USE CVP FORMULAS FOR A SINGLE PRODUCT, EXCEPT

$$\text{Weighted average contribution margin per unit} = \frac{\text{Total expected contribution margin}}{\text{Total expected number of units}}$$

$$\text{Weighted average contribution margin ratio} = \frac{\text{Total expected contribution margin}}{\text{Total expected revenue}}$$

SUMMARY

| L04 | Describe the assumptions and limitations that managers consider when using CVP analysis |

CVP ASSUMPTIONS

▶ Operations within a relevant range of activity
▶ Linear cost function
  – Fixed costs remain fixed
  – Variable costs per unit remain constant
▶ Linear revenue function
  – Sales mix remains constant
  – Prices remain constant

IN LIGHT OF ASSUMPTIONS AND BUSINESS RISK, NEED TO EVALUATE

▶ Quality of data used in CVP analyses
▶ Suitability of CVP analysis for the setting
▶ Sensitivity of CVP results to changes in data for important risks

BUSINESS RISK

▶ Actual future volumes, revenues, and costs are unknown
▶ CVP assumptions might not hold

| L05 | Assess operational risk using margin of safety and operating leverage |

MARGIN OF SAFETY

$$\text{Margin of safety in units} = \text{Actual or estimated unit of activity} - \text{Units at breakeven point}$$

$$\text{Margin of safety in revenues} = \text{Actual or estimated revenue} - \text{Revenue at breakeven point}$$

$$\text{Margin of safety percentage} = \frac{\text{Margin of safety in unit}}{\text{Actual or estimated unit}} = \frac{\text{Margin of safety in revenues}}{\text{Actual or estimated revenues}}$$

DEGREE OF OPERATING LEVERAGE

In terms of contribution margin:

$$\text{Degree of operating leverage} = \frac{\text{Contribution margin}}{\text{Earnings}} = \frac{TS - TVC}{\text{Earnings}} = \frac{(S - V) \times Q}{\text{Earnings}}$$

In terms of fixed costs:

$$\text{Degree of operating leverage} = \frac{F}{\text{Earnings}} + 1$$

Sensitivity of profits to changes in sales (units or revenues):

$$\% \text{ change in earnings} = \% \text{ change in sales} \times \text{Degree of operating leverage}$$

RELATIONSHIP BETWEEN MARGIN OF SAFETY AND DEGREE OF OPERATING LEVERAGE

$$\text{Margin of safety percentage} = \frac{1}{\text{Degree of operating leverage}}$$

HIGHER OPERATING LEVERAGE (LOWER MARGIN OF SAFETY) LEADS TO

▶ Greater risk of loss
▶ Accelerated profits above the breakeven point

L06   Analyze the difference between contribution margin and gross margin

CONTRIBUTION MARGIN FORMAT		GROSS MARGIN FORMAT	
Revenues	$ xxxx	Revenues	$ xxxx
Variable costs	(xxx)	Cost of goods sold	(xxx)
Contribution margin	xxxx	Gross margin	xxxx
Fixed costs	(xxx)	Nonmanufacturing expenses	(xxx)
Earnings before taxes	$ xxx	Earnings before taxes	$ xxx

3-1 solution to self-study problem

A. To estimate the cost function, we use judgment to classify costs as fixed, variable, or mixed. For a typical retail business, rent and wages are likely to be fixed. We estimate fixed costs as the sum of these two costs ($500 + $1,000 = $1,500). It seems reasonable that the costs of beverages and snacks ($2,000) and napkins, straws, and so on ($500) would vary with revenues. We use the revenues as the cost driver to estimate variable costs as $2,500 ÷ $5,000 = 0.50, or 50% of revenues. Thus, the cost function is calculated:

$$TC = \$1,500 + (50\% \times Revenue)$$

B. We use income-tax expense and pretax earnings from last month to estimate the tax rate:

$$Tax\ rate = Taxes \div Pretax\ earnings = \$250 \div \$1,000 = 25\%$$

C. We first calculate the amount of pretax earnings needed to achieve after-tax earnings of $1,500:

$$Targeted\ pretax\ earnings = \$1,500 \div (1 - 0.25) = \$2,000$$

The contribution margin ratio is

$$(5,000 - 2,500) \div 5,000 = 0.50,\ or\ 50\%$$

We then perform the CVP calculation for revenues

$$Revenues = (\$1,500 + \$2,000) \div 0.50 = \$3,500 \div 0.50 = \$7,000$$

D. We use the results of our previous computations to calculate the contribution margin, and we then calculate the degree of operating leverage:

$$Contribution\ margin = \$5,000 - \$2,500 = \$2,500$$
$$Degree\ of\ operating\ leverage = Contribution\ margin \div Earnings$$
$$Degree\ of\ operating\ leverage = \$2,500 \div \$1,000 = 2.50$$

E. Before calculating the margin of safety, we need to calculate the breakeven point. Note that the margin of safety must be calculated in revenue dollars. We do not have unit or product mix information. The breakeven point is calculated:

$$\$1,500 \div 0.50 = \$3,000\ in\ revenues$$

Current revenues are $5,000, so the margin of safety is calculated as

$$Margin\ of\ safety = \$5,000 - \$3,000 = \$2,000$$

F. We use the formula to calculate margin of safety percentage:

$$Margin\ of\ safety\ percentage = \$2,000 \div \$5,000 = 40\%$$

Note that we can check our previous degree of operating leverage computation as follows:

Degree of operating leverage = 1 ÷ Margin of safety percentage = 1 ÷ 0.40 = 2.50

G. The expected and actual costs at $8,000 revenue are calculated:

Expected costs = $1,500 + (50% × $8,000) = $5,500
Actual costs = $8,000 − $2,000 = $6,000

Actual costs are $500 higher than expected.

H. When any costs are volatile, predicting them is problematic. Worldwide coffee prices are uncertain for many reasons, such as weather conditions in coffee-growing areas, the ability of farmers to increase crops, and coffee demand patterns. In addition, broader factors such as changes in economies and political upheaval influence costs. All these factors reduce our ability to develop a cost function that accurately predicts future costs, which means that the quality of the cost function is diminished.

3-2 solution to self-study problem

A. Accountants and managers will explore changes in more assumptions and vary the values within the spreadsheet more readily if it is easy to do. When these changes are made and the results are analyzed, managers better understand how unplanned changes in future operations might affect profitability. This knowledge allows them to more readily evaluate results and adjust operating plans.

B. Exhibit 3.13 provides relevant parts of the spreadsheet with the changes. With increased sales of youth bikes from 10,000 to 13,000 and an increased variable cost from $75 to $100, expected pretax earnings increase to $700,000. Comparing $700,000 to $650,000, Magik can spend up to $50,000 on advertising to maintain its current level of profitability.

C. Many different scenarios could occur. No single answer is always correct. Your answer depends on the assumptions that you make. Following are some examples of assumptions for the best and worst cases. Your most likely case should be between these two values.

One best case is that the new strategy is very popular with customers. More than 13,000 of the bikes are sold. The managers discover that customers are willing to pay a higher price for the bike, so they raise the price. In addition, manufacturing efficiency improves with the greater volume, reducing variable cost per unit. Also, fixed costs are lower than expected because the managers found some costs that could be reduced.

One worst case is that the helmets fail to attract customers. In fact, sales fail to meet original expectations; fewer than 10,000 are sold. Because the company produced extra bikes, expecting an increase in demand, the managers lower the selling price to encourage additional sales. In addition, the company hired extra workers to meet the expected demand, and other costs such as insurance and electricity costs are higher than expected. These changes caused both the variable and fixed costs to be higher than originally planned.

Your memo to the managers should include the following:

- Explain the assumptions for the best- and worst-case scenarios.
- Explain the reasoning behind the most likely case.
- Ask managers to consider beforehand how they would respond to the best- and worst-case scenarios.
- Make suggestions for monitoring the results for the youth bike.
- Encourage the managers to evaluate the advertising and product results and make suggestions for improving the operation or dropping the new helmet, if plans are unsuccessful.

▶ EXHIBIT 3.13

Spreadsheet for Magik Bicycles Youth
Helmet Decision

	A	B	C	D	E
1					
2	**Input section**	Youth Bikes	Road Bikes	Mtn. Bikes	
3	Expected sales volume-units	13,000	18,000	12,000	
4	Price per unit	$200	$700	$800	
5	Variable cost per unit	$100	$250	$300	
6					
7	Fixed costs	$14,700,000			
8	Desired after-tax profit	$100,000	(enter zero for breakeven)		
9	Income tax rate	30%			
10					
11					
12	**Contribution Margin**	Youth Bikes	Road Bikes	Mtn. Bikes	Total Bikes
13	Units	13,000	18,000	12,000	43,000
14	Revenue	$2,600,000	$12,600,000	$9,600,000	$24,800,000
15	Variable costs	1,300,000	4,500,000	3,600,000	9,400,000
16	Contribution margin	$1,300,000	$8,100,000	$6,000,000	$15,400,000
17					
18	Contrib. margin per unit	$100.00	$450.00	$500.00	$358.14
19	Contrib. margin ratio	50.00%	64.29%	62.50%	62.10%
20					
21	Expected sales mix in units	30.23%	41.86%	27.91%	100.00%
22	Expected sales mix in revenues	10.48%	50.81%	38.71%	100.00%
23					
24	**Expected Income**				
25	Contribution margin (above)				$15,400,000
26	Fixed costs				14,700,000
27	Pretax income				700,000
28	Income taxes				210,000
29	After-tax income				$490,000

QUESTIONS

3.1 If a firm has a mixed cost function, a 10% increase in sales volume should increase income by more than 10%. Explain why.

3.2 Explain how to calculate a weighted average contribution margin per unit.

3.3 An organization experiences a 20% increase in pretax profits when revenues increase 20%. Assuming linearity, what do you know about the organization's cost function?

3.4 What is the effect on a firm's breakeven point of a lower income tax rate?

3.5 To estimate revenues, costs, and profits across a range of activity, we usually assume that the cost and revenue functions are linear. What are the specific underlying assumptions for linear cost and revenue functions, and how reasonable are these assumptions?

3.6 Explain the relationship between margin of safety percentage and degree of operating leverage.

3.7 How do volume discounts from suppliers affect our assumption that the cost function is linear? Explain how we incorporate this type of cost into a CVP analysis.

3.8 Explain the term *sales mix* in your own words. How does sales mix affect the contribution margin?

3.9 How are CVP analysis and breakeven analysis related?

3.10 Can the margin of safety ever be negative? Explain your answer.

3.11 Describe three uses for CVP analysis.

3.12 Explain how CVP analysis can be used to make decisions about increases in advertising costs.

3.13 Under what circumstances will managers want sensitivity analysis around results from a CVP analysis?

3.14 Explain how the optimism bias affects the use of CVP analysis. Be very specific in your answer, listing the types of cash flows that are apt to be overestimated or underestimated.

3.15 Suppose average costs were used in a CVP analysis instead of fixed costs and variable costs. Explain the circumstances in which costs would be overestimated or underestimated.

MULTIPLE-CHOICE QUESTIONS

3.16 If total fixed costs doubled and contribution margin per unit was cut in half, what would happen to the breakeven point?
- **a.** It would decrease by half.
- **b.** It would double.
- **c.** It would triple.
- **d.** It would quadruple.

Use the following information to answer Questions 3.17 to 3.20: BioTec's fixed cost and breakeven in sales are $30,000 and $75,000, respectively.

3.17 What is BioTec's contribution margin ratio?
- **a.** 60%
- **b.** 40%
- **c.** 30%
- **d.** 20%

3.18 What is the variable cost if the sale price per unit is $40?
- **a.** $8.00
- **b.** $16.00
- **c.** $24.00
- **d.** $40.00

3.19 What is the degree of operating leverage if the sales volume is 2,000 units?
- **a.** 16
- **b.** 8
- **c.** 4
- **d.** 1

3.20 What are the sales needed to obtain earnings before tax of $6,000?
- **a.** $ 60,000
- **b.** $ 90,000
- **c.** $120,000
- **d.** $180,000

EXERCISES

3.21 Target Profit, Not-for-Profit Breakeven

 LO1, LO2

REQUIRED

A. The variable cost per gift basket is $2, fixed costs are $5,000 per month, and the selling price of a basket is $7. How many baskets must be produced and sold in a month to earn pretax earnings of $1,000?

B. The Community Heritage Centre (a not-for-profit organization providing language and arts and crafts programs for children) received a lump-sum grant from the City of Moncton of $460,000 this year. The fixed costs of the centre are expected to be $236,000. The average variable cost per child visit is expected to be $7.64, and the average fee collected per child visit is $4.64. What is the breakeven volume in child visits?

3.22 CVP Graph

 LO2

REQUIRED

A. Create a CVP graph using the information in Exercise 3.21, Part A. Explain the information in the graph.

B. Create a CVP graph using the information in Exercise 3.21, Part B. Explain the information in the graph.

3.23 Cost Function, Breakeven

LO2

REQUIRED

A. The average cost per unit was $234 at a volume of 1,200 units and $205 at a volume of 1,400 units. The earnings were $24,000 at the lower volume. Estimate the variable cost per unit.

B. Sparkle Car Wash Supplier sells a hose washer for $0.25 that it buys from the manufacturer for $0.12. Variable selling costs are $0.02 per hose washer. Breakeven is currently at a sales volume of $10,600 per month. What are the monthly fixed costs associated with the washer?

C. Monthly fixed costs are $24,000 when volume is at or below 200 units and $36,000 when monthly volume is above 200 units. The variable cost per unit is $200, and the selling price is $300 per unit. What is the breakeven quantity?

3.24 Profit, Price for Target Profit The Martell Company has recently established operations in a competitive market. Management has been aggressive in its attempt to establish market share. The price of the product was set at $5 per unit, well below that of the company's major competitors. Variable costs were $4.50 per unit, and total fixed costs were $600,000 during the first year.

LO2

REQUIRED **A.** Assume that the firm was able to sell 1 million units in the first year. What was the pretax earning (loss) for the year?

B. Assume that the variable cost per unit and total fixed costs do not increase in the second year. Management has been successful in establishing its position in the market. What price must be set to achieve pretax earnings of $25,000? Assume that sales remain at 1 million units.

3.25 CVP, Solve for Unknowns Parts (A) through (D) are four different CVP analyses, but some information is missing from each analysis. Each part contains a separate analysis.

LO2

REQUIRED Fill in the unknowns for each part.

Part	Sales	Fixed Costs	Variable Costs	Total Costs	Contribution Margin %	Operating Income
A	$3,000	$1,300	$?	$?	60%	$?
B	4,000	2,800	?	4,000	?	?
C	6,000	900	?	?	?	600
D	?	?	1,000	1,600	?	2,400

3.26 CVP, Before and After Tax, Return on Sales Canterman Company manufactures a single product. Canterman normally produces and sells 500 units per month at $110 each. The company's income tax rate is 28%. Estimated monthly costs are as follows:

LO2

	Manufacturing	Nonmanufactuing
Variable	$10,000	$5,000
Fixed	12,500	7,500

REQUIRED **A.** What is the contribution margin per unit?
B. What is the contribution margin ratio?
C. How many units must Canterman sell to break even?
D. If the company desires an after-tax profit of 22% on the selling price, what is the equivalent pretax return on sales?
E. The accountant at Canterman is an optimistic person. What problems would you anticipate with her estimates? Be specific about the direction of bias for various CVP items.

3.27 Profit, Price for Target Profit Gift4U produces one single product, a small reading tablet, and sells it at $120 per unit. Its current annual sales are $240,000. Its annual fixed costs include factory rent, $43,400; depreciation expense, equipment, $12,000; utilities, $22,000; insurance, $8,400. Its variable costs include materials, $36 per unit, and direct labour, $48 per unit. Gift4U's income tax rate is 20%.

LO1, LO3, LO5

REQUIRED **A.** What is the contribution margin per unit?
B. What is the contribution margin ratio?
C. How many units must Gift4U sell to break even?
D. If Gift4U would like to earn a profit after tax of $12,000, what should the sales be? At this sales level, what is the degree of operating leverage? What is the margin of safety in units?
E. If Gift4U would like to earn a profit after tax that is 8% of sales, what should the sales be? How many units does Gift4U need to increase from the current sales level?

3.28 Cost Function, Breakeven Data for the most recent three months of operations for the RainBeau Salon appear
LO2 here:

	March	April	May
Number of appointments	1,600	1,500	1,900
Hairdresser salaries	$14,000	$14,000	$18,000
Manicurist salaries	12,000	12,000	16,000
Supplies	900	750	950
Utilities	600	480	400
Rent	1,000	1,000	1,000
Miscellaneous	3,500	3,450	3,580
Total costs	$32,000	$31,680	$39,930

A general cost-of-living salary increase occurred at the beginning of May.

REQUIRED **A.** What is the total cost function for RainBeau Salon?
B. If the average fee per appointment is $25, estimate the appointments required in June to break even.

3.29 Breakeven, Target Profit, ROI Target Profit Madden Company, which is subject to a 40% income tax rate,
LO2 projected its income before taxes for next year as shown here:

Sales (160,000 units)	$8,000,000
Cost of sales	
Variable costs	2,000,000
Fixed costs	3,000,000
Pretax earning	$3,000,000

REQUIRED **A.** What is Madden's breakeven point in units sold for the next year?
B. If Madden wants $4.5 million in pretax earning, what is the required level of sales, in dollars?
C. If Madden's net assets are $36 million, what amount of revenue must be achieved for Madden to earn a 10% after-tax return on assets?
D. If Madden wants after-tax earnings of 30% of sales, what is the required level of sales in dollars and in units?

3.30 Breakeven, Target Profit, Cost Changes, Selling Price Laraby Company produces a single product. It sold 25,000
LO1, LO2 units last year, with the following results:

Sales	$625,000
Variable costs	375,000
Fixed costs	150,000
Income before taxes	100,000
Income taxes (45%)	45,000
After-tax earnings	$ 55,000

In an attempt to improve the company's product, Laraby's managers are considering replacing a component part that costs $2.50 with a new and better part that costs $4.50 per unit during the coming year. A new machine would also be needed to increase plant capacity. The machine would cost $18,000 and have a useful life of six years, with no salvage value. The company uses straight-line depreciation on all plant assets.

REQUIRED   **A.** What was Laraby Company's breakeven point in units last year?
B. How many units of product would Laraby Company have had to sell in the past year to earn $77,000 in after-tax earnings?
C. If Laraby Company holds the sales price constant and makes the suggested changes, how many units of product must be sold in the coming year to break even?
D. If Laraby Company holds the sales price constant and makes the suggested changes, how many units of product will the company have to sell to make the same after-tax earnings as last year?
E. If Laraby Company wishes to maintain the same contribution margin ratio, what selling price per unit of product must it charge next year to cover the increased materials costs?

3.31 **Target Profit, Progressive Income Tax Rates, CVP Graph** Dalton Brothers pays 15% in taxes on income between $1 and $40,000. All income above $40,000 is taxed at 40%. The firm's variable costs as a percentage of revenues are 60%. Annual fixed costs are $250,000.

LO3

REQUIRED   **A.** What level of sales must the firm achieve to earn income after taxes of $150,000?
B. Prepare a CVP graph for Dalton Brothers.

3.32 **Breakeven, Selling Price, Target Profit with Price and Cost Changes** All-Day Candy Company is a wholesale distributor of candy. The company services grocery, convenience, and drug stores in a large metropolitan area. All-Day Candy Company has achieved small but steady growth in sales over the past few years, but candy prices have also been increasing. The company is reformulating its plans for the coming fiscal year. The following data were used to project the current year's after-tax income of $100,400:

LO1, LO2, LO3

Average selling price	$4.00 per box
Average variable costs	
Cost of candy	$2.00 per box
Selling costs	0.40 per box
Total	$2.40 per box
Annual fixed costs	
Selling	$160,000
Administrative	280,000
Total	$440,000
Expected annual sales (390,000 boxes) = $1,560,000	
Tax rate = 40%	

Candy manufacturers have announced that they will increase prices of their products an average of 15% in the coming year because of increases in raw material (sugar, cocoa, peanuts, and so on) and labour costs. All-Day Candy Company expects that all other costs will remain the same as during the current year.

REQUIRED   **A.** What is All-Day Candy Company's breakeven point in boxes of candy for the current year?
B. What average selling price per box must All-Day Candy Company charge to cover the 15% increase in the variable cost of candy and still maintain the current contribution margin ratio?
C. What volume of sales in dollars must All-Day Candy Company achieve in the coming year to maintain the same after-tax income as projected for the current year if the average selling price of candy remains at $4.00 per box and the cost of candy increases 15%?

3.33 Breakeven, Operating Leverage, Cost Function Decision You are the advisor of a Junior Achievement group in a local high school. You need to help the group make a decision about fees that must be paid to sell gardening tools at the Home and Garden Show. The group sells a set of tools for $20.00. The manufacturing cost (all variable) is $6 per set. The Home and Garden Show coordinator allows the following three payment options for groups exhibiting and selling at the show:

LO1, LO2, LO5

1. Pay a fixed booth fee of $5,600.
2. Pay a fee of $3,800 plus 10% of all revenue from tool sets sold at the show.
3. Pay 15% of all revenue from tool sets sold at the show.

REQUIRED A. Compute the breakeven number of tool sets for each option.
B. Which payment plan has the highest degree of operating leverage?
C. Which payment plan has the lowest risk of loss for the organization? Explain.
D. At what level of revenue should the group be indifferent to options 1 and 2?
E. Which option should Junior Achievement choose, assuming that sales are expected to be 1,000 sets of tools? Explain.

3.34 ROI Target Profit, Foreign Exchange Rates Borg Controls, a Canadian company, has a net investment in its German subsidiary of $2.68 million. The firm attempts to earn a 15% pretax return on its investment. Variable costs for the German subsidiary are 60% of revenues. Annual fixed costs are €321,000. For the current year, the manager of the German subsidiary anticipates revenues of €1.7 million. The exchange rate is expected to be €1 = CAD $1.50.

LO3

REQUIRED A. If operations meet expectations, what is the rate of return that Borg Controls will earn from its German subsidiary? (*Hint:* Calculate the rate of return by dividing pretax income by the net investment.)
B. What level of revenue in euros would be required of the subsidiary for the parent to earn exactly a 15% rate of return in dollars, assuming no changes in the exchange rate?

3.35 Target Profit, Margin of Safety, Operating Leverage, Contribution Margin, and Gross Margin The following budget data apply to Newberry's Nutrition:

LO2, LO5, LO6

Sales (100,000 units)		$1,000,000
Costs		
Direct materials	$300,000	
Direct labour	200,000	
Fixed factory overhead	100,000	
Variable factory overhead	150,000	
Marketing and administration	160,000	
Total costs		$ 910,000
Budgeted pretax income		$ 90,000

Direct labour workers are paid hourly wages and go home when there is no work. The marketing and administration costs include $50,000 that varies proportionately with production volume. Assume that sales and production volumes are equal.

REQUIRED A. Compute the number of units that must be sold to achieve a target after-tax income of $120,000, assuming a tax rate of 40%.
B. Calculate the margin of safety in both revenues and units.
C. Calculate the degree of operating leverage.
D. Prepare Newberry's Nutrition income statements in contribution margin format and gross margin format.

3.36 Breakeven, Target Profit, Margin of Safety, Operating Leverage Pike Street Taffy makes and sells taffy in a variety of

LO2, LO5 flavours in a shop located in the local public market. Data for a recent week are as follows:

Revenue (2,000 kgs @ $4.80 per kg)		$9,600
Cost of ingredients	$3,200	
Rent	800	
Wages	4,800	8,800
Pretax income		800
Taxes (20%)		160
After-tax income		$ 640

All employees work standard shifts, no matter how much taffy is produced or sold.

REQUIRED
A. Calculate the breakeven point in units and in revenue.
B. Calculate the number of units and the amount of revenues that would be needed for after-tax income of $3,000.
C. Calculate the margin of safety in units and the margin of safety percentage.
D. Calculate the degree of operating leverage.

3.37 Breakeven, Target Profit, Margin of Safety Vines and Daughter manufactures and sells swimsuits for $40 each. The

LO2, LO5 estimated income statement for 2017 is as follows:

Sales	$2,000,000
Variable costs	1,100,000
Contribution margin	900,000
Fixed costs	765,000
Pretax earnings	$ 135,000

REQUIRED
A. Compute the contribution margin per swimsuit and the number of swimsuits that must be sold to break even.
B. What is the margin of safety in the number of swimsuits?
C. Suppose the margin of safety was 5,000 swimsuits in 2016. Are operations more or less risky in 2017 as compared to 2016? Explain.
D. Compute the contribution margin ratio and the breakeven point in revenues.
E. What is the margin of safety in revenues?
F. Suppose next year's revenue estimate is $200,000 higher. What would be the estimated pretax earnings?
G. Assume a tax rate of 30%. How many swimsuits must be sold to earn after-tax earnings of $180,000?

3.38 CVP Analysis with Taxes, Margin of Safety Pineridge Kennels charges $32 per day to board a dog. The variable

LO5 cost to feed and handle a dog is $5 per day. The fixed costs for maintaining the kennel are $160,000 per year, and the company's income tax rate is 30%. The measure of volume is dog-days. For example, 3 dogs boarded for 4 days plus 1 dog boarded for 6 days yields 18 dog-days of service (and revenue).

REQUIRED
A. If the firm expects an annual volume of 8,400 dog-days of boarding, what is the expected after-tax profit?
B. If the firm anticipates an annual volume of 7,200 dog-days of boarding, what is the margin of safety in terms of dog-days?
C. The owner believes that an after-tax profit of $108,000 is needed to justify being in business. How many dog-days are required to meet this goal?
D. Calculate the percentage increase in dog-days between parts (A) and (C). Then list the assumptions that might no longer hold for Pineridge Kennels for the volume in part (C). What information would you need from the owner to evaluate whether the target volume calculated in part (C) is achievable?

3.39 CVP with Variable Amount of Earning Mr. Thuet owns a food truck selling Vietnamese food around a university.
LO2 His monthly fixed cost for operating the truck is $3,000, and variable cost is 70% of the revenue. The business generated revenue of $110,000 during the first year of operation. He sets his second year's earnings target before tax to be 5% of revenue.

REQUIRED **A.** What is the earning before tax for the first year's operation?
B. What should the target revenue be in order to achieve his goal?
C. By how much will his revenue have to increase in the second year?

3.40 Sales Mix, Multiple-Product Breakeven, Multiple-Product Target Income BabeMobile manufactures 3 types of baby
LO2, LO3 strollers: Lite, Elite, and Polite. The current information on sales and cost structure for the three products are as follows:

	Lite	Elite	Polite
Unit Selling Price	$110	$180	$240
Unit Variable Cost	50	110	120

The sale mix ratio for the three models is 2:3:5 for Lite, Elite and Polite. BabeMobile's fixed costs for the year are $660,000.

REQUIRED **A.** Calculate the unit contribution margin for each model of stroller.
B. Assuming that the sales mix remains constant, calculate the contribution margin for the composite.
C. What is the breakeven in units for each model of stroller?
D. If BabeMobile sets its target income before taxes at $180,000, how many units of each model of stroller should be sold to achieve its target?

PROBLEMS

3.41 Cost Function, Breakeven, Quality of Information, Relevant Range Premier Lobsters traps and packs
LO2, LO4 lobsters and then sells them wholesale to fine restaurants across Canada. The income statement for last year follows:

Revenue (based on sales of 2,000 cases of lobsters)		$200,000
Expenses:		
Wages for fishermen and packers	$100,000	
Packing materials	20,000	
Rent and insurance	25,000	
Administrative and selling	45,000	190,000
Pretax income		10,000
Taxes (20%)		2,000
After-tax income		$ 8,000

Fishermen and packers are employed on an hourly basis and can be laid off whenever necessary. Salespeople mostly deliver the product and are paid on a salaried basis; their salaries are included in administrative and selling expenses.

REQUIRED **A.** Estimate the cost function for Premier Lobsters.
B. What is the breakeven point in cases for Premier Lobsters?
C. The manager thinks that the company will sell 3,000 cases of lobsters next year. Estimate the after-tax income.
D. Premier Lobsters sold 2,000 cases in each of the past several years. What does this suggest about the quality of the income information you calculated in Part C?
E. Describe reasons why the cost function developed for the relevant range up to 2,000 cases might not hold for 2,001 to 3,000 cases.

3.42 **Relevant Information, Breakeven, Target Profit, Price, Business Risk** Francesca would like to lease a coffee cart in Whistler, B.C. The lease is $800 per month, and a city licence to sell food and beverages costs $20 per month. The lessor of the stand has shown Francesca records indicating that gross revenues average $32 per hour. The out-of-pocket costs for ingredients are generally about 40% of gross revenues. Last year she paid 25% of her income in taxes.

LO1, LO3, LO4

Francesca pays $1,000 per month for her condominium. She could store the cart overnight in the condo's garage, which is currently unused. Real estate developers in Whistler estimate that about 20% of the rental cost of a residential building is for the garage.

At present, Francesca is earning $2,400 per month as a ski instructor for one of the big ski areas. In the summertime, she earns about the same income by working as a kayaking instructor.

REQUIRED
A. List each piece of quantitative information in this problem. For each item, indicate whether it is relevant to Francesca's decision and explain why.
B. If Francesca leases the cart and works 30 days in a month, how many hours will she have to work each day, on average, to be at least as well off financially as she is in her current job?
C. If Francesca wants to work only 25 days per month, how much will revenues have to increase for her to work 4 hours per day and be as financially well off as she is in her current job?
D. Can Francesca be certain that her revenues will average $32 per hour? Why or why not?
E. What other information might help Francesca with this decision?

3.43 **Sales Mix, Multiple-Product Breakeven, Business Risk, Quality of Information** Keener produces two products: regular boomerangs and premium boomerangs. Last month 1,200 units of regular and 2,400 units of premium were produced and sold. Average prices and costs per unit for the month are displayed here:

LO2, LO3, LO4

	Regular	Premium
Selling price	$22.15	$45.30
Variable costs	4.31	6.91
Product line fixed costs	8.17	24.92
Corporate fixed costs	5.62	5.62
Operating earnings	$ 4.05	$ 7.85

Product line fixed costs can be avoided if the product line is dropped. Corporate fixed costs can be avoided only if the firm goes out of business entirely. You may want to use a spreadsheet to perform calculations.

REQUIRED
A. Assuming that the sales mix remains constant, how many units of premium will be sold each time a unit of regular is sold?
B. What are the total fixed product line costs for each product?
C. What are the total corporate fixed costs?
D. What is the overall corporate breakeven in total revenue and for each product, assuming that the sales mix is the same as last month's?
E. What is the breakeven in revenues for regular boomerangs, ignoring corporate fixed costs?
F. Why is the breakeven for regular boomerangs different when we calculate the individual product breakeven versus the combined product breakeven?
G. When managers monitor the profitability of regular boomerangs, are corporate fixed costs relevant? Explain.
H. CVP analysis assumes that the sales mix will remain constant. Explain why managers generally cannot know for certain what their sales mix will be.
I. What is the effect of uncertainty about the sales mix on the quality of the information obtained from CVP analyses?

3.44 **Cost Function, Marginal Cost, Opportunity Cost, Usefulness of CVP** A neighbour asked for your help preparing a grant for a not-for-profit, after-school art program that would benefit elementary-school children in the neighbourhood. He wants to charge low fees for most children but also offer some scholarships for low-income children. He needs to have one staff person for every six children to meet governmental regulations. He can use high-school student volunteers for two of these positions but is concerned about potential absences on their part if he relies on them for the governmental count. He would like the program to serve at least 30 children—and more, if possible.

LO1, LO2

Your neighbour wants you to help him decide on the fees to charge and also to determine how many students could receive scholarships.

REQUIRED **A.** Think about the costs involved in an after-school program. Assume that your neighbour can use the local public school for free.

　　1. List costs that will be incurred for the program and categorize them as fixed, variable, or mixed.
　　2. For each variable cost, choose a potential cost driver. Explain your choice.

B. Do you think the cost structure would be primarily fixed or primarily variable? Explain. Remember, even though staff work only part time, they will have a regular schedule to meet the governmental regulations of six children per staff member.

C. Suppose one of the staff members has only one child to help. What is the marginal cost for three scholarships?

D. Suppose the program is fully subscribed by fee-paying children. What is the opportunity cost per scholarship?

E. Will CVP analysis help your neighbour choose a fee that would cover at least 10 scholarships? Explain how you would set up a spreadsheet so that your neighbour could perform sensitivity analysis to make more informed decisions.

3.45 **Breakeven, CVP, Potential Cost Structure Change, Employee Reaction** Ersatz manufactures a single product. The following income statement shows two different levels of activity, which are assumed to be within Ersatz's relevant range. You may want to use a spreadsheet to perform calculations.

LO1, LO2, LO4

Ersatz, Inc.
Income Statement

	Activity Levels	
Volume	1,000 units	1,500 units
Sales @ $100 each	$ 100,000	$ 150,000
Less variable expenses		
Manufacturing @ $40 each	40,000	60,000
Selling @ $10 each	10,000	15,000
Administration @ $6 each	6,000	9,000
Contribution margin	44,000	66,000
Less fixed expenses		
Manufacturing	10,000	10,000
Selling	11,000	11,000
Administration	20,000	20,000
Pretax income	$　3,000	$ 25,000

REQUIRED **A.** What is Ersatz's breakeven point, in units?

B. Draw a CVP chart that shows the two levels of activity and the breakeven point.

C. If Ersatz plans to sell 1,300 units, what will pretax income be?

D. Your boss asked you to draft an e-mail response to Ersatz's major shareholder, who wants to know why pretax income increases by more than 800% when sales increase by just 50%. Both your boss and the shareholder are busy people and expect short answers.

E. Management expects that variable costs and selling prices will rise by 3% but fixed costs will not change. What will the new breakeven point be? Explain the result.

F. Management wants to change the way that sales representatives are paid. At present, sales representatives are paid $11,000 per year + $10 per unit. Management will replace this formula with a payment of $20 per unit. At what level of sales will it make no difference in income which cost function is used?

G. Add the new cost function to the preceding CVP chart.

H. Which of the two cost functions will minimize selling expenses, assuming that sales are above the indifference level calculated in Part F?

I. How would sales representatives be likely to respond to the new payment system?

J. Discuss the pros and cons to the company of changing the way sales representatives are paid.

3.46 CVP Analysis, Bonus, Taxes Sally Nuzum recently took over the presidency of J & J Products. The firm sells a single product for $30 per unit. Its cost function has been estimated as $200,000 per year plus $10 per unit. J & J Products is subject to a combined provincial and federal income tax rate of 35%. Ms. Nuzum has been offered a bonus equal to 10% of the firm's net income after tax. Sally has her eyes on a new car that will cost $36,000. Her personal tax rate will average 30%.

LO2

REQUIRED **A.** Determine the amount of bonus required so that Sally has $36,000 after paying her taxes on the bonus.
B. Determine how much after-tax income J & J will need for Sally to receive the bonus calculated in Part A.
C. Solve for the number of units sold for Sally to get her bonus.
D. In what ways might the bonus influence Sally's behaviour as president of J & J?

3.47 Contribution Margin vs. Gross Margin FongFone Ltd. manufactures cell phones, which are priced at $250. Mr. Fong, the president of FongFone, has come to you for help in terms of the company's cost structure. You are troubled because the data produced by the accounting system of FongFone do not distinguish between variable and fixed costs.

LO2, LO3, LO5, LO6

After some analysis, you have identified various cost behaviour patterns. You have determined that the margin of safety is $75,000 and sales in breakeven units are 2,700; your analysis was made easier by the fact that it is FongFone's policy *not* to carry any inventories. Instead, the company finishes pending orders sometime in December and gives employees vacations that end in early January of the following year.

You have also collected the following information for the 2017 fiscal year:

	2017
Direct labour	$170,000
Direct material	210,000
Variable manufacturing overhead	80,000
Gross margin %	22.50%
Contribution margin %	30.00%
Income-tax rate	25.00%

REQUIRED **A.** Calculate the following costs for 2017:
1. Sales in dollars
2. Variable selling and administrative expenses
3. Fixed manufacturing overhead
4. Fixed selling and administrative expenses
5. Earnings (income) before taxes

B. Determine the sales volume in dollars and in units that FongFone must achieve to earn a $36,000 income after taxes. Calculate the degree of operating leverage. If sales increase by 8%, what is the impact on the operating income?

3.48 Breakeven, Avoidable Fixed Costs, Price, CVP Assumptions, Operating Risk Last year's income statement for King Salmon Sales follows:

LO1, LO2, LO4, LO5

Revenue (100,000 kg)		$800,000
Expenses		
Fish	$200,000	
Smoking materials	20,000	
Packaging materials	30,000	
Labour (wages)	300,000	
Administrative	150,000	
Sales commissions	10,000	
Total expenses		710,000
Income		$ 90,000

The fishing season is only three to four months long, so labour costs (wages) are for employees who are college students and work in the summer. They are hired only as needed.

REQUIRED **A.** The government curtailed fishing because of low fish counts. Because of this restriction, King Salmon Sales can buy only 50,000 kilograms. Assume that the administrative cost is incurred only if the company sells salmon. Assuming that the managers will decide to operate if the company can at least break even, should they operate this year? (*Hint:* Calculate the breakeven quantity.) Provide calculations and explain your answer.

B. Now assume that the administrative costs continue, regardless of whether the company sells salmon. Assuming that the managers will decide to operate if the company can at least break even, should they operate this year? Provide calculations and explain your answer.

C. Because of the salmon shortage, suppose that retail salmon prices are increasing. What is the breakeven price for King Salmon? Assume that administrative costs continue, regardless of whether the company sells salmon.

D. Suppose the managers rely on the preceding CVP analysis to decide whether to operate the business. What assumptions are they making?

E. How reasonable are the CVP assumptions you listed for Part D?

F. Suppose the owner of King Salmon Sales asked you about the company's cost structure. Because volumes of fish fluctuate a great deal from one year to the next, the owner is wondering if some way can be found to reduce the risk of an operating loss. Write a brief memo to explain how the proportion of fixed and variable costs affects the risk of loss when operations are close to the breakeven point.

3.49 **Cost Function, Breakeven, Target Profit, Business Risk and Bias, Interpretation** Joe Greco is thinking about starting a company to produce carved wooden clocks. He loves making the clocks and sees an opportunity to be his own boss, making a living doing what he likes best.

LO1, LO2, LO4

Joe paid $300 for the plans for his first clock, and he has already purchased new equipment costing $2,000 to manufacture the clocks. He estimates that it will cost $30 in materials (wood, clock mechanism, and so on) to make each clock. If he decides to build clocks full time, he will need to rent office and manufacturing space, which he thinks would cost $2,500 per month for rent plus another $300 per month for various utility bills. Joe would perform all the manufacturing and run the office, and he would like to pay himself a salary of $3,000 per month so that he would have enough money to live on. Because he does not want to take time away from manufacturing to sell the clocks, he plans to hire two salespeople at a base salary of $1,000 each per month plus a commission of $7 per clock.

Joe plans to sell each clock for $225. He believes that he can produce and sell 300 clocks in December for Christmas, but he is not sure what the sales will be during the rest of the year. However, he is fairly sure that the clocks will be popular because he has been selling similar items as a sideline for several years. Overall, he is confident that he can pay all his business costs, pay himself the monthly salary of $3,000, and earn at least $4,000 more than that per month. (Ignore income taxes.)

The following questions will help you analyze the information for this problem. Do not turn in your answers to these questions unless your instructor asks you to do so.

REQUIRED **INFORMATION ANALYSIS**

A. Perform analyses to estimate the number of clocks Joe would need to manufacture and sell each year for his business to be financially successful:
   1. List all the costs described and indicate whether each cost is (a) a relevant fixed cost, (b) a relevant variable cost, or (c) not relevant to Joe's decision.
   2. Calculate the contribution margin per unit and the contribution margin ratio.
   3. Write down the total cost function for the clocks and calculate the annual breakeven point, in units and in revenues.
   4. How many clocks would Joe need to sell annually to earn $4,000 per month more than his salary?

B. Identify business risks concerning the CVP calculations:
   1. Explain why Joe cannot know for sure whether his actual costs will be the same dollar amounts that he estimated. In your explanation, identify as many business risks as you can. (*Hint:* For each of the costs Joe identified, think about reasons why the actual cost might be different than the amount he estimated.)
   2. Identify possible costs for Joe's business that he has not identified. List as many additional types of costs as you can.
   3. Explain why Joe cannot know for sure how many clocks he will sell each year. In your explanation, identify as many business risks as you can.

C. Discuss whether Joe is likely to be biased in his revenue and cost estimates.

D. Explain how business risk and Joe's potential biases might affect interpretation of the breakeven analysis results.

REQUIRED   WRITTEN ASSIGNMENT

Suppose Joe has asked for your advice. Turn in your answers to the following.

E. Use the information you learned from the preceding analyses to write a memo to Joe with your recommendations. Attach to the memo a schedule showing relevant information. As appropriate, refer to the schedule in the memo.

3.50 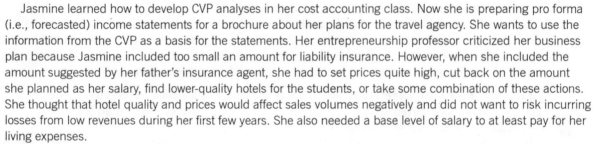 **CVP Sensitivity Analysis, Bias, Quality of Information** Jasmine Krishnan has been taking entrepreneurship courses as part of her business degree. She developed a plan to start a travel agency specializing in spring-break trips for students.

LO1, LO4

Jasmine learned how to develop CVP analyses in her cost accounting class. Now she is preparing pro forma (i.e., forecasted) income statements for a brochure about her plans for the travel agency. She wants to use the information from the CVP as a basis for the statements. Her entrepreneurship professor criticized her business plan because Jasmine included too small an amount for liability insurance. However, when she included the amount suggested by her father's insurance agent, she had to set prices quite high, cut back on the amount she planned as her salary, find lower-quality hotels for the students, or take some combination of these actions. She thought that hotel quality and prices would affect sales volumes negatively and did not want to risk incurring losses from low revenues during her first few years. She also needed a base level of salary to at least pay for her living expenses.

Jasmine decided to ask friends and relatives to invest in her travel agency to ensure that she had enough capital for the first few years. Once her reputation was well established, she assumed that higher customer volumes would cover all her expected costs. She was confident that her planned trips would attract enough students each year to cover most of her costs. From focus groups on campus, she learned which types of trips were most appealing to other students. Now she planned to use sensitivity analysis to solve for volumes that would make the pro forma statements look attractive to investors.

REQUIRED   A. In general, what information do we hope to gain from performing sensitivity analyses? Explain.

B. Explain how bias might enter into Jasmine's sensitivity analyses.

C. How might Jasmine's bias affect the quality of the investment brochure information?

D. Identify a potential ethical problem for Jasmine.

E. When you consider the well-being of Jasmine's family and friends, how would you recommend that Jasmine use sensitivity analysis for her brochure? Explain.

3.51 **Small Business Owners, CVP Research on the Internet** The Internet provides many resources to help small business owners successfully manage their businesses. Resources include information about common techniques used for planning and managing operations.

LO1, LO2, LO4

REQUIRED   A. Why are small business owners often unaware of common business techniques such as CVP analysis?

B. Why might CVP analysis be even more useful to small business owners than to managers of large organizations? (*Hint:* Consider whether information about the margin of safety and size of potential losses might be especially important for people who own small businesses.)

C. Use an Internet search engine to locate websites that provide information about the terms *breakeven analysis* and *cost-volume-profit analysis.* Also search for these terms on websites designed explicitly to help small business owners, such as the Canada Business Services for Entrepreneurs (www.canadabusiness.ca). Summarize what your research tells you about the uses and usefulness of breakeven and CVP analysis.

D. Suppose you are trying to help a small business owner learn to use breakeven and CVP analysis. Write a memo to the owner, explaining what you think the owner should do, and include appropriate references to Internet resources that would be useful to the owner. Assume that you have already had a brief conversation with the owner about breakeven and CVP analysis, and the owner expressed an interest in learning more. Focus on communicating effectively by avoiding unnecessarily technical language and concentrating on the most important points.

3.52 **Cost Function, Target Profit, Operating Leverage, CVP Graph, Owner Goals** Elina Siljander owns Elina's Stained

LO1, LO2, LO3, LO4, LO5

Glass in Helsinki, Finland. The business produces and sells three different types of stained glass windows: small, medium, and large. Elina has two full-time employees who work regular schedules to cut glass and assemble the windows. She borrowed money from the bank to start the business and pay living expenses. She is concerned that her cash flows might not be high enough either to pay herself or to repay the bank loan. She would like to generate approximately €10,000 in pretax earnings each month to cover her living expenses and repay the loan.

The following revenue and cost information covers the past four months:

	June	July	August	September
Revenues	€9,050	€10,531	€12,946	€16,116
Raw materials and supplies	1,745	2,433	3,074	4,029
Labour	3,880	4,041	4,246	4,282
Rent	2,000	2,000	2,000	2,200
Miscellaneous	525	701	747	793
Profit	€ 900	€ 1,356	€ 2,879	€ 4,812

REQUIRED **A.** Develop a cost function for Elina's Stained Glass.

B. Determine the level of revenue Elina's Stained Glass must generate to achieve the targeted profit of €10,000 per month.

C. Calculate Elina's degree of operating leverage for September.

D. Interpret Elina's degree of operating leverage.

E. Create a CVP graph that shows the breakeven point, target profit, and margin of safety.

F. Write a memo to Elina with recommendations about ways she might achieve her goals.

3.53 **Building and Using a CVP Financial Model** Toddler Toy Company sells baby dolls, teddy bears, and toy cars. The

LO1, LO2, LO3, LO4

managers established a preliminary budget, using the following assumptions:

Toddler Toy Company

Assumptions for Coming Year

	Baby Dolls	Teddy Bears	Toy Cars
Volume	200,000	125,000	225,000
Sale price	$3.50	$2.75	$3.15
Variable costs	$2.05	$1.75	$2.45
Fixed costs	$65,000	$125,000	$35,000

Target pretax income = $0

Investment = $2 million

Capacity = 1 million units

The managers of Toddler Toy Company would now like to evaluate the sensitivity of budgeted results to different sets of assumptions.

REQUIRED **A.** Create a spreadsheet that the managers can use for sensitivity analysis. (*Hint:* Use the Magik Bicycles spreadsheet in Exhibit 3.3 and Appendix 3A to help set up a spreadsheet with a data input box.) Modify input data in the spreadsheet to answer the following parts of this problem. You might want to add cell references for percentage changes in prices, volumes, and costs.

B. Assume that the volume of dolls sold increases to 225,000 units, with no change in fixed or variable costs. What is the new pretax income? Does the number produced by your financial model appear to be reasonable? (Manually estimate the increase in pretax income if volume increases and fixed costs remain constant. Compare this figure to your spreadsheet result.)

C. Based on the original assumptions, what is the effect on pretax income if variable costs increase by 5% for each of the three product lines? Assume that nothing else changes.

D. Return to the original assumptions. Assume that a sales manager proposed a new advertising campaign to boost sales volume. The campaign would cost $30,000 and is estimated to increase the volume of each product as follows:

> Baby doll sales increase by 20,000 units.
> Teddy bear sales increase by 7,500 units.
> Toy car sales increase by 30,000 units.

What would be the effect on pretax income if this plan were adopted?

E. Return to the original assumptions. Now assume that, due to competition, Toddler Toys must cut prices on each of its three products by 20%. In addition, a new advertising campaign costing $45,000 must be instituted to counteract bad publicity. Given these assumptions, what is the new breakeven point?

F. Return to the original assumptions. What would be the pretax income if Toddler Toys increased the price of all three products by 10% and the volume of each product line decreased by 5%?

G. Given the same assumptions as in Part F, how many units must Toddler Toys sell to earn a target pretax income of $100,000? a target pretax income of $150,000? a pretax return on investment (ROI) of 10%? (*Hint:* To determine the target pretax income, multiply 10% by the amount invested.)

H. Spreadsheets for financial modelling allow sensitivity analysis of revenues, costs, and quantities such as estimated product volumes.

> **1.** Explain why it is not possible to perfectly estimate revenues, costs, and quantities.
> **2.** Explain how sensitivity analysis can help managers evaluate the pros and cons of alternatives.
> **3.** Explain how manager bias might influence estimates of revenues, costs, and quantities.

3.54 Building and Using a CVP Financial Model The following information for Pet Palace, a large retail store that sells pet-related merchandise, was recorded for the first quarter:

L01, L02,
L03, L04

Input Data	Food	Toys	Pets	Other	Total
Revenue	$500,000	$150,000	$75,000	$200,000	$925,000
Variable cost	200,000	50,000	60,000	50,000	360,000
Fixed cost					550,000
Tax rate					25%

The store tracks merchandise according to product type. The category "Other" includes accessories such as dog beds, leashes, kitty litter boxes, bird cages, and so on. The company is considering several different strategies to improve operations for the next quarter.

REQUIRED

A. Create a spreadsheet that Pet Palace managers can use for sensitivity analysis. Modify information in the data input section and answer the questions in the following parts.

B. What is Pet Palace's breakeven point? What total revenue is necessary for a target after-tax income of $100,000?

C. Pet Palace managers are considering their advertising campaign for the next period. They believe they could spend an additional $10,000 on advertising for a product line and increase sales by 10%. One manager wants to increase advertising on pets because that product line is currently the smallest. Another manager believes the ads should promote the most profitable products but is not sure which products those would be. What is the after-tax income if pets are promoted? What is the most profitable product? What is the after-tax income if the most profitable product is promoted?

D. What factors, other than the quantitative results, might influence managers' decisions to increase advertising?

3.55 Contribution Margin versus Gross Margin, Degree of Operating Leverage Arcadia, Inc. manufactures souvenirs and sells the products to souvenir shops across Canada. Lisa McKay is the new owner, and is concerned about the low margins. She would like to find a way to improve the company's profitability. The accountant provides her the following financial information: sales are $250,000, of which 60% is cost of goods sold. Cost of goods sold consists of direct materials (20%), direct labour (30%), and fixed manufacturing overhead (50%). Operating expenses consist of variable expenses (40%) and fixed expenses (60%). Arcadia pays a 40% tax rate and the net income is $15,000.

L02, L03,
L05, L06

To reduce the company's operating risks, McKay would like to review the company's operations from another perspective. She would like to know how much the company needs to generate in order to break even. Based on the current cost structure, how sensitive is the profit to a sale volume increase of 5%.

REQUIRED   **A.** Prepare an income statement in the gross margin format.
B. Prepare an income statement in the contribution margin format.
C. What is the break even in sales?
D. At the current sales level, what is the margin of safety and the degree of operating leverage?
E. Explain to Lisa the impact of a 5% sales increase. Looking at the current cost structure, what would you recommend to Lisa to improve the company's financial performance?

3.56 Breakeven, CVP with Variable Amount of Earning, Margin of Safety, Degree of Operating Leverage Lynn Lin rented a cart in a mall to sell covers for cell phones and tablets. The mall charges $2,250 per month for rent, cart rental, and utilities. In addition, the mall takes 2% from the total revenue. Lynn decided to pay herself 18% commission based on sales. On average, the cost of the covers is 20% of the sales price. Lynn pays a tax rate of 20%.

LO2, LO5

REQUIRED   **A.** What is the break even in sales?
B. If Lynn would like to earn a net income equal to 12% of revenue for the next year, what should the annual sales be?
C. Based on the calculation from Part B, what is the margin of safety?
D. Calculate the degree of operating leverage based on the sales from Part B.
E. Interpret the degree of operating leverage.

3.57 Sales Mix, Multiple-Product Breakeven, Multiple-Product with Target Income, Sensitivity Analysis Royal Bikes (RB) manufactures and sells two models of bike, Ezee and Focus. Of RB's sales, 60% are for EZee and 40% for Focus. RB incurs $918,000 fixed costs, and pays taxes at a rate of 40%.

LO2, LO3, LO6

Sheldon Wright, the owner of RB, anticipates that the labour and material costs will increase next year. He is considering upgrading the existing machine, which will cost $72,000. However, the variable costs will reduce from $500 to $400 for Ezee and from $900 to $800 for Focus.

REQUIRED   **A.** Assuming the sales mix is constant, calculate the contribution margin for the composite.
B. How many units of each model of bike should be sold to break even?
C. If RB's target after-tax income is $135,000, how many units of each model of bike should be sold?
D. In preparing a budget for next year, if RB proceeds with the new cost structure, calculate the contribution margin for the composite. What is the sales break even in units for each model?
E. With the new cost structure, if RB's target after-tax income is $135,000, how many units of each model of bike should be sold?
F. Based on the above information, does the degree of operating leverage increase or decrease after the change in the cost structure? What insights do you gain from the change of the cost structure? Should RB proceed with the change of the cost structure?

MINI-CASES

3.58 Cost Function, Operating Leverage, Keeping or Dropping a Business The university's Wildcat Lair caters to students and serves sandwiches and beverages. It has been reporting losses in past months. In July, for example, the loss was $5,000:

LO1, LO2, LO3, LO4, LO5

Revenue		$ 70,000
Expenses		
Purchases of prepared food	$21,000	
Serving personnel	30,000	
Cashiers	5,500	
Administration	10,000	
University surcharge	7,000	
Utilities	1,500	$ 75,000
Loss		$ (5,000)

The Lair purchases prepared food directly from University Food Services. This charge varies proportionately with the number and kind of meals served. Personnel paid by the Lair serve the food, tend the cash register, bus and clean tables, and wash dishes. The staffing levels rarely change; the existing staff can usually handle daily fluctuations in volume. Administrative costs are primarily the salaries of the manager and her office staff. Because the university provides support services for the Lair, such as payroll, human resources, and other administrative support, the university charges a surcharge of 10% of its revenues. Utility costs are the costs of cooling, heating, and lighting during its normal operating hours.

The university's management is considering closing the Wildcat Lair because it has been operating at a loss.

REQUIRED   INFORMATION ANALYSIS

The following questions will help you analyze the information for this problem. Do not turn in your answers to these questions unless your professor asks you to do so.

A. What is the breakeven point for Wildcat Lair from the university's perspective (including the university surcharge)? What is the breakeven point from Wildcat Lair's perspective (excluding the university surcharge)?

B. Define and calculate the degree of operating leverage for the Lair, ignoring the university surcharge.

C. From the perspective of university management, is the university surcharge a relevant cost in deciding whether to close the Lair? Why or why not?

D. Identify possible ways that operations could be modified so that some of the fixed costs become variable costs.

E. Given the Lair's cost function and operating leverage, describe possible benefits of modifying operations so that some of the fixed costs become variable costs.

REQUIRED   WRITTEN ASSIGNMENT

Turn in your answers to the following.

F. From the perspective of university management, describe the pros and cons of closing the Wildcat Lair.

G. Suppose you are the manager of the Wildcat Lair. Write a memo to persuade the university management to keep the club open.

3.59 Not-for-Profit Breakeven Price, Budget Alternatives The Little Beaver Daycare Centres, a not-for-profit organization, provides daycare services to low-income families in 20 communities in Alberta. The manager's summary report for the past four months of operations is reproduced here:

	March	April	May	June	Total
Number of children	849	821	778	842	3,290
Daycare fees	$ 4,230	$ 4,180	$ 3,875	$ 4,260	$ 16,545
Daycare staff salaries	13,254	13,256	13,254	14,115	53,879
Daycare supplies used	3,182	3,077	2,934	3,175	12,368
Administrative salaries	3,197	3,198	3,197	3,412	13,004
Rent	1,000	1,000	1,000	1,100	4,100
Utilities	532	378	321	226	1,457
Other expenses	2,854	2,776	2,671	2,828	11,129
Total expenses	24,019	23,685	23,377	24,856	95,937
Operating surplus (loss)	$(19,789)	$(19,505)	$(19,502)	$(20,596)	$(79,392)

The daycare receives an operating subsidy from the city, but, unfortunately, the operating loss incurred through June ($79,392) is larger than anticipated. Part of the problem is the salary increases that went into effect in June, which were overlooked when the budget was submitted to the city last year. To compound the problem, the warm summer months traditionally bring with them an increase in additional summer outdoor activities. Thus, the daycare experiences additional costs during July.

The accountant made the following assumptions in developing the cost function:

- Salaries are fixed, and June values are used.
- Daycare supplies vary with seasonal activities.
- Rent and utilities are fixed, and last period's costs are used.
- Other expenses are mixed and, using regression, fixed cost is $702 and variable cost is $2.53 per child.

REQUIRED The centre management is considering an increase in daycare fees to reduce losses.

A. Develop a cost function for these data. You may have done this for Chapter 2, and in that case, use that cost function. Using the cost function you developed, solve for the average daycare fee necessary to break even, assuming that there are 940 children. Compare this new fee with the average daycare fee charged during March through June.

B. Suppose the centre raises its daycare fees to break even. What problems do you see from the families' perspective if the fee is raised?

C. In this setting, would an increase in fees be likely to affect number of children attending the daycare? What problems do you see from the centre's perspective if the fee is raised?

D. Other than raising the fee, what ideas might the centre consider to balance the budget?

3.60 **Integrating Across the Curriculum: Economics and Marketing** *Nonlinear revenue, maximize profits, CVP*

L01, L02, L04 *assumptions* Hollis Company manufactures and markets a regulator used to maintain high levels of accuracy in timing clocks. The market for these regulators is limited and highly dependent upon the selling price.

Based upon past relationships between the selling price and the resulting demand, as well as an informal survey of customers, management derived the following demand function, which is highly representative of the actual relationships:

$$D = 1,000 - 2 P$$

where

$$D = \text{Annual demand in units}$$
$$P = \text{Sale price per unit}$$

The estimated manufacturing and selling costs for the coming year are as follows:

Variable costs	
Manufacturing	$75 per unit
Selling	$25 per unit
Fixed costs	
Manufacturing	$24,000 per year
Selling	$6,000 per year

REQUIRED **A.** Write the function for total revenue. [*Hint:* Recall that total revenue equals price times quantity ($P \times Q$) and the demand function determines the quantity sold (Q).]

B. Write the total cost function, substituting the demand function for Q.

C. Perform a search on the Internet to find a quadratic equation calculator. Use the calculator to find the breakeven points. (*Hint:* Set the revenue function equal to the cost function and algebraically convert the equation to quadratic form: $aP^2 + bP + c = 0$.)

D. Draw a graph with total revenue and total cost for Q between zero and 1,000 units. Mark the breakeven points.

E. Determine the selling price that Hollis Company should charge per regulator and the number of regulators the company should sell to maximize the company's profits for the coming year. (*Hint:* Recall that profit is maximized when marginal revenue equals marginal cost. You must be able to differentiate a simple function to answer this question.)

F. Which CVP assumption does this situation violate? Explain.

G. Assume that for the past several years, the company sold regulators at the price you calculated in Part E and that volume varied between 375 and 425 units per year. In this situation, discuss whether it would be appropriate to use CVP analysis to estimate the company's profits.

4
Relevant Information for Decision Making

in brief Managers make a variety of decisions about operations over the next period, including special orders, outsourcing, keeping or dropping a product line or customer, and constrained resource management. Identifying relevant information such as revenues and costs is an important part of making these decisions. However, strategic fit and other qualitative factors are also important, sometimes overriding cost considerations. Managers must weigh the business risks of alternatives when choosing the best course of action. ■

After studying this chapter, you should be able to do the following:

LO1 Identify and use relevant information in decision making

LO2 Analyze the quantitative and qualitative information used in keep or drop decisions

LO3 Analyze the quantitative and qualitative information used in outsourcing (make or buy) decisions

LO4 Analyze the quantitative and qualitative information used in special order decisions

LO5 Analyze the quantitative and qualitative information used in product emphasis and constrained resource decisions

LO6 Describe factors that affect the quality of operating decisions

Should it Stay or Should it Go?

Bernard Weil/Toronto Star via Getty Images

SOURCES: Drake Bennett, "How Canada Goose Parkas Migrated South," Bloomberg Businessweek, March 13, 2015; "Canada Goose Acquires New Toronto Manufacturing Facility to Meet Global Demand," Canada Goose news release, January 13, 2015; ArminaLigaya, "Made-in-Canada Still Key for Canada Goose after Sale to U.S. Private-Equity Firm Bain, CEO Says," Financial Post, December 10, 2013; Stefania Moretti, "Canada Goose Soars with Unique Model," Sun News, October 21, 2011; Jason Buckland, "Is Outsourcing Essential for Canadian Companies?," MSN Canada, November 6, 2010; "Maintaining Local Production in the Outerwear Industry," Ethipedia, retrieved from http://ethipedia.net/canadagoose; Grant Robertson, "Year of the Goose," CTV News, no date.

Canada Goose has been producing extreme-weather outerwear for over 55 years. Canada Goose is an authentic Canadian success story of hard work and determination. Over a decade ago, as other Canadian apparel manufacturers were moving production offshore to cut costs, Canada Goose had a hard decision to make. Should the company follow suit and move to cheaper offshore locations or continue manufacturing products within Canada? Canada Goose made the unique decision to stay, keeping virtually all its production at home. "To me, a Canada Goose jacket is like a Swiss watch. You can't make a Swiss watch in China. You can't make a Canada Goose jacket in China either," says third-generation president and CEO Dani Reiss.

In order to become the premier global brand of Canadian-made, down insulated outerwear for extreme climates, Canada Goose decided consumers would value quality, authenticity, and functionality and would pay for the best. "Without being the best, it's hard to be more expensive," says Reiss. "For Canadian manufacturers it's important to look at value-added." Consumers appreciate the quality, as Canada Goose jackets retail for about $600 and up. Canada Goose jackets are designed to be worn in some of the coldest places imaginable and are equally popular on the trendy and much warmer streets of New York, Stockholm, Munich, Toronto, Paris, and Tokyo.

The luxury outerwear market has spread to the more than 50 countries they're sold in, and Canada Goose products are seen on such celebrities as actors Matt Damon, Drake, Maggie Gyllenhaal, and Hilary Duff. In the past decade, Canada Goose's sales grew from about $5 million to around $200 million a year.

To better control quality, the company owns several of the Canadian factories that produce the jackets. It bought its third factory in 2015—a 4,200 square metre (45,000 square foot) Toronto facility that had been making Canada Goose jackets on contract. In deciding to buy the factory from the supplier (for an undisclosed amount) and take over its employees, the company wanted more control over the supply chain and increased efficiency. The company continues to expand production and upgrade its existing facilities, making more than 500,000 jackets a year.

It has also invested heavily in training its 1,000 workers and is preparing for a shortage of qualified sewers through educational programs in the face of the country's apparel industry shrinking. A percentage of factory workers have been with Canada Goose for over 20 years.

In 2013, Canada Goose was purchased by a U.S.-based private-equity firm, Bain Capital, which has a reputation for outsourcing. Reiss says he made the decision to sell his family's company to Bain, retaining a 10% stake in Canada Goose, only because Bain promised to retain production in Canada. "Made in Canada is extremely important, and extremely important to Canada Goose, and we've chosen partners to whom it is also extremely important to," Reiss says. "We have chosen partners who will make the right decision for the business, and the right decision for Canada Goose is to be made in Canada. And that is a sentiment that did not exist until we proved it was possible."

Relevant Information for Decision Making

LO1   Identify and use relevant information in decision making

Relevant information is important to each of us when we make decisions. A decision as simple as choosing a restaurant for dinner involves analysis of relevant information. What is the estimated cost? What is the quality of the food? Is the atmosphere pleasing? What are the opportunity costs (e.g., forgone experiences at other restaurants and money used in other ways)?

This chapter focuses on identifying and analyzing relevant information for making sound business decisions. As we learned in Chapter 1, accounting systems include a great deal of information, and managers and accountants must identify that which is relevant for a particular decision. They also consider a variety of factors, including organizational strategies and business risks, before choosing a course of action.

The concepts introduced in this chapter apply to a wide range of business decisions. However, we will concentrate on judgment in identifying and analyzing relevant information for the following types of operating decisions:

▶ Whether to commit resources for a special order
▶ Whether to use internal resources or to outsource some activities
▶ Whether to discontinue a product line or business subunit or segment
▶ How to manage limited resources

Process for Identifying and Analyzing Relevant Information

Many management decisions are unique, requiring use of a decision-making process rather than a "cookbook" approach that could be memorized over time. Appendix 1B introduced Steps for Better Thinking, which is an example of a decision-making process that leads to higher-quality decisions. Exhibit 4.1 demonstrates how Steps for Better Thinking relates specifically to the use of relevant information for decision making.

Identifying and Envisioning the Problem and Alternatives. We do not know which information is relevant to decision making until we know the type of decision to be made. We address problems more correctly and efficiently by clarifying the type of problem before jumping into an analysis. For example, if you need to make a decision about buying a new car or keeping the one you own, some costs are not relevant, such as parking fees at the

▶EXHIBIT 4.1

Strategic Use of Relevant Information for Decision Making

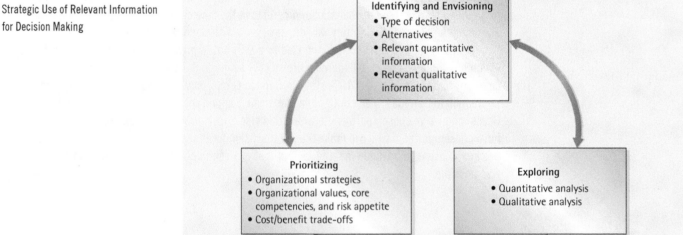

university. However, you need to know the brand, year, and model of the car you are considering in order to identify the relevant cash flows, as there are differences in fuel consumption, insurance rates, and so on among brands and models. You might also wish to consider qualitative factors such as colour, trunk size, or reliability.

Until you choose a specific car to consider, you cannot accurately identify relevant cash flows or qualitative factors. You might also want to consider other options or approaches to resolving the situation. If it's the colour of your current car you dislike, you could perhaps repaint rather than replace it. Another option could be to lease rather than purchase a new car. Higher-quality decision making often involves seeking new approaches by thinking "out of the box."

Identifying Relevant Quantitative Information. Most business decisions require analysis of both quantitative and qualitative information. **Quantitative information** is numerical information that is available for addressing a problem. In Chapter 1, we learned about relevant and irrelevant cash flows. To be relevant, cash flows must (1) arise in the future and (2) vary with the action taken. We identify relevant cash flows by first analyzing the decision alternatives and then selecting cash flows that are unique to each alternative. We ignore irrelevant (unavoidable) cash flows—those that do not differ among alternatives. Sunk costs (i.e., costs that were incurred in the past) are always irrelevant.

Where do we find quantitative information? We obtain some of the relevant information, such as past revenues and costs, from the accounting system. In addition, each decision requires specific kinds of information gathered from outside the accounting system. Such information could include bids from other companies to provide services such as payroll and telemarketing, or to manufacture parts prior to final assembly. If some of the quantitative information is unknown, we might need to estimate it. For example, we can use regression analysis as shown in Chapter 2 to estimate the fixed and variable portions of a mixed cost.

Identifying Relevant Qualitative Information. Rarely in the business world do decisions rely solely on the results of quantitative analysis. **Qualitative information**—factors that are not valued in numerical terms—is vital to good decision making. Qualitative factors can be difficult to identify, because no formula assures us that we have considered the important issues. Qualitative information might be identified from experience with similar past decisions, through research into business risks and other factors that might affect the outcomes of a decision, or by means of discussions with managers or other personnel. When outsourcing is being considered, several qualitative factors could override quantitative factors, such as the ability of the outside vendor to provide a good or service at the same level of quality and in a timely manner.

Performing Quantitative and/or Qualitative Analyses. Quantitative calculations usually focus on comparing the relevant cash flows across alternatives. Sometimes we use cost-volume-profit (CVP) analysis, as learned in Chapter 3. In this chapter, we will learn another quantitative technique—linear programming. We select one or more techniques that provide the appropriate information needed for making a specific decision. Qualitative factors are incorporated into our analysis using judgment, although sometimes they can be analyzed using simulation or other quantitative techniques. Occasionally, the qualitative factors are so important that they override the need to perform quantitative analysis. For example, many students live off campus, even though it is usually more expensive, because the benefits of a sense of independence and increased freedom in lifestyle choices outweigh the increased costs in the minds of these students.

Prioritizing Issues to Arrive at a Decision. We learned in Chapter 1 that operating decisions should be guided by organizational strategies in conjunction with the organization's vision, core competencies, and risk appetite. Before conducting detailed analysis for a decision, managers should consider whether or how the decision might affect progress toward long-term goals. Sometimes strategic and risk considerations take priority over other factors. For example, concerns about the reliability of a supplier's parts might lead managers to eliminate that vendor from consideration. The managers would then explore alternatives such as purchasing from other vendors or manufacturing the parts in-house. As shown by the arrows in Exhibit 4.1, strategic concerns can influence all aspects of the decision-making process.

Each operating decision introduced in this chapter employs a guideline, a quantitative decision rule, to make the decision. Using quantitative analysis, we identify the decision alternative that maximizes short-term cash flows. However, we do not always choose that option. Managers often make trade-offs among important issues when deciding on a course of action. In addition, we evaluate the quality of the information used, relying more on higher-quality information than on lower-quality information. When decision makers fail to consider the quality of information, they may make poor decisions. For example, in a study of German firms, researchers Gorzig and Stephan found that outsourcing improved employee productivity, yet it decreased return on sales because transaction costs for transportation, contracting, and monitoring for outside vendors overwhelmed the savings.[1] Assuming that the managers expected to achieve cost savings, the authors concluded that it might be difficult for managers to identify and evaluate the transaction costs that offset savings from purchasing outsourced products or using offshore labour, suggesting that the quality of information related to transaction costs is low, hampering the ability of managers to make optimal decisions.

Operating Decision Examples

The remainder of the chapter illustrates the following types of non-routine operating decisions:

- ▶ Keep or drop
- ▶ Insource or outsource (make or buy)
- ▶ Special orders
- ▶ Constrained resources
- ▶ Product emphasis—multiple resource constraints and multiple products

Product Line and Business Segment (Keep or Drop) Decisions

LO2 Analyze the quantitative and qualitative information used in keep or drop decisions

When organizations provide multiple products (goods or services), they periodically review operating results for each product, group of products (product line), or business segment and decide whether to keep or drop the product or segment. If financial statement data are used in these calculations, average costs are often mistakenly included as relevant information. However, managers need to separate relevant and irrelevant cash flows. Therefore, they may need to develop distinct cost functions for each product, product line, or segment.

General Rule for Keep or Drop Decisions

The general rule is that we want to be at least as well off after we discontinue a product or business segment as we were before we dropped it. Usually, this means that we discontinue a product or segment when the incremental profit from keeping it is negative. Thus, the decision rule is to drop if

Contribution margin < Relevant fixed costs + Opportunity cost

To apply this decision rule, we first separate costs into fixed and variable. We next consider whether the cost is avoidable if we drop the product or segment or unavoidable whether we do or not. To identify and estimate avoidable costs, we analyze the nature of the cost and its relation to the two alternatives (keep or drop). Variable costs are often avoidable and therefore relevant to the decision, whereas fixed costs usually include both avoidable and unavoidable

---

[1] B. Gorzig and A. Stephan, "Outsourcing and Firm-level Performance," German Institute for Economic Research, Discussion Paper 39, 2002.

costs. For example, dropping a product might mean that an employee in accounting or marketing could be laid off. The labour costs and fringe benefits for that employee are relevant to the keep or drop decision, because they are avoidable if the product is dropped. Alternatively, the lease cost for a manufacturing facility that produces a number of products is irrelevant because it is unavoidable if only one product is dropped. Opportunity costs include the potential contribution margin forgone when resources are devoted to an existing product or segment instead of to alternatives. For example, managers of grocery stores continuously monitor the contribution earned by different products in order to maximize profits earned from limited shelf space. When shelf space is devoted to one product, the company forgoes the potential contribution margin from another product.

The following Home Aide Services illustration provides an opportunity to practise making a keep or drop decision.

home aide services
KEEP OR DROP

Home Aide Services is a not-for-profit organization that provides a variety of services for people who prefer to live at home but need assistance. The organization has several lines of service, including housekeeping, meals, and shopping and transportation services. Lately, the organization has suffered a decline in surplus. The manager, Justin Krawczyk, wants to drop one of the services to increase profitability. Following are the monthly cash flows for each service:

example

Kristian Sekulic/iStockphoto

Cash Flow	Housekeeping	Meals	Shopping	Total
Revenues	$ 30,000	$15,000	$10,000	$55,000
Variable costs	15,000	3,000	1,000	19,000
Contribution margin	15,000	12,000	9,000	36,000
Fixed costs	20,000	6,000	5,000	31,000
Surplus (deficit)	$ (5,000)	$ 6,000	$ 4,000	$ 5,000

Quantitative Analysis

When Justin tells Elizabeth Klein, the accountant, that housekeeping services should be dropped to save the organization $5,000, Elizabeth says she needs to analyze costs further. The next day she reports to Justin that instead of having an overall surplus of $5,000, Home Aide Services would incur a deficit of $2,000 if housekeeping were dropped. She presents the following information about what would happen to the remaining product lines if housekeeping were discontinued:

Cash Flow	Meals	Shopping	Total
Revenues	$15,000	$10,000	$25,000
Variable costs	3,000	1,000	4,000
Contribution margin	12,000	9,000	21,000
Fixed costs	13,000	10,000	23,000
Surplus (deficit)	$(1,000)	$(1,000)	$(2,000)

Justin asks how this could be. Elizabeth explains that when she analyzed the costs in more detail, she found that the fixed costs for housekeeping included benefits for the housekeepers. The cost of benefits would be avoided if housekeeping were dropped. These costs are $8,000. Total fixed costs are now $23,000 ($31,000 − $8,000). These fixed costs are unavoidable

continued…

[2] "Kellogg's London Officially Ends Cereal Production Today." CBC News, December 20, 2014. Accessed July 24, 2015 at www.cbc.ca/news/canada/windsor/kellogg-s-london-officially-ends-cereal-production-today-1.2867538.

and are allocated to the remaining departments. They include the cost of amortization on cars as well as administrative costs for the entire organization that had been allocated to housekeeping.

Labour costs are a small part of the meals department's total cost. Only $1,000 of fixed costs would be avoided if meals were dropped; the employees who prepare meals also help with administrative work. Shopping and transportation includes $4,000 in avoidable fixed costs. This amount represents salary and benefits costs for drivers who are available all hours that the service is open.

Cash Flow	Housekeeping	Meals	Shopping	Total
Revenues	$30,000	$15,000	$10,000	$55,000
Variable costs	15,000	3,000	1,000	19,000
Contribution margin	15,000	12,000	9,000	36,000
Avoidable fixed costs	8,000	1,000	4,000	13,000
Department surplus	$ 7,000	$11,000	$ 5,000	23,000
Unavoidable fixed costs				18,000
Overall surplus				$ 5,000

Elizabeth prepares the following report for Justin:

Relevant Benefits and Costs	Housekeeping	Meals	Shopping
Revenue forgone	$(30,000)	$(15,000)	$(10,000)
Savings in labour and overhead	23,000	4,000	5,000
Net benefit (cost)	$ (7,000)	$(11,000)	$ (5,000)

With this new information, Justin analyzes the costs again. He realizes that all of the services are contributing to the unavoidable fixed costs and should be continued. This leads to the issue that the common fixed costs should not be allocated to each service to determine profitability and, therefore, not to the keep or drop decision making either. In fact, for decision making, common fixed costs should be subtracted from the combined contribution margin.

Cash Flow	Housekeeping	Meals	Shopping	Total
Revenues	$30,000	$15,000	$10,000	$55,000
Variable costs	15,000	3,000	1,000	19,000
Contribution margin	15,000	12,000	9,000	36,000
Fixed costs				31,000
Surplus (deficit)				$ 5,000

Qualitative Factors

Elizabeth observes that competitors provide all three services (housekeeping, meals, and shopping). Therefore, dropping housekeeping could affect demand for the other services. Clients might not want to deal with two separate organizations, when one could provide all the different services they need. Even if housekeeping were just breaking even, it should not be eliminated if dropping it would alienate current customers and cause demand for the other services to decrease. In addition, employee morale could suffer if a number of workers were laid off.

Strategic Prioritization

Given the new cost analysis and the qualitative factors, Justin decides to retain all of the current services. However, he decides to investigate alternative ways that the organization could improve its surplus. First, he considers any opportunity costs. If housekeeping were dropped, could Home Aide add nursing or other services instead? Would the surplus added from nursing be higher than housekeeping? ▪

> STRATEGIC RISK MANAGEMENT: HOME AIDE SERVICES

THE BUSINESS RISK OF DROPPING A PRODUCT If one of the services had actually resulted in a loss, would the manager of Home Aide Services make a different decision? Before dropping that service, the manager would need to consider whether some clients might drop all services and find another organization that could provide them. Most likely, the manager would need more information to evaluate this risk. For example, accounting records could be examined to determine the proportion of customers using multiple services. Existing customers could be surveyed about their preferences. Competitor service offerings could be investigated.

Customer Profitability

As the business environment becomes increasingly dynamic, organizations often obtain strategic benefit from developing more flexible operations. Customers are increasingly demanding additional services, such as timely delivery of small amounts of inventory or large amounts of support. Sometimes, the seller's costs to maintain these relationships are larger than the benefits. In addition, changes in the economic environment or strategic goals may require re-evaluation of customer relationships. Managers need to decide whether to keep, drop, or add individual customers or groups of customers. For example, Castle Key (formerly Allstate Floridian) decided to reduce its insurance risk in the State of Florida by dropping commercial coverage and 95,000 homeowner policies.[3] The process and decision rule for these decisions are similar to other keep or drop decisions. A customer should be dropped if

$$\text{Customer contribution margin} < \text{Relevant fixed costs} + \text{Opportunity cost}$$

Relevant cash flows include the revenues that will be forgone if the customer is dropped along with the costs to maintain the customer and deliver products or services. Potential relevant costs include the following:

- ▶ Avoidable costs of products manufactured or services provided
- ▶ Marketing, sales-order, and delivery costs
- ▶ Cost for equipment or other assets devoted to particular customers
- ▶ Product technical support, warranty costs, and product return handling
- ▶ Inventory carrying costs such as material handling, warehousing, and insurance
- ▶ Avoidable administrative costs for labour, facility, or other resources needed to satisfy customer demands
- ▶ Alternative uses for capacity devoted to customers

For a book publisher, relevant customer costs include costs related to book return policies. The publisher delivers the number of books requested by a book store, but the store typically has the right to return books that do not sell within a specified period of time. If returned books remain in inventory for long periods, the cost of providing the books could easily outweigh the revenues from small book store customers.

> RISK OF BIASED DECISIONS: CONFIRMATION BIAS

CONFIRMATION BIAS is a tendency to seek and interpret information to corroborate preconceptions. This bias may cause managers to misidentify or misinterpret relevant quantitative or qualitative information that would support choosing an alternative different than the one they prefer. For example, a manager who favours keeping a product may overlook opportunity costs, underestimate the product's relevant costs, or disregard negative market signals about the product's long-term viability. Considerable judgment is used in many business decisions, making it difficult to detect a manager's confirmation bias. Nevertheless, organizations can reduce the risk of biased decisions by pursuing contrary evidence and by vigorously debating the pros and cons of proposed actions.

> **CHAPTER REFERENCE**
Many customer-related costs vary with activities that are performed to satisfy customer needs. In Chapter 7, we will learn about identifying these activities, their costs, and cost drivers.

> **CHAPTER REFERENCE**
In Chapter 15, we will learn about just-in-time inventory practices, which eliminate most inventory carrying costs.

[3] "Allstate Floridian Applies to Scale Back, Drop 95,000 Homeowners," *Insurance Journal*, June 6, 2005, available at www.insurancejournal.com/magazines/southeast/2005/06/06/features/56495.htm.

Costs of Carrying Inventory

The costs of carrying inventory are often avoidable if a firm drops a customer or product. Thus, these costs can be relevant to keep or drop decisions. As we will learn in the next section of the chapter, inventory carrying costs may also be relevant to make or buy (outsourcing) decisions. When deciding how much inventory to keep on hand, managers consider the cost of carrying additional inventory, along with the order and transportation costs.

Inventory carrying costs are sometimes difficult to identify and separate from general overhead costs. However, these costs often include the following:

- ► Costs to process purchase orders
- ► Avoidable costs invested in the inventory, such as direct materials, direct labour, variable overhead, or fixed overhead
- ► Opportunity cost for alternative uses of cash, such as short-term investments or reductions in debt
- ► Costs to handle, warehouse, insure, and maintain inventory
- ► Opportunity cost of forgone sales from inventory shortages (stock-outs)
- ► Costs for tracking inventory and determining appropriate inventory levels
- ► Inventory shrinkage or value decline from breakage, theft, deterioration, or obsolescence

For book publishers, carrying costs would include material-handling costs of labour; forklifts, cranes, and any other equipment needed to handle cases of books in the warehouse; insurance on the warehouse facility and its contents; property taxes; resources devoted to the inventory, including direct materials, direct labour, and variable overhead; and costs to handle direct material purchase orders. In this industry, the costs of forgone sales from insufficient inventories of bestseller books can be large. However, the carrying costs of inventory for books that do not become bestsellers are also large.

Qualitative and Risk Factors for Keep or Drop Decisions

Relevant qualitative factors include any nonquantitative issues that managers should consider before making a decision. Here are examples of questions managers could ask to help them identify relevant qualitative factors, including business risks, for a keep or drop decision:

- ► How strategically important is this product, segment, or customer?
- ► Will dropping one product or customer affect the sales of other products?
- ► Will potential layoffs affect worker morale?
- ► How achievable are the revenue and cost estimates?
- ► What kinds of products and prices are competitors offering?
- ► How would dropping this product or customer affect overall organizational risk?

Exhibit 4.2 summarizes the information and decision rule used to determine if a company should keep or drop a product, service, branch, or division.

► EXHIBIT 4.2

Summary of Information Used and Decision Rule for the Keep Versus Drop Decision

Relevant Costs and Benefits	Irrelevant Costs	Decision Rule
• Contribution margin lost if dropped • Fixed costs avoided if dropped • Contribution margin loss or gain on other products/ segments	• Allocated common costs • Sunk costs	• Keep if— Contribution margin loss > fixed costs avoided + Contribution margin gain on other products/ segments • Drop if— Contribution margin lost < fixed costs avoided + Contribution margin gain on other products/ segments

Insource or Outsource (Make or Buy) Decisions

Outsourcing, the practice of finding outside vendors to supply products and services, has become increasingly common. Insourcing is the practice of providing a good or service from internal resources. For manufacturers, outsourcing decisions are often called make or buy decisions—should the company make the product or provide the service internally, or should the company buy it from the outside? Potential cost savings as well as organizational strategies drive such decisions. Some managers outsource any activity they view as unrelated to the organization's core competencies.

> **LO3** Analyze the quantitative and qualitative information used in outsourcing (make or buy) decisions

General Rule for Make or Buy Decisions

The general rule for insource or outsource decisions is to choose the option with the lowest relevant cost. Thus, the decision rule is to outsource (i.e., buy) if

> Cost to outsource < Cost to insource, or
>
> Cost to outsource < Relevant variable costs + Relevant fixed costs + Opportunity cost

To apply this decision rule, we first separate costs into fixed and variable. The variable costs are usually relevant. Existing fixed costs are relevant only if they can be avoided through outsourcing. The costs for insourcing also include opportunity costs. Sometimes, extra space or capacity from outsourcing can be converted to other uses. Another product could be manufactured or the space rented out. The forgone benefits (contribution margin from the new product or rent payments) are an opportunity cost for insourcing. The following Roadrunner Publishers (Part 1) illustration provides an opportunity to practise making an outsourcing decision.

roadrunner publishers, part 1
INSOURCE OR OUTSOURCE

Roadrunner Publishers produces the book covers for its hardbound books. Recently, Marliss Book Binders purchased new robotic equipment that cuts, trims, and prints book covers in one process. Marliss offered to provide book covers for Roadrunner at $2.00 per book. Mark Bonaray, the cost accountant for Roadrunner Publishers, analyzes the cost information for internally producing hardbound book covers as follows:

alterfalter/Shutterstock

	Total Costs for 100,000 Book Covers	Cost per Unit
Direct materials	$ 75,000	$0.75
Direct labour	50,000	0.50
Manufacturing overhead	100,000	1.00
Foreman's salary	50,000	0.50
Total cost	$275,000	$2.75

After summarizing the costs for producing the book covers in-house, Mark needs to identify costs that are relevant and irrelevant to the decision. First, he gathers more information. He learns from the production manager that the foreman could be laid off if the book covers are outsourced. As a cost accountant, Mark already knows that manufacturing overhead is an indirect cost. In this case, it is allocated to books based on the number of direct labour hours used in each production process. Overhead costs will be incurred even if the book covers are outsourced. However, after examining past utility bills, Mark estimates that closing off the part of the plant where book covers are produced would save about $30,000, or $0.30 per book cover.

continued...

example

Quantitative Analysis

Although outsourcing would save $30,000 of the manufacturing overhead, the remaining $70,000 (or $0.70 per book cover) will be incurred under each alternative and is, therefore, irrelevant to the decision. The relevant production and outsourcing costs for this decision are as follows:

	Cost per Unit		Total Cost for 100,000 Book Covers	
Relevant Costs	Make	Buy	Make	Buy
Purchase book covers		$2.00		$200,000
Direct materials	$0.75		$ 75,000	
Direct labour	0.50		50,000	
Manufacturing overhead	0.30		30,000	
Foreman's salary	0.50		50,000	
Total relevant costs	$2.05	$2.00	$205,000	$200,000

Based only on the preceding cost information, Roadrunner would save $5,000 by outsourcing the book covers. Alternatively, we can use the incremental or differential approach to calculate the benefit or cost of outsourcing. Because Roadrunner is currently producing the book covers, we then take the outsourcing position to calculate which option has lower costs:

	Total Cost for 100,000 Book Covers
Cost of purchasing book covers (Relevant costs)	$(200,000)
Cost savings of not producing:	
Direct materials	$ 75,000
Direct labour	50,000
Manufacturing overhead	30,000
Foreman's salary	50,000
Total cost savings	$ 205,000
Net benefit (cost) of purchase	$ 5,000

Calculations using the incremental or differential approach show a positive $5,000, which means that the cost savings is greater than the cost of purchase, and therefore, Roadrunner should proceed with the outsourcing decision.

Mark has not yet considered potential opportunity costs of continuing to produce the book covers in-house. If Roadrunner Books has an alternative use for the space that houses the book-cover operations, the contribution margin from the use of that space would be relevant to the decision. For simplicity, we assume that Roadrunner's management has no alternative use for the space and, therefore, no opportunity costs to consider for this decision.

Qualitative Analysis

Another factor Mark considers is the quality of the book covers, which is emphasized in Roadrunner's book production process. Roadrunner's sales managers believe that high-quality covers are important to sales. The quality of Marliss's sample covers appears to be high, possibly even higher than Roadrunner's current level of quality.

Mark is also concerned about the timeliness of delivery. He speaks with Roadrunner's book-cover supervisor, who explains that the department is able to respond to changes in production volumes if given lead time. It has been relatively easy to have Roadrunner's employees

[4] "Bombardier Grants Authority to Offer CSeries—The New Generation Five-Abreast Commercial Aircraft," company news release, February 22, 2008; "Bombardier *CSeries* Aircraft Program Reaches Another Milestone," company news release, March 25, 2010.
[5] "International Association of Outsourcing Professionals' 2011 Trends Forecast Shows Industry Redefined," association news release, December 23, 2010.

work overtime or to hire part-time employees when a book appears to be a best seller, causing production levels to rise. When Mark asks Marliss about its ability to manage a very large order caused by unanticipated demand, the sales representative cannot guarantee that such an order could be produced quickly. This response concerns Mark, who is aware that when books are bestsellers, large volumes must be produced quickly.

Strategic Prioritization

When Mark summarizes the relevant information for the decision, he concludes that the savings from outsourcing and the quality differences are relatively small. In addition, he decides that being able to meet demand is worth the additional cost. Based on his analysis, he recommends that the company continue producing its own book covers. ■

Quality and Outsourcing Decisions

Product or service quality is often a major factor in outsourcing decisions. To ensure high quality, organizations typically negotiate outsourcing contracts that stipulate specific performance criteria, such as product specifications and timeliness. Some organizations use multiple outsource vendors to avoid overreliance on any one vendor. However, few outside vendors may be available for some activities, increasing the risk of quality problems.

On the other hand, organizations sometimes outsource because they find it difficult to or do not want to ensure high quality internally. Sometimes, rapid growth prevents an organization from developing sufficient expertise in house. Or the organization's managers do not consider an activity to be a core competency; they do not expend sufficient resources internally to achieve both cost effectiveness and high quality. For example, many e-commerce retailers outsource their warehouse operations to distribution companies that hold and deliver inventories for them. Unfortunately, many distribution companies are not equipped to fill many small orders, and they might be unable to handle an increasingly large number. Thus, some e-commerce retailers have been dissatisfied with the quality of distribution company performance.

As international outsourcing has become increasingly popular, organizations need to consider a variety of qualitative factors. Research conducted by the Centre for Outsourcing Research & Education (CORE) (www.core-outsourcing.org) reported that although many Canadian companies still see outsourcing as a tactic in achieving business targets (such as cost savings), larger organizations increasingly view outsourcing as a strategic response to the difficulty experienced in accessing skills in a wide range of operational and administrative areas.

Exhibit 4.3 summarizes the information and decision rule used to determine if a company should make or buy a product component, product, service, etc.

Relevant Costs and Benefits	Irrelevant Costs	Decision Rule
• Cost of purchase	• Unavoidable fixed costs	• Make if—
• Saving on variable costs + avoidable fixed costs	• Sunk costs	Cost of purchase > Cost savings of not making + Opportunity cost (contribution margin gain from other projects)
• Opportunity cost (contribution margin gain from other projects)		• Buy if—
		Cost of purchase < Cost savings of not making + Opportunity cost (contribution margin gain from other projects)

▶ EXHIBIT 4.3

Summary of Information Used and Decision Rule for Make Versus Buy Decision

> **EXHIBIT 4.4**
Examples of Financial Institution Considerations for International IT Outsourcing

- Corporate and cultural differences
- Potential language barriers
- Legal jurisdiction for contract disputes
- Political and economic stability
- Impact on existing employee morale
- Currency exchange rate risk

- Privacy, data protection, and security breach laws
- Intellectual property rights
- Employment laws
- Partner financial viability

Source: Adapted from BITS Financial Services Roundtable, www.icba.org/files/PDFs/bits2003framework.pdf, p. 63. Used by permission.

> **BUSINESS PRACTICE**
In late 2009, **Toyota** began recalling more than 8 million vehicles due to mechanical problems. University of Utah professor Lyda Bigelow says what is likely to blame is Toyota's outsourcing of specialized components during a period of rapid expansion to suppliers with few incentives to maintain quality. "Generating an in-house infrastructure to accommodate increased production would've taken years," she says.[6]

Exhibit 4.4 presents a list of factors that financial institutions would consider in their decisions to outsource information technology.

Following are examples of questions managers could ask to help them identify relevant qualitative factors, including business risks, for an outsourcing (make or buy) decision:

- ► Is this activity a core competency?
- ► Would outsourcing this activity increase managerial attention devoted to core activities?
- ► Does this activity involve highly sensitive information?
- ► If we outsource this activity, will our organization lose strategic skills?
- ► How important are high quality and timeliness?
- ► Is it easier to ensure high quality and timeliness via insourcing or outsourcing?
- ► Do reliable measures exist for monitoring the supplier's performance?
- ► Will the supplier meet contractual obligations? Can we easily monitor compliance?
- ► How would outsourcing affect our labour relations?
- ► Will the supplier use acceptable worker conditions and environmental practices?

●● > FOCUS ON ETHICAL DECISION MAKING: MEDICAL TOURISM

Dmitry Strizhakov/Shutterstock

One of the most visible examples of resource constraints in Canada is the public health system. A shortage of funds, medical personnel, and facilities add up to longer wait times for procedures and care. Provincial health systems will sometimes approve Canadians to go abroad for surgeries and other treatments, which can sometimes happen more quickly and cheaply than at home. The wait time for bariatric surgery, for example, is estimated at over five years in Canada.

But even the option of sending Canadians out of the country for medical care has become a less attractive way to relax resource constraints. Starting around 2006, Canadian governments have been reducing the volume of foreign medical services it pays for, while the costs of these services have more than doubled. In 2008–09, Canada spent more than $220 million on some 375,000 foreign medical services.

Canada is part of an estimated U.S. $40-billion annual global trend toward "medical tourism," where people travel for treatment that is cheaper, faster, or better than what they can get at home. Some people choose to have an elective procedure, such as cosmetic surgery, done in an exotic locale to combine it with a vacation. There is inbound

---

[6] "Outsourcing May Lead to Failure in Tough Times and in Good, Shows University of Utah Research," news release, University of Utah's David Eccles School of Business, August 5, 2010.

medical tourism, too. The British Columbia government is exploring making B.C. an international destination for medical procedures to gain much-needed revenues. Some private clinics have opened in Canada, targeting Americans by offering services at rates drastically lower than in the United States.

Sources: *Evolving Medical Tourism in Canada: Exploring a New Frontier,* Deloitte Center for Health Solutions, 2011; "Canadians Warming up to Idea of 'Medical Tourism,'" CTV News online, May 21, 2011.

THE ETHICS OF MEDICAL TOURISM

Medical tourism allows provincial health care systems to provide timely care to citizens, sometimes at a cost savings. But the trend raises a host of ethical questions. Should a public health care system support medical services in another country? Should a public health care system divert resources from its own citizens to serve medical tourists from abroad? How can a public health care system ensure the quality of services provided to its citizens overseas? When a Canadian pays for elective surgery abroad, develops complications, and then has to get follow-up care at home, should the public systems pay for that care?

Special Orders

Managers need to determine whether to accept a customer's special order—one that is not part of the organization's normal operations. This type of decision has no long-term strategic impact, because it involves a one-time sale of a specified quantity of goods or services, often at a reduced price. For example, Right Print has been asked by the local Boys and Girls Club to print postcards inviting potential donors to a silent auction fundraiser. The club would like a discounted price for the printing. If Right Print has idle capacity—that is, if machine and labour time are not fully occupied with other orders—the incremental (relevant) cost of taking the order is only the variable costs of postcard paper and ink. Therefore, Right Print could accept the order as long as the price at least covers the cost of the paper and ink.

L04 Analyze the quantitative and qualitative information used in special order decisions

ALTERNATIVE TERMS
Some people use the term *one-time-only order* instead of *special order.*

General Rule for Special Order Decisions

The quantitative decision rule for special orders is that we want to be at least as well off after accepting the order as we were before we accepted it. Thus, the decision rule is to accept the special order if

Price ≥ Relevant variable costs + Relevant fixed costs + Opportunity cost

The variable costs of delivering the product or service are usually relevant. However, variable selling costs such as commissions are often irrelevant if the company requesting the special order places it directly. Most fixed costs, such as rent and depreciation on plant and equipment, are unavoidable, making them irrelevant. Some fixed costs, such as the lease cost for a piece of equipment needed for the special order, are relevant because they are unique to the special order. Labour costs are relevant if the special order causes them to change. If the order replaces regular business, then the opportunity cost (i.e., forgone contribution margin) is also relevant. On the other hand, if idle capacity is available, the special order is acceptable if the organization at least breaks even.

The following Barkley Basketballs illustration provides an opportunity to practise making a special order decision.

CHAPTER REFERENCE
Chapter 2 defines *opportunity costs* as the benefits we forgo when we choose one alternative over the next best alternative.

barkley basketballs
SPECIAL ORDER

© Niwat Chaiyawoot/Shutterstock

Barkley Basketballs manufactures high-quality basketballs at its plant, which has a production capacity of 50,000 basketballs per month. Current production is 35,000 per month. The manufacturing costs of $24.00 per basketball are categorized as follows:

	Variable Cost per Unit	Fixed Cost per Unit (at 35,000 per month)	Total Cost per Unit
Manufacturing Costs:			
Direct materials	$12.00	$0.00	$12.00
Direct labour	2.00	0.00	2.00
Manufacturing overhead	0.50	9.50	10.00
Total cost to manufacture	$14.50	$9.50	$24.00
Sales commission	$ 1.00	$0.00	$ 1.00

Jack Chang operates not-for-profit basketball camps for disadvantaged youths on First Nations reserves and throughout inner cities in large urban areas. Jack asks Billie Park, CFO at Barkley Basketballs, to sell him 5,000 basketballs at $23.00 per ball, or $115,000 for the entire order.

Billie speaks to the cost accountant and then goes to the production floor to speak to several supervisors to gather information for this decision. She determines that the direct labour cost is variable. Workers are paid an hourly wage and are sent home when there are no balls to manufacture. These workers have no guaranteed salary, but demand is stable, so they always work at least half-time, and often 40 hours per week.

Billie asks about the manufacturing overhead and finds that it consists of variable and fixed costs incurred to run the plant where the basketballs are manufactured. Overhead includes insurance, property taxes, amortization, utilities, and various other plant-related costs. She finds that all of the fixed costs are related to a capacity level of 50,000 and will not change if she uses part of the idle capacity of 15,000 units. The foreman warns her, however, that once production exceeds 40,000 basketballs, bottlenecks occur, and the production process will slow down and cause inventory levels to congest the plant, sometimes requiring the company to pay overtime.

Quantitative Analysis

With the 5,000 basketballs produced for Jack, total production for the month would be 40,000 basketballs. Bottlenecks and slowdowns do not occur until production exceeds 40,000. Therefore, the special order is within the relevant range of production; the fixed costs should remain fixed. The relevant revenues and costs per basketball are as follows:

Selling price	$23.00
Variable costs (materials, labour, and overhead)	$14.50

In deciding whether to accept this special order, fixed costs are irrelevant because they are unavoidable. They will be incurred whether 35,000 or 40,000 basketballs are produced, with a total fixed cost of $332,500 ($9.50 × 35,000). However, the fixed cost per unit will be $8.31 instead of $9.50 if Barkley produces 40,000 basketballs. The variable cost of $1.00 sales commission per ball is also irrelevant because no sales representatives are involved in this particular transaction. Therefore, the contribution margin for each special order basketball would be $23.00 − $14.50 = $8.50. For 5,000 basketballs, the additional total contribution margin would be $42,500.

Qualitative Analysis

Based on the preceding quantitative analysis, Billie wants to accept the order. However, she still needs to consider the qualitative aspects of the decision. If she sells the basketballs at this lower price, other customers might demand lower prices, too, causing Barkley Basketballs to get into a pricing war with itself. However, Jack's organization is a not-for-profit; Billie doubts that other customers would object to giving it a discount.

Billie also believes that the company could enhance its reputation if Jack publicizes Barkley's support of the basketball camps. To evaluate the value of such publicity, she meets with the marketing manager, Mark Jordan. Mark cannot quantify the value, but he suggests that the publicity would definitely help promote the Barkley Basketballs brand name. In addition, the company has funded basketball camps in the past, in keeping with its policy of supporting the community.

Strategic Prioritization

After considering all of these factors, Billie discusses the special order with Jack. She offers to lower the price even further than $23.00. Jack is pleasantly surprised and offers to publicize Barkley's generosity. Billie and Jack settle on a price of $20.00 per ball. The contribution margin of the special order is reduced from $42,500 to $27,500 (5,000 balls at $20.00 − $14.50).

In this situation, Billie is willing to reduce the price of the special order even further for several reasons. In the past, the company donated money to not-for-profit basketball camps, so providing basketballs at a discount fits with management's desire to act in a socially responsible manner. She also believes the company will benefit from additional publicity. In addition, the company will still earn a profit from the special order. Although Billie has agreed to a lower price than usual, the special order meets the general rule: ample capacity is available, and the price is greater than the relevant costs (variable production costs).

Evaluating the Decision Process

Later that week, Billie is reviewing the decision to sell Jack Chang basketballs at $20.00 each. She visits with Mark Jordan, who insists that the value of the publicity exceeds the reduction of $15,000 in contribution margin. Billie concludes that the decision to sell the balls at a discount was appropriate.

Note the process used to make this decision. Billie first identified the type of decision (special order). She knew that she needed to know the relevant costs to make this decision. She determined whether enough capacity was available for the special order without causing fixed and variable costs to change. She categorized costs as fixed and variable to help identify relevant information. Next, she determined which costs were relevant and irrelevant to the special order. In this case, all of the variable production costs and none of the fixed costs or sales commissions were relevant. In manufacturing settings such as this one, where the same product is made repeatedly, manufacturing costs can be estimated with high accuracy. Billie had good reason to be confident in her quantitative analysis. She then weighed the quantitative and qualitative factors and decided that, overall, it was best for Barkley Basketballs to offer the special order at a price of $20.00 per ball.

Billie categorized costs and factors as shown in Exhibit 4.5.

	Fixed Costs	Variable Costs	Qualitative
Relevant	May increase if $Q > 40,000$ per month (beyond the relevant range)	Direct material + Direct labour + Variable overhead = $12 + $2 + $0.50 as long as $Q < 40,000$ per month	Potential publicity for selling ball at a discount
Irrelevant	Manufacturing overhead	Sales commission per ball (not paid on this special order)	Price concerns of other customers

▶ EXHIBIT 4.5

Relevant Costs and Qualitative Factors for Barkley Basketballs

▶EXHIBIT 4.6

Summary of Information Used and Decision Rule for Special Order

Relevant Costs and Benefits	Irrelevant Costs	Decision Rule
• Incremental revenues from the order	• Allocated common costs	• Accept if
	• Sunk costs	Incremental revenues > Total relevant costs
• Incremental costs (including variable and fixed costs) of filling the order		• Reject if
• Opportunity cost of filling the order		Incremental revenues < Total relevant costs

Exhibit 4.6 summarizes the information and decision rule used to determine if a company should accept a special order.

●● > STRATEGIC RISK MANAGEMENT: BARKLEY BASKETBALLS

SPECIAL ORDER DECISION PROCESS Note the process used to make the Barkley Basketballs decision. Billie first identified the type of decision (special order). To identify relevant costs, she (1) determined whether enough capacity was available for the special order without causing fixed and variable costs to change, and (2) categorized costs as fixed and variable. In this case, all of the variable production costs and none of the fixed costs or sales commissions were relevant. In manufacturing settings such as this one, where the same product is made repeatedly, manufacturing costs can be estimated with high accuracy. Billie had good reason to be confident in her quantitative analysis. She then identified qualitative factors related to the decision, and summarized the relevant information, as shown in Exhibit 4.5. How did Billie reach a conclusion that the special order was appropriate? She determined that the benefits of the special order included earning incremental profit, gaining publicity, and contributing to the community. Billie weighed these benefits against the cost of offering a discount from the company's usual selling price.

Special Orders and Pricing Policies

▶ **CHAPTER REFERENCE**

Chapter 14 addresses general pricing policies.

Under the quantitative decision rule, managers are willing to accept a special order as long as the selling price is at least equal to incremental costs—in other words, as long as the incremental contribution margin is zero, or positive. If excess capacity exists, the minimum acceptable selling price is the sum of the per-unit relevant variable and fixed costs. Typical prices charged by most organizations are higher than this minimum price, as prices are usually set so that the organization will earn a profit. Why would an organization be willing to accept a special order at a price that covers only incremental costs? By definition, a special order is not part of the organization's normal operations. If excess capacity exists, and if the price on a special order will not affect prices on regular business, then the organization is better off accepting special orders that generate at least some incremental profit.

▶ **BUSINESS PRACTICE**

It's Show Time!

What is the minimum acceptable price for a theatre seat on the day of the performance? Regular ticket prices are set to cover fixed and variable costs, plus provide profit. However, on the day of a performance, seats often cannot be sold at regular prices. Almost all of the costs for a theatre performance are fixed, so the incremental cost to seat another patron is very small—probably near zero. As the time of a performance approaches, the opportunity cost becomes zero because an unsold seat would provide no revenue. Thus, tickets sold at any price provide an incremental contribution.

Theatres use several methods to sell discounted tickets on the day of a performance. Theatregoers to the Stratford Shakespeare Festival in Ontario, for example, can purchase same-day tickets two hours before the performance in person or over the phone for discounts ranging from 20 to 50%. Various Toronto productions use a ticket consolidator such as T.O. Tix, which sells rush seats online and at its downtown booth from noon to 5 p.m. on the day of the performance at various discounts.

Source: "Rush Tickets," Stratford Shakespeare Festival, available at www.stratfordfestival.ca; T.O. Tix website, www.totix.ca/.

Qualitative and Risk Factors for Special Order Decisions

Relevant qualitative factors for a special order include any nonquantitative issues that managers should consider before making a decision. These factors vary across organizations and across orders. Here are examples of questions managers could ask to identify relevant qualitative factors, including business risks, for a special order:

- ► Does this order help achieve a strategic goal, such as improved brand recognition or social responsibility?
- ► Will this order take attention away from orders that are more important strategically?
- ► If we give this customer a discount, will other customers also expect a lower price?
- ► How accurate are our capacity estimates? Can we deliver this order without disrupting schedules for more profitable, regular business?
- ► Will this order lead to additional orders from a potential new customer?
- ► Will this order help retain the business of an existing profitable customer?
- ► If we ask employees to work overtime, could this order lead to labour problems?

Product Emphasis Decisions

Instead of simply responding to demand and advertising products that sell well, managers may want to focus consumer attention on products that contribute more to profitability. Managers choose to emphasize particular products in their product mix through promotions and advertising campaigns or by providing incentives for salespersons. Deciding which products to emphasize requires a short-term decision.

> **L05** Analyze the quantitative and qualitative information used in product emphasis and constrained resource decisions

General Rule for Product Emphasis Decisions

When no capacity constraints apply or alternative uses of fixed resources are available, the products with the highest contribution margins per unit are emphasized. The general rule is to rank products by contribution margin per unit and then emphasize products with higher contribution margins. This approach assumes that fixed costs are unaffected by product mix or customer requirements.

> ▣ **ALTERNATIVE TERMS**
> The following pairs of terms are synonymous: *product-mix decision* and *product emphasis decision*; *scarce resources* and *constrained resources*.

Theory of Constraints and Constrained Resources

According to the Theory of Constraints, managers will always face a constraint in their operations. Constraints are resource limitations and can be shortages of direct material or labour, or bottlenecks in the manufacturing process. A bottleneck is any resource or process that limits overall capacity. Constraints can be managed through a sequential four-step process. First, managers identify the constraint. If the constraint is materials or labour, managers may need to acquire additional resources and possibly pay more for them. If the constraint is a bottleneck, it must be identified. Because manufacturing and service delivery processes include a number of dependent events, it can sometimes be difficult to find the bottleneck. Second, the pace of manufacturing throughput or service delivery is set at the same pace as the bottleneck. This step usually means slowing down the production process. The slowdown reduces the costs of congestion that arise when products or services are waiting for the next step in production. Third, managers need to find improvements for the bottleneck to increase throughput. Fourth, when this link is no longer a constraint, managers identify the next constraint and repeat the process. Demand sets the throughput pace within this process. And when production is balanced with demand and no more bottlenecks exist, demand becomes the constraint. Then, managers should focus on increasing demand until a new constraint arises within the system. Therefore, according to the Theory of Constraints, managers will always face a constraint.

Internal constraints include limits in capacity, materials, or labour. For example, in the insource-outsource illustration, Roadrunner Publishers needed cardboard to make book covers. The company could face a shortage of direct materials, or a *direct materials constraint*. A shortage of labour to run machines or to load books into packing crates would be a *labour constraint*. Similarly, a shortage of machines to bind the covers onto the books would be a *capacity constraint*. When faced with one or more constrained resources, managers have several options. They may

1. Emphasize products to maximize the contribution margin within the constraint.

2. Relax the constraint by

   ▸ Purchasing goods or services from an outside supplier.
   ▸ Increasing the speed and constancy of bottlenecks by operating them during breaks and meals.
   ▸ Increasing internal capacity by using overtime, outsourced labour or processes, and buying new equipment.
   ▸ Redesigning products and processes to use existing capacity more efficiently.
   ▸ Offloading some products that use high-technology bottleneck resources to older, less-efficient equipment that performs the same task.

Managers can also maximize the contribution margin while simultaneously adopting one or more ways to relax the constraint.

Exhibit 4.7 summarizes the information and decision rule used to determine which product or service should be emphasized under the resources constraint.

▸ **CHAPTER REFERENCE**

Chapter 17 discusses increasing throughput, the rate at which product moves through the manufacturing process to the point of sale, or the rate at which services are produced.

▸ **BUSINESS PRACTICE**

Eliahu Goldratt developed the Theory of Constraints, a formal method used to analyze organizational constraints and to improve operations. For more information, go to www.goldratt.com/.

▸ **BUSINESS PRACTICE**

Companies around the world face the constraint of growing demand and therefore rising prices for natural resources as up to 3 billion more consumers will join the middle class by 2030, according to a report by business researchers at the McKinsey Global Institute. The report estimates that demand for steel, for example, will rise by 80% over the next two decades.[7]

▸ **EXHIBIT 4.7**

Summary of Information Used and Decision Rule for Constraint Resource Decision

Relevant Costs and Benefits	Irrelevant Costs	Decision Rule
• Contribution margin per unit of the constrained resources (profitability index [PI])	• Contribution margin per unit	• Allocate the most constrained resources to the product with the highest contribution margin per unit of the constrained resources (PI)

---

[7] McKinsey Global Institute, "Report Explores How to Meet Growing Demands for Natural Resources over the Next Twenty Years," news release issued on CNW Newswire, November 22, 2011.

General Rule for Choosing the Product Mix When Resources Are Constrained

When resources are constrained, we need to emphasize products and services that maximize the contribution margin per unit of constrained resource. For example, Fabulous Furniture produces teak tables and chairs for outdoor use. Normally, the company sells about 100 tables and 800 chairs per month. Because of a strike at the local shipyards, it is unable to purchase enough lumber locally to meet current demand.

The sales manager wants to know which product to emphasize—the tables or the chairs—to maximize profits. To make this decision, the accountant calculates the contribution margin per board foot for tables and chairs. The contribution margin per table is $400, and the contribution margin per chair is $150. A table requires 4 board feet of teak, and a chair requires 2 board feet. The contribution margin per board foot for tables is $100 ($400 ÷ 4 board feet) and for chairs is $75 ($150 ÷ 2 board feet). To maximize the contribution margin, the sales manager should emphasize tables and sell as many as possible. If the demand for tables is filled, then the sales manager should emphasize chairs.

General Rule for Relaxing Constraints for One or Two Products

The general rule for relaxing a short-term constraint for direct materials, direct labour, or capacity is that managers should be willing to pay not only what they are already paying but also some or the entire contribution margin per unit of constrained resource. Their goal is to acquire added capacity, thereby eliminating the constraint.

In the furniture example, Fabulous Furniture is currently paying $50 per board foot for teak. When the company has manufactured as many tables and chairs as possible with the limited supply of teak, it will still experience demand for chairs. Customers will buy elsewhere if they cannot purchase chairs from Fabulous. Fabulous forgoes $75 in contribution margin per board foot on each chair that customers would have purchased had teak been available. Consequently, Fabulous can afford to pay what it currently pays ($50), plus up to the entire contribution margin per board foot ($75) to buy more teak. If Fabulous can find a source of teak for $125 ($50 + $75) or less per board foot, it can meet customer demand for chairs.

As the variable cost per unit (including the new cost of materials or labour) approaches the selling price of the product or service, managers become indifferent to purchasing more of the constrained resource for continued production. This general rule is valid under the following assumptions:

▶ The organization will forgo sales if the resource constraint is not relaxed.
▶ Fixed costs are unaffected by short-term decisions made to relax constraints.
▶ The managers want to maximize profits in the short term.
▶ Sales of one product do not affect sales of other products.

Capacity constraints are time constraints; that is, we have limited time available for processing products because one or more bottlenecks slow production. Any process, part, or machine that limits overall capacity is a bottleneck. To maximize use of bottleneck resources, we emphasize products that have the highest contribution margin per bottleneck hour. We calculate the relevant contribution margin in terms of time needed at the bottleneck resource.

For example, suppose Fabulous has only one three-axis milling machine (a computerized piece of equipment that cuts and routs unusual shapes). The milling machine processes all of the tables and chairs, but it can process only 4 tables per hour or 12 chairs per hour. The contribution margin per machine hour for tables is $1,600 (4 × $400) and for chairs is $1,800 ($150 × 12). Chairs should be emphasized because they have the highest contribution per hour at the bottleneck resource.

Roadrunner Publishers, Part 2, provides an opportunity to practise making a constrained resource decision.

alterfalter/Shutterstock

example

roadrunner publishers, part 2
CONSTRAINED RESOURCE

Suppose the managers of Roadrunner Publishers decide that the company should continue to make its own book covers. In performing his analysis, Mark assumes that ample capacity and materials are available. However, one of Roadrunner's children's books, *Barry Plotter, Mathematical Wizard*, sells many more copies than expected. This increase in demand leads to a shortage of the special cardboard needed for the book covers. In turn, Roadrunner is unable to publish enough books to meet current demand. Customers, both children and their parents, are becoming quite frustrated.

Qualitative Analysis

Mark discusses the cardboard shortage with the sales manager, Cathy Nakamura, who thinks the company will, in all likelihood, forgo sales if demand cannot be met in a timely manner. In addition, the sales manager believes Roadrunner must continue to build positive brand name recognition for the *Barry Plotter* series so that further books in the series will be well received. Given this information, Mark would like to find some way to produce enough books to meet customer demand.

Quantitative Analysis

The books that have already been produced and sold covered all of the company's fixed costs related to developing, editing, and designing the books and their covers. The wholesale price of the books is $10.00 each. The direct materials ($0.75) and direct labour ($0.50) costs for the covers total $1.25. The remaining variable costs for each book are $1.50 for paper and $1.50 royalty to the author. Therefore, total variable costs per book are $4.25, and the contribution margin per book is $5.75.

At Mark's request, the purchasing agent, Miguel Costa, researches alternative cardboard suppliers. Although Miguel locates a supplier, he is concerned because the lowest-cost supplier is demanding a price of $4.00 per cover for timely delivery.

Strategic Prioritization

Mark decides that, in the short run, he is willing to give up some of the contribution margin for this title to build long-term customer satisfaction. Therefore, he is willing to pay as much as the original cost of the cardboard ($0.75 per book) and the original contribution margin ($5.75 per book), or $6.50 per book. He recommends that Miguel purchase additional cardboard at the asking price of $4.00 per book. The variable costs for this additional printing now include $4.00 (book cover materials), $0.50 (book cover labour), $1.50 (paper), and $1.50 (royalty), for a total of $7.50 per book. Thus, the contribution margin from each additional book that Roadrunner produces and sells will be $2.50 ($10.00 − $7.50). Even though this amount is lower than the original contribution margin of $5.75, Roadrunner continues to earn at least some contribution margin through its effort to relax the constrained resource of the book cover cardboard. ■

●● > STRATEGIC RISK MANAGEMENT: ROADRUNNER PUBLISHERS
(PART 2)

REDUCING THE RISK OF LOST SALES Why did the manager in Roadrunner Publishers (Part 2) decide to relax the book cover constraint? He believed the company faced a risk of lost current and future sales. He decided to reduce this risk by accepting a lower contribution margin in the short term. What other options were available for relaxing the constraint? The company probably could not satisfy demand by increasing the efficiency with which it uses cardboard to make book covers. However, Roadrunner might have been able to outsource the book covers if other companies had cardboard stock on hand. Or Roadrunner could have purchased a less expensive cardboard stock to meet immediate demand.

The preceding illustration is simplistic compared to most business environments. Most organizations have capacity constraints that affect more than one resource and more than one product.

General Rule for Relaxing Constraints with Multiple Constraints and Multiple Products

The general rule is that managers want to maximize profits in the short term by selecting the product mix that achieves the highest contribution margin per set of constrained resources. When multiple resource constraints and multiple products are involved, managers must find the product mix that maximizes the contribution margin.

To find this mix, simultaneous equations are solved using linear programming, a mathematical technique that maximizes a linear objective function (such as the sum of contribution margins from multiple products) subject to linear constraints (such as the number of hours available for different manufacturing or services processes). Optimal solutions can be computed using linear programming software packages such as Excel Solver and Vanguard DecisionPro.

Quantitative Analysis for Multiple Products and Multiple Constraints

When multiple products use different amounts of multiple resources, we set up the equations needed to solve the linear programming problem as follows:

1. Determine the contribution margin for each product and lay out the objective (target) function to be maximized.

2. List the amount of constrained resources required per product and the total amount of constrained resource available (often measured in hours).

3. Solve for the optimal product mix, using Excel Solver or other software.

4. Interpret the output.

The output from Excel Solver and other programs provides information about binding constraints and slack resources. A binding constraint is a resource that limits production, such as the number of hours available for inspection. Slack resources do not limit production and could be used if no other constraints limit production. Slack resources reflect idle capacity.

Excel Solver output also provides a "shadow price" that tells us the contribution margin per constrained resource, given the other constraints in the problem. In addition, Excel Solver gives information about points at which the optimal product mix would change if changes occurred in contribution margins or constrained resources. The following Bertram Golf Carts illustration demonstrates these details.

bertram golf carts
MULTIPLE CAPACITY CONSTRAINTS
AND MULTIPLE PRODUCTS

Bertram Golf Carts manufactures regular and premium golf carts. The company's managers want to determine the mix of products that will maximize their contribution margin, so they will know which products should be emphasized.

Regular carts sell for $8,000, have a variable cost per unit of $5,600, and require 20 hours for assembly. Premium carts sell for $10,000, have a variable cost of $6,500, and require 50 hours for assembly. Because of the quality controls built into the assembly process, premium carts take only 2.5 hours to inspect and test, whereas regular carts take 5 hours to test and inspect. Bertram has 10,000 hours available for assembly and 1,200 hours for testing and inspection. In addition, a shortage of leather for seat covers limits production to only 150

shawshot/iStockphoto

continued...

example

premium carts. We next describe the output from Excel Solver for this problem. Instructions for using Excel Solver are presented in Appendix 4A.

The Excel Solver Answer Report gives the optimal solution (see Exhibit 4.8). For Bertram, the optimal product mix is 175 regular carts and 130 premium carts (under Final Value in the Adjustable Cells section). The total contribution margin for this product mix is $875,000 (under Final Value in the Target Cell section). The optimal product mix uses all the available hours in both assembly and testing; these resources are binding because they limit further production. However, the amount of leather material available is not binding; only 130 premium carts are made. Enough leather is available for an additional 20 premium carts. The unused leather is considered a slack resource.

The product mix having the highest contribution margin can be determined using a graph and calculations as shown in Exhibit 4.8. First, graph each of the three constraints. Then determine the feasible solution area, in which all constraints are satisfied (shaded area in Exhibit 4.8). Then, calculate the total contribution margin for each corner of the feasible solution area (points A, B, C, D, and E in Exhibit 4.8). Point C (130 premium golf carts and 175 regular golf carts) is the optimal solution, because it would result in the highest total contribution margin. The total contribution margin for this product mix is $875,000 (under Final Value in the Target Cell section). The optimal product mix uses all of the available hours in both assembly and testing; these resources are binding because they limit further production. However, the amount of leather material available is not binding; only 130 premium carts are made. Enough leather is available for an additional 20 premium carts. The unused leather is considered a slack resource. Notice that the results in Exhibit 4.9 are the same as in Exhibit 4.8.

The graphical solution approach works when the number of products and constraints is small, but this method is cumbersome for only two products and three constraints. An easier approach is to use an optimization software program such as Excel Solver for this type of problem. Instructions for using Excel Solver are presented in Appendix 4A.

> **EXHIBIT 4.8**

Graphical Solution to Bertram Golf Cart Product Emphasis Problem

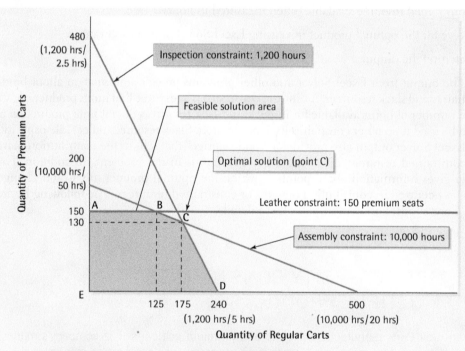

Contribution margin at corner points of feasible solution area:

	Number of carts		Total
	Premium	Regular	Contribution Margin
A	150	0	$525,000
B	150	125	825,000
C	130	175	875,000 Optimal solution
D	0	240	576,000
E	0	0	0

The Sensitivity Report provides sensitivity analysis around the product mix, contribution margins, and constrained resources (Exhibit 4.10). In the first section, for adjustable cells, the objective coefficient represents the contribution margin per product: $2,400 for regular carts and $3,500 for premium carts. The "allowable increase" and "allowable decrease" values are the amount the contribution margin per unit could change before the product mix would change (holding everything else constant). For Bertram, the optimal product mix would change if the regular cart contribution margin increased to more than $7,000 ($2,400 + $4,600) or decreased to less than $1,400 ($2,400 − $1,000). Similarly, the contribution margin for premium carts could increase by $2,500 or decrease by $2,300 before affecting the optimal product mix.

The lower section of the Sensitivity Report gives similar information for the constraints. The optimal product mix would change if total assembly time increased by more than 800 hours, to greater than 10,800 hours. The product mix would also change if total assembly time dropped by more than 5,200 hours, to less than 4,800 hours. Similarly, the testing constraint could increase by 1,300 hours or decrease by 200 hours before changing the optimal product mix.

The shadow price provides the contribution margin per constrained resource. Following the general rule for constrained resources, Bertram's managers would be willing to pay up to $57.50 per hour in addition to what they are already paying to relax the constraint in assembly. Similarly, they would be willing to pay up to $250.00 per hour in addition to what they are already paying to relax the constraint in testing and inspection. The shadow price for leather is zero, because the leather resource constraint is not binding. ■

> **EXHIBIT 4.9**
Solver Output for Bertram Golf Carts: Answer Report

Target Cell (Max)

Cell	Name	Original Value	Final Value
$B$8	Target cell: contribution margin for product mix	$0	$875,000

Adjustable Cells

Cell	Name	Original value	Final Value
$B$5	Regular	0	175
$C$5	Premium	0	130

Constraints

Cell	Name	Cell Value	Formula	Status	Slack
$C$11	Assembly hours used	10000	$C$11<=$D$11	Binding	0
$C$12	Testing hours used	1200	$C$12<=$D$12	Binding	0
$C$13	Leather seats used	130	$C$13<=$D$13	Not Binding	20

> **EXHIBIT 4.10**
Solver Output for Bertram Golf Carts: Sensitivity Report

Adjustable Cells

Cell	Name	Final Value	Reduced Cost	Objective Coefficient	Allowable Increase	Allowable Decrease
$B$5	Regular	175	0	2400	4600	1000
$C$5	Premium	130	0	3500	2500	2300

Constraints

Cell	Name	Final Value	Shadow Price	Constraint R.H. Side	Allowable Increase	Allowable Decrease
$C$11	Assembly hours used	10000	57.5	10000	800	5200
$C$12	Testing hours used	1200	250	1200	1300	200
$C$13	Leather seats used	130	0	150	1E+30	20

●● > STRATEGIC RISK MANAGEMENT: BERTRAM GOLF CARTS

RISKY ASSUMPTIONS In Bertram Golf Carts, the optimal product mix relied on several key assumptions. For example, the analysis assumed that the company could sell all of the golf carts produced. In a stable economy with a regular customer base, the company might be able to accurately forecast product demand. However, business shifts such as a financial crisis and ongoing globalization might reduce overall demand or increase competition. Managers need to continuously monitor the economic environment for these types of shifts. The analysis also assumed that no changes would occur in selling prices or in the cost function. Managers could evaluate the effects of this risk using the Sensitivity Report produced by Solver. As discussed in the next section, the company may be able to use constrained resources more efficiently even if the product mix assumptions are reasonable.

L03   **4-1** self-study problem   Product Emphasis, Solver, and Graphing

Power Tools manufactures engines for a broad range of commercial and consumer products. At its plant in Calgary, it assembles two engines—a rototiller engine and a riding lawn mower engine. Following is information for each product line:

	Rototiller Engine	Riding Lawn Mower Engine
Selling price	$800	$1,000
Variable costs per unit	560	625
Contribution margin per unit	$240	$ 375
Contribution margin ratio	30%	37.5%

Rototiller engines require 2 machine hours each, and riding lawn mower engines require 5 machine hours each. Only 600 machine hours are available each day for assembling engines. Additional capacity cannot be obtained in the short run. Power Tools has demand for only 200 rototiller engines but can sell as many riding lawn mower engines as it produces.

required

A. Which product should Power Tools emphasize? Explain and support your answer with quantitative information.
B. Using the general decision rule, what premium per machine hour would the managers of Power Tools be willing to pay to increase the number of machine hours available?
C. Use Excel Solver or a similar program to determine the optimal product mix. From the Sensitivity Report, determine the amount per machine hour that Power Tools would be willing to spend to relax the constraint in assembly.
D. Develop an answer by graphing the solution area.

See the solution on page 181.

Methods for Relaxing Constraints

Managers analyze operations and make decisions about the use of resources. Scarce resources, such as capacity constraints, must be carefully managed. We can use quantitative techniques to choose the product mix that maximizes the contribution margin for bottleneck resources. Alternatively, we can relax or elevate the constraint. Because each setting is unique, managers choose among a number of different techniques.

Use Constrained Resources More Efficiently

In the Bertram Golf Carts illustration, managers could analyze the assembly and testing/inspection processes to find ways to use constrained resources most efficiently. One possibility would be to change when inspection takes place. If golf carts were inspected earlier and more often during assembly, spoiled units would be removed from the line earlier in the assembly process. Fewer resources would then be needed in assembly and testing, helping to alleviate both assembly and testing constraints. Also, improvements in quality (lower defect rates) would ensure that only good units go through all processes.

In addition, workers from non-bottleneck resources can be reassigned to the bottleneck resources to increase the speed and constancy of the process. This reassignment is especially important during breaks and meals. To maximize output, bottleneck resources should be running as many hours as possible, regardless of the production team's schedule. Chapter 15 discusses increasing throughput, the rate at which product moves through the manufacturing process to the point of sale, or the rate at which services are produced.

Alternatively, efforts such as process re-engineering (redesigning the manufacturing or service delivery process) can be undertaken to reduce use of the constrained resources. For example, Bertram could redesign its assembly process and outsource the assembly of the seats and seat covers to reduce the amount of time each cart spends in the assembly department.

Increase Available Resources

Another possibility is to increase available resources. For example, managers can ask employees to work overtime. They can also increase capacity by buying new equipment or hiring new employees. Increasingly, companies use temporary labour or other outsourcing arrangements to increase available resources on an as-needed basis. Thus, resources might be increased either internally or externally.

Qualitative Factors for Constrained Resource Problems

As highlighted earlier in the Roadrunner Publishers illustration, managers might work to relax a constraint to protect customer loyalty or brand name recognition when the organization cannot deliver goods or services quickly. This factor, which has long-term effects, might outweigh cost considerations in some situations, especially if failure to deliver product would encourage new competition or customers to seek product substitutes. Another qualitative factor is the effect that any relaxation of the constrained resource could have on the price of that resource. A permanent increase in cost will decrease the contribution margin in the future. Product quality and timeliness of delivery from suppliers are also important if additional resources are used to relax a constraint.

Quality of Operating Decisions

Exhibit 4.11 summarizes the relevant information commonly used for making non-routine operating decisions, as illustrated in this chapter.

Managers make higher-quality decisions when they use higher-quality information and higher-quality decision processes. It is not sufficient for managers to identify relevant information when making non-routine operating decisions. They must also consider the quality of information, and they must evaluate alternatives objectively and thoroughly.

L06 Describe factors that affect the quality of operating decisions

Quality of Information

Three major factors affect the quality of information for non-routine operating decisions: business risk, information timeliness, and analysis technique assumptions.

Business Risk. Business risk prevents managers from accurately anticipating all of the quantitative and qualitative effects of a decision. Future revenues, costs, and qualitative factors

> **CHAPTER REFERENCE**
> See Exhibit 1.13 for the path to higher-quality decisions.

▶EXHIBIT 4.11

Summary of Information Used in Non-Routine Operating Decisions

Information	Special Order	Product Line and Business Segment (Keep or Drop)	Insource or Outsource (Make or Buy)	Product Emphasis (Under Constraints)	Relax Constrained Resource
			Type of Decision		
General decision rule	Accept if price is greater than or equal to the sum of variable cost, relevant fixed costs, and opportunity cost	Drop if contribution margin is less than the sum of relevant fixed costs and opportunity cost	Outsource if buy cost is less than or equal to the sum of variable cost and relevant fixed costs minus opportunity cost	Emphasize product with highest contribution margin per unit unless resources are constrained, then emphasize product with highest contribution margin per unit of constrained resource	Incur cost to relax constraint if cost is less than or equal to the sum of the contribution margin per unit of constrained resource and the current variable cost of the resource
Relevant fixed costs	Only new fixed costs associated with the special order	Only fixed costs that can be avoided if "drop"	Only fixed costs that can be avoided if "buy"		Only new fixed costs to relax the constraint
Opportunity cost	Contribution margin of any regular business replaced	Benefits from using released capacity for other purposes	Benefits from using released capacity for other purposes		
Examples of qualitative factors	• Will regular customers expect lower prices? • Will this order lead to improved brand name recognition? • Can we deliver without disrupting current schedules?	• Will dropping one product affect sales of other products? • Will layoffs affect worker morale?	• Is it easier to ensure high quality via insourcing or outsourcing? • Will delivery be timely? • Are there business risks about the supplier's ability to meet contractual obligations? • Is this activity a core competency?	• Does the product emphasis agree with strategic plans? • Are sales of one product likely to affect sales of other products?	• Are there other ways to relax the constraint? • How would brand recognition be affected by delivery delays? • Will the decision affect future supply costs?
Examples of major business risks	• How accurate are the cost estimates? • Are we operating in the relevant range? • Will fixed costs increase at higher capacity levels?	• How accurate are the revenue and cost estimates? • How will customers respond to the dropped product?	• How accurate are the cost estimates? • Is our measure of quality appropriate? • How reliable is the vendor or resource supplier?	• How accurate are the contribution margin estimates? • How reliable are the product demand forecasts?	• How accurate are the contribution margin estimates? • How accurate are the contribution use estimates?

can vary depending on changes in the economic environment, customer demand, competition, government regulation, vendor quality, technology, and so on. The degree of risk varies from decision to decision. For example, less risk comes with a special order from a long-time customer than from a new customer. Similarly, less risk accompanies outsourcing with a nearby company than with a company on another continent. In addition, decisions having a shorter time horizon, such as a special order that can be completed within one week, are less risky than decisions having a longer impact, such as dropping a product.

Information Timeliness. Many non-routine operating decisions must be made quickly and rely on up-to-date information. For example, a customer might require a prompt reply to a special order request, or managers may need to change production plans to emphasize different products as circumstances change. Access to timely information is particularly important in industries such as computer manufacturing, where technology, demand, and prices change rapidly. In such industries, cost information that is only one month old may be irrelevant. Thus, the accessibility and currency of the information system affect the quality of decisions.

Analysis Technique Assumptions. The reasonableness of assumptions affects the quality of information generated from an analysis technique. For example, regression analysis is useful for estimating costs only within a relevant range of activity. CVP analysis assumes that the revenue and cost functions are linear and that operations remain in a relevant range of activity. Although the validity of assumptions cannot be known with certainty, the validity of assumptions in a rapidly changing business environment is more uncertain than in a stable environment.

The general decision rules we learned in this chapter assume that the organization's goal is to maximize short-term profits. This assumption ignores qualitative factors that might be more important than short-term profits for some decisions.

Strategic Alignment

Operating plans are designed to help achieve an organization's long-term strategies. In turn, the strategies depend on an organization's vision, core competencies, and risk appetite. When addressing any operating decision, managers should consider whether each option is consistent with the organization's strategies, vision, core competencies, and risk appetite. For example, organizations such as Honda have established a market position based on high product reliability, making that characteristic an important strategic issue. Some organizations, such as Walmart, place strategic importance on low costs and prices. Ben & Jerry's strategy includes protecting the environment. Many organizations reduce the effects of raw material price fluctuations by entering into long-term purchase contracts or through hedging. By considering these types of qualitative issues, managers avoid taking actions that conflict with the organization's long-term interests.

> ▶ **CHAPTER REFERENCE**
> Exhibit 1.1 in Chapter 1 provides more details about the relationships among vision, core competencies, and strategies.

Decision-Maker Bias

Sometimes, decision makers are influenced by predispositions for a course of action, which reduces their ability to objectively and thoroughly analyze relevant information. The closure of Target after having invested $2 billion in Canada illustrates how biased information let to poor business decisions and significant losses. Biases can also cause managers to develop distorted forecasts (e.g., confirmation bias) or include irrelevant information such as sunk costs or unavoidable fixed costs in their analyses.

Another type of bias involves having a preference for either quantitative or qualitative information. Some people tend to rely primarily on quantitative analyses, because they are more comfortable with what they view as precise answers. Others, recognizing the risks in quantitative analyses, prefer to rely on qualitative factors to make decisions. The best approach is to weigh carefully both quantitative and qualitative factors, taking into account the strengths and weaknesses of information for a particular decision.

Opportunity Costs

Opportunity costs arise whenever decisions are made, because another alternative is always a possibility. For example, when you picked your current college or university, you decided to forgo attending alternative institutions. Furthermore, the time you spend in class or studying could be spent on other activities, such as working or leisure activities. These alternatives are relatively easy to identify and to value, either quantitatively or qualitatively. However, managers and accountants may overlook opportunity costs because they do not have time to adequately explore alternatives within a decision-making scenario. Moreover, the accounting system may not provide information about alternatives, or the available cost information may be inaccurate because of allocated costs that are not relevant to a decision.

In Roadrunner Publishers (Part 1), we assumed for simplicity that the managers had no alternative use for the space used by book covers and, therefore, no opportunity costs to consider. In Roadrunner Publishers (Part 3), we relax this assumption and explore how opportunity costs affect the outsourcing decision.

example

roadrunner publishers (part 3)
INSOURCE OR OUTSOURCE
WITH OPPORTUNITY COSTS

alterfalter/Shutterstock

Mark Bonaray, the cost accountant for Roadrunner Publishers, learns that the CEO would like to launch a new line of comic books. The comic books could potentially be produced in the physical space currently used for book covers. Therefore, Mark decides to modify his book cover outsourcing analysis to incorporate possible opportunity costs.

Mark begins by estimating the contribution margin that could be obtained from comic books. Because this is a new product line, the accounting system does not contain information about revenues or costs for this alternative. The sales manager tells Mark that breaking into this market would require an author and artist who could develop intriguing story plots and charismatic characters. Assuming an appropriate author and artist can be obtained, she estimates sales of 10,000 comic books for the first few issues produced. If successful, demand could be as high as several hundred thousand books. Because this is a new product and the firm will most likely hire a relatively new author and artist, Mark estimates sales of only 10,000 comic books. He next calls several bookstores and learns that comic books retail for about $2.99 each. Bookstores pay about half of the retail price to publishers. Therefore, Mark assumes that Roadrunner could sell the comic books for $1.50 each.

Mark next estimates the relevant comic book costs. One of the production managers estimates that variable costs would be $0.75 each. The fixed costs relating to the plant and equipment are sunk costs, but the author and artist would be paid a flat fee of $3,000 per book, plus royalties of $0.10 per comic book sold. Thus, the contribution margin per book would be $0.65 ($1.50 − $0.75 − $0.10), and the total contribution would be (10,000 books × $0.65) − $3,000, or $3,500.

Mark now adds the opportunity cost of $3,500 to his earlier cost analysis for outsourcing the book covers. The revised cost analysis is as follows:

Relevant Costs for 100,000 Book Covers

	Make	Buy
Purchase book covers		$200,000
Direct materials	$ 75,000	
Direct labour	50,000	
Manufacturing overhead	30,000	
Foreman's salary	50,000	
Opportunity cost	3,500	
Total Relevant Costs	$208,500	$200,000

Mark had previously estimated that the company could save $5,000 if book covers were outsourced. He now estimates that the savings could be $8,500 ($5,000 + $3,500). If the comic books are successful, his estimate of the opportunity cost might be low. However, comic books would be a new product line, subject to considerable business risk. Also, Mark continues to believe that problems may arise if the book cover outsourcer fails to make timely deliveries. Roadrunner could experience lost sales from book cover shortages, harming short-term profits as well as long-term relationships with authors. Successful authors could move to other publishers if book production shortages become a problem. Mark plans to discuss these issues with the CEO, who will make the final decision. ■

In Roadrunner Part 3, Mark could have subtracted the opportunity cost from the cost to buy instead of adding it to the cost to make. Either approach is correct, but opportunity costs from using capacity released by outsourcing a product or service should increase the cost to make or decrease the cost to buy.

Business Risk and Sensitivity Analysis

One way to improve decisions in light of low information quality and potential biases is to perform one or more sensitivity analyses. Sensitivity analysis helps managers evaluate how quantitative results would change with changes in various pieces of information. For example, estimates of incremental costs could be increased to evaluate the potential effects of risk. Sometimes, the degree of risk in the quantitative estimates for one option might exceed the organization's appetite for risk, making that option less desirable than another option having less risk.

Control System Incentive and Behavioural Effects

We learned in Chapter 1 that organizations adopt diagnostic control systems to encourage employees to achieve preset goals. These systems often include financial measures that can discourage optimal decision making. For example, managers may receive a bonus if operations achieve a targeted gross profit percentage. Managers with this reward might be unwilling to accept a special order that increases gross profit but decreases the gross profit percentage. Ideally, control systems should be designed to avoid such *unintended consequences*.

> ⊠ **CHAPTER REFERENCE**
> Chapters 18 and 19 explore the incentive effects of various performance measures.

Using Excel Solver for Product Emphasis and Constrained Resource Decisions

APPENDIX 4A

Linear programming problems can be solved using a spreadsheet application. This appendix provides detailed instructions for using Solver, a tool within Excel, to solve a product emphasis problem with resource constraints. We use data from the chapter's Bertram Golf Carts illustration to demonstrate the instructions. The exhibits in this appendix were prepared using Excel. Following is a summary of the steps you will learn in this appendix:

1. Determine the objective (target) function.

2. Create formulas for the resource constraints.

3. Set up an Excel spreadsheet.

4. Use Excel Solver to maximize the objective function.

5. Interpret the Solver output.

Determine the Objective (Target) Function

The general decision rule for a product emphasis problem when resources are constrained is to emphasize the product with the highest contribution margin per unit of constrained resource. The goal is to maximize the organization's total contribution margin. Therefore, the objective function for the linear programming problem is to maximize the sum of contribution margins. In Excel Solver, the objective function is called the target function.

For Bertram Golf Carts, the objective (target) function is to maximize the total contribution margin from its two types of golf carts. Regular golf carts sell for $8,000 and have a variable cost per unit of $5,600. Premium carts sell for $10,000 and have a variable cost of $6,500.

Objective (target) function

= Total contribution margin

= Regular carts × ($8,000 − $5,600) + Premium carts × ($10,000 − $6,500)

= Regular carts × $2,400 + Premium carts × $3,500

Create Formulas for the Resource Constraints

The next step is to identify and write a function for each resource constraint. The function is the sum of the quantity of the resource used by each product, which must be less than or equal to the maximum available amount of the resource. In the Bertram Golf Carts illustration, three constrained resources are assembly hours, testing and inspection hours, and leather for seat covers. Bertram has 10,000 hours available for assembly. Regular carts require 20 assembly hours, while premium carts require 50 hours. For assembly, the constraint function is

(Regular carts × 20 hours) + (Premium carts × 50 hours) ≤ 10,000 hours

Bertram has 1,200 hours for testing and inspection. Regular carts take 5 hours to test and inspect, while premium carts take only 2.5 hours. For testing and inspecting, the constraint function is

(Regular carts × 5 hours) + (Premium carts × 2.5 hours) ≤ 1,200 hours

Bertram has only enough leather for 150 seat covers. Regular carts do not have leather seat covers, so this constraint relates to only premium carts.

Premium carts × 1 seat cover ≤ 150 seat covers

Set Up an Excel Spreadsheet

Exhibit 4A.1 (a) provides a general Excel spreadsheet format for a product emphasis problem with resource constraints. A spreadsheet using this format for Bertram Golf Carts is shown in Exhibit 4A.1 (b). The following instructions describe how to create the spreadsheet.

Insert a title for the spreadsheet in cell B1. Then insert labels that will be useful later when using Solver: type "Changing Cells:" in cell A5, "Target Cell:" in cell A8, and "Constraints:" in cell A11. Next, insert headings for the product data: type "Product Mix" in cell B3 and then type product names in cells B4 and C4. If more than two products are

> EXHIBIT 4A.1

Excel Spreadsheets for Product Emphasis with Constrained Resources

(a) General Spreadsheet Format

(b) Bertram Golf Carts

involved, enter product names in additional columns of row 4. If desired, enter the word "units" after the product name to indicate that Solver calculates the optimal number of units to be sold. Bertram Golf Carts produces only two products, so only cells B4 and C4 contain product names.

Rename the cells to the right of Changing Cells and under the product names. Solver uses these cells to enter the number of units for the optimal product mix. These cells (B5, C5, and so on) must be given names that are used later in the spreadsheet for the target function formula and the constraint formulas. To assign a name to a given cell, first place the cursor in that cell. Next, find the cell number in the formula bar (if the formula bar is not visible, click View, Formula Bar). When you click on the cell number in the formula bar, the number will be highlighted. You can then replace the cell number with a name for the cell. This name will appear in Solver output reports, so you should choose a name that is recognizable. For Bertram Golf Carts, cell B5 is renamed "Regular," and cell C5 is renamed "Premium." Now enter a 0 in each of the renamed cells. For Bertram, "0" is entered in cells B5 (renamed Regular) and C5 (renamed Premium). After Solver is run, Excel will replace these entries with the optimal number of units.

Insert a heading above the target cell: type "Contribution Margin for Product Mix" in cell B7. In cell B8, enter "=" followed by the formula for the target function (i.e., the sum of the product contribution margins). When typing the formulas, use the names for cell references to the number of units for each product. If desired, format this cell as a dollar amount. For Bertram Golf Carts, the target function was determined in Step 1. The formula is entered in cell B8 as:

$$= Regular*2400 + Premium*3500$$

Because the initial units of regular and premium were entered as zeros in cells B5 and C5, Excel computes an initial value in cell B8 of $0.

Insert headings above the resource constraint cells: type "Constrained Resources:" in cell B10, "Used" in cell C10, and "Maximum" in cell D10. In column B, type a name for each constraint beginning in row 11. For Bertram Golf Carts, three constraints are named "Assembly hours" in cell B11, "Testing hours" in cell B12, and "Leather seats" in cell B13. The left- and right-hand sides of each resource constraint formula are entered in columns C and D, respectively. When typing the formulas, use the names for cell references to the renamed cells. For example, the formula for the Bertram assembly hours constraint was determined in Step 2 as

$$= Regular\ carts*20\ hours + Premium\ carts*50\ hours \leq 10,000\ hours$$

Substituting the product cells' names and omitting units of measurement, the formula becomes

$$Regular*20 + Premium*50 \leq 10000$$

Then, the left-hand side of the formula is entered in cell C11 as

$$= Regular*20 + Premium*50$$

and the right-hand side of the formula (the maximum amount of the resource available) is entered in cell D11 as 10,000. Because the initial number of regular and premium units was entered as zero in cells B5 and C5, Excel computes an initial value of 0 for the number of constrained resources used in cell C11. Make similar entries for all the constraints. Check to be sure the spreadsheet is similar to the ones in Exhibits 4A.1 (a) and (b).

Use Excel Solver to Maximize the Objective Function

Once all information is entered in the spreadsheet, select Tools, Solver in Excel. If Solver is not on the Tools menu, add it by using the Add-Ins feature on the Tools menu. Once Solver is selected, a Solver Parameters dialogue box like the first one shown in Exhibit 4A.2 will appear.

▶EXHIBIT 4A.2

Solver Dialogue Boxes

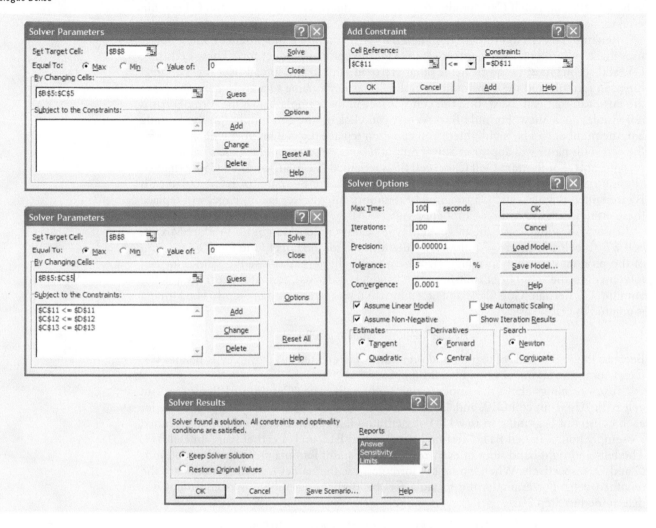

The Solver Parameters dialogue box is used to select calculation options and to define the target function, product mix (i.e., change) variables, and constraints. First, define the target function in Solver by entering a reference in the Set Target Cell area of the dialogue box to the target function in the spreadsheet (cell B8). You can either (1) type "B8" in the Set Target Cell area of the dialogue box or (2) click in the Set Target Cell area of the dialogue box and then click on the target function cell (B8) in the spreadsheet. (Excel will automatically convert "B8" to "$B$8.") Second, ensure that Solver will maximize the target function by verifying that the button next to Max is selected. Third, define the variables that Solver will change to maximize the target function by entering a reference to the cells that contain the number of units for each product (cells B5 and C5 for Bertram). You can either (1) type the cell range "B5:C5" in the By Changing Cells area of the dialogue box or (2) click in the By Changing Cells area of the dialogue box and then highlight the range of cells (B5 through C5) in the spreadsheet. Fourth, add constraints by clicking on the Add button, which will cause the Add Constraint dialogue box shown in Exhibit 4A.2 to appear.

The constraints are defined one at a time in the Add Constraint dialogue box. The Cell Reference area is used for the constraint formula, while the Constraint area is used for the maximum quantity available of each resource. The following instructions refer to the first constraint for Bertram. To set the Cell Reference, you can either (1) type "C11" in the Cell Reference area of the dialogue box or (2) click in the Cell Reference area of the dialogue box and then click on constraint formula cell (C11) in the spreadsheet. Ensure that the constraint mathematical operation in the middle area shows as "<= ". To set the Constraint, you can either (1) type "D11" in the Cell Reference area of the dialogue box or (2) click in the Cell Reference area of the dialogue box and then click on constraint formula cell (D11) in the spreadsheet. Click on the add button. The dialogue box will then clear, and you can follow the preceding directions for the next constraint. After adding values for the last constraint, click OK. You will then return to the Solver Parameters dialogue box (Exhibit 4A.2). Notice that all constraints appear in the Subject to the Constraints area of the dialogue box.

Next, click on Options in the Solver Parameters dialogue box, and the Solver Options dialogue box will appear (Exhibit 4A.2).

In the Solver Options dialogue box, select Assume Linear Model and Assume NonNegative. Then click OK. You will return to the Solver Parameters dialogue box. Now click on Solve. Solver will perform its calculations and then open the Solver Results dialogue box (Exhibit 4A.2). An explanation will appear at the top of the dialogue box. If Solver ran successfully, the wording will appear.

When Solver runs successfully, the Solver Results dialogue box contains three reports: Answer, Sensitivity, and Limits. Highlight the report names to save them as separate sheets in the spreadsheet file. Then Click OK. When Solver is finished, the spreadsheet for Bertram appears as shown in Exhibit 4.A3. The following results are shown in the spreadsheet:

▶ Number of units in the optimal product mix for each product
▶ Total contribution margin at the optimal product mix
▶ Quantity used for each constrained resource at the optimal product mix

If you use Solver again on the same spreadsheet, you must reset the Changing Cells (B5 and C5 for Bertram) to 0. Otherwise, the Solver solution may not be the optimum solution for the new variables.

Interpret the Solver Output

Refer to the Bertram Golf Carts illustration in the chapter for discussions of the Answer Report (Exhibit 4.9) and Sensitivity Report (Exhibit 4.10).

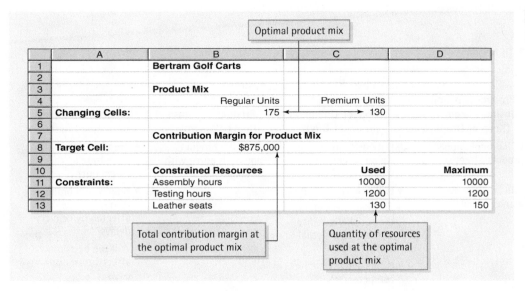

EXHIBIT 4A.3
Spreadsheet After Solver Tool Is Run

SUMMARY

DECISION PROCESS

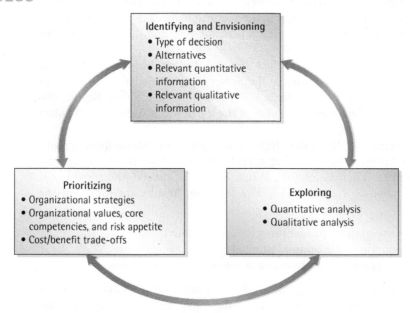

Identifying and Envisioning
- Type of decision
- Alternatives
- Relevant quantitative information
- Relevant qualitative information

Prioritizing
- Organizational strategies
- Organizational values, core competencies, and risk appetite
- Cost/benefit trade-offs

Exploring
- Quantitative analysis
- Qualitative analysis

GENERAL DECISION RULE

Take the action that maximizes current-period income (or minimizes current-period losses).

TO APPLY THE GENERAL DECISION RULE

Identify and calculate relevant revenues and costs

▶ Contribution margin per unit
▶ Contribution margin per unit of constrained resource
▶ Fixed costs that differ across alternatives
▶ Opportunity costs

EXAMPLES OF QUALITATIVE FACTORS

	Type of Decision			
Special Order	**Product Line and Business Segment (Keep or Drop)**	**Insource or Outsource (Make or Buy)**	**Product Emphasis (Under Constraints)**	**Relax (Alleviate) Constrained Resource**
• Will regular customers expect lower prices? • Will this order lead to improved brand name recognition? • Can we deliver without disrupting current schedules?	• Will dropping one product affect sales of other products? • Will layoffs affect worker morale?	• Is it easier to ensure via insourcing or outsourcing? • Will delivery be timely? • Are there risks about the supplier's ability to meet contractual obligations? • Is this activity a core competency?	• Does the product emphasis agree with strategic plans?	• Are there other ways to relax the constraint? • How would brand recognition be affected by delivery delays? • Will the decision affect future supply costs?

LO2   Analyze the quantitative and qualitative information used in keep or drop decisions

APPLIES TO

Products, product lines, segments, customers, customer groups

QUANTITATIVE DECISION RULE

Drop if—

$$\text{Contribution margin} < \text{Relevant fixed costs} + \text{Opportunity cost}$$

RELEVANT COSTS

Avoidable

► Service or product production costs
► Marketing, sales-order, delivery costs
► Dedicated equipment or other assets

► Technical support, warranty costs, product return handling
► Inventory carrying costs
► Administrative costs

OPPORTUNITY COST

Benefits from using released capacity for other purposes

QUALITATIVE AND RISK FACTORS

► Strategic goals and plans
► Effect on other services, products, customers
► Worker layoff effects
► Achievability of revenue and cost estimates
► Competitor offerings
► Effect of customer or sales mix on organizational risk

LO3   Analyze the quantitative and qualitative information used in outsourcing (make or buy) decisions

QUANTITATIVE DECISION RULE

Outsource if—

$$\text{Cost to outsource} < \text{Cost to insource}$$

Where—

$$\text{Cost to insource} = \text{Relevant variable costs} + \text{Relevant fixed costs} + \text{Opportunity cost}$$

RELEVANT COSTS

► Variable costs not always relevant
► Fixed costs relevant if avoidable

OPPORTUNITY COST

Benefits from using released capacity for other purposes

QUALITATIVE AND RISK FACTORS

► Strategic goals and plans
► Core competencies; strategic skills
► Highly sensitive information involved in activity
► Importance of quality and timeliness
► Availability of measures for monitoring performance
► Ability to monitor contractual compliance
► Effects on labour relations
► Supplier worker conditions and environmental practices

LO4   Analyze the quantitative and qualitative information used in special order decisions

QUANTITATIVE DECISION RULE

Accept if—

$$\text{Price} \geq \text{Relevant variable costs} + \text{Relevant fixed costs} + \text{Opportunity cost}$$

RELEVANT COSTS

► Variable costs not always relevant
► Fixed costs relevant if associated with the special order

OPPORTUNITY COST

Contribution margin of any regular business replaced

SPECIAL ORDERS AND PRICING POLICIES

QUALITATIVE AND RISK FACTORS

► Strategic goals and plans
► Prices for other customers
► Disruption of schedules for regular business
► Potential new, profitable customer
► Retain existing, profitable customer
► Labour overtime problems

LO5 — Analyze the quantitative and qualitative information used in product emphasis and constrained resource decisions

TYPES OF CONSTRAINED RESOURCE PROBLEMS

► Product emphasis
► Product mix when resources are constrained
► Relaxing constraints for two or fewer products
► Relaxing constraints for multiple products and multiple constraints

QUANTITATIVE DECISION RULE

Product Emphasis: Emphasize product with highest contribution margin per unit unless resources are constrained, then emphasize product with highest contribution margin per unit of constrained resource

Constrained Resource: Incur cost to relax constraint if cost is less than or equal to the sum of contribution margin per unit of constrained resource and the current variable cost of the resource

RELEVANT FIXED COSTS

Constrained Resource: Only new, fixed costs to relax the constraint

RELAXING CONSTRAINTS

► Use constrained resources more efficiently
► Increase available resources

THEORY OF CONSTRAINTS

Iterative process for eliminating constraints and increasing throughput of the manufacturing or service delivery system

INTERNAL CONSTRAINTS

Limits in capacity, materials, labour

LINEAR PROGRAMMING

► Binding constraints
► Slack resources
► Shadow price

QUALITATIVE AND RISK FACTORS

► Strategic goals and plans
► Other factors such as environmental impact or product safety
► Effect on other services, products, customers
► Competitor product offerings
► Existence of high customer loyalty
► Other options for relaxing a constraint
► Effects of delivery delays
► Cost changes near capacity constraints
► Effects of actions on future resource prices
► Effect of product emphasis on organizational risk

LO6   Describe factors that affect the quality of operating decisions

QUALITY OF INFORMATION

► Business risk
► Information timeliness
► Analysis technique assumptions
  - Managers would like to maximize short-term profits
  - CVP assumptions (see Chapter 3)
  - Additional assumptions for constrained resource decisions:
    • The organization will forgo sales if the resource constraint is not relaxed.
    • Fixed costs are unaffected by short-term decisions made to relax constraints.
    • Sales of one product do not affect sales of other products.

STRATEGIC ALIGNMENT

DECISION-MAKER BIAS

OPPORTUNITY COSTS

BUSINESS RISK AND SENSITIVITY ANALYSIS

CONTROL SYSTEM INCENTIVE AND BEHAVIOURAL EFFECTS

EXAMPLES OF BUSINESS RISK

	Type of Decision			
Special Order	**Product Line and Business Segment (Keep or Drop)**	**Insource or Outsource (Make or Buy)**	**Product Emphasis (Under Constraints)**	**Relax (Alleviate) Constrained Resource**
• How accurate are the cost estimates? • Are we operating in the relevant range? • Will fixed costs increase at higher capacity levels?	• How accurate are the revenue and cost estimates? • How will customers respond to the dropped product?	• How accurate are the cost estimates? • Is our measure of quality appropriate? • How reliable is the vendor or resource supplier?	• How accurate are the contribution margin estimates? • How reliable are the product demand forecasts?	• How accurate are the contribution margin estimates? • How accurate are the constraint use estimates?

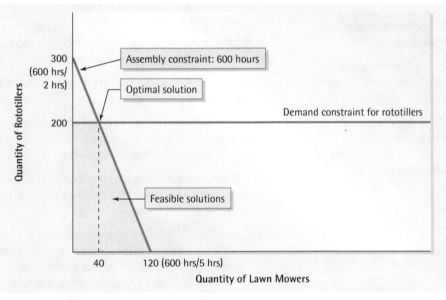

► **EXHIBIT 4.12**

Graphical Solution to Power Tool Product Emphasis Problem

4-1 solution to self-study problem
Product Emphasis, Solver, and Graphing

A. The contribution margin per unit of constrained resource for each engine is (MH = machine hour):

$$\text{Rototiller:} \quad \$240 \div 2\ \text{MH} = \$120\ \text{per MH}$$
$$\text{Lawn mower:} \quad \$375 \div 5\ \text{MH} = \$75\ \text{per MH}$$

For this constrained resource problem, Power Tools should emphasize the product having the highest contribution margin per unit of constrained resource. In this case, the company should emphasize the rototiller.

B. If Power Tools can sell more rototillers, it can spend up to $120 per machine hour plus whatever it spends now on variable production costs to increase machine hours. When the demand for rototiller engines has been met, Power Tools can spend up to $75 per machine hour plus what it spends now on variable production costs to increase machine hours for the production of lawn mower engines.

C. Using Excel Solver, the optimal product mix is 200 rototiller engines and 40 lawn mower engines. The shadow price is $75 for lawn mower engines, so Power Tools would be willing to spend $75 per machine hour plus whatever it spends now on variable production costs. Notice that this answer is the same as calculated in Part B.

D. The graphical solution for the problem is shown in Exhibit 4.12.

To create the graph:

- Each axis represents the volume of a product.
- Draw a line for each constraint.
- Find the feasible solution area, where all constraints are met.
- Calculate the total contribution margin at each corner point.
- Find the optimal sales mix by finding the corner with the highest contribution margin.

Notice that the optimal product mix in Exhibit 4.12 is the same as in Part C: 200 rototiller engines and 40 lawn mower engines.

QUESTIONS

4.1 When making an operating decision, are all future costs relevant? Explain.

4.2 Identify several ways in which confirmation bias might affect a manager's special order decision.

4.3 An organization is currently operating at capacity. Should it accept a request for a special order based on variable cost plus 40%? Explain.

4.4 Refer to the quantitative decision rule for special orders. Would this same general decision rule apply to a decision to sell last-minute event tickets at a discounted price? Explain. Identify two other businesses with a similar pricing situation.

4.5 Describe several methods that can be used to relax constrained resources.

4.6 In your own words, distinguish between quantitative and qualitative information.

4.7 Grover Nursery is a large nursery that has always raised the bedding plants it sells. The managers recently decided to buy bedding plants from a wholesale nursery in another province. List several quantitative factors that might encourage the managers to buy from another grower. List several qualitative factors that might encourage the managers to grow their own plants.

4.8 List two business risks that often need to be considered when making a decision about whether to outsource a product or service.

4.9 Explain how managers decide which products in a sales mix to emphasize in the short term.

4.10 Explain how opportunity costs arise in make or buy and keep or drop decisions.

4.11 List at least three different types of decisions that you studied in this chapter, and give an example of each one for a retail clothing factory outlet store.

4.12 List two business risks that often need to be considered when making a decision about whether to accept a special order.

4.13 Critique the following statement made by a company's sales manager: "I insist that my sales representatives avoid selling our products at a discount. How can I justify accepting a special order at a price below the standard price?"

4.14 List four different customer support costs that software companies such as Microsoft and Intuit incur after their products have been sold.

4.15 List four potential resource constraints faced by organizations in a service industry such as higher education, hospitals, or public accounting. Explain how each constraint could be relaxed.

MULTIPLE-CHOICE QUESTIONS

4.16 Which of the following statements is true?
   a. In a special order decision, additional fixed costs are irrelevant costs.
   b. In a keep or drop decision, allocated fixed costs are relevant costs.
   c. In a product emphasis decision due to constrained resources, the contribution margin per unit is irrelevant.
   d. In a make or buy decision, opportunity cost is irrelevant.

4.17 In a make or buy decision, which costs are usually irrelevant?
   a. Direct material costs
   b. Fixed costs that will not change, regardless of the decision
   c. Variable sales and administrative costs
   d. Variable production costs

Use the following information to answer Questions 4.18–4.20:

A manufacturer of skating equipment has met all its production requirements for the current month and has the opportunity to produce additional skates with its excess capacity. There is sufficient demand for the additional production of any model of the product line. The selling prices and unit costs of the four models of skates are as follows:

	Junior	Teen	International	Pro
Selling price	$75	$100	$140	$250
Direct materials	25	30	40	55
Direct labour	20	30	50	110
Variable overhead*	10	15	25	55
Fixed overhead**	26	26	30	60

*Applied on the basis of direct labour hours at a rate of $10 per hour
**Applied on the basis of machine hours at a rate of $30 per machine hour

4.18 If the manufacturer has excess machine capacity and can add as much labour as needed, which model should be manufactured with the excess production capacity?
  a. Junior
  b. Teen
  c. International
  d. Pro

4.19 If the manufacturer has excess machine capacity but limited labour hours, which model should be manufactured with the excess production capacity?
  a. Junior
  b. Teen
  c. International
  d. Pro

4.20 If the manufacturer can add labour as needed but has limited machine capacity, which model should be manufactured with the excess production capacity?
  a. Junior
  b. Teen
  c. International
  d. Pro

EXERCISES

4.21 Make or Buy, Qualitative Factors Yoklic Corporation currently manufactures a subassembly for its main product.
LO1, LO3   The costs per unit are as follows:

Direct materials	$ 4.00
Direct labour	30.00
Variable overhead	15.00
Fixed overhead	25.00
Total	$74.00

Regina Corp. has contacted Yoklic with an offer to sell it 5,000 subassemblies for $55.00 each.

REQUIRED   **A.** Should Yoklic make or buy the subassemblies? Create a schedule that shows the total quantitative differences between the two alternatives.
  B. The accountant decides to investigate the fixed costs to see whether any incremental changes will occur if the subassembly is no longer manufactured. The accountant believes that Yoklic will eliminate $50,000 of fixed overhead if it accepts the proposal. Does this new information change the decision? Show your calculations.
  C. What qualitative factors are important for accountants and managers to consider for Yoklic's make or buy decision?

4.22 Constrained Resource, Qualitative Factors Johnson and Sons Inc. produces organic cranberry juice from
LO1, LO5   cranberries it farmed. Unfortunately, it has been a bad year for cranberries because of severe cold weather. Johnson has only 10,000 litres of juice. It usually sells 15,000 litres at $3 per litre. The variable costs of farming the cranberries are $0.50 per litre. Johnson has loyal customers, but its managers are worried that the company will lose customers if it does not have juice available for sale when people stop by the farm. A neighbour is willing to sell 5,000 litres of extra cranberry juice at $2.95 per litre.

REQUIRED   **A.** Which type of non-routine operating decision is involved here? What are the managers' decision options?
  B. Using the general decision rule, what is the most per litre that Johnson's managers would be willing to pay for additional juice?

C. Why would Johnson be willing to pay the amount calculated in Part B for more juice?

D. Is the quality of the neighbour's juice a concern to Johnson's managers in making this decision? Why or why not?

E. List another qualitative factor that might affect the managers' decision.

4.23 Cumulative Exercise (Chapter 3): CVP, Single Constrained Resource Snowbird Snowboards converts regular snowboards by adding outriggers and seats so that people who use wheelchairs can snowboard. The income statement for last year, in which 500 snowboards were produced and sold, appears here:

Revenue		$150,000
Expenses:		
Variable production costs	$60,000	
Fixed production costs	25,000	
Variable selling and administration	10,000	
Fixed selling and administration	35,000	130,000
Income		$ 20,000

REQUIRED

A. What volume of snowboards must be sold to earn pretax profits of $30,000?

B. Snowbird's supplier of snowboards is unable to ship more than 500 boards for the upcoming season. Snowbird has been paying the supplier $85 for each snowboard. (The cost of the snowboards is included in variable production costs.) More expensive snowboards are available from other manufacturers for conversion. If Snowbird's managers expect to sell more than 500 converted snowboards in the upcoming season, what is the most they would be willing to pay outside suppliers for each additional snowboard?

C. Suppose Snowbird pays the price you calculated in Part B and sells an additional 200 snowboards. What is the company's incremental profit on the 200 snowboards?

4.24 Multiple Products, Multiple Resource Constraints, Sensitivity Mrs. Meadows sells two popular brands of cookies: Chip Dip and Soft Chunk Chocolate Chip. Both cookies go through the mixing and baking departments, but Chip Dip is also dipped in chocolate in the dipping department.

Frank Roman, vice president for sales, believes that Mrs. Meadows can sell all of its daily production of Chip Dip and Soft Chunk. Both cookies are made in batches of 600 cookies. The batch times for producing each type of cookie and the minutes available per day are as follows:

	Mixing	Baking	Dipping
Minutes required per batch			
Chip Dip	20	40	15
Soft Chunk	30	20	0
Minutes available per day	4,000	6,000	2,000

Revenue per batch for Chip Dip is $150, and the variable costs per batch are $100. Fixed costs of $2,350 are allocated to Chip Dip. Revenue per batch for Soft Chunk Chocolate Chips is $175, and the variable costs per batch are $135. Allocated fixed costs are $1,500.

Set up the target function (contribution margin function) and the constraints for this problem. Enter these constraints and the target function into Excel Solver or another linear programming package and print out a formula sheet and all of the reports.

REQUIRED

A. What is the optimal product mix?

B. What is the total contribution margin for that product mix?

C. Following the general decision rule, what would the managers of Mrs. Meadows be willing to pay to relax each constraint?

D. Which constraints are binding?

E. By how much could the contribution margin for Soft Chunk increase before the optimal product mix changes?

4.25 Keep or Drop and Constrained Resource The income statement for King Salmon Sales, which produces smoked
LO1, LO5   salmon, follows:

Revenue (100,000 kg)		$800,000
Expenses		
Fish	$200,000	
Smoking materials	20,000	
Packaging materials	30,000	
Labour (paid by hours)	300,000	
Administration	150,000	
Sales commissions	10,000	
Total expenses		710,000
Pretax income		$ 90,000

Assume that the administrative costs are fixed and that all the other costs are variable.

REQUIRED   A. Suppose the provincial government curtails fishing because of low fish counts. As a result, King Salmon Sales
can buy only 50,000 kg of salmon this year. Assume that the selling price, the fixed costs, and the variable
costs remain the same as last year. Using only quantitative information, should King Salmon operate this year?
Explain your answer, using calculations. (*Hint:* Before you begin, identify the type of non-routine operating
decision, the decision options, and the relevant information for this decision.)

B. Assume that King Salmon can buy up to 70,000 kg of fish at $2.00/kg and that the remainder of the fixed and
variable costs remain the same as last year. Also assume that the selling price remains the same as last year
and that the market will purchase all of the additional fish. If the managers of King Salmon wish to sell more
salmon, what should they be willing to pay to purchase more fish? (*Hint:* This type of decision is different from
the one in Part A. Before you begin, identify the type of non-routine decision, the decision options, and the
relevant information for this decision.)

4.26 Product Emphasis and Constrained Resource Emily developed an innovative computer game, called Home By
Myself (HBM). It was so successful that she quickly followed up with two sequels: Home By Myself II (HBM2) and
LO5   Home By Myself III (HBM3). The costs of developing the games were $95,000 for HBM, $10,000 for HBM2, and
$15,000 for HBM3.

The production process consists of using her computer to copy the games to blank DVDs and then packing
them with printed instructions in a display box. It takes longer to copy the original game than it takes to copy the
sequels. Emily can produce, ready for shipping, about 20 copies of HBM, 30 copies of HBM2, or 45 copies of
HBM3 in an hour, and she normally works 8 hours per day.

	HBM	HBM2	HBM3
Selling price	$49.00	$29.00	$29.00
Costs			
Blank DVD	1.00	0.50	0.50
Instructions and packaging	4.00	2.00	2.00
Prorated development costs*	19.00	2.00	3.00
Margin	$25.00	$24.50	$23.50
Daily demand	120 games	120 games	90 games

*The prorated development costs were determined for each game by dividing the
game's development costs by 5,000, the estimated minimum total demand for each
game.

REQUIRED   A. What is the contribution margin per hour of Emily's time for each game?

B. In what order should Emily produce the games?

C. Using the general decision rule for constrained capacity, what is the most Emily should be willing to pay per
hour for a worker to duplicate and pack DVDs after her normal working hours? (Assume that the worker would
work at the same pace as Emily.)

4.27 Multiple Products and Resource Constraints, Sensitivity Analysis Wildlife Foods prepares wild birdseed mixes and

L05

sells them to local pet stores, grocery stores, and wild bird stores. Two types of mixes have been most successful: Flight Fancy and Multigrain. Flight Fancy generates a contribution margin of $12 per 50 kg bag, and Multigrain contributes $9 per 50 kg. Because Wildlife Foods has been very thorough in its sterilization process, the birdseed never germinates and grows. Therefore, it is a top seller, and the company can sell all the birdseed it produces.

The seed is processed in three stages: mixing, sterilization, and packaging. The time requirements for each batch of 100 bags of Flight Fancy and 5,000 kg of Multigrain (which is sold in bulk rather than bags) follow:

	Minutes Required		
	Mixing	Sterilization	Packaging
Flight Fancy	200	200	100
Multigrain	100	300	0 (sold in bulk)
Minutes Available	6,000	12,000	4,500

REQUIRED A. Using a spreadsheet program such as Excel Solver, find the optimal product mix, given the current constraints and contribution margins.
B. Which constraints are binding?
C. What happens if minutes available for mixing are doubled? Does another constraint become binding? What is the optimal product mix in this case?

4.28 Special Order The Cone Head House sells ice cream cones in a variety of flavours. Data for a recent week appear here:

L04

Revenue (1,000 cones @ $1.50 each)	$1,500
Cost of ingredients	530
Rent	300
Store attendant	600
Income	$ 70

The Cone Head House's manager received a call from a university student club, requesting a bid on 100 cones to be picked up in three days. The cones could be produced in advance by the store attendant during slack periods and then stored in the freezer. Each cone requires a special plastic cover that costs $0.05.

REQUIRED A. What are the managers' decision options?
B. What quantitative information is relevant for this decision?
C. Using the general decision rule, what is the minimum acceptable price per cone for this special order?
D. Explain why Cone Head House's managers might be willing to sell cones at the price you calculated in Part C.

4.29 Special Order, Qualitative Factors Cute Cookies (CC) sells cookies, brownies, and beverages to small local shops. The

L01, L04

selling price per brownie is $1.25 and the variable cost is $0.75. The principal of an elementary school asked CC to provide 10 dozen brownies for its spring picnic. The principal wants to buy the brownies at CC's cost. Unlike with regular sales, each special order brownie must be delivered in a plastic container to protect it from dust. The containers cost $0.05 each. The brownies can be prepared ahead of time when workers are not busy.

REQUIRED A. Under the general decision rule for special orders, what is the minimum price per brownie that CC's management should accept?
B. If the principal can pay no more than $0.80 per brownie, should CC take the order? Why or why not?
C. List several qualitative factors that could affect CC's decision if the special order price for brownies is $0.80.

4.30 Outsourcing Computations, Business Risks Saguaro Systems produces and sells speakers and CD players.

L03, L06

The following information has been collected about the costs related to the systems:

Selling price per unit	$70
Production costs per unit	
Direct materials	$22
Direct labour	16
Variable overhead	2
Total fixed overhead	$360,000

Saguaro normally produces 25,000 of these systems per year.

The managers have recently received an offer from a Mexican company to produce these systems for $48 each. The managers estimate that $260,000 of Saguaro's fixed costs could be eliminated if they accept the offer.

REQUIRED **A.** Which type of non-routine operating decision is involved here? What are the managers' decision options? What quantitative information is relevant to the decision?

B. Perform a quantitative analysis for the decision, and present your results in a schedule.

C. Under the general decision rule for this type of decision, what production level is required for Saguaro's managers to be indifferent?

D. List as many business risks as you can for this decision.

4.31 **Special Order Computations, Qualitative Factors** The Feed Barn packages and distributes three grades of animal feed. The material cost per tonne and estimated annual sales for each of the products are listed here:

L01, L04

Product	Material Cost	Estimated Sales
Super Premium	$10.00	2,000 tonnes
Premium	8.00	3,000 tonnes
Economy	7.00	5,000 tonnes

The fixed cost of operating the machinery used to package all three products is $10,000 per year. In the past, prices have been set by allocating the fixed operating cost to products on the basis of estimated sales in tonnes. The resulting full costs (material costs plus allocated fixed operating cost) are then marked up 100%. The Feed Barn has received an offer from a foreign firm for 1,000 tonnes of the premium-grade feed. Sales to the foreign firm would not affect domestic sales but would require a $2,000 increase in fixed production costs.

REQUIRED **A.** Which type of non-routine operating decision is involved here? What are the managers' decision options?

B. What relevant quantitative information is required for this type of decision?

C. Using only quantitative information, what is the minimum price that the Feed Barn's managers should be willing to accept from the foreign firm?

D. What types of qualitative factors would the Feed Barn's managers typically consider before agreeing to the sale? Explain.

4.32 **Cumulative Exercise (Chapter 3): Keep or Drop, Multiple Product Breakeven, Qualitative Factors** Horton and Associates produces two products named Loser and Big Winner. Last month 1,000 units of Loser and 4,000 units of Big Winner were produced and sold. Average prices and costs for the two products for last month follow:

L01, L02

	Loser	Big Winner
Selling price	$95	$225
Direct materials	40	95
Direct labour	5	25
Variable overhead	5	15
Product line fixed costs	10	40
Corporate fixed costs	25	25
Average margin per unit	$10	$ 25

The production lines for both products are highly automated, so large changes in production cause very little change in total direct labour costs. Workers who are classified as direct labour monitor the production line and are permanent employees who regularly work 40 hours per week.

All costs other than corporate fixed costs listed under each product line could be avoided if the product line were dropped. Corporate fixed costs totalled $125,000, and the total sales amounted to 5,000 units, producing the average cost per unit of $25. About $10,000 of the corporate fixed costs could be avoided if Loser were dropped, and about $15,000 of the corporate fixed costs could be avoided if Big Winner were dropped. The remaining $100,000 could be avoided only by going out of business entirely.

REQUIRED **A.** What is the overall corporate breakeven in total sales revenue, assuming that the sales mix is the same as last month's?

B. What is the breakeven sales volume (in units produced and sold) for Loser? (In other words, what is the sales volume at which Horton should be financially indifferent between dropping and retaining Loser?)

C. List at least two qualitative factors that would affect the decision to keep or drop Loser.

4.33 Product Emphasis and Keep or Drop, Product Breakeven, Relevant Information The income statement information for Waterford Ginseng Growers follows:

LO1, LO2, LO5

	Premium	Regular	Royal	Total
Sales units	100 kg	100 kg	100 kg	300 kg
Sales	$2,200	$1,600	$1,800	$5,600
Variable costs	1,400	1,000	1,080	3,480
Contribution margin	800	600	720	2,120
Production line fixed costs*	640	725	520	1,885
Corporate costs (allocated)**	90	80	105	275
Total fixed costs	730	805	625	2,160
Operating income (loss)	$ 70	$ (205)	$ 95	$ (40)

* If the company drops the product, these fixed costs are no longer incurred.
** None of these corporate costs are expected to change if a product line is dropped.

REQUIRED **A.** Using the general decision rule, which product should the corporation emphasize? Support your answer with calculations.
B. Using the general decision rule, should the corporation drop Regular (assuming no changes in demand for other products)? Support your answer with calculations. Show how operating income would change if Regular were dropped.
C. At what point (in kg) would the managers be indifferent to dropping Regular? In other words, what is the breakeven point for Regular?
D. What other information do you want before you make a decision about whether to drop Regular?

4.34 Product Emphasis, Opportunity Cost, Special Order A fire recently destroyed a substantial portion of Manley Company's production capacity. It will be many months before capacity can be restored. During this period, demand for the firm's products will exceed the company's ability to produce them. Per-unit data on the firm's three major products is summarized as follows:

LO4, LO5

Product	A	B	C
Selling price	$80	$95	$70
Variable costs	40	30	25
Fixed costs	15	20	10
Operating profit	$25	$45	$35

Fixed costs have been allocated to the products on the basis of the labour hours required to produce each product. The major capacity constraint is the availability of time on a processing machine. Each unit of Product A and Product C requires 2 hours of processing on the machine, whereas Product B requires 3 hours.

REQUIRED **A.** If demand for each of the products is greater than the firm's ability to meet that demand, which product should the firm produce first? If enough capacity exists to produce two products, which product should be produced second?
B. Assume that the firm has enough capacity to meet the demand of the two products you identified in Part A. If estimated demand for the next product to be produced exceeds capacity by 1,000 units, what is the maximum amount the firm would be willing to pay to increase capacity?
C. Management adopted your plan from Part A. Shortly thereafter, a strategically important customer requested that the firm supply 500 units of Product D, which has been discontinued but could be produced again if needed. Management wants to meet the customer's request to maintain goodwill but wants to know the cost before making the decision. In the past, Product D sold for $40, incurred $22 in variable costs, was allocated $4 of fixed costs, and required 1.5 hours of processing on the machine. Assuming that Manley has the capacity to produce two products, what is the opportunity cost of accepting the order?

4.35 Cumulative Exercise (Chapter 2): Two-Point Method, Multiple Products with Multiple Constraints The Terrell Company can manufacture three products—Alpha, Beta, and Zeta—which sell for $20, $25, and $40, respectively. The materials cost for one unit is $4 for Alpha, $12 for Beta, and $10 for Zeta. Labour is paid by the hours worked, and the factory overhead is allocated based on labour cost. Labour costs per unit are $5 for Alpha, $7 for Beta, and $15 for Zeta. When total labour costs are $20,000, factory overhead amounts to $80,000. When total labour costs are $30,000, factory overhead is $85,000.

LO5

Factory output is constrained by the time available on two machines. The firm has only 10,000 hours of time available on its grinding machines and 8,000 hours available on the polishing machine. Alpha requires 2 hours of grinding per unit, 4 units of Beta can be ground per hour, while Zeta requires 30 minutes of grinding time per unit. Two units of Alpha can be polished per hour, each unit of Beta requires 1 hour of polishing, while Zeta requires 2 hours of polishing per unit.

REQUIRED   **A.** Calculate the contribution margin per unit per product and set up the target (contribution margin) function for this problem. (*Hint:* First use the high-low method to estimate the cost function for factory overhead costs.)
B. List the constraint formulas, including the hours of constraint.
C. Set up a spreadsheet for Excel Solver or another linear programming package, and solve for the optimal product mix.
D. Now suppose that Beta's selling price increased by $1.26, and the contribution margin, therefore, increases by $1.26. Re-solve this problem for the optimal product mix. Did the product mix change? Explain the results.

4.36 **Make or Buy, Alternative Cost Functions, Qualitative Factors** Fielder Company is currently purchasing a component for $13 but is considering making the part internally. The plant engineer has suggested two alternatives. The first alternative would increase fixed costs by $12,000 per month and incur variable costs of $9 per part. The second alternative would increase fixed costs by $20,000 and incur variable costs of $7 per part.
LO3

REQUIRED   **A.** What level of volume is necessary to justify making the part?
B. Over what relevant ranges of volume is each alternative optimal?
C. At a level of output of 3,500 units, which alternative is most profitable?
D. List two qualitative or risk factors that could affect this decision.

4.37 **Cost of Inventory Stock-Out** Babe's Bats manufactures baseball bats and often receives orders for bats with special logos. Currently, the managers have more orders than they can fill and have sent out letters telling customers that their orders will be delayed. Records show that when there is a delay in shipping, 35% of those orders are refused by customers when the bats are finally delivered; however, bats are not refused when no backorders exist. The company incurs an incremental cost of $1.50 to prepare a backorder. The product sells for $20, and variable production costs are $12 per unit. Because the equipment is seasonal and the bats usually have special logos, managers assume that they will not be able to easily re-sell the bats in the orders that have been refused.
LO5

REQUIRED   Calculate the expected cost of being out of stock when a customer places an order for 25 bats.

4.38 **Cumulative Exercise (Chapter 2): Savings from Inventory Reduction** Waldon Company is considering dropping a product. The firm currently carries inventory valued at $4,500,000. Dropping the product would reduce inventory value to $1,600,000. Accounting records reveal that past warehousing costs were $320,000 when inventory levels were maintained at $1,000,000 and $845,000 when inventory increased to $4,500,000. The firm has several very large bank loans outstanding and pays interest of 12% on these loans.
LO2

REQUIRED   Estimate the annual savings in inventory carrying costs if the product was dropped. (*Hints:* Use the high-low method to estimate the cost function for warehousing costs. Assume the loan would be reduced, resulting in interest savings.)

4.39 **Keep or Drop, Customer Profitability, Qualitative Factors** Ross and Jones CAs is a well-established accounting firm with two partners and four staff in a small, rural town. The firm performs financial statement reviews and compilations and prepares tax returns for local companies and individuals. One partner is concerned that several long-time individual clients may not be profitable and should be dropped. One of these customers is Mabel Farley. Her documentation is highly disorganized, and she brings it into the firm five days before the filing deadline. Her tax return requires about 6 hours of staff time and 1 hour of partner time. She has been paying a flat fee of $300 each year.
LO2
A more recent customer is John Crowe. His documentation is well organized, and he brings it into the firm three months before the filing deadline. His financial dealings require a fairly complex tax return. His return requires 1 hour of staff time and 2 hours of partner time. John pays based on time at a rate of $140 per hour.
The firm is operating at capacity during tax season, and partners and staff work 14- to 18-hour days in March and April to complete all the returns before the April 30 deadline. Staff members are paid $20 per hour, and partners are paid $100 per hour. Fixed overhead costs such as rent are allocated to each job at a rate of $50 per partner labour hour.

REQUIRED   **A.** Which customer is more profitable?
B. At what flat fee for Mabel's return would the firm be indifferent between the two clients, assuming no time constraints for completing the returns?
C. Ross and Jones can drop Mabel as a client, increase her fee, or not change anything. List two qualitative factors that could affect this decision.

4.40 Outsourcing, Qualitative Factors, Strategic Priorities Two different retail companies, S-Mart and Galatea, are

LO1, LO3 investigating potential outsource partners to manufacture clothing. S-Mart operates a large chain of discount retail stores, and competes based on low prices, convenience, and a wide selection of consumer goods. Galatea is a boutique clothing store owned and operated by a major fashion designer, and competes based on fashion design, high-quality materials and construction, and personal customer relationships.

REQUIRED **A.** From the viewpoint of each company, rank the following list of outsource partner characteristics from 1 (highest priority) to 9 (lowest priority).

S-Mart	Galatea	
_____	_____	Reasonable worker conditions and labour standards
_____	_____	Low worker turnover
_____	_____	Precise quality standards
_____	_____	Short transportation time (nearby physical location)
_____	_____	Lowest price
_____	_____	On-time delivery
_____	_____	Ability to satisfy rush orders
_____	_____	Compliance with intellectual property rights
_____	_____	Sufficient capacity for the customer's entire clothing manufacturing needs

B. Explain how you decided which factors were most important for each company. Also identify the assumptions you made.

PROBLEMS

4.41 Special Order, Capacity Constraint, Relevant Information, Qualitative Factors Rightway Printers, a book printing

LO1, LO4, LO5 shop, is operating at 95% capacity. The company has been offered a special order for book printing at $8.50 per book; the order requires 10% of capacity. No other use for the remaining 5% idle capacity can be found. The average cost per book is $8.00, and the contribution margin per book for regular sales is $1.50.

REQUIRED **A.** Which type of non-routine operating decision is involved here? What are the managers' decision options?
B. What information is relevant for this decision? Does the problem give you all of the information the manager needs to make a decision? What other information is needed?
C. Using the general decision rule, what premium is the manager willing to pay (per book) to relax the constrained capacity, assuming that no qualitative factors are relevant?
D. Explain how capacity affects the quantitative analysis for this decision.
E. What qualitative factors could affect this decision?

4.42 Make or Buy, Qualitative Factors The Vernom Corporation produces and sells to wholesalers a highly successful

LO1, LO3 line of summer lotion and insect repellents. Vernom has decided to diversify to stabilize sales throughout the year. A natural area for the company to consider is the production of winter lotions and creams to prevent dry and chapped skin.

After considerable research, a winter products line has been developed. However, because of the conservative nature of company management, Vernom's president has decided to introduce only one of the new products for this coming winter. If the product is a success, further expansion in future years will be initiated.

The product selected is a lip balm to be sold in a lipstick-type tube. The product will be sold to wholesalers in boxes of 24 tubes for $8.00 per box. Because of available capacity, no additional fixed charges will be incurred to produce the product. However, a $200,000 fixed charge will be assigned to allocate a fair share of the company's fixed costs to the new product. The remaining overhead costs are variable.

Using estimated sales and production of 100,000 boxes of lip balm as the standard volume, the accounting department has developed the following costs per box of 24 tubes:

Direct labour	$ 4.00
Direct materials	6.00
Total overhead	3.00
Total	$13.00

Vernom approached a cosmetics manufacturer to discuss the possibility of purchasing the tubes for the new product. The purchase price of the empty tubes from the cosmetics manufacturer would be $1.80 per 24 tubes. If Vernom accepts the purchase proposal, it is estimated that direct labour and variable overhead costs would be reduced by 10%, and direct materials costs would be reduced by 20%.

REQUIRED
A. Should the Vernom Corporation make or buy the tubes? Show calculations to support your answer.
B. What would be the maximum purchase price acceptable to Vernom for the tubes? Explain.
C. Instead of sales of 100,000 boxes, revised estimates show sales volume at 125,000 boxes. At this new volume, additional equipment at an annual rental of $20,000 must be acquired to manufacture the tubes. However, this incremental cost would be the only additional fixed cost required, even if sales increased to 300,000 boxes. (The 300,000 level is the goal for the third year of production.) Under these circumstances, should Vernom make or buy the tubes? Show calculations to support your answer.
D. The company has the option of making and buying at the same time. What is your answer to Part C if this alternative is considered? Show calculations to support your answer.
E. What qualitative factors should Vernom managers consider in determining whether they should make or buy the lipstick tubes?

4.43 Special Order, Capacity Constraint, Relevant Information Yoshi Co. manufactures three different models of colour plasma screens: PS1, PS2, and PS3. Data on the three models is presented below:

LO4, LO5

	PS1	PS2	PS3
Selling price	$360	$540	$480
Unit variable cost	$240	$360	$340
Annual production units	4,800	3,200	4,200
Machine-hours per unit	6	12	8
Avoidable fixed costs, if product line is eliminated	$46,800	$38,200	$52,500

Yoshi's production capacity is 90,000 machine-hours per year.

Chiyo Co. has offered to purchase 4,800 units of a simpler version of PS3 for $435. Yoshi estimates that this version of the PS3 would result in variable costs of $305 per unit to manufacture and 7 machine hours per unit, but an additional fixed cost of $62,000 for a new assembly machine. The order has to be either taken in full or rejected totally. If Yoshi takes the special order, it will *not* produce and sell PS3 to compete with Chiyo.

REQUIRED
A. Compute the profitability index for each model and rank the order of priority for the models to be produced.
B. Given the machine hour constraint, for which model should production be reduced and by how many units? If Yoshi can purchase additional machine hours from another plant, how much would Yoshi be willing to pay to meet its production requirement?
C. Should Yoshi accept the special order from Chiyo? What is the incremental operating income/loss for accepting this order?
D. Given the machine hour constraint, what is the impact, if any, on the production of PS1 or PS2?

4.44 Special Order Computations and Decision Jackson Whitecrow operates a small machine shop. He manufactures one standard product that is available from many other similar businesses, and he also manufactures custom-ordered products. His accountant prepared the following annual income statement:

LO1, LO4, LO6

	Custom Sales	Standard Sales	Total
Sales	$50,000	$25,000	$75,000
Costs			
Material	10,000	8,000	18,000
Labour	20,000	9,000	29,000
Amortization	6,300	3,600	9,900
Power	700	400	1,100
Rent	6,000	1,000	7,000
Heat and light	600	100	700
Other	400	900	1,300
Total costs	44,000	23,000	67,000
Income	$ 6,000	$ 2,000	$ 8,000

The amortization charges are for machines used in the respective product lines. The power charge is apportioned based on an estimate of power consumed. The rent is for the building space, which has been leased for 10 years at $7,000 per year. The rent and the heat and lighting are apportioned to the product lines based on the amount of floor space occupied. All other costs are current expenses identified with the product line causing them.

A valued custom-parts customer has asked Jackson if he would manufacture 5,000 special units for her. Jackson is working at capacity and would have to give up some other business to take this order. He cannot renege on custom orders already agreed to, but he would have to reduce the output of his standard product by about one-half for a year while producing the specially requested customer part. The customer is willing to pay $7.00 for each part. The material cost will be about $2.00 per unit, and the labour will be $3.60 per unit. Jackson will have to spend $2,000 for a special device that will be discarded when the job is done.

REQUIRED **A.** Calculate and present the following costs related to the 5,000-unit custom order:
   1. The incremental cost of the order
   2. The full cost of the order (incremental plus allocated fixed costs, such as amortization, rent, etc.)
   3. The opportunity cost of taking the order
   4. The sunk costs related to the order
   B. Should Jackson take the order? Explain your answer.

4.45 Foreign Versus Domestic Production and Comparative Advantage Scott Mills was originally a producer of fabrics, but several years ago, intense foreign competition led management to restructure the firm as a vertically integrated cotton garment manufacturer. Scott purchased spinning firms that produce raw yarn and fabricators that produce the final garment. The firm has both domestic and international operations.

LO1, LO2, LO3, LO5, LO6

The domestic spinning and knitting operations are highly automated and use the latest technology. The domestic operations are able to produce cotton fabric for $1.52/kg. The domestic fabricating operations are located exclusively in rural areas. Their locations keep total average labour costs to $16.40/hr (including fringe benefits). The cost to ship products to the firm's distribution centre is $0.10/kg.

The firm's foreign subsidiary is a fabricating operation located in the Maldives, a group of islands near India. The average wage rate there is $0.70/hr. The subsidiary purchases cotton fabric locally for $1.60/kg. The finished products are shipped to Scott Mills' distribution centre in New Orleans at a cost of $1.80/kg. The domestic plant and foreign subsidiary use the same amount of fabric per product. Scott Mills has been producing three products for the private label market: sweatshirts, dress shirts, and lightweight jackets. In the past, the firm processed a new order at whichever fabricating plant had the next available capacity. However, projections for the next few years indicate that orders will far exceed capacity. Management wants each plant to specialize in one of the products.

The plants are constrained by the amount of sewing time available in each. The domestic plant has 8,000 hours of sewing machine time available per week, while the foreign subsidiary has 10,000 hours available per week. The domestic plant's variable overhead is charged to products at $4.00 per machine hour, while the subsidiary's variable overhead averages $1.00 per machine hour.

The sweatshirts require 1 kg of cotton fabric to produce, the dress shirts use 250 g of fabric, and the jackets require 1 kg of fabric. The domestic plant has special-purpose equipment that allows workers to sew a sweatshirt in 6 minutes, a shirt in 15 minutes, and a jacket in 1 hour. The foreign plant's equipment constrains production to 5 sweatshirts per hour, 3 dress shirts per hour, or 2 jackets per hour. The wholesale prices are $8.76 each for the sweatshirts, $7.50 for the dress shirts, and $37.00 for the jackets.

REQUIRED **A.** Using only quantitative information, should the firm close its domestic operations and expand the foreign subsidiary?

B. Assuming that wages in the domestic operations remain constant, at what level of wages in the foreign subsidiary would the managers be indifferent between producing sweatshirts at one location versus the other?

C. Discuss qualitative factors, including ethical issues, that might influence the decision in Part A.

D. Discuss whether production quality is likely to be a bigger concern for products produced at the foreign subsidiary than for products produced in the domestic operation.

E. If demand for each product exceeds capacity, in which product should each plant specialize?

F. Management insists on manufacturing all three products to maintain good customer relations. If demand for each product exceeds capacity, management would prefer to specialize according to your answer to Part E. At which plant should management produce the third product?

4.46 **Outsource, Relevant Costs, Qualitative Factors, Risks, Biases** Falco Services processes mortgage loan applications. The cost of home appraisals is included in its service fee, but Falco uses an outside appraisal service. The cost of appraisals has been increasing rapidly over the past several years, reaching $180 per appraisal last year. Falco's CFO asked one of the accountants to estimate the cost of doing the appraisals in-house. Several of Falco's mortgage brokers worked previously as real estate agents and have performed informal appraisals; however, none have professional appraisal experience. The accountant's son-in-law owns the firm that currently performs most of the appraisals.

LO1, LO3, LO6

The accountant prepares a report for the CFO that includes the following estimates for 1,000 appraisals. Appraisers would have to be hired, but no additional computer equipment, space, or supervision would be needed. The report states that the total costs for 1,000 appraisals would be $195,000, or $195.00 per appraisal. The current appraisal price is $180, so the report recommends that Falco continue to outsource the appraisal services.

Costs:	
Supplies and paper	$ 5,000
Professional labour	100,000
Overhead	90,000
Total costs	$195,000
Cost per appraisal	$ 195

Professional labour is the cost of hiring two appraisers. Overhead consists of fixed overhead, which is allocated at 50% of the cost of professional labour, and variable overhead (mostly fringe benefits), which is 40% of the cost of professional labour. Falco's CFO has to decide whether to continue to use the appraisal service or to hire appraisers and provide the service in-house.

REQUIRED **A.** Which type of non-routine operating decision is involved here? What are the managers' decision options?

B. What is the expected total incremental cost for 1,000 appraisals?

C. Which costs in the accountant's report are not relevant? Prepare a revised report that includes only relevant costs.

D. Using the general decision rule, should Falco outsource appraisal services or provide this service itself?

E. List risk factors about Falco's ability to begin a new appraisal service at or below the cost calculated. List as many risks as you can.

F. List possible qualitative factors, as many as you can, that Falco's CFO should consider in making this decision.

G. Explain why the accountant might have been biased, and explain what effects that might have on the cost report.

H. What are the costs to Falco of relying on the accountant's report for this decision? What are the costs to the accountant of admitting that he might be biased in preparing information for this decision?

4.47 Keep or Drop Business Risks, Relevant Information, Qualitative Factors Gourmet Fast Foods produces and sells many products in each of its 35 different product lines. Occasionally a product or an entire product line is dropped because it ceases to be profitable. The company does not have a formalized program for reviewing its products on a regular basis to identify products that should be eliminated.

LO1, LO2, LO6

At a recent meeting of Gourmet's top management, the head of operations stated that several products or possibly an entire product line were currently unprofitable. After considerable discussion, management decided that Gourmet should establish a formalized product discontinuance program. The purpose of the program would be to review the company's individual products and product lines on regular and ongoing bases to identify problem areas.

The vice president of finance proposed that a person be assigned to the program on a full-time basis. This person would work closely with the marketing and accounting departments to determine the factors that indicate when a product's importance is declining and to gather the information that would be required to evaluate whether a product or product line should be discontinued.

REQUIRED **A.** Explain why the managers of Gourmet Fast Foods cannot know for sure when a product or product line should be discontinued.

B. What factors might indicate the diminishing importance of a product or product line? List as many factors as you can.

C. If you were assigned to this position, what information would you want from the accounting system?

D. If you were assigned to this position, would you want any information other than that produced by the accounting system? If so, what type of information would be useful, and where would you be likely to obtain it?

E. List several benefits of assigning an employee full-time responsibility for a product discontinuance program.

F. If you were assigned to this position, describe the steps you would take in analyzing a given product.

4.48 Outsource Computations, Qualitative Factors, Cost of Quality Mills and Vines just received a bid from a supplier for 6,000 motors per year used in the manufacture of electric lawn mowers. The supplier offered to sell the motors for $88 each. Mills and Vines' estimated costs of producing the motor follow:

LO1, LO3, LO6

Direct materials	$40
Direct labour	20
Variable overhead	20
Fixed overhead	64

Prior to making a decision, the company's CEO commissioned a special study to see whether any decreases were possible in fixed overhead costs. The company would avoid two setups, which would reduce total spending by $10,000 per setup. One inspector would be laid off, at a savings of $28,000. A person in materials handling could also be laid off, at a savings of $20,000. Engineering work would be reduced by 500 hours at $15 per hour. Although the work would decrease by 500 hours, the engineer assigned to the motor line also spends time on other products.

REQUIRED **A.** Ignore the information from the special study. Using the general decision rule, determine whether the motor should be produced internally or purchased from the supplier.

B. Repeat the analysis, using the information from the special study.

C. Identify and discuss any qualitative factors that would affect the decision, including strategic implications.

D. After reviewing the special study, the controller made the following remark: "This study ignores the additional activity demands that purchasing the motor would cause. For example, although the part would no longer be inspected on the production floor, we will need to inspect the incoming parts in the receiving area. Will we actually save any inspection costs?" Discuss whether you agree with the controller. Identify and explain other costs that might increase if the part is outsourced.

4.49 Product Emphasis with Constrained Resource, Cost Function, Business Risks Riteway currently produces and sells five different products. Total demand for the products exceeds the firm's capacity to produce all of them. The constraint on production is the time available on a special machine. Data on the products and time required on the special machine are summarized in the following table.

LO5, LO6

	Product				
	A	**B**	**C**	**D**	**E**
Selling price	$12	$15	$18	$24	$32
Variable manufacturing cost	$ 8	$ 9	$11	$12	$18
Variable marketing cost	$ 1	$ 1	$ 3	$ 2	$ 6
Machine hours needed per unit	0.2	0.3	0.25	0.5	0.4
Maximum unit demand per period	10,000	7,500	20,000	1,500	2,000

The firm has only 5,500 hours of time available on the special machine per period. Fixed costs are $110,000 per period.

REQUIRED
A. How many units of each product should the firm produce and sell to maximize income?
B. On further analysis, it is determined that while fixed costs do not vary as production volumes change, they do vary based on the number of different product lines. If only two types of products are produced, these costs are $60,000, but if all five types of products are produced, these costs will be $135,000. Using the two-point method, determine a linear cost function for the cost of product lines.
C. Describe possible business reasons for the cost behaviour described in Part B.
D. Using the results from Part A and the cost function you developed for Part B, prepare an income statement for the firm by product line and by total products.
E. Review the results in Part D. Prepare a new product line income statement that reflects any changes that should be made in the production plans to maximize income.
F. Identify reasons why the managers cannot be certain that they have accurately estimated the following for each product: selling price, variable costs, machine hours needed per unit, and maximum unit demand per period.
G. Discuss how the business risks in Part F might affect the managers' production decisions.

4.50 **International Outsourcing of CPA Services, Service Quality** During late 2003, the chair of the Texas Society of CPAs, Nita Clyde, wrote a letter to Scott Voynich, chair of the American Institute of CPAs (AICPA). The letter expressed concerns about the professional responsibilities of CPAs who outsource work internationally and asked the AICPA to study the issue. Specific concerns included whether clients should be informed that work is sent to foreign locations and whether client privacy was breached.

LO1, LO3, LO6

At the time, outsourcing was used increasingly for all types of goods and services. The accounting profession was no exception. Years earlier, CPAs had begun outsourcing by hiring part-time staff who sometimes worked at home. As staff shortage problems increased and CPAs looked for new ways to reduce costs, they entered into international outsourcing arrangements. Usually the type of work outsourced was routine, such as transaction processing or tax return preparation. Proponents argued that these arrangements reduced costs, improved efficiency, and freed CPAs to focus on more value-added client services.

Voynich responded that CPAs already had several professional standards relating to international outsourcing. In particular, AICPA ethics rulings required CPAs to ensure that client confidentiality was maintained and that work was performed competently and with due professional care. Confidentiality included using encryption software and other controls when transmitting data. Voynich also asked the AICPA staff to provide additional guidance to CPAs.

SOURCES: Nita J. Clyde, Chairman, Texas Society of CPAs, letter to S. Scott Voynich, Chairman of Board of Directors, AICPA, November 11, 2003, accessed at www.accountingweb.com; S. Scott Voynich, Chairman of Board of Directors, AICPA, letter to Nita J. Clyde, Chairman, Texas Society of CPAs, in "Foreign Outsourcing Expected to Grow, but Tough Issues Abound," *Accounting WEB*, December 10, 2003, accessed at www.accountingweb.com.

REQUIRED Exhibit 4.4 provides examples of issues that financial institutions should consider when they engage in international outsourcing of information technology (IT). Refer to these issues as you answer the following questions. Suppose a CPA is thinking about outsourcing the preparation of routine income tax returns to an accounting firm in another country.

A. Discuss whether the CPA can be sure that services are performed competently and with due professional care. Does it matter whether the services are performed by local staff or in another country? Why or why not?
B. Discuss whether the CPA can be sure that client data will remain confidential. Does it matter whether the services are performed by local staff or in another country? Why or why not?
C. If the CPA decides to outsource, should clients be informed that their tax returns are prepared in another country? Why or why not?
D. Describe the pros and cons of outsourcing to the CPA.

4.51 Product Emphasis, Behavioural Effects, Strategic Objectives Retley Manufacturing makes three products: Gizmos, Whizmos, and Gadgets. The products sell for $50, $90, and $100, respectively. Each product requires processing on each of two machines. The grinding machine is operated 8 hours a day for 25 days a month. Gizmos require 2 hours of grinding. Whizmos require 3 hours, and Gadgets require 6 hours. The finishing machine can theoretically be operated 8 hours per day for 25 days, but the firm usually loses 25% of this time due to breakdowns. Gizmos and Gadgets each use 2 hours of finishing time, and Whizmos use 4 hours.

L01, L05, L06

Final assembly is done by hand. Four Gizmos can be assembled by a labourer per hour, while it takes 2 hours to put together one Whizmo, and 30 minutes to assemble a Gadget. All three products use the same raw materials. Each Gizmo needs 3 kg, each Whizmo needs 5 kg, and a Gadget requires 8 kg. Labour is paid $14 per hour, and raw materials cost $6 per kg. The firm used regression analysis to estimate the following cost function for overhead: Overhead = $200 + $6 per direct labour hour.

REQUIRED
A. Write out the target cell equation and the constraint equations to solve for the optimal product mix.
B. Use Excel Solver or other linear programming software to solve for the optimal product mix.
C. Assume that the firm's sales representative is paid $1,000 per month, plus a sales commission of 10% of sales revenue. Thus, the sales representative has an incentive to maximize sales revenue. Revise the target cell equation and solve for the product mix that maximizes sales revenue. What is the estimated cost to Retley if its sales representative maximizes sales revenue instead of contribution margin?
D. Ignore part (C). Assume that Retley has a strategic objective to gain total market share (based on number of units sold) as quickly as possible. Revise the target cell equation to solve for the product mix that maximizes total number of units sold. What is the estimated operating income of this product mix?
E. Ignore parts (C) and (D). Assume that Retley's marketing division insists that the company will develop greater product and brand recognition by producing and selling at least 10 units of each product per month. Revise the target cell equation and the constraint equations, and solve for the optimal product mix under this new constraint. What is the estimated opportunity cost of this action?

4.52 Make or Buy, Cost Allocation Freedom Company manufactures medical scooters for people who need assistance in mobility. Facing rising utilities expenses and labour costs, Freedom is contemplating outsourcing the production of one of its product lines, FreeMe. Currently, Freedom makes 3,000 units of FreeMe annually. The cost structure for one unit of FreeMe is as follows:

L01, L03

Direct Materials	$150
Direct Labour	180
Variable Overhead	50
Fixed Overhead	120

Freedom's cost accountant analyzed the fixed overhead and found that several overhead costs are allocated to FreeMe at a rate of 40% of the total of each overhead cost. Freedom's total corporate fixed overhead costs consist of Testing & Inspection, $120,000; Design & Engineering, $180,000; Rent (Factory), $105,000; and Machine-Related Costs, $420,000. In addition, Freedom pays $30,000 per year to rent a warehouse to store the finished product before shipping to customers.

A Chinese manufacturer offers to produce FreeMe at $450 per unit. A further study of the fixed overhead costs finds that once FreeMe is outsourced, FreeMe will no longer incur the costs for Testing & Inspection. Freedom will be able to reduce the Design & Engineering cost by half, and thus the cost saving will be passed on to FreeMe. The space and machine used for making FreeMe will be freed up to produce other product. However, there is no demand to increase the production of other product lines.

REQUIRED
A. Calculate the total cost per unit for FreeMe.
B. Should Freedom outsource FreeMe? Show calculations to support your answer.
C. Suppose there is a demand for other product lines, and the Rent – Factory and Machine related costs allocated to FreeMe now can be allocated to another product line. Should Freedom outsource FreeMe?

4.53 **Keep or Drop, Qualitative Factors** Sushime has been operating two profitable restaurants in Vancouver and Toronto for several years. A year ago, Sushime expanded its business to Montreal, and the Montreal restaurant has been suffering losses since its opening. The annual income statement for last year for the three restaurants is as follows:

LO1, LO2

	Vancouver	Toronto	Montreal	Total
Revenue	$1,200,000	$1,800,000	$ 800,000	$3,800,000
Cost of food	$ 480,000	$ 720,000	$ 360,000	$1,560,000
Rent (renewal yearly)	132,000	180,000	140,000	452,000
Utilities	72,000	90,000	85,000	247,000
Labour costs (paid hourly)	200,000	380,000	185,000	765,000
Allocated corporate overhead	160,000	160,000	160,000	480,000
Total costs	$1,044,000	$1,530,000	$ 930,000	$3,504,000
Operating income (loss)	$ 156,000	$ 270,000	$(130,000)	$ 296,000

A big portion of the corporate overhead is related to marketing and advertisement. The total overhead costs doubled when French was added to the marketing and advertisement materials. The corporate overhead costs were evenly allocated to three locations, when the Montreal restaurant was newly added a year ago.

Mr. Yamamoto, the owner of Sushime, is considering his options. The first option is to close down the Montreal restaurant. The second option is to keep the Montreal restaurant and open another restaurant of similar size to the operation of the Montreal restaurant in a French-language or bilingual location, such as Moncton, New Brunswick.

REQUIRED **A.** Analyze option 1: Closing the Montreal restaurant independently. By closing down the Montreal restaurant, the total corporate overhead will be reduced by half to the previous level. Should Sushime close the restaurant in Montreal? Show your calculations to support your answer.

B. Analyze option 2: Opening the Moncton restaurant independently. By adding a new restaurant in Moncton, the financial information is similar to the Montreal restaurant, except the cost of food will be $300,000, due to the volume discount, and the rent in Moncton will be $100,000 annually. Sushime does not expect to incur additional corporate overhead and the total corporate overhead costs will be evenly allocated to four restaurants. Should Sushime open a restaurant in Moncton? Show your calculations to support your answer.

C. Which option should Mr. Yamamoto take? What are the non-financial factors he should consider?

4.54 **Relevant Information, Special Order, Breakeven** Pinto Company manufactures printers and sells them for $150 each. Pinto's capacity is 20,000 units per year. The following are the costs for making one unit:

LO1, LO4

Direct materials	$25.00
Direct labour	55.00
Variable manufacturing overhead	13.00
Fixed manufacturing overhead*	18.00
Variable marketing and selling	12.00
Fixed marketing and selling*	4.50

*Fixed costs per unit are based on the total capacity of 20,000 units.

Tinto Printer Wholesaler would like to place a special one-time order of 5,000 printers, and offers to pay $120 per unit. This special order will incur one-time manufacturing fixed costs of $45,000. Since Tinto places the order directly with Pinto, there will be no variable marketing or selling expenses incurred.

REQUIRED **A.** Consider Tinto's special order alone, what is the breakeven point in sales units?

B. Suppose Pinto is working at 75% of its capacity. Should Pinto accept this special order in full?

C. Suppose Pinto is working at 85% of its capacity. Should Pinto accept this special order in full?

D. Suppose Pinto is working at 90% of its capacity. Should Pinto accept this special order in full?

4.55 **Relevant Information, Capacity Constraint, Product Emphasis, Keep or Drop** Easton Company manufactures and

sells three models of baby cribs – Angel, Bella, and Cutie. The information on these three products is as follows:

	Angel	Bella	Cutie
Selling Price	$800	$680	$450
Variable costs	440	340	270
Machine-hour per unit	12	10	7.5
Demand (units)	500	800	1,200
Product line fixed costs	$90,000	$102,000	$72,000

Easton's production capacity is 20,000 machine-hours per year. Product line fixed costs can be eliminated if the product is not produced.

REQUIRED **A.** Compute the profitability index for each model and rank the order of priority for the models to be produced.
  B. Given the machine hour constraint, how many hours should Easton purchase to meet all the product demand. What is the maximum price that Easton would pay for each additional hour purchased?
  C. Suppose Easton cannot purchase more hours from outside. Also suppose that one of the machines breaks down and it will take a couple of months to replace a part. As a result, the capacity is down to 16,550 hours. Should Easton make all three models? If not, which model should Easton drop? What is the impact on the operating income if Easton drops this model?

4.56 **Special Order, Product Emphasis, Break-even, Opportunity Cost** Winner Gifts manufactures and sells earphones.

The unit selling price for a set of earphones is $18, and the variable cost is $8. The annual fixed cost is $360,000. The machine hour capacity is 32,000 hours. Currently, Winner Gifts is working at 95% of this capacity. The machine can make 2.5 units per hour.

A credit union would like to purchase 6,500 simplified earphone sets for promotional purposes. They request the credit union logo be incorporated into the design of the earphones. They offer to pay $12 per unit. Winner Gifts has to take the full order or nothing. Winner Gifts' cost accountant has calculated costs associated with this special order: variable cost for the simplified earphone is $4 each, and the additional fixed costs incurred to make the credit union design and to rent a machine to make the logo are $40,000, in addition to the current fixed costs of $360,000. The machine can make 3.25 units of simplified earphones per hour.

REQUIRED **A.** If Winner Gifts has the capacity to make both products, which product should be the priority? Please show your calculation.
  B. What is the break-even in sales units for taking this special order?
  C. What is the operating income that this special order will bring to Winner Gifts, ignoring the constraint on machine hours?
  D. Is there an opportunity cost for taking this special order?
  E. Based on the above calculations, should Winner Gifts take this special order?

MINI-CASES

4.57 **Special Order, Qualitative Factors, Risks, Sensitivity** Jazzy Cases manufactures several different styles of jewellery

cases. Management estimates that during the first quarter of this year, the company will operate at about 80% of normal capacity. Two special orders have been received, and management is making a decision about whether to accept either or both orders.

The first order is from Penny-Wise Department Stores. The manager would like to market a jewellery case similar to one of Jazzy's current models. Penny-Wise wants its own label on the cases and is willing to pay $5.75 per case for 20,000 cases to be shipped by April 1. The cost data for Jazzy's case that is similar to the requested case follow:

Selling price per unit	$9.00
Cost per unit	
Raw materials	$2.50
Direct labour (0.25 hr. × $12)	3.00
Overhead (0.25 machine hr. × $4)	1.00
Total cost per unit	$6.50

According to the specifications supplied by Penny-Wise, the special order case requires less expensive raw materials. Therefore, the raw materials for the special order will cost $2.25 per case. Management believes that the rest of the costs, labour time, and machine time will remain the same as for Jazzy's case.

The second order is from the Star-Mart Company. Its managers want 8,000 cases for $7.50 per case. These jewellery cases, to be marketed under the Star-Mart label, would also need to be shipped by April 1. However, these cases are somewhat different from any cases currently manufactured by Jazzy. Following are the estimated unit costs:

Cost per unit	
Raw materials	$3.25
Direct labour (0.25 hr. × $12)	3.00
Overhead (0.5 machine hr. × $4)	2.00
Total cost per unit	$8.25

In addition to these per-unit costs, Jazzy would incur $1,500 in setup costs and would need to purchase $2,500 in special equipment to manufacture these cases. Currently, Jazzy would have no other use for the equipment once this order was filled.

Jazzy's capacity constraint is total machine hours available. The plant capacity under normal operations is 90,000 machine hours per year, or 7,500 hours per month. Fixed manufacturing overhead costs are allocated to production on the basis of machine hours at $4.00 per hour and are budgeted at $360,000 per year.

Jazzy can work on the special orders throughout the entire first quarter, in addition to performing its normal production. Jazzy's managers do not expect any repeat sales to be generated from either special order.

REQUIRED   **INFORMATION ANALYSIS**

The following questions will help you analyze the information for this problem. Do not turn in your answers to these questions unless your professor asks you to do so.

A. What is the excess capacity of machine hours available in the first quarter? Explain how machine hour capacity affects the special order decision.
B. Ignore the Star-Mart order. Using the general decision rule, what is the minimum acceptable price for the Penny-Wise order?
C. Ignore the Penny-Wise order. What is the contribution margin per case for the Star-Mart order? What would be the total expected profit (loss) incurred by accepting this order?
D. Using only quantitative information, decide which special orders Jazzy should accept.
E. What qualitative factors are likely to be important to this decision?
F. Identify and explain risks that affect Jazzy's decision.
G. What might happen to costs if Jazzy's production exceeds 95% of its capacity? Discuss how increased use of capacity from a special order might affect the company's costs. (*Hint:* Think about whether bottlenecks could arise and how they might affect costs.)

REQUIRED   **WRITTEN ASSIGNMENT**

Suppose you are the cost accountant for Jazzy. Turn in your answers to the following.

H. Write a memo to Jazzy's management, recommending whether the company should accept each of the special orders. Attach to the memo a schedule that shows your computations. As appropriate, refer to the schedule in the memo.
I. Write one or two paragraphs explaining how you decided what information to include in your memo.

4.58 **Keep or Drop Decision, Relevant Costs, Qualitative Factors** Elder Services is a not-for-profit organization that has three departments in three separate locations, in addition to the headquarters. The organization provides services for elderly clients who are still living at home. One department provides meals, one department provides cleaning services, and one department provides health care services. Elder Services relies on client fees and a small grant from the region to provide services. Following are the results from last year's operations:

LO1, LO2, LO6

Departments	Meals	Cleaning	Health	Total
Visits	10,000	10,000	10,000	30,000
Revenues	$ 50,000	$100,000	$150,000	$300,000
Variable cost (labour and supplies)	30,000	50,000	120,000	200,000
Fixed overhead costs	4,000	8,000	10,000	22,000
Transportation				
($4,000 fixed + $5,000 variable)	9,000			9,000
($10,000 fixed + $2,000 variable)		12,000		12,000
($5,000 variable*)			5,000	5,000
Headquarter costs allocated (based on revenues)	10,000	20,000	30,000	60,000
Total expenses	53,000	90,000	165,000	308,000
Surplus (deficit)	$ (3,000)	$ 10,000	$(15,000)	$ (8,000)

*Nurses use their own cars.

In the past, the region provided small grants each year to cover losses for Elder Services. However, due to an economic downturn and decreased tax funds in the current year, the region will not be able to provide any support next year. In light of these changes, the managers of Elder Services are trying to decide how to balance the budget.

REQUIRED **A.** What is the contribution margin per visit for each department?

Consider the following three situations independently.

B. To eliminate losses, the director of Elder Services would like to close the department that provides health services for clients. Assume that no alternative uses are planned for the health services building and no change would occur in headquarters costs. Estimate the surplus (deficit) if the health services department is closed.

C. What would be the estimated total surplus (deficit) if cleaning services increase by 2,000 clients, assuming no changes in fixed costs?

D. What would be the estimated total surplus (deficit) if Elder closes the meals division and that space is leased to another organization for $2,000 per month?

Suppose you are hired to help Elder's managers decide what to do about the lack of funding from the region this year. Ignore Parts B, C, and D and answer the following questions as part of your analysis.

E. Which type of non-routine operating decision does Elder Services need to make? What are the managers' decision options?

F. Perform quantitative analyses to help decide whether one or more of the options listed in Parts B, C, and D would be beneficial to the finances of Elder Services.

G. Now assume that the options in Parts B, C, and D are available. List risks about Elder Services' ability to achieve the quantitative results for each option, B, C, and D. List as many risks as you can.

H. List qualitative factors that the managers of Elder Services need to consider in making this decision. List as many factors as you can.

I. As a consultant to Elder Services, how might you go about acquiring qualitative information?

J. Suppose you decide to interview Elder Services employees to help gather qualitative information. Identify possible reasons that information you obtain from employees might be biased. List as many reasons as you can.

K. Describe possible trade-offs the managers of Elder Services might need to make in deciding what to do.

4.59 Integrating Across the Curriculum—Finance: *Special order, exchange rate options* General Robotic has received an order from an English firm to produce 10 robots that will perform welding tasks on the customer's assembly line. General Robotic's managers estimate that it will take four months to produce and deliver the robots. The total variable costs to produce the robots will be $600,000. The selling price to the customer is £64,000 each. Typically, payment is made at the time of delivery.

LO4, LO6

Currently the exchange rate between the British pound and the Canadian dollar is £1 = $1.58. Management is uncertain about whether or not the loonie will weaken against the pound between now and four months from now. Three alternatives for dealing with this potential problem have been proposed:

1. Do nothing and hope for the best.
2. Offer the customer a $10,000 price reduction if the customer will pay one-half of the selling price now with the remainder due on delivery.
3. Buy a four-month option that gives General Robotic the right to sell £640,000 for $1,400,000. The cost of the option would be $30,000.

REQUIRED **A.** Write an equation for the pretax profit the company will earn under each option. Use "R" to represent the exchange rate four months from now. (Ignore any interest on the money.)
B. What would the exchange rate need to be four months from now for the company to earn the same pretax profit on options 1 and 2?
C. What would the exchange rate need to be four months from now for the company to earn the same pretax profit on options 2 and 3?
D. What would the exchange rate need to be four months from now for the company to earn the same pretax profit on options 1 and 3?
E. Prepare a schedule that shows the best action for every possible exchange rate that might occur four months from now.
F. Assume that the managers chose option 3, and the actual exchange rate turns out to be £1 = $2.30 four months from now. How much profit did the company lose by choosing option 3 instead of option 1?
G. Assume the same information as in Part F. Were the managers wrong to choose option 3? Why or why not?

4.60 **Integrating Across the Curriculum (Operations Management):** *Product emphasis, simulation, risk appetite* The
L01, L05 managers of MGAF Specialty Products are considering shifting their product emphasis to create a new sales mix. The new sales mix has greater risk; the potential profits and losses are larger than under the current sales mix. The managers have gathered marketing and cost data and have run a computerized simulation of expected operating results under the current sales mix and under the proposed sales mix. Below are distributions of the income for each period based on 5,000 trials of the simulation.

Current Sales Mix				Proposed Sales Mix			
Range of Income			Probability	Range of Income			Probability
(10,000)	to	(5,000)	6%	(30,000)	to	(20,000)	1%
(5,000)	to	0	8	(20,000)	to	(10,000)	3
0	to	5,000	8	(10,000)	to	0	6
5,000	to	10,000	10	0	to	10,000	6
10,000	to	15,000	10	10,000	to	20,000	42
15,000	to	20,000	12	20,000	to	30,000	16
20,000	to	25,000	30	30,000	to	40,000	14
25,000	to	30,000	10	40,000	to	50,000	6
30,000	to	35,000	4	50,000	to	60,000	4
35,000	to	40,000	2	60,000	to	70,000	2
			100%				100%

REQUIRED **A.** Which sales mix should the managers select assuming they are risk neutral? *(Hint:* Calculate the expected value for each option, assuming income at the mid-point within each range.)
B. Which sales mix should the managers select under each of the following decision rules? Explain.
  1. Minimize the maximum potential loss.
  2. Minimize the probability of operating at less than breakeven.
  3. Maximize the potential amount of income.
  4. Maximize the probability of earning $20,000 or more each period.
  5. Maximize the probability of earning $30,000 or more each period.

C. Identify possible reasons why one sales mix might be riskier than another.
D. Explain how the company's risk appetite would affect the managers' decision rule.

Job Costing

in brief Custom products and services, which are produced singly or in small batches, need to be valued for financial statements, tax reporting, and management monitoring. Job costing is an accounting method used to assign product costs to *custom products or services*. In job costing, direct costs are traced and overhead costs are allocated to individual jobs. Sometimes, defects occur in custom products, and while defective units can sometimes be reworked, the costs for both spoilage and rework need to be accounted for, as does the cost of scrap that arises from production. ■

After studying this chapter, you should be able to do the following:

LO1 Explain product costs and cost flows through the manufacturing process

LO2 Describe how costs are assigned to customized goods and services

LO3 Allocate overhead costs to individual jobs

LO4 Discuss how job costing information affects managers' incentives and decisions

LO5 Explain how spoilage, rework, and scrap are handled in job costing

LO6 Appreciate the quality and behavioural implications of spoilage

Bombardier: Custom Manufacturing

Clement Sabourin/AFP/Getty Images

The iconic Canadian company **L'Auto-Neige Bombardier Limitée** began manufacturing tracked vehicles for snow-covered terrain in 1942. (In English, *l'auto-neige* means "snow car.") These vehicles were early models of what later became snowmobiles. Over time, the company developed expertise in building engines and expanded into other markets, such as personal watercraft, aircraft, subway cars, buses, and jet boats.

The company, now known as **Bombardier Inc.**, continued to expand, often by acquiring existing companies such as **Canadair** (the leading Canadian aircraft manufacturer), **Pullman Railcars** in the United States, and an Irish manufacturer of civil and military aircraft and defence systems.

In 1990, Bombardier acquired **Learjet Corporation**, a U.S. manufacturer of high-performance business jets with interiors designed for personal comfort and convenience. Often referred to as the limousines of the skies, these jets are built at Bombardier's plant in Wichita, Kansas. Models include the Learjet 31A (light jet), Learjet 45 (super-light jet), and Learjet 60 (midsize jet).

Bombardier operates Learjet completion centres in Wichita and Tucson, Arizona. The completion centres provide customized services such as exterior painting and installation of cabinetry and furniture. Corporate jet customers often order specialized interiors, including unique fabric, carpet, wood, and colour; ergonomic seating; sound, video, and satellite communication systems; distinctive galleys; water systems; custom wiring; bulkhead reinforcements; and soundproofing. Different types of work are performed in different areas of the facility. The facility includes two paint booths, two sand-and-strip areas, four preparation areas, and an interior mockup room. The centre in Wichita completes approximately 120 Learjet 45 aircraft per year.

Deciding what to charge for a custom manufacturing job requires considering many quantitative and qualitative factors. Even when manufacturing to standard specifications takes place over several continents, job costing can be complicated. Bombardier is designing and building a new CSeries of jets that carry 100 to 149 passengers due to be delivered to airlines around the world in 2016. The jets were being be assembled at the company's plant in Mirabel, Quebec, but components were being built by thousands of suppliers across the globe, including the wings in Northern Ireland, the fuselage in China, the landing gear in Germany, and the wheels and brakes in Ohio.

SOURCES: "Bombardier Celebrates the Completion of its CS100 Aircraft's Certification Flight Test Program," company news release, November 17, 2015; Yan Barcelo, "Fasten Your Seatbelts," *CPA Magazine*, January 1, 2014; Jens Flottau, "Bombardier Temporarily Reassigns CSeries Fuselage Work," Aviation Daily, July 6, 2012; "Bombardier Gears Up for CSeries Assembly," CompositesWorld, April 4, 2011; "Bombardier CSeries Aircraft Program Continues to Move Forward," company news release, July 19, 2010; John Sopinski, "Where in the World Are the C Series' Parts Being Made?", *The Globe and Mail*, October 1, 2010; Bombardier corporate website, http://businessaircraft. bombardier.com.

Product Costs and Cost Flows

There are three types of businesses: service, merchandising, and manufacturing companies. Chapter 2 discusses product costs and period costs. **Product costs** are those involved in either making or purchasing a product, and they are called *manufacturing* or *inventoriable costs*. Period costs are the operating costs that are not part of making or purchasing a product, such as sales and administrative expenses. Service companies, which provide services or intangible products, do not incur product costs and do not have inventory. Merchandising companies purchase merchandise for resale as a part of their business operations and, therefore, incur merchandise costs, and they may have leftover inventory, if all the merchandise purchased during the period was not sold by the end of the accounting period. Manufacturing companies, on the other hand, purchase raw materials and components and process them, making them into finished goods. Therefore, manufacturing companies may have leftover inventories in the raw materials account, the work-in-process (partially finished products) account, and the finished goods account at the end of an accounting period.

As a part of preparing the income statement, managers in merchandising companies need to prepare the schedule of cost of goods sold (see Exhibit 5.1). Managers in manufacturing companies also need to prepare the schedule of cost of goods sold, and the schedule of cost of goods manufactured as well. To do this, they consider the three main components to a product: (1) direct materials that become part of a product (cost object), (2) direct labour that includes the wages paid to the operator or assembly workers, and (3) manufacturing overhead, which includes all indirect expenses of making the product, such as utilities, machine amortization, plant insurance, maintenance and repair, indirect materials, indirect labour, etc. Direct materials and direct labour combined are referred to as *prime cost*. Direct labour and manufacturing overhead combined are referred to as *conversion cost*, reflecting the fact that these two costs convert materials into finished goods. The calculation of cost of goods sold for manufacturing companies is similar to that for merchandising companies, except that instead of merchandise inventory and purchases, manufacturing companies *produce* the products and have finished goods inventory. See Exhibit 5.2.

Product Cost Flows

In order to calculate the cost of goods manufactured, managers need to know the flow of cost in a manufacturing company and how costs are incurred and accumulated.

As shown in Exhibit 5.3, raw materials purchased for production are first recorded in the raw materials inventory account. When the raw materials are used directly in production, they are moved into the work-in-process inventory account. On the other hand, when

►EXHIBIT 5.1

Cost of Goods Sold Calculation for Merchandise Companies

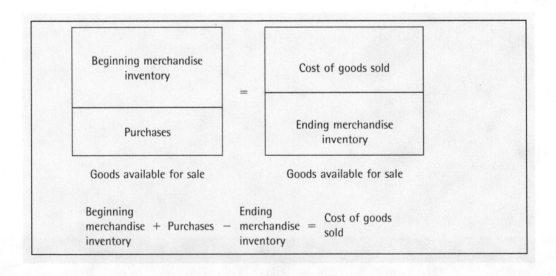

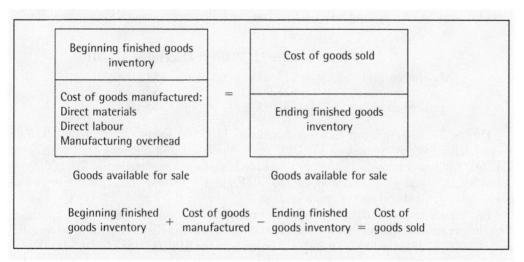

Cost of Goods Sold Calculation for
Manufacturing Companies

raw materials are used indirectly, they are moved into the manufacturing overhead control
account, which is an expense account. The costs of operation or assembly-line workers are
part of converting raw materials into finished goods; therefore, this direct labour cost goes
directly into the work-in-process inventory account. On the other hand, like the indirect
material costs, the indirect labour costs are accumulated in the manufacturing overhead
control account. Once a product or a cost object is completed, manufacturing overhead is
assigned to the product based on a rate. At the end of a period, the fully completed products
are transferred from the work-in-process inventory account to the finished goods account.
When the products are sold, the total costs are transferred from the finished goods account
to the cost of goods sold account.

To illustrate how the cost of goods manufactured and cost of goods sold are calculated
for manufacturing companies, consider Aluminum Benders Inc., a producer of aluminum

►EXHIBIT 5.3

Cost Flows and Accumulation of Direct
and Indirect Costs using T-accounts

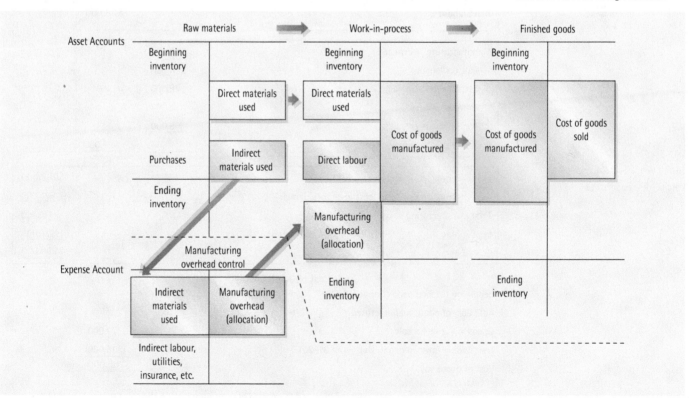

vents for heating and cooling systems that has the following balances for its three inventory accounts:

	December 31, 2016	December 31, 2017
Material control	$15,000	$12,000
Work-in-process	$28,000	$26,000
Finished goods	$32,000	$36,000

During 2017, Aluminum Benders purchased $105,000 worth of raw materials. The direct labour costs amounted to $88,000, and supervision and cleaning staff costs were $24,000. Additional manufacturing costs included machine amortization of $28,000, utilities of $32,000, and plant insurance of $8,000. Exhibit 5.4 shows the schedule of cost of goods manufactured and cost of goods sold.

Prime costs consist of direct materials and direct labour, and conversion costs consist of direct labour and manufacturing overhead. Therefore, Aluminum Benders' prime costs for 2017 are $196,000 ($108,000 + $88,000) and conversion costs are $180,000 ($88,000 + $92,000).

Measuring and Monitoring Product Costs

Managers necessarily measure past costs when producing financial statements and other reports of an organization's profits. Outsiders, such as shareholders, use profitability to

▶ **EXHIBIT 5.4**

Schedule of Cost of Goods Manufactured and Cost of Goods Sold

Schedule of Cost of Goods Manufactured

Direct Material Used:		
Beginning raw material inventory, January 1, 2017	$15,000	
Add: Purchases of materials	105,000	
Raw materials available for use	120,000	
Less: Ending raw materials inventory, December 31, 2017	(12,000)	
Direct materials used in production		$108,000

Direct labour		$88,000

Manufacturing Overhead:		
Indirect labour	$24,000	
Machine amortization	28,000	
Utilities	32,000	
Plant insurance	8,000	
Total manufacturing overhead*		$92,000

Manufacturing costs incurred in 2017	$288,000
Add: Beginning work-in-process inventory, January 1, 2017	$28,000
Total manufacturing costs inventory	$316,000
Less: Ending work-in-process inventory, December 31, 2017	($26,000)
Cost of goods manufactured	$290,000

Cost of Goods Sold

Beginning finished goods, January 1, 2017	$32,000	
Add: Cost of goods manufactured	290,000	
Goods available for sale		$322,000
Less: Ending finished goods, December 31, 2017		($36,000)
Cost of goods sold		$286,000

*Assume that the company uses actual costing and there is no over- or under-costing amount to be adjusted at the end of the period.

evaluate management performance and to make investment and other decisions. Managers also use past cost information to monitor operations, develop estimated costs for bids, and sometimes to make long-term decisions such as whether to introduce a new product. To enable these various uses for cost information, we need to distinguish between product costs and other costs that are not directly related to production.

Next, we focus on measuring and monitoring the product costs of customized goods and services. Customized products pose special problems, because the nature and levels of costs vary from product to product. Therefore, the accounting systems must be designed to capture costs for individual units or batches of goods or services as the manufacturing or service delivery process unfolds.

Assigning Product Costs to Individual Goods or Services

Cost information is used in various ways by managers. Financial accounting requires the matching of production costs with revenues on the income statement. The variable and fixed production costs associated with ending inventory are recorded as an asset on the balance sheet. To assign total direct and indirect manufacturing costs to all of the units produced during a period, accountants use *absorption costing*, as dictated by financial accounting rules (Canadian ASPE and IFRS). Several different absorption costing methods exist, reflecting differences in manufacturing processes. We will learn here about assigning costs to custom products, and in later chapters we will learn about assigning costs to mass-produced units (Chapter 6) and joint products (Chapter 9). Managers frequently rely on past production cost information to develop costs for bids, or sometimes to make decisions such as whether to introduce, keep, or drop a product. Distinguishing between product costs and other costs that are not directly related to production enables these various uses for cost information.

Product Costs

Product costs are the direct and indirect costs of producing goods or services. For the production of a Bombardier Learjet, direct costs include materials such as metal, wiring, and cabinetry, as well as labour directly involved in the production of an individual jet. In addition to direct materials and direct labour costs, product costs also include overhead costs related to production, which at Bombardier includes costs related to the manufacturing facility, such as amortization of equipment and insurance costs. Product costs exclude the costs of operating activities that are not directly related to production, such as sales and administration.

> **LO 2** Describe how costs are assigned to customized goods and services

The ease with which production costs are traced to individual products or services often depends on the degree of customization. As illustrated in Exhibit 5.5, some goods and services are one of a kind, and some are uniform. Other products require a hybrid process in which most of the product is uniform but select features are customized. Bombardier's Learjet 45 model is a hybrid product. It has a single, uniform aircraft design and manufacturing process, but the exterior paint and interior furnishings are customized at the completion centre.

> **⊠ CHAPTER REFERENCE**
> Chapter 2 defines *overhead costs* as all production costs except direct materials and direct labour.

Process Costing

When goods or services are uniform and mass produced, tracing product costs to individual units is generally inefficient, if not impossible. For example, it would be impractical to trace the cost of food ingredients to a single box of breakfast cereal that is mass produced. Process costing allocates both direct and overhead costs to continuous-flow processing lines; it is the approach generally used for mass-produced products. Direct and indirect costs are traced and allocated to production departments and then allocated to units. Industries that use process costing include food and beverage manufacturers, petroleum refiners, and plastic and metal manufacturers. The details of process costing are found in Chapter 6.

Product or Service	Customized	Hybrid	Uniform
Automobiles	One-of-a-kind vehicle (e.g., a race car)	Produced on an assembly line but customer chooses colours and amenities	Produced on a continuous-flow assembly line, without customer specifications
Jewellery	Hand designed and fabricated	Setting a specific diamond into a mass-produced gold ring	Uniform pieces of jewellery produced continuously
Accounting and tax services	Income tax research performed for a specific client	Tax services offered by the hour	Mass-produced tax returns
Health care	Hospitals, where each patient receives treatment using different resources	Blood donation centre	Flu vaccinations

Job Costing

When goods or services are customized, many costs are easily traced to individual products. For example, the interiors of Bombardier's Learjets are customized to suit each customer. Costs of direct materials such as carpeting or handcrafted cabinetry can easily be traced to an individual jet. It is also easy to trace the cost of direct labour to install the carpet and cabinetry. Other production costs, such as the completion facility manager's salary or the building insurance, are indirect and are allocated as part of overhead to an individual jet.

When a customer with specific product or service requirements places an order, we call the order a *job*. For example, if a famous diva orders a custom Learjet with a pink-and-white lace interior, Bombardier would consider this order a job. Orders placed for batches of product, such as a batch of a particular style and size of men's running shoes sold under the brand name of a retail shoe store, would be considered a job by the shoe manufacturer. Orders are also placed for services, such as the preparation of tax returns. When a client brings his tax records to an accountant, the accounting firm considers this order a job.

Job costing is the process of assigning costs to custom products or services. Direct materials and direct labour are traced to individual jobs, and production overhead is allocated. Manufacturers that use job costing include aircraft builders, custom motorcycle and automobile manufacturers, and custom jewellers, among others. Job costing is also frequently used in service industry organizations, such as hospitals, accounting firms, and repair shops. You'll first learn about job costing in a manufacturing setting. Later in the chapter, you'll learn about job costing for services.

Job Costing in Manufacturing

One of the purposes of measuring current and past product costs is to provide information for financial statements. Under financial accounting rules for IFRS and Canadian ASPE, product costs must be assigned to inventory. Then, when products are sold, these costs are transferred to cost of goods sold. This practice allows inventory to be reported at cost on the balance sheet and cost of goods sold to be matched against revenues on the income statement. Thus, job costing in a manufacturing organization assigns costs first to inventory and then to cost of goods sold when jobs are completed and sold. Exhibit 5.6 shows the flow of costs for Snow-Blade Snowboards, the example from Chapter 1.

To measure the cost of individual jobs, job costing systems typically include a subsidiary ledger. As shown in Exhibit 5.7, direct costs are traced and overhead costs are allocated to each job. Total work in process (WIP) is equal to the sum of the accumulated costs for all jobs in the subsidiary ledger.

▶EXHIBIT 5.6

Cost Flows in a Manufacturing Job Costing System

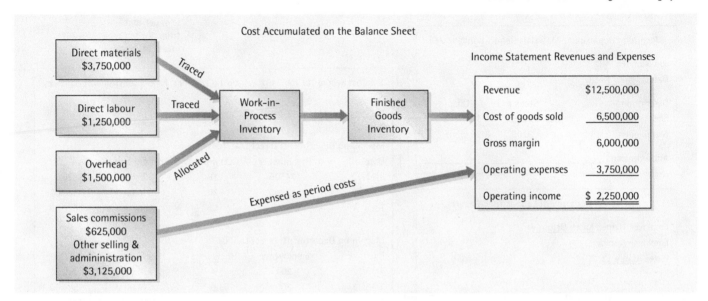

▶EXHIBIT 5.7

Tracing and Allocating Product Costs to Jobs

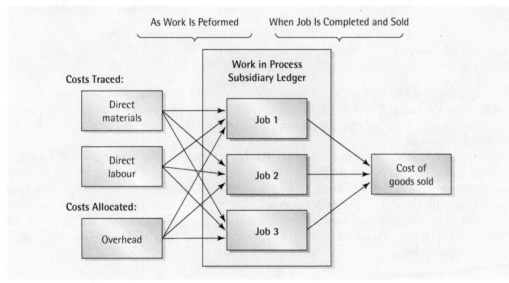

Assigning Direct Costs

Accounting records are used to trace the costs of direct materials and direct labour to each job. For example, suppose that Aluminum Benders Inc. works with contractors on large commercial buildings. Each job requires different styles and lengths of vents and joints; therefore, the company uses job costing. Work is performed in two different departments: machining and assembly.

Source documents are manual or electronic records created to capture and provide information about transactions or events. For example, the direct labour employees at Aluminum Benders create daily time reports that show the time they spend on individual jobs. The accounting department uses the time reports to calculate employee pay and to trace direct labour hours to individual jobs. As shown in Exhibit 5.8, each time report may include several different jobs. Similarly, when materials such as sheet metal or metal joints are requisitioned for each job, they are tracked in the accounting system, using the materials requisition form also shown in Exhibit 5.8.

The cost and activity information gathered from source documents is used to record costs in a subsidiary ledger for each new job. This record, called a **job cost record**, contains all the costs traced and assigned to a specific job, as shown in Exhibit 5.8. At Aluminum

> ▷ **ALTERNATIVE TERMS**
>
> Some organizations use the terms *job sheet* or *job record* instead of *job cost record*.

▶EXHIBIT 5.8
Job Cost Record for Aluminum Benders

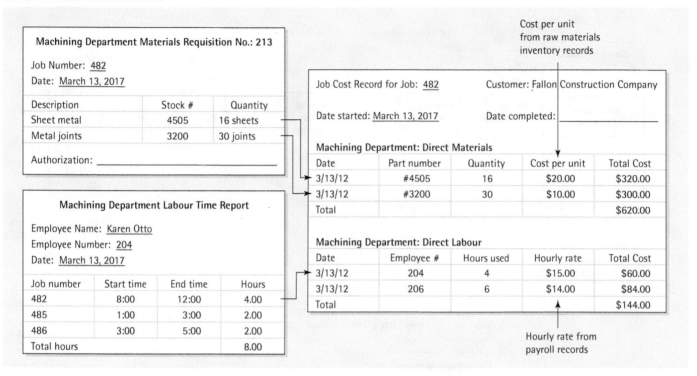

Benders, the cost per unit of direct materials is obtained from the company's raw materials inventory records. The hourly rate of pay for each employee is obtained from payroll records. Other companies may use an estimated, budgeted, or standard cost for direct materials and direct labour.

The sample job cost record shown in Exhibit 5.8 includes the direct costs of work performed on Job 482 in Aluminum Benders' machining department. The record is not yet complete; only some materials and labour have been recorded thus far, and the indirect costs have not yet been allocated. Aluminum Benders' job costing system calculates summary costs (totals for direct materials, direct labour, and manufacturing overhead by department) on each job cost record. The detailed information in the job cost record and the totals in work-in-process inventory are updated as new costs are incurred until the job is completed.

Computerized and Manual Job Costing Systems

▶CHAPTER REFERENCE
For more information on standard costs, see chapters 6 and 11.

Maintaining the detailed job cost records shown in Exhibit 5.8 can be time consuming and prone to clerical error. Therefore, job cost records are often part of a software package. Direct labour and direct material data are entered into electronic source documents (online time records and material requisitions). From there, the data are automatically posted into the job cost record and the general ledger system. This approach allows managers to immediately view job costs, even before the job is completed. Specialized software packages are most likely to be used in large organizations and in businesses where jobs are complex or require many resources.

In small businesses, job cost records may be tied less formally to the general ledger system. Instead of using source documents to track direct costs, organizations may use a manual job cost record to track direct costs for individual jobs. The job sheet is physically attached to an individual job. As materials and direct labour hours are added to the job, the amounts are recorded on the sheet. An artist might use this method when producing crafts and art pieces. Carpenters and home contractors also frequently use this method to monitor direct costs. Amounts from the job cost sheet are recorded in the job cost record in the subsidiary ledger on a periodic basis, when the job is complete, or sometimes as resources are used.

▶BUSINESS PRACTICE
FedEx Kinko stores use a manual job sheet to keep track of the work performed and prices charged to customers for individual print jobs.

Allocating Overhead

Overhead includes all production costs except direct materials and direct labour. Allocating overhead to individual products is a two-stage process. In the first stage, a variety of overhead costs are collected in an overhead cost pool, a group of individual costs that are accumulated for a particular purpose. In the second stage, costs are allocated from the cost pool to individual jobs.

L03   Allocate overhead costs to individual jobs

Steps in Allocating Overhead

Successful completion of the two stages of allocating overhead requires four steps:

1. Identify the relevant cost object.
2. Identify one or more overhead cost pools and allocation bases.
3. For each overhead cost pool, calculate an overhead allocation rate.
4. For each overhead cost pool, allocate costs to the cost object.

1. Identify the relevant cost object. In a job costing system, the cost object is a job. Sometimes a job consists of an individual product, and sometimes it consists of a batch of products. For example, a job at a Bombardier completion centre consists of the exterior and interior completion of one Learjet. A job at Aluminum Benders consists of a large number of aluminum vents required for a specific building.

2. Identify one or more overhead cost pools and allocation bases. Overhead costs are accumulated in one or more cost pools. Some organizations use a single company-wide or plant-wide cost pool for all fixed and variable overhead costs. Other organizations use separate cost pools for fixed and variable overhead costs. Fixed overhead includes costs such as production management salaries and space rental. Variable overhead includes any cost that varies with activity levels, such as supplies and, sometimes, electricity. If work is performed in separate departments or work areas, separate overhead cost pools may be designated for each department or activity. Accountants use judgment in choosing the number and type of overhead cost pools for a given organization.

The choice of overhead cost pools depends on the organization of production, the nature of overhead costs, and the usefulness of different types of overhead information to management. For example, Bombardier's Wichita completion centre has two paint booths, two sand-and-strip areas, four preparation areas, and an interior mock-up room. Each work area might be under the supervision of a different manager who is responsible for controlling costs. The use of separate overhead cost pools for each area would help top management monitor the performance of area managers. Alternatively, a single manager might oversee multiple work areas. If one manager is responsible for the exterior paint operation, overhead costs might be combined for the two paint booths. Organizations are also more likely to use different overhead cost pools for different types of work activities. For example, exterior painting is a different type of activity from preparation work such as installing carpeting, seating, and wiring. It is appropriate to use different cost pools when the nature or level of overhead costs differs across activities.

For each overhead cost pool, an **allocation base** is chosen to assign overhead costs to cost objects. If some portion of an overhead cost pool varies with a cost driver, it can be used as the allocation base. For example, the cost of some employee benefits varies with labour hours and labour costs. Indirect costs such as supplies in a paint area may vary with machine use. For cost pools that consist only of variable costs or a mixture of fixed and variable costs, accountants use allocation bases that are likely to affect at least a portion of the costs. For a *fixed overhead cost pool*, accountants choose an allocation base that is related to activities even though fixed costs are not expected to vary with the allocation base. Manufacturing job costing systems frequently allocate overhead using one of the following bases:

▶ Direct labour hours
▶ Direct labour costs
▶ Machine hours

HELPFUL HINT

In process costing systems, overhead is allocated to departments and then to units. In ABC systems (Chapter 7), overhead is allocated to activities and then to units, batches, product lines, or other cost objects.

CHAPTER REFERENCE

In Chapter 2, a *cost driver* is defined as some input or activity that causes changes in total cost for a cost object.

ALTERNATIVE TERMS

The terms *cost application base* and *application base* mean the same as *allocation base*.

3. For each overhead cost pool, calculate an overhead allocation rate. The allocation rate is the dollar amount per unit of allocation base used to allocate overhead to each cost object. (In a job costing system, each job is a cost object.) If we know the total amount of overhead cost and the total quantity of the allocation base, the actual overhead allocation rate is calculated as follows:

$$\text{Actual allocation rate} = \frac{\text{Actual overhead cost}}{\text{Actual quantity of allocation base}}$$

The actual overhead cost and actual quantity of allocation based are only available at the end of an accounting period. Calculating the total job cost for a particular job once it is completed or providing a quote for job will have to wait until the end of the accounting period. Alternatively, overhead may be allocated using an estimated allocation rate. To compute an estimated rate for the next period, we estimate total overhead costs and the total quantity of the allocation base and then calculate the rate as follows:

$$\text{Estimated allocation rate} = \frac{\text{Estimated overhead cost}}{\text{Estimated quantity of allocation base}}$$

Suppose we estimate overhead costs for Bombardier's exterior painting areas as $216,000 for the next three months and the hours paint employees will work as 5,400. If we use direct labour hours to allocate overhead costs, then the overhead allocation rate will be

$$\$216,000 \div 5,400 \text{ hours} = \$40 \text{ per direct labour hour}$$

The overhead cost can be over-budgeted or under-budgeted, which leads to over-allocated or under-allocated overhead amount. As a result, the actual overhead amount and the allocated amount can be different. The difference will need to be adjusted by the end of an accounting period.

4. For each overhead cost pool, allocate costs to the cost object. We allocate overhead costs by multiplying the overhead allocation rate by the actual quantity of the allocation base used by each job. In the previous example, we calculated the painting area's overhead allocation rate to be $40 per direct labour hour. When an exterior painting job requires 64 direct labour hours, the overhead cost allocation is

$$64 \text{ direct labour hours} \times \$40 \text{ per direct labour hour} = \$2,560$$

The overhead rate is also useful when completion centre managers need to prepare bids for new jobs. Once the labour hours are estimated for a bid, the estimated allocation rate is used to estimate overhead cost for the job.

Software packages that trace direct costs to jobs can also automatically allocate overhead. Suppose labour cost is used to allocate overhead. As the software package records labour costs in specific job cost records, overhead is allocated to each job at the same time. However, the accounting department might need to create a source document to gather the allocation base information (such as machine hours) needed to allocate overhead costs. Data for direct labour hours and direct labour costs are automatically collected for payroll calculations, but specific details about each job's use of labour or machine hours need to be recorded by job in a job costing system. Appropriate data about machine hour usage might not be available unless special records are maintained.

For Aluminum Benders, suppose overhead in the machining department is allocated using machine hours. The company's accountants created an online system so that the machine operator records the machine hours used for each job. If three machine hours are recorded for Job 482 and the overhead is allocated based on an estimated allocation rate of $56.00 per machine hour, then the computer automatically allocates $168.00 in machining department overhead to Job 482, as shown in Exhibit 5.9.

[1] M. Lucas, "Absorption Costing for Decision Making," *Management Accounting (CIMA)*, October 1997, pp. 42–44.

ALTERNATIVE TERMS

The *estimated allocation rate* is also called the *estimated application rate*, *standard overhead rate* (see Chapter 11), *budgeted application rate*, *predetermined application rate*, or simply *allocation rate*.

INTERNATIONAL

In Japan, fixed overhead is allocated using labour hours because accountants and managers believe that this allocation base encourages the substitution of capital for labour in advanced manufacturing technology.[1]

► EXHIBIT 5.9

Partial Job Cost Record Showing Overhead Allocation for Aluminum Benders

Job Cost Record for Job: <u>482</u>			Customer: Fallon Construction Company	
Date started: <u>March 13, 2017</u>			Date completed: _____	
Machining Department: Overhead				
Date	Allocation Base	Hours Used	Allocation Rate per Hour	Allocated Overhead
3/13/17	Machine hours	3	$56.00	$168.00
Total				$168.00

► EXHIBIT 5.10

Similarities and Differences Between Actual and Normal Costing

	Actual Costing	**Normal Costing**
Direct costs recorded	Actual cost of direct materials and labour	Actual cost of direct materials and direct labour
Overhead cost allocation rate	$\dfrac{\text{Actual overhead cost}}{\text{Actual quantity of allocation base}}$	$\dfrac{\text{Estimated overhead cost}}{\text{Estimated quantity of allocation base}}$
Overhead allocation	Actual allocation rate × Actual quantity of allocation base	Estimated allocation rate × Actual quantity of allocation base

Actual and Normal Costing

Under **actual costing**, overhead is allocated using the actual volume of the allocation base multiplied by the actual allocation rate. Because managers often need cost information before total actual cost and resource use information is available at the end of the period, estimates are typically used to allocate overhead. When the estimated allocation rate and actual quantity of the allocation base are used to allocate overhead, as in the preceding example, the method is called **normal costing**. Information from normal costing systems is used to prepare interim income statements, manage costs, and estimate costs for bids throughout a period. Exhibit 5.10 compares actual costing and normal costing. Under both methods, actual direct materials and direct labour are traced to each job. Following is a more complete example of the normal costing method for Aluminum Benders.

aluminum benders, part 1
ALLOCATING OVERHEAD COSTS IN JOB COSTING

Sean Rousseau, recently hired as the accountant for Aluminum Benders, is responsible for producing annual financial statements for the owners, creditors, and employees. He knows that product costs must be allocated to each job for the financial statements and also for preparing the organization's income tax returns. Sean is also responsible for preparing cost reports to help management monitor direct and indirect job costs. Because he is new to the company, Sean needs to learn about the company's past job costing methods. He also plans to evaluate the quality of the methods to determine whether changes are needed.

Evaluating Overhead Cost Pools and Allocation Bases

Sean learns that the company consists of two departments: machining and assembly. Separate overhead cost pools are used in each department, but fixed and variable costs are combined in each pool. In the machining department, overhead is allocated to production jobs using machine hours as the allocation base. In the assembly department, direct labour cost is used as the allocation base. In addition, the company uses a normal costing method to allocate an estimated overhead rate to each job.

Sean meets with the supervisor of each department to discuss the best allocation bases to use. In machining, he learns that the machines require little direct labour. A large portion of cost in the overhead pool relates to operating the machines, such as amortization,

© zhu difeng/iStockphoto

example

continued...

maintenance, and replacement parts. Thus, Sean concludes that machine hours are a reasonable allocation base.

The assembly department has few machines, but labour is used heavily. The labour mix is varied, with both skilled and unskilled workers. Sean agrees that direct labour cost is a reasonable allocation base because some overhead expenses, such as vacation and sick leave pay, vary with labour cost.

Understanding the Overhead Cost Allocation Method

The following estimates were developed by Sean's predecessor for all manufacturing during 2017:

	Machining	Assembly
Production overhead	$1,400,000	$2,400,000
Direct labour cost	$ 700,000	$1,000,000
Direct labour hours	35,000	100,000
Machine hours	25,000	10,000

Sean uses this information to verify computations for the estimated overhead allocation rate for each department:

Machining: $1,400,000 ÷ 25,000 machine hours = $56.00 per machine hour

Assembly: $2,400,000 ÷ $1,000,000 direct labour cost = 240% of direct labour cost

Sean wants to be sure he understands how the company's job costing system allocates overhead cost, so he recalculates the allocations for Job 482. This job was completed this week and shipped to a large office building construction site. He obtains the following information from the job cost record for Job 482:

	Machining	Assembly
Direct materials requisitioned	$40,000	$70,000
Direct labour cost	$28,000	$10,000
Direct labour hours	200	1,000
Machine hours	100	500

Using the allocation rates computed previously, Sean recalculates the amount of overhead for Job 482 as follows:

Machining: 100 machine hours × $56.00 per machine = $5,600

Assembly: $10,000 direct labour cost × 240% of direct labour cost = $24,000

Next, Sean queries the job costing system to create a report for management of the total costs for Job 482, as follows:

	Machining	Assembly	Total
Direct materials requisitioned	$40,000	$ 70,000	$110,000
Direct labour cost	28,000	10,000	38,000
Overhead allocated	5,600	24,000	29,600
Total cost	$73,600	$104,000	$177,600

Sean believes it would be helpful to management if the report also included the revenue and profit, as well as the original job bid. However, the job costing system currently cannot access those pieces of information. Sean decides to investigate ways to link the job costing system with revenue and job bid data. ■

General Ledger Entries for a Manufacturer

The general ledger in a manufacturer's job costing system typically includes separate inventory accounts for raw materials, work in process, and finished goods. These accounts are illustrated in Exhibit 5.11, which shows the entries that would be used by Aluminum Benders for Job 482.

Purchases of raw materials (not illustrated) are recorded in the raw materials inventory account (refer to Exhibit 5.3). As direct materials are traced to a job, the cost of the materials is transferred to work-in-process inventory (entries 1 and 4). Some types of direct materials, such as supplies, are not traced to individual jobs when they are used; these costs are

> **EXHIBIT 5.11**
>
> T Accounts and Journal Entries for Job 482

Raw Material Inventory		Job 482 Work in Process Inventory		Finished Goods Inventory		Cost of Goods Sold
40,000 1	1 40,000		7 177,600	177,600 8	8 177,600	
70,000 4	2 28,000					
	3 5,600					
	4 70,000					
	5 10,000					
	6 24,000	177,600 7				
	0					

Wages Payable		Machining Department Overhead Cost Control		Assembly Department Overhead Cost Control	
28,000 2		5,600 3		24,000 6	
10,000 5					

Journal Entries:

1	Work in process (Job 482)	40,000	
	Raw material inventory		40,000
	To record direct materials requisitioned for Job 482 in machining		
2	Work in process (Job 482)	28,000	
	Wages payable		28,000
	To record direct labour used for Job 482 in machining		
3	Work in process (Job 482)	5,600	
	Machining department overhead cost control		5,600
	To record overhead allocated to Job 482 in machining		
4	Work in process (Job 482)	70,000	
	Raw material inventory		70,000
	To record direct materials requisitioned for Job 482 in assembly		
5	Work in process (Job 482)	10,000	
	Wages payable		10,000
	To record direct labour used for Job 482 in assembly		
6	Work in process (Job 482)	24,000	
	Assembly department overhead cost control		24,000
	To record overhead allocated to Job 482 in assembly		
7	Finished goods inventory (Job 482)	177,600	
	Work in process (Job 482)		177,600
	To record completion of Job 482		
8	Cost of goods sold	177,600	
	Finished goods inventory (Job 482)		177,600
	To record the delivery of Job 482		

transferred into an overhead cost pool (not illustrated, refer to Exhibit 5.3). As direct labour employees report their work time, the cost of their wages is debited to the jobs they work on, and wages payable is credited for the wages earned (entries 2 and 5).[2]

Many organizations use overhead cost control accounts to monitor the costs for each overhead cost pool. As actual overhead costs are incurred, they are debited to the control account. For example, the assembly department supervisor's salary would be debited to the assembly department overhead cost control and credited to wages payable. Overhead allocated to individual jobs is debited to work in process and credited to the control account (entries 3 and 6).

When a job is complete, the work-in-process account includes all of the direct material, direct labour, and overhead costs that have been assigned to the job. The total cost can then be transferred to finished goods inventory (entry 7). Finally, when revenue for the job is earned, the total cost is transferred from finished goods to cost of goods sold (entry 8).

Overapplied and Underapplied Overhead

Under normal costing, periodic adjustments need to be made to reconcile the actual overhead cost with the amount of overhead that has been allocated to jobs. When we determine the overhead allocation rate, we estimate both the cost of overhead (numerator) and the volume of the allocation base (denominator). At the end of the period, the amounts of overhead in the inventory accounts (work in process, finished goods, and cost of goods sold) are either too little or too much, and so adjustments need to be made. Overapplied overhead occurs when actual costs are less than the total amount of overhead allocated to inventory accounts. In contrast, underapplied overhead occurs when actual costs are more than the amount of overhead allocated.

To correct for overapplied or underapplied overhead, we first compare the amount of overhead allocated to actual overhead cost. Suppose it is the end of the fiscal year at Aluminum Benders. Balances in the overhead cost control accounts for the machining department and assembly department cost pools are shown in Exhibit 5.12 (a). Machining department overhead costs incurred totalled $1,600,000, while costs allocated to jobs totalled $1,120,000 (20,000 machine hours × $56). Assembly department overhead costs incurred totalled $2,700,000, while costs allocated to jobs totalled $2,880,000 ($1,200,000 direct labour cost × 240%). The combined amount of overapplied (underapplied) overhead is

	Overapplied or (Underapplied) Overhead
Machining	$(480,000)
Assembly	180,000
Net underapplied overhead	$(300,000)

We then record an adjusting entry so that the balance of overapplied or underapplied overhead is removed at the end of the accounting period. We can think about the adjustment the same way as we close the expense accounts. Exhibit 5.3 shows that the manufacturing overhead control account is an expense account. At the end of an accounting period, we need to close the expense account, regardless of whether it has a debit or a credit balance. As shown in Exhibit 5.12, when the manufacturing overhead control account has a debit balance, it means that the overhead account has not been applied enough to the jobs. When the manufacturing overhead control account has a credit balance, it means that the overhead account has been applied too much to the jobs. If the amount is immaterial, it is simply assigned to cost of goods sold. If the amount of the adjustment is material, its treatment depends on production volumes. In general, a material adjustment is prorated among work in process, finished goods (if any), and cost of goods sold. However, financial accounting rules (Canadian ASPE and IFRS) require that fixed production overhead costs be allocated

---

[2] The direct labour entries in Exhibit 5.11 show only the part of employee wages payable that relates to Job 482. The total amount of an individual employee's wages would be credited to wages payable, and debit entries would be made to all of the jobs the employee worked on during the pay period.

▶ EXHIBIT 5.12

Overhead Cost Control Accounts
for Aluminum Benders

	Machining Department Overhead Cost Control Account				Assembly Department Overhead Cost Control Account		
Total costs incurred	1,600,000	1,120,000	Total costs allocated	Total costs incurred	2,700,000	2,880,000	Total costs allocated
Underapplied overhead	480,000					180,000	Overapplied overhead

(a) Before Adjustment

	Machining Department Overhead Cost Control Account				Assembly Department Overhead Cost Control Account		
Total costs incurred	1,600,000	1,120,000	Total costs allocated	Total costs incurred	2,700,000	2,880,000	Total costs allocated
		480,000	Adjustment	Adjustment	180,000		
Balance	0			Balance	0		

(b) After Adjustment

to inventory based on normal capacity. **Normal capacity** is the range of production volumes that is expected to occur under ordinary circumstances. If actual volume is less than normal capacity, then fixed overhead costs related to the excess capacity must be recorded as a loss in cost of goods sold. For simplicity, in this chapter we will assume that production volumes are within the normal range. In Chapter 17, we will relax that assumption.

Because the method of adjusting for overapplied or underapplied overhead depends on *materiality*, we need to decide whether the $300,000 amount for Aluminum Benders is material. One way to evaluate materiality is to calculate the net overapplied or underapplied overhead as a percent of actual overhead costs. For Aluminum Benders, this calculation follows:

$$\$300,000 \div (\$1,600,000 + 2,700,000) = 7\%$$

Many accountants view amounts smaller than 10% as immaterial. If we decide that the adjustment for Aluminum Benders is immaterial, we adjust the cost of goods sold total. Because overhead was underapplied, cost of goods sold would be increased, as follows:

Cost of goods sold	300,000	
Assembly department overhead cost control	180,000	
Machining department overhead cost control		480,000

If we decide that the adjustment for Aluminum Benders is material, it must be prorated among work in process, finished goods, and cost of goods sold. There are two proration methods: (1) use the ending balances in the work-in-process, finished goods, and cost of goods sold accounts as the basis for proration; (2) if the amounts of overhead allocated and remaining overhead in each of the work-in-process, finished goods, and cost of goods sold accounts at the end of the period are known, then the balances of the overhead amounts in each account should be used as the basis for proration.

Taking the first method as an example, suppose the balances in these accounts before the adjustment are

▶ HELPFUL HINT

Some accountants might use cost of goods sold to determine materiality.

	Account Balance	%
Ending work in process	$ 100,000	0.99%
Finished goods	20,000	0.20%
Cost of goods sold	10,000,000	98.81%
Total	$10,120,000	100.00%

The adjustment of $300,000 would be prorated among these accounts based on each account's proportion of the total. The adjusting journal entry would be

Ending work in process ($100,000 ÷ $10,120,000 × $300,000), or 0.99% × $300,000	2,964	
Finished goods ($20,000 ÷ $10,120,000 × $300,000), or 0.20% × $300,000	593	
Cost of goods sold ($10,000,000 ÷ $10,120,000 × $300,000), or 98.81% × $300,000	296,443	
Assembly department overhead cost control	180,000	
Machining department overhead cost control		480,000

The balances before and after the adjustment would be

	Before Adjustment	Adjustment	After Adjustment
Ending work in process	$ 100,000	$ 2,964	$ 102,964
Finished goods	20,000	593	20,593
Cost of goods sold	10,000,000	296,443	10,296,443
Total	$10,120,000	$300,000	$10,420,000

Whether the adjustment is considered material or immaterial, zero balances are left in both overhead cost control accounts after the adjustment, as shown in Exhibit 5.12 (b).

Another alternative is to recalculate the difference of the overhead cost for each job and adjust the amount to each job. This is a more time-consuming approach; however, this method will provide a more accurate result.

Exhibit 5.13 summarizes how overhead costs are assigned to jobs using normal costing.

> EXHIBIT 5.13
Overview of Overhead Allocation
Using Normal Costing

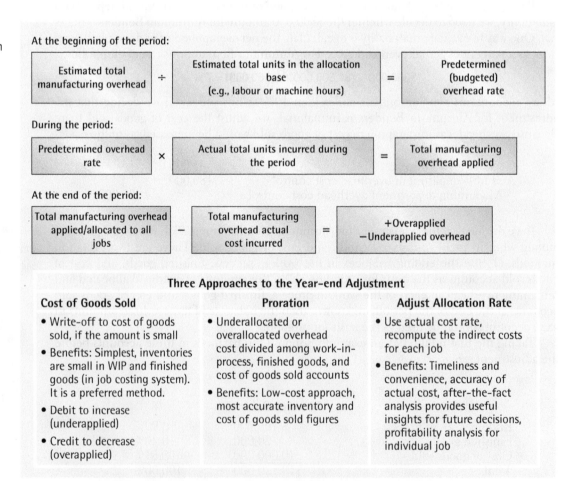

5-1 self-study problem   Normal Costing with Two Overhead Cost Pools

LO2, LO3

William Felix & Sons uses an estimated overhead rate for allocating production overhead to job orders. The rate is on a machine hour basis for the machining department and on a direct labour cost basis for the finishing department. The company estimated the following for 2017:

	Machining	Finishing
Production overhead cost	$10,000,000	$8,000,000
Machine hours	200,000	33,000
Direct labour hours	30,000	160,000
Direct labour cost	$ 900,000	$4,000,000

During the month of January, the cost record for job order No. 806 shows the following:

	Machining	Finishing
Direct materials requisitioned	$14,000	$3,000
Direct labour cost	$ 600	$1,250
Direct labour hours	30	50
Machine hours	130	10

Total costs and machine hours for 2017, recorded at year end, were as follows:

	Machining	Finishing
Production overhead incurred	$10,200,000	$7,900,000
Direct labour cost	$ 950,000	$3,900,000
Machine hours	220,000	32,000

A. What is the estimated overhead rate that should be used in the machining department? In the finishing department?
B. What is the total overhead allocated to Job 806?
C. Assuming that Job 806 manufactured 200 units of product, what is the unit cost of Job 806?
D. What is the total amount of overapplied or underapplied overhead in each department at the end of 2017?
E. Provide reasons why Felix uses two different overhead application bases. Also, discuss why Felix might use machine hours and labour costs to allocate overhead costs.

See the solution on page 231.

Service Sector Job Costing

Many different kinds of organizations provide customized services for their clientele; for example, hospitals, accounting firms, law firms, architecture firms, and print shops. A major difference between job costing for service organizations and job costing for manufacturing organizations is that service companies typically do not carry product inventory on the balance sheet. Under generally accepted accounting principles, service revenues are usually earned as the services are performed. Therefore, both revenue and product costs are recorded on the income statement as services are performed. Although job costing information is not required for inventory record keeping, many service organizations use job costing systems to help managers measure and monitor job costs and profits. In addition, the customer's price for a service is often calculated based on a percentage above cost. Costs in these contracts often include direct costs as well as allocated overhead costs. Thus, the allocation of overhead costs can directly affect revenues.

Job costing systems for service organizations are similar to the ones used by manufacturers. Source documents are used to trace direct costs to a specific job, and overhead costs are allocated. For example, in hospitals, physicians order treatments directly on computers at nurses' stations. From these treatment orders, materials are requisitioned and costs and patient charges are recorded as part of each patient's stay. Charges and costs are also accumulated for resources such as the number of meals served, X-rays taken, and minutes in the operating room. When the patient is sent home, the bill is sent to the provincial or private insurance organization, and the costs (direct and allocated overhead) are recorded in a subsidiary ledger identified with the patient's medical number and a hospital episode number.

When allocating overhead, service organizations often use the labour hours of their professional employees as an allocation base. For example, accountants and lawyers record professional labour hours and other direct costs to specific jobs. Overhead cost is then allocated on the basis of the professional labour hours used for each specific job.

Service organizations often use information from their job costing systems to facilitate cost management, productivity measurement, and billing. Consulting firms and other organizations that manage large projects often track job costs in conjunction with their project management systems. Following is an example of job costing in a service organization.

Uses and Limitations of Job Cost Information

L04 Discuss how job costing information affects managers' incentives and decisions

Job costing systems measure the cost of products, primarily for customized goods and services. The information from a job costing system can be used for several purposes, including the following:

- ▸ Reporting inventory and cost of goods sold values on financial statements and income tax returns
- ▸ Developing cost estimates to assist in bidding on potential future jobs
- ▸ Measuring actual costs to compare to estimated costs
- ▸ Developing cost estimates for short-term or long-term decisions

Adam Gregor/Shutterstock

example

nighthawk law company
JOB COSTING IN A LAW FIRM

Nighthawk Law Company specializes in copyright protection for authors. A client approached the law firm about handling his lawsuit against a large film company that he believes stole the plot from one of his novels for a made-for-TV movie.

Estimated Job Costs and Price

The law partners estimated that the case would require 500 hours of professional labour. Nighthawk's accountant estimated the following direct costs:

Direct professional labour (500 hours)	$ 75,000
Direct support labour	20,000
Fringe benefits for direct labour	15,000
Photocopying	1,000
Telephone calls	1,000
Total direct costs	$112,000

Last year, Nighthawk's overhead totalled $450,000. The two law partners worked about 5,000 professional labour hours. The accountant developed an estimated overhead allocation rate of $90 per direct labour hour ($450,000 ÷ 5,000). Therefore, the estimated overhead cost for this case is $90 × 500 hours = $45,000, and the total estimated cost is $157,000 ($45,000 + $112,000). The law firm's policy is to mark up cost by 20% for the estimated price. Using this mark-up, the estimated profit for the case is $31,400 ($157,000 × 20%). Using all of this information, the partners estimate the client's service price as follows:

Direct professional labour (500 hours)	$ 75,000
Direct support labour	20,000
Fringe benefits for direct and professional labour	15,000
Photocopying	1,000
Telephone calls	1,000
Total direct costs	112,000
Overhead ($90 × 500 hours)	45,000
Total costs	157,000
Margin ($157,000 × 20%)	31,400
Total estimated service price	$188,400

Competitor's Job Costs and Price

A competing law firm traces only the direct professional labour hours as a direct cost and considers all other costs to be indirect (overhead). These overhead costs are allocated at an estimated rate of $160 per professional labour hour. The accountant for this firm estimates this copyright case to cost $75,000 + $80,000 ($160 × 500) = $155,000. The competitor uses the same mark-up rate as Nighthawk: 20% of estimated total cost, or $31,000 ($155,000 × 20%). The partner in the competitor firm estimates the client's service price as follows:

Direct professional labour (500 hours)	$ 75,000
Overhead ($160 × 500 hours)	80,000
Total costs	155,000
Margin ($155,000 × 20%)	31,000
Total estimated service price	$186,000

Monitoring Job Costs

The prices estimated by the two law firms are very close in amount. However, the costs that are used to estimate the price are also used to monitor costs in the law firm. Nighthawk separately accounts for direct costs such as fringe benefits, photocopying, and telephone calls. The competitor includes these costs in overhead. Each approach has pros and cons.

Nighthawk's accounting system incurs additional costs to separately accumulate and assign fringe benefits, photocopying, and telephone calls to individual jobs. Each of these costs is accumulated in a separate cost pool. Fringe benefits are allocated to jobs based on information that is already available about professional and support labour hours or costs. To allocate photocopying costs, the firm needs a system, such as the use of client codes, to record photocopying usage for each job. Telephone costs are traced using telephone logs. The accuracy of records for photocopying and telephone costs depends on the ability and desire of professional and support staff to maintain good records.

The benefit of separately accumulating and assigning fringe benefits, photocopying, and telephone call costs is improved monitoring of costs. The overhead cost pool is considerably smaller and includes fewer different types of costs. As the proportion of costs that can be directly traced to individual jobs increases, the accuracy of the costing system increases. Therefore, systems with lower proportions of overhead more accurately capture the flow of resources to individual jobs. ■

> ●● > STRATEGIC RISK MANAGEMENT: NIGHTHAWK, LLP

RELEVANCE OF FIXED COSTS In creating their bid for a new client, the Nighthawk partners included both fixed and variable costs in their calculations. The following costs were probably fixed: direct professional labour, direct support labour, fringe benefits, and overhead costs, such as rent. In Chapter 4, we learned that fixed costs are often irrelevant for short-term decisions. Should the partners ignore fixed costs when developing a job bid? Relevant costs include the opportunity costs of any other jobs that the law firm will forgo if it accepts this client. Assuming that other clients would be willing to pay fees that include a mark-up of 20% on total costs, then the partners' calculations are appropriate. They plan to charge this client the same fees they would charge another client. However, the law partners may be willing to accept a lower price if accepting this job is strategically important to the law firm. Conversely, they may bid a higher price than usual if this job is strategically unimportant or if alternative clients are willing to pay higher rates.

Differences in business operations and accounting systems lead to differences in the quality of job cost information. Before using job cost information for controlling operations or making decisions, managers need to consider whether their job cost information is relevant and reliable. In addition, overhead allocations may distort costs for financial statements, income tax returns, cost-based customer contracts, or other uses.

Allocated Overhead Costs and Decision Making

Overhead costs are allocated to jobs to match revenues and product costs. However, allocated overhead costs are not relevant information for most short-term decisions, such as special orders or the use of constrained resources. Many overhead costs are fixed; they do not change with changes in the allocation base or any other measure of activity. Nevertheless, managers may mistakenly assume that these allocated costs are variable, particularly when the job costing system uses several cost pools and allocation bases. Another problem occurs if the allocation base used to allocate variable overhead costs is not a cost driver, which means it does not accurately reflect the use of variable cost resources.

▶ CHAPTER REFERENCE
See Chapter 4 for more information on short-term decision making.

Managers within an organization often do not understand how costs are allocated to individual jobs. They may misinterpret cost information and rely on irrelevant information. Accountants must not only produce relevant information for each decision but also help educate managers about appropriate uses of cost information.

The next illustration, Aluminum Benders, Part 2, demonstrates the accountant's role in providing managers with relevant information for internal decision making.

example

aluminum benders, part 2
JOB COSTS RELEVANT FOR DECISION MAKING

Suppose Aluminum Benders receives two new orders from two different contractors. Because of previous commitments, the company has only enough capacity during the next few weeks to accept one of the new orders.

Sean estimates the direct costs for the new orders and the amount of overhead that will be allocated to each job. These figures allow him to estimate the contribution margin and operating income as follows:

	For Contractor A	For Contractor B
Estimated selling price	$150,000	$230,000
Less variable costs:		
Direct materials	55,000	100,000
Direct labour		
Machining	5,000	10,000
Assembly	10,000	20,000
Estimated contribution margin	80,000	100,000
Less allocated overhead:		
Machining:		
For Contractor A (85 hours × $56)	4,760	
For Contractor B (150 hours × $56)		8,400
Assembly (direct labour cost × 240%)	24,000	48,000
Estimated operating income	$ 51,240	$ 43,600

© zhu difeng/iStockphoto

Sean initially thinks that the company should accept the job from contractor A because that job is expected to generate higher operating income. However, he realizes that operating income includes a reduction for allocated overhead. He knows that the contribution margin for each job is relevant to the decision; he is less sure whether overhead is relevant.

Sean studies the types of costs included in the overhead cost pools and learns that most of the overhead costs are fixed. Direct labour employees are guaranteed a 40-hour work week, so the overhead costs of fringe benefits are likely fixed. The machine-related costs are also primarily fixed, although repair costs probably increase as volumes increase. Sean would like to break overhead into fixed and variable portions but does not have time right now.

Given his quick analysis of the costs for each job, Sean believes he should present only the incremental costs in his report because managers may assume that allocated overhead costs actually vary with machine hours and labour cost and choose contractor A's job, with an estimated operating income of $51,240. Thus, Sean plans to recommend that the company accept the job from contractor B. He expects the company to earn $20,000 more ($100,000 − $80,000) in incremental contribution margin from this job than from contractor A's job.

Qualitative Factors

Sean asks the controller, Monisha Patel, for her advice. She agrees that only incremental costs should be presented. She tells Sean that he also needs to discuss some qualitative factors with the managers. For example, contractor A is a profitable, ongoing customer who would become dissatisfied if the order were turned down. The job from contractor B involves special machining that the company does not ordinarily perform, reducing the accountant's confidence in the job cost estimate. However, contractor B is a new customer with whom Aluminum Benders would like to work in the future. These types of qualitative factors sometimes weigh more heavily than the estimated incremental contribution margin when managers make these types of decisions. ■

Judgment and Uncertainties in Job Costing System Design

The tendency is to mistakenly believe that job costs are measured accurately. However, job costing systems are subject to uncertainties and require judgment when deciding which costs to trace directly, the types of overhead cost pools, and the allocation base for each overhead cost pool.

Little uncertainty tends to surround the direct costs assigned to a job, because those costs are traced to each job. However, accountants use judgment to decide which direct costs will be traced. Occasionally direct costs are quite small, and the cost of creating a system to track them is greater than the benefit achieved. In these cases, costs that might potentially be traced are instead included with indirect costs in a pool of overhead costs. However, changes in technology sometimes allow accountants to trace costs that were previously too costly to trace. For example, most large photocopiers today include security systems that track the number of copies made to specific account codes.

Accountants also choose the type and number of overhead cost pools. For example, overhead costs were pooled at the department level in Aluminum Benders, and they could have been broken down further. For example, fixed and variable overhead could have been separated, or overhead could have been pooled for individual activities within each department. On the other hand, fewer cost pools could have been used by combining all overhead at the plant level. When deciding how many cost pools to use, accountants consider the costs and benefits from identifying and tracking more detailed information about overhead costs.

Ideally, we would prefer that the overhead allocation process reflect the flow of overhead resources to each job. Thus, an ideal overhead allocation base would be a cost driver. However, fixed overhead is not expected to vary with any allocation base, and it is not always possible to identify or to accurately measure a cost driver for variable overhead. Thus, allocated overhead generally does not accurately measure the overhead resources used by a job.

Measuring Job Costs for Diagnostic Control

Managers use job cost estimates to establish a bid for a job or decide whether to accept a job. They then monitor operations by comparing actual job costs to the original estimate and analyze the differences between actual and estimated job costs to evaluate the efficiency of operations and to improve future job cost estimates.

In diagnostic control systems, job costs may be tracked so that managers and employees can be held responsible for controlling costs. These systems are most effective when costs are measured accurately and personal performance can be linked clearly to costs. However, even direct costs are sometimes measured inaccurately. For example, employees may accidentally report time to the wrong job code or intentionally manipulate time reports to avoid recording more cost to a job that is over budget.

When overhead costs from many departments are pooled, managers and employees within each department have little incentive to control costs. In addition, different departments usually perform different tasks, so their costs may be quite different. Costs allocated on a department level provide better control and may more accurately reflect the flow of resources. In addition, this practice may encourage managers to redesign products to use fewer resources from costly departments.

Allocated Overhead and Relevant Costs

Because a job costing system accumulates and reports costs for individual jobs, managers may mistakenly believe that the costs assigned to a job are incremental—that is, would not be incurred if the job were not undertaken. However, analysis is required to identify the job costs that are relevant to a given decision.

CHAPTER REFERENCE

Chapter 7 introduces ABC, GPK, and RCA, which use a larger number of overhead cost pools.

CHAPTER REFERENCE

Chapter 2 introduces several techniques for evaluating whether a potential cost driver explains the variation in a cost.

CHAPTER REFERENCE

Chapter 11 introduces variance analysis, which is used to evaluate differences between estimated and actual costs.

●●◉ RISK OF BIASED DECISIONS: HINDSIGHT BIAS

HINDSIGHT BIAS is a tendency to view uncertain past events as being relatively inevitable and predictable. When the memory of a past event is reconstructed, people often fill in the gaps so that the outcome appears to be foreseeable. The hindsight bias is also known as the 'I-knew-it-all-along' effect. Hindsight bias is reduced when people stop to think carefully about the causes of events.

Business decisions including job budgets are based on estimates, so managers frequently have doubts about the success of a project. Hindsight bias encourages managers to erroneously recall that they had greater confidence in projects that turn out to have good results, but greater doubts about projects that have bad results. This bias inhibits managers from carefully evaluating the circumstances that lead to good or poor results, and, thus, they fail to learn sufficiently from past experiences.

Professionals such as accountants, lawyers, architects, and management consultants often bill their clients for reimbursement of expenses in addition to professional fees. Reimbursable expenses might include travel, printing, research, or other costs. Clients expect to pay for only actual costs. However, questions sometimes arise about whether professionals overbill their clients for expenses.

For example, the U.S. Justice Department investigated the four largest public accounting firms for overbilling their travel expenses. Allegedly, the firms billed the U.S. government for the full cost of airline tickets, hotels, and car rentals, even though the firms had received rebates and volume discounts amounting to hundreds of millions of dollars. During 2005, **PricewaterhouseCoopers** settled the charges by paying the government $41.9 million without admitting any wrongdoing. The government later reached an agreement for a combined $25.5-million payment from **BearingPoint**, **Booz Allen Hamilton**, **Ernst & Young**, and **KPMG**. These settlements followed an earlier class-action lawsuit in which five accounting and consulting firms were court-ordered to pay $104 million on behalf of corporate clients for travel cost overbillings.

Source: J. Weil and C. Bryan-Low, "Travel-Billing Probe Has a Bigger Scope," *The Wall Street Journal Online*, September 26, 2003; Staff reporter, "Pricewaterhouse Settles Charges," *The Wall Street Journal Online*, July 12, 2005; T. Johansmeyer, "Major Firms Settle Expense Lawsuit," *Big Four Alumni Magazine*, Vol. 1, No. 1, January 2006; "NPR Recoveries Total $104 million Against Accounting Industry," Nix, Patterson & Roach, LLP.

Sawayasu Tsuji/iStockphoto

TRACING REBATES AND DISCOUNTS DIRECTLY TO JOBS

Professional service firms use job costing systems to trace reimbursable expenses directly to each client. Do firms have an ethical responsibility to also trace rebates and volume discounts to individual clients? Would it matter if the amount of rebates and discounts depend upon total annual volumes that are not yet known at the time a client is billed for travel costs? Should the same ethical standards apply to accounting firms and other types of professional firms?

Spoilage, Rework, and Scrap in Job Costing

No matter how carefully goods are manufactured, occasionally some units do not meet quality standards; they are spoiled. Spoilage refers to units of product that are unacceptable and are discarded, reworked, or sold at a reduced price. Examples of spoilage in job costing include

| L05 | Explain how spoilage, rework, and scrap are handled in job costing |

> ▶ Units in batches of clothing that have flaws in the material or sewing
> ▶ Several valves in a batch that do not function properly when tested at the end of production
> ▶ A custom-ordered birdhouse that has an off-centre round hole

Different types of spoiled products are handled in different ways. For example, if the material flaws are not too noticeable, the clothing can be sold as irregular. Perhaps the birdhouse can be sold at a discount, but the valves probably cannot be sold and must be discarded or reworked.

Spoilage is typically identified through some type of inspection process. Sometimes inspection occurs at the end of the production process, immediately before units are moved to finished goods inventory. Other times, inspection occurs at one or more intermediate stages during production. Inspection can also occur at the beginning of the process.

For example, denim fabric can be checked for flaws before it is introduced into the production process for manufacturing jeans. Other practices, such as conducting preventive maintenance on equipment rather than waiting for machinery problems to develop, help minimize spoilage.

To determine the cost of a partially complete spoiled unit, we add up all direct materials and labour costs used, and allocate overhead according to the amount of work completed before the unit was removed from production. The way spoilage cost is handled depends on whether the spoilage is considered normal or abnormal.

Normal and Abnormal Spoilage

Normal spoilage consists of defective units that arise as part of regular operations. If normal spoilage arises from the requirements of a specific job, the cost of the spoiled units is charged to the job. For example, suppose one of Bombardier's completion centre customers wants leather interior walls. If the leather is more difficult to install than other materials and part of the leather is spoiled in the installation process, then the cost of the spoilage would be charged to that job. Normal spoilage also occurs periodically as a regular part of all jobs. For example, suppose that the safety lighting system installed along the carpeting in a Learjet sometimes twists and breaks as it is being installed, no matter how carefully it is handled. This loss has nothing to do with any specific order; instead, it is a normal part of operations. The cost of normal spoilage common to all jobs is charged to overhead and is allocated with other overhead costs to all jobs.

Abnormal spoilage is spoilage that is not part of everyday operations. It occurs for reasons such as the following:

▶ Out-of-control manufacturing processes
▶ Unusual machine breakdowns
▶ Unexpected electrical outages that result in a number of spoiled units

Some abnormal spoilage is considered avoidable; that is, if managers monitor processes and maintain machinery appropriately, little spoilage will occur. To highlight these types of problems so that they can be monitored, abnormal spoilage is recorded in a loss from abnormal spoilage account in the general ledger and is not included in the job costing inventory accounts (work in process, finished goods, and cost of goods sold).

The following illustration demonstrates normal and abnormal spoilage for Aluminum Benders.

example

aluminum benders, part 3
ASSIGNING SPOILAGE COSTS

When Job 512 was being processed in the machining department, a piece of sheet metal was off centre in the bending machine and two vents were spoiled. This problem occurs periodically, is considered normal spoilage, and is recorded as an overhead cost. Because this step comes first in the procedure for making the vents, the only costs incurred were for direct materials ($25). The following journal entry records normal spoilage as an overhead cost, assuming the sheet metal cannot be sold at a discount and its cost has been recorded in work-in-process inventory.

Overhead cost control (normal spoilage)	25	
Work-in-process inventory (cost of spoiled sheet metal)		25

If these costs had been abnormal spoilage, they would have been recorded to a loss from abnormal spoilage account instead of the overhead cost control account.

Job 489 required an especially thin sheet metal to reduce the weight of the vents. When two of the vents were being assembled, they were spoiled because the metal twisted and could not be joined properly. Because the thin metal was a specific requirement for this job, the costs for the spoiled units were recorded as a cost for Job 489. Direct materials cost $100 and direct labour cost $150 for the vents up to the time they were spoiled. The metal can be sold to a recycler at a discounted price of $50. The journal entries for the use of direct materials and labour are the same as if the direct materials and labour were not spoiled, because these are additional costs for this specific job. However, the following journal entries record the value of the sheet metal at the time it is spoiled and the subsequent sale of the metal.

Raw material inventory (metal to be sold to recycler)	50	
Work-in-process inventory (Job 489)		50
Cash	50	
Raw material inventory		50

© zhu difeng/iStockphoto

Rework

Rework consists of spoiled units that are repaired and sold as if they were originally produced correctly. For example, electronic equipment that is special ordered, such as computers or batches of cell phones, are reworked when defects are discovered during the manufacturing process or through inspection at the end of the process. If the cost of rework is tracked, it is recorded in the same manner as spoilage; normal rework is charged to overhead or to a specific job, and abnormal rework is recorded as a line item loss. Rework costs are often not tracked, however.

Units are sometimes reworked and then sold at a regular price through regular marketing channels. Other times, reworked units remain flawed and must be sold at a reduced price. Costs and benefits are analyzed to decide whether to rework a spoiled unit. Suppose a clothing manufacturer discovers several jeans with back pockets sewn on upside down. If the pockets are carefully removed and then sewn on correctly, it may be difficult to tell that there was ever a problem. However, additional cost is added for the labour time to fix the pockets. Furthermore, the pockets might rip more easily because the material has been weakened. The managers need to evaluate whether the costs of reworking the pockets outweigh the benefits.

Scrap

Scrap consists of the bits of direct material left over from normal manufacturing processes. Sometimes it has value and can be sold, and sometimes it is discarded. New technology affects whether something is considered scrap. For example, for many years, lumber mills burned sawdust, for which they had no alternative uses, in teepee-shaped silos that glowed red at night. As trees became a scarce resource, sawdust became more valuable. With improved glues and new manufacturing processes, products such as specialty logs for fireplaces and chipboard were developed. A process was developed to turn sawdust into pulp for paper mills. Sawdust is no longer scrap but has become an important by-product of milling lumber.

Some manufacturers track scrap to measure whether resources are being used efficiently. Scrap is also tracked if it has value and could be stolen. Often it is recorded in

CHAPTER REFERENCE

Accounting for joint products and by-products is covered in Chapter 9.

physical terms: for example, gold scraps from jewellery manufacture are weighed, the weight is recorded, and the scraps are stored in a safe.

From an accounting standpoint, we need to plan for and sometimes guard scrap by setting up control systems. We also need to determine the effect of the value of scrap on inventory costing and the income statement. If scrap can be sold, the revenue is recorded either at the time it is produced or at the time it is sold. When the value of scrap is immaterial, it is simply recorded as part of other revenues in the income statement.

In job costing, scrap sometimes arises as part of specific jobs. If we can trace it to individual jobs, revenue from the scrap is credited to the specific job in work in process. Scrap revenue reduces the cost of the job with which it is associated. If scrap is common to all jobs, or if it is not worth tracing to individual jobs, the scrap revenue offsets overhead cost for the period. This entry reduces overhead cost for all jobs produced.

If scrap is held for a period of time before it is reused as direct material or sold, we need to estimate its net realizable value so that the value of the scrap can be used to offset overhead costs in the same period in which the overhead costs and associated revenues are recognized. When the price of scrap is volatile (e.g., gold in the previous example), estimating its value is more difficult.

Some organizations develop creative ways to use scrap to benefit employees and others. For example, print shops sometimes bind scrap paper into scratch pads and give them to employees, customers, or public schools. Employees working for a U.S. defence contractor near the Mexican border remove the nails and staples from lumber the company receives as packing crates for parts. The company then transports the lumber across the border for use by impoverished families living in homes made from cardboard. Such uses of scrap improve employee satisfaction, enhance the firm's reputation, and provide social value.

Production Quality and Behaviour Implications

LO6 Appreciate the quality and behavioural implications of spoilage

In the preceding section, you learned about methods used to account for the direct costs of spoilage, rework, and scrap. Although the direct costs can be significant, managers need to consider several other issues related to the quality of their production processes.

Spoilage Opportunity Costs

The opportunity costs of spoilage and rework can be large. Opportunity costs include the following:

- ▶ Forgone profit
- ▶ Loss of reputation and market share

An organization forgoes the normal profit from resources that are used to produce spoiled units. Forgone profit is a bigger problem when capacity limits are involved, because the organization forgoes the profit on resources employed as well as the contribution margin from good units that might have been produced. In addition, some proportion of spoiled units is likely to mistakenly pass inspection. As the number of spoiled units increases, a larger number of spoiled units will inevitably be sold to customers. The sale of these defective units leads to loss of market share because consumers switch brands. The company eventually loses its reputation for quality products, leading to further erosion of market share, including customers who never had direct quality problems. These opportunity costs, which are often much greater than the cost of the spoiled units, are not tracked by the accounting system.

5-2 self-study problem   Normal and Abnormal Spoilage   LO5

Flockhart Company produces custom-made garden sheds using recycled materials. Currently two jobs are in process, numbers 689 and 690. During production of Job 689, lightning hit the factory and caused an electrical surge followed by an outage. Lightning strikes are relatively unusual in the region where the factory is located. At the time of the strike, wood was being sawed to fit Job 689. The rip-saw malfunctioned and ruined a large piece of lumber that originally cost $175. During production of Job 690, two pieces of lumber had sawing errors and were scrapped. These pieces of lumber originally cost $80 and $75; they could be sold as scrap for $20 and $30. Sawing errors occur for many different jobs on a regular basis.

required

A. Consider the spoilage for Job 689. Should it be categorized as normal or abnormal spoilage? Explain.
B. Consider the spoilage for Job 690. Should it be categorized as normal or abnormal spoilage? Explain.
C. Describe the actual and opportunity costs of spoilage.

See the solution on page 231.

Investing in Quality

Some organizations position themselves as high-quality producers and work toward continuous improvement in quality. For example, Bombardier's Learjets have a reputation for high quality. In addition, customers may demand higher quality or may be willing to pay a premium price for quality. To improve quality, many organizations adopt a variety of business practices, such as total quality management, Six Sigma, lean manufacturing, and kaizen costing. Quality efforts can dramatically reduce spoilage, rework, and related opportunity costs.

However, measuring the costs and benefits of such improvements is difficult. Quality costs are often measured imprecisely. Employees often work on quality issues in addition to their other responsibilities, so time spent on quality is not tracked but estimated. Measuring loss of market share due to quality problems is also difficult. Therefore, exactly identifying the costs and benefits of quality improvement measures is an uncertain process. Although managers may not be able to prove that their quality efforts are cost effective, other qualitative benefits result from investments in quality.

> **BUSINESS PRACTICE**
> Organizations may voluntarily agree to comply with ISO 9000 standards, which are designed to improve quality management and facilitate business-to-business transactions.[3]

> **CHAPTER REFERENCE**
> To learn more about kaizen costing, see Chapter 15.

> **BUSINESS PRACTICE**
>
> #### Quality as a Public Issue
>
> The effects of quality go beyond the costs for individual organizations. Quality is often a public issue. In 2008, listeria bacteria was confirmed in some meat packaged at a **Maple Leaf Foods** plant. The next day, the company recalled all 220 packaged meats coming from the plant and shut it down. The outbreak killed nine people across Canada, with another 11 suspected deaths.
>
> The recall and advertising by CEO Michael McCain apologizing for the outbreak cost the company at least an estimated $20 million. His candour and swift action resulted in the Canadian Press naming him its business newsmaker of 2008.[4]

---

[3] The ISO 9000 standards are available at the International Organization for Standardization (ISO) website, www.iso.org.
[4] "How Maple Leaf Foods Is Handling the Listeria Outbreak," CBC News online, August 28, 2008; Tony Wilson, "The Best Legal Advice Is Often an Apology," *Globe and Mail*, August 24, 2011.

Effect of Accounting on Manager Behaviour

Accounting practices influence manager behaviour, especially when managers are compensated based on accounting earnings. Only some types of spoilage and rework costs are reflected in the accounting records. For example, the following accounting procedures may not provide incentives that encourage managers to control spoilage:

- ▶ Spoilage opportunity costs are not measured or recorded in the accounting records, which discourages management attention.
- ▶ Normal spoilage may seem insignificant because it is often a relatively small part of the total overhead cost pool.
- ▶ Judgment is used to determine normal spoilage, which influences the portion of spoilage costs included in the overhead cost pool versus the portion reported as a separate operating loss.
- ▶ Rework costs are not usually tracked, giving managers an incentive to inappropriately rework units to avoid recognizing abnormal spoilage.

To control for the potentially adverse effects of these accounting practices, some organizations institute systems to monitor defects and establish defect rates as part of management compensation criteria. Still other organizations prohibit rework to emphasize initial quality and to avoid the potential waste of additional resources.

External Monitoring

✉ INTERNATIONAL

Some organizations strategically adopt a zero-defect policy, with normal spoilage expected to be zero. Japanese companies frequently implement zero-defect policies, and this pressures competing North American firms to adopt similar policies.

External stakeholders such as shareholders typically do not have access to explicit information about an organization's spoilage rates or costs. Although abnormal spoilage is recorded in a separate loss account in the general ledger, it is typically combined with other financial statement items. Thus, spoilage rarely appears as a line item on published financial statements. Exceptions tend to be large catastrophes, such as damage caused by an earthquake, that are publicly known before financial statements are issued. Therefore, external stakeholders must use indirect ways to analyze the quality of an organization's production processes. An organization with a high spoilage rate might have a lower-than-average gross profit margin, higher-than-average warranty liabilities, or a poor reputation for product quality.

SUMMARY

LO1   Explain product costs and cost flows through the manufacturing process

PRODUCT OR SERVICE COSTS

- ▶ Direct materials
- ▶ Direct labour
- ▶ Overhead costs

COST FLOWS IN MANUFACTURING COMPANIES

Cost flows in manufacturing companies go through three stages:

Raw materials → Work-in-process → Finished goods

These are inventory accounts. Indirect materials used, indirect labour costs, and other manufacturing expenses are accumulated in an expense account called the manufacturing overhead control account. This overhead is applied or allocated to the work-in-process account once a job (product or service) is completed.

LO2   Describe how costs are assigned to customized goods and services

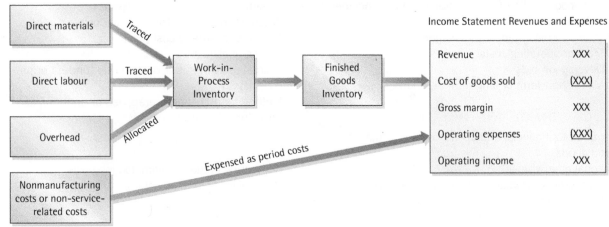

Cost Flows in Manufacturing Job Costing Accounting System

Cost Accumulated on the Balance Sheet

ACCOUNTING SYSTEM

▶ Source documents (e.g., employee time reports, material requisitions)
▶ Job cost record
▶ Job cost software

LO3   Allocate overhead costs to individual jobs

PROCEDURES FOR ALLOCATING OVERHEAD COSTS TO JOBS

1. Identify the relevant cost object.

2. Identify one or more overhead cost pools and allocation bases

3. For each overhead cost pool, calculate an overhead allocation rate

4. For each overhead cost pool, allocate costs to the cost object

ACTUAL COSTING

Actual quantity of allocation base for job × Actual allocation rate

NORMAL COSTING

Actual quantity of allocation base for job × Estimated allocation rate

TYPES OF OVERHEAD COST POOLS

▶ Company-wide
▶ Plant-wide
▶ Separate departments
▶ Separate activities, processes, or resources
▶ Separate fixed and variable

ADJUSTMENT FOR OVERAPPLIED OR UNDERAPPLIED OVERHEAD

Overapplied (underapplied) overhead = Allocated overhead − Actual overhead

If material: Prorate among work in process, finished goods, and cost of goods sold

If actual production < range of normal capacity: Assign excess fixed overhead to cost of goods sold.

If not material: Assign to cost of goods sold

LO4　Discuss how job costing information affects managers' incentives and decisions

USES OF JOB COST INFORMATION

- ► Assign costs to work in process, finished goods, and cost of goods sold for financial statement and income tax returns
- ► Provide information to help managers
  - – Monitor operating costs
  - – Develop job bids
  - – Make short-term or long-term decisions

ALLOCATION OF OVERHEAD COSTS

- ► Required for financial and tax accounting of manufactured goods
- ► Optional otherwise
- ► Fixed overhead allocation generally not relevant for short-term decisions

ACCOUNTING JUDGMENTS

- ► Which estimated job costs are relevant for decision making
- ► Whether and how to trace direct costs
- ► Choice of overhead cost pools
- ► Choice of allocation bases
- ► Estimated overhead allocation rate (under normal costing)
- ► Method for adjusting overapplied or underapplied overhead (under normal costing)

DIAGNOSTIC CONTROL

- ► Comparing actual to estimated job costs
- ► Responsibility for cost control

LO5　Explain how spoilage, rework, and scrap are handled in job costing

Type of Spoilage, Rework, or Scrap	Accounting Treatment
Normal spoilage arising from the requirements of a specific job	Charge to the individual job
Normal spoilage occurring periodically as a regular part of all jobs	Charge to overhead
Abnormal spoilage	Charge to separate loss account
Opportunity costs of spoilage	Not measured
Rework for defects arising from the requirements of a specific job	Charge to individual job
Rework for defects occurring periodically during normal production	Charge to overhead
Rework for abnormal defects	Charge to separate loss account
Sale of scrap	Record at time of production or at time sold. If not material: Record as other income
Scrap traced to individual jobs	Credit to individual job
Scrap common to all jobs or difficult-to-trace to jobs	Credit to overhead

LO6　Appreciate the quality and behavioural implications of spoilage

SPOILAGE OPPORTUNITY COSTS

- ► Forgone profit
- ► Loss of reputation and market share

INVESTING IN QUALITY

EFFECT OF ACCOUNTING ON MANAGER BEHAVIOUR

EXTERNAL MONITORING

5-1 solution to self-study problem

A. Overhead rates should be calculated using estimated costs and allocation bases:

   Machining: $10,000,000 ÷ 200,000 = $50 per machine hour

   Finishing: $8,000,000 ÷ $4,000,000 = 200% of direct labour cost

B. Using the overhead rates from Part A, the total overhead allocated to Job 806 should be as follows:

Machining department: $50 × 130 machine hours	$6,500
Finishing department: 200% × $1,250 direct labour cost	2,500
Total overhead allocated to Job 806	$9,000

C. To calculate per-unit costs, first calculate the total cost for the batch and then divide by the number of units:

	Machining	Finishing
Direct materials	$14,000	$3,000
Direct labour	600	1,250
Overhead allocated	6,500	2,500
Total	$21,100	$6,750

Total costs: $21,100 + $6,750 = $27,850

Cost per unit: $27,850 ÷ 200 unit = $139.25 per unit

D.

Machining department overhead allocated (220,000 × $50)	$11,000,000
Actual overhead in machining	10,200,000
Overapplied overhead	$ 800,000
Finishing department overhead allocated ($3,900,000 × 200%)	$ 7,800,000
Actual overhead in finishing	7,900,000
Underapplied overhead	$ (100,000)

E. Felix must believe that the overhead costs in each department are related to different allocation bases. Machining is likely to have more overhead expense for buying, maintaining, and using machines, and therefore, machine hours are likely to reflect the activities involved in running machines. In the finishing department, more labour-related costs are incurred, and therefore, it is logical to use labour dollars as an allocation base. Although accountants attempt to choose allocation bases that are related to the activities in a cost centre, the allocations are still arbitrary. Changes in volumes do not result in proportionate changes in costs. A portion of the costs is often fixed and unaffected by changes in the level of the allocation bases. In other words, allocation bases are not necessarily cost drivers. Instead, they are simply measures of activity used to allocate costs logically.

5-2 solution to self-study problem

A. The spoilage for Job 689 is abnormal spoilage because it occurred from an unusual force of nature. Abnormal spoilage is not part of normal operations and occurs because systems are out of control or an unusual event occurs, such as loss of electricity from an unusual storm. Abnormal spoilage is recorded as a loss for the period.

B. The spoilage for Job 690 is normal spoilage because it arises as a part of ongoing operations. If it occurs because of the requirements of a specific job, it is recorded as a cost for that job. If it occurs as part of operations, it is recorded as an overhead cost.

solution to self-study problem

5-2

C. The actual costs of spoilage include the dollar amounts for direct materials, direct labour, and overhead that have been incurred up to the point that the spoiled units are removed from production. The opportunity costs of spoilage include warranty and return costs and potential loss of reputation and market share. It is difficult to estimate these costs, but they can be considerable.

QUESTIONS

5.1 List three examples of job cost records you recently received for services provided to you. (*Hint:* Itemized bills made out to you are usually job cost records.)

5.2 Will underapplied and overapplied overhead arise under both actual and normal costing? Explain your answer.

5.3 Within the area where you live, work, or attend school, name three businesses that would likely use job costing and three that would likely use process costing.

5.4 How does the point of inspection (and therefore completion) affect the cost of spoilage?

5.5 Part of a contract between a union and a company guarantees that all manufacturing employees earn 5 hours of overtime each week. In the company's job costing system, should overtime be treated as a direct or indirect cost?

5.6 Compare actual and normal cost systems. Discuss the ways in which they are similar and the ways they differ.

5.7 Exquisite Furniture designs and manufactures custom furniture from exotic materials. Explain why spoilage is sometimes recorded as a cost for a specific job and other times as overhead for this company.

5.8 Explain how manufacturing overhead cost pools and cost allocation are related.

5.9 Describe the procedures used in job costing.

5.10 List the most common allocation bases used in job costing, and explain under what circumstances each base would be most appropriate.

5.11 List several different sources of information used in job costing and explain why this information is required.

5.12 Explain the process of assigning overapplied and underapplied overhead.

5.13 List the kinds of costs that are recorded in job cost records.

5.14 List at least five different costs that would be accumulated in the overhead cost pool for an accounting firm.

5.15 Develop a diagram similar to Exhibit 5.3 that presents an overview of the cost flows for the manufacturing costs in the job costing system used by William Felix & Sons in self-study problem 1. Your diagram should ignore revenue and nonmanufacturing costs.

MULTIPLE-CHOICE QUESTIONS

5.16 Which of the following statements is true if the overhead control account has a debit balance at the end of the period?
   a. Overhead is overapplied, and the difference should be credited to the appropriate accounts.
   b. Overhead is overapplied, and the difference should be debited to the appropriate accounts.
   c. Overhead is underapplied, and the difference should be debited to the appropriate accounts.
   d. Overhead is underapplied, and the difference should be credited to the appropriate accounts.

 Use the following information to answer Questions 5.17 to 5.20:

The following information is selected from the accounting records of Walmer Company:

	January 1, 2017	December 31, 2017
Direct materials	$ 35,000	$ 38,000
Work-in-process	42,000	28,000
Finished goods	32,000	27,000
Direct materials purchased		$120,000
Direct labour		$ 96,000
Direct labour rate per hour		$ 12
Manufacturing overhead rate per direct labour hour		$ 10

5.17 What was the manufacturing overhead cost for the year?
  a. $ 8,000
  b. $ 9,600
  c. $ 80,000
  d. $115,200

5.18 What was the prime cost for the year?
  a. $176,000
  b. $197,000
  c. $213,000
  d. $293,000

5.19 What was the cost of goods manufactured for the year?
  a. $339,000
  b. $307,000
  c. $296,000
  d. $293,000

5.20 What was the cost of goods sold for the year?
  a. $339,000
  b. $312,000
  c. $307,000
  d. $302,000

EXERCISES

5.21 **Schedule of Cost of Goods Manufactured, Cost of Goods Sold, Income Statement** Canton Ltd. manufactures hand-
L01 bags. Selected account balances for the year ended December 31, 2017, are presented below:

Depreciation—factory	$ 28,500
Beginning direct materials inventory	13,200
Beginning finished goods inventory	65,800
Beginning work-in-process inventory	24,800
Direct labour	88,200
Direct material purchases	98,200
Ending direct materials inventory	16,200
Ending finished goods inventory	52,500
Ending work-in-process inventory	35,200
Factory insurance	8,400
Factory maintenance	25,300
Factory utilities	14,500
General and administrative expenses	62,800
Indirect labour	19,500
Indirect materials	7,800
Sales	482,000
Selling expenses	70,400

REQUIRED **A.** Prepare a schedule of cost of goods manufactured.
  B. Calculate the prime cost and conversion cost.
  C. Prepare a schedule of cost of goods sold.
  D. Prepare a single-step income statement for Canton Ltd. for the year.

5.22 **Custom Versus Mass Production** The following chart lists several different products:
L02

Custom	Mass	Product
		Jewellery
		Rolls Royce automobiles
		Honda automobiles
		Tax services in an accounting firm
		Haircuts
		Personal shopping services
		Breakfast cereal production

REQUIRED Check the appropriate boxes to identify whether the products can be custom produced or mass produced. Some products, such as house construction, can be either mass manufactured or custom built. In such cases, both boxes would be checked.

5.23 Job Costing, Service Sector Consider the following budgeted data for the client case of Thanh Ng's accounting firm. The client wants a fixed-price quotation.

LO2, LO3, LO4

Direct professional labour	$20,000
Direct support labour	10,000
Fringe benefits for direct labour	13,000
Photocopying	2,000
Telephone calls	2,000
Computer lines	6,000

Overhead is allocated at the rate of 100% of direct labour cost.

REQUIRED **A.** Prepare a schedule of the budgeted total costs for the client. Show subtotals for total direct labour costs and total costs as a basis for mark-up.
B. Assume that the partners' policy is to quote a fixed fee at 10% above the total costs. What fee would be quoted?
C. Explain why the listed estimates for costs might not be similar to the actual costs for the job. What factors could affect the accuracy of these estimates? List as many factors as you can.

5.24 Job Costing, Over- and Underapplied Overhead, Journal Entries, Service Quote Bibby Auto Shop uses a normal job-costing system to allocate overhead on the basis of labour hours. For the current year, Bibby estimated that the total overhead costs would be $72,000 and that the total labour hours would be 2,400. At the end of the year, Bibby obtained the actual overhead costs from the ledger and found that the shop had incurred $65,800 and had worked 2,350 labour hours.

LO2, LO3, LO4

REQUIRED **A.** Compute the predetermined (budgeted) overhead rate.
B. Compute the overhead amount that was applied for the year. Was overhead underapplied or overapplied?
C. Prepare the journal entry to close the overhead account. Assume that the underapplied and overapplied overhead was not material.
D. A customer brings her car to be fixed. She wants an estimate before she decides to have her car fixed. Bibby estimates that the parts would cost $250, labour costs $40/hour for 2.5 hours. What is the cost of this job?
E. To provide a quote to a customer, Bibby adds a 40% mark up on the full costs. What is the quote for the job in (D)?

5.25 Job Costing, Service Sector Mercy Hospital uses a job costing system for all patients who have surgery. The hospital uses a budgeted overhead rate for allocating overhead to patient stays. In March, the operating room had a budgeted allocation base of 1,000 operating hours. The budgeted operating room overhead costs were $66,000.

LO2, LO3

Patient Dwight Schuller was in the operating room four hours during March. Other costs related to Schuller's four-hour surgery include

Patient medicine	$250
Cost of nurses	3,500
Cost of supplies	800

Physician cost is not included because physicians bill the government separately from the hospital billing system.

REQUIRED **A.** Explain why the hospital uses a job costing system instead of a process costing system.
B. Determine the budgeted (i.e., estimated) overhead rate for the operating room.
C. Determine the total costs of Schuller's four-hour surgery.

5.26 **Job Costing, Over- and Underapplied Overhead, Journal Entries** Shane's Shovels produces small, custom earth-moving equipment for landscaping companies. Manufacturing overhead is allocated to work in process, using an estimated overhead rate. During April, transactions for Shane's Shovels included the following:

LO2, LO3, LO4

Direct materials issued to production	$180,000
Indirect materials issued to production	30,000
Other manufacturing overhead incurred	250,000
Overhead allocated	225,000
Direct labour costs	75,000

Beginning and ending work in process were both zero.

REQUIRED **A.** What was the cost of jobs completed in April?
B. Was manufacturing overhead underapplied or overapplied? By how much?
C. Write out the journal entries for these transactions, including the adjustment.

5.27 **Job Costing, Underapplied Overhead, Solve For Unknowns** Traco manufactures tracked vehicles. Budgeted and actual fixed overhead for the year was $800,000. Overhead is allocated at the rate of 80% of direct labour cost. Overhead was underapplied by $12,000.

LO2

REQUIRED **A.** Determine the original budget for direct labour cost.
B. What is the total fixed overhead that was allocated for the year?
C. Calculate the actual direct labour cost for the year.

5.28 **Job Costing, Over- and Underapplied Overhead, Journal Entries** Huber and Sons uses job costing in a manufacturing setting. The firm began the month with $123 of work-in-process and completed jobs that moved to finished goods was $1,233. A summary of this month's transactions follows.

LO1, LO2

Direct materials requisitioned	$167
Direct labour	224
Actual overhead	899
Allocated overhead	922

REQUIRED **A.** Prepare journal entries for costs added to WIP this month.
B. Determine the amount of overapplied or underapplied overhead and prepare the journal entry to close it to cost of goods sold.
C. What is the value of ending work in process?

5.29 **Job Costing, Service Sector, Fixed and Variable Overhead Costs, Over- and Underapplied Overhead** Opinion Research, a marketing research firm, has a cost function for overhead costs of $60,000 per month plus $50 per client hour. In July its overhead allocation rate was calculated assuming 3,000 client hours. Actual overhead costs for July were $220,000, and client hours amounted to 2,800.

LO1, LO2

REQUIRED **A.** Determine the total cost for Job 717 if direct costs were $52,000 and 850 hours were worked for the client.
B. Provide examples of possible overhead costs for Opinion Research that are (1) fixed and (2) variable.
C. Determine the amount of overapplied or underapplied overhead for July.

5.30 **Job Costing, Service Sector, Return on Revenue** Trainor and Associates is a CA firm that specializes in helping clients with complex tax problems. The firm charges its clients by applying a mark-up rate to job costs so that operating income is equal to 15% of revenues. Trainor allocates overhead costs such as computer systems and human resources using a single cost pool with direct labour costs as the allocation base. Direct labour costs consist of the cost for partners at $100 per hour and the cost for associates at $50 per hour. Following is the budget for the current year.

LO1, LO2

Revenues	$ 3,500,000
Direct costs: Professional labour	1,000,000
Overhead costs	1,975,000
Operating income	$ 525,000

REQUIRED
A. Calculate the overhead cost allocation rate for the current year.
B. A potential client, Max Krzepkowski, has asked for a bid for completing his taxes. After examining his documentation, a partner estimates that the work would require 20 hours of partner time and 45 hours of associate time. If the firm wants to earn operating income of 15% of revenues for this client, what will the bid be?

5.31 Job Costing, Price Quote, Over- and Underapplied Overhead Home Contracting Company builds additions and
L01, L02 remodels homes. The firm's pricing policy is to estimate the direct costs of the job, allocate overhead as a percentage of the direct costs, and then add 40% to this as profit. For the next year, direct costs are estimated at $8,000,000 and overhead costs are estimated at $11,120,000.

REQUIRED
A. Determine the company's overhead allocation rate.
B. Calculate the price that will be quoted to a customer for a remodelling job that is expected to have direct materials costs of $25,000 and direct labour costs of $15,000.
C. If actual direct costs next year are $7,200,000, what would be the amount of overapplied or underapplied overhead?

5.32 Normal and Abnormal Spoilage Franklin Fabrication produces custom-made security doors and gates. Currently
L05 two jobs are in process, 359 and 360. During production of Job 359, the supervisor was on vacation, and the employees made several errors in cutting the metal pieces for the two doors in the order. The spoiled metal pieces cost $20 each and had zero scrap value. In addition, an order of five gates that had been manufactured for Job 360 required a fine wire mesh that sometimes tore as it was being mounted. Because a similar wire could be used that was much easier to install, the customer had been warned that costs could run over the bid if any difficulty was encountered in installing the wire. One of the gates was spoiled during the process of installing the wire. The cost of the materials and direct labour for the gate was $150. The gate and metal were hauled to the dump and discarded.

REQUIRED
A. Should the spoilage for Job 359 be categorized as normal or abnormal spoilage? Explain.
B. Should the spoilage for Job 360 be categorized as normal or abnormal spoilage? Explain.
C. Prepare spoilage journal entries for both jobs.

5.33 Direct Costs and Overhead Job 87M had direct material costs of $400 and a total cost of $2,100. Overhead is
L02, L03 allocated at the rate of 75% of prime cost (direct material and direct labour).

REQUIRED
A. How much direct labour was used?
B. How much overhead was allocated?

5.34 Analysis of WIP T Account Jeeter Company uses a job costing system. Overhead is allocated based on 120% of
L02, L03 direct labour cost. Last month's transactions in the work-in-process account are shown here:

Work in Process

Beginning balance	$ 48,000		
Direct materials	160,000	To finished goods	$442,000
Direct labour	120,000		
Factory overhead	150,000		

Only one job, #850, was still in process at the end of the month. Job 850 was charged with $9,000 in overhead for the month.

REQUIRED
A. What is the ending balance in the WIP account?
B. How much direct labour cost was used for Job 850?
C. What is the amount of direct materials used for Job 850?

5.35 Journal Entries Langley Ltd. uses a job costing system. At the beginning of the month of June, two orders were in process, as follows:

LO2, LO3, LO4

	Order 88	Order 105
Direct materials	$1,000	$900
Direct labour	1,200	200
Overhead allocated	1,800	300

There was no inventory in finished goods on June 1. During the month of June, orders numbered 106 through 120, inclusive, were put into process.

Direct materials requirements amounted to $13,000, direct labour costs for the month were $20,000, and actual manufacturing overhead recorded during the month amounted to $28,000.

The only order in process at the end of June was Order 120, and the costs incurred for this order were $1,150 of direct materials and $1,000 of direct labour. In addition, Order 118, which was 100% complete, was still on hand as of June 30. Total costs for this order were $3,300. The firm's overhead allocation rate in June was the same as that used in May and is based on labour cost.

REQUIRED
A. Prepare journal entries, with supporting calculations, to record the cost of goods manufactured, the cost of goods sold, and the closing of the overapplied or underapplied overhead to cost of goods sold.
B. Describe the two different approaches to closing overapplied or underapplied overhead at the end of the period. How do you choose an appropriate method?

5.36 Cost of Goods Sold Schedule The Rebecca Corporation is a manufacturer of machines made to customer specifications. All production costs are accumulated by means of a job order costing system. The following information is available at the beginning of the month of October 2017:

LO2, LO3

Raw materials inventory October 1	$16,200
Work in process October 1	5,100

A review of the job order cost sheets revealed the composition of the work-in-process inventory on October 1 as follows:

Direct materials (assuming no indirect labour materials this month)	$1,320
Direct labour (300 hours)	3,000
Factory overhead allocated	780
	$5,100

Activity during the month of October was as follows:

Raw materials costing $20,000 were purchased.
Direct labour for job orders totalled 3,300 hours at $10 per hour.
Factory overhead was allocated to production at the rate of $2.60 per direct labour hour.

On October 31, inventories consisted of the following:

Raw materials inventory	$17,000
Work-in-process inventory:	
Direct materials	4,320
Direct labour (500 hours)	5,000
Factory overhead	1,300

REQUIRED Prepare in good form a detailed schedule showing the cost of goods manufactured for the month of October.

5.37 Cumulative Exercise (Chapter 4): *Job costing, special order, over- and underapplied overhead* Vern's Van Service customizes light trucks according to customers' orders. This month the company worked on five jobs, numbered 207 through 211. Materials requisitions for the month were as follows:

L02, L03, L04

Ticket	Carpet	Paint	Electronics	Other	Total
207	$ 40	$350	$580	—	$ 970
208	75	200	375	—	650
209	200	400	200	—	800
210	30	150	770	—	950
211	60	—	50	—	110
Indirect	—	—	—	$750	750
Total costs					$4,230

An analysis of the payroll records revealed the following distribution for labour costs:

Job	207	208	209	210	211	Other	Total
Direct labour	$1,400	$1,200	$800	$1,700	$400	—	$5,500
Indirect labour	—	—	—	—	—	$2,200	2,200
Total costs							$7,700

Other overhead costs (consisting of rent, amortization, taxes, insurance, utilities, etc.) amounted to $3,600. At the beginning of the period, management anticipated that overhead costs would be $6,400 and total direct labour would amount to $5,000. Overhead is allocated on the basis of direct labour dollars.

Jobs 207 through 210 were finished during the month; Job 211 is still in process. Jobs 207 through 209 were picked up and paid for by customers. Job 210 is still on the lot, waiting to be picked up.

REQUIRED   **A.** Calculate the total cost for each job for this month.
B. Calculate the overapplied or underapplied overhead.
C. Suppose that a customer who has just started a catering service wants to customize her truck but has a limited budget for the job. Estimated paint, electronics, and materials for containers to keep food cold or warm amounts to $1,700. Direct labour is estimated to be $1,100. The customer's budget is $3,000, but she is hoping that the delivery service will be successful so that she can order more trucks in the next several years. Calculate the minimum price that would be acceptable if there is ample capacity to accept the job.

5.38 Job Costing Journal Entries, Close Over- or Underapplied Overhead Costs for Vern's Van Service are shown in Exercise 5.37.

L01, L02

REQUIRED   **A.** Prepare the journal entries to reflect the incurrence of materials, labour, and overhead costs; the allocation of overhead; and the transfer of units to finished goods and cost of goods sold.
B. Close overapplied or underapplied overhead to cost of goods sold.

5.39 Allocating Overhead, Over- and Underapplied Overhead, Spoilage The Futons for You Company sells batches of custom-made futons to customers and uses predetermined rates for fixed overhead, based on machine hours. The following data are available for last year:

L03, L04, L05

Budgeted and actual fixed factory overhead cost	$160,000
Budgeted machine hours	100,000
Actual machine hours used	110,000

	Machine Hours Used
Job 20	11,000
Job 21	16,000
Job 22	14,000
Job 23	9,000

REQUIRED   **A.** Compute the estimated overhead allocation rate to be used for the year.
B. Determine the overhead to be allocated to Job 21.

C. Determine total overapplied or underapplied overhead at the end of the year.
D. Should cost of goods sold be increased or decreased at the end of the year? Why?
E. If the amount of overapplied or underapplied overhead is material, how is it assigned?
F. Suppose Job 21 required a special fabric cover for the futon pads. This type of fabric dulls the blades of the cutting machine, and a number of fabric covers were unusable. Should this spoilage be recorded for Job 21 or for all jobs processed this period? Explain your answer.

5.40 Job Costing, Close Over- or Underapplied Overhead At the beginning of the accounting period, the accountant for ABC Industries estimated that total overhead would be $80,000. Overhead is allocated to jobs on the basis of direct labour cost. Direct labour was budgeted to cost $200,000 this period. During the period, only three jobs were worked on. The following summarizes the direct materials and labour costs for each:

 LO2, LO3, LO4

	Job 1231	Job 1232	Job 1233
Direct materials	$45,000	$70,000	$30,000
Direct labour	70,000	90,000	50,000

Job 1231 was finished and sold, Job 1232 was finished but is waiting to be sold, and Job 1233 is still in process. Actual overhead for the period was $82,000.

REQUIRED   **A.** Calculate the cost of each job completed.
B. Calculate the cost of goods sold.
C. Calculate the amount of overapplied or underapplied overhead that will be prorated to the ending balances in work in process, finished goods, and cost of goods sold.

5.41 Job Costing Journal Entries Costs for ABC Industries are shown in Exercise 5.40.

REQUIRED   Prepare journal entries for ABC as follows:
A. Cost recorded during production

LO1, LO2   **B.** Cost of jobs completed
C. Cost of goods sold
D. Overapplied or underapplied overhead prorated to the ending balances in work in process, finished goods, and cost of goods sold

5.42 Spoilage Journal Entries Portofino Company manufactures custom doors. When Job 186 (a batch of 14 custom doors) was being processed in the machining department, one of the wood panels on a door split. This problem occurs periodically and is considered normal spoilage. Direct materials and labour for the door, to the point of spoilage, were $35. In addition, a storm caused a surge in electricity, and a routing machine punctured the wood for Job 238. This incident occurred at the beginning of production, so spoilage amounted to only the cost of wood, at $200.

LO5, LO6

REQUIRED   **A.** Prepare the journal entries for normal and abnormal spoilage.
B. Now suppose that the wood from abnormal spoilage can be sold for $25. Record the journal entries for the disposal value.
C. Portofino Company is considering hiring someone to inspect all wood after it arrives at the plant but prior to production. Discuss the pros and cons of hiring an inspector.

PROBLEMS

5.43 Collecting Overhead Cost Information A family member has asked you to review the accounting system used for Hanna's, a custom stained glass manufacturing business. The owner currently uses a software package to keep track of her chequing account, but she does not produce financial statements. The owner seeks your help in setting up a costing system so that financial statements can be produced on a monthly basis.

LO2, LO3, LO4

REQUIRED   **A.** What kind of costing system is needed for this setting?
   B. You plan to categorize the chequebook data for entry into the financial statement records. List the categories you might use for these entries. (List only broad categories here; see Parts C, D, and E for more details.)
C. List several costs that might be included in a fixed overhead category.

D. List several costs that might be included in a variable overhead category.

E. List several costs that might be included in direct materials.

F. Write a memo to the owner, discussing the alternative choices for the costing system. Include an explanation of the type of information that would need to be captured to support the costing system.

5.44 Cost of Rework, Control of Scrap, Accounting for Scrap Dapper Dan Draperies manufactures and installs custom-
LO5, LO6 ordered draperies.

REQUIRED   A. For all drapes, occasionally the sewing equipment malfunctions and a drape must be reworked. Explain how to account for the cost of rework when it is needed.

B. Explain how to account for the cost of rework when customers choose a fabric that is known to require rework.

C. Explain why scrap will always arise in this business.

D. Dapper Dan can sell scraps to quilting groups or just throw them away. List several factors that could affect this decision.

E. If Dapper Dan decides to sell scraps, explain the accounting choices for recording the sales value.

5.45 Accounting for Scrap You are helping a friend, Jonah, set up a new accounting system for a small start-up con-
LO5, LO6 struction company. He specializes in custom, energy-efficient homes that are built on a cost-plus basis. Cost-plus
means that his customers pay a fixed percentage above the sum of direct and overhead costs.

As he goes through the accounts, Jonah asks why you set up a separate account for scrap. He does not believe that scrap should be recorded anywhere in his accounting system because it is worth little, and theft is no problem. He makes weekly trips to a recycling plant, where he receives a small sum for the scrap. Most of the time Jonah is working on only one house and the scrap is only for that house. However, once in a while he is working on several houses, and the scrap for all of the houses is recycled at once.

REQUIRED   A. Explain the two ways that scrap can be recorded in a job costing system.

B. Choose the appropriate method for Jonah and explain your choice.

C. Suppose you are a prospective homeowner. Explain to Jonah why you believe the revenue from scrap associated with your home should be recorded as a reduction in your costs rather than his overall costs.

D. Write a brief (and diplomatic) paragraph to convince Jonah that he needs to account for the revenues from scrap.

5.46 Job Costing, Overhead Rates The Eastern Seaboard Company uses an estimated rate for allocating factory over-
LO2, LO3, head to job orders based on machine hours for the machining department and on a direct labour cost basis for
LO4 the finishing department. The company budgeted the following for last year:

	Machining	Finishing
Factory overhead	$5,000,000	$3,000,000
Machine hours	250,000	14,000
Direct labour hours	15,000	16,000
Direct labour cost	$ 225,000	$2,400,000

During the month of December, the cost record for Job 602 shows the following:

	Machining	Finishing
Direct materials requisitioned	$7,000	$2,000
Direct labour cost	$ 300	$6,750
Direct labour hours	20	300
Machine hours	35	5

REQUIRED   A. What is the estimated overhead allocation rate that should be used in the machining department? In the finishing department?

B. What is the total overhead allocated to Job 602?

C. Assuming that Job 602 consisted of 200 units of product, what is the unit cost for this job?

D. What factors affect the volume of production in a period? Can we know all the factors before the period begins? Why or why not?

E. Explain why Seaboard would use two different overhead allocation bases.

5.47 Job Costing, Service Sector Hawk and Eagle Co., a law firm, had the following costs last year:

LO2, LO3, LO4

Direct professional labour	$15,000,000
Overhead	21,000,000
Total costs	$36,000,000

The following costs were included in overhead:

Fringe benefits for direct professional labour	$ 5,000,000
Paralegal costs	2,700,000
Telephone call time with clients (estimated but not tabulated)	600,000
Computer time	1,800,000
Photocopying	900,000
Total overhead	$11,000,000

The firm recently improved its ability to document and trace costs to individual cases. Revised bookkeeping procedures now allow the firm to trace fringe benefit costs for direct professional labour, paralegal costs, telephone charges, computer time, and photocopying costs to each case individually. The managing partner needs to decide whether more costs than just direct professional labour should be traced directly to jobs to allow the firm to better justify billings to clients.

During the past year, more costs were traced to client engagements. Two of the case records showed the following:

	Client Cases	
	875	876
Direct professional labour	$20,000	$20,000
Fringe benefits for direct labour	3,000	3,000
Secretarial costs	2,000	6,000
Telephone call time with clients	1,000	2,000
Computer time	2,000	4,000
Photocopying	1,000	2,000
Total costs	$29,000	$37,000

Three methods are being considered for allocating overhead this year:

1. Allocate overhead based on direct professional labour cost. Calculate the allocation rate using last year's direct professional labour costs of $15 million and overhead costs of $21 million.
2. Allocate overhead based on direct professional labour cost. Calculate the allocation rate using last year's direct professional labour costs of $15 million and overhead costs of $10 million ($21 million less $11 million in direct costs that are traced this year).
3. Allocate the $10 million overhead based on total direct costs. Calculate the allocation rate using last year's direct costs (professional labour of $15 million plus other direct costs of $11 million).

REQUIRED   **A.** Compute the overhead allocation rate for method 1.
B. Compute the overhead allocation rate for method 2.
C. Compute the overhead allocation rate for method 3.
D. Using each of the three rates computed in Parts A, B, and C, compute the total costs of Cases 875 and 876.
E. Explain why the total costs allocated to Cases 875 and 876 are not the same under the three methods.
F. Explain why method 1 would be inappropriate.
G. Would method 2 or method 3 be better? Explain.
H. Explain how job costing in a service business is different from job costing in a manufacturing business.

5.48 Plant-wide Versus Production Cost Pools Flexible Manufacturers Inc. produces small batches of customized products. The accounting system is set up to allocate plant overhead to each job using the following production cost pools and overhead allocation rates:

LO2, LO3, LO4

Labour-paced assembly	$25 per direct labour hour
Machine-paced assembly	$18 per machine hour
Quality testing	$2 per unit

The following actual resources were used for Job 75:

Direct labour hours	3 hours
Machine hours	1.25 hours
Number of units	36 units

The plant accountant wants to simplify the cost accounting system and use a plant-wide rate. If the preceding costs are grouped into a single cost pool and allocated based on labour hours, the rate would be $35 per direct labour hour.

REQUIRED **A.** What cost should be allocated to Job 75, using the plant-wide overhead rate?
B. What cost should be allocated to Job 75, using the production cost pool overhead rates?
C. Why do the allocated amounts in Parts A and B differ?
D. Which method would you recommend? Explain your choice.

5.49 T account Job Costing Entries S-F Manufacturing Company performs a variety of activities for custom products. This week the following transactions took place.

LO1, LO2

1. Received 600 units of material at $12 per unit.
2. Issued 120 units of material for Job 26M and 80 units for Job 27N.
3. Received miscellaneous supplies for $420. The costs are recorded as overhead.
4. Job 26M required 110 hours of direct labour and Job 27N required 80 hours. Direct labour is paid at $22 per hour.
5. Overhead is allocated at the rate of 120% of direct labour.
6. Other costs included $500 for utilities, $900 in depreciation, and $1,200 for supervision.
7. Beginning work in process for Job 26M was $2,400.
8. Job 26M was completed during the week.
9. Delivered Job 26M to the customer.

REQUIRED **A.** Set up all of the T accounts needed to record this information. Use titles similar to those in Exhibit 5.11.
B. Record all of the transactions for the week.

5.50 Solve for Unknowns, Job Costing, Over- and Underapplied Overhead Following is information about consulting jobs for a company that is increasing in sales, but has not yet become profitable. The owner keeps financial records on yellow sticky notes stuck to the wall behind his desk. He has asked you to help him set up a costing system so that he can better understand his costs. The owner said that job 140 was completed, job 141 was started and completed, and job 142 was started this month. Professional labour hours for contracts in process consist of job 140 with 120 hours, job 141 with 240 hours, and job 142 with 140 hours. Professional labour was paid $25,000 for the month, and the professional employees are all paid the same rate per hour. Overhead is allocated using an estimated rate based on professional labour hours. The total cost for job 141 is $30,000. Actual overhead cost for the month was $48,000.

LO1, LO2

REQUIRED **A.** What is labour paid per hour? What is the estimated rate per labour hour used to allocate overhead?
B. What are the total costs (before adjusting for overapplied or underapplied overhead) for Jobs 141, 142, and 143?
C. What are the amounts in cost of goods sold and work-in-process at the end of the month?
D. What amount of overhead was overapplied or underapplied this month?
E. If this month is typical, what is a reasonable overhead rate?

5.51 Allocating Variable and Fixed Overhead in the Service Sector Prime Personal Trainers is a personal training service in Belgium for people who want to work out at home. Prime offers two different types of services: Setup and Continuous Improvement. Setup services consist of several home visits by a personal trainer who specializes in determining the proper equipment for each client and helping the client set up a home gym. Continuous Improvement services provide daily, weekly, or bi-weekly home visits by trainers.

Prime's accountant wants to create a job costing system for Setup services. She decides to use direct labour cost as the allocation base for variable overhead costs and direct labour hours for fixed overhead cost. To estimate normal capacity, she calculates the average direct labour cost over the past several years. She estimates overhead by updating last year's overhead cost with expected increases in rent, supervisors' salaries, and so on. Following are her estimates (given in euros) for the current period:

Direct labour hours (based on 250 normal hours per month)	3,000
Direct labour cost	€ 75,000
Indirect labour cost	25,000
Variable overhead (primarily fringe benefits)	150,000
Fixed overhead (office-related costs)	120,000

Inventories consist of exercise equipment and supplies that Prime uses for new clients. The following information summarizes operations during the month of October. A number of new jobs were begun in October, but only two jobs were completed: Job 20 and Job 22.

Account balances on October 1:

Equipment and supplies (raw materials)	€5,000
Client contracts in process (Job 20)	3,500
Client contracts in process (Job 22)	1,500

Purchases of equipment and supplies:

Equipment	€54,000
Supplies	500
Total	€54,500

Equipment and supplies requisitioned for clients:

Job 20	€ 1,000
Job 21	500
Job 22	4,000
Job 23	5,000
Other jobs	40,000
Indirect supplies	500
Total	€51,000

Direct labour hours and cost:

	Hours	Cost
Job 20	10	€ 250
Job 21	18	450
Job 22	15	375
Job 23	6	150
Other clients	180	4,500
Total	229	€5,725

Labour costs:

Direct labour wages	€ 5,725
Indirect labour wages (160 hours)	1,920
Manager's salary	6,250
Total	€13,895

Office costs:

Rent	€1,000
Utilities	100
Insurance and taxes	900
Miscellaneous	1,000
Total	€3,000

REQUIRED **A.** What are the estimated allocation rates for fixed and variable overhead for the current period?
B. What is the total overhead cost allocated to Job 20 in October?
C. What is the total cost of Job 20?
D. Calculate the amounts of fixed and variable overhead allocated to jobs in October.
E. Why would the accountant choose to use two cost pools instead of one? Will this method make a difference in client bills when a job includes more equipment and less labour than other jobs?

5.52 Job Costing, Service Sector Ava Advertising Agency (AAA) uses a job costing system for all its advertising projects.

LO2, LO3, LO4 Since the advertising agency is a labour-intensive business, AAA sets a policy to allocate/apply overhead costs to each job (advertisement) based on labour hours.

On January 1, 2017 AAA *estimated* its 2017 total overhead costs to be $120,000, and also estimated the total labour hours to be 6,000 hours for 2017. By December 31, 2017, AAA had incurred and accumulated $127,600 *actual* total overhead costs and 5,800 actual labour hours worked (at $45/hr). The following are a list of four advertisements completed during 2017.

	Job #1501	Job #1502	Job #1503	Job #1504
Work schedule	Jan – May	March – June	Aug – Oct	Sep – Dec
Material costs	$65,000	$32,000	$43,000	$52,000
Labour hours	1,800	1,200	1,500	1,300

REQUIRED **A.** What is the budgeted overhead rate?
B. What is the cost for Job# 1502 on June 30?
C. Compute the ending balance in the total overhead account. Was overhead underapplied or overapplied?
D. Prepare the journal entry to close the overhead account. Assume that the underapplied and overapplied overhead was not material.
E. A client would like to get a quote for an advertising project before she decides to have her advertisement done by AAA. The cost accountant estimates that the project would take 1,000 labour hours and $45,000 of material costs. What is the cost of this job?
F. If AAA's mark-up percentage is 40% of its full costs (i.e., add 40% of profit on its full cost), what is the quote that AAA should give to this client?

5.53 Cost Flows, Cost Allocation, Over- or Underapplied Delmar Ltd. manufactures industrial kitchen equipment. Delmar

LO1, LO2, LO3 uses a normal job-costing system to allocate manufacturing overhead cost, based on the machine hours. The selected account balances are as follows:

	January 1	December 31
Direct materials	$72,000	$55,000
Work-in-process	24,000	35,000
Finished goods	48,000	26,000
Direct manufacturing labour		124,000
Indirect manufacturing labour		50,000
Factory Insurance		8,000
Factory Utilities		30,000
Factory Maintenance		25,000
Depreciation—Machine		42,000

The budgeted manufacturing overhead costs and machine hours were $126,000 and 5,600 hours. The actual machine hours worked was 6,200 hours.

REQUIRED
A. Calculate the budgeted overhead rate per machine hour and the actual overhead rate per machine hour?
B. What was the manufacturing overhead amount applied to the work-in-process? Was the amount over- or underapplied?
C. The material requisition records showed that $94,500 of materials was used in the production. What is the amount of material purchased?
D. Prepare all journal entries related to the production, including the year-end adjustment for over- or underapplied manufacturing overhead.
E. Prepare a schedule of cost of goods manufactured, using the amount of actual manufacturing overhead incurred.

What is the amount of cost of goods sold after the adjustment?

5.54 Cost Flows, Job Costing, Cost Allocation, Over- and Underapplied Overhead Phillies Company manufactures custom-made awnings. Phillies uses a normal job-costing system, based on the direct labour cost. The direct labour rate is $25 per hour. The budgeted labour hours for the quarter are 2,000 hours. The actual overhead rate for this past quarter is $32.50 per labour hour. The cost information for work-in-process and finished goods is shown as follows:

LO1, LO2, LO3, LO4

Work-in-Process			Finished Goods		
Beginning Balance	0	106,000	Beginning Balance	21,500	?
Direct materials	31,500			106,000	
Direct labour	52,000		Ending Balance	59,500	
Manufacturing Overhead	65,000				

The ending balance in the Work-in-Process account consists of three incomplete jobs. An analysis shows that 600 labour hours and overhead costs have been charged to these jobs.

REQUIRED
A. Calculate the ending balance of work-in-process and the amount of cost of goods sold.
B. Calculate the actual labour hours worked for the quarter. What is the budgeted manufacturing overhead rate per labour hour? What are the total budgeted overhead costs?
C. Is the overhead over- or underapplied? Prepare an adjusting entry for the difference, assuming the amount is immaterial.
D. Calculate the amount of direct materials, direct labour, and manufacturing overhead charged to the three incomplete jobs.

5.55 Cost Flows, Job Costing, Cost Allocation, Over- and Underapplied Overhead Lucien Ltd. manufactures custom-made

LO1, LO2, LO3, LO4 doors and uses a normal job costing system to allocate overhead costs, based on labour hours. The direct labour rate is $40 per hour. Direct materials used in the production amounted to $145,000.

The additional cost information for last year is as follows:

Budgeted manufacturing overhead	$240,000	Budgeted labour hours	8,000
Actual manufacturing overhead	$255,000	Actual labour hours	7,500

Inventory balances were:

	January 1	December 31
Work-in-Process	$155,000	$120,000
Finished Goods	175,000	155,000

REQUIRED **A.** Calculate the applied manufacturing overhead costs and the direct labour costs for last year.
B. Calculate (1) the total manufacturing costs for last year, (2) the cost of goods manufactured for last year, and (3) the cost of goods sold.
C. Is the overhead over- or underapplied? Prepare an adjusting entry for the difference, using the proration method.

5.56 Job Costing, Cost Allocation, Service Sector Avant-garde Architects (AGA) specializes in industrial properties.

LO2, LO3, LO4 It has five architects who work on the projects directly with clients, and each of the architects' annual salary is $231,000 based on 2,200 hours per year. The architect will not be paid more, if he or she works more than 2,200 hours per year. The architect's hours are traced and charged to the project directly. The overhead costs include staff members' salary, supplies, office related expenses, etc. The overhead costs are allocated to projects based on the architects' hours. The budgeted overhead cost for the year is $1,980,000. The actual overhead cost for the year is $2,002,500, and the architect worked 2,250 hours this year.

Rubin Developer Ltd. was working on an industrial park, and commissioned AGA to be the architect for the project. AGA estimated the project would take 3,600 hours. At the end of the project, the project took architects 3,620 hours to complete.

REQUIRED **A.** What is the architect's hourly rate? What is the budgeted overhead rate?
B. What is the quote for Rubin's project, if AGA uses normal job costing, with a 50% mark up on the total costs?
C. What is the actual job cost for Rubin's project? What is the amount of over- or underapplied overhead?

5.57 Cost Flows, Schedule of Cost of goods manufactured, Schedule of Cost of Goods Sold, Job Costing, Cost Allocation

LO2, LO3, LO4 Halton Inc. manufactures kitchen cabinets to customer order. Halton uses a normal job-costing system to allocate manufacturing overhead cost, based on the direct labour hour. The direct labour rate is $20 per hour. Last month, the work-in-process account was charged $48,000 for direct labour and $27,000 direct materials. Additional information about work-in-process, finished goods, and manufacturing overhead control accounts is as follows:

	Beginning	Ending
Work-in-process	$28,000	$25,000
Finished goods	25,000	15,000
Equipment depreciation		24,000
Factory Utilities		18,000
Factory Rent		12,000
Factory maintenance		9,000

The record also showed that manufacturing overhead was over-applied by $9,000 to the work-in-process account.

REQUIRED **A.** What is the manufacturing overhead amount applied to the work-in-process account?
B. What is the manufacturing overhead rate per direct hour?
C. What are the manufacturing costs, using normal job costing, for last month? What was the cost of goods manufactured? What is the cost of goods sold?

D. Prorate the amount of over-applied manufacturing overhead based on the ending balance of work-in-process, finished goods, and cost of goods sold. Prepare the adjusting journal entry. What are the balances in the work-in-process, finished goods, and cost of goods sold accounts after the adjustment?

E. The ending balance of the work-in-process account consists of two incomplete jobs – Job 207 and Job 214. Job 207 was charged $2,500 and Job 214, $3,750 of direct materials. Job 207 and Job 214 were charged 150 and 225 direct labour hours and manufacturing overhead. Present the job costs for each incomplete job.

MINI-CASES

5.58 Effects of Robotic Equipment on Overhead Rates "Our costs are out of control, our accounting system is screwed up, or both!" fumed the sales manager. "We are simply noncompetitive on a great many of the jobs we bid on. Just last week we lost a customer when a competitor underbid us by 25%! And I bid that job at cost because the customer has been with us for years but has been complaining about our prices."

LO2, LO3, LO4

This problem, raised at the weekly management meeting, has been getting worse over the years. The Tufbuilt Tool Company produces parts for specific customer orders. When the firm first became successful, it employed nearly 500 skilled machinists. Over the years, the firm has become increasingly automated, and it now uses a number of different robotic machines. The firm currently employs only 75 production workers, but output has quadrupled.

The problems raised by the sales manager can be seen in the portions of two bid sheets brought to the meeting (shown below). The bids are from the cutting department, but the relative sizes of these three types of manufacturing costs are similar for other departments.

The cutting department charges overhead to products based on direct labour hours. For the current period, the department expects to use 4,000 direct labour hours. Departmental overhead, consisting mostly of amortization on the robotic equipment, is expected to be $1,480,000.

An employee can typically set up any job on the appropriate equipment in about 15 minutes. Once machines are operating, an employee oversees five to eight machines simultaneously. All that is required is to load or unload materials and monitor calibrations. The department's robotic machines will log a total of 25,000 hours of run time in the current period.

For Bid 74683, the firm was substantially underbid by a competitor. The firm did get the job for Bid 74687, but the larger jobs are harder to find. Small jobs arise frequently, but the firm is rarely successful in obtaining them.

Cutting Department

Bid # 74683	Machine Run Time 3 Hours
Materials	
Steel sheeting	$280.25
Direct labour	
Equipment setup (0.25 hours @ $12.50)	3.13
Equipment tending (1 hour @ $12.50)	12.50
Overhead (1.25 hours @ $370)	462.50
Total costs	$758.38

Cutting Department

Bid # 74687	Machine Run Time 11 Hours
Materials	
Steel sheeting	$2,440.50
Direct labour	
Equipment setup (0.25 hours @ $12.50)	3.13
Equipment tending (1.25 hours @ $12.50)	15.63
Overhead (1.5 hours @ $370)	555.00
Total costs	$3,014.26

REQUIRED   **A.** Critique the cost allocation method used within the current cost accounting system.

B. Suggest a better approach for allocating overhead. Allocate costs by using your approach and compare the costs of the jobs under the two systems.

C. Discuss the pros and cons of using job costs to determine the price for a job order.

5.59 **Classification of Rework Costs, Uncertainties, Critique of Rework and Scrap Policy** Fran Markus is in the cost account-
LO5, LO6 ing group at Boats Galore, a large manufacturing company that produces customized boats and yachts. The company sometimes experiences quality problems with its fibreglass raw material, causing flawed areas in boat hulls. The problem is often fixed by reworking the flawed areas. Other times, the hull is scrapped because it is too flawed, and a new hull is fabricated. The spoilage policy at Boats Galore is to charge the cost of rework and spoilage to overhead unless it arises because a hull design is particularly complicated. In those cases, the cost is assigned to the job.

Two boats currently under construction require triple the usual amount of materials and labour time to enhance boat security. The customer wants each hull to be able to withstand the explosion of a small bomb. It is the company's first order with this hull construction. Because of the new design and fibreglass process, the customer has agreed to a cost-plus contract and will pay cost plus a fixed percentage of cost. This contract assures that Boats Galore does not incur a loss from developing the enhanced security hull. This week, the third layer on one of the boat hulls had a flaw in the fibreglass. The area was reworked, after which it met the security requirements.

Fran receives weekly data on labour and materials for each boat under construction. For regular production, workers estimate the time and materials used to rework flawed fibreglass areas, and Fran adds those costs to overhead instead of recording them as a cost of the particular job. Now she needs to decide how to record the cost of rework for the enhanced security hulls. The production people are not sure whether the flaw was due to poor-quality fibreglass or to the triple hull design. If Fran adds the cost to the job order, the customer will pay for the labour and supplies as part of the cost-plus price. If she adds the cost to overhead, the cost will be spread across all jobs, and only part of it will be allocated to the job involving the enhanced security hulls.

REQUIRED   **INFORMATION ANALYSIS**

The following questions will help you analyze the information for this problem. Do not turn in your answers to these questions unless your professor asks you to do so.

A. Critique the company's accounting policy for rework and scrap.

B. Describe uncertainties about the accounting treatment for the rework costs on the enhanced security hull job.

C. Discuss the pros and cons of alternative accounting treatments for the rework costs on this job.

REQUIRED   **WRITTEN ASSIGNMENT**

Suppose you are an accounting intern at Boats Galore. Fran asks you to recommend an accounting treatment for the rework costs on the enhanced security hull job. Turn in your answers to the following.

D. Write a memo to Fran with your recommendation. As you write the memo, consider what information Fran will need from you to help her make a final decision.

E. Write one or two paragraphs explaining how you decided what information to include in your memo.

5.60 **Integrating Across the Curriculum—Financial Accounting and Auditing:** *Research financial accounting rules,*
LO2, LO3, *evaluate overhead allocation policy* Refer to the information in Problem 5.48. Suppose you work for a CA firm
LO4 and are part of the team auditing the financial statements of Flexible Manufacturers. You have been assigned the responsibility for auditing the allocation of overhead costs.

REQUIRED   **A.** Assume that the company uses separate overhead allocation rates for labour-paced assembly, machine-paced assembly, and quality testing.

1. Research financial accounting rules and determine whether the company's method for allocating overhead cost to inventory complies with IFRS.

2. Use T accounts to document your understanding of the company's overhead cost allocation method. (*Hint:* Prepare a schedule similar to Exhibit 5.11.)

B. Suppose you learn that the company plans to change its method of accounting for overhead to use a single plant-wide overhead allocation rate. Research financial accounting rules and determine the following:

    1. Whether a plant-wide overhead allocation rate complies with IFRS.

    2. The conditions under IFRS that must be met for the company to change its accounting method from using separate department overhead allocation rates to a single plant-wide allocation rate.

C. Suppose the company's policy is to include all overapplied or underapplied overhead as part of cost of goods sold on the income statement. As an auditor, would you consider this policy to be acceptable? Why or why not?

CHAPTER 6

Process Costing

in brief Some products are mass produced, making it impractical to trace costs to individual units. Process costing provides a way to overcome this challenge by assigning costs to production departments and then allocating the costs from a department to individual units. The practice of process costing is complicated by the fact that some physical units are likely to be partially complete at the beginning and end of the accounting period. Furthermore, organizations typically produce some proportion of defective or spoiled units. To assign costs appropriately to all of the units processed (completed, partially complete, and spoiled), accountants must understand both the production process and the various methods for applying process costing. ■

After studying this chapter, you should be able to do the following:

LO1 Assign costs to mass-produced products by applying equivalent units to the production process

LO2 Apply and compare the FIFO and weighted average methods in process costing

LO3 Apply alternative methods in mass production for multiple departments

LO4 Describe how spoilage costs are handled in process costing

LO5 Explain how process costing information affects managers' incentives and decisions

Fruit d'Or—Growing Business Through Innovation

© Steffen Hauser/botanikfoto/Alamy

SOURCES: H. Schultz, "Fruit d'Or Launches Organic Cranberry Powders Featuring Nutrient-Preserving Drying Technique," Nutraingredients-usa. com, October 27, 2015; "Fruit d'Or Launches Cran Bella for Beauty and Health," Nutraceuticalsworld.com, March 23, 2015; "Fruit D'Or Inc.," http://listings.ftb-companies-ca. com/l/111992220/Fruit-D-Or-Inc-in-Lourdes-QC; www.canadianbusiness. com; "Government of Canada Lends Financial Support to Fruit d'Or Inc.," Canada Economic Development for Quebec Regions news release, October 11, 2011; Y. Poisson, "Fruit d'Or Investit 1,6 million $," La Tribune, October 14, 2011; D. Kucharsky, "Happy in the Red: How Fruit d'Or Married Organics with Innovative Processing Methods to Build Quebec's Cranberry King," Profit, June 2006; and www.fruit-dor.ca.

In the early 1990s, Mario Carrier, founding partner of **Fruit d'Or Inc.**, started drying fruits and vegetables on a small scale. Having previously worked with the Canadian Food Inspection Agency to develop a new drying process that was free of food preservatives, Carrier's goal was to develop organic-only products.

In 1993, his founding partner, Martin Le Moine, started cranberry farming as a hobby. The ardent environmentalists went organic before doing so was in vogue, and in the process, their company became North America's first large-scale organic cranberry producer, dedicated to preserving the fruit's colour, shape, and nutritional value. "I wanted to do something good," says Le Moine, "not just grow cranberries for the sake of growing cranberries."

Fruit d'Or is now riding a cranberry wave powered by frequent media reports of the red berry's health benefits. In fact, the company has become the continent's largest processor of organic cranberry products. Fruit d'Or supplies a wide range of products to food processors, from dried and frozen cranberries and blueberries. It makes ingredients used in cosmetics, such as cranberry seed oil. It also supplies fresh fruit, concentrates, and a full range of dried, sweetened products. Its latest products are a dried cranberry juice powder and a cranberry gum. Fresh products are sold in supermarkets and grocery stores in the fall. Dried and frozen products are largely used by food manufacturers such as bakeries, cereal and juice companies, and food distributors and manufacturers. Cranberry and sweet blueberry products are mostly used to make cereal bars, dried fruit snacks, and breakfast cereals.

Organics make up 30% of sales at Fruit d'Or, whose heavy investment in a high-tech processing plant permits it to outproduce its rivals by far. In addition, from the field to the plant, Fruit d'Or applies a vertical quality control system when choosing its cranberry producers. The company also uses a complete tracking system that covers production from the fields to shipping to the customer.

In 2011, the firm announced it was investing a further $1.6 million, much of it acquired through government loans, to buy state-of-the-art specialized equipment to reduce its operating costs by $300,000 a year, improve production control, and enhance the quality of its products. Le Moine said the company needed to update and automate its drying process.

Exports to more than 35 countries on four continents generate about 85% of Fruit d'Or's revenues. As a private company, it does not have to publicly report its financial information, but one source reported that Fruit d'Or had $49.1 million in sales in a recent year. The firm's decision to go organic has paid off.

Accounting for the Cost of Mass-Produced Goods

LO1 Assign costs to mass-produced products by applying equivalent units to the production process

The accounting approach for assigning product costs to mass-produced products is called process costing. The purpose of process costing is to assign costs to each unit of a good or service. However, it is time consuming and costly to trace costs directly to individual units when products or services are identical and mass produced. Thus, production costs are traced to cost pools that reflect the production process (usually departments) and then allocated to individual units in a two-stage process. Examples of products for which process costing is used include beverages, food, chemicals, petroleum, plastic products, and pharmaceuticals. Examples of services that use process costing include coupon sorting and bank cheque processing.

In many organizations, the production process consists of work performed in a sequence of departments. Thus, costs are assigned to each production department and then allocated to all units that pass through the department. Consider the flow of work and costs for a cranberry processor. Fresh cranberries are received and washed in the first department. At this point in the process, some of the cranberries are sold on the market as fresh cranberries. Other cranberries will be processed further. In the second department, the cranberries are placed in vats and then covered with a syrup solution, brought to a boil, and then prepared for canning or drying. Most of the cranberries are canned in the second department, but some are transferred to a third department, where the syrup is drained and the berries are dried and packaged. Notice that each department incurs a variety of costs. Costs in the first department include the purchase price of the cranberries and the costs of labour, equipment amortization and maintenance, water, electricity, and supplies. It would be impossible to directly measure the cost of water used to clean each kilogram (unit) of cranberries. However, costs such as water are allocated to each kilogram of cranberries by dividing the total cost of water by the total volume of cranberries processed.

Assigning Direct Materials and Conversion Costs

Similarly to job costing, costs in a process costing system, as was already mentioned, are assigned to products using a two-stage process. In process costing, however, all costs are first assigned to departments. Costs are then allocated from departments to individual product units, as shown in Exhibit 6.1(a).

In a traditional process costing system, the two categories of product cost are direct materials and conversion costs. Conversion costs are direct labour and production overhead costs. Direct materials and conversion costs are allocated separately because they are usually incurred at different points in the production process. Exhibit 6.1(b) shows the cost flow within a department. Other costs, such as indirect materials and indirect labour, are traced to departments through materials and payroll records, while the costs for a shared production facility, such as rent and insurance, are allocated to departments.

Exhibit 6.2 illustrates how costs are incurred for the cranberry production process. In the cleaning department, the direct materials (cranberries) are added at the beginning of the process. In the cooking and canning department, some direct materials (water and syrup) are added at the beginning of the process, and others (jars and lids) are added at the end of the process. In the drying department, packaging materials are used at the end of the process. The conversion costs are added throughout processing in all three departments.

Work in Process and Equivalent Units

When the production process covers a span of time, organizations are likely to have partially complete units of goods or services at the beginning and end of an accounting period. The cranberry processing example would probably not have beginning or ending work-in-process

BUSINESS PRACTICE

The **Winnipeg Mint**, a part of the Royal Canadian Mint, is the powerhouse of Canada's high-volume coin production. It uses the technologically advanced processes and equipment to produce up to 15 million plated coins each day for Canadian and foreign circulation.[1]

HELPFUL HINT

In both process costing and job costing, overhead costs are allocated using a two-stage approach (first allocated or traced to cost pools, then allocated to units). Direct costs are handled differently.

---

[1] See The Royal Canadian Mint/Coin Production, *High Volume Production*, http://www.mint.ca/store/mint/learn/coin-production-1200012.

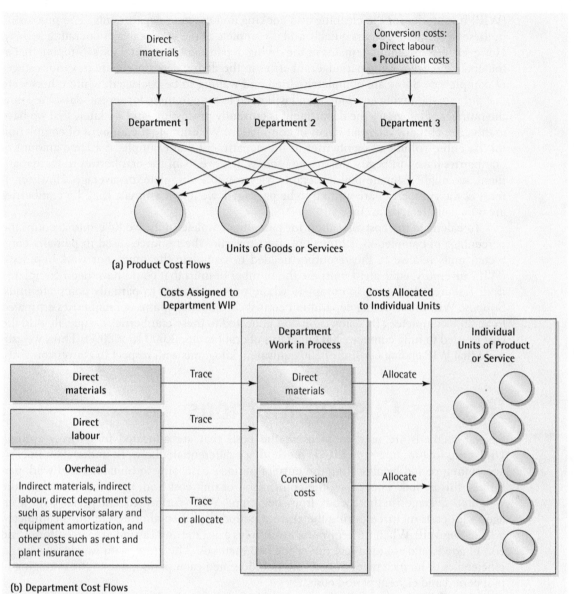

(a) Product Cost Flows

(b) Department Cost Flows

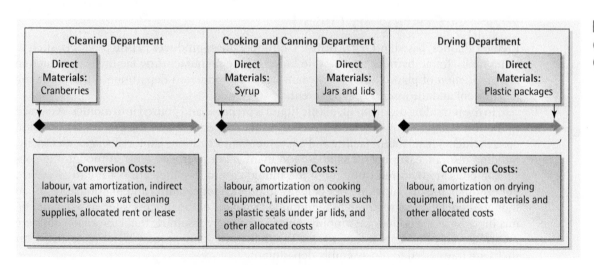

▶ EXHIBIT 6.2
Cost Flows for Producing
Cranberries

(WIP) inventories for the cleaning and cooking and canning departments. The processing in these departments occurs quickly and is complete at the end of a day's operating activity. However, WIP inventory remains in the drying department for several days. Suppose that at the end of an accounting period, cranberries in the drying department are in various stages of completion. Some are completely dried and waiting to be packaged, while others were just put into the drying equipment and will need to remain there for several days. We know the number of kilograms the department is currently processing, and we know that we have cranberries at many different stages of completion. We estimate the amount of completion for the entire volume of cranberries in the department. For example, if a large amount of cranberries have just begun the drying process, relative to all the cranberries in the department, we might estimate that the cranberries are 20% complete, on average. However, if most of the cranberries are waiting to be packaged, we might estimate that the cranberries are 80% complete, on average.

To calculate the cost allocation for partially complete units, we take into account the percentage of completion. **Equivalent units** measure the resources used in partially completed units relative to the resources needed to complete the units. For work-in-process (WIP) inventory, equivalent units are the number of units that could have been completed if all resources had gone to complete whole units instead of to partially complete units. Suppose WIP in the drying department consists of 1,000 kilograms of cranberries estimated to be 20% complete. The conversion cost allocated to these cranberries is equivalent to the cost needed to fully compete 200 kilograms of cranberries (1,000 kg × 20%). Thus, we estimate that WIP ending consists of 200 equivalent kilograms with respect to conversion costs.

Process Costing Methods

LO 2   Apply and compare the FIFO and weighted average methods in process costing

Several methods are used to measure the costs that are allocated for process costing. Under the **first-in, first-out (FIFO) method**, we differentiate the work undertaken in each accounting period by allocating the current period's costs only to units that had work performed this period. This allows the comparison of unit cost from period to period. In the **weighted average method**, costs from beginning WIP (performed last period) are averaged with costs incurred during the current period, and then allocated to units completed and ending WIP. When no beginning inventories exist, the costs assigned to inventories and cost of goods sold are identical under the two methods. Therefore, with weighted average, efficiencies or inefficiencies in costs are not identified each period, due to the averaging of past period and current period costs.

In the following example, the month of March has no beginning or ending inventories, while April has ending inventories but no beginning inventories. The costs for these two months under the weighted average and FIFO methods are identical.

Process Costing in Detail

Premier Plastics, based in Delta, British Columbia, mass-produces plastic products, such as water tanks, traffic barriers, and bicycle lockers. One manufacturing facility is dedicated to the production of plastic filters. The plant has two production departments: the moulding department and the assembly department.

In the moulding department, plastic liquid is prepared and poured into moulds. As shown in Exhibit 6.3, plastic mix ingredients are added at the beginning of the process. Conversion costs include direct labour, facility and equipment amortization, janitorial wages, electricity, building insurance, supervisor salaries, and many other overhead costs. Although the conversion costs are incurred throughout the moulding process, they are not incurred evenly. For example, the machines are periodically shut down for cleaning and maintenance. Even though more labour is required to monitor certain parts of the process, such as when plastic mix ingredients are added, we simplify the accounting by assuming that conversion costs are incurred evenly throughout the process. When the moulding process is complete, the outer shells are transferred to the assembly department.

➤EXHIBIT 6.3
Cost Flows for Producing Plastic Filter
Units

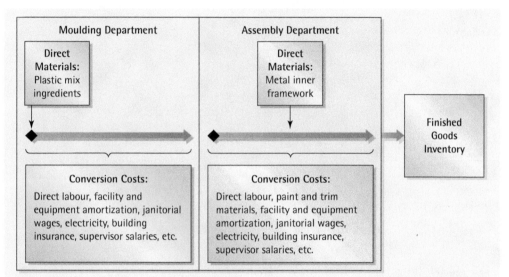

In the assembly department, machines remove any rough edges and then smooth the outer and inner surfaces. Next, a metal inner framework for holding filters is inserted. Thus, direct materials are added partway through this process. Finally, details are painted on each unit. Because the cost for paint and trim for each filter unit is small, those costs are considered indirect and are included in conversion costs. The completed units are transferred to finished goods inventory. As orders are processed, the units are transferred to the shipping department for packing and delivery.

In the following calculations, we focus on process costing for the moulding department over the course of three months of production activities. The first month portrays the simplest scenario, with no beginning or ending work in process. During the second month, the computations become slightly more complex, with the addition of ending WIP. The third month includes both beginning and ending WIP. For each month, we prepare cost reports to summarize and compare the results for the FIFO and weighted average methods.

Process Cost Reports Without Beginning or Ending WIP. During March, 10,000 units are started, completed, and transferred to the assembly department. The cost of direct materials used during March is $30,000, and conversion costs incurred are $70,000. When no WIP is involved, the equivalent unit cost is the average cost per unit for the period, calculated by dividing total cost for direct materials and conversion by the total units produced. Therefore, the equivalent unit cost for direct materials is $3.00 ($30,000/10,000 units) and for conversion is $7.00 ($70,000/10,000 units). The total equivalent unit cost is $10.00 ($3.00 + $7.00). When no beginning or ending inventories exist, the costs under the weighted average and FIFO methods are identical, as shown in the cost report for March (Exhibit 6.4). As Exhibit 6.4 shows, the summary of physical units and equivalent units manufactured during March is simple. Because no beginning or ending WIP need be accounted for, the number of physical units is equal to the number of equivalent units for both direct materials and conversion costs. The finished units are transferred into finished goods at $10.00 per unit, and the total costs incurred this period are transferred into finished goods inventory with the 10,000 units produced. Notice that all of the cost reports in this chapter first summarize total costs, separating direct materials costs from conversion costs. The physical units are summarized; again, separated into direct materials and conversion activities. Next, an equivalent unit cost for direct materials and conversion cost is calculated. And finally, the costs are allocated to the units that were completed or are in inventories at the end of the period.

➤ BUSINESS PRACTICE
Ethanol is a renewable high-octane
fuel made from corn. The "dry mill"
method for making ethanol includes the
following major processes: grinding,
cooking, fermenting, and centrifugal
separation.[2]

---

[2] See Renewable Fuels Association, *How Ethanol Is Made*, http://www.ethanolrfa.org/pages/how-ethanol-is-made.

> **EXHIBIT 6.4**
Process Cost Reports Without Beginning and Ending WIP

Assumptions for March
Work performed:
  10,000 units started, completed, and transferred out

Costs added during the month
Direct materials	$ 30,000
Conversion costs	70,000
Total costs to account for	$100,000

Summarize Physical and Equivalent Units

		Work This Period				
	① +	②			=	③
		(a) +	(b) +	(c) =		
	Beginning WIP	Beginning WIP Competed this period	Started & Completed this period	Ending WIP Started/not completed	Total Work Performed this period	Total Units to Account For
Physical units	0	0	10,000	0	10,000	10,000
Equivalent units						**Total Work**
Direct materials	0	0	10,000	0	10,000	10,000
Conversion costs	0	0	10,000	0	10,000	10,000

Calculate Cost per Equivalent Unit

First-in, first-out:

$$\text{Direct materials} : \frac{\text{Direct materials costs}}{\text{Equivalent units for total work performed this period}} = \frac{\$30,000}{10,000} = \$3.00$$

$$\text{Conversion costs} : \frac{\text{Conversion costs}}{\text{Equivalent units for total work performed this period}} = \frac{\$70,000}{10,000} = \underline{7.00}$$

Total cost per equivalent unit: $\underline{\underline{\$10.00}}$

Weighted average: Computations are the same as for FIFO because there is no beginning WIP.

Process Cost Reports for Moulding Department: March

	First-In, First-Out			Weighted Average		
	Computation	Units	Costs	Computation	Units	Costs
New units started, completed, and transferred out	10,000$ × $10.00	10,000	$100,000			
Total units completed and transferred out		10,000	100,000	10,000 × $10.00	10,000	$100,000
Total accounted for		10,000	$100,000		10,000	$100,000

FIFO and Weighted Average Methods. Because no beginning WIP is involved in Exhibit 6.4, the costs per unit are the same under both the FIFO and weighted average methods. These methods differ only when beginning WIP must be taken into account. As shown in the exhibit, the direct material cost is $3.00 per unit, and the conversion cost is $7.00 per unit. Total cost per unit is $10.00. Thus, the cost for the 10,000 units produced is $100,000, which is equal to the total costs to account for.

Comparison. Without beginning WIP, no cost difference arises between the FIFO and weighted average methods.

►EXHIBIT 6.5
Process Cost Reports with Ending WIP

Assumptions for April:

Work performed:

Units started	0
Units completed and transferred out	10,000
Ending WIP	2,000
% complete direct materials	100%
% complete conversion costs	30%

Costs added during the month:

Direct materials	$ 36,000
Conversion costs	74,200
Total costs to account for	$110,200

Summarize Physical and Equivalent Units

	Beginning WIP ①	(a) Beginning WIP Competed this period	(b) Started & Completed this period	(c) Ending WIP Started/not completed	Total Work Performed this period ②	Total Units to Account For ③
Physical units	0	0	10,000	2,000	12,000	12,000
Equivalent units						Total Work
Direct materials (% completed)	0	0	10,000	2,000 (100%)	12,000	12,000
Conversion costs (% completed)	0	0	10,000	600 (30%)	10,600	10,600

Calculate Cost per Equivalent Unit

First-in, first-out:

$$\text{Direct materials}: \frac{\text{Direct materials cost}}{\text{Equivalent units for total work performed this period}} = \frac{\$36,000}{12,000} = \$3.00$$

$$\text{Conversion costs}: \frac{\text{Conversion costs}}{\text{Equivalent units for total work performed this period}} = \frac{\$74,200}{10,600} = 7.00$$

Total cost per equivalent unit: $10.00

Weighted average: Computations are the same as for FIFO because there is no beginning WIP.

Process Cost Reports for Moulding Department: April

	First-In, First-Out Computation	Units	Costs	Weighted Average Computation	Units	Costs
New units started, completed, and transferred out	10,000 × $10.00	10,000	$100,000			
Total units completed and transferred out		10,000	100,000	10,000 × $10.00	10,000	$100,000
Ending WIP:		2,000			2,000	
Direct materials	2,000 × $3.00		6,000	2,000 × $3.00		6,000
Conversion costs	600 × $7.00		4,200	600 × $7.00		4,200
Total ending WIP cost			10,200			10,200
Total accounted for		12,000	$110,200		12,000	$110,200

Process Cost Reports with Ending WIP. Exhibit 6.5 presents the data and computations for the month of April, which has ending WIP but no beginning WIP. During April, 10,000 units are started, completed, and transferred out. An additional 2,000 units are started but only 30% complete at the end of the month. The cost of direct materials used during April is $36,000, and conversion costs are $74,200.

The total work performed during April is the sum of the units that were started, completed, and transferred out and the equivalent units in ending WIP. Direct materials in the moulding department are added at the beginning of production, so the 2,000 units in ending WIP are 100% complete with respect to direct materials, and equivalent units for direct materials equal 2,000. The total amount of work performed during April for direct materials is 12,000 equivalent units. However, we assume that conversion costs in the moulding department are incurred evenly throughout production. Therefore, the 2,000 physical units in ending WIP are counted as 600 equivalent units (2,000 units × 30%) for conversion costs. The total amount of work performed during April for conversion costs is 10,600 equivalent units.

FIFO and Weighted Average Methods. Because Premier began April with no beginning WIP, the costs per unit are again the same under the FIFO and weighted average methods. However, because we have ending WIP, we now use equivalent units rather than actual units to calculate the per-unit cost. As shown in Exhibit 6.5, direct material cost remains $3.00 per unit, and conversion cost is $7.00 per unit. So, the total equivalent unit cost remains $10.00. Thus, the cost allocated to the 10,000 units completed is $100,000. For ending WIP, the cost of direct materials is $6,000, and the conversion cost is $4,200. We can double-check our computations by verifying that the sum of costs accounted for ($110,200) is equal to the sum of beginning WIP plus the costs incurred during April ($0 + $36,000 + $74,200 = $110,200).

Comparison. As before, with no beginning WIP, no cost difference occurs between the FIFO and weighted average methods.

Process Cost Reports with Beginning and Ending WIP. Exhibit 6.6 presents the data and computations for the month of May, which has beginning WIP as well as ending WIP. For May, beginning WIP includes 2,000 units; 9,000 units are started, completed, and transferred to the assembly department; and another 1,000 units are started and 40% complete in ending WIP. The cost of direct materials used during May is $30,500, and conversion costs incurred are $76,680. Because beginning inventory exists this month, the cost report under weighted average differs from the cost report under FIFO.

▷ **INTERNATIONAL**

Fibria is the world's largest producer of eucalyptus pulp, which is used in paper products. Its pulp production includes the following major processes: wood chipping, cooking, purifying/bleaching, drying, and packaging.[3]

▷ **EXHIBIT 6.6**
Process Cost Reports with Beginning and Ending WIP

Assumptions for May:

Work performed:		Costs:	
Beginning WIP	2,000	Beginning WIP (FIFO and Weighted Average)	
% complete direct materials	100%	Direct materials	$ 6,000
% complete conversion costs	30%	Conversion costs	4,200
Units started	9,000	Total beginning WIP costs	10,200
Units completed and transferred out	11,000	Costs added this month	
Ending WIP	1,000	Direct materials	30,500
% complete direct materials	100%	Conversion costs	76,680
% complete conversion costs	40%	Total costs added	107,180
		Total costs to account for	$117,380

[3] Source: Fibria's Pulp Production Process, www.fibria.com/shared/midia/fibria-infographic-september-3-2012a.pdf.

▶EXHIBIT 6.6

continued

Summarize Physical and Equivalent Units

| | ① + | (a) + | (b) + | (c) = | = | ③ |
		Work This Period		②		
	Beginning WIP	Beginning WIP Completed this period	Started & Completed this period	Ending WIP Started/not completed	Total Work Performed this period	Total Units to Account For
Physical units	2,000	0	9,000	1,000	10,000	12,000
Equivalent units						**Total Work**
Direct materials (% completed)	2,000 (100%)	0	9,000	1,000 (100%)	10,000	12,000
Conversion costs (% completed)	600 (30%)	1,400 (70%)	9,000	400 (40%)	10,800	11,400

Calculate Actual Cost per Equivalent Unit

First-in, first-out:

$$\text{Direct materials}: \frac{\text{Direct materials cost}}{\text{Equivalent units for total work performed this period}} = \frac{\$30,500}{10,000} = \$3.05$$

$$\text{Conversion Costs}: \frac{\text{Conversion cost}}{\text{Equivalent units for total work performed this period}} = \frac{\$76,680}{10,800} = \underline{7.10}$$

Total cost per equivalent unit: $\underline{\$10.15}$

Weighted average:

$$\text{Direct materials}: \frac{\text{Beginning WIP} + \text{Direct materials cost}}{\text{Equivalent units for total work}} = \frac{\$36,500}{12,000} = \$3.04$$

$$\text{Conversion costs}: \frac{\text{Beginning WIP} + \text{Direct materials cost}}{\text{Equivalent units for total work}} = \frac{\$80,880}{11,400} = \$7.09$$

Total cost per equivalent unit: $\underline{\$10.13}$

Process Cost Reports for Moulding Department: May

	First-In, First-Out			Weighted Average		
	Computation	Units	Costs	Computation	Units	Costs
Beginning WIP	(from April cost report)	2,000	$10,200			
Costs to complete beginning WIP						
Direct materials	0 × $3.05		0			
Conversion costs	1,400 × $7.10		9,940			
Total costs added this period			9,940			
Total cost of beginning WIP transferred out		2,000	20,140			
New units started, completed, and transferred out	9,000 × $10.15	9,000	91,350			
Total units completed and transferred out		11,000	111,490	(2,000 + 9,000) × $10.1364	11,000	$111,500
Ending WIP		1,000			1,000	
Direct materials	1,000 × $3.05		3,050	1,000 × $3.0417		3,042
Conversion costs	400 × $7.10		2,840	400 × $7.0947		2,838
Total ending WIP cost			5,890			5,880
Total accounted for		**12,000**	**$117,380**		**12,000**	**$117,380**

The total units to account for during May (12,000) include both beginning WIP and the units started during the month. In Exhibit 6.6, the total work performed during the month is the sum of work performed to complete beginning WIP units, the units both started and completed, and the work performed on units started but not yet completed. Because direct materials are added at the beginning of the process, no additional direct materials were needed to complete beginning WIP, meaning it is 100% complete with respect to direct materials. Conversion costs are added throughout the process, so part of the conversion costs for beginning WIP were incurred last period and part were incurred this period. The beginning WIP consisted of 2,000 units that were 30% complete, or 600 equivalent units with respect to conversion costs. Conversion cost work performed during May consisted of completing the beginning WIP of 1,400 [2,000 units × (1 – 30%)] equivalent units, plus the 9,000 units started and completed, plus 400 equivalent units in ending WIP (1,000 units × 40%), for a total of 10,800 units.

FIFO Method. Only the current period work and costs are included in the equivalent unit calculations under the FIFO method. Therefore, the difference between weighted average and FIFO is in the treatment of beginning units. To determine the equivalent unit cost under FIFO, current period costs are divided by the number of equivalent units for total work performed this period. During May, equivalent unit costs are calculated as shown in Exhibit 6.6: $3.05 for direct materials and $7.10 for conversion costs. These costs are allocated to the work performed to complete beginning WIP, to the units started and completed, and to the equivalent units in ending WIP. We can double-check our computations by verifying that the sum of costs accounted for ($117,380) is equal to the sum of beginning WIP plus costs incurred during May ($10,200 + $30,500 + $76,680 = $117,380).

Weighted Average Method. Under the weighted average method, the costs from beginning WIP are averaged with the costs incurred during the period. Average costs— rather than current period costs alone—are then allocated to the units completed and in ending WIP. As shown in Exhibit 6.6, the weighted average cost per equivalent unit is $3.0417 for direct materials and $7.0947 for conversion costs. Because beginning WIP and current period costs are averaged under the weighted average method, average cost per unit is simply allocated to the total units completed and transferred out and to the equivalent units in ending WIP.

Comparison. During the month of May, the per-unit costs differ between FIFO and weighted average. FIFO reflects only the current period costs ($3.05 for direct materials and $7.10 for conversion), while weighted average blends last period's and this period's costs ($3.0417 for direct materials and $7.0947 for conversion). Most organizations experience at least some fluctuation in costs between accounting periods, leading to differences in the per-unit costs between weighted average and FIFO. For Premier, the costs per unit under weighted average are lower than the FIFO costs, indicating that costs increased in May.

●●◉ RISK OF BIASED DECISIONS: LAKE WOBEGON EFFECT

THE LAKE WOBEGON EFFECT is a tendency to overrate one's own performance. The bias takes its name from the town in *A Prairie Home Companion*, a radio show hosted by Garrison Keillor. The show describes life in the fictional U.S. Midwestern town of Lake Wobegon, where all of the children are above average. When researchers survey individuals such as drivers, investors, students, and CEOs about their performance, the majority claim to be above average. Managers of mass-production operations may also believe that their operations are above average. However, most industries publish benchmark information that can be accessed to provide a more realistic assessment about operations relative to the industry average.

►EXHIBIT 6.7

Process Costing General Ledger Accounts for Producing Plastic Filter Units

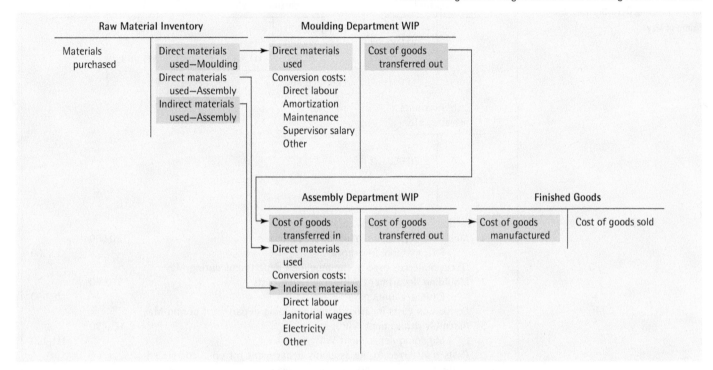

General Ledger Accounts for Process Costing

In process costing, separate WIP accounts are maintained for each production department. Pools of product costs are accumulated in WIP and then allocated to the individual units. In a traditional system, two cost pools are used for costs incurred within a department: direct material costs and conversion costs. As units are completed in the first department, their costs are transferred to WIP for the second department. The costs for transferred-in units are pooled separately from other costs in the second department. Then, additional direct material (if any) and conversion costs are added. At the end of production in the second department, the three categories of cost (transferred-in costs, direct materials costs, and conversion costs) are assigned to units, and the costs are transferred out. This process continues for each department until the products are transferred into finished goods.

Exhibit 6.7 shows the general ledger accounts and inventory cost flows for the two production departments at Premier Plastics. First, direct materials move from raw material inventory to the moulding department. Conversion costs are accumulated in the WIP account for each department. The costs for the completed units in the moulding department are transferred to the assembly department WIP account. In the assembly department, additional direct material and conversion costs are added. When assembly work is completed, costs are transferred from the assembly department WIP to finished goods inventory.

Journal entries for process costing are similar to those for job costing. The main difference is that materials, labour, and overhead costs are assigned to departments rather than to specific jobs. The costs are then allocated from each department to individual units. Exhibit 6.8 provides the general journal entries for FIFO process costing for the moulding department of Premier Plastics during the month of May.

The following illustration, Premier Plastics, Part 1, compares FIFO and weighted average cost information for use in monitoring costs.

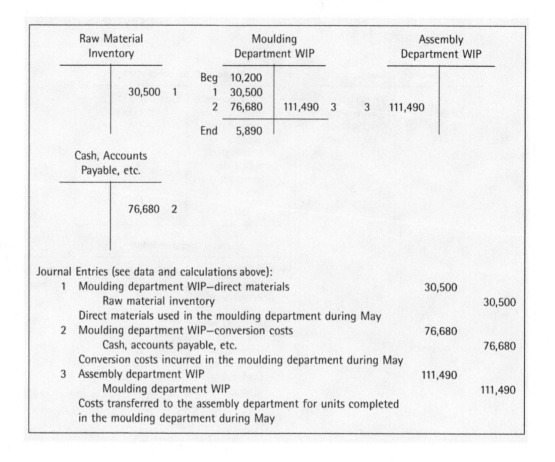

Journal Entries (see data and calculations above):

1	Moulding department WIP—direct materials	30,500	
	Raw material inventory		30,500
	Direct materials used in the moulding department during May		
2	Moulding department WIP—conversion costs	76,680	
	Cash, accounts payable, etc.		76,680
	Conversion costs incurred in the moulding department during May		
3	Assembly department WIP	111,490	
	Moulding department WIP		111,490
	Costs transferred to the assembly department for units completed in the moulding department during May		

example

premier plastics, part 1
CHOOSING A PROCESS COSTING METHOD

Nancy Redhouse is the cost accountant for Premier Plastics, a manufacturer of plastic water tanks, traffic barriers, bicycle locks, etc. To reduce costs, the company's managers installed new machines in the moulding department to reduce waste. Direct materials costs are expected to decrease and the machines will use less labour and time, thereby reducing conversion costs. Nancy wants to help the managers monitor costs for the new equipment, so she is reconsidering the method used for process cost reports. The head of the moulding department also wants to use cost information to motivate employees operating the machines to identify potential process improvements that could further reduce cost or increase quality.

The process cost reports are prepared using the weighted average method, but Nancy is concerned that this method might not provide managers with the most current cost information. The FIFO method provides more current cost information. Nancy decides to prepare process cost reports for the month of June using both methods so that she can discuss the results with the managers and obtain feedback for the final decision on which method to use.

FIFO and Weighted Average Process Cost Reports

Nancy gathers information about June production and costs. During June, 12,000 units were started, 3,000 units in ending WIP were 50% complete, and 9,000 units were transferred out. Direct material cost was $33,600, and conversion costs were $74,925. Beginning work

example

in process consisted of 1,000 units. Nancy obtains the weighted average costs from May's accounting records and calculates the values that would have been used for FIFO. The costs for beginning WIP are as follows:

	FIFO	Weighted Average
Direct materials: 1,000 equivalent units	$3,050	$3,042
Conversion costs: 400 equivalent units	2,840	2,838
Total beginning WIP	$5,890	$5,880

Nancy uses a four-step process to prepare the process cost report under each method:

1. Summarize total costs to account for.
2. Summarize total physical and equivalent units.
3. Compute cost per equivalent unit.
4. Account for cost of units completed and cost of ending WIP.

The first step is to summarize total costs for which an accounting is necessary, as shown in Exhibit 6.9. Nancy uses the beginning WIP costs and adds costs incurred during June. The total costs to account for are different under FIFO than under the weighted average method because the costs assigned to beginning WIP are different (see the May computations in Exhibit 6.6).

The second step is to summarize the total physical and equivalent units. Nancy prepares only one schedule for FIFO and weighted average, as shown in Exhibit 6.9. However, she knows that under the FIFO method she needs only the equivalent units for work performed during June, whereas under weighed average she needs the equivalent units for total work during June and in beginning WIP. The equivalent units for work performed during June includes work to complete beginning WIP, work on units started and completed during June, and work on units started but not completed during June.

The third step is to compute the cost per equivalent unit for direct materials and conversion costs, as shown in Exhibit 6.9. The computations for FIFO use only the costs and equivalent units for work performed during June, while the computations for weighted average use the costs and equivalent units in beginning WIP plus the work performed during June.

The fourth step is to prepare the process cost reports, as shown in Exhibit 6.9. Nancy prepares the FIFO and weighted average reports side-by-side, to easily compare the results.

HELPFUL HINT
Carry enough decimal places, typically four or more, or use a spreadsheet with cell references to avoid rounding errors.

EXHIBIT 6.9
Premier Plastics Moulding Department Process Cost Report for June

1. Summarize Total Costs to Account For

First-in, first-out:

	Direct Materials	Conversion Costs	Total Cost
Beginning WIP	$ 3,050	$ 2,840	$ 5,890
Current period costs	33,600	74,925	108,525
Total costs to account for	$36,650	$77,765	$114,415

Weighted average:

	Direct Materials	Conversion Costs	Total Cost
Beginning WIP	$ 3,042	$ 2,838	$ 5,880
Current period costs	33,600	74,925	108,525
Total costs to account for	$36,642	$77,763	$114,405

continued…

►EXHIBIT 6.9
continued

2. Summarize Physical and Equivalent Units

		Work This Period				
	① +	②			=	③
		(a) +	(b) +	(c) =		
	Beginning WIP	Beginning WIP Competed this period	Started & Completed this period	Ending WIP Started/not completed	Total Work Performed This Period	Total Units to Account For
Physical units	1,000	0	9,000	3,000	12,000	13,000
Equivalent units:						**Total Work**
Direct materials (% completed)	1,000 (100%)	0	9,000	3,000 (100%)	12,000	13,000
Conversion costs (% completed)	400 (40%)	600 (60%)	9,000	1,500 (50%)	11,100	11,500

3. Calculate Cost per Equivalent Unit

First-in, first-out:

$$\text{Direct materials}: \frac{\text{Direct materials cost}}{\text{Equivalent units for total work performed this period}} = \frac{\$33,600}{12,000} = \$2.80$$

$$\text{Conversion costs}: \frac{\text{Conversion costs}}{\text{Equivalent units for total work performed this period}} = \frac{\$74,925}{11,100} = \underline{6.75}$$

Total cost per equivalent unit: $\underline{\underline{9.55}}$

Weighted average:

$$\text{Direct materials}: \frac{\text{Beginning WIP} + \text{Direct materials cost}}{\text{Equivalent units for total work}} = \frac{\$36,642}{13,000} = \$2.8186$$

$$\text{Conversion costs}: \frac{\text{Beginning WIP} + \text{Conversion cost}}{\text{Equivalent units for total work}} = \frac{\$77,763}{11,500} = \underline{6.7620}$$

Total cost per equivalent unit: $\underline{\underline{\$9.5806}}$

4. Process Cost Reports for Moulding Department: June

	First-In, First-Out			Weighted Average		
	Computation	Units	Costs	Computation	Units	Costs
Beginning WIP	(from May cost report)	1,000	$5,890			
Costs to complete beginning WIP:						
Direct materials	0 × $2.80		0			
Conversion costs	600 × $6.75		4,050			
Total costs added this period			4,050			
Total cost of beginning WIP transferred out		1,000	9,940			
New units started, completed, and transferred out	9,000 × $9.55	9,000	85,950			
Total units completed and transferred out		10,000	95,890	(1,000 + 9,000) × $9.5806	10,000	$95,806
Ending WIP:		3,000			3,000	
Direct materials	3,000 × $2.80		8,400	3,000 × $2.8186		8,456
Conversion costs	1,500 × $6.75		10,125	1,500 × $6.7620		10,143
Total ending WIP cost			18,525			18,599
Total accounted for		**13,000**	**$114,415**		**13,000**	**$114,405**

example

Comparison of FIFO and Weighted Average

As Nancy reviews her work, she notices that the weighted average method requires fewer computations than the FIFO method. However, she thinks the extra work for FIFO is not a problem, because she plans to use a spreadsheet to create future reports. From a management perspective, she thinks that FIFO is probably a better method, because it provides more precise information about any changes in per-unit cost between periods. During June, the difference in per-unit cost between weighted average and FIFO was small ($9.5806 versus $9.55). However, she believes it is large enough that managers will prefer the more current data provided by FIFO. When Nancy discusses the two methods with the managers, they agree that the FIFO method provides them with the best information for monitoring monthly costs. ■

6-1 self-study problem   Weighted Average and FIFO Process Cost Reports

L01, L02

Evergreen Kit Company produces kits for plastic airplanes and car models. The company uses process costing to assign costs to its inventory and has always used the weighted average method. Jussi, the company's new accountant, is thinking about recommending changing to the FIFO method. He plans to prepare inventory cost reports for March using both methods so that he can compare the results.

The company has only one production department. Direct materials are introduced at the beginning of the process, and conversion costs are incurred evenly throughout the manufacturing process. Once each unit is completed, it is transferred to finished goods inventory. Jussi collected the following data for the month of March:

Beginning inventory:		
Work in process (40% complete)		10,000 units
Costs:		
Direct material costs	$ 8,000	
Conversion costs	2,220	
Total cost of beginning WIP	$10,220	
Units completed and transferred out during March		48,000 units
Units started during March		40,000 units
Ending WIP inventory (50% complete)		2,000 units
Direct material costs used during March	$44,000	
Conversion costs incurred during March	$36,000	

required

A. Prepare a process cost report using the weighted average method:
   1. Summarize total costs to account for.
   2. Summarize total physical units and equivalent units.
   3. Compute costs per equivalent unit.
   4. Prepare a process costing report.
B. Following the same procedures as in Part A, prepare a process cost report using the FIFO method.
C. Prepare a table to compare the total costs and cost per equivalent unit under the weighted average and FIFO methods. Provide possible explanations for the difference between FIFO and weighted average costs.

See the solution on page 282.

tukkata/Shutterstock

Alternative Systems for Costing Mass Production

L03 Apply alternative methods in mass production for multiple departments

In the preceding section, we performed process costing computations under the following assumptions:

- ► Direct materials added at the beginning of the process
- ► Conversion costs incurred evenly throughout the process
- ► Conversion costs accumulated in a single cost pool
- ► No costs transferred in from another department
- ► Fluctuations between beginning WIP and current period cost per unit

Now we consider the effects of different organizational settings on process costing.

Direct Materials Added During the Process

For manufactured products, the cost of direct materials is often a large proportion of the total cost per unit. If the point when direct materials are added is correctly identified, accuracy is increased in the equivalent unit calculations and cost for WIP inventories. In many processes, direct materials are added at the beginning, and WIP is always 100% complete with respect to direct materials. However, direct materials are sometimes added later during the process, as shown in the assembly department in Exhibit 6.3. Direct materials may also be added at more than one point during the process, as shown for the cooking and canning department in Exhibit 6.2. Alternatively, direct materials are not added at all in some processes. For example, if cranberries were dried and packaged in separate departments, no direct materials would be added during the drying process. Because the process of adding direct materials varies, accountants must analyze the production process before performing process costing calculations.

Nonuniform Conversion Costs and Multiple Cost Pools

Accountants analyze production processes to determine how conversion costs are incurred. We often assume that conversion costs are incurred evenly throughout the process in each department, but this is often not the case. In addition, for some processes, it might be easier to match costs to the work performed if conversion costs are separated into two or more cost pools.

For example, direct labour costs might be incurred in one pattern and other types of conversion costs might be incurred in a different pattern. In the cranberry drying department portrayed in Exhibit 6.2, labour is used to load the cranberries onto drying frames, and then the cranberries sit for several days while drying. Few labour hours are needed to monitor the drying process. On the other hand, electricity and equipment are used evenly throughout the drying process. If it is relatively easy to track labour separately, the accountants may find it beneficial to allocate labour and overhead costs separately.

Costs Transferred from Another Department

As illustrated in Exhibits 6.2 and 6.3, many processes are organized around multiple departments. Process costing for each department is performed separately, but costs for work done in one department are transferred to the next department as units are transferred. Completed units and costs are transferred from department to department until the last production department transfers completed units to finished goods inventory. After the first department, the number of units started consists of units transferred in from the preceding department. In addition, the total costs to account for include a new cost category for costs transferred in.

In the following illustration, units and costs are transferred into Premier Plastics' assembly department. In addition, direct materials are added in the middle of the process. Both FIFO and weighted average methods are illustrated.

premier plastics, part 2
COSTS TRANSFERRED FROM ANOTHER DEPARTMENT AND DIRECT MATERIALS ADDED LATER IN THE PROCESS

After hearing that the managers in the moulding department were pleased with their new FIFO process cost report, the managers in the assembly department asked Nancy to prepare a similar report for their department for the month of June.

Nancy first refers to the cost flows she previously developed for the assembly department, shown in Exhibit 6.3. The assembly department smoothes and finishes the plastic filters and adds a metal framework for the filters. The metal frames are direct materials that are added when the filters are about 50% complete. Nancy assumes that conversion costs are added evenly throughout the assembly process.

Next, Nancy gathers information about June's operations. Beginning WIP inventory (1,000 units) was 20% complete. The cost of beginning WIP includes the costs transferred in from the moulding department in May under FIFO ($10.15 per unit) and weighted average ($10.1364 per unit). In addition, conversion costs in May were $10.00 per unit under FIFO (total cost of $10 × 200 = $2,000) and $9.95 per unit under weighted average (total cost of $9.95 × 200 = $1,990):

© Shotshop GmbH/Alamy

continued...

example

Beginning WIP:		FIFO	Weighted Average
Transferred in: 1,000 equivalent units		$10,150	$10,136
Direct materials: 0 equivalent units		0	0
Conversion costs: 200 equivalent units		2,000	1,990
Total beginning WIP		$12,150	$12,126

During June, 10,000 units were transferred in from the moulding department. The total cost of units transferred in under weighted average costing was $9.5806 per unit, or $95,806 total (Exhibit 6.9). Nancy calculates that the cost would have been $95,890 total under FIFO, or an average of $9.589 per unit. Of the 10,000 units transferred in, 8,000 units were completed and transferred out to finished goods inventory. The remaining 2,000 units in ending WIP inventory were 60% complete.

Nancy follows the same four steps she used for the moulding department to create a cost report for the assembly department, as shown in Exhibit 6.10. The procedures to prepare the process cost reports for the assembly department are similar to those performed previously for the moulding department, except for the transferred-in costs and timing for the addition of direct materials.

Transferred-in costs are treated as a third category of cost, similar to the treatment of direct materials and conversion costs. However, as units are transferred from moulding to assembly, they are always 100% complete.

> **EXHIBIT 6.10**
>
> Premier Plastics Assembly Department Process Cost Report for June

1. Summarize Total Costs to Account For

First-in, first-out:

	Transferred In	Direct Materials	Conversion Costs	Total Cost
Beginning WIP	$ 10,150	$ 0	$ 2,000	$ 12,150
Current period costs	95,890	22,000	98,000	215,890
Total costs to account for	$106,040	$22,000	$100,000	$228,040

Weighted average:

	Transferred In	Direct Materials	Conversion Costs	Total Cost
Beginning WIP:	$ 10,136	$ 0	$ 1,990	$ 12,126
Current period costs:	95,806	22,000	98,000	215,806
Total costs to account for:	$105,942	$22,000	$99,990	$227,932

2. Summarize Physical and Equivalent Units

Work This Period

	① +	(a) + Beginning WIP Competed this period	(b) + Started & Completed this period	(c) = Ending WIP Started/not completed	② Total Work Performed this Period	=	③ Total Units to Account For
	Beginning WIP						
Physical units	1,000	0	8,000	2,000	10,000		11,000
Equivalent units							**Total Work**
Transferred in	1,000	0	8,000	2,000 (100%)	10,000		11,000
Direct materials (% completed)	0	1,000 (100%)	8,000	2,000 (100%)	11,000		11,000
Conversion costs (% completed)	200 (20%)	800 (80%)	8,000	1,200 (60%)	10,000		10,200

3. Calculate Cost per Equivalent Unit

First-in, first-out:

$$\text{Transferred in :} \quad \frac{\text{Transferred-in costs}}{\text{Equivalent units for total work performed this period}} = \frac{\$95,890}{10,000} = \$9.589$$

$$\text{Direct materials :} \quad \frac{\text{Direct materials cost}}{\text{Equivalent units for total work performed this period}} = \frac{\$22,000}{11,000} = 2.000$$

$$\text{Conversion costs :} \quad \frac{\text{Conversion costs}}{\text{Equivalent units for total work performed this period}} = \frac{\$98,000}{10,000} = 9.800$$

Total cost per equivalent unit: $\quad\quad \$21.389$

Weighted average:

$$\text{Transferred in :} \quad \frac{\text{Beginning WIP + Transferred-in costs}}{\text{Equivalent units for total work}} = \frac{\$105,942}{11,000} = \$9.6311$$

$$\text{Direct materials :} \quad \frac{\text{Beginning WIP + Transferred-in costs}}{\text{Equivalent units for total work}} = \frac{\$22,000}{11,000} = 2.000$$

$$\text{Conversion costs :} \quad \frac{\text{Beginning WIP + Conversion cost}}{\text{Equivalent units for total work}} = \frac{\$99,990}{10,000} = 9.8029$$

Total cost per equivalent unit: $\quad\quad \$21.4340$

4. Process Cost Reports for Assembly Department: June

	First-In, First-Out			Weighted Average		
	Computation	Units	Costs	Computation	Units	Costs
Beginning WIP	(from May cost report)	1,000	$12,150			
Costs to complete beginning WIP:						
Direct materials	1,000 × $2		2,000			
Conversion costs	800 × $9.8		7,840			
Total costs added this period			9,840			
Total cost of beginning WIP transferred out		1,000	21,990			
New units started, completed, and transferred out	8,000 × $21.389	8,000	171,112			
Total units completed and transferred out		9,000	193,102	(1,000 + 8,000) × $21.434	9,000	$192,906
Ending WIP:		2,000			2,000	
Transferred in	2,000 × $9.589		19,178	2,000 × $9.6311		19,262
Direct materials	2,000 × $2		4,000	2,000 × $2		4,000
Conversion costs	1,200 × $9.8		11,760	1,200 × $9.8029		11,764
Total ending WIP cost			34,938			35,026
Total accounted for		11,000	$228,040		11,000	$227,932

Because direct materials are added when units are 50% complete and beginning WIP was only 20% complete, none of the units in beginning WIP included direct materials. Then, 100% of the direct materials were added to beginning WIP during June. Ending WIP was 60% complete, so 100% of the direct materials to those units were added during June.

After finishing the cost reports, Nancy compares the equivalent cost per unit in the assembly department using weighted average and FIFO. The weighted average equivalent unit cost is $21.434, and the FIFO cost is $21.389.

Nancy notices that the cost per equivalent unit that is added in assembly is similar under both methods, which means that costs during June were similar to May's costs. She asks the

continued...

example

managers whether costs in the assembly department fluctuate much from month to month. The managers tell her that a long-term contract with suppliers guarantees prices for at least a one-year period, and labour contracts are negotiated annually, so the costs do not fluctuate much from month to month. In addition, volumes do not fluctuate a great deal.

Because costs in the department rarely fluctuate and volumes are reasonably stable, the costs added will be similar under both methods, so either method would be appropriate. However, because moulding is now using FIFO, units are transferred in at FIFO cost. To be consistent, Nancy decides that the assembly department should also use FIFO. ■

In recent years, several developments have affected the manufacturing environment and costing practices. Organizations have concentrated on reducing the amount of inventory in their systems and also on increasing their abilities to customize mass-produced goods. In addition, managers have sought better ways to monitor costs and motivate higher levels of performance. The costing systems used by organizations vary, depending on the information needs of the managers, the production processes used, and the nature of the organization's products or services. Next, we discuss three types of alternative systems.

Standard Costing

> **► CHAPTER REFERENCE**
> Accounting entries in a standard process costing system are similar to the allocation of overhead using an estimated rate, introduced in Chapter 5.

A **standard cost** is a cost that managers expect to incur for production of goods or services under operating plan assumptions. Under a standard costing system, accounting entries for direct materials, conversion costs, and transferred-in costs are recorded at standard, or expected, rather than actual costs. Actual costs are accumulated in a control account, and then costs are allocated to WIP using a standard rate per equivalent unit. At the end of the period, adjustments are made for the differences between actual and standard costs.

Standard costs are used for a variety of reasons. For example, they simplify the process of making accounting entries during the period; actual costs need not be compiled for product costs to be recorded. Standards also provide a benchmark against which actual costs can be compared. Managers and operating employees can then be rewarded based on whether the standards are achieved or exceeded. These rewards provide motivation for monitoring operations and maintaining higher productivity levels.

> **► CHAPTER REFERENCE**
> Developing and using standard costs are discussed in more detail in Chapter 11.

Standard costs are allocated to units in a manner similar to FIFO process costing. The difference is that no equivalent cost per unit is calculated. Instead, a standard cost is used to allocate costs to inventory. In Exhibit 6.11, the standard costs for the moulding department of Premier Plastics in May are $3.00 for direct materials and $7.00 for conversion costs, or $10.00 per unit. Assuming no change from the prior month in the standard costs, the cost of beginning WIP is carried over from the previous month at the costs per equivalent unit. Therefore, beginning WIP includes direct materials cost of $6,000 (2,000 × $3.00) and conversion costs of $4,200 (600 × $7.00), for a total of $10,200. During May, standard costs are first allocated to the equivalent units of work performed to complete beginning WIP: $0 for direct materials and $9,800 for conversion costs. Next, standard costs of $90,000 ($10 × 9,000 units) are allocated to the units started, completed, and transferred out. Finally, standard costs of $3,000 for direct materials and $2,800 for conversion costs are allocated to ending WIP. The total amount of standard cost to account for (beginning WIP plus costs allocated during May) is $115,800. Details of the cost report are presented in Exhibit 6.11.

When standard costs are used as benchmarks, they are compared to actual costs calculated using either weighted average or FIFO. In this example for Premier Plastics, Nancy could compare the standard cost of $10 per unit with the actual weighted average cost per equivalent unit in May of $10.1364 or to the FIFO cost of $10.15. From these comparisons, it appears that actual costs are higher than standard costs. When actual costs are higher than standard costs, managers investigate the causes and analyze ways to improve operations. If actual costs are lower, the causes may also be analyzed so that managers better understand the improvements that have taken place.

Premier Plastics Moulding Department Standard Process Cost Report for May

Assumptions for May:

Direct materials standard cost = $3.00

Standard cost for conversion = $7.00

Work performed:

Beginning WIP	2,000
% complete direct materials	100%
% complete conversion costs	30%
Units started	9,000
Units completed and transferred out	11,000
Ending WIP	1,000
% complete direct materials	100%
% complete conversion costs	40%

1. Summarize Total Costs to Account For

Direct materials: 12,000 equivalent units at standard cost of $3.00 per unit	$ 36,000
Conversion costs: 11,400 equivalent units at standard cost of $7.00 per unit	79,800
Total standard costs to account for	$115,800

2. Summarize Physical and Equivalent Units

		Work This Period				
	① +	②			=	③
		(a) +	(b) +	(c) =		
	Beginning WIP	**Beginning WIP Competed this period**	**Started & Completed this period**	**Ending WIP Started/not completed**	**Total Work Performed this Period**	**Total Units to Account For**
Physical units	2,000	0	9,000	1,000	10,000	12,000
Equivalent units:						**Total Work**
Direct materials (% completed)	2,000 (100%)	0	9,000	1,000 (100%)	10,000	12,000
Conversion costs (% completed)	600 (30%)	1,400 (70%)	9,000	400 (40%)	10,800	11,400

3. Calculate Cost per Equivalent Unit (This step is not needed for standard costs.)

4. Process Cost Report for Moulding Department: May

	Standard Cost		
	Computation	**Units**	**Cost**
Beginning WIP	(from April cost report)	2,000	$ 10,200
Costs to complete beginning WIP:			
Direct materials	0 × $3.00		0
Conversion costs	1,400 × $7.00		9,800
Total costs added this period			20,000
Total cost of beginning WIP transferred out		2,000	20,000
New units started, completed, and transferred out	9,000 × $10.00	9,000	90,000
Total units completed and transferred out		11,000	110,000
Ending WIP:		1,000	
Direct materials	1,000 × $3.00		3,000
Conversion costs	400 × $7.00		2,800
Total ending WIP cost			5,800
Total accounted for		**12,000**	**$115,800**

Just-in-Time and Long-Term Procurement Contracts

Some organizations have few or no units in beginning or ending WIP inventories because the organization substantially completes processing at the end of each accounting period or because the organization uses just-in-time (JIT) production methods. With little or no WIP inventory, process costing is simple because beginning and ending inventories are small or nonexistent, making the computations similar to those shown in Exhibit 6.4. In essence, an average cost for the period is calculated by dividing total current costs incurred by total units completed. In addition, the choice between FIFO and weighted average method is unimportant because the dollar amounts in the two types of process cost reports are similar.

When organizations adopt JIT inventory practices, they often also alter their production processes so that work occurs in small teams rather than in departments. In such cases, the traditional cost pools for direct materials and conversions costs may no longer be appropriate.

Some organizations enter into long-term procurement contracts with suppliers, so the cost of raw materials is relatively stable over long periods of time. When few changes occur in costs between accounting periods, FIFO and weighted average process costing reports are similar.

Hybrid Costing Systems and Operation Costing

As manufacturing systems incorporate more technology, organizations become more flexible in meeting the diverse needs of their customers. Products that were once mass produced are now customized. Although most of the manufacturing process might be performed identically for all units, at some point individual units are customized. For example, Harley-Davidson customizes its motorcycles with special accessories and colours. Flexible manufacturing systems are used in many industries, such as computers, cars, and bicycles. Customers order these products with specific features. The manufacturing process is a combination of mass-produced components, but during assembly the products are customized. Hybrid costing is the accounting approach used to assign product costs by applying a combination of both job and process costing. Often, process costing is used up to the point of customization, after which the direct costs are traced to each specific job.

Operation costing is a particular type of hybrid method used when similar batches of identical products are manufactured. Units in each batch are identical, but the processing of each batch is different and may not include the same steps. For example, consider the production of notebook computers that have different configurations. Some batches go through the same processes but differ based on type of memory chip or size of hard drive installed. Some batches go through fewer processes than others. For example, some notebook computers are sold with only one installed battery, while others have both an installed battery and an extra battery.

Operation costing systems track costs by using work orders for each batch. These work orders include detailed information about the direct materials required and the steps needed in the manufacturing operation. Direct materials are traced to each batch through the work orders and then allocated to units. In addition, all units within a batch are allocated uniform amounts of overhead. Unlike traditional process costing, operation costing usually includes more than two types of cost pools. The cost pools are designed to match the separate processes that may be allocated to batches of products. This matching of processes and cost pools improves the accuracy of cost assignment to individual products. Managers are better able to focus on the control of physical processes within a given production system because their financial information more accurately matches the flow of resources through specific processes.

▶ CHAPTER REFERENCE
For more information about JIT systems, see Chapter 15.

▶ HELPFUL HINT
Just-in-time operations minimize inventory buildup during production. Raw materials and partially complete units are received just before they are needed for the next step in the manufacturing process.

▶ ALTERNATIVE TERMS
In flexible manufacturing, *batches* are often called *production runs*.

▶ BUSINESS PRACTICE
Honda of Canada Mfg. announced in 2011 that it would build its popular CR-V compact sports utility vehicle at its plant in Alliston, Ontario. It will be Honda's first plant in North America to build four types of vehicles on one assembly line, bringing it up to its near capacity of making 390,000 vehicles a year.[4]

---

[4] Scott Deveau, "Honda to Make Compact SUVs in Ontario," *Financial Post*, November 17, 2011.

Accounting for Spoilage in Process Costing

Production processes often create spoilage—units of product that are unacceptable and are either discarded or sold at a reduced price. Sometimes, spoiled units are reworked or repaired and sold as if they were originally produced correctly. The costs of spoilage include resources that are wasted due to spoilage, including the full amount of product costs for units that are discarded and the rework costs for units that are repaired. From an accounting perspective, decisions are made about how to record the costs of spoilage. Should they be included in the product cost of all good units sold, or should they be recognized as a separate loss? The accounting treatment depends on whether the spoilage is a normal part of the production process.

Normal spoilage consists of defective units that arise as part of regular operations. Because normal spoilage is considered an ordinary and inherent part of operations, the cost of normal spoilage is included in the costs of all good units produced under Canadian Accounting Standards for Private Enterprises (ASPE) and International Financial Reporting Standards (IFRS). The cost of normal spoilage is considered necessary for producing good units. For example, if Premier Plastics finds that one out of every 1,000 plastic filters fails to work properly when tested at the end of production, then that proportion of spoilage will be treated as normal. If the managers modify operations to reduce product failures, then a new lower rate of spoilage will become normal.

Abnormal spoilage is spoilage that is not part of everyday operations. Because abnormal spoilage is considered unusual and is not an inherent part of operations, the cost of abnormal spoilage is excluded from product costs and is recorded as a separate loss. Abnormal spoilage occurs because of events such as strikes and natural disasters, but it also occurs when operations are out of control. For example, at Premier Plastics, an equipment malfunction that ruins a large number of plastic filters would be considered abnormal spoilage.

To properly account for spoilage in a process costing system, accountants need to identify the point in the production process where spoiled units are removed. Different organizations establish different procedures for inspection and removal of spoiled units. Spoilage caused by poor-quality raw materials can sometimes be identified before materials are added to production. Inspection could also occur in the middle of production, at the end of the process in one department, or when processing in all departments is complete. If spoiled units are removed before they are 100% complete, the costs of direct materials and conversion need to be estimated at the point at which the units are removed from production.

The costs of spoilage are accounted for in a two-step process. First, all product costs are accumulated in the departmental WIP account, as usual. The computation of cost per equivalent unit includes all work performed, regardless of whether the units are spoiled. If spoiled units are 100% complete at the time they are removed from production, they are treated the same as any other unit. If they are less than 100% complete, the calculation of equivalent units depends on their completion percentage, similarly to ending WIP. Second, the costs of normal spoilage are allocated to the good units produced, and the costs of abnormal spoilage are written off as a loss for the accounting period. Therefore, the cost of each good unit includes an allocation for the cost of normal spoilage. The cost per good unit transferred out is computed as follows:

$$\text{Cost per good unit transferred out} = \frac{\text{Total cost of good units transferred out} + \text{Cost of normal spoilage}}{\text{Total good units transferred out}}$$

Following is a numerical illustration of spoilage using the FIFO method.

LO4 Describe how spoilage costs are handled in process costing

▷ **INTERNATIONAL**
Bridgestone Corporation incurred ¥162 billion (over $1.7 billion Canadian) in recall and litigation costs relating to claims that the tread on certain Firestone tires peeled off, causing numerous rollover accidents.[5]

▷ **INTERNATIONAL**
Ball Packaging Europe uses a camera system on its beverage-can production line to test for unit defects. A computer compares images from five cameras to image specifications.[6]

---

[5] Combined losses recorded during 2000 and 2001 on the income statement of Bridgestone Corporation and Subsidiaries Annual Report, December 31, 2002.
[6] Ball Packaging Europe, *Production Process*, Station: Testing for Internal Defects, www.ball-europe.com/Production-process-of-beverage-cans.htm.

premier plastics, part 3
FIFO COST REPORT WITH NORMAL AND ABNORMAL SPOILAGE

© Shotshop GmbH/Alamy

While collecting information to prepare the Premier Plastics moulding department process cost report for July, Nancy learns that 1,000 units were spoiled and discarded. The previous month, there was no spoilage. She is puzzled by the large amount of spoilage during July.

Nancy discusses the spoilage with the manager of the moulding department. He tells her that 300 units were spoiled because of a problem that occurs three or four times a year with the quality of the plastic raw material. The problem causes a slight discolouration in a number of units. In addition, a new employee accidentally programmed the moulding machine incorrectly, spoiling 700 units during July. All spoilage is discovered when units are turned out of the moulds at the end of the moulding processing (when they are 100% complete).

After further discussion with the department manager, Nancy learns that approximately 2% of units throughout the year are spoiled because of discolouration. Thus, she decides that for the raw material problem, up to 2% of units produced should be accounted for as normal spoilage. She decides that the spoilage caused by the incorrect equipment setting should be accounted for as abnormal spoilage because in a department with little employee turnover, the manager tells her, this problem rarely occurs.

Nancy finds that during July, 3,000 units in beginning WIP were completed, and 9,000 units were started and completed. Ending WIP consisted of 1,200 units that were 70% complete. Total costs added this period are $28,560 in direct materials and $86,184 in conversion costs.

FIFO Process Cost Report and Journal Entries with Spoilage

Because a decision was made last month to adopt the FIFO method, Nancy prepares this month's cost report using only FIFO. She obtains the beginning WIP cost from the June FIFO cost report (Exhibit 6.9): $18,525 ($8,400 direct materials and $10,125 conversion costs). Given this information, she follows the same four steps as before to prepare the July cost report shown in Exhibit 6.12.

Nancy summarizes the total costs to account for, as usual. However, the summary of physical and equivalent units takes into account the spoiled units. She first summarizes the work performed in terms of physical and equivalent units and then adds a column showing the 1,000 spoiled units. Because spoiled units were identified and removed when they were 100% complete, they represent 1,000 equivalent units for both direct materials and conversion costs. Nancy next separates the spoilage into normal and abnormal. She calculates the maximum normal spoilage for July as 240 units (12,000 units completed during July × 2%), which is less than the 300 units spoiled due to discolouration.[7] Therefore, she considers 240 units as normal spoilage. She classifies the remaining 60 discoloured units plus the 700 units spoiled from the incorrect machine setting as abnormal spoilage (total 760 units). ■

> **EXHIBIT 6.12**
Premier Plastics Moulding Department FIFO Cost Report with Spoilage for July

1. Summarize Total Costs to Account For

First-in, first-out:

	Direct Materials	Conversion Costs	Total Cost
Beginning WIP	$ 8,400	$ 10,125	$ 18,525
Current period costs	28,500	86,184	114,744
Total costs to account for	$ 36,960	$ 96,309	$ 133,269

[7] In the cost report, total units completed = 3,000 beginning WIP + 8,000 good units started and completed + 1,000 spoiled units = 12,000 units.

►EXHIBIT 6.12
continued

2. Summarize Physical and Equivalent Units

	Work This Period						
	① +	②			=		③
	Beginning WIP	(a) + Beginning WIP Competed this period	(b) + Started & Completed this period	(c) = Ending WIP Started/not completed	Total Work Performed This Period	Total Units to Account For	Spoiled Units (100%)
Physical units	3,000	0	9,000	1,200	10,200	13,200	(1,000)
Equivalent units:						Total Work	
Direct materials (% completed)	3,000 (100%)	0	9,000	1,200 (100%)	10,200	13,200	(1,000)
Conversion costs (% completed)	1,500 (50%)	1,500 (50%)	9,000	840 (70%)	11,340	12,840	(1,000)
Total spoilage							1,000
Less: Normal spoilage		$(3,000 + 9,000) \times 2\%$					240
Abnormal spoilage							760

3. Calculate Cost per Equivalent Unit

First-in, first-out:

$$\text{Direct materials} : \frac{\text{Direct material cost}}{\text{Equivalent units for total work performed this period}} = \frac{\$28,560}{10,200} = \$2.80$$

$$\text{Conversion costs} : \frac{\text{Conversion costs}}{\text{Equivalent units for total work performed this period}} = \frac{\$86,184}{11,340} = 7.60$$

Total cost per equivalent unit: $\$10.40$

4. Process Cost Report for Moulding Department: July

	First-In, First-Out		
	Computation	Units	Cost
Beginning WIP	(from June cost report)	3,000	$ 18,525
Costs to complete beginning WIP:			
Direct materials	0 × $2.80		0
Conversion costs	1,500 × $7.60		11,400
Total costs added this period			11,400
Total cost of beginning WIP transferred out		3,000	29,925
New units started, completed, and transferred out	(9,000 − 1,000) × $10.40	8,000	83,200
Normal spoilage	240 × $10.40		2,496
Total units completed and transferred out		11,000	115,621
Abnormal spoilage	760 × $10.40		7,904
Ending WIP:		1,200	
Direct materials	1,200 × $2.80		3,360
Conversion costs	840 × $7.60		6,384
Total ending WIP cost			9,744
Total good units accounted for	**13,200 − 1,000**	12,200	
Total costs accounted for			$133,269

When Nancy prepares the cost report, she calculates the cost of good units started, completed, and transferred out. She then adds the cost of normal spoilage to arrive at the total cost transferred to the assembly department ($115,621). Abnormal spoilage is added below this subtotal to reconcile the total cost.

Nancy's journal entries are presented in Exhibit 6.13. Notice that normal spoilage costs are included in the cost of WIP transferred out. Abnormal spoilage costs are no longer associated with units but are written off as a loss.

►BUSINESS PRACTICE
The accounting treatment shown in the textbook agrees with financial accounting rules under Canadian ASPE and IFRS; normal spoilage is allocated to inventory, while abnormal spoilage is assigned to cost of goods sold.

> **EXHIBIT 6.13**

FIFO Process Costing Journal Entries
with Spoilage

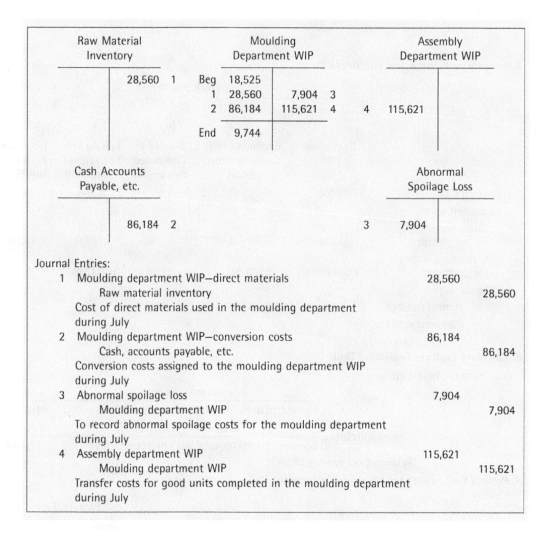

Journal Entries:

1	Moulding department WIP—direct materials	28,560	
	Raw material inventory		28,560
	Cost of direct materials used in the moulding department during July		
2	Moulding department WIP—conversion costs	86,184	
	Cash, accounts payable, etc.		86,184
	Conversion costs assigned to the moulding department WIP during July		
3	Abnormal spoilage loss	7,904	
	Moulding department WIP		7,904
	To record abnormal spoilage costs for the moulding department during July		
4	Assembly department WIP	115,621	
	Moulding department WIP		115,621
	Transfer costs for good units completed in the moulding department during July		

Using Spoilage Cost Information

Nancy is concerned about the total costs for spoilage this period. The 1,000 spoiled units cost $10,400 ($2,496 + $7,904). However, Nancy is even more concerned about other problems that arise when spoilage is high. Sometimes inspectors miss some spoiled units, which are then sold as good units. When defective filters are sold, return costs increase, and customers are less satisfied. The special filters are expensive, and Premier's reputation suffers when units are less than perfect. Nancy knows that Japanese competitors have zero-defect-tolerance policies, so their customers rarely receive flawed filters. She decides to meet with the plastics department manager to emphasize the need for lower levels of spoilage.

●● > STRATEGIC RISK MANAGEMENT: PREMIER PLASTICS, PART 3

ACCEPTABILITY OF NORMAL SPOILAGE In Premier Plastics, Part 3, Nancy concluded that 2% of the units produced each year are spoiled because of a discoloration problem that occurs three or four times per year, caused by raw material problems. She then classified this cost as normal spoilage. How will this classification affect management control of spoilage costs? Managers are not likely to focus on the reduction of normal spoilage costs because those costs are combined with other costs to arrive at a total cost per unit. As long as the total cost per unit is close to budgeted amounts, managers are likely to ignore normal spoilage. In Chapter 20, we will learn about *material flow cost accounting*, which emphasizes wasted resources and encourages managers to reduce normal spoilage.

Costs of Spoilage	Quality Costs to Prevent and Detect Spoilage
• Direct materials and conversion costs wasted	• Labour and other resources to inspect:
• Rework costs	– Raw materials when purchased
• Loss of contribution margin for units that cannot be sold	– Units during/after production
• Disposal of spoiled units that cannot be reworked	• Design and implementation of quality process improvements
• Warranty costs to repair or replace defective units sold	• Preventive equipment maintenance
• Defective product return costs	• Higher prices for raw materials and for ensuring high quality
• Loss of product quality reputation, leading to lower future revenues	• Higher labour costs for hiring and training qualified employees

> **EXHIBIT 6.14**
Costs of Spoilage and Quality

Quality-Related Costs

When manufactured products are spoiled, the organization loses the resources used to create the spoiled units as well as the potential contribution margin that might have been earned from selling a good product. To minimize spoilage losses, managers often expend additional resources to rework defective units. For example, if the metal racks are improperly installed in Premier Plastic's assembly department, the racks in the spoiled units could be taken out and the unit sent back through the process for reworking. The cost of rework is usually not tracked separately. Because reworked units go through processes twice, they use more resources than good units. The costs for the extra use of resources are allocated to all the units produced and, therefore, rework costs cannot be easily tracked and monitored.

Managers also implement procedures to reduce or eliminate the occurrence of spoilage. Sometimes, however, spoiled units are not detected and are instead sold to customers. Sales of defective units lead to additional costs, such as warranty expenditures and customer dissatisfaction. Exhibit 6.14 provides a summary of the various types of spoilage and quality-related costs. Although some of these costs are impossible to measure, they could be large, making the difference between an organization's success or failure.

Managers make trade-offs between the costs spent to ensure quality and the costs of spoilage. Some managers adopt a strategy of achieving low or zero defect rates. Motorola, for example, developed a Six Sigma defect policy (limiting defects to no more than 3.4 defective parts per million). Motorola's managers believe that the costs to ensure high quality are lower than the costs of manufacturing and selling defective units.

> **CHAPTER REFERENCE**
The opportunity costs of spoilage and other issues related to product quality are discussed in Chapter 5.

●● > FOCUS ON ETHICAL DECISION MAKING:
      COST OVERRUNS AT BOEING

During 2002, Boeing settled, without admitting guilt, a securities fraud lawsuit. The lawsuit, which was settled for $92.5 million, claimed that the company had improperly failed to report abnormal production losses on its income statement during the first half of 1997. The company's production had been out of control. The company's audit firm, Deloitte & Touche, notified the board of directors' audit committee that the company experienced negative trends during 1996 in "overtime, parts shortages, rework, defective parts, and out-of-sequence work."

In most companies, production problems of this nature would have been reflected in inventory and then in cost of goods sold as units were sold. However, Boeing uses a practice called *program accounting*, a long-term standard costing system. Instead of assigning actual costs to each plane built, the company allocates an expected cost. Actual product costs are accumulated in a cost pool that is recorded as an asset. The asset is reduced for costs allocated to planes built. However, no adjustment is made each period for the amount of cost that has been underapplied or overapplied. Instead, the company depends on the reliability of its long-term cost estimates. Boeing uses this accounting method because it experiences a learning curve when it launches a new type of plane; the company expects higher production costs early in a program and lower production costs later. Thus, program accounting allows the company to allocate an average cost to planes throughout the life of a program.

Nathan Denette/The Canadian Press

> FOCUS ON ETHICAL DECISION MAKING:
COST OVERRUNS AT BOEING (*CONTINUED*)

As production problems grew, Boeing's managers estimated during May 1997 that total production costs would exceed estimates by $1 billion. The lawsuit claimed that the abnormal costs should have been recognized during the second quarter of 1997, in a manner similar to the treatment of abnormal spoilage presented in this chapter. However, Boeing's lawyer argued that the costs were typical for periods in which production levels were unusually high and that costs were expected to even out over the life of the project. The company ultimately announced an abnormal production loss in October 1997, when production on two product lines was temporarily halted.

Why should it matter whether the loss was reported in May 1997 versus October 1997? In August 1997, Boeing completed its acquisition of McDonnell-Douglas and paid for the acquisition through a stock swap. "If investors had understood the scope of the problems, the stock would probably have tumbled and the McDonnell deal—a stock swap that hinged on Boeing's ability to maintain a lofty share price—would have been jeopardized."

Source: S. Holmes and M. France, "Boeing's Secret: Did the Aircraft Giant Exploit Accounting Rules to Conceal a Huge Factory Snafu?" *BusinessWeek*, May 20, 2002, pp. 110–120; and Boeing Company Annual Report for the year ended December 31, 2002, available under Investor Relations at www.boeing.com.

PRACTISING ETHICAL DECISION-MAKING

In Chapter 1, you learned about a process for making ethical decisions (Exhibit 1.14). You can address the following questions for this ethical dilemma to improve your skills for making ethical decisions. Think about your answers to these questions and discuss them with others.

Ethical Decision-Making Process	Questions to Consider About This Ethical Dilemma
Identify ethical problems as they arise.	Was Boeing's delay in recognizing losses for its program an ethical issue? Why or why not?
Objectively consider the well-being of others and society when exploring alternatives.	Describe a McDonnell-Douglas shareholder's viewpoint and a Boeing shareholder's viewpoint about whether Boeing should have recognized the losses earlier. What assumptions lie behind each viewpoint?
Clarify and apply ethical values when choosing a course of action.	When managers are faced with long-term uncertainties about their costs, as in this situation, what criteria should they use to decide how to report costs publicly? What values did you use to arrive at the solution?
Work toward ongoing improvement of personal and organizational ethics.	How might Boeing continuously improve its public reporting of product costs?

Process Cost Information and Managers' Incentives and Decisions

LO5 Explain how process costing information affects managers' incentives and decisions

Process costing systems measure the cost of products, primarily for mass-produced goods. The product costs are used to value inventory and cost of goods sold for external reports, such as financial statements and income tax returns. Managers also use them to monitor operations and develop estimates of future costs for decision making. When managers use process costing information, they need to be aware that it measures the costs of processes, which are then allocated to individual units. Thus, process costing is useful for measuring and monitoring processes. However, process costing is also subject to a number of limitations.

Diagnostic Control of Process Quality and Costs

An organization's profitability and long-term success often depend on the ability of managers to control processes and costs. Organizations frequently compete based on both product quality and cost. Managers use process cost information to help evaluate whether production processes are operating as expected. They compare actual process costs to budgets, standards, or prior periods to identify potential production problems. For example, in Premier Plastics, Part 3, units were spoiled during July when an employee improperly programmed the moulding equipment. This type of event causes actual costs to be higher than expected. If the managers had not already been aware of this production problem, the calculation of process costs at the end of the month would have alerted them to it.

Managers do not rely on process costing systems alone to monitor quality and cost. They also implement quality control systems, and they separately monitor resource use, such as direct materials and direct labour costs. Quality systems can include inspection to identify spoiled units. Information about normal and abnormal spoilage can then be integrated into the process costing system to help managers measure and monitor the cost of resources wasted due to spoilage.

Process Costing Information and Decision Making

Product costs developed in a process costing system are average costs and might not adequately represent relevant costs for many types of decisions, such as product pricing, outsourcing, product emphasis, or special orders. Sometimes, process costing systems can be modified to do a better job of providing managers with estimates of relevant information, such as marginal (or incremental) cost per unit. For example, conversion costs could be divided into fixed and variable cost pools. Managers could then estimate marginal cost using the direct material cost per unit plus the variable conversion cost per unit. Production costing systems often include multiple cost pools representing different activities in the production process. More precise categorizations of cost improve the ability of managers to monitor operations as well as to estimate information for decisions.

Mismeasurement of Cost Flows

It is rarely possible to determine exactly how costs are incurred during process costing. For example, in the moulding department at Premier Plastics, more labour might be used during the beginning of the process, when plastic ingredients are added, and at the end of the process, when units are turned out of the moulds. Equipment and electricity use might be greater during the middle of the processing. However, it is difficult to exactly measure how and when costs such as labour, equipment amortization, maintenance, and utilities are incurred. Accordingly, at least some mismeasurement typically occurs in the allocation of costs in a process costing system.

Also, mismeasurement occurs when accounting for spoilage. Normal spoilage is based on an estimate. Any errors in identifying normal spoilage quantities automatically cause mismeasurement in abnormal spoilage. Therefore, abnormal spoilage costs may be overestimated or underestimated, with an opposite mismeasurement in the cost of good units.

Mismeasurement is likely to be greatest in organizations that have little experience producing a product. Over time, greater knowledge is gained about production processes, and the cost allocations become more accurate. However, little benefit may come from developing an accounting system to more accurately allocate process costs. Often, the simple assumptions used throughout this chapter provide sufficiently accurate costs.

Work-in-Process Units at Different Stages of Completion

At the end of each period, the percentage of completion for work in process needs to be estimated. Depending on the process, all the units in work in process inventories might be at different stages of completion. For example, in the assembly department at Premier Plastics, some units of WIP will have the rough edges removed but still be awaiting smoothing. Some will

> **INTERNATIONAL**
> The **British Plastics Federation** provides comparative product cost information for different types of plastics production processes. The lowest-cost process (injection moulding) can be used only for large production volumes.[8]

> **INTERNATIONAL**
> Low cost is not always the most important production goal. For example, the British **Clay Roof Tile Council** supports the production of tiles by hand "using methods passed down through the centuries."[9]

> **CHAPTER REFERENCE**
> See Chapter 4 for information on short-term decisions and Chapter 14 for information on pricing.

---

[8] British Plastics Federation, *Comparative Production Costs for a Typical Component*, Process Costing Guide, http://www.bpf.co.uk/plastipedia/processes/injection_moulding.aspx#Costings.
[9] Clay Roof Tile Council, *Preferred Roofing Material*, http://www.rooftileassociation.co.uk.

have been smoothed but be awaiting the next step within assembly. Others will have the metal framework added but be awaiting final paint and trim work.

When work is at many different stages of completion, estimating the average percentage of completion for ending inventories involves some guesswork. However, these estimates affect the equivalent unit costs for both the current period and next period. If the percentage of completion is overestimated this period, the number of units in the denominator is too large, causing cost per equivalent unit to be too low this period. Because ending WIP is completed during the next period, an overestimate this period will cause an underestimate of the work performed next period. If ending inventories are a small part of the total costs allocated this period, inaccurate estimates are less of a problem. But if ending inventories are relatively large, inaccurate estimates could distort process cost reports this period and next.

SUMMARY

LO1   Assign costs to mass-produced products by applying equivalent units to the production process

COST FLOW IN PROCESS COSTING

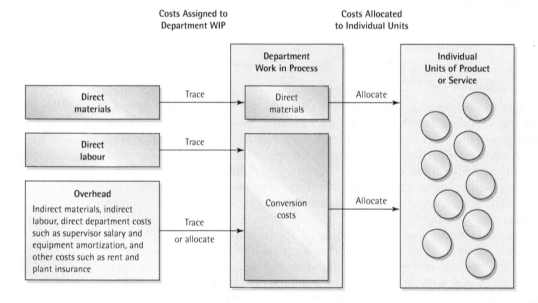

STEPS FOR PREPARING A PROCESS COST REPORT

1. Determine total costs to account for

2. Summarize total physical and equivalent units, including spoilage (if any)

3. Compute cost per equivalent unit

4. Account for cost of units completed and cost of ending WIP

EQUIVALENT UNITS

Measure of the resources used in partially completed units relative to the resources needed to complete the units

EQUIVALENT UNITS AND PATTERN OF COST FLOW

► Direct materials:
  – Added at the beginning of the process
  – Added during the process
► Conversion costs:
  – Incurred evenly throughout the process
  – Incurred unevenly
► Identification of spoiled units:
  – Inspection at the end of the process
  – Inspection during the process

SUMMARY

LO2   Apply and compare the FIFO and weighted average methods in process costing

FIRST-IN, FIRST-OUT (FIFO) METHOD

The current period's costs are used to allocate cost to work performed this period

WEIGHTED AVERAGE METHOD

Costs from beginning WIP (performed last period) are averaged with costs incurred during the current period and then allocated to units completed and ending WIP

CALCULATION OF COST PER EQUIVALENT UNIT

$$\frac{\text{Current period costs}}{\text{Equivalent units for work performed this period}}$$

CALCULATION OF COST PER EQUIVALENT UNIT

$$\frac{\text{Beginning WIP} + \text{Current period costs}}{\text{Equivalent units for total work}}$$

LO3   Apply alternative methods in mass production for multiple departments

ADAPTATIONS OF TRADITIONAL PROCESS COSTING

Match equivalent units calculations to actual process

Separate conversion costs into multiple pools

TRANSFERRED-IN COSTS

These are the costs of processing performed in a previous department

Transferred-in costs are pooled separately from other costs

STANDARD COSTING

ALTERNATIVE PRODUCTION SYSTEMS

Just-in-time

Hybrid costing systems and operation costing

LO4   Describe how spoilage costs are handled in process costing

NORMAL SPOILAGE

Defective units arising as part of regular operations

Cost is allocated to good units produced

ABNORMAL SPOILAGE

Spoilage that is not part of everyday operations

Cost is recorded as a loss for the period

LO5   Explain how process costing information affects managers' incentives and decisions

USES OF PROCESS COST INFORMATION

▸ Measure costs of mass-produced products
▸ Assign costs to inventory and cost of goods sold for financial statements and income tax returns
▸ Monitor operations and costs
▸ Develop estimates of future costs for decision making
▸ Analyze the costs and benefits of quality improvements
▸ Identify potential areas for process improvements

MISMEASUREMENT IN PROCESS COSTING

▸ Actual cost flows might not be known:
  – When are direct materials added?
  – When are conversion costs incurred?
  – How complete are the units in ending work in process?
▸ What amount of spoilage is normal?
▸ How achievable are standard costs?

6-1 solution to self-study problem

A. Weighted average

1. Summarize total costs to account for:

	Direct Materials	Conversion Costs	Total Cost
Beginning WIP	$ 8,000	$ 2,220	$10,220
Current period costs	44,000	36,000	80,000
Total costs to account for	$52,000	$38,220	$90,220

2. Summarize total physical units and equivalent units:

Because direct materials are added at the beginning of the process, all 2,000 WIP units are 100% complete with respect to direct materials. However, these 2,000 units are only 50% complete with respect to conversion costs, which translates to 1,000 equivalent units in ending WIP for conversion costs (50% × 2,000).

		Work This Period				
	① +	②			=	③
		(a) +	(b) +	(c) =		
	Beginning WIP	Beginning WIP Completed this period	Started & Completed this period	Ending WIP Started/not completed	Total Work Performed this period	Total Units to Account For
Physical units	10,000	0	38,000	2,000	40,000	50,000
Equivalent units						**Total Work**
Direct materials (% completed)	10,000 (100%)	0	38,000	2,000 (100%)	40,000	50,000
Conversion costs (% completed)	4,000 (40%)	6,000 (60%)	38,000	1,000 (50%)	45,000	49,000

3. Compute costs per equivalent unit:

$$\text{Weighted average}: \frac{\text{Beginning WIP} + \text{Current period costs}}{\text{Equivalent units for total work}}$$

Direct materials	$52,000 ÷ 50,000	$1.04
Conversion costs	$38,220 ÷ 49,000	0.78
Total cost per equivalent unit		$1.82

4. Prepare a process cost report (i.e., account for cost of units completed and cost of ending WIP):

	Computations	Units	Costs
Completed and transferred out	(10,000 + 38,000) × $1.82	48,000	$87,360
Ending WIP		2,000	
Direct materials	2,000 × $1.04		2,080
Conversion costs	1,000 × $0.78		780
Total ending WIP			2,860
Total accounted for		50,000	$90,220

B. FIFO

Steps 1 and 2 are identical to the schedules presented in Part A. Because the problem did not provide separate beginning WIP costs for weighted average and FIFO, we use the same beginning WIP values for Parts A and B.

3. Compute cost per equivalent unit:

FIFO: $\dfrac{\text{Current period costs}}{\text{Equivalent units for work performed this period}}$

Direct materials	$44,000 ÷ 40,000	$1.10
Conversion costs	$36,000 ÷ 45,000	0.80
Total cost per equivalent unit		$1.90

4. Prepare a FIFO cost report (i.e., account for cost of units completed and cost of ending WIP):

First-In, First-Out

	Computation	Units	Costs
Beginning WIP		10,000	$10,220
Costs to complete beginning WIP:			
Direct materials	0 × $1.10		0
Conversion costs	6,000 × $0.80		4,800
Total costs added this period			4,800
Total cost of beginning WIP transferred out		10,000	15,020
New units started, completed, and transferred out	38,000 × $1.90	38,000	72,200
Total units completed and transferred out		48,000	87,220
Ending WIP:		2,000	
Direct materials	2,000 × $1.10		2,200
Conversion costs	1,000 × $0.80		800
Total ending WIP cost			3,000
Total accounted for		50,000	$90,220

C. Compare weighted average and FIFO

The following table compares total costs and equivalent unit costs under weighted average and FIFO. Remember, the total costs accounted for are equal in this problem *only* because we used the same beginning WIP costs for both methods:

	Weighted Average	FIFO
Costs transferred out	$87,360	$87,220
Ending WIP	2,860	3,000
Total costs accounted for	$90,220	$90,220
Costs per equivalent unit:		
Direct materials	$1.04	$1.10
Conversion costs	0.78	0.80
Total	$1.82	$1.90

The weighted average costs include both current period and prior period costs, while the FIFO costs include only current period costs. Because the costs per unit for FIFO are higher than for weighted average, average production costs during March were higher than during the previous month. An increase occurred in both direct materials and conversion costs. These increases might have been caused by inflation in the cost of resources, a decline in production volume, production inefficiencies, or other factors.

QUESTIONS

6.1 Under what conditions will weighted average and FIFO process costing consistently produce similar equivalent unit costs?

6.2 Under what conditions could a process complete more units during the period than it started?

6.3 "We treat spoiled units as fully completed regardless of when the spoiled units are detected. This method makes unit costing much simpler." What is wrong with this approach?

6.4 In a continuous processing situation (such as an oil refinery), the beginning and ending WIP inventories are frequently the same. How does this simplify determination of equivalent units completed?

6.5 Although process costing appears to use precise measurements, it requires several estimates. Discuss where judgment is needed in collecting information for process costing.

6.6 Suppose the percentage completion of ending WIP is overestimated at the end of year one. How does this measurement error affect the process costing results in year one and year two?

6.7 Explain the difference between the weighted average and FIFO methods for process costing. Explain why an organization might choose one method over the other.

6.8 Describe the differences between mass production and custom production of goods and services. Explain how these differences influence the costing method.

6.9 A department within a processing operation has some finished units physically on hand. Should they be counted as completed units or as ending inventory in the department? Explain.

6.10 In processes involving pipeline operations or assembly line operations, if the pipeline or assembly line is always full, then beginning and ending WIP inventories are always 50% complete with regard to conversion costs. Explain.

6.11 When units are transferred from one department to another, how are normal spoilage costs recorded?

6.12 A firm has one machine through which is drawn a standard type of wire to make nails. With minor adjustments, different sizes of nails are produced with different sizes of wire. Would you recommend that the firm employ job or process costing methods? Explain.

6.13 Identify and explain two factors that could affect managers' choices for the number of times and points in processing to inspect units.

6.14 List and explain three factors that managers might consider in deciding whether to expend resources to reduce spoilage.

6.15 Describe the Lake Wobegon effect and explain why it could be a problem for managers when monitoring results in a process costing system.

MULTIPLE-CHOICE QUESTIONS

6.16 In process costing, if the units in beginning inventory are at less than 100% completion, what will be the cost of production per equivalent unit for the period under weighted average costing during periods of rising prices?
a. The same as the cost per equivalent unit under FIFO
b. Higher than the cost per equivalent unit under FIFO
c. The relationship is indeterminate
d. Lower than the cost per equivalent unit under FIFO

6.17 In process costing, the journal entry to record factory overhead applied would include which of the following?
a. A debit to work in process
b. A credit to work in process

c. A debit to cost of goods sold
d. A credit to cost of goods sold

Use the following information to answer Questions 6.18 to 6.20. The information below pertains to production activities in the refining department of Burn Corporation. All units in work in process (WIP) were costed using the FIFO cost flow assumption.

Refining Department	Units	Percentage of Completion	Conversion Costs
WIP, February 1	25,000	80%	$22,000
Units started and cost incurred during February	135,000		$143,000
Units completed and transferred to the mixing department	100,000		
WIP, February 28	?	50%	$?

6.18 What were the conversion costs per equivalent unit of production last period and this period, respectively?
a. $1.10 and $1.30
b. $1.10 and $1.45
c. $1.30 and $1.30
d. $1.30 and $1.43

6.19 What was the conversion cost in the WIP inventory account at February 28?
a. $39,000
b. $39,600

c. $42,500
d. $45,000

6.20 What was the per-unit conversion cost of the units started last period and completed this period?
a. $0.86
b. $1.14
c. $1.25
d. $1.30

EXERCISES

6.21 Equivalent Units, No Beginning WIP Carina Medical Supplies manufactures syringes and other medical supplies. Direct materials are added at the beginning of the process, and conversion costs are incurred evenly throughout production. No WIP inventory existed on February 1. The total manufacturing costs for the syringe manufacturing departments during February follow:

LO1

Direct materials	$360,000
Conversion costs	380,000
Total costs	$740,000

REQUIRED **A.** Suppose 200,000 units were started and completed in February. Calculate the equivalent unit costs for direct materials and conversion costs and the total cost per equivalent unit.
B. Now suppose 200,000 units were started, but 20,000 units remained in WIP at the end of February. These units were 100% complete with respect to direct materials, but only 50% complete for conversion costs. Calculate the equivalent unit costs for direct materials and conversion costs and the total cost per equivalent unit.
C. Explain why the answers in part A and part B are different.

6.22 Equivalent Units Under Weighted Average Francisco's mass-produces folding chairs in Mexico. All direct materials are added at the beginning of production, and conversion costs are incurred evenly throughout production. The following production information is for the month of May:

LO1, LO2

	Physical Units
Beginning WIP (40% complete)	9,000
Started in May	50,000
Completed in May	47,000
Ending WIP (30% complete)	12,000

REQUIRED Calculate the equivalent units used to calculate cost per unit under the weighted average method.

6.23 Equivalent Units, FIFO Refer to the information in Exercise 6.22.

LO1, LO2

REQUIRED Calculate the equivalent units used to determine cost per unit under the FIFO method.

6.24 Equivalent Unit Cost Under Weighted Average Fine Fans mass-produces small electric fans in Taiwan for home use. All direct materials are added at the beginning of production, and conversion costs are incurred evenly throughout production. The following production information is for the month of October (currency is New Taiwan dollars):

LO1, LO2

	Physical Units
Started in October	100,000
Completed in October	94,000
Ending WIP (60% complete)	15,000
Beginning WIP (20% complete)	9,000

	Costs
Beginning work in process costs	
Direct materials	NT$18,000
Conversion costs	36,000
Costs added this period	
Direct materials	100,000
Conversion costs	200,000

REQUIRED Calculate the equivalent cost per unit using the weighted average method.

6.25 Equivalent Unit Cost, FIFO Refer to the information in Exercise 6.24.

L01, L02

REQUIRED Calculate the equivalent cost per unit using the FIFO method.

6.26 Cumulative Exercise (Chapter 5): Abnormal Spoilage Calculation Rejected castings in a foundry are treated as spoilage. During the current period, 80 castings (costing $200 each to produce) were spoiled and sold at a net realizable value of $25 each.

L04

REQUIRED Calculate the cost of spoilage, assuming it is abnormal.

6.27 Abnormal Spoilage Journal Entry Refer to the information in Exercise 6.26.

L04

REQUIRED **A.** Prepare the journal entry for normal spoilage.
B. Prepare the journal entry, assuming that the spoilage was abnormal.

6.28 Normal and Abnormal Spoilage, Solve for Unknown A department started 10,000 units last month, and the total cost per equivalent unit was $5.00. The department completed and transferred 8,000 units to finished goods inventory. There was no beginning or ending WIP inventories.

L04

REQUIRED Calculate the number and cost of spoiled units.

6.29 Journal Entries for Normal and Abnormal Spoilage Refer to the information in Exercise 6.28.

L04

REQUIRED **A.** Prepare journal entries for the spoilage if it is all considered normal.
B. Prepare journal entries for the spoilage if it is all considered abnormal.

6.30 Solving for Unknowns, Equivalent Units, FIFO Reliable Fittings had 6,000 units 60% complete for conversion costs in beginning WIP. During the month 20,000 units were completed. Ending WIP consisted of 8,000 units 40% complete for conversion costs. Direct materials are added at the beginning of the process, and conversion costs are incurred evenly throughout production.

L01, L02

REQUIRED **A.** Calculate the number of units started during the month.
B. Calculate the equivalent units for direct materials and conversion costs under the FIFO method.

6.31 Solving for Unknowns, Equivalent Units, Weighted Average Refer to the information in Exercise 6.30.

L01, L02

REQUIRED **A.** Calculate the equivalent units for direct materials and conversion costs under the weighted average method.

6.32 Cost per Equivalent Unit Under Weighted Average Felix and Sons is a toy maker that produces Flying Flingbats, a soft foam rubber weapon. All direct materials are added at the beginning of production, and conversion costs are incurred evenly throughout production. Conversion was 75% complete for the 8,000 units in WIP on December 1 and 50% complete for the 6,000 units in WIP on December 31. During the month, 12,000 Flingbats were completed and transferred out as finished goods. Following is a summary of the costs for the period:

L01, L02

	Direct Materials	Conversion Costs
Work in process, December 1	$19,200	$ 7,200
Costs added in December	31,200	21,600

REQUIRED Using the weighted average method, prepare a schedule calculating the total cost per equivalent unit for December.

6.33 Account for Costs Under Weighted Average Refer to the information presented in Exercise 6.32.

LO1, LO2

REQUIRED Prepare a process cost report under the weighted average method.

6.34 Cost per Equivalent Unit Under FIFO Refer to the information presented in Exercise 6.32.

LO1, LO2

REQUIRED Using the FIFO method, prepare a schedule calculating the cost per equivalent unit for December.

6.35 Account for Costs Under FIFO Refer to the information presented in Exercise 6.32.

LO1, LO2

REQUIRED Prepare a process cost report under the FIFO method.

6.36 Equivalent Units, Weighted Average, Production Pattern Wilson Company manufactures its product on an assembly line. The firm began production in year one. During the year, work was begun on 45,000 units. The assembly line has 1,000 "slots," so at the end of year one, WIP ending consisted of 1,000 units 50% complete. In year two, the firm started 50,000 units and ended the year with a full assembly line estimated to be 50% complete. A slowdown occurred during year three, so the firm started only 25,000 units. Nonetheless, year three ended with the assembly line full, and the units were estimated to be 50% complete. Direct materials are added at the beginning of the process, and conversion costs are incurred evenly throughout production.

LO1, LO2

REQUIRED **A.** Calculate a summary of physical units by determining the beginning WIP, units started, ending inventory, and units completed for each year.
B. Determine the equivalent units for direct materials and conversion costs for each of the three years under the weighted average method.
C. Describe the relationship between beginning and ending WIP inventory in years two and three.

6.37 Cost Report, No Beginning WIP A department began the month with no beginning WIP. During the month, 15,000 units were started and 10,000 units were completed. The 5,000 units in ending WIP were 80% complete for direct materials and 60% complete for conversion. Total costs for the month were $29,400 for direct materials and $23,350 for conversion. Direct materials are added at the beginning of the process, and conversion costs are incurred evenly throughout production.

LO1

REQUIRED Prepare a process cost report for this month.

6.38 Units Transferred In, No Direct Material, No Beginning WIP Department O receives material from department N for further processing. It does not add any material to the product. Conversion costs are incurred evenly throughout production. No WIP existed at the beginning of the month. During the month, 6,000 units costing $9,000 were transferred in. At the end of the period, 5,000 were completed and transferred to department P. Ending WIP inventory was 50% complete. Processing costs in department O for the current period were $17,050.

LO2, LO3

REQUIRED **A.** Calculate the cost for equivalent units completed during the period.
B. Calculate the cost for ending WIP.

6.39 Weighted Average, Cost Report, Labour and Overhead Allocated Separately Germain Company uses weighted average process costing to determine product costs. At the beginning of last month 8,000 units were 60% complete. An additional 70,000 units were started. At the end of the month, 12,000 units were still in process and were 40% complete. Materials are added at the beginning of the process. Labour is incurred when the units are one-half complete, and overhead costs are incurred uniformly. Costs for beginning WIP were $18,000 for materials, $38,000 for labour, and $12,000 for overhead. Costs incurred during the month were $138,000 for materials, $292,000 for labour, and $200,400 for overhead.

LO1, LO2

REQUIRED Prepare a process cost report under the weighted average method.

6.40 FIFO, Cost Report Yellow Crate Company makes soft drink containers. Direct materials are added at the beginning of the process, and conversion costs are incurred evenly throughout production. The firm had 6,000 units in beginning WIP that were 75% complete. During the period, 98,000 units were started. Ending WIP consisted of 10,000 units that were 30% complete. Costs for beginning WIP were $2,000 for direct materials and $600 for conversion. Costs added during the period were $29,400 for materials and $13,875 for conversion.

LO1, LO2

REQUIRED Prepare a cost report using the FIFO method.

6.41 Weighted Average, Cost Report Red Dog Products manufactures toys for dogs and cats. The most popular toy is a ball containing a smaller ball that dispenses tiny treats. To get the treats, dogs must roll the balls around until the treats fall out. These balls are mass-produced from plastic. Direct materials are introduced at the beginning of the process, and conversion costs are incurred evenly throughout the manufacturing process. Once each unit is completed, it is transferred to finished goods. Data for the month of March are as follows:

LO1, LO2

Beginning WIP (30% complete):	
Direct material	$25,000
Conversion costs	3,000
Total	$28,000
Units started during March	80,000 units
Units completed and transferred out during March	88,000 units
Ending WIP inventory (50% complete)	12,000 units
Direct material cost added during March	$220,000
Conversion costs added during March	$74,000

REQUIRED Prepare a process cost report using the weighted average method.

6.42 FIFO, Cost Report Refer to the information in Exercise 6.41.

LO1, LO2

REQUIRED Prepare a process cost report using the FIFO method.

6.43 Direct Materials Added During the Process, Equivalent Units, Weighted Average, FIFO On June 30, Linda Lou Chemicals Limited has 18,000 units in its ending work-in-process account. These units are 80% complete with respect to conversion costs. Conversion costs are added uniformly throughout the process, but the production process adds materials in stages as follows:

LO1, LO3, LO5

Process Stage	Percent of Materials Added
0% completion	10%
40% completion	30%
75% completion	45%
95% completion	15%

The company introduced 57,000 units to production during June and completed 54,000 units in the month. On June 1, the work in process was 70% complete with respect to conversion costs.

REQUIRED **A.** Assuming that the company uses the weighted average method, what would be the equivalent units of production with regard to conversion costs?
B. Assuming that the company uses the FIFO method, what would be the equivalent units of production for June with regard to materials?

6.44 Spoilage, Equivalent Units Rose Flour Company makes flour from high-protein lentils. It uses a process costing system. In the monthof January, the company started 11,350 units and completed and transferred out 8,000 units. The inspection process occurs at the 60% point and the process results in normal spoilage of 13.5% of the good units passed. There were no beginning inventories in January. January's ending inventories were 75% complete with respect to labour and overhead and 100% complete with respect to materials. There was no abnormal spoilage during January. The company incurred $20,620 in conversion costs and $22,700 indirect materials cost during January.

REQUIRED **A.** What is the number of spoiled units?
B. What will be the cost per equivalent unit for labour and overhead costs?

6.45 Equivalent Units, No Beginning WIP At the end of April, department A at Carson Company transferred all production to finished goods inventory. During May, the department started and fully completed 80 units. The month-end work in process (WIP) was 100% complete with respect to direct materials and 0% complete with respect to conversion costs. Manufacturing costs for May were as follows:

LO1

Direct materials (DM)	$12,125,000
Conversion	$ 9,750,000

The cost per equivalent unit for direct materials was $97,000.

REQUIRED **A.** How many units are in the ending work in process inventory at the end of May?
B. What is the cost per equivalent unit for conversion costs?

6.46 Equivalent Units, FIFO, Weighted Average Last month, the painting department of Surfaces Company started 20,000 units into production. The department had 6,000 units in process at the beginning of the month and these were 30% complete with respect to conversion costs. There were 8,000 units in process at the end of the month, which were 40% complete with respect to conversion costs. A total of 18,000 units were completed and transferred to the next department during the month.

LO1, LO2

REQUIRED **A.** Under the weighted average method, what would the equivalent units of production for conversion costs for the month be?
B. Under the FIFO method, what would the equivalent units of production for conversion costs for the month be?

6.47 Equivalent Units, FIFO, Weighted Average Marsa Co. uses a weighted average process costing system. The following data are for the production department for the month of February.

LO1, LO2

	Units	Materials (% complete)	Conversion (% complete)
Work in process, beginning	2,000	$4,500 (60%)	$4,800 (60%)
Units started into production	34,000		
Costs added in February		$70,000	$70,000

The February ending work-in-process inventory was 75% complete with respect to both materials and conversion costs.

REQUIRED **A.** What is the number of units in the February ending work-in-process inventory, assuming that 30,000 units were transferred out?
B. Assume that 30,000 units were transferred out and the number of units in the February ending work-in-process inventory was 8,000. What is the equivalent number of units produced for materials for the month of February?
C. Assume that the equivalent number of units produced for materials for the month of February was 35,550. What is the unit cost of production for February (rounded to the nearest cent)?

PROBLEMS

6.48 Costs and Journal Entries Under Weighted Average and FIFO Humphrey Manufacturing produces automobile parts and batteries. All direct materials are added at the beginning of production, and conversion costs are incurred evenly throughout production. The following production information is for the month of April:

LO1, LO2

Units:
   Work in process, March 31: 6,000 units (40% complete)
   Units started in April: 42,000
   Units completed during April: 40,000
   Work in process April 30: 8,000 units (25% complete)

Costs in beginning WIP:	
Direct materials	$7,500
Conversion costs	2,125
Total	$9,625
Costs added this period	
Direct materials added in April	$ 70,000
Conversion costs added in April	42,500
Total	$112,500

REQUIRED   **A.** Using the weighted average method, assign costs to production for this period.
B. Using the FIFO method, assign costs to production for this period.
C. Write out the journal entries for either the weighted average or FIFO methods.

6.49 **Process Costing for a Service** Your father is on the board of directors of a not-for-profit organization, For Seniors
LO1 Only. One of its services is to prepare simple tax returns for senior citizens. Each return takes about the same
amount of time and effort. Student volunteers from a local university help prepare returns. A small staff of part-
time accountants is employed throughout the tax season. The busiest time is just before the returns are due in
April, when student volunteers are busy with final exams. Because of this schedule conflict, additional help is
hired for several weeks. To predict costs for the month of April, the board would like to know the average cost for a
tax return prepared by paid employees. Some returns will be in process at the beginning and end of each month.

REQUIRED   **A.** Is process costing appropriate in this situation? Explain your answer.
B. What information do you need to determine the cost of preparing tax returns for the month of April?
C. List and explain the procedures you would use to determine the average cost per tax return prepared by paid
employees.

6.50 **FIFO Process Costing, Transferred-In Costs, Direct Materials Added During Process** Benton Industries began the
LO1, LO2, year with 15,000 units in department 3 beginning WIP. These units were one-third complete, with $40,470
LO3 transferred-in cost for prior departments' work and $14,322 for department 3 conversion costs. During the year,
93,000 additional units were transferred into department 3 from department 2, at a cost of $224,130. Department
3 incurred materials costs of $166,840 and conversion costs of $315,228 during the year. Department 3 ended
the year with 11,000 units in WIP ending. These units were 40% complete.

REQUIRED   Determine the cost of goods completed and the cost of ending WIP in department 3 using FIFO process costing.
Assume that conversion costs are incurred evenly and that materials are added in department 3 when units are
60% complete.

6.51 **Process Costing Under Weighted Average, Spoilage, Journal Entries** Victoria's Closet mass-produces luxurious
LO1, LO2, sleepwear for women. Consider the following data for the flannel nightgown department for the month of January.
LO4 All direct materials are added at the beginning of production in the department, and conversion costs are incurred
evenly throughout production. Inspection occurs when production is 100% completed. Normal spoilage is 6,600
units for the month.

	Physical Units
Beginning WIP (25% complete)	11,000
Started during January	74,000
Total to account for	85,000
Good units completed and transferred out during current period:	
From beginning work in process	11,000
Started and completed	50,000
Spoiled units	8,000
Ending WIP (75% complete)	16,000
Total accounted for	85,000

Costs	
Beginning WIP:	
Direct materials	$220,000
Conversion costs	30,000
Total beginning WIP	250,000
Costs added during current period:	
Direct materials	1,480,000
Conversion costs	942,000
Costs to account for	$2,672,000

REQUIRED **A.** Prepare a process cost report using the weighted average method.
B. Write out the journal entries for this period's work.

6.52 Process Costing Under FIFO, Spoilage Refer to the information provided in Problem 6.51.

LO1, LO2,
LO3, LO4

REQUIRED Prepare a process cost report using the FIFO method.

6.53 Standard Costing, Spoilage Refer to the information from Problem 6.51.

LO1, LO3,
LO4

REQUIRED **A.** Explain how a standard cost report would differ from a FIFO cost report.
B. Under what circumstances would a standard cost report be preferable to a FIFO cost report? Explain your answer.

6.54 Cumulative Problem (Chapter 4): Normal and Abnormal Spoilage, Quality Decision Kim Mills produces yardage

LO4 for knitwear. The knit cloth is sold by the bolt. November data for its milling process follow. Beginning WIP was 20,000 units. Good units completed and transferred out during the current period totalled 90,000. Ending WIP was 17,000 units. Inspection occurs at the 100% stage of completion regarding conversion costs, which are incurred evenly throughout the process. Total spoilage is 7,000 units. Normal spoilage is 3,600 units. Direct materials are added at the beginning of the process.

REQUIRED **A.** Compute abnormal spoilage in units.
B. Assume that the manufacturing cost of a spoiled unit is $1,000. Compute the amount of potential savings if all spoilage were eliminated, assuming that all other costs would be unaffected.
C. Discuss the additional costs of spoilage and why it might be important to require low defect rates in a manufacturing process.

6.55 Spoilage with Inspection Point Other Than 100% Use the information for Kim Mills from Problem 6.49. Now

LO4 assume that inspection occurs when units are 40% complete.

REQUIRED **A.** Calculate total spoilage for conversion cost calculations.
B. If normal spoilage is 1,800 units instead of 3,600, what is abnormal spoilage this period for conversion costs?
C. List several costs and benefits from moving inspection to an earlier point in the manufacturing process.

6.56 Normal and Abnormal Spoilage, Quality Improvements Empire Forging produces small plumbing valves.

LO4 January data for its valve-making process follow. Beginning WIP was 60,000 units. Good units completed and transferred out during the current period totalled 420,000. Ending WIP was 68,000 units. Inspection occurs

at the 100% stage of completion with respect to conversion costs, which are incurred evenly throughout the process. Total spoilage is 36,000 units. Normal spoilage is 12,600 units. Direct materials are added at the beginning of the process.

REQUIRED **A.** Compute abnormal spoilage in units for January.

B. Compute the number of units started in January.

C. Calculate the percentage of units produced that is considered normal spoilage, and calculate the total percentage of units spoiled this period. List several potential business risks related to dramatic increases in spoilage rates.

D. Provide arguments for the manager of the valve department about the trade-offs between investing in quality improvements and incurring the costs of undetected spoiled units.

6.57 **Process Costing Under Weighted Average and FIFO, Spoilage, Journal Entries** The Rally Company operates under a process cost system and uses the weighted average method. All direct materials are added at the beginning of production in the department, and conversion costs are incurred evenly throughout production. Inspection occurs when production is 100% completed.

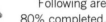

LO1, LO2, LO4

Following are data for July. All unfinished work at the end of July is 25% completed. The beginning inventory is 80% completed.

Beginning inventories	
Direct materials	$ 4,000
Conversion costs	3,200
Costs added during current period	
Direct materials	$36,000
Conversion costs	32,000
Physical units	
Units in beginning inventory	2,000
Units started this month	18,000
Total units completed and transferred out	14,800
Normal spoilage	1,000
Abnormal spoilage	1,000

REQUIRED **A.** Prepare a spreadsheet that uses a data input box, calculates information necessary for a weighted average process cost report, and presents the cost report in an easily understood format.

B. Write out the journal entries for this period's work.

C. Copy the spreadsheet into a new range or new worksheet. If you use a new worksheet, highlight the tab and rename the worksheet "FIFO." Now alter the weighted average calculations so that the spreadsheet uses data from the input box to calculate the information necessary for a FIFO process cost report and presents the cost report in an easily understood format.

D. Describe factors that would affect an accountant's choice of process costing method and make a recommendation for a process costing method for Rally. Explain your choice.

6.58 **Choice of Costing Method, Process Cost Report, Transferred-In Units, Spoilage** Toddler Toys produces toy construction vehicles for young children. Plastic pieces are moulded in the plastics department. These pieces are transferred to the assembly department where direct materials are added after some assembly has been done. For example, plastic pieces of road graders are put together, then the blades and wheel assemblies are added, and finally some details are painted on the sides and back. The direct materials are added in the assembly department when the process is 75% complete. Beginning inventory is 80% complete, and ending inventory is 25% complete. Following are data for August:

LO1, LO2, LO3 LO4, LO5,

Beginning inventory costs for the assembly department:	
Transferred in	$4,000
Direct materials	2,000
Conversion costs	1,600
Total cost	$7,600
Costs incurred in the assembly department during current period:	
Transferred in	$36,000

Direct materials	18,000
Conversion costs	16,000
Total cost	$70,000
Physical units in the assembly department:	
Units in beginning inventory	2,000
Units started this month	18,000
Total units completed and transferred out	14,800
Normal spoilage	1,000 (100% complete)
Abnormal spoilage	1,000 (100% complete)

REQUIRED **A.** Choose a process costing method for the assembly department. Explain your choice and describe its pros and cons.

B. Prepare a cost report using the method you chose in Part A.

C. Write out journal entries for the cost report you prepared in Part B.

6.59 **Process Costing Under Weighted Average and FIFO, Spoilage, Rework** The accountant at Cellular Advantage needs to close the books at the end of January, using the following information. Direct materials are added at the start of production. Conversion costs are incurred evenly throughout production. Inspection occurs when production is 75% completed. Normal spoilage is 13,200 units per month.

LO1, LO2, LO4

Physical Units	
Work in process, beginning (30% complete)	22,000
Started during the month	148,000
Total units to account for	170,000
Good units completed and transferred out during current period:	
From beginning work in process	22,000
Started and completed	100,000
Total good units completed	122,000
Spoiled units	16,000
Work in process, ending (60% complete)	32,000
Total units accounted for	170,000
Costs	
Beginning inventory:	
Direct materials	$440,000
Conversion costs	60,000
Total beginning inventory	500,000
Costs added during current period:	
Direct materials	2,960,000
Conversion costs	1,884,000
Total costs to account for	$5,344,000

REQUIRED **A.** Prepare a process cost report using the weighted average method.

B. Prepare a process cost report using the FIFO method.

C. Explain why an organization might specify limits for normal spoilage, after which spoilage is considered abnormal.

D. To reduce spoilage, units are sometimes reworked. How are rework costs recorded?

6.60 **Two Departments, Two Periods, FIFO and Weighted Average, Estimate Accuracy** Rausher Industries began a new product line this year. Management wants a cost report for the current year and a budget for next year. The product requires processing in two departments. Materials are added at the beginning of the process in department 1. Department 2 finishes the product but adds no direct materials.

LO1, LO2, LO3, LO5

During the year, work was begun on 12,000 units in department 1, and 9,000 of these units were transferred to department 2. The remaining 3,000 units were 60% complete with regard to conversion costs in department 1, which incurred $36,000 in material costs and $14,040 in conversion costs.

Department 2 completed and sent 7,000 units to the finished goods warehouse. It ended the period with 2,000 units 40% complete with regard to department 2's conversion costs, which were $32,760 for the period.

The plan for next year is to begin an additional 15,000 units in department 1. Management expects to finish the year with 5,000 units one-half converted in department 1. Department 2 is expected to complete 14,000 units, and its ending inventory is expected to be 70% complete. Materials are expected to be $48,600, and conversion costs for departments 1 and 2 are expected to be $14,545 and $59,075, respectively.

REQUIRED **A.** Prepare cost reports for the current year and a budgeted cost report for next year, assuming that the firm uses FIFO process costing.

B. Prepare cost reports for the current year and a budgeted cost report for next year, assuming that the firm uses weighted average process costing.

C. The employee responsible for estimating the percentage completion had experience estimating completion percentages for one of Rausher's other product lines. However, she is wondering whether she could improve the accuracy of her estimates. A colleague in another department suggested that she consider using techniques such as timing one unit through each department and identifying points in the production process where units appear to be 25% complete, 50% complete, and so on.

1. Comment on whether the suggested method is likely to provide an accurate estimate of work in process.

2. List two advantages of improving the accuracy of the estimate. What might be a disadvantage?

MINI-CASES

6.61 **Costs of Workplace Health and Safety** Britain's Health and Safety Commission (HSC) provides information and
L01, L05 proposes regulations to protect workers against health and safety risks. In its Strategic Statement, issued in June 2000, HSC established the following national targets, to be achieved by 2010:

- Reduce the number of working days lost per 100,000 workers from work-related injury and ill health by 30%
- Reduce the incidence rate of fatal and major injury incidents by 10%
- Reduce the incidence rate of cases of work-related ill health by 20%

To achieve these targets, the HSC's Strategic Plan for 2001–2004 placed priority on reducing incidents in the following areas that have historically high risks:

- Falls from height
- Workplace transport accidents
- Musculoskeletal disorders
- Work-related stress, anxiety, and depression
- Construction injuries and ill health
- Agriculture injuries
- Health services accidents, violence, and sickness
- Slips and trips

SOURCE: Health and Safety Commission, *HSC Strategic Plan 2001–2004*, http://www.hse.gov.uk/aboutus/strategiesandplans/hscplans/strategicplan0104/misc319.pdf.

REQUIRED **A.** Employers incur many costs because of health and safety issues, including
- Lost worker time
- Employer-paid medical costs
- Training to replace workers who are ill or injured
- Record-keeping to comply with governmental regulation

How would each of these costs be recognized in a process costing system?

B. Who is responsible for workplace health and safety? Discuss the responsibilities for each of the following groups:
- Employers
- Managers

- Workers
- Customers
- Governments

C. What goal should an individual company establish for workplace health and safety? Should the goal be to meet government regulations? Should the goal be to experience zero health and safety incidents, or is some other goal appropriate? What values did you use to arrive at your answer?

6.62 **Comparison of Actual to Standard Processing Costs, Use in Bonus Decisions** Tiffany Vanderburg is the cost

accountant at a small manufacturing company, Computer Components Inc. (CC). CC produces components for one of the large computer manufacturers. Its strategy is to provide highly reliable components at the lowest possible price. To help maintain cost competitiveness, Tiffany produces two process cost reports each month, one based on the FIFO method and the other based on the standard cost method. When the reports are complete, costs from the two systems are compared. If actual costs are under control (i.e., within the standard costs) for a particular division, the manager receives a small bonus. If costs have been under control throughout the year, a larger bonus is given at the end of December.

This month, Tiffany investigates the results for Kevin Meledrez's division. Actual direct material costs are higher than standard cost, so the equivalent unit cost is higher than the standard. When Tiffany speaks to Kevin about the direct material costs in his division, he argues that the standard cost needs to be changed because the current supplier has increased the cost of a particular part. Kevin believes that he should not be held responsible for costs that are not under his control; when prices change, the standard should also change.

Tiffany asks Kevin whether he had investigated other vendors who sell the same part to see whether the price change was across the board for all vendors. Kevin says that he has used this vendor for a number of years and is satisfied with the quality and timeliness of delivery. He does not believe that another vendor would provide the same quality and service, so he does not want to consider changing suppliers at this time.

REQUIRED   **INFORMATION ANALYSIS**

The following questions will help you analyze the information for this problem. Do not turn in your answers to these questions unless your professor asks you to do so.

A. Identify a variety of reasons why actual costs are likely to be different from standard costs for CC.
B. Discuss whether Kevin would be likely to make the same argument about changing the standard if the supplier's price had decreased.
C. Describe the pros and cons of changing vendors.
D. Explain the benefit to the company of giving managers bonuses based on comparisons of actual to standard costs.
E. Discuss the advantages and disadvantages of adopting a policy of adjusting the standard cost for changes in vendor prices.

REQUIRED   **WRITTEN ASSIGNMENT**

Suppose Tiffany asks for your advice. Turn in your answers to the following.

F. Use the information you learned from the preceding analyses to write a memo to Tiffany with your recommendation. As you write the memo, consider information that Tiffany needs from you to help her make a final decision.

6.63 **Integrating Across the Curriculum—Production Management:** *Batch versus continuous processing, usefulness of*

process costing Techtra makes electronic components used by other firms in a wide variety of end products. Initially, the firm bid for any type of electronic assembly work that became available (mostly subcontract work from other firms experiencing temporary capacity problems). But over the years, the firm has narrowed its focus. It now produces essentially three products, although minor variations within each product line yield a large number of different models.

Each of the products goes through three separate operating departments: assembly, soldering, and testing. When an order is received, it goes to production scheduling. Personnel there schedule time in each of the three departments. The availability of parts usually determines when a job can be started in the assembly department. If parts are not in stock, they are usually received from suppliers within a week. On the appropriate day, the computerized scheduling program places the job on the assembly department's job list. Simultaneously, an electronic materials requisition goes to the stores department. Materials handling people then deliver the parts to the assembly department. The assembly operation is semiautomatic. When the department is ready to begin a new job, a worker inserts the appropriate guides into the equipment and adjusts the various settings. Parts are then loaded into the machines, which do the actual assembly. Because a worker keeps several machines running simultaneously, each order is processed using several (sometimes all) of the machines available in the department. Once the units for an order are assembled, an assembly department worker enters its completion in the computerized production system. The system then adds the job to the soldering department's job list. Materials handling personnel load assembled product onto racks and take them to the soldering department.

Soldering processes the jobs on a first-in, first-out basis unless production scheduling asks for priority treatment for a particular job. For each job, the soldering machines must be set up for the appropriate product, but thereafter the operation is totally automatic. Once a job is completed, an entry is made in the production system, which adds it to the testing department's job list. The products are then reloaded onto racks and transported to the testing department.

By the time the products get to the testing department, many of the jobs are near or past their promised delivery date. Thus, the production scheduling system directs the testing department to work on jobs in the order of promised delivery date. Normally, the firm expects 3% to 5% of the products to be defective and plans its lot size for each order accordingly. However, from time to time, an entire order must be scrapped due to faulty assembly or soldering on every unit. When an order is scrapped, it is noted in the production system, and a rush replacement order is sent to the assembly department. Completed jobs that pass testing are immediately shipped to customers.

Workers in the assembly, soldering, and testing departments each enter in the production system information detailing the amount of time spent working on specific jobs. This information plus the materials requisitions are used by the cost accounting system to track the cost of each job. The cost accounting system allocates departmental overhead to each job, using overhead allocation rates based on budgeted overhead costs and budgeted hours for each department. General factory overhead, which includes production scheduling, materials handling, property taxes, and so on, is charged to each job based on total materials costs. Within each of the three product types, the average cost per unit varies primarily with the size of each job order because of setup costs. The cost data are used to update the firm's pricing sheets and determine the efficiency with which each order was produced.

Management is considering a change in the organization of the plant floor. Instead of arranging the organization into functional departments, there will be manufacturing "cells" for each product; that is, the company would establish clusters of assembly machines, soldering machines, and test equipment, and each cluster would be dedicated to making only one type of product. Under this arrangement, when an order is processed, individual units would proceed one by one through the assembly, soldering, and testing of equipment in the appropriate cell. Most jobs would be completed within a day, but large jobs would sometimes take up to a week. Management is also considering a change in the way it orders parts from suppliers. The company would place orders for each job, requesting delivery of parts on the day production is scheduled to begin.

REQUIRED **A.** Describe how the proposed changes would likely affect each of the following:
   1. Size of work in process and raw materials inventories
   2. Material handling and machine setup costs
   3. Cost of defective units
   4. Ratio of units produced to units ordered
   5. Production scheduling costs and machine utilization rates
   6. Average cost per unit of product
   7. Ability to fulfill a customer's rush order

B. Consider the effects of proposed manufacturing changes:
   1. What would be the advantages of adopting a process costing system?
   2. The company would no longer carry significant inventories. How would this change affect the cost accounting?

## CHAPTER 7

Activity-Based Costing and Management

After studying this chapter, you should be able to do the following:

LO1	Differentiate activity-based costing (ABC) from traditional costing
LO2	Use cost hierarchy to help assign costs to activities
LO3	Apply an ABC system in assigning costs
LO4	Describe the characteristics and use of activity-based management (ABM)
LO5	Explain GPK and RCA
LO6	Describe how ABC, GPK, and RCA affect managers' incentives and decisions

in brief Activity-based costing (ABC) is a system that assigns costs to the specific activities performed in a manufacturing or service delivery process. ABC attempts to trace costs more accurately to products or other cost objects than is done by traditional costing methods. The costs of the various activities then become the building blocks used to compile costs for products or other cost objects. Activity-related costs are collected, and cost drivers are chosen for each pool. Direct and indirect costs are then assigned to products or services using these activity-based cost pools and cost drivers. The information derived from ABC can be used with activity-based management (ABM) to improve operations and minimize activities that do not add value to the organization. ■

The ABC's of Better Cost Allocation

Hero Images/Getty Images

SOURCE: J. Gurowka, "Sun Life Insurance—A Case Study—Activity Based Costing Implementation," *Focus Magazine*, www.focusmag.com/ back_issues/issue_04/pages/bpbpte. htm; "Object Technology Opens New Costing Horizons for Pratt & Whitney Canada," 3C Software case study, accessed October 6, 2015, at http://www.3csoftware.com/clients/ success-stories/success-story-pratt- whitney/; "Pratt & Whitney Canada to Invest Over $1 Billion in Research & Development Over 4.5 Years," company news release, December 8, 2014.

Activity-based costing (ABC) has been a catalyst for change at many companies. For example, ABC has been implemented with success at **Sun Life Assurance** Company of Canada, a wholly owned subsidiary of Sun Life Financial Services Inc., which is an international insurance company that provides individual and group life insurance, group retirement services, and benefit management services. Several issues led Sun Life to implement an ABC analysis. Increased competition, new computing technology, and increasing client demands caused margins to decrease and costs to rise. The increased costs and decreased per-unit revenue pressured management to seek to reduce costs significantly.

Competition and customer demands forced Sun Life to dramatically reduce the time to process a claim, while also increasing the due diligence performed on each claim. Each processing centre performed tasks using different operational processes and standards with greatly differing processing times for various types of claims. The organization needed to identify and implement best practices for each process.

A cross-functional team of eight Sun Life employees representing all locations was formed. After a thorough training on ABC, the team conducted activity analysis on all positions in the group claims area. It then created a cost flow diagram with all activities and processes and mapped the flow of activities throughout. The team collected resource and activity driver information and entered it into ABC software. Activity, process, and unit activity costs were obtained and validated by the team and then by senior division management.

Significant differences in activity cost, process cost, cycle time, transaction volumes, and unit costs were found both within locations and between the different locations. In some cases, unit costs for the same activity varied by over 300%. The ABC analysis led to a review of the activities, tasks, and work flow in each location, with a view toward standardizing process steps as much as possible. Some activities that were performed did not add any value to the process and were eliminated. The ABC system implemented in the group claims division at Sun Life helped to realize significant reductions in operational costs.

ABC was also implemented with success at **Pratt & Whitney Canada**, which develops and manufactures airplane engines. Under its previous traditional costing system, the Montreal-based company would allocate production overhead for each engine component based on how long it spent in a machine. So if a washer took as long to make as an engine case, it would be allocated the same overhead cost, even though the actual production costs were vastly different.

Pratt & Whitney Canada switched to using ABC software to allocate costs, and found that the traditional costs used for some items were off by 100%. ABC allows the company to much more accurately calculate the actual costs of production, including machine time, materials, and energy use. As a private company, Pratt & Whitney doesn't divulge its sales figures, but it did publicly state in late 2014 that it planned to invest more than $1 billion in research and development over four and a half years. With so much at stake, the company needs to ensure it can recoup its R&D investment and earn a profit by charging customers accurate amounts that reflect the actual costs of its products.

In this chapter, we learn about costing systems that use multiple cost pools and multiple cost drivers, including ABC, GPK (*grenzplankostenrechnung*, a German costing system), and RCA (resource consumption accounting). These costing systems aim to improve the mapping between resource use and cost flows. We will compare cost information under alternative costing methods using several company examples, including a door and window manufacturer, a watch manufacturer, and an MRI scanner operation. We will also explore ways in which more accurate cost information can motivate and support improved business operations.

Activity-Based Costing (ABC)

Many cost accounting systems were originally developed primarily to assign costs to products for financial reporting purposes. Little consideration was given to the usefulness of cost accounting information for management. Today's managers want more from their cost accounting systems. Managers want their cost accounting systems to provide better information for decision making. They need accurate information about the costs of alternative products so that they can focus on the most profitable products and improve gross margins. As the business environment becomes increasingly competitive, managers of many organizations call for greater accuracy from their cost accounting systems. In their efforts to cut costs, they also need to identify activities that contribute the most and least value to the organization.

Traditional Cost Accounting Systems

► CHAPTER REFERENCE
Chapters 5 and 6 provide details about traditional methods of allocating product costs. Chapter 8 addresses traditional methods for allocating nonmanufacturing overhead costs.

Traditional cost accounting systems, such as job costing and process costing, assign manufacturing production costs to individual products in inventory and cost of goods sold, while nonmanufacturing costs are recognized as period costs on the income statement. Traditional cost accounting methods are also used to allocate nonmanufacturing costs for some types of contractual reporting. For example, hospitals prepare cost reports for the government in which they allocate overhead to patient services. Also, defence contractors allocate nonmanufacturing overhead costs to products for cost reimbursement reports.

As discussed in chapters 5 and 6 and illustrated in Exhibit 7.1, traditional cost accounting systems trace direct costs and allocate overhead costs to each individual product. Cost allocation is a two-stage process whereby overhead costs are grouped into one or more cost pools in the first stage and then allocated using an allocation base—such as direct labour cost or hours, machine hours, or number of units—in the second stage. Labour has been a common allocation base, because it was historically a significant driver of manufacturing costs. As manufacturing has become less labour intensive, labour-related allocation bases are increasingly viewed as arbitrary. Allocation bases such as machine hours and number of units are also viewed as arbitrary, because they may not reflect a product's use of resources. Some organizations attempt to increase cost allocation relevance by using more than one overhead cost pool. For example, fixed and variable overhead costs or overhead in different production departments might be pooled separately.

► CHAPTER REFERENCE
As discussed in Chapter 5, a *cost pool* is a group of individual costs that are accumulated for a particular purpose.

Even with multiple cost pools, traditional allocation bases rarely reflect the flow of resources to products of different complexity. Suppose that a computer manufacturer uses robotic equipment to assemble custom-ordered computers. Most of the manufacturing overhead costs (e.g., amortization, insurance, maintenance, software maintenance) are related to the robotic equipment. If the company lacks an information system that tracks time on the robotic machines or the number of new setups required, direct labour hours are likely to be used to allocate the fixed overhead related to the machines. However, direct labour might be used only to test and package the machines for shipping, and the times needed for these tasks are the same for every machine produced. As a result, fixed overhead costs are distributed equally among all the computers, regardless of the actual time spent by the robotic machines or the number of new machine setups required.

In this setting, the traditional system understates the cost of more complex computers that require more assembly time and machine setups in the robotic manufacturing process. At the

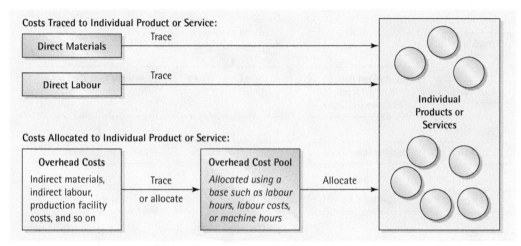

Traditional Overhead Cost Allocation System

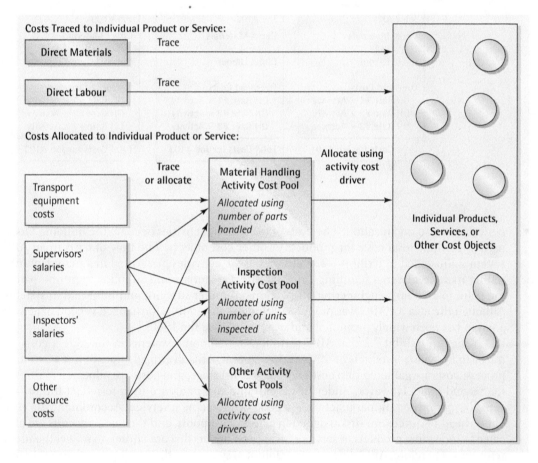

▶EXHIBIT 7.2

ABC Cost Allocation System

same time, the system overstates the cost of simple computers requiring little robotic assembly time and few changes in setup. If the information generated by this traditional cost system is used for product decisions, the simple product could be de-emphasized relative to more complex products. Yet it is highly unlikely that this emphasis would reflect the optimal sales mix.

Activity-Based Costing Systems

Activity-based costing (ABC) is a system that assigns overhead costs to the specific activities performed in a manufacturing or service delivery process. It attempts to trace costs more accurately to products or other cost objects. An **activity** is a type of task or function

▶EXHIBIT 7.3
ABC: Overview of Overhead Cost
Allocation

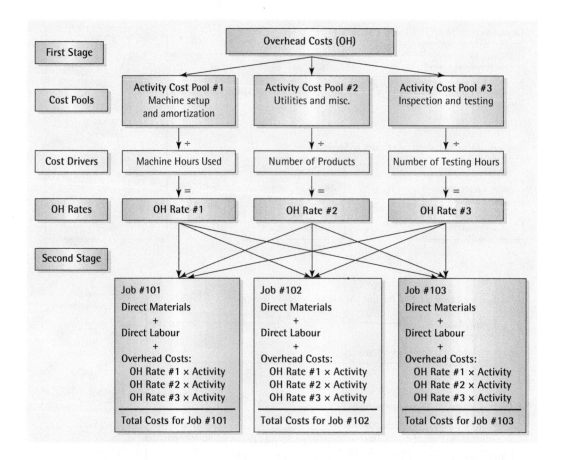

▶EXHIBIT 7.3
ABC: Overview of Overhead Cost
Allocation

performed in an organization. The costs of the various activities become the building blocks used to compile total costs for products or other cost objects. The flow of costs in an ABC system is illustrated in Exhibit 7.2. Examples of the activities performed in a manufacturing setting include material handling (moving direct materials and supplies from one part of the plant to another), engineering, inspection, customer support, and information systems. Although the idea for ABC was proposed as long ago as 1949, a formalized version of activity analysis has been widely promoted and used only since the 1980s.[1]

Notice in Exhibit 7.2 that ABC is similar to traditional systems in that direct costs are traced to individual products or services. In addition, ABC overhead allocation is a two-stage process: costs are gathered into cost pools in the first stage, and costs are allocated to units in the second stage. However, under ABC, multiple cost pools are used to reflect the various activities performed in manufacturing a good or providing a service. Accordingly, the costs of overhead resources are first assigned to activity cost pools, and then activity costs are allocated to individual products or services, using cost drivers that are chosen to reflect the use of resources. Therefore, ABC differs from traditional systems in that multiple activity cost pools and cost drivers are used to allocate overhead costs, as shown in Exhibit 7.3. For example, if material handling is defined as an activity, the cost of buying and maintaining equipment for material handling, such as forklifts or conveyor belts, is traced directly to an activity cost pool for material handling. Other costs, such as supervisors' salaries, may be allocated to a number of different activity cost pools, including material handling. A cost driver such as number of parts handled is used to allocate material handling costs to individual products. In this example, products that use more parts would be allocated higher material handling costs than products that use fewer parts.

[1] B. Goetz, *Management Planning and Control: A Managerial Approach to Industrial Accounting* (New York: McGraw-Hill, 1949), p. 142.

ABC Cost Hierarchy

Accountants often use a cost hierarchy to help identify activities, and then they assign costs to these activities. ABC developers identified a number of general categories for the cost hierarchy based on different levels of operation. These categories include the following:

> L02 Use cost hierarchy to help assign costs to activities

- ▶ Organization sustaining
- ▶ Facility sustaining
- ▶ Customer sustaining
- ▶ Product sustaining
- ▶ Batch level
- ▶ Unit level

A general description of each category, with examples of costs and cost drivers, is provided in Exhibit 7.4. Accountants are not restricted to these categories; other categories can

Level of Activities	Examples of Costs	Examples of Cost Drivers
Organization-sustaining activities are related to the overall organization and are unaffected by number or types of facilities and customers or by volumes of products, batches, or units.	• Administrative salaries • Headquarters housekeeping • Information system salaries • Accountant salaries and equipment	These costs are typically not allocated because they do not vary with activity volumes.
Facility-sustaining activities are related to the overall operations of a facility and unaffected by the number of customers served or by quantities of products, batches, or units.	• Facility janitorial service • Retail store insurance and heating • Manufacturing plant manager's salary • Amortization and liability insurance for individual hospitals in a hospital system	These costs are typically not allocated except when the organization needs to allocate all product costs for a particular purpose.
Customer-sustaining activities are related to individuals or groups of past, current, and future customers and are not driven by total sales volumes and mix.	• Customer sales representative salaries • Technical support salaries and supplies • Customer market research • Special tools for a customer's order	• Number of sales calls • Hours of technical support (not tied to a specific product) • Number of customers
Product-sustaining activities support the production and distribution of a single product or line of products.	• Production-line supervisor salary • Product advertising • Product design engineer salaries • Amortization of equipment used to manufacture one type of product	• Number of engineering change orders • Number of advertisements • Machine hours
Batch-level activities are performed for each batch of product and are not related to the number of units in the batch.	• Labour cost for new setup at the beginning of a batch • Utility costs for heating a kiln for batches of pottery • Shipping costs for batches	• Setup hours • Number of batches • Weight of orders shipped
Unit-level activities produce individual units of goods or services; a resource cost is proportional to production volumes or sales volumes.	• Material handling wages • Production workers paid based on quantity produced • Supplies used to provide services	• Machine hours • Units processed • Materials quantity processed

▶ EXHIBIT 7.4

General Hierarchy of ABC Costs and Cost Drivers

also be used to analyze costs when organizations want to focus on different facets of their operations. For example, costs could be categorized by business segment or by strategic emphasis, such as quality or protection of the environment.

Organization-Sustaining Activities

Organization-sustaining activities are tasks or functions undertaken to oversee the entire entity. These activities occur no matter the number of facilities operated, customers served, products sold, batches processed, or units produced. For example, the world headquarters for Sun Life are located in Toronto, Ontario. Headquarters office activities and costs are considered organization sustaining because they occur regardless of customer, product line, batch, or unit volumes. The salaries and office costs of the chief executive officer and chief financial officer would be considered organization-sustaining costs. In addition, costs such as information technology services are organization-sustaining costs if they are performed for the entire organization.

Because many of these costs, such as administrative salaries, amortization, and rent or lease costs, are fixed, usually no cause-and-effect relationships exist between organization-sustaining costs and the activities performed at this level. Therefore, these activity costs are typically assigned to the entire organization and not allocated to specific product lines, batches, or units.

Facility-Sustaining Activities

Facility-sustaining activities are tasks or functions undertaken to provide and manage an area, location, or property. These activities occur no matter the number of customers served, products sold, batches processed, or units produced. Therefore, they are assigned to the facility and not allocated to product lines, batches, or units. Manufacturing incurs costs that do not vary with levels of activity in the facility, such as facility manager salary, building amortization, insurance, and telephone services. These costs would also be considered facility-sustaining costs. Occasionally, managers want to know the full costs of production on a per-unit basis, in which case all manufacturing facility-sustaining costs are allocated.

Customer-Sustaining Activities

INTERNATIONAL
Customer-sustaining costs can be large. For example, large conglomerate manufacturers spend up to 25% of gross sales on incentives to acquire and maintain retail customers, such as grocery chains.[2]

Customer-sustaining activities are tasks or functions undertaken to service past, current, and future customers. These costs tend to vary with the needs of individual customers or groups of customers. Sun Life operates sales offices in the United States, United Kingdom, India, China, Hong Kong, the Philippines, etc. The sales division sells insurance and financial products through distributors and agents. The commissions and fees paid to sales representatives and agents would be classified as customer-sustaining costs.

Product-Sustaining Activities

ALTERNATIVE TERMS
The term *product sustaining* means the same as *product level*. Similarly, the term *customer sustaining* means the same as *customer level, facility sustaining* means the same as *facility level*, and *organization sustaining* means the same as *organization level*.

Product-sustaining activities are tasks or functions undertaken to support the production and distribution of a single product or line of products. These activities are not related to units or batches but to individual products or product lines. For example, Reichhold, the world's largest producer of polyester resins, is organized around two major divisions that represent its major product lines. The coating and performance resins division manufactures powder-coating resins, alkyds, acrylics, urethanes, epoxy resins, epoxy curing agents, and radiation-cured solutions. The composites division manufactures mixtures, including unsaturated polyester resins and gel coats. Some costs, such as division headquarters, research and development, and some types of marketing costs, are incurred exclusively for each product line and do not vary with levels of production or other activities. These costs would be classified as product-sustaining costs. Some of the

[2] "Retailing: Trouble in Store," *The Economist*, May 17, 2003, pp. 55–56.

product-sustaining costs apply to all of the products within a particular division, while other product-sustaining costs relate to only a single product, such as a type of gel coat. Thus, numerous different ways can be used to define product-sustaining activities at a company such as Reichhold.

Batch-Level Activities

Batch-level activities are tasks or functions undertaken for a collection of goods or services that are processed as a group. Batch-level costs do not relate to the number of units in the batch but instead to the number of batches processed. Thus, batch costs increase as the number of batches increases. The manufacture of resins at Reichhold is performed in batches, similar to cooking a pot of stew. Workers measure and put specific quantities of powdered and liquid chemicals into a reactor vessel and then set the equipment to "cook" the mixture. Periodically, quality control personnel test the mixture to determine whether the appropriate chemical reactions have occurred. Once the resin is complete, it is transferred to a storage tank. The reactor vessel must then be cleaned before the next batch can be started. The batch-related costs include those related to the reactor equipment and its maintenance and the supplies used to clean the reactor vessels.

Unit-Level Activities

Unit-level activities are undertaken to produce individual units manufactured or services produced. Unit-level activities need to be performed for every unit of good or service, and, therefore, the cost should be proportional to the number of units produced. Reichhold sells resin in standard containers such as 55-gallon (200-litre) drums and railroad tankers. Unit-level costs include the costs to use and maintain the equipment for filling containers.

Assigning Costs Using an ABC System

In an ABC system, the process of assigning costs is a two-stage process similar to the process used in other cost accounting methods we have studied: overhead costs are gathered into cost pools in the first stage and then allocated to the cost objects, such as product line, batch, or units, in the second stage. ABC differs from other cost accounting methods in that overhead costs are assigned to a larger number of activity-based cost pools, and cost drivers are used as allocation bases. The following procedures are followed for the ABC method:

1. Identify the relevant cost object.

2. Identify activities.

3. Assign costs to activity-based cost pools.

4. For each ABC cost pool, choose a cost driver.

5. For each ABC cost pool, calculate an allocation rate.

6. For each ABC cost pool, allocate activity costs to the cost object.

1. Identify the Relevant Cost Object

Different managers have different purposes for implementing an ABC system. The design of the system begins with identification of one or more cost objects that are relevant to managers. For example, managers might want to assign manufacturing costs to products when they adopt

> **BUSINESS PRACTICE**
> To reduce batch-level costs, Timken invested $150 million in a sophisticated new industrial bearings factory. Setup that used to require half a day now takes only 15 to 30 minutes.[3]

L03 Apply an ABC system in assigning costs

---

[3] A. Aston and M. Arndt, "The Flexible Factory," *BusinessWeek*, May 5, 2003, pp. 90–91.

an ABC system. In this case, direct manufacturing costs are traced to products, and manufacturing overhead costs are allocated using ABC. However, the cost object could be customers, customer orders, a product line, batches, or any other aspect of operations in which managers are interested. In this part of the chapter, we focus on assigning manufacturing costs first to batches and then to units of product. Later in the chapter, we will discuss assigning costs to other cost objects and assigning other types of costs, such as costs of quality, to cost objects.

Suppose the managers at Keener Doors and Windows want to improve their ability to measure the production costs of various types of windows. This information will help them identify potential improvements in the manufacturing process. In this case, the production costs of individual windows are the cost object. The accountant developing an ABC system would focus only on manufacturing activities and not on other activities, such as marketing, distribution, or research and development.

2. Identify Activities

To identify the activities performed within the production process, the use of resources must be tracked and, in many cases, additional information must be gathered from employees. For example, accountants may ask production managers about the types of tasks and functions performed in each production area. At this time, an accountant would categorize activities into unit, batch, product, customer, facility, and organization levels. This task might seem simple, but considerable judgment is needed to identify and choose the best set of cost pools for an ABC system. The goal is to account for separate activities in a way that provides managers useful information for decision making. In general, accountants try to identify activities so that the costs within each cost pool are homogeneous. **Homogeneous activities** are related in a logical manner and consume similar resources. Sometimes a cost driver helps establish whether activities should be combined or separated.

For Keener Doors and Windows, the accountant would identify all the activities involved in window manufacturing, including glass and framing material handling and transportation, glass cutting, window framing, and distribution preparation. The accountant must also decide whether to establish separate cost pools for each activity or whether to combine some activities into a single activity cost pool.

An appropriate cost driver for glass cutting might be the number of windows produced, especially if each window requires a similar amount of equipment and employee time. In this case, the window-cutting activities are homogenous, the window-cutting tasks are all related in a logical manner, and the tasks require similar amounts of time and equipment per window. If each window requires the same amount of time to frame, the accountant might conclude that the number of windows also drives the framing activity. In this case, both glass cutting and window framing have the same cost driver, and no benefit is likely to be gained by using separate cost pools for these two tasks. The accountant could combine the costs into one cost pool. Glass cutting and window framing are logically related, in that the glass is cut for a particular size frame and the activities take place sequentially, with glass cutting occurring first. In addition, the cost driver for both is number of windows produced, because each window takes about the same amount of time and supplies to cut and frame. These activities could be considered homogeneous.

However, different windows might require different amounts of time and effort to cut. Each type of window would require the same amount of time to frame, but combining the activity costs in a single cost pool and using the same cost driver (number of windows processed) would not accurately reflect the cost of cutting resources. In this case, the two activities are not homogenous, because they require different amounts of time and effort. Therefore, the accountant would probably separate glass cutting and window framing into two separate cost pools and choose time spent cutting as the cost driver for the cutting activity and number of windows framed for framing activities.

3. Assign Costs to Activity-Based Cost Pools

Costs related to each activity are identified and pooled. Some costs are directly traced to the cost pools. Indirect material costs are often traced directly to batch or unit cost pools, whereas costs such as property taxes, insurance, and lease or amortization are directly traced to the facility. Similarly, costs such as amortization on equipment used for only one product line are traced to a cost pool for that product line.

Suppose the accountant for Keener Doors and Windows identifies glass cutting as a separate activity. The supplies used to cut glass, such as blades and oil for the glass-cutting equipment, are traced directly to the cost pool for this activity. Amortization on the glass-cutting equipment is also traced directly to the glass-cutting activity. However, other overhead costs, such as the salary of a supervisor who oversees several different activities in the window department, need to be allocated to the cost pools for these activities.

4. For Each ABC Cost Pool, Choose a Cost Driver

Ideally, activity costs are allocated to cost objects using a driver that explains changes in activity cost. (Examples of cost drivers for various activities are listed in Exhibit 7.4.) The terms *cost driver* and *allocation base* are sometimes used interchangeably. However, *cost driver* refers to some measure of activity that causes costs to fluctuate, whereas *allocation base* refers to the base used to allocate costs in an accounting system. Many allocation bases are not cost drivers. For example, in traditional costing systems, square footage is often used as an allocation base for building-related costs such as property taxes and insurance, but no cause-and-effect relationship connects these costs with square footage in any specific work area or department. Therefore, the allocation base of square footage is not a cost driver. In contrast, the amount of time Keener employees spend cutting windows causes the cost of glass cutting to increase. Therefore, time spent cutting is a cost driver that can be used to allocate the cost pool for the glass-cutting activity. Cost drivers are a special kind of allocation base.

A cost driver is the best allocation base choice for an ABC cost pool. In other words, a cause-and-effect relationship should be evident between the allocation base and activity costs. Often, information about potential cost drivers is elicited from employees involved in the activities. They may suggest several potential drivers, and accountants must choose the most appropriate one.

The accountant for Keener Doors and Windows needs to determine a cost driver for window-framing costs. The best choice depends on the accountant's analysis of the variation in cost (increases and decreases). If windows are framed in batches by robotic equipment, the number of batches is a likely choice for a cost driver. If windows are framed individually, time spent framing and number of windows are potential cost drivers. If each window takes a different amount of time, then time spent framing is a more accurate cost driver. However, if roughly the same amount of time and supplies are used per window, the number of windows may be nearly as accurate and easier to track.

> **CHAPTER REFERENCE**
> See Chapter 2 for details about choosing and evaluating potential cost drivers.

5. For Each ABC Cost Pool, Calculate an Allocation Rate

An allocation rate is calculated by dividing activity costs by some measure of volume for the cost driver. The choice of data for the activity costs and the volume of the cost driver depend on the purpose of the ABC analysis. Sometimes managers are interested in measuring or analyzing past costs. In this case, the allocation rate is determined by dividing prior-period cost by the prior-period volume. Alternatively, managers may be interested in estimating future costs. In this case, estimated costs and estimated volumes could be used.

The accountant for Keener Doors and Windows might calculate an estimated allocation rate for window framing costs as follows:

$$\text{Estimated allocation rate} = \frac{\text{Estimated total cost of window framing}}{\text{Estimated number of batches}}$$

Suppose that the estimated total cost for framing windows is $5,000 this month, and the estimated number of batches of windows framed is 100. The estimated allocation rate for window framing is then $50 per batch ($5,000 ÷ 100 batches).

One of the potential benefits of ABC is that it can be used to measure the cost of an organization's capacity. **Practical capacity** is maximum capacity under typical operating conditions, assuming that some downtime is unavoidable for maintenance and holidays. If an estimated allocation rate is calculated using practical capacity in the denominator, then the allocation rate measures the cost of supplying the organization's production capacity. When this allocation rate is used to allocate costs, the ABC system will measure the cost of unused capacity as well as the cost of capacity used.

6. For Each ABC Cost Pool, Allocate Activity Costs to the Cost Object

Costs are allocated to the cost object based on the actual volume of activity for the cost driver. In the Keener example, the cost object is individual window units. The cost of an individual window includes the unit-level costs as well as allocated batch-level costs. For the window-framing activity, suppose 95 batches are processed during the month. Using the estimated batch-level allocation rate of $50 per batch, the total batch costs for the month are estimated as $4,750 (95 batches × $50 per batch). Assuming that each batch includes 10 windows, the total number of windows produced during the month is 950 (95 batches × 10 windows per batch). Thus, the allocated framing cost per window would be $5 ($4,750 ÷ 950). The total cost of an individual window would be estimated as the $5 cost for framing plus the per-unit cost of all other activities involved in producing the windows.

ABC provides a more accurate picture of the flow of overhead resources than do traditional costing methods. This accuracy is useful when organizations need to determine which products to emphasize or whether their pricing schemes adequately reflect resources used. The illustration that follows compares costs assigned using a traditional system and an ABC system.

example

keener doors and windows, part 1
COMPARISON OF ABC AND TRADITIONAL JOB COSTING

Keener Doors and Windows Company produces two types of wooden doors. Regular doors are high volume and use standard parts and manufacturing processes. Premium doors are lower volume and are considered a customized, specialty item. Managers are considering the pricing policies for both doors, because their major competitor recently lowered prices on regular doors. Premium doors have been selling well, because they are priced lower than the competitor's specialty doors. The managers are concerned about the effects on profit margins if they reduce the price of regular doors to match the competition. Although they consider only variable costs in their pricing decisions, they would like to have more information about each product's use of overhead resources.

The cost accountant, Valerie Bradley, suggested that Keener consider implementing an ABC system to better understand the costs for all the manufacturing activities needed to produce the doors. She believes that the regular doors use fewer overhead resources, because all the regular doors go through routine processes, whereas the premium doors require special processes. Both doors are produced in batches of 100. However, each premium door is processed further to add custom features, such as special routing effects in the wood or special window treatments. Currently, overhead is allocated based on direct labour hours, but machines perform much of the work. Valerie believes that labour hours do not reflect the two products' different use of plant overhead resources.

An ABC team is assembled to analyze the manufacturing activities and costs for individual doors in both product lines. The team consists of Valerie, a product designer, and several employees from the manufacturing process. They want to compare costs under the current

© Nick Moore/Alamy

job costing system and a new ABC system. As they consider the task, they realize that ABC allocations typically ignore facility-related costs, while job costing allocations include them. For purposes of comparison, they decide to ignore facility-sustaining costs in their calculations for job costing so that the results from the two systems are comparable. From the general ledger, Valerie identifies overhead costs of $18,270,000 (not including any facility costs) that were assigned to regular and premium doors last period.

Product Costs Using Job Costing

The team re-creates the products' job costs, using information from the general ledger. Each regular door requires $65 of direct materials and 2.5 hours of direct labour. Each premium door requires $100 of direct materials and 3 hours of direct labour. The job costing system allocates overhead using a factory-wide estimated allocation rate of $32.05 per direct labour hour, based on a single cost pool for door production of $18,270,000 and direct labour hours of 570,000 for the year. The following schedule summarizes the costs of the two types of doors:

	Regular Doors	Premium Doors
Direct materials	$65.00	$100.00
Direct labour	$50.00 ($20 × 2.5 hours)	$60.00 ($20 × 3 hours)
Factory overhead	$80.13 ($32.05 × 2.5 hours)	$96.15 ($32.05 × 3 hours)
Total cost	$195.13	$256.15

The team members notice that the overhead allocation for premium doors is $16.02, or 20%, greater than for regular doors under the job costing system. However, the shop supervisor believes that premium doors use two to three times more resources than regular doors because of extra processing the premium doors receive on the most expensive equipment.

Product Costs Using ABC

The managers want to know whether their current pricing policy reflects any differences in resources used by regular doors compared to premium doors. Therefore, the ABC team decides that the relevant cost objects are individual doors and the activities involved in production must be analyzed.

When the team members visit the production area, they ask about the activities performed for each type of door. They learn that the first activity is delivery of materials to work stations. They identify a material handling cost pool for this activity.

The next steps involve work done in batches, such as the initial cutting, sanding, and smoothing of doors. The team learns that two different activities are required: setting up machines for the next batch and monitoring the machines as batches are processed. Some team members believe that these two activities could be combined into one cost pool, allocated on the number of batches run. Valerie asks whether these activities differ between regular doors and premium doors. She learns that the setup for premium door batches is more complex and takes more time than for regular doors. The batches take the same amount of time, no matter what type of door is produced. Therefore, the team identifies two activity pools—one for setup costs and one for batch monitoring costs—because the activities in these pools are not homogeneous and cannot be allocated using a single cost driver.

After the doors are cut and sanded, they are processed through routing machines. The team discovers that premium doors require more routing machine hours because the designs are more complex. An activity pool for machining is identified.

The last activity is inspection. The inspectors explain that premium doors take longer to inspect because of their greater detail. The team identifies inspection as a cost pool.

Now that the cost pools are identified, costs need to be traced or allocated to each pool. Valerie uses annual accounting records and information from employees about supplies used and the amount of time they spend performing different tasks. Material handling costs are easy to trace, because workers perform only material handling duties, so their wages are traced directly to the cost pool. Equipment amortization accounts are analyzed, and the cost

continued...

of material handling equipment is separated. Workers estimate fuel costs and some supply costs, because detailed records are not kept for these expenses. Employees who set up and monitor batches estimate the amount of time spent in each activity. The employees performing the machining estimate the time and indirect materials used on each type of door, as do the inspectors.

The team's next step is to select cost drivers. They decide to use number of parts as the cost driver for material handling because each part is handled separately. The setup for each batch varies with the complexity of the door design. Regular doors are processed using three simple designs. The machines automatically cut the doors to size and rout simple designs on the doors. Premium door setup requires more time because the door designs are more complex and usually include windows. The robotic machines cut holes for and insert windows. Setup for this process is more time intensive. The team decides to use setup time as the cost driver for this activity. Each batch requires about the same amount of monitoring, so the team selects number of batches as the cost driver for monitoring costs. Premium doors require more machine hours than regular doors because the routing designs are more complex, so machine hours are chosen as the cost driver for machining costs. Each door requires a different amount of time to inspect, so the team selects inspection labour time as the cost driver for inspection.

Before calculating the allocation rates, team members estimate the volume for each cost driver. They have complete records for machine hours and labour hours but are not sure about information for number of parts, because that statistic is not tracked. The material handling employees estimate the number of parts they handled last year. Records are maintained for the number of batches, so that information is readily available. Employees are asked to estimate time spent in setup. The number of doors inspected is available, as is total time spent inspecting. However, time per regular versus premium door has not been tracked, so inspectors estimate those figures.

Next, the team gathers information about the amount of each cost driver used by regular and premium doors last month as follows:

	Regular Doors	Premium Doors
Number of doors per batch	100	100
Number of batches	1,200	900
Number of parts per door	10	20
Machine setup time	1/2 hour per batch	1 hour per batch
Machine hours per door	1	3
Inspection time per door	1/2 hour	1 hour

Exhibit 7.5 summarizes the steps thus far, showing the activities, related cost drivers, overall costs, estimated volume for each cost driver, and estimated allocation rates.

Machine setup time is one-half hour per batch for regular doors. At $100 per hour, the cost is $50 per batch. Because each batch consists of 100 doors, the cost per regular door is $0.50. Similarly, the cost per premium door is $1.00.

The total ABC overhead cost for each type of door is calculated as follows:

		Regular Door		Premium Door
Material handling	(10 × $1.00)	$10.00	(20 × $1.00)	$ 20.00
Machine setup	(1/2 × $100 ÷ 100)	0.50	(1 × $100 ÷ 100)	1.00
Monitoring of batches	($200 ÷ 100)	2.00	($200 ÷ 100)	2.00
Machine hours	(1 × $30)	30.00	(3 × $30)	90.00
Inspections	(0.5 × $20)	10.00	(1 × $20)	20.00
Total overhead		$52.50		$133.00

Using ABC Product Cost Information

The team believes that the calculations under ABC costing confirm their intuition that the job costing system did not accurately reflect each product's use of resources. Under the job costing system, $80.13 in overhead was allocated to regular doors, and under ABC, regular doors are allocated only $52.50. For the premium doors, $96.15 in overhead cost was allocated by the job costing system compared to $133.00 under activity-based costing. These results suggest that the old system overstated the cost of regular doors and understated the cost of premium doors. The team believes that the ABC costs are more accurate because they better map the use of resources to each type of product.

When the team presents its results to the company's managers, they decide that the regular door price can be reduced to match competitors' prices and that the premium door price can be increased. Valerie reminds the managers that this ABC information contains some allocated fixed costs, such as salaries for supervisors and equipment amortization, and that these costs probably will not change proportionately with changes in production volumes. Therefore, these ABC costs should be used only as a guide for pricing decisions. After any pricing changes are made, the managers need to monitor sales volumes to determine the effects of price changes on demand and determine whether profitability actually improves. ■

example

►EXHIBIT 7.5

Estimated Volumes and Costs Developed by the ABC Team at Keener Doors and Windows

Volume	Estimated Cost	Cost Driver	Cost Drivers: Estimated Volume			Estimated Allocation Rate
			Regular Doors	Premium Doors	Total	
Number of doors			120,000	90,000	210,000	
Number of batches			1,200	900	2,100	
Activity						
Material handling	$ 3,000,000	Number of parts	1,200,000	1,800,000	3,000,000	$1.00 per part
Setting up machines	150,000	Time spent	600	900	1,500	$100 per setup hour
Monitoring batch operations	420,000	Number of batches	1,200	900	2,100	$200 per batch
Machining doors	11,700,000	Machine hours	120,000	270,000	390,000	$30 per machine hour
Inspecting doors	3,000,000	Time spent	60,000	90,000	150,000	$20 per inspection hour
Total cost	$18,270,000					

●● > STRATEGIC RISK MANAGEMENT: KEENER DOORS AND WINDOWS, PART 1

PRODUCT COST INFORMATION BIAS In Keener Doors and Windows, Part 1, the managers learned that their traditional costing system consistently assigned too much overhead cost to one product and too little cost to another product. Why did it matter whether overhead costs were assigned accurately? Inaccurate product cost information could encourage managers to make inappropriate decisions, such as emphasizing less-profitable products, dropping profitable products, outsourcing products that could be produced internally at lower cost, or accepting special orders that would generate negative marginal profit.

ABC generally provides more accurate cost information than traditional costing, thus reducing the risk of some types of decision errors. However, ABC does not measure costs perfectly. For Keener, the ABC overhead cost per door included at least some fixed costs, such as employee salaries, that do not vary proportionately with volume of activity. Thus, the ABC costs are likely to overstate relevant costs for many short-term decisions.

LO3   **7-1** self-study problem   Compute Unit ABC Costs

The Fallon Company manufactures a variety of handcrafted bed frames. The company's manufacturing activities and related data for the current year follow:

Manufacturing Activity	Estimated Cost	Cost Driver Used as Allocation Base	Estimated Volume for Cost Driver
Material handling	$ 400,000	Number of parts	800,000 parts
Cutting	1,200,000	Machine hours	40,000 hours
Assembly	3,000,000	Direct labour hours	150,000 hours
Wood staining	1,320,000	Number of frames stained	60,000 frames

Two styles of bed frames were produced in July: a wood frame needing fewer direct labour hours and a metal frame that required no staining activities. Direct labour is paid at $25 per hour. Quantities, direct material costs, and other data follow:

	Units Produced	Direct Material	Machine Hours	Number of Parts	Direct Labour Hours
Wood frames	5,000	$600,000	5,000	100,000	6,000
Metal frames	1,000	200,000	500	10,000	3,000

required

A. Compute the ABC cost allocation rates and then calculate total manufacturing costs and unit costs of the wood and metal frames.
B. Suppose nonmanufacturing activities, such as product design, were analyzed and allocated to the wood frame at $10 each and to the metal frame at $15 each. Moreover, similar analyses were conducted of other nonmanufacturing activities, such as distribution, marketing, and customer service. The support costs allocated were $50 per wood frame and $80 per metal frame. Compute the product cost per unit, including the nonmanufacturing costs.

See the solution on page 333.

ABC for Nonmanufacturing Costs

In the Keener Doors illustration, ABC was used to allocate product manufacturing costs. ABC can also be used to allocate nonmanufacturing costs such as the costs of marketing and accounting. To allocate nonmanufacturing costs, the nonmanufacturing activities need to be analyzed, and cost pools and cost drivers need to be set up in the same manner as described for manufacturing costs.

For example, suppose the managers at Reichhold are interested in re-evaluating some of their distributor relationships. An ABC analysis could be used to determine which distributor relationships are the most and least profitable. Similarly, the company could use ABC analysis to estimate the profitability of individual products, taking into account nonmanufacturing product-level costs, such as research and development and marketing.

ABC in Service Organizations

ABC is used to assign costs not only to physical products but also to services, as in the case of Sun Life Assurance and Pratt & Whitney Canada. Often, service organizations analyze cost performance by comparing their actual costs to budgeted costs each year. These types of comparisons do not provide information about cost per activity or service provided, which

[4] Anne Fortin, Hamid Haffaf, and Chantal Viger, "The Measurement of Success of Activity-Based Costing and Its Determinants: A Study within Canadian Federal Government Organizations," Accounting Perspectives 6, August 2007, pp. 231–262.

is needed to measure an organization's efficiency in providing services. To better understand the effects of activities on their costs, service organizations may benefit from developing ABC systems. By analyzing activities, these organizations may be able to improve efficiency or quality of service, which may help them control or reduce costs. Service organizations follow the same process as manufacturing organizations for implementing an ABC system. Self-Study Problem 2 provides practice using ABC in a service setting.

L02, L03   **7-2** self-study problem   ABC Activities and Cost Drivers, Measure-ment Error, Usefulness

You have been asked to analyze your sister's preschool operation to determine in what ways she can improve quality and reduce costs. You decide to analyze the activities provided by the preschool and use an ABC system to assign costs to the activities. The following list contains potential activities from which to choose:

- *Learning activities* At times during the day, children are listening to stories, learning to sing simple songs, following simple directions as part of games or art activities, and playing interactively with special toys developed to enhance hand–eye coordination or understanding of spatial relations.
- *Resting* The children rest on mats during this activity, while one teacher monitors and the other teachers prepare lesson plans.
- *Snack and meal activities* Snacks and meals are prepared by teachers and one food service employee. Sometimes the students prepare their own snacks and practise following directions.
- *Free play activities* While children play either inside or outside, a few teachers monitor their prog-ress while others prepare learning activities to be used later.
- *Art and craft activities* These daily activities promote some of the same skills as the learning activi-ties, but children are encouraged to be more creative.
- *Miscellaneous* These activities include greeting the children, helping them with their coats, help-ing them use the restroom, interacting with parents, and conferencing with parents.
- *Music activity* This weekly activity encourages the children's interest in music and dance.
- *Conferencing with parents* This quarterly activity consists of the head teacher (your sister) meet-ing with each child's parents for half an hour.

required

A. Choose several activities to use for cost pools. Explain your choices.
B. Choose cost drivers for these pools. Explain your choices.
C. Identify possible reasons measurement error might exist in the ABC costs.
D. How would you estimate the increase in future costs if your sister plans to expand her operations?

See the solution on page 333.

Activity-Based Management

Activity-based management (ABM) is the process of using ABC information to evaluate the costs and benefits of production and internal support activities, and to identify and implement opportunities for improvements in profitability, efficiency, and quality within an organization. ABM relies on accurate ABC information. Next, we discuss five major uses of ABM:

L04 Describe the characteristics and use of activity-based management (ABM)

- ► Managing customer profitability
- ► Managing product and process design
- ► Managing environmental costs
- ► Managing quality
- ► Managing constrained resources

Managing Customer Profitability

ABC can be used to identify characteristics that cause some customers to be more costly than others. Customer-sustaining activities include sales and technical support supplied to specific customers or groups of customers, costs of holding inventory for just-in-time deliveries, and costs of customizing orders. For example, Canadian Imperial Bank of Commerce (CIBC) uses ABC for customer profitability analysis, re-engineering of its business processes, product profitability analysis, and capacity planning.[5] Exhibit 7.6 lists characteristics of customers having high and low costs.

As the costs of serving specific customers are determined, managers can choose different strategies for different types of customers. For example, some customers need very little service but are quite price sensitive. Although margins for these customers are low, these customers are profitable when service costs are also kept low. Customers with high service costs are also profitable when their net margins are high enough to account for the extra service costs. Alternatively, the company can price its extra services and let customers choose the services they are willing to pay for.

The most valuable customers are those who order high-margin products but have low service requirements. Managers can identify these customers by using ABC information, and then monitor their sales volumes. The organization can then compete for the best customers by offering discounts, special services, or other sales incentives, when necessary.

Customers requiring the most creative approaches are those who order low-margin products but require costly services. Customer ordering patterns can be analyzed and the information shared with these customers to improve predictability of orders, reduce engineering and delivery changes, reduce demand for technical or sales support, and increase standardization of product and delivery requirements. In addition, pricing arrangements can be modified to increase margins and to introduce a pricing system for specialized services.

Managing Product and Process Design

▶ CHAPTER REFERENCE

Chapter 15 provides more information about value-added and non-value-added activities and improvements to business processes.

An advantage of ABC is its focus on activities. As an organization's activities are analyzed more closely, managers improve their understanding of how resources are used. In turn, this analysis enables managers to improve operations and profits. They can focus resources on value-added activities, which increase the worth of an organization's goods or services to customers. Conversely, they can reduce or eliminate non-value-added activities, which are unnecessary and, therefore, waste resources.

For example, Keener Doors and Windows incurs costs for warranty work on its doors. Sometimes warranty problems are addressed by rework that is performed during idle times. Although no incremental labour cost is incurred in this situation, the rework requires additional materials. In addition, some defective doors are replaced, and the company forgoes

▶ EXHIBIT 7.6
Characteristics of Customers with High and Low Service Costs

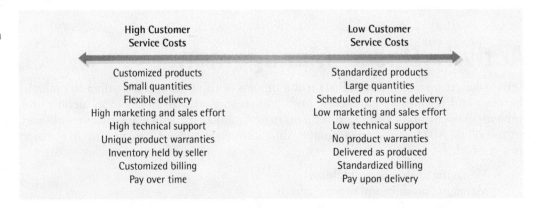

High Customer Service Costs	Low Customer Service Costs
Customized products	Standardized products
Small quantities	Large quantities
Flexible delivery	Scheduled or routine delivery
High marketing and sales effort	Low marketing and sales effort
High technical support	Low technical support
Unique product warranties	No product warranties
Inventory held by seller	Delivered as produced
Customized billing	Standardized billing
Pay over time	Pay upon delivery

---

[5] "CIBC—Using Activity-Based Costing in Canada," *Financial World*, April 2002, p, xiv.

the cost of labour and materials in addition to the contribution margin on good doors that could be sold. Therefore, warranty costs are non-value-adding; that is, no real value is added for incurring these costs. If warranty activities could be reduced or eliminated, overall costs at Keener Doors and Windows would be reduced.

Under ABM, non-value-added activities are identified and eliminated when possible. As ABC systems are implemented, activities can be categorized as follows:

- ► Required to produce a good or service and cannot be improved at this time
- ► Required but the process could be improved or simplified
- ► Not required to produce a good or service and can eventually be eliminated
- ► Not required and can be eliminated by changing a process or procedure

The following illustration shows managers analyzing an activity to improve operations and reduce cost.

keener doors and windows, part 2
USING ABM TO REDUCE NON-MANUFACTURING COSTS

example

The managers at Keener Doors and Windows are pleased with the ABC cost information for door production and ask for additional analysis of marketing and warranty costs for doors. They feel that they can reduce these costs if they better understand marketing and warranty activities and their related costs.

ABC Costs for Marketing and Warranty

Because marketing and warranty services are similar for regular and premium doors, the ABC team concludes that these costs can be analyzed using doors as a single product line and windows as the other product line. Thus, they plan to identify activities related to marketing and warranty costs and then separate the costs for doors from the costs for windows.

Product-sustaining marketing costs consist of advertising, marketing department employee costs, sales commissions, and marketing department supplies. The cost of advertising is relatively easy to assign, because either doors or windows are featured in advertisements. Marketing department employees estimate the amount of time spent per product line, and any sales commissions are traced to each product line. Miscellaneous supplies are allocated according to employee time spent.

To analyze costs for product-sustaining warranty work, the ABC system needs to separate the costs for warranty work on doors from the warranty work on windows. Depending on the problem, sometimes doors are replaced. In these cases, detailed cost records are kept. Other times, the doors are reworked. Tracking the costs of rework is difficult because employees take time from their regular tasks to rework and often complete rework tasks during idle times when batches are in process and do not need monitoring. Monthly rework costs rely on employee estimates of time and materials used for rework. The team concludes that the warranty work cost pool is probably measured with error. They decide to develop a tracking system for the time and materials used for rework to get better estimates of warranty costs in the future.

The final estimates of the per-door costs for marketing and warranty follow:

Marketing	$20.00 per unit
Warranty work	$18.00 per unit

© Nick Moore/Alamy

[6] S. Layne, "Warranty Chain Management Is Real," *Line56.com*, January 27, 2004.

Applying Activity-Based Management

The team members are surprised that warranty costs are nearly as large as marketing costs. They invite the product design team to meet with customer service representatives to discuss possible product changes to reduce warranty costs. The data for last period indicate that more than half of the warranty costs—about $10 per door sold—resulted from hinge problems; the whole door must be replaced when a hinge fails. The team immediately begins to solve this problem.

The first suggestion is to reinforce the door around the hinge, but the team learns that this procedure costs $15 per door. One team member researches the newest technology in hinges and finds one that would eliminate 90% of the problem at a cost of $14.50 per door, whereas the current hinges cost $12 per door. After discussing a number of other alternatives, the team recommends the new hinges. Although this increases the cost of each door by $2.50, it is likely that overall warranty costs will be reduced by $9 per door ($10 × 90%). In addition, the team believes that Keener's reputation for high quality has been hurt by the hinge problem, resulting in a loss of market share. Management accepts the team's recommendation and issues engineering change orders for the new hinges to improve quality, reduce warranty work, and eventually increase market share. ▪

Target and Kaizen Costing. ABC and ABM are often combined with other techniques as activities and processes are analyzed. Target costing is a cost control method by which products and their manufacturing processes are designed to meet specific target costs, based on expected product selling prices. ABC information helps the product and manufacturing process design teams within an organization understand the cost effects of their design choices. ABC improves the accuracy of product cost estimates, and ABM helps managers identify and remove non-value-added activities. Kaizen costing is a cost reduction and quality improvement process that occurs when a product has been manufactured for a while. Once again, ABM helps managers identify non-value-added activities and redesign products and manufacturing processes to reduce cost and improve quality.

▶ **CHAPTER REFERENCE**
Chapter 15 provides full discussions of target costing and kaizen costing.

Managing Environmental Costs

Many managers are concerned about the effects of their organizations' manufacturing processes on the environment. In addition, many shareholders are concerned with the "green" reputations of companies in which they invest. Federal and provincial regulations may require organizations to reduce pollution levels. The direct costs of reducing pollution are often easily tracked, but identifying the costs and benefits of protecting the environment within traditional accounting systems is difficult. ABC systems can be designed to identify the activities involved in environmental protection and to develop costs for those activities. Analyzing overhead activities also helps managers identify opportunities for improved environmental performance.

Suppose a high-quality printing company used inks that were detrimental to the environment. The cost of ink disposal was traditionally recorded as part of overhead cost. When management developed an ABC system, however, the disposal cost became part of an activity cost pool for the printing process that used these inks. As the activity was analyzed, the high cost of disposal became more noticeable. Managers realized that they could invest in an incinerator that used high temperatures to burn the ink so thoroughly that it left little airborne or solid residual. Thus, the ABC process identified the cost effects of pollution, waste, and other environmental activities, thereby motivating managers to make investments that improve environmental performance. With these improvements, costs associated with pollution or waste are reduced, and in addition, many non-value-added activities are eliminated, such as disposal or cleaning activities.

Although identifying activities and costs related to environmental quality can be difficult, organizations are increasingly concerned with valuing the costs and benefits of developing environmentally friendly practices. The number of Japanese corporations that publish environmental reports listing environmental costs and benefits has been increasing rapidly. Japan's Ministry of the Environment has published *Environmental Report Guidelines*, and the Ministry of Economy, Trade and Industry has published the *Environmental Reporting*

Guideline for Stakeholders. According to the Ministry of Environment, environmental accounting procedures identify costs and benefits of environmental conservation activities.[7] For examples of environmental accounting reports, go to the website of Pioneer (Japan) (http://pioneer.jp/index-e.html) or Panasonic (http://panasonic.net/index.html).

Managing Quality

Part of organizational strategy is the choice of product-quality levels. Some organizations strive to maintain reputations for high-quality products, while other companies seek only to match the quality of their competitors. ABC can be used to determine the costs of quality and to help refine quality strategies. Exhibit 7.7 defines four categories of quality activities—prevention, appraisal, production, and postsales—and provides examples of activities performed within each category. These actions are taken to minimize the opportunity costs that arise when customers have problems with defective units or poor-quality services. When quality failures occur, reputations suffer, and market share is lost. These losses are difficult to value and are, therefore, often ignored when accountants and managers consider the costs and benefits of maintaining high-quality processes.

> **CHAPTER REFERENCE**
>
> Chapter 5 provides a more complete discussion of product quality opportunity costs.

Sometimes the costs of quality failures are extremely high, such as the loss of reputation and market share that occurs when a great deal of publicity is generated about defective goods or processes. Consumer confidence and profitability of Maple Leaf Foods suffered whenever a death from *listeriosis* bacterial contamination occurred.[8] Firestone and Ford lost market share and experienced lower stock market prices when news was released about an increased rollover and fatality rate in Ford Explorers that was associated with Firestone tires. One of Firestone's plants in which a strike had occurred and inexperienced workers had been hired to replace the striking employees has been implicated as a source of defective tires.[9] The cost of quality failures such as these catastrophes is nearly impossible to value yet is extremely important to consider in measuring the costs and benefits of proposed quality improvement initiatives.

Managers make decisions about the trade-offs of investing in the different categories of quality activities. As organizations increasingly invest in prevention activities, competitors are forced to maintain equally high levels of quality. The following illustration shows ABC information and ABM practices being used to reduce cost and improve quality.

> **EXHIBIT 7.7**
>
> Quality-Related Activities

Term and Definition	Examples
Prevention activities	Design and process engineering
Activities performed to ensure defect-free production.	Routine equipment maintenance
	Inspection of incoming raw materials
	Quality training and meetings
Appraisal activities	Inspection of products
Activities performed to identify defective units.	Inspection of manufacturing process
	Monitoring of service delivery process
	Testing
Production activities	Production of spoiled units
Activities undertaken in the production or rework of failed units.	Reworking of spoiled units
	Repair of machine and equipment
	Re-engineering and redesigning
Postsales activities	Product recalls (replacing both good and defective units)
Activities undertaken after a product has been sold to remedy problems caused by defects and failed units.	Warranty repair work
	Replacement of defective units
	Liability lawsuits

---

[7] Ministry of the Environment, Japan, *Understanding Environmental Accounting*, September 2002.

[8] See R. Rampton, *Maple Leaf's Future Seen at Risk Amid Food Recall*, August 26, 2008, www.reuters.com/article/marketsNews/idCAN2634042620080826?rpc = 44.

[9] A. Merrick, "Bridgestone Tire Issue Clouds Labour Negotiations," *Wall Street Journal* (Eastern edition), September 1, 2000, p. A4.

example

Noa/Getty Images

swiss watch
ABM AND THE COST OF QUALITY

Swiss Watch, located in Switzerland, is a watch manufacturer with a reputation for producing high-quality watches. Lately, however, a competitor has advertised both quality improvements and price reductions in its line of watches. Pierre Borgeaud, the head of cost accounting at Swiss Watch, conducted a study to determine whether costs could be reduced. His initial focus was on activities related to quality. Although the managers want to maintain high quality, they also want to reduce costs and, in turn, prices. The study categorized quality costs into four activities: prevention, appraisal, production, and postsales.

Estimating the Costs of Quality

Using information gathered from the general ledger, last year's quality activity costs were estimated as follows (amounts in Swiss francs):

Prevention costs (inspecting materials from suppliers)	SFr 10,000
Appraisal costs (inspection)	20,000
Production costs (spoiled units)	5,000
Postsales costs (warranty)	8,000
Total costs of quality	SFr 43,000

When Pierre reviews these costs, he believes that they are too low. He decides to seek more information than is provided by the general ledger accounts. He speaks with employees both individually and in their work teams and finds that informal inspections occur frequently. He asks employees to estimate time spent on *quality-related activities*. He learns that when defect rates begin to increase, employees respond by spending more time on quality-related activities. He estimates that it cost an additional SFr 50,000 last year in prevention costs for the informal inspections that occurred when defect rates increased. In addition, employees would spend time analyzing and correcting the process to improve quality. He estimates the cost of these activities to be about SFr 2,000 and categorizes the cost as prevention related. He also discovers additional production costs of SFr 6,000 incurred for rework that had not been included in the original estimates. Finally, he discovers an additional SFr 7,000 in postsales service costs for handling returns. He summarizes his revised estimate of the costs of quality as follows:

	First Estimate	Additional Costs	Total Costs
Prevention costs	SFr 10,000	SFr 50,000 + SFr 2,000	SFr 62,000
Appraisal costs	20,000		20,000
Production costs	5,000	6,000	11,000
Postsales costs	8,000	7,000	15,000
Total costs of quality	SFr 43,000	SFr 65,000	SFr 108,000

Using Quality Cost Information to Better Manage Operations

Pierre reports his revised cost estimate to managers, who share the information with a team of production employees. The team members are surprised at the high cost, and they discuss ways to reduce it. The team believes that the company can reduce quality costs by identifying and removing defective units earlier in the production process. Therefore, they recommend tracking the number of defective units discovered by employees on the line versus those found by the inspectors.

Production employees also recommend analyzing the types of defects discovered by inspectors, to help the employees identify and correct potential problems earlier in the production process. The team believes that some of the inspectors could be assigned to other activities, decreasing the overall costs of quality. In addition, the team recommends tracking the types of warranty problems that occur to determine changes in the design or manufacturing process that would minimize the cost of warranty work and, simultaneously, improve customer satisfaction. ■

●● > STRATEGIC RISK MANAGEMENT: SWISS WATCH

QUALITY AND REPUTATION The strategy at Swiss Watch depended on the company's ability to produce high-quality watches. What would happen if defective units were sold to customers? The company might lose its reputation for high quality, resulting in loss of reputation and market share.

Sometimes the costs of quality failures are extremely high. The reputation and profitability of companies suffer whenever product quality problems are publicized. Mattel was highly criticized when it recalled toys due to a design flaw that increased the risk of small children accidentally swallowing a magnet. Other toys from suppliers in China contained lead paint. Following vehicle acceleration problems and massive worldwide recalls during 2010, Toyota lost market share and experienced lower stock market prices. Questions were raised about the company's ability to regain its previous reputation for high quality. The cost of quality failures such as these catastrophes is nearly impossible to value, yet is extremely important to consider in measuring the costs and benefits of proposed quality improvement initiatives.

SOURCES: "Plenty of Blame to Go Around," *The Economist*, September 27, 2007; "Trouble in Toyland: New Challenges for Mattel—and 'Made in China'," Knowledge@Wharton, August 22, 2007, available at knowledge.wharton.upenn.edu/article.cfm?articleid=1796; and J. Green and A. G. Keane, "Americans Saying 'No' to Toyota; Ford Most Popular," *Bloomberg Businessweek*, March 25, 2010, available at www.businessweek.com.

Managing Constrained Resources

If an organization faces capacity constraints, ABC can help identify each product's use of constrained resources. By analyzing the activities within the constraints, efficiency improvements can be proposed and tested. Thus, ABC information can help managers identify the best way to relax constraints. ABC information can also be used in designing products and manufacturing or service delivery processes that minimize use of constrained resources.

In addition, by developing an ABC system that separates committed from flexible costs, managers would have more accurate information to determine the contribution margin per constrained resource. When products with the highest contribution margin per constrained resource are emphasized, profits are maximized.

> ▷ **CHAPTER REFERENCE**
> For more details about maximizing constrained resources, see Chapter 4.

Benefits, Costs, and Limitations of ABC Systems

Accountants need to consider cost-benefit trade-offs when choosing activities and cost drivers for an ABC system. They must estimate the costs of alternative ABC systems and anticipate the potential benefits from alternative system designs. They also need to recognize that an ABC system might fail to meet expectations.

Benefits of an ABC System. ABC systems enable managers to focus on measurement at the activity level. Once activities are identified and cost drivers are chosen, employees are more aware of cause-and-effect relationships. This awareness prompts employees to search for ways to improve performance simply because they have more information about the cost effects of an activity. The importance and materiality of some non-value-added costs become apparent with a more careful analysis of activity costs, and motivation to reduce those costs increases. In an ABC system, activities that do not add value to customers are more likely to be identified and eliminated from operations. Examples include holding excess levels of inventories, unnecessary motion and transportation, waste in the setup process, and inspection inefficiencies.

More than other costing systems, ABC systems measure the flow of resources in an organization. They reduce the arbitrariness in cost measurement by more closely matching cost allocations to the actual use of resources by operating activities. Compared to the allocation bases used in a traditional costing system, those used in an ABC system are more likely to be cost drivers and related to costs rather than just used to allocate cost. For example, when the Keener ABC team used ABC to allocate overhead costs to regular and premium doors, the flow of resources was more accurately reflected, and the allocated costs were different from the job costing system because more cost pools were used, and each cost pool was allocated using a cost driver that better reflected the use of the resources in the activity cost pool.

Costs of an ABC System. Many costs are associated with designing and using an ABC system, including the following:

- System design costs, such as costs of employee time and consulting fees
- Accounting and information system modifications needed to gather and report activity and cost driver information
- Employee training to use the ABC system effectively

Sometimes, the cost of developing ABC information is low, especially in cases where the activity cost is readily available and the number of times the activity is performed can easily be tracked. Suppose the activity is inspection of units. The cost consists of the salary and fringe benefits of the inspector and the number of units being inspected. Identifying salary costs in an accounting system is easy, and fringe benefit costs can be estimated. The number of units produced should be readily available from production records, and the capacity of the inspection area can be easily estimated. Thus, developing an activity-based cost for inspection may be as simple as dividing the salary-related costs by a chosen measure of unit volume.

Other times, ABC information is more costly to develop. Suppose the activity is the setup process. This process often includes labour, supplies, and other resources. Because cost tracing is one of the components of cost assignment under ABC, it takes time and analysis to identify costs that can be traced and those that should be allocated. In addition, data for the cost driver, such as the number of setups, must be tracked.

In general, the costs of an ABC system are higher when more activities or more complex activities are involved, as it is more difficult to accurately trace costs to activities as their complexity and number increase. Increased employee training is often required. Also, the process of ABC system development bogs down if too much complexity is introduced at one time. However, a failure to sufficiently break down activities might prevent the system from providing useful information.

Accounting researchers questioned whether the costs of implementing ABC systems were worth the benefits received. They found that although ABC use was associated with higher quality and improved cycle time, for the average firm, no significant association was found between ABC use and return on assets. However, ABC appeared to be related to profitability for firms using advanced manufacturing techniques that combine information technology with more flexible manufacturing practices.[10] Researchers who document successful implementations suggest that important factors include top management support and performance evaluations.[11] In addition, researchers have found that for small manufacturing firms, simple ABC systems with few activities and cost drivers are best. These systems are inexpensive yet efficient, and they are easier for managers to understand and implement.[12]

Uncertainties in ABC and ABM Implementation. Managers face many uncertainties about how best to implement an ABC system as well as how useful an ABC system will be. Thus, they face uncertainties about the costs and benefits of using ABC and ABM systems.

---

[10] C. Ittner, W. Lanen, and D. Larcker, "The Association Between Activity-Based Costing and Manufacturing Performance," *Journal of Accounting Research*, June 2002.

[11] M. Shields, "An Empirical Analysis of Firms' Implementation Experiences with Activity-Based Costing," *Journal of Management Accounting Research* 7, 1995, pp. 148–166; and G. Foster and D. Swenson, "Measuring the Success of Activity-Based Cost Management and Its Determinants," *Journal of Management Accounting Research* 7, 1997, pp. 109–141.

[12] K. L. Needy, H. Nachtmann, N. Roztocki, R. C. Warner, and B. Bidanda, "Implementing Activity-Based Costing Systems in Small Manufacturing Firms: A Field Study," *Engineering Management Journal*, March 2003, pp. 3–10.

Managers use judgment to decide which activities and cost drivers to include in an ABC system, because of uncertainty about the set of activities and drivers that would provide the best information. As the number of activities increases, measurement error also tends to increase, because a greater number of allocations are used to assign costs to activity cost pools. In addition, it is not always possible to determine the best cost driver. Information for some cost drivers may be readily available, whereas information for a potentially superior driver might be costly to accumulate. When designing an ABC system, accountants cannot foresee all the various ways in which the new information could be used in ABM to reduce costs or improve decision making. For example, until activities and costs are evaluated, we may not be able to identify non-value-added activities. Accordingly, the ability to identify the most valuable activities to measure and track is uncertain.

Uncertainties are also part of choosing an appropriate denominator value to determine the allocation rate. The accuracy of estimates used in the denominator affects the allocation of cost. We overstate or understate cost when the denominator estimate is too large or small. Although ABC information is more detailed, measurement errors also increase because of estimates. Thus, the additional detail does not necessarily improve the quality of information.

Accountants also face uncertainties about how an organization's employees will respond to the design and implementation of an ABC system. In some cases, employees are afraid of major system changes, especially when their jobs might be viewed as non-value-added jobs. As a result, some employees will fail to provide adequate information for designing the system; they might even provide misleading or incorrect information. If employees believe that their performance will be evaluated using ABC information, they may provide biased information to show better performance. Once the new system is designed, they may try to undermine implementation and training efforts. Even when employees fully embrace the new ABC system, they might misunderstand it and make inappropriate decisions. Furthermore, if an ABC system is overly complex, even the most enthusiastic employees might not be able to take full advantage of it.

Drawbacks of ABC

Although ABC and ABM are used widely by a range of businesses worldwide, major concerns exist about mismeasurement of costs assigned to ABC activities and misuse of ABC data for decision making.

Mismeasurement of Costs Assigned to ABC Activities. As illustrated in Exhibit 7.2, costs must be assigned to each ABC cost pool. Errors may creep into the process of tracing or allocating individual costs, leading to mismeasurement in ABC costs. The allocation process often introduces a degree of measurement error. For example, costs such as supplies and employee benefits might be allocated to a number of activities, such as setup, maintenance, and monitoring of production. It is impossible to identify the exact amount of cost associated with each activity when we use allocated costs.

In addition, errors are sometimes made in assigning costs directly to ABC pools. In the case of Keener Doors and Windows, suppose windows are periodically pulled from the production line for quality testing, and the direct cost of employee labour for this activity is traced to the inspection activity. If a defect is found, inspection activities probably increase, temporarily drawing labour resources away from other production activities. This type of event causes mismeasurement in the assignment of costs across ABC cost pools. The accounting system is unlikely to capture a temporary change in the type of work that employees perform. Because of the measurement error, allocations from the activity cost pools will not reflect the actual flow of resources. However, if the inspection activity is pooled with other production activities, then the temporary reassignment of employees within production will not cause mismeasurement.

In general, the risk of measurement error increases under the following circumstances:

- ► If uncertainties exist about the activity to which costs relate
- ► When costs are allocated to ABC cost pools instead of traced
- ► When the number of ABC cost pools increases

Relevant ABC Costs for Decision Making. When making decisions about short- or long-term uses of resources, decision makers need to identify relevant costs. Therefore, they need to understand how alternative decisions will change costs. Managers sometimes use ABC cost allocation rates as if they are variable costs—that is, as if costs change proportionately as the activity increases or decreases. However, the activity pools often contain costs that do not vary with activity levels, such as fixed costs. Therefore, ABC cost information is often irrelevant or misleading for decision making.

To address this problem, the costs within an activity can be categorized as flexible or committed. Flexible costs vary with activity levels, and committed costs remain fixed, regardless of activity levels. Committed costs are related to capacity and do not change in the short term. Therefore, they do not change proportionately with volume changes. When managers use ABC cost allocation rates for decision making without distinguishing between flexible and committed costs, their estimates of relevant costs are biased upward or downward. The direction of bias depends on how the volume after alternative decisions are implemented compares to the volume on which the current rates are based.

Suppose ABC cost rates were established at Keener Doors and Windows by estimating monthly ABC cost information. Machine setup costs for glass cutting in the window department were estimated to be $6,720 per month, and the practical capacity was estimated to be 320 batches. In other words, it costs $6,720 per month to supply enough capacity to handle 320 batches of windows. Given this information, the ABC cost allocation rate is set at $21 per batch ($6,720 ÷ 320 batches). If the $6,720 cost is committed, total costs will be $6,720, even when the number of actual batches run is less than 320 during the month. If the managers incorrectly assume that the $21 ABC cost per batch is a variable cost, they are likely to overestimate or underestimate actual costs. For example, if they plan for 200 batches, they would underestimate cost at $4,200 ($21 × 200 batches). If they plan for 400 batches, they would estimate cost at $8,400 ($21 × 400 batches). In this case, depending on potential extra costs, such as employee overtime, costs that the company incurs when actual production exceeds practical capacity might be overestimated or underestimated. ABC allocation rates do not provide accurate cost estimates when they include committed costs or when production levels move to a new relevant range of activity.

To provide managers with information that is more useful for decision making, the ABC system can be set up with separate activity pools and cost rates for

- ▶ Different levels of the ABC cost hierarchy, and
- ▶ Committed and flexible costs within each hierarchy.

⊳ **ALTERNATIVE TERMS**

In earlier chapters, we used the terms *variable costs* and *fixed costs* related to product or sales volumes. Because ABC costs relate to activity levels, we use the terms *flexible* and *committed*.

●● > FOCUS ON ETHICAL DECISION MAKING:
PROMOTING INAPPROPRIATE USES OF ABC

When ABC was first developed, consultants sometimes promoted it for inappropriate uses. Many consulting services focused on using ABC information for short-term decisions, such as pricing and product emphasis. Yet in the early stages of ABC and ABM development, both flexible and committed costs were included in ABC cost pools and were not tracked separately. As a result, ABC unit costs included both fixed and variable costs, even when the fixed costs were irrelevant for decision making. ABC promoters suggested that all costs were variable in the long run, and they ignored criticism of their methods.

If the ABC cost rates include fixed costs, their unquestioned use in setting prices is detrimental to operations. If demand falls, then production volumes may fall, too, first causing cost per unit to increase and then causing prices to increase. This type of pricing policy can lead to a death spiral, in which prices increase inappropriately as volumes decline.

Pressmaster/Shutterstock/Getty Images

After ABC was developed, it was quickly added to cost accounting curricula at many universities. However, a few academics were highly critical of ABC and eventually provided evidence that overhead costs included a large portion of fixed costs, even in the long run. As research evidence accumulated, ABC consultants suggested that organizations not allocate facility-level costs and that costs within each activity cost pool be categorized as flexible and committed. Then total costs could be used to analyze processes and improve operations, but flexible cost information could be retrieved for decision making.

Currently, "incremental ABC cost analysis" services are being promoted. These services are sometimes called *predictive accounting*. Because consulting services can be expensive, and judging the outcome of new ideas can be difficult, managers need to incorporate healthy scepticism when considering the potential costs and benefits of products and services promoted by consultants.

Source: E. Noreen and N. Soderstrom, "Are Overhead Costs Strictly Proportional to Activity? Evidence from Hospital Service Departments," *Journal of Accounting & Economics*, January 1994, pp. 255–279.

ETHICS OF CONSULTANT SERVICES

Perform a web search for two articles written by consultants or consulting firms about activity-based costing. Consider the following questions. Did you find articles promoting the use of ABC for pricing and other short-term decisions? If so, did the article stipulate that fixed and variable costs should be separated when analyzing relevant costs? When consultants write articles about a technique such as ABC, are the articles likely to be biased? How can consultants increase the likelihood that clients will benefit from their consulting services?

> **CHAPTER REFERENCE**
> See Chapter 14 for more information on pricing and the death spiral.

Ethical Decision-Making Process	Questions to Consider About This Ethical Dilemma
Identify ethical problems as they arise.	Did you find articles promoting the use of • ABC for pricing and other short-term decisions? • incremental ABC or predictive accounting? When consultants develop management techniques such as ABC, do uncertainties always remain about whether the technique will benefit clients? Does selling ABC consulting services create an ethical problem? Why or why not?
Objectively consider the well-being of others and society when exploring alternatives.	In light of uncertainties about whether consulting services will benefit clients, • Why do consultants promote them? • Why do clients purchase the services? • What are the pros and cons to the clients? Did your articles appear to promote appropriate or inappropriate uses of costs for decision making? How do you know? When consultants write articles about a technique such as ABC, are the articles likely to be biased? Why or why not?
Clarify and apply ethical values when choosing a course of action.	What are consultants' ethical obligations when selling consulting services that have uncertain outcomes? What values did you use to arrive at your conclusions?
Work toward ongoing improvement of personal and organizational ethics.	How can consultants increase the likelihood that clients will benefit from their consulting services?

Other Multi-Pool, Multi-Driver Cost Accounting Systems[13]

The problems with typical ABC systems motivated accountants and managers to seek alternatives to both traditional costing and ABC methods. In recent years, the cost accounting community has explored new types of multi-pool, multi-driver systems. This section introduces the following methods:

- ▶ Grenzplankostenrechnung (GPK)
- ▶ Resource consumption accounting (RCA)

These methods focus not only on measuring costs, but also on encouraging managers to use resources more efficiently. The capacity definitions shown in Exhibit 7.8 are used throughout this section.

Grenzplankostenrechnung (GPK)

▣ BUSINESS PRACTICE

About 3,000 companies have adopted the GPK approach, including **Siemens**, **IBM Germany**, **Mobil Oil**, **Michelin**, and **Porsche**.

Survey results revealed that U.S. managerial accountants were largely dissatisfied with current cost accounting approaches.[14] Ninety-eight percent claimed that cost data were distorted, primarily due to overhead cost allocation methods. In contrast, similar surveys of German accountants using a method called Grenzplankostenrechnung found that most respondents were quite satisfied.[15]

The literal translation of Grenzplankostenrechnung is grenz (marginal) plan (planned) kosten (costing) rechnung (accounting), so a close description would be "marginal planning and cost accounting." Under GPK, each cost is traced to a **cost centre**, which is typically smaller than a department, performs a single repetitive activity, and is the responsibility of one manager. Planned costs and volumes are used to develop a standard cost function for each cost centre, using one or a few output measures as cost drivers. An **output measure** tracks the volume of resource use, usually measured in time. For example, the output measure for a machine would be the number of machine hours. Instead of variable costs, the cost function includes **proportional costs**, which are attributable to changes in volume of resource use. The standard cost function is used to develop budgets and to assign costs to units of product or other cost centres. Practical capacity is typically used for estimated denominator volume when assigning fixed costs, allowing managers to track and analyze the cost of idle capacity. The use of standard costs also allows managers to monitor and analyze variances between budgeted and actual costs for each cost centre. Because of its focus on marginal costs, GPK provides relevant cost information for short-term decisions such as product emphasis, make or buy, use of constrained resources, and minimum selling prices.

▣ CHAPTER REFERENCE

See Chapter 11 for more information about standard costs and cost variances.

▣ EXHIBIT 7.8

Capacity Definitions

Theoretical capacity	Maximum capacity limit assuming continuous, uninterrupted operations 365 days per year
Practical capacity	Maximum volume of a resource under typical operating conditions, assuming that some downtime is unavoidable for maintenance, holidays, etc.
Budgeted capacity	Expected volume for the upcoming time period
Idle/excess capacity	Difference between actual capacity used and one of the above measures of capacity

---

[13] The authors gratefully acknowledge the assistance of B. Douglas Clinton and Anton van der Merwe in developing the GPK and RCA materials in this textbook. The authors are responsible for any errors or omissions.

[14] A. Garg, D. Ghosh, J. Hudick, and C. Nowacki, "Roles and Practices in Management Accounting Today," *Strategic Finance* 85, July 2003, pp. 30–35.

[15] G. Friedl, "Lessons from German Cost Accounting," Presentation at CAM-I Quarterly Meeting, Phoenix, December 12, 2006.

Resource Consumption Accounting (RCA)

Resource consumption accounting (RCA) builds on GPK and ABC principles. It attempts to accurately measure resource costs, which become the building blocks used to compile fixed and proportional costs for activities, products, or other cost objects. Therefore, each cost is initially assigned to a resource cost pool, which is a grouping of homogeneous resources. Judgment is used to decide which types of resources belong in the same cost pool. Labour and machinery are often placed in separate cost pools, because they are different types of resources. In addition, different pieces of equipment are often placed in different cost pools. Like GPK, RCA involves a significantly larger number of cost pools than traditional accounting systems. For example, the number of cost pools for only four departments increased from 29 to 97 when The Hospital for Sick Children in Toronto implemented a combined GPK/ABC system as a pilot study preceding implementation of RCA.[16] Fixed and proportional cost rates for each resource cost pool are developed using one output measure as the cost driver. Theoretical rather than practical capacity is used as estimated volume for fixed costs, and fixed and proportional costs are accounted for separately throughout the accounting system. An RCA system can create reports summarizing information at different levels of detail. Depending on the information needed by management, RCA can provide timely, relevant information for short-, mid-, or long-term decisions.

▶ BUSINESS PRACTICE
Although GPK has its roots in manufacturing, it has been increasingly adopted by service organizations such as Deutsche Bundesbank, Deutsche Post, Lufthansa, and Deutsche Telekom.

Cost Pool Calculations Under GPK and RCA

To illustrate cost assignment to products under GPK and RCA, consider the magnetic resonance imaging (MRI) scanner at Prescott Imaging Clinic. The clinic's managers are analyzing the profitability of the scanner and considering whether to extend the hours of operation.

The MRI scanner operation consists of a single MRI scanner machine, located in a dedicated area of the clinic building. Costs for the scanner under GPK and RCA are shown in Exhibit 7.9. Primary costs are traced directly to a cost pool. For the scanner,

▶ EXHIBIT 7.9
MRI Scanner Cost Rates Under GPK and RCA[17]

GPK			RCA		
Cost Centre: MRI Scanner			Resource Cost Pool: MRI Scanner		
	Fixed	Proportional		Fixed	Proportional
Output measure – MRI hours:	2,400	2,200	Output measure – MRI hours:	8,760	2,200
Practical capacity			Theoretical capacity		
Budgeted capacity			Budgeted capacity		
Primary costs:			Primary costs:		
Depreciation	$350,000	$ 0	Depreciation	$350,000	$ 0
Supplies	1,000	680,000	Supplies	1,000	680,000
Electricity	3,000	50,000	Electricity	3,000	50,000
Total primary costs	354,000	730,000	Total primary costs	354,000	730,000
From other cost pools (i.e., Secondary costs):			From other resources (i.e., Secondary costs):		
Labour (technician)	0	200,000	Labour (technician)	0	200,000
Maintenance – equipment	120,000	25,000	Maintenance – equipment	120,000	25,000
Maintenance – facilities	27,600	2,000	Maintenance – facilities	27,600	2,000
Fully assigned resource costs	$501,600	$957,000	Attributable resource costs	$501,600	$957,000
Fully assigned cost rate per hour	$209.00	$435.00	Attributable cost rate per hour	$57.2603	$435.00

---

[16] P. Sharman, "Merging GPK and ABC on the Road to RCA," *Strategic Finance*, November 2006.
[17] This exhibit does not portray all of the differences that would typically exist between cost calculations for a GPK system versus an RCA system. In particular, the costs assigned from other cost/resource centres would usually differ because of differences in the capacity volume used to calculate the attributable fixed cost rate (theoretical capacity in RCA and practical capacity in GPK) and possibly also due to differences in the type and number of cost pools used.

CHAPTER REFERENCE

In this example, costs are assigned directly from one cost centre to another. Chapter 8 introduces other allocation methods that can be used when cost centres simultaneously use each other's resources.

ALTERNATIVE TERMS

Accountants often use the terms *proportional costs* or *marginal costs* instead of *variable costs* in GPK and RCA systems to emphasize that costs vary in proportion to output of a cost pool, not necessarily to final units of product.

primary costs include equipment and space depreciation, supplies, and electricity. **Secondary costs** are assigned based on resource use from separate cost pools. For the scanner, secondary costs include technician labour, equipment maintenance, and facility maintenance.

Under both GPK and RCA, costs assigned from other cost pools are classified as fixed or proportional, based on how the costs behave with respect to scanner activity—that is, hours of scan use. For example, the clinic pays electricity on a strictly variable basis. However, a certain amount of electricity is used by the scanner to keep the equipment in a ready state. This portion of electricity use is classified as fixed, while electricity used to run scans is classified as proportional. The clinic's accounting system must be able to track and assign each of these costs to the scanner cost pool based on resource use. For example, a meter could be used to measure electricity use. Similarly, supplies requisitions could be used to trace costs such as intravenous chemicals that boost MRI visibility.

Under both GPK and RCA, a cost function is developed for the resources used in each cost pool, and it is updated annually or when major changes occur to costs or operations. Managers use the cost function for budgeting and periodic monitoring of actual costs compared to budget. The hours of scan use is likely to explain changes in proportional costs and is also an appropriate output measure for the scanning resource, so "hours" is used as the output measure for both cost systems. If all scans require about the same amount of time and require the same quantities of proportional resources, such as electricity and supplies, then a generic output measure like number of scans might be adequate.

The fixed and proportional costs are also converted into *attributable cost rates* per scanner hour. The proportional cost rate is based on budgeted capacity, or the expected volume of scanner hours. The fixed cost rate is based on practical capacity under GPK and theoretical capacity under RCA. Similar cost analyses were performed for other cost pools, and the resulting cost rates in support areas were used to assign costs to the MRI cost pool. The MRI cost rates are used to assign resource costs to individual patient services or other activities. For example, the fixed and proportional rates could be used to analyze profitability for different types of patients, or the proportional cost rate could be used in a decision about minimum prices to charge for an MRI.

Idle/Excess Capacity Analysis

The preceding MRI cost analyses address a major flaw in traditional accounting systems—the allocation of idle capacity fixed costs to cost objects. In RCA, GPK, and some event-driven ABC systems, the fixed cost rate would be used to assign costs to idle/excess capacity. The calculations shown in Exhibit 7.10 compare costs for the MRI using three alternative capacity volumes and assuming that actual scanner use was 2,150 hours.

Exhibit 7.10 illustrates how different capacity choices significantly affect the fixed costs assigned to individual patients. Should individual patient costs be affected by the budgeted number of scans needed by other patients (budgeted capacity), or by the number of maintenance and other downtime hours expected this year (practical capacity)? Proponents of RCA argue that theoretical capacity should be used to allocate fixed costs for physical assets, such as plant and equipment, to avoid arbitrary cost differences caused by these factors. In addition, the use of theoretical capacity is likely to focus more manager attention on reducing idle and non-productive MRI time.

CHAPTER REFERENCE

In GPK and RCA, internal-use income statements are often called *product* or *service profit and loss statements*. Chapter 17 provides more information about internal-use income statements.

Multi-Level Income Statement

Accountants using GPK and RCA systems typically produce income statements for internal use that are layered to provide margins at the product, product group, business unit, and entire organization levels. Exhibit 7.11 illustrates a monthly multi-level income statement for the Prescott Imaging Clinic for the month of June.

The clinic's operations are divided into two product groups: imaging equipment and physician services. The equipment group is responsible for providing images using the

	Budgeted Capacity	Practical Capacity	Theoretical Capacity
Estimated volume – MRI hours	2,200	2,400	8,760
Fixed cost rate per scan	$228.00*	$209.00	$57.2603
Fixed costs allocated to patient services			
(2,150 hours × fixed cost rate)	$490,200	$449,350	$123,110
Allocated to idle capacity:			
Unplanned idle capacity			
(2,200 − 2,150) hours × fixed cost rate	11,400	10,450	2,863
Planned idle capacity			
(2,200 − 2,200) hours × $228.00	0		
(2,400 − 2,200) hours × $209.00		41,800	
(8,760 − 2,200) hours × $57.2603			375,627
Total fixed costs assigned	$501,600	$501,600	$501,600

*$501,600 fixed costs ÷ 2,200 budgeted capacity = $228.00

> EXHIBIT 7.10
Budget Capacity Analysis for MRI Scanner

clinic's MRI, X-ray, and ultrasound equipment. The physician services group provides analyses of imaging results. RCA margin 1 is equal to revenues minus proportional costs for individual products, so it would be relevant for making and monitoring many short-term decisions. Fixed costs that are relevant to only one product, including idle/excess capacity, are subtracted to determine RCA margin 2. Notice that sometimes more capacity is used than planned, leading to negative values for excess capacity. This margin would be relevant for decisions such as whether to keep or drop a piece of equipment. Fixed costs that are relevant to an entire product group are subtracted to calculate RCA margin 3. Because the physician group has only one type of product, no additional fixed costs are subtracted at this point. Fixed costs that are relevant to the entire clinic are subtracted to determine clinic profit. The multi-level income statement also provides useful information for evaluating actual versus planned performance at each level within the clinic's operations.

In GPK and RCA systems, each cost centre is analyzed to determine its classification within the multi-level income statement. For example, an advertising cost pool might be categorized as product, product group, division, or company, depending on the nature of advertisements created. Advertising costs for a single product would be attributed to product fixed costs and would reduce RCA margin 2 in Exhibit 7.11, while advertising costs for an entire division's products would be attributed to division fixed costs. Similarly, a particular production cost pool might include equipment depreciation, labour, supplies, and other costs. If the cost pool tasks relate to only one product, then its costs would be classified as fixed and proportional product costs. If the cost pool's tasks relate to a group of products, then the proportional costs related to each product would be classified as product costs, while the fixed costs would be classified as group fixed costs. This method for separately assigning fixed and proportional costs avoids the arbitrary allocations of fixed costs that are common in traditional and ABC systems.

Drawbacks of GPK and RCA

The effect of GPK and RCA on management decisions and incentives will be discussed in more detail in the next section of the chapter. Although these costing systems address major problems in traditional and ABC costing, concerns arise about the costs to implement these systems. GPK and RCA are comprehensive accounting systems in which the

> EXHIBIT 7.11

RCA Monthly Multi-Level Income Statement for Prescott Imaging Clinic

Month of June	Imaging Equipment Group			Physician Services Group
	X-ray	MRI	Ultrasound	
Revenues	$108,793	$523,312	$273,901	$506,781
Proportional costs	21,430	289,676	30,444	76,312
RCA margin 1	87,363	233,636	243,457	430,469
Fixed costs, product	22,041	57,434	29,677	322,471
Excess capacity – unplanned	488	(1,191)*	512	(2,946)*
Excess capacity – planned	14,295	45,552	39,688	51,493
RCA margin 2	50,539	131,841	173,580	59,451
Fixed costs, product group		99,432		n/a
RCA margin 3		256,528		59,451
Fixed costs, clinic			283,194	
Clinic profit			$32,785	

*Unplanned excess capacity is negative for the MRI and physician services group because actual volume exceeded budgeted volume during June.

general ledger, planning, and operational systems are integrated. Full implementation can entail ongoing detailed analysis of resource use in large numbers of cost pools. However, these systems are facilitated by *enterprise resource planning (ERP)* software, such as SAP ERP and Microsoft Dynamics NAV, significantly reducing the cost of maintenance.

Despite the high implementation cost of GPK systems, research reveals increased adoption, with few adopters abandoning the approach.[18] Nevertheless, some German accounting experts anticipate future modifications. Today's more advanced manufacturing systems create higher consistency in operations, reducing the need for after-the-fact cost control. In the future, GPK systems may become less complex. For example, Rasselstein, a German packaging steel producer, calculates variances for 400 cost centres, but focuses analyses on the five centres having the largest variances.[19] Beiersdorf, producer of body-care products such as Nivea, uses a simplified GPK system. All costs other than raw materials, labour, and energy are treated as fixed costs.[20] At the same time, managers are calling for more non-production information, such as customer profitability. GPK systems are likely to be expanded to include more activity-based data.[21]

Overall, some experts argue that the costs of GPK systems outweigh the benefits, and similar arguments can be made for RCA systems. This conclusion might be particularly true in the United States, where managers express dissatisfaction with the quality of cost accounting information, yet place relatively low priority on implementing new cost management tools.[22] In contrast, research suggests that German managers are willing to invest in and maintain their GPK systems. Differences in managers' attitudes toward developing more detailed, comprehensive costing systems might be caused by differences in values, culture, training, availability of knowledgeable consultants, or other factors.[23]

[18] G. Friedl, op cit.

[19] K. R. Krumwiede, "Rewards and Realities of German Cost Accounting," *Strategic Finance*, April 2005, pp. 27–34.

[20] K. R. Krumwiede, op cit.

[21] For an example of customer profitability analysis using GPK, see P.A. Sharman, "Bring on German Cost Accounting," *Strategic Finance*, December 2003.

[22] See, for example, P.A. Sharman, "The Case for Management Accounting," *Strategic Finance*, October 2003, p. 2.

[23] See, for example, J.B. MacArthur, "Cultural Influences on German Versus U.S. Management Accounting Practices," *Management Accounting Quarterly*, Winter 2006.

Multi-Pool, Multi-Driver Systems, Decision Making, and Incentives

Traditional costing is often referred to as *peanut butter costing* because it spreads overhead costs without regard to products' use of resources. Thus, the cost information provided by traditional accounting systems is of low quality for decision making. In addition, traditional costing often leads to product-cost cross-subsidization, which distorts the costs of individual products and leads to poor decisions. The multi-pool, multi-driver systems discussed in this chapter—ABC, GPK, and RCA—seek to address these problems. Exhibit 7.12 presents a comparison of some of the key features of ABC, GPK, and RCA, including the types of decisions that are appropriate for each method.

LO6 Describe how ABC, GPK, and RCA affect managers' incentives and decisions

Benefits of ABC, GPK, and RCA Systems

The benefits of all three costing methods include the following:

- As managers and employees analyze the use of resources to better map them to costs, they gain a better understanding of value-added and non-value-added activities, and often improve the processes and use of resources to become more efficient.
- Cost assignments more closely measure the flow of resources in an organization.
- Cost accuracy usually increases as the number of appropriate cost pools increases and cost drivers are identified.
- Managers become more aware of the cause-and-effect relationships for activities.
- The costs of idle capacity and constrained resources can more easily be identified.

A problem with ABC is that costs are not typically separated into fixed and variable categories, so ABC is not very useful for short-term decision making. GPK and RCA address this problem and their use includes the following additional benefits.

- Cost information is categorized and summarized according to its behaviour as fixed or proportional at the resource level.
- Relevant cost information is produced for many types of short-term decisions.
- Budgeting, monitoring, and control are enhanced through the development of appropriate cost functions.
- The use of cost functions allows budgets and cost rates to be updated easily.
- With the use of ERP systems, resources are assigned as they are used, resulting in greater cost measurement accuracy.
- Reports are multi-level, starting with detailed operational data that is summarized at the bottom line.

▶ EXHIBIT 7.12
▶ EXHIBIT 7.12

Comparison of ABC, GPK, and RCA

	ABC	GPK	RCA
Character of cost accounting system	Full costing	Marginal costing	Full and marginal costing
Location of data	Database separate from the general ledger	Comprehensive accounting system	Comprehensive accounting system
Primary decision relevance	Mid- to long-term decisions	Short-term decisions	Short-, mid-, and long-term decisions
Allocation of overhead based on:	Activities	Cost centres	Resources and/or activities
Cost drivers	Activity-based	Resource output-related	Resource output and/or activity-based
Fixed cost allocation rate denominator	Actual, budgeted, or practical capacity	Budgeted or practical capacity	Theoretical capacity
Cost responsibility/cost consciousness	Activity owners across cost centres	Cost centre managers, product managers, product group managers	Potentially all managers at various organization levels

Adapted from G. Friedl, H. Kupper, and B. Pedell, "Relevance Added: Combining ABC with German Cost Accounting," *Strategic Finance*, June 2005, p. 59.

► Managers can be held responsible for results at the cost centre level in performance evaluation.
► The cost of unused capacity is automatically calculated and reported.

Proponents of RCA believe that the following factors provide improvements over GPK systems.

► RCA includes both resource and activity information, which increases its flexibility in assigning and reporting costs.
► RCA uses theoretical capacity to calculate fixed cost rates for physical assets such as plant and equipment, which provides more transparent capacity usage information and reduces cost distortions caused by arbitrary allocations of idle capacity costs to products or other cost objects.
► Variance analysis information by cost centre is available for both resources and processes.
► RCA supports a variety of analysis approaches including throughput analysis, traditional contribution analysis, activity-based analysis, and value-stream analysis.

Costs of ABC, GPK, and RCA Systems

Many costs are associated with designing and using these costing systems, including the following:

► System design costs, such as employee time and consulting fees
► Accounting and information system modifications needed to gather and report activity and cost driver information
► Employee training for effective system use

As the complexity of operations increases, the costs to implement and maintain ABC, GPK, and RCA systems increase. For some organizations, the costs to implement and maintain these systems may outweigh the benefits derived from more accurate cost information.

U.S. accounting researchers have questioned whether the costs of implementing ABC systems were worth the benefits received. They found that although ABC use was associated with higher quality and improved cycle time, for the average firm no significant association was found between ABC use and return on assets. However, ABC appeared to be related to profitability for firms using advanced manufacturing techniques that combine information technology with more flexible manufacturing practices.[24] Researchers who document successful implementations suggest that important factors include top management support and performance evaluations.[25] In addition, researchers have found that for small manufacturing firms, simple ABC systems with few activities and cost drivers are best. These systems are inexpensive yet efficient, and easier for managers to understand and implement.[26] More research is needed to help managers evaluate the cost-benefit trade-offs for GPK and RCA systems.

SUMMARY

L01 Differentiate activity-based costing (ABC) from traditional costing

TRADITIONAL COSTING SYSTEM

Few cost pools, allocated using traditional allocation bases

ACTIVITY-BASED COSTING SYSTEM

Multiple cost pools, reflecting activities and cost drivers for allocation bases

L02 Use cost hierarchy to help assign costs to activities

ACTIVITY

A type of task or function performed in an organization

ACTIVITY IDENTIFICATION

► Tracking the use of resources
► Using the cost hierarchy
► Grouping homogeneous costs

COST HIERARCHY

► Organization-sustaining activities
► Facility-sustaining activities
► Customer-sustaining activities
► Product-sustaining activities
► Batch-level activities
► Unit-level activities

L03 Apply an ABC system in assigning costs

ABC PROCEDURES

1. Identify the relevant cost object
2. Identify activities
3. Assign (trace and allocate) costs to activity-based cost pools
4. For each ABC cost pool, choose a cost driver
5. For each ABC cost pool, calculate an allocation rate

   Allocation rate = Activity cost ÷ Volume of cost driver

6. For each ABC cost pool, allocate activity costs to the cost object

SELECTION OF COST DRIVERS

► Cause-and-effect relationship between cost driver and activity costs
► Judgment in choosing and evaluating potential cost drivers

---

[24] See C. Ittner, W. Lanen, and D. Larcker, "The Association Between Activity-Based Costing and Manufacturing Performance," *Journal of Accounting Research*, June 2002.

[25] See M. Shields, "An Empirical Analysis of Firms' Implementation Experiences with Activity-Based Costing," *Journal of Management Accounting Research* 7, 1995, pp. 148–166; and G. Foster and D. Swenson, "Measuring the Success of Activity-Based Cost Management and Its Determinants," *Journal of Management Accounting Research* 7, 1997, pp. 109–141.

[26] See Needy, Nachtmann, Roztocki, Warner, and Bidanda, "Implementing Activity-Based Costing Systems in Small Manufacturing Firms: A Field Study," *Engineering Management Journal*, March 2003, pp. 3–10.

LO4 Describe the characteristics and use of activity-based management (ABM)

ACTIVITY-BASED MANAGEMENT

Using ABC information to evaluate the costs and benefits of production and internal support activities and to identify and implement opportunities for improvements in profitability, efficiency, and quality within an organization.

APPLICATIONS OF ABM

- Customer profitability
- Product and process design:
  - Focus resources on value-added activities
  - Reduce or eliminate non-value-added activities
  - Target and kaizen costing

- Environmental costs
- Quality:
  - Prevention activities
  - Appraisal activities
  - Production activities
  - Postsales activities
- Constrained resources

LO5 Explain GPK and RCA

GRENZPLANKOSTENRECHNUNG (GPK)

- Cost centres
  - Smaller than a department
  - Performs single repetitive activity
  - Responsibility of one manager
- Output measure: Usually volume of time
- Estimated volume: Practical or budgeted capacity
- Focus on marginal costs for short-term decisions

RESOURCE CONSUMPTION ACCOUNTING (RCA)

- Resource cost pools
  - Separate resources in separate pools
- Output measure: Usually volume of time
- Estimated volume: Theoretical capacity
- Focus on short-, mid-, and long-term decisions

COMPREHENSIVE ACCOUNTING SYSTEMS

COST POOL COST FUNCTION

- Use for budgeting and planning
- Monitor and analyze variances
- Update at least annually

RCA FIXED AND PROPORTIONAL COST RATES

Attributable fixed resource costs ÷ theoretical capacity
Attributable proportional resource costs ÷ budgeted capacity

IDLE/EXCESS CAPACITY

- Planned
- Unplanned

LO6 Describe how ABC, GPK, and RCA affect managers' incentives and decisions

KEY ISSUES

- Increasing relevance of cost information for short-, mid-, and long-term decisions
- Reducing arbitrariness in cost measurement
- Optimizing use of constrained resources
- Increasing manager awareness of cause-and-effect relationships
- Identifying non-value-added activities

- Motivating cost reduction
- Identifying and reducing cost of idle/excess capacity
- Balancing costs and benefits of complex costing systems

STRENGTHS AND WEAKNESSES OF EACH METHOD

LO3 **7-1** solution to self-study problem

A.

Resource or Activity	Wood Frames		Metal Frames	
Direct materials		$ 600,000		$200,000
Direct labour	6,000 × $25	150,000	3,000 × $25	75,000
Material handling	100,000 × $0.50	50,000	10,000 × $0.50	5,000
Cutting	5,000 × $30	150,000	500 × $30	15,000
Assembly	6,000 × $20	120,000	3,000 × $20	60,000
Wood staining	5,000 × $22	110,000	0 × $22	0
Total		$1,180,000		$355,000
Per unit	$1,180,000 ÷ 5,000 = $236 per unit		$355,000 ÷ 1,000 = $355 per unit	

B. **Product cost per unit, including manufacturing and nonmanufacturing costs:**

Wood frame = $236 + $10 + $50 = $296

Metal frame = $355 + $15 + $80 = $450

LO2, LO3 **7-2** solution to self-study problem

A. First, consider the activity hierarchy. Some costs can be allocated to the organization, such as rent, insurance, and licences. Greeting and helping children with coats may be considered part of the organization-sustaining costs, or they may be viewed as a separate activity cost pool. This reasoning is also true for interacting with parents. However, time greeting and interacting with parents varies on a daily basis but is not necessarily dependent on the number of children or number of classes. Therefore, these activities will most likely be considered part of the facility-sustaining costs.

No product-sustaining costs are evident because the organization has only one product.

In this organization, we can consider each class a batch when the children are all involved in a similar activity. Resting and free play could be combined into a single batch-level cost pool, because no supplies are used in these activities, and fewer teachers are interacting with the children. Learning, art, and music activities could be combined as a second batch-level cost pool, because they require similar numbers of teachers and supplies.

Snacks and meals can be considered a unit-level cost pool that varies with number of children. For this cost pool, flexible and committed costs could be tracked separately. Parent conferences could also be a unit-level cost pool because gathering information about each child and meeting with each child's parents would require about the same amount of time per child.

Notice that the choices of activities are somewhat arbitrary. As an alternative to the preceding set of activities, a separate pool could be established for each activity described in the problem.

B. The cost driver for resting and play could be measured in time or in days if the same times are used each day. Teacher time might be used as a cost driver for learning activities because most of the teachers are involved in these activities. Number of meals served or number of children could drive the costs of snacks and meals. Number of children would be a likely cost driver for conferencing with parents.

C. We discuss only two possible types of measurement error in this solution; there are many other possible answers. Measurement error might occur if some of the teachers use unpaid time to prepare activities. These potential costs are not measured. The willingness to spend extra time on preparation varies among teachers. If a new teacher is hired who does not want to spend unpaid time, then labour costs could increase, or the quality of the program could decrease. Another type of measurement error occurs if different groups of children require different levels of monitoring for play time and nap time. For groups that require more time, labour costs could be understated if teachers require more preparation time, or the quality of the program could suffer if no more time is spent in preparation.

D. Because this organization relies heavily on labour, the best predictor for expansion costs is to determine the desired ratio of children to teachers. Facility-sustaining cost changes also need to be predicted. Meal and snack costs probably contain both flexible and committed components, taking into consideration the food service worker who is employed. The cost of raw materials, such as art supplies, would need to be separated from the activity cost pool to predict costs for more children.

QUESTIONS

7.1 Mannon Company's accountant exclaimed, "Our cost accounting system allocates overhead based on direct labour hours, but our overhead costs appear to be more related to setup activities than to the use of direct labour. It seems as though our costing system allocates too much cost to large batches of product and not enough cost to small batches." Explain what she means.

7.2 Describe the six ABC cost hierarchies.

7.3 The results from allocations using ABC are usually different from the results using traditional cost systems. Explain why these differences arise.

7.4 Does increasing the number of cost pools always increase the accuracy of allocations under an ABC system? Explain your answer.

7.5 Is an ABC system appropriate for every industry and every type or organization? Explain your answer.

7.6 Should ABC be used in service industries? Why or why not?

7.7 Does measurement error increase or decrease when ABC systems are implemented? Explain your answer.

7.8 List several costs and several benefits of implementing an ABC system.

7.9 Suppose that you are part of a student consulting team working for your university. You need to analyze accounting department activities and set up cost pools for these activities. Explain how you would identify the activities and pools.

7.10 Is ABC appropriate for an organization that sells a wide range of customized products manufactured using flexible manufacturing systems? Why or why not?

7.11 Explain how traditional and ABC cost systems differ.

7.12 Explain the difference between activity-based costing and activity-based management.

7.13 Why might ABC and ABM be useful in reducing environmental costs?

7.14 In your own words, describe the four types of quality-related activities.

7.15 List the similarities and differences among ABC, GPK, and RCA.

MULTIPLE-CHOICE QUESTIONS

7.16 Which of the following statements best describes the objective of kaizen costing?
a. To accumulate costs that are associated with a short-term or long-term project.
b. To determine all costs related to the quality of a product.
c. To reduce costs and improve quality through continuous improvement.
d. To simplify cost accounting in a just-in-time environment.

7.17 Which of the following statements best describes activity-based management?
a. ABM is an approach developed in response to the competitive pressures of today's global market.
b. ABM does not use activity-based costing to improve a business.
c. ABM is designed to set the goals and objectives of an organization.
d. ABM focuses on functional areas and products.

Use the following information to answer questions 7.18 to 7.20. Viva Electronics produces and sells two products, VE1 and VE2. Viva incurred $168,000 overhead costs in a single cost pool. Viva allocates the overhead cost to each product based on the machine hours. The cost accountant gathered the following additional information about the overhead costs:

	Cost	Cost Driver
Machine-related costs	$62,000	Machine hours per unit
Supervision and scheduling costs	48,000	Scheduling hours
Engineering costs	32,000	Engineering hours
Inspection and testing costs	26,000	Inspection and testing hours
Total costs	$168,000	

	VE1	VE2
Units produced	1,000	1,500
Machine hours per unit	2	4
Scheduling hours	140	180
Engineering hours	240	260
Inspection and testing hours	320	200

7.18 Which of the following statements is correct?
a. Machine-related costs are batch-level activities.
b. Engineering costs are unit-level activities.
c. Inspection and testing costs are organization-sustaining activities.
d. Supervision and scheduling costs are facility-sustaining activities.

7.19 What is the overhead cost per unit using activity-based costing?

	VE1	VE2
a.	$42.00	$84.00
b.	$67.86	$66.76
c.	$77.00	$61.00
d.	$84.00	$56.00

7.20 What is the overhead cost per unit using traditional costing?

	VE1	VE2
a.	$42.00	$84.00
b.	$67.20	$66.20
c.	$73.50	$63.00
d.	$80.64	$58.24

EXERCISES

7.21 **Mapping Costs to the Cost Hierarchy** Each of the following is a cost incurred by Fairgood & Hernandez, a small
LO2 CA firm.

REQUIRED Identify whether each of the following costs most likely relates to a(n) (1) organization-sustaining activity, (2) facility-sustaining activity, (3) customer-sustaining activity, (4) product-sustaining activity, (5) batch-level activity, or (6) unit-level activity. For each item, explain your choice.
___ A. Receptionist salary
___ B. Financial forecasting software
___ C. Photocopy machine rental
___ D. Janitorial service
___ E. Audit manager salary
___ F. Long-distance telephone charges
___ G. Meal costs for entertaining clients
___ H. Costs of annual employee golf party
___ I. Office supplies, such as paperclips and tablets of paper
___ J. Annual subscription for income tax regulations

7.22 **Identifying Costs Using the ABC Cost Hierarchies** Steam Whistle Brewing is a successful brewery engaged
LO2, LO3 in the development and production of specialty microbrews. It uses an activity-based costing system. During the past year, it has incurred $1,250,000 of product development costs; $850,000 of materials handling costs; $2,500,000 of production line labour costs; $700,000 for production setup costs; $500,000 in power costs for cooling beer and running equipment; and $1,500,000 for manufacturing facility management.

REQUIRED In an ABC cost hierarchy, calculate the total cost that would be classified as
    A. Facility sustaining
    B. Product sustaining
    C. Batch level
    D. Unit level

7.23 ABC Cost Hierarchy In ABC systems, activities are often separated into a hierarchy of six categories.

LO 2

REQUIRED In your own words, define and give examples of the following types of activities and costs in an ABC system for an international car rental company such as Hertz or Enterprise:
    A. Unit-level activities and costs
    B. Batch-level activities and costs
    C. Product-sustaining activities and costs
    D. Customer-sustaining activities and costs
    E. Facility-sustaining activities and costs
    F. Organization-sustaining activities and costs

7.24 Cost Pools and Cost Drivers Following are lists of potential cost pools and cost drivers:

LO 3

Cost Pool	Cost Driver
_____ Machining	A. Number of employees
_____ Purchasing activities	B. Number of parts per unit
_____ Inspection	C. Kilograms of laundry processed
_____ Assembly	D. Number of invoices
_____ Payroll	E. Number of batches
_____ A special quick-freezing process for food	F. Number of machine hours
_____ Laundry in a hospital	G. Number of units

REQUIRED Match each cost driver to the most appropriate cost pool. Use each cost driver only once. Explain your choices.

7.25 Traditional Versus ABC Costing Kalder Products manufactures two component parts: AJ40 and AJ60. AJ40 components are being introduced currently, and AJ60 parts have been in production for several years. For the upcoming period, 1,000 units of each product are planned for manufacturing. Assume that the only relevant overhead cost is for engineering change orders (any requested changes in product design or the manufacturing process). AJ40 components are expected to require four change orders and AJ60 only two. Each AJ40 requires 1 machine hour, and each AJ60 requires 1.5 machine hours. The cost of a change order is $300.

LO 1, LO 3

REQUIRED **A.** Estimate the cost of engineering change orders for AJ40 and AJ60 components if Kalder uses a traditional costing method and machine hours as the allocation base.
    B. Now suppose that Kalder uses an ABC system and allocates the cost of change orders by using as cost driver the number of change orders. Estimate the cost for change orders for each unit of AJ40 and AJ60.
    C. Calculate the difference in overhead allocated to each product. This figure represents an amount by which one product cross-subsidizes the other product. Explain what that means.

7.26 ABC Cost Hierarchy, Traditional Versus ABC Costing Yonex Company produces two products: MB-R and MB-X. Currently, Yonex allocates overhead based on direct labour hours. Overhead is estimated at $400,000. The cost accountant realizes that there are some differences in how resources are being used in producing these two components and is considering the use of ABC to allocate overhead. She determines that overhead is caused by testing and inspections, $120,000; machine setup, $80,000; machine stamping, $160,000; and plant maintenance, $40,000. Yonex estimates the following activities related to the overhead costs:

LO 1, LO 2, LO 3

Activity	Cost Driver	MB-R	MB-X
Testing and inspections	Number of testing and inspections	400	400
Machine setup	Number of setups	120	80
Machine stamping	Number of machine hours	25,000	15,000
Plant maintenance	Direct labour hours	1,500	2,500

REQUIRED   **A.** Use ABC cost hierarchy to classify each activity.
B. Compute the amount of overhead assigned to each product using the traditional (i.e., direct labour hours) costing method.
C. Compute the amount of overhead assigned to each product using ABC.
D. Which product is overcosted using the traditional costing method? What insights do ABC costing provide?

7.27 Traditional Versus ABC Costing CompuTrain Learning Centre delivers two services, IT training and Office
L01, L03 training, in the same location. Last month, the centre experienced the following costs and results:

	IT Training	Office Training	Total
Direct materials (books & courseware)	$ 9,000	$ 6,000	$ 15,000
Direct labour (instructors)	15,000	9,000	24,000
Overhead (300% of labour)	45,000	27,000	72,000
Total cost	$69,000	$42,000	$111,000
Number of students registered	120	280	
Average cost per student	$ 575	$ 150	

The IT training manager felt that his line of business was overcharged due to the overhead allocation based on the direct labour cost. He approached the cost accounting department for help in understanding activity-based costing. His specific request was that ABC be applied to see whether the average cost per student had significantly changed. The following additional information is extracted from the accounting records for the month:

- The overhead cost for registration was $10,000. The cost driver is the number of students registered.
- The overhead cost for computer depreciation was $36,000. The cost driver is hours of use. The computers were used 1,400 hours for IT training and 1,000 hours for office training.
- The overhead cost for rent was $26,000. The cost driver for this cost is classroom utilization. Sixteen classrooms were for IT training and 10 classrooms were for office training.

REQUIRED   **A.** Assign the overhead cost to each type of training using ABC.
B. Determine the average cost per student for the two types of training using direct materials, direct labour, and overhead allocated under ABC.
C. Compare and explain the average cost per student under ABC to the average cost per student found in the data section of this problem.

7.28 ABC Costing, ABM Applewood Electronics manufactures two large-screen, high-definition television (HDTV)
L01, L03, models—the Monarch, which has been produced since 2010 and sells for $900, and the Regal, a model
L04 introduced in early 2012 that sells for $1,140. Applewood's CEO, Harry Hazelwood, suggested that
the company concentrate its marketing resources on the Regal model and begin to phase out the
Monarch model.

Applewood currently uses a traditional costing system. The following cost information has been used as a basis for pricing decisions over the past year:

Per-Unit Data	Monarch	Regal
Direct materials	$208	$584
Direct labour hours	1.5	3.5
Machine hours	8.0	4.0
Units produced	22,000	4,000

The direct labour cost is $12 per hour, and the machine usage cost is $18 per hour. Manufacturing overhead costs were estimated at $4,800,000 and were allocated on the basis of machine hours.

Martin Alecks, the new company controller, suggested that an activity-based costing analysis first be run to get a better picture of the true manufacturing cost. The following data were collected:

Activity Centre	Cost Driver	Traceable Costs
Soldering	Number of solder joints	$ 942,000
Shipments	Number of shipments	860,000
Quality control	Number of inspections	1,240,000
Purchase orders	Number of orders	950,400
Machining	Machine hours	57,600
Machine setups	Number of setups	750,000
Total traceable costs		$4,800,000

Number of Events

Activity	Monarch	Regal	Total
Soldering	1,185,000	385,000	1,570,000
Shipments	16,200	3,800	20,000
Quality control	56,200	21,300	77,500
Purchase orders	80,100	109,980	190,080
Machining	176,000	16,000	192,000
Machine setups	16,000	14,000	30,000

Selling, general, and administrative expenses per unit sold are $265.00 for Monarch and $244.60 for Regal.

REQUIRED   **A.** Calculate the manufacturing cost per unit for Monarch and Regal under
   1. A traditional costing system
   2. An ABC system
B. Explain the differences in manufacturing cost per unit calculated in Part A.
C. Calculate the operating profit per unit for Monarch and Regal under
   1. A traditional costing system
   2. An ABC system
D. Should Applewood concentrate its marketing efforts on Monarch or on Regal? Explain how the use of ABC affects your recommendation.

7.29 ABC Costing, ABM Palmer Company uses an activity-based costing system. It has the following manufacturing
LO3, LO4 activity areas, related drivers used as allocation bases, and cost allocation rates:

Activity	Cost Driver	Cost Allocation Rate
Machine setup	Number of setups	$50.00
Material handling	Number of parts	0.50
Machining	Machine hours	26.00
Assembly	Direct labour hours	22.00
Inspection	Number of finished units	12.00

During the month, 100 units were produced, requiring two setups. Each unit consisted of 19 parts and used 1.5 direct labour hours and 1.25 machine hours. Direct materials cost $100 per finished unit. All other manufacturing costs are classified as conversion costs. ABC costs for research and marketing costs are $140. All other nonmanufacturing ABC costs are $320 per unit.

REQUIRED   **A.** Calculate the manufacturing cost per unit for the period.
B. Calculate the total cost (manufacturing and nonmanufacturing costs) per unit for the period.
C. Suppose Palmer Company's managers want to implement target costing. Under target costing, the managers need to determine the amount of cost savings that must be achieved to earn a desired level of profit. If they must set a competitive price of $650 and require a 10% profit based on the total cost calculated in Part B, how much cost savings must they generate?

7.30 ABC in Job Costing, ABM, Non-Value-Added Activities Kestral Manufacturing has identified the following overhead costs and cost drivers for the current period. Kestral produces customized products that move through several different processes. Materials and intermediate products are moved among several different work stations. Custom features are designed by engineers.

Activity	Cost Driver	Estimated Cost	Estimated Activity Level
Machine setup	Number of setups	$ 40,000	400
Material handling	Number of times materials are moved	160,000	16,000
Product design	Design hours	100,000	2,000
Inspection	Number of inspections	260,000	13,000
Total cost		$560,000	

Information for three of the jobs completed during the period follows:

	Job 42	Job 43	Job 44
Direct materials	$10,000	$24,000	$16,000
Direct labour	$ 4,000	$ 4,000	$ 8,000
Units completed	200	100	400
Number of setups	2	4	8
Number of materials moves	60	20	100
Number of inspections	40	20	60
Number of design hours	20	100	20

REQUIRED
A. If the company uses ABC, how much overhead cost should be assigned to Job 42?
B. If the company uses ABC, calculate the cost per unit for Job 43.
C. Kestral would like to reduce the cost of its overhead activities. Describe non-value-added activities and explain why reducing these specific activities would also reduce cost.

7.31 Design ABC System, Per-Unit ABC Costs, Uncertainties Suppose that Elite Daycare provides two different services: full-time childcare for preschoolers, and after-school care for older children. The director would like to estimate an annual cost per child in each of the daycare programs, ignoring any facility-sustaining costs. She is considering expanding the services and wants to know whether full-time or after-school care is more profitable.

The following activities and annual costs apply to the daycare centre. Salaries and wages are $100,000. Full-time children arrive between 8:00 and 9:00 a.m. Older children arrive about 3:00 p.m. All the children are gone by 6:00 p.m. Employees estimate that they spend about 20% of their time on meal-related activities, 20% supervising naps or recreation, 10% in greeting children or sending them home, and the rest of the time presenting educational experiences to the children. Meals and snacks cost about $20,000. Preschoolers receive two snacks and one meal per day, and the older children receive one snack per day. On average, snacks and meals do not differ in cost. Supplies cost $10,000 for the full-time childcare program and $8,000 for the after-school program.

Currently, 30 children participate in full-time care and 10 children in after-school care. Because Elite Daycare maintains a waiting list for openings in its programs, the number of children in each program remains steady.

REQUIRED
A. Identify a cost object and then choose a set of activities and cost drivers for Elite Daycare's ABC system. Explain your choices.
B. Using the activities you chose in Part A, estimate the annual cost per child in each program.
C. Do uncertainties exist about the proportion of salaries and wages that should be allocated to full-time care versus after-school care? Why or why not?

7.32 ABM, Customer Profitability Suppose that you are asked for suggestions about increasing profitability for a customer that purchases low-margin products and requires costly services.

L04

REQUIRED
A. In your own words, define activity-based management (ABM).
B. In your own words, describe high-cost and low-cost customers.
C. Prepare a brief paragraph, suggesting methods to improve profitability for a high-cost customer.

7.33 Quality Costs Using ABC Versus Traditional Costing New-Rage Cosmetics uses a traditional cost accounting system to allocate quality control costs uniformly to all products at a rate of 14.5% of direct labour cost. The monthly direct labour cost for Satin Sheen makeup is $27,500. In an attempt to more equitably distribute quality control costs, New-Rage is considering activity-based costing. The following monthly data have been gathered for Satin Sheen makeup:

L01, L03, L04

Incoming material inspection:
    Cost driver—type of material
    Cost allocation rate—$11.50 per type of material
    Quantity—12 types of material
In-process inspection:
    Cost driver—number of units
    Cost allocation rate—$0.14 per unit
    Quantity—17,500 units
Product certification:
    Cost driver—per order
    Cost allocation rate—$77 per order
    Quantity—25 orders

REQUIRED
A. Calculate the amount of quality control cost assigned to each order of Satin Sheen makeup, using
  1. Activity-based costing (*Hint:* Total all the ABC costs for one month and divide by the number of orders.)
  2. Traditional cost accounting
B. Explain the difference in quality control costs assigned under the two methods.

7.34 Categorizing Quality Activities Following is a list of quality-related activities:

L04

Type	Quality Activity
_____	1. Inspection of units when they are 100% complete to remove defective units
_____	2. Design of a process with as few parts as possible to reduce the chance of defects
_____	3. Warranty costs for defective products returned to the factory for rework
_____	4. Reworking of spoiled units before they leave the factory
_____	5. Costs to defend the company against lawsuits for damages caused by defective products
_____	6. Tracking number of defects for each manufacturing team and posting of daily defect rates on a plant-wide bulletin board
_____	7. Redesign of a manufacturing process to reduce the rate of defects

REQUIRED   Mark each activity according to whether it pertains to the internal costs of prevention (P), appraisal (A), production (PR), or postsales (PS) costs.

7.35 GPK Multi-Level Income Statement Last year, the Krishnan Manufacturing Plant, part of Johnson's Global Corporation, earned revenues of $800,000. Direct materials and direct labour were $200,000, product-line fixed costs were $150,000, and company-level fixed costs were $200,000. Krishnan's accountant aggregates the idle capacity costs, and finds they were $75,000.

L05

REQUIRED   Develop a multi-level income statement using a GPK approach.

7.36 GPK, RCA, Cost Rates Budgeted information for this year's operations of the X-ray resource cost pool at Diagnostic
L05 Services follows.

Theoretical capacity	8,760 X-ray hours
Practical capacity	5,600 X-ray hours
Budgeted capacity	5,000 X-ray hours
Costs traced directly:	
X-ray supplies cost function	$3,000 + $2.10 per X-ray hour
Electricity at $0.10	6,000 kWh + 4 kWh per hour of
per kilowatt hour (kWh)	X-ray equipment use
X-ray equipment depreciation	$93,100 per year
Other resource pool cost rates:	
Technician proportional cost rate	$45 per labour hour
Maintenance proportional cost rate	$20 per maintenance hour
Facilities fixed cost rate	$25 per square foot

The X-ray department uses 1,000 square feet of facility space. The technician and maintenance resource pools
have only proportional cost rates. However, the X-ray department requires some of these resources regardless of
the number of X-ray hours. Budgeted X-ray department use of these resources follows:

- X-ray technician resources: 300 technician hours + 1 technician hour per hour of X-ray equipment use
- Maintenance resources: 100 maintenance hours + 0.0424 maintenance hour per hour of X-ray equipment use

REQUIRED **A.** Calculate the fixed and proportional cost rates for the X-ray department using GPK.
B. Calculate the fixed and proportional cost rates for the X-ray department using RCA.
C. Calculate the total cost under GPK and RCA that would be assigned to patient services for a patient who
required X-rays taking half hour of time.
D. Which costing system (GPK or RCA) would assign higher cost in Part (C)? Explain why.
E. Explain why part of the X-ray technician and maintenance costs are treated as fixed in the X-ray department,
even though these resources have only a proportional cost rate.

7.37 GPK, RCA, Capacity Analysis Budget information for this year's operations of the X-ray resource cost pool at
L05 Diagnostic Services is shown in Exercise 7.36. Actual X-ray hours totalled 5,200 during the year.

REQUIRED Prepare a capacity analysis similar to the one in Exhibit 7.10, comparing the assignment of fixed X-ray
department costs using budgeted, practical, and theoretical capacities.

PROBLEMS

7.38 Setting Up an ABC System, Uncertainties Following is a list of steps that must be performed in setting up an ABC
L03, L04 system:

_____ Identify and sum the costs into activity-based cost pools.
_____ Choose a cost driver for each activity.
_____ For each ABC cost pool, allocate overhead costs to the product or service.
_____ Identify the relevant cost object.
_____ Identify the activities necessary for production or service delivery.
_____ For each ABC cost pool, calculate a cost allocation rate.

REQUIRED **A.** Number the steps from 1 through 6 to indicate the sequence in which they are performed.
B. For each step, explain whether uncertainties are likely.
C. Choose the step that you think would require the greatest use of judgment (i.e., would include the most
uncertainties). Explain your choice.

7.39 ABC Cost Hierarchy, Uncertainties In ABC systems, activities are often separated into a hierarchy of categories.

LO2, LO4

REQUIRED **A.** In your own words, explain what is meant by a cost hierarchy in ABC.

B. Explain why uncertainty is possible in classifying costs within the cost hierarchy.

C. Explain how categorizing costs into a hierarchy helps accountants determine how costs behave.

7.40 Cumulative Problem (Chapter 5): ABC Versus Traditional Job Costing, Cost Driver Uncertainties, Advantages and Disadvantages Vines Corporation produces custom machine parts on a job order basis. The company has two direct product cost categories: direct materials and direct labour. In the past, *indirect manufacturing costs* were allocated to products using a single indirect cost pool, allocated based on direct labour hours. The indirect cost rate was $115 per direct labour hour.

LO1, LO3, LO4

The managers of Vines Corporation decided to switch from a manual system to software programs that release materials and that signal machines when to begin working. Simultaneously, the company adopted an activity-based costing system. The manufacturing process has been organized into six activities, each with its own supervisor who is responsible for controlling costs. The following list indicates the activities, cost drivers, and cost allocation rates:

Activity	Cost Driver	Cost per Unit of Cost Driver
Material handling	Number of parts	$ 0.40
Milling	Machine hours	20.00
Grinding	Number of parts	0.80
Assembly	Hours spent in assembly	5.00
Inspection	Number of units produced	25.00
Shipping	Number of orders shipped	1,500.00

The company's information system automatically collects the necessary data for these six activity areas. The data for two recent jobs follow:

	Job Order 410	Job Order 411
Direct materials cost	$9,700	$59,900
Direct labour cost	$ 750	$11,250
Number of direct labour hours	25	375
Number of parts	500	2,000
Number of machine hours	150	1,050
Number of job orders shipped	1	1
Number of units	10	200
Number of hours in assembly	2	30

REQUIRED **A.** Suppose the company had not adopted an ABC system. Compute the manufacturing cost per unit for job orders 410 and 411 under the old, traditional costing system.

B. Under the new ABC system, compute the manufacturing cost per unit for job orders 410 and 411.

C. Compare the costs per unit for job orders 410 and 411 as computed. Explain why the cost per unit under the traditional costing system is different from the cost per unit under the ABC system.

D. Explain why uncertainties may arise about the choice of cost drivers for each activity.

E. Identify and explain to Vines Corporation's managers the possible advantages and disadvantages of adopting the ABC system.

7.41 Cumulative Problem (Chapter 6): ABC Versus Traditional Process Costing, ABM Kim Mills produces three different types of fabric, using two departments. In department 1, machines weave the cloth. In department 2, the cloth is dyed a variety of colours. Information for the combined use of resources in both departments for the three types of fabric follows:

LO1, LO3, LO4

Bolts of cloth are 20 metres each. All fabric is inspected during production. Robotic equipment inspects the fabric for obvious flaws as the bolts are wound up. Each bolt spends about 5 minutes in the inspection process.

	Denim	Lightweight Cotton	Heavyweight Cotton	Total
Monthly production in units (bolts of fabric)	1,000 bolts	4,000 bolts	2,000 bolts	7,000 bolts
Direct materials costs	$8,000	$24,000	$20,000	$52,000
Direct labour costs	$ 660	$ 1,320	$ 920	$ 2,900
Direct labour hours	33 hours	66 hours	46 hours	145 hours
Machine hours	500 hours	1,333.3 hours	1,500 hours	3,333.3 hours
Number of setups for dye	10 setups	30 setups	20 setups	60 setups
Colour changes				
Inspection time	83.3 hours	333.3 hours	166.6 hours	583.2 hours

Combined overhead costs for the two departments follow:

Cost to operate and maintain machines	$40,000
Setup costs	11,000
Inspection costs	6,996
Total	$57,996

Previously, Kim Mills used a process costing system that allocated direct materials to each product separately but allocated direct labour and conversion costs as if they were incurred equally across the units produced. Under the process costing system, the overhead cost for department 1 is $19,332, and for department 2 it is $38,664. Direct labour hours and costs in department 1 are 55 hours at $1,100, and the rest are in department 2. Direct materials for department 1 are $6,000 for denim, $16,000 for lightweight cotton, and $15,000 for heavyweight cotton. The remaining direct materials are added in department 2. No beginning or ending inventory or abnormal spoilage is recorded for Kim Mills this period.

REQUIRED **A.** Set up a spreadsheet to perform the following calculations. Use a data input section and cell referencing.
  1. Use traditional process costing to allocate the direct materials and conversion costs per department to total bolts produced. Develop a cost per bolt for each type of fabric. (*Hint:* You will need to first calculate the equivalent cost per bolt for conversion costs for each department.)
  2. Using activity-based costing, develop a cost per bolt.
B. Compare the process costing and ABC results. Identify the products with overstated costs and those with understated costs. Explain why the costs are misstated under traditional process costing.
C. How could managers use the ABC information to improve operations?

7.42 **ABC Costs, Uncertainties, ABM, Non-Value-Added Activities** The Pond Kit Company manufactures kits for fish ponds. The managers recently set up an ABC system to identify and reduce non-value-added activities. The ABC system includes the following cost pools, cost drivers, and estimated costs for manufacturing activities:

LO3, LO4

Activity	Cost Driver	Cost Allocation Rate
Material handling	Number of parts	$1.00 per part
Forming	Moulding hours	40.00 per hour
Moulding setup	Number of batches	50.00 per batch
Packing and shipping	Weight	1.30 per kg
Inspection	Finished kits	10.00 per kit
Direct labour	Finished kits	20.00 per kit
Direct materials	Finished kits	100.00 per kit

The company manufactures 10 kits per batch. Each kit requires 20 parts and two hours in moulding, and each weighs 30 kg.

REQUIRED **A.** Calculate the total ABC manufacturing cost per batch.

B. Calculate the total ABC cost per finished kit.

C. Suppose that Pond Kit's managers also want to allocate marketing costs and customer service to each product. Total marketing costs for the period were $15,000, and customer service costs were $25,000. The number of batches produced was 1,000. Calculate the total ABC cost per unit and cost per kit, including the costs of marketing and customer services.

D. Are the activities listed likely to be the only possible set of activities for Pond Kit Company? Why or why not?

E. Describe how the managers and accountants of Pond Kit Company might use this new ABC system to identify non-value-added activities.

7.43 **Uncertainties, Actual Versus Estimated Costs, Practical Capacity** Data Processors performs credit card services for banks. The company uses an ABC system. The following information applies to the past year:

LO2, LO3, LO4

Activity	Estimated Cost	Actual Cost	Cost Driver
Processing transactions	$2,000,000	$2,200,000	Number of transactions
Issuing monthly statements	1,000,000	1,300,000	Number of statements
Issuing new credit cards	500,000	400,000	Number of new credit cards
Resolving billing disputes	90,000	100,000	Number of disputes
Total	$3,590,000	$4,000,000	

Cost Driver	Estimated Activity Level	Actual Activity Level
Number of transactions	5,000,000	5,800,000
Number of statements	250,000	270,000
Number of new credit cards	100,000	110,000
Number of disputes	3,000	3,500

REQUIRED **A.** Are the activities listed likely to be the only possible set of activities for the ABC system? Why or why not?

B. Using estimated values for costs and activity, calculate an ABC allocation rate for each activity.

C. Explain why actual costs and activity levels are likely to be different from estimated amounts.

D. Is practical capacity likely to be higher or lower than the estimated activity levels? Explain.

7.44 **Cumulative Problem (Chapter 4): ABC, ABM, Customer Profitability, Keep or Drop** The sales manager of Flying Carpets, a carpet manufacturer and wholesaler, is analyzing the profitability of two of the company's customers. One customer, a boutique store, purchases small orders for individual clients and often wants a custom-run carpet. The other customer, a discount retailer, buys large lots of standard carpets. The sales manager is concerned that providing services for the boutique store is costing more than the contribution margin from its business. The accountant has gathered the following relevant information for the past year. All employees are guaranteed a 40-hour work week. Sales representatives are paid $20 per hour, and the production line supervisor is paid $18 per hour. Employee benefits and human resource services amount to approximately 50% of hourly wages. The discount retailer picks up large lots of carpets four times a year. Deliveries to customers of the boutique store must be made as the carpets are completed.

LO3, LO4

	Boutique Store	Discount Retailer
Revenues	$135,000	$850,000
Direct costs (DM and DL)	$80,000	$400,000
Sales representatives	60 hours	24 hours
Production line supervisor	90 hours	36 hours
Delivery costs	$20,000	$8,000

REQUIRED **A.** Calculate the profitability for each customer.

B. Flying Carpets would like to retain the boutique store as a customer because its clients' homes are often featured in the local lifestyle magazine and the publicity is free advertisement. What suggestions can you make for negotiations with the customer about service costs?

C. If Flying Carpets can replace either customer with other business, what is your recommendation? Explain.

7.45 Cumulative Problem (Chapter 4): ABC, RCA, Cost Rates, Capacity Analysis, Special Order Flightways, a flight
training academy, owns several flight simulators. The flight simulators usually have a significant amount of idle
time because customers do not want to use them in the middle of the night. However, a competitor has
contacted the sales manager about a special arrangement to use Flightways' B7X7 flight simulator during idle
times over the next month. The competitor's B7X7 simulator experienced a malfunction, and repairs cannot
be completed until new parts arrive. The competitor is offering to pay $400 per hour for 250 hours during the
next month.

LO3, LO4, LO5, LO6

Budget information for this year's operations of the B7X7 flight simulator follows.

Theoretical capacity	8,760 hours
Budgeted capacity	3,400 hours
Costs traced directly:	
Simulator supplies cost function	$1,000 + $4.50 per simulator hour
Electricity at $0.10 per kilowatt hour (kWh)	6,000 kWh + 165 kWh per hour of simulator use
Simulator depreciation	$1,505,160 per year
Other resource pool cost rates:	
Maintenance variable cost rate	$70 per maintenance hour
Facilities fixed cost rate	$15 per square foot
Usage of resources from other cost pools:	

Facility resources: 2,000 square feet
Maintenance resources: 50 maintenance hours regardless of the volume of simulator use + 0.06
maintenance hours per hour of simulator use

REQUIRED
A. Calculate the ABC-estimated allocated rate per hour of simulator use. (*Hint*: Assume that all of the costs listed
above would be included in the ABC cost pool, and use budgeted capacity.)
B. Based on your ABC calculations in Part A, should the sales manager accept the competitor's offer? Explain and
identify your assumptions about relevant costs.
C. Calculate the RCA fixed and proportional cost rates per hour of simulator use.
D. Based on your RCA calculations in Part C, should the sales manager accept the competitor's offer? Explain and
identify your assumptions about relevant costs.
E. Which costing method provides better information for making this decision? Explain.
F. Identify several qualitative factors that might affect this decision.
G. Assume it is late during the fiscal year, and actual total hours are estimated to be 3,300 if the competitor's
offer is not accepted. Prepare a capacity analysis under the RCA costing system comparing the following two
options. (*Hint*: Prepare a schedule with a column for each option.)
   1. The competitor's offer is not accepted.
   2. The competitor's offer is accepted.

7.46 Traditional Costing versus ABC Costing, ABM Azure Ltd., manufactures boat engines and propellers. Azure has
been accumulating manufacturing overhead costs into one cost pool, and charged $120 overhead cost to each
unit of product. Azure made 4,800 units of engines and 3,200 units of propellers last year. The cost accountant
believes that there are significant differences in how each product line uses resources, and is considering
using the ABC costing method to allocate the manufacturing overhead costs. She analyzes the manufacturing
overhead costs and gathers the following information:

LO1, LO3, LO4

Activity Costs	Cost Driver
25% of the overhead costs is for machine amortization	Number of units
45% of the overhead costs is for material handling	Number of times material moves
30% of the overhead costs is for testing	Number of tests

The Engine Department has materials moved 200 times and 120 tests done, while the Propeller Department has
materials moved 400 times and 180 tests done.

REQUIRED **A.** What are the manufacturing overhead costs allocated to the Engine Department and the Propeller Department?

B. What are the overhead rates for machine amortization, material handling, and testing?

C. Based on each of the overhead rates calculated in (B), what are the total overhead costs allocated to the Engine Department and the Propeller Department?

D. Which department has over-allocated the overhead costs using the traditional method? Explain why this is the case.

7.47 Cost Hierarchy, ABC Costing, ABM Sonica Ltd., manufactures medical ultrasound products. The ultrasound

products require high precision and rigorous testing before they are sold. The annual overhead cost for quality control is $650,000, and all units produced have to be tested for quality control. Sonica makes 4 product lines. The quality control is set up to test 200 batches and 5,000 units a year.

REQUIRED **A.** What is the overhead rate based on the product-level allocation base? How much of the overhead cost for quality control should be allocated to Product A, if 1,350 units are produced in 45 batches, using the product level as the allocation base?

B. What is the overhead rate based on the batch-level allocation base? How much of the overhead cost for quality control should be allocated to Product A, if 1,350 units are produced in 45 batches, using the batch level as the allocation base?

C. What is the overhead rate based on the unit-level allocation base? How much of the overhead cost for quality control should be allocated to Product A, if 1,350 units are produced in 45 batches, using the unit level as the allocation base?

D. If you were the manager for Product A, which level of allocation base would you prefer?

E. If you were the cost accountant for Sonica, which level of allocation base would you recommend that Sonica uses? Explain.

7.48 Traditional Costing, Cost Hierarchy Classification, ABC Costing, ABM Weston Ltd. manufactures two models of

automotive parts—LD and XD. Weston has been using the normal costing based on machine hours to allocate manufacturing overhead. Last year, the manufacturing overhead was $960,000, and machine hours used were 40,000 hours. Forty-five percent of the machine hours were used for LD. Weston produced 12,000 units of LD, and 8,000 units of XD.

Weston is concerned that their costs may be too high for XD, as XD is priced higher than their main competitor, and the sales volume is significantly lower than LD. The sales manager is in discussions with the production manager and the cost accountant to see if there is another way to cost the manufacturing overhead. The cost accountant suggests using ABC costing, and gathers the following information from the production manager:

	Activity Cost	Cost Driver	LD	XD
Product design	$ 210,000	number of designs	125	175
Equipment setup	180,000	number of setups	500	700
Machine process	500,000	number of units	12,000	8,000
Inspection & testing	70,000	number of inspections	220	180
	$ 960,000			

REQUIRED **A.** Identify the cost hierarchy level for each activity.

B. What is the overhead rate based on the machine hours? How much total overhead cost was allocated to LD and XD? What is the unit overhead cost for LD and XD?

C. What is the overhead rate for each activity, using ABC costing? How much total overhead cost was allocated to LD and XD? What is the unit overhead cost for LD and XD?

D. Comparing the findings from (B) and (C), what should Weston do to address the costing issue of XD? Provide explanations to support your recommendations.

7.49 Traditional Costing, Cost Hierarchy Classification, ABC Costing, ABM Appleby Community Centre (ACC) offers

various courses for residents in the area. One of the biggest overhead costs is the administration cost, which includes registration, coordinating with the instructors and students, and room bookings. ACC runs the courses three terms a year, using 30 classrooms each term, and offers 1,750 course sections. ACC groups the courses into three departments—Arts & Design, Languages, and Technology—with a total enrolment of 3,600 students a year. The total administration costs were $126,000 last year. An accounting co-op student was hired to help AAC better understand how the resources were used to support delivering these courses and to determine whether the overhead costs could be reduced, especially the administration costs. The additional information for ACC's operation is as follows:

Department	Courses Offered	Students	Room Usage
Arts & Design	350	1,440	10%
Languages	525	900	20%
Technology	875	1,260	70%

REQUIRED **A.** Classify each of the activities as unit-level, batch level, product/service sustaining, or organization sustaining level.

Cost Driver	Cost Hierarchy Classification
Departments	
Classrooms	
Courses	
Students	

B. ACC would like determine the fee for the courses offered to see whether the fee would be able to cover the cost. The director of ACC believes that the number of students is the main cost driver for the administration cost. What is the rate that should be charge to each student? How much should each department be charged for the administration costs based on students as the cost driver?

C. After some investigation, the co-op student found that 60% of administration costs are related to the registration, 25% to coordination, and 15% to room booking. What is the overhead cost allocated for each of these activities? If the number of students is the cost driver for registration, courses for coordination, and number of rooms for room booking, what is the overhead rate for each activity? Using ABC costing, what amount should be allocated to each department?

D. Based on parts B and C, which costing method should the co-op student recommend? Some researchers say that the cost of using the ABC system may outweigh the benefit. Do you agree that the main cost driver is students, since all the activities are to support students in the learning program? Do you see any significant differences in allocating the overhead? Provide your arguments to justify your recommended costing approach.

MINI-CASES

7.50 Design ABC Cost System, Usefulness for ABM The town of Jefferson owns and operates an animal shelter that

performs three services: housing and finding homes for stray and unwanted animals, providing health care and neutering services for the animals, and training pets. One facility is dedicated to housing animals waiting to be adopted. A second facility houses veterinarian services. A third facility houses the director, his staff, and several dog trainers. This facility also has several large meeting rooms that are frequently used for classes given by the animal trainers. The trainers work with all of the animals to ensure that they are relatively easy to manage. They also provide dog obedience classes for adopting families.

Estimated annual costs for the animal shelter and its services are as follows:

Director and staff salaries	$ 60,000
Animal shelter employees' salaries	100,000
Veterinarians and technicians	150,000
Animal trainers	40,000
Food and supplies	125,000
Building-related costs	200,000

On average, 75 animals per day are housed at the facility, or about 27,375 (75 × 365) animal days in total. The number of animals housed during the year totalled 4,500. In addition, the trainers offer about 125 classes during about 30 weeks throughout the year. On average, 10 families attend each class. Last year the veterinarian clinic experienced 5,000 animal visits.

One of the director's staff members just graduated from an accounting program and would like to set up an ABC system for the shelter so that the director can better understand the cost for each of the shelter's services. He gathers the following information:

Square footage for each facility:

Animal shelter	5,000 square feet
Director and training	3,000 square feet
Veterinary clinic	2,000 square feet
Percentage of trainer time used in classes	50%
Supplies used for veterinarian services	$75,000

REQUIRED **A.** Identify cost pools and assign costs to them, considering the three cost objects of interest.
B. Determine a cost driver for each cost pool and explain your choice.
C. Calculate the allocation rates for each cost pool and cost driver. Interpret the allocation rate for each cost pool (i.e., explain what it means).
D. Suppose that the director is concerned about an increase in the number of adopted dogs returned to the shelter because of behaviour problems. When dogs are returned, the shelter incurs extra animal intake and adoption costs, in addition to extra costs for board, room, and more training for the dogs. In addition, the director is concerned that adopting families may not want another dog because of their unhappy experience. The director views this as a quality problem and wants to improve quality in adoption services and reduce costs at the same time.
  1. List the four types of quality activities presented in the chapter. What type of quality problem is the shelter experiencing? Explain your answer.
  2. Will the current ABC system help managers determine costs for their quality activities? Explain.
  3. List one new cost pool and cost driver that could be used to improve the director's ability to analyze quality.

7.51 **ABC Costs, Benefits, and Popularity** In January 2003, *CFO.com* featured an article titled "Where Are They Now? From Corporate Raiders to Earnings Management to Activity-Based Costing, We Take a Look at Some of Finance's Greatest Hits." The author, David Katz, examined eight ideas that have been big news in corporate finance and accounting practitioner journals over the past two decades. He rated these ideas using gold stars ("the idea is still peaking"), silver stars ("percolating along just fine"), and bronze stars ("the idea is gone"). Most of the ideas, including activity-based costing, were awarded silver stars.

When Robert Kaplan and other academics published their first papers explaining ABC in the late 1980s, business managers were highly interested. ABC involves identifying activities and cost drivers that should reflect a cause-and-effect relationship with cost for many of the resources used to produce goods. Kaplan and other consultants extolled the advantages of ABC for understanding product profitability. They suggested that managers did not really understand how products used resources in the manufacturing process.

By the mid-1990s, some business experts argued that ABC was being replaced with tools such as economic value-added (see Chapter 18) and the balanced scorecard (see Chapter 19). However, a large number of organizations continued to use ABC. For example, consulting firm Bain & Company found that 50% of the 708 companies it surveyed during 2002 used ABC. Bain & Company also found that companies were using multiple analytical tools; they were not relying on any single tool, such as ABC, to meet all of their needs.

"Some observers contend that ABC will come back in vogue—if the recession continues," says Katz. ABC provides information about customer profitability and could help companies develop ways to raise profits without raising prices.

Sources: D. M. Katz, "Where Are They Now?" *CFO.com*, January 5, 2003, www.cfo.com; D. M. Katz, "Activity-Based Costing (ABC)," *CFO.com*, December 31, 2002, www.cfo.com; and D. Rigby, "Management Tools Survey 2003: Usage Up as Companies Strive to Make Headway in Tough Times," *Strategy & Leadership 31*, no. 5 (2003), pp. 4–11.

REQUIRED **A.** Why might accountants believe that ABC information would be useful?
B. What uncertainties do managers face when they adopt ideas that are new and for which there is little data about effectiveness?

C. Given uncertainties about whether a new method will be effective, why might managers consider adopting it?

D. Discuss possible reasons for a method losing favour over time.

E. How might a recession affect the popularity of ABC?

7.52 **Integrating Across the Curriculum: Corporate Social Responsibility,** *Environmental accounting reports, ABC and ABM*
for environmental costs Many countries provide incentives for businesses to produce environmental accounting reports. For example, the Association of Chartered Certified Accountants (ACCA) in the United Kingdom developed the European Environmental Reporting Awards program in 1997. Currently 12 countries, including the United Kingdom, Denmark, the Netherlands, Belgium, France, and Germany, participate in this program. In Japan, the Global Environmental Forum and the National Association for the Promotion of Environmental Conservation have given Environmental Report Awards since 1997. In addition, Toyo Keizai and Green Reporting Forum have given the Green Reporting Award since 1998. These awards encourage businesses to take responsibility for environmental conditions that affect society's well-being.

Conduct research about corporate environmental disclosures. Choose one company located in Japan and a competitor located in Canada. Go to each company's website and search for information about environmental policies and procedures. Two possible companies are Toyota (www.toyota.ca) and Magna (www.magna.com).

Also conduct research to find governmental guidelines for environmental accounting. Go to the website of *Environment Canada* (www.ec.gc.ca) and search for information about environmental accounting. Now perform a similar search on the website of *Japan's Ministry of the Environment* (www.Env.go.jp/en/). Skim through the information that you find on each website. These links are also available at www.wiley.com/go/eldenburgcanada.

In its "Environmental Accounting Guidelines 2002," Japan's Ministry of the Environment identified the following environmental conservation cost categories:

Category	Content
Business area cost	Environmental conservation cost to control environmental impacts that result from key business operations within the business area
Upstream/downstream cost	Environmental conservation cost to control environmental impacts that result from key business operations upstream or downstream
Administration cost	Environmental conservation cost stemming from administrative activities
R&D cost	Environmental conservation cost stemming from research and development activities
Social activity cost	Environmental conservation cost stemming from social activities
Environmental remediation cost	Cost incurred for dealing with environmental degradation
Other cost	Other costs related to environmental conservation

REQUIRED

A. Is environmental accounting an ethical issue? Why or why not?

B. Which of the companies you researched provides the easiest-to-find and most understandable information about environmental policies and procedures? Explain.

C. Discuss a company's responsibilities for reporting environmental information to various stakeholders, including shareholders, managers, employees, other companies, government regulators, product customers, and the general public.

D. If one company provides better reporting than a competitor of its environmental behaviour, policies, and procedures, does that mean the company is more responsible than its competitor toward the environment? Why or why not?

E. What factors are likely to affect a company's willingness to publish an environmental accounting report?

F. Discuss possible reasons the governments of different countries place different degrees of emphasis on environmental accounting reports.

G. Discuss ways in which ABC systems could be used to capture information for environmental accounting reports.

H. Discuss ways in which the process of preparing and publishing an environmental accounting report is likely to help a company reduce its environmental costs.

I. Should all governments require companies to publish environmental accounting reports? What values did you use to arrive at your conclusion?

Measuring and Assigning Support Department Costs

in brief When managers and accountants consider the cost of their goods and services, they typically focus on operating costs. However, it is sometimes useful to measure and monitor the cost of all resources used to create a product or service. When all of an organization's costs are allocated, each unit's cost includes not only allocated operating costs but also allocated costs of internal support, such as accounting, purchasing, and marketing. These costs are particularly important when measuring and monitoring the cost of services provided by private and public not-for-profit organizations. They also help determine reimbursements under cost-based contracts, such as those with the Canadian government. However, sometimes costs that include support department allocations are used inappropriately in decision making. ▣

After studying this chapter, you should be able to do the following:

LO 1 Define support departments, and explain why their costs are allocated to other departments

LO 2 Explain the process that is used to allocate support department costs

LO 3 Explain how the direct method is used to allocate support costs to operating departments; calculate cost allocations using the direct method

LO 4 Explain how the step-down method is used to allocate support costs to operating departments; calculate cost allocations using the step-down method

LO 5 Explain how the reciprocal method is used to allocate support costs to operating departments; calculate cost allocations using the reciprocal method

LO 6 Explain the difference between single- and dual-rate allocations

LO 7 Identify how support cost allocations and information quality impact management decision making

Helping Canada's Universities and Colleges with Indirect Research Costs

Shutterstock

Prior to 2001, Canadian federal research grant programs did not cover indirect costs of administering and managing top-quality research activities. This situation decreased Canada's competitiveness in the academic research area, as research grants in the United States, Great Britain, and Australia all covered indirect costs. To begin to address this disadvantage, in the December 2001 budget, the federal government provided a one-time payment of $200 million to cover past indirect costs incurred by universities. The permanent Indirect Costs Program was then established in 2003 with an initial budget of $225 million.

The program was renamed the Research Support Fund and has since grown to over $342 million, and the program is accessed by more than 126 post-secondary institutions nationwide. To receive funds, an eligible institution submits a request to the program secretariat. Funding is given on a yearly basis and is calculated using a predetermined formula that is based on total federal research funding. The formula provides decreasing rates of funding as the total federal research funding increases. An institution must meet specific interim reporting deadlines, and only eligible costs are covered.

Eligible costs are classified into five categories: research facilities, research resources, management and administration of an institution's research enterprise, regulatory requirements and accreditation, and intellectual property and knowledge mobilization. The guidelines further specify the types of eligible costs by subdividing each category into subcategories and listing specific costs that are not covered. On a yearly basis, institutions must report, by category, how they spent their awarded funds. During the fiscal year 2008–2009, funds allocated to each area were facilities 36%, resources 15%, management and administration 34%, regulatory requirements and accreditation 9%, and intellectual property 6%.

In the Briefing Report to the Minister for April 1, 2008, to March 31, 2009, the Steering Committee for the then Indirect Costs program stated, "Institutions regard the Program's funding as crucial, but it covers only a portion of the actual amount of the indirect costs of research supported by the federal government. The impact of expenditures is thus hard to evaluate because it is in general diffuse and spread over several years."

SOURCE: Research Support Fund website, www.rsf-fsr.gc.ca/apply-demande/index-eng.aspx#information; "Indirect Costs Program: Briefing Report to the Minister for April 1, 2008 to March 31, 2009," http://www.indirectcosts.gc.ca/publications/Brief09_e.pdf; "Indirect Costs of Federally-funded University Research," Association of Universities and Colleges of Canada, Rev. 10-2006, http://www.aucc.ca/_pdf/english/reports/2006/indirect_costs_10_19_e.pdf; "Indirect Costs Program: About the Program," Government of Canada, http://www.indirectcosts.gc.ca/about/index_e.asp.

Support Department Cost Allocation

Overhead costs are considered necessary for universities to conduct research. However, much of a university's overhead costs would be incurred with or without a particular research project. Thus, it is possible to argue that only incremental overhead costs should be reimbursable as part of a research grant. However, the federal government's policy is to reimburse overhead costs for many different types of contracts, including university research grants, defence contracts, and health care reimbursements. Overhead is reimbursed under these contracts, because overhead costs represent the common costs for a variety of activities necessary to produce goods and services, including support services such as accounting, administration, human resources, and so on. In this chapter, you will learn methods for allocating costs for these support services. You will also learn that in some circumstances the allocation of such costs is useful for measuring, monitoring, and motivating performance within an organization.

A **common cost** is the cost for a resource that is shared among two or more departments, activities, products, or other cost objects. In this chapter, we focus on methods for allocating the common costs of support departments to operating departments. **Operating departments** are the departments or divisions within an organization that manufacture goods or produce services for external customers or clients. In manufacturing businesses, operating departments produce goods for sale. In service organizations, operating departments produce services for clients or customers. In a retail or distribution business, operating departments sell merchandise to customers. Government agencies provide services such as police, fire, and emergency medical response; maintenance and repair of city streets; parks and recreational facilities; and special interest classes. Other not-for-profit organizations—such as food banks, arts and cultural groups, and child care centres—also provide services.

Support departments provide services internal to the organization that support the operating departments. For example, a large auto manufacturer may operate a cafeteria for its employees and have a human resources department that hires employees and keeps track of employee benefits for all departments. These services are provided as support for departments that produce parts, subassemblies, and autos for sale to external customers, which generates revenues for the auto manufacturer. Typical support departments include accounting, information systems, human resources, marketing, research and development, and general administration.

Exhibit 8.1 provides examples of operating and support departments for various types of organizations.

Objectives for Support Department Cost Allocation

Support department costs are generally treated as period expenses when preparing financial statements under IFRS and Canadian ASPE. Therefore, support department costs are allocated for objectives other than financial statements reporting, as summarized in Exhibit 8.2.

Some organizations must allocate support service costs when reporting to outsiders. For example, universities allocate a portion of their overhead costs to federally funded programs. Hospitals prepare annual health care cost reports in accordance with the Canada Health Act. These reports identify the costs incurred by hospitals to treat patients, including identified support costs. Government defence contractors are often paid based on cost, including costs related to support departments. Sometimes consulting firms are paid according to savings that result from their work. To fully value these savings, costs from support services may need to be allocated. In the Melodious Notes (MN) example on the next page, the owners are required to submit an annual cost report to the local credit union as part of the debt covenants on a loan.

Type of Organization	Operating Departments	Support Departments
Apparel manufacturer	Dresses, suits	Customer services
		Product design
Retail sales	Departments: housewares, appliances	Custodial services
	Individual stores	Purchasing
Breakfast cereal manufacturer	Processed cereals	Maintenance and repair
	Cereal bars	Shipping
Electronic commerce and payment services	Electronic transaction processing	Transaction dispute resolution
	Credit card issuance	Data processing
Chartered accountant firm	Accounting and auditing	Word processing
	Income taxes	Reception
Not-for-profit organization for visually impaired persons	Audio book recordings	Accounting
	Community education	Fundraising
University	University academic departments	Library
	On-campus housing	Buildings and grounds
Ministry of Natural Resources	Licences	Accounting
	Wildlife management	Research
Fitness centre	Aerobics classes	Advertising
	Café	General management

> **EXHIBIT 8.1**
Production and Support Departments

Objective	Example
External reporting	Cost reports for government contracts
	Income tax returns
	Reports prepared for reimbursement purposes
Motivation	Provide incentives for efficient production of support services
	Provide incentives for appropriate use of support services
	Monitor use and production of support services
Strategic and operating decisions	New product/market introductions
	Insource or outsource
	Pricing

> **EXHIBIT 8.2**
Objectives for Allocating Support Department Costs

melodious notes, part 1
SUPPORT DEPARTMENT COSTS

Melodious Notes (MN) is a local business that sells musical instruments and offers lessons. The owners would like to set prices that are as attractive as possible and need to be sure they are covering all their costs. The local credit union from which the owners have a small business loan requires them to submit an annual cost report that shows total costs, including support department cost allocations. The credit union does not require particular methods or bases for the allocations.

The accounting department at the local university sponsors an internship program, in which accounting students develop their professional skills and contribute to the community by working as volunteers for small businesses. This year, a team of accounting students has been assigned to MN. The students have been asked to help allocate all of MN's costs to products (i.e., sales and lessons). MN's owners plan to use this information to help set prices. The students will also prepare the annual cost report for the credit union. ■

example

mkm3/Shutterstock

Some organizations allocate support department costs in order to motivate managers to improve cost control and efficiency. Managers of departments that provide support services are held responsible for their department costs, whereas managers of other departments are held responsible for their departments' use of support services. An effective allocation system motivates both sets of managers to be efficient. Suppose an organization has a motor fleet department that manages all of the organization's vehicles. Each department using motor vehicles incurs a charge or cost allocation from the motor fleet department, based on its vehicle usage. Usage charges depend on the motor fleet department's budget. If the budget increases, charges also increase. The managers of departments that use the vehicles are responsible for monitoring and controlling their departmental cost budgets. Therefore, they have incentives to ensure that vehicle use is monitored and controlled. Meanwhile, the manager of the motor fleet department is motivated to provide cost-effective support. Otherwise, the other managers will argue in favour of outsourcing vehicle use to a lower-cost provider.

Sometimes allocated support department costs are used in making strategic or operating decisions, such when to enter a new market, where to outsource an activity, and how much to charge for services provided. Support costs are relevant to such decisions only if they would be affected by the decision. For example, avoidable support costs would be relevant to an outsourcing decision. However, support department allocations often include fixed costs that are less likely to be relevant for decision making. Accountants need to help managers understand the uses and limitations of allocated cost information.

The Process for Allocating Support Department Costs

L02 Explain the process that is used to allocate support department costs

As shown in Exhibit 8.3, the process for allocating support department costs to operating departments is similar to the allocation methods discussed in chapters 5, 6, and 7. The process involves the following steps:

1. Clarify the purpose of the allocation.

2. Identify support and operating department cost pools.

3. Assign costs to cost pools.

4. For each support department cost pool, choose an allocation base.

5. Choose and apply a method for allocating support department costs to operating departments.

6. If relevant, allocate support costs from the operating departments to units of goods or services.

⊠ BUSINESS PRACTICE

By implementing technology enhancements on July 12, 2010, the UPS Billing Centre "provides faster access to bills and supports streamline cost allocation . . .," which results in improved invoice payment processes.[1]

Clarifying the Purpose of Allocation

Before you begin the allocation process, you need to know the purpose of the allocation. As shown in Exhibit 8.2, a variety of reasons prompt the allocation of support department costs to operating departments. The choices made in the following steps must be consistent with the purpose.

---

[1] "Technology Takes Off at UPS to Simplify International Shipping," *Canada NewsWire* [Ottawa], August 4, 2010.

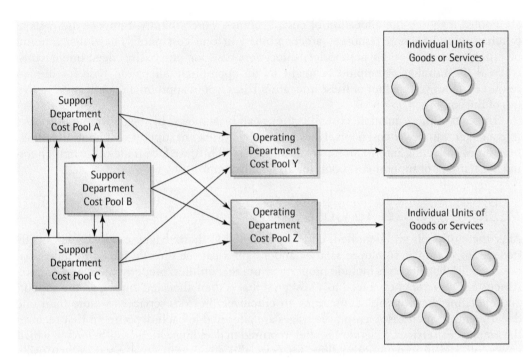

> EXHIBIT 8.3

Allocation of Support Department Costs

Identifying Support and Operating Department Cost Pools

You consider the purpose for allocating support department costs as you decide the type and number of support and operating department cost pools that will be used. For example, for Canadian universities, the purpose is to allocate overhead costs to federally funded grant programs. A university is likely to have at least one operating cost pool for the direct costs of each grant, as well as many indirect cost pools with costs separated by functional area, such as accounting, human resources, information technology, and general administration. The choice of support department cost pools to be allocated would depend on the types of indirect costs permitted under federal guidelines. The Melodious Notes case later in this chapter provides additional examples.

Because many organizations already accumulate costs by department within their organizational structure, departments are often used as cost pools. Larger organizations usually have more support departments providing specific services. For example, a large organization may have a purchasing department that is responsible for receiving materials, for requisitions, and for ordering everything required by other departments. In smaller organizations, the purchasing function may be performed by a single person in the administration department who may also be responsible for several other functions, such as preparing the paperwork for hiring a new employee and making copies of reports for meetings.

The choice of cost pools is also influenced by the design of the accounting system. Some organizations have detailed accounting systems that make different types of costs more accessible. In others, it may be difficult and costly to identify only specific types of support costs. For example, assume that accounting, purchasing, and human resources are aggregated with general administration into a single support cost pool in the general ledger. The cost of the time and effort involved in isolating only one of these costs (e.g., purchasing) may exceed the benefit derived from the more accurate cost information. Sometimes fixed and variable support costs are allocated separately. However, if fixed and variable costs have not been assigned to separate cost pools in the accounting system, it might be time consuming and costly to separately allocate them.

Another factor influencing the number and type of support department cost pools is the ability to identify an appropriate allocation base. When too many different types of costs are pooled together, the allocation of costs becomes more arbitrary. Suppose the costs of purchasing and human resources are combined in one cost pool. The dollar amount of purchases might be an appropriate allocation base for purchasing department costs, whereas the number of employees might be an appropriate allocation base for human resources. However, neither of these allocation bases would appropriately reflect the activities of the combined cost pool.

In general, more accurate cost allocations can be achieved by separating support costs into a larger number of cost pools. However, as the number of support cost pools increases, the cost of collecting information may also increase. Thus, we face trade-offs when choosing the number of support cost pools for an organization.

Assigning Costs to Cost Pools

After the cost pools are identified, costs are assigned to them. Many costs can be directly traced. For example, employee salaries and supplies can be directly traced to individual departments. Facility costs include property insurance, utilities, property taxes, and maintenance, and they are often traced to a cost pool that is then allocated among all the support and operating departments. Sometimes an employee provides services to more than one department. In such cases, employee wages are allocated to each department that receives the employee's services. Judgment is often required in deciding which costs belong to which cost pools and in making estimations for costs allocated among cost pools. When using judgment to assign costs to support cost pools, accountants must consider not only technical definitions but also perceived fairness.

Choosing Allocation Bases

A cause-and-effect relationship is desirable between the support costs and the allocation base that is used to allocate them. Thus, the best allocation base is a cost driver. In a hospital, kilograms of laundry would be an appropriate cost driver for the laundry department, because costs increase as the kilograms of laundry increase. However, it may be difficult or impossible to find an appropriate cost driver if the department cost pool includes many different activities. In these cases, an allocation base is chosen to reflect some of the activities provided. Number of employees might be an appropriate allocation base for a department cost pool that includes both human resources and accounting activities, even if it does not reflect the use of accounting time, except perhaps in payroll. If accounting department employees track the time they spend on activities for all other departments, time spent would be an appropriate allocation base.

example

melodious notes, part 2
ALLOCATION OF SUPPORT DEPARTMENT COSTS

Cost Object, Cost Pools, and Cost Assignment

MN provides two different types of products: instrument sales and music lessons. Because costs probably differ by the type of product provided, the students decide to treat each type of product as a cost object. Therefore, they calculate costs separately for each of the two operating departments and set up a cost pool for each. They learn from an interview with the accountant that the music store has two support departments: administration and custodial services. The students set up a cost pool for each of these departments.

The accountant helps the students trace the direct costs to each department cost pool. In addition, costs for the entire facility, such as rent and electricity, are gathered into a cost pool and then allocated to all the departments based on the physical size (area in square metres) of each.

example

The students prepare a summary of the costs assigned to each department, as follows:

Cost	Administration	Custodial Services	Instrument Sales	Music Lessons	Total
Salaries	$80,000	$40,000	$200,000	$80,000	$400,000
Supplies	15,000	20,000	35,000	10,000	80,000
Facility costs	3,240	360	28,800	3,600	36,000
Total	$98,240	$60,360	$263,800	$93,600	$516,000

Choosing Allocation Bases

Before the students allocate support department costs, they need to choose allocation bases for the services provided by the custodial services and administration departments. One student suggests that area is a good base for allocating custodial costs. Another student thinks that hours spent in each department would be a better basis because the departments have different kinds of equipment and different volumes of service. They agree that hours spent is a better choice, but then learn that custodial services does not keep records of hours by department, so they return to their alternate choice and use area (square metres) for allocating custodial costs.

For the administration allocation base, the accountant suggests using either the direct costs for each operating department or the number of employees. When the students study the administration department activities, they find that many services relate to employees, such as recruiting, training, benefits, and payroll. Other services include purchasing and maintenance. The students decide that number of employees in each department is more representative than direct costs for the overall activities in administration, and they, therefore, choose it as the allocation base for administration.

The students gather the following information for the allocation bases:

	Administration	Custodial Services	Instrument Sales	Music Lessons	Total
Number of employees	2	2	5	3	12
Square metres	90	10	800	100	1,000

Having calculated the total costs for each cost pool and chosen an allocation base for each support cost pool, the student interns are now ready to begin allocating support department costs to operating departments. ■

The cost of obtaining accurate allocation base information is an important consideration. Tracking time spent on different activities may cost more than the benefit gained from using it as an allocation base. As a result, accountants often use less accurate allocation bases for which data are available. Exhibit 8.4 presents a list of support departments and possible allocation bases.

Choosing and Applying Allocation Methods

Three allocation methods are used to allocate support department costs to operating departments:

- ► Direct method
- ► Step-down method
- ► Reciprocal method

▣ **BUSINESS PRACTICE**

When the municipalities in the **Essex-Windsor Solid Waste Authority** region generated 6,600 tonnes less waste, the general manager needed to reassess landfill charges. He is considering changing from the current tipping fee of $97.50 per tonne to an allocation of the 2011 budgeted amount of $10.1 million based on each municipality's share of the residential garbage in 2010.[2]

---

[2] Gary Rennie, "Where Has the Garbage Gone? Region 6,600 Tonnes Lower Than usual." *The Windsor Star* [Windsor, ON] February 2, 2011, C.9.

> **EXHIBIT 8.4**
Support Departments and Possible
Allocation Bases

Support Departments	Possible Allocation Bases
Administration	Direct costs of other departments
	Number of employees
	Revenue of operating departments
Accounting	Direct costs of other departments
	Number of accounting transactions
	Time spent
Housekeeping	Time spent
	Square metres cleaned
Purchasing	Number of requisitions
	Number of items ordered
	Total cost of items ordered
Employee training	Hours of training
	Number of employees
	Number of classes provided

> **BUSINESS PRACTICE**
Health Canada's **Health Products &
Foods Branch** assigns both direct and
indirect program costs to activities
based on use of resources.[3]

Each of these methods is formally introduced and illustrated in the following sections.

The Direct Method of Allocation

> **L03**
Explain how the direct
method is used to allocate
support costs to operating
departments; calculate
cost allocations using the
direct method

The **direct method** allocates the costs of all support departments to the operating departments only. Because no costs are allocated among support departments, none of the interactions among support departments are reflected under this method. The use of the direct
method is illustrated in the Melodious Notes (MN) example. The accountants for MN have
identified two support departments, custodial services and administration, and two operating
departments, retail sales and lessons. As shown in Exhibit 8.5, the direct method uses each
support department's allocation base to allocate the costs for that department to each of the
operating departments. Calculations for MN are shown in Melodious Notes, Part 3.

> **EXHIBIT 8.5**
The Direct Method of Allocation

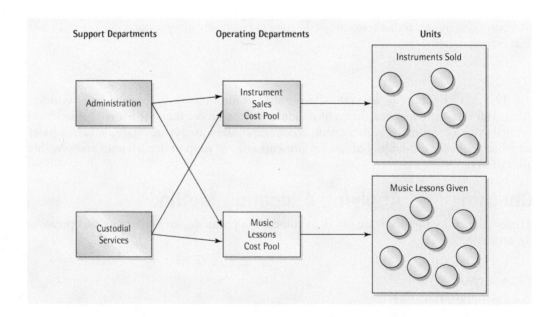

---

[3] Health Canada, *2014 Review of the Fees in Respect of Drugs and Medical Devices Regulations* (October 31, 2014),
www.hc-sc.gc.ca/dhp-mps/finance/fdmdr-rpdim-eng.php# a3-1-1.

example

melodious notes, part 3
DIRECT METHOD ALLOCATION

The accountant tells the students that they can use any reasonable method for allocating support costs to operating departments. The students want to learn more about different methods and their effects on allocated costs. Therefore, they decide to perform calculations using the direct, step-down, and reciprocal methods.

Direct Method Calculations

The students begin with the direct method, which is the easiest to perform. They first draw a diagram similar to the one in Exhibit 8.5 to clarify how they will perform calculations. They next calculate the percentage of each support department's costs allocated to each operating department. Costs for custodial services are allocated based on area. One student observes that the area used by administration is not relevant to the direct method because custodial services costs are not allocated to another support department. Of the 900 square metres used by the operating departments, the retail space uses 800 square metres, or 89%. Accordingly, 89% of the custodial services costs will be allocated to instrument sales, and the remaining 11% (100 square metres/900 square metres) will be allocated to music lessons.

Costs for administration are allocated based on number of employees. The instrument sales area employs five of the eight employees who work for operating departments, so 62.5% of the administration costs will be allocated to instrument sales. The remaining 37.5% (3 employees/8 employees) will be allocated to music lessons.

The students prepare a report that summarizes their allocations, as shown in Exhibit 8.6. The line for department cost reflects the costs that the students had previously assigned to each department. Of the $60,360 custodial services cost, 89% ($53,720) is allocated to instrument sales, and 11% ($6,640) is allocated to music lessons. Similarly, the administrative cost of $98,240 is allocated 62.5% ($61,400) to instrument sales and 37.5% ($36,840) to music lessons. The costs allocated from the support departments are added to each operating department's costs. Thus, the total allocated costs are $378,920 for the instrument sales and $137,080 for music lessons. Notice that the total costs of $516,000 have not been affected by the allocation.

mkm3/Shutterstock

HELPFUL HINT
The examples in this chapter involve only a handful of departments. Organizations often have many departments, making the allocation procedure considerably more complex than illustrated here.

		Support		Production	
	Administration	Custodial Services	Instrument Sales	Music Lessons	Total
Allocation Bases					
Square metres			800	100	900
			89%	11%	100%
Number of employees			5	3	8
Costs					
			62.5%	37.5%	100%
Department cost	$98,240	$60,360	$263,800	$ 93,600	$516,000
Custodial services		(60,360)	53,720	6,640	0
Administration	(98,240)		61,400	36,840	0
Total allocated cost	$ 0	$ 0	$378,920	$137,080	$516,000

EXHIBIT 8.6
Direct Method Cost Allocation Report for Melodious Notes

The Step-Down Method of Allocation

The **step-down method** allocates support department costs one department at a time to remaining support and operating departments in a cascading manner until all support department costs have been allocated. This method goes beyond the direct method in recognizing that support departments provide support not only for the operating departments but also for other support departments. The step-down method begins by ranking each support department according to the amount of service provided to other support departments. Then, as shown in Exhibit 8.7, the costs for the first support department chosen are allocated to the remaining departments, both support and operating. The process continues, and costs for the remaining support departments are allocated one at a time to the remaining departments until no support department costs remain. For example, in Exhibit 8.7, costs are allocated from administration to custodial services but not from custodial services to administration.

► EXHIBIT 8.7

Step-Down Method

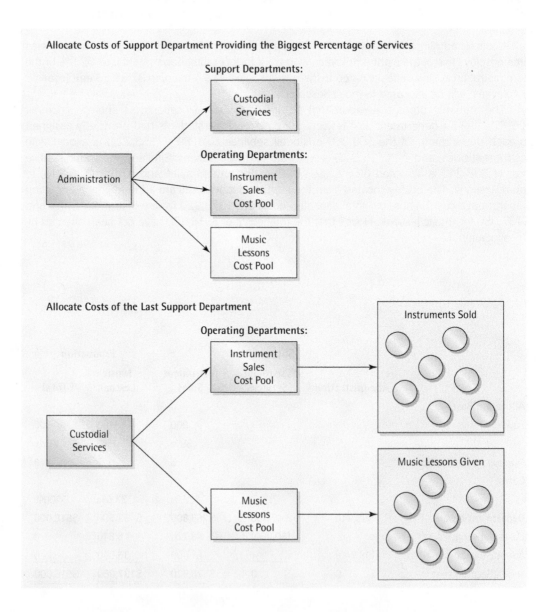

In this method, support department costs are allocated sequentially, beginning with the support department that provided the most service to other support departments and ending with the support department that provided the least service to other support departments. The ranking can be based on any reasonable criteria, such as a quantitative measure like the dollar amount of services provided to other support departments. Alternatively, sometimes a qualitative judgment must be made about the degree of services. Calculations for the step-down method are illustrated in Melodious Notes, Part 4.

▶ **ALTERNATIVE TERMS**
The *step-down method* is sometimes called the *sequential method*.

melodious notes, part 4
STEP-DOWN METHOD ALLOCATION

example

After the student interns allocate MN's costs using the direct method, they recalculate the allocations using the step-down method. For the step-down method, the support departments are ranked based on the quantity of services provided to other support departments. The students decide to rank administration first because it probably provides more support to custodial services than vice versa. For example, administration purchases supplies and provides employee support, such as payroll and benefits, for the custodial services department.

The students draw a diagram similar to the one in Exhibit 8.7 to clarify how they will perform calculations. They first allocate administration department costs to all the remaining departments—the other support department (custodial services) and the two operating departments. Therefore, in determining the percentage of costs for each department, they factor in the two custodial services employees with the operating department employees. After the administrative costs are allocated, the students allocate custodial costs to the two operating departments, using the same percentages used for the direct method because only the two operating departments remain. The students summarize their calculations in the report shown in Exhibit 8.8.

In the first step, 20% of the administration department's $98,240 cost goes to custodial services ($19,648), 50% to instrument sales ($49,120), and 30% to music lessons ($29,472). In the second step, the custodial costs are now $80,008 ($60,360 + $19,648) because they include an allocation from administration. Therefore, 89% of $80,008 is allocated to instrument sales ($71,207), and the remaining 11% ($8,801) is allocated to music lessons. ■

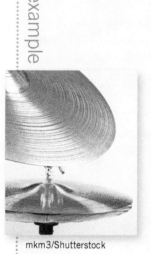

mkm3/Shutterstock

	Administration	Support Custodial Services	Instrument Sales	Production Music Lessons	Total
Allocation Bases					
Number of employees		2	5	3	10
		20%	50%	30%	100%
Square metres			800	100	900
			89%	11%	100%
Costs					
Total department cost	$98,240	$60,360	$263,800	$ 93,600	$516,000
Step 1: Administration	(98,240)	19,648	49,120	29,472	0
Step 2: Custodial services	0	(80,008)	71,207	8,801	0
Total allocated cost	$ 0	$ 0	$384,127	$131,873	$516,000

▶ **EXHIBIT 8.8**
Step-Down Method Cost Allocation Report for Melodious Notes

The Reciprocal Method of Allocation

The **reciprocal method** simultaneously allocates costs among support departments and then from support departments to operating departments. Because the reciprocal method allows for all the interactions among departments, it is widely used. This method reflects support department interactions more accurately than either the direct method, which does not address the interactions at all, or the step-down method, which addresses only part of the interactions.

The reciprocal method is performed in two phases. First, support department costs are allocated among each other. These interactions for Melodious Notes are shown in Exhibit 8.9(a). To capture the cost effects of these interactions, a set of equations is created and solved simultaneously. The exhibit shows the simple two-department case, which can easily be performed manually. However, when more than two support departments are involved, the reciprocal method becomes mathematically complex and is more easily performed using software such as spreadsheet functions that solve simultaneous equations. Thus, the computations for the reciprocal method are the most complex among the three methods introduced in this chapter.

After the simultaneous equations are solved, the allocated cost for each support department includes costs allocated from the other support departments. Next, this new total cost per support department is allocated to all the other departments (support and operating), as shown in Exhibit 8.9(b). The reciprocal method is illustrated in Melodious Notes, Part 5.

EXHIBIT 8.9
Reciprocal Method

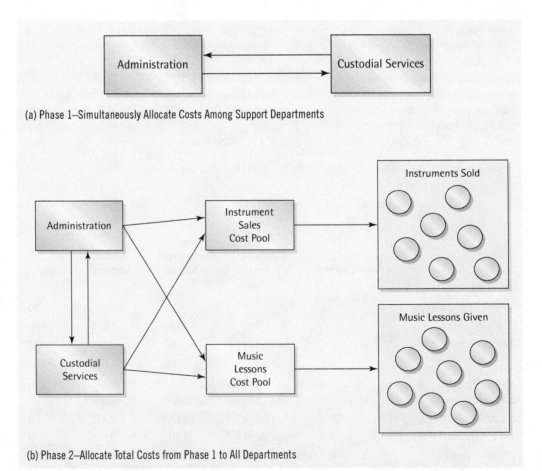

(a) Phase 1—Simultaneously Allocate Costs Among Support Departments

(b) Phase 2—Allocate Total Costs from Phase 1 to All Departments

melodious notes, part 5
RECIPROCAL METHOD ALLOCATION

mkm3/Shutterstock

After completing the step-down method calculation, the student interns are ready to apply the reciprocal method to MN's support costs. The students adopt the same allocation bases they used previously, and they draw diagrams similar to the ones in Exhibit 8.9 to clarify how they will perform calculations.

Allocating Support Costs Among Support Departments

The students first simultaneously allocate each support department's costs to all other support departments. To simultaneously compute costs between support departments, the students need to set up and solve simultaneous equations. The cost of each support department is written as a sum of directly assigned costs plus costs allocated from the other support department. Administration is allocated based on number of employees. MN has 10 employees outside the administration department; 2 of them work in custodial services, the other support department. For the purpose of allocating administration costs, the custodial services portion of employees is 2/10, and:

$$\text{Custodial services} = \$60{,}360 + 0.2 \,(\text{Administration})$$

Similarly, custodial services is allocated based on area. Of the 990 square metres that are not in custodial services, 90 square metres are in administration. Thus, for the purpose of allocating custodial costs, administration's portion of the area is 90 ÷ 990 square metres, and

$$\text{Administration} = \$98{,}240 + 0.09 \,(\text{Custodial services})$$

Because only two support departments are involved, only two equations need to be solved simultaneously. The students decide to use the substitution method to solve them. They substitute the administration equation into the custodial services equation and solve for the total cost of custodial services:

$$\text{Custodial services} = \$60{,}360 + 0.2 \times (\$98{,}240 + 0.09 \times \text{Custodial services})$$

$$\text{Custodial services} = \$60{,}360 + \$19{,}648 + 0.018 \times \text{Custodial services}$$

$$0.982 \times \text{Custodial services} = \$80{,}008$$

$$\text{Custodial services} = \$81{,}475$$

Next, they substitute the result for custodial services into the administration equation and solve for the total cost of administration:

$$\text{Administration} = \$98{,}240 + 0.09 \times \$81{,}475$$

$$\text{Administration} = \$105{,}573$$

When an organization has three or more support departments, the simultaneous equations are set up in the same way. Each equation includes the total cost for the department plus a term for each of the other support departments. The simultaneous calculations become more complex but can easily be solved with computer programs or repeated algebraic substitution.

Allocating Support Costs to Operating Departments

The calculations performed using simultaneous equations provide a total cost for each support department that includes cost allocations from other support departments. These totals are the new amount that the students next allocate to all other departments (support and operating). The new total cost for custodial services is $81,475, which includes the original department cost of $60,360 plus an allocation of $21,115 from administration. In Exhibit 8.10, the students allocate this new custodial cost based on area, with 9% to administration, 81% to instrument sales, and 10% to music lessons.

> **HELPFUL HINT**
> Melodious Notes, Part 6, illustrates the reciprocal method with three support departments. Appendix 8A provides details for using Excel Solver.

continued...

example

Similarly, the new cost for administration of $105,573 includes the original cost of $98,240 plus an allocation of $7,333 from custodial services. The students allocate this new administration amount based on number of employees, with 20% to custodial services, 50% to instrument sales, and 30% to music lessons. The students create a report to summarize their allocations and demonstrate that zero cost remains in each support department after the allocations are complete, as shown in Exhibit 8.10.

Comparing Results and Choosing an Allocation Method

When the students finish their calculations for the three allocation methods, they create the following schedule to compare their results:

	Instrument Sales	Music Lessons	Total
Direct method	$378,920	$137,080	$516,000
Step-down method	384,127	131,873	516,000
Reciprocal method	382,581	133,419	516,000

MN's owners and managers want to know the cost for each of their products. Therefore, the students also calculate the average allocated cost per product. The accountant tells them that instrument sales usually stocks and sells 12,000 instruments, and music lessons provides 10,000 lessons. Dividing the total allocated costs by these volumes, the total allocated cost per product under each method is:

	Instrument Sales	Music Lessons
Direct method	$31.58	$13.71
Step-down method	32.01	13.19
Reciprocal method	31.88	13.34

The students notice that the fully allocated costs do not vary significantly across methods. They ask their accounting professor whether this result is always true. She tells them that the variation depends on the data and number of departments for a given setting. With a larger number of support departments, the differences are usually greater. She also tells them that the step-down and reciprocal methods often yield similar results when only two support departments are involved. She adds that the reciprocal method is the most accurate because it takes into account all interactions.

▶ **EXHIBIT 8.10**

Reciprocal Method Cost Allocation Report for Melodious Notes

		Support		Operating		
	Administration	Custodial Services	Instrument Sales	Music Lessons	Total
Cost Allocation Bases					
Square metres	90		800	100	990
	9%		81%	10%	100%
Employees		2	5	3	10
		20%	50%	30%	100%
Costs					
Total department cost	$ 98,240	$ 60,360	$263,800	$ 93,600	$516,000
Custodial services	7,333	(81,475)	65,995	8,147	
Administration	(105,573)	21,115	52,786	31,672	
Total allocated cost	$ 0	$ 0	$382,581	$133,419	$516,000

example

The students discuss the effort that each method takes. They agree that the direct method requires the least amount of effort and that the reciprocal method requires the most. However, they also agree that they could easily set up a spreadsheet to calculate MN's allocations. After concluding that computational difficulty is not a major issue, they recommend the reciprocal method to the music store owners and managers. ■

Comparing the Direct, Step-Down, and Reciprocal Methods

As shown in the Melodious Notes case, different allocation methods result in different values. Each method has pros and cons. The direct method is the easiest to calculate, but computer programs reduce the importance of this issue. An advantage of the direct and step-down methods is that the calculation methods are easier to explain to managers. However, the reciprocal method most accurately considers support department interactions.

Single- Versus Dual-Rate Allocations

The practice of using only one base to allocate both fixed and variable costs is called **single-rate allocation,** For example, at Melodious Notes, area was used to allocate custodial services costs. Area might be appropriate for allocating custodial services fixed costs, such as depreciation (amortization) on any cleaning equipment used, but some custodial services costs vary with the type of work required in a given area. The time custodial services workers spend in each department might be a more appropriate allocation base for the variable costs. Thus, single-rate allocation likely mismeasures resources used. In addition, managers may believe that all support costs are variable, even when they include a large proportion of fixed costs.

Under **dual-rate allocation,** support costs are separated into fixed and variable cost pools and cost drivers are identified for the variable cost pools to more accurately reflect the flow of resources. Exhibit 8.11 presents the dual-rate allocation process under the reciprocal method. Compared to single-rate allocation, the variable cost allocations reflect a more accurate estimation of the incremental costs of providing support services. Some organizations use variable costs to measure use of a department's services and assign the fixed costs as part of a department's formally adopted budget.

The dual-rate system also has drawbacks. It costs more to develop and maintain. Furthermore, uncertainties about how to classify costs as fixed and variable can introduce additional mismeasurement.

Melodious Notes, Part 6, demonstrates the use of dual-rate allocation.

| LO 6 | Explain the difference between single- and dual-rate allocations |

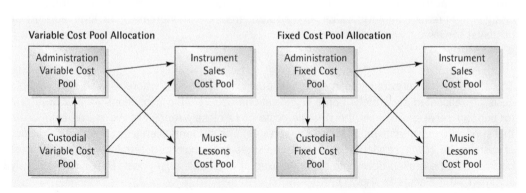

▷ EXHIBIT 8.11
Dual-Rate Allocation

melodious notes, part 6
DUAL-RATE AND RECIPROCAL
METHOD WITH THREE SUPPORT DEPARTMENTS

After the students finish allocating administration and custodial costs to MN's operating departments, the accountant asks them whether that information could be used to charge departments for their use of other departments' services. The accountant believes that by charging for support department services, employees in the user departments will be motivated to manage their use of the support services more cost consciously, and some support costs might be reduced. The charges can then become part of the current budgeting system in which employees are held responsible for their budgets. Employees receive performance bonuses if costs are maintained at or under budgeted levels.

Charges Based on Single-Rate Allocation

The students obtain the total allocated costs for each support department from their previous reciprocal method calculations: $105,573 for administration and $81,475 for custodial services. Their goal is to calculate a charge representing the use of these services by other departments. Previously, they used number of employees as the allocation base for administration and square metres as the allocation base for custodial services. They decide to use the allocation bases to calculate a charge for the use of each department's services. For administration services, other departments would be charged a cost per employee. MN has 12 employees, 2 of whom work in administration. The students calculate the charge for administration costs based on the 10 non-administration employees:

$105,573 administration costs ÷ 10 employees = $10,557 per employee

For custodial services, other departments would be charged a cost per square metre. MN has 1,000 total square metres, of which 10 are devoted to custodial services. The students calculate the charge for custodial services based on the 990 non-custodial square metres:

$81,475 custodial costs ÷ 990 square metres = $82.29 per square metre

The students discuss whether the charges they calculated are reasonable. They think that the administration charge seems high, based on their research of costs at other music stores. They wonder whether other departments should be charged $10,557 for administrative costs for each employee in the department. The charge might encourage managers in the operating departments to inappropriately reduce the number of employees. For example, the managers might replace an employee with services from a temporary labour agency, which would cost MN more overall. When the students review the custodial services charge, they believe that an average annual charge of $82.29 per square metre is reasonable, based on their research on custodial charges in local retailing establishments. However, one student asks whether it is reasonable for the custodial cost rate for administration to be the same as the cost rate for instrument sales and music lessons. The retailing and lesson areas require special cleaning supplies and greater effort than the administration area. In addition, employees in·other departments might feel that they have no control over a fixed charge of $82.29 per square metre. A fixed charge might reduce their motivation to keep work areas clean, increasing the time required by custodial services.

Analyzing Cost Behaviour and Revising Cost Pools

The students had previously learned about dual-rate allocation, whereby fixed and variable costs are allocated separately. Some organizations use variable allocations as a charge rate for support services because the variable costs more closely represent the incremental costs that support departments incur to provide services. The students plan to analyze the behaviour of costs in the administration and custodial services cost pools to determine whether the cost pools should be broken down into separate fixed and variable cost pools. They had previously summarized the costs as shown here.

example

Cost	Administration	Custodial Services
Salaries	$80,000	$40,000
Supplies	15,000	20,000
Facility costs	3,240	360
Total	$98,240	$60,360

The students focus first on administration costs. Most of these costs are for salaries of the managers and the accountant. The managers are responsible for general management of sales and lessons while the accountant is responsible for accounting and billing functions. The accountant says she spends much more time on billing functions for the sales and lessons than on general functions for the whole organization. These functions include receiving information about each credit sale and lesson plan from the operating departments and then billing customers, receiving and depositing payments, and following up on bad debts. One student points out that the functions of the managers are different from those of the accountant. He argues that the costs for these employees should not be combined in a single cost pool if other departments will be charged for the services. The other students agree that accuracy of the cost allocations will improve if they separate accounting costs from other administration costs, so they decide to establish a separate cost pool called accounting. The accountant helps the students identify the costs that should be assigned to the accounting cost pool, and she summarizes the time she usually spends on activities for each department.

When the students study the custodial services department cost records, they find that custodial services employees are paid an hourly wage, and part of the department's costs vary with time spent working in each department. Therefore, the students think that the variable part of custodial services costs could be allocated to other departments, based on the time spent cleaning each department. However, custodial services employees do not currently keep track of their time by department. The accountant agrees to establish a new record-keeping system for custodial services employees to keep track of the hours they spend in each department.

Based on their discussions with the accountant and their investigation of the types of costs in each cost pool, the students conclude that costs for all three support departments could be broken down into fixed and variable components. The students and the accountant examine past accounting records and other information to identify fixed and variable costs. The accountant estimates the cost of supplies and postage for accounting and billing activities and the amount of her salary that should be considered a fixed cost of the accounting department. Variable costs in administration include payroll costs that vary by employee, such as fringe benefits, and supplies and record-keeping costs for employees. The costs are summarized as follows:

	Administration	Accounting	Custodial Services	Total
Variable costs	$11,052	$9,210	$30,180	$50,442
Fixed costs	50,348	27,630	30,180	108,158
Total cost	$61,400	$36,840	$60,360	$158,600

Charges Based on Variable Cost Allocation

The students discuss with the accountant the effects of the new support cost pool on the calculation of charges to other departments. They conclude that other departments should be charged only for variable support costs. Thus, the cost object for each support department is the variable cost of support services provided to other departments.

They next discuss the allocation bases for the variable cost pools. They plan to use the accountant's time to allocate accounting costs. They decide to continue using number of employees for administration. They want to use the time spent in various departments for custodial services, but they lack recorded information about the amount of time spent in each area. However, the custodial services employees estimate that they spend 10% of their time cleaning the administration department, 5% in the accounting area, 55% in the instrument sales area, and 30% in the lesson area.

continued...

The new variable cost allocation base amounts for all departments are as follows:

	Administration	Accounting	Custodial Services	Instrument Sales	Music Lessons	Total
Employees		1	2	5	3	11
Time spent accounting	15%		10%	50%	25%	100%
Time spent cleaning	10%	5%		55%	30%	100%

To apply the reciprocal method, the students must first calculate the total support department variable costs, including interactions. They set up simultaneous equations for the interactions among administration, accounting, and custodial services:

$$\text{Administration} = \$11{,}052 + 15\% \times \text{Accounting} + 10\% \times \text{Custodial services}$$

$$\text{Accounting} = \$9{,}210 + (1/11) \times \text{Administration} + 5\% \times \text{Custodial services}$$

$$\text{Custodial services} = \$30{,}180 + (2/11) \times \text{Administration} + 10\% \times \text{Accounting}$$

The students use Excel Solver to find the solutions to this set of simultaneous equations. Instructions for using Solver are presented in Appendix 8A. The Solver results for each department's total variable cost (including interactions) to be allocated are

Administration	$16,354
Accounting	$12,416
Custodial services	$34,395

Given the total allocated variable cost for each support department, the students calculate the support charge per unit of allocation base. The charge for variable administration cost is based on the number of employees:

$$\$16{,}345 \div 11 \text{ employees} = \$1{,}486 \text{ per employee}$$

The charge for accounting is based on the time spent by the accountant. The accountant works full-time. Allowing two weeks of vacation and eight holidays, her estimated work hours per year are

$$[40 \text{ hours per week} \times (52 - 2) \text{ weeks}] - (8 \text{ days} \times 8 \text{ hours per day}) = 1{,}936 \text{ hours}$$

Thus, the charge for variable accounting cost is

$$\$12{,}416 \div 1{,}936 \text{ hours} = \$6.41 \text{ per hour}$$

The charge for custodial services is based on time spent cleaning. The custodial services employees work full time, or an estimated 1,936 hours per year each. Based on the two custodial services employees, the estimated total hours are 3,872 per year. The charge for variable custodial cost is

$$\$34{,}395 \div 3{,}872 \text{ hours} = \$8.88 \text{ per hour}$$

The students discuss these rates with the accountant. The administration charge per employee seems low, so department managers would probably not consider these charges in making decisions about employment levels. Many administrative costs are fixed, so the variable portion is small.

The accounting charges also seem low, reflecting the high proportion of fixed costs in salary for the accountant. At the same time, charging each department for variable accounting costs helps the department managers recognize that they are using accounting resources.

The custodial services charges are similar to costs that would be paid if an outside custodial service were used, so the department managers are likely to think that these charges

example

are fair. At the same time, charging the departments for custodial services based on time spent in each department provides the managers with incentives to keep work areas clean to reduce the number of hours that custodial services spends in them. The accountant recommends that the fixed costs be assigned to other departments as part of their annual budgets. This way, all costs will be allocated, but only variable costs will be charged based on some measure of usage.

Dual-Rate Allocation

The accountant reminds the students that they need to allocate costs for the regulatory reports that are filed with the province. For these reports, all support costs—not just the variable costs—must be allocated. The students can separately allocate the fixed support costs and then sum the fixed and variable allocations for provincial reporting.

The students discuss allocation bases for the fixed costs. They use number of employees as the allocation base for administration, time spent for accounting, and area (square metres) for custodial services. The fixed cost allocation base amounts for all departments are:

	Administration	Accounting	Custodial Services	Instrument Sales	Music Lessons	Total
Employees		1	2	5	3	11
Accounting	15%		10%	50%	25%	100%
Square metres	60	30		800	100	990

Once again, the students use Excel Solver to simultaneously allocate the costs among the support departments. (The simultaneous equations and instructions for Excel Solver are shown in Appendix 8A.)

The students prepare a schedule summarizing the variable and fixed cost allocations and calculating the total allocated costs for operating departments, as shown in Exhibit 8.12.

The students discuss how much they enjoyed helping the music business and gaining experience using three different methods of allocating support department costs, including the use of Solver. They feel the internship was a worthwhile experience. The accountant is glad that the student interns helped her with this task. She now knows how to use Solver and can revise the allocation scheme over time as MN's needs and cost estimates change. ■

▶EXHIBIT 8.12
Dual-Rate Support Cost
Allocations for Melodious Notes

	Support Departments			Operating Departments		
	Administration	Accounting	Custodial Services	Instrument Sales	Music Lessons	Total
Directly assigned costs	$ 61,400	$ 36,840	$ 60,360	$263,800	$ 93,600	$516,000
Variable Cost Allocation:						
Administration	(16,354)	1,486	2,973	7,434	4,460	0
Accounting	1,862	(12,416)	1,242	6,208	3,104	0
Custodial services	3,440	1,720	(34,395)	18,917	10,319	0
Fixed Cost Allocation:						
Administration	(58,164)	5,287	10,575	26,438	15,863	0
Accounting	5,138	(34,256)	3,426	17,128	8,564	0
Custodial services	2,678	1,339	(44,181)	35,702	4,463	0
Total allocated costs	$ 0	$ 0	$ 0	$375,627	$140,373	$516,000

Support Cost Allocations, Information Quality, and Decision Making

L07   Identify how support cost allocations and information quality impact management decision making

As discussed throughout this chapter, allocated support cost information can be low quality because of the judgment involved in the allocation process. For example, the administrative department cost pool in small organizations often includes costs related to the accounting and human resources functions, in addition to general management. No allocation base will accurately reflect other departments' use of administration because such a wide variety of services are pooled together. Even in organizations that maintain separate fixed and variable cost pools for each type of support services, the allocation base for a particular cost pool may not be a cost driver—either because no cost driver exists or because the cost of gathering reliable data for a cost drive would exceed the benefit.

The quality of support cost information affects how well support cost allocations achieve the objectives outlined in Exhibit 8.2. Next, we learn about several problems that may arise from use of allocated support costs. We also learn several techniques for addressing these problems.

Relevant Support Costs for Decision Making

Support costs are relevant for some types of business decisions, including decisions to outsource support services and operating decisions such as those discussed in Chapter 4. However, relevant support costs are often difficult to measure, so the allocations are often used instead of relevant cost analysis.

In Chapter 4 we identified relevant costs for outsourcing decisions. Variable support cost allocations under a dual-rate system probably reflect the incremental costs of support services. However, relevant fixed costs must be identified by analyzing costs and determining which would be avoidable if the department services were outsourced. Identification of relevant costs is further complicated by interactions among support departments. For example, the custodial costs allocated to instrument sales in Melodious Notes (Part 6) included the fixed and variable costs of the custodial department, as well as fixed and variable allocations of administration and accounting costs to custodial. Which of these costs would be relevant if the managers wanted to consider outsourcing the custodial services? Because it is difficult to track the behaviour of resource costs, identifying relevant support cost information requires careful analysis.

Support cost allocations also tend to be inaccurate when measuring relevant costs for operating department decisions. When evaluating costs for a keep-or-drop decision, support costs that are allocated to an operating department might not be eliminated if the operating department is dropped. Similarly, allocated support costs might be irrelevant when evaluating incremental costs for a special order, product emphasis, or other decision.

Support Department Allocations as Transfer Prices

When support departments provide services without charge to user departments, the user departments tend to use the support services inefficiently. In turn, inefficient use tends to encourage support departments to grow unnecessarily large. To reduce this type of inefficiency, many organizations use transfer prices to charge user departments for the cost of support services. Support costs are then included in user department budgets, which are often the basis for evaluating manager performance. However, transfer prices introduce a variety of incentive problems.

Transfer prices are often based on fully allocated costs and, therefore, include fixed support department costs as well as allocations from other support departments. As a result, the transfer prices can be high, which can encourage user departments to outsource the support services. However, outsourcing is not always beneficial to the organization as a whole as it can cause internal services to be duplicated, resulting in excess capacity and inefficient use of resources. For example, total custodial costs for Melodious Notes would probably increase if instrument sales hired an outside company for its custodial services while music lessons continued to use the internal service.

Setting Transfer Prices for Support Services

Ideally, transfer prices should be set to motivate efficient use of support services. The best transfer price policy is an opportunity cost approach. Each department is charged an amount that reflects the value of any opportunities forgone by not using the service for its next best alternative use.

Consider a manufacturing company with a maintenance department. The manufacturing equipment needs routine maintenance to prevent downtime during regular hours of operation. The maintenance department schedules its repair and maintenance time during lunch hours and at the end of each production shift. Currently, the maintenance department is operating close to capacity. Other departments need to schedule non-routine tasks, such as painting walls and repairing damaged flooring, well in advance. If a department wants maintenance workers to hang pictures in an office, the value of the opportunity forgone might be the cost of hiring a contractor to provide routine maintenance on equipment or to paint walls. However, if the maintenance department has extra capacity and workers are idle part of the time, the opportunity cost of hanging pictures would be zero.

Implementing a transfer price policy based on opportunity costs is problematic because opportunities change over time with changes in demand and capacity. In addition, identifying and valuing alternative uses for some services can be difficult. Therefore, organizations often adopt either a cost-based or a market-based transfer pricing policy. Cost-based transfer prices range from variable costs to fully allocated costs. Market-based transfer prices are set at amounts that would be paid if the service were outsourced. Some organizations establish a price per job for each task, keep prices low on jobs they want to have performed internally, and set prices high on jobs that are considered unnecessary or inappropriate. If managers believe that maintenance workers should not spend time hanging pictures, they could set the transfer price for hanging pictures high enough to discourage other departments from asking the maintenance department to perform this service.

Uncertainties in Support Cost Allocations

Support cost allocations are subject to the same uncertainties as other types of cost allocations. As discussed throughout this chapter, the process of allocating support costs involves many uncertainties, such as the following:

- Identifying appropriate cost pools for support and operating departments.
- Whether to establish separate pools for fixed and variable costs.
- How to assign costs to cost pools.
- Identifying the most appropriate allocation bases for each cost pool.
- Identifying the most appropriate allocation method.
- Whether the benefits exceed the costs of establishing a more detailed support cost allocation system.

Because the process of measuring and allocating support costs is uncertain and requires judgment, allocated support cost information can be low quality. The quality of allocated support cost information can be improved in many ways. Accountants, managers, and operational personnel can work together to identify more appropriate cost pools and allocation bases. Accounting systems can be redesigned to more accurately trace costs to activities and gather better allocation base data. In addition, accountants can adopt allocation

> **BUSINESS PRACTICE**
> As **NB Power** and **Hydro-Quebec** combined their resources to provide cost-efficient electricity to their customers, questions arose about the 7.35 cent per kWh bundled price. The fundamental principle is one of paying the costs of the services used; however, "This cost allocation process is not simple . . . ."[4]

---

[4] William Marshall, "Inside the Power Deal," *Telegraph-Journal* [Saint John, N.B.], January 30, 2010, A8.

methods to more closely match the purpose of an allocation. Earlier in the chapter, you learned about one type of improvement—dual-rate allocations. Other improvements can also be made.

Estimated Versus Actual Support Costs and Rates

If the goal is to measure the value of support resources actually used, then actual costs and actual allocation base volumes are appropriate. Sometimes, however, it is appropriate to use estimates rather than actual values. The use of estimated rates simplifies and expedites the calculation of allocated support costs. However, the appropriateness of using estimated versus actual costs depends on the purpose of the allocation (see Exhibit 8.2).

For external reporting, estimated support costs can be used only if permitted by the external party. For example, some not-for-profit funding providers allow these organizations to use a "predetermined" support cost allocation rate. The support cost allocation is calculated by multiplying either actual direct labour costs or actual total direct costs by a predetermined rate, which is based on estimates of support costs. The difference between actual and estimated support costs is typically included as an adjustment when negotiating future predetermined rates. Actual support costs are subject to audit even when a predetermined rate is negotiated.

When the purpose of support cost allocation is motivation, the goal is to charge other departments in a way that will encourage managers to use support services efficiently. Several possible methods can be used to measure support cost allocations within an organization. The general formula for charges to other departments is as follows:

$$\text{Allocation rate} = \frac{\text{Total support costs}}{\text{Total volume of allocation base}}$$

$$\text{Charge} = \text{Allocation rate} \times \text{Volume of support services used}$$

Each of the two components of the charge—the allocation rate and the volume of support services used—may be based on actual or estimated values. Estimated values are typically used only when an organization formally adopts a budget.

An advantage of using budgeted values for the entire calculation is that managers of other departments know the support charge in advance, and this charge is not affected by the amount of support service actually used. However, this practice provides little incentive to use support services efficiently. An advantage of using actual values for the entire calculation is that department managers are held responsible for the actual cost of the support services they use. However, this practice can lead to additional problems. For example, if one department uses much less of a support service than anticipated, the charge to the remaining departments increases to cover the total cost of the support department. Under this system, managers feel they have little control over the charges incurred by their departments. One way to address this concern is to charge departments by using a budgeted allocation rate and actual usage. These factors need to be considered when choosing budgeted or actual rates and usage.

For strategic or operating decisions, managers are interested in estimating future costs. Therefore, if they are relevant to a decision, support cost allocations should be based on future estimated costs and volumes of the allocation base. To simplify and expedite decision making, however, actual costs and volumes are often used to estimate future costs and volumes.

Fairness and Allocation Methods

The direct, step-down, and reciprocal methods introduced earlier in this chapter assume that all operating departments should be allocated costs based on their use of support services, and no one operating department is inherently more responsible for support costs than any other operating department. These assumptions are not always appropriate. Sometimes

▷ CHAPTER REFERENCE

Chapter 14 discusses additional methods and issues related to charges between units within an organization, also called transfer prices.

other criteria, such as perceived fairness, are used to allocate common costs such as support department costs.

The perceived fairness of an allocation system depends on the circumstances and sometimes on the ability to bear costs. Suppose costs are being allocated from corporate headquarters to business segments, divisions, or departments. The organization's CEO and CFO want divisions to be aware that corporate costs must be covered for the organization to be profitable. In this case, they might choose revenues as an allocation base because divisions with more revenues are likely to have increased ability to bear the headquarter's support costs. Division or department managers probably believe that revenues are a fair allocation base.

Another way to address perceived fairness is to base common cost allocations on estimates of the costs that would be incurred if the services were not shared. Two methods rely on estimates of separately incurred costs: the stand-alone method and the incremental cost method.

Under the **stand-alone method**, common costs are allocated using weights based on information about the individual users of a cost object. Suppose a professor located in Vancouver travels to present some new research at two different universities—one located in Calgary, and one in Toronto. The total airfare for the trip from Vancouver to Calgary, on to Toronto, and then back to Vancouver, is $944. If the professor were to travel only to each location and back, the round trip to Calgary would cost $448, and the round trip to Toronto would cost $763. Under the stand-alone method, the university in Calgary would pay its proportion of the total ticket cost of $944 based on its stand-alone airfare relative to the total stand-alone airfares. The amount allocated to Calgary is $[\$448/(\$448 + \$763)] \times \$944 = \$349$. The university in Toronto would pay the rest ($595).

Sometimes one user (cost object) is viewed as being more responsible for common costs than other users. Under the **incremental cost allocation method**, the most responsible user is allocated the cost that would have been incurred had the services not been shared with other users. Then, the next most responsible user is allocated the incremental cost to use the shared resource. Suppose the professor had first been invited to Toronto. Under the incremental cost allocation method, Toronto would pay the equivalent of a full-fare ticket to Toronto, or $763, and Calgary would pay the incremental cost to add the extra flight, or $181 ($944 – $763).

▷ **BUSINESS PRACTICE**
The **Saint John Common Council** is wrestling with changes to water rates to balance the need to attract residential and commercial customers but also raise funds to cover the costs of a much-needed water treatment plant. One approach to raising funds is through the general tax base. However, this is perceived as unfair to the households that do not use the municipal water supply.[5]

▷ **CHAPTER REFERENCE**
Chapter 9 introduces several types of revenue-based allocation methods for the common costs of production.

●●◉ RISK OF BIASED DECISIONS: FAIRNESS BIAS

The **FAIRNESS BIAS** is a tendency to reject benefits when offers are perceived as unfair. This bias has been demonstrated in behavioural experiments. Researchers give Player 1 a sum of money and ask that it be split with Player 2. If Player 2 rejects the split, neither player will receive any money. From an economic perspective, Player 2 should accept any amount above zero. However, research has shown that offers of less than 30% are routinely rejected by Player 2. Decision scientists believe that emotional responses to unfair offers are involved in this type of decision making. In business settings, managers may overuse or underuse support services if they believe that cost allocations are unfair.

Cost-Based Contracting

Organizations typically conduct business with other organizations using fixed-price contracts, whereby the vendor provides products or services at a specific price. Alternatively, organizations sometimes use cost-based contracts, where the vendor is reimbursed based on the costs incurred to produce the good or service. For example, the federal government awards cost-plus contracts for some defence equipment. The government allows support costs, such as administration and research and development, to be allocated to defence contracts.

---

[5] Stephen Chase, "Turn Down the Tap on Water Rates," *Telegraph-Journal* [Saint John, N.B.], July 2, 2010, A7.

Cost-based contracts have two major incentive problems. First, managers have little encouragement to control costs when they know that costs will be reimbursed. Second, when allocating costs, managers might be motivated to inappropriately shift costs from other types of contracts to cost-based contracts.

To reduce the likelihood of costs being inappropriately shifted to cost-based contracts, the government often requires contractors to follow specific rules for measuring costs. Contractors with the Canadian government must abide by rules established by Public Works and Government Services Canada. Nongovernmental agencies that award grants also establish detailed guidelines for cost measurement. Accountants must study and use judgment in applying the guidelines for a particular cost-based contract. However, as you have learned throughout this chapter, uncertainties arise in measuring and allocating support costs. Thus, no set of cost accounting rules completely eliminates discretion and bias.

▶ BUSINESS PRACTICE

You can find more information about Public Works and Government Services Canada and contract cost principles at https://buyandsell.gc.ca/ policy-and-guidelines/standard-acquisition-clauses-and-conditions-manual/3/1031-2/6.

Alternatives to Cost-Based Contracting

Some contract-granting organizations have developed approaches to reduce incentive problems by moving away from cost-based contracting. The new approaches have come about, in part, because incentives under cost-based payment systems do not encourage cost containment. Instead, some funding organizations choose to reimburse using a per diem payment while others pay a flat fee per month for each service provided.

8-1 self-study problem   Direct, Step-Down, and Reciprocal Methods: Using Allocation Information

LO1, LO2, LO3, LO4, LO5

Pet Protection is a veterinary clinic that is subsidized by the local humane society. A not-for-profit organization, it was set up to encourage low-income pet owners to neuter and vaccinate their pets. The humane society would like to know the cost per animal visit to use in its fund-raising campaign literature. The information for a recent period follows:

	Support Departments		Operating Departments		
Costs before allocation:					
Direct costs:	**Janitorial**	**Administration**	**Neuter**	**Vaccinations**	**Total**
Salaries	$25,000	$40,000	$100,000	$ 75,000	$240,000
Supplies	5,000	5,000	15,000	25,000	50,000
Building-related costs	2,400	3,600	12,000	6,000	24,000
Total	$32,400	$48,600	$127,000	$106,000	$314,000
Some possible allocation bases:					
Square metres	20	30	100	50	200
Employees	1	1	5	3	10

required

A. Allocate the support department costs to the operating departments by using the following:
   1. Direct method
   2. Step-down method
   3. Reciprocal method
B. Assume that the neuter clinic handles 2,400 pet visits and vaccinations handles 5,000 pet visits. Calculate the cost per visit for each department under the three methods.
C. A local TV station has contacted the head veterinarian at Pet Protection. The station will provide free advertising to encourage low-income pet owners to neuter their pets using Pet Protection's services. The veterinarian estimates the cost of a 10% increase in business volume using the total allocated costs developed in Part A and becomes alarmed at the large total cost. Describe the calculation of total allocated costs and explain why these costs should not be used to estimate future costs.

See the solution on page 379.

●●> FOCUS ON ETHICAL DECISION MAKING:
COST RECOVERY RESPONSIBILITY

In 2000, the province of British Columbia assented to the Tobacco Damages and Health Care Costs Recovery Act, which allowed the provincial government to sue tobacco manufacturers for the costs incurred to treat the tobacco-related illnesses of tobacco products users. Shortly thereafter, British Columbia filed action against Imperial Tobacco Canada Ltd., to recover $10 billion in costs of treatment. On June 5, 2003, the Supreme Court of British Columbia found that the Tobacco Damages and Health Care Costs Recovery Act was unconstitutional, which meant that the province would not be able to recover health care costs of tobacco-related illnesses. In May 2004, the Court of Appeals of British Columbia overturned the Supreme Court decision, and this cleared the way for British Columbia to proceed with legal action against Imperial Tobacco Canada. However, on June 22, 2004, Imperial Tobacco Canada was joined by the British American Group, the R.J. Reynolds Group, the Philip Morris Group, the Rothmans Group, and the Canadian Tobacco Manufacturers Council in an appeal to the Supreme Court of Canada to overturn this ruling. Unfortunately for the tobacco industry, the Supreme Court of Canada, on September 29, 2005, upheld the decision of the Court of Appeals of British Columbia.

Gabrielle Revere/Getty Images

The Act defines the *cost of health care benefits* as

(a) the present value of the **total** [emphasis added] expenditure by the government for health care benefits provided for insured persons resulting from tobacco-related disease or the risk of tobacco-related disease, and

(b) the present value of the **estimated total** [emphasis added] expenditure by the government for health care benefits that could reasonably be expected will be provided for those insured persons resulting from tobacco-related disease or the risk of tobacco-related disease.

The Act defines *health care benefits* as

(a) benefits as defined under the Hospital Insurance Act,

(b) benefits as defined under the Medicare Protection Act,

(c) payments made by the government under the Continuing Care Act, and

(d) other expenditures, made directly or through one or more agents or other intermediate bodies, by the government for programs, services, benefits or similar matters associated with disease.

Further, the Act states that population-based evidence may be used to quantify the costs. In this case, statistical information, results from relevant scientific studies, and information derived from sampling processes are acceptable evidence to quantify the cost of health care benefits.

Steve Maich of *Maclean's* rallied for the tobacco industry by pointing out that a 2002 study indicated that almost 72% of the cost of cigarettes is taxes paid to the federal and provincial governments. A 2000 study indicated that direct health care costs due to tobacco were approximately $2.68 billion per year, while the federal and provincial governments were collecting $7.69 billion per year in cigarette taxes. He asked, "Is the government now trying to double dip? Did British Columbia (and other provinces with copycat legislation) write a law to 'virtually guarantee a windfall at the expense of consumers and shareholders'?" He went on to further question "What industry will be next? Will automakers be held responsible for smog-related illness costs? Will fast-food chains be responsible for obesity-related costs? What about the liquor companies for liver disease costs?"

Source: British Columbia v. Imperial Tobacco Canada Ltd, [2005] 2 S.C.R. 473, 2005 SCC 49; *Tobacco Damages and Health Care Costs Recovery Act [SBC 2000] CHAPTER 30* and S. Maich, "Pity Poor Big Tobacco," *Maclean's* 118 (July 18, 2005), p. 32.

THE ETHICS OF ACCURATE COST CLASSIFICATION

Does the accurate assignment of costs on federal or provincial cost reports create an ethical problem for accountants? What are the costs and benefits of using estimates in accounting? Was it appropriate in this situation for British Columbia to use estimates in its claim? What is the role of the accounting system and procedures in helping an organization meet its responsibilities to various stakeholder groups?

APPENDIX 8A

Using Solver to Calculate Simultaneous Equations for the Reciprocal Method

Solver, a tool within Excel, can be used to solve simultaneous equations. See Appendix 4A for an introduction to using Solver. In this appendix, you'll learn to use Solver for allocating support costs under the reciprocal method.

In Melodious Notes, Part 6, the student interns increased the number of support department cost pools from two to three. Therefore, they decided to use Solver to calculate the support department allocations under the reciprocal method. Before using Solver, it is necessary to specify the simultaneous equations. For MN's fixed cost allocation, the simultaneous equations are as follows:

$$\text{Administration} = \$50{,}348 + 15\% \times \text{Accounting} + (60/990) \times \text{Custodial services}$$
$$\text{Accounting} = \$27{,}630 + (1/11) \times \text{Administration} + (30/990) \times \text{Custodial services}$$
$$\text{Custodial services} = \$30{,}180 + (2/11) \times \text{Administration} + 10\% \times \text{Accounting}$$

Exhibits 8A.1 and 8A.2 provide results and formulas using Solver for this set of simultaneous equations. The change cells are given the names Admin, Acct, and Custodial. Solver manipulates these cells to solve the simultaneous equations for each department's cost. The solution includes allocations from the other two support departments. The target function is the sum of the three change cells and is given the following formula:

$$= \text{Admin} + \text{Acct} + \text{Custodial}$$

Notice in cells B15, B16, and B17 that the simultaneous equations are listed so that they can be entered into Solver as constraints. When adding each constraint in the Solver dialog box, set the simultaneous equation (by selecting the equal sign in the pull-down menu) equal to the change cell that represents the department for which cost you are solving. For example, the cell with the simultaneous equations for administration should contain

$$= \text{B3} + \text{B7}*\text{Acct} + (\text{B8/G8})*\text{Custodial}$$

Click Add next to the constraints box. The cell with this formula will be entered on the left-hand side, under Cell Reference. Click on the box under Constraint and then highlight the department for the simultaneous equation in the cell reference, in this case Admin.

▶EXHIBIT 8A.1

Fixed Cost Allocation Spreadsheet for Using Solver

	A	B	C	D	E	F	G
1	Melodious Notes						
2	Departments	Administration	Accounting	Custodial Services	Instrument Sales	Music Lessons	Total
3	Costs	$50,348	$27,630	$30,180	$263,800	$93,600	$465,558
4							
5	Allocation Bases						
6	Employees	0	1	2	5	3	11
7	Accounting time spent	15%	0%	10%	50%	25%	100%
8	Square metres	60	30	0	800	100	990
9							
10	Change cells for solver						
11		Admin	Acct	Custodial			
12		$58,164	$34,256	$44,181			
13							
14	Simultaneous equations						
15	Administration	$58,164					
16	Accounting	$34,256					
17	Custodial Services	$44,181					
18							
19	Target function						
20	136601.5012						
21							
22	Allocation	Administration	Accounting	Custodial Services	Instrument Sales	Music Lessons	Total
23	Department Cost	$50,348	$27,630	$30,180	$263,800	$93,600	$465,558
24	Administration Allocation	($58,164)	$5,287	$10,575	$26,438	$15,863	$0
25	Accounting Allocation	$5,138	($34,256)	$3,426	$17,128	$8,564	$0
26	Custodial Allocation	$2,678	$1,339	($44,181)	$35,702	$4,463	$0
27	Total Allocated Cost	$0	$0	$0	$343,068	$122,490	$456,558

	A	B	C	D	E	F	G
1	Melodious Notes						
2	Departments	Administration	Accounting	Custodial Services	Instrument Sales	Music Lessons	Total
3	Costs	50348	27630	30180	263800	93600	=SUM(B3:F3)
4							
5	Allocation Bases						
6	Employees	0	1	2	5	3	=SUM(B6:F6)
7	Accounting time spent	0.15	0	0.1	.5	0.25	=SUM(B7:F7)
8	Square metres	60	30	0	800	100	=SUM(B8:F8)
9							
10	Change cells for solver						
11		Admin	Acct	Custodial			
12		58164.1018577537	34256.4619090369	44180.9374373239			
13							
14	Simultaneous equations						
15	Administration	=B3+B7*Acct+(B8/G8)*Custodial					
16	Accounting	=C3+(C6/G6)*Admin+(C8/G8)*Custodial					
17	Custodial Services	=D3+(D6/G6)*Admin+D7*Acct					
18							
19	Target function						
20	=Admin+Acct+Custodial						
21							
22	Allocation	Administration	Accounting	Custodial Services	Instrument Sales	Music Lessons	Total
23	Cost	=B3	=C3	=D3	=E3	=F3	=SUM(B23:F23)
24	Administration Allocation	=-B15	=(C6/$G$6)*$B$15	=(D6/$G$6)*$B$15	=(E6/$G$6)*$B$15	=(F6/$G$6)*$B$15	=SUM(B24:F24)
25	Accounting Allocation	=B7*B16	=-B16	=D7*$B$16	=E7*$B$16	=F7*$B$16	=SUM(B25:F25)
26	Custodial Allocation	=(B8/$G$8)*$B$17	=(C8/$G$8)*$B$17	=-B17	=(E8/$G$8)*$B$17	=(F8/$G$8)*$B$17	=SUM(B26:F26)
27	Total Allocated Cost	=SUM(B23:B26)	=SUM(C23:C26)	=SUM(D23:D26)	=SUM(E23:E26)	=SUM(F23:F26)	=SUM(G23:G26)

► EXHIBIT 8A.2

Fixed Cost Allocation Spreadsheet for Using Solver with Formulas

In the spreadsheet shown in Exhibits 8A.1 and 8A.2, solution values from Solver feed into the bottom part of the spreadsheet that performs the allocation process. You may need to go back and forth between these two spreadsheets to understand how to set up your own spreadsheet for this problem. Notice that the values for costs and allocation bases are at the top of the spreadsheet. If you change any of these values, you will need to run Solver again to determine the new amounts for the three support departments. Use the formula spreadsheet as a guide to set up this problem. If you need a reminder on how to use Solver, go back to Appendix 4A for details.

SUMMARY

LO1 Define support departments, and explain why their costs are allocated to other departments

OPERATING DEPARTMENTS

The departments or divisions within an organization that manufacture goods or produce services for external customers or clients.

SUPPORT DEPARTMENTS

Provide services, internal to the organization, to the operating departments.

OBJECTIVES FOR ALLOCATING SUPPORT DEPARTMENT COSTS

Objective	Example
External reporting	Cost reports for government contracts
	Income tax returns
	Reports prepared for reimbursement purposes
Motivation	Provide incentives for efficient production of support services
	Provide incentives for appropriate use of support services
	Monitor use and production of support services
Strategic or operating decisions	Insource or outsource
	Pricing

LO2   Explain the process that is used to allocate support department costs

PROCESS FOR ALLOCATING SUPPORT DEPARTMENT COSTS

1. Clarify the purpose of the allocation.

2. Identify support and operating department cost pools.

3. Assign costs to cost pools.

4. For each support department cost pool, choose an allocation base.

5. Choose and apply a method for allocating support department costs to operating departments.

6. If relevant, allocate support costs from the operating departments to units of goods or services.

LO3   Explain how the direct method is used to allocate support costs to operating departments; calculate cost allocations using the direct method

DIRECT METHOD

Each support department's cost is allocated to only the operating departments.

PROS AND CONS OF THE DIRECT METHOD

► Is the easiest method computationally, but computers make this factor less important.
► Is easy to explain to managers and others.
► Ignores interactions among support departments.

LO4   Explain how the step-down method is used to allocate support costs to operating departments; calculate cost allocations using the step-down method

STEP-DOWN METHOD

Support department costs are allocated one department at a time to remaining support and operating departments in a cascading manner until all support department costs have been allocated.

PROS AND CONS OF THE STEP-DOWN METHOD

► Requires ranking of support departments in terms of services provided to other support departments.
► Has moderately easy computations, depending on the number of support departments.
► Is moderately easy to explain to managers and others.
► Takes into account some of the interactions among support departments.

LO5   Explain how the reciprocal method is used to allocate support costs to operating departments; calculate cost allocations using the reciprocal method

RECIPROCAL METHOD

► First, support department costs are simultaneously allocated among support departments.
► Next, support department costs, including interactions, are allocated to operating departments.

PROS AND CONS OF THE RECIPROCAL METHOD

► Is computationally the most complex, but computers simplify the process.
► May be difficult to explain to managers and others.
► Is the most accurate allocation method because it takes into account all the interactions among support departments.

SUMMARY

LO6   Explain the difference between single- and dual-rate allocations

SINGLE-RATE ALLOCATION

Uses only one base to allocate both fixed and variable costs.

DUAL-RATE ALLOCATION

Accumulates fixed and variable costs in separate cost pools and uses different allocation bases for these cost pools.

PROS AND CONS OF DUAL-RATE ALLOCATION

► Reduces mismeasurement of allocations.
► Reduces misunderstandings about the behaviour of support costs.
► Costs more to develop and maintain.
► May introduce additional mismeasurement from problems classifying costs as fixed and variable.

LO7   Identify how support cost allocations and information quality impact management decision making

UNCERTAINTIES

► Identifying support and operating cost pools.
► Assigning costs to cost pools.
► Selecting allocation bases.

WAYS TO IMPROVE THE QUALITY OF INFORMATION

► Dual-rate allocations
► Redesign of accounting system for cost pools and allocation bases
► Choices regarding estimated versus actual support costs and rates

► Consideration of perceived fairness
► Choice of an allocation method that measures the degree of services provided among support departments (step-down and reciprocal methods)
► Use of alternative criteria for allocation:
  – Stand-alone method
  – Incremental cost allocation method
► Imposition of allocation rules by contracting parties
► Replacement of cost-based payments with fixed-fee payments

8-1 solution to self-study problem

A. Two assumptions are used in making these calculations: (1) the administration costs will be allocated using number of employees and janitorial costs will be allocated using square metres, and (2) the administration support department provides more services to the janitorial support department than the other way around.

1. Direct Method Allocation

| | Support Departments | | Operating Departments | | |
	Janitorial	Administration	Neuter	Vaccinations	Total
Allocation base percentages:					
Administration					
Employees			5	3	8
Percent			62.5%	37.5%	100%

(Continued)

	Support Departments		Operating Departments		
	Janitorial	Administration	Neuter	Vaccinations	Total
Janitorial					
Square metres			100	50	150
Percent			66.6667%	33.3333%	100%
Departmental costs	$ 32,400	$ 48,600	$127,000	$106,000	$314,000
Allocations:					
Administration		(48,600)	30,375	18,225	
Janitorial	(32,400)		21,600	10,800	
Total allocated cost	$ 0	$ 0	$178,975	$135,025	$314,000

2. Step-Down Method Allocation

For the step-down allocation method, administrative costs are allocated first because they are largest:

	Support Departments		Operating Departments		
	Janitorial	Administration	Neuter	Vaccinations	Total
Allocation base percentages:					
Administration					
Employees	1		5	3	9
Percent	11.1111%		55.5556%	33.3333%	100%
Janitorial					
Square metres			100	50	150
Percent			66.6667%	33.3333%	100%
Departmental costs	$ 32,400	$ 48,600	$127,000	$106,000	$314,000
Allocations:					
Administration	5,400	(48,600)	27,000	16,200	
Janitorial	(37,800)		25,200	12,600	
Total allocated cost	$ 0	$ 0	$179,200	$134,800	$314,000

3. Reciprocal Method Allocation

The first task in the reciprocal method is to set up and solve simultaneous equations for the interactions among the support departments. The interactions are calculated using the allocation base percentages. When only two support departments are involved, the substitution method can be used to solve the simultaneous equations.

	Support Departments		Operating Departments		
	Janitorial	Administration	Neuter	Vaccinations	Total
Allocation base percentages:					
Administration					
Employees	1		5	3	9
Percent	11.1111%		55.5556%	33.3333%	100%
Janitorial					
Square metres		30	100	50	180
Percent		16.6667%	55.5556%	27.7777	100%

Simultaneous Equations:
The equation for the total costs of each support department is equal to the costs assigned to the departmental cost pool plus an allocation of the costs from the other support department:

$$\text{Janitorial} = \$32,400 + (1/9) \times \text{Administration}$$

$$\text{Administration} = \$48,600 + (30/180) \times \text{Janitorial}$$

The cost for the janitorial department is calculated by substituting the administration equation into the janitor equation:

$$\text{Janitorial} = \$32,400 \times (1/9) \times (48,600 + (30/180) \times \text{Janitorial})$$

$$0.98148148 \times \text{Janitorial} = \$37,800$$

$$\text{Janitorial} = \$38,513$$

The cost for the administration department is calculated by substituting the result for the janitorial cost into the administration equation:

$$\text{Administration} = \$48,600 + (30/180) \times \$38,513$$

$$\text{Administration} = \$55,019$$

Next, costs are allocated from each support department to the other support departments and to the operating departments. The amounts allocated are based on the computations from the simultaneous equations. The use of simultaneous equations ensures that zero cost remains in each support department after the allocations are complete. In other words, the total cost allocated from janitorial ($38,513) is equal to the costs assigned to the janitorial cost pool ($32,400) plus the costs allocated to janitorial from administration ($6,113). Similarly, the total cost allocated from administration ($55,019) is equal to the costs assigned to the administration cost pool ($48,600) plus the costs allocated to administration from janitorial ($6,419):

| | Support Departments | | Operating Departments | | |
	Janitorial	Administration	Neuter	Vaccinations	Total
Departmental costs	$ 32,400	$48,600	$127,000	$106,000	$314,000
Allocations:					
Administration	6,113	(55,019)	30,566	18,340	0
Janitorial	(38,513)	6,419	21,396	10,698	0
Total allocated cost	$ 0	$ 0	$178,962	$135,038	$314,000

B. The cost per visit is calculated by dividing each operating department's total direct and allocated costs by the number of pet visits per year:

	Neuter	Vaccinations
Direct method	$178,975 ÷ 2,400 = $74.57 per visit	$135,025 ÷ 5,000 = $27.01 per visit
Step-down method	$179,200 ÷ 2,400 = $74.67 per visit	$134,800 ÷ 5,000 = $26.96 per visit
Reciprocal method	$178,962 ÷ 2,400 = $74.57 per visit	$135,038 ÷ 5,000 = $27.01 per visit

C. The costs per visit are calculated as follows. First, all clinic costs are assigned to departments. Some costs are traced directly to departments (salaries and supplies), and some (building-related costs) are gathered together in a general cost pool and distributed (allocated) among all the departments. Then, the support department costs (administration and janitorial) are allocated to each other and then to the operating departments (neuter and vaccinations). Many of these costs are fixed and will not change as volumes increase (e.g., salaries, building-related costs such as the lease).

Through the allocation process, all the fixed costs become an average cost per unit. The cost per visit is accurate only at the level of visits used in the denominator. When the veterinarian multiplies the per-visit rate by a larger number of visits, the total cost is overestimated because the per-visit cost is an average cost that includes a portion of fixed cost. These fixed costs do not increase proportionately as volumes increase but remain constant across a relevant range. To increase the accuracy of future cost estimates, past costs need to be separated into fixed and variable categories, and a cost function needs to be developed. In addition, some of the information used in the cost function should be updated to reflect any anticipated price changes.

QUESTIONS

8.1   Explain the differences and similarities among the direct, step-down, and reciprocal methods.

8.2   Explain the similarities and differences between support department costs and manufacturing overhead costs.

8.3   What should determine the choice of cost allocation method (direct, step-down, or reciprocal), as discussed in this chapter?

8.4   Sometimes costs that include support department allocations are used in short-term decision making. List several limitations of these costs when used in decision making and discuss ways to address the limitations.

8.5   What factors should be considered when choosing allocation bases?

8.6   A product is started in Department 1 and completed in Department 2. Is Department 1 a support department or an operating department? Explain.

8.7   Explain the difference between operating departments and support departments.

8.8   List at least two advantages of the dual-rate method.

8.9   Explain several problems that arise when allocated costs are used to charge for support services.

8.10   What kinds of incentive problems arise when information from a single-rate allocation system is used as a transfer price for the use of support department services?

8.11   Would better decisions be made with information from single-rate or dual-rate cost allocation systems? Explain your reasoning.

8.12   What are the advantages and disadvantages of using estimated support cost allocation rates?

8.13   List at least three possible allocation bases that could be used to allocate accounting department costs to other departments. List one advantage and one disadvantage of using each allocation base.

8.14   Describe IFRS and Canadian ASPE as it applies to
   a. Manufacturing overhead
   b. Support department costs

8.15   Sometimes it is more appropriate to use actual support cost allocations, but at other times it is better to use estimated allocations. Explain when each type of allocation is more appropriate.

8.16   Is the cafeteria at your university a support department or a revenue-generating department? Explain.

MULTIPLE-CHOICE QUESTIONS

8.17 A business uses the step-down method to allocate service department costs to the manufacturing departments. There are two service departments and two manufacturing departments, as shown here:

	Service Departments		Manufacturing Departments	
	Plant Administration	Custodial Services	Cutting	Polishing
Costs	$360,000	$90,000	$261,000	$689,000
Labour hours	25,000	6,000	18,000	30,000
Space occupied (m²)	10,000	1,000	5,000	45,000

Plant administration costs are allocated based on labour hours, and custodial services costs are allocated based on space occupied. The total costs of the cutting and polishing departments (rounded to the closest 1,000), after allocating all the service department costs, starting with the largest service provider, are which of the following?

a. Cutting, $396,000; polishing, $914,000
b. Cutting, $405,000; polishing, $995,000
c. Cutting, $381,000; polishing, $889,000
d. Cutting, $394,000; polishing, $1,006,000
e. Cutting, $380,000; polishing, $892,000

8.18 The managers of ACME Manufacturing are discussing ways to allocate the cost of service departments, such as quality control and maintenance, to the production departments. To aid them in this discussion, the controller has provided the following information:

	Quality Control	Maintenance	Machining	Assembly	Total
Budgeted overhead costs before allocation	$350,000	$200,000	$400,000	$300,000	$1,250,000
Budgeted machine hours	–	–	50,000	–	50,000
Budgeted direct labour hours	–	–	–	25,000	25,000
Budgeted hours of service: Quality control	–	7,000	21,000	7,000	35,000
Maintenance	10,000	–	18,000	12,000	40,000

Using the direct allocation method, the total amount of overhead allocated to each machine hour would be which of the following?

a. $9.35
b. $5.25
c. $2.40
d. $8.00
e. $15.65

8.19 Which of the following methods of allocating service department costs results in the most accurate product cost?

a. Direct method
b. Step-down method
c. Reciprocal method
d. Activity-based costing method

The following information is relevant to Questions 8.20 and 8.21:

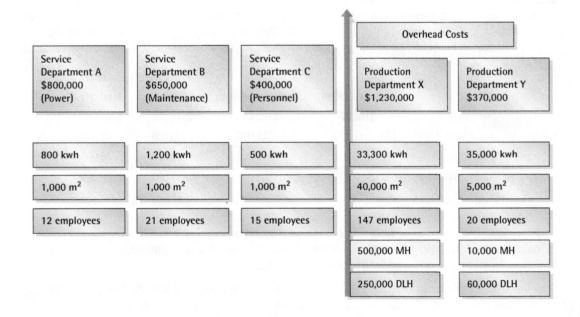

Assume that the cost drivers for each department are as follows:

Department A	Kilowatt hours (kwh)
Department B	Square metres (m²)
Department C	Number of employees
Department X	Machine hours (MH)
Department Y	Direct labour hours (DLH)

8.20 Which service department should be allocated first, based on the amount of service provided (determined by costs), using the step-down method of allocation?

a. Department A
b. Department B
c. Department C
d. Department X or Y

8.21 Assume that the service departments' costs were allocated in alphabetical order. What is the approximate overhead rate for Department C?
a. $1,860
b. $2,308
c. $2,429
d. $2,516

EXERCISES

8.22 Estimated Versus Actual Allocation Rates A custodial support department budgets its costs at $40,000 per month plus $12 per hour. For November, the custodial support department provided the following estimated and actual hours to three operating departments:

LO2, LO7

	Estimated Hours Spent Cleaning	Actual Hours Spent Cleaning
Department A	1,600	1,500
Department B	1,400	1,600
Department C	2,000	1,800
Total	5,000	4,900

REQUIRED **A.** What is the support department's allocation rate if estimated activity is the allocation base?
B. What is the support department's allocation rate if actual activity is the allocation base?
C. List one advantage and one disadvantage of each type of allocation rate.

8.23 Allocating Support Costs to Units A local hospital is required to account for the total cost of patient care, including support costs. Patients are assigned all direct costs. Support costs are $240,000 per month plus $90 per patient day. This 120-bed hospital averages 80% occupancy.

LO2

REQUIRED Calculate the average daily charge per patient for support costs, assuming 30 days in a month.

8.24 Direct Method Cedar Hill Manufacturing produces wooden outdoor furniture. Cedar Hill uses the direct method to allocate service department costs to the production departments. There are two service departments: administration and custodial services, and two production departments: cutting and assembly. Administration costs are allocated based on labour hours, and custodial services costs are allocated based on space occupied.

LO3

			Production Departments	
	Administration	Custodial Services	Cutting	Assembly
Direct costs	$160,000	$100,000	$345,000	$731,000
Labour hours	12,000	10,000	30,000	50,000
Space occupied (m²)	5,000	5,000	20,000	30,000
# units produced			50,000	90,000

REQUIRED **A.** Using the direct method
    1. Allocate the administration costs to the production departments.
    2. Allocate the custodial services costs to the production departments.
B. Calculate the total costs (direct plus allocated) for each production department.
C. Calculate a cost per unit produced for cutting and assembly.

8.25 Step-Down Method Refer to Exercise 8.24. Assume instead that Cedar Hill Manufacturing uses the step-down method and allocates administration costs first followed by custodial services costs.

LO4

REQUIRED A. Using the step-down method (round to 2 decimals):
  1. Allocate the administration costs to the production departments.
  2. Allocate the custodial services costs to the production departments.
  B. Calculate the total costs (direct plus allocated) for each production department.
  C. Calculate a cost per unit produced for cutting and assembly.

8.26 Direct Method Ridgeway Associates rents space to landscape design business and an environmental consulting
LO3 business. Ridgeway Associates provides payroll/tax reporting services and custodial services as part of the rental
contract. To determine the monthly rental fee, Ridgeway Associates must allocate the payroll/tax reporting costs
and the custodial services costs to the landscape design business and the environmental consulting. Payroll/tax
reporting services are allocated based on number of employees and custodial services are allocated based on
space occupied. Costs reported are for the year.

	Payroll/Tax Reporting Services	Custodial Services	Pet Store	Grooming
Direct costs	$60,000	$40,000	$72,000	$90,000
# employees	2	3	5	7
Space occupied (m²)	1,000	1,000	3,000	5,000

REQUIRED If Ridgeway Associates uses the direct method to allocate costs, what are the monthly rental charges for the
landscape design business and the environmental consulting business? (*Hint:* First, allocate the payroll/tax
reporting services costs and the custodial services costs to the landscape design business and the environmental
consulting business. Then, add the direct costs and allocated costs together and divide by 12 (months in a year).)

8.27 Step-Down Method Refer to Exercise 8.26. Assume that Ridgeway Associates uses the step-down method.
LO4

REQUIRED A. Starting with payroll/tax reporting services, calculate the costs to be allocated to the landscape design business
and the environmental consulting business. Assuming that the above costs are for one year, what are the
monthly costs charged to the landscape design business and the environmental consulting business?
  B. Starting with custodial services, calculate the costs to be allocated to the landscape design business and the
environmental consulting business. Assuming that the above costs are for one year, what are the monthly costs
charged to these businesses?

8.28 Direct and Step-Down Methods Donaldson Company has two service departments (personnel and financial) that provide
LO3, LO4 services for one another as well as for two production departments, assembly and finishing. Data for the month follow:

	Personnel	Financial	Assembly	Finishing
Employees	6	8	20	15
Payroll	$15,000	$14,000	$30,000	$27,000

Personnel department costs were $86,000, and financial department costs were $41,000. Donaldson uses
employees as the allocation base for personnel department costs and payroll costs for financial department costs.

REQUIRED A. Allocate support costs using the direct method.
  B. Allocate support costs using the step-down method, with personnel costs allocated first.

8.29 Single-Rate Versus Dual-Rate A factory averages total employment of 700 people. The administrative department
LO6, LO7 averages 150 people. The company operates a cafeteria with capacity to serve all employees. The cafeteria's
monthly costs are $12,000 plus $2.50 per meal served. In July, the factory was closed for retooling. During July,
the cafeteria provided 3,200 meals to administrative personnel and 1,000 meals to factory employees.

REQUIRED A. Using the single-rate method, allocate the cafeteria costs to factory and administration based on actual meals
served during July.
  B. Using the dual-rate method, allocate the cafeteria costs to factory and administration based on actual meals
served during July.
  C. List the pros and cons of using the single-rate allocation method.
  D. Would the managers of the administrative department prefer the single-rate method or the dual-rate method? Explain.
  E. Should the fixed costs for the cafeteria be allocated in July if it causes the administrative department's costs to
exceed its budget?

8.30 Stand-Alone and Incremental Cost Methods, Fairness A graduate student interviewing for a full-time teaching

LO7 position has just returned from visiting three organizations in a single trip costing $950. Each school has offered to reimburse the student its "fair share." If the schools had been visited individually, travel costs and time would have been as follows:

Public University	$ 500	2 days
City College	250	1 day
Private University	750	3 days
Total	$1,500	6 days

REQUIRED **A.** Allocate the costs using the stand-alone method.
B. Allocate the costs using the incremental cost method.
C. Which method is most "fair?" Explain.

8.31 Single-Rate Versus Dual-Rate, Estimated and Actual Volumes Use the information given in Exercise 8.22.

LO6, LO7

REQUIRED **A.** Assume that the single-rate method is used, and calculate the cost allocation to each department for housekeeping services if estimated hours are used.
B. Assume that the dual-rate method is used, estimated hours are used to allocate fixed costs, and actual hours are used to allocate variable costs. Calculate the cost allocation to each department for housekeeping services.
C. List one advantage and one disadvantage for each type of allocation method.

8.32 Direct Method Using Estimated Costs, Benchmarking Devon allocates support department costs using the direct

LO1, LO3, LO7 method and estimated costs. The support department costs are budgeted at $88,000 for Department A, $63,000 for Department B, and $40,000 for Department C. These costs are allocated using the proportion of total cost the firm would pay to an outside service provider:

	Support Departments			Operating Departments	
	Dept. A	Dept. B	Dept. C	Casting	Machine
Direct costs	$88,000	$63,000	$40,000	–	–
Labour hours				6,000	4,000
Machine hours				2,000	10,000
Costs if support services were purchased externally:					
Department A				$50,000	$60,000
Department B				$40,000	$20,000
Department C				$30,000	$30,000

REQUIRED **A.** Allocate budgeted support department costs using the direct method, first using labour hours and then with the outside cost proportions as the allocation bases.
B. Could Devon use the cost of purchasing externally as an efficiency benchmark for the cost of both the support departments and the user departments? List several advantages and disadvantages of this approach.

8.33 Direct and Step-Down Methods with Dual Rates Enviro-Go uses the direct method for allocating both fixed and

LO2, LO3, LO4, LO6 variable costs from the physical plant and equipment maintenance support departments to operating departments Echo and Golf. The bases for allocation are as follows:

Physical plant	Fixed costs on the basis of square metres occupied
	Variable costs on the basis of number of employees
Equipment maintenance	Fixed costs on the basis of budgeted machine hours
	Variable costs on the basis of expected maintenance hours

Costs for physical plant and equipment maintenance follow:

	Physical Plant	Equipment Maintenance
Fixed costs	$39,000	$75,000
Variable costs	$18,000	$60,000

Allocation bases for all four departments are

	Support Departments		Operating Departments	
	Physical Plant	Equipment Maintenance	Department Echo	Department Golf
Square metres	1,600	3,900	5,000	8,000
Number of employees	10	12	40	50
Budgeted machine hours	0	100	10,000	15,000
Budgeted maintenance hours	10	20	200	400

REQUIRED
A. Assign the support department costs to Departments Echo and Golf using the direct method.
B. Assign the support department costs to Departments Echo and Golf using the step-down method, with the physical plant costs allocated first.
C. Assign the support department costs to. Departments Echo and Golf using the step-down method, with equipment maintenance costs allocated first.
D. Under the step-down method, what criterion should be used to decide which support department costs to allocate first?

8.34 Reciprocal Method The Brown and Brinkley Brokerage firm is organized into two major sales divisions: institutional clients and retail clients. The firm also has two support departments: research and administration. The research department's costs are allocated to the other departments based on a log of hours spent on tasks for each user. The administration department's costs are allocated based on the number of employees in each department.

Records are available for last period as follows:

	Support Departments		Operating Departments	
	Research	Administration	Institutional	Retail
Payroll costs	$350,000	$300,000	$400,000	$550,000
Other costs	$230,000	$150,000	$120,000	$240,000
Research hours	100	200	500	300
Number of employees	7	10	8	10

REQUIRED Using the reciprocal method, determine the total cost of operations for each sales division. Use either simultaneous equations or Excel Solver.

8.35 Reciprocal Method Paul's Valley Protection Service has three support departments (S1, S2, and S3) and three operating departments (P1, P2, and P3). The direct costs of each department are $30,000 for S1, $20,000 for S2, and $40,000 for S3. The proportions of service provided by each support department to the others are given in the following table:

	Support Departments			Operating Departments		
	S1	S2	S3	P1	P2	P3
S1	–	0.4	0.1	0.2	0.2	0.1
S2	0.1	–	0.2	0.2	–	0.5
S3	0.2	0.2	–	0.1	0.4	0.1

REQUIRED Using the reciprocal method, allocate the support department costs to the operating departments.

8.36 Step-Down, Direct, and Reciprocal Methods, Accuracy of Allocation Up, Up, and Away Ltd. create flight and driving simulations and games for personal computers. The president has a complaint about the accounting for support department costs. He points to the following table, which describes the use of various support departments in the company, and says, "According to this table, every department receives services from all the support departments. But I understand that only some of the support departments are bearing costs from the other support departments. Why is that?"

Percentage Use of Services

Support Department	Cost	Administration	Maintenance	Information Systems	Games Manufacturing	Simulation Manufacturing
Administration	$40,000	0%	10%	40%	20%	30%
Maintenance	20,000	20	0	10	40	30
Information systems	50,000	30	10	0	40	20

REQUIRED
A. What method has Up, Up, and Away Ltd. been using to allocate support costs? Explain how you know.
B. Which method would ignore all interactions among support departments? Explain.
C. Which method would consider all interactions among support departments? Explain.
D. Allocate the support department costs to games and simulations using the step-down method. Explain how you decided which department's costs to allocate first.
E. Allocate the support department costs using the direct method.
F. Allocate the support department costs using the reciprocal method.
G. In your own words, explain how the step-down method improves on the direct method.
H. In your own words, explain how the reciprocal method improves on the step-down method.

8.37 Direct, Step-Down, and Reciprocal Methods, Assigning Costs to Departments Cost information for Red Oak Town Library is as follows:

LO2, LO3, LO4, LO5

	Support Departments		Operating Departments		
Direct Costs	Janitorial	Administration	Books	Other Media	Total
Salaries	$20,000	$40,000	$70,000	$50,000	$180,000
Supplies	10,000	5,000	15,000	20,000	50,000
Allocation Base Volumes					
Square metres	50	50	120	30	250
Employees	1	1	2	1	5

REQUIRED In addition to directly traceable costs, the library incurred $24,000 for a building lease.
A. Allocate to departments any costs that have not been traced and then calculate total costs assigned to each department.
B. Allocate the support department costs to the operating departments using the direct method.
C. Allocate the support department costs to the operating departments using the step-down method. Allocate first the costs for the support department that has the largest direct costs.
D. Allocate the support department costs to the operating departments using the reciprocal method. Use either simultaneous equations or Excel Solver.

8.38 Stand-alone and Incremental Cost Allocation Methods Monty is the CFO of a large organization with fast-food outlets in London, Paris, and Frankfurt. When the manager at an outlet asks for his help, he flies out and discusses matters such as the controls that are in place for each outlet and any expected upcoming changes in costs or procedures that will affect productivity. The outlets are charged for the airfare for these trips. Shortly after Monty was contacted by the Frankfurt outlet, the Paris outlet also called to set up a visit. Monty's airfare from London to Frankfurt to Paris to London is €300. If he travels round trip from London to Frankfurt, the cost would be €250, and if he travels round trip from London to Paris, the fare would be €200.

LO7

REQUIRED
A. Calculate the charge for Monty's airfare to each outlet using the stand-alone allocation method.
B. Calculate the charge for Monty's airfare to each outlet using the incremental cost allocation method.
C. Which allocation method is most fair? Explain your reasoning.

8.39 Step-Down and Reciprocal Methods, Uncertainties, Pricing Kovacik manufactures two types of piggy banks in two different departments: a plain piggy bank and a metallic bank. The plant is highly automated and contains only two other departments: (1) engineering and design and (2) information systems. Kovacik allocates support department costs according to estimated service use. Estimated information for next year is as follows:

LO2, LO4, LO5, LO7

	Support Departments		Operating Departments	
	Engineering and Design	Information Systems	Plain Bank	Metallic Bank
Direct costs	$2,700	$8,000	$10,000	$20,000
Services used				
Engineering and design		10%	40%	50%
Information systems	20%		30%	50%
Production volume			8,000	4,000

Total allocated costs are assigned to individual units using the production volume.

REQUIRED
A. Determine the estimated total allocated costs for the operating departments using the step-down method.
B. Determine the estimated total allocated cost per unit of the plain piggy bank and the metallic piggy bank using the step-down method, allocating the department with the largest direct costs first.
C. Explain why actual total allocated costs will turn out to be different from the estimated total allocated costs.
D. Determine the estimated total allocated costs for the operating departments using the reciprocal method. Use either simultaneous equations or Excel Solver.
E. Determine the estimated total allocated cost per unit of the plain piggy bank and the metallic piggy bank under the reciprocal method.

PROBLEMS

8.40 **Step-Down and Reciprocal Methods, Uncertainties, Pricing** Howard Inc. manufactures two types of skateboards
LO2, LO4, in two different departments: a basic board and an exclusive model. The plant is highly automated and contains
LO5, LO7 only two other departments: (1) engineering and design and (2) information systems. Howard's allocates
support department costs according to estimated service use. Estimated information for next year is as follows:

	Support Departments		Operating Departments	
	Engineering and Design	Information Systems	Basic Board	Exclusive Model
Direct costs	$40,500	$120,000	$150,000	$300,000
Services used				
Engineering and design		10%	20%	70%
Information systems	20%		30%	50%
Production volume			120,000	60,000

Total allocated costs are assigned to individual units using the production volume.

REQUIRED
A. Determine the estimated total allocated costs for the operating departments using the step-down method.
B. Determine the estimated total allocated cost per unit of the basic skateboard and the exclusive skateboard using the step-down method, allocating the department with the largest direct costs first.
C. Explain why actual total allocated costs will turn out to be different from the estimated total allocated costs.
D. Determine the estimated total allocated costs for the operating departments using the reciprocal method. Use either simultaneous equations or Excel Solver.
E. Determine the estimated total allocated cost per unit of the basic skateboard and the exclusive skateboard under the reciprocal method.
F. Explain the differences in the results from the different allocation methods. When would managers use each method?

8.41 **Direct, Step-Down, and Reciprocal Methods, Accuracy of Allocation** Sight and Sound Ltd. produces televisions and
LO2, LO3, stereo systems. The managers of production departments have a complaint about the accounting for support
LO4, LO5, department costs. Based on the following table they point out that every department receives services from all
LO7 the support departments; but, only some of the support departments are bearing costs from the other support
departments. They believe that means that the production departments are bearing more cost than they use.

Percentage Use of Services

Support Department	Cost	Administration	Maintenance	Information Systems	Television Manufacturing	Stereo Manufacturing
Administration	$80,000	0%	20%	20%	30%	30%
Maintenance	40,000	25	0	15	30	30
Information systems	100,000	40	10	0	25	25

REQUIRED

A. What method has Sight and Sound Ltd. been using to allocate support costs? Explain this approach to the managers.

B. Which method would ignore all interactions among support departments? Explain.

C. Which method would consider all interactions among support departments? Explain.

D. Allocate the support department costs using the direct method.

E. Allocate the support department costs to television and stereo using the step-down method. Explain how you decided which department's costs to allocate first

F. Allocate the support department costs using the reciprocal method. Use either simultaneous equations or Excel Solver.

G. In your own words, explain how the step-down method improves on the direct method.

H. In your own words, explain how the reciprocal method improves on the step-down method.

I. Make a recommendation to the President of Sight and Sound Ltd. for an allocation method. Be sure to consider the managers concerns as well as the cost of implementing the different allocation methods.

8.42 Department Allocations, Decision Making

LO1, LO2, LO3, LO4, LO5, LO6, LO7

In 2016, JacLyn's Bookstore devoted 400 square metres to the display and sale of paperback books, 100 square metres to children's books, and 50 square metres to rare books. The store is 600 square metres, and 50 square metres were unused. The cost to maintain the store was $68,750, which was allocated among the three departments based on 550 square metres of occupied space. In 2017, management put a specialty coffee shop in the previously unused space. However, the allocation was not updated for this change. In 2017, the four departments' contribution margins before the allocation of building costs were

Paperback Books	$48,000
Children's Books	34,000
Rare Books	13,000
Coffee	5,000

During 2018, the four department managers all requested that they be allowed to expand their floor space. Each argued that the floor space of one of the other departments should be reduced so that their own department could be expanded.

REQUIRED

A. Determine earnings after the building costs have been allocated for 2017 for each department (remember that the firm allocated costs to only three departments).

B. After seeing the results, the managers of the paperback books, children's books, and rare books point out that the coffee shop was not contributing toward covering the building costs. Determine the earnings after the building costs have been allocated for 2017 using all four departments.

C. Suppose the managers mistakenly used the earnings after building costs were allocated to determine the contribution per unit of constrained resource (per square metre) for each department. Which department would be allowed to expand, and which one should be reduced or dropped?

D. Suppose that managers properly calculated the contribution margin per unit of constrained resource (per square metre) for Part C by ignoring allocated costs. Which department would be allowed to expand, and which one would be reduced?

E. Explain why the method in Part D is better for making this decision. What are the qualitative factors related to this decision?

F. Assume instead that during 2018, a small 200 square metre adjacent shop becomes available. The cost to open the adjoining wall to connect the two spaces is estimated to be $8,000. Based on the information that you have, would you recommend that JacLyn's bookstore expand into this space? Which departments should expand? Justify your recommendation.

8.43 **Direct, Step-Down and Reciprocal Methods, Decision-Making** The managers of ACME Manufacturing are discussing ways to allocate the cost of service departments, such as quality control and maintenance, to the production departments. To aid them in this discussion, the controller has provided the following information:

LO3, LO4, LO5, LO7

	Quality Control	Maintenance	Machining	Assembly	Total
Budgeted overhead costs before Allocation	$350,000	$200,000	$400,000	$300,000	$1,250,000
Budgeted machine Hours	–	–	50,000	–	50,000
Budgeted direct labour hours	–	–	–	25,000	25,000
Budgeted hours of service: Quality Control	–	7,000	21,000	7,000	35,000
Maintenance	10,000	–	18,000	12,000	40,000

REQUIRED **A.** Using the direct method, allocate the Quality Control and Maintenance costs to Machining and Assembly.
B. Using the step-down method allocate the Quality Control and Maintenance costs. Allocate the Quality Control costs first.
C. Using the step-down method allocate the Quality Control and Maintenance costs. Allocate the Maintenance costs first.
D. Using the reciprocal method allocate the Quality Control and Maintenance costs. Use either simultaneous equations or Excel Solver.
E. Based on your results and your understanding of the different allocation methods, which method do you recommend ACME Manufacturing implement? Explain your choice.

8.44 **Direct, Step-Down, and Reciprocal Methods, Decision-Making** The managers of Alphabet Co. are investigating the allocation of service department costs. They have gathered the following information to help in the analysis of their options.

LO3, LO4, LO5, LO7

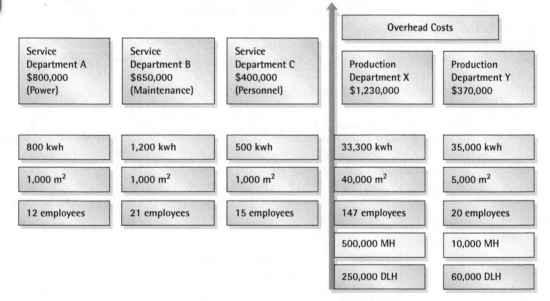

The cost drivers for each department are as follows:

Department A	Kilowatt hours (kwh)
Department B	Square metres (m²)
Department C	Number of employees
Department X	Machine hours (MH)
Department Y	Direct labour hours (DLH)

REQUIRED   **A.** Allocate the service department costs using the direct method.

B. Allocate the service department costs using the step-down method. Choose the order of allocation based on the amount of service provided (determined by costs).

C. Allocate the service department costs using the reciprocal method. Use either simultaneous equations or Excel Solver.

D. Explain each method to the managers. Provide the pros and cons of each method.

E. Identify which managers, if any, will be upset using each of the allocation methods. Explain why this manager might feel that s/he is being unfairly treated.

8.45 **Department Allocations, Decision Making** In 2016, Haley's Department Store devoted 600 square metres to the

LO1, LO2, LO3, LO4, LO5, LO6, LO7

display and sale of clothing, 150 square metres to linens and bedding, and 200 square metres to jewellery and cosmetics. The store is 1,000 square metres, and 50 square metres were unused. The cost to maintain the store was $95,000, which was allocated among the three departments based on 950 square metres of occupied space. In 2017, management put a confectionery shop in the previously unused space. However, the allocation was not updated for this change. In 2017, the four departments' contribution margins before the allocation of building costs were

Clothing	$72,000
Bedding	19,500
Jewellery	40,000
Confections	4,000

During 2018, the four department managers all requested that they be allowed to expand their floor space. Each argued that the floor space of one of the other departments should be reduced so that their own department could be expanded.

REQUIRED   **A.** Determine earnings after the building costs have been allocated for 2017 for each department (remember that the firm allocated costs to only three departments).

B. Suppose the managers mistakenly used the earnings after building costs were allocated to determine the contribution per unit of constrained resource (per square metre) for each department. Also assume the confections department was allocated store maintenance costs based on its use of 50 square metres. Which department would be allowed to expand, and which one should be reduced or dropped?

C. Suppose that managers properly calculated the contribution margin per unit of constrained resource (per square metre) for Part B by ignoring allocated costs. Which department would be allowed to expand, and which one would be reduced?

D. Explain why the method in Part C is better for making this decision. What are the qualitative factors related to this decision?

8.46 **Single Versus Dual Rates, Manager Incentives, Transfer Pricing** Cheng and Gonzales operate a trucking company

LO6, LO7

that hauls produce from British Columbia to the East Coast. There are three departments: West Coast, Prairies, and East Coast. A number of support services for the departments are provided in B.C. One of these is truck maintenance. When a driver returns to B.C. to pick up produce, trucks may be washed and serviced, and any repairs may be undertaken. The maintenance department's operating costs per month are $16,000, plus $35 per labour hour for the hours worked on each truck. Last year's demand was as follows:

Department	Budgeted	Actual
West Coast	300 hours	270 hours
Prairies	350 hours	380 hours
East Coast	400 hours	400 hours

REQUIRED   **A.** Allocate total costs based on the single-rate method using budgeted hours.

B. Allocate total costs based on the single-rate method using actual hours.

C. Allocate total costs based on the dual-rate method using budgeted hours for fixed costs and actual hours for variable costs.

D. Describe the optimal use of the maintenance department by the three trucking departments.

E. Suppose these allocations are considered part of each manager's department costs, and the managers are rewarded for reducing costs. Describe managers' incentives for determining a budgeted amount and then for their actual usage under

  1. Single-rate method, budgeted hours
  2. Single-rate method, actual hours
  3. Dual-rate method

F. Recommend a transfer pricing policy for the maintenance department, and list several advantages and disadvantages for that policy.

8.47 **Step-Down and Reciprocal Methods, Choosing Methods, Cost Pools, Uncertainties** Your brother is a physician and has decided to start a home health care agency. The provincial government will reimburse treatment costs for about half of the patients under a new province-sponsored health insurance program for low-income residents. Your brother has asked you to explain the cost report that the provincial government requires. He tells you that he can use either the step-down method or the reciprocal allocation method. He has several choices in allocation bases but has little choice in the type of cost pools that are allowed.

LO2, LO4, LO5, LO7

REQUIRED **A.** Explain to your brother the differences between the two allocation methods. Remember that your brother is not familiar with accounting; use language he will understand.

B. Your brother wants to know how to choose the best allocation method and bases for his business. List some of the factors your brother should consider as he makes these decisions.

C. One of the cost pools allowed by the province is a pool for transportation-related costs. Your brother asked colleagues at other home health care agencies to list the costs they include in this pool. The organizations have some costs that are identical, such as amortization (depreciation) on vehicles, gas, and repairs. However, other costs in the pool are different; some include facilities-related costs, and others do not. Why would cost pools for the same activity include different types of costs?

8.48 **Cost Pools and Allocation Bases** You are an accountant for a defence contractor. The federal government is considering a change of rules for the allocation of research and development costs. The government is asking contractors to submit a list of potential cost pools and allocation bases for activities within research and development. The government wants defence contractors to separate their research and development activities into several smaller cost pools with separate allocation bases.

LO2

Your research department performs a variety of different duties, including developing new designs for products, developing and testing new materials for use in these products, designing the manufacturing processes for new products, and redesigning old products and their manufacturing processes. In addition, the research and development department creates commercial uses for new technologies that have been developed under government contracts.

REQUIRED **A.** List at least four potential research and development activities that could be used as the basis for separate cost pools within the research and development department.

B. List two or more potential cost allocation bases for each cost pool listed in Part A.

C. List factors that you might consider in making a choice about the cost pools and the allocation bases.

8.49 **Step-Down Method, Choosing Allocation Order and Bases** Space Products manufactures commercial and military satellites. Under its defence contracts, the company is permitted to allocate administrative and other costs to its military division. These costs are then reimbursed by Public Works and Government Services Canada (PWGSC). Assume that under PWGSC guidelines, administrative costs can be allocated using either the direct costs incurred in the operating divisions or the number of employees as an allocation base. Management information systems (MIS) costs can be allocated either on the basis of direct costs incurred in the operating divisions or on the basis of CPUs (a measure of computer resources used). Data concerning the company's operations are as follows:

LO2, LO4, LO7

	Support Departments		Operating Departments	
	Administrative	MIS	Commercial	Military
Direct costs	$600,000	$200,000	$2,000,000	$4,000,000
Employees	20	10	40	50
CPUs (millions)	20	50	30	70

The MIS department is responsible for computer equipment and systems, and it maintains databases for the entire organization.

REQUIRED **A.** Suppose Space Products uses the step-down method for allocating support department costs. Administrative costs are allocated first on the basis of the number of employees, and then MIS costs are allocated on the basis of CPUs. How much support department cost will be allocated to the military division?

B. Space Products produced 100 military satellites in the period considered in this problem. Assuming that the company uses the allocations calculated in Part A, what is the average cost per military satellite?

C. Is the average cost that you calculated in Part B most likely an underestimate, overestimate, or unbiased estimate of the incremental cost of producing one more military satellite? Explain.

D. Suppose Space Products uses the direct method of allocating support department costs. What is the maximum amount of support department cost that can be allocated to the military division under PWGSC rules?

E. Suppose the management of Space Products always calculates its support department cost allocations to maximize the amount of contribution received from the PWGSC. Management uses this policy because it allows the company to be more competitive in its commercial markets.

   1. Discuss possible reasons why the PWGSC does not specify a single, unambiguous support cost allocation method.

   2. From a taxpayer's point of view, discuss whether you agree with Space Products' policy.

   3. From a competitor's point of view, discuss whether you agree with Space Products' policy.

8.50 **Categorization of Support Costs** The Better Business Bureau (BBB), through its BBB Wise Giving Alliance, provides

LO1, LO2, LO7

www.wiley.com/go/
eldenburgcanada

information on the Internet about charitable organizations in the United States and Canada (see http://give.org or go to www.wiley.com/go/eldenburgcanada). On the BBB website, charitable organizations are evaluated based on whether they meet the standards for charitable solicitations established by the Council of Better Business Bureaus. The finances standards state, "This section of the standards seeks to ensure that the charity spends its funds honestly, prudently and in accordance with statements made in fundraising appeals." The three individual standards in this section outline specific requirements for how much of the expenses should be for supported programs and how much should be spent on administration and fundraising activities. These standards reflect the desire of donors to be sure that an organization devotes its resources primarily to programs rather than to administration and fundraising.

Suppose a charitable organization called Food on Wheels provides meals for low-income individuals who are unable to leave their homes. To support its services, it solicits contributions from individuals and businesses. The organization's director would like the organization to be listed on the BBB Wise Giving Alliance website. Food on Wheels needs to submit financial statements in which its expenses are assigned to the following cost pools: administrative, fundraising, and programs.

The bookkeeper for Food on Wheels is a volunteer taking accounting classes at the local college. He knows that all the costs to prepare and deliver meals should be assigned to the program. However, he is not sure how to assign some of the costs. In particular, he is concerned about the following two items:

- **Costs for printing and mailing a monthly newsletter.** The newsletter is sent out to donors and clients and asks for donations. It also describes the organization's activities, provides information for obtaining meal services, and provides recipes for some of the meals that are served. The director of the organization wants the cost of the newsletter to be classified as a program cost. She maintains that the program information and recipes should be considered educational material. Not-for-profit organizations typically classify educational materials as program expenses.

- **Director's salary and benefits.** The director of Food on Wheels spends much of her time raising funds, meeting with the board of directors, and performing other administrative duties. She also manages the cooks and drivers, purchases food and delivery supplies, and schedules the food deliveries. The director has instructed the bookkeeper to allocate her salary and benefit costs as follows: 50% to the program, 25% to fund-raising, and 25% to administration.

REQUIRED **A.** Identify and discuss uncertainties about how each of the following costs should be classified:

   1. Costs to print and mail the newsletter

   2. Director's salary and benefits

B. Does this situation involve an ethical dilemma for the bookkeeper? Why or why not?

C. Explain why the director has a preference for costs to be assigned to program expenses.

D. Explain how you think donors would prefer for the costs in Part A to be assigned.

E. Suppose you are reviewing cost information for another organization reported on the Better Business Bureau website. Would you expect the organization's program costs to be biased upward, biased downward, or unbiased? Explain.

F. How would you classify the costs in Part A if you were the bookkeeper for Food on Wheels? Explain your reasoning.

8.51 Direct, Step-Down, and Reciprocal Methods Using Dual-Rate and Three Departments In the Melodious Notes, Part 6, example, the students did not perform direct or step-down methods for the dual-rate costs. Following are the allocation bases for these costs. See the example for the support cost data.

LO2, LO3, LO4, LO5, LO6

	Administration	Accounting	Custodial Services	Instrument Sales	Music Lessons	Total
Number of employees	1	1	2	5	3	12
Square metres	60	30	10	800	100	1,000
Time spent accounting	15%		10%	50%	25%	100%
Time spent cleaning	10%	5%		55%	30%	100%

REQUIRED **A.** Draw a diagram of the direct method for the Melodious Notes allocations for three support departments.
B. Allocate the support department costs using dual rates and the direct method.
C. Draw a diagram of using the step-down method for the three support departments.
D. Allocate the support department costs using dual rates and the step-down method.
E. Write out the simultaneous equations for the reciprocal allocation.
F. Set up a spreadsheet that uses Excel Solver to solve the simultaneous equations and then allocates support costs using dual rates and the reciprocal method. Ensure that your solution matches the solution in the text.

8.52 Total Cost Under Alternative Allocation Bases, Special Order Price Danish Hospital recently installed an RAP Scanner, which is a diagnostic tool used both in suspected cancer cases and for detecting certain birth defects while the fetus is still in the womb. The scanner is leased for $5,000 per month, and a full-time operator is paid $3,000 per month. Data concerning use of the scanner for a typical month follow:

LO1, LO2, LO7

	Cancer Detection	Birth Defect Detection
Revenue per scan	$600	$400
Direct costs per scan	$100	$50
Minutes required per scan	30	10
Number of scans performed	20	40

The direct costs consist primarily of supplies that are consumed in the scanning process. Currently, less than 20% of the machine's capacity is used.

REQUIRED **INFORMATION ANALYSIS**

The following questions will help you analyze the information for this problem. Do not turn in your answers to these questions unless your professor asks you to do so.

A. If the lease cost and the operator salary are allocated on the basis of minutes on the scanner, what is the total cost of a cancer scan?
B. Suppose the cancer scans are experimental. Rather than charging $600 per scan, the hospital costs are reimbursed under a federally funded program. The federal government will reimburse direct costs as well as an allocated share of the lease cost and operator's salary. As an allocation base, the federal government allows either the number of scans or total minutes on the machine. What is the maximum reimbursable cost per cancer scan?
C. The hospital is bidding on a provincial contract to supply birth defect scans to low-income pregnant women. The hospital would provide up to 14 scans per month for a fixed fee per scan. Assuming that the hospital does not want to lose money on this contract, what is the minimum acceptable fee? Explain how you decided which costs are relevant.
D. Identify uncertainties about which costs should be included in bidding for the contract described in Part C.
E. Discuss the pros and cons of using total allocated costs, including administrative overhead, in bidding for the contract described in Part C.

REQUIRED **WRITTEN ASSIGNMENT**

Suppose the hospital is bidding on the contract described in Part C. You have been asked to prepare a report of the hospital's expected costs for the contract. Turn in your answers to the following.

F. Write a memo to the chief accountant, recommending the costs you think should be included in the expected costs. Attach to the memo a schedule showing your computations. As appropriate, refer to the schedule in the memo.

8.53 Support Cost Allocation Uncertainties and Fairness Andy Rich is an agent for Steve Kurl, a basketball player who has been on a number of championship professional teams over the past 10 years. Steve has complained to Andy that his compensation does not seem to be what was promised. In addition to salary, Steve was promised a percentage of the gate receipts after deduction of expenses for each game. However, the organization's accountants told Steve that little profit is left after all the expenses have been deducted.

LO2, LO4, LO7

Andy asks to review the financial reports from the last five games. As he reviews the reports, Andy notices that the expenses for each game include large amounts for administration and public relations. He asks the accountant about these expenses and is told that these costs are allocated using revenue as the allocation base. The rate is calculated by dividing estimated total administrative and public relations costs by estimated total revenue for all the games played during the regular season.

Because Steve played in a number of championship games, Andy asks for the financial reports for those games, too. It appears that the same rate was used to allocate administration and public relations for postseason games. He brings this practice to the attention of the accountant, who responds that each game has to have a share of the expenses and that it has always been done this way.

REQUIRED **A.** Discuss uncertainties about how to measure the profit for each game. (Think about this question: Why is there no single way to calculate profit for each game?)
B. Is this scenario an ethical dilemma? Why or why not?
C. The team allocates its administration and public relations costs using an estimated allocation rate. Is this method likely to be biased? In other words, are allocated costs likely to be higher or lower than actual costs for the year? Explain.
D. Provide arguments in favour of allocating administration and public relations costs as an expense of each game.
E. Provide arguments against allocating administration and public relations costs as an expense of each game.
F. Brainstorm ideas and recommend a method for calculating the profits for each game that you think would be fair to both the owners and players. Explain how your conclusion addresses all important stakeholders.

8.54 Allowable Costs Under a Cost-Based Contract, Accountant Ethical Responsibility Accountants often consider it a part of their job to help their organizations succeed. Often, this assistance means developing strategies to maximize the organization's cash flows. For example, accountants promote income tax strategies to help companies minimize income tax payments. Similarly, accountants might promote strategies to maximize reimbursements under cost-based contracts. This type of strategy might encourage accountants to include a cost in an indirect cost pool when there is uncertainty about whether it is allowed.

LO1, LO7

REQUIRED **INFORMATION ANALYSIS**

The following questions will help you analyze the information for this problem. Do not turn in your answers to these questions unless your professor asks you to do so.

A. Explain why accountants must often use judgment to decide whether a particular cost is reimbursable under a cost-based contract.
B. Discuss whether maximizing reimbursements under cost-based contracts is an ethical issue for accountants.
C. Is your answer to Part B affected by the size of a potential overcharge? Why or why not?
D. Identify the major groups of stakeholders for this problem. From the perspective of each major stakeholder group, discuss the pros and cons when accountants help their organizations maximize reimbursements under cost-based contracts.
E. What trade-offs must accountants make when deciding whether to help their organizations maximize reimbursements under cost-based contracts?

REQUIRED **WRITTEN ASSIGNMENT**

Turn in your answer to the following.

F. Use the information you learned from the preceding analyses to help you write an essay in response to the following question: Is it ethical for accountants to help their organizations maximize reimbursements under cost-based contracts?

MINI-CASES

8.55 Step-Down Method, Multiple- Versus Single-Pool Allocations, Manager Incentives The Gleason Company, a

LO1, LO2, LO4, LO7

Canadian division of a large international company, has prepared estimated costs for next year that can be traced to each department as follows:

Building and grounds	$ 41,010
Factory administration	78,270
Cafeteria–operating loss	4,920
Machining	104,100
Assembly	146,700
Total	$375,000

Management would like to know the estimated total allocated product cost per unit. This cost will be used as a benchmark for future-period operations. The following information is available and can be used as possible allocation bases. The difference between direct labour hours and total labour hours represents hours of supervisory labour or labour hours that are used indirectly for manufacturing. The cost of these hours in machining and assembly is part of manufacturing overhead:

Department	Direct Labour Hours	Number of Employees	Square Metres	Total Labour Hours	Number of Purchase Orders
Factory administration	2,000	3	50	2,000	1,000
Cafeteria	1,000	2	100	1,000	4,000
Machining	3,000	4	350	8,000	2,000
Assembly	6,000	5	500	10,000	1,000
Total	12,000	14	1,000	21,000	8,000

REQUIRED
A. Allocate the building and grounds costs to all other departments using square metres as the allocation base. Add the allocated costs to direct costs to arrive at the total costs assigned to each department.
B. Explain whether each remaining department is a support department or an operating department.
C. Select a reasonable allocation base for the costs of each support department. Justify your choices.
D. Compute allocated overhead costs for each operating department. Given the allocation bases you selected in Part C, allocate support department costs to each operating department using the step-down method. Then calculate an overhead rate per direct labour hour for each operating department.
E. Calculate overhead rates for the operating departments, assuming that Gleason uses an average, plantwide factory overhead allocation rate based on direct labour hours. That is, aggregate the support department overhead costs into one cost pool and use direct labour hours as the allocation base to determine the overhead rate per direct labour hour.
F. What causes the difference between the rates you calculated in Parts D and E?
G. Assume that factory administration costs are allocated based on total labour hours and that the total allocated cost is used to charge other departments for administrative services. List one advantage and one disadvantage of this charge system.
H. Suppose you are the manager of the machining department at Gleason. You can outsource some of your department's work. Outsourcing would reduce direct labour hours and, therefore, reduce the amount of overhead allocated to your department. What factors should you consider in deciding whether to outsource?
I. Now suppose you are the director of finance for Gleason. The manager of the machining department has decided to outsource some tasks. When you analyze the current-period results, you notice that while direct labour costs decreased in machining, outsourcing costs are slightly higher this period than the prior period's direct labour costs. When you ask the manager about these costs, he replies that the outsourcing does cost more than using direct labour, but because the amount of overhead for the department decreases, this solution is more profitable. What happened to the overhead that is no longer allocated to machining? Is the manager's decision beneficial to Gleason Company as a whole? Explain.

8.56 Comprehensive Problem, Dual Versus Single Rates, Purpose of Allocation Vines Company is a manufacturer of women's and men's swimsuits. The company uses a dual-rate system to allocate support costs. Last year's support departments' fixed and variable costs are as follows:

LO1, LO2, LO3, LO4, LO5, LO6, LO7

	Accounting	Human Resources	Janitorial	Total
Variable costs	$18,420	$22,104	$60,360	$100,884
Fixed costs	55,260	100,696	60,360	216,316
Total cost	$73,680	$122,800	$120,720	$317,200

Allocation base amounts for all the departments are as follows:

	Accounting	Human Resources	Janitorial	Women's	Men's	Total
Employees	2	2	4	10	6	24
Time spent for accounting	15%	10%	20%	30%	25%	100%
Time spent cleaning	5%	10%	15%	30%	40%	100%
Square metres	80	100	120	500	500	1,300
Direct costs	$73,680	$122,800	$120,720	$800,000	$500,000	$1,617,200

REQUIRED   **A.** Use the following allocation bases for fixed support costs: direct costs for accounting, number of employees for human resources, and square metres for janitorial.
   1. Allocate fixed support costs using the direct method.
   2. Allocate fixed support costs using the step-down method.
   3. Allocate fixed support costs using the reciprocal method.
B. Use the following allocation bases for variable support costs: time spent for accounting, number of employees for human resources, and time spent for janitorial.
   1. Allocate variable support costs using the direct method.
   2. Allocate variable support costs using the step-down method.
   3. Allocate variable support costs using the reciprocal method.
C. Suppose support costs were not broken down into fixed and variable cost pools. What allocation base would you use to allocate the costs for each support department? Explain.
D. Describe several possible reasons why the managers of Vines Company allocate support costs to operating departments.
E. Discuss whether a dual-rate support cost allocation system is likely to be better for Vines Company than a single-rate system.

8.57 Integration of Information and Information Technology This chapter does not directly address how to leverage technology to develop and enhance an accountant's ability to provide useful business advice. However, the chapter introduces two major uses of technology that are related to accountants' responsibilities:

LO1, LO2

1. Use of accounting information systems to accumulate cost and allocation base data.
2. Use of Excel Solver for simultaneous equations.

As you address the following questions, focus on how technology assists accountants in the process of allocating support department costs.

REQUIRED   **A. 1.** What types of decisions are addressed in this chapter? List business decisions as well as decisions about accounting methods.
   2. For the decisions you identified above, list relevant information that might be stored in an electronic database.
B. Accountants are expected to communicate orally and in writing both the processes and results of decision making. Considering this requirement, perform the following:
   1. Create a spreadsheet for allocating costs from more than two support departments using the reciprocal method. Include in your spreadsheet information documenting the work performed.

2. Show the spreadsheet to someone else and ask him or her to explain the work documented in the spreadsheet. Make a list of items that the other person does and does not understand.

3. Given the lists you created in Part B-2, modify the spreadsheet to improve its ability to document the work performed.

C. Think about situations in which you have adopted new technologies. What strategies do you use to decide whether or when to adopt a new technology? Think about the following types of questions to help identify strategies: Do you wait until you are required to use a new technology (such as in a course)? Do you seek information about new technologies on your own? How do you decide whether a new technology is worthwhile? How do you go about learning and adopting a new technology? Do you tend to be either reluctant or overly eager about new technologies? If so, how do you compensate for your tendencies?

8.58 **Integrating Across the Curriculum: Not-for-Profit Accounting—*Allocating common costs to programs*** Many not-for-profit organizations use the restricted fund method of accounting. Under this approach, a set of separate self-balancing accounts is set up for each fund that is established by legal, contractual, or voluntary agreement. The use of the resources in each fund is either internally or externally restricted. Common funds include endowment, capital, and operating. Within the operating fund, cost accumulation accounts collect costs that are associated with services provided to support the many different functions and programs of the not-for-profit organization. For example, the Canadian Cancer Society of Saskatchewan reports cost accounts for bulletins and reports, computers and services, conferences and meetings, exhibits, displays and posters, insurance, office stationery and supplies, postage and courier, publicity, salaries and benefits, telephone and fax, travel and volunteer development, and so on. Each type of cost is collected in an account and then allocated to the functions carried out by the society (e.g., research, advocacy, prevention, information, support for people living with cancer, fundraising, management, and general). In addition, the Canadian Cancer Society's national office allocates a share of its costs to the provincial societies (i.e., national office assessment).

LO1, LO7

Source: Financial Statements for the Canadian Cancer Society in Saskatchewan, 2006–2007 and 2007–2008; www .cancer.ca/Saskatchewan/About%20us/SK-Financial%20statements.aspx?sc_lang=en.

REQUIRED

A. Conduct research on the Internet to locate information about the restricted funds used by a not-for-profit organization and how common costs are allocated to functions and/or programs supported by the organization. What restricted funds are used? What is the description of each fund? What costs are allocated to other functions?

B. How are the uses of restricted funds similar to the uses of support cost allocations in a business organization?

C. "Failure to allocate inter- and intradepartmental costs overstates the cost of general administration and management, making a not-for-profit appear to be inefficient and understating the cost of other activities." Explain what these arguments mean.

D. As a citizen and taxpayer, what do you think are the benefits of not-for-profit organizations using a restricted fund approach? Explain your reasoning.

CHAPTER 9

Joint Product and By-product Costing

After studying this chapter, you should be able to do the following:

LO1 Describe a joint process, and explain the difference between a by-product and a main product

LO2 Allocate joint costs

LO3 Explain the factors that are considered in choosing a joint cost allocation method

LO4 Identify the relevant information for deciding whether to process a joint product beyond the split-off point

LO5 Apply the methods that are used to account for the sale of by-products

LO6 Explain how a sales mix affects joint cost allocation

LO7 Evaluate the uses and limitations of joint cost information

in brief Some products are produced jointly with other products. For example, when crude oil is processed, gasoline, diesel, and heating oil are produced. For external reports, such as financial statements and tax returns, the common costs incurred to produce joint products are allocated to the resulting products. Accountants choose among several methods to allocate joint costs.

Managers and accountants also make decisions about when to sell joint products. Some goods and services are sold when joint production ends, while others are processed further and then sold. For example, managers of a food manufacturer must decide how much of the wheat they purchase to sell as flour and how much to process further into pasta or other food products. They must also identify relevant costs when making this type of decision. ■

Creating a Diversion: City of Hamilton Rethinks Its Waste

Courtesy of the City of Hamilton

Due to decreasing space in the city's one operating landfill, the **City of Hamilton**, Ontario, undertook a massive recycling program in 2006. The goal of the program was to divert at least 65% of household waste out of landfills. A significant part of this initiative was the Green Cart Program. Residents are asked to separate their household organic waste—such as food waste, paper coffee cups, and dryer lint—from the rest of their garbage and place it in a green cart. Green cart waste is then collected on the same days as the other garbage and sent to the Central Composting Facility, where it is processed into compost. Collection of garbage and organic waste is accomplished using the same truck—a dual-compartment truck with one side for garbage and one side for organic waste.

At the end of a route, trucks hold garbage that must be taken to distant landfills and organic waste that must be taken to the Central Composting Facility. The city's Waste Management 2012 Annual Report indicated that Hamilton had achieved a 49% diversion rate with a 6% decrease in metric tonnes delivered to landfills. Landfills assess dumping fees based on quantity of waste disposed. The decrease in waste going to landfills combined with the household waste recycled in blue boxes and gold boxes was expected to put the city over the stated 65% diversion goal by 2021.

The environmental benefits of composting are high on the list of benefits associated with separating organic waste. An added benefit is the free compost available for Hamilton residents in exchange for a small monetary donation that goes to the United Way charity. In addition, with less household waste thrown out in the regular garbage, the city is hoping to move to bi-weekly regular garbage collection, which could save about $2.4 million a year. If the city achieves a 65% diversion by 2021, it predicts that it could extend the life of its existing landfill to 2044, saving millions in building costs of a new site.

SOURCE: City of Hamilton—Garbage & Recycling home page, www.hamilton. ca/garbage-recycling (accessed October 19, 2015); "City of Hamilton Solid Waste Management Master Plan Review, 2012 Solid Waste Management Master Plan: Final Report," City of Hamilton, March 2012.

Joint Products and Costs

The success of the City of Hamilton Green Cart Program depended on the coordination of two separate products—waste disposal and compost processing. When the production of two or more products is co-dependent, it becomes more difficult for managers to measure and monitor operations. In this chapter, you will learn methods for measuring the cost of such products. You will also learn the uses and limitations of costs that are allocated across interdependent products.

Some industries simultaneously produce a group of products through a single process. Consider a fish farm where products include fresh fish, frozen fish, frozen fish entrees, and fish fertilizer. In the process of making one product, one or more other products or services are created, called **joint products**. Joint products fall into two categories. A **main product** has high sales value compared to the other joint products. At the fish farm, fresh fish, frozen fish, and fish entrees are main products. A **by-product** has low sales value compared to the other joint products. Fish fertilizer is an example of a by-product. Exhibit 9.1 presents a list of industries that manufacture joint products and gives examples of main products and by-products.

Joint costs are all the costs incurred to jointly produce a group of goods. These costs are common to all the joint products and are incurred prior to the **split-off point**, the point at which individual products are identified. At the fish farm, the split-off point is the point at which the fish are caught and cleaned. The joint costs include the costs to maintain the fish ponds, such as labour, fish food, insurance, and property taxes, plus all the costs to clean fish and prepare them for further processing.

Separable costs are the costs incurred after the split-off point. These incremental costs can be easily traced to each specific product. At the fish farm, separable costs are incurred for packaging fresh fish, freezing fish, preparing entrees, and pulverizing and emulsifying the waste and bottling it for fertilizer. Exhibit 9.2 shows the common and separable activities involved in raising fish, and lists several of the costs for these activities.

Allocating Joint Costs

An organization commits to joint costs when managers decide to produce joint products. For the City of Hamilton, the costs of the dual-compartment garbage trucks and the labour costs associated with collecting household waste are joint costs. Joint costs must be allocated to each product for reporting inventory and cost of goods sold on financial statements, income tax returns, and other types of reports. Joint costs must also be allocated for government regulatory reports when companies that sell to both government agencies and commercial organizations seek reimbursement of costs on government-funded projects. Occasionally, legal processes scrutinize joint cost allocations, such as when an organization must support the transfer price used between divisions located in high-tax and low-tax countries. A tax

Industry	Main Products	By-products	Example Company
Petroleum (crude oil)	Gasoline, diesel, jet fuel	Asphalt	Petro-Canada
Copper mining	Copper, silver, lead, zinc	Malachite, azurite	Astral Mining
Cheese production	Fresh cheese, butter	Buttermilk	Amalgamated Dairies Limited
Lumber (logs)	Lumber, veneer, plywood	Bark dust, sawdust	Canfor
Beef production	Cuts of meat, leather	Dog bones, bone meal for gardens	Maple Leaf

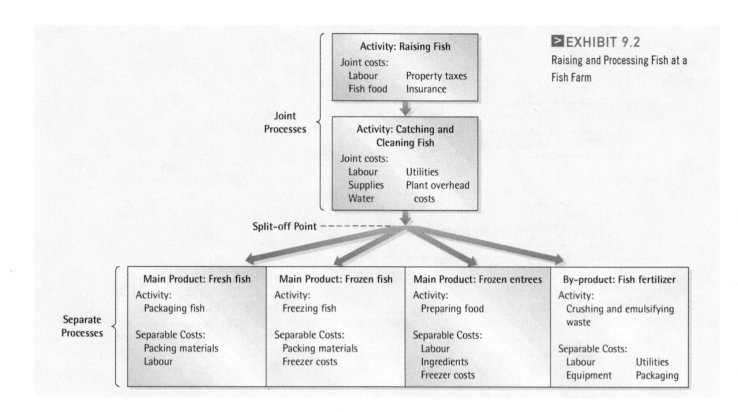

audit or corporate or government litigation may also require joint cost allocation information. However, joint costs should be used cautiously internally when evaluating division or segment performance or product profitability.

In the City of Hamilton Green Cart Program, joint costs are allocated between the collection of household waste and the production of compost. The allocation of joint costs assists in matching revenues and costs. Therefore, the allocated costs of compost would be expensed in the accounting period when compost is provided to residents, and the allocated costs of any undistributed compost would be included in inventory on the balance sheet. Similarly, the allocated cost of collecting household waste would be recorded on the income statement in the same period in which the revenues are recorded.

Several different methods are used to allocate joint costs to main products. In this chapter, you will learn about the following methods:

► CHAPTER REFERENCE
Transfer prices and policies are discussed further in Chapter 14.

- ► Physical output method
- ► Market-based methods
  - – Sales value at split-off point
  - – Net realizable value (NRV)
  - – Constant gross margin NRV

To illustrate these methods, we use a sawmill example. LeRoy Family owns and operates a sawmill in northern Saskatchewan. The company hires loggers who cut timber and bring it to the mill, where the logs are sawed into lumber. In addition, sawdust and wood chips from the sawmill operation are glued and pressed into chipboard. Exhibit 9.3 presents the costs and revenues from this operation. The joint costs of cutting trees, debarking logs, and sawing logs into lumber are $220 per log, which LeRoy Family commits to when a tree is cut down and sent to the sawmill. Revenue from lumber, the main product, is $400 per log. The company could sell the sawdust and wood chips, a by-product, to a pulp mill for $40. However, LeRoy Family currently processes the sawdust and wood chips further by gluing and pressing them into chipboard, which is considered another main product. The cost of this additional processing is $46, and the chipboard sells for $146.

kozmoat98/Getty Images

> **EXHIBIT 9.3**
LeRoy Family Revenues and Costs for
Processing One Log

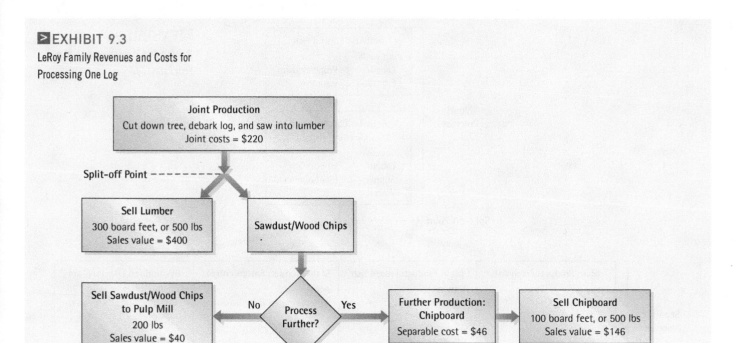

Physical Output Method

The **physical output method** allocates joint costs using the relative proportion of physical output for each main product. This method is used only when output for all main products can be expressed using the same physical measure, such as metres, kilograms, or litres. Each main product is allocated a proportion of joint costs, based on that product's physical output divided by the total physical output of all main products. When the output for the main products is expressed in different measures, such as kilograms and litres, then one of the other monetary allocation methods must be used.

For LeRoy Family, either pounds or board feet could be used as an allocation base.[1] Suppose the company uses pounds of final product as the physical volume allocation base. Each log processed results in 500 lbs of chipboard and 500 lbs of lumber. Thus, the relative weight of chipboard is 500 lbs/1,000 lbs. The joint costs of $220 are multiplied by this proportion to calculate the amount of joint costs allocated to chipboard:

$$(500 \text{ lbs}/1,000 \text{ lbs}) \times \$220 = \$110$$

A similar set of calculations leads to allocation of $110 of joint costs to lumber, as follows:

	Main Products		
	Chipboard	Lumber	Total
Base: Pounds of final product	500 lbs	500 lbs	1,000 lbs
Proportion	500 lbs/1,000 lbs	500 lbs/1,000 lbs	
Allocated joint costs	$110	$110	$220

Suppose LeRoy Family instead uses the number of board feet of final product as the allocation base. For each log processed, the company produces 100 board feet of chipboard and

---

[1]Natural Resources Canada reports Canadian sawmill capacities in cubic metres but notes that the industry regularly uses board feet as the unit of measure. The conversion formulas are 1 cubic metre = 424 board feet and 1,000 board feet = 2.36 cubic metres. See http://cfs.nrcan.gc.ca/terms/1347

300 board feet of lumber. In this case, the joint costs allocated to each main product are calculated as follows:

	Main Products		
	Chipboard	Lumber	Total
Base: Board feet of final product	100 bd ft	300 bd ft	400 bd ft
Proportion	100 bd ft/400 bd ft	300 bd ft/400 bd ft	
Allocated joint costs	$55	$165	$220

Sales Value at Split-off Point Method

Market-based methods use some proportion of the profit contribution for each main product to determine the joint cost allocation rate. Under the sales value at split-off point method, joint costs are allocated based on the relative sales value of main products at the point where joint production ends. For LeRoy Family, joint production of a log creates lumber that can be sold for $400 and sawdust and wood chips that can be sold, without further processing, for $40. The relative proportions of sales values at the split-off point are used to allocate the joint costs of each main product as follows:

	Main Products		
	Chipboard	Lumber	Total
Base: Sales value at split-off point	$40	$400	$440
Proportion	$40/$440	$400/$440	
Allocated joint costs	$20	$200	$220

Net Realizable Value Method

The net realizable value (NRV) method allocates joint costs using the relative value of main products, taking into account both the additional sales value that is created and costs that are incurred after joint production ends. NRV for each main product is calculated as the final selling price minus separable costs. For LeRoy Family, lumber is not processed further, so its net realizable value is equal to its sales value at the split-off point, or $400. The NRV for chipboard is expected to be $100 ($146 − $46) after further processing. The joint cost allocation calculations are as follows:

	Main Products		
	Chipboard	Lumber	Total
Base: Net realizable value	$100	$400	$500
Proportion	$100/$500	$400/$500	
Allocated joint costs	$44	$176	$220

Constant Gross Margin NRV Method

The constant gross margin NRV method allocates joint costs so that the gross margin percentages for the main products are identical. This method involves two sets of computations. First, the combined gross margin percentage for main products is calculated. Second, joint costs are allocated to each main product to achieve a constant gross margin.

Calculating the Combined Gross Margin Percentage. To calculate the combined gross margin, we create an income statement for the main products. The gross margin is determined by subtracting the joint and separable costs from the sales. Then the gross margin is divided by sales to determine the gross margin percentage. Continuing with the LeRoy Family example:

Determine sales:		
Sales: Lumber		$400
Chipboard		146
Combined sales		546
Determine costs:		
Joint costs	$220	
Separable costs: Lumber	0	
Chipboard	46	
Combined product costs		266
Combined gross margin		$280
Combined gross margin percentage ($280 ÷ $546)		51.3%

Allocating Joint Costs to Achieve a Constant Gross Margin. The desired gross margin, based on the preceding calculation, is first subtracted from the sales value to determine the desired amount of total product cost for each main product. Next, separable costs are subtracted from total product costs to determine the amount of joint costs to be allocated to each main product:

	Main Products		
	Chipboard	Lumber	Total
Sales	$146	$400	$546
Less gross margin (51.3% × sales)	75	205	280
Total product costs	71	195	266
Less separable costs	46	0	46
Allocated joint costs	$ 25	$195	$220

Choosing an Appropriate Joint Cost Allocation Method

LO3   Explain the factors that are considered in choosing a joint cost allocation method

Although each of the joint cost allocation methods is logical, the allocation process itself is arbitrary. We cannot trace joint costs to each product because we always incur all the joint costs to produce any one product. Therefore, no method for allocating joint costs develops a true cost per product.

Each method of joint cost allocation simply assigns a different proportion of cost to products and, therefore, results in a different allocated cost per product. In turn, different allocation methods result in different measures of profitability for each product. Consider the following comparison of the gross margin for LeRoy Family under different allocation methods for each log processed and sold:

Main Product	Physical Output (weight)	Sales Value at Split-off Point	Net Realizable Value	Constant Gross Margin NRV
Lumber:				
Sales value	$400	$400	$400	$400
Allocated joint costs	(110)	(200)	(176)	(195)
Separable costs	(0)	(0)	(0)	(0)
Product gross margin	290	200	224	205

Main Product	Physical Output (weight)	Sales Value at Split-off Point	Net Realizable Value	Constant Gross Margin NRV
Chipboard:				
Sales value	146	146	146	146
Allocated joint costs	(110)	(20)	(44)	(25)
Separable costs	(46)	(46)	(46)	(46)
Product gross margin	(10)	80	56	75
Total gross margin	**$280**	**$280**	**$280**	**$280**

Notice that the total gross margin per log is not affected by the joint cost allocation method. The cost allocation affects only the relative gross margins for the individual products. Accordingly, the joint cost allocation method used by a company affects the apparent profitability of different products. Sometimes a product can give the appearance that it is sold at a loss, when in fact the company profits from producing the joint product.

Pros and Cons of Alternative Allocation Methods

An allocation method should be chosen to avoid giving the mistaken impression that one or more products are sold at a loss. Under the physical output method, such distortions are likely to occur when the incremental contribution (incremental revenues less incremental costs) of some products is relatively high compared to that of other products. For example, if LeRoy Family uses the physical output method, using weight as the allocation base, the gross margin for chipboard is negative. If the managers make product-related decisions with this information, they might decide to quit producing chipboard. However, chipboard's incremental revenues exceed its incremental costs. If the company were to sell the sawdust and wood chips for $40 (the sales value at the split-off point), it would forgo the $100 incremental contribution from producing and selling chipboard ($146 revenue less $46 in separable costs). Thus, if chipboard is dropped, profit drops by $60 per log ($100 – $40). To avoid this problem, market value methods are generally superior to the physical output method.

Nevertheless, the physical volume method is commonly used in some industries because all units are similar in size and have comparable net realizable values. Suppose a company grows tomatoes and then manufactures different products, such as ketchup and salsa. The company incurs joint costs of raising, picking, cleaning, and chopping tomatoes. Possible physical output measures include weight, fluid millilitres, or number of same-sized bottles. If the incremental contributions of the different products are similar, a physical output measure would provide approximately the same cost allocation as the other methods. In addition, the physical output method is the easiest to calculate.

If most or all products are sold at the split-off point, then the sales value at split-off point method is generally most appropriate. This method avoids the physical output method problem of negative contribution for some products. As long as the total gross margin at the split-off point is positive, expected revenues always exceed allocated costs under the sales value at split-off point. However, some products may need further processing before they can be sold and have no value at the split-off point, or the net realizable value of each joint product may change greatly after further processing. In these cases, this method could distort the relative profitability of products. For example, at LeRoy Family, the net realizable value of the chipboard increases from $40 at the split-off point to $100 ($146 – $46) after processing.

The two NRV methods are generally preferred because they are based on the ability of each product to "pay" for its allocated cost. Using these methods, products appear profitable as long as their revenues are greater than their separable costs. Because the constant gross margin NRV method is more complicated, the NRV method is often chosen. However, the constant gross margin NRV method allocates joint costs so that all joint products appear to have equal profitability, and this approach best reflects the inseparability of the joint production process.

It is important to keep in mind that with all these methods, joint costs are allocated to final product costs. Including these joint costs in internal product-related decisions could result in discontinuing a product that contributes to overall profitability. For internal decisions, it is best to double-check any product-related decision against an incremental analysis of the separable costs and benefits (as described later in this chapter).

Each of the allocation methods is illustrated in the following LeRoy Family example.

example

leroy family, part 1
CHOOSING AN APPROPRIATE ALLOCATION METHOD

kozmoat98/Getty Images

Lacy Rudy, an accounting major at the local college, is working as an intern for LeRoy Family. When Lacy prepares financial statements for the company, she needs to choose an allocation base for assigning joint costs to products. First, she examines the differences in the allocations and margins for chipboard under the different methods. The following table summarizes her findings:

Allocation Method	Joint Cost Allocated to Chipboard	Chipboard Gross Margin
Physical output (using weight)	$110	$(10)
Sales value at split-off point	20	80
Net realizable value	44	56
Constant gross margin NRV	25	75

Lacy wants to find the simplest method that most fairly values the contribution of chipboard, since it is the joint product with least value. First, she eliminates the physical output method using weight as the allocation base. Weight distorts the profitability of chipboard because the allocated amount is higher than its revenue. With this allocation method, LeRoy Family appears to lose money on each sale, and Lacy knows that the sale of chipboard contributes to overall profitability. Next, she eliminates the constant gross margin NRV method because she thinks the calculations would be more difficult to explain to the mill owners and managers. Because the sales value at split-off point method does not reflect the increased value of separately producing chipboard, Lacy, in the end, decides that the NRV method would be the best choice. This method takes into account information about revenues and separable costs for the chipboard. ▪

Processing a Joint Product Beyond the Split-off Point

LO4 Identify the relevant information for deciding whether to process a joint product beyond the split-off point

▶ **CHAPTER REFERENCE**
More details about product emphasis decisions are provided in Chapter 4.

Managers often have a choice about whether to sell a product at the split-off point or to process it further. For example, LeRoy Family can sell the sawdust and wood chip scraps as a product, or they can use the scraps to produce and sell chipboard. When making decisions about whether to process a joint product beyond the split-off point, the joint costs are irrelevant because they are sunk costs. Once managers decide to produce a group of joint products, the joint costs are unavoidable and therefore irrelevant for making product-emphasis decisions that identify the final products from a joint process. The product with the highest incremental contribution is the most profitable and should be emphasized. No allocation method is necessary for this type of decision because allocated joint costs are sunk costs. A decision-making example for LeRoy Family (Part 2) follows.

example

leroy family, part 2
JOINT PRODUCT DECISION MAKING

LeRoy Family currently produces chipboard from its sawdust and wood chip scraps. A local pet store approached LeRoy Family and wants to buy sawdust and wood chip scraps. The pet store plans to use the scraps for pet bedding. The pet store is willing to pay $60 for 200 pounds (the quantity produced from one log) of sawdust and wood chips, which is more than the $40 the company would receive from a pulp mill. The managers of LeRoy Family are deciding whether to accept this offer. If they sell sawdust and wood chips to the pet store, they will no longer produce chipboard.

The managers ask Lacy to prepare an analysis for this decision. Lacy begins her analysis by accessing sales, production, and cost records. Using this information, she creates a cost flowchart (Exhibit 9.4). Lacy recalls learning in her cost accounting course that incremental revenues and costs are relevant for decision making. As Lacy works on the flowchart, she realizes that the revenues from sale of the lumber of $400 and the joint costs of $220 are irrelevant to her analysis. The costs and revenues of cutting a tree down and sawing it into lumber occur whether sawdust and wood chip scrap is sold to the pet store or pulp mill or is converted into chipboard.

Flander/iStockphoto

► EXHIBIT 9.4

LeRoy Family Decision for Use of Sawdust and Wood Chips

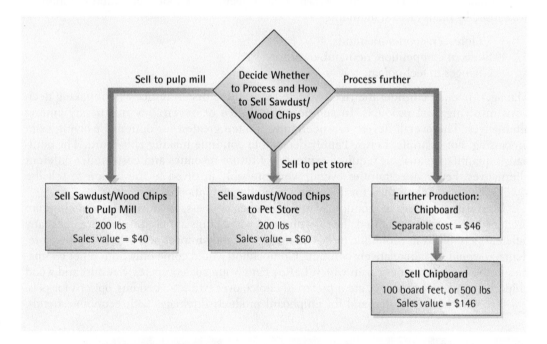

Accordingly, only the incremental revenues and costs for the scraps and chipboard are relevant. Using this information, Lacy presents the LeRoy Family management with the following analysis:

	Sell Sawdust and Wood Chips		
	Pulp Mill	Pet Store	Produce Chipboard
Incremental revenues	$40	$60	$146
Incremental (separable) costs	0	0	46
Incremental contribution	$40	$60	$100

Quantitative and Qualitative Factors

After Lacy explains her analysis to the managers, they decide to continue producing chipboard. They expect to earn $40 ($100 – $60) more profit per log by producing chipboard than by selling scrap to the pet store. In addition, LeRoy Family prefers this option because it avoids employee layoffs that would be detrimental to individual employees and to the small town's economy. ■

> STRATEGIC RISK MANAGEMENT: LEROY FAMILY (PART 2)

RELEVANT INFORMATION FOR PRODUCT LINE DECISIONS In LeRoy Family (Part 2), the managers decided to continue producing and selling chipboard rather than selling sawdust and wood chips through other channels. Would the managers have changed their decision if chipboard was not expected to provide the highest contribution? Managers make product line decisions such as this one after considering the strategic fit of each alternative. To analyze strategic fit, managers consider whether and how each product helps the organization take advantage of competitive strengths and achieve overall strategic goals while they manage costs. They also consider qualitative factors, such as the impact on employees and the local economy, and also social/environmental concerns in light of the company's mission and values.

Uncertainty and Bias in Incremental Revenue and Cost Estimates

Any estimate of future revenues and costs includes uncertainties about achievability. Changes are caused by many factors, including:

- ▶ Unforeseen economic trends
- ▶ Shifts in competition, demand, or supply
- ▶ Changes in technology

Managers need to consider the risk associated with these uncertainties when making decisions involving joint products. In addition, the degree of uncertainty might vary among alternatives. The overall degree of uncertainty is often greatest for options involving extra processing. For example, LeRoy Family decided to continue making chipboard. The company's quantitative analysis required estimates of future revenues and costs under different alternatives. Fewer uncertainties overall were probably involved in the option to sell the sawdust and wood chips than for the option to produce chipboard.

Even with advances in technology in the lumber business, sawdust and wood chips are produced when trees are milled. The sawdust and wood chips are used in bedding for many different pets. Shifts in economic trends do not significantly impact pet ownership; therefore, demand would remain relatively constant. Competition would come only from other companies in the lumber business, with which LeRoy Family already competes. Sawdust and wood chips, being natural products, are a preferred choice over synthetic bedding options for pets. On the other hand, the demand for chipboard products fluctuates with economic trends.

●●● > RISK OF BIASED DECISIONS: JOINT-VERSUS-SEPARATE PREFERENCE REVERSALS

The JOINT-VERSUS-SEPARATE PREFERENCE REVERSAL is a tendency to react emotionally to a decision when only one option exists but to use a more objective decision rule when multiple options exist. In economic market experiments involving the split of money between two players, a player who is given only one option—to accept or reject a split of money offered by another player—is likely to reject any split that is not approximately equal. As we learned in Chapter 8, the fairness bias prevents the player from accepting an economically beneficial offer. However, when given a choice between two or more splits of money, players tend to choose the offer that is most economically beneficial, even when it is an unequal split. Decision scientists believe that when we are presented with one option at a time, we make a quick comparison and decisions are heavily affected by emotions. When we have multiple options, we take time to assess each option more carefully and place less weight on the emotional aspects of the decision. When making joint product decisions, managers may be less biased when evaluating two or more options (such as in LeRoy Family Part 2) than when deciding whether to accept or reject only one option.

Competition could come from companies not directly in the sawmill business, and substitute products are always a threat. Changes in technology could impact the production of chipboard and change the form of substitute products. Thus, the managers might have been less confident in the data used to estimate their incremental profit under the chipboard option.

Joint Products and By-products

By definition, by-products have low sales values compared to the other products. In the LeRoy Family example, lumber is the main product and scrap (sawdust and wood chips) is the by-product. If scrap is processed further into chipboard, it becomes a main product because the sales value of chipboard is relatively high. Deciding whether a product is a main product or by-product often requires judgment.

Sometimes products that were previously by-products become main products and vice versa. A by-product can become valuable when new technologies or markets emerge. For example, when the LeRoy family first began their lumber mill, sawdust and wood chips were burned in large teepee-shaped metal incinerators. As the gluing and pressing processes improved and logs became a scarce natural resource, producing chipboard became technologically and economically feasible. Lumber scraps are now used in a wide variety of products in addition to chipboard. For example, pulp mills pulverize the scraps and add liquid to make wood pulp that can be further processed into paper goods, cardboard, and building materials.

Accounting for By-products

Sometimes by-products of a joint process are disposed of at a net cost, such as when metal scraps are hauled to a recycling centre, or when a joint process results in hazardous material by-products that require special handling and disposal. In such cases, the costs of disposal are part of the joint costs of production. If the by-products have zero value, such as paper trimmings in a print shop, no accounting is needed for the by-product. However, if the by-product contributes to profits, a decision is made about accounting for the by-product.

By-products would not exist if an organization were not already producing one or more main products. Theoretically, then, it is reasonable to reduce joint costs by the net realizable value of by-products. The sale of a by-product reduces the cost of producing the main products. To achieve the best matching against the cost of main products, the value of by-products should be recorded at the time of production. However, by-products by definition have little value relative to main products, so they are typically immaterial to financial statements or other reports. Therefore, by-products may not be recorded in what is theoretically the most correct way; a great deal of variation occurs in practice.

In general, the selection of an accounting method depends on whether managers want to establish control over by-products. Although by-products are not material relative to main products, they may have considerable absolute value and managers might want to establish controls to reduce the likelihood of theft or other loss. In this case, by-products are usually recorded at the time of production. When the value is so small that theft concerns are not a problem, by-products are often recorded at the time of sale.

The following income statements for LeRoy Family use the two methods of accounting for by-products, assuming that sawdust and wood chips are sold to a pulp mill at the split-off point and are viewed as by-products. The selling price is $40 for 200 pounds of scrap, or $0.20 per pound. We assume that 1,000 logs are processed during March, resulting in 300,000 board

LO5 Apply the methods that are used to account for the sale of by-products

BUSINESS PRACTICE
BC Hydro and a number of British Columbia technology companies generate megawatts of energy from wood chips and other organic waste.[2]

BUSINESS PRACTICE
Dakota Gasification ships about 8,000 metric tonnes of CO_2 emissions, a by-product previously considered waste, daily to oil companies who use it in oil recovery processes.[3]

[2]Power Generation Options, BC Hydro, 2015, www.bchydro.com/energy-in-bc/meeting_demand_growth/generation-options.html; P. Severinson, "Watts for Wood Chips," *BCBusinessOnline* (May 2008), www.bcbusinessonline.ca/bcb/business-sense/2008/05/01/watts-wood-chips.
[3]Dakota Gasification Company, CO_2 Capture and Storage: The greatest CO_2 story ever told, www.dakotagas.com/CO2_Capture_and_Storage/index.html

feet (1,000 logs × 300 bd ft per log) of lumber and 200,000 pounds (1,000 logs × 200 lbs per log) of sawdust and wood chip scrap. Sales during the month totalled 270,000 bd ft of lumber and 190,000 lbs of scrap. Refer to Exhibit 9.3 for the per-log cost and sales value information.

	Beginning Inventory	Production	Sales	Ending Inventory
Lumber (board feet)	0	300,000	270,000	30,000
Sawdust and wood chips (kilograms)	0	200,000	190,000	10,000

By-product Value Recognized at the Time of Production

When by-product value is recognized at the time of production, the joint costs of the main product are reduced by the net realizable value of the by-product. Later, when the by-product is sold, no gain or loss is recorded. For LeRoy Family, the net realizable value of the by-product is equal to its sales value at the split-off point ($0.20 per pound). This amount is subtracted from the joint cost and reduces the product cost of lumber. In turn, this computation reduces the per-unit cost of lumber in cost of goods sold and in ending inventory. Notice that ending inventory includes lumber at cost and by-product at net realizable value. This method allows managers to monitor both the quantity and value of by-products.

INTERNATIONAL

Under International Accounting Standards (IAS) No. 2, the net realizable value of by-products is often deducted from the cost of main products.

Production costs for the main product:	
Joint product costs incurred (1,000 logs × $220)	$220,000
Less NRV of by-product (200,000 lbs × $0.20)	40,000
Net joint product cost	$180,000
Product cost per log ($180,000 ÷ 1,000 logs)	$ 180
Product cost per lumber board foot ($180 ÷ 300 bd ft)	$0.60
Income statement:	
Revenue [270,000 bd ft × ($400 ÷ 300 bd ft)]	$360,000
Cost of goods sold (270,000 bd ft × $0.60)	162,000
Gross margin	$198,000
Ending inventory at March 31:	
Lumber (30,000 bd ft × $0.60)	$18,000
By-product (10,000 lbs × $0.20)	2,000
Total inventory	$20,000

ALTERNATIVE TERMS

The terms *net realizable value approach* and *offset approach* mean the same as *recognizing by-product value at the time of production.*

By-product Value Recognized at the Time of Sale

When by-product value is recognized at the time of sale, the value may be recorded as sales revenue, other income, or a reduction of cost of goods sold. Because by-products are viewed as immaterial, the choice of accounting treatment is considered unimportant. Until they are sold, by-products are not accounted for in the general ledger. For LeRoy Family, this practice means that no inventory value is recorded for sawdust and wood chips. In the following example, we assume that the sales value of by-products is reported as part of revenue on the income statement:

Income statement:	
Revenue:	
Lumber [270,000 bd ft × ($400 ÷ 300 bd ft)]	$360,000
Sawdust (190,000 lbs × $0.20)	38,000
Total revenue	398,000
Cost of goods sold [270,000 bd ft × ($220 ÷ 300 bd ft)]	198,000
Gross margin	$200,000
Ending inventory at March 31:	
Lumber [30,000 bd ft × ($220 ÷ 300 bd ft)]	$ 22,000

ALTERNATIVE TERMS

The terms *realized value approach* and *income approach* mean the same as *recognizing by-product value at the time of sale.*

For the LeRoy Family example, the difference between gross margins under the two methods is $2,000 ($198,000 − $200,000). This amount is offset by the difference in the total values of ending inventory [$20,000 − $22,000 = $(2,000)], which is true only in cases where beginning inventory is zero. In general, the difference between gross margins under the two methods is equal to the difference in the change during the period in the values of total inventory. As long as by-product values are immaterial, the choice of method has little effect on the income statement and balance sheet.

Joint Product Costing with a Sales Mix

In the LeRoy Family examples, the concepts and calculations for joint product costing are illustrated using simple products. However, in most settings, joint product costing is more complex. Complexity increases as the number of products, all with different units of measure, increases. Cost behaviour introduces complexity when the joint costs include both fixed and variable costs, or step costs. Some production processes include multiple split-off points. Differential market demand for end products also increases the complexity of the analysis. In addition, the different allocation methods will impact employee behaviours. If allocated joint costs are considered in performance evaluation or compensation, managers are likely to modify their decisions in order to maximize their performance. In the following example, costs are allocated to multiple products when multiple units are involved. The impact on managers' behaviours is also discussed.

> **LO6** Explain how a sales mix affects joint cost allocation

premier maple syrup
JOINT PRODUCT COSTING WITH A SALES MIX

example

Premier Maple Syrup, located in Quebec, processes maple sap into maple syrup, maple sugar, and maple butter. The company has three product managers, one for each of the three main products. The managers receive bonuses based on the profitability of their individual products. Lately, some of the managers have been concerned about the allocations of joint costs and the effect these allocations have on the profitability of each of the product lines. They approached the accountant, Jacqueline Dubois, about this problem. Jacqueline explained that several different allocation methods could be used and that the gross margin of each product would change with each method. The managers wanted Jacqueline to prepare their usual reports using each of these methods. She agreed to provide the managers with information about product profitability using each of the acceptable joint product cost allocation methods (Exhibit 9.5).

First, she gathered data from the current period. During the most recent spring, the joint costs of processing maple sap were $2,000,000 ($2M). The company had no beginning or ending inventories for the season. Production and sales value information for the season were as follows:

Product	Cases	Sales Value at Split-off Point	Separable Costs	Selling Price
Syrup	90,000	$24 per case	$12 per case	$38 per case
Sugar	20,000	$26 per case	$16 per case	$46 per case
Butter	10,000	$32 per case	$14 per case	$50 per case

Sales value at split-off for each product varies because the grade and kilograms of sap required for each option vary. In addition, the case is used as the common unit of measure, because syrup is measured in millilitres while sugar and butter are measured in grams.

ritajaco/iStockphoto

continued...

example

Physical Output Method

The number of cases is used as the measure of physical output.

1. Determine the number of cases sold, by product, and sum them:

	Number of Cases:
Syrup	90,000 cases
Sugar	20,000
Butter	10,000
Total	120,000 cases

2. Use each product's relative proportion of cases to allocate the joint costs.

Allocate joint costs:

Syrup [(90,000/120,000) × $2M]	$1,500,000
Sugar [(20,000/120,000) × $2M]	333,333
Butter [(10,000/120,000) × $2M]	166,667
Total allocated joint costs	$2,000,000

Sales Value at Split-off Point Method

Each product's proportion of the total sales value at the split-off point is used.

> **EXHIBIT 9.5**
>
> Summary of Alternative Gross Margins for Premier Maple Syrup

	Allocation Method			
	Physical Output	Sales Value at Split-off Point	Net Realizable Value	Constant Gross Margin NRV
Syrup:				
Sales	$3,420,000	$3,420,000	$3,420,000	$3,420,000
Separable costs	1,080,000	1,080,000	1,080,000	1,080,000
Incremental contribution	2,340,000	2,340,000	2,340,000	2,340,000
Allocated joint costs	(1,500,000)	(1,440,000)	(1,418,182)	(1,421,405)
Gross margin	840,000	900,000	921,818	918,595
Sugar:				
Sales	920,000	920,000	920,000	920,000
Separable costs	320,000	320,000	320,000	320,000
Incremental contribution	600,000	600,000	600,000	600,000
Allocated joint costs	(333,333)	(346,667)	(363,636)	(352,893)
Gross margin	266,667	253,333	236,364	247,107
Butter:				
Sales	500,000	500,000	500,000	500,000
Separable costs	140,000	140,000	140,000	140,000
Incremental contribution	360,000	360,000	360,000	360,000
Allocated joint costs	(166,667)	(213,333)	(218,182)	(225,702)
Gross margin	193,333	146,667	141,818	134,298
Combined gross margin	$1,300,000	$1,300,000	$1,300,000	$1,300,000

example

1. Determine each product's total sales value at split-off and calculate its relative proportion:

Syrup (90,000 × $24)	$2,160,000
Sugar (20,000 × $26)	520,000
Butter (10,000 × $32)	320,000
Total sales value at split-off point	$3,000,000

2. Use each product's relative proportion of sales value at split-off to allocate the joint cost:

Allocate joint costs:

To syrup [($2.16M/$3M) × $2M]	$1,440,000
To sugar [($0.52M/$3M) × $2M]	346,667
To butter [($0.32M/$3M) × $2M]	213,333
Total allocated joint costs	$2,000,000

Net Realizable Value Method

The net realizable value (NRV) is the selling price minus separable costs.

1. Determine each product's net realizable value and sum them:

Syrup [90,000 × ($38 − $12)]	$2,340,000
Sugar [20,000 × ($46 − $16)]	600,000
Butter [10,000 × ($50 − $14)]	360,000
Total net realizable value	$3,300,000

2. Use each product's relative proportion of net realizable value to allocate the joint costs:

Allocate joint costs:

To syrup [($2.34M/$3.3M) × $2M]	$1,418,182
To sugar [($0.6M/$3.3M) × $2M]	363,636
To butter [($0.36M/$3.3M) × $2M]	218,182
Total allocated joint costs	$2,000,000

Constant Gross Margin NRV Method

The constant gross margin NRV method uses the gross margin for all products in the joint cost allocation process.

1. Calculate the combined gross margin percentage:

Combined sales	
Syrup ($38 × 90,000)	$3,420,000
Sugar ($46 × 20,000)	920,000
Butter ($50 × 10,000)	500,000
Total combined sales	$4,840,000
Less combined product costs:	
Joint costs	2,000,000
Syrup ($12 × 90,000)	1,080,000
Sugar ($16 × 20,000)	320,000
Butter ($14 × 10,000)	140,000
Total combined product costs	3,540,000
Combined gross margin	$1,300,000
Combined gross margin percentage ($1.3M/$4.84M)	26.86%

continued...

example

2. Allocate the joint costs to achieve a constant gross margin:

	Syrup	Sugar	Butter	Total
Sales	$3,420,000	$920,000	$500,000	$4,840,000
Less gross margin (.2686 × sales)	918,595	247,107	134,298	1,300,000
Total product costs	2,501,405	672,893	365,702	3,540,000
Less separable costs	1,080,000	320,000	140,000	1,540,000
Allocated joint costs	$1,421,405	$352,893	$225,702	$2,000,000

Comparing Methods

Jacqueline prepared the schedule shown in Exhibit 9.5 so that the managers could see the effects of the allocation system on their products' profitability. The syrup manager prefers the net realizable value measure method because it shows the greatest profit for his products. The managers of the sugar division and the butter division object because their profits were lower under this method. They want to use the physical output method, where their profits appear higher.

Jacqueline realizes that at least one manager will always be unhappy with the allocations and shows them that regardless of each product's profits, the overall benefit to the company is $1,300,000 (NRV – Joint costs = $3,300,000 – $2,000,000). The managers agree that all these methods arbitrarily divide up the contribution and that for determining bonus amounts, none of the methods is fair to every manager.

When the managers speak to the director of finance, he addresses the bonus issue from the perspective of responsibility. He points out that the managers are responsible for sales of their product lines and costs of further processing. He suggests that their bonuses should be based on each product's contribution to total profitability, before any allocations of joint costs have been made. In addition, to provide incentives for them to increase sales and contain costs, he believes that changes in the contribution over time should be as important as the total contribution. The director of finance points out that the demand for each product and the market share captured by each manager also are important factors to consider in performance evaluation. ■

●● > STRATEGIC RISK MANAGEMENT: PREMIER MAPLE SYRUP

RESPONSIBILITY FOR SALES AND COSTS To provide incentives for increasing sales and containing costs, the product managers at Premier Maple Syrup received bonuses based on the profitability of their individual products. Why did the director of finance recommend removing joint cost allocations from the bonus computations? The managers had no control over the joint costs and did not need to coordinate activities such as quantities of separate products produced by the joint process, production methods, or capacity usage. Thus, no benefit would be gained by including joint costs in their bonus computations. Furthermore, holding the product managers accountable for joints costs might lead to dysfunctional behaviour. For example, the product managers might devote a scarce company resource—manager attention—to unproductive arguments with finance staff about the allocation methods used. In addition, the allocations might encourage the managers to consider irrelevant joint costs when making decisions about how best to generate additional contribution margins.

Uses and Limitations of Joint Cost Information

Joint costs are allocated to individual products primarily to meet requirements for financial accounting, income tax, government regulatory, or other external reporting. All product costs must be assigned to inventory and cost of goods sold. By definition, it is not possible to directly trace joint costs to individual products. Instead, an allocation method must be adopted. Several potential methods may be used, and most of the methods involve estimation of one or more of the following: physical quantities, sales values at the split-off point, sales price if processed further, and separable costs. Anytime estimates are used, the potential arises for bias and other distortions caused by uncertainties. Ultimately, joint cost allocations are often chosen to avoid the appearance that some main products are unprofitable whereas others are profitable.

Because joint costs are assigned to products for external reporting, managers tend to use them in making decisions. However, allocated joint costs are irrelevant for most decisions. For example, joint cost allocations should not be used to decide whether to process a joint product beyond the split-off point or in evaluating individual product manager performance. Accountants assist managers by helping them understand whether joint costs are relevant to a particular decision.

> **LO 7** Evaluate the uses and limitations of joint cost information

Diagnostic Control of Joint Processes and Costs

Although joint cost allocations generally should not be used for management control of individual products, other aspects of joint processes can and should be controlled. In this section, we focus on two aspects of diagnostic control systems related to joint products: manager performance and bonus incentives, and control over physical quantities.

Manager Performance and Bonus Incentives. The performance of product line or sub-unit managers often depends on the accounting profits of the products they manage. Sometimes, the allocation of joint costs is included in the calculation of these profits, and some managers may perceive the allocation as unfair. If managers have no control over common costs, each joint cost allocation method distributes income in a different manner that is not related to managerial efforts. When joint costs are large, the resulting profit measure may provide little information about individual manager performance.

As organizations focus on strategic business processes, product line or sub-unit managers need to coordinate activities. For example, optimal decisions about joint product emphasis may depend on input from individual managers about the prospects of their product markets. Similarly, the organization as a whole may benefit when managers share information about production innovations. In these situations, therefore, it may be appropriate to include profit of the entire joint process in the individual manager's performance evaluation.

> **► CHAPTER REFERENCE**
> Performance measures and managerial incentives are discussed further in Chapter 18.

Physical Quantity Data. Operations management typically includes control of the physical quantities of materials for manufacturing processes. All physical products can be measured using weight, volume, or some other physical measure. Ideally, evaporation, waste, or other losses in physical quantities should be measured and controlled. Through regular monitoring of these data in a diagnostic control system, managers can quickly learn about and correct problems such as

- ► Out-of-control production processes
- ► Theft of materials or inventories
- ► Failure to dispose of waste in accordance with environmental laws or company policies

Because manufacturing companies tend to maintain records of physical quantities, these data are readily available for other management or accounting purposes. Accordingly, companies might want to use the physical output method for allocating joint costs, unless this method causes serious distortions of main product profitability.

> **► CHAPTER REFERENCE**
> Chapter 5 discusses process costing procedures for waste and spoilage. Chapter 20 introduces material flow accounting, which tracks all physical flows.

9-1 self-study problem   Four Allocation Methods, Further Processing Decision, and Uncertainties

L02, L04   Atlantic Sand and Gravel Corp. produces two grades of sand: coarse and fine. Both grades are used to manufacture industrial abrasives. The results of operations for the last year were as follows:

	Coarse	Fine	Total
Production	4,000 tonnes	6,000 tonnes	10,000 tonnes
Sales value at split-off point	$40,000	$ 50,000	$ 90,000
Revenue	$90,000	$150,000	$240,000
Separable costs	$20,000	$ 15,000	$ 35,000

Joint product costs were $100,000. There were no beginning inventories.

required

A. Allocate the joint costs, using the physical output method.
B. Allocate the joint costs, using the sales value at split-off point method.
C. Allocate the joint costs, using the net realizable value method.
D. Allocate the joint costs, using the constant gross margin NRV method.
E. Discuss the pros and cons of each method.
F. Suppose fine sand can be processed further by mixing in colour. The cost of adding colour is $15 per tonne, and the sand can then be sold for $35 per tonne. Should fine sand be processed further?
G. What uncertainties do managers face in making the decision in Part F?
H. Which of the options in Part F involves greater uncertainties and, therefore, greater risk for the company? Explain.

See the solution on page 421.

Laurin Rinder/Shutterstock

●● > FOCUS ON ETHICAL DECISION MAKING
HAZARDOUS WASTE

Manufacturing and industrial processes often produce more than main products and by-products. They can also produce significant quantities of hazardous materials that must be disposed of, including the following:

• Acids and bases from chemical manufacturing

• Ink sludge containing heavy metals from the printing industry

• Wastewater containing benzene and other hydrocarbons from petroleum refining

• Paint waste and solvents from construction

The annual quantity of industrial hazardous waste produced in Canada is significant. In 2006, the Canadian Institute for Environmental Law and Policy estimated the total amount at 6 million tonnes of hazardous and liquid industrial waste. It is estimated that Ontario hazardous waste producers alone account for 2.8 million tonnes of the total waste.

Historically, Ontario was known as a "dumping ground for hazardous waste." Liquid hazardous waste produced in Ontario was shipped to U.S. firms for use as fuel in cement kilns. However, Ontario was a net importer of all other types of hazardous waste. Minimum regulations compared to increasing regulation in the United States made it cost beneficial for hazardous waste producers to ship their waste to Ontario, where it could be landfilled with no pretreatment—and, hence, no additional cost. However, beginning in 2000, the Ontario government started to step up hazardous waste disposal regulations. Since January 1, 2002, the Ontario Ministry of the Environment has required all hazardous waste producers to register the type and quantity of waste produced. A yearly fee is assessed, based on the type and quantity of waste. Starting in 2005, Ontario implemented pretreatment standards equivalent to those in the United States for waste going into landfills. One of the intentions was to discourage U.S. hazardous waste producers from shipping their waste across the border. Unfortunately, as of 2006, 30 percent of all hazardous waste producers had not complied with the existing regulations. In an attempt to change the situation, more stringent reporting requirements were implemented on January 1, 2007.

Other issues in the spotlight include minimal or lack of operating and emission standards for companies that burn hazardous waste (e.g., in cement kilns), small-quantity producers that individually operate below the levels of the existing monitoring guidelines, and specific types of hazardous waste (e.g., fluorescent light bulbs, electronic waste). Also, one report indicated that there was "no substantial reduction in the amounts of hazardous waste generated overall in Ontario over the years 2000 to 2005." Ultimately, the best solution is one that makes it more costly to generate and dispose of hazardous waste than to develop processes that are environmentally friendly.

ETHICS AND HAZARDOUS WASTE

This case highlights increasing environmental concerns about hazardous waste (a by-product of production) disposition. It raises important issues about record keeping and regulation, as well as ethical debates. Some companies, like cement manufacturers, burn hazardous waste in the normal course of their production processes. For these companies, hazardous waste is an inexpensive and perhaps free input to the manufacturing process. As such, hazardous waste used in this way does not fall under the existing regulations. The result is a potentially provocative situation between managers, shareholders, regulators, and the local population. What assumptions lie behind the viewpoints of each? What criteria should companies use when deciding how to dispose of hazardous waste? What is the best overall solution for society?

Source: Guy Crittenden, "Hazardous Waste in Ontario," *Lake Ontario Waterkeeper*, February 5, 2008, at http://old-www.waterkeeper.ca/2008/02/05/hazardous-waste-in-ontario; and Canadian Institute for Environmental Law and Policy, *Understanding Hazardous Waste in Ontario*, 2006, www.cielap.org/pdf/hwfactsheet.pdf; Government of Ontario, Hazardous waste management: business and industry, www.ontario.ca/environment-and-energy/hazardous-waste-management-business-and-industry.

SUMMARY

LO1   Describe a joint process, and explain the difference between a by-product and a main product

JOINT PROCESS

- More than one product can be jointly produced.
- Joint costs cannot be traced to individual products.
- Joint production ends at the split-off point.
- Individual products might or might not be processed beyond the split-off point.
- Main products have high relative sales value.
- By-products have low relative sales value.

| Joint Production and Joint Costs |
Split-off Point - - - - - - - -
| Main Products Relatively High Value | | By-products Relatively Low Value |

LO2   Allocate joint costs

PHYSICAL OUTPUT METHOD

- Allocate joint costs in proportion to the physical output for each main product.

- Examples of physical measures: metres, kilograms, litres.
- All main products must be expressed in the same physical measure.

SALES VALUE AT SPLIT-OFF POINT METHOD

▸ Allocate joint costs in proportion to the sales value for each main product at the point where joint production ends.

▸ Not always possible to measure sales value at the split-off point.

NET REALIZABLE VALUE (NRV) METHOD

▸ Allocate joint costs in proportion to the net realizable value for each main product, taking into account the final selling price and separable costs.

▸ Same as the sales value at split-off method if no additional production occurs beyond the split-off point.

CONSTANT GROSS MARGIN NRV METHOD

▸ Allocate joint costs so that the gross margin percentage for all main products is the same:
  - First, calculate combined gross margin percentage for all main products.
  - Second, calculate joint cost allocation that will result in the same gross margin percentage for all main products, taking into account the final selling price and separable costs.

LO3   Explain the factors that are considered in choosing a joint cost allocation method

MAJOR GOAL

Avoid distortion of individual main product values.

PHYSICAL OUTPUT METHOD

▸ May inappropriately give impression that a main product is unprofitable, even when it has a positive incremental value.

▸ Appropriate when units of all main products are similar in size and have comparable NRVs.

MARKET-BASED METHODS

▸ Sales value at split-off point method
  - Generally appropriate if most or all products are sold when joint production ends.
  - Sales values must exist at the split-off point.

▸ NRV methods generally preferred because allocation is based on the ability of each main product to "pay" for its allocated cost.
  - Constant gross margin NRV method best reflects the inseparability of the joint production process.

LO4   Identify the relevant information for deciding whether to process a joint product beyond the split-off point

GENERAL DECISION RULE (SEE CHAPTER 4)

Process further if the incremental revenue is greater than the incremental cost, including any relevant fixed costs and opportunity costs.

ASSUMPTIONS

▸ Cost-volume-profit assumptions.
▸ Managers want to maximize profits in the short term.

▸ Sales of one product do not affect sales of other products.

UNCERTAINTY AND BIAS IN FUTURE REVENUE AND SEPARABLE COST ESTIMATES

CONSIDER QUANTITATIVE AND QUALITATIVE FACTORS TO REACH DECISION

LO5   Apply the methods that are used to account for the sale of by-products

ACCOUNTING FOR NRV OF BY-PRODUCTS

▸ If net cost, include NRV in joint costs.
▸ If net profit
  - Method often considered unimportant because by-product values are immaterial.
▸ Record at time of production

  - Subtract NRV from joint costs.
  - By-product inventory carried at NRV.
  - Establishes control over by-product inventory.
▸ Record at time of sale
  - Recognize sales revenue or other income, or
  - Subtract NRV from cost of goods sold.

SUMMARY

LO6   Explain how a sales mix affects joint cost allocation

EFFECT OF SALES MIX ON CALCULATIONS

The sales mix is incorporated into the calculations for each allocation method.

LO7   Evaluate the uses and limitations of joint cost information

USES OF JOINT COST INFORMATION

► Financial statements
► Income tax returns
► Government regulatory reports
► Other external reports

ESTIMATES USED IN ALLOCATION COMPUTATIONS

► Physical quantities
► Sales value at split-off point
► Sales price if processed further
► Separable costs

IMPROPER USE OF JOINT COST INFORMATION

Joint costs are irrelevant for many types of decisions.

DIAGNOSTIC USES OF JOINT COST INFORMATION

► Manager performance evaluation and bonus incentives in business process (team) environments.
► Control over use of physical quantities.

9-1 solution to self-study problem

A. Allocate the joint costs, using the physical output method.
   Joint costs allocated:

To coarse [(4,000 tonnes/10,000 tonnes) × $100,000]	$ 40,000
To fine [(6,000 tonnes/10,000 tonnes) × $100,000]	60,000
Total joint costs allocated	$100,000

B. Allocate the joint costs, using the sales at split-off point method.
   Joint costs allocated:

To coarse [($40,000/$90,000) × $100,000]	$ 44,444
To fine [($50,000/$90,000) × $100,000]	55,556
Total joint costs allocated	$100,000

C. Allocate the joint costs, using the net realizable value method:
Total net realizable value:

Coarse ($90,000 – $20,000)	$ 70,000
Fine ($150,000 – $15,000)	135,000
Total NRV	$205,000

Joint costs allocated:

To coarse [($70,000/$205,000) × $100,000]	$ 34,146
To fine [($135,000/$205,000) × $100,000]	65,854
Total joint costs allocated	$100,000

D. Allocate the joint costs, using the constant gross margin NRV method.
Calculate the combined gross margin percentage:

Total revenue	$240,000
Separable costs	(35,000)
Joint costs	(100,000)
Total combined gross margin	$105,000
Combined gross margin percentage ($105,000/$240,000)	43.75%

Allocate joint costs to achieve a constant gross margin.

	Coarse	Fine	Total
Revenue	$90,000	$150,000	$240,000
Less gross margin (Revenue × 0.4375)	(39,375)	(65,625)	(105,000)
Total product costs	50,625	84,375	135,000
Less separable costs	(20,000)	(15,000)	(35,000)
Allocated joint costs	$30,625	$ 69,375	$100,000

E. The physical output method is the simplest to calculate. It is usually easy to identify the information needed because quantities of each product are often routinely
measured during regular production and accounting activities. However, the contributions of different joint products are distorted unless all the joint products have similar
contributions. Some products could be allocated more joint cost than their contribution, and would appear to be losers when actually a contribution can be realized
by selling them. If all joint products have a similar physical output per unit and a
similar contribution per unit, this method is the simplest and, therefore, would likely
be preferred.

The sales value at split-off point method is relatively easy to calculate. If all joint
products have a value at the time of split-off, this method requires less information
and fewer calculations than the NRV methods. If all products are sold at split-off, this
method is often the best. However, split-off values may not be available for some types
of products.

The net realizable value method provides the least distortion of incremental contribution
because the allocation is based on each product's incremental revenue and incremental

solution to self-study problem

9-1

cost. It requires a little more information and a few more calculations than the sales value at split-off point method. The allocations reflect each product's incremental contribution in the allocation scheme when products are processed after the split-off point.

The constant gross margin NRV method uses the contribution margin to allocate joint costs, so no product will be allocated more cost than its incremental revenue. It also considers the products' contributions after further processing. However, it is more complex to explain and requires more calculations than the net realizable value method. With spreadsheets and allocation software programs, the extra calculations are unlikely to be a problem.

F. This question involves a decision about additional processing beyond the split-off point. Joint costs are irrelevant for this decision, so no joint cost allocation is needed. Instead, we calculate the incremental contribution for each option. Currently, fine sand sells for $25 per tonne, and separable costs are $2.50 per tonne, so the contribution per tonne is $22.50. If the sand is processed further, it sells for $35 per tonne but costs an additional $15 to process. The contribution for this option is $17.50 ($35 – $15 – $2.50). Ignoring any possible qualitative factors, the managers should decide not to colour the sand. They would rather receive $22.50 per tonne than $17.50 per tonne.

G. Many uncertainties, including the following, are involved in this decision:

- Future revenues are uncertain under both options; the managers cannot know with certainty that future prices will be equal to current prices.
- Additional costs for adding colour are uncertain; the managers cannot know how much it will cost because they do not have experience creating this type of product. In addition, future costs might not be the same.
- The managers cannot know with certainty how their decision might affect sales of regular fine sand. Will the sale of coloured sand replace the sale of regular fine sand? Is the demand for coloured sand a short-term occurrence? Would the coloured sand market create other opportunities for the company?

H. Two main reasons explain why uncertainties and risk for the coloured sand option are probably greater than uncertainties and risk for the regular fine sand option. First, the company does not have experience creating coloured sand. Accordingly, it faces greater uncertainty about production methods and customer markets. Second, products requiring more processing usually entail greater risk. The company must expend more resources before selling the product.

QUESTIONS

9.1 In your own words, explain what determines whether a product is a main product or by-product.

9.2 One of the products from a joint process, Product A, can be sold at the split-off point for $10. The other products can all be sold at the split-off point for $200 or more. Would you categorize Product A as a main product or by-product? Explain.

9.3 In your own words, explain the two methods for recognizing revenue from a by-product.

9.4 Describe a group of main products and by-products for an industry located near your home or university.

9.5 How are joint product costs and indirect costs similar? How are separable costs and direct costs similar?

9.6 Describe the split-off point, and explain its significance for joint product costing.

9.7 Give an example of joint products in a service industry, and describe the main products and by-products.

9.8 A decision about processing a product further should not be influenced by joint cost allocation but should be based on incremental costs and qualitative factors. Explain.

9.9 "The allocation of a joint cost among joint products is essentially an arbitrary process." If this statement is true, then why allocate?

9.10 The owner of a business says, "I cannot uniquely determine the profitability of one of my joint products, but I can uniquely determine its contribution to joint costs and profit." Explain.

9.11 A specialty chemical company obtains 73 different products of relatively equal value from processing a single input. Should these products be treated as main products or by-products?

9.12 What estimates are required to perform market-based joint cost allocations? Where would accountants obtain the information needed for these estimates?

9.13 Provide three or more examples of qualitative factors that might influence a decision to process a joint product beyond the split-off point.

9.14 Information about some by-products is not recorded in the accounting system. However, for other by-products, control systems are instituted and accounting records are kept. How do accountants identify by-products that need control systems and record keeping and those that do not?

9.15 Why would the perceived fairness of a joint cost allocation method be important to some managers?

MULTIPLE-CHOICE QUESTIONS

9.16 SMT Ltd. manufactures three products. Production begins with a joint process, and the three outputs of the joint process are processed further to produce products L, M, and N. The outputs at split-off have no market value. Last year, the joint costs amounted to $600,000. Other data for last year are as follows:

	Product L	Product M	Product N
Selling price per unit	$160	$300	$400
Costs per unit after split-off point to complete and sell	$100	$200	$350
Total output at split-off point used in production	16,400 kg	10,000 kg	8,400 kg
Production in units	20,000	10,000	7,000
Sales in units	18,000	8,000	7,000

Using the estimated (approximate) net realizable value method of joint costing, the inventory cost per unit of product M is
a. $226.91
b. $223.53
c. $221.52
d. $220.00
e. $217.24

The following information pertains to Questions 9.17 and 9.18:

Omega Company manufactures three chemicals in a joint process. The manufacturing costs of the joint process include $25,000 of direct materials and $35,000 of conversion costs. All three chemicals can be sold in their unrefined form immediately after the split-off point, or they can be further refined before they are sold. During May, all three chemicals were further refined. The following table shows data regarding production for the month of May:

	Chemical		
	A	B	C
Sales price per litre before refining	$20	$25	$10
Sales price per litre after refining	$35	$40	$18
Cost of refining	$28,000	$10,000	$12,000
Total output of chemical at split-off	2,500 L	1,600 L	3,000 L
Total output of chemical after refining	2,300 L	1,500 L	2,700 L

9.17 Using the sales value at split-off method, the total joint cost allocated to chemical A in May (rounded to the nearest hundred dollars) is
a. $21,100
b. $25,000
c. $22,600
d. $25,500
e. $33,600

9.18 Now assume that Omega Company uses the physical measures method, that the refining process for chemical C also produces a hazardous by-product that must be disposed of at a cost of $5/L, and that refining 1,000 L of chemical C results in 100 L of this by-product. For the month of May, what effect would refining chemical C have on Omega Company's profits as compared with its profits if chemical C was sold at split-off without being further refined (rounded to the nearest $100)?

a. $17,100 more profits by refining
b. $20,300 less profits by refining
c. $8,100 more profits by refining
d. $5,100 more profits by refining
e. $8,400 less profits by refining

The following information pertains to Questions 9.19 and 9.20:

Omega Company manufactures three chemicals in a joint process. The manufacturing costs of the joint process include $25,000 of direct materials and $35,000 of conversion costs. All three chemicals are then processed further before they are sold. Other pertinent data are as follows:

Chemicals	Sales Value at Split-off	Separable Costs	Final Sales Value
A	$50,000	$28,000	$100,000
B	40,000	10,000	60,000
C	30,000	12,000	40,000

9.19 Using the estimated net realizable value method, the joint costs allocated to chemical A would be
a. $16,800
b. $25,000
c. $28,800
d. $30,000
e. $33,600

9.20 The decision to process all three chemicals beyond the split-off point is suboptimal. If the optimal decision had been made, the income of Omega Company would have improved by
a. $2,000
b. $10,000
c. $30,000
d. $60,000
e. $12,000

EXERCISES

9.21 Identifying Joint Products
LO1

REQUIRED **A.** Which of the following related products would be considered joint products? Explain your choices.
1. Sand produced with three levels of fineness
2. Automobiles and trucks
3. Milk, yogurt, butter, and cheese
4. Motorcycles and mopeds
5. Various lines of clothing manufactured for a discount department store
6. An airline that provides first class, business class, and economy class service

B. List two additional product groups that could be considered joint products.

9.22 Identifying Joint and Separable Costs Cowboy Cattle Company raises cattle and sells beef products. Following is a list of costs for the operation.
LO1

1. Veterinary costs for the calves
2. The cost of grinding hamburger
3. The cost of feed for the cattle
4. Labour cost to manage the cattle while they grow
5. Labour cost to prepare the cowhide for sale as leather
6. The cost for packaging steaks and roasts
7. The amortization on the sheds that provide shelter for the cattle

REQUIRED Identify whether each cost is most likely a (J) joint cost or a (S) separable cost. For each item, explain why.

9.23 Profitability of Joint Products Larry Dean raises registered Labrador retrievers. Dean's prize dog has just given birth

LO2 to six puppies. The litter consisted of two chocolate males, two yellow males, and two yellow females. The stud fee, veterinary bills, and other costs associated with the dog's pregnancy amounted to $700. The puppies were kept with their mother for 12 weeks before they could be sold. During this time, feeding and medical bills for each of the puppies amounted to $160. In addition, the two chocolate males required additional veterinary costs of $40 each. At 12 weeks, the two chocolate males were sold for $300 each, the two yellow males were sold for $400 each, and the females were sold for $450 each.

REQUIRED **A.** Using the NRV method, allocate the joint costs.
B. Determine the gross profit that would be recognized from the sale of each dog.

9.24 By-product Further Processing Decision For a given by-product, 100 units can be sold at the split-off point for $8

LO4 each or processed further at a cost of $12 each and sold for $19.

REQUIRED Should the by-product be processed further? Provide calculations, and explain your answer.

9.25 NRV Method, Contribution Margin, Further Processing for a Service Deluxe Tours, a tour organizer, leased a cruise

LO2, LO3, liner for a special around-the-world tour. The lease cost is $200,000. Two classes of passengers are booked on
LO4 the tour: first class and economy class. The total revenue from the 100 first-class passengers is $200,000 and from the 200 economy-class passengers is $200,000. Other costs for the two classes of passengers amount to $30,000 for first class and $30,000 for economy class.

REQUIRED **A.** How much of the lease cost will be allocated to first-class passengers if the net realizable value method is used?
B. What is the contribution margin generated by first-class passengers?
C. When the cruise liner managers are deciding whether to increase the number of first-class rooms, which joint cost allocation method is best to use? Explain.

9.26 Four Joint Cost Allocation Methods with Sales Mix, Further Processing Decision The Palm Oil Company buys crude

LO2, LO4, coconut and palm nut oil. Refining this oil results in four products at the split-off point: soap grade, cooking
LO6 grade, light moisturizer, and heavy moisturizer. Light moisturizer is fully processed at the split-off point.
Soap grade, cooking grade, and heavy moisturizer can individually be refined into fine soap, cooking oil, and premium moisturizer. In the most recent month (June), the output at the split-off point was as follows:

Soap grade	100,000 L
Cooking grade	300,000 L
Light moisturizer	50,000 L
Heavy moisturizer	50,000 L

The joint costs of purchasing the crude coconut and palm nut oil and processing it were $100,000. There were no beginning or ending inventories. Sales of light moisturizer in June were $50,000. Total output of soap, cooking oil, and heavy moisturizer was further refined and then sold. Data relating to June are as follows:

Product	Separable Costs	Sales
Fine soap	$200,000	$300,000
Superior cooking oil	80,000	100,000
Premium moisturizer	90,000	120,000

Palm Oil Company had the option of selling the soap grade, cooking grade, and heavy moisturizer at the split-off point. This alternative would have yielded the following sales for the June production:

Soap grade	$50,000
Cooking grade	30,000
Heavy moisturizer	70,000

REQUIRED **A.** Allocate the joint costs, using each of the following methods:
  1. Sales value at split-off point
  2. Physical output
  3. Net realizable value
  4. Constant gross margin NRV

B. Could Palm Oil Company have increased its June operating income by making different decisions about further refining the soap grade, cooking grade, or heavy moisturizer palm nut oil? Show the effect on the contribution margin of any changes you recommend.

9.27 **Sales Value at Split-off, Physical Output, NRV Methods, Further Processing Decision** Flowering Friends is a small

L02, L04 nursery. The company grows rhododendrons and azaleas. The plants are dug up and potted after three years of growth. Some of them are considered premium because they are taller and have more bloom buds than the rest. They are placed in a greenhouse for several months, fertilized heavily, and then sold when they are in bloom. The others are sold at the time they are dug. Joint costs for raising the plants are $15,000. Following is information about potential allocation bases for the joint costs of growing the plants:

Allocation Base	Premium	Regular
Number of pots	2,000 pots	8,000 pots
Sales value per pot at the time they are dug	$5	$3
Net realizable value (NRV) per pot	$25	$10

REQUIRED **A.** Allocate the joint cost using the following methods:
  1. Sales value at split-off point
  2. Physical output
  3. Net realizable value

B. If the premium plants are repotted in ceramic pots just before Mother's Day, they can be sold for $35. Labour (plus fringe benefits) for repotting costs $20 per hour, and 4 plants can be repotted by an employee each hour. The ceramic pots cost $3 each. Should Flowering Friends process these plants further?

9.28 **NRV and Physical Output Methods, Further Processing Decision** Click and Clack Recyclers buys used motor oil for

L02, L04 $0.75/L from shops that specialize in oil changes and other minor services for cars. The cost of transporting and refining the motor oil is $1.25/L. The refined oil becomes commercial-grade motor oil and a thick residual fuel oil. Each litre of used motor oil yields 0.7 L of commercial-grade motor oil and 0.3 L of residual fuel oil. Commercial-grade motor oil is sold for $3/L, and residual fuel oil is sold for $1.50/L.

REQUIRED **A.** If the costs of purchasing and processing the used motor oil were allocated on the basis of their net realizable value, what would be the inventory cost per litre of residual fuel oil?

B. If the costs of purchasing and processing the used motor oil were allocated on the basis of physical output, what would be the inventory cost of residual fuel oil?

C. With additional processing, residual fuel oil can be converted into special fuel oil. The additional processing costs $0.40/L. What would be the minimum acceptable price for the special fuel oil?

9.29 **By-product Value Recognized at Time of Production Versus Time of Sale** Following is information about log

L05 production at Mile High Lumber Mill, with joint costs of $600,000:

	Production	Sales	Inventory
Lumber (board feet)	300,000	270,000	30,000
Scraps (per log)	1,000 logs	900 logs	100 logs

The lumber can be sold for $3/ bd ft. The scraps per log can be sold for $10/ log.

REQUIRED **A.** Create an income statement, using the by-product value recognized at the time of sale method.

B. Create an income statement, using the by-product value recognized at the time of production method.

9.30 Physical Output, NRV, and Constant Gross Margin NRV Methods, Further Processing Decision The Paint Palette

LO2, LO4 Company produces two products, premium paint and regular paint, through a joint process. Joint costs amount to $10,000 per batch of output. Each batch totals 4,000 litres: 30% premium and 70% regular. Both products are processed further.

Separable processing costs:	
Premium	$1.00/L
Regular	$0.25/L
Selling price:	
Premium	$20.00/4 L can
Regular	$10.00/4 L can

REQUIRED
A. Allocate the joint costs according to the physical output method.
B. Allocate the joint costs according to the net realizable value method.
C. Allocate the joint costs according to the constant gross margin NRV method.
D. The company has discovered an additional process by which the regular paint can be made into paint that dries extremely quickly. The new selling price would be $22/4 L can. Additional processing would increase separable costs by $11 (in addition to the $1 separable cost required to yield a 4 L can of regular paint). Assuming no other changes in cost, determine whether the company should begin producing quick-drying paint. Create a schedule that shows how you made the decision.

9.31 Calculate Missing Information for Sales Value at Split-off Point Method The Chile Salsa Company manufactures

LO2 three different types of salsa—mild, medium, and spicy hot—from a joint process. The following information is available:

	Mild	Medium	Spicy Hot	Total
Units produced	24,000	?	?	48,000
Joint costs	$24,000	?	?	$ 60,000
Sales value at split-off point	?	?	$25,000	$100,000
Additional cost if processed further	$ 9,000	$ 7,000	$ 5,000	$ 21,000
Sales value if processed further	$55,000	$45,000	$30,000	$130,000

REQUIRED Assuming that joint product costs are allocated using the sales value at split-off point method, what was the sales value at the split-off for mild and medium salsa?

9.32 Further Processing Profit and Decision Conrad Miller owns a small sheet metal business. He produces three

LO2, LO4 different types of sheet metal. Their sizes are similar, but they have different degrees of flexibility. Costs are allocated based on the sales value at split-off point method. Additional information for March production follows:

	Stiff	Flexible	Very Flexible	Total
Units produced	100,000	80,000	20,000	200,000
Joint costs	?	?	?	$ 900,000
Sales value at split-off point	$840,000	$540,000	$120,000	$1,500,000
Additional cost if processed further	$ 88,000	$ 30,000	$ 12,000	$ 130,000
Sales value if processed further	$948,000	$565,000	$135,000	$1,648,000

REQUIRED
A. Assuming that the 20,000 units of Very Flexible were processed further and sold, what would be the gross margin on this sale?
B. Would you recommend that Miller process the Very Flexible sheet metal further? Show your calculations.

9.33 Accounting for Main Products and By-products Georgette Rheingold owns and operates a fruit smoothie

L05 manufacturing operation, Nutri-smoothie. She processes fruit and adds it to yogurt to produce fruit smoothies, the main product. She sells the rinds and other waste to a recycling organization that turns the waste into compost. Neither product requires processing after the split-off point. Information for last month's operations follows:

Joint costs of smoothie production	$12,000
Smoothie production (in ½ L bottles)	20,000
Price per bottle	$2
Sales last month (bottles)	18,000
Compost production	10,000 kg
Compost sales	8,000 kg
Compost revenue	$2,000

REQUIRED **A.** What is Nutri-smoothie's gross margin for last month if the by-product value is recognized at the time of production?

B. What is Nutri-smoothie's gross margin for last month if the by-product value is recognized at the time of sale?

C. Calculate the inventory value for both smoothies and compost on the balance sheet under the methods used in Parts A and B.

PROBLEMS

9.34 Identifying Joint Costs, Choice of Allocation Method Roses to Go is a flower farm that specializes in fragrant roses

L01, L03 for florist shops.

REQUIRED **A.** List five joint costs that Roses to Go is likely to incur in raising roses.

B. The roses are sold by the dozen, with no difference in price for any of the bouquets. Which joint cost allocation method would be most appropriate? Explain your choice.

C. Now assume that Roses to Go raises two different types of roses, fragrant roses and regular roses. The growing requirements for the two types of roses do not differ. However, fragrant roses sell for twice as much as regular roses. Which joint cost allocation method would be most appropriate? Explain your choice.

9.35 Identifying Joint Costs, Choice of Allocation Method Captain Fred's is a fish hatchery that raises two different types

L01, L03 of trout for release into local lakes as part of a restocking program. These small 5 to 10 cm juvenile fish are known as fingerlings.

REQUIRED **A.** List five joint costs that Captain Fred's is likely to incur in raising fingerlings.

B. The fingerlings are sold for $100 per 100 fish. Which joint cost allocation method would be most appropriate? Explain your choice.

C. Now assume that Captain Fred's begins to raise catfish in addition to the trout. The hatchery requirements for the two types of fish do not differ. However, catfish are less desirable and mist be grown to a larger size (10 to 20 cm) before they are sold for $50 per 100 fish. Which joint cost allocation method would be most appropriate? Explain your choice.

9.36 NRV, Processing Further Decision Deepa Company manufactures two products using a joint process. The cost of

L02, L04 materials used during a typical period is $55,000, while labour and overhead are $65,000. This level of operations results in 10,000 kilograms of product 1 and 30,000 kilograms of product 2. Product 1 can be sold "as is" for $4/kg. Product 2 requires further processing costs of $2/kg and is eventually sold for $3/kg.

REQUIRED **A.** Determine gross margin by product line if Deepa sells 7,000 kg of product 1 and 26,000 kg of product 2 in a particular period. Deepa uses the NRV method to allocate joint costs.

B. Assume the firm does not sell product 1 "as is" but instead incurs separate processing costs of $20,000 per batch of 10,000 kg to finish the product. The finished products sell for $5/kg. Assume that Deepa sold 10,000 kg of product 1 and 30,000 kg of product 2. What is the gross margin by product line for the period using the NRV method?

C. Assume that Deepa could sell the same number of kilograms of product 1 "as is." Should the company finish the product or sell it "as is"? Why?

9.37 NRV, Processing Further Decision Feed 'N Grow manufactures three types of plant food using a joint process. The

cost of materials used during a typical period is $100,000, while labour and overhead are $150,000. This level of operations results in 35,000 kilograms of PF1, 10,000 kilograms of PF2, and 5,000 kilograms of PF3. PF1 can be sold "as is" for $8/kg. PF2 can be sold "as is" for $3/kg. or processed further at a cost of $1.50/kg. and then sold for $4.5/kg (identify this end product as PF4). PF3 requires further processing costs of $1/kg and is eventually sold for $2.50/kg.

REQUIRED **A.** Determine gross margin by product line if Feed 'N Grow sells 30,000 kg of PF1, 7,000 kg. of PF2, and 5,000 kg of PF3 in a particular period. Feed 'N Grow uses the NRV method to allocate joint costs.
B. Assume the firm does not sell PF2 "as is" but instead incurs separate processing costs of $15,000 per batch of 10,000 kg to finish the product. The finished products sell for $4.5/kg. Assume that Feed 'N Grow sold 30,000 kg of PF1, 5,000 kg. of PF 4, and 5,000 kg. of PF3. What is the gross margin by product line for the period using the NRV method? Explain to management why processing PF2 further to PF4 caused the profitability of PF1 and PF3 to decline.
C. Assume that Feed 'N Grow could sell the same number of kilograms of PF2 or PF4. Should the company process PF2 further into PF4 or sell it "as is"? Why?

9.38 Accounting for Main Products and By-Products A chemical process product produces two main products (Delta
LO5, LO7 and Echo) and one by-product (Golf) from a joint product (Beta). None of the products require processing after the split-off point. Information for last month's operations follows:

Joint costs of production	$15,000
Delta production (grams)	15,000
Price per 10 gram package	$3.00
Sales last month (grams)	13,500
Echo production (litres)	10,000
Price per 4 L bottle	$5.50
Sales last month (4 L bottles)	2,250
Golf production (grams)	1,500
Sales last month (grams)	1,250
Golf revenue	$125

REQUIRED **A.** What is the gross margin for last month if the by-product value is recognized at the time of production?
B. What is the gross margin for last month if the by-product value is recognized at the time of sale?
C. Calculate the inventory value for Delta, Echo, and Golf on the balance sheet under the methods used in Parts A and B.
D. Research and Development has suggested that Delta can be processed further into high-quality Indigo. The additional processing will cost $1.50 per 10 grams and there will be a 10% loss in the processing (i.e., 100 grams of Delta will yield 90 grams of Indigo). Indigo sells for $6.00 per 10 gram package. Should Delta be processed further?

9.39 Physical Output, NRV, and Constant Gross Margin NRV Methods, Further Processing Decision The We Care Pharmaceutical Company produces two pain relievers, premium and regular, through a joint process. Joint costs amount to $2,000 per batch of output. Each batch totals 5,000 grams: 75% premium and 25% regular. Both products are processed further.

Separable processing costs:	
Premium	$0.025 per gram
Regular	$0.010 per gram
Selling price:	
Premium	$10.00/10g
Regular	$6.00/10g

REQUIRED **A.** Allocate the joint costs according to the physical output method.

B. Allocate the joint costs according to the net realizable value method.

C. Allocate the joint costs according to the constant gross margin NRV method.

D. Explain the advantages and disadvantages of each method, including the reactions of the product line managers.

9.40 NRV The Ali Chemical Company processes a liquid mixture into two products: SLX-241 and QY-58. A batch of mixture yields 400 litres of SLX-241 and 800 kilograms of QY-58. The cost to obtain a batch of the liquid mixture is $5,000, and the cost to process it into the two products is $1,500. The SLX-241 must be filtered prior to sale at a cost of $2/L. The filtered product can then be sold for $8/L. Two hundred kilograms of an inert substance are mixed with the 800 kilograms of QY-58 to reduce its toxicity. The inert substance costs $0.50/kg. The diluted QY-58 is then sold for $6/kg.

LO2

REQUIRED **A.** What are the joint costs for the process yielding the two products?

B. What are the separable costs for each product?

C. What is the total cost per unit of each product if joint costs are allocated using the NRV method?

9.41 Separable and Joint Costs, NRV, Operating Income, By-product Doe Corporation grows, processes, cans, and sells three main pineapple products: sliced pineapple, crushed pineapple, and pineapple juice. The outside skin, which is removed in the cutting department and processed as animal feed, is treated as a by-product.

LO1, LO2, LO5, LO6

Doe's production process is as follows: Pineapples are first processed in the cutting department. The pineapples are washed, and the outside skin is cut away. Then the pineapples are cored and trimmed for slicing. The three main products (sliced, crushed, juice) and the by-product (animal feed) are recognizable after processing in the cutting department. Each product is then transferred to a separate department for final processing.

The trimmed pineapples are forwarded to the slicing department, where they are sliced and canned. Any juice generated during the slicing operation is packed in the cans with the slices. The pieces of pineapple trimmed from the fruit are diced and canned in the crushing department. Again, the juice generated during this operation is packed in the can with the crushed pineapple. The core and surplus pineapple generated from the cutting department are pulverized into a liquid in the juicing department. An evaporation loss equal to 8% of the weight of the good output produced in this department occurs as the juices are heated. The outside skin is chopped into animal feed in the feed department.

Doe Corporation uses the net realizable value method to assign costs of the joint process to its main products. The by-product is inventoried at its net realizable value. The NRV of the by-product reduces the joint costs of the main products.

A total of 270,000 kilograms of pineapple entered the cutting department in May. The schedule shows the costs incurred in each department, the proportion by weight transferred to the four final processing departments, and the selling price of each product.

May Processing Data and Costs

Department	Costs Incurred	Proportion of Product by Weight Transferred to Departments	Selling Price per Kilogram of Final Product
Cutting	$60,000	–	None
Slicing	4,700	35%	$0.60
Crushing	10,580	28	0.55
Juicing	3,250	27	0.30
Animal feed	700	10	0.10
Total	$79,230	100%	

REQUIRED **A.** How many kilograms of pineapple result as output for pineapple slices, crushed pineapple, pineapple juice, and animal feed?

B. What is the net realizable value of each of the main products?

C. What is the amount of the cost of the cutting department (joint costs) assigned to each of the main products and the by-product using Doe's allocation method?

D. What is the gross margin for each of the three main products?

E. How valuable is the gross margin information for evaluating the profitability of each main product?

F. If no market exists for the outside skin as animal feed and, instead, it must be disposed of at a cost of $800, what effect will this cost have on the costs allocated to the main products?

9.42 **Sales Value at Split-off, Physical Output, NRV Methods, Further Processing Decision** Apples Galore, a local orchard, grows and sells apples and apple pies. At harvest time, apples are sorted into saleable apples and defective apples. The defective apples are considered a by-product and are sold as animal feed to local hog farmers. The saleable apples are sorted by size. The larger, visually appealing apples are sold as eating apples. The smaller apples could be sold as seconds or processed further into apple pies, which are then sold at farmers' markets. Apples Galore makes 4 pies from each bushel of apples. Joint costs for the apple orchard are $180,000. Additional information is as follows:

LO2, LO4, LO6

Allocation Base	Animal Feed	Eating	Seconds	Pies
Bushels of Apples	5,000	27,000	8,000	
Sales value per bushel at harvest	$2	$8	$5	
Additional processing costs				$10/pie
Net Realizable Value	$2 per bushel	$8 per bushel	$5 per bushel	$15 per pie

REQUIRED

A. Determine the net income for Apples Galore if all of the apples are sold at the split-off point.

B. Allocate the joint cost using the following methods:
   1. Sales value at split-off point
   2. Physical output
   3. Net realizable value

C. What qualitative factors must be considered when deciding whether to sell seconds or make apple pies?

D. Historical records indicate that demand for pies at the local farmers' markets totals 10,000 pies. Should Apples Galore sell seconds or make apple pies? (Hint: You do not have to choose one or the other.)

E. The local grocery stores are willing to sell Apples Galore pies for $15; however, they want a $2.50 commission per pie. Should Apples Galore sell pies through the grocery stores? What other factors must Apples Galore consider when making this decision?

9.43 **Cumulative Problem (Chapter 4): Optimal Product Mix, Joint Cost Allocation Using Three Methods** Aromasoaps is a bulk buyer of soap by-products. These by-products are combined with secret-recipe essences to develop three products. Joint costs for processing the soaps are $90,000. Aromasoaps treats all of its products as main products. Data for the products follow:

LO2, LO4

		Further Processing Data		
Product	Number of Units Produced	Selling Price per Unit at Split-off	Separable Costs	Total Revenues After Processing
Relaxation	3,000	$2	$ 8,000	$15,000
Energizer	12,000	4	20,000	72,000
Harmony	33,000	2	10,000	73,000

REQUIRED

A. Which of the products should be further processed? Explain.

B. If Aromasoaps pursues the optimal product mix, what is the maximum profit that can be achieved?

C. If Aromasoaps allocates the joint costs based on the physical volume method (number of units), how much joint cost will be allocated to each product?

D. If Aromasoaps allocates the joint costs based on the NRV method, how much joint cost will be allocated to each product?

E. Now suppose that Aromasoaps incorrectly uses the final sales value of each product without considering separable costs to allocate joint costs. How much joint cost will be allocated to each product? Why is this method inappropriate?

F. Suppose managers incorrectly use gross margin after allocations to make the decision about processing further. How would each of the allocations in Parts C, D, and E affect your answer to B? Explain.

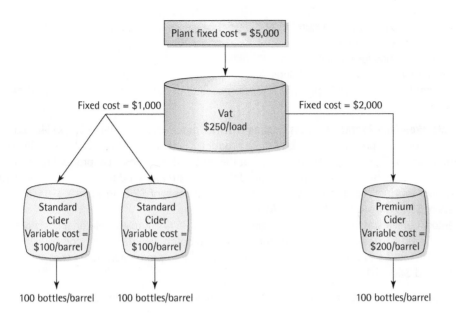

EXHIBIT 9.6
Production Costs for Jumping
Juice

9.44 Physical Output Method, Drop a Product, Special Order Jumping Juice Ltd. produces two grades of sparkling

apple juice (cider). A diagram of the production process appears in Exhibit 9.6. The process begins when the vat is loaded with apples. The incremental cost of raw materials and processing one load is $250. Each load produces one barrel of premium raw apple juice and two barrels of standard raw apple juice. The variable cost of carbonating and bottling the cider is $200 per barrel for premium cider and $100 per barrel for standard cider. Each barrel of raw juice produces 100 bottles of finished sparkling juice. The fixed costs for one month are $5,000 for the plant, $2,000 for handling and bottling premium, and $1,000 for handling and bottling standard. Premium cider sells for $5 per bottle and standard cider for $3 per bottle, both wholesale. In a normal month, 100 loads are processed and converted into 20,000 bottles of standard cider and 10,000 bottles of premium cider.

REQUIRED **A.** In a normal month, what is the total allocated cost (fixed plus variable) per bottle of premium cider if the costs of the manufacturing operation are allocated on the basis of physical output measured by volume?

B. In a normal month, what is the variable cost per bottle of premium cider if the joint variable costs of the juice company are allocated on the basis of physical output measured by volume?

C. Assuming that the $1,000 in fixed costs for standard handling and bottling could be avoided, what would be the impact on the profit of the company in a normal month if the company discontinued the standard brand and treated all raw cider as premium grade?

D. Explain to the CEO of the company why the variable cost per bottle of premium cider you calculated in Part B should or should not be used in pricing special orders for the premium cider.

9.45 Identify Joint Costs in Complex Process, Income Statement, By-product, Opportunity Cost Goodman and Sons manufactures a number of joint products. The process begins in department 1 with 100,000 kilograms, of which 30% goes to department 2, 60% goes to department 3, and the remainder is waste. From department 2, five-sixths goes to department 4 and one-sixth goes to department 5.

There is no market for intermediate products; only the end products of department 3 (a by-product), department 4 (a main product), and department 5 (a main product) are sold. Goodman uses the net realizable value method to allocate joint costs, and the by-product value is recognized at the time of sale. Cost and sales data are as follows:

Department	Costs	Sales	Product
1	$10,000		
2	10,000		
3	2,000	$10,000	C
4	25,000	40,000	A
5	5,000	6,000	B

REQUIRED **A.** In this problem, the joint costs result from a number of different processes. What are the joint costs for products A and B (the two main products)?

B. What are the joint cost allocations for products A and B?

C. Develop an income statement for Goodman and Sons.

D. What opportunity cost could be assigned to product B for purposes of determining whether it should be processed further?

9.46 Joint Product, By-products, Weighted-Average Process Costing S-T Inc. processes material in 1,000-litre batches. **LO2, LO5** Each batch results in 400 L of main product X, 500 L of main product Y, and 100 L of by-product Z. Material is added at the start of the process. The joint products emerge at the end of the process. By-product revenues are treated as a reduction of joint costs at the time of production. Joint costs are assigned to main products using the net realizable value method. Product X sells for $8/L and has separable costs of $2/L. Product Y sells for $11/L and has separable costs of $3/L. By-product Z sells for $1/L.

The beginning inventory consists of two batches averaging 30% and 80% complete. Material costs are $8,550, and conversion costs are $3,007. The ending inventory consists of one batch, which is 50% complete. During the week, 20 batches were completed and transferred out. Materials placed into production had a cost of $71,250, and conversion costs totalled $40,470.

REQUIRED Using the weighted-average process costing method, what is the unit cost to be assigned to each of the completed products X, Y, and Z?

MINI-CASES

9.47 Profit at Split-off Point and After Further Processing, Manager Incentives and Decisions The Champion Chip **LO2, LO3,** Company produces three grades of computer chips—deluxe, superior, and good—through a joint process. **LO6, LO7** Although the chips are manufactured in plants in several international locations, each grade is considered a separate product line, and each product line manager earns a bonus based on the reported profit of his or her line. To calculate income on which the bonuses are based, Champion allocates joint costs according to percentage of revenue. If all of the products are sold at the split-off point, this method would be the sales value at split-off point method. If products are processed further, each product's percentage of total revenues (without subtracting separable costs) is used as the allocation base.

The management office for the deluxe line is located outside London, UK. The management office for the superior line is located in Hong Kong. The management office for the good line is located in Calgary. Assume that the exchange rates are as follows.

	Canadian Dollars
British pounds (£)	$2.00
Hong Kong dollars (HK$)	$0.125

A batch of chips costing $1,000 yields chips with the following market values at the split-off point:

	Deluxe	Superior	Good
Sales value	£400	HK$3,200	CAD$200

Alternatively, each manager could process the chips further, in which case the new sales values and further processing costs would be as follows:

	Deluxe	Superior	Good
Sales value	£550	HK$4,800	CAD$800
Separable costs	£200	HK$800	CAD$500

REQUIRED **A.** Determine product line and company-wide pretax income in Canadian dollars if each product is sold at the split-off point. (Use the sales value at split-off point method to allocate joint costs.)

B. Each product line manager decides whether to process chips further. In making that decision, each manager assumes that the other two managers will sell their products at the split-off point. Analyze each manager's decision choices and predict their decisions (translate all dollars to Canadian dollars first). Allocate the joint costs, using each division's percentage of total revenues. Show your calculations.

C. If optimal decisions were made for the entire firm (not just for each product line), what decision should each manager make about processing chips further?

D. Develop income statements by product line and for the entire organization, assuming that managers make the decisions you predicted in Part B. Now develop income statements, assuming that managers make the best decisions for the overall organization from Part C.

E. Recast the income statements, using the NRV method to determine the decisions managers would make.

F. Explain why the individual managers might make decisions that are not optimal for the company.

G. Recommend a bonus scheme that could reduce the problem of suboptimal decision making.

9.48 **NRV Method, Division Manager Incentives, Qualitative Factors** Hudziak Industries has two separate profit centres: Chemicals and Cosmetics. The firm acquires its major ingredient for both divisions jointly. Currently, this material is purchased in 1,000-kg lots for $2,000. The material is passed through an exclusive separator process. After separation, Chemicals receives 300 L of chemical J-52A, and Cosmetics receives 200 kg of quitoban. The Chemicals division must process chemical J-52A further before it can be sold. Additional processing costs $150 per lot, and the chemical is then sold for $5/L. The Cosmetics division bottles and packages quitoban as an antiperspirant at a cost of $250 per lot. The antiperspirant is sold for $7/kg.

LO2, LO3, LO7

REQUIRED **INFORMATION ANALYSIS**

The following questions will help you analyze the information for this problem. Do not turn in your answers to these questions unless your professor asks you to do so.

A. Determine the income per lot that each division would report if joint costs were allocated on a net realizable value basis.

B. Hudziak has the opportunity to buy higher-quality lots of raw materials for $3,000. Some questions have been raised about the health effects of certain ingredients in antiperspirants, and the higher-quality raw material does not contain any of these ingredients. If Hudziak buys the new material, Chemical's processing costs will increase to $400 per lot, but the selling price of its product will remain the same. Cosmetics' selling price will increase to $15/kg, and its separable costs will remain the same. Managers provide input to the decision-making process for such decisions, but the president of the firm makes the final decision.

   1. If you were the manager of Chemicals, would you want the firm to buy the higher-quality material? Show your calculations, and explain your position.

   2. If you were the manager of Cosmetics, would you want the firm to buy the higher-quality material? Show your calculations, and explain your position.

   3. Describe the pros and cons to the company as a whole from purchasing the higher-quality material.

C. Explain why top management faces uncertainties about how to handle situations such as the purchase described in Part B.

D. What methods can be used to encourage managers who have conflicting interests to take actions that are in the best interests of the company as a whole?

E. What are the advantages and disadvantages of the methods you identified in Part D?

REQUIRED **WRITTEN ASSIGNMENT**

Suppose you are the cost accountant for Hudziak Industries. Turn in your answers to the following.

F. Write a memo to the president, recommending a decision for the purchase described in Part B. Attach to the memo a schedule showing your computations. As appropriate, refer to the schedule in the memo.

G. Include in your memo for Part F your recommendations for avoiding potential conflicts for similar types of future decisions in a way that is fair to both managers.

9.49 **Use of Joint Cost Information; Strategic** In this chapter, we discussed the fact that managers sometimes use joint

LO7   cost accounting information inappropriately in making decisions.

REQUIRED   In a memo to your professor:

Explain what is meant by the above statement.

A. Give an example of how joint cost information could inappropriately affect decision making. Support your answers with references to actual products or businesses.

B. Give an example of how joint cost information could improve decision making. Support your answers with references to actual products or businesses.

C. Develop a strategy, and describe how it could be implemented, to prevent the misuse of cost accounting information, and explain how cost accounting information should be used to support strategic objectives.

9.50 **Integrating Across the Curriculum—Economics and Governmental Regulation:** *Beef by-products in animal feed,*

LO1   *by-product economics, regulator responsibilities* May 2003 was the beginning of a crisis for the Canadian beef industry. Alberta officials confirmed that a sick cow sent to slaughter in January was infected with bovine spongiform encephalopathy (BSE), commonly known as mad cow disease. The cow had been considered substandard and had been removed from processing as food for humans or other animals. However, this did not prevent the resulting public scare as the United States, Japan, South Korea, and Australia temporarily banned imports of Canadian beef and live cattle. The crisis escalated when in early 2004 it was discovered that an infected dairy cow in Washington State came from a Canadian herd 11 years prior to slaughter. Government regulators and consumer groups were alarmed because humans who eat contaminated beef may become ill with a fatal brain-wasting disease. The finding of mad cow disease caused prices paid to cattle ranchers to drop considerably. The ban cost the Canadian beef industry an estimated $11 million per day. Mad cow disease virtually destroyed the British beef industry during the 1990s, and industry groups wanted to avoid a similar fate in Canada.

The only known cause of mad cow disease was the ingestion of infected animal parts. For many years, cattle had routinely been fed by-products from the beef rendering industry. Before the 1990s, this practice was viewed as an economic and ecological success. In the rendering process, the remains were ground up and then cooked, which removed the water. The residue could be turned into fats, oils, or meat and bone meal. The rendering process provided beef by-product revenues, reduced the cost of protein in cattle feed, and avoided the need to dispose of the beef by-products because 99% of the slaughtered cattle was used. The concern about mad cow disease and changes in regulations related to beef by-products resulted in lost sales from Canadian beef by-products totalling approximately $84 million per year.

Following an outbreak of mad cow disease in Britain, scientists determined the manner in which the disease spread. With this new information, regulators throughout the world banned the use of beef by-products in cattle feed. However, these 1997 changes did not prohibit the use of beef by-products in feed for other types of animals, such as poultry, pigs, and pets. Canada also allowed the use of by-products from other types of livestock to be used in cattle feed.

Most European countries do not allow the parts of the cow that can pass on BSE (e.g., brain, spine) to be used in any animal feed. Some consumer activists called for a complete ban on the use of mammal by-products in animal feed. Others called for expanded testing of cattle, which presently could be done only on dead animals. Cattle industry groups argued that these measures were not economical because they would dramatically increase the cost of beef, since the unused parts would need to be disposed of, which would be costly, especially in light of possible BSE contamination concerns.

Sources: CBC News Online, "Indepth: Mad Cow—Mad Cow in Canada: The Science and the Story" August 24, 2006; CBC News Online, "Indepth: Mad Cow—Canada, the United States and Japan: What's the Beef?" December 29, 2003; D. Le Roy, K. K. Klein, and T. Klvacek, "The Losses in the Beef Sector in Canada from BSE," *CATPRN Trade Policy Brief 2006-4,* October 2006, www.catrade.org.

REQUIRED   Conduct research on the Internet to find articles and other information that discusses the pros and cons of using beef by-products in animal feed. Answer the following questions:

A. What is likely to happen to Canadian beef by-products if they are not sold for use in animal feed?

B. Suppose the Canadian government bans the use of all types of animal by-products in livestock feed.

   1. How would the ban most likely affect the cost of main products in the cattle industry? Explain.

   2. How would the ban most likely affect the cost of main products in other livestock industries, such as pigs and chicken? Explain.

C. Besides the effects in Part B, describe the likely economic effects on the Canadian cattle industry if the use of beef by-products is banned for all types of animal feed.

D. What responsibilities do Canadian regulators have to various stakeholders in this issue? Consider the following types of stakeholders:
- Canadian cattle industry
- Other Canadian livestock industries, such as pigs and chicken
- Other Canadian food manufacturers
- Consumers of Canadian beef (both national and international)

E. Industry representatives argue that consumers of Canadian beef face no serious risk from mad cow disease. How valid is this argument?

F. In your opinion, should Canada ban the use of all types of animal by-products in livestock feed? What values did you use to reach your conclusion?

Static and Flexible Budgets

After studying this chapter, you should be able to do the following:

LO1   Discuss the relationships among budgets, long-term strategies, and short-term operating plans

LO2   Describe a master budget and explain how it is prepared; explain how operating budgets are prepared

LO3   Explain how a cash budget is developed

LO4   Discuss the differences between static and flexible budgets

LO5   Explain budget variances and how they are calculated

LO6   Discuss how budgets are used to monitor and motivate performance

LO7   Describe other approaches to budgeting

in brief An organization's long-term strategies are communicated and advanced through short-term and long-term budgets. In addition, budgets provide a mechanism for monitoring an organization's progress toward its goals. Comparisons of actual to budgeted revenues and costs help managers evaluate performance, leading to improved operations and more accurate planning. Some organizations provide employee incentives for meeting or exceeding budget-based benchmarks. Accordingly, budgets are used in planning, monitoring, and motivating performance. ■

Going with the budgeting flow

Highmountainphotography/Getty Images

Like many municipalities, the **City of Welland**, Ontario, funds its water and sewer infrastructure entirely through user rates. In other words, homes and businesses are billed for the amount of water they use, and those revenues cover the cost of providing the water and wastewater services. No property tax dollars are used to fund these services. That means municipalities such as Welland need to carefully budget water and wastewater revenues so that they cover expenses.

Welland ran into budgeting trouble starting in 2008, when the amount it was collecting from water and wastewater users fell short of costs. As of 2013, Welland had an accumulated water and wastewater deficit of $2.4 million. While its staff was studying how much to raise water rates to cover costs in future years, the city froze its rates in its 2013 budget. That year's budget included a capital expense of approximately $5 million to replace some of the 80-year-old watermains, made of cast iron that caused water to be discoloured, and another $2 million to replace sanitary sewers (those that carry sewage).

Two years later, city engineers estimated that future infrastructure costs would be a total of $28 million to replace all the necessary watermains and $37 million to replace all the necessary sewer lines. "We're not replacing old water and sewer pipes fast enough, because we simply can't afford to do it," said Welland Mayor Frank Campion. The city was considering transferring money from its 2015 capital budget to help cover part of the pipe replacement costs.

When setting its water budget, Welland needs to estimate water use for the coming year. Its forecasts include the fact that many residents and businesses have been stepping up efforts to conserve water. For example, lawn-watering use has declined The city used nearly 2.5 million cubic metres of water in the summer of 2001, but only about 1.6 million cubic metres in the summer of 2012, despite it being hot and dry. The city is expecting water use to continue to decline, which would further reduce revenues from water users.

A municipality has fixed and variable costs involved in providing water services, for which it needs to budget. The watermains and sewers, along with debt charges to finance this infrastructure, are examples of fixed costs, while the cost of treating both the water and wastewater are variable costs that change with consumption. Welland passes most of these fixed and variable costs on to users in their water bills. "Each customer account is charged a fixed rate for water and for wastewater. In addition, the customer is billed volumetric rates for water and wastewater based on the amount of water used," the city said in a memo to its council seeking approval for the 2013 water rates. City staff recommended that the fixed rates be raised gradually over five to 10 years to help pay for watermain and sewer replacement.

SOURCES: A. Benner, "Welland's Leaking Pipes Will Cost Millions," *The Welland Tribune*, March 14, 2015; S. Henschel, "Welland Water Bills on the Rise in 2015," *Niagara this Week*, March 12, 2015; "Report from Financial Management Services, Accounting: 2013 Water and Wastewater Budget and Associated Rates," City of Welland, March 8, 2013.

Budgeting

LO1 Discuss the relationships among budgets, long-term strategies, and short-term operating plans

With increased environmental awareness and an aging infrastructure, the City of Welland Water Department is facing new challenges in budget preparation. Freezes on rate increases have city personnel looking for other ways to raise the capital necessary to upgrade water infrastructure systems. As you will learn in this chapter, struggles like these are reflected in budgets, documents that communicate decisions to stakeholders, and are used to monitor operating performance and motivate employees to work toward the strategic goals envisioned by managers.

University students routinely anticipate both school-related expenses, such as tuition and books, and living expenses, such as rent and food. Before each term begins, they develop financial plans that consider both expenses and incoming funds, such as scholarships, bursaries, loans, and wages. At the end of each month or term, students might compare their actual expenditures to those they had planned. They use these comparisons to adjust their plans for future spending or financing. For example, if expenses are outpacing revenues, students have several choices. They can lower their living expenses, transfer to a less expensive university, switch from full-time to part-time status, or take fewer courses. Or they might increase funds by applying for more scholarships or loans or by increasing their work hours.

Every organization faces budgetary problems similar to the ones that students face. For the upcoming fiscal period, plans must be developed to anticipate revenues, expenses, and cash flows. These plans help the organization coordinate the activities needed to carry out the plan. At the end of the period, actual results are compared to the plans to identify gaps, or variances, from the plan. The formalized financial plan for operations of an organization for a specified future period is called a budget. A budget is an organization's financial roadmap; it reflects management's forecast of the financial effects of an organization's plans for one or more future time periods.

As shown in Exhibit 10.1, organizations use budgets as part of their strategic management process. Budgets for capital expenditures and long-term financing help managers implement organizational strategies. Budgets for revenues, costs, and cash flows help managers plan for and carry out short-term operating plans. In preparing budgets, managers forecast a number of events, such as the volume of goods or services they will sell. Using these estimates, they develop plans to determine the resources an organization needs, including employees, raw materials and supplies, cash, and anything else necessary to the future operations. To monitor organizational performance and to motivate employees, managers compare actual results to budgets and use variance information to improve operations.

▶EXHIBIT 10.1

Budgeting and the Strategic Management Process

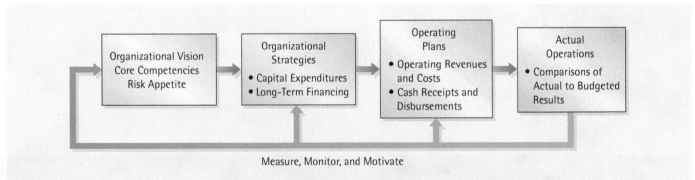

> **EXHIBIT 10.2**
Budgets and Levers of Control

Belief Systems

- Communicate organizational strategies and goals for the entire organization as well as for each segment, division, or department
- Motivate managers to plan in advance and to coordinate operating activities

Boundary Systems

- Authorize employees to engage in only planned business activities and to spend within budget limits
- Ensure sufficient cash to maintain financial viability

Interactive Control Systems

- Engage in organizational learning by investigating the strategic opportunities and threats revealed by differences between planned and actual performance
- Re-evaluate and revise strategies and operating plans as conditions change

Diagnostic Control Systems

- Motivate managers to provide appropriate estimates, meet expectations, and use resources efficiently
- Monitor expected versus actual performance to maintain control over preset goals
- Assign responsibility and reward employees for achieving budget targets

Budgets and Levers of Control

When budgets are used to measure, monitor, and motivate performance, they become part of the organization's control system. As shown in Exhibit 10.2, budgets provide valuable information for a number of different control points. Budgets enhance belief systems by communicating organizational strategies and goals. Budgets also encourage managers throughout the organization to clarify their plans and to coordinate activities, such as sales and production. In addition, budgets provide a mechanism for defining the responsibilities and financial decision-making authority, or **decision rights**, of individual managers. For example, separate budgets are often developed for each department within an organization. The manager of each department is then given authority to use the organization's resources in accordance with the budget (a boundary system) and is also responsible for meeting budgeted goals (a diagnostic control system). Managers may use comparisons of budgeted to actual results to identify changes in the business environment that might require revisions to strategies or operating plans (an interactive control system).

Budget Cycles

A **budget cycle** is a series of steps that organizations follow to develop and use budgets, as summarized in Exhibit 10.3. Managers typically begin the process by revisiting and possibly revising the organizational vision and core competencies. The opening case in this chapter describes this part of the process for the City of Welland Water Division as the city faces declining revenues from home owners. The next part of the budget cycle reconsiders long-term strategies in light of the aging infrastructure. After long-term strategies are reviewed and revised, the current period's operating plans are developed. For the City of Welland, this plan needed to include a plan to replace the infrastructure.

The rest of this chapter addresses the other steps in the budget cycle. You'll first learn to translate operating plans into a master budget and then learn how managers monitor actual results, investigate differences between actual and budget, and evaluate and reward performance.

> **EXHIBIT 10.3**
Budget Cycle

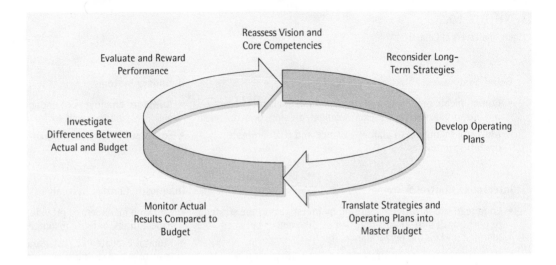

Master Budgets

A **master budget** is a comprehensive plan for an upcoming financial period, usually a year.

As shown in Exhibit 10.4, the master budget for a manufacturing organization begins with organizational strategies and operating plans, which lead to an **operating budget**— management's plan for revenues, production, and operating costs. The master budget also includes a **financial budget**—management's plan for capital expenditures, long-term financing, cash flows, and short-term financing. Master budgets are often summarized in a set of **budgeted financial statements**, which are forecasts of the future income statement, balance sheet, and cash flows.

Developing a Master Budget

The master budget is developed using a set of **budget assumptions**, which are plans and predictions about next period's operating activities. Budget assumptions often begin with a sales forecast and pricing plans, leading to the revenue budget. Next, the volume of production is forecast using beginning inventory levels, sales forecasts, and desired ending inventory levels. The production budget leads to budgets for direct materials, direct labour, and manufacturing overhead. These budgets are used to create budgets for ending inventory and cost of goods sold. The operating budget also includes budgets for costs of nonproduction departments such as sales, human resources, research and development, and general administration. Expected operating cash receipts and disbursements are combined with planned capital expenditures and long-term financing to develop a short-term financing budget. Finally, the components of all the preceding budgets are combined to create budgeted financial statements. Master budgets are often broken down into monthly or quarterly time periods to allow managers to monitor cash flows and operating results throughout the year. Some businesses, such as retail stores, may prepare budgets for weekly time periods.

Although the master budget is usually developed in the sequence shown in Exhibit 10.4, some organizations develop the production and support department budgets simultaneously with the revenue budget. Also, some parts of the production and support department budgets might be developed independently of the revenue budget. For example, the City of Welland's water budget is highly dependent upon the revenues received from home owners' water bills. However, the City managers were trying to find a way to develop a long-term budget to replace the infrastructure that was not tied to the short-term water bill revenues.

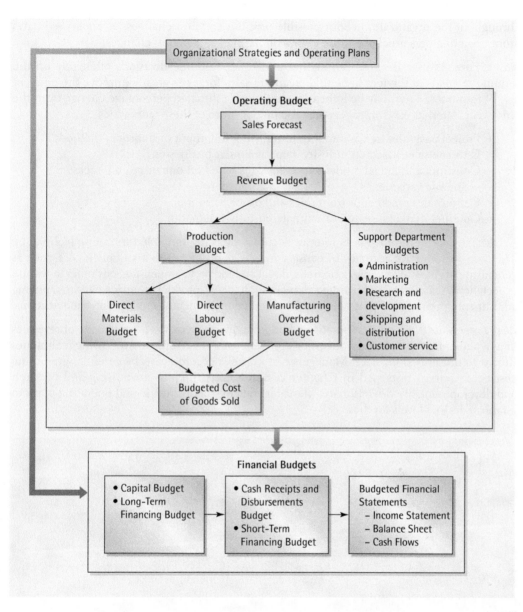

▶ EXHIBIT 10.4
Developing a Manufacturer's
Master Budget

The process of developing a master budget becomes increasingly complex in larger organizations or those that operate internationally. Communication can be more time-consuming when international business segments participate in the budgeting process. Cultural and legal differences influence both internal and external operations and need to be considered. The economies of different countries rarely move in tandem, and forecasting sales can be difficult. In addition, currency translations and differences in inflation and deflation rates greatly increase uncertainty in the planning and budgeting process.

Forecasting

Accountants assist managers in the process of developing budget assumptions. They may analyze past revenue and cost trends and behaviour, gather information from personnel

▶ CHAPTER REFERENCE
See Chapter 13 for details about capital budgeting.

▶ INTERNATIONAL
Budget factors vary internationally. For example, employees in Germany receive a legal minimum vacation of 20 working days per year, while vacation in most of Canada is at least 10 working days a year in the first six consecutive years of service for the same employer, with specified increases for additional years of service.[1]

¹ Invest in Germany, *Terms of Employment*, http://www.gtai.de/GTAI/Navigation/EN/Invest/Investment-guide/Employees-and-social-security/terms-of-employment.html; and Department of Justice, *Canada Labour Code* (R.S., 1985, c. L-2), Part III: Standard Hours, Wages, Vacations, and Holidays, Division IV Annual Vacations, http://laws-lois.justice.gc.ca/eng/acts/L-2/page-80.html#h-73

throughout the organization about possible revenue and cost changes, or obtain estimates from operating personnel about the effects of planned production changes.

Sales Forecasting. Because production and other resource decisions often rely on the volume of goods or services to be sold, accurate sales forecasts greatly improve the efficient use of resources. Sales may be forecast assuming an estimated percentage change from the prior year. Alternatively, managers may use one or more of these techniques:

- ► Project past sales trends into the future using judgment or statistical methods.
- ► Estimate sales based on industry data for similar businesses.
- ► Construct a financial model to predict sales based on one or more forecasted economic variables.
- ► Gather sales predictions from sales and other personnel.
- ► Conduct market research to estimate customer demand.

Managers can improve sales forecast accuracy by using multiple forecasting techniques. They can also improve accuracy by considering the many factors that influence sales, such as general and industry economic conditions, direct and indirect competition, customer tastes and expectations, seasonality, and planned changes such as new product or service offerings, pricing adjustments, promotional efforts, distribution method revisions, and credit policy modifications.

Cost Forecasting. Managers sometimes budget individual costs as a percentage of revenues or as a percentage change from the prior year. They may also forecast costs using techniques similar to those used for sales. Managers can improve cost forecasts by carefully evaluating cost behaviour, as discussed in Chapter 2. Some costs, such as advertising and research and development, are discretionary. Managers rely on their strategic and operating plans to establish desired levels for these costs.

●●◉❯ RISK OF BIASED DECISIONS: RECENCY EFFECT

THE RECENCY EFFECT is a bias in which people rely too heavily on recent experiences or information. This bias may cause managers to discount longer-term evidence of change and make inappropriate assessments of current business conditions. When analyzing information about changes in the economic environment, the recency effect causes managers to weigh the most recently received information more heavily than information received earlier. The recency effect increases the risk of overly optimistic or pessimistic budgets. For example, a manager who has recently experienced a significant downturn in sales may plan for lower production levels and then suffer lost sales due to unavailable product or long lead times. Organizations can reduce the risk of poor decisions by seeking multiple sources of information and by varying the sequence in which information is considered and presented.

Cash Flow Forecasting. Accurate cash flow forecasts can be critical to financial viability, particularly for small organizations. For example, Glen Herriman, the owner of Herriman's Stationery Supplies, blamed his past financial troubles on a failure to manage finances. He stated in a radio interview, "I figured that the finance could sort itself out as long as I was making the sales and the profit was right."[2]

Cash flow forecasting includes not only identifying the expected sources and uses of cash but also estimating the timing of receipts and disbursements. To forecast cash flows, managers consider questions such as these: How quickly will customers pay their bills? How quickly must we pay our vendors, employees, other suppliers, and tax authorities? Are our business plans or other economic changes likely to alter the cash flow patterns? When do we plan to purchase new equipment, pay dividends, issue stock, or buy back stock? Should

---

[2] J. Carleton, transcript of radio interview with Glen Herriman and others, "Small to Medium Business: Money," Open Learning Australia and ABC Radio National (producers), February 5, 2006, available online at www.abc.net.au/radionational/programs/lifelonglearning/small-to-medium-business-money/3432054.

we arrange to borrow money, as needed, to cover short-term cash shortages? Should excess cash be invested?

In Mountain High Bikes, the accountant develops a master budget by creating individual budgets in the following order:

1. Revenue budget
2. Production budget
3. Direct materials budget
4. Direct labour budget
5. Manufacturing overhead budget
6. Inventory and cost of goods sold budget
7. Support department budgets
8. Financial budgets

mountain high bikes, part 1
DEVELOPING THE OPERATING BUDGETS

Sanjay Rajakrishnan is an accountant for Mountain High Bikes, a manufacturer of sturdy mountain bikes for intermediate-level bikers. The company's managers are forecasting an increase in sales because of the success of their current advertising campaign. They ask Sanjay to create a master budget for the upcoming year, given the forecasted sales increase.

To gather information needed for the budget, Sanjay first accesses relevant data about revenues, inventories, and production costs from last period's accounting records. Next, he obtains information from every department and meets with top management to identify changes in sales volumes and prices, production processes, manufacturing costs, and support department costs.

maxpro/Shutterstock

Developing the Revenue Budget

Sanjay prepares the revenue budget first, because he needs the volume of bike sales to develop the production and variable cost budgets. The managers forecasted that 100,000 bikes would be sold at a price of $800 each. Approximately, one-half of the sales occur in the fourth quarter due to the holiday season, one-quarter of the sales occur in the second quarter due to the onset of nicer weather, and the remainder of the sales are spread evenly throughout the other two quarters. Based on this information, Sanjay develops the following sales forecast and revenue budget for Mountain High Bikes:

REVENUE BUDGET

	Quarter 1	Quarter 2	Quarter 3	Quarter 4	Year in Total	Quarter 1, Year 2
Sales Forecast (units)	12,500	25,000	12,500	50,000	100,000	12,500
Selling Price	$ 800.00	$ 800.00	$ 800.00	$ 800.00	$ 800.00	
Sales Revenue	$10,000,000.00	$20,000,000.00	$10,000,000.00	$40,000,000.00	$80,000,000.00	

Developing the Production Budget

Sanjay next develops the production budget. According to prior accounting records, beginning finished goods inventory consists of 2,500 bikes at a cost per unit of $454.75, or $1,136,875 in total. Given the anticipated increase in sales volume and the expected sales trends, the managers want ending finished goods inventory in quarters 1 and 3 to be 5% of sales in the following quarter and ending finished goods inventory in quarters 2 and 4 to be 3% of sales in the following quarter. Sanjay calculates the number of bikes that will be manufactured for each quarter and the year in total.

continued...

PRODUCTION BUDGET

	Quarter 1	Quarter 2	Quarter 3	Quarter 4	Year in Total	Quarter 1, Year 2
Sales	12,500	25,000	12,500	50,000	100,000	12,500
Add: Desired Ending Inventory	1,250	375	2,500	375	375	1,250
Total bikes needed	13,750	25,375	15,000	50,375	100,375	13,750
Less: Beginning Inventory	2,500	1,250	375	2,500	2,500	375
Production	11,250	24,125	14,625	47,875	97,875	13,375

Developing the Direct Materials Budget

Now Sanjay can determine the amount of direct materials that must be purchased. The beginning materials inventory consists of the following:

Beginning direct material inventories:

Wheels and tires (2,000 @ $10)	$ 20,000
Components (1,000 @ $70)	70,000
Frames (1,000 @ $50)	50,000
Total	$140,000

The cost per unit of direct materials is expected to be as follows:
Direct materials (cost per unit):

Wheels and tires	$10
Components	70
Frame	50

The managers want ending material inventories to be as follows:

Wheels and tires – 3% of the following month's production needs
Components – 5% of the following month's production needs
Frames – 2% of the following month's production needs

Given these assumptions, Sanjay prepares the following direct materials budgets.

DIRECT MATERIALS BUDGET—WHEELS

	Quarter 1	Quarter 2	Quarter 3	Quarter 4	Year in Total	Quarter 1, Year 2
Production	11,250	24,125	14,625	47,875	97,875	13,375
Number of wheels	22,500	48,250	29,250	95,750	195,750	26,750
Add: Desired Ending Inventory	1,448	878	2,873	803	803	
Total wheels needed	23,948	49,128	32,123	96,553	196,553	
Less: Beginning Inventory	2,000	1,448	878	2,873	2,000	
Purchases—wheels	21,948	47,680	31,245	93,680	194,553	
Cost	$219,475.00	$476,800.00	$312,450.00	$936,800.00	$1,945,525.00	

DIRECT MATERIALS BUDGET—COMPONENTS

	Quarter 1	Quarter 2	Quarter 3	Quarter 4	Year in Total	Quarter 1, Year 2
Production	11,250	24,125	14,625	47,875	97,875	13,375
Add: Desired Ending Inventory	1,206	731	2,394	669	669	-
Total components needed	12,456	24,856	17,019	48,544	98,544	
Less: Beginning Inventory	1,000	1,206	731	2,394	1,000	
Purchases—components	11,456	23,650	16,288	46,150	97,544	
Cost	$801,937.50	$1,655,500.00	$1,140,125.00	$3,230,500.00	$6,828,062.50	

DIRECT MATERIALS BUDGET—FRAMES

	Quarter 1	Quarter 2	Quarter 3	Quarter 4	Year in Total	Quarter 1, Year 2
Production	11,250	24,125	14,625	47,875	97,875	13,375
Add: Desired Ending Inventory	483	293	958	268	268	
Total frames needed	11,733	24,418	15,583	48,143	98,143	
Less: Beginning Inventory	1,000	483	293	958	1,000	
Purchases—frames	10,733	23,935	15,290	47,185	97,143	
Cost	$536,625.00	$1,196,750.00	$764,500.00	$2,359,250.00	$4,857,125.00	

Developing the Direct Labour Budget

The quantity and cost of direct labour per unit is expected to be as follows:

Direct Labour	Hours	Cost per Hour
Assembly	1.5	$25
Testing	0.15	15

Sanjay prepares the direct labour budget, which forecasts the number of labour hours and the total direct labour costs for producing bikes each quarter and for the year in total:

DIRECT LABOUR BUDGET

	Quarter 1	Quarter 2	Quarter 3	Quarter 4	Year in Total
Assembly Hours	16,875	36,188	21,938	71,813	146,813
Assembly Costs	$421,875.00	$904,687.50	$548,437.50	$1,795,312.50	$3,670,312.50
Testing Hours	1,687.50	3,618.75	2,193.75	7,181.25	14,681.25
Testing Costs	$ 25,312.50	$ 54,281.25	$ 32,906.25	$ 107,718.75	$ 220,218.75
Total Labour Hours	18,562.50	39,806.25	24,131.25	78,993.75	161,493.75
Total Labour Costs	$447,187.50	$958,968.75	$581,343.75	$1,903,031.25	$3,890,531.25

Developing the Manufacturing Overhead Budget

In addition to the direct costs of production, overhead costs need to be included in the budgeting process. Sanjay uses information that he collected from last year's operations and updates it with current prices. The cost per unit of variable manufacturing overhead is expected to be as follows:

Variable overhead (cost per unit):

Supplies	$20.00
Indirect labour	37.50
Maintenance	10.00
Miscellaneous	7.50
Total	$75.00

Sanjay expects $20,200,000 to be spent on fixed manufacturing overhead costs. He calculates the fixed overhead allocation rate by dividing budgeted fixed overhead costs by the budgeted volume of production:

$$\$20,200,000 \div 97,875 \text{ units} = \$206.39 \text{ per unit}$$

Sanjay prepares the manufacturing overhead budget by quarter and for the year in total:

MANUFACTURING OVERHEAD BUDGET

	Quarter 1	Quarter 2	Quarter 3	Quarter 4	Year in Total
VARIABLE OVERHEAD					
Supplies	$ 225,000.00	$ 482,500.00	$ 292,500.00	$ 957,500.00	$ 1,957,500.00
Indirect labour	$ 421,875.00	$ 904,687.50	$ 548,437.50	$1,795,312.50	$ 3,670,312.50
Maintenance	$ 112,500.00	$ 241,250.00	$ 146,250.00	$ 478,750.00	$ 978,750.00
Miscellaneous	$ 84,375.00	$ 180,937.50	$ 109,687.50	$ 359,062.50	$ 734,062.50
Total Variable Overhead	$ 843,750.00	$1,809,375.00	$1,096,875.00	$3,590,625.00	$ 7,340,625.00
FIXED OVERHEAD					
Amortization	$1,010,000.00	$1,010,000.00	$1,010,000.00	$1,010,000.00	$ 4,040,000.00
Property taxes		$ 505,000.00		$ 505,000.00	$ 1,010,000.00
Insurance	$ 707,000.00		$ 707,000.00		$ 1,414,000.00
Plant supervision	$1,262,500.00	$1,262,500.00	$1,262,500.00	$1,262,500.00	$ 5,050,000.00
Fringe benefits	$1,767,500.00	$1,767,500.00	$1,767,500.00	$1,767,500.00	$ 7,070,000.00
Miscellaneous	$ 404,000.00	$ 404,000.00	$ 404,000.00	$ 404,000.00	$ 1,616,000.00
Total Fixed Overhead	$5,151,000.00	$4,949,000.00	$5,151,000.00	$4,949,000.00	$20,200,000.00
Total Overhead	$5,994,750.00	$6,758,375.00	$6,247,875.00	$8,539,625.00	$27,540,625.00

continued...

Developing the Inventory and Cost of Goods Sold Budgets

To prepare the cost of goods sold budget, Sanjay needs forecasted costs for ending inventories. Using the fixed and variable production costs, he prepares the ending inventory budget, summarized as follows:

ENDING INVENTORY BUDGET

	Quarter 1	Quarter 2	Quarter 3	Quarter 4	Year in Total
Wheels	$ 14,475.00	$ 8,775.00	$ 28,725.00	$ 8,025.00	$ 8,025.00
Components	$ 84,437.50	$ 51,187.50	$ 167,562.50	$ 46,812.50	$ 46,812.50
Frames	$ 24,125.00	$ 14,625.00	$ 47,875.00	$ 13,375.00	$ 13,375.00
Bikes					
Materials	$175,000.00	$ 52,500.00	$ 350,000.00	$ 52,500.00	$ 52,500.00
Labour	$ 49,687.50	$ 14,906.25	$ 99,375.00	$ 14,906.25	$ 14,906.25
Variable Overhead	$ 93,750.00	$ 28,125.00	$ 187,500.00	$ 28,125.00	$ 28,125.00
Fixed Overhead	$257,982.12	$ 77,394.64	$ 515,964.24	$ 77,394.64	$ 77,394.64
Total Finished Goods Ending Inventory	$576,419.62	$172,925.89	$1,152,839.24	$172,925.89	$172,925.89

Using information from the preceding budgets, Sanjay prepares the cost of goods sold budget for the forecasted sale of 100,000 units:

COST OF GOODS SOLD BUDGET

	Quarter 1	Quarter 2	Quarter 3	Quarter 4	Year in Total
Beginning Finished Goods	$1,152,839.24	$ 576,419.62	$ 172,925.89	$ 1,152,839.24	$ 1,152,839.24
Add:					
Direct Materials Used	$1,575,000.00	$ 3,377,500.00	$2,047,500.00	$ 6,702,500.00	$13,702,500.00
Direct Labour	$ 447,187.50	$ 958,968.75	$ 581,343.75	$ 1,903,031.25	$ 3,890,531.25
Manufacturing Overhead	$3,165,589.08	$ 6,788,429.92	$4,115,265.80	$13,471,340.20	$27,540,625.00
Total Goods Available	$6,340,615.82	$11,701,318.29	$6,917,035.44	$23,229,710.69	$46,286,495.49
Less: Ending Finished Goods	$ 576,419.62	$ 172,925.89	$1,152,839.24	$ 172,925.89	$ 172,925.89
Cost of Goods Sold	$5,764,196.20	$11,528,392.40	$5,764,196.20	$23,056,784.80	$46,113,569.60

Developing the Support Department Budgets

Having completed the production cost budgets, Sanjay next estimates other operating costs—that is, the budgeted costs for all the support departments. In this illustration, the support costs are all fixed. In other situations, support costs could contain a mixture of fixed and variable costs. Support department information is gathered from each department manager. The support department budget is summarized as follows:

SUPPORT DEPARTMENT COSTS BUDGET

	Quarter 1	Quarter 2	Quarter 3	Quarter 4	Year in Total
Administration	$4,119,553.75	$4,119,553.75	$4,119,553.75	$4,119,553.75	$16,478,215.00
Marketing	$2,471,732.25	$2,471,732.25	$2,471,732.25	$2,471,732.25	$ 9,886,929.00
Distribution	$1,235,866.25	$1,235,866.25	$1,235,866.25	$1,235,866.25	$ 4,943,465.00
Customer Service	$ 411,955.25	$ 411,955.25	$ 411,955.25	$ 411,955.25	$ 1,647,821.00
Total Support Department Costs	$8,239,107.50	$8,239,107.50	$8,239,107.50	$8,239,107.50	$32,956,430.00

Budgeting in Nonmanufacturing Organizations

The individual budgets shown in Exhibit 10.4 are for a manufacturing organization. The specific types of budgets that comprise a master budget depend on the nature of an organization's goods or services and its accounting system. For example, some service organizations do not carry inventory; the direct costs of producing services are recognized as a period cost in the income statement. Thus, budgets for these organizations generally would not include inventory computations and might not include direct materials. Other service industries, such as retailers, would carry inventory. The categories chosen for individual budgets are based on the categories that managers use to plan and monitor operations.

In the not-for-profit sector, budgets are often a primary source of information about the operations of the organization. Although donors request financial statements, budgets provide much of the operating information that managers use. In governmental organizations, budgets must often be legally adopted, which means there are restrictions on spending authority.

BUSINESS PRACTICE

The province of Alberta provides the *Citizens Guide to the Alberta Legislature*. Part IV, "Getting the Business Done," includes the chapter "Putting Your Tax Dollars to Work," which discusses the provincial budgeting process. The entire budget and the highlights of the budget are available on the provincial government's website.[3]

Developing a Cash Budget

A cash budget reflects the effects of management's plans on cash and summarizes information that accountants gather about the expected amounts and timing of cash receipts and disbursements. Cash budgets may be prepared quarterly, monthly, weekly, or even daily to help management plan the organization's short-term borrowing or investing.

L03 Explain how a cash budget is developed

Operating Cash Receipts and Disbursements

Operating cash receipts are estimated from budgeted revenues, taking into account the nature of customer transactions. For example, if sales are made on account, then forecasts must be made for bad debts and for the timing of customer payments. Mountain High Bikes, Part 2, includes a simple timing difference for accounts receivables. Several problems at the end of this chapter feature more variation in the timing of receivables and discounts and the effects of bad debts on the cash budget.

Operating cash disbursements are estimated from the budgets for direct materials, direct labour, manufacturing overhead, and support departments. The timing of cash disbursements for these items depends on the payment terms with employees and vendors. For example, the organization might pay employees on the fifteenth and last day of each month. Payments to vendors might be made in the month after the purchase of goods or services. Some expenses, such as amortization, do not require a cash payment.

Other Planned Cash Flows

In addition to operating cash flows, organizations have many other types of cash flows, including the following:

- Purchasing or selling property, plant, and equipment
- Borrowing or repaying long-term debt
- Paying interest on debt[4]
- Issuing or redeeming capital stock
- Paying dividends to shareholders

[3] Legislative Assembly of Alberta, *Citizens Guide to the Alberta Legislature*, https://www.assembly.ab.ca/pub/gdbook/CitizensGuide.pdf and Alberta Government, *Provincial Budget*, www.finance.alberta.ca.

[4] Financial accounting standards require interest to be classified under operations on the statement of cash flows. However, interest expense arises from financing rather than operating decisions.

Although the purchase or sale of property, plant, and equipment is planned in the capital budget, the cash effects of borrowing and repaying are reflected in cash budgets. Similarly, cash flows related to long-term debt and capital stock are planned in the long-term financing budget, but the changes in cash flows need to be reflected in the cash budget.

Short-Term Borrowing or Investing

Managers typically use short-term loans or investments to balance the cash budget, taking into account the desired cash balance. Short-term loans may be prearranged as a line of credit with a financial institution so that the organization can borrow up to a specified amount as needed to cover cash shortages. Organizations often use excess cash to repay short-term debt, with any remainder placed in liquid investments.

The purpose of the cash budget is to ensure adequate levels of cash for day-to-day operations. If an organization lacks the necessary cash to fund its operations at any given moment, then it is insolvent. Successful new, fast-growing companies, especially franchise companies or companies growing by acquisition, sometimes fail because they have no liquid assets and cannot pay their employees. At the same time, companies such as Air Canada are able to continue operating, even when they are legally bankrupt and are incurring losses, because their assets are liquid; they are able to sell nonliquid assets for cash, or they are able to obtain the additional financing needed to stay in business while they restructure.[5]

To prepare a cash budget, three types of cash transactions are planned:

1. Cash receipts

2. Cash disbursements

3. Short-term borrowings or investments

Mountain High Bikes, Part 2, demonstrates the preparation of a cash budget.

example

maxpro/Shutterstock

mountain high bikes, part 2
DEVELOPING A CASH BUDGET

The managers tell Sanjay that they plan to invest $8 million in new equipment during the second quarter. This expenditure means that the company may not have enough cash and short-term investments to cover operating cash requirements. Sanjay decides to prepare a quarterly cash budget to estimate the company's borrowing needs.

Cash Receipts

To develop the cash receipts portion of the budget, Sanjay creates a quarterly schedule showing the timing of cash receipts expected from customers during the year. Because the company sells merchandise to its customers on account, he needs to forecast the time it will take customers to pay their accounts. He analyzes prior accounting records to estimate the sales and collection patterns. He then asks the marketing and credit managers whether they anticipate any changes in sales or collection patterns.

Sanjay knows that about half of the company's $80 million in sales occur in the fourth quarter because of holiday sales, about one quarter of the sales occur in the second quarter,

[5] See, for example, Simon, Bernard, "Air Canada Is Granted Bankruptcy Court Protection," NY Times online, April 2, 2003, http://www.nytimes.com/2003/04/02/business/air-canada-is-granted-bankruptcy-court-protection.html; "Air Canada granted bankruptcy protection," CBC News online, Dec. 4, 2003, http://www.cbc.ca/news/business/air-canada-granted-bankruptcy-protection-1.366723.

CASH COLLECTIONS

	Quarter 1	Quarter 2	Quarter 3	Quarter 4	Year in Total
Quarter 4, prior year	$10,000,000.00				$10,000,000.00
Quarter 1	$ 6,700,000.00				$ 6,700,000.00
					$ –
Quarter 1		$ 3,300,000.00			$ 3,300,000.00
Quarter 2		$13,400,000.00			$13,400,000.00
					$ –
Quarter 2			$ 6,600,000.00		$ 6,600,000.00
Quarter 3			$ 6,700,000.00		$ 6,700,000.00
					$ –
Quarter 3				$ 3,300,000.00	$ 3,300,000.00
Quarter 4				$26,800,000.00	$26,800,000.00
Total	$16,700,000.00	$16,700,000.00	$13,300,000.00	$30,100,000.00	$76,800,000.00

EXHIBIT 10.5

Cash Receipts from Customers at Mountain High Bikes

example

with the remainder spread evenly between the first and third quarters. Given this information, Sanjay forecasts sales revenues as follows:

First quarter (25% × $80,000,000 ÷ 2 quarters)	$10,000,000
Second quarter (25% × $80,000,000)	20,000,000
Third quarter (25% × $80,000,000 ÷ 2 quarters)	10,000,000
Fourth quarter (50% × $80,000,000)	40,000,000
Total budgeted revenue	$80,000,000

Customers usually pay in 30 days, and sales are uniform within each quarter, so Sanjay forecasts that two-thirds of each quarter's sales will be received in cash during the quarter and one-third in the next quarter. Therefore, first-quarter receipts will include collection of accounts receivable from the prior year. Fourth-quarter revenues from the prior year were expected to be $30 million, so first-quarter receipts should include $10 million (1/3 × $30,000,000). Mountain High sells to the same bicycle dealers every year and has eliminated those that do not pay on time. Therefore, bad debts are usually immaterial; Sanjay assumes that all accounts receivable will be collected. The managers do not anticipate any other receipts, such as new long-term borrowings, during the year. Sanjay's forecast of cash receipts is presented in Exhibit 10.5. The total estimated amount received from customers ($76,800,000) is less than the budgeted amount of revenues ($80,000,000) because accounts receivable at the end of the year ($40,000,000 – $26,800,000 = $13,200,000) are greater than accounts receivable at the beginning of the year ($10,000,000).

Cash Disbursements

Next, Sanjay analyzes prior accounting records and supplier contracts to identify the normal timing of cash payments to vendors, employees, and others. He also asks the production and other department managers whether they anticipate any changes in purchasing or payment patterns.

Sanjay notes from the production budget that production matches the pattern of sales. Based on the direct materials budgets, Sanjay summarizes purchases as follows:

SUMMARY OF PURCHASES

	Quarter 1	Quarter 2	Quarter 3	Quarter 4	Year in Total
Wheels	$ 219,475.00	$ 476,800.00	$ 312,450.00	$ 936,800.00	$ 1,945,525.00
Components	$ 801,937.50	$1,655,500.00	$1,140,125.00	$3,230,500.00	$ 6,828,062.50
Frames	$ 536,625.00	$1,196,750.00	$ 764,500.00	$2,359,250.00	$ 4,857,125.00
Total	$1,558,037.50	$3,329,050.00	$2,217,075.00	$6,526,550.00	$13,630,712.50

continued...

example

► EXHIBIT 10.6
Disbursements for Direct
Materials Purchases at
Mountain High Bikes

		CASH DISBURSEMENTS			
	Quarter 1	Quarter 2	Quarter 3	Quarter 4	Year in Total
Quarter 4, prior year	$2,000,000.00				$ 2,000,000.00
Quarter 1	$1,043,885.13				$ 1,043,885.13
Quarter 1		$ 514,152.38			$ 514,152.38
Quarter 2		$2,230,463.50			$ 2,230,463.50
Quarter 2			$1,098,586.50		$ 1,098,586.50
Quarter 3			$1,485,440.25		$ 1,485,440.25
Quarter 3				$ 731,634.75	$ 731,634.75
Quarter 4				$4,372,788.50	$ 4,372,788.50
Total	$3,043,885.13	$2,744,615.88	$2,584,026.75	$5,104,423.25	$13,476,951.00

Payments for direct materials are made a month after purchase. As a result, two-thirds of the purchases are paid during each quarter, and one-third are paid during the following quarter. Fourth-quarter purchases for the prior year were expected to be $6 million, so payments for these purchases of $2 million (1/3 × $6,000,000) are expected in the first quarter. Sanjay uses this information to prepare the quarterly schedule for direct material disbursements in Exhibit 10.6. The total amount paid ($13,476,951) is less than the budgeted amount of direct material purchases ($13,630,712.50) because accounts payable at the end of the year ($6,526,550 − $4,372,788.50 = $2,153,761.5) are greater than accounts payable at the beginning of the year ($2,000,000).

Sanjay forecasts that the remaining variable costs are incurred in the same pattern as production. He learns that property taxes are due in the second and fourth quarters, and insurance payments are due in the first and third quarters. He also knows that amortization will not be paid because it is a noncash expense, so he removes it from the list of expenses. Sanjay forecasts that the remaining fixed costs are incurred uniformly across the four quarters. He assumes that all costs other than direct material purchases are paid in the quarter in which they are incurred. In addition, he learns from management that the company will spend $8 million on new equipment during the second quarter. Given these forecasts and assumptions, Sanjay completes the cash disbursements section of the cash budget in Exhibit 10.7.

Short-Term Investments and Borrowings

Sanjay expects cash and short-term investments at the beginning of the period to total $9 million. The managers want to maintain a minimum cash balance of $200,000. Any cash deficiencies are financed with the company's line of credit and require quarterly interest payments at an annual rate of 6%. The company's policy is to budget zero earnings on short-term investments.

Sanjay uses this information to complete the short-term financing portion of the cash budget. He realizes that the company will need to liquidate its short-term investments during the second quarter. It will also have to borrow $205,997.25 in the second quarter and an additional $3,345,442,96 in the third quarter. These short-term borrowings, totalling $3,551,440.21, can then be repaid during the fourth quarter, when sales increase. Total interest costs on the line of credit are estimated to be $53,271.60. A summary of the short-term financing budget is shown in Exhibit 10.8.

Developing the Budgeted Income Statement

Finally, Sanjay combines the information from all the individual operating budgets to prepare the budgeted income statement on page 456. The company's managers do not anticipate any nonoperating income statement items, so no additional items must be included in the budgeted income statement except for income taxes at the expected rate of 30%.

CASH BUDGET

	Quarter 1	Quarter 2	Quarter 3	Quarter 4	Year in Total
Beginning Cash Balance	$ 9,000,000.00	$ 8,985,069.88	$ 200,000.00	$ 200,000.00	$ 9,000,000.00
Cash Collections	$16,700,000.00	$16,700,000.00	$13,300,000.00	$30,100,000.00	$76,800,000.00
Total Cash Available	$25,700,000.00	$25,685,069.88	$13,500,000.00	$30,300,000.00	$85,800,000.00
Cash Disbursements					
Direct Materials Purchases	$ 3,043,885.13	$ 2,744,615.88	$ 2,584,026.75	$ 5,104,423.25	$13,476,951.00
Direct Labour	$ 447,187.50	$ 958,968.75	$ 581,343.75	$ 1,903,031.25	$ 3,890,531.25
Variable Overhead					
Supplies	$ 225,000.00	$ 482,500.00	$ 292,500.00	$ 957,500.00	$ 1,957,500.00
Indirect labour	$ 421,875.00	$ 904,687.50	$ 548,437.50	$ 1,795,312.50	$ 3,670,312.50
Maintenance	$ 112,500.00	$ 241,250.00	$ 146,250.00	$ 478,750.00	$ 978,750.00
Miscellaneous	$ 84,375.00	$ 180,937.50	$ 109,687.50	$ 359,062.50	$ 734,062.50
Fixed Overhead					
Property taxes	$ –	$ 505,000.00	$ –	$ 505,000.00	$ 1,010,000.00
Insurance	$ 707,000.00	$ –	$ 707,000.00	$ –	$ 1,414,000.00
Plant supervisor	$ 1,262,500.00	$ 1,262,500.00	$ 1,262,500.00	$ 1,262,500.00	$ 5,050,000.00
Fringe benefits	$ 1,767,500.00	$ 1,767,500.00	$ 1,767,500.00	$ 1,767,500.00	$ 7,070,000.00
Miscellaneous	$ 404,000.00	$ 404,000.00	$ 404,000.00	$ 404,000.00	$ 1,616,000.00
Administration	$ 4,119,553.75	$ 4,119,553.75	$ 4,119,553.75	$ 4,119,553.75	$16,478,215.00
Marketing	$ 2,471,732.25	$ 2,471,732.25	$ 2,471,732.25	$ 2,471,732.25	$ 9,886,929.00
Distribution	$ 1,235,866.25	$ 1,235,866.25	$ 1,235,866.25	$ 1,235,866.25	$ 4,943,465.00
Customer Service	$ 411,955.25	$ 411,955.25	$ 411,955.25	$ 411,955.25	$ 1,647,821.00
Equipment	$ –	$ 8,000,000.00	$ –	$ –	$ 8,000,000.00
Total Cash Disbursements	$16,714,930.13	$25,691,067.13	$16,642,353.00	$22,776,187.00	$81,824,537.25
Excess receipts and (disbursements)	$8,985,069.88	($5,997.25)	($3,142,353.00)	$7,523,813.00	$3,975,462.75

> **EXHIBIT 10.7**
Summary of Cash Receipts and Disbursements for Mountain High Bikes

CASH BUDGET

	Quarter 1	Quarter 2	Quarter 3	Quarter 4	Year in Total
Excess receipts and (disbursements)	$8,985,069.88	($ 5,997.25)	($3,142,353.00)	$7,523,813.00	$3,975,462.75
Line of Credit					
Borrowing	$ –	$205,997.25	$3,345,442.96	$ –	$3,551,440.21
Interest on borrowing		$ –	$ 3,089.96	$ 50,181.64	$ 53,271.60
Repayment		$ –	$ –	$3,551,440.21	$3,551,440.21
Ending Cash Balance and Short-Term Borrowing	$8,985,069.88	$200,000.00	$ 200,000.00	$3,922,191.15	$3,922,191.15

> **EXHIBIT 10.8**
Short-Term Financing Budget for Mountain High Bikes

continued...

example

BUDGETED INCOME STATEMENT

	Quarter 1	Quarter 2	Quarter 3	Quarter 4	Year in Total
Sales Revenue	$10,000,000.00	$20,000,000.00	$10,000,000.00	$40,000,000.00	$80,000,000.00
Cost of Goods Sold	$ 5,764,196.20	$11,528,392.40	$ 5,764,196.20	$23,056,784.80	$46,113,569.60
Gross Margin	$ 4,235,803.80	$ 8,471,607.60	$ 4,235,803.80	$16,943,215.20	$33,886,430.40
Operating Costs					
Administration	$ 4,119,553.75	$ 4,119,553.75	$ 4,119,553.75	$ 4,119,553.75	$16,478,215.00
Marketing	$ 2,471,732.25	$ 2,471,732.25	$ 2,471,732.25	$ 2,471,732.25	$ 9,886,929.00
Distribution	$ 1,235,866.25	$ 1,235,866.25	$ 1,235,866.25	$ 1,235,866.25	$ 4,943,465.00
Customer Service	$ 411,955.25	$ 411,955.25	$ 411,955.25	$ 411,955.25	$ 1,647,821.00
Total Operating Costs	$ 8,239,107.50	$ 8,239,107.50	$ 8,239,107.50	$ 8,239,107.50	$32,956,430.00
Operating Income/ Loss	($ 4,003,303.70)	$ 232,500.10	($ 4,003,303.70)	$ 8,704,107.70	$ 930,000.40
Interest Expense					$ 53,271.60
Income Taxes					$ 263,018.64
Net Income					$ 613,710.15

Sanjay reviews the budgeted income statement information with the company's controller. The budgets are then presented at a meeting with the CEO and the various department heads. ■

10-1 self-study problem   Constructing a Master Budget

LO2

Summer Select Patio Furniture is a manufacturer of patio furniture. The patio table department produces table sets. Each table set consists of four chairs, a table, and an umbrella. The accountant at Summer Select gathered the following information from all the departments in the organization so that she can prepare next year's budget. No change occurred in costs from last period to this period. Support department costs are allocated between two separate production departments. Following is information about costs for the patio table department:

MANUFACTURING COSTS

Direct materials	Chairs	$75
	Table	$42
	Umbrella	$20
Direct labour		
Hours	Assembly	2
	Packing	0.2
Cost per hour	Assembly	$20.00
	Packing	$10.00
Cost per unit	Assembly	$40.00
	Packing	$ 2.00

INVENTORIES

	Beginning	Target Ending
Direct materials		
Chairs	$15,000	$20,000
Tables	$10,000	$12,000
Umbrellas	$5,000	$7,000
Finished goods	1,000 units at $304 per unit	1,200 units

REVENUE ASSUMPTIONS

Selling price	$500
Table sets sold	50,000

ESTIMATED VARIABLE MANUFACTURING OVERHEAD COSTS

Supplies	$ 422,000
Indirect labour	627,500
Maintenance	80,000
Miscellaneous	125,500
Total	$1,255,000

ESTIMATED FIXED MANUFACTURING OVERHEAD COSTS

Amortization	$1,004,000
Property taxes	251,000
Insurance	351,400
Plant supervision	1,255,000
Fringe benefits	1,757,000
Miscellaneous	401,600
Total	$5,020,000

ESTIMATED SUPPORT DEPARTMENT COSTS

Department	Fixed Costs
Administration	$4,819,200
Marketing	2,891,520
Distribution	1,445,760
Customer service	481,920
Total	$9,638,400

required

Prepare the following budgets: revenue, production, direct materials, direct manufacturing labour, manufacturing overhead, ending inventory, cost of goods sold, and support department. Then prepare a budgeted income statement, assuming an income tax rate of 35%.

See the solution on page 473.

Flexible Budgets

The master budget illustrated in Mountain High Bikes, Part 1, is a static budget, or a budget based on forecasts (point estimates) of specific volumes of production or services. All variable revenues and costs are calculated for a specific volume of operations. The information in a static budget is biased when compared to results for a different volume of operations. In particular, budgeted variable costs and budgeted cash inflows are overstated when fewer units or services are produced than were budgeted. Similarly, budgeted variable costs and budgeted cash inflows are understated if more units or services are produced.

LO4 Discuss the differences between static and flexible budgets

In contrast to a static budget, a flexible budget is a set of revenue and cost relationships that can be used to estimate costs and cash flows for any level of operations, within the relevant range. As such, a flexible budget uses the variable revenue and cost information from the master budget but adjusts sales information and variable costs to reflect actual volumes. Because fixed costs are not expected to change, these values are carried over from the static budget.

Budget Sensitivity Analysis

One benefit of creating a flexible budget is that managers and accountants can easily perform sensitivity analysis to estimate the effects of deviations from budget assumptions. For example, the owner of Mountain High Bikes might want to know how profits or cash flows would be affected if direct material prices increase or if sales volumes fall. Budget sensitivity analysis can be performed using spreadsheets with an input area containing budget assumptions. Similar spreadsheets were shown for cost-volume-profit analysis in Chapter 3.

Mountain High Bikes, Part 3, illustrates the preparation of a flexible budget and its use in performing sensitivity analysis.

▶ CHAPTER REFERENCE

Chapters 2 and 3 emphasize the importance of the relevant range for estimating a cost function and evaluating the effects of volume on costs and profits.

example

mountain high bikes, part 3
DEVELOPING AND USING A FLEXIBLE BUDGET

Due to increased environmental awareness, overall demand for bikes has increased, creating a shortage of raw materials. As a result, direct material prices for frames and wheels have increased by 5% and 10%, respectively. To maintain profit margins, Mountain High Bikes will need to increase their selling price. Sanjay expects that, depending on the increase in selling price, Mountain High Bikes may experience a slight, 2%, decrease in sales volume, or in a worst case scenario, sales may go down 4%. In addition, Sanjay expects the distribution of sales to change to 10% in the first quarter, 25% in the second quarter, 15% in the third quarter, and 50% in the fourth quarter. For now, he expects the following year's sales distribution to follow the new pattern.

Developing a Flexible Budget

Sanjay decides to create a spreadsheet for the flexible budget that will allow changes to the budget assumptions. First, he creates an input section to capture the budgeting assumptions.

maxpro/Shutterstock

INPUT SECTION–THIRD QUARTER BUDGET ASSUMPTIONS

SALES FORECAST	% Estimate	Units
Base amount	100,000	
Quarter 1	12.50%	12,500
Quarter 2	25.00%	25,000
Quarter 3	12.50%	12,500
Quarter 4	50.00%	50,000
Quarter 1, Year 2	12.50%	12,500

SALES PRICE per UNIT	$800.00
DIRECT MATERIALS COSTS per UNIT	
Wheels	$ 10.00
Components	$ 70.00
Frames	$ 50.00
Material cost per unit	$ 140.00

BEGINNING INVENTORY	
Bikes	2,500
Wheels	2,000
Components	1,000
Frames	1,000

DESIRED ENDING INVENTORY	
Bikes	
Qtr. 1	5.00%
Qtr. 2	3.00%
Qtr. 3	5.00%
Qtr. 4	3.00%
Qtr. 1, Yr. 2	5.00%
Wheels	3.00%
Components	5.00%
Frames	2.00%

PARTS PER UNIT

Wheels	2
Components	1
Frames	1

DIRECT LABOUR	Hours	Costs	Cost per Unit
Assembly	1.5	$25.00	$37.50
Testing	0.15	$15.00	$ 2.25
Total cost per unit			$39.75

VARIABLE OVERHEAD COSTS per UNIT

Supplies	$20.00
Indirect labour	$37.50
Maintenance	$10.00
Miscellaneous	$ 7.50
Total cost per unit	$75.00

BUDGETED FIXED OVERHEAD

	per year
Amortization	$ 4,040,000.00
Property taxes	$ 1,010,000.00
Insurance	$ 1,414,000.00
Plant supervision	$ 5,050,000.00
Fringe benefits	$ 7,070,000.00
Miscellaneous	$ 1,616,000.00
Total budgeted fixed overhead	$20,200,000.00
Total budgeted production	97,875
Fixed overhead allocation rate	$ 206.39

SUPPORT DEPARTMENT COSTS

Administration	$16,478,215.00
Marketing	$ 9,886,929.00
Distribution	$ 4,943,465.00
Customer service	$ 1,647,821.00

CASH COLLECTIONS

Month of sale	67%
Month following sale	33%
Outstanding accounts receivable	$10,000,000.00

CASH DISBURSEMENTS

Month of purchase	67%
Month following purchase	33%
Outstanding accounts payable	$2,000,000.00

EQUIPMENT

Qtr. 1	
Qtr. 2	$8,000,000.00
Qtr. 3	
Qtr. 4	

BEGINNING CASH BALANCE	$9,000,000.00
MINIMUM CASH BALANCE	$ 200,000.00
ANNUAL INTEREST RATE	6%
TAX RATE	30%

Sanjay assumes that the revenue and cost functions do not change as sales volume declines (i.e., that operations remain within the relevant range). This assumption means that changes in sales volume will cause total variable costs to change but will have no effect on total fixed costs.

Flexible Budget

Sanjay now programs the spreadsheet to allow computation of all budgets based on the new materials costs and sales assumptions.

Sanjay uses the spreadsheet budgets to analyze and compare the impact of the possible 2% and 4% decline in sales volume, holding the selling price at $800. The budgeted income statements at the base level and at each of the levels of decreased sales are compared.

BUDGETED INCOME STATEMENT

	Base Level	2% Decrease	4% Decrease
Sales revenue	$80,000,000.00	$78,400,000.00	$ 76,800,000.00
Cost of goods sold	$46,113,569.60	$46,055,833.72	$ 45,548,558.28
Gross margin	$33,886,430.40	$32,344,166.28	$ 31,251,441.72
Operating costs			
Administration	$16,478,215.00	$16,478,215.00	$ 16,478,215.00
Marketing	$ 9,886,929.00	$ 9,886,929.00	$ 9,886,929.00
Distribution	$ 4,943,465.00	$ 4,943,465.00	$ 4,943,465.00
Customer service	$ 1,647,821.00	$ 1,647,821.00	$ 1,647,821.00
Total operating costs	$32,956,430.00	$32,956,430.00	$ 32,956,430.00
Operating income/loss	$ 930,000.40	$ (612,263.72)	$(1,704,988.28)

From these analyses, Sanjay estimates that operating income would decrease between $1,303,851.04 and $2,176,049.97 without a price increase. He can now use the spreadsheet to analyze the impact of different selling prices on resource needs, cash flow, and net income.

Using the Flexible Budget for Planning

Sanjay provides the CEO with his analyses and shows him how to make changes to the spreadsheet. The CEO is pleased to have this new planning model. He can use it to anticipate the effects of changes in sales and to investigate the effects of potential tactics. ▪

> ●● > STRATEGIC RISK MANAGEMENT: MOUNTAIN HIGH BIKES, PART 3
>
> **FLEXIBLE BUDGET AND QUALITY OF INFORMATION** Sanjay created a flexible budget. How was the quality of information in the flexible budget better than the information in the static budget? The flexible budget provided a better target against which to compare actual results. The static budget would overestimate revenues, variable costs, and cash inflows if the sales volume dropped. The flexible budget will improve the CEO's ability to effectively monitor whether costs are under control.

Budgets as Performance Benchmarks

Managers and accountants use budgets to monitor operations by comparing actual results to the original budget forecasts. These comparisons serve as *benchmarks* for performance and help managers and accountants evaluate whether strategies and operations are meeting expectations. For example, managers learn whether desired sales volumes are achieved or whether costs are under control. In addition, accountants monitor budgets to improve the quality of the budgeting process over time.

| L05 | Explain budget variances and how they are calculated |

Budget Variances

Differences between budgeted and actual results are called budget variances. If actual revenues are larger than the budget, or if actual costs are lower than the budget, the variance is categorized as a favourable variance. Conversely, an unfavourable variance occurs when actual costs are greater than budgeted or when actual revenues are less than budgeted.

> ▷ **CHAPTER REFERENCE**
> In Chapter 11, you'll learn more about the reasons for variances and the actions that managers take, if any, after analyzing variances.

Budget variances occur for two general reasons. First, actual activities might not follow plans. For example, the Wii produced by Nintendo was previewed at Toronto's Ontario Place by Ron Bertram, vice president and general manager of Nintendo Canada, and then became a "hot item" during the 2006 Christmas season. It sold out at electronics stores immediately, with people standing on line for hours in the early morning, waiting for new shipments.[6] Actual volumes of production might have increased greatly above budgeted amounts.

> ▷ **HELPFUL HINT**
> Budget variances can be calculated based on either a static budget (static budget *variance*) or a flexible budget (flexible budget *variance*).

Second, unanticipated increases or decreases in the purchase prices of direct materials or other input factors can cause a budget to be an inappropriate benchmark for performance. Accordingly, revision of a budget benchmark would take into account new information about costs.

Determining the underlying reasons for a variance is sometimes complicated. Suppose the City of Welland has a favourable wastewater treatment cost variance. This variance could occur because residents used water saving devices resulting in less waste water to be treated. However, it could also occur because shortcuts were taken in the wastewater treatment process, which raises other serious concerns.

Variances are used to monitor actual results compared to the budget, as indicated in Exhibit 10.3. Managers and accountants gain improved understanding of the organization's progress toward objectives and goals when they investigate the reasons for variances. Variances can also be part of a diagnostic control system used to evaluate and reward performance. In addition, variances can be part of an interactive control system; as managers investigate factors causing variances, they might reassess the organization's vision and core competencies, reconsider strategies, and develop improved operating plans.

Variances may be calculated by comparing actual results to a static budget, a flexible budget, or a budget that has been adjusted to create a better benchmark for performance. As shown in Mountain High Bikes, Part 3, different benchmarks are appropriate for different purposes.

---

[6] Marketnews, "Wii Rocks Canada," *Marketnews*, November 14, 2006; and "FutureShop/Best Buy Gears up for Gaming," *Marketnews*, November 15.

> **BUSINESS PRACTICE**

Software vendors such as **SAP**, **Oracle**, **Sage** (Simply Accounting and ACCpAC), **Intuit** (QuickBooks), and **Microsoft** (Dynamics) provide budgeting packages that allow changes in underlying assumptions.

When evaluating actual results at the end of a period, a flexible budget is set at the actual sales or production volume and used as a benchmark for analyzing variances. An organization that uses a static budget transforms it into a benchmark by adjusting its variable costs to reflect actual volume. However, because fixed costs are not expected to vary with volume, they are not adjusted for any differences between budgeted and actual volumes. Therefore, a flexible budget uses actual volume for variable costs and the budgeted fixed costs. Mountain High Bikes, Part 4, illustrates variances for static and flexible budgets.

example

mountain high bikes, part 4
STATIC VERSUS FLEXIBLE BUDGET VARIANCES

At the end of the budget cycle, Sanjay compares actual results for the period to the budget and is excited to see that sales greatly exceeded expectations. He plans to create a budget variance report for management.

Static Budget variances

Sanjay creates the summary shown in Exhibit 10.9, comparing revenues and costs under the static budget with the actual income statement. He uses the budgeted variable costs for this period. Variable costs per bike include the following:

Direct materials:

Wheels/tires	$ 20.00
Components	70.00
Frame	50.00
Total direct materials	140.00
Direct labour	39.75
Variable overhead	75.00
Total cost per bike	$254.75

maxpro/Shutterstock

Sanjay includes the total budgeted fixed manufacturing overhead costs ($20,200,000) and the budgeted support department costs ($32,956,430). He calculates variances for sales volume, revenue, and each of the cost categories. When Sanjay compares the actual results to the budget, he is pleased with the organization's performance during the period. The overall variance was favourable by over $2.6 million, and the revenue variance was positive and large—$10.5 million. However, he is concerned about the large unfavourable cost variances.

> **EXHIBIT 10.9**

Static Budget Variances at Mountain High Bikes

	Static Budget	Actual	Variance	
Bikes sold	100,000	113,500	13,500	Favourable
Revenue	$80,000,000	$90,500,000	$10,500,000	Favourable
Production costs				
Variable	25,475,000[a]	29,492,408	(4,017,408)	Unfavourable
Fixed overhead	20,200,000	19,400,000	800,000	Favourable
Support department costs	32,956,430	37,565,337	(4,608,907)	Unfavourable
Income	$ 1,368,570[b]	$ 4,042,255		
Total variance			$ 2,673,685	Favourable

[a]Budgeted variable costs × 100,000 = $254.75 × 100,000 = $25,475,000.

[b]Differs from budgeted income statement because some fixed overhead costs were removed from inventory. A decrease of 2,125 bikes in ending inventory was budgeted this period. This reduction in inventory results in $438,569.60 (2,125 × (20,200,000/97,875)) additional fixed overhead costs on the budgeted income statement, which is prepared using absorption costing. The budgeted income statement used for variance analysis is prepared using variable costing. Chapter 17 discusses these differences in greater detail.

	Flexible Budget	Actual	Variance	
Bikes sold	113,500	113,500		
Revenue	$90,800,000[a]	$90,500,000	$ (300,000)	Unfavourable
Production costs:				
Variable	28,914,125[b]	29,492,408	(578,283)	Unfavourable
Fixed overhead	20,200,000	19,400,000	800,000	Favourable
Support department costs	32,956,430	37,565,337	(4,608,907)	Unfavourable
Income	$ 8,729,445	$ 4,042,255		
Total variance			$(4,687,190)	Unfavourable

[a]Actual quantity sold multiplied by budgeted selling price per bike of $800.

[b]Actual quantity sold multiplied by this period's budgeted variable cost per unit of $254.75.

►EXHIBIT 10.10
Flexible Budget Variances
at Mountain High Bikes

As Sanjay thinks more about the cost variances, he realizes that he would expect to see unfavourable variable production cost variances because the sales volume was higher than planned. Because he used a static budget in his schedule, the cost variances did not reflect the actual volume of sales. Therefore, the schedule gave him poor-quality information for analyzing last period's costs.

Flexible Budget Variances

Sanjay decides to create a new budget variance analysis that reflects the actual volume of sales. Using the spreadsheet that he developed during the budgeting process, he transforms the static budget into a flexible budget by recalculating budgeted revenues using actual sales volumes (113,500) and budgeted selling price ($800). He then recalculates budgeted variable production costs by multiplying the actual sales volume (113,500) by the budgeted variable cost per unit of $254.75. Because fixed costs are not expected to vary with changes in volume, no adjustments are made to either budgeted fixed production costs or support costs. Finally, Sanjay recalculates the variances. Exhibit 10.10 summarizes his revised variance schedule.

Based on the new schedule, Sanjay realizes that the company's performance was worse than he previously thought. After accounting for the higher sales volume, the total flexible budget variance is unfavourable by more than $4.6 million. These variances indicate the following:

▶ The average selling price per bike was lower than the budget.
▶ The average variable production cost per bike was higher than the budget.
▶ Total fixed production costs were lower than the budget.
▶ Total fixed support costs were significantly higher than the budget.

Sanjay plans to investigate the reasons for the large unfavourable fixed support department cost variance. He also knows that at least part of the fixed overhead variance is due to producing more bikes than planned in order to meet the increased sales. However, he is unsure whether the other variances are significant enough to justify spending time investigating them. He decides to meet with the controller to discuss how to proceed. This discussion is presented later in the chapter, in Mountain High Bikes, Part 5. ■

Variances and Budgeting Uncertainties

Because budgets are based on forecasts about the future, it is impossible to prevent variances by exactly achieving budgeted revenues and costs. The degree of forecast uncertainty varies across organizations and across time. Some organizations have fairly predictable revenues and costs, especially organizations that purchase and sell under fixed-price, long-term contracts. Other organizations have volatile or unpredictable revenues and costs. Budgets are likely to be less accurate—significant variances are more likely to occur—in highly competitive industries, when selling newly developed goods and services, or when subject to fluctuating raw material costs such as petroleum prices.

Budgets, Incentives, and Rewards

LO6 Discuss how budgets are used to monitor and motivate performance

Budgets are used to assign decision rights to individual managers within an organization. Managers are given authority over resources and then held responsible for meeting budget benchmarks, such as producing units at the budgeted cost per unit. Many organizations monitor individual manager performance by comparing actual results to the budget. Bonuses based on meeting or exceeding budget goals help motivate performance. Sometimes broader employee groups receive profit sharing, cash, or other bonuses based on achieving or exceeding budgeted income levels. For example, manufacturing plant workers who meet production volume, cost, and quality goals could be entitled to share in profits or receive cash bonuses. Sales representatives who meet target sales volumes may be rewarded with family trips to resort destinations or awards dinners to celebrate their good performance. These practices raise questions about how information is gathered for budgets and what levels of responsibility should be included.

Participative Budgeting

Budget plans can be developed from the top down, using information that has been gathered from the bottom up. In other words, top management provides strategies and suggested organizational targets for the coming period. These strategies and targets are communicated "top down" to division and department managers, who incorporate them into the budgeted operating plans. Departmental budget requests are then communicated "bottom up" to members of top management who are responsible for final budget approval. Although top managers approve the final budget, they rely on the knowledge and experience of individual managers to help them establish reasonable departmental budgets. When managers in the field have more knowledge about future operations than top management, budgets are often developed from the bottom up. For example, sales representatives at Mountain High Bikes could submit their forecasts for next year to the marketing department. Participative budgeting occurs when managers who are responsible for meeting budgets also prepare the initial budget forecasts, setting targets for themselves. Theoretically, participative budgeting motivates employees to meet budget targets because they buy in to the target-setting process. However, when employees set targets, incentives exist to set them low so that goals can be met easily, a practice known as budgetary slack. In contrast, when top management sets targets, incentives exist to raise targets to induce greater productivity. This practice is known as budget ratcheting. If targets are either too low or too high—easily met or unachievable—employees have little motivation to improve performance. Therefore, negotiations are often required over a period of time prior to setting a final budget. Because uncertainties exist about future revenues and costs, top managers, shareholders, and others cannot easily identify and remedy budgets that have been manipulated. However, several methods are used to minimize budgetary slack. For example, independent sources such as consultants or market experts may prepare forecasts. These forecasts are compared to budgeted estimates so that employees providing budget information realize their estimates are being scrutinized. Also, bonuses can be given for accurate forecasts as well as for operating within the budget.

Incentives to manipulate budgets often increase in larger organizations, where managers tend to focus only on the resources and performance of their own departments. As a result, they are less likely to consider the organization as a whole and more likely to submit biased budget requests. These requests lead to misallocations of resources among competing departments or projects. To address this problem, some organizations give bonuses based on

▶ EXHIBIT 10.11
Challenges in Appropriately
Assigning Decision Rights

Challenges	Why They Arise	Specific Examples
Resentment	Department managers held responsible for costs over which they have no control	Allocated support department costs may be high because of poor management in support departments
Isolating the performance of individual managers	Interdependency among divisions and departments	Quality of customer service department affects ability of the sales department to meet future sales targets
Manager turnover	New manager is responsible for old manager's budget decisions	After the production manager is promoted to vice president, the new production manager faces unrealistic budget targets
Employee turnover	Employees are promoted, let go, or leave	Delays arise in hiring process or a hiring freeze occurs
Uncontrollable external factors	Unanticipated changes in volumes, costs, or prices	Oil price and availability change because of broken pipelines

a combination of department results and overall organization profitability, which reduces incentives to build in slack while at the same time motivating managers to support each other by directing resources toward the best projects.

Budgets give managers authority over the use of an organization's resources. Accordingly, it seems reasonable to hold managers responsible for meeting budget benchmarks. However, when budget variances are used in performance evaluation, a number of challenges arise for the managers being evaluated as well as for the managers conducting the evaluation. Exhibit 10.11 provides examples of these challenges. Notice that most of these problems relate to holding managers responsible for results when they lack control over factors that affect their variances.

Budget and Variance Adjustments

Because managers' budgets often include items not under their control, the following adjustments should be made when budgets are used to measure managers' performance:

- ▶ Use a flexible budget to determine expected revenues based on budgeted prices and actual volumes.
- ▶ Use a flexible budget to determine expected variable costs based on budgeted variable cost rates and actual volumes.
- ▶ Remove allocated costs that are not controllable by managers in the departments receiving allocations.
- ▶ Update costs for any anticipated price changes in direct materials, direct labour, and overhead-related resources.

Mountain High Bikes, Part 5, provides an example of these adjustments.

▷ CHAPTER REFERENCE
You will learn more about performance evaluation and manager responsibility in Chapter 18.

mountain high bikes, part 5
BUDGET ADJUSTMENTS FOR PERFORMANCE EVALUATION

Sanjay knows that the sales and production managers receive bonuses if their departmental performances exceed the budget. Before his planned meeting with the controller, Sanjay creates a performance schedule for each manager.

example

maxpro/Shutterstock

example

Sanjay reviews his flexible budget variance schedules (Exhibit 10.10). Because the sales department is responsible for the level of sales as well as prices, he decides that managers should be rewarded for the level of sales above the static budget, but any effects from sales discounts should also be included. Therefore, he prepares the following summary for the sales department:

SALES VARIANCES

Volume variance		
Budgeted sales		100,000 bikes
Actual sales		<u>113,500</u>
Favourable variance		<u>13,500</u> bikes
Sales price variance		
Actual sales at budgeted prices	$90,800,000	
Actual sales at actual prices	<u>90,500,000</u>	
Unfavourable variance	<u>$ (300,000)</u>	

The production department sets manufacturing volumes according to information provided by the sales department. Therefore, the production department manager does not have control over production volumes. Sanjay decides that the flexible budget variances should reflect costs over which managers have control. The production manager is responsible for the fixed and variable costs in the manufacturing plant, so only those costs are included in his performance evaluation. Sanjay finds these details in the flexible budget he had earlier prepared and summarizes them for the controller. As he prepares the summary, he checks with the purchasing department to see if any price changes occurred this period. He finds that the prices of wheels and frames have increased by $4.50 per bike, but all other prices have remained unchanged. He adds $510,750 to the adjusted flexible budget variable production costs to account for the additional $4.50 cost for each of the 113,500 bikes manufactured. The payroll department has had no changes in budgeted labour rates. Sanjay also removes the support department costs because they were not under the production manager's control. Sanjay's summary is presented in Exhibit 10.12.

> **CHAPTER REFERENCE**
In Chapter 11 you'll learn to calculate and analyze additional types of variances.

Evaluating Department Manager Performance

Sanjay presents the variance summaries to the controller. He tells the controller that the sales manager probably should receive a bonus for an increased level of sales. However, some bikes were sold at a discount, and this fact needs to be investigated further because the discount resulted in $300,000 less in revenues than expected, given actual sales. Sanjay believes that the unfavourable variable production costs variance and the favourable fixed production costs variance should be investigated. In addition, he decides that the support department heads should meet to determine the reasons for the large unfavourable variance in their department costs. ■

> **EXHIBIT 10.12**
> Adjusted Production Flexible Budget Variances at Mountain High Bikes

	Flexible Budget, Adjusted for Price Changes	Actual	Variance	
Variable production costs	$29,424,875[a]	$29,492,408	$ (67,533)	Unfavourable
Fixed production costs	<u>20,200,000[b]</u>	<u>19,400,000</u>	800,000	Favourable
Total costs	<u>$49,624,875</u>	<u>$48,892,408</u>		
Total variance			<u>$732,467</u>	Favourable

[a]Flexible budget at old price ($28,914,125) plus the effects of $4.50 price increase ($4.50 × 113,500 bikes), totalling $29,424,875.
[b]These are the original estimated fixed overhead costs, not the applied fixed overhead costs that appear on the income statements.

Zero-Based Budgeting

To plan for the next period, some managers simply add an adjustment that increases last year's budget. This type of budgeting practice can result in biased decision making as a result of recency (Chapter 10) and anchoring (Chapter 11) and discourages managers from seeking ways to use the organization's resources more efficiently. In addition, many organizations adopt policies so that departments lose authority over unspent budgeted costs and receive lower future budgets if actual costs are lower than the current budget. This policy encourages department managers to spend all their budgeted funds to avoid future cutbacks. To reduce these types of problems and encourage more strategic use of scarce resources, organizations may adopt zero-based budgeting, in which managers justify budget amounts as if no information about budgets or costs from prior budget cycles were available. This system encourages managers to manage costs and improve decision making. A disadvantage is that it is time-consuming, and may represent a shift in organization culture, which would need to be carefully managed.

▶ **BUSINESS PRACTICE**
The **Public Service Commission of Canada** stated that to become a model organization in financial and human resources management, it has introduced the use of zero-based budgeting.[7]

10-2 self-study problem   Comparing Actual Results to a Flexible Budget

LO4, LO5

Suppose that the manager of Summer Select Patio Furniture is evaluated based on budgeted expectations. She is responsible for both sales and production costs. This period, the company produced and sold more units than budgeted, and the manager expects to get a bonus. Refer to Self-Study Problem 10-1 for Summer Select Patio Furniture's static budget. The company's actual results for the period were as follows:

Sales volume	54,000 table sets
Sales revenue	$25,500,000
Variable production costs	10,980,000
Fixed production costs	5,000,000
Fixed support department costs	9,415,300

required

A. Prepare a flexible budget based on actual sales volumes and then calculate the flexible budget revenue and cost variances.
B. Review the variances from Part A. For each variance, briefly describe the types of operating or budgeting problems that might have caused these variances.
C. Compose at least three questions the accountant could ask the manager, to better understand how the largest variances arose.

See the solution on page 476.

Beyond Traditional Budgeting

In addition to the more traditional methods, other budgeting approaches can be taken. Budgets are sometimes used for long- or short-term plans. As software systems have become increasingly complex, real-time information has become more easily accessible, and it is used in updating budgets.

LO7   Describe other approaches to budgeting

---

[7] Audit of Budgeting, Public Service Commission of Canada, approved April 27, 2009, http://www.psc-cfp.gc.ca/abt-aps/inta-veri/2009/ab-vb/index-eng.htm.

Long-Term Budgets

As illustrated in Exhibit 10.3, long-term strategies are an important consideration in the budget process. Therefore, budgets are often prepared for periods beyond one year. Frequently, organizations prepare budgets to forecast five or 10 years into the future. Such budgets improve long-term planning and communication. They are also used to motivate performance consistent with long-term strategic goals. However, uncertainties increase when managers forecast further into the future, making long-term budgets less reliable than short-term budgets. Accordingly, organizations often revise their long-term budgets each year.

Rolling Budgets

The business environment has become increasingly dynamic, requiring quick managerial response to change. A rolling budget, which is prepared monthly or quarterly, reflects planning changes going forward, often through the next 12 to 18 months. Many organizations use rolling budgets because they incorporate more current information than either static or flexible budgets. Rolling budgets reflect the most recent results and also incorporate significant changes in business strategy, operating plans, and the economy. With current information at hand, managers can quickly increase or decrease costs and inventory levels during economic upturns or downturns. In addition, production can more easily be resumed or expanded when the economy picks up.

As technology advances, more and more budget software solutions are offered to businesses. High-tech solutions allow continuous monitoring of both internal and external data. These data are then used to update budgets and make operating decisions. For some business operations, this continual updating is important to ongoing success. Unfortunately, in some situations, the additional data creates or contributes to an already dysfunctional management environment. When considering a technological solution, managers need to consider whether the additional data are necessary to solve a problem or whether the problem is a result of incorrect or inappropriate uses of the existing data. Increasing the quantity of data available for decision making does not necessarily improve the decision. Some companies pursue innovative implementations of rolling budgets by updating their budgets on a monthly or quarterly basis or using advanced technology and continuous updating only in time-critical areas.[8]

> **ALTERNATIVE TERMS**
>
> Some companies use the term *continuous budget* instead of *rolling budget.*

Activity-Based Budgets

Traditional budget models are developed around a few cost drivers that are primarily output based. For example, in the Mountain High Bikes case, production costs were separated into direct materials, direct labour, and variable and fixed overhead. Activity-based budgeting uses activity cost pools and their related cost drivers to anticipate the costs for individual activities. A budget is developed for each activity in an organization's activity-based system.

---

[8] See Marc P. Lynn, Roland L. Madison, "A Closer Look at Rolling Budgets," *Management Accounting Quarterly* 6 (Fall 2004); p. 60.

Suppose that Mountain High Bikes used activity-based budgeting. Its key production cost drivers might then include frame assembly, wheel attachment, painting, accessory attachment, inspection, and packaging. In addition, activities would be developed for the support departments. For example, the marketing department might include personal customer contacts and website customer maintenance as well as other activities. The costs for each activity would be budgeted separately, as shown in Exhibit 10.13.

Activity-based budgeting provides a number of advantages over traditional budgeting methods. When operational budgets are prepared before financial budgets, managers are assured that the budget is operationally feasible. Under traditional budgeting systems, the operational budget is usually prepared separately from the financial budget. In budget systems such as the one illustrated for Mountain High Bikes, the accountant might inadvertently base the financial budget on a forecast of production volume exceeding the company's capacity. Also, activity-based budgets incorporate more factors, such as unit, batch, facility, and customer drivers, into the planning process. These additional factors improve the quality of information for planning, promoting better allocation of resources. Finally, activity-based budgets improve communication with lower-level operating personnel, who are more likely to understand budgets set in operational terms.

CHAPTER REFERENCE
ABC was presented in Chapter 7.

The disadvantages of activity-based budgeting are similar to those for activity-based costing (ABC) as discussed in Chapter 7. To use activity-based budgeting, organizations must have an activity-based information system in place. Such systems can be costly to develop and maintain.

GPK and RCA Budgets

CHAPTER REFERENCE
See Chapter 7 for more details about the strengths and weaknesses of GPK and RCA.

Although activity-based budgets can lead to improved planning, a problem with activity-based costing is that some fixed costs are treated as variable once activity pools and cost drivers have been identified. This practice introduces measurement error into budget estimates.

In contrast, GPK (grenzplankostenrechnung) and RCA (resource consumption accounting) identify cost functions for fixed and variable costs at the resource centre level. Firms that use GPK and RCA cost accounting systems typically use these systems to develop flexible budgets based on resource usage. Accordingly, compared to traditional and ABC budgets, GPK and RCA systems are likely to provide more accurate cost forecasts. However, GPK and RCA systems are expensive to implement, and benefits from added accuracy in planning may not be worth the costs of implementing and maintaining these systems.

EXHIBIT 10.13

Activity-Based Budgeting (ABB) for Marketing Department at Mountain High Bikes

Activity	Budgeted Cost	Cost Driver	Budgeted Volume	Budgeted Cost per Unit of Cost Driver
Customer-Related Costs:				
Personal customer contacts	$ 48,000	Number of contacts	2,400 contacts	$20 per customer contact
Website customer maintenance	30,000	Web service hours	2,000 hours	$15 per hour
Other activities	9,808,929			
Total marketing activities	$9,886,929			

Kaizen Budgets

Kaizen costing, a system developed in Japan, is used for products that tend to have decreasing prices or increasing quality across time, such as home entertainment centres, cell phones, and computers. **Kaizen budgets** set targeted cost reductions across time, anticipating market price reductions across the life of a product. In addition to cost reductions, quality improvements are also targeted. When kaizen budgeting is performed, cost reduction and quality improvement goals are explicitly embedded in the budgets. For example, Mountain High Bikes could budget for cost reductions of 15% for direct labour and 10% in assembly time to meet cost and production targets in anticipation of competitors' price decreases. In addition, the company could budget an increase in the quality of components. If the costs of quality improvements are less than the savings from reduced labour and cycle time, overall costs are reduced. Therefore, a kaizen budget for Mountain High Bikes would reduce the cost of each bike while improving quality.

> ▷ **CHAPTER REFERENCE**
>
> See Chapter 15 for more details about kaizen costing.

Beyond Budgeting: Relative Performance Evaluation

Some business groups believe that planning should be separate from performance evaluation because the adverse behavioural effects of traditional budgeting are so severe.[9] Promoters of an approach called **beyond budgeting** argue that manager or employee performance should be evaluated relative to internal or external benchmarks. Internal benchmarks might include actual performance of other departments or business units. External benchmarks might include performance of close competitors.

As shown in Exhibit 10.14 relative performance evaluation differs from flexible budget variances, which are based on actual sales or production volumes.[10] When managers are evaluated under a relative performance system, they may still use traditionally developed budgets and variances as part of an interactive control system to search for challenges and opportunities arising from changing economic conditions.

Benchmarks have several advantages over static or flexible budget variances for performance evaluation. The most important advantage is that benchmarks focus manager attention on creating value rather than on manipulating the budget or taking inappropriate actions to achieve budget targets. Benchmarks also increase the accuracy and fairness of performance

> ▷ **EXHIBIT 10.14**
>
> Relative Performance Compared to Static and Flexible Budget Variances

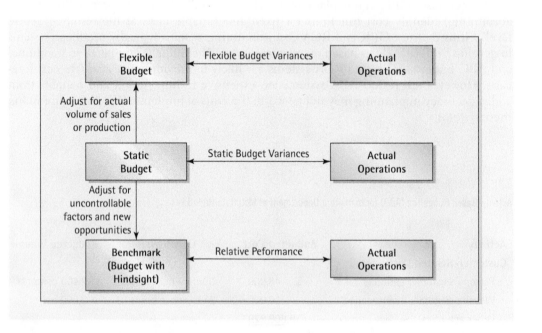

---

[9] See, for example, S. C. Hansen, D. T. Otley, and W. A. Van der Stede, "Practice Developments in Budgeting: An Overview and Research Perspective," *Journal of Management Accounting Research* (15), 2003, pp. 95–116.

[10] A. Garg, D. Gosh, J. Hudick, and C. Nowaki, "Roles and Practices in Management Accounting Today," *Strategic Finance*, July 2003, pp. 30–36.

evaluation. Relative performance evaluation automatically removes uncontrollable changes, such as general or industry economic conditions. The benchmark approach also holds managers accountable for initiatives by competing firms, such as the adoption of new business opportunities or cost-reduction practices. Relative performance evaluation might also increase motivation, if benchmarks are perceived as challenging but achievable.

A major drawback of relative performance evaluation systems is that organizations may lack the necessary benchmark data. Insufficient data is most likely to be a problem in the rapidly changing environments that would benefit most from this approach. In addition, as discussed in Chapter 18, simpler approaches may be available for reducing the dysfunctional behaviours associated with traditional budgeting practices.

●● > FOCUS ON ETHICAL DECISION MAKING: TIMELY REPORTING OF BUDGET PROBLEMS

A dilemma that individuals face is whether to be truthful when it appears that a project is over budget. Being over budget typically means that actual costs exceed budgeted costs or that a planned timeline will not be met. People often delay reporting an over-budget condition, either because they believe they can catch up later or because they want to delay negative repercussions. Unfortunately, information delays prevent managers from responding rapidly and decisively to delays in project timing and cost overruns, leading to additional dissatisfaction and inefficiencies.

Suppose a CPA firm establishes a budget of professional hours for a particular audit job. The hours are broken down by audit area, and one area is the valuation of inventory and cost of goods sold. During the past year, the audit client adopted new procedures for assigning product costs to individual units. The audit budget includes extra hours for the estimated time needed to document and assess the reasonableness of the new method. Many factors could cause this part of the audit to be over budget. Consider the following two scenarios:

1. The client failed to establish appropriate records needed to easily audit the new method, and this part of the audit will require more than the budgeted time to complete.

2. The auditor assigned to this part of the audit is inexperienced and unable to complete the work in the budgeted time.

Regardless of the reason for an overage, managers in charge of an audit need to be notified as soon as possible so that they can consider possible ways to realign staff and complete the total job on time. In addition, in the first scenario, the audit firm might be able to bill the client for the extra work involved if the audit contract includes a provision for such price adjustments. However, this scenario would most likely require the client to be notified promptly, while the work is still being performed. In the second scenario, the overage may result in a poor performance evaluation, especially if the auditor has similar problems in other audit areas. Yet the overage may be considered reasonable in light of the auditor's inexperience. Even so, the auditor should be able to accomplish the following:[11]

- Design appropriate procedures based on the assignment's scope, risk, and materiality guidelines.

- Assign staff to carry out the engagement.

- Execute the work plan.

- Modify the program, as necessary.

The auditor must quickly recognize an impending overage and formulate appropriate strategies for completing the task as efficiently as possible. The auditor also needs to keep her supervisor apprised of the situation and seek help, when needed.

ETHICS AND BUDGET PROBLEMS

When audit engagements are over budget, the auditor may have to make difficult decisions. Have you ever failed to meet a deadline on a group project? If so, what were the reasons for the delay? When and how did you report the delay to your team members? In your future career, how can you work toward developing your professional responsibility as a member of a work team?

Monkey Business Images/Shutterstock

---

[11] These elements of Assurance (a specific competency) are defined in the CPA Competency Map (Elective Module 3 – Assurance, Competency 4.3 Internal Audit Projects and External Assurance Engagements).

SUMMARY

L01   Discuss the relationships among budgets, long-term strategies, and short-term operating plans

BUDGET OBJECTIVES

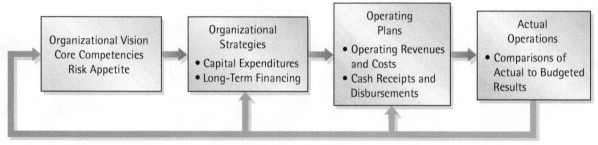

Measure, Monitor, and Motivate

BUDGETS AND LEVERS OF CONTROL

BUDGET CYCLE

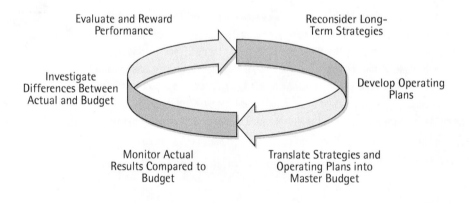

MASTER BUDGET OVERVIEW

L02   Describe a master budget and explain how it is prepared; explain how operating budgets are prepared

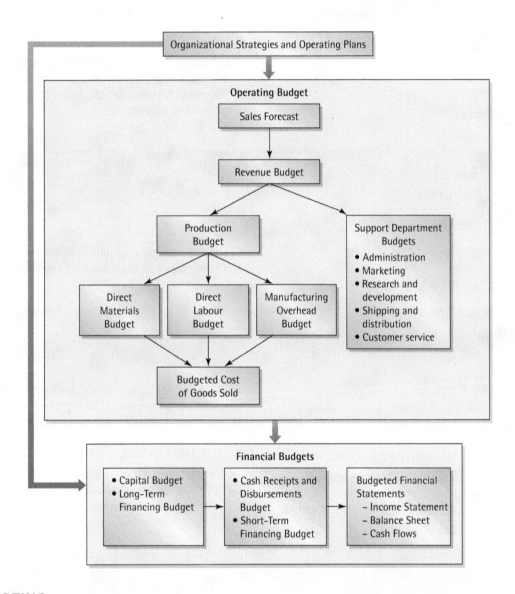

FORECASTING

► Sales Forecasting
► Cost Forecasting
► Cash Flow Forecasting

LO3   Explain how a cash budget is developed

OPERATING CASH RECEIPTS AND DISBURSEMENTS
- Forecast timing of cash receipts from customers
- Forecast timing of cash payments for direct materials, direct labour, variable and fixed overhead, and support department costs

BALANCING THE CASH BUDGET
- Desired cash balance

- Purchase or liquidation of short-term investments
- Proceeds or repayments of short-term debt
- Interest on short-term debt

OTHER PLANNED CASH FLOWS
- Purchase or sale of property, plant, and equipment
- Proceeds or repayments of long-term debt
- Proceeds or redemption of capital stock
- Dividends to shareholders

LO4   Discuss the differences between static and flexible budgets

STATIC BUDGET
- Based on point estimates of future activity

FLEXIBLE BUDGET
- Set of revenue and cost relationships that can be used to estimate costs and cash flows for any level of operations

LO5   Explain budget variances and how they are calculated

BUDGET VARIANCES
- Differences between budgeted and actual results
- May be favourable or unfavourable

FLEXIBLE BUDGET VARIANCES
- Variances are based on the budget that is adjusted for actual sales or production volume
- Variable costs are adjusted for actual volume of activity

- Flexible budget variances are useful for measuring performance of individuals/departments *not* responsible for achieving budgeted volume of activity

MAJOR REASONS FOR VARIANCES
- Actual activities do not follow plans
- Budget may be an inappropriate benchmark (i.e., budget assumptions may be incorrect)

LO6   Discuss how budgets are used to monitor and motivate performance

- As benchmarks
- To reward performance

PARTICIPATIVE BUDGETING
- Budgetary slack
- Budget ratcheting

BUDGET ADJUSTMENTS FOR PERFORMANCE EVALUATION
- Use flexible budget to adjust for actual volumes
- Remove costs not under managers' control
- Update costs for anticipated price changes

ZERO-BASED BUDGETING

SUMMARY

L07   Describe other approaches to budgeting

▶ Long-Term Budgets
▶ Rolling Budgets
▶ Activity-Based Budgets
▶ GPK and RCA Budgets
▶ Kaizen Budgets
▶ Beyond Budgeting: Relative Performance Evaluation

10-1 solution to self-study problem

Revenue Budget

The revenue budget calculates forecasted revenues, given forecasted sales volume and price:

	Selling Price	Units Sold	Total Revenues
Table sets	$500	50,000	$25,000,000

Production Budget (units)

The production budget calculates the number of units that need to be produced, given current and targeted ending inventory levels and budgeted sales:

	Table Sets
Sales	50,000
Target ending inventory	1,200
Total finished units needed	51,200
Less beginning inventory	1,000
Production	50,200

Direct Materials Budget

The direct materials budget calculates the budget for purchases of raw materials, given the beginning and targeted ending inventory levels and budgeted production volume:

Budgeted usage:	
Chairs (50,200 sets × $75 per set)	$3,765,000
Tables (50,200 sets × $42 per set)	2,108,400
Umbrellas (50,200 sets × $20 per set)	1,004,000
Total direct materials used	6,877,400
Add target ending inventory	39,000
Deduct beginning inventory	(30,000)
Total purchases	$6,886,400

Direct Manufacturing Labour Budget

The direct manufacturing labour budget calculates the amount of direct labour hours needed for budgeted production and then determines the cost:

Labour hours budget	
Assembly (50,200 sets × 2 hours)	100,400
Packing (50,200 sets × 0.2 hours)	10,040
Total labour hours	110,440
Labour cost budget	
Assembly (100,400 hours × $20 per hour)	$2,008,000
Packing (10,040 hours × $10 per hour)	100,400
Total labour cost	$2,108,400

Manufacturing Overhead Budget

The manufacturing overhead budget summarizes the expected fixed and variable overhead costs:

Variable manufacturing overhead costs	
Supplies	$ 422,000
Indirect labour	627,500
Maintenance	80,000
Miscellaneous	125,500
Total variable overhead	1,255,000
Fixed manufacturing overhead costs	
Amortization	1,004,000
Property taxes	251,000
Insurance	351,400
Plant supervision	1,255,000
Fringe benefits	1,757,000
Miscellaneous	401,600
Total fixed overhead	5,020,000
Total overhead	$6,275,000
Manufacturing overhead allocation rates	Cost per Set
Variable ($1,255,000 ÷ 50,200 sets)	$25
Fixed ($5,020,000 ÷ 50,200 sets)	$100

Ending Inventory Budget

The ending inventory budget determines the unit costs and then forecasts the cost of ending inventory units:

Unit costs (cost per table set):	
Direct materials	Cost per Unit
Chairs	$ 75.00
Table	42.00
Umbrellas	20.00
Total direct materials	137.00
Direct labour	
Assembly	40.00
Packaging	2.00
Total direct labour	42.00

Overhead		
Variable		25.00
Fixed		100.00
Total overhead		125.00
Total unit cost		$304.00

Cost of Goods Sold Budget

The cost of goods sold budget calculates the cost of inventory available for sale during the period and the cost of goods sold:

Beginning finished goods (1,000 sets × $304 per set):		$ 304,000
Cost of goods manufactured		
Direct materials	$6,877,400	
Direct labour	2,108,400	
Manufacturing overhead	6,275,000	
Total cost of goods manufactured		15,260,800
Total goods available for sale		15,564,800
Less ending finished goods (12,00 sets × $304 per set)		(364,800)
Cost of goods sold		$15,200,000

Support Department Costs Budget

The support department costs budget forecasts the total nonmanufacturing costs for the period:

Department	Fixed Costs
Administration	$4,819,200
Marketing	2,891,520
Distribution	1,445,760
Customer service	481,920
Total	$9,638,400

Budgeted Income Statement

When all the budget schedules have been prepared, the budgeted income statement is created. Revenue is drawn from the revenue budget, and cost of goods sold is drawn from the cost of goods sold budget. Then the operating costs from the support department costs budget are subtracted to determine operating income:

Revenues		$25,000,000
Cost of goods sold		15,200,000
Gross margin		9,800,000
Operating costs:		
Administration	$4,819,200	
Marketing	2,891,520	
Distribution	1,445,760	
Customer service	481,920	9,638,400
Operating income		161,600
Income tax expense ($161,600 × 35%)		56,560
Net income		$ 105,040

10-2 solution to self-study problem

A. To create a flexible budget for evaluating the department manager's performance, we modify the static budget to reflect the actual volume of sales and remove any costs not under the manager's control. This requires a recalculation of budgeted variable costs to reflect actual volume. Because fixed costs remain fixed within a relevant range, we assume that they will not change with the changes in volume. However, we remove the support department costs because they are allocated and not under control of the manager:

	Static Budget	Flexible Budget	Actual	Variance F = Favourable U = Unfavourable
Sales volume	50,000	54,000	54,000	
Revenue	$25,000,000	$27,000,000ᵃ	$25,500,000	$1,500,000 U
Variable production costs	10,200,000ᵇ	11,016,000ᶜ	10,980,000	36,000 F
Fixed production costs	5,020,000ᵈ	5,020,000	5,000,000	20,000 F
Fixed support costs	9,638,400	Not applicable	Not applicable	Not applicable
Forecasted operating income	$ 141,600	$10,964,000	$ 9,520,000	$1,444,000 U

ᵃ54,000 × $500.
ᵇ50,000 × ($137 + $42 + $25).
ᶜ54,000 × ($137 + $42 + $25).
ᵈTotal budgeted fixed costs.

B. Following are possible explanations for each of the variances (you may have thought of others):

- The revenue variance is the biggest problem for Summer Select. Instead of selling the furniture for $500 per set, the company got average revenue of $472.22 ($25,500,000 ÷ 54,000). It is possible that weather or economic factors reduced demand, and so the furniture was discounted during the season. It is also possible that sales volumes were better than expected because of the discounted price. The volume is larger than budgeted, but with the reduced selling price, a large unfavourable revenue variance occurred.

- Variable production costs might be lower than the flexible budget because prices for direct materials, direct labour, or variable overhead costs were lower than budget. Or, the use of materials or labour might have been more efficient than in the budget. For example, less scrap might have occurred, or employees might have been more productive than anticipated. Other types of variable production costs might also have been lower than budget. For example, machinery might have required fewer repairs than expected. Also, economies of scale may have been introduced, such as fewer setup costs because production runs were longer, or direct materials costs may have been lower because of volume discounts. However, the favourable variance could possibly signal a reduction in quality, which could create a problem with future sales.

- Fixed production costs were slightly less than expected. The $20,000 variance is a small percentage of the budgeted fixed production costs, so it might be a random variation in cost.

- Fixed support costs might have been lower than the budget for many different reasons: unexpected decreases in the costs of fixed items such as computer software, better purchase prices for office supplies, or outsourcing of services. It is important to keep in mind that the variances in Part A are net amounts. Most likely, each cost category includes some favourable and some unfavourable variances. A relatively small net variance could consist of two or more large offsetting items.

C. The following list contains possible questions (you may think of others):

1. Why were prices discounted, and will the new price carry over to the next period?
2. Is the favourable variance in variable production costs due to changes in the quality of materials? How did the savings arise?
3. Were any fixed production costs either much larger or much smaller than expected?

QUESTIONS

10.1 Explain how the following budgets relate to each other: revenue budget, production budget, and direct materials budget.

10.2 Explain the relationship between an organization's budget and its vision, core competencies, risk preferences, strategies, and operating plans.

10.3 What are the objectives of participative budgeting?

10.4 What distinguishes zero-based budgeting from other types of budgeting?

10.5 How are a master budget and a flexible budget related?

10.6 What methods do organizations use to minimize budgetary slack?

10.7 What adjustments should be made to static budgets before they are used for management performance evaluation?

10.8 What are some of the challenges that organizations face when allocating budget authority and responsibility?

10.9 Snow Blowers produces and sells snow blowers. Production levels are high in the summer and beginning of fall and then taper off through the winter. Sales are high in the fall and early winter and then taper off in the spring. Explain why preparing a cash budget might be particularly important for Snow Blowers.

10.10 Describe the types of information that managers use to develop budgets.

10.11 Discuss the similarities and differences between annual budgets and rolling budgets.

10.12 How are budgets related to organizational strategies?

10.13 Define in your own words budgetary slack and budget ratcheting.

10.14 Why does preparation of a master budget often begin with the sales forecast?

10.15 What tensions could arise if top management set unrealistically high goals?

MULTIPLE-CHOICE QUESTIONS

10.16 Sawdust Inc. wants to reduce its inventory of a particular direct material by 40%. The inventory at the beginning of the budget period is 120,000 litres at $9.90 per litre. The production budget requires the company to manufacture 84,000 units of output next month. Each of these units requires 2.5 litres of the direct material. If the budgeted cost of this direct material is $10.00 per litre, what amount should the purchases budget include for this direct material for next month?
a. $ 900,000
b. $1,632,000
c. $1,380,000
d. $1,620,000
e. $2,580,000

10.17 The most important difference between a master budget and a flexible budget is that the master budget is
a. Prepared by the head office while flexible budgets are prepared in each division.
b. Based on planned volume while the flexible budget is based on actual volume.
c. Based on actual volume while the flexible budget is based on planned volume.

d. Based on standard price while the flexible budget is based on actual price.
e. Based on actual price while the flexible budget is based on standard price.

10.18 Lynn Company uses a standard cost system. Overhead is applied on the basis of direct labour hours (DLH), and the annual practical capacity of 42,000 DLH is used in establishing the standard overhead rates. The following summarizes budget and actual data for the past year:

	Budget	Actual
Units produced	100,000	92,000
Direct materials (kg)	50,000	47,840
Direct labour hours (DLH)	40,000	37,720
Production costs:		
Direct materials	$200,000	$188,968
Direct labour	$500,000	$471,500
Variable factory overhead	$ 80,000ᵃ	$ 84,640
Fixed factory overhead	$160,000ᵃ	$162,000

ᵃApplied

During the year, 90,000 units were sold. There were no beginning or ending work-in-process inventories, but there were 3,000 units of finished goods on hand at the end of the year.

The direct materials flexible budget variance is
a. $11,032 favourable
b. $ 8,968 unfavourable
c. $ 4,968 unfavourable
d. $ 2,968 unfavourable
e. $ 0

10.19 Bluebird Company uses a standard cost system under which overhead is applied on the basis of direct labour hours (DLH). The following information is summarized from its preliminary budget on manufacturing costs:

Production activity	45,000 DLH	50,000 DLH
Factory overhead:		
Indirect materials	$135,000	$150,000
Indirect labour	96,000	100,000
Utilities	10,000	11,000
Rent	80,000	80,000
Amortization	25,000	25,000
Miscellaneous	24,500	26,500
Total factory overhead	$370,500	$392,500

The flexible budget for total factory overhead can be expressed as
a. $ 17,250 + $7.85 per DLH
b. $105,000 + $5.90 per DLH
c. $105,000 + $5.75 per DLH
d. $105,000 + $4.40 per DLH
e. $172,500 + $4.40 per DLH

10.20 DeBerg Company has developed the following sales projections for its second and third quarters:

May	$100,000
June	120,000
July	140,000
August	160,000
September	150,000
October	130,000

Normal cash collection experience has been that 50% of sales are collected during the month of sale and 45% in the month following sale. The remaining 5% of sales is never collected. DeBerg's budgeted cash collections for the third calendar quarter are
a. $360,000
b. $427,500
c. $414,000
d. $440,000
e. $450,000

EXERCISES

10.21 **Revenue Budget, Services** The Evergreen Children's Clinic provided 20,000 doctor visits and 15,000 flu vaccinations last year. The average fee per doctor visit was $20, and the average fee for flu shots was $10. The manager of the clinic believes that by advertising in local School Advisory Council bulletins, doctor visits could increase by 10%, but flu shots would probably be unaffected.

LO2

REQUIRED   A. Prepare a revenue budget assuming that no advertising will be done.
B. Prepare a revenue budget assuming that the advertising campaign will be undertaken.

10.22 **Sales Forecasts** Golden Oldies sells CDs of formerly popular singers and groups. Its customers tend to be middle age or older, so the firm advertises on TV, in magazines, and through direct mailing of catalogues. On average, it sells to four customers for every 1,000 people watching a TV commercial. These customers reply within two weeks of the time the commercial is shown. Catalogues are always sent out at the end of each month because people tend to pay their bills at that time. Research shows that 0.5% of the catalogues will result in a purchase during the month following the mailing. Magazine advertisements generate about 25 responses per 10,000 subscribers in the month the magazine is published, 6 responses per 10,000 subscribers in the month after publication, and 1 response per 10,000 in the second month following publication.

LO2

Golden Oldies is currently marketing the rock group "Beancounters." Advertisements will be placed in the February issue of magazines having total subscribers of 6,500,000. It will also send out 800,000 catalogues in February. In addition, 20 late-night TV commercials will air in the first two weeks of February. The commercials should reach 18 million viewers.

REQUIRED   Calculate the budgeted number of Beancounters CDs sold per month for February through April, assuming no other sales in March and April.

10.23 Production Budget The sales forecast for birdhouses built by Ryan Enterprises follows. Beginning inventory for the year is expected to be 10,000 birdhouses, and the production manager prefers to maintain an ending inventory of 20% of the next quarter's sales.

Quarter	Number of Birdhouses
First	10,000
Second	30,000
Third	35,000
Fourth	50,000

REQUIRED Prepare a quarterly production budget. Assume that the sales forecast for the first quarter of the following year is the same as the first quarter forecast for this year.

10.24 Retail Inventory Purchases Budget Chang's Jeans 'n Tees is a retailer specializing in designer jeans and T-shirts. The company expects to sell 10,000 pairs of jeans each quarter in the first two quarters, 20,000 pairs in the third quarter, and 15,000 in the fourth quarter. For T-shirts, sales are expected to be 20,000 each quarter for the first two quarters, 35,000 in the third quarter, and 25,000 in the fourth quarter. Managers would like to maintain an ending inventory equal to 25% of next quarter's sales, but they expect to have only 2,000 pairs of jeans and 3,000 T-shirts in beginning inventory.

REQUIRED Prepare a quarterly purchases budget for jeans and T-shirts. Assume that the sales forecast for the first quarter of the following year is the same as the first quarter forecast for this year.

10.25 Direct Materials Purchases Budget The manager of Parton's Pottery Company believes that the company will sell 800 place settings of pottery dinnerware next month. She expects to have 100 place settings in finished goods inventory at the beginning of the month and would like to have 200 place settings in ending inventory. Each place setting requires 3 kilograms of clay. The manager expects to have 700 kilograms of clay on hand at the beginning of the month, but she would like to decrease ending inventory to 600 kilograms.

REQUIRED How many kilograms of material will need to be purchased to meet these requirements?

10.26 Production Budget Upward Inc. has projected sales to be 10,000 units in January; 12,000 units in February; 8,000 units in March; 10,000 units in April; and 12,000 units in May. There are 900 units on hand on January 1. Management has determined that it needs to carry 5% of the following month's sales in ending inventory.

REQUIRED Prepare a production budget for the first quarter, by month and in total.

10.27 Direct Materials Budget Refer to Upward Inc. in Exercise 10.26. Assume that each unit requires 4 litres of raw materials. There are 6,000 litres of raw materials on hand at January 1. Management has decided that raw materials ending inventory should be 15% of next month's production needs. Upward Inc. pays $1.50 per litre for raw materials.

REQUIRED Prepare a raw materials budget for the first quarter, by month and in total. Include quantity of materials to purchase and cost for the purchases.

10.28 Production Budget Sharpe Co. has projected sales as follows:

Month	Units
July	40,000
August	50,000
September	70,000
October	50,000
November	30,000

Sharpe Co. always holds 4% of the next month's sales in ending inventory.

REQUIRED Prepare a production budget for the third quarter, by month and in total.

10.29 Direct Materials Budget Refer to Sharpe Co. in Exercise 10.28. Assume that each unit produced uses 3 grams of raw materials and that Sharpe Co. maintains ending inventory equal to 5% of next month's usage. Sharpe Co. pays $2.50 per gram for the raw materials.

REQUIRED Prepare a raw materials budget for the third quarter, by month and in total. Include quantity of materials to purchase and the cost of the purchasing.

10.30 Production, Direct Materials, and Direct Labour Budgets Seer Manufacturing has projected sales of its product for the

LO 2   next six months as follows:

January	40 units
February	90 units
March	100 units
April	80 units
May	30 units
June	70 units

The product sells for $100, variable expenses are $70 per unit, and fixed expenses are $1,500 per month. The finished product requires three units of raw material and 10 hours of direct labour. The company tries to maintain an ending inventory of finished goods equal to the next two months of sales and an ending inventory of raw materials equal to half of the current month's usage.

REQUIRED **A.** Prepare a production budget for February, March, and April.

B. Prepare a forecast of the units of direct materials required for February, March, and April.

C. Prepare a direct labour hours budget for February, March, and April.

10.31 Production, Labour, Materials, and Sales Budgets Bullen & Company makes and sells high-quality glare filters for

LO 1, LO 2   microcomputer monitors. John Crane, controller, is responsible for preparing Bullen's master budget and has assembled the following data for 2016.

The direct labour rate includes wages and all employee-related benefits and the employer's share of Canada Pension Plan (CPP) and Employment Insurance (EI). Labour-saving machinery will be fully operational by March. Also, as of March 1, the company's union contract calls for an increase in direct labour wages that is included in the direct labour rate.

Bullen expects to have 10,000 glare filters in inventory at December 31, 2015, and has a policy of carrying 50% of the following month's projected sales in inventory.

	2016			
	January	**February**	**March**	**April**
Estimated unit sales	20,000	24,000	16,000	18,000
Sales price per unit	$80	$80	$75	$75
Direct labour hours per unit	4.0	4.0	3.5	3.5
Direct labour hourly rate	$15	$15	$16	$16
Direct materials cost per unit	$10	$10	$10	$10

REQUIRED **A.** Prepare the following budgets for Bullen & Company for the first quarter of 2016. Be sure to show supporting calculations: (1) production budget in units, (2) direct labour budget in hours, (3) direct materials budget, and (4) sales budget.

B. Calculate the total budgeted contribution margin for Bullen & Company for the first quarter of 2016. Be sure to show supporting calculations.

C. Discuss at least three behavioural considerations in the profit-planning and budgeting process.

10.32 Production Budget, Direct Material Resource Requirements Ryan Manufacturing must budget a particular direct

LO 2   material very carefully because of its scarcity and its cost. One unit of this material is used to produce one unit of finished product, and all direct material is added at the beginning of production. Beginning inventory data are as follows:

Direct materials	1,200 units
Work in process	400 units
Finished goods	2,000 units

The CEO developed a strategic plan to increase sales this period to 14,000 units. To protect against inventory shortages, she would like to double finished goods, work-in-process, and direct materials inventories.

REQUIRED **A.** How many units must be completed to achieve these goals?

B. How many units must be placed into production to achieve these goals?

C. How many units of direct materials must be purchased to achieve these goals?

D. Assume that Ryan's purchasing agent is certain that only 12,000 units of this material can be acquired next period. If the firm holds to its goal for ending inventories, how many units can be sold?

10.33 Cash Collections Schedule Downward Inc. has budgeted sales for the second quarter of $400,000 for April; $525,000 for May; and $600,000 for June. Normally, 20% are cash sales and 80% of sales are on account. As well, 30% of the sales on account are normally collected during the month of sale, 50% in the following month, and 20% in the second month following sale. The accounts receivable balance as of April 1 is $250,000.

L03

REQUIRED   Prepare the schedule of cash collections for the second quarter by month and in total.

10.34 Cash Collections Schedule DeBerg Company has the following sales projections for its second and third quarters:

L03

April	$100,000
May	$120,000
June	$140,000
July	$160,000
August	$150,000
September	$130,000

Normal cash collection experience has been that 50% of sales are collected during the month of sale, 30% in the month following sale, and 15% in the second month following sale. The remaining 5% of sales is never collected.

REQUIRED   Prepare the schedule of cash collections for the third quarter, by month and in total.

10.35 Static and Flexible Budgets, Variances, Information Quality The photocopying department in a community college has budgeted monthly costs at $40,000 per month plus $7 per student. Normally 800 students are enrolled. During January there were 730 students (which is within the relevant range). At the end of the month, actual fixed costs were $42,000, and variable costs were $3,650.

L02, L04, L05

REQUIRED   **A.** Develop a static budget for photocopying costs based on 800 students.
B. Calculate the January static budget variance for fixed and variable photocopying costs.
C. Develop a flexible budget for the actual volume of students in January.
D. Calculate the January flexible budget variance for fixed and variable photocopying costs.
E. Which variance information—Part (B) or (D)—is of higher quality? Explain.

10.36 Cumulative Exercise (Chapter 2): Flexible Budget, Regression Analysis The CEO of Central Industries has requested a forecast for next month's maintenance costs. Three possible levels of operations and potential cost drivers are as follows (all within the relevant range):

L04

www.wiley.com/
go/eldenburgcanada

Units of output	1,350	1,710	2,000
Direct labour hours	215	330	270
Machine setups	50	62	70

Refer to the information in Exercise 2.41. Data are available on the Wiley website at www.wiley.com/go/eldenburgcanada.

REQUIRED   **A.** If you have not already done so, perform a regression analysis using the most appropriate cost driver for estimating maintenance costs. Write the cost function.
B. Use the cost function from Part A to develop a flexible budget for the three possible levels of operations.

10.37 Meals Budget, Zero-Based Budgeting Explore your personal meals costs by examining your bank account records, credit card bills, or other financial information for the last month.

L03, L06

REQUIRED   **A.** Use your last month's financial information to develop an estimate for the cost of meals (groceries and meals eaten away from home) for next month.
B. Develop an estimate for next month's meals costs using zero-based budgeting. Decide the kinds of food and types of meals you will eat and then develop estimated costs for the groceries and meals eaten away from home.
C. Explain what happened to your budget when you used zero-based budgeting. List one advantage and one disadvantage of using zero-based budgeting for your meals costs.

10.38 Cash Receipts Budget Celina is developing a forecast for cash receipts for the first quarter of the year. Credit sales for the quarter are estimated to be $640,000. The accounts receivable balance from the fourth quarter of the prior year is $600,000. All other accounts receivable from the prior year have been collected or written off. On average, collections of 50% occur during the quarter, 30% in the next quarter, and 15% two quarters after a sale. At the end of the year, 5% are written off as uncollectible.

L03

REQUIRED   Calculate the budgeted cash receipts for the first quarter from credit sales.

10.39 Flexible Budget Variances, Profit Effect of Market Share Decline Here are data for the stove division of Appliances Now, which produces and sells a complete line of kitchen stoves:

LO2, LO3, LO4

(In thousands)	Budget	Actual
Revenue	$16,491	$17,480
Variable production costs	5,892	6,451
Fixed manufacturing costs	1,977	2,032
Variable selling expenses	456	550
Fixed selling expenses	1,275	1,268
Administrative expenses	4,773	5,550
Operating income	$2,118	$1,629

The budget, set at the beginning of the year, was based on estimates of sales and costs. Administrative expenses include charges by corporate headquarters for providing strategic guidance. These fixed costs are allocated to divisions using revenues as the allocation base.

REQUIRED
A. Assume that a different volume of stoves was sold than was budgeted, and prepare a flexible budget using the change in revenue to adjust the variable costs. Calculate budget variances.

B. Due to a booming economy, the stove division's unit sales were higher than anticipated, even though the division's share of the stove market fell from 22% to 20% during the year. Using information from the flexible budget, estimate the impact on profits of the decline in market share. (*Hint*: First estimate what the total sales should have been.)

10.40 Purchase, Cost of Goods Sold, and Cash Collection Budgets The Zel Company operates at local flea markets. It has budgeted the following sales for the indicated months:

LO2, LO3

	June	July	August
Sales on account	$1,500,000	$1,600,000	$1,700,000
Cash sales	200,000	210,000	220,000
Total sales	$1,700,000	$1,810,000	$1,920,000

Zel's success in this specialty market is due in large part to the extension of credit terms and the budgeting techniques implemented by the firm's owner, Barbara Zel. Ms. Zel is a recycler; that is, she collects her merchandise daily at neighbourhood garage sales and sells the merchandise weekly at regional flea markets. All merchandise is marked up to sell at its invoice cost (as purchased at garage sales) plus 25%. Stated differently, cost is 80% of selling price. Merchandise inventories at the beginning of each month are 30% of that month's forecasted cost of goods sold. With respect to sales on account, 40% of receivables are collected in the month of sale, 50% are collected in the following month, and 10% are never collected.

REQUIRED
A. What is the anticipated cost of goods sold for June?
B. What is the beginning inventory for July expected to be?
C. What are the July purchases expected to be?
D. What are the forecasted July cash collections?

10.41 Direct Materials Budgeted Payments New Ventures intends to start business on January 1. Production plans for the first four months of operations are as follows:

LO2, LO3

January	20,000 units
February	50,000 units
March	70,000 units
April	70,000 units

Each unit requires 2 kilograms of material. The firm would like to end each month with enough raw material inventory on hand to cover 25% of the following month's production needs. The material costs $7 per kilogram. Management anticipates being able to pay for 40% of the purchases in the month of purchase. The firm will receive a 10% discount for these early payments. Management anticipates having to defer payment to the next month on 60% of the firm's purchases. No discount will be taken on these late payments. The business starts with no inventories on January 1.

REQUIRED Determine the budgeted payments for purchases of materials for each of the first three months of operations.

10.42 Cash Budget for Revenues and Expenses Myrna Manufacturing, located in France, has projected sales in units for
LO2, LO3 four months of operations as follows:

January	25,000
February	30,000
March	32,000
April	35,000

The product sells for €18 per unit. Twenty-five percent of the customers are expected to pay in the month of sale and take a 3% discount; 70% are expected to pay in the month following sale. The remaining 5% will never pay.

It takes 2 kilograms of materials to produce a unit of product. The materials cost €0.75 per kilogram. In January, no raw materials are in beginning inventories, but managers want to end each month with enough materials for 20% of the next month's production. The firm pays for 60% of its materials purchases in the month of purchase and 40% in the following month.

It takes 0.5 hour of labour to produce each unit. Labour is paid €15.00 per hour and is paid in the same month as worked. Overhead is estimated to be €2.00 per unit plus €25,000 per month (including amortization of €12,000). Overhead costs are paid as they are incurred.

Myrna will begin January with no finished goods or work-in-process inventory. The managers want to end each month with 25% of the following month's sales in finished goods inventory. They will end each month with no work in process.

REQUIRED Prepare a cash budget listing cash receipts and disbursements for February. The firm will begin February with a cash balance of €80,000.

10.43 Flexible Budget and Variances, Performance Measurement, Reasons for Variances Play Time Toys is organized into
LO1, LO4, two major divisions: marketing and production. The production division is further divided into three departments:
LO5, LO6 puzzles, dolls, and video games. Each production department has its own manager.

The company's management believes that all costs must be covered by sales of the three product lines. Therefore, a portion of headquarters, marketing, and production division costs are allocated to each product line.

The company's accountant prepared the following performance report for the manager of the dolls production department:

PERFORMANCE REPORT—DOLLS PRODUCTION DEPARTMENT
(Volumes and total dollar amounts are in thousands)

	Cost Forecasts	Budget	Actual	Variance
Sales volume	1,000	1,000	1,100	100 F
Revenue	$12.00/unit	$12,000	$12,400	$ 400 F
Direct materials	2.00/unit	2,000	2,100	(100) U
Direct labour	1.00/unit	1,000	1,225	(225) U
Variable factory overhead	1.00/unit	1,000	1,100	(100) U
Fixed factory overhead	0.80/unit	800	1,020	(220) U
Production division overhead	0.10/unit	100	105	(5) U
Headquarters	0.20/unit	200	220	(20) U
Marketing	0.50/unit	500	550	(50) U
Operating income	$ 6.40/unit	$ 6,400	$ 6,080	$(320) U

REQUIRED **A.** Is Play Time using a static budget or a flexible budget to calculate variances? Explain. Do you agree with using this approach? Why or why not?

B. Develop an appropriate benchmark for evaluating the performance of the dolls production department. Decide whether to include or exclude each cost category and explain your decisions.

C. Use the benchmark you created in Part B to calculate variances.

D. Review the variances from Part C. Briefly describe the types of operating or budgeting problems that might have caused these variances.

10.44 Prepare Cash Budget A university student, Brad Worth, plans to sell atomic alarm clocks with CD players over the
LO3 Internet and by mail order to help pay his expenses during the fall semester. He buys the clocks for $32 and sells them for $50. If payment by cheque accompanies the mail orders (estimated to be 40% of sales), he gives

a 10% discount. If customers include a credit card number for either Internet or mail order sales (30% of sales), customers receive a 5% discount. The collections are estimated:

One month following	15%
Two months following	6%
Three months following	4%
Uncollectible	5%

Sales forecasts are as follows:

September	120 units
October	220 units
November	320 units
December	400 units
January	out of the business

Brad plans to pay his supplier 50% in the month of purchase and 50% in the following month. A 6% discount is granted on payments made in the month of purchase; however, he will not be able to take any discounts on September purchases because of cash flow constraints. All September purchases will be paid for in October.

He has 50 clocks on hand (purchased in August and to be paid for in September) and plans to maintain enough end-of-month inventory to meet 70% of the next month's sales.

REQUIRED   **A.** Prepare schedules for monthly budgeted cash receipts and cash disbursements for this venture. During which months will Brad need to finance purchases?

B. Brad planned simply to write off the uncollectibles. However, his accounting professor suggested that he turn them over to a collection agency. How much could Brad let the collection agency keep so that he would be no worse off?

10.45 **Production Budget, Flexible Budget, Rolling Budget** The sales forecast for ceramic pottery handcrafted by Fergie Industries follows. Beginning inventory for the year is expected to be 1,000 ceramic bowls, and the production manager prefers to maintain an ending inventory of 10% of the next quarter's sales.

LO2, LO4, LO7

Quarter	Number of Ceramic Bowls
First	2,000
Second	3,000
Third	4,500
Fourth	6,750

REQUIRED   **A.** Prepare a production budget by quarter and for the year in total. Assume that the sales forecast for the first quarter of the following year is expected to be 10% higher than the first quarter of this year.

B. If actual first quarter sales were 5% higher than forecasted, should the production manager be concerned? Evaluate ending inventory requirements.

C. Prepare an adjusted production budget for the remaining three quarters based on the actual sales. (*Hint:* The original forecast is based on sales increasing by 50% each quarter.)

10.46 **Direct Materials Purchases Budget, Flexible Budget** The manager of Safe Keeping Wallets believes that the company will sell 500 designer credit card safe wallets next month. She expects to have 50 wallets in finished goods inventory at the beginning of the month and would like to have 100 wallets in ending inventory. Each wallet requires 0.25 metres of leather. The manager expects to have 75 metres of leather on hand at the beginning of the month, but she would like to decrease ending inventory to 25 metres. The estimated cost per metre of leather is $30.

LO2, LO4, LO5

REQUIRED   **A.** How many metres of leather will need to be purchased to meet these requirements? What is the estimated cost?

B. During the month, 480 wallets were sold. Prepare a direct materials purchases budget for this level of sales.

C. Ninety metres of leather were purchased at a total cost of $2,430 (10% per metre discount based on quantity and cash payment). Compare these results to the budgets prepared in A. and B. Be sure to consider ending inventory requirements and the cost of the leather.

10.47 **Sales, Materials, Production, and Labour Budgets, Flexible Budgets, Motivation** Mike's Bikes makes and sells high-quality replacement gears for mountain bikes. Mike Speedway, controller, is responsible for preparing the master budget and has assembled the following data for 2016.

LO1, LO2, LO4, LO6

The direct labour rate includes wages and all employee-related benefits and the employer's share of Canada Pension Plan (CPP) and Employment Insurance (EI). Labour-saving machinery will be fully operational by February. Also, as of March 1, the company's union contract calls for an increase in direct labour wages that is included in the direct labour rate.

Mike's Bikes expects to have 100 gear units in inventory at December 31, 2015, and has a policy of carrying 5% of the following month's projected sales in inventory during the first quarter of the year.

	2016			
	January	**February**	**March**	**April**
Estimated unit sales	800	1,000	2,000	2,400
Sales price per unit	$30	$30	$25	$25
Direct labour hours per unit	0.75	0.5	0.5	0.5
Direct labour hourly rate	$16	$16	$18	$18
Direct materials cost per unit	$5	$5	$5	$5

Required **A.** Prepare the following budgets for Mike's Bikes for the first quarter of 2016. Be sure to show supporting calculations: (1) sales budget, (2) production budget in units, (3) direct materials budget in units and cost, and (4) direct labour budget in hours.

B. Calculate the total budgeted contribution margin for Mike's Bikes for the first quarter of 2016. Be sure to show supporting calculations.

C. Assume that due to decreasing gas prices, more people are expected to drive (not bike) during the first quarter of 2016. The revised estimated sales for replacement gear units is 10% lower. Prepare new budgets based on this revised estimate.

D. If the actual sales in January are 750 gears, which budget would you use to evaluate performance? Using a rolling budget approach, what adjustments would you make to the remaining budgets?

E. Discuss at least three behavioural considerations in the profit-planning and budgeting process.

10.48 **Cash Budget for Revenues and Expenses** Hammocks and Swings, Ltd. has projected sales in units for four months of operations as follows:

LO2, LO3, LO4, LO6

April	20,000
May	25,000
June	35,000
July	40,000
August	30,000

The hammocks sell for $35 each. Fifty-five percent of the customers are expected to pay in the month of sale and take a 3% discount; 30% are expected to pay in the month following the sale; 13% are expected to pay two months following the sale. The remaining 2% will never pay. February sales totaled $70,000 and March sales totaled $350,000.

It takes 3 metres of material to produce a hammock. The material cost is $5 per metre. In April, 10,000 metres of material are in beginning inventory; managers want to end each month with enough materials for 5% of the next month's production. The firm pays for 75% of its material purchases in the month of purchase and 25% in the following month. Materials paid for within the month of purchase are eligible for a 2% discount.

It takes hours of 0.75 hours of labour to produce each hammock. Labour is paid $18 per hour and is paid in the same month as worked. Overhead is estimated to be $1.50 per unit plus $15,000 per month (including depreciation of $6,500). Overhead costs are paid as they are incurred.

Hammocks and Swings will begin April with 2,000 hammocks in finished goods inventory and no work-in-process inventory. The managers want to end each month with 10% of the following month's sales in finished goods inventory. They will end each month with no work in process.

Selling and administrative expenses are estimated to be $0.50 per hammock sold plus $20,000 per month (including depreciation of $7,500).

Required   **A.** Prepare a cash budget listing cash receipts and disbursements for the second quarter of the year by month and in total. The firm will begin April with a cash balance of $65,000. (*Hint:* It would be helpful to use Excel to prepare this budget. Use an input section for the basic information. Then, this section can be changed to answer the following requirements.)

B. In March, the long range weather forecasts call for an early spring with unseasonably warm temperatures. As a result, the managers of Hammocks and Swings revised the sales forecast to the following:

April	30,000
May	40,000
June	35,000
July	30,000
August	25,000

Prepare a new cash budget to help managers plan for this change.

C. As a result of the expected increase in sales, managers expect the following changes: Forty-five percent of customers will pay in the month of sale and take the 3% discount, 30% will pay in the month following the sale; 18% will pay in the second month following the sale; 5% will pay in the third month following the sale; and 2% will remain uncollectible. Adjust the cash budget to reflect this additional information.

D. What advice will you give to the managers of Hammocks and Swings?

E. In the past, Hammocks and Swings has negotiated a line of credit with their bank. The terms of this agreement state an annual interest rate of 3%, borrowing must occur at the start of a month and repayment is accepted only at month-end; a minimum cash balance of $25,000 must be maintained to qualify for the line of credit. There are no restrictions on the amount that can be borrowed; however, there is a minimum repayment amount of 1% of the outstanding loan. Include this information in a cash budget for Hammock and Swings managers. What advice will you give?

PROBLEMS

10.49 **Cumulative Problem (Chapter 3): Budgeted Financial Statements, Bad Debts, Breakeven** Walker Products fell behind in paying its vendors, and it now has a poor credit rating. Consequently, all suppliers demand cash on delivery (even employees are paid on a daily basis). The firm has a note payable on which principal payments have been suspended. The firm must pay interest on this note at the rate of 1.5% of the beginning balance. If Walker misses even one interest payment, the bank will initiate bankruptcy proceedings. The following is Walker's balance sheet as of October 1.

Assets		Liabilities and Equity	
Cash	$ 7,000	Notes payable	$ 90,000
Accounts receivable (net)	24,000	Common stock	75,000
Inventory	39,000	Retained earnings (deficit)	(15,000)
Plant & equipment (net)	80,000	Total liabilities and equity	$150,000
Total assets	$150,000		

Walker sells its product for $25 per unit. The purchase cost is $15 per unit. Budgeted sales for October are 2,500 units, and ending budgeted inventory is 2,000 units. Typically, 60% of Walker's customers pay in the month of sale, 35% in the month following purchase, and 5% never pay.

Walker's employees are paid strictly on commission, based on 10% of sales. The firm depreciates its fixed assets at the rate of $2,000 per month. All other selling and administrative costs amount to $15,000 per month.

REQUIRED   **A.** Prepare a cash receipts and disbursements budget for October.

B. Prepare a budgeted income statement for October.

C. Prepare the budgeted balance sheet as of the end of October.

D. Is the firm operating at a profit or loss? What level of sales is needed to break even? (*Hint:* Treat commissions and expected bad debts as variable costs.)

10.50 **Master Budget, Budgeted Financial Statements, Solve for Unknown** Anchor Manufacturing has forecasted sales of

5,000 units of its product at $75 each for the next month. Beginning inventory consists of 800 grams of direct materials and 300 units of finished goods. The managers would like to end the month with 1,200 grams of raw materials, no units in work in process, and 500 units in finished goods. The firm accounts for inventory using the first-in, first-out (FIFO) method.

   Three grams of materials are required per unit of product manufactured. Each unit also requires two hours of direct labour time. Materials cost $0.50 per gram, and labour is paid $15 per hour. Forecasted overhead is $20,000 plus $2 per unit manufactured. Sales commissions are paid at the rate of $1 per unit, and administrative costs are estimated to be $15,000 for the month.

   The firm's customers usually pay 25% of their bill in the month of the sale and 73% in the next month (the other 2% are generally uncollectible). The firm pays its materials suppliers 70% in the month of purchase and 30% in the following month. Labourers, sales personnel, administrators, and all overhead purchases are paid in the month that services are received. Overhead costs include $5,000 of depreciation on plant and equipment. Sales last month were $240,000, and direct materials purchases were $6,000. A partially complete balance sheet as of the beginning of the month is given here.

Assets		Liabilities and Equity	
Cash	$3,000	Accounts payable	$?
Accounts receivable	?	Common stock	200,000
Direct materials inventory	400	Retained earnings	?
Work-in-process inventory	0	**Total liabilities**	
Finished goods inventory	4,650	**and equity**	$?
Plant & equipment (net)	245,000		
Total assets	**$?**		

REQUIRED   **A.** Complete the beginning balance sheet.
   B. Prepare a master budget, including budgeted financial statements, for next month.
   C. Analyze the income statement, cash budgets, and balance sheet—particularly the changes in receivables and inventory. What changes would you suggest to improve Anchor's performance?

10.51 **Budgeting for Next Semester, Assumptions, Monitoring** Suppose a friend asks you to help her prepare a budget for

the next semester.
   A. Assuming that you followed a process similar to that presented in this chapter, which budgets would you help your friend prepare? Explain your choices.

REQUIRED   **B.** Create a list of information needed to complete the various budgets. Identify which pieces of information need to be estimated.

   C. Create a list of the assumptions your friend will need to make for estimating the necessary information.
   D. How should your friend monitor her budget performance throughout the semester? Write an explanation that your friend, who is not familiar with accounting, will understand.

10.52 **Performance Benchmark, Variances, and Analysis** Central City Clinic is an outpatient clinic that provides visiting

nurses for elderly patients in their homes. A homemaker who cleans and performs other household tasks accompanies each nurse. When the nurses are not visiting clients, they work at the office, preparing for visits. When the homemakers complete their visits, they go home.

   Each year, the clinic receives a budget allotment from Central City. The city does not allow the clinic to spend more than this allotment. The clinic, in turn, allocates its budget among its various programs. The visiting nurse program was authorized (and spent) $250,396 in 2015 and $279,476 in 2016, as follows:

	2015	2016
Nurses	$135,378	$145,019
Homemakers	60,046	71,500
Medical supplies	18,197	21,402
Cleaning supplies	6,894	9,216
Transportation	9,068	11,144
Clinic general overhead	20,813	21,195
Total expenditures	$250,396	$279,476
Home visits	4,312	5,101
Average cost per home visit	$58.07	$54.79

The nursing staff received a 5% increase in salary one-third of the way through 2014. The homemakers did not receive an increase in wages in 2015 or in 2016. The prices of medical supplies increased about 2% during 2016 compared to 2015. The prices of cleaning supplies were relatively constant across the two years.

Transportation is provided by the nurses, who are reimbursed $0.40 per kilometre. The clinic's general overhead is allocated to programs on the basis of budgeted program salaries.

REQUIRED **A.** In this problem, you are not given a budget for 2016. If you want to evaluate performance of the 2016 clinic, what can you use as the basis of a flexible budget to develop a benchmark?

B. Prepare a schedule to evaluate the performance of this program in 2016, using the benchmark suggested in Part A.

C. If you were the general manager of the clinic, what would you like to discuss with the head of the visiting nurse program concerning the 2016 results? Explain.

D. How many patients would have been served in 2016 for $279,476 if costs had been under control?

10.53 **Comprehensive Manufacturing Master Budget Problem** The accountant at Fighting Kites has always prepared a budget that is calculated using only one estimated volume of sales. He has asked you to help him set up a spreadsheet that can be used for sensitivity analysis in the budgeting process. This year, it appears that the company may not meet expectations, which could result in a loss. The accountant is concerned that the company will incur a loss again next year and wants to develop a budget that will easily reflect changes in the assumptions. After gathering information about next year's operations, he will provide information using a what-if sensitivity analysis.

PART 1: SPREADSHEET WITH INPUT BOX, REVENUE AND PRODUCTION BUDGETS

LO2 Following are the assumptions regarding revenues, direct materials and labour costs, and inventory levels:

Direct materials per kite:

Nylon	$10
Ribs	$ 5
String	$ 2

Direct labour:

Hours	Assembly	0.5
	Packing	0.1
Cost per hour	Assembly	$30.00
	Packing	$15.00
Cost per kite	Assembly	$15.00
	Packing	$ 1.50

Inventory information:

	Beginning	Target Ending
Direct materials:		
Nylon	$5,000	$7,000
Ribs	$3,000	$3,200
String	$1,000	$1,200
Finished goods (units)	2,000 kites	2,200 kites
Finished goods (cost)	$97,850	

Revenue assumptions:

Selling price	$75
Volume of kite sales	80,000

REQUIRED **A.** Create a spreadsheet with a data input box at the top. Into this box put all the relevant assumption data. This box should be formatted with a border to separate the input data from the cell-referenced data. Set up each schedule with cell references to information in the data input box. Any changes made to information in this box should be reflected through all the schedules that you set up. As you proceed through Parts 2 and 3 of this problem, more information will be given that needs to be located in the assumptions box, such as next year's estimated variable and fixed manufacturing overhead, as well as support department costs. You will need to leave space in the data input box for this information or add more rows as you develop the spreadsheet.

B. Prepare a revenue budget.

C. Prepare a production budget in units.

D. Prepare the direct materials usage budget and a direct materials purchases budget.

E. Prepare a direct labour budget (in hours and cost).

PART 2: OVERHEAD, ENDING INVENTORY, AND COST OF GOODS SOLD BUDGETS

LO2 Refer to the information for Part 1. Following are estimated manufacturing overhead costs. Both fixed and variable overhead will be allocated based on the number of kites produced:

Estimated variable manufacturing overhead costs:	
Supplies	$160,250
Indirect labour	200,650
Maintenance	80,200
Miscellaneous	40,100
Total variable overhead costs	$481,200
Estimated fixed manufacturing overhead costs:	
Amortization	$211,728
Property taxes	28,872
Insurance	67,368
Plant management	240,600
Fringe benefits	336,840
Miscellaneous	76,992
Total fixed overhead costs	$962,400

REQUIRED **F.** Prepare a manufacturing overhead budget and determine variable and fixed overhead allocation rates by dividing the budgeted overhead by budgeted labour hours for the fixed overhead, and by units for the variable overhead.

G. Prepare a schedule that calculates the unit costs of ending inventory in finished goods, and then prepare the ending inventories budget.

H. Prepare a cost of goods sold budget.

PART 3: BUDGETED INCOME STATEMENT

LO2, LO3 Refer to the information for Parts 1 and 2. Following is the information that the accountant collected about support department costs:

Support department:	Fixed Costs
Administration	$1,034,580
Marketing	620,748
Distribution	310,374
Customer service	103,458
Total support department costs	$2,069,160

REQUIRED **I.** Prepare a support department costs budget.

J. Prepare a budgeted income statement. Assume an income tax rate of 25%.

PART 4: CASH BUDGET WITH BAD DEBTS AND BORROWING

LO3 Refer to the information for Parts 1, 2, and 3. The company's managers budget cash flows on a quarterly basis so that they can plan short-term investments and borrowings.

Kite sales are highest during the spring and summer. Sales are fairly even within each quarter, but sales vary across quarters as follows:

January–March	10%
April–June	50%
July–September	30%
October–December	10%

Accounts receivable at the end of the prior year, consisting of sales made during December, totalled $90,000. Payments from customers are usually received as follows:

Pay during the month goods are received	50%
Pay the next month	47%
Bad debts	3%

The managers plan to maintain beginning inventory quantities during January and February but to increase inventories to the targeted levels by the end of March and maintain those levels throughout the rest of the year. The company pays its vendors 10 days after raw materials are received, so approximately two-thirds of all purchases are paid in the month of production and one-third are paid the following month. Accounts payable at the end of the prior year totalled $13,000. Employee wages and other production costs are paid during the month incurred. Property taxes are paid in two equal installments on March 31 and September 30, and insurance is paid annually on June 30. Support costs are paid evenly throughout the year. Estimated income tax payments are made at the end of each quarter, based on 25% of total estimated taxes for the year.

In addition to customer receipts, the company expects to receive $10,000 in proceeds from the sale of equipment during January. The company also plans to purchase and pay for new equipment costing $50,000 during January.

The company finances its short-term operations with a line of credit from the bank, which had a balance of $150,000 at the end of the prior year. The line of credit agreement requires the company to maintain a minimum cash balance of $100,000 (non-interest-bearing). The company's line of credit requires quarterly interest payments at an annual rate of 5.5%. (For simplicity, assume that all borrowings and repayments occur on the last day of each quarter.)

REQUIRED   **K.** Prepare quarterly budgets for cash receipts, cash disbursements, and short-term financing.

10.54   **Budget Planning Sensitivity Analysis** Refer to the information from Problem 10.49, Parts 1, 2, and 3. The budget

L01, L02, L04

indicates that the company is likely to incur a loss during the next period. The accountant asks you to assist him in developing sensitivity analyses that will help the manager identify possible ways to avoid a loss. To perform sensitivity analysis, you will alter volume of production, volume of sales, selling prices, direct material prices, wage rates, and overhead and support department costs.

REQUIRED   **A.** Identify the assumptions that are relevant for sensitivity analysis. Relevant assumptions are assumptions that the manager could potentially influence by changing the company's operating plans.

B. Identify possible changes in budget assumptions that might eliminate the forecasted loss (i.e., that would lead to a breakeven).

C. Perform sensitivity analysis, using the input section of your spreadsheet to determine a set of assumption changes that would cause budgeted income to break even. Explain your choices.

D. Describe uncertainties and their effects on the assumptions you made in Part A.

10.55   **Comprehensive Restaurant Master Budget Problem**

You are the accountant for Wok and Egg Roll Express. Following are assumptions about sales for the coming month. Wok offers three basic meals: noodle bowls, egg rolls, and rice bowls. Each meal can be prepared with several different meats or with vegetables only. Costs and prices are similar for all varieties of each meal. Prices for noodle bowls are $4.00 each, egg roll meals are $3.00 each, and rice bowls are $3.50 each. Estimated sales for the next month are 200 noodle bowls, 100 egg roll meals, and 500 rice bowls per day.

L01, L02   **PART 1: REVENUE BUDGET, UNCERTAINTIES, REVENUE STRATEGIES**

REQUIRED   **A.** Prepare a revenue budget for the next month, assuming that the month is 30 days long.

B. Discuss factors that affect the budgeted volumes of meals.

C. Identify possible ways the owner could increase total revenues. Discuss the pros and cons of each of your ideas.

L01, L02   **PART 2: DIRECT MATERIALS BUDGET, UNCERTAINTIES, COST CONTROL STRATEGIES**

The owner of Wok and Egg Roll Express has studied the cost of direct materials for each type of meal. He estimates that noodle bowls use about $1.00 in direct materials, egg roll meals use about $0.75, and rice bowls use about $0.90. Food is purchased daily to ensure high quality. Beginning and ending inventory amounts are minimal.

REQUIRED   **D.** Explain why you would not need to prepare a production budget for Wok and Egg Roll Express.

E. Prepare a direct materials usage budget and a direct materials purchases budget.

F. Discuss reasons why actual costs might be different from budgeted costs in Part E.

G. Suppose the prices of food ingredients increase. Identify possible ways the owner could keep food costs within the budget. Discuss drawbacks for each of your ideas.

L01, L02   **PART 3: DIRECT LABOUR BUDGET, UNCERTAINTIES, COST CONTROL STRATEGIES**

The owner of Wok and Egg Roll Express employs cooks and cashiers. The cashiers take orders and collect payment, transfer food from the cooks to customers, and clean tables. Cooks are paid $10 per hour, and cashiers are paid $8 per hour. Wok operates four shifts, and weekdays and weekends are staffed similarly. Following are the shifts and required workers:

Shift	Cooks	Cashiers
10 a.m. to 2 p.m.	2	2
11 a.m. to 2 p.m.	3	3
2 p.m. to 10 p.m.	2	2
5 p.m. to 8 p.m.	3	3

REQUIRED   **H.** Prepare a labour budget showing hours and costs for a month. (Assume 30 days per month.)

I. Discuss reasons why actual labour costs might turn out to be different from budgeted costs in Part H.

J. Identify possible ways the owner could reduce labour costs. Discuss possible drawbacks for each of your ideas.

L01, L02   PART 4: OVERHEAD BUDGET, UNCERTAINTIES, COST CONTROL STRATEGIES

Wok and Egg Roll Express does not separately account for production versus general overhead. Fixed overhead includes production overhead as well as support services and general administration. Variable overhead includes labour-related costs such as payroll taxes and employee benefits. Wok has estimated variable overhead costs as $2.50 per direct labour hour. Following are the estimated fixed overhead costs for one month:

Fixed overhead costs:	
Utilities	$ 1,300
Manager	5,000
Lease	2,000
Miscellaneous	2,500
Total	$10,800

REQUIRED   **K.** Prepare an overhead costs budget for one month.

L. Discuss reasons why actual overhead costs might turn out to be different from budgeted costs in Part K.

M. Identify possible ways the owner could reduce overhead costs. Discuss possible drawbacks for each of your ideas.

L01, L02   PART 5: BUDGETED INCOME STATEMENT, UNCERTAINTIES, PROFIT STRATEGIES

Refer to the information from the preceding budgets. The income statement for Wok and Egg Roll Express consists of revenues less direct costs (direct materials and direct labour) to determine the gross margin. Then the overhead costs are deducted to determine operating income.

REQUIRED   **N.** Prepare a budgeted income statement, ignoring income taxes.

O. What are the major uncertainties in Wok's budget? Explain.

P. Wok's owner would like to increase profits from the store. Suggest several possible ways to accomplish this goal. Explain your reasoning.

10.56   **Preparing Cash Budget from Financial Statements** The Red Midget Company processes and distributes beans. The

L03   beans are packed in 1-kilogram plastic bags and sold to grocery chains for $0.50 each, in boxes of 100 bags. During March, the firm anticipates selling 16,000 boxes (sales in February were 14,000 boxes). Typically, 80% of the firm's customers pay within the month of sale, 18% of the customers pay the month after, and 2% of sales are never collected.

The firm buys beans from local farmers. The farmers are paid $0.20 per kilogram, in cash. Most of the processing is done automatically. Consequently, most ($80,000) of the firm's factory overhead is amortization expense.

The firm advertises heavily. For March, managers expect to publish $75,000 worth of advertisements in popular magazines. This amount is up from February's $60,000 of advertisements. The firm pays for 10% of its advertising in the month the ads are run and 90% in the following month. March's budgeted income statement and statement of cost of goods manufactured and sold follow. All costs and expenses are paid for as incurred, unless specifically indicated otherwise. The firm will begin March with a cash balance of $25,000, and it pays a monthly dividend of $15,000 to the owners.

INCOME STATEMENT

Sales	$800,000
Cost of goods sold	540,000
Gross margin	260,000
Administrative salaries	80,000
Sales commissions	69,000
Advertising	75,000
Bad debts expense	16,000
Operating income	$ 20,000

STATEMENT OF COST OF GOODS MANUFACTURED AND SOLD

Beginning balance direct materials	$ 20,000
Direct materials purchases	330,000
Materials available for use	350,000

Ending balance direct materials	30,000
Direct materials used	320,000
Labour costs incurred	90,000
Overhead costs	115,000
Cost of goods manufactured	525,000
Beginning finished goods balance	45,000
Goods available for sale	570,000
Ending finished goods balance	30,000
Cost of goods sold	$540,000

REQUIRED   From the information provided, prepare a cash budget for March.

10.57 **Traditional Budget Versus Relative Performance Evaluation** Games 'N More operates a chain of retail stores that sell primarily puzzles, board games, and video games. The manager of each store receives a bonus based on annual store results. The company's CEO, Amanda Hryiuk, is currently evaluating last year's performance. Most stores experienced lower than expected sales because of increasing competition from Internet retail companies. In the past, the managers were evaluated based on store results compared to budgets. However, the company's CFO recently attended a seminar on relative performance evaluation and recommended that Amanda consider evaluating manager performance based on how well each store performed relative to other stores in the chain.

LO4, LO5, LO6

Managers are required to place all inventory orders through the corporate purchasing department, to enable the company to take advantage of quantity discounts. However, managers make their own decisions about selling prices, product mix, sales promotions, and staffing levels. The corporate office conducts marketing research, and the store managers meet quarterly to discuss customer purchasing trends and competition. Amanda negotiates with each store manager to develop annual budgets, but she insists on setting challenging budget targets to encourage managers to continuously improve store results. For example, the current year's budgets assumed a 10% increase in sales over the prior year even though the company faced greater competition. In addition, the cost of goods sold budget was set at 60% of sales even though the prior year's average was 65%. Amanda believed the managers could meet this target by increasing their emphasis on higher-margin products.

Amanda decided to investigate the idea of relative performance evaluation by considering the performance of three stores with below-average, average, and above-average results. All 20 of the company's stores have roughly the same amount of retail space. Store occupancy, selling, and administration are primarily fixed costs. Corporate overhead is allocated to each store based on sales revenue. Budgets and results for these stores were as follows for the past year:

	Below-Average		Average		Above-Average	
	Budget	Actual	Budget	Actual	Budget	Actual
Sales	$495,000	$464,000	$737,000	$688,000	$902,000	$926,000
Cost of goods sold	297,000	287,680	442,200	433,440	541,200	620,420
Store occupancy, selling, and administration	150,000	144,000	180,000	169,000	210,000	192,000
Corporate overhead	24,750	32,480	36,850	48,160	45,100	64,820
Income (loss)	$ 23,250	$ (160)	$ 77,950	$ 37,400	$105,700	$ 48,760

REQUIRED   **A.** Analyze the performance of the managers of these three stores under the current performance evaluation system (actual compared to budget):

   1. Should each manager be held responsible for sales plus all of the costs for his or her store? Explain your reasoning.

   2. Calculate variances that would be appropriate for evaluating the performance of each manager.

   3. Based on the variance calculations, which, if any, of the managers should receive a bonus? Explain your reasoning.

   B. Analyze the performance of the managers of these three stores using the following relative performance evaluation system:

   1. Calculate the prior year's actual sales, and then calculate the percent change in actual sales for each store. What does this information suggest about each manager's performance?

   2. Calculate actual cost of goods sold as a percent of sales for each store. What does this information suggest about each manager's performance?

3. Identify several possible reasons why actual fixed costs are different across the three stores. (Assume that all costs other than cost of goods sold are fixed costs.) What do differences in fixed costs suggest about each manager's performance?

4. Based on your preceding analysis, which, if any, of the managers should receive a bonus? Explain your reasoning.

C. Describe the strengths and weaknesses of each performance evaluation system.

MINI-CASES

10.58 **Time Budget, Uncertainties, Performance Evaluation, Priorities** Patricia sighed and briefly closed her eyes. She was frustrated with the reconciliation she was working on. She was sure that she was missing something, but she could not determine what it was. And she felt the clock ticking. Patricia knew that the time budget for this assignment was only three hours, and she had already worked on it for two hours.

LO1, LO4, LO5, LO6

Patricia started with a CPA firm after graduation, three months ago. Her first few assignments had been stressful. She had been a good student in school, and she expected to do well at work, too. But she often felt inadequate here, as though she was supposed to know more than she did. Her supervisor, Ron, told her not to worry too much. He said that her job was to learn and that she would be performing well soon. "All new-hires are slow to begin with," he told her. "Just let me know if you have questions." However, Patricia felt that she had pestered him with enough questions. Most of the time, the answers to her questions seemed so obvious . . . after Ron had answered her.

She looked at the reconciliation again.

REQUIRED **INFORMATION ANALYSIS**

The following questions will help you analyze the information for this problem. Do not turn in your answers to these questions unless your professor asks you to do so.

A. Explain why it might be difficult to establish accurate time budgets for accounting tasks.

B. Provide possible reasons why Patricia's time on this assignment could exceed the budget.

C. Explain why Patricia is reluctant to seek Ron's help on this assignment.

D. Describe how Ron might evaluate Patricia's performance, assuming the following:

1. She seeks his help and completes the assignment in four hours.

2. She does not seek his help and completes the assignment in eight hours.

E. Suppose Patricia does not seek Ron's help and completes the assignment in eight hours.

1. What priorities has Patricia used in making this choice?

2. Has Patricia behaved ethically? Why or why not?

F. What could Patricia learn from this experience that will improve her performance in the future?

Suppose Patricia asked for your advice. Turn in your answers to the following.

REQUIRED **WRITTEN ASSIGNMENT**

G. Use the information you learned from the preceding analyses to write a memo to Patricia with your recommendation. Refer in your memo to the information that would be useful to Patricia.

H. Write one or two paragraphs explaining how you decided what information to include in your memo.

10.59 **Budgeting for a Bequest in a Not-for-Profit Organization, Participative Budgeting** During late 2003, National Public Radio (NPR) in the U.S. announced a $200-million bequest from the estate of Joan B. Kroc. Mrs. Kroc, widow of McDonald's founder Ray A. Kroc, was a long-time supporter of public radio. NPR is a not-for-profit organization that produces and distributes news, talk, and entertainment programming for a worldwide network of more than 770 independent public radio stations.

LO1, LO2, LO6, LO7

At the time of the announcement, NPR management stated that most of the bequest would be placed in an endowment fund, and only the annual earnings would be spent. However, NPR's board of directors had not yet made specific plans about how the funds would be used. The bequest would significantly affect NPR's finances. The current endowment fund contained $35 million, and the organization's annual budget was around $104 million. NPR and its affiliate stations were continually faced with tight operating budgets.

The announcement triggered speculations about how NPR would spend the money. Some people argued that NPR should re-evaluate its strategies, with possible expansion into the Internet or other platforms. A number of public radio station managers wanted part of the funds to support their operations, perhaps through a reduction in NPR programming fees. Approximately half of NPR's annual budget was financed through programming fees. An independent producer wanted to see pay increases for the freelance workers who create NPR programming. Various groups voiced opinions about ways to improve the quality of NPR programming. Some observers were concerned that the large bequest might cause the organization's management to become overly conservative, reducing the likelihood of innovative new programming.

Some people were concerned that the bequest would discourage listener and other support for NPR and its affiliate stations. Others believed that the bequest would have the opposite effect.

Sources: "What Is NPR?" www.npr.org (click "about"); "NPR Receives a Record Bequest of More Than $200 Million," November 6, 2003, www.npr.org/about/press/031106.kroc.html; M. Jurkowitz, "'Extraordinary' $200M Bequest Stuns, Elates NPR Staff," *The Boston Globe*, November 7, 2003; M. Janssen, "Kroc's $200 Million Gift Frees PubRadio's Dreams," November 17, 2003, http://current.org/files/archive-site/npr/npr0309kroc.shtml; and T. Lowry, J. Weber, and C. Yang, "Can NPR Bear the Burden of Wealth?" *BusinessWeek*, December 15, 2003, p. 77.

REQUIRED
A. Discuss why NPR's management should clarify the organization's vision, core competencies, and strategies (see Chapter 1 and Exhibit 1.1) before deciding how to budget the bequest funds.

B. Participative budgeting usually relates only to participation within an organization; however, it might also apply to NPR's negotiations with affiliate stations and freelance workers. Discuss the pros and cons of a participative budgeting approach for NPR's use of the bequest.

C. Suppose NPR decides to use the funds primarily to improve programming quality. Describe how this strategy might be translated into specific items in an annual master budget.

10.60 **Cumulative Mini-Case (Chapter 4): Cash Budget, Sensitivity Analysis, Keep or Drop Customer** Riley Instruments, a rapidly

L01, L02, L03, L04

expanding electronic parts distributor, is in the process of formulating plans for next year. Bill Stockton, the firm's director of marketing, has completed his sales forecast and is confident that sales estimates will be met or exceeded. The following sales figures show the growth expected and will provide the planning basis for other corporate departments.

Month	Forecasted Sales	Month	Forecasted Sales
January	$1,800,000	July	$3,000,000
February	2,000,000	August	3,000,000
March	1,800,000	September	3,200,000
April	2,200,000	October	3,200,000
May	2,500,000	November	3,000,000
June	2,800,000	December	3,400,000

Samantha Carlson, assistant controller, has been given the responsibility for formulating the cash flow projection, a critical element during a period of rapid expansion. The following information will be used in preparing the cash analysis.

1. Riley has experienced an excellent record in accounts receivable collection and expects this trend to continue. Sixty percent of billings are collected in the month after the sale and 40% in the second month after the sale. Uncollectibles are nominal and can be ignored in the analysis.

2. The purchase of electronic parts is Riley's largest expenditure: the cost of these items is equal to 50% of sales. Sixty percent of the parts are received by Riley one month prior to sale and 40% are received during the month of sale.

3. Historically, 80% of accounts payable have been cleared by Riley one month after receipt of purchased parts and the remaining 20% have been cleared two months after receipt.

4. Hourly wages, including fringe benefits, are a function of sales volume and are equal to 20% of the current month's sales. These wages are paid in the month incurred.

5. General and administrative expenses are projected to be $2,640,000 for the next period. These include $480,000 in salaries, $660,000 in product promotions, $240,000 in property taxes, $360,000 for insurance, $300,000 in utilities, and $600,000 in depreciation. All expenses except property taxes are incurred uniformly throughout the year, and property taxes are paid in four equal instalments in the last month of each calendar quarter.

6. Riley makes income tax payments in the first month of each quarter based on the income for the prior quarter. Riley is subject to an effective income tax rate of 40%. Riley's pretax income for the first quarter of the next year is projected to be $612,000.

7. Riley has a corporate policy of maintaining an end-of-month cash balance of $100,000. Cash is invested or borrowed monthly, as necessary to maintain this balance.

REQUIRED   A. Prepare a spreadsheet with the cash receipts and disbursements budget for Riley Instruments by month for the second quarter. Be sure that all receipts, disbursements, and borrowing/investing are presented on a monthly basis. Ignore the interest expense and/or income associated with borrowing/investing.

B. Although this industry has experienced rapid growth over the last few years, competition from outside the country has also increased markedly and is beginning to affect prices. In fact, an offshore electronics manufacturer recently contacted Riley's largest customer and has offered the same electronic product at a lower price. The customer would prefer to stay with Riley, but only if Riley will cut prices by 20%. Assume that half of all sales are to this customer. Perform sensitivity analysis using the cash budget as a flexible budget to determine whether Riley would be better off to reduce prices or to drop the customer. (*Hint:* Adjust costs that vary with sales to reflect the new level and keep fixed costs at the static budget level.)

C. Consider the decision that needs to be made from the following viewpoints: (1) vendors who supply Riley with the parts, (2) direct labour employees, and (3) managers. Would any of these stakeholders be willing to make concessions to help Riley meet the 20% price reduction? Explain. (*Hint:* Consider whether each group would be better off by having sales cut by half or by reducing costs to minimize the effects of the price reduction.)

D. Write a memo detailing your findings and making a recommendation to the CEO of Riley about the decision to drop the customer or to lower prices.

10.61 Integrating Across the Curriculum: Financial Accounting and Attestation: *Prospective Financial Statements,*
LO1, LO2 *Types of Attestation, Assumptions* Delanna's, a privately owned, high-end women's clothing store, has been successful since it was opened five years ago. The owner, Delanna Ricci, wants to open a second store in a nearby city. She has talked with her banker about a possible loan to cover the costs of opening the store. The banker wants Delanna to submit a business plan, including estimated income statements for the first three years for both stores. Delanna already has a line of credit agreement with the bank. During part of each year, she borrows money to finance inventory purchases. She has always paid off the loans by late December, which is the store's busiest time of year.

Last year's income statement for the existing store was as follows. The business is a sole proprietorship, so it does not include a salary expense for Delanna, who manages the store.

Revenues		$632,000
Cost of goods sold		350,000
Gross margin		282,000
Operating expenses		
Employee wages and commissions	$82,000	
Occupancy costs	58,000	
Store supplies	6,000	
Office and miscellaneous expenses	18,000	
Interest expense (line of credit loan)	5,000	
Total operating expenses		169,000
Pretax income		$113,000

Delanna has contacted her CPA firm to help her create estimated income statements that will be submitted to the bank. You have performed quarterly compilations of Delanna's financial statements, which are submitted to the bank under the line of credit agreement. Thus, you are assigned the job of helping Delanna develop financial statements for the new bank loan.

You have not helped a client develop estimated financial statements, but you find the following definitions in one of your old textbooks:

Financial forecast: Prospective financial statements that present expected results based on assumptions about conditions expected to exist and the course of action the entity expects to take. *Financial projection:* Prospective financial statements that present expected results, given one or more hypothetical courses of action.

Conduct research into financial accounting and attestation standards, as needed, to answer the following questions.

REQUIRED
A. Will Delanna's estimated income statements be considered financial forecasts or financial projections? Explain.
B. What alternative types of attestation services can a CPA perform for prospective financial statements? Briefly describe the CPA'S responsibilities for each type of attestation service.
C. Suppose Delanna engaged your firm to perform a compilation. Write a list of questions to ask Delanna to help you gather the information necessary to create the estimated income statements.
D. Discuss how you would use the prior year's income statement to help prepare estimated future income statements for the two stores.
E. The preparation of prospective financial statements requires a set of assumptions, similar to the assumptions needed when preparing a budget. Write a list of assumptions that will be needed to create the estimated income statements.
F. Explain why Delanna is likely to be biased when she provides you with information for the estimated financial statements. Discuss whether you would be able to detect bias as you compile the estimated financial statements.

CHAPTER 11

Standard Costs and Variance Analysis

in brief Accountants produce information that managers use to monitor operations. Standard costs and variances from budgets are an important part of that information. Variances are calculated by comparing standard revenues and costs with actual revenues and costs. Through the analysis of variances, managers identify operating processes that need to be investigated and possibly improved. They also learn whether planned improvements in operations have been achieved. Variance information helps managers create more accurate plans for future operations. In addition, variance analysis provides information for evaluating employee performance. ■

After studying this chapter, you should be able to do the following:

LO1 Explain the role of variance analysis in the strategic management process

LO2 Describe a standard costing system and how it is used

LO3 Calculate and journalize direct cost variances

LO4 Analyze and use direct cost variance information

LO5 Calculate and journalize variable and fixed overhead variances

LO6 Analyze and use overhead variance information

LO7 Journalize closing entries for manufacturing cost variances

Medication Shortages: Labour Time Demands

racorn/Shutterstock

SOURCE: "Canadians Paying the Price for Drug Shortages: Survey," news release, Canadian Medical Association, Canadian Pharmacists Association, and Canadian Society of Hospital Pharmacists, January 14, 2013; "Position Statement on Prescription Drug Shortages in Canada," Canadian Medical Association, 2013; A. Pellett, "Pharmacists Report Drug Shortages," Associated Press, CBC News, December 16, 2010; A. K. Woodend, J. Poston, and K. Weir, "Drug Shortages—Risk or Reality?" CPJ/RPC, February 2005, Vol. 138, No. 1, pp. 27–30.

A survey of Canadian pharmacists and physicians in 2012 indicated that 94% had encountered medication shortages in the past week. Two thirds of physicians said that drug shortages had become worse since 2010.

The Canadian Medical Association (CMA), which conducted the survey along with the Canadian Pharmacists Association and the Canadian Society of Hospital Pharmacists, said that drug shortages can happen at any point along the drug supply chain, which takes medications from approval by health regulators to pharmaceutical manufacturers, wholesalers or provincial drug plans, and finally to consumers. Medication shortages are attributable to a variety of factors, including raw material shortages, production problems, changes in formulation, limited manufacturing capacity, just-in-time delivery, regulatory delays, and communication breakdowns. "Disruptions in the supply of an active or key ingredient contribute to drug shortages and this is exacerbated when the active ingredient is produced by a single raw material supplier. If the supplier is unable to meet demand then all manufacturers relying on that supply become vulnerable to disruptions," the CMA said. "In addition, procurement strategies that lead to sole source contracts for bulk purchases has been identified as the single most avoidable cause of drug shortages." The resultant shortages have health-related repercussions and productivity-related effects on the pharmacist and doctor.

When pharmacists encounter a medication shortage, their time required to fill prescriptions increases. Three quarters of pharmacists surveyed in 2012 said that drug shortages had a "significant" impact on their workload. Results from a similar survey in 2010 indicate that the increased time could range from 10 to 20 minutes per shift, or more, to deal with medication shortages. Although this labour time variance seems small, when it is considered for all of the shifts worked in a month or year, it becomes significant. When extended to a larger medical facility with multiple pharmacists, it is even more significant. In analyzing the increased time usage, it was discovered that the increased time demand extends to the entire pharmacy staff.

Two thirds of physicians surveyed in 2012 said that drug shortages increased their workload, taking up more of their time to research or consult with colleagues to find alternative drugs, to meet with patients to address medication substitution concerns, or to fill out additional insurance forms. With health care professional shortages and overwork already an issue in Canada, these unfavourable labour time variances contribute to this concerning situation.

Variance Analysis and the Strategic Management Process

Variance Analysis

L01   Explain the role of variance analysis in the strategic management process

When managers create operating plans for the next period, they often establish preset goals such as budgets for revenues and costs. These plans reflect organizational strategies and include expectations about employee productivity and other factors that affect revenues and costs. Managers then monitor actual operations to determine whether operating targets are met. By studying differences between planned and actual results, managers also identify ways to improve future operations and to establish more realistic goals. In this chapter, we learn the process that managers use to establish expectations for production costs and to analyze variances for major categories of revenues and costs.

Variance analysis is the process of calculating variances and investigating their causes. This information is then used for decision making, as shown in Exhibit 11.1. Simply calculating the dollar amount of a variance is not useful for decision making. Variance analysis is valuable because managers identify the reasons for the variances and use that information to improve future strategies or operating plans. However, variance investigation can be time consuming. Therefore, managers monitor and perform detailed investigation only for variances they consider important. The types of variances that are likely to be important depend on a variety of factors, including whether the analysis will be performed as part of a diagnostic or interactive control system.

> ⊠ **CHAPTER REFERENCE**
> Chapter 10 defined a *budget variance* as a difference between budgeted and actual results.

Variance Analysis in a Diagnostic Control System

In a diagnostic control system, managers throughout an organization regularly monitor variances to determine whether operations are proceeding according to plan. Managers use variance analysis to decide whether actions should be taken to bring operations back under control. Because management time is limited, only variables that are critical to success should be monitored regularly. In addition, managers at different levels in the organization focus on different degrees of detail. An audit manager in a CPA firm might analyze detailed variances for each component of the time budget for an audit engagement. The partner in charge of the office might focus primarily on office-level summary data.

> ⊠ **CHAPTER REFERENCE**
> Chapter 1 defined *preset goals* as targets that must be achieved for the organization's strategy to be successful.

Investigating Variances

Because variance investigation and decision making is time consuming, managers perform detailed investigations only for variances they consider important. Importance is decided in two ways. First, the variances that will be calculated and monitored need to be chosen. Second, for variances that are measured and monitored, managers decide whether a particular amount of variance is large enough or consistent enough to justify investigation. Managers may decide that a variance is important only if it is larger than a given dollar amount or a given percentage of the budget. When variances show a consistent trend, managers may want to know what causes the trend so that it can be managed.

> ⊠ **CHAPTER REFERENCE**
> Chapter 10 defined a *flexible budget* as a budget that reflects a range of operations.

> ⊠ **BUSINESS PRACTICE**
> **Trimac**, a Canadian transportation and logistic services company, monitors the performance of individual truck hauls using standards such as distance and loading time.[1]

For Chartered Professional Accounting (CPA) firms, it is strategically critical to achieve audit engagement time budgets; therefore, time spent on each stage of the audit engagement is monitored. Suppose an unfavourable variance of 1,000 hours occurred last year in an audit engagement—actual hours exceeded budgeted hours by 1,000. The audit manager would investigate this variance by asking questions like the following. Did unanticipated issues encountered during the audit cause this variance? Were staff auditors inexperienced, so that they spent more time than expected on assigned work? Was staff turnover higher than

---

[1] J. Caplan, "Applying a Little Business Intelligence," *CFO.com*, July 22, 2003.

► EXHIBIT 11.1
Variance Analysis

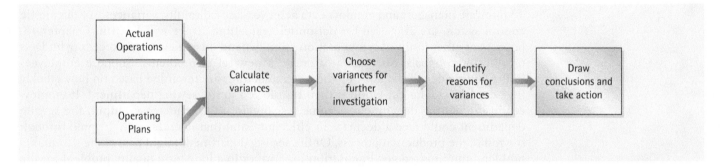

usual, reducing productivity? Did the audit supervisor fail to adequately monitor staff while the work was being performed? Was the original time budget insufficient given the client's needs? The answers to these questions will guide management actions.

Conclusions and Actions

Once managers identify the reasons for variances, they draw conclusions about what has occurred and consider whether some type of corrective action is needed. Suppose the audit manager finds that the unfavourable time variance was caused primarily by an unanticipated audit issue. The manager would want to know whether the additional time required was temporary or expected to continue on future audits. If the audit issue will be encountered in the future, the manager might decide to bring costs back under control by developing a more efficient audit method for this area. Or the manager might decide that next year's audit staff time budget should be increased to reflect the new issue. If the audit issue was temporary, the manager might decide that no action should be taken. Sometimes, a variance investigation uncovers an error in the accounting records, causing the appearance of a variance when none exists. In this case, managers might take action to correct the accounting system to avoid similar future errors. Exhibit 11.2 provides a summary of the general conclusions about variances and related management actions.

Separating Variances into Components

Identifying the reasons for variances can be time consuming. When variances are aggregated, the sum of favourable and unfavourable variances can hide production problems that need to be investigated. Identifying categories in the accounting system to separate variances into component parts makes the process easier, and more useful information is produced. In this chapter, we will calculate separate components of revenue and cost variances, a process that highlights specific areas that need further investigation and improves decision making.

General Conclusion About Variance	General Management Action
Operations are out of control.	Take action to correct operations.
Operations are better than expected.	Monitor quality to ensure that it is maintained.
Operations are better than expected, and quality is maintained.	Modify future operating plans to take advantage of gains.
Benchmark is inappropriate.	Revise benchmark to improve the accuracy of future plans.
Error made is in accounting records.	Take action to correct accounting system.
Variance is random or is not expected to recur.	Do nothing.

► EXHIBIT 11.2

General Conclusions About Variances and Management Actions

Behavioural Implications of Variances in a Diagnostic Control System

To motivate managers and employees to achieve planned results, variances in a diagnostic control system are also used for personnel evaluation. As we will learn in Chapter 18, bonuses or other forms of compensation often depend on achieving or exceeding budgets or other preset goals. Such rewards create a new set of problems. Suppose employees in the cutting department of a clothing manufacturer are rewarded based on how quickly they cut fabric. The cut fabric is then transferred to the sewing department. If employees in the cutting department become less precise as they increase output, the sewing department could face a decrease in efficiency, and that decrease could ripple through the rest of the production process. Or the sewing department might pass along the quality problem into finished goods, contributing further to a long-term quality problem for the company. If the sewing department is also rewarded based on meeting efficiency standards, employees in that department will be penalized for fixing a problem created by the cutting department. Only when variances are analyzed can managers identify whether the incentives are working as expected to promote overall organizational success.

Variance Analysis in an Interactive Control System

In an interactive control system, top managers regularly monitor a small number of crucial variables to identify and explore strategic opportunities and threats. Some variances might be included in an interactive control system if they provide information about strategic uncertainties. For example, managers may investigate the variance between budgeted and actual sales to identify possible changes in customer preferences, shifts in competition, or other factors that may influence future strategies and operating plans.

The process for analyzing variances in an interactive control system is similar to that shown in Exhibit 11.1. However, in an interactive system, variances are analyzed in face-to-face meetings with top managers and subordinates. This format encourages managers to challenge and debate their underlying assumptions, interpretations, and appropriate actions. The goal is to decide whether strategies remain appropriate or should be modified.

Standard Costs

LO2 Describe a standard costing system and how it is used

To improve the ability of managers to plan operations and monitor performance, organizations often establish a set of standards for expected costs. You learned in Chapter 6 that a standard cost is the cost managers expect to incur to produce goods or services under operating plan assumptions. Key assumptions include the following:

- ▶ Volume of production activity
- ▶ Production processes and efficiency
- ▶ Prices and quality of inputs

As shown in Exhibit 11.3, the total standard cost for a unit of output is the sum of standard costs for the resources used in production. Typical resources include direct materials, direct labour, fixed overhead, and variable overhead. Standards are also established for the cost of each resource.

For example, the standards for direct costs include the price of the direct costs and the expected quantity of input for each unit of output. Suppose Benny's, a wholesale gourmet ice cream manufacturer, uses a standard cost system. Frozen blackberries are one of the direct materials used in Benny's Purple Madness ice cream. The company's managers determine that 125 grams of frozen blackberries should be included in every litre of ice cream. They forecast that the cost of frozen blackberries this year will be $8.00 per kilogram.

> **EXHIBIT 11.3**
Typical Cost Standards for Production

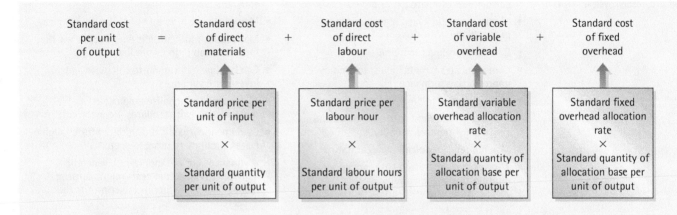

Keeping in mind that 1 kilogram = 1,000 grams, we can describe the standard cost of frozen blackberries as follows:

Standard price per unit of input:

$8.00 per kg = $8.00 per 1,000 grams = $0.008 per gram

Standard quantity of input per unit of output:

125 grams of blackberries per litre of ice cream

Standard cost of blackberries per unit of output:

125 grams of blackberries per litre of ice cream × $0.008 per gram

= $1.00 per litre of ice cream

Standard Costing System and Variances

Under a **standard costing system** for a manufacturer, inventory and cost of goods sold are initially recorded at standard costs rather than actual costs. Actual costs are recorded through cash disbursements, payroll, purchases, fixed assets, and other components of the accounting system. The **standard cost variances** reconcile standard costs to actual costs. As we will learn later in the chapter, IFRS (International Financial Reporting Standards) and Canadian ASPE require that standard cost variances be closed to cost of goods sold and/or ending inventory when preparing financial statements.

Although standard costing systems often motivate greater productivity, systems suffer from many of the problems discussed in Chapter 10 regarding the use of budgets. Exhibit 11.4 summarizes the major advantages and disadvantages associated with the use of standard costing and analysis of standard cost variances.

▶ **CHAPTER REFERENCE**
Chapter 7 provides information about GPK and RCA systems, which provide standard costs and track variances at the resource consumption level.

Standard Cost Categories

In this chapter, we focus on measuring and monitoring the standard costs for direct materials, direct labour, variable overhead, and fixed overhead. These cost categories are traditionally the ones used for manufactured goods. The cost categories that are measured and monitored in a given organization depend on the following:

▶ Nature of goods or services
▶ Cost accounting system used
▶ Costs that managers consider important
▶ Cost-benefit trade-off for monitoring individual costs

▶ EXHIBIT 11.4

Advantages and Disadvantages
of a Standard Costing System

System Advantages	Disadvantages
• Provides information that can be used to easily calculate or estimate job or project costs • Monitors labour, which may increase productivity • Can monitor direct material • Communicates targets (goals) to employees, improving performance • May improve planning • Provides information used to analyze and continually improve operations • May improve organizational learning • Allows for standardized costs/prices across multiple business locations	• Allows employees to build extra time into the standards • May cause waste to be built into the standards • May reduce motivation if employees view the targets as too high or too low • Can be time consuming to calculate and investigate variances • May reward or penalize employees inappropriately if standards are incorrect • Could be incorrect if not updated for changing prices, production processes, etc. • If variances are not monitored, year-end adjustments to actual costs might surprise managers (e.g., higher or lower profits than expected)

▶ BUSINESS PRACTICE

Syncrude's business management
system has the ability to drill down
to the team level and monitor cost
variances. At month end, there are no
unexpected issues with respect to cost
control.[2]

For example, consider the cost of a clothing item sold by a retail store. The managers of the store might consider it unimportant to allocate and monitor labour and overhead costs for individual pieces of clothing sold. They might instead choose to focus only on the direct cost of the clothing. Professional service organizations, such as accounting firms, might primarily track direct labour costs. Organizations that use activity-based costing monitor overhead costs for individual activities. In practice, accountants and managers measure and monitor many variations of specific costs. Although we focus in this chapter on traditional cost categories, the methods introduced here can be adapted to many different settings.

Developing Standard Costs

Standards are set for the price of direct materials, as well as for the amount of direct materials that should be used to produce each unit. Similarly, standards are set for the price per direct labour hour and for the number of hours needed per unit of output. In addition, standards are set for overhead costs. No exact rules are prescribed for developing these standard costs. Sometimes, managers simply use the most recent year's data, while at other times they evaluate and incorporate historical trends. To set a standard for the next period, they update historical data for expected changes in costs or processes. For new products, standards are often set with the assistance of industrial engineers, who estimate quantities and costs for direct materials, direct labour, and production overhead. Managers might also seek the periodic assistance of industrial engineers to find ways to improve efficiency, modify output quality, or identify cost-reduction opportunities for existing products. Production plans include expected efficiency and quality, which means the normal cost of waste and defects is included in standard costs.

Standard costs are reviewed periodically. Depending on organizational strategy, cost-reduction goals may be incorporated into the standards, or quality improvements might require that standards be changed. Standards should serve as achievable targets. Working with current suppliers or investigating alternative suppliers for lower prices could lead to reduced direct materials price standards. As technology improves the productivity of robotic and labour processes, efficiency standards will also change.

▶ CHAPTER REFERENCE

Chapter 18 addresses ways that
organizations evaluate and compensate
employees for meeting or exceeding
budgets and standards.

Managers use standard costs not only to help plan future costs but also to monitor and motivate employee performance. To encourage employees to achieve planned productivity, standards are often set at a level that is attainable but without much slack. Sometimes tightening standards can promote productivity improvements.

Creaciones Concretas, Part 1, demonstrates the setting of standard costs for a manufacturer.

---

[2] R. Colman, "Better Controls, Better Business," CMA *Management* 80 (December 2006/January 2007), p. 40.

creaciones concretas, part 1
SETTING STANDARD COSTS

Creaciones Concretas manufactures concrete blocks at its plant in Mexico. When Josephina Gonzales, the company's new accountant, started work last month, she learned that the company had never used standard costs. She decided to implement a standard cost system to help the managers monitor operating performance.

Josephina toured the production facilities with Jorge, the labour supervisor. She learned that workers combine cement mix, sand, and water, and then they pour the mixture into block forms. The blocks are turned out of the forms and allowed to dry in the sun. When the blocks are dry, they are stacked on pallets and loaded on trucks for shipment to customers. Workers can be sent home if no work is scheduled; therefore, direct labour cost is variable.

© Steven Frame/Alamy Stock Photo

Setting Cost Standards

Because the company had not previously used standard costs, Josephina decided to set next month's standards based on past experience, adjusted for expected changes in activities or costs. To gather information for creating cost standards, Josephina first studied the accounting and production records for the past year. Then, she reviewed the next month's production schedule, which showed a planned volume of 90,000 blocks. After conducting interviews to learn about next month's production activities and costs, she did not expect any changes from prior costs.

Josephina identified the following potential direct costs for producing the blocks: cement mix, sand, water, and direct labour. Sand and water are readily available on the company's land, so the company does not incur any costs for them.[3] Therefore, the only direct materials cost is the cement mix. Based on past accounting and production records, Josephina set a standard cost for cement mix of 10 pesos per kilogram. She also estimated that it should take about 1 kg of cement mix per block. In addition, Josephina set the direct labour cost standard at 10 pesos per hour and the standard for quantity of labour at 100 blocks per labour hour.

Josephina next turned to the production overhead costs and determined that some costs were variable and others were fixed. Variable costs consisted of the cost of supervisors; as the number of direct labour hours increases, the number of supervisor hours also increases. Josephina set the variable overhead standard at 2 pesos per labour hour. She then classified all remaining overhead costs as fixed and estimated next month's spending at 180,000 pesos. After considering several allocation bases for the fixed overhead costs, Josephina decided that this volume of production would be appropriate. With planned production of 90,000 blocks, she set the standard fixed overhead allocation rate at 2 pesos (180,000 pesos ÷ 90,000 blocks) per block.

Summary of Direct and Overhead Cost Standards

The following is a summary of the standards Josephina established for the next month:

Direct materials:	
Cost of cement mix	10 pesos per kg
Quantity of cement mix	1 kg per block
Standard cost per block (10 pesos per kg × 1 kg per block)	10 pesos
Direct labour:	
Labour pay rate	10 pesos per hour
Quantity of direct labour	100 blocks per labour hour
Standard cost per block (10 pesos per hour × 1 hour per 100 blocks)	0.10 pesos

continued...

---

[3] In reality, some costs could most likely be incurred for these resources; however, this illustration avoids complication by assuming no cost.

example

Variable overhead:

Spending per labour hour	2 pesos
Standard cost per block (2 pesos ÷ 100 blocks)	0.02 pesos
Total standard cost per block (10 + 0.10 + 2 + 0.02)	12.12 pesos

Fixed overhead:

Planned spending	180,000 pesos
Volume of allocation base (blocks produced)	90,000 blocks
Standard cost per block (180,000 pesos ÷ 90,000 blocks)	2 pesos

Cost Budget

Based on the standards she set and the expected production volume of 90,000 blocks, Josephina created the following budget for next month's production costs:

Direct materials (90,000 blocks × 10 pesos per block)	900,000 pesos
Direct labour (90,000 blocks × 0.10 pesos per block)	9,000
Variable overhead (90,000 blocks × 0.02 pesos per block)	1,800
Fixed overhead	180,000
Total standard production costs	1,090,800 pesos
(90,000 blocks × 12.12 pesos per block)	

●●● > RISK OF BIASED DECISIONS: ANCHORING TRAP

The **ANCHORING TRAP** is a bias in which estimates are developed by focusing on an initial piece of information called an anchor. This anchor may be based on irrelevant or only partially relevant information. Suppose you are asked to estimate the grade you will receive in a course that you have not yet taken. You would probably pick the same grade that you received in a prior similar course, regardless of differences between the courses that might affect your performance.

Managers often use prior period results as an anchor when establishing standard costs or other budgets. This practice may build slack into budgets and discourage employees from searching for operational improvements. In Chapter 10, we discussed several methods to reduce budgetary slack, including participative budgeting, zero-based budgeting, and external benchmarking. These methods may reduce anchoring bias and encourage managers to identify more efficient operating plans.

●● > STRATEGIC RISK MANAGEMENT: CREACIONES CONCRETAS (PART 1)

STANDARD COSTS IN A DIAGNOSTIC CONTROL SYSTEM Josephina, the accountant at Creaciones Concretas, planned to use the standard costs to monitor production costs for the next month—that is, she planned to use the standard costs as a diagnostic control to ensure that operations proceeded according to plan. How confident could Josephina be that her standard cost estimates were appropriate benchmarks? The standard costs were based on prior year actual costs and, thus, might have suffered from an anchoring bias. Currently, higher prices are plaguing the cement industry. Unfortunately, Josephina did not anticipate these increased cement prices when setting her standards. Also, she assumed that prior manufacturing procedures provided a good benchmark—that is, no efficiency improvements or other modifications should be planned.

Direct Cost Variances

Recall from Exhibit 11.3 that standard costs for direct materials and direct labour consist of a standard price multiplied by a standard quantity for each of the direct resources that should be used in production. As a result, as shown in Exhibit 11.5, the total variance for direct costs can be broken down into two components:

> ▸ Price variance
> ▸ Efficiency variance

> **LO3** Calculate and journalize direct cost variances

Price Variances

A **price variance** is the difference between standard and actual prices paid for resources purchased and used in the production of goods or services. We informally calculate price variances frequently in our daily lives. For example, we may compare the advertised prices of groceries with a standard price (the price we usually pay) and then decide to purchase certain items. Suppose pop usually costs $5.00 for a 12-pack but is on sale at $2.50. After comparing the sale price to the $5.00 standard, we may decide to purchase more than the usual amount. Our standard price for two 12-packs of pop would have been $10.00 ($5.00 per pack × 2 packs), and our actual cost would be $5.00 ($2.50 per pack × 2 packs). By taking advantage of the sale, we achieve a favourable price variance of $5.00 ($10.00 − $5.00).

This example illustrates several limitations of a price variance. The price variance does not take into account whether sufficient cash flows, storage space, or usage requirements justify and accommodate purchasing resources in larger quantities. Perhaps our kitchen lacks sufficient space to store extra groceries if we purchase more than our weekly usage. If we purchase large quantities of perishable foods, they may spoil before they are needed. Also, the price variance does not reflect possible quality differences between resources purchased at higher or lower prices. Suppose the brand of pop that is on sale is not the brand we prefer. We may be willing to pay a higher price for our preferred brand. In a business organization, it might be inefficient to use lower-quality direct materials even when they are less expensive.

> ▷ **ALTERNATIVE TERMS**
> Some people use the term *rate variance* instead of *price variance*, and *expected price* or *budgeted price* instead of *standard price*.

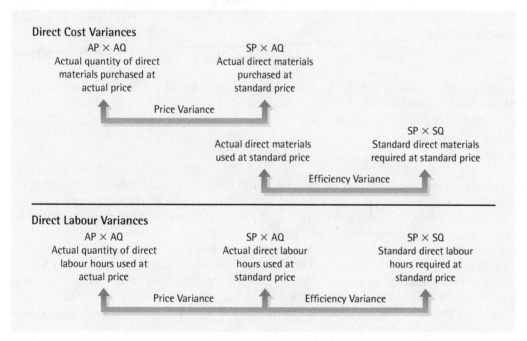

> ▷ **EXHIBIT 11.5**
> Direct Cost Variances

Direct Materials Price Variance. A **direct materials price variance** compares the standard price for direct materials to the actual price, for the amount of direct materials purchased. Direct materials price variances are calculated using the following formula:

$$\text{Direct materials price variance} = \left(\text{Actual price} - \text{Standard price}\right) \times \text{Quantity purchased}$$

Suppose that Benny's purchased 13.75 kilograms (13,750 grams) of frozen blackberries at $10 per kg ($0.01 per gram). The standard cost is $0.008 per gram ($1.00 per 125 grams). Therefore, the price variance for these berries is

$$(\$0.01 \text{ per gram} - \$0.008 \text{ per gram}) \times 13{,}750 \text{ grams} = \$27.50 \text{ U}$$

This variance is unfavourable (U) because the actual price paid for the frozen blackberries is higher than the standard price. Similar calculations would be made for each of the other direct materials used to produce Purple Madness ice cream.

The direct materials price variance is usually calculated at the time direct materials are purchased. Therefore, direct materials are recorded in raw material inventory at the standard cost rather than at the actual cost. This practice has two advantages. First, it reduces bookkeeping complexity; because all units of direct material are recorded at the same standard cost, the actual cost of individual batches of direct material purchases need not be tracked. Second, this approach allows managers to identify the price variance during the period in which the variance occurred—at the time direct materials are purchased. Purchasing department personnel are often held accountable for price variances, so it is more appropriate to measure the variance at the time of purchase than at the time the direct materials are used. Depending on how quickly inventory is used, a delay in recognition could prevent managers from rapidly taking any needed action.

Direct Labour Price Variance. A **direct labour price variance** compares the standard price with the actual price for labour. Direct labour price variances are calculated using the following formula:

$$\text{Direct labour price variance} = \left(\text{Actual labour price per hour} - \text{Standard labour price per hour}\right) \times \text{Actual hours used}$$

Suppose that Benny's paid $9 per hour for 9.5 hours of work packing 100 litres of Purple Madness ice cream. The standard labour rate is $8.00 per hour. The direct labour price variance is calculated as

$$(\$9 \text{ per hour} - \$8 \text{ per hour}) \times 9.5 \text{ hours} = \$9.50 \text{ U}$$

This variance is unfavourable because Benny's paid more for labour per hour than the standard called for. Similar computations would be made for other types of direct labour used to produce Purple Madness ice cream.

Efficiency Variances

An **efficiency variance** provides information about how economically direct resources such as materials and labour were used. We informally assess our own efficiency in our daily lives. For example, when we plan a bicycle ride on the weekend, we might believe that it will take two hours to ride 45 kilometres. When we finish the ride, we compare the actual length of time to our estimate. We might use this information to gauge our effort on the ride or to change our estimate for future trips. The variance calculation does not consider any factors that might have affected efficiency; instead, we must consider those factors when investigating the variance. For example, suppose one of the tires on our bicycle is faulty and becomes flat during the ride. The time needed to fix the tire would cause us to take longer than expected to complete the trip.

Direct Materials Efficiency Variance. The **direct materials efficiency variance** compares the standard amount of materials that should have been used to the amount of materials actually used. This difference is valued at the standard price. The formula is as follows:

$$\text{Direct materials efficiency variance} = \left(\begin{array}{c} \text{Actual quantity} \\ \text{for actual output} \end{array} - \begin{array}{c} \text{Standard quantity} \\ \text{for actual output} \end{array} \right) \times \begin{array}{c} \text{Standard} \\ \text{price} \end{array}$$

Assume that Benny's produced a batch of 100 litres of Purple Madness ice cream using 11,250 grams of blackberries. (Recall that the standard quantity is 125 grams per litre.) Here are calculations for the variance:

$$[11,250 \text{ grams} - (125 \text{ grams per litre} \times 100 \text{ litres})] \times \$0.008 \text{ per gram}$$
$$= [11,250 \text{ grams} - 12,500 \text{ grams}] \times \$0.008 \text{ per gram} = \$10 \text{ F}$$

This variance is favourable (F) because fewer direct materials were used than called for at standard. Although we call this variance favourable, using fewer blackberries likely affects the quality of Benny's ice cream, so this variance may be investigated. Similar efficiency variance computations would be performed for each of the direct materials used to produce Purple Madness ice cream.

Direct Labour Efficiency Variance. The **direct labour efficiency variance** compares the standard number of labour hours that should have been used to the number actually used; it values this difference at the standard labour price per hour:

$$\text{Direct labour efficiency variance} = \left(\begin{array}{c} \text{Actual hours for} \\ \text{actual output} \end{array} - \begin{array}{c} \text{Standard hours} \\ \text{for actual ouput} \end{array} \right) \times \begin{array}{c} \text{Standard} \\ \text{price} \end{array}$$

Suppose one group of employees at Benny's is responsible for hand-packing ice cream into 1-litre containers. The standard amount of time to pack 1 litre of ice cream is 0.1 hour, and 9.5 hours were used to pack 100 litres. The direct labour efficiency variance is calculated as

$$[9.5 \text{ hours} - (100 \text{ litres} \times 0.1 \text{ hour per litre})] \times \$8 \text{ per hour}$$
$$= [9.5 \text{ hours} - 10 \text{ hours}] \times \$8 \text{ per hour} = \$4.00 \text{ F}$$

This variance is favourable because actual hours were less than standard hours. Similar computations would be performed for other types of direct labour used to produce Purple Madness ice cream.

Journal Entries for Direct Costs and Variances

In a standard cost system for a manufacturer, inventory accounting entries are recorded using standard costs. Differences between actual and standard costs are recorded in variance accounts. Later in this chapter, you'll learn to close variance accounts at the end of an accounting period. Exhibit 11.6 summarizes the variances and journal entries used by Benny's for the frozen blackberries direct material and the direct labour for packing 100 litres of Purple Madness ice cream.

When 13,750 grams of frozen blackberries are purchased, they are recorded in raw material inventory at standard cost ($110.00), and the price variance is recorded ($27.50 U). Then, 11,250 grams are removed from raw materials inventory at standard cost ($90.00). The direct materials price and efficiency variances account for the difference between actual and standard costs.

The labour journal entry is also presented in Exhibit 11.6. The entry for work-in-process inventory is made at the standard quantity and standard cost. Wages payable is credited for the actual wages owed to employees. The direct labour price and efficiency variances account for the difference between actual and standard costs.

Creaciones Concretas, Part 2, demonstrates the calculation of direct cost variances and direct cost journal entries.

▶ **BUSINESS PRACTICE**

Between 2009 and 2013, labour productivity in the manufacturing sector increased 2.0% per year on average compared to the Canadian economy, which increased 0.9% per year. This variance may be the result of businesses using more capital- and technology-intense approaches to increase output while decreasing the labour force or keeping it on par with prior years.[4]

---

[4] Industry Canada, Canadian Industry Statistics, Labour Productivity Manufacturing (NAICS 31-33), https://strategis.ic.gc.ca/app/scr/sbms/sbb/cis/labourProductivity.html?code=31-33.

> **EXHIBIT 11.6**
Direct Cost Variances for Benny's
Purple Madness Ice Cream

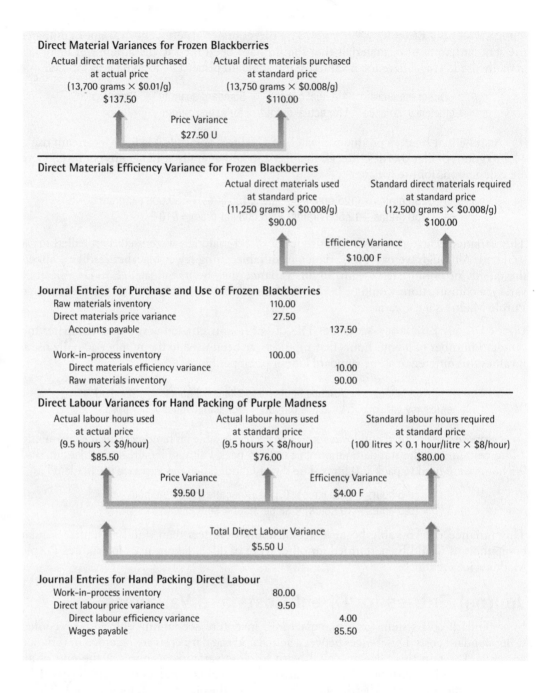

Direct Material Variances for Frozen Blackberries

Actual direct materials purchased at actual price (13,700 grams × $0.01/g) $137.50		Actual direct materials purchased at standard price (13,750 grams × $0.008/g) $110.00
	Price Variance $27.50 U	

Direct Materials Efficiency Variance for Frozen Blackberries

	Actual direct materials used at standard price (11,250 grams × $0.008/g) $90.00	Standard direct materials required at standard price (12,500 grams × $0.008/g) $100.00
	Efficiency Variance $10.00 F	

Journal Entries for Purchase and Use of Frozen Blackberries

Raw materials inventory	110.00	
Direct materials price variance	27.50	
Accounts payable		137.50
Work-in-process inventory	100.00	
Direct materials efficiency variance		10.00
Raw materials inventory		90.00

Direct Labour Variances for Hand Packing of Purple Madness

Actual labour hours used at actual price (9.5 hours × $9/hour) $85.50	Actual labour hours used at standard price (9.5 hours × $8/hour) $76.00	Standard labour hours required at standard price (100 litres × 0.1 hour/litre × $8/hour) $80.00
Price Variance $9.50 U	Efficiency Variance $4.00 F	

Total Direct Labour Variance
$5.50 U

Journal Entries for Hand Packing Direct Labour

Work-in-process inventory	80.00	
Direct labour price variance	9.50	
Direct labour efficiency variance		4.00
Wages payable		85.50

example

creaciones concretas, part 2
VARIANCES FOR DIRECT MATERIALS
AND DIRECT LABOUR

At the end of the first month of operations after Josephina developed the cost standards, she collected the following data needed to perform a direct cost variance analysis:

▶ The company produced 100,000 cement blocks.
▶ The company purchased 130,000 kg of cement mix for 975,000 pesos.
▶ The company used 120,000 kg of cement mix.
▶ Direct labour employees were paid 16,500 pesos and worked 1,100 hours.

© Steven Frame/Alamy Stock Photo

example

Direct Materials Price Variance

Josephina first calculates the direct materials price variance. The purchase price last month for the cement mix was 975,000 pesos for 130,000 kg, or 7.5 pesos per kg. The standard cost is 10 pesos per kg. She calculates the direct materials price variance as follows:

$$[\text{Actual price} - \text{Standard price}] \times \text{Quantity purchased}$$
$$= [7.50 \text{ pesos} - 10 \text{ pesos}] \times 130,000 \text{ kg} = 325,000 \text{ pesos F}$$

Because the price per kg that Creaciones Concretas paid last month is less than expected, the direct materials price variance is favourable.

Direct Labour Price Variance

Josephina now calculates the direct labour price variance. During the month, Creaciones Concretas paid its employees 16,500 pesos for 1,100 hours of work. Thus, the actual price for labour was 15 pesos per hour (16,500 pesos/1,100 hours). The standard cost is 10 pesos per hour, so 11,000 pesos should have been paid for 1,100 hours of work. Therefore, the direct labour price variance is as follows:

$$[\text{Actual labour price per hour} - \text{Standard labour price per hour}]$$
$$\times \text{Number of labour hours used}$$
$$= [15 \text{ pesos} - 10 \text{ pesos}] \times 1,100 \text{ hours} = 5,500 \text{ pesos U}$$

Because the company paid more than the standard labour wage, the direct labour price variance is unfavourable.

Direct Materials Efficiency Variance

After completing the direct cost price variances, Josephina calculates the direct cost efficiency variances. Efficiency variances are calculated based on actual production volume (i.e., the quantity of concrete blocks produced). During the last month, the company produced 100,000 blocks, using 120,000 kg of cement mix. The standard quantity of direct materials is 1 kg per block, for a total of 100,000 kg of cement mix. Josephina calculated the direct materials efficiency variance as follows:

$$(\text{Actual quantity for actual output} - \text{Standard quantity for actual output}) \times \text{Standard price}$$
$$= [120,000 \text{ kg} - (1 \text{ kg per block} \times 100,000 \text{ blocks})] \times 10 \text{ pesos per kg}$$
$$= (120,000 \text{ kg} - 100,000 \text{ kg}) \times 10 \text{ pesos per kg} = 200,000 \text{ pesos U}$$

The materials efficiency variance is unfavourable because more materials than the standard quantity were used.

Direct Labour Efficiency Variance

To calculate the direct labour efficiency variance, Josephina first determines the amount of labour that should have been used to produce 100,000 blocks and then compares it to the amount of labour actually used—1,100 direct labour hours. The standard quantity of labour is 100 blocks per hour. The direct labour efficiency variance is calculated as follows:

$$(\text{Actual hours for actual output} - \text{Standard hours for actual output}) \times \text{Standard price}$$
$$= [1,100 \text{ hours} - (100,000 \text{ blocks} \times 1 \text{ hour per 100 blocks})] \times 10 \text{ pesos per hour}$$
$$= (1,100 \text{ hours} - 1,000 \text{ hours}) \times 10 \text{ pesos per hour} = 1,000 \text{ pesos U}$$

Because actual hours exceeded standard hours, the direct labour efficiency variance is unfavourable.

Summary of Direct Cost Variances

After calculating the individual direct cost variances, Josephina creates a summary that shows all the variances (see Exhibit 11.7).

continued...

example

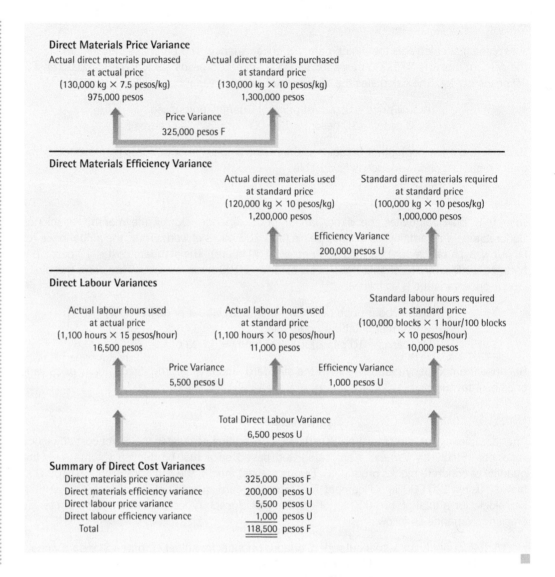

Direct Materials Price Variance

Actual direct materials purchased at actual price (130,000 kg × 7.5 pesos/kg) 975,000 pesos	Actual direct materials purchased at standard price (130,000 kg × 10 pesos/kg) 1,300,000 pesos

Price Variance
325,000 pesos F

Direct Materials Efficiency Variance

Actual direct materials used at standard price (120,000 kg × 10 pesos/kg) 1,200,000 pesos	Standard direct materials required at standard price (100,000 kg × 10 pesos/kg) 1,000,000 pesos

Efficiency Variance
200,000 pesos U

Direct Labour Variances

Actual labour hours used at actual price (1,100 hours × 15 pesos/hour) 16,500 pesos	Actual labour hours used at standard price (1,100 hours × 10 pesos/hour) 11,000 pesos	Standard labour hours required at standard price (100,000 blocks × 1 hour/100 blocks × 10 pesos/hour) 10,000 pesos

Price Variance 5,500 pesos U	Efficiency Variance 1,000 pesos U

Total Direct Labour Variance
6,500 pesos U

Summary of Direct Cost Variances

Direct materials price variance	325,000	pesos F
Direct materials efficiency variance	200,000	pesos U
Direct labour price variance	5,500	pesos U
Direct labour efficiency variance	1,000	pesos U
Total	118,500	pesos F

> **EXHIBIT 11.7**
Direct Cost Variances for Creaciones Concretas

Analyzing Direct Cost Variance Information

LO4 Analyze and use direct cost variance information

Direct cost variances are analyzed using the process introduced in Exhibit 11.1. The analysis begins with calculating the variances. For variances that are to be investigated further, the reasons for the variances are identified. Breaking the variances into price and efficiency components, as illustrated in Exhibit 11.5, helps to identify why actual direct costs differ from standard costs.

Identifying Reasons for Direct Cost Variances

In the Creaciones Concretas example, a favourable direct materials price variance of 325,000 pesos arises for cement. The combined direct cost variances are 118,500 pesos, favourable. Does this result mean that operations are performing better than expected? What about the 200,000-peso unfavourable direct materials efficiency variance for cement? Is some type of corrective action needed? Before addressing these types of questions, it is necessary to discover the reasons for the direct cost variances.

Exhibit 11.8 lists examples of circumstances that can cause direct cost variances. Some types of variances are relatively easy to discover. For example, accountants would know whether

> **EXHIBIT 11.8**
Examples of Reasons for Direct Cost Variances

Direct Materials Variances	Direct Labour Variances
Price:	**Price:**
• Change in price paid for materials, caused by	• Change in average wages paid to employees, caused by
– A change in the quality of materials purchased	– A new union contract
– A change in quantity purchased, leading to a change in purchase discount	– A change in average experience or training of workers
– A new supplier contract	– A change in the government-mandated minimum wage
• Unreasonable materials price standard	• Unanticipated overtime hours
• Error in the accounting records for the actual price of materials	• An unreasonable labour price standard
	• Error in the accounting records for the actual price of direct labour
Efficiency:	**Efficiency:**
• Normal fluctuation in materials usage	• Normal fluctuation in labour hours
• Change in production processes, causing a change in the quantity of materials used	• Change in average labour time, caused by
• Change in proportion of materials spoiled, caused by	– A change in equipment, technology, or other aspect of production processes
– A change in quality of materials	– A change in average worker experience or training caused by:
– A change in equipment, technology, or other aspect of production processes	• Improved performance from effective training programs
– Equipment malfunction	• Change in employee turnover
– Intentional worker damage	– International work slowdown
• Theft of raw materials	• Intentional or unintentional over- or underreporting of labour hours
• Unreasonable materials quantity standard	• Unreasonable labour hours standard
• Error in the accounting records for the quantity of materials used	• Error in the accounting records for the quantity of labour hours

the company negotiated a pay increase with a labour union, as well as the amount of the pay increase. To determine whether the pay increase explains an unfavourable direct labour price variance, accountants could simply compare the amount of the variance with the expected amount of the pay increase. Some types of variances are more difficult to discover. For example, it would not be easy to determine that workers intentionally worked more slowly than expected. Theft and fraud are difficult to discover because the perpetrators deliberately try to hide them. Determining that a standard is incorrect, especially for price variances, may be relatively easy. For other types of variances, however, the process is more difficult because of uncertainties about the reasonableness of standard prices and quantities.

Recognizing Resource and Quality Trade-offs

Sometimes trade-offs are made between price and efficiency or between different inputs. For example, it may be possible to hire more proficient workers at a higher wage per hour. Similarly, higher-quality direct materials with a higher price might produce less spoilage during production. Consider the cost of producing Purple Madness ice cream at Benny's. The company usually purchases frozen blackberries that have been cleaned and can be added directly to the ice cream. During fresh blackberry season, the company could pay a lower price for fresh blackberries that have not been cleaned. However, the company would incur greater direct labour time for cleaning the berries. Thus, the trade-off is made between the price paid for the blackberries and the labour time required. Quality differences also affect this decision. Suppose managers believe that fresh blackberries are better flavoured than frozen blackberries. They may purchase fresh blackberries to achieve better flavour, even if the cost is higher overall.

When analyzing variances, it is necessary to consider possible trade-offs. A favourable variance in one area might be partially or completely offset by an unfavourable variance in another area. Creaciones Concretas, Part 3, demonstrates the analysis of direct cost variances.

© Steven Frame/Alamy Stock Photo

example

creaciones concretas, part 3
ANALYZING DIRECT COST VARIANCE INFORMATION

Josephina examines the total favourable variance of 118,500 pesos (Exhibit 11.7). In some cases, an overall favourable variance means that the organization has no problems—operations performed better than expected. However, Josephina is concerned about the large unfavourable efficiency variance for cement mix, and she is puzzled by its large favourable price variance. In addition, the unfavourable direct labour price variance seems high relative to total labour costs. However, Josephina decides to focus her attention on only the two largest variances because they explain most of the total direct cost variance.

First, Josephina considers the favourable price variance for cement mix. She speaks with Ricardo, who purchases direct materials. He has found a new supplier with better prices. Because he receives a bonus based on reducing the company's costs, he is looking forward to a sizeable bonus. Josephina tentatively thinks that the future standard cost for cement mix should be reduced to reflect the new lower price.

Next, Josephina investigates the unfavourable efficiency variance for cement mix. She speaks with Jorge, the labour supervisor. He is very upset about a decrease in the quality of the cement mix from the new supplier; the mix contains inadequate quantities of an ingredient that prevents the blocks from slumping, or losing shape, when they are turned out of the forms. Of the 120,000 blocks produced, 20,000 of them were rejected because of the slumping problem. In addition, more labour hours were needed, leading to overtime payments. These factors explain the unfavourable direct labour price variance. Jorge is concerned that some of the blocks shipped to customers are not the correct shape. Some customers might become dissatisfied and no longer purchase cement blocks from the company.

Josephina plans to recommend to management that the company pay a higher price (the original standard) for the higher-quality cement mix. Although it appeared that the company saved money overall last month from the lower-priced mix, most of the savings were offset by unfavourable variances elsewhere caused by the lower quality. Furthermore, she believes that just the risk of lost sales in the future outweighs the cost savings. Josephina also plans to work with management to design a better reward system that avoids any further adverse effects resulting from the purchasing agent's bonus plan. ■

Overhead Variances

LO5 Calculate and journalize variable and fixed overhead variances

Organizations use standard cost systems to monitor overhead costs in addition to direct costs. To monitor overhead costs, a **standard overhead allocation rate** is created at the beginning of each period. Overhead is typically allocated using an allocation base such as production units, direct labour costs, direct labour hours, or machine hours. Separate allocation bases and rates are often used for fixed and variable overhead costs.

The **standard variable overhead allocation rate** is determined by estimating the variable amount of overhead cost per unit of an allocation base as follows:

$$\text{Standard variable overhead allocation rate} = \frac{\text{Estimated variable overhead cost}}{\text{Estimated volume of an allocation base}}$$

▶ **CHAPTER REFERENCE**
To learn more about the accounting choices for estimated volumes of allocation bases, see Chapter 5.

For example, the accountant at Benny's estimated the variable overhead cost as $150,000 and the labour hours as 75,000, so the cost function for variable overhead costs is $2.00 per direct labour hour.

Accountants choose allocation bases for variable overhead that reflect the use of variable resources. Indirect labour costs, such as maintenance wages, might be related to direct labour costs; as the number of employees providing direct labour increases, the number of maintenance worker hours increases. When the proportion of labour-related costs in the variable overhead cost pool is high, direct labour hours or direct labour cost is an appropriate allocation base. Alternatively, indirect materials cost—such as costs of paint, plastic stripping, and decals applied to toy cars—could be a large proportion of the variable overhead cost pool. In this case, the estimated volume of units would be the most appropriate allocation base.

Although fixed costs do not vary with volume, we need to develop an allocation rate to assign these costs to inventory and cost of goods sold. The **standard fixed overhead allocation rate** is determined as follows:

$$\text{Standard fixed overhead allocation rate} = \frac{\text{Estimated fixed overhead cost}}{\text{Estimated volume of an allocation base}}$$

For example, if the estimated fixed overhead cost for Benny's is $200,000 and the company allocates fixed overhead based on units produced using a normal volume of 500,000 litres of ice cream during the year, the standard fixed overhead allocation rate is $200,000 ÷ 500,000 litres, or $0.40 per litre. Therefore, standard fixed overhead of $0.40 will be allocated to the cost of each litre of ice cream.

At the end of the period, variances between standard allocated overhead costs and actual costs are analyzed. The **variable overhead budget variance** is the difference between allocated variable overhead cost and actual variable overhead cost. The **fixed overhead budget variance** is the difference between allocated fixed overhead cost and actual fixed overhead cost. As shown in Exhibit 11.9, the **overhead variances** can be broken down into the following components:

- ► Variable overhead budget variance:
  - ► Spending variance
  - ► Efficiency variance
- ► Fixed overhead budget variance:
  - ► Spending variance
  - ► Production volume variance

Variable Overhead Spending Variance

The **variable overhead spending variance** is the difference between the total expected variable overhead costs for the actual output and the actual variable overhead costs for that level of output. The variable overhead spending variance helps managers monitor whether the organization spent the planned amount on overhead. Because variable overhead costs are expected to vary with activity, the calculation for the spending variance takes into account the actual volume of activity.

For Benny's, the allocation base for variable overhead is direct labour hours. The normal volume of direct labour hours is 500,000 litres × 0.15 hours per litre, or 75,000 hours. The standard variable overhead allocation rate is $2.00 per direct labour hour. Suppose actual

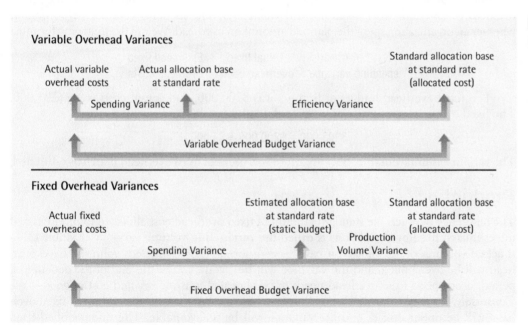

► EXHIBIT 11.9
Overhead Cost Variances

variable overhead costs total $147,000 and actual labour hours are 74,000. The variable overhead spending variance is calculated as follows:

$$\text{Variable overhead spending variance} = \text{Actual variable overhead cost} - \left(\text{Actual volume of allocation base} \times \text{Standard variable overhead allocation rate}\right)$$

$$= \$147,000 - (74,000 \text{ hours} \times \$2.00 \text{ per hour})$$

$$= \$147,000 - \$148,000 = \$1,000 \text{ F}$$

The variance is favourable because actual variable overhead costs were less than expected, given the actual volume of output.

Variable Overhead Efficiency Variance

The difference between the flexible budget for variable overhead cost and the standard amount of variable overhead for the actual volume of the allocation base is called the **variable overhead efficiency variance** (Exhibit 11.9). This variance is favourable if the actual volume of the allocation base is less than expected given actual production levels, and it is unfavourable if the actual volume of the allocation base is more than expected. It is calculated as follows:

$$\text{Variable overhead efficiency variance} = \left(\text{Actual volume of allocation base} - \text{Standard volume of allocation base for actual output}\right) \times \text{Standard variable overhead allocation rate}$$

For Benny's, assume that 498,000 litres of ice cream were produced. The standard number of direct labour hours for actual production is 74,700 hours (498,000 litres × 0.15 hours per litre), and 74,000 actual hours were used. The standard variable overhead allocation rate is $2.00 per direct labour hour. Therefore, the variable overhead efficiency variance calculation is as follows:

$$(74,000 \text{ hours} - 74,700 \text{ hours}) \times \$2.00 \text{ per hour} = \$1,400 \text{ F}$$

The variance is favourable because actual direct labour hours are less than expected, given actual production of 498,000 litres of ice cream.

Fixed Overhead Spending Variance

CHAPTER REFERENCE
Chapter 10 defined a *static budget* as a budget that is not altered to reflect actual volume levels during the budget period.

The **fixed overhead spending variance** is the difference between estimated fixed overhead costs and actual fixed overhead costs. Fixed overhead costs are not expected to fluctuate with levels of activity. Thus, the spending variance is not affected by the volume of activity; it reflects the amount by which the actual spending on fixed overhead differs from the estimated fixed overhead (the static budget), as shown in Exhibit 11.9. The spending variance helps monitor whether an organization spent the planned amount on overhead. We use the following formula:

$$\text{Fixed overhead spending variance} = \text{Actual fixed overhead costs} - \text{Estimated fixed overhead costs}$$

The fixed overhead budget at Benny's was $200,000, and actual costs were $203,000. The fixed overhead spending variance is calculated as follows:

$$\$203,000 - \$200,000 = \$3,000 \text{ U}$$

The variance is unfavourable, because more was spent of fixed overhead than was estimated.

Production Volume Variance

The difference between the standard amount of fixed overhead cost allocated to products and the estimated fixed overhead costs is called the **production volume variance** (Exhibit 11.9). If actual volumes of the allocation base exceed normal (i.e., estimated) volumes, fixed overhead will be overapplied, and the variance will be favourable. At the end of the accounting period, overapplied fixed overhead needs to be allocated to inventory and cost of goods sold. Conversely, if actual volumes of the allocation base are less than normal volumes, fixed overhead will be underapplied, and the variance will be unfavourable. The underapplied fixed overhead amount is expensed in cost of goods sold at the end of the accounting period. The production volume variance is calculated only for fixed overhead. This variance is used for bookkeeping purposes. The variance is calculated as follows:

$$\begin{array}{c}\text{Production} \\ \text{volume variance}\end{array} = \left(\begin{array}{c}\text{Estimated volume} \\ \text{of allocation base}\end{array} - \begin{array}{c}\text{Standard volume of allocation} \\ \text{base for actual output}\end{array}\right) \times \begin{array}{c}\text{Standard fixed overhead} \\ \text{allocation rate}\end{array}$$

For Benny's, suppose estimated fixed overhead was $200,000 and the estimated volume of the allocation base was 500,000 litres (normal production). The standard allocation rate is $200,000 ÷ 500,000 litres = $0.40 per litre. Actual production was 498,000 litres. The production volume variance is calculated as follows:

$$(500{,}000 \text{ litres} - 498{,}000 \text{ litres}) \times \$0.40 \text{ per litre} = \$800 \text{ U}$$

Because actual production was less than normal, Benny's fixed overhead is underapplied, causing an unfavourable variance. This variance is expensed in cost of goods sold at the end of the accounting period. These overhead variance computations are shown in Exhibit 11.10.

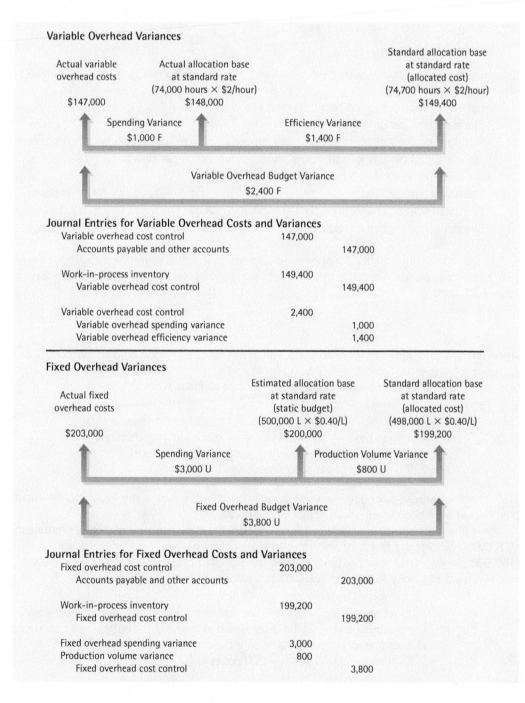

Variable Overhead Variances

Actual variable overhead costs	Actual allocation base at standard rate (74,000 hours × $2/hour)	Standard allocation base at standard rate (allocated cost) (74,700 hours × $2/hour)
$147,000	$148,000	$149,400

Spending Variance $1,000 F

Efficiency Variance $1,400 F

Variable Overhead Budget Variance $2,400 F

Journal Entries for Variable Overhead Costs and Variances

Variable overhead cost control	147,000	
Accounts payable and other accounts		147,000
Work-in-process inventory	149,400	
Variable overhead cost control		149,400
Variable overhead cost control	2,400	
Variable overhead spending variance		1,000
Variable overhead efficiency variance		1,400

Fixed Overhead Variances

Actual fixed overhead costs	Estimated allocation base at standard rate (static budget) (500,000 L × $0.40/L)	Standard allocation base at standard rate (allocated cost) (498,000 L × $0.40/L)
$203,000	$200,000	$199,200

Spending Variance $3,000 U

Production Volume Variance $800 U

Fixed Overhead Budget Variance $3,800 U

Journal Entries for Fixed Overhead Costs and Variances

Fixed overhead cost control	203,000	
Accounts payable and other accounts		203,000
Work-in-process inventory	199,200	
Fixed overhead cost control		199,200
Fixed overhead spending variance	3,000	
Production volume variance	800	
Fixed overhead cost control		3,800

Journal Entries for Overhead Costs and Variances

Organizations often use an overhead cost control account to keep track of actual and allocated overhead costs. As actual overhead costs are incurred, they are debited to the account. The account is then credited for the standard amount of overhead costs allocated to inventory. The remaining balance in the overhead cost control account is the total variance. This balance for fixed overhead costs is closed to separate spending and volume variance accounts, while the balance for variable overhead costs is closed to separate spending and efficiency variance accounts. The journal entries for Benny's are shown in Exhibit 11.10.

Creaciones Concretas, Part 4, demonstrates the calculation of fixed and variable overhead variances.

© Steven Frame/Alamy Stock Photo

example

creaciones concretas, part 4
OVERHEAD VARIANCES

Josephina had previously established the following standard costs for fixed and variable overhead:

Variable overhead (allocated based on direct labour hours):

Standard cost per direct labour hour	2 pesos
Standard quantity of allocation base per block (1 hour per 100 blocks)	0.01 hours
Standard cost per block (0.01 hours per block × 2 pesos per hour)	0.02 pesos

Fixed overhead (allocated based on units):

Estimated cost	180,000 pesos
Estimated volume of allocation base (blocks produced)	90,000 blocks
Standard cost per block (180,000 pesos ÷ 90,000 blocks)	2 pesos

At the end of the month, Josephina determines that actual fixed overhead costs were 175,000 pesos. Actual variable overhead costs were 2,500 pesos, and 1,100 actual labour hours were used.

Variable Overhead Spending and Efficiency Variances

Josephina analyzes variable overhead costs, which are allocated based on direct labour hours. Actual variable overhead costs were 2,500 pesos, and actual direct labour hours were 1,100. She calculates the variable overhead spending variance as follows:

$$\text{Actual variable overhead cost} - \left(\text{Actual volume of allocation base} \times \text{Standard variable overhead allocation rate} \right)$$
$$= 2{,}500 \text{ pesos} - (1{,}100 \text{ hours} \times 2 \text{ pesos per labour hour})$$
$$= 2{,}500 - 2{,}200 \text{ pesos} = 300 \text{ pesos U}$$

The variable overhead spending variance is unfavourable because more was actually spent than should have been spent, given actual labour hours.

Next she calculates the variable overhead efficiency variance. Based on actual production of 100,000 blocks, the standard volume of the allocation base is 1,000 direct labour hours (100,000 blocks × 0.01 hour per block). Given the standard cost of 2 pesos per hour, the variable overhead efficiency variance is calculated as follows:

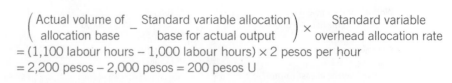

$$\left(\text{Actual volume of allocation base} - \text{Standard variable allocation base for actual output} \right) \times \text{Standard variable overhead allocation rate}$$
$$= (1{,}100 \text{ labour hours} - 1{,}000 \text{ labour hours}) \times 2 \text{ pesos per hour}$$
$$= 2{,}200 \text{ pesos} - 2{,}000 \text{ pesos} = 200 \text{ pesos U}$$

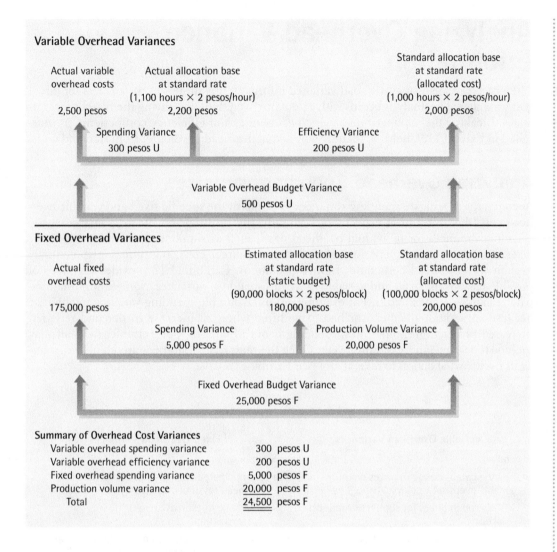

Variable Overhead Variances

Actual variable overhead costs	Actual allocation base at standard rate (1,100 hours × 2 pesos/hour)		Standard allocation base at standard rate (allocated cost) (1,000 hours × 2 pesos/hour)
2,500 pesos	2,200 pesos		2,000 pesos

Spending Variance
300 pesos U

Efficiency Variance
200 pesos U

Variable Overhead Budget Variance
500 pesos U

Fixed Overhead Variances

Actual fixed overhead costs	Estimated allocation base at standard rate (static budget) (90,000 blocks × 2 pesos/block)	Standard allocation base at standard rate (allocated cost) (100,000 blocks × 2 pesos/block)
175,000 pesos	180,000 pesos	200,000 pesos

Spending Variance
5,000 pesos F

Production Volume Variance
20,000 pesos F

Fixed Overhead Budget Variance
25,000 pesos F

Summary of Overhead Cost Variances

Variable overhead spending variance	300 pesos U
Variable overhead efficiency variance	200 pesos U
Fixed overhead spending variance	5,000 pesos F
Production volume variance	20,000 pesos F
Total	24,500 pesos F

➤**EXHIBIT 11.11**
Overhead Variances for
Creaciones Concretas

The variable overhead efficiency variance is unfavourable because actual labour hours used in production exceeded the standard number of labour hours (see Exhibit 11.11).

Fixed Overhead Spending and Production Volume Variances

Josephina calculates the fixed overhead spending variance as follows:

$$\text{Actual fixed overhead costs} - \text{Estimated fixed overhead costs}$$
$$= 175{,}000 \text{ pesos} - 180{,}000 \text{ pesos} = 5{,}000 \text{ pesos F}$$

The fixed overhead spending variance is favourable because less was spent than expected, as is shown in Exhibit 11.11.

Next, Josephina calculates the production volume variance as follows:

$$\left(\begin{array}{c}\text{Estimated volume} \\ \text{of allocation base}\end{array} - \begin{array}{c}\text{Standard volume of allocation} \\ \text{base for actual output}\end{array}\right) \times \begin{array}{c}\text{Standard fixed} \\ \text{overhead allocation rate}\end{array}$$
$$= (90{,}000 \text{ blocks} - 100{,}000 \text{ blocks}) \times 2 \text{ pesos per block} = 20{,}000 \text{ pesos F}$$

Estimated production volume was 90,000 blocks, but 100,000 blocks were actually produced. Therefore, 10,000 more blocks were produced than expected, resulting in a favourable production volume variance; that is, fixed overhead costs were overapplied by 20,000 pesos (2 pesos per block × 10,000 blocks). ■

Analyzing Overhead Variance Information

The process of analyzing overhead variance information is similar to the process for direct cost variances. The analysis begins with calculating and then identifying the reasons for variances. Breaking the variances into spending, volume, and efficiency components, as illustrated in Exhibit 11.9, helps to identify why actual overhead costs differ from standard costs.

Analyzing Overhead Spending Variances

Accountants investigate spending variances to pinpoint the specific fixed and variable overhead costs that differ from expectations. Usually, the investigation includes analyzing the spending variances for individual overhead costs, such as supplies, depreciation, property taxes, insurance, and supervision salaries. As with direct costs, many reasons potentially explain why overhead costs differ from expectations. Exhibit 11.12 provides examples of possible reasons for fixed and variable overhead spending variances. Sometimes, unanticipated changes occur in costs. For example, an unfavourable spending variance might arise because an additional supervisor had to be hired when an increase in demand required increased production. Sometimes, spending is out of control. For example, the staff may include too many janitorial employees. Once the reasons for variances are identified, managers decide what action to take, if any (see Exhibit 11.2).

> **EXHIBIT 11.12**
>
> Examples of Reasons for Overhead Variances

Variable Overhead Variances	Fixed Overhead Variances
Spending:	**Spending:**
• Unanticipated change in prices paid for variable overhead resources, caused by	• Unanticipated change in prices for fixed overhead resources, caused by
— Variation in prices for supplies or indirect labour	— Change in estimated asset life for depreciation
— New supplier or labour contract	— Change in electricity, other utility, insurance, or property tax rates
• Out-of-control or improved efficiency in variable overhead cost spending	• Out-of-control or improved efficiency in fixed overhead cost spending
• Change in type or extent of variable overhead resources used, such as	• Change in activity level to a new relevant range, requiring change in fixed resources such as
— Change from in-house to outsourced equipment maintenance services	— Hire or lay off a supervisor
— Increase or decrease in normal spoilage, rework, or scrap	— Increase or decrease fixed hours of janitorial staff
• Unreasonable standard variable overhead allocation rate, caused by	— Depreciation change from purchase or disposal of property, plant, and equipment
— Inappropriate allocation base	• Unreasonable estimate for fixed overhead costs
— Poor estimate of variable overhead costs	• Error in the accounting records for actual fixed overhead costs
— Poor estimate of allocation base volume	
• Error in the accounting records for actual variable overhead costs	
Efficiency:	**Production Volume:**
• Fluctuation in efficiency of the allocation base (e.g., labour hours, labour costs, machine hours, units produced)—see efficiency examples in Exhibit 11.8	• Normal fluctuation in volume of allocation base (usually caused by changes in demand)
	• Improved production processes
	• Unreasonable estimate of volume of the allocation base
	• Error in the accounting records for actual output

Interpreting the Variable Overhead Efficiency Variance

Variable overhead costs are allocated to production based on an estimated volume of an allocation base. The allocation base used for variable costs is typically some type of resource input (such as labour hours, labour costs, or machine hours) or the volume of output. Because the direct cost efficiency variances already provide information about the efficiency of inputs and outputs, overhead efficiency variances provide no new information. For example, consider the Creaciones Concretas case. Recall that direct labour hours were used to calculate the standard variable overhead allocation rate. The variable overhead efficiency variance of 200 pesos was unfavourable because actual labour hours exceeded standard labour hours (see Exhibit 11.11). However, the inefficient use of labour hours was already reflected in the 1,000- peso unfavourable direct labour efficiency variance (see Exhibit 11.7). Thus, the variable overhead efficiency variance provides no new information; for monitoring purposes, it is meaningless. However, this variance must be calculated for bookkeeping reasons; it helps to explain why variable overhead costs allocated are different from actual variable overhead costs.

Interpreting the Production Volume Variance

By definition, fixed overhead costs are not expected to vary with volume of production. However, a production volume variance exists because fixed overhead costs are allocated to production based on an estimated level of an allocation base. In turn, the estimated level of the allocation base depends on the estimated level of production. We usually produce more or less than estimated, and so we allocate more or less of our estimated fixed cost than we expected. At the end of each accounting period, we adjust the accounting records for this difference. Exhibit 11.10 shows the adjusting journal entries for Benny's.

As shown in Exhibit 11.12, actual production volume (and volume of the allocation base) may differ from estimated volume because of normal fluctuations, production problems, improved production processes, unreasonable estimates, or accounting errors. Managers need to analyze the reasons for actual production volume differing from estimated volume to determine what type of action, if any, is needed. In general, we would expect production volume to vary with sales levels. Thus, the investigation of production volume variances tends to focus on the deviation between actual and estimated sales (see Chapter 12). Although managers want to know why production volume deviates from the budget, the dollar amount of the production volume variance does not require investigation. The production volume variance also provides information about capacity utilization. Therefore, it can be monitored to achieve long-term goals of operating at optimal capacity levels. The relationship between capacity and demand can be monitored to find the optimum capacity levels where throughput (the rate at which products are manufactured) is equal to demand.

11-1 self-study problem   Direct Cost and Overhead Variances, Variance Analysis

LO1, LO3, LO4, LO5, LO6

Latiefa is the cost accountant at Hallet and Sons, manufacturer of exquisite glass serving bowls. The materials used for the bowls are inexpensive, but the process is labour intensive. The supervisor decided to use less costly labour this period to see whether costs could be reduced. Latiefa needs to prepare a report for her supervisor about how effective operations had been during the month of January. She had set the following standards:

		Cost per Unit
Direct materials	3 kg @ $2.50 per kg	$ 7.50
Direct labour	5 hours @ $15.00 per hour	75.00
Factory overhead:		
Variable	$3.00 per direct labour hour	15.00
Fixed	$20.00 per unit	20.00

Variable overhead is allocated by labour hours, and fixed overhead is allocated by unit. Estimated production per month is 40,000 standard direct labour hours.

self-study problem

11-1

Records for January based on production of 7,800 units indicated the following:

Direct materials purchased	25,000 kg @ $2.60
Direct materials used	23,100 kg
Direct labour	40,100 hours @ $14.60
Variable overhead	$119,000
Fixed overhead	$180,000

required

The company's policy is to record direct material price variances at the time materials are purchased.

A. Prepare a simple, meaningful variance report for direct materials, direct labour, and variable and fixed overhead that Latiefa could present to her supervisor.

B. Attach to the variance report a discussion of the variances and a recommendation about whether some of them should be investigated further.

See the solution on page 527.

Cost Variance Adjustments

LO7 Journalize closing entries for manufacturing cost variances

When all the production entries and variances are recorded for an accounting period, an additional entry is made to eliminate the variance accounts. If the total variance is favourable, fewer resources were used than estimated, so we need to decrease the costs in inventory and cost of goods sold. If the total variance is unfavourable, more resources were used than estimated, so the costs in inventory and cost of goods sold need to be increased.

The type of adjustment made typically depends on whether variances are material, which is a matter of judgment. Amounts are generally viewed as material if their treatment would affect the decisions made by people who rely on reported values. If the net amount of variances is deemed immaterial, the adjustment is usually made only to cost of goods sold. However, the existence of material variances means that the standard costs assigned to product units do not fairly represent the actual cost of the units. Thus, if the net amount of variances is material, a more accurate adjustment procedure is needed. A proportionate share of the variance should be allocated to work in process, finished goods inventory, and cost of goods sold.

Consider the production cost variances for Creaciones Concretas. The combined variances are as follows:

Direct costs (see Exhibit 11.7)	118,500 pesos F
Overhead costs (see Exhibit 11.11)	24,500 pesos F
Total	143,000 pesos F

To evaluate materiality, we compare the combined variance amount with the total amount of actual production costs:

Actual direct material costs (see Exhibit 11.7)	975,000 pesos
Actual direct labour costs (see Exhibit 11.7)	16,500 pesos
Actual variable overhead costs (see Exhibit 11.11)	2,500 pesos
Actual fixed overhead costs (see Exhibit 11.11)	175,000 pesos
Total	1,169,000 pesos

The combined variances amount to 143,000 pesos ÷ 1,169,000 pesos, or 12.2% of actual production costs. If we decide this amount is not material, we can simply close the variances to cost of goods sold; that is, we can decrease cost of goods sold by 143,000 pesos.

As a general rule, accountants often consider amounts larger than 10% to be material. Therefore, the combined variance for Creaciones Concretas would most likely be considered material. In this case, the variances would be closed to the general ledger accounts that contain the current period's standard production costs. For Creaciones Concretas, standard costs allocated to production during the period totalled 100,000 blocks × 12.12 pesos standard cost per block (see Creaciones Concretas, Part 1), or 1,212,000 pesos. Assume that these costs are included in the following general ledger accounts at the end of the accounting period:

	Pesos	Percentage
Work-in-process inventory	0 pesos	0%
Finished goods inventory (5,000 blocks × 12.12 pesos per block)	60,600	5
Cost of goods sold (95,000 blocks × 12.12 pesos per block)	1,151,400	95
Total	1,212,000 pesos	100%

Of the standard costs allocated during the accounting period, 5% remain in finished goods inventory, and 95% are recognized in cost of goods sold. Therefore, we decrease each of these accounts—finished goods by 7,150 pesos (5% of 143,000) and cost of goods sold by 135,850 pesos (95% of 143,000). The journal entry to record the adjustment is as follows:

Direct materials price variance	325,000 pesos[5]	
Fixed overhead spending variance	5,000 pesos	
Production volume variance	20,000 pesos[6]	
Direct materials efficiency variance		200,000 pesos
Direct labour price variance		5,500 pesos
Direct labour efficiency variance		1,000 pesos
Variable overhead spending variance		300 pesos
Variable overhead efficiency variance		200 pesos
Finished goods inventory		7,150 pesos
Cost of goods sold		135,850 pesos

After this adjustment is made, the actual production costs are recorded in the inventory and cost of goods sold accounts, as required by generally accepted accounting principles for financial reporting.

●● > FOCUS ON ETHICAL DECISION MAKING: WASTED SOUP

While she was watching operations at a food processing plant, a consultant noticed a large amount of soup on the floor under a filling machine. An operator washed this soup away each day. When asked about the loss of soup, the production manager replied that no losses occurred. In this manager's view, no problem existed because the production line operating costs were below budgeted costs. Later, a productivity team analyzed the amount of soup wasted over a given time period. The team estimated the cost of the leak to be $750,000 per year. To correct the problem, the company installed a set of valves that cost $50,000, and the new valves eliminated the loss of soup.

Instead of measuring performance against expected budget levels, managers could compare actual profits to ideal profits that could be earned if operations were to run at their true potential. By focusing on the gap between ideal and actual profits, managers are encouraged to identify lost profit potential and to reconsider critical processes. Once gaps are identified, managers rank them according to their value to the organization and correct them in priority order.

© RosaIreneBetancourt 7/Alamy Stock Photo

Source: I. Thompson and C. Rosen, "Accounting for Higher Profits," *Optimize*, January 2003, pp. 29–34.

ETHICS AND CONTINUOUS IMPROVEMENT
Organizations forgo opportunities for improvement when employees fail to alert managers about waste that is built into standard costs. This opportunity cost reduces shareholder value and potentially prevents reduction of consumer prices. Why it is common for employees to do nothing when they observe inefficiencies? How does everyone benefit when companies and individuals seek continuous improvement?

---

[5] This example is a simplified version of the adjustment for the direct materials price variance. Technically, if the variance were material, it would be prorated to direct materials and production, with the production amount added to the other production variances and closed in aggregate as shown in the full entry.

[6] The production volume variance is favourable. This means that fixed overhead is overapplied to the units of production. In an overapplied situation, IFRS/Canadian ASPE requires that the value of inventory be adjusted to reflect actual cost. This is the necessary journal entry to make this adjustment. If the production volume variance is unfavourable due to low production, the entire variance is written off to cost of goods sold.

SUMMARY

L01   Explain the role of variance analysis in the strategic management process

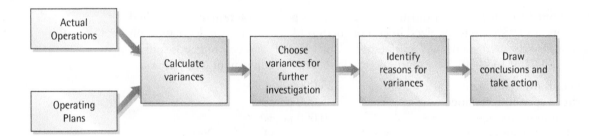

VARIANCE ANALYSIS IN A DIAGNOSTIC CONTROL SYSTEM

- ► Monitor variances for preset goals
- ► Factors influencing further investigation of variances
  - – Size of variance
  - – Trends in variances
- ► Management conclusions and actions
- ► See Exhibit 11.2
- ► Behavioural implications

VARIANCE ANALYSIS IN AN INTERACTIVE CONTROL SYSTEM

- ► Monitor variances for strategic uncertainties
- ► Discuss in face-to-face meetings with top management
- ► Decide whether strategies should be changed

L02   Describe a standard costing system and how it is used

STANDARD COSTS FOR MANUFACTURED PRODUCTS

$$\text{Standard cost per unit of output} = \text{Standard cost of direct materials} + \text{Standard cost of direct labour} + \text{Standard cost of variable overhead} + \text{Standard cost of fixed overhead}$$

DEVELOPING STANDARD COSTS

- ► Information used
  - – Historical costs and trends
  - – Expected changes in costs or processes
  - – Estimates from industrial engineers
- ► Key assumptions
  - – Volume of production activity

- – Production processes and efficiency, including expected waste and defects
- – Prices and quality of inputs
- ► Attainability
  - – To motivate performance, set standards with little slack

SUMMARY

LO3   Calculate and journalize direct cost variances

A standard cost variance is a difference between standard costs and actual costs.

DIRECT COST VARIANCES

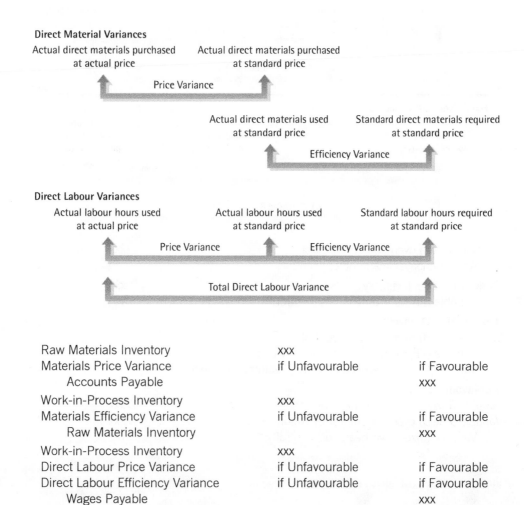

Direct Material Variances

Actual direct materials purchased at actual price — Price Variance — Actual direct materials purchased at standard price

Actual direct materials used at standard price — Efficiency Variance — Standard direct materials required at standard price

Direct Labour Variances

Actual labour hours used at actual price — Price Variance — Actual labour hours used at standard price — Efficiency Variance — Standard labour hours required at standard price

Total Direct Labour Variance

Raw Materials Inventory	xxx	
Materials Price Variance	if Unfavourable	if Favourable
Accounts Payable		xxx
Work-in-Process Inventory	xxx	
Materials Efficiency Variance	if Unfavourable	if Favourable
Raw Materials Inventory		xxx
Work-in-Process Inventory	xxx	
Direct Labour Price Variance	if Unfavourable	if Favourable
Direct Labour Efficiency Variance	if Unfavourable	if Favourable
Wages Payable		xxx

LO4   Analyze and use direct cost variance information

IDENTIFYING REASONS FOR DIRECT COST VARIANCES – SEE EXHIBIT 11.8

RESOURCE AND QUALITY TRADE-OFFS REFLECTED IN DIRECT COST VARIANCES

► Price and efficiency
► Different inputs

SUMMARY

L05 Calculate and journalize variable and fixed overhead variances

OVERHEAD VARIANCES

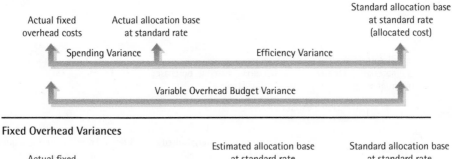

Variable Overhead Variances

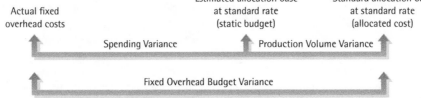

Fixed Overhead Variances

Variable (Fixed) overhead cost control	xxx	
Accounts payable and other accounts		xxx
Work-in-Process Inventory	xxx	
Variable (Fixed) overhead cost control		xxx

If Favourable Variances

Variable (Fixed) overhead cost control	xxx	
Variable (Fixed) overhead spending variance		xxx
Variable (Fixed) overhead efficiency (volume) variance		xxx

If Unfavourable Variances

Variable (Fixed) overhead spending variance	xxx	
Variable (Fixed) overhead efficiency (volume) variance	xxx	
Variable (Fixed) overhead cost control		xxx

L06 Analyze and use overhead variance information

For examples of reasons for overhead variances, see Exhibit 11.12.

L07 Journalize closing entries for manufacturing cost variances

IMMATERIAL VARIANCES

- Amount would not affect information users' decisions
- Closed to cost of goods sold

MATERIAL VARIANCES

- Standard costs do not fairly represent the actual cost of the units
- Prorate among
  - Work in process
  - Finished goods
  - Cost of goods sold

11-1 solution to self-study problem

A. Latiefa could present the following variance report to her supervisor:

	Favourable (F) or Unfavourable (U) Variance		
	Price/Spending	Volume/Efficiency	Total
Direct materials	$ 2,500 U	$ 750 F	$ 1,750 U
Direct labour	16,040 F	16,500 U	460 U
Total direct cost variance			2,210 U
Variable overhead	1,300 F	3,300 U	2,000 U
Fixed overhead	20,000 U	4,000 U	24,000 U
Total overhead cost variance			26,000 U
Total variance			$ 28,210 U

Computation check:

Standard costs allocated based on actual production

[7,800 units × ($7.50 + $75.00 + $20.00 + $15.00)] $916,500

Less actual costs:

Direct materials:

Materials used at standard cost

(23,100 kg × $2.50) $57,750

Unfavourable price variance for material purchases

[25,000 kg × ($2.60 − $2.50)]   2,500

Total direct material cost   60,250

Direct labour (40,100 hours × $14.60)   585,460

Variable overhead   119,000

Fixed overhead   180,000

Total actual costs   944,710

Total variance $ 28,210 U

Details of the calculations are shown in Exhibit 11.14.

B. Discussion of most significant variances:

- Because the supervisor hired less-expensive labour this month, it is not surprising that the direct labour price variance is large and favourable ($16,040). However, this positive variance is more than offset by a large unfavourable direct labour efficiency variance ($16,500). It appears that more hours were required to compensate for less-skilled labour. This variance should be investigated to verify the conjectures.
- If less-skilled labour has a negative effect on quality, sales could be lost. Any potential change in the quality of output needs to be investigated.
- The fixed overhead spending variance was very large and unfavourable ($20,000). These costs might be out of control, and they need to be investigated.

Discussion of less significant variances:

- Given the unfavourable direct materials price variance ($2,500) and the favourable direct materials efficiency variance ($750), it is possible that the quality purchased this period has improved because less was used than expected. However, a price increase is also a possible explanation. These variances should be investigated to determine whether either or both of the standards should be changed.
- We need to determine whether a favourable variable overhead spending variance ($1,300) was due to improvements made in variable overhead costs and whether such improvements can be sustained (i.e., whether the standard should be changed).

▶EXHIBIT 11.14

Calculation of Premier Gift Basket Revenue Variances

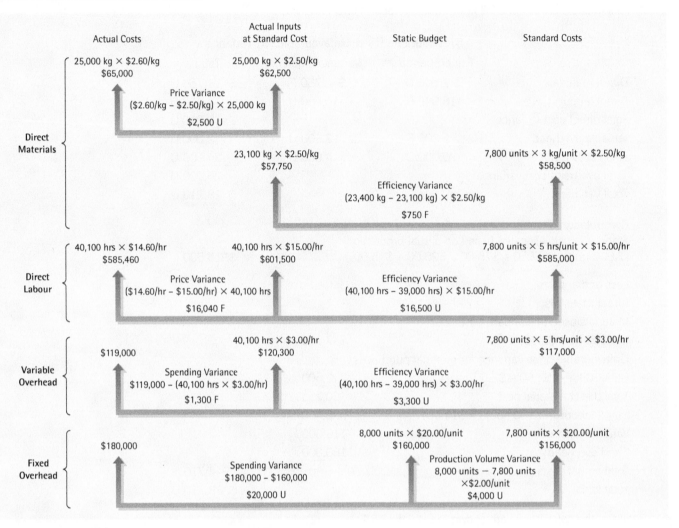

QUESTIONS

11.1 Explain why variances for direct material and direct labour are separated into price and efficiency variances.

11.2 Suppose that utilities are considered a fixed cost for a retail clothing outlet. Why might we expect a variance to occur for the cost of utilities?

11.3 How might variance analysis contribute to a diagnostic control system?

11.4 Explain why the variance accounts need to be closed at the end of the period.

11.5 Fly-a-Kite Company manufactures a variety of kite kits. The company's production manager has asked you to prepare a simple but meaningful variance report for product costs so that she can identify areas in need of improved cost control. List all the variances you would present in the variance report for production costs, and explain why each is useful.

11.6 Identify the common variances needed to reconcile a manufacturing organization's accounting records at the end of the period. How are these variances treated if the total variance is immaterial? if the total variance is material?

11.7 Discuss factors that affect accountants' decisions to investigate the reasons for variances.

11.8 Explain how accountants and managers decide which cost variances to monitor.

11.9 How are standard costs determined?

11.10 List several ways that variances can be used to improve future operations.

11.11 Suppose the direct materials price variance is large and favourable, and the direct materials efficiency variance is large and unfavourable. What questions are you likely to ask when investigating these variances further?

11.12 Why are direct materials price variances usually recorded at the time of purchase?

11.13 What is an anchoring bias and how does it affect the process of setting new standards at the end of an accounting period?

11.14 What does the production volume variance tell managers?

11.15 How are standard quantities for materials, labour, and variable overhead calculated?

11.16 Explain the relationship between the labour variances and variable overhead variances when variable overhead is applied based on direct labour hours.

MULTIPLE-CHOICE QUESTIONS

11.17 Generico Ltd. uses an injection device to regulate the flow of raw materials into moulds in its production process. When the injector device is "out of control," the entire production line must be shut down.

The production data for the past month indicated an unfavourable raw material cost variance as follows:

Budgeted production volume	40,000 units
Actual production volume	39,000 units
Budgeted raw materials (40,000 × 2 grams @ $10 per gram)	$ 800,000
Actual raw materials (39,000 × 2.2 grams @ $12 per gram)	1,029,600
Variance (unfavourable)	$ 229,600

The variance was either caused by the injector device being out of control or by random factors that would disappear on their own. The production manager must decide whether to shut down production to investigate the cause of the variance or wait another month.

Data regarding investigation of the cause of the variance are as follows:

Cost to inspect injector device (10 hours @ $300)	$3,000
Cost to repair injector device (20 hours @ $300)	$6,000
Lost contribution margin during downtime	$1,000 per hour

Based on past experience, there is a 10% chance that the injector device is out of control. If it is out of control and not corrected right away, the net cost to the company until the next regularly scheduled maintenance adjustment will be $90,000.

Which of the following represents the materials efficiency variance?
a. $ 93,600 unfavourable
b. $ 69,600 unfavourable
c. $ 78,000 unfavourable
d. $ 58,000 unfavourable
e. $156,000 unfavourable

11.18 Casey's Photography expected to work 400 hours per year taking wedding photos for 50 weddings. Casey's standard labour rate for photographers is $25 per hour. During the last year, Casey actually worked 420 hours for 50 weddings and paid photographers $10,815. The labour rate and labour efficiency variances are:
a. $315 favourable; $500 favourable
b. $815 favourable; $500 unfavourable
c. $315 favourable; $815 favourable
d. $315 unfavourable; $500 unfavourable

11.19 Cozy Creatures expected to produce 5,000 Hazel the Hedgehog bed warmers. Hazel was so popular that Cozy Creatures sold 5,750 Hazels. Each Hazel requires 0.5 metres of cotton flannel. Cozy Creatues purchased

3,000 metres of cotton flannel and used 2,900 metres. The standard price for cotton flannel is $9.00 per metre. Cozy Creatures paid $13,500 for the cotton flannel. The materials price and materials quantity variances are:

a. $ 13,500 favourable; $1,125 unfavourable
b. $ 900 favourable; $900 unfavourable
c. $ 450 unfavourable; $225 favourable
d. $ 13,500 favourable; $225 unfavourable

11.20 Lynn Company uses a standard cost system. Overhead is applied on the basis of direct labour hours (DLH), and the annual practical capacity of 42,000 DLH is used in establishing the standard overhead rates. The following summarizes budget and actual data for the past year:

	Budget	Actual
Units produced	100,000	92,000
Direct materials (kg)	50,000	47,840
Direct labour hours (DLH)	40,000	37,720
Production costs:		
Direct materials	$200,000	$188,968
Direct labour	$500,000	$471,500
Variable factory overhead	$ 80,000ᵃ	$ 84,640
Fixed factory overhead	$160,000ᵃ	$162,000
ᵃapplied		

During the year, 90,000 units were sold. There were no beginning or ending work-in-process inventories, but there were 3,000 units of finished goods on hand at the end of the year.

The variable factory overhead flexible budget variance is which of the following?

a. $12,640 unfavourable
b. $ 4,560 unfavourable
c. $ 9,200 unfavourable
d. $11,040 unfavourable
e. $ 4,600 unfavourable

11.21 Up North's managers expected to produce 20,000 units of product in March. The standard cost for the materials used for 20,000 units is $173,600 and the standard cost per unit is $2.80 per litre. Actual production in March was 19,100 units. The company purchased and used 57,300 litres of materials costing $163,305. What is the standard quantity of litres per unit?

a. 3.1 litres
b. $2.80 per litre
c. 8.68 litres
d. 3 litres

EXERCISES

11.22 Direct Labour Variances To help control operations, Sisyphus Company developed a standard costing system in its
LO3   job shop. Data for a recent job follows.

	Standard	Actual
Direct labour hours	950	920
Direct labour dollars	$1,900	$1,850
Units produced	380	380

REQUIRED Calculate the direct labour price and efficiency variances and determine whether they are favourable or unfavourable. Provide one possible explanation for each variance.

11.23 Journal Entries Refer to 11.22. Prepare the journal entries for the direct labour price and efficiency variances.
LO3   Assume that Sisyphus Company uses a Wages Payable account to record direct labour.

11.24 Direct Labour Variances Following is information about Forester's Furniture's direct labour hours and wages last period.

LO3

Actual labour hours at the standard price per hour	$2,184
Actual labour hours at the actual price per hour	2,278
Standard labour hours at the standard price per hour	2,275
Standard labour hours at the actual price per hour	2,373

REQUIRED
A. Calculate the direct labour efficiency variance.
B. Calculate the direct labour price variance.
C. Provide one possible explanation for each variance.

11.25 Journal Entries Refer to 11.24. Prepare the journal entries for the direct labour price and efficiency variances. Assume that Forester's Furniture uses a Wages Payable account to record direct labour.

LO3

11.26 Direct Material Variances Delicata's managers expected to produce 30,000 units of product in November. The standard cost for the materials used for 30,000 units is $260,400 and the standard cost per unit is $4.20 per litre. Actual production in November was 28,650 units. The company purchased and used 85,950 litres of materials costing $244.957.50

LO3

REQUIRED
A. What was the standard quantity of litres per unit?
B. What was the direct materials efficiency variance for November?
C. What was the direct materials price variance for November?

11.27 Journal Entries Refer to 11.26. Prepare the journal entries for the materials price and efficiency variances for November. Assume that Delicata records the materials price variance at the time materials are purchased.

LO3

11.28 Fixed Overhead Variances, Solve for Unknown Country Pet Clinic charges its patients on the basis of actual direct costs incurred plus fixed costs at the rate of $40 per hour. The fixed cost rate of $40 per hour is based on the assumption of 6,000 patient hours monthly, assuming that each patient requires a half hour. During September, 11,000 patients were seen and the following costs were recorded.

LO5

Fixed overhead costs allocated to patients	$248,000
Fixed overhead spending variance	24,000 unfavourable

REQUIRED
A. How many patient hours were recorded?
B. What was the budgeted fixed cost?
C. What was the production volume variance?
D. What was the actual fixed overhead?

11.29 Fixed and Variable Overhead Variances Kirkpatrick Consulting uses a standard costing system to allocate overhead costs. The accountant estimated 7,650 hours as the volume to develop standard overhead rates. Budgeted costs were $17,213 for fixed overhead and $13,770 for variable overhead. The following results were reported.

LO5

Actual hours	7,380
Standard hours	7,470
Actual fixed overhead	$17,100
Actual variable overhead	$12,600

REQUIRED
A. Calculate the spending variances for fixed and variable overhead.
B. Calculate the overhead allocation rates for fixed and variable overhead.
C. Calculate the production volume variance for fixed overhead.
D. Calculate the efficiency variance for variable overhead.

11.30 Journal Entries Refer to 11.24. Prepare the journal entries to record the variable and fixed overhead. Then, prepare the journal entries to record the allocation of variable and fixed overhead into work in process. Then, record the overhead variances.

LO5

11.31 Direct Labour Variances, Overhead Spending Variance The following data for Kitchen Tile Company relate to the production of 18,000 tiles during the past month. The company allocates fixed overhead costs at a standard rate of $19 per direct labour hour:

LO3, LO5

Direct labour:
   Standard cost is 6 tiles per hour at $24.00 per hour
   Actual cost per hour was $24.50
   Labour efficiency variance was $6,720 F

Fixed overhead costs:
Estimated = $60,000
Actual = $58,720

REQUIRED   **A.** How many actual labour hours were worked to produce the 18,000 tiles?
B. What is the price variance for direct labour?
C. What is the budget variance for fixed costs?

11.32 Direct Materials and Labour Variances, Variances to Investigate The managers of Nakatani Enterprises established the following standards for Model 535:

LO2, LO3, LO4

	Quantity Standard	Price Standard
Direct materials	0.8 kg per unit	$ 2.00 per kg
Direct labour	0.2 hours per unit	$17.00 per hour

Last month, 15,342 units of Model 535 were produced at a cost of $26,870 for direct materials and $47,000 for direct labour. A total of 13,252 kilograms of direct materials was used. Total direct labour hours amounted to 2,730 hours. During the same period, 11,000 kilograms of direct material were purchased for $21,730. The company's policy is to record materials price variances at the time materials are purchased.

REQUIRED   **A.** What is the total standard cost for direct materials and direct labour for the output this period?
B. What was the direct materials price variance?
C. What was the direct materials efficiency variance?
D. What was the direct labour price variance?
E. What was the direct labour efficiency variance?
F. Identify any variances that are material (greater than 10% of total direct cost at standard). Discuss whether you would investigate these variances.

11.33 Direct Materials and Direct Labour Variances, Journal Entries The following information pertains to Nell Company's production of one unit of its manufactured product during the month of June. The company recognizes the materials price variance when materials are purchased:

LO3

Standard quantity of materials	5 kg
Standard cost per kilogram	$0.20
Standard direct labour hours	0.4 hr
Standard wage rate per hour	$7.00
Direct materials purchased	100,000 kg
Cost of direct materials purchased per kilogram	$0.17
Direct materials consumed for manufacture of 10,000 units	60,000 kg
Actual direct labour hours required for 10,000 units	3,900
Actual direct labour cost per hour	$7.20

REQUIRED   **A.** Calculate the price and efficiency (quantity) variances for materials and labour.
B. Record the journal entries for purchase and use of direct materials, and the journal entries for direct labour.
C. Provide one possible explanation for each variance.

11.34 Direct Labour Variances, Solve for Unknowns The Chase Company's budget for April called for production of 7,000 units. At that level of activity, direct labour was budgeted at $168,000. During April, 7,200 units were produced. Labour was paid $12.20 per hour, resulting in an unfavourable labour price variance of $2,860. The total direct labour variance was $1,660 unfavourable.

LO3

REQUIRED   **A.** What was the standard pay rate per direct labour hour?
B. What was the standard number of direct labour hours per unit?
C. What was the actual total number of direct labour hours during April?
D. What was the direct labour efficiency variance for April?
E. Record the journal entries for direct labour.

11.35 Variable and Fixed Overhead Variances, Journal Entries Derf Company allocates overhead on the basis of direct labour hours. Two direct labour hours are required for each unit of product. Planned production for the period was set at 9,000 units. Manufacturing overhead is estimated at $135,000 for the period (with 20% of this cost being fixed). The 17,200 hours worked during the period resulted in the production of 8,500 units. The variable manufacturing overhead cost incurred was $108,500, and the fixed manufacturing overhead cost was $28,000.

LO5, LO6, LO7

REQUIRED
A. Determine the variable overhead spending variance.
B. Determine the variable overhead efficiency (quantity) variance.
C. Determine the fixed overhead spending (budget) variance.
D. Determine the production volume (fixed overhead volume or denominator) variance.
E. Prepare journal entries to close these variances at the end of the period.

11.36 Direct Materials and Labour Variances, Variances to Investigate The following standard cost card is available for product S141.

LO2, LO3, LO4

	Quantity Standard	Price Standard
Direct materials	2.4 ml per unit	$ 0.75 per ml
Direct labour	0.25 hours per unit	$18.00 per hour

Last month, 12,580 units of S141 were produced at a cost of $24,800 for direct materials and $69,064 for direct labour. A total of 33,513 millilitres of direct materials were used. Total direct labour hours amounted to 3,774 hours. During the same period, 34,000 millilitres of direct material were purchased for $25,160. The company's policy is to record materials price variances at the time materials are purchased.

REQUIRED
A. What is the total standard cost for direct materials and direct labour for the output this period?
B. What was the direct materials price variance?
C. What was the direct materials efficiency variance?
D. What was the direct labour price variance?
E. What was the direct labour efficiency variance?
F. Identify any variances that are material (greater than 10% of total direct cost at standard). Discuss whether you would investigate these variances.

11.37 Direct Cost and Overhead Variances, Decision to Automate Plush pet toys are produced in a largely automated factory in standard lots of 100 toys each. A standard cost system is used to control costs and to assign cost to inventory:

LO3, LO4, LO5, LO6

	Price Standard	Quantity Standard
Plush fabric	$ 2 per metre	15 metres per lot
Direct labour	$10 per hour	2 hours per lot

Variable overhead, estimated at $5 per lot, consists of miscellaneous items such as thread, a variety of plastic squeakers, and paints that are applied to create features such as eyes and whiskers. Fixed overhead, estimated at $24,000 per month, consists largely of depreciation on the automated machinery and rent for the building. Variable overhead is allocated based on lots produced. The standard fixed overhead allocation rate is based on the estimated output of 1,000 lots per month.

Actual data for last month follow:

Production	2,400 lots
Sales	1,600 lots
Plush fabric purchased	30,000 metres
Cost of fabric purchased	$62,000
Fabric used	34,000 metres
Direct labour	4,200 hours
Direct labour cost	$39,000
Variable overhead	$12,000
Fixed overhead	$24,920

The company's policy is to record materials price variances at the time materials are purchased.

REQUIRED
A. Compute the commonly used direct cost and overhead variances.
B. Management is considering further automation in the factory. Robotized forklifts could reduce the standard direct labour per lot to 1.5 hours.
   1. Estimate the savings per lot that would be realized from this additional automation.
   2. Assume that the company would be able to generate the savings as calculated. Considering only quantitative factors, calculate the maximum price the managers would be willing to pay for the robotized forklifts. Assume that the company's management requires equipment costs to be recovered in five years, ignoring the time value of money.

11.38 Journal Entries for Closing Variances Following are the variances for Fine Products Manufacturing Company for the month of March. Assume that the price variance for direct materials is calculated at the time of purchase and that the amount of direct materials purchased is equal to the amount of direct materials used, with no beginning or ending inventories for direct materials (F = favourable and U = unfavourable).

L07

Direct materials price variance	$2,000 U
Direct materials efficiency variance	1,500 F
Labour price variance	5,000 U
Labour efficiency variance	2,000 U
Fixed overhead spending variance	200 U
Variable overhead spending variance	1,000 F
Variable overhead efficiency variance	1,200 U

Fine Products considers anything greater than $5,000 as a material variance. Following are end-of-period inventory balances:

Work in process	$ 2,000
Finished goods	6,000
Cost of goods sold	24,000

REQUIRED **A.** Determine whether the total variance amount is material.

B. Prepare a journal entry to close the variances at the end of March.

11.39 Journal Entries for Closing Variances Following are the variances for Caldera Cooking Company for the month of July. Assume that the price variance for direct materials is calculated at the time of purchase and that the amount of direct materials purchased is equal to the amount of direct materials used, with no beginning or ending inventories for direct materials (F = favourable and U = unfavourable).

L07

Direct materials price variance	$1,500 F
Direct materials efficiency variance	1,000 F
Labour price variance	800 U
Labour efficiency variance	1,500 F
Fixed overhead spending variance	200 U
Variable overhead spending variance	1,000 F
Variable overhead efficiency variance	500 F

Caldera Cooking considers anything greater than $3,000 as a material variance. Following are end-of-period inventory balances:

Work in process	$ 2,000
Finished goods	6,000
Cost of goods sold	42,000

REQUIRED **A.** Determine whether the total variance amount is material.

B. Prepare a journal entry to close the variances at the end of July.

PROBLEMS

11.40 Cost Variances, Variance Analysis, and Employee Motivation Raging Sage Coffee is a franchise that sells cups of coffee from carts in shopping centres. A computerized standard costing system is provided as a part of the franchise package. A portion of the standard cost data follows:

L02, L03, L04, L05, L06

	Price	Quantity
Coffee beans	$ 6 per kg	0.04 kg per cup
Clerks/brewers	$10 per hour	0.05 hours per cup

In its first month of operation, the Winnipeg franchise recorded the following data:

Coffee sold	8,260 cups
Coffee beans used	224 kg
Coffee beans purchased	240 kg
Cost of coffee beans purchased	$1,800
Clerks'/brewers' total hours	600 hours
Clerks'/brewers' total wages	$6,000

The company's policy is to record materials price variances at the time materials are purchased.

REQUIRED
A. Are direct labour hours for the cart most likely fixed or variable? Explain.
B. Given your answer to Part A, should a direct labour efficiency variance be calculated? Why or why not?
C. Calculate the direct materials price and efficiency variances.
D. How many cups of coffee did the franchise owners expect to sell this period? Compare this estimate to the number actually sold.
E. Provide possible explanations for the drop in sales.
F. Suppose the clerks/brewers currently receive a bonus based on their ability to control costs as measured using cost variances. Recommend a bonus system that might help the owners contain costs and also increase sales.

11.41 **Cost Standards, Cost Variances, Improving Cost Variance Information** Sunglass Guys produces two types of wraparound sunglasses on one assembly line. The monthly fixed overhead is estimated at $235,707, and the variable overhead is estimated at $8.15 per Regular Wrap and $12.32 per Deluxe Wrap.

 LO1, LO2, LO5, LO6

The company set up a standard costing system and follows the common practice of basing the overhead rate on the total standard direct labour hours required to produce the estimated volume. The company uses only one overhead rate for fixed and variable overhead costs. Data concerning these two products appear here:

	Regular	Deluxe
Estimated monthly volume	4,300 units	1,400 units
Standard direct labour	0.2 hours per unit	0.3 hours per unit

Last month, actual production volume was 4,500 units of the Regular Wraps and 1,300 units of the Deluxe Wraps. Actual variable overhead was $54,238, and actual fixed overhead was $237,859. The nine full-time employees who are classified as direct labour worked regular schedules for a total of 1,564 hours.

REQUIRED
A. Compute the standard overhead rate per direct labour hour.
B. Explain why the company's overhead cost variances would provide poor information for monitoring and controlling costs.
C. Using the information available to you in this problem, suggest a method of allocating overhead costs that would provide better variance information. Using this method, calculate relevant variances for monitoring and controlling overhead costs.
D. For bookkeeping purposes, Sunglass Guys needs to calculate a production volume variance and a variable overhead efficiency variance. Calculate these variances, assuming that overhead costs are allocated using the method in Part C.
E. Because employees work regular schedules, direct labour costs tend to be fixed. Also, variable overhead consists primarily of indirect materials and facility-level costs (such as building rent, assembly line equipment, and utilities). These costs do not differ between Regular Wraps and Deluxe Wraps. Given this information, recommend a better cost allocation base for variable overhead. Explain your choice.

11.42 **Developing Direct Cost Standards, Cost Variances, Using Variance Analysis** The Mighty Morphs produces two popular games: Powerful Puffs (PP) and Mini-Mite Morphs (MMM). Following are standard costs.

LO1, LO2, LO3, LO4

	Powerful Puffs		Mini-Mite Morphs	
	Standard Quantity	Standard Price	Standard Quantity	Standard Price
DVDs	1.08 DVD/unit	$0.35/DVD	1.08 DVD/unit	$ 0.35/DVD
Documentation	1.03 book/unit	$3.00/book	1.03 book/unit	$ 5.00/book
Assembly labour	0.01 hour/unit	$15.00/hour	0.03 hour/unit	$15.00/hour

The standards call for more than one DVD and documentation book per unit because of normal waste due to faulty DVDs and poor binding.

Actual costs for last week follow:

DVDs purchased (@ $0.39)	$780
DVDs used	2,025
PP games produced	1,000
PP documentation printed (@ $2.95)	$4,425
PP documentation used	1,005
MMM games produced	800
MMM documentation printed (@ $4.75)	$4,750
MMM documentation used	825
Assembly labour cost (55 hours)	$795

Management decided that it would require too much effort to keep track of how many DVDs and hours are used for each of the games separately. Accordingly, the DVD materials and labour variances are combined. The price variances are recorded at the time of purchase.

REQUIRED
A. What is the documentation price variance for MMM?
B. What is the efficiency variance for DVDs?
C. What is the sum of all variances for assembly labour for both games?
D. Calculate last week's estimated cost of waste for DVDs and documentation.
E. Discuss the pros and cons of building waste into the standards.

11.43 Cost Variance Analysis The following information is available for ConcertWearShirts:

	Standard Quantity	Standard Cost	Total Standard Cost
Direct Materials	3 metres	$12.00/metre	$36.00
Direct Labour	2 hours	$10.00/hour	$20.00
Variable Overhead	2 machine hours	$3.00/machine hour	$6.00
Fixed Overhead	2 machine hours	$1.00/machine hour	$2.00
			$64.00

The normal production level is 300 shirts. This production period ConcertWear produced 280 shirts. ConcertWear purchased 900 metres of fabric for $9,720. The variances for the production period are:

Materials Price Variance	?
Materials Quantity Variance	$ 336 U
Labour Rate Variance	$ 532 U
Labour Efficiency Variance	$ 280 F
VOH Spending Variance	$ 98 F
VOH Efficiency Variance	$ 210 F
FOH Budget Variance	$ 110 F
FOH Volume Variance	$ 40 U

REQUIRED
A. How many metres of fabric were used? (Hint: Metres used was not the same as the metres purchased.)
B. What was the materials price variance?
C. What was the actual direct labour rate?
D. What was the actual variable overhead rate?
E. How many machine hours were used?
F. What was the master budget amount for fixed overhead?

11.44 Cost Variance Analysis Fragrances Unlimited provided the following information.

Actual materials (purchased and used)	200,000 ml @ $0.30 per ml
Actual direct labour	735 hours @ $14 per hour
Actual variable overhead	980 machine hours @ $4.90 per machine hour
Actual fixed overhead	$20,000

Materials Price Variance	$10,000 U
Materials Quantity Variance	$2,000 U
Labour Rate Variance	$735 F
Labour Efficiency Variance	$225 U
Variable Overhead Spending Variance	$98 F
Variable Overhead Efficiency Variance	$100 U
Fixed Overhead Budget Variance	$1,250 U

Normal capacity is 5,000 bottles of fragrance. Actual production this quarter was 4,800 bottles of fragrance.

REQUIRED
A. Develop the standard cost card for Fragrances Unlimited. Include materials, labour, variable overhead, and fixed overhead.
B. What was the master budget amount for fixed overhead?
C. What was the applied fixed overhead?
D. What is the fixed overhead volume variance? Explain why it is favourable/unfavourable.
E. Was fixed overhead over or under applied? By how much?

11.45 Cost Variance Analysis, Using Variance Information Baker Street Animal Clinic routinely uses a particular

serum in its vaccination program. Veterinarian technicians give the injections. The standard dose is 10 cc per injection, and the cost has been $100 per 1,000 cc. According to records, 2,000 injections were administered last month at a serum cost of $2,270. The veterinarian noted that the serum for the injections should have cost $2,000 [($0.10 per cc) × (10 cc per injection) × (2,000 injections)]. Moreover, she noted some carelessness in handling the serum that could easily have led to unnecessary waste. When this issue was brought to the attention of the technicians, together with the $270 discrepancy in costs, they claimed that the $270 excess costs must be due to the inflated prices charged by the veterinarian supply company. Purchasing records reveal that the price for the serum used last month had indeed increased to $105 per 1,000 cc.

REQUIRED
A. Provide variance calculations to help you evaluate the technicians' argument.
B. Discuss whether a significant waste of serum occurred last month. Include quantitative and qualitative information in your discussion.
C. If you were the manager for the Baker Street Animal Clinic, how would you use the results of your analyses in Parts A and B? Explain.

11.46 Direct Labour, Variable and Fixed Overhead Variances, Solve for Unknowns At both Phi and Pho Companies,

overhead is applied to production based on standard labour hours.

	Phi Company	Pho Company
Number of labour hours budgeted	A	5,000
Standard variable overhead rate per labour hour	$2	J
Standard labour hours allowed per unit	5	2
Actual labour hours used per unit	B	2.1
Actual variable overhead rate per hour	C	K
Fixed overhead allocation rate per hour	$4	L
Actual total variable overhead costs	D	$15,372
Actual total fixed overhead costs	E	$23,750
Budgeted variable overhead	$21,000	M
Budgeted fixed overhead	$40,000	N
Fixed overhead allocated to production	F	$25,000
Variable overhead spending variance	$540 F	O
Variable overhead efficiency variance	$840 F	$720 U
Fixed overhead volume variance	G	$1,000 F
Total fixed overhead budget variance	$600 U	P
Number of budgeted units for this period	H	Q
Number of actual units produced this period	I	R

REQUIRED   Find the values of missing information for letters A through R in the columns for Phi and Pho Companies.

11.47 **Normal and Abnormal Waste, Adjustment of Variances** Damson Products prepares monthly financial statements. It closes its variance accounts at that time. For the month of May, the firm's accounting records reveal the following variances (the comments were supplied by appropriate operating personnel):

LO6, LO7

Variance	Amount	Percentage of Standard	Comment
Direct material price	$ 658 U	0.04%	Normal fluctuation
Direct material efficiency	12,600 U	11.38%	$13,000 lost in spring flood
Direct labour price	376 F	0.11%	Normal fluctuation
Direct labour efficiency	9,700 U	9.62%	$9,000 for days plant was closed during flood
Variable overhead spending	507 F	0.21%	Normal fluctuation
Variable overhead efficiency	412 U	0.18%	Normal fluctuation
Fixed overhead spending	782 F	0.07%	Normal fluctuation
Production volume	10,400 U	11.29%	$10,200 due to time lost in flood; the rest represents normal decreased spring operations

The firm uses a standard fixed overhead allocation rate based on annual operations. The firm was closed several days when a nearby stream flooded after heavy rains. The firm did not have flood insurance, and the lost material and labour costs were charged to production. At month end, the firm had no raw material and no work-in-process inventories. The standard cost of finished goods inventory was $34,000, and the standard cost of goods sold was $305,000.

REQUIRED   **A.** For each variance, explain whether the total amount of the variance should all be closed as a production variance or whether part of the amount should be closed to a separate flood loss account.

B. Prepare journal entries to close out the variances.

C. What is the cost of finished goods and cost of goods sold after the variance accounts are closed?

11.48 **Evaluating Grading Scheme, Professional Responsibilities** Variance analysis reflects information about actual performance relative to a standard. Variance analysis reports provide managers with information about the performance of employees, from direct labour to supervisors and managers.

LO1, LO2, LO4

Grades provide similar information for recruiters who want to hire graduating students. Following is information about Professor E. Z. Grader's performance measurement system.

Professor Grader is popular; almost all of his students receive A's. This phenomenon is widely attributed to Professor Grader's superior teaching skills. Grades for this professor's courses are determined as follows:

Item	Points
Midterm exam	200
Attendance	200
Term paper	200
Final exam	400
Total	1,000

A student needs 700 points for an A, 600 points for a B, 500 for a C, and 400 for a D. From the 200 points given for perfect attendance, a student loses 5 points for every class missed (out of 40 class meetings); however, attendance is seldom taken.

If the term paper is 20 pages or longer, 200 points are earned; 10 points are lost for each page less than 20 (thus, a 12-page paper is worth 120 points).

Professor Grader has given the same midterm exam for the past 20 years. To reduce the number of exam copies in students' files, Professor Grader does not return the exams; grades are simply reported to individual students. A popular business fraternity obtained a copy of the exam 15 years ago. It has chosen not to share the exam with any person not a member of the fraternity; thus, Professor Grader usually observes that grades on this exam are nearly normally distributed.

The final exam is a take-home exam that the students have two weeks to complete.

REQUIRED   **A.** Is it possible to develop a perfect system for measuring student performance in a course? Why or why not?

B. How much variation is likely in student performance for each of the four graded items? Explain.

C. Describe the weaknesses in Professor Grader's grading system as a performance measurement system.

D. What are Professor Grader's professional responsibilities to the various stakeholders in this situation?

E. Discuss whether Professor Grader has acted ethically in this situation. Describe the ethical values you use to draw your conclusions.

F. Is it ethical for students in this situation to access a copy of the prior midterm exam or to seek assistance in completing take-home assignments? Does Professor Grader's system affect the students' responsibilities? Describe the ethical values you use to draw your conclusions.

11.49 Evaluating a Proposal for Measuring Performance Benerux Industries has been in business for 30 years. The firm's major product is a control unit for elevators. The firm has a reputation for manufacturing products of exceptionally high quality, resulting in higher prices for its units than competitors charge. Higher prices, in turn, have meant that the firm has been comfortably profitable. A major reason for the high product quality is a loyal and conscientious workforce. Production employees have been with the firm for an average of 18 years.

LO1, LO2, LO4

Recently the firm hired a cost accountant from the local university. After a few months at the firm, the new accountant proposed a performance measurement report consisting of two parts. The first part will report the actual number of units started during each month, the target number of units that should have been started, and a variance. The second part will calculate an actual cost per good unit completed during each month, the target cost per unit, and a variance.

The new accountant provided the following additional information concerning the performance report. The first part of the report concentrates on units started because many units are scrapped in the manufacturing process (to maintain high quality). Therefore, the best measure of effort expended is the number of units on which work was begun. The target number of units to be started in a month is the number of units started in the corresponding month of the previous year, plus 5%. In the second part of the report, actual costs per unit will be calculated by dividing total production cost incurred during the month by the number of good units completed during the month. The *target cost* per unit is the average cost for manufacturing this kind of product, as determined from industry newsletters.

The proposal concluded with the following comments: "This report should be prepared and distributed quarterly. For maximum benefit, I suggest that a bonus be awarded whenever units started exceeds target and costs are below target. This system will result in substantially improved profits for the firm. It should be implemented immediately."

REQUIRED
A. Is it possible to develop a perfect system for monitoring and motivating worker performance? Why or why not?

B. Explain what the managers might learn by monitoring each of the variances in the proposed performance measurement system.

C. Discuss possible reasons why the company did not previously use a variance system to monitor and motivate worker performance.

D. Describe weaknesses in the proposed performance measurement system.

E. If you were the CFO of Benerux Industries, how would you respond to the new cost accountant's proposal? Discuss whether you agree with the proposal, and explain how you would communicate your response.

11.50 Direct and Overhead Cost Variance Analysis, Closing Accounts at End of Period Jennifer has just been promoted to manager of the piston division of Auto Parts Co. The division, which manufactures pistons for hydraulic drives, uses a standard cost system and calculates the standard cost of a completed piston as $85.00, as follows:

LO2, LO3, LO4, LO5, LO6, LO7

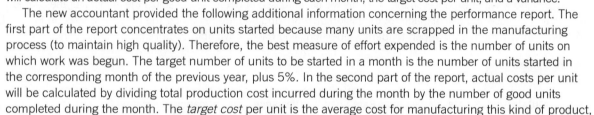

	Quantity	Price	Cost per Piston
Piston shaft	1	$35/piston shaft	$35.00
Shaft housing	1	$20/housing	20.00
Direct labour	0.4 hours	$15/hour	6.00
Variable factory overhead	0.4 hours	$10/hour	4.00
Fixed factory overhead	0.4 hours	$50/hour	20.00
Total standard cost			$85.00

The fixed overhead rate is based on an estimated 1,000 units per month. Direct labour is nearly a fixed cost in this division. Selling and administrative costs are $50,000 per month plus $10 per piston sold.

The following information is for production during April:

Number of pistons manufactured	950
Purchase of 1,000 piston shafts	$34,950
Piston shafts used	954
Purchase of 1,000 shaft housings	$20,000
Shaft housings used	950

Direct labour costs (397 hours)	$ 6,120
Variable factory overhead costs	$ 3,677
Fixed factory overhead costs	$18,325
Selling and administrative costs	$59,101

The company's policy is to record materials price variances at the time materials are purchased. You may want to use a spreadsheet to perform calculations.

REQUIRED **A.** Prepare a flexible cost budget for the month of April.

B. Calculate all the common direct cost variances. (*Note:* There are no variances for shaft housings.)

C. Calculate all common factory overhead variances.

D. Calculate a total variance for the selling and administrative costs.

E. Prepare a complete, yet concise, report that would be useful in evaluating control of production costs for April.

F. Prepare a report that sums all the variances necessary to prepare the reconciling journal entry at the end of the period. Explain how you would close the total variance; that is, identify the account or accounts that would be affected and whether expenses in the accounts will be increased or decreased to adjust the records for the total variance.

G. Suppose you are manager of the piston division, and you are reviewing the report prepared in Part E. Use information in the report to identify questions you might have about April's production costs.

MINI-CASES

11.51 **ABC Costing, Single- Versus Dual-Rate Spending Variances, Performance Evaluation** Data Processors Inc. performs
LO1, LO2, LO3, LO4, LO7   credit card services for banks. The company uses an ABC system. Following is information for the past year:

Activity	Estimated Cost	Actual Cost	Cost Driver	Estimated Activity Level	Actual Activity Level
Processing transactions	$2,000,000	$2,200,000	Number of transactions	5,000,000	5,800,000
Issuing monthly statements	1,000,000	1,300,000	Number of statements	250,000	270,000
Issuing new credit cards	500,000	400,000	Number of new credit cards	100,000	110,000
Resolving billing disputes	90,000	100,000	Number of disputes	3,000	3,500
Total	$3,590,000	$4,000,000			

INFORMATION ANALYSIS

REQUIRED The following questions will help you analyze the information for this problem. Do not turn in your answers to these questions unless your professor asks you to do so.

A. Using standard values for costs and activity, calculate an ABC allocation rate for each activity.

B. Prepare an operating cost statement for Data Processors that compares the static budget, flexible budget, and actual costs.

C. Calculate the spending variance for the cost of processing transactions.

(*Hint:* Treat this activity the same way you would treat variable overhead costs.)

D. Suppose the costs for processing transactions include some fixed and some variable costs, as shown here:

	Estimated Cost	Actual Cost
Fixed costs	$1,000,000	$1,300,000
Variable costs	1,000,000	900,000
Total	$2,000,000	$2,200,000

Given this new information, calculate spending variances for the cost of processing transactions.

E. Discuss possible reasons for the variances calculated in Part D.

WRITTEN ASSIGNMENT

REQUIRED The CEO and CFO of Data Processors Inc. want your opinion about whether and how ABC variance information should be used in departmental manager performance evaluations. Turn in your answer to the following.

F. Use the information you learned from the preceding analyses to write a memo to the CEO and CFO, presenting your evaluation of (1) whether the use of ABC cost variances in departmental manager performance evaluations would likely improve organizational performance and (2) which spending variance—the one from Part C or Part D—would provide better information for evaluating the credit card transaction processing manager's ability to control costs. As you write the memo, consider what information the CEO and CFO will need from you to help make a final decision.

11.52 **Cost-Volume-Profit Pricing and Standard Cost Variances** Bramlett Company has several divisions and just built a new plant with a capacity of 20,000 units of a new product. A standard costing system has been introduced to aid in evaluating managers' performance and for establishing a selling price for the new product. At the present time, Bramlett faces no competitors in this product market, and managers priced it at standard variable and fixed manufacturing cost, plus 60% mark-up. Managers hope this price will be maintained for several years.

LO3, LO5, LO6

During the first year of operations, 1,000 units per month will be produced. During the second year, production is estimated to be 1,500 units per month. In the first month of operations, employees were learning the processes, so direct labour hours were estimated to be 20% greater than the standard hours allowed per unit. In subsequent months, employees were expected to meet the direct labour hours standards.

Experience in other plants and with similar products led managers to believe that variable manufacturing costs would vary in proportion to actual direct labour dollars. For the first several years, only one product will be manufactured in the new plant. Fixed overhead costs of the new plant per year are expected to be $1,920,000, incurred evenly throughout the year.

The standard variable manufacturing cost (after the break-in period) per unit of product has been set as follows:

Direct materials (4 pieces @ $20 per piece)	$ 80
Direct labour (10 hours @ $25 per hour)	250
Variable overhead (50% of direct labour cost)	125
Total	$455

At the end of the first month of operations, the actual costs incurred to make 950 units of product were as follows:

Direct materials (3,850 pieces @ $19.80)	$ 76,230
Direct labour (12,000 hours @ $26)	312,000
Variable overhead	160,250
Fixed overhead	172,220

Bramlett managers want to compare actual costs to standard to analyze and investigate variances and take any corrective action.

REQUIRED **A.** What selling price should Bramlett set for the new product according to the new pricing policy? Explain.

B. Using long-term standard costs, compute all direct labour and manufacturing overhead variances.

C. Is it reasonable to use long-term standard costs to calculate variances for the first month of operations? Why or why not?

D. Revise the variance calculations in Part B, using the expected costs during the first month of operations as the standard costs.

E. Provide at least two possible explanations for each of the following variances:
   1. Direct labour price variance
   2. Direct labour efficiency variance
   3. Variable overhead spending variance
   4. Fixed overhead spending variance

F. As shown in Exhibit 11.1, the reasons for variances must be identified before conclusions and actions are decided upon. For two of the variance explanations you provided in Part E, explain what action(s) managers would most likely take.

G. Would it most likely be easier or more difficult to analyze the variances at the new plant compared to analyzing the variances at Bramlett's other plants? Explain.

11.53 **Integrating Across the Curriculum—Auditing:** *Auditor evaluation of variances for error and fraud, accounting principles for variances* CICA *Handbook* Section 5135, "The Auditor's Responsibility to Consider Fraud," requires auditors to plan and perform an audit to obtain reasonable assurance about whether the financial statements are free of material misstatements, which may be caused by either error or fraud. Errors are unintentional misstatements caused by factors such as mistakes in processing accounting data, misinterpretation of facts, and confusion about accounting principles. Fraudulent financial reporting and misappropriation of assets are the only two types of financial statement fraud. Fraudulent financial reporting consists of intentional misstatements caused by factors such as manipulation of accounting data, misrepresentation of facts, and intentional misapplication of accounting principles. Misappropriation of assets includes stealing assets such as inventory and causing an organization to pay for goods or services that were not received.

LO1, LO2, LO6, LO7

Auditors perform a variety of procedures to gather and evaluate information that will help them identify possible material misstatement. One potential audit procedure is to analyze a company's cost variances, which might be caused by error or fraud.

REQUIRED   **A.** For each of the following variances, describe *in detail* a possible error that could cause a variance even when no variance actually exists: direct materials price, direct materials efficiency, direct labour price, direct labour efficiency, variable overhead spending, variable overhead efficiency, fixed overhead budget, and production volume.

B. Suppose a material amount of raw materials inventory theft took place during the past year. Which of the variances in Part A would most likely reflect this fraud? Explain.

C. Discuss possible reasons why variance analysis might not uncover the theft described in Part B.

D. Suppose a production manager fraudulently entered a fictitious employee into the payroll system during the past year. The fictitious employee's paycheques are deposited directly into a bank account that is then accessed by the production manager. Which of the variances in Part A would most likely reflect this fraud? Explain.

E. During the current year, suppose an accountant accidentally records a large equipment repair as an addition to property, plant, and equipment. Assume that equipment repairs and equipment depreciation are both recorded in variable overhead costs. Which of the variances in Part A would most likely reflect this accounting error? Discuss how this error would affect the variance during the current year. Discuss how this error would affect the variance during the next year.

F. Suppose a company's managers want to report higher earnings on the income statement. Describe in detail a possible way that the managers could improve reported earnings by intentionally misapplying accounting principles for variances.

12

More Variances: Revenue, Contribution Margin and Advanced Production Variances

After studying this chapter, you should be able to do the following:

LO1 Calculate and analyze sales price and sales volume variances

LO2 Calculate and analyze sales mix and sales quantity variances

LO3 Calculate and analyze market share and industry volume variances

LO4 Calculate and analyze production mix and yield variances

LO5 Calculate and analyze productivity measures (Appendix 12A)

in brief Standards are a business' benchmarks—the expectations to guide future decision making and evaluation. Variances are the difference between what actually happened and the standard. Production cost variances are internally focused and analyze the use of input resources used to produce a product. The mix and yield variances provide information for management decisions about the trade-offs between substitutable inputs. Revenue and profit variances focus on the effect of changes in selling price and shifts in sales mix. The profit variances also provide information about the business' position in the external market. ■

Smartphone Market Share

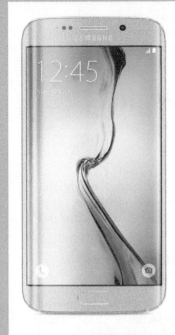

© STANCA SANDA/Alamy Stock Photo

Smartphone vendors like Samsung, Apple, LG, Lenovo, and others monitor market size and growth patterns as they develop and introduce new products and product features. In August 2015, IDC (International Data Corporation) released its market share analysis indicating that the smartphone market grew 13.1% year over year in the second quarter of 2015. This growth resulted in 341.5 million shipments of smartphones. Each of the smartphone vendors monitor their share of this overall market and then analyze the various segments of the market.

Although Samsun maintained its number 1 position with 21.4% of the market, managers will analyze the decline from 24.8% in 2014 and 31.9% in 2013. A sales mix analysis shows that the underperformance of the Galaxy S6 and Galaxy S6 Edge was offset by increased sales of lower-end models and growth in specific geographic regions (e.g., Southeast Asia, the Middle East, and Africa). Further analysis of the IDC report indicates that while Samsung is losing market share, Apple, Huawai, Xiaomi, and others are gaining market share.

To understand the details of changing market share, smartphone vendors analyze specific geographic markets. The digital data firm comScore reported that 81% of Canadian wireless subscribers have a smartphone. Samsung captures 32.4% of this market, second to Apple which captures 38.3% of the Canadian smartphone market. One way analysts segment this market is by operating system. With 32.4% of the smartphone market, Samsung leads the Android segment, which is 50.5% of the smartphone market. This segment grew by 5.5% from 2014 to 2015. The next largest segment is Apple's iOS system.

Even within these segments, the data are further decomposed. Smartphone providers track numbers of first device owners versus repeat purchases; the age category of smartphone owners, how smartphones are used ("on the go," "at home," and "at work"), application use, and frustrations. These trends influence future of product offerings—larger screen sizes are better for the increasing "at home" activities like watching video and reading articles. In the ever-changing smartphone market, these trends and variances provide insights into the future and the performance of companies like Samsung and Apple.

SOURCES: Smartphone Vendor Market Share, 2015 Q2, IDC (International Data Corporation), www.idc.com/prodserv/smartphone-market-share.jsp; I. Hardy, "Apple Tops Samsung in Canadian Smartphone Market Share: comScore," MobileSyrup, March 27, 2015, http://mobilesyrup.com/2015/03/27/comscore-canada-smartphone-android-apple-os-market-share/; "With Growth Comes Change: The Evolving Mobile Landscape in 2015," Catalyst, http://catalyst.ca/2015-canadian-smartphone-market.

As you learned in Chapter 11, variances help managers understand current results and plan for future performance. Managers of smartphone vendors like Samsung and Apple are concerned with production variances (those presented in Chapter 11), as well as revenue and market-related variances like those in the chapter opener. Samsung will need to understand why the Galaxy S6 and Galaxy S6 Edge models have not performed up to expectations. Segmenting the market by product line, by geographic region, or by customer helps managers to explain variances and make decisions aligned with strategic goals.

Revenue and Contribution Margin Variances

Revenue Variances

LO1 Calculate and analyze sales price and sales volume variances

Before managers estimate revenues for the next period, they assess market conditions, develop marketing strategies, and establish the type and quality of goods or services they want to sell. Given assumptions and plans for these factors, they set the following standards for operating revenue performance:

$$\frac{\text{Standard (or budgeted)}}{\text{revenues}} = \frac{\text{Standard (or budgeted)}}{\text{selling price}} \times \frac{\text{Standard (or budgeted)}}{\text{sales volume}}$$

When actual revenues are compared to standard revenues, the difference is called a **revenue budget variance**. Revenue variances are caused by a number of factors, such as changes in demand, sales price, and discounting practices. In addition, because total revenue is based on a projected sales mix among products, changes in the mix cause changes in revenues. Managers are often concerned about variances between planned and actual revenues; therefore, accountants produce and analyze several variances that reflect the success of marketing efforts.

Sales Price and Revenue Sales Quantity Variances

As shown in Exhibit 12.1, the revenue budget variance can be broken down into two types of variances. The **sales price variance** reflects the difference between standard and actual selling prices for the volume of units actually sold. The sales price variance is calculated as:

Sales price variance = (Actual price − Standard price) × Actual volume sold

This variance is favourable if the actual selling price exceeds the standard price, and it is unfavourable if the reverse is true. When an organization sells more than one product or service, the combined variance is calculated as the sum of sales price variances for all products and services.

The **revenue sales quantity variance** reflects the difference between the standard and actual quantity of units sold at the standard selling price. The revenue sales quantity variance is calculated using the following formula:

Revenue sales quantity variance = (Actual volume sold − Standard volume sold) × Standard price

This variance is favourable when actual sales quantities exceed standard quantities, and it is unfavourable otherwise. When an organization sells more than one product or service, the combined variance is calculated as the sum of revenue sales quantity variances for all products and services.

▶EXHIBIT 12.1
Revenue Budget Variances

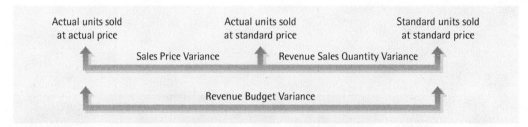

Actual units sold at actual price		Actual units sold at standard price		Standard units sold at standard price
	Sales Price Variance		Revenue Sales Quantity Variance	
		Revenue Budget Variance		

Suppose that Benny's sells both Purple Madness and French Vanilla ice cream. Following is information about the standard and actual sales for the period:

Product	Standard Price	Standard Volume	Actual Price	Actual Volume
Purple Madness	$7.00 per litre	1,000 litres	$6.50 per litre	1,500 litres
French Vanilla	$6.00 per litre	2,000 litres	$5.75 per litre	1,700 litres

Actual revenues are $19,525: ($9,750 (1,500 litres × $6.50 per litre) for Purple Madness ice cream and $9,775 (1,700 litres × $5.75 per litre) for French Vanilla ice cream. Total standard revenues are $19,000: $7,000 (1,000 litres × $7.00 per litre) for Purple Madness ice cream and $12,000 (2,000 litres × $6.00 per litre) for French Vanilla ice cream.

As shown in Exhibit 12.2, the revenue budget variance is calculated as follows:

$$(1{,}500 \text{ litres} \times \$6.50 \text{ per litre}) + (1{,}700 \text{ litres} \times \$5.75 \text{ per litre})$$
$$- [(1{,}000 \text{ litres} \times \$7.00 \text{ per litre}) + (2{,}000 \text{ litres} \times \$6.00 \text{ per litre})]$$
$$= \$19{,}525 - \$19{,}000$$
$$= \$525 \text{ F}$$

This variance is favourable because revenues are higher than standard. However, sales prices for both products were lower than expected. Benny's managers want to understand the influence of the price changes separately from the volume changes, so their accountant breaks this variance into the sales price variance and the revenue sales volume variance.

The sales price variance for Purple Madness ice cream is $750 U [($6.50 per litre – $7.00 per litre) × 1,500 litres], and the sales price variance for French Vanilla is $425 U [($5.75 per litre – $6.00 per litre) × 1,700 litres]. The total sales price variance of $1,175 U ($750 U + $425 U) is unfavourable because both prices were lower than standard.

The revenue sales volume variance for Purple Madness of $3,500 F [(1,500 litres – 1,000 litres) × $7.00 per litre] is favourable because Benny's sold more than standard. The variance for French Vanilla of $1,800 U [(2,000 litres – 1,700 litres) × $6.00 per litre] is unfavourable because Benny's sold less than standard. The total variance of $1,700 F ($3,500 F – $1,800 U) is favourable because the largest variance ($3,500) was favourable. The combined sales price and revenue sales quantity variance is $525 F ($1,700 F – $1,175 U), the same value as the revenue budget variance that we calculated earlier.

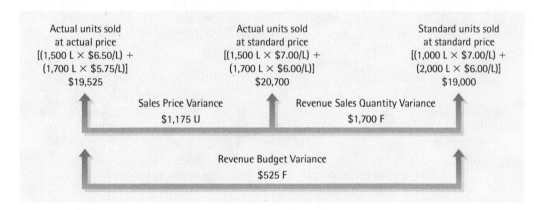

EXHIBIT 12.2
Revenue Budget Variances for Benny's (Two Products)

---

[1] See Maria Altman, "World Series Cash Brings Relief to St. Louis," NPR, October 26, 2011, http://www.npr.org/2011/10/26/141712558/world-series-cash-brings-relief-to-st-louis.

Contribution Margin-Related Variances

For organizations that sell more than one product, analysis of the total contribution margin is often useful, especially when a company's products are substitutes for each other. The **contribution margin budget variance** reflects the difference between standard and actual contribution margins. At Benny's, some ice cream flavours are more expensive than others because of the cost of special ingredients. For customers who are price sensitive, a less expensive flavour is probably a good substitute for a more expensive flavour. When the economy is down, Benny's probably sells more of the less expensive ice cream. When the economy recovers, expensive ice creams sell better. Because the contribution margin of each flavour affects profitability, plans are made for a specific sales mix with specific contribution margins. At the end of a period, managers analyze the contribution margin budget variance. This analysis helps them know which products to advertise and provides guidance for future budgeting tasks.

Suppose that Benny's has standard contribution margins for Purple Madness and French Vanilla ice cream as follows:

	Standard Contribution Margin	Actual Contribution Margin
Purple Madness	$1.00 per litre	$1.15 per litre
French Vanilla	$1.25 per litre	$1.00 per litre

The standard contribution margin is $3,500 [(1,000 litres × $1.00 per litre) + (2,000 litres × $1.25 per litre)]. However, actual sales were 1,500 litres of Purple Madness at a contribution margin of $1.15 each, and 1,700 litres of French Vanilla at a contribution margin of $1.00 each. The actual contribution margin for this sales mix and contribution margin per product is $3,425 [(1,500 litres × $1.15 per litre) + (1,700 litres × $1.00 per litre)]. The contribution margin budget variance is $75 U ($3,500 − $3,425), which is unfavourable, because the total actual contribution margin is lower than the total standard contribution margin.

Contribution Margin Variance and Contribution Margin Sales Volume Variance

The contribution margin budget variance of $75 U can be broken into the contribution margin variance and the contribution margin sales volume variance, as shown in Exhibit 12.3. The **contribution margin variance** indicates the effects of changes in contribution margins, given the actual level of sales. This variance is calculated as follows:

$$\text{Contribution margin variance} = \left(\text{Actual contribution margin} - \text{Standard contribution margin} \right) \times \text{Actual volume sold}$$

▶ EXHIBIT 12.3
Contribution Margin Budget Variances

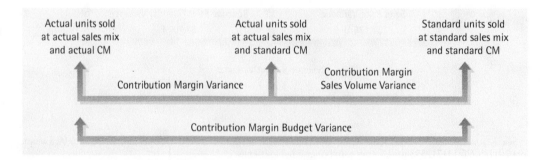

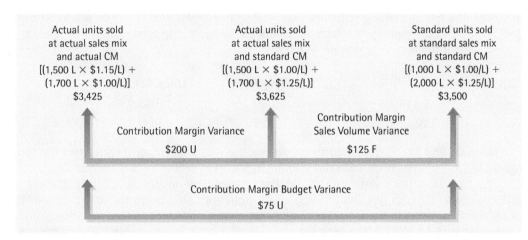

▶ EXHIBIT 12.4
Contribution Margin Budget Variances for Benny's (Two Products)

This variance is favourable when the actual contribution margin is higher than the standard contribution margin, and it is unfavourable otherwise. When an organization sells more than one product or service, the combined variance is calculated as the sum of contribution margin variances for all products and services.

The **contribution margin sales volume variance** indicates the effects of changes in units sold, given the standard contribution margins. The variance is calculated as follows:

$$\text{Contribution margin Sales vlolume variance} = \left(\text{Actual volume sold} - \text{Standard volume sold} \right) \times \text{Standard contribution margin}$$

This variance is favourable when actual sales quantities exceed standard quantities, and it is unfavourable otherwise. When an organization sells more than one product or service, the combined variance is calculated as the sum of contribution margin volume variances for all products and services.

For Benny's, the contribution margin variance for Purple Madness is $225 F [1,500 × ($1.00 − $1.15)], and for French Vanilla it is $425 U [1,700 × ($1.00 − $1.25)]. The total contribution margin variance is $200 U ($425 − $225), as shown in Exhibit 12.4. In other words, the company achieved a lower average contribution margin per litre than standard. Although the actual contribution margin per litre for Purple Madness ice cream was higher than standard, it was more than offset by the reduction in contribution margin on French Vanilla ice cream. The contribution margin sales variance for Purple Madness is $500 F [(1,500 litres − 1,000 litres) × $1.00 per litre] and for French Vanilla is $375 U [(1,700 litres − 2,000 litres) × $1.25 per litre]. The total contribution margin sales volume variance is $125 F ($500 F − $375 U). Benny's sold more total units of ice cream than planned, resulting in a favourable contribution margin sales volume variance. The sum of the contribution margin variance of $200 U and the contribution margin sales volume variance of $125 F reflects the contribution margin budget variance of $75 U.

outdoor cooking, part 1
REVENUE VARIANCES

Annie Kidd and Jane Earp, the accountant and sales manager for Outdoor Cooking, were reviewing the most recent sales results for backyard grills. Outdoor Cooking features a line of gas grills for those who wanted a fast, easy solution to outdoor cooking and a line of traditional charcoal grills for those who savor the aroma of an old fashioned barbeque.

The master budget indicated expected sales of 1,500 gas grills and 750 charcoal grills. The gas grills have an average selling price of $450 and an average contribution margin of

example

$292.50. The average selling price and contribution margin for charcoal grills are $150 and $82.50. Due to the combined effects of a slow economy, a long winter, and recent warm, sunny weather the actual sales were as follows:

	Selling Price	Units Sold
Gas Grills	$390	1,350
Charcoal Grills	$125	950

Ms. Kidd and Ms. Earp started by calculating the revenue budget variance and the two related variances, sales price and sales volume, as shown in Exhibit 12.5.

The total sales price variance is $104,750 unfavourable including unfavourable sales price variances for both gas and charcoal grills. Both grills sold below the expected selling price, most likely due to the slow economy. Although the total sales volume variance is also unfavourable ($37,500 U), the variance consists of a large unfavourable variance for gas grills ($67,500 U) but a significant favourable variance for charcoal grills. This indicates that the sales for the more expensive gas grills were negatively impacted by the economy but sales in units exceeded expectations for the less expensive charcoal grills.

Because gas and charcoal grills are substitutes for each other, Ms. Kidd suggested analyzing the contribution margin variances. The actual contribution margin for gas grills is $227.75 and for charcoal grills is $57.50. The contribution margin budget variances are calculated in Exhibit 12.6.

Ms. Kidd observed that these variances are in the same direction as the revenue budget variances. A further analysis of the differences between the contribution margin budget variances and the revenue budget variances reveals that the unit sales for the gas grills were less than planned at a selling price below budget; however, the analysis also reveals that the variable costs had increased ($450 – $390 = $60 decline in selling price; $292.50 – $227.75 = $64.75 decline in contribution margin, which is higher due to an increase in variable costs).

A similar analysis of the charcoal grills reveals that although there was a decline in selling price, there was an increase in units sold. However, the sales price variance and the contribution margin variance are the same, indicating that the difference between the actual and standard price and the difference between the actual and standard contribution margin are the same, which means that the variable costs did not change.

Ms. Kidd and Ms. Earp considered the impact of this information. In view of the slow economy but the good weather, the sales price for both grills had been reduced. Evan at the reduced price, the number of gas grills sold was below expectations; however, the number of charcoal grills sold exceeded expectations. The contribution margin for both grills is below standard; however, the decline in contribution margin for gas grills is greater than the decline in sales price. ■

▶ EXHIBIT 12.5

Outdoor Cooking Revenue Budget Variances

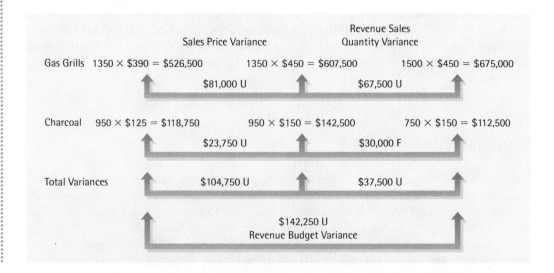

		Sales Price Variance		Revenue Sales Quantity Variance	
Gas Grills	1350 × $390 = $526,500		1350 × $450 = $607,500		1500 × $450 = $675,000
		$81,000 U		$67,500 U	
Charcoal	950 × $125 = $118,750		950 × $150 = $142,500		750 × $150 = $112,500
		$23,750 U		$30,000 F	
Total Variances		$104,750 U		$37,500 U	

$142,250 U
Revenue Budget Variance

example

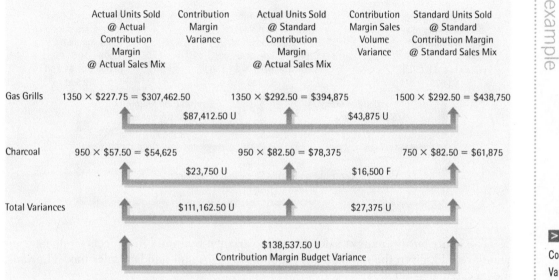

	Actual Units Sold @ Actual Contribution Margin @ Actual Sales Mix	Contribution Margin Variance	Actual Units Sold @ Standard Contribution Margin @ Actual Sales Mix	Contribution Margin Sales Volume Variance	Standard Units Sold @ Standard Contribution Margin @ Standard Sales Mix
Gas Grills	1350 × $227.75 = $307,462.50		1350 × $292.50 = $394,875		1500 × $292.50 = $438,750
		$87,412.50 U		$43,875 U	
Charcoal	950 × $57.50 = $54,625		950 × $82.50 = $78,375		750 × $82.50 = $61,875
		$23,750 U		$16,500 F	
Total Variances		$111,162.50 U		$27,375 U	

$138,537.50 U
Contribution Margin Budget Variance

> **EXHIBIT 12.6**
> Contribution Margin Budget Variances

Sales Volume Variances

Contribution Margin Sales Mix Variance and Contribution Margin Sales Quantity Variance

When an organization sells more than one product or service, the contribution margin sales volume variance can be broken into two more variances, the contribution margin sales mix variance and the contribution margin sales quantity variance, as shown in Exhibit 12.7. The contribution margin sales mix variance examines the effects of changes in the sales mix, given the standard contribution margin and actual quantity of units sold. The variance is calculated as follows, where actual sales volume is the number of units sold for a specific product and total actual sales volume is the combined actual volume for all products:

> **L02**   Calculate and analyze sales mix and sales quantity variances

$$
\begin{array}{l}
\text{Contribution} \\
\text{margin sales} \\
\text{mix variance}
\end{array}
=
\begin{array}{l}
\text{Sum} \\
\text{for all} \\
\text{products of}
\end{array}
\left\{
\left[
\begin{array}{c}\text{Actual}\\\text{sales}\\\text{volume}\end{array}
-
\left(
\begin{array}{c}\text{Total}\\\text{actual sales}\\\text{volume}\end{array}
\times
\begin{array}{c}\text{Standard}\\\text{sales mix}\\\text{percentage}\end{array}
\right)
\right]
\times
\begin{array}{c}\text{Standard}\\\text{contribution}\\\text{margin}\end{array}
\right\}
$$

The standard sales mix percentage is the standard number of units for the specific product as a percent of the total standard number of units for all products. This variance is favourable when a shift occurs in sales mix toward products having a higher standard contribution margin.

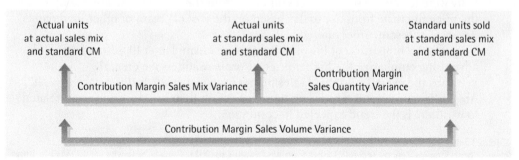

> **EXHIBIT 12.7**
> Contribution Margin Sales Volume Variances

▶EXHIBIT 12.8
Contribution Margin Sales Volume
Variances for Benny's (Two Products)

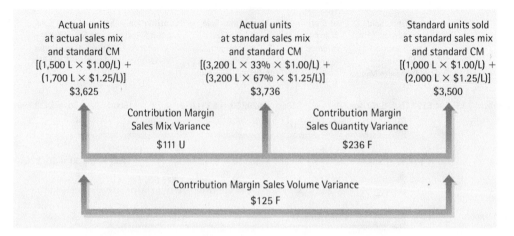

The **contribution margin sales quantity variance** examines the effects of changes in quantities sold, given the standard contribution margins and standard sales mix. The variance is calculated as follows:

$$
\begin{array}{c}
\text{Contribution} \\
\text{margin sales} \\
\text{quantity variance}
\end{array}
=
\begin{array}{c}
\text{Sum} \\
\text{for all} \\
\text{products of}
\end{array}
\left\{
\left[
\left(
\begin{array}{c}
\text{Total} \\
\text{sales} \\
\text{volume}
\end{array}
\times
\begin{array}{c}
\text{Standard} \\
\text{sales mix} \\
\text{percentage}
\end{array}
\right)
-
\begin{array}{c}
\text{Standard} \\
\text{sales mix}
\end{array}
\right]
\times
\begin{array}{c}
\text{Standard} \\
\text{contribution} \\
\text{margin}
\end{array}
\right\}
$$

The standard sales mix percentage is the standard number of units for the specific product as a percentage of the total standard number of units for all products. This variance is favourable if the total actual sales volume for the organization is greater than standard.

The calculations of these variances for Benny's are presented in Exhibit 12.8. The standard proportion (i.e., sales mix) of litres sold for Purple Madness is 33% [1,000 litres ÷ (1,000 litres + 2,000 litres)], and the standard proportion for French Vanilla is the remaining 67%. The contribution margin sales volume variance ($125 F) is broken into two other contribution margin variances. The contribution margin sales mix variance is $111 U [(1,500 litres − (3,200 litres × 0.33)) × $1.00 per litre + (1,700 litres − (3,200 litres × 0.67)) × $1.25 per litre]. The variance is unfavourable because a larger proportion of PurpleMadness was sold than expected, and Purple Madness has a lower standard contribution margin than French Vanilla. The sales quantity variance is $236 F [((3,200 litres × 0.33) − 1,000 litres) × $1.00 per litre + ((3,200 litres × 0.67) − 2,000 litres) × $1.25 per litre]. The favourable variance arose because Benny's expected to sell 3,000 litres and actually sold 3,200 litres.

Analyzing Revenue and Contribution Margin Variance Information

The process of analyzing these variances is similar to the process used for cost variances. After variances have been computed, the reasons for variances are investigated. For example, after analyzing the variances in Exhibits 12.2, 12.4, and 12.8, Benny's managers might investigate the following questions:

- ▶ Why were ice cream selling prices different from standard prices? For example, does the price fluctuate from day to day based on the cost of cream or other ingredients? Are discounts sometimes offered?
- ▶ Why was the proportion of Purple Madness ice cream larger than standard? Did advertising emphasize the higher-priced Purple Madness ice cream?
- ▶ Why was the overall volume of sales higher than expected? Is this part of a trend? Are particular customers ordering more ice cream than usual? Is this event related to weather? Is the trend expected to continue?

[2] S. John Tilak, "Sears Canada Records Loss Amid Sales Decline," Reuters, August 16, 2011, http://ca.reuters.com; Press Release, "Sears Canada Reports Second Quarter Earnings," August 16, 2011, Canada Newswire via COMTEX, http://phx.corporate-ir.net.

▶ Will the increased contribution margin for Purple Madness ice cream continue? It appears that costs were reduced because prices decreased and contribution margin increased. Will the cost reduction continue into the next period?

▶ Can cost reductions be found for French Vanilla to compensate for the reduced price?

▶ Should advertising emphasize Purple Madness even more because it now has the largest contribution margin?

▶ What do the answers to all the preceding questions suggest about ways to increase profits for Benny's?

After considering these types of questions, the managers would decide what action, if any, to take.

outdoor cooking, part 2

Ms. Kidd continued the analysis of the sales for gas grills and charcoal grills by decomposing the contribution margin sales volume variance into the contribution margin sales mix variance and the contribution margin sales quantity variance. The calculation of these variances is presented in Exhibit 12.9.

This analysis indicates that although overall sales are slightly greater than expected (2,300 grills versus 2,250 grills), there was a significant shift in the sales mix away from the higher contribution margin gas grills to the lower contribution margin charcoal grills. The original estimate was for gas grills to account for 2/3 (66.67%) of total sales; the actual result was that gas grills were only 58.7% (i.e., 1350/2300) of total sales. The percentage of charcoal grills in the sales mix increased from 1/3 (33.33%) to 41.3% (i.e., 950/2300).

Ms. Earp and Ms. Kidd planned to use this information to respond to the following questions:

• Should advertising emphasize the benefits of the gas grills to try to boost sales?
• What caused the costs of the gas grills to increase?
• Are there ways to reduce the costs of gas grills and charcoal grills to improve the contribution margins?
• How long is the downturn in the economy expected to last?
• How can Outdoor Cooking best position itself to improve sales as the economy comes out of the slump? ■

Lauri Patterson/iStockphoto

▶ EXHIBIT 12.9
Contribution Margin Sales Volume Variances

	Actual Units Sold @ Standard Contribution Margin @ Actual Sales Mix	Contribution Margin Sales Mix Variance	Actual Units Sold @ Standard Contribution Margin @ Standard Sales Mix	Contribution Margin Sales Quantity Variance	Standard Units Sold @ Standard Contribution Margin @ Standard Sales Mix
Gas Grills	1350 × $292.50 = $394,875	$53,625 U	2300 × 2/3 × $292.50 = $448,500	$9,750 F	1500 × $292.50 = $438,750
Charcoal	950 × $82.50 = $78,375	$15,125 F	2300 × 1/3 × $82.50 = $63,250	$1,375 F	750 × $82.50 = $61,875
Total Variances		$38,500 U		$11,125 F	

$27,375 U
Contribution Margin Sales Volume Variance

12-1 self-study problem   Profit-Related Variances, Variance Analysis

Gift Baskets Galore (GBG) sells gift baskets at a kiosk in a mall. Exhibit 12.10 contains information about standard and actual sales for the first quarter. A competitor has changed its prices, and GBG has been forced to lower the price on its premium basket. The price for the regular basket was increased in an attempt to compensate for revenue that might be lost from the price decrease for premium baskets. The owner has asked her accountant to help her determine how the price changes have affected revenues.

> **EXHIBIT 12.10**

Data for Self-Study Problem 2

Sales and Contribution Margin (CM) Forecasts for First Quarter

Product	Standard Unit Price	Standard Unit CM	Standard Volume	Standard Revenue	Standard CM	Standard Volume Mix
Premium basket	$10.00	$1.00	4,500	$45,000	$4,500	75%
Regular basket	5.00	0.50	1,500	7,500	750	25%
Totals			6,000	$52,500	$5,250	100%

Actual Sales and Contribution Margin (CM) for First Quarter

Product	Actual Unit Price	Actual Unit CM	Actual Volume	Actual Revenue	Actual CM	Actual Volume Mix
Premium basket	$9.75	$0.75	4,756	$46,371	$3,567	80%
Regular basket	5.50	0.55	1,189	6,540	654	20%
Totals			5,945	$52,911	$4,221	100%

required

A. For the premium basket, calculate the two revenue budget variances: sales price variance and revenue sales quantity variance.
B. Calculate all the contribution margin variances: the contribution margin budget variance composed of the contribution margin variance and contribution margin sales volume variance. Then decompose the contribution margin sales volume variance into the contribution margin sales mix variance and the contribution margin sales quantity variance.
C. Write a paragraph discussing these variances. Examine the current pricing policy and explain any changes you think the manager should consider.

See the solution on page 565.

Market-Related Volume Variances

LO3   Calculate and analyze market share and industry volume variances

In addition to using variances to understand operations and support internal decision making, variances are also used to analyze the external market and a company's position in that market. Exhibit 12.11 summarizes the internally focused revenue-side variance analyses and indicates the next step: to provide an analysis of the market.

When analyzing the contribution margin sales quantity variance, some of the questions that managers ask are market related, for example:

> CHAPTER REFERENCE

Chapter 3 discusses how changes in the sales mix affect a cost volume profit analysis.

► How have changes in the market affected our sales?
► Have changes in the market caused our sales mix to shift?
► Have sales been impacted by market growth or contraction?

Answers to these questions have both strategic and operational impacts on a company.

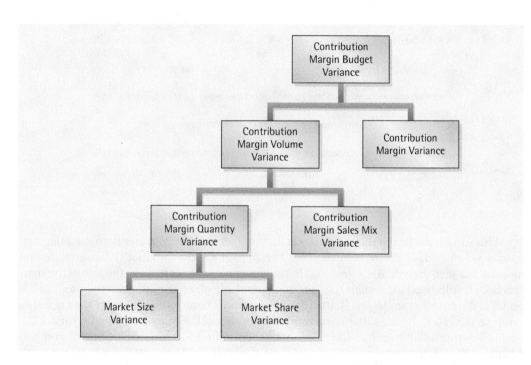

►EXHIBIT 12.11
Contribution Margin Variances

►EXHIBIT 12.12
Market Share and Market Size
Variances

The contribution margin quantity variance can be analyzed from an external perspective by calculating the market share variance and the market size variance as seen in Exhibit 12.12. The **market share variance** reflects the difference between the budgeted market share percentage and the actual market share percentage achieved for the standard contribution margin. The market share variance is calculated as follows:

Market Share Variance =
Sum for all products [(Actual market share percentage – Standard market share percentage) ×
Actual industry sales volume × Standard contribution margin]

This variance is favourable when the actual market share percentage is greater than the budgeted market share percentage. This result indicates that the company has increased its share of the available market. An unfavourable variance reflects a decreased share of the market. Both results need to be analyzed in terms of strategic objectives and stage in the product life cycle.

The other market-related variance that is analyzed is the **market size variance**. The market size variance is calculated as follows:

Market Size Variance =
Sum for all products [(Actual market volume – Standard market volume) ×
Standard market share percentage = Standard contribution margin]

► ALTERNATIVE TERMS
Market size variance is also known as
the **industry volume variance**.

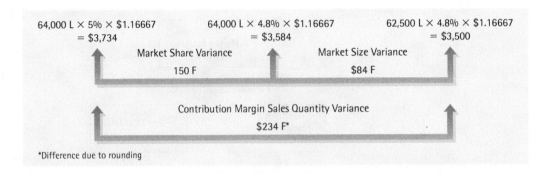

▶ EXHIBIT 12.13

Benny's Market Share and Market Size Variances

This variance is favourable when the actual market volume is greater than the budgeted market volume. This result indicates that the market for the product(s) has grown—the industry has seen growth. An unfavourable variance reflects a decrease in the size of the market. Both results need to be analyzed in terms of strategic objectives, stage in the product life cycle, and marketing strategies. Remember that Benny's contribution margin sales quantity variance is $236 F. Benny's managers want to understand the market impact on their business. They recall that they had forecast a market size of 62,500 litres of ice cream and had estimated that Benny's would capture 4.8% of this market. Their market research reveals that the market was actually 64,000 litres of ice cream and at sales of 3,200 litres, Benny's had captured 5% of this market. With a quick review of this information, you will see that the market size is larger than Benny's managers had predicted (64,000 L > 62,500 L) and Benny's share of the market has increased (5% > 4.8%). To provide information for decision making, Benny's managers calculate the market share variance as follows:

$$\text{Market share variance} = [(5\% \times 64,000 \text{ L}) - (4.8\% \times 64,000 \text{ L})] \times \$1.16667$$
$$= [(.05 - .048) \times 64,000 \text{ L}] \times \$1.6667$$
$$= \$150 \text{ F}$$

Notice that this calculation uses the weighted average contribution margin for Purple Madness and French Vanilla ice cream [($1.00 \times 1/3) + ($1.25 \times 2/3) = $1.6667]. You would get the same result (within in rounding differences) if you calculated the market share variance individually for Purple Madness and French Vanilla ice cream separately and summed them. The market size variance is calculated as follows:

$$\text{Market size variance} = [(4.8\% \times 64,000 \text{ L}) - (4.8\% \times 62,500 \text{ L})] \times \$1.16667$$
$$= [(64,000 \text{ L} - 62,500 \text{ L}) \times .048] \times \$1.16667$$
$$= \$84 \text{ F}$$

This analysis, which is summarized in Exhibit 12.13 shows Benny's managers that $84 of the $236 (approximately 35.5%) favourable contribution margin sales quantity variance is the result of growth in the relevant ice cream industry. As a relatively small player in this industry, Benny's may or may not have had much impact on this market growth. Of more interest to Benny's managers is the increase in their share of the market. Although this seems like a small change (0.2% points), Benny's managers will want to understand the factors that may have contributed to this growth in order to continue to maintain and improve their market share.

outdoor cooking, part 3

As Ms. Earp and Ms. Kidd consider strategies to weather the economic slump and position their company for an economic recovery, they decide to calculate the market share and market size variances for Outdoor Cooking. First, they calculate the weighted average standard contribution margin for grills: ($292.50 × 2/3) + ($82.50 × 1/3) = $222.50. Then, they do some market research and determine that the current market is 23,000 grills. Comparing this to the estimates that they used to budget, Ms. Kidd determines that her estimate was to capture 7.5% of a 30,000 grill market. Instead, the economic slowdown resulted in a much smaller market (23,000 vs. 30,000), but Outdoor Cooking captured 10% (2,300 grills out of 23,000 grills) of the market. To better understand the financial impact of these changes Ms. Kidd calculated the market share and market size variances as follows and in Exhibit 12.14.

$$\text{Market share variance} = [(23{,}000 \text{ grills} \times 10\%) - (23{,}000 \text{ grills} \times 7.5\%)] \times \$222.50$$
$$= [(0.10 - 0.075) \times 23{,}000 \text{ grills}] \times \$222.50$$
$$= \$127{,}937.50 \text{ F}$$

$$\text{Market size variance} = [(23{,}000 \text{ grills} \times 7.5\%) - (30{,}000 \text{ grills} \times 7.5\%)] \times \$222.50$$
$$= [(23{,}000 \text{ grills} - 30{,}000 \text{ grills}) \times 0.075] \times \$222.50$$
$$= \$116{,}812.50 \text{ U}$$

Ms. Kidd and Ms. Earp have learned that although the market for grills has shrunk by 23% [(30,000 − 23,000)/30,000], Outdoor Cooking's share of the market has increased by 2.5%, resulting in overall increased sales of grills. The decline in the market size resulted in a decrease in contribution margin of $116,812.50; however, this was offset by the increase in market share, which resulted in a $127,937.50 increase in contribution margin. They now need to ask important questions about how to maintain this increased market share when the market recovers from its current slump. A next step would be to break down the information by product: gas grills and charcoal grills. They know from their previous analysis that their sales mix has shifted. Was this shift in line with changes in the industry? Is the shift in sales mix expected to persist? How should they position their grills in the future? ■

Lauri Patterson/iStockphoto

▶**EXHIBIT 12.14**
Outdoor Cooking's Market Share and Market Size Variances

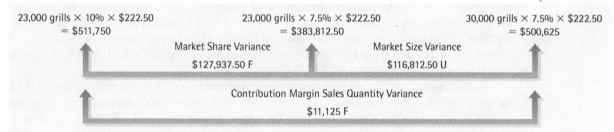

23,000 grills × 10% × $222.50 = $511,750	Market Share Variance $127,937.50 F	23,000 grills × 7.5% × $222.50 = $383,812.50	Market Size Variance $116,812.50 U	30,000 grills × 7.5% × $222.50 = $500,625

Contribution Margin Sales Quantity Variance
$11,125 F

●● > STRATEGIC RISK MANAGEMENT

Understanding Outdoor Cooking's market position is an important step in strategically positioning the company to take advantage of its strengths and opportunities. SWOT analyses helps businesses understand their strengths, weaknesses, opportunities and threats. Market size and market share variances are part of these analyses. What other external factors should Ms. Kidd and Ms. Earp consider in their analysis? Ms. Kidd and Ms. Earp are aware of the impact of the busy lives of consumers and have included top of the line gas grills. The other perspective that might impact sales of grills is growing environmental awareness among consumers.

Production Quantity Variances

In Chapter 11, we considered the simple case of one material or one type of labour used to produce a product. To help a business understand better the use of input resources, we learned to calculate the material and labour efficiency variances. In practice, many products are produced from a mixture of interchangeable input resources. Businesses determine the most efficient and cost effective combination of these input resources to produce the

LO4   Calculate and analyze production mix and yield variances

quality product desired. Although these standards are the goal, ongoing business operations may result in deviations from these standards. Now, to understand the fluctuations in the interchangeable input resources, we further analyze the efficiency variance by calculating mix and yield variances.

In general, the **mix variance** explains trade-offs between the quantities used of the different inputs by comparing the actual mix of the inputs used to the standard mix for the inputs. The mix variance is calculated as follows:

Mix Variance =
Sum for all products (Actual total quantity used × Actual production mix percentage ×
Standard price of input) − (Actual total quantity used ×
Standard production mix percentage × Standard price of input)

The mix variance gets a favourable when the actual percentage used for an input resource is less than the standard percentage for that input. Managers must be careful in interpreting this favourable variance because it may indicate that less of a higher quality input was used, which may result in a lower quality final product. An unfavourable mix variance indicates that the actual percentage used of an input is greater than the standard percentage allowed. Both favourable and unfavourable mix variances must be analyzed with respect to the company's strategy: for example, is the company a high quality producer? a low cost producer? focused on low-skilled jobs or on encouraging further education and advanced skills?

Recall that in Chapter 11 we calculated the direct materials efficiency variance for a batch of 100 litres of Purple Madness ice cream. Now, Benny's managers turn to the French Vanilla ice cream to analyze the use of whipping cream and half and half, which are substitutable inputs. The standards call for 250 mL of each material for each litre of French Vanilla ice cream. Benny's knows that the actual use of these two inputs may vary from batch to batch and they would like to understand what happened with a particular recent batch. In the batch of interest, 20 litres of whipping cream and 32.5 litres of half and half were used to produce 100 litres of ice cream. The standard cost for whipping cream is $4.00 per litre and for half and half is $2.00 per litre. The calculation of the mix variance for the French Vanilla ice cream is presented in Exhibit 12.15.

Benny's managers can see that this change in proportion of inputs resulted in a $12.50 F variance overall. This total variance is the result of a $25 favourable mix variance for whipping cream because less cream was used than specified in the standards and a $12.5 unfavourable mix variance for half and half because more half and half was used than specified in the standards.

In general, the **yield variance** analyzes the output achieved for the inputs used. The yield variance holds the product mix percentages constant at the standard percentages; thereby, focusing on the difference between the standard amount of inputs required to make the actual output and the actual amount of inputs used to make the actual output. The calculation of the yield variance is:

Yield Variance = Sum for all products =
(Actual total quantity used × Standard production mix percentage ×
Standard price of input) − (Standard total quantity allowed ×
Standard production mix percentage × Standard price of input)

▶EXHIBIT 12.15
Benny's Direct Materials Mix Variances

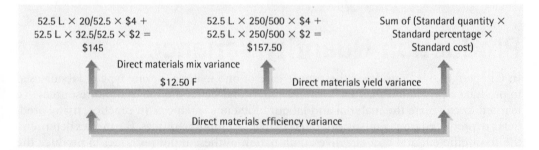

52.5 L × 20/52.5 × $4 + 52.5 L × 32.5/52.5 × $2 = $145	52.5 L × 250/500 × $4 + 52.5 L × 250/500 × $2 = $157.50	Sum of (Standard quantity × Standard percentage × Standard cost)

Direct materials mix variance
$12.50 F

Direct materials yield variance

Direct materials efficiency variance

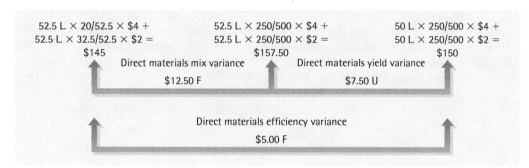

$$52.5 \text{ L} \times 20/52.5 \times \$4 +$$
$$52.5 \text{ L} \times 32.5/52.5 \times \$2 =$$
$$\$145$$

$$52.5 \text{ L} \times 250/500 \times \$4 +$$
$$52.5 \text{ L} \times 250/500 \times \$2 =$$
$$\$157.50$$

$$50 \text{ L} \times 250/500 \times \$4 +$$
$$50 \text{ L} \times 250/500 \times \$2 =$$
$$\$150$$

Direct materials mix variance
$12.50 F

Direct materials yield variance
$7.50 U

Direct materials efficiency variance
$5.00 F

The yield variance is favourable when the actual amount of the input is less than the standard amount allowed for the actual quantity of final product produced. The yield variance is unfavourable when more input is used than specified by the standard for the actual quantity of final product produced. Both of these situations must be considered in terms of strategic goals for the company including, in some situations, concerns about the integrity of the product.

For Benny's French vanilla ice cream, the standards indicate that 500 mL of cream and half and half should be used to produce 1 litre of French vanilla ice cream. For the batch of 100 litres, that means that 50 litres of liquid ingredients should be used. However, when making the batch of ice cream, Benny's used 52.5 litres of liquid ingredients. This will result in an unfavourable variance. The calculation of the yield variance is presented in Exhibit 12.16.

The yield variance tells Benny's that they overused liquid ingredients in making this batch of French Vanilla ice cream. Although in this example the dollar value of the overuse of materials is rather small, the extra quantity of materials used could have implications for purchasing and production of subsequent batches if not enough materials ae available to produce the next batch.

creaciones concretas, part 5

Recall from Chapter 11 that Josephina analyzed the direct cost variances for the cement mix after observing a large favourable price variance and a large unfavourable efficiency variance. The analysis revealed that the cement mix from the new supplier contained an inadequate quantity of the ingredient that prevents the cement blocks from slumping. As a result, after investigating other options, Creaciones Concretas implemented a new process that gave them more control over the cement mix used in producing their blocks. A new supplier was engaged. In the new process, Creaciones Concretas mixes the cement mix with the slumping agent. The standard mix is 4 parts cement mix to 1 part slumping agent. If more cement mix is added, the resulting blocks may be slightly deformed. If more slumping agent is added, the blocks become difficult to remove from the molds.

After working with these new materials, Josephina has collected the following information.

▶ The company produced 110,000 cement blocks
▶ The company purchased 100,000 kg of cement mix for 950,000 pesos
▶ The company purchased 25,000 kg of slumping mix for 200,000 pesos
▶ The company used 95,000 kg of cement mix
▶ The company used 20,000 kg of slumping agent
▶ The standard cost for cement mix is 8 pesos/kg
▶ The standard cost for slumping agent is 5 pesos/kg

Based on this information, she has calculated the materials efficiency variance for both cement mix and slumping agent and has broken down this variance into the mix and yield variances. Her calculations are shown in Exhibit 12.17.

Josephina is concerned. These results indicate that more cement mix was used than called for by the standard mix. Less slumping agent was used than called for by the standard

example

© Steven Frame/Alamy Stock Photo

continued...

example

mix. Further, more materials were used than was allowed for the number of bricks produced. Josephina believes that the workforce is conscientious; therefore, these results seem to indicate that the workers did not adequately understand the new process and perhaps there were unforeseen problems in implementing it. Josephina has scheduled a meeting with Jorge, the labour supervisor, to consider additional training. ■

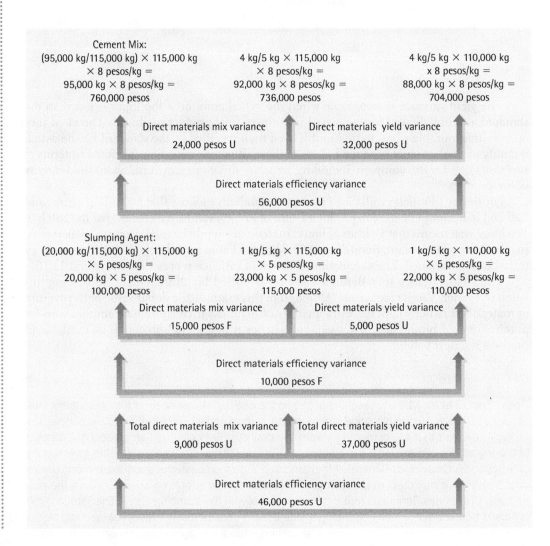

> EXHIBIT 12.17

Creaciones Concretas' Mix and Yield Variances

●● > STRATEGIC RISK MANAGEMENT

After using standard costs as a diagnostic control system, Josephina discovered problems with the cement mix from the new supplier. As a result, she made changes to the production processes and identified a new supplier. With an improved standard cost control system in place, Josephina is better able to monitor production variances and respond more quickly to variances that will damage Creaciones Concretas' reputation. What factors other than the accounting numbers has Josephina considered in current decisions? It is important to recognize the behavioural aspects of decisions based on control systems. Josephina believes that she has a competent, dedicated work force. Her next steps will rely on their commitment to Creaciones Concretas.

Accounting fraud is more prevalent than is expected or reported (Khalilieh 2015). Ernst & Young's (EY) *Annual Global Fraud Survey* (2015) reported on the frequency of the occurrence of fraud. Over 10% of respondents to the survey reported that their company had experienced a significant fraud in the past two years. Fraud can have a significant impact on both short and long term profitability and on the reputation of a business. Consequently, detecting and deterring fraud in organizations requires both management attention and resources. The development of internal controls and procedures to compel adherence to anti-fraud policies and to detect and deter accounting fraud is a regrettable but necessary function of business.

An effective internal control system necessarily incorporates the calculation and evaluation of variances from prior years and from budgeted amounts. In fact, a lack of variance analysis signals a material weakness in internal controls (Zack 2012). Variances are apt to occur normally given changes in industry and market trends, in assumptions and expectations inherent in the budget process, and in interrelationships among budget variables (Zack 2012). As such, there are legitimate reasons such as changes in prices, in economic factors and in corporate strategy which explain the occurrence of variances (Raiborn et al 2013). If variances, in whole or part, are unexplained, further investigation is warranted and necessary. Unexplained or unexpected variances occurring between periods or between budget and actual results may be an indicator of manipulation in the accounting records.

As a means of deception, an employee may attempt to conceal fraudulent activity within various general ledger accounts (Khalilieh 2015). Consequently, uncovering fraud through an investigation of unexplained accounting variances is a viable approach. For example, unexplained increases in property and equipment may signal improper expense capitalization, especially if the increase is not correlated with growth or expansion activities (Zack 2012). Also, large increases in sales in conjunction with a large increase in accounts receivable could signal that fictitious revenue has been recorded (Zack 2012). Vigilance in assessing both the variance and its explanation is critical in the detection and deterrence of fraud. Unexplained variances are signals of fraudulent activity which require corporate attention.

Sources: Khalilieh, Kelly (2015), Recognizing the Signs of Accounting Fraud, *D&A Magazine*, Chartered Professional Accountants: ON; Raiborn, Cecily A., (2013), Butler, Janet B., and Zelazny, Lucian, Standard Costing Variances: Potential Red Flags of Fraud, *Cost Management* 27(3), pp. 16-27; Zack, Gerard M. (2012), *Financial Statement Fraud: Strategies for Detection and Investigation*. John Wiley & Sons: Toronto.

ETHICS AND VARIANCES ANALYSIS

Unexplained variances capture changes that occurred during a given reporting period. Those variances also provide insight into possible fraudulent activities. How might an employer discourage fraudulent activity among employees? Would the approach to discouraging fraudulent activity among employees differ if the employees are professional accountants (e.g., CPA)?

Productivity

APPENDIX 12A

LO5 Calculate and analyze productivity measures

Chapters 11 and 12 illustrate the calculation of various variances between budgets (expectations) and actual results. The variance calculations presented in these two chapters rely on the use of a standard costing system and comparison of actual results with standards, and focus on whether the actual results are greater or less than expected for a single time period. Businesses also need to monitor performance over time and ask questions about the efficiency of operations in achieving the actual output.

Productivity is the ratio of outputs achieved for the inputs used. Businesses adapt this basic measure to indicate the efficiency of operations. **Technical efficiency** occurs when a business produces the maximum quantity of outputs for the minimum quantity of inputs. **Allocative efficiency** considers the costs of the input mix and the price paid by the consumer for the output. The optimal mix of inputs is achieved at the point at which the customers are willing to pay for the output produced. From a strategic decision-making perspective, this represents the lowest cost for the optimal mix of the input resources and provides insight into the numerous trade-offs that must be made when allocating scarce resources.

Partial Productivity Measures

A **partial productivity measure** is an assessment of the output achieved for each individual input, one input at a time. Therefore,

$$\text{Partial productivity} = \frac{\text{Output produced}}{\text{Input used}}$$

Partial productivity can be expressed in either physical units (e.g., litres, kilograms, or hours) or financial measures (e.g., dollars). By themselves, partial productivity measures tell managers only part of the story. They do not provide a basis for answering questions about whether the productivity has improved from a previous time period or whether operational improvements have been successful. To begin to analyze this type of question, partial productivity measures must be compared over time.

The time period chosen for comparison must be relevant to the decision. For example, if a manager is interested in analyzing the productivity improvement of a change in materials, the base time period productivity measure should be before the new materials were introduced while the comparator productivity measure should be after the new materials are introduced. The interval between might be relatively short—perhaps, one week or one month. Alternatively, if a production process improvement technique is being analyzed, a longer time period may be necessary to allow for learning curve effects that might diminish productivity.

The advantage of using partial productivity measures is that they focus on maximizing the use of each individual input resource to achieve the most benefit from that resource. Partial productivity measures can be short term, providing immediate feedback to operations-level personnel. As a result, necessary changes can happen more quickly. The disadvantage of using partial productivity measures is that, because they are based on a single input resource, they do not consider the trade-offs between resource usages that are part of most operating decisions. This narrow perspective may cause managers to miss important opportunities to better achieve strategic goals.

Total Productivity Measure

To provide managers with a more holistic view of operations, a **total productivity measure** is calculated. Total productivity measures the output achieved for all of the combined inputs. It is not always feasible to include all inputs, in which case total productivity includes all of the combined resources that management has deemed relevant to and important for achieving organizational goals. Two approaches to a total productivity assessment are possible: a portfolio approach and a total factor approach.

The portfolio approach considers of the whole collection of partial productivity measures simultaneously. Each partial productivity measure is calculated and the change in productivity is assessed. Then, managers use their knowledge of the operations to determine how the individual changes in productivity have impacted the overall productivity of the organization. A good deal of professional judgment is involved; however, the impact of the partial productivity measures on the whole is directly considered. This consideration of the partial productivity measures in light of the whole organization addresses the weakness associated with these measures.

The total factor approach calculates total factor productivity as:

$$\text{Total factor productivity} = \frac{\text{Quantity of output produced}}{\text{Costs of all inputs used}}$$

Although this calculation affords an aggregate productivity measure, it provides little useful information for operational decision making or insights into achievement of specific organizational goals.

In conclusion, productivity measures, whether partial or total, are additional tools that can be used to understand operations, the impact of changes on operations, and progress toward achieving certain goals. Like most of the measures presented throughout this text, including variances, productivity measures should not be used in isolation. They are single pieces of information that should raise and help answer important questions.

creaciones concretas, part 6

Recall the following information from part 5, which Josefina collected after working with the new materials (cement mix and slumping agent), Josephina collected the following information.

- ► The company produced 110,000 cement blocks
- ► The company purchased 100,000 kg of cement mix for 950,000 pesos
- ► The company purchased 25,000 kg of slumping mix for 200,000 pesos
- ► The company used 95,000 kg of cement mix
- ► The company used 20,000 kg of slumping agent
- ► The standard cost for cement mix is 8 pesos/kg
- ► The standard cost for slumping agent is 5 pesos/kg

In addition, Josephina learns that 1,200 hours of labour were worked at 15 pesos per hour. Josephina decides to calculate the partial productivity factors for each of the materials and labour.

© Steven Frame/Alamy Stock Photo

$$\text{Cement mix productivity} = \frac{110{,}000 \text{ cement blocks}}{95{,}000 \text{ kg cement mix}} = 1.158 \text{ blocks/kg}$$

$$\text{Slumping agent productivity} = \frac{110{,}000 \text{ cement blocks}}{20{,}000 \text{ kg slumping agent}} = 5.5 \text{ blocks/kg}$$

$$\text{Labour productivity} = \frac{110{,}000 \text{ cement blocks}}{1{,}200 \text{ labour hours}} = 91.67 \text{ blocks/hr}$$

Then, she calculates the total productivity factor as follows:

$$\text{Total productivity factor} = \frac{110{,}000 \text{ cement blocks}}{\left(95{,}000\text{kg} \times 9.5\frac{\text{pesos}}{\text{kg}}\right) + \left(20{,}000\text{kg} \times 8\frac{\text{pesos}}{\text{kg}}\right) + \left(1{,}200 \text{ hrs} \times 15\frac{\text{pesos}}{\text{hour}}\right)}$$

$$= 0.1018 \text{ blocks/peso}$$

To assess productivity using this information, Josephina decided to collect the same information for the next operating period.

- ► The company produced 105,000 cement blocks
- ► The company used 95,000 kg of cement mix (purchased at 9.5 pesos per kg)
- ► The company used 22,000 kg of slumping agent (purchased at 8 pesos per kg)
- ► The company worked 1,100 labour hours at 15 pesos per hour

The partial productivity factors for this period are:

$$\text{Cement mix productivity} = \frac{105{,}000 \text{ cement blocks}}{88{,}000 \text{ kg cement mix}} = 1.193 \text{ blocks/kg}$$

$$\text{Slumping agent productivity} = \frac{105{,}000 \text{ cement blocks}}{22{,}000 \text{ kg slumping agent}} = 4.77 \text{ blocks/kg}$$

$$\text{Labour productivity} = \frac{105{,}000 \text{ cement blocks}}{1{,}100 \text{ labour hours}} = 95.45 \text{ blocks/hr}$$

Then, she calculates the total productivity factor as follows:

$$\text{Total productivity factor} = \frac{105{,}000 \text{ cement blocks}}{\left(88{,}000\text{kg} \times 9.5\frac{\text{pesos}}{\text{kg}}\right) + \left(22{,}000\text{kg} \times 8\frac{\text{pesos}}{\text{kg}}\right) + \left(1{,}100 \text{ hr} \times 15\frac{\text{pesos}}{\text{hour}}\right)}$$

$$= 0.1021 \text{ blocks/pes}$$

In analyzing these results, Josephina concludes that the productivity efficiency improved for usage of the cement mix and labour hours but declined for usage of the slumping agent. As a result, the total productivity factor improved very slightly. Josephina is still concerned about the mixing of the cement mix and the slumping agent. She will talk with the production manager about the quality of the cement blocks and concerns about the workforce. She will also check with the sales force to follow up on customer satisfaction. ■

SUMMARY

LO1 Calculate and analyze profit related variances

REVENUE VARIANCES

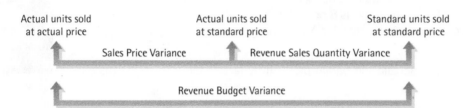

Actual units sold at actual price		Actual units sold at standard price		Standard units sold at standard price
	Sales Price Variance		Revenue Sales Quantity Variance	
		Revenue Budget Variance		

CONTRIBUTION MARGIN VARIANCES

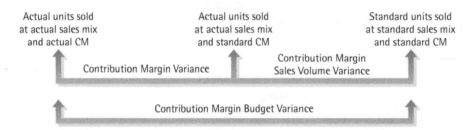

Actual units sold at actual sales mix and actual CM		Actual units sold at actual sales mix and standard CM		Standard units sold at standard sales mix and standard CM
	Contribution Margin Variance		Contribution Margin Sales Volume Variance	
		Contribution Margin Budget Variance		

LO2 Calculate and analyze sales mix and sales quantity variances

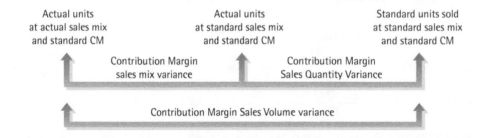

Actual units at actual sales mix and standard CM		Actual units at standard sales mix and standard CM		Standard units sold at standard sales mix and standard CM
	Contribution Margin sales mix variance		Contribution Margin Sales Quantity Variance	
		Contribution Margin Sales Volume variance		

LO3 Calculate and analyze market share and industry volume variances

Actual market share % of actual market sales in units at standard CM		Standard market share % of actual market sales in units at standard CM		Standard market share % of standard market sales in units at standard CM
	Market Share Variance		Market Size Variance	
		Contribution Margin Sales Quantity Variance		

SUMMARY

LO4   Calculate and analyze production mix and yield variances

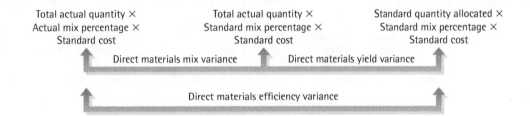

Total actual quantity × Actual mix percentage × Standard cost	Total actual quantity × Standard mix percentage × Standard cost	Standard quantity allocated × Standard mix percentage × Standard cost
	Direct materials mix variance	Direct materials yield variance
	Direct materials efficiency variance	

LO5   Calculate and analyze productivity measures (Appendix 12A)

PRODUCTIVITY = OUTPUT/INPUT

PARTIAL PRODUCTIVITY MEASURES

TOTAL FACTOR PRODUCTIVITY

12-1 solution to self-study problem

A. See Exhibit 12.18.

B. See Exhibit 12.19.

C. For the premium baskets, the price decrease is reflected in the unfavourable sales price variance ($1,189). However, the price variance is more than offset by a favourable revenue sales quantity variance ($2,560). The contribution margin budget variance for Gift Baskets Galore is $1,029 U. This variance is composed of the contribution margin variance of $1,130 U (reflecting only the effect of the changes in contribution margin for each product) and the contribution margin sales volume variance of $101 F (reflecting the effects of the changes in number of units sold). The contribution margin sales volume variance ($101 F) can be broken into the contribution margin sales mix variance of $149 favourable (reflecting the effects of the change in sales mix on contribution margin) and the contribution margin sales quantity variance of $48 favourable (reflecting the effects of the changes in units sold).

More premium baskets were sold, and this variance favourably affected the revenue sales quantity variance. However, the contribution margin on premium baskets was lower than expected, resulting in an unfavourable contribution margin variance. Managers will want to investigate reasons for the price decrease of premium baskets and consider controlling costs to maintain the expected contribution margin.

▶EXHIBIT 12.18

Calculation of Premium Gift Basket
Revenue Variances

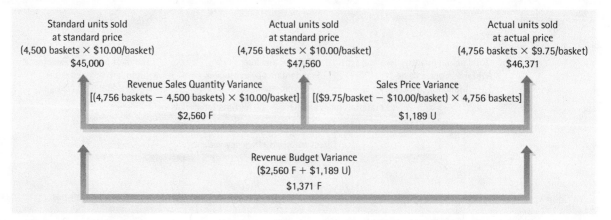

▶EXHIBIT 12.19

Calculation of Gift Baskets Galore
Contribution Margin Variances

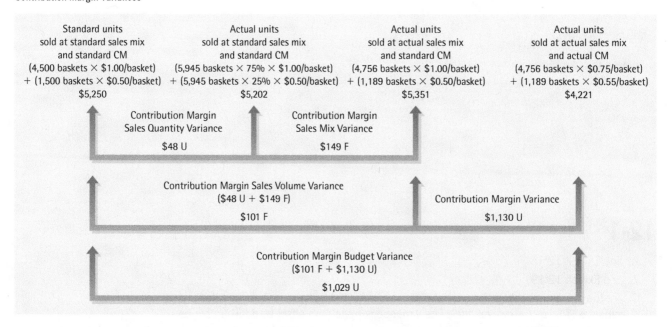

QUESTIONS

12.1 Describe the revenue-related variances, and explain why managers might monitor them.

12.2 How is the sales price variance calculated? What does it tell managers?

12.3 How is the revenue sales quantity variance calculated? What does it tell managers?

12.4 Describe the contribution margin budget variances, and explain why managers might monitor them.

12.5 How is the contribution margin variance calculated? What does it tell managers?

12.6 How is the contribution margin sales volume variance calculated? What does it tell managers?

12.7 Describe the contribution margin sales volume variances that an organization may calculate if it provides more than one product or service. Explain why managers might monitor these variances.

12.8 How do you calculate the standard sales mix percentage?

12.9 How do you calculate the contribution margin sales mix variance? What does this variance tell managers?

12.10 How do you calculate the contribution margin sales quantity variance? What does this variance tell managers?

12.11 How do changes in sales mix affect contribution margin variances?

12.12 Identify two variances that an organization can use to understand the sales volume variance from an external focus. What do these variances tell managers?

12.13 How do you calculate the market share variance? What does this variance tell managers?

12.14 How do you calculate the industry volume variance? What does this variance tell managers?

12.15 When an organization uses interchangeable inputs (either materials or labour), the production cost quantity/efficiency variance can be further analyzed. What are the two additional variances that can be calculated? Why would managers want to monitor these variances?

12.16 How do you calculate the materials (labour) mix variance? What does this variance tell managers?

12.17 How do you calculate the materials (labour) yield variance? What does this variance tell managers?

MULTIPLE-CHOICE QUESTIONS

12.18 The budget and actual results for Acme Co. Inc. for the first quarter of the year are as follows:

		Static Budget	Actual Results
Unit sales:	Regular	40,000	15,000
	Deluxe	60,000	65,000
	Total	100,000	80,000
Unit selling price:	Regular	$6	$6
	Deluxe	$12	$13
Unit variable costs:	Regular	$4	$3
	Deluxe	$7	$9
Market size (total units of both products)		500,000	480,000

The total sales (contribution margin) mix variance for the first quarter (rounded to the nearest thousand) is which of the following?

a. Zero
b. $102,000 unfavourable
c. $ 75,000 unfavourable
d. $ 17,000 unfavourable
e. $ 64,000 unfavourable

12.19 Restco Beds Inc. produces two models of beds: Regular and Majestic. Budget and actual data were as follows:

	Budget		Actual	
	Regular	Majestic	Regular	Majestic
Selling price per unit	$300	$800	$325	$700
Sales volume in units	4,500	5,500	7,200	4,800
Variable costs per unit	$220	$590	$238	$583

	Master Budget	Actual
Sales revenue	$5,750,000	$5,700,000
Variable costs	4,235,000	4,512,000
Contribution margin	1,515,000	1,188,000
Fixed costs	882,500	919,500
Operating income	$ 632,500	$ 268,500

Market Data

Expected total market sales of beds	500,000 beds
Actual total market sales of beds	666,667 beds

Which of these is the sales price variance?
a. $437,500 unfavourable
b. $300,000 unfavourable
c. $ 50,000 unfavourable
d. $660,000 unfavourable
e. $ 69,000 favourable

12.20 The Moose Co. expects to capture 35% of the moose chocolate market. In a typical year, this market averages 600,000 units. This year sales reached an all-time high of 725,000 units. Moose Co. sold 282,750 units. The standard contribution margin per unit for moose chocolate is $4.35. What are the market share variance and the market size variance?
a. $126,150 U; $190,312.50 U
b. $190,312.50 F; $126,150 U
c. $126,150 F; $190,312.50 U
d. $126,150 F; $190,312.50 F
e. $190,312.50 U; $126,150 U

12.21 Bison Burt's uses two different grade scales of labour, GS4 and GS5. In the last production period they used 2,500 hours of GS4 and 1,500 hours of GS5. The standard pay rates are $11 per GS4 hour and $15 per GS5 hour. At Bison Burt's the standard is to use 2 hours of labour per unit produced; 60% GS4 and 40% GS5. During this production period 2,100 units were produced. What are the total mix and yield variances?

a. $2,700 U; $2,520 U
b. $400 F; $2,520 F
c. $1,500 F; $1,200 F
d. $2,700 F; $120 U
e. $2,700 U; $1,200 U

12.22 Bison Burt's uses two different grade scales of labour. In the last production period they used 2,500 hours of GS4 and 1,500 hours of GS5. The standard pay rates are $11 per GS4 hour and $15 per GS5 hour. At Bison Burt's the standard is to use 2 hours of labour per unit produced; 60% GS4 and 40% GS5. During this production period 2,100 units were produced. What are the mix and yield variances for GS4?

a. $1,100 U; $1,320 F
b. $1,500 F; $1,200 F
c. $1,100 F; $1,320 U
d. $400 F; $2,520 F
e. $1,100 U; $1,500 F

EXERCISES

12.23 Profit-Related Variances Following is information for the Sunflower Company:

LO1

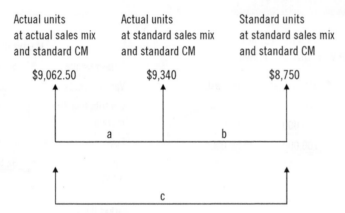

Actual units at actual sales mix and standard CM	Actual units at standard sales mix and standard CM	Standard units at standard sales mix and standard CM
$9,062.50	$9,340	$8,750

a   b

c

REQUIRED   **A.** Identify, by name, each of the labelled variances.
   B. Calculate each variance and indicate whether it is favourable or unfavourable.

12.24 Profit-Related Variances Slumber Cozy Inc. produces two models of beds: Regular and Majestic.

LO1, LO3

	Budget		Actual	
	Regular	Majestic	Regular	Majestic
Selling price per unit	$300	$800	$325	$700
Variable costs per unit	$220	$590	$238	$583
Sales volume in units	4,500	5,500	7,200	4,800

	Master Budget	Actual
Sales revenue	$5,750,000	$5,700,000
Variable costs	4,235,000	4,512,000
Contribution margin	1,515,000	1,188,000
Fixed costs	882,500	919,500
Operating income	$ 632,500	$ 268,500

The expected total market sales were 500,000 beds. The actual total market sales were 666,667 beds.

REQUIRED   **A.** Calculate the sales quantity variance.
   B. Calculate the market size variance.
   C. Explain why the budgeted operating income for Slumber Cozy Inc. was less than expected.

12.25 Profit-Related Variances Following is information for the Mitchellville Products Company for the month of July:

LO1, LO2

	Master Budget	Actual
Units	4,000	3,800
Sales revenue	$60,000	$53,200
Variable manufacturing costs	16,000	19,000
Fixed manufacturing costs	15,000	16,000
Variable selling and administrative expense	8,000	7,600
Fixed selling and administrative expense	9,000	10,000

REQUIRED
A. Determine the revenue budget variance.
B. Determine the sales price variance.
C. Determine the revenue sales quantity variance.
D. Determine the contribution margin sales quantity variance.

12.26 Profit-Related Variances Afos Sofas Inc. produces two models of sofas: Standard and Deluxe.

LO1, LO3

	Budget		Actual	
	Standard	Deluxe	Standard	Deluxe
Selling price per unit	$400	$900	$425	$850
Variable costs per unit	$260	$670	$275	$685
Sales volume in units	4,000	6,000	6,800	4,200

	Master Budget	Actual
Sales revenue	$7,000,000	$6,460,000
Variable costs	5,060,000	4,747,000
Contribution margin	1,940,000	1,713,000
Fixed costs	867,500	938,500
Operating income	$1,072,500	$ 774,500

The expected total market sales of sofas were 250,000 sofas. The actual total market sales of sofas were 220,000 sofas.

REQUIRED
A. Calculate the sales quantity variance.
B. Calculate the market size variance.
C. Explain why the budgeted operating income for Afos Sofas Inc. was less than expected.

12.27 Contribution Margin Variances, Analysis Metropolitan Motors is an auto retailer. Salespeople have the authority to negotiate with customers for price, but they are given target profits. The firm classifies the cars it sells into one of three broad groups: economy, family, and luxury. Target sales and average expected contribution margins per unit for March were estimated as follows:

LO2

Class	Unit Sales	Average Contribution Margin
Economy	10	$400
Family	20	800
Luxury	5	1,300

During March, the auto manufacturer ran a special promotion to reduce an overstock of economy cars. The manufacturer offered to pay directly to the salespeople a bonus of $75 for each economy car sold. Actual sales and total contribution margin earned by Metropolitan Motors for March turned out to be as follows:

Class	Unit Sales	Total Contribution Margin Earned
Economy	25	$5,625
Family	10	$7,500
Luxury	3	$4,200

REQUIRED **A.** Calculate the contribution margin budget variance.

B. Calculate the contribution margin variance and contribution margin sales volume variance.

C. Calculate the contribution margin sales mix variance and the contribution margin sales quantity variance.

D. Should the management of Metropolitan Motors be pleased or upset with the manufacturer for running the special promotion? Why?

12.28 **Profit-Related Variances** Pet Toys Inc. expected to sell one plush toy for each two Frisbees sold.

L01, L02

	Frisbees	Plush Toys	Total
Sales (100,000 Frisbees)	$300,000	$150,000	$450,000
Variable costs	175,000	50,000	225,000
Contribution margin	$125,000	$100,000	$225,000

During the year, a competitor came out with a similar plush toy at a lower price. Management reacted by dropping its selling price for plush toys, but the results were disappointing. Actual sales were as follows:

Frisbees (95,000 @ $3.30)	$313,500
Plush toys (40,000 @ $2.40)	96,000
Total sales	$409,500

REQUIRED **A.** Determine the revenue budget variance, the sales price variance, and the revenue sales quantity variance.

B. Determine the contribution margin budget variance, the contribution margin variance, and the contribution margin sales volume variance.

C. Determine the contribution margin sales mix variance and the contribution margin sales quantity variance.

12.29 **Market Share and Market Size Variances** Geysers Unlimited expects to capture 55% of the flavoured water market. In a typical year, this market averages 2,500,000 units. This year sales reached an all-time high of 2,800,000 units. Geysers Unlimited sold 1,820,000 units. The standard contribution margin per unit for flavoured water is $1.25.

L03

REQUIRED **A.** Calculate the market share variance.

B. Calculate the market size variance.

C. Write a memo explaining the results to management.

12.30 **Mix and yield variances** Flathead Music uses two different types of labour. In the last production period, they used 4,600 hours of technician I time and 2,200 hours of technician II time. The standard pay rates are $15 per technician I hour and $18 per technician II hour. At Flathead Music the standard is to use 1.5 hours of labour per unit produced; 1 hour of technician I and ½ hour of technician II time. During this production period 4,500 units were produced.

L04

REQUIRED **A.** Calculate the mix and yield variances for technician I.

B. Calculate the mix and yield variances for technician II.

C. Calculate the total mix and yield variances.

D. Write a brief report to management explaining what happened during this production period.

12.31 **Mix and yield variances** Blitz Inc. uses three different substitutable products in the production process. In the last production period, they used a total of 555,000 litres: 138,750 litres of solution E, 222,000 litres of solution T; and 194,250 litres of solution A. The standard cost card follows:

L04

	Quantity	Cost	Standard
Solution E	10 litres	$0.50 per litre	$ 5.00
Solution T	21 litres	$0.10 per litre	$ 2.10
Solution A	19 litres	$0.35 per litre	$ 6.65
			$13.75

During this production period, 11,000 batches were produced.

REQUIRED   **A.** Calculate the materials quantity variance.
B. Calculate the mix and yield variances for each solution.
C. Calculate the total mix and yield variances.
D. Write a memo explaining to management what happened during this production period.

12.32 Market share and market size variances Fairy Flats Ltd. expects to capture 28% of the glitter market. In a typical year, this market averages 8,000,000 units. This year sales were 7,800,000 units. Fairy Flats sold 1,716,000 units. The standard contribution margin per unit for glitter is $2.40.

LO3

REQUIRED   **A.** Calculate the market share variance.
B. Calculate the market size variance.
C. Write an explanation of the results for management.
D. Make a recommendation to management for the upcoming production period.

PROBLEMS

12.33 Reconciling Standard to Actual Income, Performance Evaluation, Budget Software Development Company produces computer programs on DVDs for home computers. This business is highly automated, causing fixed costs to be very high, but variable costs are minimal. The company is organized along three product lines: games, business programs, and educational programs. The average standard selling price for each is $16 for games, $55 for business programs, and $20 for educational programs. The standard variable cost consists solely of one DVD per program at $2.00 per DVD, without regard to the type of program. Fixed costs for the period were estimated at $535,000. For the current period, standard sales are 40,000 games, 2,000 business programs, and 10,000 educational programs. Actual results are as follows:

LO1, LO2

Sales:		
Games	(35,000 DVDs)	$ 616,000
Business	(4,000 DVDs)	198,000
Educational	(11,000 DVDs)	220,000
Total sales		1,034,000
Variable costs	(50,750 DVDs)	106,575
Fixed costs		533,500
Pretax income		$ 393,925

REQUIRED   **A.** Calculate standard pretax income and then reconcile it to actual pretax income by calculating the contribution margin sales mix variance, revenue sales quantity variance, sales price variance, materials price and quantity variances, and fixed cost spending variance.
B. A new marketing manager was hired during the period. The manager changed prices and redirected sales efforts.
   1. Discuss whether one or more of the preceding variances are relevant to evaluating the performance of the new marketing manager.
   2. What do the variances suggest about the new manager's performance? Explain.
C. An analysis reveals that the company will have to pay $1.80 per DVD next period. Prepare next period's master budget. Assume a standard of one DVD per program, total unit sales of 55,000, and the actual sales mix and sales prices from this period.
D. Discuss possible reasons why the company might not meet its budget for next period.

12.34 Contribution margin variances Tile Floors produces a variety of tiles used for kitchen flooring. Two of Tile Floors lines are particularly popular with local home builders. The standard grade is a 6-inch (15 cm) square, high-glass tile. The high grade is an 8-inch (20 cm) square tile with a rough sandstone finish. When the housing market gets tight, home builders use more of the standard grade to keep the overall cost of the house lower. The following information is available for sales during the last six-month period.

LO1, LO2

	Standard Price	Standard Contribution Margin	Standard Volume	Actual Price	Actual Contribution Margin	Actual Volume
6-inch	$24/case	$ 9.60	250,000	$22/case	$ 6.00	225,000
8-inch	$60/case	$30.00	50,000	$55/case	$25.00	65,000

REQUIRED **A.** Calculate the contribution margin sales volume variance.
B. Calculate the contribution margin sales mix variance.
C. Calculate the contribution margin sales quantity variance.
D. Explain what has happened in these 2 product lines in the last 6 months.

12.35 Contribution margin variances Jersey Knits sells two types of fabric that are used interchangeably in the production of lawn chairs. The following information about each fabric is available:

L01, L02

	Standard Contribution Margin	Standard Volume	Actual Contribution Margin	Actual Volume
Fabric A	$1.75/metre	50,000 metres	$1.80/metre	45,000 metres
Fabric B	$5.00/metre	10,000 metres	$4.75/metre	12,000 metres

REQUIRED **A.** Calculate the contribution margin sales volume variance.
B. Calculate the contribution margin sales mix variance.
C. Calculate the contribution margin sales quantity variance.
C. Explain what has happened.

12.36 Direct Material Variances, Mix and Yield Variances Rainbow Bubbles' managers expected to produce 30,000 units of product in March. Two materials are used to produce the bubble product: Material A is the soap that makes the bubbles and determines the size of the bubbles; Material B is the colour agent that determines the brightness of the colours. The standard cost for the materials used for 30,000 units is $156,240 for material A and $104,160 for material B and the standard cost per unit is $4.20 per litre for material A and $2.10 per litre for material B. Actual production in March was 28,650 units. The company purchased and used 33,750 litres of material A costing $143,436.22 and 49,736.4 litres of material B costing $99,472.80.

L04

REQUIRED **A.** What was the standard quantity of litres for material A and material B per unit?
B. What were the direct materials price variances for materials A and B for March?
C. What were the direct materials efficiency variances for materials A and B for March?
D. Calculate the materials mix and yield variances for materials A and B for March.
E. Identify possible causes for the variances.
F. Rainbow Bubbles is known for producing very large, colourful bubbles. Discuss possible business concerns arising from of these variances.

12.37 Direct Labour Variances, Mix and Yield Variances Following is information about Nature's Song direct labour hours and wages last period.

L04

Actual labour hours for guides at the standard price per hour	$2,760
Actual labour hours for guides at the actual price per hour (240 hours x $12/hr)	2,880
Standard labour hours for guides at the standard price per hour	2,300
Standard labour hours for guides at the actual price per hour	2,400
Actual labour hours for naturalists at the standard price per hour	$7,200
Actual labour hours for naturalists at the actual price per hour (360 hours × $18/hr)	6,480
Standard labour hours for naturalists at the standard price per hour	8,000
Standard labour hours for naturalists at the actual price per hour	7,200

REQUIRED **A.** Calculate the direct labour price variances.
B. Calculate the direct labour efficiency variances.
C. Calculate the direct labour mix and yield variances.
D. Provide one possible explanation for each variance.
E. At Nature's Song, guides answer questions and provide basic information; naturalists provide educational programming. One of Nature's Song's strategic goals is to educate visitors about the natural environment they are visiting. Based on the variances that you calculated, assess whether Nature's Song is supporting this strategic goal. Make suggestions for future use of labour hours assuming that Nature's Song has a total labour budget of $10,000.

12.38 Direct Labour Variances, Mix and Yield Variances To help control operations, Cabo Company developed a standard costing system in its job shop. Data for a recent job follows.

L04

	Standard	Actual
Direct labour hours (G1)	1,900	1,840
Direct labour dollars (G1)	$38,000	$37,000
Direct labour hours (G2)	475	560
Direct labour dollars (G2)	$11,875	$15,400
Units produced	380	380

REQUIRED   **A.** Calculate the direct labour price variances.
B. Calculate the direct labour efficiency variances.
C. Calculate the direct labour mix and yield variances.
D. Provide one possible explanation for each variance.
E. Are these results consistent with Cabo Company's low-cost product strategy? Why or why not? Make recommendations for future labour scheduling.

12.39 **Market size and market share variances** Marisa has recently opened Rapid Oil Change, a service station in a small but growing community. Her strategy is to provide a low cost, high quality service in a customer-friendly atmosphere. Marisa estimated that there are approximately 5,000 families in the community each with an average of two cars. Given the average commuting distance driven in these cars, she estimates that each car will need an oil change approximately every four months. Marisa hopes to capture 40% of this market. After four months of operation, Marisa has serviced 4,335 cars and 100 new families (each with 2 cars) have moved into the area. The average contribution margin is $15 per oil change.

LO3

REQUIRED   **A.** Calculate the industry market size.
B. Calculate the market share variance.
C. Explain what has happened to Marisa.
What other key performance indicators would you recommend Marisa monitor to be sure she is achieving her goals?

12.40 **Productivity (Appendix 12A)** Quick-start, Inc. produces fire starters for starting charcoal grills. The fire starters are made from wood chips and paraffin. If there is not enough paraffin, the fire starters are more difficult to light; if there is too much paraffin, the fire starters burn too quickly and don't light the charcoal. Management are concerned about productivity and have collected the following information.

LO5

		Cost per unit	Month 1	Month 2
Wood chips	kg	$ 3.50	500	650
Paraffin	kg	$10.00	100	120
Labour	hrs	$15.00	240	280
Total fire starters			5400	7200

REQUIRED   **A.** Calculate partial productivity measures.
B. Calculate the total factor productivity measure.
C. Analyze Quick-start, Inc.'s productivity from month 1 to month 2.

12.41 **Productivity (Appendix 12A)** Green Elements, Ltd. uses three chemical inputs, one labor grade, and major scientific equipment. Management tracks productivity be input and in total. The following information is available.

LO5

	Unit	Cost	Week 1	Week 2	Week 3
Chemical 1	Litres	$ 3.50	10000	10500	12000
Chemical 2	Grams	$ 7.75	450	400	500
Chemical 3	Millilitres	$25.00	15	15	20
Labour	Hours	$32.00	16	18	16
Equipment	Machine hours	$18.00	8	9	10
Output	Litres		9500	9800	11500

REQUIRED   **A.** Calculate the partial productivity measures.
B. Calculate the total factor productivity measure.
C. Analyze the changes in productivity.

MINI-CASE

12.42 Market changes and effect of sales price changes Dig We Must, Inc. produces three different grades of shovels. The differences among the shovels are due to the materials and construction of the handles. These differences result in cost and selling price differences. DWM's product strategy is to provide high quality, long-lasting tools. Originally, the target market was construction and landscape design companies. They introduced the low-price model when home renovation enthusiasts started asking for DWM products but seemed reluctant to pay the price for professional-grade tools. Estimated sales information for the upcoming 6 months is as follows (assume an even distribution over the 6 months).

LO3

	Market Size (shovels)	DWM Sales (shovels)	Selling Price	Variable Costs
Professional Grade	30,000	25,000	$150	$50
Performance Grade	20,000	5,000	$ 90	$40
Home Repairs	50,000	10,000	$ 30	$15

Due to an upturn in the housing market and a stronger economy, 3 months into this 6-month planning period, actual sales information indicated the following.

	Market Size (shovels)	DWM Sales (shovels)	Selling Price	Variable Costs
Professional Grade	20,000	18,000	$150	$50
Performance Grade	8,000	1,800	$ 90	$40
Home Repairs	35,000	10,000	$ 30	$15

REQUIRED **A.** Analyze the market share and market size variances.

B. Analyze the actual results in terms of DWM's product differentiation goals. Make suggestions to DWM management.

As a result of the results for the first 3 months, DWM increased the selling price of the professional-grade shovel to $160 and the home repairs shovel to $35. Further, the selling price of the performance grade shovel was reduced to $85. The sales results for the second 3 months are as follows.

	Market Size (shovels)	DWM Sales (shovels)	Selling Price	Variable Costs
Professional Grade	20,000	18,000	$160	$50
Performance Grade	10,000	2,000	$ 85	$40
Home Repairs	40,000	15,000	$ 35	$15

REQUIRED **A** Analyze the market changes and the effect of the sales price change.

B Make recommendations to DWM management for next year's peak 6-month season.

13

Strategic Investment Decisions

in brief Managers periodically make decisions about long-term investments for new projects or replacement of old assets. These decisions focus on creating long-term value consistent with organizational strategies. The outcomes from these decisions are generally more uncertain than shorter-term decisions because we forecast further into the future. In addition, the time value of money becomes important. ■

After studying this chapter, you should be able to do the following:

LO1 Explain how strategic investment decisions are made

LO2 Identify relevant cash flows and perform net present value (NPV) analysis for capital investment decisions

LO3 Identify the uncertainties of NVP analysis

LO4 Apply alternative methods in analyzing strategic investment decisions

LO5 Identify additional issues to be considered for strategic investment decisions

LO6 Explain how income taxes affect strategic investment decision cash flows (Appendix 13A)

LO7 Explain how real and nominal methods are used to address inflation in an NPV analysis (Appendix 13A)

SolarShare: Harnessing the Power of Financial Analysis

© iStockphoto/Ryan Morgan

SOURCES: R. Blackwell, "SolarShare Grows as 'Green Bonds' Heat Up," *The Globe and Mail*, September 14, 2014; P. Gipe, "Project Analysis for Toronto Renewable Energy Co-operative's SolarShare: A Community Power Photovoltaic Project Financial Model," October 16, 2007; M. Brigham and P. Gipe, "Feasibility Analysis for a SolarShare Co-operative in the City of Toronto," September 27, 2007; Toronto Renewable Energy Co-operative website, www.trec.on.ca.

The **Toronto Renewable Energy Co-operative (TREC)** is a not-for-profit, cooperative environmental organization. Its mission is to develop cooperatively owned renewable energy projects and energy efficiency/conservation projects, and to educate both citizens of Toronto and visitors about renewable energy, energy conservation, and the community power model:

Renewable energy + Cooperative ownership = Community power

TREC had great success installing the WindShare turbine at Toronto's Exhibition Place. It then sought to duplicate that success with SolarShare, a cooperative producing electricity from solar photovoltaic (PV) cells on rooftops of existing buildings or on the ground. SolarShare sells "green bonds" to the public, raising $5 million over three years to finance the electricity-generating projects. SolarShare bondholders, or "members," get a guaranteed 5% return on their bonds, which they can't cash for five years.

TREC and SolarShare identified potential PV projects in Toronto's urban core totalling nearly 4 megawatts of power production. In 2007, TREC studied the economic feasibility of these projects. With a responsibility to its members, TREC and SolarShare needed to ensure that there would be a return on their investment.

To help analyze the potential projects, the SolarShare project team created both an economic model and a financial model. The economic model is a simple tool for examining the influence of various parameters. This model is also useful for determining the tariffs necessary to make solar projects profitable under varying conditions. The detailed financial model examines individual elements of a cooperative solar PV project. The analysis uses techniques such as internal rate of return (IRR), net present value (discounted cash flows), profitability index, and payback period.

After a thorough study, TREC concluded that it could not profitably develop the solar energy projects in the more costly Toronto urban core under current conditions. A simple economic analysis of feasibility gave results that closely agreed with those of the more detailed financial model that TREC developed for this project. The model yields a negative NPV, a very low IRR, and a payback beyond the 20-year project life. Returns from the SolarShare project were expected to remain negative until the 26th year, when the project would finally fully pay for itself. The assumptions used in the analysis were conservative, and revenues beyond 20 years were considered extremely uncertain. Such projects would not be economically feasible without a radical drop in the installed cost, a substantial increase in Ontario's standard-offer contract solar PV tariff, or a substantial up-front subsidy. SolarShare has since built several PV generators in various Ontario communities, but the Toronto urban core has remained not economically feasible.

Strategic Investment Decisions

Compared to decisions that affect operations in the short term, strategic investment decisions have long-term effects. As we learned in Chapter 1, organizational strategies lead to the tactics that managers use to take advantage of core competencies while working toward the organizational vision. Strategies guide long-term investment flows over a number of years. These investments fall into two general categories of projects:

- Developing or expanding products or services
- Replacing or reorganizing assets or services

For example, managers may wish to acquire another company to expand existing services. Or they may wish to install new technology or reorganize operations to improve profitability. The objective of strategic investment decisions is to increase the long-term value of the organization.

Capital Budgeting

Capital budgeting is a process that managers use when they choose among strategic investment opportunities. Exhibit 13.1 demonstrates how the strategic management process introduced in Chapter 1 relates specifically to the identification and analysis of capital budgeting projects.

The capital budgeting process is similar to the process for making non-routine operating decisions (Chapter 4). The major difference is that capital budgeting decisions affect cash flows in future years. Therefore, strategic priorities become more critical. Another important factor is the time value of money, which refers to the idea that a dollar received today is worth more than a dollar received in the future.

Identifying and Prioritizing Investment Opportunities

Organizations identify new projects, products, and services through a variety of methods. Individuals, teams, and whole departments are responsible for identifying future investment opportunities. Organizational strategies are reflected in long-term decisions about products, services, and acquiring new business segments. For example, organizations with reputations for low-cost, high-quality products want to invest in new technology to improve quality while reducing cost.

L01 | Explain how strategic investment decisions are made

▶ EXHIBIT 13.1
Process for Identifying and Analyzing Strategic Investments

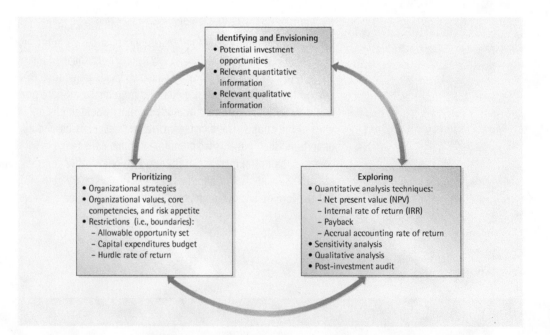

Identifying and Envisioning
- Potential investment opportunities
- Relevant quantitative information
- Relevant qualitative information

Exploring
- Quantitative analysis techniques:
  - Net present value (NPV)
  - Internal rate of return (IRR)
  - Payback
  - Accrual accounting rate of return
- Sensitivity analysis
- Qualitative analysis
- Post-investment audit

Prioritizing
- Organizational strategies
- Organizational values, core competencies, and risk appetite
- Restrictions (i.e., boundaries):
  - Allowable opportunity set
  - Capital expenditures budget
  - Hurdle rate of return

Sometimes, organizational strategies require consideration of new product lines or business segments to expand the organizational scope. Once projects that align with company strategies are identified, capital budgeting analysis is performed to determine their financial viability.

Some organizations encourage large groups of employees to search actively for new business ideas. For example, Google allows its engineers to spend 20% of their time on projects of their own choice.[1] To provide greater focus, many organizations use belief systems to inspire and direct employees to search for strategically desirable investment opportunities. Vision, mission, or core value statements frequently communicate the organization's strengths and strategies, which guide selection of potential investment opportunities. To prevent waste of organizational resources on inappropriate investment opportunities, top managers often establish boundary systems. Common boundary systems include clear definitions of allowed versus disallowed types of projects, spending limits based on capital expenditures budgets, and minimum required rates of return. Managers may also develop a 5- or 10-year comprehensive capital project plan to guide the direction of annual strategic investments.

Relevant Cash Flows

The process of identifying relevant cash flows for capital budgeting decisions is similar to the process for any other type of decision. We learned in Chapter 1 that relevant cash flows must arise in the future and differ among decision alternatives (possible courses of action). The cash flows associated with capital projects are usually estimated using techniques such as those described in Chapter 2 (Cost Concepts, Behaviour, and Estimation), Chapter 4 (Relevant Information for Decision Making), and Chapter 10 (Static and Flexible Budgets).

Exhibit 13.2 presents timelines and also lists common types of cash flows associated with capital budgeting decisions. Cash flows must be estimated for all future periods affected by the potential investment. We usually begin by creating a timeline to help us think about the nature and timing of relevant cash flows.

At the beginning of the project, at time 0, the company faces initial cash outflows—such as the purchase of new property, plant, equipment—and other costs required to make assets ready for use in operations. Sometimes, these outflows include initial contractual payments, such as signing bonuses, or additions to working capital, such as inventories. Initial cash inflows or outflows may also come from the disposal of old assets which can be viewed as a trade-in value, at the beginning of a project.

During years 1 through n, the life of the project, there are annual, incremental operating cash flows and/or cost savings for the project. For a new or an expanded product or service, these cash flows and/or cost savings may include new revenues as well as new fixed and variable costs. When replacing or reorganizing assets, revenues and costs may increase or decrease because of improved product quality, increased capacity, or greater efficiency.

Any terminal cash flows appear at the end of the project's life (time n). Terminal cash flows typically include proceeds from the sale of assets at the end of the project (e.g., salvage value). However, assets such as equipment may be obsolete and have zero terminal value. Some projects require terminal cash outflows, such as the costs to reinstate the quality of land (called land reclamation) at the end of a mining operation.

Quantitative Analysis Techniques

This chapter describes the four methods listed in Exhibit 13.1 for quantitatively analyzing potential strategic investment projects. The first two methods, net present value (NPV) and

> **CHAPTER REFERENCE**
> Chapter 1 introduced four types of control systems: belief, boundary, diagnostic, and interactive.

> **BUSINESS PRACTICE**
> Consistent with their strategy to sustain high-quality seafoods, the managers at **Clearwater Seafoods** established a capital budget of $100 million for capital spending on a modern fishing fleet that can freeze the catch at sea when it's fresh.[2]

> **ALTERNATIVE TERMS**
> The terms *residual value*, *salvage value*, and *disposal value* mean the same as *terminal value*.

---

[1] According to "The Engineer's Life at Google," www.google.com/intl/en/jobs/lifeatgoogle/englife/.
[2] Clearwater Seafoods, Annual Report 2006. www.clearwater.ca/site/media/Parent/ClearwaterAR06(1).pdf.

Common Cash Flows for Long-Term Decisions

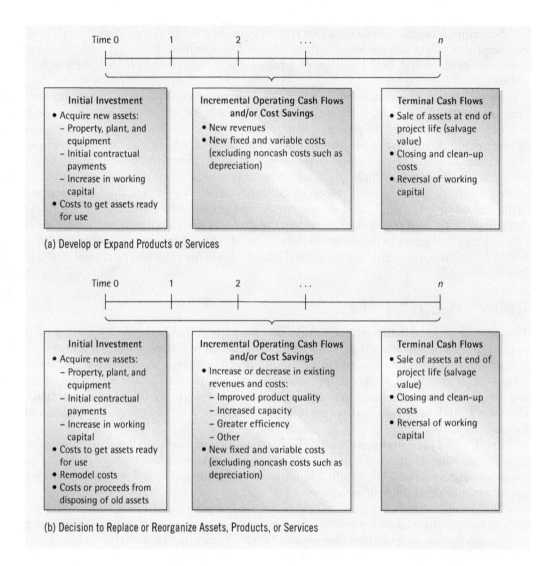

(a) Develop or Expand Products or Services

(b) Decision to Replace or Reorganize Assets, Products, or Services

internal rate of return (IRR), explicitly take into account the time value of money, making them preferred methods. However, many managers still use the other, less-preferred methods: payback and accrual accounting rate of return. Therefore, we introduce all these methods, covering the advantages and disadvantages of each. We also address sensitivity analyses that help managers evaluate the potential effects of uncertainties about quantitative results.

Managers consider both quantitative and qualitative information when considering strategic investments. Later in the chapter, we introduce a number of qualitative factors that influence capital budgeting decisions.

When deciding whether to accept or reject proposals, managers analyze capital budgeting projects as if they were stand-alone projects. However, they may face capital constraints, so that accepting one project would eliminate another. In these cases, alternative investments are analyzed simultaneously so that they can be compared.

Discounted Cash Flow Methods

The two quantitative analysis techniques discussed below—net present value (NPV) and internal rate of return (IRR)—which take into consideration the time value of money, are called discounted cash flow methods.

Net Present Value Method

In business, although we value a project today, the cash flows occur in the future, and therefore, we discount the future dollars to determine their value in today's dollars. Appendix 13B provides tables with factors that when multiplied by cash flows will determine either a **future value**—the amount received in the future, for a given number of years at a given interest rate, for a given investment today—or a **present value**, the value in today's dollars of a sum received in the future.

Suppose you want to buy a $20,000 sports car two years from now. Assume that you can invest money today and earn a rate of return of 10% per year. How much would you have to invest today so that in two years you will have $20,000? In other words, at an annual interest rate of 10%, what present value is needed to create a future value of $20,000? To calculate the present value, we multiply the future value ($20,000) by the present value factor for 10% and two time periods. Using Table 13B.1 in Appendix 13B, we locate the 10% column and go down to the row representing two periods. The factor is 0.826. We multiply this factor by the future value of $20,000 and find that you need $16,520 today to have enough money in two years to buy the car.

LO2   Identify relevant cash flows and perform net present value (NPV) analysis for capital investment decisions

Present Value of a Series of Cash Flows

Managers are often involved in evaluating projects that have different time horizons. One project might end in 5 years and another in 10 years. The future values of such projects are not strictly comparable, because a dollar received 5 years from now is not worth a dollar received 10 years from now. For this and other reasons, the cash flows for projects are generally converted to their present values. The projects can then be compared on a common basis.

The **net present value (NPV) method** determines whether an organization would be better off investing in a project, based on the net amount of discounted cash flows for the project. The net present value of a project is calculated as follows:

$$\text{NPV} = \sum_{t=0}^{n} \frac{\text{Expected cash flow}_t}{(1+r)^t}$$

where

$t = \text{time period (year)}$

$n = \text{life of the project}$

$r = \text{discount rate}$

The expected cash flows include the initial investment, incremental operating cash flows and/or cost savings, and terminal cash flows. If the NPV is positive, the project is generally considered acceptable, because it is expected to increase the organization's value. If investment resources are limited, we should invest in the project(s) having the highest NPV. Following is an example of the NPV method.

Suppose Gordon wants to convert a 30,000-square-foot motel into apartments that he will rent to university students. The initial investment is $1,400,000. Gordon expects to rent the apartments for $1.00 per square foot per month and to pay a management company fees representing 15% of rents. He forecasts that property taxes and insurance will be about $30,000 per year. Therefore, the incremental cash flows are $276,000 = [$1 per sq ft × 30,000 sq ft × 12 months) × (1 − 0.15)] − $30,000. Gordon expects to be able to sell the building at the end of 10 years for $400,000. (We will ignore income taxes for these calculations.) Gordon's discount rate is 14%. The cash flows for this project are shown in Exhibit 13.3. The total discounted cash flow after the initial investment is the sum of individual present values, as follows:

Period	Interest Rate	Present Value Factor (PVF)	Cash Flow	Discounted Cash Flow
1	14%	0.877	$276,000	$ 242,052
2	14	0.769	276,000	212,244
3	14	0.675	276,000	186,300
4	14	0.592	276,000	163,392
5	14	0.519	276,000	143,244
6	14	0.456	276,000	125,856
7	14	0.400	276,000	110,400
8	14	0.351	276,000	96,876
9	14	0.308	276,000	85,008
10	14	0.270	276,000	74,520
		5.216	276,000	1,439,892
10	14	0.270	400,000	108,000
		Total discounted cash flows		$1,547,892

Notice that the incremental operating cash flows during years 1 through 10 are identical. In other words, Gordon expects to receive an annual annuity of $276,000 per year for 10 years, and in year 10, he also receives the terminal value of $400,000. In the case of an annuity, we can simplify the present value calculation by using Table 13B.2 in Appendix 13B, as follows:

PV = $276,000 × (PVFA 10 years, 14%) + $400,000 × (PVF 10 years, 14%)
   = $276,000 × 5.216 + $400,000 × 0.270
   = $1,439,616 + $108,000
   = $1,547,616

Notice that we obtain the same present value for the project cash flows (the difference between $1,547,892 and $1,547,616 is due to rounding) regardless of the method we use. However, if we are performing these calculations manually, we can often save time by using an annuity table.

Net Present Value of a Project

Once we calculate the present value of a series of cash flows for Gordon's project, we can compare the net present value to the investment amount, because both amounts are now valued in today's dollars. We use the following formula to calculate NPV for Gordon's apartment project:

NPV = Initial investment cash outflow + PV of cash inflows
    = −$1,400,000 + $1,574,616
    = $174,616

►EXHIBIT 13.3

Timeline for Gordon's Apartment Building Project

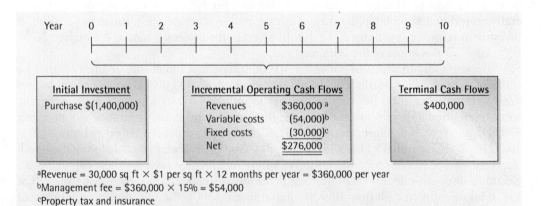

Year   0   1   2   3   4   5   6   7   8   9   10

Initial Investment	Incremental Operating Cash Flows		Terminal Cash Flows
Purchase $(1,400,000)	Revenues	$360,000 [a]	$400,000
	Variable costs	(54,000)[b]	
	Fixed costs	(30,000)[c]	
	Net	$276,000	

[a]Revenue = 30,000 sq ft × $1 per sq ft × 12 months per year = $360,000 per year
[b]Management fee = $360,000 × 15% = $54,000
[c]Property tax and insurance

At the end of 10 years, we estimate that Gordon will have realized $174,616 in today's dollars. Because this net present value amount is greater than zero, the general rule is that Gordon would want to invest in this project.

Profitability Index

If Gordon were considering more than one investment, he could calculate the profitability index for each project. The profitability index is the ratio of the present value of the cash inflows to the present value of the investment cash outflows. The decision rule for a solitary investment is that the investment should be undertaken if the index is equal to or greater than one. For example, Gordon's profitability index would be

$$\text{Profitability index} = \frac{\text{Present value of cash inflows}}{\text{Present value of investment cash outflows}} = \frac{\$1,574,616}{\$1,400,000} = 1.125$$

If Gordon were comparing a number of different projects and could not undertake all of them, he would consider both today's dollar amount and the profitability index. The profitability index and the NPV method always accept and reject the same project, but the index allows managers to rank-order projects. It provides a simple way to identify which projects are expected to earn higher rates of return.

Identifying a Reasonable Discount Rate

A discount rate, r, must be selected to apply the NPV formula. The discount rate is the interest rate that is used across time to reduce the value of future dollars to today's dollars. Many decision makers simply set the discount rate at the organization's weighted average cost of capital (WACC), which is the weighted average rate for the costs of the various sources of financing, such as debt and stock. (Mini-Case 13.55 at the end of this chapter provides practice at calculating the weighted average cost of capital.) However, this method ignores variations in risk among projects. If a project involves little risk, then a lower discount rate might be appropriate. Conversely, a higher discount rate is appropriate for projects having higher risk.

Judgment is required to incorporate an estimate of project risk. One way to think about project risk is to consider the opportunities for return on other investments that appear to be of similar risk. For example, the stock market has returned, on average, about 11% from 1928 through to 2010, and 3.54% from 2001 to 2010. The Credit Suisse Global Investment Yearbook reports that stock markets in the developed world delivered an annualized return of 8.5% over the last 112 years.[3] We can think about how the risk of a particular project compares with the risk of investing long term in the stock market. If the project seems more (less) risky than investing in the market, a discount rate of greater (less) than 11% might be appropriate.

> **ALTERNATIVE TERMS**
> Managers often choose a specific discount rate for all projects and call it the *required rate of return* or *hurdle rate.*

Uncertainties and Sensitivity Analysis

When we perform NPV analysis, the general rule is to accept the project if NPV is greater than zero. Many assumptions are built into this general rule. For example, we assume that we know each of the following:

> **LO3**   Identify the uncertainties of NVP analysis

- Cost of the initial investment
- Timing and dollar amounts of incremental revenues and costs
- Terminal values
- Project life
- Appropriate discount rate

However, we cannot know any of these factors with absolute certainty. Also, uncertainties grow with the number of years being forecast, as shown for TREC's SolarShare project at the beginning of the chapter. A 20-year project has more uncertainties than a project completed in 5 years.

---

[3] Credit Suisse, website, www.credit-suisse.com/investment_banking/doc/cs_global_investment_returns_yearbook.pdf.

Cash Flow Risks

The preceding illustration for Gordon's apartment building decision includes little uncertainty about the initial investment cash flows. Gordon knows for certain the purchase price of the motel and negotiates a final bid with a building contractor for converting the motel into apartments. Some uncertainty may be involved in the cost of renovation. As long as the specific nature of the renovations is known and the project can be completed fairly quickly, before costs change, the cost estimate from the contractor should be reasonably close to the final cost. However, renovation of Gordon's motel could rise dramatically if contractors discover unforeseen problems, such as asbestos needing to be removed.

We always encounter uncertainty when estimating future revenues, costs, and terminal values. However, our ability to accurately estimate cash flows decreases as we forecast further into the future. Long time frames reduce our ability to anticipate customer tastes, changes in technology, productivity, competition, availability of resources, and changes in regulation. For example, certain organizations, such as health care providers, rely completely on reimbursement from the government. Changes in reimbursement rates or changes in the basis of reimbursement greatly affect the expected revenues of these organizations. As another example, unexpected spikes in fuel prices affect transportation companies and the organizations that use them, such as produce haulers and grocery stores.

Estimating cash flows for projects involving new products or services is more difficult than for projects involving changes or expansions of existing products and services. Revenues must sometimes be based on a market that does not currently exist. It is nearly impossible to anticipate all potential costs. Substantial errors are likely in these types of predictions.

Estimating Project Life and Discount Rate

The expected life of a project is uncertain. Difficulties in estimating the life of a project are often related to difficulties in estimating revenues and costs. Managers are likely to continue a project longer if it is profitable. The reverse is true if a project is unprofitable. Managers may also change how they define an organization's core competencies. Such changes increase or decrease the strategic importance of a project, leading to an extension or cancellation of the project.

Several factors affect the discount rate for NPV analysis, including interest rates, inflation, and the riskiness of the project. However, none of these factors are known, and the length of time for capital projects increases the uncertainty.

▶ BUSINESS PRACTICE

The risk of capital projects being cancelled, delayed, or over budget was one of the top five business risks facing the world's mining and metals industry in 2011–2012, according to consultants Ernst & Young. Scarce natural resources require "tight management and execution"; otherwise capital projects could cost companies millions more than budgeted.[4]

Estimating Risks

Because of the many uncertainties involved, managers use considerable judgment in making capital project estimates. However, those responsible for forming the estimates are often the ones who originated the idea for the project. Intentionally or not, these managers are likely to form estimates that favour adoption of the project. In addition, they are more likely to fail to identify all possible project costs than to anticipate costs that will not occur— another estimation bias that favours project adoption.

Sensitivity Analysis

Sensitivity analysis helps managers evaluate how their NPV results would change with variations in the input data. When spreadsheets are set up appropriately, the discount rate, cash flows, and any other underlying assumptions can be easily varied. Decision makers can then consider the results of alternative scenarios under different sets of assumptions. For example, what is the change in NPV if we reduce our revenue estimates by 10%? What if we increase the discount rate by 1%? What if the terminal value is zero? The sensitivity of results to variations in assumptions helps managers evaluate the risk of investments.

---

[4] "Business Risks Facing Mining and Metals 2011–2012," Ernst & Young, 2011.

●●● > RISK OF BIASED DECISIONS: OVERCONFIDENCE TRAP

THE OVERCONFIDENCE TRAP is a bias in which people overestimate their own performance. Managers may be even more prone to an overconfidence bias because of past success. Managers who view project outcomes optimistically may overlook negative data about a project and focus on positive information.

When performing sensitivity analyses, overconfident managers may choose a best-case scenario that minimizes potential negative influences. For example, the developer of the Olympic Village that housed athletes at the 2010 Winter Games in Vancouver overestimated demand for the units when they were later sold as condos. The developer went into receivership in 2009, leaving the City of Vancouver on the hook for more than $700 million. In 2011, the units were discounted by 30%. The developer likely did not forecast weakened demand due to the recession. Accountants can help managers compensate for overconfidence by performing sensitivity analyses with reduced expectations for the "average case" and by brainstorming to identify potential worst-case scenarios.

SOURCES: "Olympic Village Condos Discounted 30%," CBC News online, February 17, 2011; and E. Teach, "Avoiding Decision Traps: Cognitive Biases, and Mental Shortcuts Can Lead Managers into Costly Error of Judgment," *CFO.com*, June 1, 2004.

gordon's health club, part 1
NET PRESENT VALUE AND SENSITIVITY ANALYSIS

example

Gordon has a basement space in his building that would not be suitable for living units because it has no windows. A friend offered to rent the space from Gordon for $60,000 per year, with an increase of $2,000 after three years. She will use the space to house an upscale health spa for women. However, Gordon would like to open a health club to serve the students at his building, people living in the neighbourhood, and people who work nearby.

Relevant Cash Flows and Timeline

Gordon hires a consultant to gather information about the project and to recommend a plan of action. The fee for this service is $5,000. The following list includes the relevant information the consulting firm estimates for the project:

1. The cost of renovation and new equipment that will be purchased is $650,000. The terminal value is estimated at $100,000 after five years.
2. Promotion costs to advertise the club will be $120,000 for the first year and $50,000 per year thereafter.
3. The revenues for the health club are estimated as $300,000 in the first year, $400,000 in the second, and $500,000 in each of the third through fifth years.
4. The operating costs for the health club are estimated as $200,000 for the first year and $130,000 for each of the following years.

Gordon sets up a timeline as shown in Exhibit 13.4. Notice that he ignores sunk costs (the fee paid to the consulting firm) and includes opportunity costs (forgone rent), and he uses a 10% discount rate.

Kzenon/Shutterstock

NPV Analysis

Gordon sets up a spreadsheet, as shown in Exhibit 13.5. He organizes the spreadsheet with an input section so that any of the assumptions made for the NPV analysis can be easily varied in performing a sensitivity analysis. He includes a cell reference for changes in revenues. Based on these NPV calculations, Gordon expects to realize $1,851 in today's dollars, over and above the investment amount of $650,000, if he invests in the health club. ■

When Gordon reviews his spreadsheet calculations with the consultants, they indicate some uncertainty about the assumptions. The consulting team is concerned that the revenue estimates might be too high. The building is located in an older part of town, and people

> EXHIBIT 13.4

Timeline for Gordon's Health Club Project

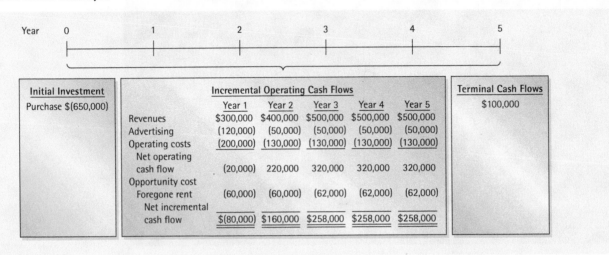

> EXHIBIT 13.5

NPV Calculations for Gordon's Health Club

	A	B	C	D	E
1	Gordon's Health Club Project				
2	Assumptions				
3	Discount rate	10%		Teminal value	$100,000
4	Initial investment	$650,000			
5	Cash Flows				
6	Period	Revenues	Operating Costs	Advertising	Foregone Rent
7	1	$300,000	$200,000	$120,000	$60,000
8	2	$400,000	$130,000	$50,000	$60,000
9	3	$500,000	$130,000	$50,000	$62,000
10	4	$500,000	$130,000	$50,000	$62,000
11	5	$500,000	$130,000	$50,000	$62,000
12	Change to Assumptions for Sensitivity Analysis:				
13	Change Revenues	0%			
14					
15					
16	PV Calculations				
17		Net Cash Flows	Discounted		
18	1	($80,000)	($72,727)		
19	2	$160,000	$132,231		
20	3	$258,000	$193,839		
21	4	$258,000	$176,217		
22	5	$258,000	$160,198		
23	Total Discounted Operating CF		$589,759		
24	Terminal value				
25	5	$100,000	$62,092		
26					
27	NPV				
28	Operating CF	$589,759			
29	Terminal value	$62,092			
30	Less				
31	Investment	($650,000)			
32	NPV	$1,851			

Examples of Excel formulas:
    Net cash flow in cell B18: $= (1+\$B\$13)*B7-(C7+D7+E7)$
    Discounted cash flow in cell C18: $=-PV(\$B\$3,A18,,B18)$

may not want to walk in the neighbourhood at night to get to the club. They suggest that Gordon reduce the revenues by 5% for sensitivity analysis. He enters 25% in the appropriate input cell. With this drop in revenues, he would incur a $79,696 loss over the five-year life of the project. Gordon decides to develop a series of spreadsheets, varying all the assumptions to reflect possible changes in future economic conditions. He will then discuss his decision further with the consulting team.

Internal Rate of Return

The **internal rate of return (IRR)** method determines the discount rate necessary for the present value of the discounted cash flows to be equal to the investment. In other words, the method solves for the discount rate at which a project's NPV equals zero. The calculation of IRR is similar to NPV analysis in that it is based on discounted cash flows. In the NPV analysis, we assumed a discount rate and solved for the NPV. In the case of IRR, we search for the discount rate that results in an NPV of zero. This discount rate is the internal rate of return.

IRR Calculations

Earlier in this chapter, Gordon analyzed a decision to invest in an apartment building for students. Suppose he is now trying to decide whether to install coin-operated vending machines in the apartment building. He knows that students eat a lot of snack foods, but the closest 24-hour grocery store is eight blocks away. Gordon thinks that the students will purchase beverages and food from vending machines if he installs them. The equipment will cost $5,000 and have a useful life of five years. He expects to net $1,500 in annual cash flows from operating the machines (revenues minus food and maintenance costs). The equipment will have no terminal value at the end of five years. Gordon thinks it could be a good investment, but he would like to know what his expected rate of return would be. The cash flows for this project are shown in Exhibit 13.6.

> **ALTERNATIVE TERMS**
> Some people use the term *time-adjusted rate of return* to describe the method called *internal rate of return*.

Gordon wants to find the discount rate at which the NPV equals zero. Recall that the NPV is calculated by subtracting the initial investment from the NPV of cash inflows. Because the cash inflows are uniform across time, Gordon can use Table 13B.2 (see Appendix 13B). Then, the IRR is the interest rate (X%) at which:

$$\text{Initial investment} = \text{NPV of cash inflows}$$
$$\$5,000 = \$1,500 \times (\text{PVFA 5 years}, X\%)$$

Gordon then solves for the present value of an annuity factor:

$$(\text{PVFA 5 years}, X\%) = \$5,000 \div \$1,500 = 3.333$$

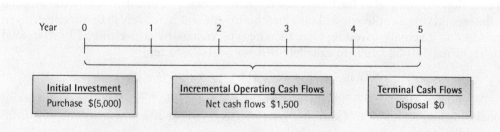

> **EXHIBIT 13.6**
> Timeline for Gordon's Coin-Operated Equipment Project

> EXHIBIT 13.7

IRR for Gordon's Coin-Operated
Equipment Project

	A	B
1	Net Cash Flows:	
2	Time 0	($5,000)
3	Year 1	$1,500
4	Year 2	$1,500
5	Year 3	$1,500
6	Year 4	$1,500
7	Year 5	$1,500
8		
9	IRR	15.24%
10	NPV	$0

Excel formula to calculate internal rate of return in cell B9: =IRR(B2:B7)
Excel formula to calculate net present value in cell B10: =B2+NPV(B9,B3:B7)

Gordon uses the table to locate the interest rate (X%) at which the present value of an annuity factor is approximately equal to 3.333 for a time period of five years. Finding the row for five time periods, he sees that the factor for 15% is 3.352. This factor is very close to 3.333, so he concludes that the IRR is close to 15%. This return is higher than the discount rate he used to calculate the net present value of the apartment complex, and this project is probably less risky, so Gordon decides it is a worthwhile investment.

The approach using Table 13B.2 can be applied only when the cash flows from a project are uniform over time. For uneven cash inflows, such as for Gordon's apartment building project, a trial-and-error approach may be used along with the present value table. We first try a discount rate and calculate the NPV of the project using that discount rate. If the NPV is greater than zero, we try a larger discount rate; if it is less than zero, we decrease the discount rate.

We can easily calculate a more precise IRR by using a spreadsheet. Using Excel's IRR function (see Exhibit 13.7), Gordon learns that the IRR for his coin-operated machine project is 15.24%. When he calculates the NPV using the IRR as the discount rate, the NPV is zero.

Comparison of NPV and IRR Methods

Certainly, without spreadsheets, the net present value method is computationally simpler than the internal rate of return method. Determining IRR can be time consuming, particularly for projects that return uneven cash flows. The use of a spreadsheet reduces the effort considerably. However, if several projects are being analyzed, their NPVs can be summed to determine the NPV for that group, or portfolio, of projects, whereas IRR can be neither summed nor averaged.

An important difference between the two methods is that the IRR method assumes that cash inflows can be reinvested to earn the same return that the project would generate. However, it may be difficult for an organization to identify other opportunities that could achieve the same rate when IRR is high. In contrast, the NPV method assumes that cash inflows can be reinvested and earn the discount rate—a more realistic assumption. If the discount rate is set equal to the organization's cost of capital, then alternative uses of cash would include paying off creditors and buying back stock. In addition, in some situations, there could be multiple IRRs, which would render this measure meaningless. For example, suppose Gordon invests $10,000 in paving a new parking lot, he expects to generate $23,000 of cash flows by the end of the first year, and he is expected to invest an additional $13,200 in the second year. Intuitively, we know that this investment is unlikely to be attractive, given that Gordon is actually investing more than he is receiving—he is investing $23,200 in total and receiving only $23,000. To calculate IRR, we set NPV to zero:

$$NPV = -10,000 + 23,000/(1 + r) + 13,200/(1 + r)^2$$

We find $r = 10\%$ and $r = 20\%$, so there are two distinct IRRs. It is difficult to draw a useful conclusion about the value of knowing that the IRR is 10% or 20% when Gordon's discount rate is 14%.

For the preceding reasons, the NPV method is preferable. Both NPV and IRR are used widely in business. One reason for the continued use of IRR is that many people find it intuitively easier to understand than NPV. In addition, managers may want to compare the IRR on prior projects to current project return rates as they consider new investment. For example, Gordon could compare the IRR for the health club with any new projects and decide whether to accept a project with a lower IRR.

Non-discounted Cash Flow Methods

The two quantitative analysis techniques discussed below—payback period and accrual accounting rate of return (AARR)—which do not take into consideration the time value of money, are called non-discounted cash flow methods.

Payback Method

In analyzing the payback period, depending on the nature of the project, we can take either of two approaches: first, assume that the amounts of the annual cash flows will be constant or uniform; or second, assume the amounts of the annual cash flows will be different or non-uniform.

Uniform Cash Flows

The **payback method** measures the amount of time required to recover the initial investment. Assuming that cash flows from the project are constant over future years, the payback period can be calculated by dividing the initial investment cash flow by the annual incremental operating cash flows. Consider Gordon's decision to install vending machines:

$$\frac{\text{Number of years to}}{\text{pay back the investment}} = \frac{\text{Initial investment}}{\text{Annual incremental operating cash flow}} = \frac{\$5,000}{\$1,500} = 3.33$$

Thus, the payback period for this example is 3.33 years.

Non-uniform Cash Flows

Suppose Gordon modifies his annual cash flow estimates as follows:

Year	Annual Cash Flows
1	$1,000
2	$1,200
3	$1,600
4	$1,800
5	$2,200

Because the cash flows are non-uniform each year, the payback period can be found by calculating the cumulative incremental operating cash flows until the initial investment amount has been fully recovered. The number of years needed to cover the initial investment is the payback period. In this case, the initial cost of investment, $5,000, will be fully recovered sometime in year 4; at the beginning of year 4, only $3,800 will have been

[5] G. Anthes, "Internal Rate of Return," *Computerworld*, February 17, 2003, p. 32.
[6] Tomonari Shinoda, "Capital Budgeting Management Practices in Japan," *Economic Journal of Hokkaido University*, Vol. 39 (2010), pp. 39–50.

BUSINESS PRACTICE
Gaylord Entertainment compares an investment's IRR to a required rate of return slightly higher than its weighted average cost of capital. Subjective assessment of risk also influences managers' decisions.[5]

L04   Apply alternative methods in analyzing strategic investment decisions

INTERNATIONAL
A survey of Japanese companies found that most prefer the payback method for capital budgeting but are starting to use a combination of the payback and NPV methods.[6]

recovered, and by the end of year 4, the cash flows will have accumulated to $5,600. To find the point when $5,000 will be recovered, we calculated the leftover amount to be covered in year 4, $1,200 ($5,000 – $3,800), and then we divide this amount by the amount to be recovered in year 4, $1,800. This tells us that it will take an additional 0.67 years, or 8 months, to recover the full amount. Therefore, the investment will have a payback period of 4.67 years, or 4 years and 8 months.

Year	Annual Cash Flows	Cumulative Cash Flows	Investment to Be Recovered at End of Year
1	$1,000	$1,000	$4,000
2	$1,200	$2,200	$2,800
3	$1,600	$3,800	$1,200
4	$1,800	$5,600	—
5	$2,200	$7,800	—

Advantages and Disadvantages of the Payback Method

The payback method has some significant disadvantages. First, it does not incorporate the time value of money. Future cash flows are not discounted to reflect the opportunity cost of using funds for other projects. This method does not value the cash flows that are received after the investment has been recovered. In addition, it imposes an arbitrary cut-off period, which favours projects with shorter payback periods. Because of these disadvantages, the payback method cannot be used to choose among several projects. However, the payback method is used extensively in many parts of the world, as it is easy to calculate and easy to understand. In addition, payback is sometimes used with NPV or IRR when meaningful estimates of relevant cash flows are lacking because the project or product is so new that it provides no historical data for reference. Longer payback periods reflect higher risk; therefore, projects with shorter payback periods are preferable because cash is not committed over long periods.

Accrual Accounting Rate of Return Method

The accrual accounting rate of return (AARR) is the expected increase in average annual operating income as a percentage of the initial increase in required investment. In Gordon's vending machine decision, the net increase in income needs to be adjusted so that it reflects accrual accounting income. For financial statements, suppose that Gordon uses straight-line depreciation. With a five-year life and no terminal value, annual financial statement depreciation is $1,000 per year ($5,000 ÷ 5 years). Assuming that depreciation is the only difference between cash flows and financial statement income, accrual accounting income is $500 ($1,500 – $1,000). The accrual accounting rate of return of 10% is the expected incremental accounting income from the project divided by the initial investment ($500 ÷ $5,000).

> **ALTERNATIVE TERMS**
>
> The terms *return on investment (ROI)*, *average rate of return*, and *unadjusted rate of return* are often used to describe the method called *accrual accounting rate of return*.

Advantages and Disadvantages of the Accrual Accounting Rate of Return Method

The AARR method presents several problems. First, it ignores the time value of money. In addition, depreciation is deducted from the numerator, but the full investment amount is the denominator, so the investment amount is essentially counted twice. The AARR method is frequently used to evaluate division or department performance because the financial information is readily available, but it is not an appropriate method for evaluating long-term investment.

13-1 self-study problem   Capital Budgeting Cash Flows, NPV, IRR, Payback, and Sensitivity Analysis

Newberry and Mills Company is considering the purchase of new robotic manufacturing equipment. The purchase price is $85,000. The cost for shipping the machine to the plant is $2,000. Another $3,000 will be spent to remodel the area in which the machine is to be installed. The purchase price includes installation costs. The company has already spent $1,500 in travel costs and employee time on the search for this equipment. The machine is expected to save $30,000 per year in labour and insurance expenses over the next four years, and it is expected to be obsolete in four years. Newberry and Mills use a 10% discount rate as the required rate of return on capital budgeting projects. Ignore income taxes.

required

A. Calculate the net present value.
B. Calculate the profitability index.
C. Calculate the internal rate of return.
D. Calculate the payback period.
E. List factors that you would vary to perform sensitivity analysis and explain why you would vary them.

See the solution on page 610.

Other Considerations for Strategic Investment Decisions

Managers consider qualitative factors as well as quantitative analyses when making a strategic investment decision. In this section, we discuss a variety of factors that affect the final capital budgeting decision. We also discuss long-term monitoring of results.

LO5 — Identify additional issues to be considered for strategic investment decisions

Qualitative Factors

Qualitative factors often influence strategic investment decisions. Sometimes, these factors cannot be quantified and other times numerical estimates would be so uncertain that decision makers would find them useless.

Estimating the future cash flows from implementing an enterprise-wide system such as those sold by Oracle, PeopleSoft, SAP, or Baan involves high uncertainty. The benefits of such systems include increased timeliness of information and increased availability of new information. Therefore, many organizations make these types of decisions based on the experience of other organizations as well as the information they receive from enterprise-wide system developers and sales representatives.

The need for a timely decision sometimes overrides the use of a formal capital budgeting process such as NPV. Timeliness can be particularly important when new opportunities arise suddenly, and an organization needs to take action before its competitors. Another related consideration is the ability of an organization to envision new products and services. Organizations often stumble when they concentrate solely on the improvement of existing products and services, because they fail to recognize changes in customer preferences, technology, and other factors that call for shifts in products and services. Innovative organizations typically focus on combining formal quantitative analysis with exploration of future trends.

Reputation, Environment, Quality, and Community

If a proposed capital project would affect the environment in a negative way, the project might harm an organization's reputation. Projects adversely affect the environment in a number of ways, such as producing hazardous waste, emitting chemicals into the air, or polluting lakes, streams, or landfills. Sometimes, the cost of environmental impact creates direct cash flow effects that are included in NPV analyses, such as permit fees for air emissions. However, many environmental costs are not borne by the emitting company but by society as a whole. For example, real estate developers are not assessed for the increases in neighbourhood noise levels that result from increased traffic to a new shopping centre. To encourage organizations to adopt environmentally friendly policies, several organizations index firms according to their pollution control practices. In addition, some mutual funds comprise strictly "green" investments.

> **BUSINESS PRACTICE**
>
> ### Innovation, Environmental Stewardship, and Reward
>
> **Clearwater Seafoods**, based in Bedford, Nova Scotia, one of Canada's largest seafood processors and an important global player, reaps rewards for its strategic investment, cost management, and innovative solutions to obstacles facing the industry.
>
> Clearwater invested in leading-edge and environmentally sound technologies and practices to harvest, process, and store its seafood, which resulted in higher quality. Among other things, the company has spent nearly $100 million on a modern fishing fleet that can freeze the catch at sea when it's fresh, instead of on land.
>
> Clearwater also profits from its investments in environmental stewardship. For example, the company pays up to $200,000 per product to be certified by the internationally recognized Marine Stewardship Council as having environmentally responsible fishing practices, a designation for which several retailers are willing to pay a premium. Its advanced technologies allow it to reduce processing costs, and the company is investing in ways to reduce fuel consumption on its fishing fleet to help offset the rising cost of fuel.
>
> The company's future cost estimates include plans to replace vessels in a few years, even though a typical vessel might have a useful life of 30 years, as it hopes to see a return on its investment in the latest technologies through higher quality and prices.[7]

Because reputation effects are difficult to value, managers typically incorporate these concerns qualitatively. An increasing number of companies are developing environmental policy statements to help guide their strategic decisions, and they may make environmental investments without formal quantitative analysis. To attract customers and investors who are concerned about the environment, some organizations advertise their "green" practices.

In recent years, companies have increased their focus on global warming. For example, HSBC became the first winner of the Financial Times FT Sustainable Banking Award. HSBC had achieved carbon neutrality by reducing its direct emissions, purchasing electricity from renewable sources, and purchasing emissions reductions from "green" projects. Among other initiatives, the bank also established environmental guidelines for lending or investing in companies and projects.[8] According to Business for Social Responsibility, a not-for-profit advisory organization, companies that fail to adopt more climate-friendly practices will be subjected to increased pressure from investors, insurers, governments, and consumers.[9]

Many organizations invest a great deal of time and money in improving product or service quality. These decisions are often made without formal quantitative consideration of the long-term costs and benefits. For some organizations, quality requirements from markets such as the European Union must be met to sell products or services. Other firms stick to high-quality standards as a part of their competitive strategies. Because measuring and

> **BUSINESS PRACTICE**
> Some people are skeptical of the benefits of implementing strategies promoted by the popular press and consultants. Research by economists and accountants fails to find increased financial performance for firms employing total quality management.[10]

[7] Adapted from Forest L. Reinhardt and James Weber, "Clearwater Seafoods," Harvard Business School Case 707-012, February 22, 2007; "Business Finds New Way to Chill Carry-on Lobster," National Public Radio, August 24, 2006; and Clearwater Annual Report 2006 at www.clearwater.ca/site/media/Parent/ClearwaterAR06(1).pdf.
[8] "2006 Awards Winners and Special Commendations," The FT Sustainable Banking Conference & Awards, *Financial Times*, www.ftconferences.co.uk/sustainablebanking/2006winners.asp?m_pid=0&m_nid=16249; "HSBC Named Sustainable Bank of the Year," June 14, 2006, HSBC, News Archive 2006, www.hsbc.com.
[9] Business for Social Responsibility, A *Three-Pronged Approach to Corporate Climate Strategy*, October 2006, www.bsr.org.
[10] See, for example, C. Ittner and D. Larcker, "Total Quality Management and the Choice of Information and Reward Systems," *Journal of Accounting Research*, 33 (Supplement 1995), pp. 1–34; J. Mathews and P. Katel, "The Cost of Quality," *Newsweek*, September 7, 1992, p. 48; and "The Cracks in Quality," *The Economist*, April 18, 1992, pp. 67–68.

predicting the costs and benefits of total quality management (TQM) practices are difficult, firms typically implement them without performing NPV analysis.

In some cases, an investment under consideration would result in a potentially negative impact on employees. If new equipment or manufacturing processes replace employees, for example, the impact needs to be evaluated for displaced employees and also on the morale of remaining employees. If job responsibilities or perceptions of job stability change as a result of the project, the remaining employees may be negatively affected. Sometimes organizations forgo or modify projects to reduce negative impacts on employees.

Some projects result in a large impact on the community. Bringing a large new facility into a small community can change the dynamics of the entire community. Closing a plant or service on which a community relies can result in a negative reputation for an organization. A negative corporate image can have far-reaching effects on the company as a whole, including loss of market share and morale problems among employees and management.

Making and Monitoring Strategic Investment Decisions

Managers consider a number of factors when making the final decision about a proposed capital budgeting project. The results of any quantitative analyses as well as the qualitative issues already discussed are taken into account. Accountants often prepare analyses of projects that align with an organization's strategic plans. Managers use these analyses to examine financial outcomes under a number of different scenarios. They often have a better grasp than the accountants on certain business factors, such as competitors' product development and prices. In addition, managers may use their own informal estimates to determine NPV.

After a project has been accepted, accountants and managers monitor its progress and compare actual performance to the capital budget expectations. Some projects are relatively simple to implement and require little monitoring (e.g., the replacement of equipment in a laundromat). Other projects are more complex, such as Gordon's new line of business through the health club. More complex projects that take longer to implement need more monitoring to reduce the probability of budget overruns.

Because these projects are long-lived, outcomes are always different from expectations. A **post-investment audit** provides feedback about whether operations are meeting expectations. When results are below expectations, processes are investigated and improvements can be implemented. In addition, the process of re-evaluating past decisions usually improves future decision making. The more we learn about factors that affect the accuracy of our forecasts, and investigate unanticipated problems or benefits, the better we can predict these occurrences in future projects.

●● > FOCUS ON ETHICAL DECISION MAKING: THE RIGHT THING TO DO

When organizations incorporate ethical values into their decision-making processes, their investment decisions reflect high ethical standards and their desire to act in a socially responsible manner. For example, Ontario's **The Beer Store** has been operating a bottle deposit return program since 1927. When the province extended deposit return to wine and liquor bottles in 2007, The Beer Store decided to invest in expanding its bottle recycling capacity to become the partner to accept all alcoholic beverage containers across Ontario. By its fourth year, the program had recycled one billion bottles—enough to reach three quarters of the way to the moon. The program diverts approximately 485,000 tonnes of waste from landfills annually, saving municipalities an estimated $40 million a year.

Source: *Responsible Stewardship Report 2010–2011,* The Beer Store; "Bag It Back," available at http://www.thebeerstore.ca/about-us/environmental-leadership/bag-it-back-odrp.

ETHICAL PRIORITIES FOR STRATEGIC INVESTMENTS

Managers weigh many factors when making strategic investment decisions. What priority should be given to ethical considerations? How do ethics contribute to long-term organizational success?

© YAY Media AS/Alamy Stock Photo

APPENDIX 13A

Income Taxes and the Net Present Value Method

L06 Explain how income taxes affect strategic investment decision cash flows

Income taxes affect an organization's cash flows and, in turn, capital budgeting decisions. Because individual provinces and countries have different income tax rules, the specific tax effects on a proposed project depend on the tax jurisdictions of the organization and the project. Even for small organizations that operate in only one province, tax laws can be complicated. Taxes become even more complex as an organization grows and expands domestically and internationally. In addition, income tax laws change periodically and capital budgeting requires current knowledge of tax laws. The capital cost allowance (CCA) is a rate of depreciation for tax purposes that Canadian tax laws allow businesses to use to calculate an annual tax deduction for the loss in value of capital assets due to wear and tear or obsolescence. In evaluating investment projects, managers should use the most current CCA regulations to calculate the after-tax cash flows, and use this information to guide their decision making. Before developing NPV analyses in a complex business, accountants consult tax experts so that their analyses reflect the cash flows that would actually take place.

Calculating Incremental Tax Cash Flows

After we forecast depreciation for the life of a project, we can calculate the incremental tax cash flow—the amount that will be paid or saved on taxes each year of the project. We combine the operating cash flow for each year with that year's depreciation and then multiply the total by the marginal income tax rate.

We also need to calculate the tax cash flow based on the terminal value of the project. This calculation requires the following steps:

1. Find the total amount of tax depreciation that accumulated from the time of the initial investment to its disposal.

2. Subtract the total depreciation from the initial investment. The remainder is the tax basis.

3. Subtract the tax basis from the disposal value. The remainder is a taxable gain or loss.

4. Multiply the taxable gain or loss by the marginal income tax rate to find the incremental tax cash flow at the end of the project.

For Gordon's apartment building decision (Exhibit 13.3), the initial investment is $1,400,000, with estimated cash flows of $276,000 annually. Gordon expects to be able to sell the building at the end of 10 years for $400,000. Suppose, for tax purposes, Gordon uses straight-line depreciation with an annual deduction of $100,000 and has a 30% marginal income tax rate. His income tax expense each year will be $52,800 [($276,000 – $100,000) × 30%]. His incremental cash flow becomes $223,200 ($276,000 – $52,800). We discount these cash flows to compare them with the initial investment as follows:

$$PV = \$223,200 \times (PVFA\ 10\ years,\ 14\%) + \$400,000 \times (PVF\ 10\ years,\ 14\%)$$
$$= \$223,200 \times 5.216 + \$400,000 \times 0.270$$
$$= \$1,164,211 + \$108,000$$
$$= \$1,272,11$$

So NPV = $1,272,211 – $1,400,000 = –$127,789. Before we considered income taxes, our previous calculations resulted in an NPV of $174,616 ($1,574,616 – $1,400,000). When income taxes are factored in, the NPV becomes negative.

Effects of Income Taxes in Capital Budgeting Decisions

Depreciation for income taxes is generally different from depreciation for financial reporting. In financial reporting, depreciation is calculated based on an asset's estimated useful life, using a method that measures the cost of the asset against the benefits received. To encourage business investment, the Canadian government allows businesses to deduct depreciation using accelerated methods for most assets when computing taxable income. Exhibit 13A.1 summarizes some of common asset classes and rates of Canadian federal income taxation that affect capital budgeting decisions.

Most cash flows associated with capital budgeting projects either increase or decrease income taxes in the year of the cash flow. However, the cost of depreciable assets—such as buildings, furniture, and equipment—acquired for use in business or professional activities cannot be deducted immediately from taxable income. Instead, depreciation can be deducted in future years as these assets wear out or become obsolete over time and are replaced. This is why the federal government created the capital cost allowance (CCA). This depreciation deduction is often referred to as a tax shield, which affects after-tax operating

▶EXHIBIT 13A.1

CCA Classes Commonly Used Assets in a Business for Capital Budgeting

Class	Rate (%)	Description
1	4	Most buildings bought after 1987, including components such as wiring, plumbing, heating, and cooling systems. The rate for eligible non-residential buildings acquired after March 18, 2007, used for manufacturing and processing in Canada of goods for sale or lease includes an additional allowance of 6% (total 10%). For all other non-residential buildings, the rate includes an additional allowance of 2% (total 6%).
3	5	Most buildings, including components bought after 1978 and before 1988. However, you may have to include part of the cost of additions made after 1987 in class 1. For more details, see IT-79, Capital Cost Allowance—Buildings or Other Structures and http://www.cra-arc.gc.ca/E/pub/tp/it79r3/README.html.
8	20	Property that you did not include in any other class. Some examples are fixtures, furniture, machinery, photocopiers, refrigeration equipment, telephones, and tools costing $500 or more. Class 8 also includes outdoor advertising signs you bought after 1987.
9	25	Aircraft, including furniture or equipment attached to the aircraft, and spare parts.
10	30	Automobiles, except those you use as a taxi or in a daily rental business, including vans, trucks, tractors, wagons, and trailers. Also, general-purpose electronic data-processing equipment (commonly called computer hardware) and systems software acquired before March 23, 2004. See also class 45.
10.1	30	A passenger vehicle.
12	100	China, cutlery, kitchen utensils that cost under $200, linens, uniforms, dies, jigs, moulds, cutting or shaping parts of a machine, tools and medical or dental instruments that cost under $200, computer software (except systems software), and videocassettes bought after February 15, 1984, that you rent and do not expect to rent to any one person for more than 7 days in a 30-day period. Under proposed changes, the cost limit for Class 12 treatment will increase to $500 from $200 for tools acquired on or after May 2, 2006, and medical and dental instruments and kitchen utensils acquired on or after May 2, 2006. Tools eligible under this class specifically exclude electronic communication devices and electronic data processing equipment.
13		Leasehold interest—You can claim CCA on a leasehold interest, but the maximum rate depends on the type of leasehold interest and the terms of the lease.
14		Patents, franchises, concessions, or licences for a limited period. Your CCA is whichever of the following amounts is less: • The total of the capital cost of each property, spread out over the life of the property • The undepreciated capital cost to the taxpayer as of the end of the tax year of property of that class
16	40	Taxis, vehicles you use in a daily car-rental business, coin-operated video games or pinball machines acquired after February 15, 1984, and freight trucks acquired after December 6, 1991, that are rated higher than 11,788 kg.
17	8	Roads, parking lots, sidewalks, airplane runways, storage areas, or similar surface construction.
43	30	Eligible machinery and equipment, used for the manufacturing and processing (M&P) in Canada of goods for sale or lease that are not included in Class 29.
45	45	Computer equipment and systems software acquired after March 22, 2004 and before March 19, 2007.
46	30	Data network infrastructure equipment and systems software for that equipment acquired after March 22, 2004 (usually included in class 8).
50	55	Computer equipment and systems software for that equipment, including ancillary data-processing equipment acquired after March 18, 2007, and not included in Class 29 or Class 52.
52	100	General-purpose electronic data-processing equipment (commonly called computer hardware) and systems software for that equipment, including ancillary data-processing equipment acquired after January 27, 2009, and before February 2011. Also see Class 50. For more information, see Class 52.

For a complete list of CCA asset classes and their CCA rates, go to the income tax regulations website, http://laws.justice.gc.ca/en/I-3.3/ C.R.C.-c.945/index.html

Source: CCA classes, http://www.cra-arc.gc.ca/tx/bsnss/tpcs/slprtnr/rprtng/cptl/clsss-eng.html; Canada Revenue Agency, 2011. Reproduced with the permission of the Minister of Public Works and Government Services Canada, 2011.

income by reducing the required payment of income taxes. In addition, operating cash flows and gains or losses on assets' terminal values affect the amount of income tax paid.

Every depreciable asset must be assigned to a classification (left column of Exhibit 13A.1) based on the type of property (right column). The classification determines the rate of depreciation (middle column) that may be used. For most asset classes, the CCA is calculated based on the declining balance method. This method applies the appropriate CCA rate to the undepreciated capital cost of an asset or group of assets of the same class at the end of each year. The CCA rate is the maximum rate of depreciation that can be applied to assets in that class in each year. Claiming CCA reduces the balance of the class by the amount of CCA claimed, and the unclaimed amount can be applied in future years.

An asset balance will never reach zero. Under the half-year convention, assets are assumed to be purchased halfway through the year of acquisition; therefore, only one-half of the normal CCA rate can be deducted in the year that an asset is acquired. Because of the half-year convention, depreciation is higher during the second year of an asset's life than during the first year. Salvage value is not taken into account.

Some asset classes are not subject to the declining balance method; the CCA is instead calculated using the straight-line method. Unlike the declining balance method, the straight-line method is calculated on an asset-by-asset basis and generates equal CCA deductions each year until the undepreciated balance reaches zero.

gordon's health club, part 2
THE EFFECT OF TAXATION ON INVESTMENT DECISION

Let's go back to Gordon's decision about investing in a health club. Suppose Gordon went to a tax seminar and learned about the depreciable assets and capital cost allowance. He would like to incorporate taxes and CCA information into his health club investment calculation.

Additional Relevant Information

Gordon hired a consultant, who gathered the following information:
1. Gordon's health club is subject to an income tax rate of 20%.
2. The after-tax discount rate is 8% [10% × (1 − 0.2)].
3. The new equipment qualifies as CCA class 8, with a CCA rate of up to 20% declining balance. Gordon's health club will take the maximum rate each year.
4. Assume that there will be no balance in the class in five years, when the equipment is sold.

Kzenon/Shutterstock

NPV with Income Tax and CCA Analysis

Gordon sets up another spreadsheet, as shown in Exhibit 13A.2. Again, he organizes the spreadsheet with an input section so that any of the assumptions made for the NPV and tax analysis can easily be varied in performing a sensitivity analysis. With the additional tax information, Gordon concludes that the investment will bring a negative NPV of $9,255 if he proceeds with the investment in the health club.

Initial Investment

The initial investment of $650,000 remains the same, because this is an investment, and it cannot be deducted as an up-front expense for tax purposes.

Annual Cash Flows

Annual cash flows are first adjusted for the effects of income taxes, and then discounted.

Terminal Cash Flow

The terminal cash flow from disposal of the equipment is adjusted for the effects of income taxes, as we assume that there will be no balance in the class, and the proceeds from sale of the equipment will be recaptured and fully taxed as ordinary income at the 20% tax rate.

▶EXHIBIT 13A.2

NPV Calculations for Gordon's Health Club, with CCA Implications

	A	B	C	D	E	F
1	Assumptions					
2	Discount rate (after tax)	8%				
3	Income Tax Rate	20%				
4	CCA Rate (Class 8)	20%				
5	Initial investment	$ 650,000				
6	Terminal cash flow	$ 100,000				
7	Annual Cash Flows					
8	Period	Revenue	Operating Costs	Advertising	Forgone Rent	
9	1	$ 300,000	$ 200,000	$ 120,000	$ 60,000	
10	2	$ 400,000	$ 130,000	$ 50,000	$ 60,000	
11	3	$ 500,000	$ 130,000	$ 50,000	$ 62,000	
12	4	$ 500,000	$ 130,000	$ 50,000	$ 62,000	
13	5	$ 500,000	$ 130,000	$ 50,000	$ 62,000	
14						
15	PV Calculations					
16		Net Cash Flows	Tax Effect (1-Tx)	After-Tax CF	8% Factor	Discounted
17	1	$ (80,000)	0.8	$ (64,000)	0.926	$ (59,264)
18	2	$ 160,000	0.8	$ 128,000	0.857	$ 109,696
19	3	$ 258,000	0.8	$ 206,400	0.794	$ 163,882
20	4	$ 258,000	0.8	$ 206,400	0.735	$ 151,704
21	5	$ 258,000	0.8	$ 206,400	0.681	$ 140,558
22	Total Discounted Operating CF					$ 506,576
23	Terminal Value					
24	5	$ 100,000	0.8	$ 80,000	0.661	$ 54,480
25						
26	PV of CCA Tax Shield	Investment	Tax	PV of Tax Shield	Half-year Rule	PV of Tax Shield
27		$ 650,000	20%	0.714	0.963	$ 89,418
28						
29						
30	Lost Tax Shield from Disposal	Terminal Value	Tax	PV of Tax Shield	8% Factor	PV of Tax Shield
31	5	$ 100,000	20%	0.714	0.681	$ 9,729
32						
33	Initial Investment	$ (650,000)				
34	PV of Annual Cash Flows	$ 506,576				
35	Terminal Value	$ 54,480				
36	PV of CCA Tax Shield	$ 89,418				
37	Lost Tax Shield from Disposal	$ (9,729)				
38	Net Present Value	$ (9,255)				

Present Value of the Tax Shield

The tax savings provided by the CCA deduction is calculated by using the following tax shield formula:

$$\text{Present value of tax savings} = \frac{\text{Investment} \times \text{Tax rate} \times \text{CCA rate}}{\text{CCA rate} + \text{Required rate of return}}$$
$$\times \frac{1 + 0.5 \times \text{Required rate of return}}{1 + \text{Required rate of return}}$$

or

$$(\text{Investment} \times \text{Tax rate}) \times [\text{CCA rate} \div (\text{CCA rate} + \text{RR rate})] \times [(1 + 0.5\ \text{RRR}) \div (1 + \text{RRR})]$$

Tax savings of the investment	PV of Annual Tax savings	Adjustment for the half-year rule

Loss of Tax Shield from the Disposal of Equipment

The tax savings calculation assumes that the savings are in perpetuity. When an asset is being sold, there is a reduction of assets in the class and thus a reduction in tax savings. The loss of tax shield is calculated based on the salvage value in the following formula:

$$\text{Loss of tax shield} = \frac{\text{Salvage value} \times \text{Tax rate} \times \text{CCA rate}}{\text{CCA rate} + \text{Required rate of return}} = \frac{1}{(1 + \text{RRR})^n}$$

example

►EXHIBIT 13A.3

Schedule of After-Tax Annual Cash Flows

Year	Investment (A)	Depreciation Amount (B)	UCC (A – B)	Tax Effect (B × 20%) (C)	Op CF (D)	Total CF (C + D)	Cumulative
1	$650,000	$65,000	$585,000	$13,000	$(64,000)	$(51,000)	$(51,000)
2	$585,000	$117,000	$468,000	$23,400	$128,000	$151,400	$100,400
3	$468,000	$93,600	$374,400	$18,720	$206,400	$225,120	$325,520
4	$374,400	$74,880	$299,520	$14,976	$206,400	$221,376	$546,896
5	$299,520	$59,904	$239,616	$11,981	$206,400	$218,381	$765,277

example

Payback Period

The payback period calculation should take into account the after-tax annual operating cash flows and the CCA tax savings. Exhibit 13A.3 shows the schedule of total annual cash flows. Because the cash flows are non-uniform each year, the payback period is found by calculating the cumulative operating cash flows until the initial investment amount has been fully covered—in this case, some months into year 5.

The cost of investment will be fully covered sometime in year 5, because by the end of year 5, the cash flows will have accumulated to $765,277. To find the point at which $650,000 will be recovered, we calculate the leftover amount to be covered in year 5 ($103,140 [$650,000 – $546,896]) and then we divide this amount by the amount to be recovered in year 5 ($218,381). Thus, we know that it will take an additional 0.47 years:

$$($650,000 – $546,896) ÷ $218,381 = 0.47 \text{ years}$$

Therefore, the investment will have a payback period of 4.47 years. ■

Other Related Issues in an NPV Analysis

Inflation and the Net Present Value Method

The NPV computations in this chapter did not take into account the fact that many revenues and costs tend to inflate or deflate over time. When these changes occur, it is inappropriate to use today's revenue and cost values when forecasting future cash flows, particularly for projects spanning many years. Some costs, such as fuel costs, may increase or decrease rapidly. Wages or supplies might increase at a slower rate over time. Still other costs, such as new technology, might actually decrease over time. Cash flows from projects in other countries sometimes are subject to much higher inflation rates than in Canada. Managers need to incorporate these types of expected differences in their NPV analyses.

Inflation is the decline in the general purchasing power of a monetary unit, meaning that more monetary units, such as dollars, are needed to purchase goods or services. Deflation is the opposite—an increase in the general purchasing power of the monetary unit. Because either can distort an NPV analysis, cash flows should be adjusted for anticipated levels of inflation or deflation.

Real and Nominal Methods for NPV Analysis

L07 Explain how real and nominal methods are used to address inflation in an NPV analysis

Two types of interest rates, as shown in Exhibit 13A.4, need to be considered when analyzing inflation. The first type, the real rate of interest, is the rate of return required on investments when inflation is not a factor. It is calculated as the sum of the risk-free rate and a risk premium. The risk-free rate is the "pure" rate of interest paid on short-term government bonds (without considering inflation). The risk premium is an element above the risk-free rate that businesses demand for undertaking risks. The second type, the nominal rate of interest,

▶EXHIBIT 13A.4

$$\text{Real rate of interest} = \text{Risk-free rate} + \text{Risk premium}$$
$$\text{Nominal rate of interest} = (1 + \text{Real rate}) \times (1 + \text{Inflation rate}) - 1$$

▶EXHIBIT 13A.4
Real and Nominal Interest Rates

is the rate of return required on investments when inflation is present. It is calculated by increasing the real rate of interest by the expected rate of inflation.

Cash flows and the discount rate should be measured using a consistent approach. In the **real method**, cash inflows and outflows are forecast in real dollars (no inflation) and discounted using a real rate. The examples we have used so far in the chapter have used real cash flows.

In the **nominal method**, cash inflows and outflows are forecast in nominal dollars (inflated) and discounted using a nominal discount rate. Real cash flows can be converted to nominal cash flows by using the following formula:

ALTERNATIVE TERMS
The *real rate of interest* is also known as the *real discount rate*. Similarly, the *nominal rate of interest* is also known as the *nominal discount rate*.

$$\text{Nominal cash flow} = \text{Real cash flow} \times (1 + i)^t$$
$$\text{where } i = \text{rate of inflation}$$
$$t = \text{number of time periods in the future}$$

Suppose Gordon hires an accountant at $35,000 per year to help with his new businesses. If the accountant's salary is valued in an NPV analysis using the real method over a five-year period, the cash flows will be uniform across time. But if the salary inflates at 2% per year, the cash flows will increase across time. Exhibit 13A.5 compares the real and nominal cash flows.

Under inflation, the real amount of annual depreciation tax savings decreases over time. Nominal cash flows can be converted to real cash flows as follows:

$$\text{Real cash flow} = \frac{\text{Nominal cash flow}}{(1 + i)^t}$$

Internal Consistency in NPV Analysis

If cash inflows and outflows are valued in real terms and then discounted using a nominal rate, or vice versa, the approach is internally inconsistent. Because nominal rates include inflation, they tend to be higher than real rates. Discounting real cash flows using a nominal rate creates a bias against the adoption of many worthwhile capital investment projects, because the discounted present value of cash inflows is understated. Discounting nominal cash flows using a real rate overstates discounted cash flows and creates a bias toward accepting projects that may have a negative NPV.

When we expect relevant cash flows to be influenced by inflation or deflation, we must select a method (real or nominal) and then use that method consistently for all calculations. We perform the NPV analysis as before, and the only differences are as follows:

▶ Cash flows must be adjusted so that they are internally consistent with the method used.
▶ Only a real discount rate should be used under the real method, and only a nominal discount rate should be used under the nominal method.

Exhibit 13A.6 summarizes the types of adjustments to cash flows that are required under the real and nominal methods. The illustration of an NPV analysis in Central Irrigation Inc., Part 1, incorporates income taxes and inflation.

▶EXHIBIT 13A.5
Real Versus Nominal Cash Flows

Period	Real Cash Flows	Nominal Cash Flows
1	$35,000	$35,000 \times 1.02 = $35,700$
2	$35,000	$35,000 \times 1.02^2 = $36,414$
3	$35,000	$35,000 \times 1.02^3 = $37,142$
4	$35,000	$35,000 \times 1.02^4 = $37,885$
5	$35,000	$35,000 \times 1.02^5 = $38,643$

▶EXHIBIT 13A.6
Cash Flow Adjustments Required Under
the Real and Nominal Methods

Cash Flow	Adjustments for Real Method	Adjustments for Nominal Method
Initial investment	No adjustment	No adjustment
Depreciation tax shield	Adjust from a nominal to a real amount for each year (deflate)	No adjustment
Remaining cash flows: • Incremental operating cash flows • Income taxes on incremental cash flows • Terminal cash flows • Income taxes on terminal gain or loss	If original cash flow estimates include inflation, then the cash flows must be adjusted from nominal to real amounts for each year; the tax cash flows must then be recalculated	If original cash flow estimates do not include inflation, then the cash flows must be adjusted from real to nominal amounts for each year; the tax cash flows must then be recalculated

Adjustment Formulas:

$$\text{Nominal cash flow} = \text{Real cash flow} \times (1 + i)^t$$

$$\text{Real cash flow} = \frac{\text{Nominal cash flow}}{(1 + i)^t}$$

where i = rate of inflation

t = number of time periods in the future

example

Cecilia Lim H M/Shutterstock

central irrigation inc.
NPV ANALYSIS WITH INFLATION

Central Irrigation manufactures new and repairs old irrigation sprinkler systems for golf courses and agricultural use. It produces metal pipes and fittings for large sprinkler systems. The company has been plagued with industrial accidents involving its old welding technology, so a new, safer welding robot has been developed that will reduce labour costs, worker insurance costs, and direct material costs. The investment will be $10 million, and the annual cash savings are estimated to be $5.75 million, but it will cost an additional $3 million per year to operate the machine. The old equipment will be disposed of, but its scrap price will equal the costs of removal, resulting in zero cash flow.

Sam Waters, CFO at Central Irrigation, believes that the robots would be used in production for six years and would then be sold for $1 million in today's dollars. He estimates inflation to be 5% per year and the risk-free rate to be 4% over the life of the project. He also estimates that a minimum risk premium of 6% is required for this project. Therefore, the real rate is 10% (4% + 6%), and the nominal rate is [(1 + 0.10) × (1 + 0.05) − 1] = 15.5%.

Sam asks the company's accountant, Georgia Taniwaki, to analyze the project. Georgia prepares the timeline shown in Exhibit 13A.7 to summarize the relevant nontax cash flows. The cash outflow for the initial investment is $10 million. The incremental operating cash flows in years 1 through 6 are $2.75 million ($5.75 − $3). The terminal value is $1 million.

Georgia knows that she also needs to consider income tax effects for the project. Suppose she determines that the robots would qualify for a CCA rate of 40% for Canadian income tax depreciation. She also estimates that Central Irrigation's marginal income tax rate will be 25% over the next 6 years.

▶EXHIBIT 13A.7
Timeline for Central Irrigation

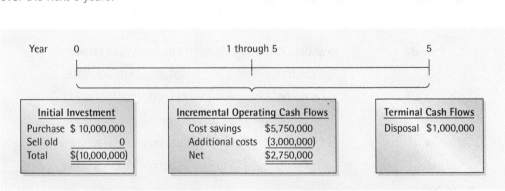

Year	0	1 through 5	5

Initial Investment		Incremental Operating Cash Flows		Terminal Cash Flows	
Purchase	$ 10,000,000	Cost savings	$5,750,000	Disposal	$1,000,000
Sell old	0	Additional costs	(3,000,000)		
Total	$(10,000,000)	Net	$2,750,000		

NPV Calculations: Real Method

Georgia's NPV calculations under the real method are presented in the spreadsheet shown in Exhibit 13A.8. The initial investment, incremental operating cash flows, and terminal cash flow are already estimated in real values, so no adjustment for inflation is needed for these amounts. The spreadsheet also provides the income tax cash flows. No tax cash flow occurs at time 0 because the initial investment is not immediately tax deductible, and the old equipment is expected to be sold at zero gain or loss.

The incremental operating cash flow is estimated to require an additional tax cash payment of $687,500 per year ($2,750,000 × 25% tax rate). The tax basis of the robots is expected to be zero at the end of year 6 ($10,000,000 cost − $10,000,000 total tax depreciation). If the robots are sold for $1,000,000, the full amount will be a taxable gain. Then, the income tax paid on the gain will be $250,000 ($1,000,000 gain × 25% tax rate).

The depreciation tax shield is calculated in three steps:
1. The annual depreciation is calculated by multiplying the initial investment by the CCA rate (Exhibit 13A.9). For example, year 3 depreciation is $1,920,000 ($10,000,000 × 19.20%).

> **EXHIBIT 13A.8**
> Real Method NPV for Central Irrigation

	A	B	C	D	E	F	G	H
1	Real interest rate	10%						
2	Inflation rate	5%						
3	Income tax rate	25%						
4	Initial investment	$ 10,000,000						
5	Terminal cash flow	$ 1,000,000						
6	Incremental operating cash flow	$ 2,750,000						
7								
8	Period		1	2	3	4	5	6
9	Incremental operating cash flows		$2,750,000	$2,750,000	$2,750,000	$2,750,000	$2,750,000	$2,750,000
10	Less income taxes		$ (687,500)	$ (687,500)	$ (687,500)	$ (687,500)	$ (687,500)	$ (687,500)
11								
12	Terminal cash flow							$1,000,000
13	Income taxes on gain							$ (250,000)
14								
15	Total		$2,062,500	$2,062,500	$2,062,500	$2,062,500	$2,062,500	$2,812,500
16								
17	Calculation of depreciation tax shield							
18	CCA rate (40%)		20.00%	32.00%	19.20%	11.52%	6.91%	4.15%
19	Depreciation deduction (nominal)		$2,000,000	$3,200,000	$1,920,000	$1,152,000	$1,152,000	$ 576,000
20	Depreciation deduction (real)		$1,904,762	$2,902,494	$1,658,568	$ 947,753	$ 902,622	$ 429,820
21	Tax savings (tax shield)		$ 476,190	$ 725,624	$ 414,642	$ 236,938	$ 225,656	$ 107,455
22								
23								
24	SUMMARY OF CASH FLOWS							
25	Incremental cash flows		$2,062,500	$2,062,500	$2,062,500	$2,062,500	$2,062,500	$2,062,500
26	Tax savings from depreciation		$ 476,190	$ 725,624	$ 414,642	$ 236,938	$ 225,656	$ 107,455
27	Total		$2,538,690	$2,788,124	$2,477,142	$2,299,438	$2,288,156	$2,919,955
28								
29	Present value		$ 2,307,900	$2,304,234	$ 1,861,113	$1,570,547	$1,420,765	$1,648,238
30								
31	PV of annual cash flows	$ 11,112,799						
32	Less initial investment	$ (10,000,000)						
33	Net present value	$ 1,112,799						

Excel formula to calculate the depreciation amount in real dollars in cell C20: =-PV($B$2,C8,,C19)
Excel formula to calculate net present value in cell D29: =-PV($B$1,D8,,D27)

> **EXHIBIT 13A.9**
> CCA Depreciation Rate Schedules

CCA Rate Declining Balance Half-Year Convention

CCA Rate

Year	50.00%	40.00%	30.00%	20.00%	10.00%
1	25.00%	20.00%	15.00%	10.00%	5.00%
2	37.50%	32.00%	25.50%	18.00%	9.50%
3	18.75%	19.20%	17.85%	14.40%	8.55%
4	9.38%	11.52%	12.50%	11.52%	7.70%
5	4.69%	6.91%	8.75%	9.22%	6.93%
6	2.34%	4.15%	6.12%	7.37%	6.23%

example

2. Because the depreciation is calculated based on the year 0 nominal cost, the next step is to convert the depreciation expense from nominal to real value. The real depreciation expense is calculated by dividing the nominal amount by $(1.05)^t$, where 5% is the inflation rate and t is the number of years in the future when the tax benefit will be received. For year 3, the real value of tax depreciation is $1,658,568 ($1,920,000 ÷ $(1.05)^3$).

3. Finally, calculate the depreciation tax shield by multiplying the real value of the tax depreciation by the marginal tax rate. For year 3, it is $414,642 ($1,658,568 × 25% tax rate).

Georgia combines the incremental cash flows with the tax shield cash flows to determine the total incremental cash flow for each year. She then uses the real interest rate of 10% to calculate the present value for each year's incremental cash flows. Finally, she sums the present values for all years and subtracts the initial investment of $10 million to determine the NPV of $1,112,799. The NPV is positive, so she concludes that the robots would be a good investment for the company.

NPV Calculations: Nominal Method

Georgia is not sure how inflation will affect her NPV calculations, so she decides to also compute the NPV using the nominal method. She prepares the spreadsheet shown in Exhibit 13A.10.

▶ **EXHIBIT 13A.10**
Nominal Method NPV for Central Irrigation

	A	B	C	D	E	F	G	H
1	Real interest rate	10%						
2	Inflation rate	5%						
3	Nominal rate	15.5%						
4	Income tax rate	25%						
5	Initial investment	$ 10,000,000						
6	Terminal cash flow	$ 1,000,000						
7	Incremental operating cash flow	$ 2,750,000						
8								
9	Period		1	2	3	4	5	6
10	Incremental operating cash flows		$2,750,000	$2,750,000	$2,750,000	$2,750,000	$2,750,000	$2,750,000
11								
12	Inflated		$ 2,887,500	$3,031,875	$3,183,469	$3,342,642	$3,509,774	$3,685,263
13	Less income taxes		$ (721,875)	$ (757,969)	$ (795,867)	$ (835,661)	$ (877,444)	$ (921,316)
14								
15	Terminal cash flow							$1,340,096
16	Income taxes on gain							$ (335,024)
17								
18	Total		$2,165,625	$2,273,906	$ 2,387,602	$2,506,982	$2,632,331	$ 3,769,019
19								
20	Calculation of depreciation tax shield							
21	CCA rate (40%)		20.00%	32.00%	19.20%	11.52%	6.91%	4.15%
22	Depreciation deduction (nominal)		$2,000,000	$3,200,000	$1,920,000	$1,152,000	$1,152,000	$ 576,000
23	Tax savings (tax shield)		$ 500,000	$ 800,000	$ 480,000	$ 288,000	$ 288,000	$ 144,000
24								
25								
26	Summary of cash flows							
27	Incremental operating cash flows		$2,165,625	$2,273,906	$ 2,387,602	$2,506,982	$2,632,331	$ 3,769,019
28	Tax savings from depreciation		$ 500,000	$ 800,000	$ 480,000	$ 288,000	$ 288,000	$ 144,000
29	Total		$2,655,625	$3,073,906	$ 2,867,602	$2,794,982	$2,920,331	$ 3,913,019
30								
31	Present value		$ 2,307,900	$2,304,234	$ 1,861,113	$1,570,547	$1,420,765	$1,648,238
32								
33	PV of annual cash flows	$ 11,112,799						
34	Less initial investment	$ (10,000,000)						
35	Net present value	$ 1,112,799						

Under the nominal method, real cash flows must be adjusted for inflation, which means that the incremental operating cash flows and terminal cash flows must be multiplied by $(1.05)^t$, where 5% is the inflation rate and t is the number of years in the future when the cash flow will occur. For example, if the nominal amount of the incremental operating cash flow grows by the inflation rate of 5% each year, then they will increase in year 3 to $3,183,469 ($2,750,000 $\times (1.05)^3$). Then, the income tax that must be paid on the incremental operating income is $795,867 ($3,183,469 $\times$ 25% tax rate).

Inflation will also cause the terminal cash flows to increase from $1 million in today's dollars to $1,340,096 at the end of year 6. Once again, the taxable gain will equal the proceeds, because the robots will be fully depreciated in year 6. The amount of income tax payable on the nominal amount of the gain will be $335,024 ($1,340,096 $\times$ 25% tax rate).

Georgia uses the nominal interest rate of 15.5% to calculate the NPV, which is again positive and $1,112,799.

Comparison of Nominal and Real Methods

Georgia notices that the NPV values under the nominal and real methods are the same. Then she remembers from her cost accounting class that these two methods give the same result when only one inflation rate is used for all cash flows. ■

example

13-2 self-study problem   NPV, IRR, Payback with Inflation, and Income Taxes (Appendix 13A)

LO2, LO4, LO5, LO6, LO7

Kestrel and Sons drills residential and commercial wells. The company is in the process of analyzing the purchase of a new drill that would cost $80,000 and have an expected useful life of 6 years. Several employees have spent $5,000 in travel expenses to locate the best drill. Operating the drill would increase revenue by $60,000 per year but cost an additional $39,000 in labour, maintenance, and other related costs. The managers estimate the salvage value of the drill to be $8,000. Kestrel's marginal income tax rate is 25%. The province requires that each well be registered and that the location of the well meet certain health requirements, such as being at least 100 metres away from septic and sewage systems. An ongoing controversy over the past 15 years centres on whether individual homeowners should be allowed to drill wells, but so far no regulation has been proposed.

required

A. Using a CCA rate of 40%, an inflation rate of 4%, a risk-free rate of 5%, and a risk premium of 8%, calculate the net present value for the purchase of the drill using the nominal method.
B. Calculate the internal rate of return.
C. Calculate the payback period using nominal cash flows.
D. What regulatory issues would Kestrel consider as qualitative factors?
E. How would the issues you identified in Part D affect your assessment of the project risk?

See the solution on page 611.

Real and Nominal Methods Under Varying Inflation Rates

Sometimes, we expect different rates of inflation for different cash flows. Suppose the managers of Central Irrigation believe that salary costs will increase at a relatively low regional wage inflation rate, overhead costs such as utilities and property taxes will increase at a higher inflation rate, and the salvage value of the equipment will decrease over time, as technology costs deflate. In these cases, we cannot use the real method, because that method assumes that all cash flows inflate at the same rate. Instead, the managers would need to use the nominal method to allow for different rates of inflation and deflation.

Present and Future Value Tables

TABLE 13B.1
Present Value of $1

Period	2%	3%	4%	5%	6%	7%	8%	9%	10%	11%	12%	13%	14%	15%	16%	18%	20%	25%
1	0.9804	0.9709	0.9615	0.9524	0.9434	0.9346	0.9259	0.9174	0.9091	0.9009	0.8929	0.8850	0.8772	0.8696	0.8621	0.8475	0.8333	0.8000
2	0.9612	0.9426	0.9246	0.9070	0.8900	0.8734	0.8573	0.8417	0.8264	0.8116	0.7972	0.7831	0.7695	0.7561	0.7432	0.7182	0.6944	0.6400
3	0.9423	0.9151	0.8890	0.8638	0.8396	0.8163	0.7938	0.7722	0.7513	0.7312	0.7118	0.6931	0.6750	0.6575	0.6407	0.6086	0.5787	0.5120
4	0.9238	0.8885	0.8548	0.8227	0.7921	0.7629	0.7350	0.7084	0.6830	0.6587	0.6355	0.6133	0.5921	0.5718	0.5523	0.5158	0.4823	0.4096
5	0.9057	0.8626	0.8219	0.7835	0.7473	0.7130	0.6806	0.6499	0.6209	0.5935	0.5674	0.5428	0.5194	0.4972	0.4761	0.4371	0.4019	0.3277
6	0.8880	0.8375	0.7903	0.7462	0.7050	0.6663	0.6302	0.5963	0.5645	0.5346	0.5066	0.4803	0.4556	0.4323	0.4104	0.3704	0.3349	0.2621
7	0.8706	0.8131	0.7599	0.7107	0.6651	0.6227	0.5835	0.5470	0.5132	0.4817	0.4523	0.4251	0.3996	0.3759	0.3538	0.3139	0.2791	0.2097
8	0.8535	0.7894	0.7307	0.6768	0.6274	0.5820	0.5403	0.5019	0.4665	0.4339	0.4039	0.3762	0.3506	0.3269	0.3050	0.2660	0.2326	0.1678
9	0.8368	0.7664	0.7026	0.6446	0.5919	0.5439	0.5002	0.4604	0.4241	0.3909	0.3606	0.3329	0.3075	0.2843	0.2630	0.2255	0.1938	0.1342
10	0.8203	0.7441	0.6756	0.6139	0.5584	0.5083	0.4632	0.4224	0.3855	0.3522	0.3220	0.2946	0.2697	0.2472	0.2267	0.1911	0.1615	0.1074
11	0.8043	0.7224	0.6496	0.5847	0.5268	0.4751	0.4289	0.3875	0.3505	0.3173	0.2875	0.2607	0.2366	0.2149	0.1954	0.1619	0.1346	0.0859
12	0.7885	0.7014	0.6246	0.5568	0.4970	0.4440	0.3971	0.3555	0.3186	0.2858	0.2567	0.2307	0.2076	0.1869	0.1685	0.1372	0.1122	0.0687
13	0.7730	0.6810	0.6006	0.5303	0.4688	0.4150	0.3677	0.3262	0.2897	0.2575	0.2292	0.2042	0.1821	0.1625	0.1452	0.1163	0.0935	0.0550
14	0.7579	0.6611	0.5775	0.5051	0.4423	0.3878	0.3405	0.2992	0.2633	0.2320	0.2046	0.1807	0.1597	0.1413	0.1252	0.0985	0.0779	0.0440
15	0.7430	0.6419	0.5553	0.4810	0.4173	0.3624	0.3152	0.2745	0.2394	0.2090	0.1827	0.1599	0.1401	0.1229	0.1079	0.0835	0.0649	0.0352
16	0.7284	0.6232	0.5339	0.4581	0.3936	0.3387	0.2919	0.2519	0.2176	0.1883	0.1631	0.1415	0.1229	0.1069	0.0930	0.0708	0.0541	0.0281
17	0.7142	0.6050	0.5134	0.4363	0.3714	0.3166	0.2703	0.2311	0.1978	0.1696	0.1456	0.1252	0.1078	0.0929	0.0802	0.0600	0.0451	0.0225
18	0.7002	0.5874	0.4936	0.4155	0.3503	0.2959	0.2502	0.2120	0.1799	0.1528	0.1300	0.1108	0.0946	0.0808	0.0691	0.0508	0.0376	0.0180
19	0.6864	0.5703	0.4746	0.3957	0.3305	0.2765	0.2317	0.1945	0.1635	0.1377	0.1161	0.0981	0.0829	0.0703	0.0596	0.0431	0.0313	0.0144
20	0.6730	0.5537	0.4564	0.3769	0.3118	0.2584	0.2145	0.1784	0.1486	0.1240	0.1037	0.0868	0.0728	0.0611	0.0514	0.0365	0.0261	0.0115
25	0.6095	0.4776	0.3751	0.2953	0.2330	0.1842	0.1460	0.1160	0.0923	0.0736	0.0588	0.0471	0.0378	0.0304	0.0245	0.0160	0.0105	0.0038
30	0.5521	0.4120	0.3083	0.2314	0.1741	0.1314	0.0994	0.0754	0.0573	0.0437	0.0334	0.0256	0.0196	0.0151	0.0116	0.0070	0.0042	0.0012
35	0.5000	0.3554	0.2534	0.1813	0.1301	0.0937	0.0676	0.0490	0.0356	0.0259	0.0189	0.0139	0.0102	0.0075	0.0055	0.0030	0.0017	0.0004
40	0.4529	0.3066	0.2083	0.1420	0.0972	0.0668	0.0460	0.0318	0.0221	0.0154	0.0107	0.0075	0.0053	0.0037	0.0026	0.0013	0.0007	0.0001
50	0.3715	0.2281	0.1407	0.0872	0.0543	0.0339	0.0213	0.0134	0.0085	0.0054	0.0035	0.0022	0.0014	0.0009	0.0006	0.0003	0.0001	0.0000

TABLE 13B.2
Present Value of an Ordinary Annuity of $1

Period	2%	3%	4%	5%	6%	7%	8%	9%	10%	11%	12%	13%	14%	15%	16%	18%	20%	25%
1	0.9804	0.9709	0.9615	0.9524	0.9434	0.9346	0.9259	0.9174	0.9091	0.9009	0.8929	0.8850	0.8772	0.8696	0.8621	0.8475	0.8333	0.8000
2	1.9416	1.9135	1.8861	1.8594	1.8334	1.8080	1.7833	1.7591	1.7355	1.7125	1.6901	1.6681	1.6467	1.6257	1.6052	1.5656	1.5278	1.4400
3	2.8839	2.8286	2.7751	2.7232	2.6730	2.6243	2.5771	2.5313	2.4869	2.4437	2.4018	2.3612	2.3216	2.2832	2.2459	2.1743	2.1065	1.9520
4	3.8077	3.7171	3.6299	3.5460	3.4651	3.3872	3.3121	3.2397	3.1699	3.1024	3.0373	2.9745	2.9137	2.8550	2.7982	2.6901	2.5887	2.3616
5	4.7135	4.5797	4.4518	4.3295	4.2124	4.1002	3.9927	3.8897	3.7908	3.6959	3.6048	3.5172	3.4331	3.3522	3.2743	3.1272	2.9906	2.6893
6	5.6014	5.4172	5.2421	5.0757	4.9173	4.7665	4.6229	4.4859	4.3553	4.2305	4.1114	3.9975	3.8887	3.7845	3.6847	3.4976	3.3255	2.9514
7	6.4720	6.2303	6.0021	5.7864	5.5824	5.3893	5.2064	5.0330	4.8684	4.7122	4.5638	4.4226	4.2883	4.1604	4.0386	3.8115	3.6046	3.1611
8	7.3255	7.0197	6.7327	6.4632	6.2098	5.9713	5.7466	5.5348	5.3349	5.1461	4.9676	4.7988	4.6389	4.4873	4.3436	4.0776	3.8372	3.3289
9	8.1622	7.7861	7.4353	7.1078	6.8017	6.5152	6.2469	5.9952	5.7590	5.5370	5.3282	5.1317	4.9464	4.7716	4.6065	4.3030	4.0310	3.4631
10	8.9826	8.5302	8.1109	7.7217	7.3601	7.0236	6.7101	6.4177	6.1446	5.8892	5.6502	5.4262	5.2161	5.0188	4.8332	4.4941	4.1925	3.5705
11	9.7868	9.2526	8.7605	8.3064	7.8869	7.4987	7.1390	6.8052	6.4951	6.2065	5.9377	5.6869	5.4527	5.2337	5.0286	4.6560	4.3271	3.6564
12	10.5753	9.9540	9.3851	8.8633	8.3838	7.9427	7.5361	7.1607	6.8137	6.4924	6.1944	5.9176	5.6603	5.4206	5.1971	4.7932	4.4392	3.7251
13	11.3484	10.6350	9.9856	9.3936	8.8527	8.3577	7.9038	7.4869	7.1034	6.7499	6.4235	6.1218	5.8424	5.5831	5.3423	4.9095	4.5327	3.7801
14	12.1062	11.2961	10.5631	9.8986	9.2950	8.7455	8.2442	7.7862	7.3667	6.9819	6.6282	6.3025	6.0021	5.7245	5.4675	5.0081	4.6106	3.8241
15	12.8493	11.9379	11.1184	10.3797	9.7122	9.1079	8.5595	8.0607	7.6061	7.1909	6.8109	6.4624	6.1422	5.8474	5.5755	5.0916	4.6755	3.8593
16	13.5777	12.5611	11.6523	10.8378	10.1059	9.4466	8.8514	8.3126	7.8237	7.3792	6.9740	6.6039	6.2651	5.9542	5.6685	5.1624	4.7296	3.8874
17	14.2919	13.1661	12.1657	11.2741	10.4773	9.7632	9.1216	8.5436	8.0216	7.5488	7.1196	6.7291	6.3729	6.0472	5.7487	5.2223	4.7746	3.9099
18	14.9920	13.7535	12.6593	11.6896	10.8276	10.0591	9.3719	8.7556	8.2014	7.7016	7.2497	6.8399	6.4674	6.1280	5.8178	5.2732	4.8122	3.9279
19	15.6785	14.3238	13.1339	12.0853	11.1581	10.3356	9.6036	8.9501	8.3649	7.8393	7.3658	6.9380	6.5504	6.1982	5.8775	5.3162	4.8435	3.9424
20	16.3514	14.8775	13.5903	12.4622	11.4699	10.5940	9.8181	9.1285	8.5136	7.9633	7.4694	7.0248	6.6231	6.2593	5.9288	5.3527	4.8696	3.9539
25	19.5235	17.4131	15.6221	14.0939	12.7834	11.6536	10.6748	9.8226	9.0770	8.4217	7.8431	7.3300	6.8729	6.4641	6.0971	5.4669	4.9476	3.9849
30	22.3965	19.6004	17.2920	15.3725	13.7648	12.4090	11.2578	10.2737	9.4269	8.6938	8.0552	7.4957	7.0027	6.5660	6.1772	5.5168	4.9789	3.9950
35	24.9986	21.4872	18.6646	16.3742	14.4982	12.9477	11.6546	10.5668	9.6442	8.8552	8.1755	7.5856	7.0700	6.6166	6.2153	5.5386	4.9915	3.9984
40	27.3555	23.1148	19.7928	17.1591	15.0463	13.3317	11.9246	10.7574	9.7791	8.9511	8.2438	7.6344	7.1050	6.6418	6.2335	5.5482	4.9966	3.9995
50	31.4236	25.7298	21.4822	18.2559	15.7619	13.8007	12.2335	10.9617	9.9148	9.0417	8.3045	7.6752	7.1327	6.6605	6.2463	5.5541	4.9995	3.9999

TABLE 13B.3

Future Value of $1

Period	2%	3%	4%	5%	6%	7%	8%	9%	10%	11%	12%	13%	14%	15%	16%	18%	20%	25%
1	1.0200	1.0300	1.0400	1.0500	1.0600	1.0700	1.0800	1.0900	1.1000	1.1100	1.1200	1.1300	1.1400	1.1500	1.1600	1.1800	1.2000	1.2500
2	1.0404	1.0609	1.0816	1.1025	1.1236	1.1449	1.1664	1.1881	1.2100	1.2321	1.2544	1.2769	1.2996	1.3225	1.3456	1.3924	1.4400	1.5625
3	1.0612	1.0927	1.1249	1.1576	1.1910	1.2250	1.2597	1.2950	1.3310	1.3676	1.4049	1.4429	1.4815	1.5209	1.5609	1.6430	1.7280	1.9531
4	1.0824	1.1255	1.1699	1.2155	1.2625	1.3108	1.3605	1.4116	1.4641	1.5181	1.5735	1.6305	1.6890	1.7490	1.8106	1.9388	2.0736	2.4414
5	1.1041	1.1593	1.2167	1.2763	1.3382	1.4026	1.4693	1.5386	1.6105	1.6851	1.7623	1.8424	1.9254	2.0114	2.1003	2.2878	2.4883	3.0518
6	1.1262	1.1941	1.2653	1.3401	1.4185	1.5007	1.5869	1.6771	1.7716	1.8704	1.9738	2.0820	2.1950	2.3131	2.4364	2.6996	2.9860	3.8147
7	1.1487	1.2299	1.3159	1.4071	1.5036	1.6058	1.7138	1.8280	1.9487	2.0762	2.2107	2.3526	2.5023	2.6600	2.8262	3.1855	3.5832	4.7684
8	1.1717	1.2668	1.3686	1.4775	1.5938	1.7182	1.8509	1.9926	2.1436	2.3045	2.4760	2.6584	2.8526	3.0590	3.2784	3.7589	4.2998	5.9605
9	1.1951	1.3048	1.4233	1.5513	1.6895	1.8385	1.9990	2.1719	2.3579	2.5580	2.7731	3.0040	3.2519	3.5179	3.8030	4.4355	5.1598	7.4506
10	1.2190	1.3439	1.4802	1.6289	1.7908	1.9672	2.1589	2.3674	2.5937	2.8394	3.1058	3.3946	3.7072	4.0456	4.4114	5.2338	6.1917	9.3132
11	1.2434	1.3842	1.5395	1.7103	1.8983	2.1049	2.3316	2.5804	2.8531	3.1518	3.4785	3.8359	4.2262	4.6524	5.1173	6.1759	7.4301	11.6415
12	1.2682	1.4258	1.6010	1.7959	2.0122	2.2522	2.5182	2.8127	3.1384	3.4985	3.8960	4.3345	4.8179	5.3503	5.9360	7.2876	8.9161	14.5519
13	1.2936	1.4685	1.6651	1.8856	2.1329	2.4098	2.7196	3.0658	3.4523	3.8833	4.3635	4.8980	5.4924	6.1528	6.8858	8.5994	10.6993	18.1899
14	1.3195	1.5126	1.7317	1.9799	2.2609	2.5785	2.9372	3.3417	3.7975	4.3104	4.8871	5.5348	6.2613	7.0757	7.9875	10.1472	12.8392	22.7374
15	1.3459	1.5580	1.8009	2.0789	2.3966	2.7590	3.1722	3.6425	4.1772	4.7846	5.4736	6.2543	7.1379	8.1371	9.2655	11.9737	15.4070	28.4217
16	1.3728	1.6047	1.8730	2.1829	2.5404	2.9522	3.4259	3.9703	4.5950	5.3109	6.1304	7.0673	8.1372	9.3576	10.7480	14.1290	18.4884	35.5271
17	1.4002	1.6528	1.9479	2.2920	2.6928	3.1588	3.7000	4.3276	5.0545	5.8951	6.8660	7.9861	9.2765	10.7613	12.4677	16.6722	22.1861	44.4089
18	1.4282	1.7024	2.0258	2.4066	2.8543	3.3799	3.9960	4.7171	5.5599	6.5436	7.6900	9.0243	10.5752	12.3755	14.4625	19.6733	26.6233	55.5112
19	1.4568	1.7535	2.1068	2.5270	3.0256	3.6165	4.3157	5.1417	6.1159	7.2633	8.6128	10.1974	12.0557	14.2318	16.7765	23.2144	31.9480	69.3889
20	1.4859	1.8061	2.1911	2.6533	3.2071	3.8697	4.6610	5.6044	6.7275	8.0623	9.6463	11.5231	13.7435	16.3665	19.4608	27.3930	38.3376	86.7362
25	1.6406	2.0938	2.6658	3.3864	4.2919	5.4274	6.8485	8.6231	10.835	13.585	17.000	21.231	26.462	32.919	40.8742	62.6686	95.3962	264.6978
30	1.8114	2.4273	3.2434	4.3219	5.7435	7.6123	10.0627	13.2677	17.449	22.892	29.960	39.116	50.950	66.212	85.8499	143.371	237.376	807.7936
35	1.9999	2.8139	3.9461	5.5160	7.6861	10.6766	14.7853	20.4140	28.102	38.575	52.800	72.069	98.100	133.176	180.314	327.997	590.668	2,465.19
40	2.2080	3.2620	4.8010	7.0400	10.2857	14.9745	21.7245	31.4094	45.259	65.001	93.051	132.782	188.884	267.864	378.721	750.378	1,469.77	7,523.16
50	2.6916	4.3839	7.1067	11.4674	18.4202	29.4570	46.9016	74.3575	117.39	184.56	289.00	450.74	700.23	1,083.7	1,670.7	3,927.4	9,100.4	70,064.9

TABLE 13B.4

Future Value of an Ordinary Annuity of $1

Period	2%	3%	4%	5%	6%	7%	8%	9%	10%	11%	12%	13%	14%	15%	16%	18%	20%	25%
1	1.000	1.000	1.000	1.000	1.000	1.000	1.000	1.000	1.000	1.000	1.000	1.000	1.000	1.000	1.000	1.000	1.000	1.000
2	2.020	2.030	2.040	2.050	2.060	2.070	2.080	2.090	2.100	2.110	2.120	2.130	2.140	2.150	2.160	2.180	2.200	2.250
3	3.060	3.091	3.122	3.153	3.184	3.215	3.246	3.278	3.310	3.342	3.374	3.407	3.440	3.473	3.506	3.572	3.640	3.813
4	4.122	4.184	4.246	4.310	4.375	4.440	4.506	4.573	4.641	4.710	4.779	4.850	4.921	4.993	5.066	5.215	5.368	5.766
5	5.204	5.309	5.416	5.526	5.637	5.751	5.867	5.985	6.105	6.228	6.353	6.480	6.610	6.742	6.877	7.154	7.442	8.207
6	6.308	6.468	6.633	6.802	6.975	7.153	7.336	7.523	7.716	7.913	8.115	8.323	8.536	8.754	8.977	9.442	9.930	11.259
7	7.434	7.662	7.898	8.142	8.394	8.654	8.923	9.200	9.487	9.783	10.089	10.405	10.730	11.067	11.414	12.142	12.916	15.073
8	8.583	8.892	9.214	9.549	9.897	10.260	10.637	11.028	11.436	11.859	12.300	12.757	13.233	13.727	14.240	15.327	16.499	19.842
9	9.755	10.159	10.583	11.027	11.491	11.978	12.488	13.021	13.579	14.164	14.776	15.416	16.085	16.786	17.519	19.086	20.799	25.802
10	10.950	11.464	12.006	12.578	13.181	13.816	14.487	15.193	15.937	16.722	17.549	18.420	19.337	20.304	21.321	23.521	25.959	33.253
11	12.169	12.808	13.486	14.207	14.972	15.784	16.645	17.560	18.531	19.561	20.655	21.814	23.045	24.349	25.733	28.755	32.150	42.566
12	13.412	14.192	15.026	15.917	16.870	17.888	18.977	20.141	21.384	22.713	24.133	25.650	27.271	29.002	30.850	34.931	39.581	54.208
13	14.680	15.618	16.627	17.713	18.882	20.141	21.495	22.953	24.523	26.212	28.029	29.985	32.089	34.352	36.786	42.219	48.497	68.760
14	15.974	17.086	18.292	19.599	21.015	22.550	24.215	26.019	27.975	30.095	32.393	34.883	37.581	40.505	43.672	50.818	59.196	86.949
15	17.293	18.599	20.024	21.579	23.276	25.129	27.152	29.361	31.772	34.405	37.280	40.417	43.842	47.580	51.660	60.965	72.035	109.687
16	18.639	20.157	21.825	23.657	25.673	27.888	30.324	33.003	35.950	39.190	42.753	46.672	50.980	55.717	60.925	72.939	87.442	138.109
17	20.012	21.762	23.698	25.840	28.213	30.840	33.750	36.974	40.545	44.501	48.884	53.739	59.118	65.075	71.673	87.068	105.931	173.636
18	21.412	23.414	25.645	28.132	30.906	33.999	37.450	41.301	45.599	50.396	55.750	61.725	68.394	75.836	84.141	103.74	128.117	218.045
19	22.841	25.117	27.671	30.539	33.760	37.379	41.446	46.018	51.159	56.939	63.440	70.749	78.969	88.212	98.603	123.41	154.740	273.56
20	24.297	26.870	29.778	33.066	36.786	40.995	45.762	51.160	57.275	64.203	72.052	80.947	91.025	102.44	115.38	146.63	186.69	342.94
25	32.030	36.459	41.646	47.727	54.865	63.249	73.106	84.701	98.347	114.41	133.33	155.62	181.87	212.79	249.21	342.60	471.98	1,054.79
30	40.568	47.575	56.085	66.439	79.058	94.461	113.28	136.31	164.49	199.02	241.33	293.20	356.79	434.75	530.31	790.95	1,181.88	3,227.17
35	49.994	60.462	73.652	90.320	111.43	138.24	172.32	215.71	271.02	341.59	431.66	546.68	693.57	881.17	1,121	1,817	2,948	9,857
40	60.402	75.401	95.026	120.80	154.76	199.64	259.06	337.88	442.59	581.83	767.09	1,014	1,342	1,779	2,361	4,163	7,344	30,089
50	84.579	112.80	152.67	209.35	290.34	406.53	573.77	815.08	1,164	1,669	2,400	3,460	4,995	7,218	10,436	21,813	45,497	280,256

SUMMARY

PROCESS FOR IDENTIFYING AND ANALYZING STRATEGIC INVESTMENTS

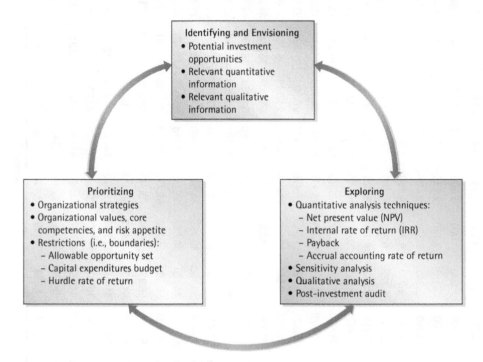

TYPES OF LONG-TERM INVESTMENT DECISIONS

▶ Developing or expanding products or services
▶ Replacing or reorganizing assets or services

COMMON TYPES OF RELEVANT CASH FLOWS

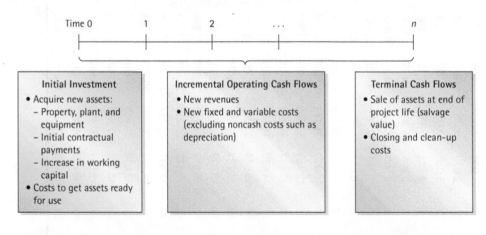

SUMMARY

CALCULATION OF NET PRESENT VALUE

$$NPV = \sum_{t=0}^{n} \frac{\text{Expected cash flow}_t}{(1+r)^t}$$

$$= \sum_{t=0}^{n} \text{Expected Cash Flow}_t \times PVF_{r,t}$$

POTENTIAL DISCOUNT RATES

► Weighted average cost of capital
► Rate reflecting project risk

GENERAL DECISION RULES

► Projects with a positive NPV are generally acceptable
► Invest in the project(s) having the highest NPV if investment resources are limited
► Projects with a profitability index greater than 1 should be accepted
► Rank order projects on profitability index

L03 Identify the uncertainties of NPV analysis

MAJOR ASSUMPTIONS AND UNCERTAINTIES

► Cost of initial investment
► Timing and dollar amounts of incremental revenues and costs
► Terminal values
► Project life
► Appropriate discount rate
► Marginal income tax rate
► Depreciation rules for income taxes

POTENTIAL MANAGER BIAS SENSITIVITY ANALYSIS

► Evaluate how NPV results change with variations in assumptions

INTERNAL RATE OF RETURN (IRR)

► Discount rate necessary for the present value of the discounted cash flows to be equal to the investment

L04 Apply alternative methods in analyzing strategic investment decisions

PAYBACK

► Measure of the amount of time required to recover the initial investment

ACCRUAL ACCOUNTING RATE OF RETURN

► Expected increase in average annual operating income as a percent of the initial increase in required investment

L05 Identify additional issues to be considered for strategic investment decisions

QUALITATIVE ISSUES

► Difficulty in estimating cash flows for new information technology
► Need for speedy decisions
► Need for innovation in new products and services
► Environmental effects
► Quality of product or service
► Employees
► Community
► Reputation

POST-INVESTMENT AUDIT

► Improve implementation, results, and accuracy of future capital budgets

LO6   Explain how income taxes affect strategic investment decision cash flows

INCOME TAX CASH FLOWS

▶ Tax on incremental operating cash flows
▶ Tax on terminal gain or loss
▶ Depreciation tax shield

CCA DEPRECIATION (APPENDIX 13A)

LO7   Explain how real and nominal methods are used to address inflation in an NPV analysis

REAL METHOD

Discount real cash flows at the real rate of interest:

Real rate of interest = Risk-free rate + Risk premium

NOMINAL METHOD

Discount nominal cash flows at the nominal rate of interest:

$$\text{Nominal rate of interest} = (1 + \text{Real rate}) \times (1 + \text{Inflation rate}) - 1$$

INTERNAL CONSISTENCY IN NPV ANALYSIS

Cash flows and interest rate must both be calculated using the same method (real or nominal)

DIFFERENT RATES OF INFLATION (OR DEFLATION) FOR THE DIFFERENT CASH FLOWS

Cannot use real method

13-1 solution to self-study problem

A. First, we summarize the cash flows across time. Notice that the $1,500 in travel and employee costs is a sunk cost and does not affect the NPV calculation. Also, no terminal cash flows occur for this project:

Time 0	Years 1–4
Investment	$30,000 savings
$85,000 purchase	
2,000 shipping	
3,000 remodel	
$90,000	

Because cash flows are equal across time, we can treat the incremental cash flows in years 1 through 4 as an annuity to calculate NPV:

$$\begin{aligned}
\text{NPV} &= -\$90,000 + \$30,000 \times (\text{PVPA 4 years, 10\%}) \\
&= -\$90,000 + \$30,000 \times 3.170 = -\$90,000 + \$95,100 \\
&= \$5,100
\end{aligned}$$

B. Profitability index = $95,100 ÷ $90,000 = 1.057.

C. IRR (calculated using the IRR function in an Excel spreadsheet) = 12.59%

D. Payback period = $90,000 ÷ $30,000 = 3 years.

E. Factors that could be varied for sensitivity analysis include all the assumptions, such as the initial investment amount, the labour and insurance savings, and the discount rate. Because we cannot know future economic conditions, and we cannot know whether technology developments will improve models more rapidly than we expect, we need to perform sensitivity analyses for all the assumptions we make. Even the initial investment could change if remodelling is more substantial than expected.

13-2 solution to self-study problem

A. Exhibit 13.8 provides a spreadsheet for Kestrel and Sons with the NPV calculation using the nominal method. This spreadsheet demonstrates a different format than shown in the chapter examples.

B. Exhibit 13.9 provides a spreadsheet for Kestrel and Sons with the IRR calculation.

C. Because the net cash flows in this problem are not uniform (i.e., are not identical) across time, the payback period must be calculated by manually determining the years it takes to recover the investment. Payback does not include the time value of money, so we analyze the cash flows before they are discounted:

	Net Nominal Cash Flow	**Balance to Recover**
Time 0		$80,000
Year 1	$16,380 + $4,000 = $20,380	$80,000 − $20,380 = $59,620
Year 2	$17,035 + $6,400 = $23,435	$59,620 − $23,435 = $36,185
Year 3	$17,717 + $3,840 = $21,557	$36,185 − $21,557 = $14,628
Year 4	$18,425 + $2,304 = $20,729	$14,628 − $14,628 = 0

The initial investment is expected to be fully recovered in more than three years but less than four. We can estimate the proportion of the fourth year needed to complete the payback as follows:

$$\$14,628 \div \$20,729 = 0.7 \text{ of year } 4$$

Thus, the payback period is estimated as 3.7 years.

D. Kestrel would have to consider the possible upcoming change in regulation that would make it impossible for homeowners to drill wells. The percentage of wells drilled that are residential would decrease greatly. If this percentage is high, Kestrel may not be able to bring in the predicted revenue.

E. The risk premium should probably be increased if residential drilling is a large (say, greater than about 30%) proportion of Kestrel's business. Sensitivity analysis can be done around the discount rate by varying the risk premium to determine the risk rate that brings the net present value to zero.

> EXHIBIT 13.8

NPV Calculation for Self-Study Problem 2

	A	B	C	D	E
1	Cash Flows:				
2	Increase in revenue	$60,000	Discount rate information:		
3	Increase in labour	($39,000)	Risk free	5.00%	
4	Total	$21,000	Project risk	8.00%	
5	Terminal value	$8,000	Inflation	4.00%	
6	Investment:				
7	Purchase equipment	($80,000)	Tax rate	25.00%	
8					
9	Nominal discount rate	17.52%			
10					
11	Incremental Cash Flows:				
12	Period	Incremental CF	Inflated	Less Tax	Discounted
13	1	$21,000	$21,840	$16,380	$13,938
14	2	$21,000	$22,714	$17,035	$12,335
15	3	$21,000	$23,622	$17,717	$10,916
16	4	$21,000	$24,567	$18,425	$9,660
17	5	$21,000	$25,550	$19,162	$8,548
18	6	$21,000	$26,572	$19,929	$7,565
19	Total PV of Incremental Cash Flow				$62,961
20					
21	Depreciation Tax Savings:				
22	Period	CCA Rate	Depreciation	Tax Savings	Discounted
23	1	20.00%	$16,000	$4,000	$3,404
24	2	32.00%	$25,600	$6,400	$4,634
25	3	19.20%	$15,360	$3,840	$2,366
26	4	11.52%	$9,216	$2,304	$1,208
27	5	11.52%	$9,216	$2,304	$1,028
28	6	5.76%	$4,608	$1,152	$437
29	Total PV of Tax Savings				$13,077
30					
31		Today's Dollars	Inflated	After Tax	Discounted
32	Terminal value	$8,000	$10,123	$7,592	$2,882
33					
34	Net Present Value:				
35	Incremental CF	$62,961			
36	Tax savings	$13,077			
37	Terminal value	$2,882			
38	Less investment	($80,000)			
39	NPV	($1,080)			

Examples of Excel formulas:

Nominal discount rate in cell B9: =(1+D3+D4)*(1+D5)−1

Inflated incremental cash flow in cell C15: =−FV($D$5,A15,,B15)

After-tax incremental cash flow in cell D15: =C15*(1−$D$7)

Present value of incremental cash flow in cell E15: =−PV($B$9,A15,,D15)

> EXHIBIT 13.9

IRR Calculation for Self-Study Problem 2

	A	B	C	D	E	F
41	Combined Cash Flows:					
42	Period	Investment	Incremental CF	Tax Savings	Terminal	Total
43	0	($80,000)				($80,000)
44	1		$16,380	$4,000		$20,380
45	2		$17,035	$6,400		$23,435
46	3		$17,717	$3,840		$21,557
47	4		$18,425	$2,304		$20,729
48	5		$19,162	$2,304		$21,466
49	6		$19,929	$1,152	$10,123	$31,203
50						
51	Internal Rate of Return	17.46%				

Excel formula to calculate internal rate of return in cell B51: =IRR(F43:F49)

QUESTIONS

13.1 Forecasting the terminal value of equipment 20 years from now is difficult to do accurately, but errors in estimation probably have a small effect on the NPV. Explain.

13.2 Suppose a company has five different capital budgeting projects from which to choose, but it has constrained funds and cannot implement all the projects. Explain why comparing the projects' NPVs is better than comparing their IRRs.

13.3 Describe the pros and cons of each of the capital budgeting methods described in this chapter: (1) net present value, (2) internal rate of return, (3) payback, and (4) accrual accounting rate of return.

13.4 "When projects have longer lives, it is more difficult to accurately estimate the cash flows and discount rates over the life of a project." Explain why this statement is true.

13.5 (Appendix 13A) The present value of a given cash flow gets smaller as the number of periods gets larger, regardless of whether cash flow is discounted with a real rate or a nominal rate. Explain why this relationship holds true and what it means from an economic perspective.

13.6 (Appendix 13A) Two methods can be used to incorporate the effects of inflation or deflation into an NPV analysis. In your own words, explain how a nominal discount rate is different from a real discount rate. Why are analyses using the nominal approach potentially more accurate than those using the real approach?

13.7 (Appendix 13A) How might inflation influence a decision to acquire an asset now rather than later?

13.8 If a firm has unlimited funds, what criterion should be used to determine which projects to invest in?

13.9 An international firm requires a rate of return of 15% domestically and in other developed countries, but it requires 25% in less-developed countries. Does this requirement mean that the firm is exploiting the less-developed countries? Explain.

13.10 When we covered CVP analysis in Chapter 3, we calculated the amount of pretax profit needed to achieve a given level of after-tax profit. We could calculate a pretax rate of return given an after-tax rate of return. Why would it be inappropriate to use a pretax discount rate in capital budgeting? (For example, if a firm requires an after-tax return of 10% and has a marginal income tax rate of 50%, why not use a 20% pretax rate of return and ignore the separate income tax calculations?)

13.11 A well-known new-immigrant language centre in Hamilton, Ontario, operates as a not-for-profit organization. Typical capital expenditure decisions involve acquiring audio-visual equipment that will provide language training for new immigrants beyond the number currently being served at the centre (hence adding revenues) and/or providing services more efficiently than currently (hence decreasing expenses). To evaluate such expenditures, the language centre uses a discount rate equal to the return on its investment trust portfolio. Explain, briefly, why it does so.

13.12 As the time period for an NPV analysis gets longer, what happens to each incremental present value factor? Refer to a present value chart. At 15% interest, beyond what year do the discount factors get so small that very little value is added by annual incremental cash flows?

13.13 Refer to the present value of an annuity table. As the time period in an analysis using annuity factors gets longer, what happens to each incremental factor? Explain why this is different from the changes for present value factors.

13.14 Explain why top managers might establish the following types of boundaries for strategic investment decisions made by subordinates: (1) required rate of return, (2) types of capital projects to consider, and (3) maximum capital budget that can be spent without top management approval.

13.15 Why is the terminal value of an asset adjusted for income taxes before it is discounted?

MULTIPLE-CHOICE QUESTIONS

13.16 In analyzing capital budgeting decisions, a number of methods are commonly used. Which of the following methods does *not* involve the measurement of cash flows?
 a. Internal rate of return method
 b. Net present value method
 c. Real method
 d. Payback method

Use the following information to answer Questions 13.17 to 13.20:
Juno Manufacturing Ltd. is considering replacing its existing equipment with an automated machine for $133,950. Juno depreciates its capital assets using the straight-line depreciation method. Juno estimates that the new machine will reduce production costs by $28,500 per year and that it has a useful life of 6 years.

13.17 What is the internal rate of return?
 a. 6.84%
 b. 7.46%

 c. 7.66%
 d. 8.14%

13.18 What is the payback period?
 a. 1.27 years
 b. 4.00 years
 c. 4.70 years
 d. 6.00 years

13.19 What is the net present value if the required rate of return is 8%?
 a. $(2,194.50)
 b. $0.00
 c. $1,909.50
 d. $37,050.00

13.20 What is the accrual accounting rate of return?
 a. 3.55%
 b. 4.61%
 c. 9.50%
 d. 21.30%

EXERCISES

13.21 Time Value of Money

LO2

 A. What is the present value of $8,000 received in 7 years' time at 8% interest?
 B. Bonnie Lee buys a savings bond for $125. The bond pays 6% and matures in 10 years. What amount will Bonnie receive when she redeems the bond?
REQUIRED **C.** Erik Peterson needs to have $10,000 at the end of 5 years to purchase a second car. His investment returns 6%. How much does he need to invest now?
 D. Conan Bardwell will receive $1,000 in 6 years from an investment that returns 12%. How much did he invest?

13.22 Capital Budgeting Process Put the following six steps for capital budgeting in the most likely order, numbering the

LO1 first activity as number 1, the second as 2, and so on.
 _____ Perform sensitivity analysis
 _____ Identify decision alternatives
REQUIRED _____ Analyze qualitative factors
 _____ Identify relevant cash flows
 _____ Apply the relevant quantitative analysis technique
 _____ Consider quantitative and qualitative information to make a decision

13.23 Payback in Months The International Netherlands Group (ING) built its new headquarters building in Amsterdam

LO4 using "green" principles to reduce energy consumption. The building used primarily passive cooling systems, made use of daylight, and applied various other energy efficiency techniques that increased the building's construction costs by about $700,000. These systems reduced energy costs by approximately $2.9 million per year.

Source: "Buildings & Land: International Netherlands Group (ING) Bank, Amsterdam, Netherlands," Rocky Mountain Institute.

REQUIRED Calculate the payback period in months for ING's energy investment.

13.24 NPV Calculations with Taxes Overnight Laundry is considering the purchase of a new pressing machine that
L02, L06 would cost $96,000 and would produce incremental operating cash flows of $25,000 annually for 10 years. The
machine has a terminal value of $6,000 and is depreciated for income tax purposes using straight-line deprecia-
tion over a 10-year life (ignore the half-year convention). Overnight Laundry's marginal tax rate is 33.3%. The
company uses a discount rate of 18%.

REQUIRED   What is the net present value of the project?

13.25 NPV and IRR Calculations Axel Corporation is planning to buy a new machine, with the expectation that this invest-
L02, L04 ment should earn a rate of return of at least 15%. This machine, which costs $150,000, would yield an estimated
net cash flow of $30,000 per year for 10 years.

REQUIRED   **A.** What is the net present value for this proposal?
B. What is the internal rate of return for this proposal?

13.26 NPV, IRR, ARR, and Payback Methods Amaro Clinic, a not-for-profit institution not subject to income taxes, is con-
L02, L04 sidering the purchase of new equipment costing $20,000 to achieve cash savings of $5,000 per year in operating
costs. The estimated useful life is 10 years, with no salvage value. Amaro's minimum expected return is 14%.

REQUIRED   **A.** What is the net present value of this investment?
B. What is the internal rate of return?
C. What is the accrual accounting rate of return based on the initial investment?
D. What is the payback period?

13.27 NPV, ARR, and Payback Methods Moosehead Community Centre, a not-for-profit organization not subject to income
L02, L04 taxes, is considering the purchase of a new snowplow costing $20,000. The estimated useful life is eight years,
with no salvage value. Moosehead's minimum expected return is 12%, and it has a four-year cut-off guideline
when evaluating an investment project. Moosehead uses straight-line depreciation. The manager estimates the
following savings in cash operating costs:

Year	Amount
1	$ 5,200
2	4,800
3	4,400
4	3,600
5	3,200
6	2,800
7	2,200
8	1,800
Total	$28,000

REQUIRED   **A.** What is the net present value of this investment?
B. What is the accrual accounting rate of return based on the initial investment? Use the average annual savings
when computing the numerator.
C. What is the payback period?
D. Based on the financial evaluation, would you recommend the investment?

13.28 Present Value and Future Value Calculations Crown Corporation agreed to sell some used equipment to one of its
L02, L04 employees. Alternative financing arrangements for the sale have been discussed, and the present and future
values of each alternative have been determined.

REQUIRED   **A.** Crown offered to accept a $1,000 down payment and set up a note receivable that calls for four $1,000
payments, one at the end of each of the next four years. What is the net present value of this note if it is
discounted at 6%?
B. The employee agrees to the $1,000 down payment but would like the note for $4,000 to be payable in full at
the end of the fourth year. Because of the increased risk associated with the terms of this note, Crown would
apply an 8% discount rate. What is the true selling price of the equipment?
C. Suppose the employee borrows the $5,000 at 8% interest for four years from a bank so that he can pay Crown
the full price of the equipment immediately. Also, suppose that Crown could invest the $5,000 for three years
at 7%. What is the selling price of the equipment? What would be the future value of Crown's investment?

13.29 NPV, IRR, Payback Methods, and ARR KTI Inc. is considering a project that would have a five-year life and require a $320,000 investment in equipment. The project will release working capital of $20,000 at the beginning of the project. At the end of five years, the project would terminate, the equipment would have $20,000 residual value, and the working capital will be increased by $20,000. The project would provide net income each year as follows:

LO2, LO3, LO4

Sales	$500,000
Less: Variable Expenses	$220,000
Contribution Margin	$280,000
Less: Fixed Expenses	$230,000
Net Income	$50,000

All of the above items, except for depreciation, represent cash flows. The depreciation is included in the fixed expenses. KTI's required rate of return is 10%, and the payback period is 2.5 years.

REQUIRED
A. What is the project's net present value?
B. What is the project's internal rate of return?
C. What is the project's payback period?
D. What is the project's accrual accounting rate of return?
E. Should KTI invest in this project? Provide your argument based on your quantitative analysis from A to D.

13.30 NPV Analysis with Taxes and CCA (Appendix 13A) A company is considering buying a new machine for $1,200,000. The new machine will replace the current machine, which can be sold now for $75,000. The company will incur installation costs of $130,000 if it buys the new machine. The company's tax rate is 35% and its cost of capital after tax is 12%.

LO2, LO3, LO6

Buying the new machine is forecast to generate the following annual savings:

Year 1	$130,000
Year 2	140,000
Year 3	150,000
Year 4	175,000
Year 5	180,000
Year 6	185,000
Year 7	195,000

If the company decides to keep the old machine for seven more years, it will have to spend $45,000 in 3 years from now for a complete refurbishment. On the other hand, if the company decides to buy the new machine, it would have to spend $40,000 for maintenance in year 5. In seven years, the salvage value of the new machine would be $120,000, and the salvage value for the old machine would be $30,000.

The capital cost allowance for this type of machine is 15%.

REQUIRED Compute the net present value for the acquisition of the new machine and state whether the company should proceed with the investment or not.

13.31 Relevant Cash Flows, NPV Analysis with Taxes and CCA (Appendix 13A) Karisma Ltd. manufactures signs and trophies. Ms. Karol is considering investing in a new machine that will save annual material costs of $14,000 and labour costs of $6,000. The new machine costs $60,000 and has a five-year life and a terminal disposal price of zero. Karisma's income tax rate is 30%, and the after-tax required rate of return is 7%. Karisma uses four years as a cut-off when evaluating an investment project. The capital cost allowance rate for this new machine is 20%, with a declining balance.

LO2, LO3, LO6

REQUIRED
A. What is the net present value for this investment?
B. What is the profitability index for this investment?
C. What is the payback period for this investment?
D. Should Karisma invest in the new machine?

13.32 Relevant Cash Flows, NPV Analysis with Taxes and Inflation (Appendix 13A) Clearwater Bottling Company sells bottled spring water for $12 per case, with variable costs of $7 per case. The company has been selling 200,000 cases per year and expects to continue at that rate, unless it accepts a special order from Blue Danube

LO2, LO3, LO6, LO7

Restaurant. Blue Danube has offered to buy 20,000 cases per year at $9 per case. Clearwater must agree to make the sales for a five-year period. Blue Danube will not take fewer than 20,000 cases but is willing to take more.

Clearwater's current capacity is 210,000 cases per year. Capacity could be increased to 260,000 per year if new equipment costing $100,000 were purchased. The equipment would have a useful life of five years and no salvage value. Maintenance on the new equipment would increase fixed costs by $20,000 each year. Variable costs per unit would be unchanged. Clearwater has a marginal income tax rate of 25%. Inflation is estimated to be 4% over each of the next five years. The risk-free rate is estimated to be 5%. Clearwater can earn a rate of 12% if it invests in an alternative investment having similar risk.

REQUIRED   **A.** Create a timeline showing the relevant cash flows for this problem.
   B. Ignoring inflation, using straight-line depreciation over five years (ignoring the half-year convention), and using a 12% discount rate, determine the NPV if 20,000 cases are sold.
   C. Ignoring inflation, using straight-line depreciation over five years (ignoring the half-year convention), and using a 12% discount rate, determine the number of cases Blue Danube would need to purchase to bring the NPV to zero.

13.33 NPV Analysis Parish County government supervisors are considering the purchase of a small, used plane to save on travel costs. The plane will cost $400,000 and can be sold in five years for 20% of the original cost.

LO2

REQUIRED If 10% is the required rate of return, what minimum annual savings in transportation costs are needed for this plane to be a good investment? Ignore income taxes.

13.34 NPV and Payback with Taxes Equipment with a cost of $60,000 will, if acquired, generate annual savings of $30,000 for six years, at which time it will have no further use or value. The firm has a marginal tax rate of 40% and requires a 10% rate of return. It uses straight-line depreciation (ignore the half-year convention). Ignore inflation.

LO2, LO4, LO6

REQUIRED   **A.** What is the after-tax cash flow for each year?
   B. What is the NPV of this investment?
   C. What is the payback period?

13.35 IRR Ferris Industries has $50,000 available to invest in new equipment. Management is considering four different equipment investments, each of which requires $50,000. The expected after-tax cash flow for each project has been estimated as follows:

LO4, LO6

	Year					
	1	2	3	4	5	6
Project 1	$10,000	$12,000	$14,000	$16,000	$16,000	$16,000
Project 2	40,000	5,000	(3,000)	40,000	5,000	1,000
Project 3	18,000	(16,000)	50,000	50,000	3,000	3,000
Project 4	30,000	—	—	30,000	30,000	30,000

REQUIRED   **A.** Rank order the projects in terms of desirability, using the internal rate of return for each project as the criterion. Use Excel or a similar spreadsheet to calculate the IRRs.
   B. What other factors should be considered in making the decision of which investment to choose?

13.36 Alternative Technologies and Capital Budgeting with Taxes Lymbo Company, Inc. must install safety devices throughout its plant or it will lose its insurance coverage. Two alternatives are acceptable to the insurer. The first costs $100,000 to install and $20,000 to maintain, annually. The second costs $150,000 to install and $10,000 to maintain annually. Each has a 5-year income tax life and a 15-year useful life. Lymbo's discount rate is 12%, its marginal tax rate is 30%, and it uses straight-line depreciation (ignore the half-year convention).

LO2, LO6

REQUIRED   **A.** Which system should be installed? Why?
   B. If Lymbo were a not-for-profit organization that does not pay income taxes on its operations, which system would be installed?

13.37 Equipment Replacement, NPV, IRR, and Payback Garco is considering replacing an old machine that is currently being
L02, L04 used. The old machine is fully depreciated, but it can be used for another five years, at which time it would have
no terminal value. Garco can sell the old machine for $60,000 on the date that the new machine is purchased.

If the purchase occurs, the new machine will be acquired for a cash payment of $1 million. Because of the
increased efficiency of the new machine, estimated annual cash savings of $300,000 would be generated during
its useful life of five years. The new machine is not expected to have any terminal value.

REQUIRED **A.** Garco requires investments to earn a 12% return. What is the net present value for replacing the old machine
with the new machine?
B. What is the internal rate of return to replace the old machine?
C. What is the payback period for the new machine?

PROBLEMS

13.38 Capital Budgeting Methods, Sensitivity Analysis, Spreadsheet Development, Uncertainties Your brother, Jackson, was
L02, L03, laid off from his job with a large and famous software company. He would like to sell his stock in the company and
L04, L05 use the proceeds to start a restaurant. The stock is currently valued at $500,000. He received a job offer from
a competitor that will pay $90,000 per year plus benefits. He asked you to help him decide the best course of
action.

REQUIRED **A.** What are the alternatives that Jackson faces?
B. Choose the most appropriate analysis technique and explain your choice.
C. If Jackson chooses to open a restaurant, what are his opportunity costs?
D. List the steps you would take to develop a spreadsheet that Jackson could manipulate to help with the
quantitative aspects of this decision. Assume that you only have time to set up a template and that Jackson will
fill in the specific information. However, you need to tell him the general categories of information he will need
to gather.
E. List as many uncertainties as you can about whether taking the job offer would turn out well for Jackson.
F. List as many uncertainties as you can about whether opening a restaurant would turn out well for Jackson.
G. Explain why it is possible for Jackson to make a good decision even though he cannot know for sure how well
his alternatives would work out.

13.39 NPV, Payback Methods, and ARR TubeFab Inc. is considering replacing its metal tubing machine acquired 2 years
L02, L03, ago at a cost of $50,000. This machine is still in good condition but management wants more flexibility and lower
L04 manufacturing costs. The actual current market value of the machine is $20,500, with a salvage value of $2,000
in 10 years.
A manufacturer is offering a new metal tubing machine at a price of $60,000. The machine would last 10 years
and has an expected salvage value of $4,000. The new machine will require an additional $5,000 in working
capital, which will be recovered at the end of the 10th year. With the new machine, management estimates an
important decrease in the manufacturing costs:

	Old Tubing Machine	New Tubing Machine
Annual expenses:		
Direct labour	$ 13,500	$ 7,900
Machinery costs	3,000	3,400
Cleaning & setup	2,500	1,200
Depreciation	4,000	5,600
Annual production (in units)	500,000	500,000

TubeFab has a minimum desired rate of return of 8% and a cutoff period of 4 years in evaluating the new project.

REQUIRED **A.** What is the net present value of this machine?
B. Calculate the point of indifference in terms of annual cost savings (or cash flow).
C. What is the payback period?
D. What is the accrual accounting rate of return (AARR)?
E. Based on your calculations above, state your conclusion on whether the new tubing machine should be
purchased. Please briefly comment on quantitative measures and qualitative issues.

13.40 **IRR, Developing a Discount Rate, Evaluating Risk** The local homeless shelter received a large donation from a

LO2, LO3, LO4

wealthy benefactor and asked you to review its decision-making process for the proposed investment choice. The shelter's financial advisor suggested using the internal rate of return (IRR) to evaluate three different projects:

- A hotel that offers rooms based on the renter's ability to pay
- An apartment complex for elderly people who receive rent subsidization from a federal agency
- A small cardboard-box manufacturing company that will serve as a job training facility for homeless clients

REQUIRED **A.** In your own words, describe the advantages and disadvantages of IRR for this decision.

B. This not-for-profit organization uses an IRR hurdle rate of 15% for most projects. Is it a good idea for an organization to use the same hurdle rate for most projects? Why or why not?

C. List information that might help you develop a hurdle rate for each project.

D. Which alternative do you believe is most financially risky for the homeless shelter? Explain your thinking.

13.41 **NPV Analysis with Taxes and CCA (Appendix 13A)** A sawmill is facing increasing costs partly due to increases in

LO6

fuel prices. Managers have been discussing different strategies to reduce these costs. They agreed to replace a machine acquired 5 years ago at a cost of $83,000. The market value of the old machine is $7,000 and it could still be used for 2 more years. The new machine costs $116,000 and is expected to last 5 years, with an expected salvage value of $10,000.

The sawmill production costs per unit are as follows:

Direct materials	$1.00
Direct labour	1.30
Overhead (fixed and variable)	0.80
Total	$3.10

The price charged by the sawmill for one unit of lumber is $6.00 and 100,000 units are sold each year. With the new machine, management expects to save 20% on all variable costs. The desired before-tax rate of return is 25%, the capital cost allocation rate is also 25%, and the company tax rate is 40%. The fixed portion of overhead costs is 60%.

REQUIRED **A.** Determine the net present value of the replacement machine.

B. Indicate whether the company should replace its old machine. Justify your answer, and identify some factors that management should consider before making a final decision.

13.42 **Real Interest Rates, Uncertainties, Effects of Time (Appendix 13A)** Managers often use the real interest rate to help

LO2, LO3, LO7

decide whether to take on a new project.

REQUIRED **A.** What two factors are included in the real interest rate?

B. What economic factors could affect the two aspects you identified in Part A? List as many factors as you can.

C. Discuss how certain you can be that interest rates will remain constant over the life of a project.

D. Does the time length of a project affect your answer to Part C? Why or why not?

13.43 **Choice of Method, Uncertainties, Addressing Company Policy** Green Jade Resorts, a Singapore company that owns

LO2, LO3, LO4, LO5

and operates golf resorts, has hired you to analyze its investment opportunities in Ontario and Quebec. The company managers have always used the payback method and have asked you to prepare an analysis comparing three different resorts, one near the town of Huntsville, Ontario; another at Charlevoix, Quebec; and a third near Mont Tremblant, Quebec.

REQUIRED **A.** List four methods that could be used to analyze this long-term decision. Describe each method in your own words.

B. In your own words, describe the advantages and disadvantages of each method you identified in Part A.

C. Explain why it is not possible to perfectly predict a project's cash flows.

D. In using quantitative results for decision making, would you place equal reliance on the results of all four analysis techniques? Explain.

E. Discuss how the managers of the Singapore company might respond to your advice if you recommend an analysis method other than the payback method.

F. Write a brief memo to the CEO of the Singapore company, recommending your choice of analysis method and explaining the most important issues for the CEO to consider when choosing an analysis method.

13.44 Timeline, Relevant Costs, NPV, Payback, Uncertainties Irrigation Supply is negotiating with a major hardware chain to supply heavy-duty sprinkler heads at $18,000 each year for five years. Irrigation Supply would need to retool at a cost of $20,000 to fill this order. Incremental costs associated with the order (in addition to the retooling costs) would be $12,000 per year. In addition, existing fixed overhead costs would be reallocated among Irrigation Supply's products, which would result in a $1,000 overhead charge against the special order. For income taxes, the retooling costs would be depreciated using the straight-line method, with no terminal value, ignoring the half-year convention. Irrigation Supply's marginal income tax rate is 25%. Assume that all cash flows (except the initial retooling costs) occur at year end. The company's discount rate is 16%.

LO2, LO3, LO4

REQUIRED
A. Create a timeline showing the relevant cash flows for this problem.
B. What is the net present value of the special order?
C. What is the payback period for this project?
D. For this problem, what do you learn from the NPV analysis, and what do you learn from the payback period?
E. The managers of the hardware store (the customers in this problem) believe that demand will ensure their ability to purchase sprinkler heads from Irrigation Supply. Explain why the hardware chain's managers cannot be certain about the future demand for sprinkler heads.
F. Discuss how uncertainties for the hardware store could lead to uncertainties for Irrigation Supply.

13.45 NPV with and Without Inflation, Tax Effects (Appendix 13A) Cy Keener, president of the Carbondale Architectural Design Group, is considering an investment to upgrade his current computer-aided design equipment. The new equipment would cost $110,000, have a five-year useful life, and have a zero terminal value. The new equipment would generate annual cash operating savings of $36,000. The company's required rate of return is 18% per year.

LO2, LO3, LO6, LO7

REQUIRED

A. Compute the net present value of the project. Assume a 25% marginal tax rate and straight-line depreciation, ignoring the half-year convention.
B. Keener is wondering whether the method in Part A provides a correct analysis of the effects of inflation. The 18% required rate of return incorporates an element attributable to anticipated inflation. For purposes of his analysis, Keener assumes that the existing rate of inflation, 5% annually, will persist over the next five years. Recalculate the NPV, adjusting the cash flows, as appropriate, for the 5% inflation rate.
C. Compare the quantitative results for Parts A and B. In general, how does inflation affect capital budgeting quantitative results?
D. Explain why managers cannot predict future inflation rates with total accuracy.
E. In your own words, explain how failure to consider the effects of inflation might bias managers' capital budgeting decisions.

13.46 NPV with Taxes and Inflation, Uncertainties, Sensitivity Analyses, Interpretation (Appendix 13A) Kelly Bucek is manager of the customer service division of a retail computer store, Quik Computers. Kelly would like to buy computer diagnostic equipment that costs $10,000. The equipment will last five years. Kelly estimates that the incremental operating cash savings from using the equipment will be $3,000 annually, measured at current prices. For income tax purposes, she will depreciate the equipment using the straight-line method, ignoring the half-year convention. Kelly requires a 10% real rate of return. The annual inflation rate is 5%, and the marginal income tax rate is 30%.

LO1, LO2, LO3, LO5, LO6, LO7

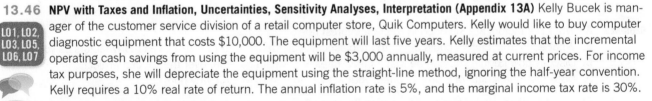

REQUIRED **INFORMATION ANALYSIS**

The following questions will help you analyze the information for this problem. Do not turn in your answers to these questions unless your professor asks you to do so.
A. Create a spreadsheet schedule showing the net present value calculations for the equipment.
B. Identify factors in your calculations that are uncertain and explain why they are uncertain.
C. Explain how changes in technology might influence the risk involved in this project.
D. Decide which of the factors you identified in Part B would likely have a significant impact on the net present value calculation. Use your spreadsheet to vary each of these factors, performing sensitivity analyses.
E. Use the quantitative results and your judgment to interpret your sensitivity analyses. Which factors seem to have the largest and smallest effects on the NPV results?
F. Describe the pros and cons of investing in the equipment.

REQUIRED **WRITTEN ASSIGNMENT**

Suppose you are the cost accountant for Quik Computers. Turn in your answers to the following.
G. Use the information you learned from the preceding analyses to write a memo to Kelly with your recommendation about whether to accept or reject this project. Refer in your memo to one or more attachments of spreadsheet

schedules that would be useful to Kelly. In your memo, address the most important factors that Kelly should consider in making the decision.

13.47 Timeline, Maximum Payment for Zero NPV, Qualitative Factors, Uncertainties The Hotshots are a professional hockey team with a long tradition of winning. However, over the past three years, the team has not won a major championship, and attendance at games has dropped considerably. A large hockey manufacturer is the team's major corporate sponsor. Carl Cliff, president of the hockey company, is also the president of the Hotshots. Cliff proposes that the team purchase the services of a star player, Bob Jackson. Jackson would create great excitement for Hotshots fans and sponsors.

LO2, LO3, LO5

Jackson's agent notifies Cliff that terms for the superstar's signing with the Hotshots are a signing bonus of $8 million payable now and a house in Toronto at a cost of $5 million. The annual salary and cost of living adjustments are under negotiation.

Cliff's initial reaction is one of shock. However, he decides to examine the cash inflows expected if Jackson is signed for a four-year contract. Net gate receipts would most likely increase by $2 million a year, corporate sponsorships would increase $2.5 million per year, television royalties would increase $0.5 million per year, and merchandise income (net of costs) would increase $1 million per year. Cliff believes that a 12% discount rate is appropriate for this investment. The Hotshots' marginal tax rate is 20%. The signing bonus can be depreciated over the four-year period for income tax purposes, providing an annual tax deduction of $2 million.

REQUIRED **A.** Create a timeline that shows the relevant cash flows for this problem.

B. Assuming that he is not willing to lose money on the contract, what is the maximum amount per year that Cliff would be willing to pay Jackson? You will need to set up a spreadsheet for this calculation and through trial and error find an amount that brings the NPV to zero, or you will need to use an algebraic approach and annuity factors.

C. Identify possible additional factors that Cliff should consider when deciding whether to sign Jackson to the four-year contract. List as many factors as you can.

D. For each of the relevant cash flows in this problem, discuss why Cliff cannot be certain about the dollar amount of the cash flow.

13.48 NPV with Taxes and CCA, Qualitative Factors (Appendix 13A) Mr. V is the director of the canoe division of Watertransport Inc. The actual net income and the total assets of the division are, respectively, $500,000 and $2,500,000. Mr. V is evaluated by Watertransport on the return on investment of the division.

LO2, LO3, LO5, LO6, LO7

The canoe division's equipment was purchased six years ago and has an expected useful life of 10 years, with no salvage value at the end of its life. The market value of the equipment is $210,000, but Mr. V wants to replace the equipment with new high-technology equipment that just came out on the market.

This high-technology equipment can be bought for $1,170,000, and Watertransport will incur a cost of $30,000 for installation. The new equipment will have a 10-year useful life, with no salvage value. The division's overhead and direct labour costs will together decrease by $250,000 per year. The company's income tax rate is 35% and its cost of capital is 14%. The CCA rate is 25%.

REQUIRED **A.** Should the company make the investment? Show your calculations and briefly explain your recommendation.

B. Briefly explain how Mr. V's return-on-investment performance will be affected by this investment. Show your calculations.

13.49 NPV, AARR, and Payback Methods Lincoln Community Centre (LCC), a not-for-profit organization, offers many recreational programs for the residents. The directors of the board would like to expand the program offerings for seniors, and are considering purchasing exercise equipment costing $30,000. They plan to use the equipment for 5 years, and sell it for 10% of its original value. The board estimates the new senior exercise program will generate the following revenues from the government subsidy and user fees:

LO2, LO4, LO5

Year 1	$ 6,000
Year 2	9,200
Year 3	11,800
Year 4	14,600
Year 5	18,400

Since LCC would like to encourage senior participation and would like to make sure the program is financially viable, the board has decided not to allocate any fixed costs to the program for the first two years. Starting from the 3rd year, the program has to contribute 50% of its revenue to cover LCC's fixed costs. LCC uses the straight-line depreciation method. LCC's required rate of return is 5%.

REQUIRED **A.** What is the payback period?
B. What is the accrual accounting rate of return, using the average annual income?
C. What is the net present value?
D. Should LCC purchase the exercise equipment and expand the program for seniors? What other non-financial factors should LCC consider?

13.50 **NPV, IRR, AARR, and Payback Methods** JuciCo is considering introducing a new fad toy, Topico. The new product is expected to generate annual revenue of $520,000, with direct materials cost of $182,000, direct labour $156,000, and overhead cost of $104,000. In order to produce Topico, JuciCo will need to purchase new equipment costing $300,000. The equipment will be used for 5 years, as JuciCo expects that interest in the toy will be stopped by then. The equipment will have no residual value after 5 years. To insure a smooth operation, JuciCo expects that the project will increase working capital by $8,000 at the beginning, which will be recovered at the end of the five years. In addition, it will cost JuciCo $8,000 to remove the equipment and clean up the facility. JuciCo's policy is to accept investment projects that have a 3-year payback period. JuciCo's required rate of return is 7%.

LO2, LO3, LO4

REQUIRED **A.** What is the payback period for this investment?
B. What is the net present value for this investment?
C. What is the internal rate of return for this investment?
D. What is the accrual accounting rate of return?
E. Should JuciCo proceed with this project? Please support your recommendation based on your calculations.

13.51 **NPV, IRR, Payback, and Accounting Income** MW Property Management (MW) owns and manages apartment buildings. Each apartment building has a dedicated room for laundry facilities. One of the laundry facilities was equipped with older laundry machines and driers that consume more electricity than the newer ones. These machines were purchased 10 years ago, and they can last for another 10 years. The management is considering replacing these old machines with new energy efficient machines. MW's accountant has gathered the following comparison for the annual expenses:

LO2, LO3, LO4, LO5

Annual Expenses	Old Machines	New Machines
Electricity	$20,000	$12,000
Water	6,000	5,200
Maintenance	4,200	5,800
Depreciation	2,800	4,000

The cost of the old machines was $56,000, and the new machines will cost $40,000. If the new machines are purchased, the old machines can be sold for $3,000 now. Both sets of machines will be disposed of in 10 years, with no residual value then. MW's required rate of return is 6%. In general, MW rejects projects with a payback period greater than 4 years.

REQUIRED **A.** What is the project's payback period?
B. What is the project's net present value?
C. What is the project's internal rate of return?
D. Suppose you are the manager for this specific building, and your performance appraisal for the current year is based on the accounting income. Would you recommend proceeding with this project to replace the machines?
E. Should MW proceed with this project? Please support your recommendation by providing quantitative and qualitative reasons.

13.52 **NPV, Payback Methods, AARR** Fusion Foods manufactures and sells frozen dinners. The packaging machine was acquired 4 years ago for $500,000, and the machine can be used for another 6 years, with a residual value of $40,000. Recently, the machine has broken down quite frequently, which caused bottleneck in production and back orders for many retailers. Many retailers have filed several complaints about unreliable delivery. The annual production and cost information is as follows:

LO2, LO4, LO5

Direct materials	$120,000
Direct labour	270,000
Manufacturing Overhead*	210,000

*Thirty percent of the manufacturing overhead is variable.

A salesperson heard about Fusion's problem and approached Fusion with a new packaging machine costing $624,000, which can last 6 years without any residual value at the end. The new machine will reduce direct materials and direct labour by 25%, and variable manufacturing overhead by 30%. In addition, Fusion will be able to reduce the working capital by $20,000 when the new machine is in operation; however, at the end of the project, $20,000 of working capital will be required. If Fusion replaces the old machine with the new machine, the old machine can be sold for $30,000. Fusion's investment policies include a 5% of required rate of return and a 3-year payback period.

REQUIRED   **A.** What is the net present value for the new packaging machine?

B. What is the payback period?

C. What is accrual accounting rate of return?

D. Should Fusion Foods proceed with the replacement of the new machine? Please support your recommendation by providing quantitative and qualitative reasons.

MINI-CASES

13.53 **Cost-Benefit Analysis, Qualitative Factors, Uncertainties** In 1977, public outcries arose when a memo written by Ford Motor Company executives was published. According to the memo, Ford continued to produce and market the Pinto automobile, even after company crash tests showed that its gas tank would burst into flames when the car was rear-ended at low speeds. The memo indicated that Ford's managers used a cost-benefit analysis to make their decision. The analysis compared the expected benefit of avoiding future lawsuits filed on behalf of burn victims with the expected cost to recall and fix the defective gas tanks.

LO1, LO2, LO3, LO5

Beginning in 1977, automobiles sold in the United States were required to meet new federal standards requiring automobiles to withstand a rear-end collision at 30 miles per hour without causing fire. The Pinto met this standard. However, following publication of the Ford memo, the U.S. media became extremely critical of Ford's actions. This criticism led to an investigation by the U.S. National Highway Transportation Safety Administration (NHTSA), which concluded that the Pinto gas tank represented a safety defect. Ford then recalled 1.4 million Pintos, including 1971–1976 models, which were built before existence of the federal standard.

A few months before the recall, a civil jury in California awarded a burn victim a record $126 million. However, a judge later reduced the award to $6.6 million. Ford was indicted for reckless homicide and criminal recklessness by an Indiana grand jury after the burning death of three teenage girls. In this case, Ford was found not guilty. Overall, Pintos were linked to more than 60 deaths.

Although Ford redesigned the fuel tank for the 1978 Pinto, sales of the model declined 45% from 1977 sales. Ford ultimately dropped the Pinto brand. Over the next decade, sales of Japanese automobiles continued to increase, causing a long-term decline in the sale of automobiles by Ford and other U.S. manufacturers. Many consumers perceived Japanese automobiles as being higher quality than U.S. autos. U.S. automobile companies were often viewed as callous and unconcerned about safety, reliability, and fuel efficiency.

In a 1998 analysis, University of Delaware sociology and criminal justice professor Matthew T. Lee pointed out that the Pinto case occurred during a time of change in federal safety regulation and public expectation. He revealed that cost-benefit analyses had commonly been used by managers of automobile companies as well as NHTSA. His research indicated that NHTSA's conclusions in the Pinto case represented two important deviations from prior regulatory practice. First, during its investigation, it held the Ford Pinto to a level of performance that was more stringent than existing federal safety guidelines. Second, NHTSA staff used the societal value of human life, rather than the commonly used average corporate payout, in their cost-benefit analysis. In addition, NHTSA staff had focused their investigation on Ford because of the public outcry over the Pinto. Other automobile companies were not held to the same safety standards.

Sources: M. Lee, "The Ford Pinto Case and the Development of Auto Safety Regulations, 1893–1978," *Business and Economic History*, Winter 1998, pp. 390–402; and D. Winter, "Together Again in the Headlines," *Ward's Auto World*, October 2000, pp. 57–58.

REQUIRED   **A.** Had you previously heard about the gas tank problems of the Ford Pinto? If so:

1. Describe your previous impressions of the Pinto problem.

2. In what ways do these impressions create potential biases as you address this case?

B. Identify several ethical issues in this case—in other words, areas of conflicts of interest between stakeholders.

C. What were the opportunity costs (qualitative and quantitative) that were apparently overlooked by Ford's managers in valuing the cost of fixing the gas tanks during their cost-benefit analysis?

D. Ford's managers measured the potential benefit of eliminating the gas tank problems by using the expected future cost of settling lawsuits filed on behalf of burn victims. NHTSA used the societal value of human life in its cost-benefit analysis. Explain how these measures are different, and describe the pros and cons of using each measure when analyzing the Pinto problem. Take into account the viewpoints of the following different stakeholders:

- Pinto crash victims and their families
- Pinto owners
- Potential Pinto owners
- Customers of other Ford vehicles
- General public
- NHTSA staff members
- Ford's managers
- Ford's employees
- Ford's shareholders
- Ford's domestic competitors
- Ford's Japanese competitors

E. What values did Ford's managers appear to use in reaching their decision to continue selling the Pinto with its existing gas tank design? Were these values reasonable under the circumstances? Why or why not?

F. What values did NHTSA staff appear to use in drawing their conclusions? Were these values reasonable under the circumstances? Why or why not?

13.54 **NPV with Taxes, Sensitivity Analysis, Minimum Volume, Minimum Selling Price** The managers of Favourite Fish are

LO2, LO3 considering a new project in which they would purchase equipment to produce canned sardines. You are to perform capital budgeting computations relating to this project.

A spreadsheet template developed to analyze the Favourite Fish decision is available at www.wiley.com/go/ eldenburgcanada. Notice that the first part of the spreadsheet computes the NPV of a project, given the information from the input box at the top of the spreadsheet. The lower portion of the spreadsheet computes the price necessary for the project to have an NPV of zero. You will manipulate the data in the data entry box as you alter

www.wiley.com/go/ eldenburgcanada

the underlying assumptions of the analysis. For example, you can change the discount rate but leave all the other information as it is in the original template. Each time you begin a new analysis, you should return to the original template values.

REQUIRED **A.** What is the NPV of the project if the discount rate is 15%?

B. What is the NPV of the project if the tax rate goes down to 30%?

C. What is the NPV if the cost of the equipment increases to $120,000?

D. What is the minimum price that must be charged to make this project acceptable, given that 10,000 cases must be sold?

E. What is the NPV of the project if 12,000 cases are sold at $5.50 per case and variable costs remain unchanged?

F. What is the NPV of the project if variable costs increase to $2.75?

G. What is the NPV of the project if variable costs increase to $2.75 and the marginal tax rate declines to 30%?

H. What is the NPV of the project if variable costs increase to $2.75, the marginal tax rate declines to 30%, and the marginal discount rate is 24%?

I. What is the minimum price that Favourite Fish must charge to make this project acceptable if the marginal tax rate becomes 50%?

J. What is the minimum price to make the project acceptable if only 9,000 cases are sold?

K. What is the minimum price if 8,000 cases are sold, the discount rate is 14%, and the tax rate is 30%?

L. To help managers perform sensitivity analysis, it is useful to gather information about competitors' prices, current and future economic factors, and any other relevant information. Where could you find information that would help you or a manager decide on the values to use for this type of sensitivity analysis?

13.55 **Integrating Across the Curriculum—Finance:** *Weighted average cost of capital, estimation problems* The weighted

LO2, LO3, LO4, LO5, LO6 average cost of capital is the weighted average rate for the costs of the various sources of financing in an organization. These sources for Tudor Industries are as follows:

Source of Capital	Market Value	Cost
Short-term debt	$300,000	8%
Bonds	900,000	6%
Leases	200,000	7%
Common shares	900,000	10%

The short-term debt represents revolving credit, which is periodically renewed. Income taxes average 25%.

REQUIRED **A.** Calculate the weighted average cost of capital (WACC) for Tudor Industries. If you need a formula, use a finance textbook or conduct an Internet search for "weighted average cost of capital." One website that provides a formula is www.investopedia.com/terms/w/wacc.asp.

B. Explain how and why income taxes affect the calculation of WACC.

C. Discuss uncertainties about the best measure to use for the discount rate in a capital budgeting problem.

D. Discuss the pros and cons of using WACC as a discount rate in capital budgeting.

E. The market value for each source of capital is used when calculating WACC. Suppose you work for Tudor and need to calculate its WACC, but you do not know the market values. Describe possible ways that you could estimate the market value for each of Tudor's sources of capital.

F. Some people use financial statement book values to calculate WACC. Discuss reasons why this approach might result in an inappropriate value for WACC.

14

Pricing Decisions

in brief Managers and accountants make decisions about long-term organizational strategies as well as short-term operating plans. These strategies and plans include mutually dependent decisions about how to control costs and price products to generate profits and achieve organizational goals. To be successful, managers must understand their competitive position, costs, and both internal and external suppliers and customers. Understanding cost measurements and pricing methods and their interrelationships helps managers make these pricing decisions. In large organizations, resources may be transferred internally from one department to another, and the prices set for these transfers also affect financial measures of performance. When these transfer prices are set appropriately, managers have incentives to increase the value of the overall organization. However, transfer prices can encourage suboptimal decisions that may be beneficial at the local level but are not in the best interests of the whole organization. ■

After studying this chapter, you should be able to do the following:

LO1	Compare the different pricing methods and calculate prices using each method
LO2	Discuss other market-based sources of pricing information
LO3	Explain the uses and limitations of cost-based and market-based pricing
LO4	Explain price elasticity of demand and its impact on pricing
LO5	Discuss the additional factors that affect prices
LO6	Compare the different pricing methods used for transferring goods and services within an organization
LO7	Discuss the uses and limitations of different transfer pricing methods
LO8	Discuss additional factors that affect transfer prices

Video Game Consoles: The Big 3 Battle It Out for Top Spot

© True Images/Alamy Stock Photo

The video gaming industry has experienced a three-way battle between **Microsoft's** Xbox, **Sony's** PlayStation (PS), and **Nintendo's** Wii.

When Wii launched in 2006, it took the market by surprise as it became almost an instant best seller, with its unique motion-sensing device and significantly lower cost. Both Sony and Microsoft had to respond with price cuts and deals to stimulate their market share. Both manufacturers slashed the prices of their units by up to 20%, which did improve sales. The price they could charge was limited by the competition. Given the huge investments in research, product design, and advertising, it is often a difficult decision for a manager of a losing video game system to decide to invest further in a product. So far, the three manufacturers have decided to continue in the race to develop the next generation of console with more features at a lower price.

With the three consoles now firmly entrenched, the manufacturers constantly come up with promotions to boost their market share. For example, in late 2015, the Xbox One and PS4 were up to 30% cheaper than when they originally launched. At that time, sales of Wii had fallen to third place. The PS4 was by far the market leader, with 29.3 million units sold since it was launched, followed by the Xbox One at just over 14 million consoles, and the Wii U at 10.5 million.

The video game console market is massive, with hardware sales of more than U.S. $190 million in the month of August 2015 alone. But more than that, video game console manufacturers rely on income from software sales to subsidize hardware costs, especially in the early years of a new console design. Because there are so many game creators, getting an industry sales total is difficult.

Industry speculators wonder whether physical standalone game consoles like the PS, Xbox, and Wii will survive the rise of cloud gaming services, games available on mobile devices, and games available on Apple TV and other big-screen devices.

SOURCES: S. Schneider, "Sony Has Sold 29 Million PlayStation 4 Consoles in Less than Two Years," Tech Times, November 2, 2015; S. Stein, "Gaming on the New Apple TV: First Impressions and Where It Can Go from Here," CNET.com, October 31, 2015; K. Stuart, "Is Now the Right Time to Buy a New Video Game Console?," The Guardian, October 5, 2015; C. Pereira, "PS4 Comes Out on Top in NPD's August 2015 US Sales Report," Gamespot.com, September 10, 2015; J. Davison, "PlayStation, Xbox, Wii U: Which Will Survive?" Gamespot.com, January 13, 2012; N. Wingfield and Y. Iwantani Kane, "Sony PlayStation 3 Revival Lifts Result," The Wall Street Journal (Eastern Edition), May 15, 2008, p. B1.

Pricing Methods

The link between costs, prices (revenues), and profits has become increasingly important with global competition. Managers and accountants must simultaneously manage both costs and revenues to successfully generate profits. Successful companies continuously improve their cost efficiency, charge competitive prices, respond to customer preferences, and focus on long-term organizational strategies.

Determining appropriate prices for an organization's products or services is an important activity, because pricing decisions have both short- and long-term consequences. The competition between products indicates that, even in markets with few competitors, prices are often based on competitors' prices, not just on production costs.

As indicated in Exhibit 14.1, pricing methods need to consider production costs, market factors, and customer expectations. The starting point for any pricing analysis depends on the goods produced or service provided and the market conditions in which the organization operates.

Cost-Based Pricing

Cost-based prices are determined by adding a mark-up to some calculation of the product's cost. To apply this method, a cost base is selected and a mark-up rate is calculated. The cost base can be calculated in several ways. Some organizations use variable cost as the base, whereas others use an average cost that includes both variable and fixed costs of production (absorption cost), and yet others use a total cost (production costs plus marketing and administration costs). Organizations frequently rely on mark-ups they have used for many years. Such mark-ups often originate from general industry practice and may be found in trade journals. For example, clothing retailers typically price using a 100% mark-up on their variable costs. If a retailer pays $10 per blouse to the wholesaler, the variable cost per blouse is $10, and the blouse would be priced at $20 ($10 cost plus 100% mark-up of another $10). Mark-up percentages are also calculated so that the organization earns a target rate of return on investment. Given differences in calculation methods and cost structures, cost-based prices vary a great deal across organizations.

> **EXHIBIT 14.1**
Pricing Considerations

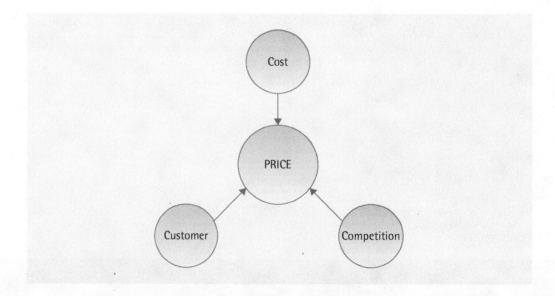

van truen nurseries
COMPARING COST-BASED PRICING APPROACHES

Van Truen Nurseries is a family-owned wholesale nursery specializing in providing mums to regional retailers. During the winter, the owners start new plants from seed and nurture them into the traditional 6-inch potted plants sold at retail greenhouses. The variable costs of production include the seeds, the potting soil, the 6-inch (15-cm) pots, fertilizer, and labour costs at a total of $2.50 per 6-inch plant. The fixed costs are those costs associated with maintaining the greenhouse, growing benches, tools, and hoses. Total fixed costs per year are $175,000. The Van Truens have a $1,500,000 investment in the greenhouse itself and desire an 8% return on their investment. Although sales of mums are seasonal, some effort and, therefore, cost is incurred throughout the year to maintain customers and cultivate new customers. The fixed costs associated with these selling activities are $60,000 per year and are predominantly salary-related costs. The variable costs associated with selling and shipping the mums are $1.75 per 6-inch plant. Annual volume totals 500,000 6-inch potted mums.

©jim plumb/iStockphoto

Alternative One: Variable Costing Approach

Assuming that the Van Truens use cost-based pricing and have decided to use variable costs as their cost base, we can calculate the mark-up percentage necessary to achieve their return on investment goal of 8% as follows:

$$\text{Mark-up percentage} = \frac{\text{Desired return on investment} + \text{Fixed costs}}{\text{Variable cost per unit} \times \text{Annual volume}}$$

$$= \frac{(8\% \times \$1,500,000) + (\$175,000 + \$60,000)}{(\$2.50/\text{plant} + \$1.75/\text{plant}) \times 500,000 \text{ plants}}$$

$$= \frac{\$120,000 + \$175,000 + \$60,000}{\$2,125,000}$$

$$= 16.71\%$$

Using this mark-up percentage, the Van Truen family would set their selling price as follows:

$$\begin{aligned}
\text{Selling price} &= \text{Variable costs} + (\text{Variable costs} \times \text{Mark-up \%}) \\
&= \text{Variable costs} \times (1 + \text{Mark-up \%}) \\
&= (\$2.50/\text{plant} + \$1.75/\text{plant}) \times (1 + 0.1671) \\
&= \$4.25/\text{plant} \times 1.1671 \\
&= \$4.96/\text{plant}
\end{aligned}$$

The variable costing approach is consistent with cost-volume-profit analysis and the general assumptions in management decision making—it draws attention to the fixed costs of being in business versus those costs that change with volume produced and sold.

Alternative Two: Absorption Costing Approach

If the Van Truens use absorption costing as their cost base, then the calculation of the mark-up percentage necessary to achieve their 8% return on investment goal is as follows:

$$\text{Mark-up percentage} = \frac{\text{Desired return on investment} + \text{Selling \& administrative costs}}{\text{Absorption cost per unit} \times \text{Annual volume}}$$

$$= \frac{(8\% \times \$1,500,000) + (\$60,000 + (\$1.75 \times 500,000))}{(\$2.50 + (\$175,000/500,000)) \times 500,000 \text{ plants}}$$

$$= \frac{\$120,000 + \$60,000 + \$875,000}{(\$2.50/\text{plant} + \$0.35/\text{plant}) \times 500,000 \text{ plants}}$$

$$= \frac{\$1,055,000}{\$1,425,000}$$

$$= 74.03\%$$

continued...

example

Using this mark-up percentage, the Van Truen family would set their selling price as follows:

$$
\begin{aligned}
\text{Selling price} &= \text{Absorption costs} + (\text{Absorption costs} \times \text{Mark-up \%}) \\
&= \text{Absorption costs} \times (1 + \text{Mark-up \%}) \\
&= (\$2.50/\text{plant} + \$0.35/\text{plant}) \times (1 + 0.7403) \\
&= \$2.85/\text{plant} \times 1.7403 \\
&= \$4.96/\text{plant}
\end{aligned}
$$

The absorption approach is consistent with external financial reporting—it is the same cost basis used for preparation of formal financial statements.

Alternative Three: Total Cost Approach

If the Van Truen family uses total cost as the cost base, the mark-up percentage and selling price are calculated as follows:

$$
\text{Mark-up percentage} = \frac{\text{Desired return on investment}}{\text{Total cost per unit} \times \text{Annual volume}}
$$

$$
= \frac{(8\% \times \$1,500,000)}{\left[(\$2.50/\text{plant} + \$1.75/\text{plant}) + \dfrac{(\$175,000 + \$60,000)}{500,000 \text{ plants}} \right] \times 500,000 \text{ plants}}
$$

$$
= \frac{\$120,000}{\left[\$4.25/\text{plant} + \dfrac{\$235,000}{500,000 \text{ plants}} \right] \times 500,000 \text{ plants}}
$$

$$
= \frac{\$120,000}{\$4.72/\text{plant} \times 500,000 \text{ plants}}
$$

$$
= 5.08\%
$$

Using this mark-up percentage, the Van Truen family would set their selling price as follows:

$$
\begin{aligned}
\text{Selling price} &= \text{Total costs} + (\text{Total costs} \times \text{Mark-up \%}) \\
&= \text{Total costs} \times (1 + \text{Mark-up \%}) \\
&= \$4.72/\text{plant} \times (1 + 0.0508) \\
&= \$4.72/\text{plant} \times 1.0508 \\
&= \$4.96/\text{plant}
\end{aligned}
$$

Notice that all of the alternative cost bases result in the same selling price; all of the alternatives cover all of the costs. The difference between these alternatives is the calculated mark-up percentage, which differs because of where in each calculation each cost is covered. The variable cost approach recognizes that fixed costs are unavoidable costs of being in business and must be covered collectively. The absorption cost approach allocates the fixed production costs to each product, recognizes selling and administrative costs separate from production costs, and is consistent with the cost accounting systems discussed in chapters 5 and 6. The total cost approach allocates all costs of being in business to the product. For Van Truen Nurseries, a single product business, this approach recognizes that each 6-inch potted mum must contribute to covering not only the variable costs of production but to all of the fixed costs as well. In a multiple product business, the total cost approach requires allocation of these unavoidable costs of being in business. As discussed in prior chapters, these allocations may adversely affect management decision making. In the pricing decision, if the allocation of unavoidable costs is too high, the selling price will be too high and there will be lost sales. If the allocation of unavoidable costs is too low, the selling price will be too low and sales may soar but profits will not achieve desired levels. The allocation of overhead was discussed in Chapter 7 and cost–volume–profit analysis of a sales mix was discussed in Chapter 3. ∎

▷ **ALTERNATIVE TERMS**
As mentioned in Chapter 1, *avoidable (incremental) cash flows* are relevant because they can be avoided depending on the course of action taken. Conversely, *unavoidable cash flows* are not relevant.

Time and Material Pricing

In service organizations, cost-based pricing is determined by calculating a labour rate and a materials loading charge. The labour rate includes (1) direct labour salaries plus benefits, (2) selling and administrative costs and related overhead costs, and (3) a desired profit amount. The materials loading charge includes (1) all costs associated with purchasing, receiving, handling, and storing materials; and (2) a desired profit percentage.

r & s automotive
CALCULATING SERVICE CHARGES USING TIME AND MATERIAL PRICING

example

Robert and Steven own and operate R & S Automotive, a Volkswagen restoration and repair shop. Their business consists of restoring older-model Volkswagen Beetles and servicing these cars. R & S Automotive uses a time and material pricing system when billing customers for work done on their VW Beetles. Costs in the past year were as follows:

Technicians' salaries and benefits	$240,000	4,000 hours
Selling, administrative, and related overhead costs	$ 20,000	
Materials invoice costs	$560,000	1,500 invoices
Purchasing, receiving, handling, and storing parts costs	$ 36,000	

©Michael Luhrenberg/iStockphoto

Robert and Steven know that a profit of $10 per hour of technician time and a 25% profit margin on materials are the industry standards for this type of specialty work.

Time per labour hour:
To calculate the time charges (labour rate), R & S Automotive adds the technicians' salaries and benefits to the selling, administrative, and related overhead costs. They divide this total by the expected number of hours to be worked. Finally, they add the desired industry average profit of $10 per hour to arrive at the labour rate they will use to calculate each customer's bill.

$$\text{Labour rate} = ([\text{Labour costs} + \text{Selling, administrative, and overhead costs}]$$
$$\div \text{Labour hours}) + \text{Profit}$$
$$= (\$260,000 \div 4,000) + \$10$$
$$= \$75$$

Materials loading charge:
To calculate the materials loading charge, R & S Automotive divides the purchasing, receiving, handling, and storage costs by the materials invoice costs. The resulting percentage is added to the industry average profit margin for parts. To calculate material costs for each customer, R & S will add the parts invoice amount and the materials loading charge, which is calculated by multiplying the parts invoice costs by the materials loading charge.

$$\text{Materials loading charge} = (\text{Purchasing, receiving, handling, and storing parts costs}$$
$$\div \text{Invoice costs}) + \text{Profit margin \%}$$
$$= (\$36,000 \div \$560,000) + 25\%$$
$$= 6.5\% + 25\%$$
$$= 31.5\% \text{ (rounded up)}$$

A customer, Henry, brings his 1971 VW Beetle to R & S Automotive for an oil change and tune up. To calculate Henry's bill, we must first know the number of hours it will take to complete the work. R & S charge 2 hours of labour for an oil change and tune up. Next, we must know the invoice cost for the needed parts. The tune up will require 4 spark plugs at $3 each, 2.5 litres of oil at $20,

continued...

example

points and a condenser at $20, and an air filter for $6. The total materials invoice costs is $58. We calculate the bill as follows:

Labour costs	2 hours × $75 =	$ 150.00
Materials invoice costs		$58.00
Materials loading charge	$58 × 31.5% =	$18.27
Total materials charges		$ 76.27
Total bill		$ 226.27

Notice that in determining its pricing formula, R & S Automotive has covered its costs and considered the industry averages. These averages are determined by factoring in the competitions' prices and a long-term history of the amounts customers are willing to pay for the specialty services being offered. ■

Market-Based Pricing

High quality and brand name are likely to be as important, if not more important, than price for specialty product companies like a custom home builder. Accordingly, a cost-based pricing scheme might not maximize profits. As company managers make pricing decisions, they need to understand competitors' prices; however, they should also consider each buyer's ability and willingness to pay for the product. To maximize profits, a specialty product company should charge the highest price possible but not such a high price that the customer buys from a competitor or decides not to buy the product (e.g., the home).

Market-based prices are determined using some measure of customer demand. Under market-based pricing, managers strive to identify what customers are willing to pay for a good or service. As illustrated in Exhibit 14.2, market prices are influenced by the degree of product differentiation and competition.

At one extreme, organizations face many competitors and cannot differentiate their products. In this case, the market price is the commodity price that customers would pay to any organization offering the good or service. For example, farmers typically sell agricultural products at a quoted market price. The same is true for mining companies selling gold or silver. In such cases, managers estimate prices by referring to published rates.

At the other extreme are monopolies that sell unique goods or services and have no competition. Monopolies such as residential water services are often owned or regulated by the government. In these cases, the organization is not allowed to establish a free market price but must charge the regulated price. Occasionally, short-term monopolies arise; for example, the only store in town with snow shovels after a blizzard can theoretically charge as much as the market will bear, until competitors receive shovel shipments. Most goods and services fall between these two extremes. Organizations can typically differentiate their product in the market because features and brand names are important. However, these organizations are subject to competition, which must be considered when setting prices. To set prices, an organization estimates consumer demand for product characteristics such as quality and functionality.

▶EXHIBIT 14.2

Market Prices, Product Differentiation, and Degree of Competition

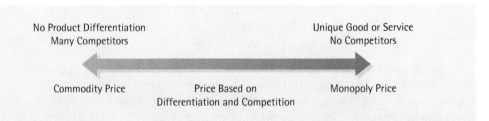

Other Market-Based Pricing Methods

Companies sometimes use competitors' prices to establish their own market prices. For common products in retail settings, competitors' prices are easily observed. However, it may be difficult to learn about competitors' prices when fewer transactions occur or they are made in nonretail settings.

LO2 | Discuss other market-based sources of pricing information

The Internet makes it possible to learn about market prices for items that were previously difficult to value, as websites such as e-Bay, Bidz, Yahoo!, and Amazon provide information on prices. Given the large range of products and prices that are readily available, these sites increase the consistency of prices, even for objects such as antiques. Because increasing numbers of organizations include product and service price information on their websites, the Internet also makes it easier for managers to monitor competitors' prices.

The Internet is likely to cause prices to become more elastic, because close substitutes are more easily found and priced. The Internet also increases the global reach of many companies. Together, the Internet and global competition have forced an increasingly large number of organizations to use market-based pricing.

Cost-Based Versus Market-Based Pricing

A major drawback of cost-based pricing is that it ignores customer demand. Prices are likely to be higher or lower than what customers are willing to pay for goods or services. For example, Motorola based the price of its global cellular phones on costs rather than by surveying the market for a competitive price. This decision resulted first in prices for the phone and calling rates that were higher than customers would pay, and it eventually contributed to the bankruptcy of the entire project. In other situations, cost-based prices are too low, and organizations forgo potential profits.

LO3 | Explain the uses and limitations of cost-based and market-based pricing

With cost-based prices, sales volumes inappropriately influence the price, causing a downward demand spiral, known as the death spiral. If production decreases because demand has decreased, then the average product cost increases and the price based on that average cost increases. When the product has an elastic demand curve, price increases cause sales to decline even more. This decline, in turn, causes average cost to increase even further, producing more price increases and more sales deterioration. This pattern persists until the product is discontinued because it cannot cover its costs.[1]

Despite these disadvantages, cost-based pricing is a commonly used method for setting at least an initial price. Surveys of manufacturers consistently report that they prefer to mark up an average cost that includes a portion of fixed cost, using a mark-up system based on desired return.[2] This preference might reflect the fact that it was difficult in the past for companies' information systems to gather the data needed to calculate profit-maximizing sales prices. The major benefit of using cost-based pricing is its simplicity. Prices are calculated from readily available cost data.

Using market-based prices to estimate revenues, managers make better decisions about sales volumes or whether to sell goods or services, leading to more success in organizational strategies. The disadvantage is that estimating market demand and prices is often difficult. However, more sophisticated information systems make it easier for managers to estimate demand, marginal costs, and revenues, leading to an increasing trend in the use of market-based pricing.

[1] S. Finkelstein and S. H. Sanford, "Learning from Corporate Mistakes: The Rise and Fall of Iridium," *Organizational Dynamics* 29, no. 2 (2000), pp. 138–148; J. N. Sheth and R. Sisodia, "Manager's Journal: Why Cell Phones Succeeded Where Iridium Failed," *The Wall Street Journal*, August 23, 1999, p. A14; I. Smolowitz, "Iridium: Lessons for all Companies," *Business Forum*, 24, no. 1/2 (2000), pp. 37–38; and J. Schack, "Iridium Splashes Down," *Institutional Investor*, January 2000, p. 98.
[2] E. Shim and E. Sudit, "How Manufacturers Price Products," *Management Accounting*, February 1995, 76, 8, pp. 37–39.

Price Elasticity

L04 Explain price elasticity of demand and its impact on pricing

Organizations with differentiated products can formally or informally incorporate consumer demand into their pricing policies. For example, contractors who build expensive houses often negotiate prices with individual buyers. The negotiations continue throughout the construction period, when unforeseen costs arise or when the home buyer makes choices for things like carpeting and wall coverings that are more expensive than anticipated. A more formal way to incorporate demand into prices is through the price elasticity of demand.

Profit-Maximizing Price

> **BUSINESS PRACTICE**
>
> There is a direct correlation between cigarette prices and the number of people under 18 years old who are moderate to below-moderate smokers. With information in hand, the federal and provincial governments have used tobacco tax hikes to deter children from trying or continuing smoking.[3]

For normal goods, as prices increase, demand usually falls (and as price decreases demand usually increases). This sensitivity of sales to price increases is called the **price elasticity of demand**. When small increases in price result in large decreases in demand, the demand for that product is considered elastic. Cigarettes are an example of a product for which changes in price have a substantial effect on sales; that is, demand is elastic. In contrast, customized homes are a product with relatively inelastic demand. Price changes have little effect on demand, and factors such as quality and the ability to customize are more important, within limits, than price. Price elasticity of demand is measured on a continuous scale, with larger numbers representing increasingly elastic demand for a product. The calculation of the price elasticity of demand for normal goods typically results in a negative number. The negative sign is usually ignored; that is, the absolute value of the number is interpreted based on the assumption that there is an inverse relationship between quantity demanded and price. Products with price elasticity numbers less than one are considered to have very inelastic demand. Understanding price elasticity of demand helps managers develop prices that will maximize contribution margin for a given level of fixed costs; thereby, maximizing profits.

In economic terms, the profit-maximizing price occurs when marginal costs equal marginal revenues. To develop a price that maximizes profit, we must have some information about how changes in price will affect the demand for a product. With this information, we can calculate the price elasticity of demand. Using the price elasticity of demand, we can determine a profit-maximizing price and a mark-up percentage for the product. The steps for these calculations are shown in Exhibit 14.3.

The first step is to calculate the price elasticity of demand. To perform this calculation, we need data to calculate the percentage change in quantity that occurs for a percentage change in price. These data are usually available in the accounting (sales) records. The second step is to determine the profit-maximizing price, a calculation that is based on the strong

> **EXHIBIT 14.3**
> Computing the Profit-Maximizing Price

Step 1: Calculate the price elasticity of demand:

$$\text{Elasticity} = \frac{\ln(1 + \% \text{ change in quantity sold})}{\ln(1 + \% \text{ change in price})}$$

where ln is the mathematical function for natural logarithm.

Step 2: Calculate the profit-maximizing price:[a]

$$\text{Profit-maximizing price} = \left[\frac{\text{Elasticity}}{(\text{Elasticity} + 1)}\right] \times \text{Variable cost}$$

[a] The profit-maximizing mark-up formula is $\left[\frac{\text{Elasticity}}{(\text{Elasticity} + 1)} - 1\right]$. We add 1 to the mark-up before we multiply it by variable cost to determine the profit-maximizing price.

[3] Euromonitor International, *Tobacco in Canada*, www.euromonitor.com/Tobacco_in_Canada.

assumption that changes in volume result *only* from changes in price. This assumption is never completely true, however, so the profit-maximizing price and the mark-up amount need to be interpreted with caution; they only provide guidance about pricing decisions.

These calculations are based on information about prices, sales volumes, and variable costs. Two factors affect the profit-maximizing price: (1) changes in the product's demand sensitivity to price and (2) changes in variable costs. Information about fixed costs is irrelevant in this calculation. The following example shows how these calculations help a company set prices.

©pavelis/iStockphoto

parfum boutique
USING PRICE ELASTICITY TO CALCULATE PRODUCT PRICES

example

Parfum Boutique produces two perfumes: Printemps and Amour de Nuit. Printemps is a well-known, inexpensive perfume, and its customers are sensitive to price. Several competitors market similar products, and close substitutes are available at discount drug and department stores. Amour de Nuit is a customized perfume sold only in small boutique stores, where few substitutes are available and where customers are less sensitive to price. Parfum Boutique's accountant, Normand, needs to develop pricing guidelines for management. He performs the following analysis.

Profit-Maximizing Prices for Printemps and Amour de Nuit

Normand calculates the variable cost of Printemps as $2 per 5 mL and $10 per 5 mL for Amour de Nuit. Based on information from historical accounting records, he believes that every 10% increase in price for Printemps results in a decrease in sales of 20% because customers for this product are so price sensitive. He calculates the price elasticity for Printemps as -2.34 $[\ln(1-0.2) \div \ln(1+0.1)]$, which indicates a more elastic demand. In turn, he uses the elasticity to calculate a profit-maximizing price per 5 mL of $3.50 $\{[-2.34 \div (-2.34+1)] \times \$2\}$.

Normand estimates that for every 10% increase in price, sales of Amour de Nuit will decrease only 12%. He calculates the price elasticity of demand for Amour de Nuit as -1.34 $[\ln(1-0.12) \div \ln(1+0.1)]$, which indicates a more inelastic demand. The profit-maximizing price per 5 mL is then $39.40 $\{[-1.34 \div (-1.34+1)] \times \$10\}$. According to these calculations, the mark-up for Printemps is 75%, and the mark-up for Amour de Nuit is 294%. Amour de Nuit's demand is less sensitive to price changes than Printemps' (indicated by the lower price elasticity of demand), so Normand knows that Amour de Nuit's demand is more inelastic. Products or services with inelastic demand have higher optimal mark-ups than products or services with more elastic demand.

Market Price Guidelines

When Normand presents his calculations to managers, he cautions them about this information. Although the calculations seem precise, they should be interpreted only as guidelines for price setting, not as absolute determinants of price. He warns them that, as with other decisions, the managers need to consider uncertainties when making pricing decisions. For example, measurement error may occur in collecting information about how price changes affect sales. He explains to the managers that these formulas are extremely sensitive to errors, and small changes in assumptions have a large effect on the calculations. Also, price elasticity can vary over time due to changes in competitor prices and customer preferences. Managers need to anticipate and monitor for changes in product demand.

Normand also explains the following assumptions underlying his calculations:

- The price elasticity of demand is constant.
- The variable cost is constant.
- The product price has no effect on other product costs or sales.

The managers know that these assumptions may not always hold, so they decide to make small incremental changes to prices and then track profitability and sales volume to refine the profit-maximizing price. ■

Estimating the Effect of Prices on Demand

Accountants use historical information to estimate the effects of price changes on sales volume. Some organizations might rely on price elasticity information published by their industries. Other organizations use optical scanners to capture historical price and volume data. The quality of this type of information improves as sales volumes increase. Companies can rapidly gather data and monitor relationships between price and volume. They can also analyze how sales behave for groups of products. For example, grocery stores often sell some products as "loss leaders," lowering the price on a specific product to bring customers into the store. In these cases, managers assume that increases in sales of other products will more than make up for the forgone profit from the loss leader.

The quality of product demand estimates based on historical data depend in part on sales volumes. Large retailers collect large amounts of sales data and conduct price experiments to learn more about how volumes respond to price changes. Organizations with lower sales volumes also collect sales and price data but less of it, and they are, therefore, likely to face more error in their estimates of product demand.

> ▶ **BUSINESS PRACTICE**
>
> Industry analysts estimate that no more than 150 retailers worldwide are using price-optimization software. Most of these companies do not freely talk about the profit gains because the limited use of this software is considered a competitive advantage. However, contrary to popular belief, the software does not always recommend a price cut to move product out of inventory. Managers at **ALDO Group Inc.**, a Canadian shoe company with stores worldwide, found out by using the software that they should hold the price of their more expensive sneaker constant and that it would sell by the specified target date.[4]

14-1 self-study problem   Cost-Based and Market-Based Prices, Minimum Acceptable Price

The OK Feed Store packages and distributes three grades of animal feed. The material costs per tonne and estimated annual sales for each of the products are listed here:

Product	Material Cost	Estimated Sales
Super Premium	$16.00	1,000 tonnes
Premium	$12.00	1,500 tonnes
Economy	$10.00	2,500 tonnes

The fixed cost of operating the machinery used to package all three products is $20,000 per year. In the past, prices have been set by allocating the fixed overhead to products on the basis of estimated sales in tonnes. The resulting total costs (material costs plus allocated fixed overhead) are then marked up by 100%.

required

A. Determine the price per tonne for each grade of feed, using the method described for setting prices.
B. Does the price in Part A take into account how much customers are willing to pay for the product? Explain.
C. Suppose a 10% increase in price would result in about a 40% decrease in the amount of the economy-grade feed sold. Estimate the price that would maximize profits on the economy-grade feed.
D. Explain how the price for economy-grade feed calculated in Part C should be used.
E. Suppose a foreign distributor would like to buy 200 tonnes of economy-grade feed and has offered to pay $2,400 for the special order.
   1. What is the relevant cost to OK Feed for this order?
   2. Considering only quantitative factors, what is the minimum acceptable price per tonne?

See the solution on page 649.

---

[4] B. Bergstein, "Pricing Software Could Reshape Retail," April 29, 2007, www.usatoday.com/tech/products/2007-04-29-2437158859_x.htm.

Additional Pricing Considerations

Regardless of the general technique used, a number of other factors influence prices for individual organizations or in specific circumstances.

LO5 Discuss the additional factors that affect prices

Other Influences on Price

Some industries charge different prices at different times to reduce capacity constraints, a practice called **peak load pricing**. For example, movie theatres charge less for movies shown early in the day than for movies shown in the evening. Telephone companies often charge less for calls made at night or on the weekend than for peak-time calls. In the airline industry, a variety of prices are offered to customers based on factors such as advance ticket purchase, whether the customer is willing to include a weekend-night stay, and whether the customer wants preferential seating and other services. During economic downturns, even organizations with set prices may negotiate with customers.

Price skimming occurs when a higher price is charged for a product or service when it is first introduced than later on. The term refers to the practice of skimming the cream off the market. When new technology is introduced (e.g., notepads that transcribe handwriting to word processing), high prices are charged to cover the initial research and development costs. Prices are then reduced as competitors enter the market.

Penetration pricing is the practice of setting low prices when new products are introduced, to increase market share. Penetration pricing is legal if its intent is to reduce customer uncertainty about product or service value. However, if the purpose is to eliminate competition, then it could be considered predatory pricing, which is illegal in Canada.

Sometimes managers take advantage of unusual circumstances to increase prices. **Price gouging** is the practice of charging a price viewed by consumers as too high. If managers can convince consumers that prices are based on costs, they avoid being labelled as price gougers.

Pricing in Not-for-Profit Organizations

Not-for-profit organizations are concerned with many objectives besides profit maximization. Their pricing methods tend to be more complex than those used by for-profit organizations. Grants, donations, and interest from endowed funds often help defray the cost of products and services. Because of these sources of funds, not-for-profits do not always expect to recover all their costs from prices or fees they charge.

Some not-for-profit organizations charge a fee based on a client's income. This fee is called a *sliding-scale fee*; as client income decreases, the fee decreases, while clients who can afford to pay more are charged more. Other not-for-profits charge high prices to everyone but then provide free services for low-income clients or discount the charges to selected clients. For example, youth sports organizations often offer reduced registration rates to families with three or more children participating. The result is that registration costs for other families tend to be inflated. Some not-for-profit organizations use price-setting policies to achieve organizational goals. For example, many universities offer grants and scholarships to students with high school averages of 85% and above in selected classes. Their goal is to improve the quality of incoming students. A stronger student body enhances these schools' reputations and may in turn increase the number of applicants and the amount of financial contributions from alumni.

Government Regulations and Pricing

Organizations are not free to establish any price they wish; some pricing practices are illegal. In Canada, illegal pricing practices are regulated under the Competition Act and include conspiracies that unduly lessen competition (e.g., price fixing), bid rigging, price maintenance, price discrimination, predatory pricing, and dumping. Courts often use costs to determine whether an organization has violated laws.

Price fixing is an agreement between competitors to sell a common product at the same price. It requires a conspiracy that will result in the mutual benefit of the sellers at the expense of the buyers. Bid rigging, considered a form of price fixing, is an agreement with another person that interferes with the bidding process. Bid rigging can happen if two or more parties agree to not bid on a specified job. Revealing the contents of a bid to another individual is also considered bid rigging.

Price maintenance occurs if a business uses its influence to encourage an increase or discourage a decrease in the price of a product in Canada. Refusal to supply product to a purchaser because of the purchaser's low pricing policies is considered price maintenance. Along the same lines, requiring a supplier to refuse to provide product to companies with low pricing policies, as a condition of doing business, is also forbidden.

Price discrimination is the practice of setting different prices for different customers. Although not-for-profit organizations charge prices according to ability to pay, Canadian regulations forbid for-profit organizations from charging some customers higher prices for the same product if the intent is to lessen or prevent competition for customers. Organizations can use cost differences as a defence against price discrimination charges.

It is also illegal for organizations to practise predatory pricing, which is the deliberate act of setting prices low to drive competitors out of the market and then raising prices. However, low prices are not considered predatory if they can be justified by cost differences.

Dumping occurs when a foreign-based company sells products in an international market at prices that are below the market value in the country where the product is produced. Anti-dumping tariffs are set so that the new price will be equivalent to the prices charged by the home country. Prior to 1995, only a few countries (e.g., Canada, the United States, Australia, and countries of the European Union) had anti-dumping laws. However, with the adoption of the World Trade Organization agreement in 1995, the number of countries with anti-dumping laws has increased to 64. These rules have been applied in a number of industries, most recently in the computer chip industry. Canada has 14 anti-dumping measures in targeted industries, such as base metals (mostly steel), chemicals, plastics, textiles, machinery and equipment, and agriculture and food. Other countries enact similar laws to protect home country manufacturers from unfair competition from foreign businesses. For example, from 1999 through 2000, steel exports from India grew by 53%. Because prices for Indian steel were much lower than domestic prices in Canada, the United States, and Europe, these governments levied anti-dumping duties on certain steel products to protect the domestic industry.[5]

Transfer Price Policies

LO6 Compare the different pricing methods used for transferring goods and services within an organization

Transfer prices are the prices charged for transactions that take place within an organization. Prices are set for the use of support departments such as human resources and accounting. In a manufacturing setting, intermediate products are often transferred to other departments where further assembly takes place before the final product is sold to external markets. These intermediate products need to be priced so that appropriate decisions can be made about the value of selling products internally or externally. Transfer price policies also have incentive and tax effects; they are discussed in more detail in the next section.

When one unit relies on other units within an organization for goods or services, a problem arises that affects the measurement of financial performance. Suppose Porcelain & More, a kitchen and bath fixtures manufacturer, operates with three departments: fixtures, sinks, and tubs. Sinks and tubs are sold as kits that include fixtures. The kits produced by the sinks and tubs departments use the faucets and handles produced by the fixture departments. Thus, these fixtures are transferred from one department to the other two departments, and the fixtures need to be priced appropriately. A transfer price is the price used to record revenue and cost when goods or services are transferred between departments within an organization.

[5] R. Krishnan, "Anti-dumping Action: Steel Industry's Bane," *Hindu Business Line* (Internet publication), January 20, 2002; Department of Finance Canada, "Anti-dumping Information Paper," www.collectionscanada.gc.ca/webarchives/20071115161602/http://www.fin.gc.ca/activty/pubs/antidmp01_e.html.

●● > FOCUS ON ETHICAL DECISION MAKING:
ALLEGED PRICE FIXING BY MAKERS OF CHOCOLATES

In November 2007, the superior court of justice in Ontario issued search warrants in support of price fixing investigations involving **Hershey Co.**, **Cadbury Schweppes PLC**, **Mars Inc.**, and **Nestlé SA**. An unidentified informant turned over evidence supporting a claim that the big chocolate makers had been involved in at least three incidents of price fixing since February 2004.

According to a statement made by a spokesperson for Canada's Competition Bureau, this action was taken "based on evidence that there are reasonable grounds to believe that a number of suppliers in the chocolate confectionery industry have engaged in activities contrary to the conspiracy provisions of the Competition Act."

Due to changing international markets for dairy products (especially milk) and unfavourable weather conditions, demand for milk has increased as supply has decreased. The result has been steady and continuous increases in the cost of milk. These increases, of approximately 5–6% per year up to 2007, hit the chocolate industry hard. The major chocolate makers took price increases repeatedly from 2004.

At question in the investigation was not the price increases themselves but how those increases were implemented in the chocolate industry. Unidentified informants claimed that the price increases were coordinated through manoeuvring at the senior management level at the big chocolate makers.

The four companies eventually paid over $23 million in total to settle class-action law suits filed in connection with the price-fixing allegations. Price fixing charges were eventually stayed against Mars and Nestlé, while Hershey pled guilty to price fixing and Cadbury was given immunity from prosecution for being the initial whistleblower.

Source: J. Jargon and J. R. Wilke, "Chocolate Makers Face Probe Over Pricing," *The Wall Street Journal* (eastern edition), December 21, 2007, p. A4; D. Belkin and J. Jargon, "Chocolate Probe Cites Canadian Pricing," *The Wall Street Journal* (eastern edition), December 22, 2007, p. A.3; and Dow Jones Newswires, *Canada Suit Accuses Chocolate Makers of Price-Fixing (DJ)*, February 20, 2008; Oliver Nieburg, "Canada chocolate price fixing saga ends as Nestlé charges stayed," Confectionerynews.com, November 19, 2015, www.confectionerynews.com/Manufacturers/Canada-chocolate-price-fixing-saga-ends-as-Nestle-charges-stayed.

©EM Arts/Shutterstock

ETHICAL PRICING DECISIONS

Did the alleged actions of the senior management at the chocolate makers create an ethical problem for the unidentified informants? What might have motivated senior management at the top chocolate makers to follow along and increase their prices? What might have motivated the informant to come forward? How can managers ensure that the prices they charge are ethical?

▣ INTERNATIONAL

In September 1996, Hurricane Fran, a category 3 hurricane with sustained winds of 190 km/h, hit the coastline of North Carolina and left more than a million people without power. In a very short time, refrigerated food and medication began to spoil. Although neighbouring towns that had not been hit by the hurricane had plenty of ice, no one brought any to the affected areas—not even to sell. Two young men finally did, and when they charged $8 per $1.75 bag of ice, they were arrested for breaking North Carolina's Anti-Gouging Law. Was it unethical to sell the ice for $8 per bag? Plenty of people were grateful for the ice and willing to pay the $8 per bag. What is the government's role in this type of situation?[6]

Setting an Appropriate Transfer Price

The perfect transfer price would be the opportunity cost of transferring goods and services internally. If external demand is zero, and the selling division has excess capacity, the transfer price would be the variable cost. Fixed cost is ignored when establishing the range of the transfer price, because fixed cost is irrelevant, as it will be incurred regardless of the transfer of the product/service or not. The variable cost is the minimum price the selling division would typically be willing to accept from an outside buyer when it has excess capacity.

---

[6] M. Munger, "They Clapped: Can Price-Gouging Laws Prohibit Scarcity?" January 8, 2007, www.econlib.org/library/Columns/y2007/Mungergouging.html.

However, if capacity is limited and goods or services can be sold externally, then the opportunity cost would be the market price. To sell internally, the department forgoes an external sale and, therefore, should charge the market price.

Although the opportunity cost is the best transfer price policy, it is rarely used because the price would vary with capacity. Most managers prefer stable transfer prices across time. In addition, selling managers may regard a price equal to variable cost as being unfair when excess capacity exists, because the purchasing department receives credit for the entire contribution margin for products that are essentially manufactured by both departments. Therefore, other transfer price policies, such as the following, are typically used in manufacturing and service organizations:

- ▶ Cost based
- ▶ Activity based
- ▶ Market based
- ▶ Dual rate
- ▶ Negotiated

Cost-Based Transfer Price The cost of the good or service transferred is used as the basis of **cost-based transfer pricing**. Cost can be computed in different ways, ranging from variable costs to fully allocated costs. If a product has no external market because it is a subcomponent of another product, some type of cost-based transfer price is commonly used.

Suppose that the fixtures department of Porcelain & More usually produces about 40,000 sets of fixtures and incurs about $200,000 in manufacturing overhead cost during an accounting period. The average fixed cost per unit would be $5 ($200,000 ÷ 40,000 units). Under a full production cost transfer price policy, Porcelain & More could set a transfer price of $15 ($10 variable cost + $5 fixed cost). This transfer price allows each department to split the contribution margin that arises when fixtures are sold as part of sink and tub kits.

Cost-based transfer prices present several disadvantages. When products have an external market, and departments are profit centres, the transfer price affects decisions about transferring internally versus purchasing externally. This can lead to suboptimal decisions, or goal incongruence between the subunits and the organization. For example, when the selling department has excess capacity, there is no opportunity cost and the fixed cost is irrelevant. If the selling department charges full cost, the buying division may be able to purchase the product/service externally at a lower price. In addition, when transfer prices include allocated fixed costs, the fact that buying department treats the selling price as a variable cost leads to the fixed cost being covered twice from the organization's perspective. Ultimately, the selling price to external customers may be too high to be competitive. Another disadvantage of using cost-based transfer prices is that managers in selling departments do not have as much incentive to reduce fixed costs. They can pass the responsibility for allocated fixed costs to another department through the transfer pricing policy.

Activity-Based Transfer Price A variation of cost-based transfer prices is **activity-based transfer prices**. Here, the purchasing unit is charged for the unit-level, batch-level, and possibly some product-level costs of products transferred, plus an annual fixed fee that is a portion of the facility-level costs. Suppose the tubs department at Porcelain & More plans to buy enough fixtures internally so that it uses 20% of the fixture department's capacity. Under activity-based transfer pricing, the tubs department could pay for the unit and batch costs of each fixture and also pay 20% of the fixtures department facility-level costs. By making this lump sum payment, the tubs department essentially reserves some of the fixture department's capacity for units it will purchase internally.

An advantage of activity-based transfer pricing is that the purchasing department has an incentive to accurately project the number of units it will purchase internally. This accuracy enhances an organization's planning abilities. Suppose managers in the fixtures department believe that external sales will be forgone by selling 20% of their fixtures to the tubs department. Because they receive a fixed price from the tubs department, they know ahead of time that they need to increase capacity to accommodate external sales, and they can more easily plan for these changes.

However, because of uncertainty in demand, organizations may sometimes need to reallocate capacity to attain the highest contribution. In a changing business environment,

▣ **CHAPTER REFERENCE**
See Chapter 18 for more details about responsibility centres, such as profit centres.

departments should be allowed to subcontract with each other so that the departments with the best opportunities are using most of the capacity.

Market-Based Transfer Prices Competitors' prices or supply-and-demand relationships are the basis for **market-based transfer prices**. They are appropriate under a restrictive set of conditions, including the presence of a highly competitive market for the intermediate product, so that the selling department can sell as much as it wants to outside customers, and the purchasing department can buy as much as it wants from outside suppliers, all without affecting the price. These conditions are rarely met. However, when they are, the market price provides an objective value for intermediate products. The problem with market-based transfer prices is that information about underlying costs is not revealed, and this lack of information encourages suboptimal decision making.

Dual-Rate Transfer Prices The selling department is credited for the market price and the purchasing department is charged the variable cost under **dual-rate transfer pricing**. The difference is charged to the organization's account. When financial statements are consolidated at the end of the accounting period, adjustments are made so that overall organizational profit is accurately reported. This method provides appropriate information and incentives when the selling department has excess capacity. Also, it is most similar to a policy that uses an opportunity cost for the transfer price. A disadvantage of the method is that it overstates profitability at the subunit level, and managers may believe that the organization as a whole is more profitable than it actually is.

Negotiated Transfer Prices **Negotiated transfer prices** are based on agreements reached between the managers of the selling and purchasing departments. This method ensures that both managers have full information about costs and market prices and that the transfer price provides appropriate incentives. A disadvantage of this method is that it usually requires extra time, because both managers prefer more contribution margin. Managers' time is valuable to the organization for other responsibilities, and negotiation time may not be a high priority for the organization as a whole.

To establish the boundary for a viable transfer price, it is necessary to consider a few factors—variable costs, incremental costs required due to the transfer, opportunity costs which are related to the capacity, and the market price for the buying unit. From the buying unit's perspective, it will be only willing pay internally up to what they pay externally. At this price, the buying unit will be indifferent as to whether to purchase internally or externally. If the internal price is higher than the external price, then the buying unit will buy externally. This establishes the maximum transfer price—it is the market price for the buying unit.

The minimum transfer price that the selling unit is willing to sell for covers the variable cost, the incremental cost required due to the transfer, and the opportunity cost. Fixed costs are ignored at this point, because fixed costs are irrelevant regardless of the transfer. When a selling unit has excess capacity, there is no opportunity cost. When a selling unit has no capacity, the opportunity cost is the contribution forgone from selling externally. When a selling unit has some capacity, the opportunity cost is the portion of the contribution forgone in exchange for selling internally. Exhibit 14.4 summarizes the minimum and the maximum of a transfer price. In between the boundary, the selling unit and the buying unit can negotiate a mutually acceptable price. The selling unit may be able to add some profit to cover its fixed cost. In some situations, both units may be able to agree to split the difference between the minimum and the maximum to reach a transfer price. The impact of the capacity on the transfer price is shown in Exhibit 14.5.

Minimum		Maximum
Seller's 1. Variable Cost + 2. Incremental Cost + 3. Opportunity Cost (CM loss ÷ Units transferred)	≤ Transfer Price ≤	Buyer's Market Price

▶**EXHIBIT 14.4**

Setting the range for a transfer price.

> EXHIBIT 14.5

Summary of the impact of the capacity on transfer price

Capacity	Transfer Price	
	Seller	Buyer
Idle Capacity	• No opportunity cost • Willing to sell at VC + incremental cost (cost recovery)	• Willing to pay below the market price
	Optimum Transfer Price: Min ≤ Transfer Price ≤ Max	
No Idle Capacity	• Opportunity cost • Willing to sell at VC + incremental cost (cost recovery) + Opportunity Cost (CM loss)	• Willing to pay as high as the market price
	Optimum Transfer Price: Transfer Price ≤ Max If Transfer Price > Market Price, then there will be no purchase internally.	
Some Idle Capacity	• Opportunity cost • Willing to sell at VC + incremental cost (cost recovery) + Opportunity Cost (CM loss ÷ # transferred)	• Willing to pay as high as the market price
	Optimum Transfer Price: Min ≤ Transfer Price ≤ Max	

computer wizards
NEGOTIATED TRANSFER PRICES

The Happy Valley-Goose Bay (HVGB) division of Computer Wizards produces computer monitors. These monitors are sold on the open market for $110 each, or the Red Deer (RD) division uses them as part of a complete computer package. When a monitor is transferred internally, the entire computer package has a contribution margin of $415 each. The organization currently uses market price plus shipping as a transfer price. Jason, the director of operations, is happy with this transfer price, but Cecilia, the RD division manager, has asked the director of finance, Renée, to consider changing the policy, because her division shows lower earnings than it should. She would prefer to purchase monitors from Jason but often purchases less-expensive and lower-quality monitors from an external vendor to improve her division's earnings.

©Fuse/Getty Images

The HVGB division has capacity to produce 10,000 monitors per month and usually operates at 70% of capacity. The following data pertain to production at this level:

	Average Cost
Direct materials	$25
Direct labour	15
Supplies	5
Total variable cost per monitor	45
Allocated fixed costs	50
Total average cost per monitor	$95

If a monitor is sold on the open market, the customer pays the shipping cost. The cost of shipping one monitor from HVGB to RD is about $10.

The HVGB division is currently operating at 50% of its capacity, substantially below normal. Jason would like to sell more monitors internally to help cover fixed costs. Both managers contact Renée, who tells them to negotiate a policy that is fair to both divisions. Jason would like to set a transfer price that is below the market price but above the variable cost so that some of the fixed costs are covered by internal transfers. Cecilia would prefer to pay only the variable cost plus the shipping charge because the HVGB division's fixed costs will not change if production increases, and workers would be idle part of the time without the internal transfers.

example

After negotiating for several weeks, the two managers go back to Renée for help. Renée has laid out the following information, based on a selling price of $950 for the computer package:

	Average Cost
Direct material	$240
Direct labour	75
Supplies	175
Total variable costs excluding monitor	490
Cost of monitor	110
Allocated fixed costs	200
Total average cost per computer package	$800

Renée explains that, from Computer Wizards' perspective, the contribution margin on monitors sold externally is $65 ($110 – $45). When a monitor is transferred internally, the relevant cost to Computer Wizards is $45, the variable cost. The relevant contribution margin for the computer package is $415 ($950 – $490 – $45). When Cecilia purchases a monitor externally for $110, the contribution margin is $350 ($950 – $490 – $110). Therefore, corporate headquarters would prefer internal transfers over purchases from outside vendors.

Renée suggests that Cecilia pay Jason a flat amount to help cover fixed costs and also pay the variable cost for each monitor transferred. Jason agrees to this policy as long as the division operates with excess capacity. However, he points out that when the division lacks enough capacity to fill both external and internal orders, he will sell externally and forgo internal transfers to increase profits for the HVGB division.

Renée calculates the difference in the company-wide contribution margin when transferring monitors internally versus purchasing them externally at $65 ($415 – $350). This difference happens to be the same as the contribution margin for the HVGB division when monitors are sold externally. Therefore, Jason and Cecilia are indifferent to whether sales take place internally or externally *when the HVGB division is at capacity*. Meanwhile, both managers agree that developing a transfer price policy that suits not only both divisions but also the overall organization is more difficult than it first appeared. Exhibit 14.6 shows the overview of the transfer prices and their impact on each unit's contribution margins and the headquarters' contribution margin. When the transfer price is at $115, which is higher than the price that RD can purchase externally, there will be no transfer from HVGB to RD. ■

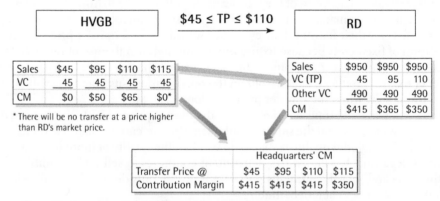

> **EXHIBIT 14.6**
> Overview of the Transfer Prices and Contribution Margins

Transfer Prices and Conflicts Among Managers

LO7 Discuss the uses and limitations of different transfer pricing methods

When compensation is tied to the financial performance of subunits, managers tend to overlook their contribution to the entire organization and focus instead on how decisions affect only their subunit's financial performance. Conflicts arise among managers, leading to suboptimal operating decisions.

Suppose that the fixtures department at Porcelain & More sells fixtures for a market price of $20 to external customers. When fixtures are sold externally, the fixtures department receives credit in its operating income for the entire contribution margin. How should the fixtures be priced, however, when fixtures are transferred internally to the sinks and tubs departments? The manager of the fixtures department would like to recognize the same revenue that is recorded for external sales. However, managers from the sinks and tubs departments would like to record in their books only the variable cost for the fixtures that are internally transferred. The managers from the sinks and tubs departments have legitimate claims, because their departments are responsible for selling kits that include fixtures. The managers from the three departments are in conflict with each other. All of them would prefer to show high profits and, therefore, to recognize most of the contribution for each product sold.

The following chart shows prices and sales for last year. Assume that the fixtures department has plenty of capacity and sells 37,000 sets of fixtures. Of these, 20,000 sets go to the external market, 12,000 to the sinks department, and 5,000 to the tubs department:

	Fixtures	Sinks	Tubs	Total
Units sold	20,000	12,000	5,000	37,000
Market price	$20	$75	$150	
Variable cost	$10	$30	$ 75	

The departments' contribution margins, assuming that fixtures are transferred at market price, are summarized as follows:

	Fixtures	Sinks	Tubs	Total
External revenue	$400,000	$900,000	$750,000	$2,050,000
Transfer price	340,000	(240,000)	(100,000)	0
Other variable costs	(370,000)	(360,000)	(375,000)	(1,105,000)
Contribution margin	$370,000	$300,000	$275,000	$ 945,000

The external market demand is for only 20,000 sets of fixtures. Suppose the sinks and tubs department managers insist on using the variable cost of $10 for the transfer price. The following calculations summarize each department's contribution margin if all departments record variable cost as the transfer price for fixtures.

	Fixtures	Sinks	Tubs	Total
Revenue	$400,000	$900,000	$750,000	$2,050,000
Transfer price	170,000	(120,000)	(50,000)	0
Other variable costs	(370,000)	(360,000)	(375,000)	(1,105,000)
Contribution margin	$200,000	$420,000	$325,000	$ 945,000

Notice that the total contribution margin to Porcelain & More is the same under either alternative, $945,000, regardless of the transfer price policy. If the fixtures department always has excess capacity, its managers may be willing to sell at variable cost, because they have no other outlets for their fixtures. However, they would prefer a transfer price that includes some portion of fixed costs because fixture production requires the use of resources such as equipment and supervisor time. If the fixtures department has no excess capacity—that is, if every set of fixtures produced can be sold on the open market—its managers will be unwilling to sell internally when the transfer price is below market price.

Now assume that the transfer price is set at the market price of $20. The fixtures department has excess capacity, but the sinks and tubs departments can buy fixtures from a supplier for $18 a set, although the quality is slightly lower than the quality of those manufactured by the fixtures department. The fixtures department continues to sell 20,000 units externally, while the sinks and tubs departments purchase from the outside supplier. Following is the contribution margin for each department:

	Fixtures	Sinks	Tubs	Total
Revenue	$400,000	$900,000	$750,000	$2,050,000
Transfer price	0	(216,000)	(90,000)	(306,000)
Other variable costs	(200,000)	(360,000)	(375,000)	(935,000)
Contribution margin	$200,000	$324,000	$285,000	$ 809,000

Compared to the results with fixtures transferred internally, the overall contribution margin for Porcelain & More is lower by $136,000 ($945,000 − $809,000). The difference is equal to the incremental cost to the company of purchasing the fixtures externally versus manufacturing them internally: 17,000 units × ($18 − $10) = $136,000. In addition, the sinks and tubs are sold with lower-quality fixtures. Yet, when fixtures are purchased externally, managers in both the sinks and tubs departments appear to be better off in an evaluation of the performance of their individual departments. Thus, a transfer price policy based on market price encourages the managers to make suboptimal decisions for the company as a whole.

Additional Transfer Price Considerations

The preceding section addresses the incentives of managers regarding transfer prices between operating units. The following additional factors affect the choice of transfer prices.

LO8 Discuss additional factors that affect transfer prices

International Income Taxes

For organizations that do business internationally, the taxable location of profit is affected by transfer price policies. An organization with subsidiaries located in high-tax and low-tax countries could potentially charge a high transfer price in the low-tax countries so that most of the contribution margin arises where taxes are lowest. To restrict firms' abilities to shift income in this manner, the Canadian government enacted legislation to regulate transfer prices. Section 247 of the Canadian Income Tax Act (the "Act") is core of the Canadian transfer pricing rules. This section of the Act, introduced in 1998, brings Canadian transfer pricing regulations in line with the Organisation of Economic Co-operation and Development (OECD) guidelines (*Transfer Pricing Guidelines for Multinational Enterprises and Tax Administrations*). Basically, the guidelines specify that the transfer price should be the same as one determined in an arm's length transaction—a transaction between unrelated parties. Taxpayers are required to keep "contemporaneous documentation" for all multinational transfer pricing agreements. Advance pricing agreements allow multinational companies to seek pre-approval from taxing authorities for predetermined transfer prices. These agreements often alleviate the possibility of becoming involved in long and sometimes expensive tax audits. The details of international tax regulation are complex and beyond the scope of this textbook. Further information is available on the Canada Revenue Agency website and in professional publications (e.g., Hill, D. C., Transfer pricing 101, *CMA Management*, March 2007, pp. 36–39.)

Transfer Prices for Support Services

Many organizations set transfer prices for support services. Their objective is to motivate efficient use and cost-effective production of internal support services such as accounting, printing, human resources, and purchasing. When support departments provide services without charge to user departments, the user departments tend to use the support services inefficiently. In turn, inefficient use tends to encourage support departments to grow unnecessarily large.

Transfer prices are often based on fully allocated costs and, therefore, include allocations of fixed support department costs and allocations from other support departments. As a result, the transfer prices can be high. High transfer prices can encourage user departments to outsource the support services. As shown in the Porcelain & More example, outsourcing is not always beneficial to an organization as a whole, as it can cause internal services to be duplicated, resulting in excess capacity and inefficient use of resources.

⊠ INTERNATIONAL

To simplify cross-border transfers when at least one European Union country is involved, in late November 2005, the European Commission adopted a code of conduct standardizing the documentation needed to substantiate the arm's-length nature of intercompany transactions.[7]

Setting Transfer Prices for Internal Services

Because top managers prefer to have support services used efficiently, they want to set transfer prices that motivate this behaviour. The best transfer price policy is an opportunity cost approach. Each department is charged an amount that reflects the value of any opportunities forgone by not using the service for its next best alternative use.

Suppose that Computer Wizards' production and assembly equipment needs routine maintenance to prevent downtime during regular hours of operation. The maintenance department schedules its repair and maintenance time during lunch hours and at the end of

⊠ CHAPTER REFERENCE

See Chapter 11 for more details about allocating service department costs.

---

[7] "Baker & McKenzie Transfer Pricing Annual Update: Part 2," *Journal of International Taxation*, 18(1), January 2007, p. 12.

each production shift. Currently, the maintenance department is operating close to capacity. Other departments need to schedule non-routine tasks, such as painting walls and repairing damaged flooring, well in advance. If a department wants maintenance personnel to hang pictures in an office, the value of the opportunity forgone might be the cost of hiring a contractor to provide routine maintenance on equipment or to paint walls. However, if the maintenance department has extra capacity, and workers are idle part of the time, the opportunity cost of hanging pictures would be zero.

Implementing a transfer price policy based on opportunity costs is problematic because opportunities change over time with changes in demand and capacity. In addition, finding and valuing alternative uses for some services can be difficult. Therefore, organizations use transfer price policies for internal services similar to those used for transferring goods. Cost-based transfer prices range from variable costs to fully allocated costs. Market-based transfer prices are set at amounts that would be paid if the service were outsourced.

Some organizations establish a price per job for each task, keep prices low on jobs they want to have performed internally, and set prices high on jobs that are considered unnecessary or inappropriate. Suppose the managers of Computer Wizards believe that the maintenance personnel should not be hanging pictures. They could set the transfer price for hanging pictures high enough to discourage other departments from asking the maintenance department to perform this service.

Transfer of Corporate Overhead Costs

A particular type of transfer price occurs when corporate overhead costs are allocated to departments. Managerial performance that is rewarded based on accounting profits can stimulate much discussion between corporate headquarters and department managers about whether allocating overhead costs is appropriate and whether the allocation plan and allocation bases are appropriate. Under responsibility accounting (discussed further in Chapter 18), managers should be held accountable only for costs they control. Because they have little or no control over corporate costs, they should not be held responsible for those costs in performance evaluations.

Many organizations do allocate corporate headquarters costs, however. Sometimes these are considered a "corporate" tax and are allocated based on revenues or profitability. In this manner, subunits operating under optimal circumstances absorb more overhead than subunits with poor results, because of economic or industry conditions that are not under managers' control.

14-2 self-study problem   Transfer Price, Excess versus Full
                                Capacity, Outsourcing

The Kamloops division of AirTemp Control (AC) produces a digital thermometer. The thermometer can be sold on the open market for $180 each, or it can be used by the Quebec City division in the production of a temperature control gauge that has a unit contribution margin of $140 (given that the digital thermometer is transferred at variable cost plus shipping).

The Kamloops division is currently operating at 70% of its capacity of 2,000 digital thermometers per month. Following are average costs per unit at this level of capacity:

	Average Cost
Direct materials	$ 50
Variable supplies	10
Fixed costs	100
Total variable cost per thermometer	$160

If a digital thermometer is sold on the open market, the customer pays the shipping cost. The cost of shipping a digital thermometer from Kamloops to Quebec City is $15.

required

A. What is the best transfer price for AC overall if a digital thermometer is transferred to Quebec City and the Kamloops division is operating at 70% of capacity?

B. What is the best transfer price for AC overall if a digital thermometer is transferred to Quebec City, but the Kamloops division is operating at full capacity and the digital thermometer could have been sold on the open market?

C. Suppose the Quebec City division can purchase a substitute for the digital thermometer from an outside supplier for $100 (including shipping costs). Under ordinary circumstances, what single transfer price would motivate the managers of both divisions to act in AC's interests at either excess or full capacity?

D. What are the potential problems with the transfer price identified in Part C? Explain.

See the solution on page 650.

▶ **CHAPTER REFERENCE**
See Chapter 10 for information about the use of flexible budgets to evaluate performance.

SUMMARY

L01   Compare the different pricing methods and calculate prices using each method

COST-BASED PRICE

$$Price = Cost \times (1 + Mark\text{-}up \%)$$

MARK-UP %

$$Mark\text{-}up \% = \frac{Desired\ return\ on\ investment + costs\ not\ covered\ in\ per\ unit\ cost}{Cost\ per\ unit \times Annual\ volume}$$

MUST CHOOSE

▶ Measure of cost (variable, fixed and variable, etc.)

TIME AND MATERIAL PRICING

Labour rate:

1. direct labour salaries plus benefits
2. selling, administrative, and related overhead costs
3. desired profit

Materials loading charge:

1. all costs associated with purchasing, receiving, handling, and storing materials
2. desired profit percentage

FACTORS AFFECTING MARKET PRICES

No Product Differentiation   Unique Good or Service
Many Competitors   No Competitors

◀————————————————————▶

Commodity Price   Price Based on   Monopoly Price
                   Differentiation and Competition

L02   Discuss other market-based sources of pricing information

Match competitors' prices using information from:

▶ Competitor retail stores
▶ Competitor websites
▶ Internet auction sites

SUMMARY

ADVANTAGES AND DISADVANTAGES

	Cost-Based Pricing	Market-Based Pricing
Advantages	• Most commonly used method	• Offers better decisions about how much or whether to sell a product
	• Simple	• Provides better success with strategies
	• Calculated from readily available cost data	
Disadvantages	• Ignores customer demand	• Difficult to estimate market demand and prices
	• Prices may be too high or too low	• Method not commonly used
	• Sales volumes inappropriately influence price if fixed costs are included	

COMPUTATIONS FOR PROFIT-MAXIMIZING PRICE

STEP 1: CALCULATE THE PRICE ELASTICITY OF DEMAND:

$$\text{Elasticity} = \frac{\ln(1 + \% \text{ change in quantity sold})}{\ln(1 + \% \text{ change in price})}$$

STEP 2: CALCULATE THE PROFIT-MAXIMIZING PRICE:

$$\text{Profit-maximizing price} = \left[\frac{\text{Elasticity}}{(\text{Elasticity} + 1)}\right] \times \text{Variable cost}$$

OTHER INFLUENCES ON PRICE

► Peak load pricing
► Price skimming
► Penetration pricing
► Price gouging

PRICING IN NOT-FOR-PROFIT ORGANIZATIONS

► Prices need not cover costs
► Different prices can be set for different customers

► Prices are often based on ability to pay
► Organizational goals influence prices

GOVERNMENTAL REGULATIONS

► Price discrimination
► Predatory pricing
► Price fixing
► Bid rigging
► Price maintenance
► Dumping

SUMMARY

LO6 Compare the different pricing methods used for transferring goods and services within an organization

IDEAL TRANSFER PRICE
- Opportunity cost

- Market based
- Dual rate
- Negotiated

TRANSFER PRICE ALTERNATIVES
- Cost based
- Activity based

SETTING THE RANGE FOR A TRANSFER PRICE

Minimum		Maximum
Seller's 1. Variable Cost + 2. Incremental Cost + 3. Opportunity Cost (CM loss ÷ Units transferred)	≤ Transfer Price ≤	Buyer's Market Price

LO7 Discuss the uses and limitations of different transfer pricing methods

USES
- Assign cost to goods and services transferred internally for financial reporting and income taxes
- Motivate efficient use of support services
- Allocate corporate overhead costs

LIMITATIONS
- Conflicts among managers

LO8 Discuss additional factors that affect transfer prices

- International income taxes
- Suboptimal decision making

- Management responsibility for costs over which they have no control

14-1 solution to self-study problem

A.

	Economy	Premium	Super Premium
Materials cost	$10.00	$12.00	$16.00
Allocated fixed overhead			
$20,000 ÷ 5,000 = $4 per tonne	4.00	4.00	4.00
Total cost	14.00	16.00	20.00
Mark-up (100% of total cost)	14.00	16.00	20.00
Price	$28.00	$32.00	$40.00

B. No. A cost-based price assumes that customers are willing to pay a set mark-up above cost. However, a price based on cost might be higher or lower than customers are willing to pay.

C. The price for economy-grade feed can be computed in two steps:

$$\text{Elasticity of demand} = \ln(1 - 0.40) \div \ln(1 + 0.10) = -5.36$$
$$\text{Profit-maximizing price} = [-5.36 \div (-5.36 + 1)] \times \$10 = \$12.30$$

D. The price in Part C is only a guideline for pricing. The elasticity formulas are sensitive to error, so the profit-maximizing prices are used only as guidelines. OK Feed could reduce the price of economy-grade feed slowly and see how volumes and profits change.

E. 1. This problem requires a special-order calculation (see Chapter 4). The relevant cost of filling the special order is the variable cost, which in this problem is the cost of materials: $10 per tonne × 200 tonnes = $2,000.

  2. Under the general quantitative decision rule for special orders, the minimum acceptable price is the variable cost. The minimum acceptable price would be $10 per tonne.

14-2 solution to self-study problem

A. When the Kamloops division has excess capacity (30% in the problem), the transfer price should be the variable cost of $75 (direct materials of $50 plus supplies of $10 and shipping of $15).

B. If the Kamloops division could sell all its thermometers on the open market, the transfer price should be the market price of $180 plus $15 shipping = $195.

C. First consider the contribution margin for each division from the perspective of the entire organization. Selling the temperature control gauge results in a contribution margin of $140 per unit. Selling the digital thermometers results in a contribution margin of $105 ($180 − $75 thermometer variable cost). When Kamloops has excess capacity, the total contribution margin is $245 ($140 + $105).

  For each unit produced with a digital thermometer from an outside supplier, the Quebec City division's contribution margin is reduced by $25 ($100 − $75), from $140 to $115. However, from the perspective of the entire organization, the contribution margin is $115 from Quebec City plus $105 from Kamloops, or $220 in total. If the internal transfer takes place, the contribution margin is only $140. Therefore, transfers should take place only when Kamloops has excess capacity. To motivate this behaviour, the transfer price should be equal to or greater than $75 and equal to or less than $100. Setting the transfer price at $90 + $10 shipping would give Quebec City incentive to purchase inside if Kamloops had capacity but purchase outside if Kamloops had no capacity because the transfer price would be the same with either purchase. In addition, Kamloops would have incentive to sell to the external market when possible because the contribution margin of $105 on external sales is greater than the $35 ($90 − $65) contribution margin for internal sales.

D. The Quebec City division might find an external vendor that could produce the digital thermometer at a cost less than the transfer price, but that would decrease AC's overall contribution margin. In addition, the Quebec City division could forgo special orders that would have a positive contribution margin for AC if the division uses the internal transfer price to determine whether to accept the order.

QUESTIONS

14.1 What factors need to be considered when setting a selling price?

14.2 Explain cost-based pricing and give an example that shows how prices would be determined using this method.

14.3 Explain market-based pricing, and explain where managers and accountants can find information that would help them set prices using this type of approach.

14.4 If fixed costs are included in the marked-up costs used in setting cost-based prices, a problem may occur when demand declines. Describe this problem.

14.5 Explain the difference between the calculation of the mark-up percentage using absorption and variable costing.

14.6 Explain why not-for-profit organizations do not always set prices so that their operating costs are recovered.

14.7 What are the components of a time and materials bill and what is included in each component?

14.8 An organization's plant in Saskatchewan manufactures a product that is shipped to a branch in the Yukon Territory for sale. Does it make any difference which branch (each is a profit centre) is charged for the cost of transportation? Explain.

14.9 A national corporation, Fast Print, decided to expand into several developing countries. The corporation has been managed under a centralized organizational form but is considering changing to a decentralized form. List the advantages and disadvantages of making this change.

14.10 Suppose transfer prices are set at market prices and a manager who previously purchased internally begins to purchase externally. Explain what it means to say that the outsourcing decision might have been suboptimal.

14.11 Describe as many different methods for setting transfer prices as you can.

14.12 Describe the restrictions that are often imposed on transfer prices by income tax regulations.

14.13 Why is it not possible for a multinational company to simply transfer income to the division in the lowest tax country through transfer pricing?

MULTIPLE-CHOICE QUESTIONS

14.14 WWL Ltd. has a target before-tax profit of $200,000. At the planned sales volume for each of its products, the variable and fixed costs are $2,000,000 and $400,000, respectively. All fixed costs are common to all products. If the selling price of one of the products is $13 per unit, and the unit has allocated to it fixed costs of $2 per unit, what is the target variable cost (to the nearest cent) to make its average mark-up over full costs?
a. $9.00
b. $9.80
c. $10.00
d. $10.15

14.15 Clay Cookery produces ceramic cookware. Variable costs include clay and glazes for each crock and selling expenses. Fixed costs include salaries for potters and the necessary equipment to produce the cookware. There are also fixed marketing and administrative costs. Clay Cookery's owner has $80,000 invested in the business and desires an 8% return on his investment. Clay Cookery sells 3,650 crocks per year.

Product Costs

Variable	$4.50 per crock
Fixed	$78,000 per year

Selling, Marketing, and Administrative Costs

Variable	$3.00 per crock
Fixed	$15,000 per year

Using the absorption approach to cost-based pricing, what are the mark-up percentage and the selling price?

	Mark-up percentage	Selling price
a.	5.32%	$34.73
b.	34.26%	$34.73
c.	27.48%	$32.98
d.	363%	$34.73

14.16 Based on the information in multiple choice question 13.15, calculate the mark-up percentage and selling price assuming that Clay Cookery uses variable cost-based pricing.

	Mark-up percentage	Selling price
a.	5.32%	$34.73
b.	34.26%	$34.73
c.	27.48%	$32.98
d.	363%	$34.73

14.17 Road Runners is a bike sales and service shop. The service division uses a time and material billing policy. Based on the following costs and desired profits, calculate the hourly rate for labour and the material loading charge for Road Runners assuming that the service technicians work 2,960 hours per year and invoice costs total $64,000 per year. Round to two decimal places.

	Labour	Materials
Technicians' salaries	$74,000	
Office supplies	$ 3,000	$ 8,000
Parts		$24,000
Overhead on equipment	$ 5,000	
Advertising costs	$ 3,000	
Desired profit	$ 7 per hour	15%

	Hourly labour rate	Materials loading charge
a.	$28.72	15%
b.	$28.72	50%
c.	$35.72	65%
d.	$35.72	50%

14.18 Ruce Ltd. has two manufacturing divisions located in the same plant. Division X is evaluated as a cost centre, and Division Y is evaluated as a profit centre.

Division X produces component X98 at a budgeted full cost of $108 per unit, of which $100 represents variable costs. Currently, Division X is operating at full capacity and transfers all of its output to the sales division at $108 per unit. The sales division sells component X98 to external customers for $133 per unit; it incurs variable costs of $9 per unit to sell the component.

Division Y purchases a component similar to X98 from an outside supplier for $125/unit plus a $2 per unit delivery charge. Ruce Ltd.'s production engineers have determined that component X98 could be used by Division Y with no adverse effects on the quality of the final product. Assume that no selling or delivery expenses would be incurred for internal transfers. What is the highest transfer price per unit that Division Y should be willing to accept for component X98?

a. $133
b. $124
c. $125
d. $108
e. $127

EXERCISES

14.19 Cost-Based Pricing Designs by Breanne is a graphic design studio specializing in logos and business stationery.
LO1 Breanne has just made a $65,000 investment in her company and desires a 12% return. Annually, she designs and prints 3,000 orders. Her costs include

	Variable	Fixed
Design costs	$ 45 per order	$50,000 per year
Production costs	$125 per order	$39,000 per year
Marketing costs		$ 2,500 per year
Shipping costs	$ 15 per order	

REQUIRED **A.** Determine the mark-up percentage using
    1. absorption cost-based pricing
    2. variable cost-based pricing
    3. total cost-based pricing
  B. Determine the selling price for each mark-up percentage calculated in Part 1.
  C. Discuss the other factors that Breanne must consider when setting her selling prices.

14.20 Cost-Based Pricing Wagon Wheels manufactures personalized wagons for toddlers. Each wagon goes through a woodworking process, painting, and assembly. Wagon Wheels produces and sells 7,200 wagons per year. Wagon Wheels' owners have invested $55,000 in the business and desire a return of 15%. Wagon Wheels costs include

L01

	Variable	Fixed
Direct labour salaries		$240,000 per year
Office staff		$ 30,000 per year
Materials	$45 per wagon	
Supplies		$ 4,000 per year
Marketing	$ 3.50 per wagon	$ 2,400 per year
Overhead	$ 1.50 per wagon	$ 850 per year

REQUIRED
A. Determine the mark-up percentage using
   1. absorption cost-based pricing
   2. variable cost-based pricing
   3. total cost-based pricing
B. Determine the selling price for each mark-up percentage calculated in Part 1.
C. Discuss the other factors that Wagon Wheels must consider when setting their selling prices.

14.21 Time and Materials Pricing Happy Homes is a house cleaning service. As a special feature, Happy Homes will supply flowers or small decorator items when they clean a home. They use a time and material billing policy. Based on the following costs and desired profits, calculate the hourly rate for labour and the material loading charge for Happy Homes, assuming that in 4,000 hours per year they clean 800 homes. Invoice costs per year are $200,000.

L01

	Labour	Materials
Maids' salaries	$60,000	
Office supplies	$18,000	$18,000
Supplies		$24,000
Overhead on equipment	$ 5,000	
Advertising costs	$ 3,000	
Desired profit	$10 per hour	20%

REQUIRED
A. Calculate the labour rate that Happy Homes uses.
B. Calculate the materials loading charge for Happy Homes.
C. Cathy, a potential new client, would like to have her home cleaned every two weeks and a large floral arrangement to be provided for the dining room table and a small arrangement for the kitchen table. Happy Homes estimates that it will take 2 maids 4 hours to clean Cathy's home and the invoice cost for the flowers will be $55. Using the rates calculated in Parts A and B, determine Cathy's bi-weekly bill.

14.22 Activity-Based Costing and Price Setting Dundas Company uses an activity-based costing system. Consider the following information:

L01, L02

Manufacturing Activity Area	Cost Driver Used as Application Base	Cost per Unit of Conversion Application Base
Machine setup	Number of setups	$180
Material handling	Number of parts	$ 15
Milling	Machine hours	$ 50
Assembly	Direct labour hours	$ 30

During the past month, 60 units of a component were produced. Three setups were required. Each unit needs 35 parts, 4 direct labour hours, and 6 machine hours. Direct materials cost $140 per finished unit. All other costs are classified as conversion costs.

REQUIRED If the company would like its gross margin to be 35% of sales, what price should it charge per unit of the component (rounded to the nearest dollar)?

14.23 Market-Based Price (Elasticity Formula) Lickety Split sells ice cream cones in a variety of flavours. The following are
L04 data for a recent week:

Revenue (1,000 cones @ $1.75 each)		$1,750
Cost of ingredients	$640	
Rent	500	
Store attendant	600	1,740
Pretax income		$ 10

REQUIRED The manager estimates that if she were to increase the price of cones from $1.75 to $1.93 each, weekly volume would be
cut to 850 cones due to competition from other nearby ice cream shops. Estimate the profit-maximizing price per cone.

14.24 Market-Based Prices (Elasticity Formula) Paulo's Flowers is a small neighbourhood florist shop. Paulo sells flowers
L04 for bouquets, and he also prepares and delivers flower arrangements.

REQUIRED **A.** Paulo is trying to decide how much to charge for a new type of rose that wholesales for $0.40 per bud. He ran
a special on a similar rose last month and discovered that a 20% discount on the usual price increased sales
by about 35%. What would you suggest as a starting price for the rose? Explain.

B. Paulo has been wondering whether he has been charging the right prices on some of his specialty bouquets.
He has been using a mark-up for all specialty items of 200% (i.e., he charges three times wholesale cost).
Paulo estimates that a 10% increase in price on such items would decrease his unit sales by about 12%.
Perform calculations to estimate a profit-maximizing mark-up. Based on your calculation, do you think he
should increase or decrease his mark-up? Explain.

14.25 Market-Based Price (Elasticity Formula), Uncertainties, Other Pricing Factors La Cabane à Sucre is a shop located in
L04, L05 Quebec. It makes and sells taffy in a variety of flavours, including the local favourite, *tire d'érable*. Revenue and
cost data for a recent week appear here:

Revenue (1,500 kg @ $6.00 per kg)		$9,000
Cost of ingredients	$2,400	
Rent	800	
Wages	3,200	6,400
Pretax income		$2,600

All employees work standard shifts, regardless of how much taffy is produced or sold. Jasmine, the shop's manager,
estimates that if she were to decrease the price of taffy by $0.60 per kilogram to a new price of $5.40 per
kilogram, weekly volume would increase by 20%.

REQUIRED **A.** Calculate the price elasticity of demand.
B. Calculate the profit-maximizing price.
C. Based on the profit-maximizing price, does it appear that Jasmine should drop the price of the taffy? Why or
why not?
D. List possible relevant factors that could influence Jasmine's price decision. List as many factors as you can.

14.26 Market-Based (Elasticity Formula) and Cost-Based Prices, Special Order Decision Malpeque Bayview shucks and
L01, L03, packs oysters and sells them on a wholesale basis to fine restaurants across the province. The income statement
L04, L05 for last year follows:

Revenue (2,000 cases)		$200,000
Expenses:		
Wages for pickers, shuckers, and packers	$100,000	
Packing materials	20,000	
Rent and insurance	25,000	
Administration and selling	45,000	
		190,000
Pretax income		$ 10,000

Pickers, shuckers, and packers are employed on an hourly basis and can be laid off whenever necessary. Salespeople merely deliver the product and so are paid on a salaried basis.

Linda Hanson, manager of Malpeque Bayview, believes that a price increase of 10% would result in a 15% decrease in sales.

The Rake and Tongs Restaurant is providing dinner for a meeting of the Pickers, Shuckers, and Packers Union in Prince Edward Island. Rake and Tongs offered to pay Malpeque Bayview $65 a case for 300 cases of oysters. This sale would not affect Malpeque Bayview's regular sales.

REQUIRED **A.** Ignoring the Rake and Tongs offer, estimate the profit-maximizing price for Malpeque Bayview.

B. Assuming that Linda is not willing to lose money on the Rake and Tongs order, what is the minimum price that she should accept for the special order (Chapter 4)?

C. What other relevant factors might Linda consider before she makes a decision about the Rake and Tongs order? List as many factors as you can.

14.27 Transfer Prices ED Electronics operates as a decentralized company. The bit division manufactures an electronic device and purchases a component, part X22, from the part division of the same company. The division managers have full authority on decisions involving transactions with internal or external customers and suppliers. Currently, the part division is operating at full capacity and the bit division is operating below its capacity of 5,000 units. Part X22 can be sold externally for $75. The costs of producing the electronic device, excluding the cost of part X22, are as follows:

L06, L07

Direct materials	$120
Direct labour	30
Variable overhead	125
Fixed overhead	100
Total	$375

The manager of the bit division has received an offer from a national distributor willing to buy 500 electronic devices at a price of $425 per unit.

REQUIRED **A.** Indicate the minimum transfer price that the manager of the part division would agree to. Justify your answer.

B. Indicate the maximum transfer price that the manager of the bit division would be willing to pay for part X22. Justify your answer.

C. Assume the full cost of part X22 is $50. Explain whether the firm as a whole would benefit if part X22 is transferred from the part division to the bit division at full cost. Justify your answer.

D. Explain whether your answer to Part C would be different if the part division is not operating at full capacity.

14.28 Transfer Prices Wood Inc. manufactures wood poles. It has two divisions, Harvesting and Sawing, which are both evaluated as profit centres. The Harvesting Division is responsible for all the harvesting operations and transfers logs to the Sawing Division, which transforms the logs into poles for external customers. Sawing can produce 10,000 poles per year. The Sawing Division is currently producing at full capacity, after management decided a year ago to manufacture a higher-demand wood pole, Pole-S, that can be sold readily. The manager of the Sawing Division suggests that the maximum price the division can pay for logs transferred from Harvesting is $61.50 per log. The following information supports this suggestion:

L06, L07

Price that external customers are willing to pay for one unit of Pole-S $122.00

Costs per unit:	
Direct labour	$35.00
Variable overhead	4.50
Fixed overhead	8.50
Direct materials (other than logs)	2.50
Total cost per unit	50.50
Target profit margin	10.00
Total cost and margin	$60.50
Maximum transfer price for one log	$61.50

The manager of the Harvesting Division disagrees with the proposed transfer price of $61.50. The division is operating at full capacity and can sell all the logs it produces to external customers for $75. Moreover, the director says: "For each unit of Pole-S my direct labour cost is $40.50, variable overhead is $9.50, and fixed overhead is $15. I cannot spend $65 to cut trees and sell them for $61.50."

REQUIRED **A.** Determine whether it would be beneficial for the company as a whole if logs were transferred to the Sawing Division at the suggested price of $61.50 per log. Show all your calculations.

B. Explain the impact of transferring the logs to the Sawing Division at $61.50 on the performance of each division and specifically on each manager.

C. Determine the minimum and the maximum transfer price that could be used to account for the transfer of logs from the Harvesting Division to the Sawing Division. Recommend an appropriate transfer price. Justify your recommendation.

14.29 ROI, Transfer Prices, Taxes, Employee Motivation Fowler Electronics produces colour plasma screens in its

L06, L07 Windsor, Ontario, plant. The screens are then shipped to the company's plant in Detroit, Michigan, where they are incorporated into finished televisions. Although the Windsor plant never sells plasma screens to any other assembler, the market for them is competitive. The market price is $750 per screen.

Variable costs to manufacture the screens are $350. Fixed costs at the Windsor plant are $2,000,000 per period. The plant typically manufactures and ships 10,000 screens per period to the Detroit plant. Taxes in Canada amount to 30% of pretax income. The Canadian plant has total assets of $20,000,000.

The Detroit plant incurs variable costs to complete the televisions of $110 per set (in addition to the cost of the screens). The Detroit plant's fixed costs amount to $4,000,000 per period. The 10,000 sets produced each period are sold for an average of $2,500 each. The U.S. tax rate is 45% of pretax income. The U.S. plant has total assets of $30,000,000. All dollar amounts are after exchange rate corrections.

REQUIRED **A.** Determine the return on investment for each plant if the screens are transferred at variable cost.

B. Determine the return on investment for each plant if the screens are transferred at market price.

C. To reduce taxes, will Fowler prefer a transfer price based on cost or market price? Explain.

D. Will the top managers in each plant prefer to use cost or market price as the transfer price? Explain.

E. How would you resolve potential conflict over the transfer price policy?

14.30 Choice of Transfer Price The following information relates to a new computer chip that Hand Held has developed for

L06, L07 its new smart phone to boost graphics capability:

Chip Division

Market price of finished chip to outsiders	$	24
Variable cost per unit		12
Contribution margin	$	12
Total contribution for 30,000 units	$360,000	

Cell Phone Division

Market price of finished products	$	128
Variable costs:		
From Chip Division		12
Other direct materials		50
Assembly		38
Packaging		20
Contribution margin	$	8
Total contribution for 20,000 units	$160,000	

The variable costs of the cell phone division will be incurred whether it buys from the chip division or from an outside supplier.

REQUIRED **A.** What is the highest price that the managers of the cell phone division would want to pay the chip division for the chip? Explain.

B. If the chip division is working at full capacity and cannot produce additional units, what transfer price for the chip would be best for the company as a whole? Explain.

C. If the chip division is not operating at capacity and has no prospect of reaching capacity, what is the lowest price its managers would typically be willing to sell chips to the cell phone division?

14.31 Minimum Transfer Price, Capacity, Contribution Margins Nexa's Division A produces a product that can be sold for $200

or transferred to Division B as a component for its product. Division B can buy the part from another suppler at $180. In the current period, Division B purchased 1,000 units from Division A. Data on a per-unit basis follows:

	Division A	Division B
Selling price	$200	$600
Variable cost	100	200
Allocated fixed cost	90	159

The variable cost in Division B does not include the cost of the component provided by Division A or the outside supplier.

REQUIRED
A. Calculate the minimum transfer price if Division A is operating at capacity.
B. Calculate the minimum transfer price if Division A is operating below capacity.
C. Calculate the effect on the company's contribution margin if Division A has excess capacity and Division B buys 1,000 units from the outside supplier.
D. Calculate the contribution margin for the company for 1,000 units if Division A is required to sell to Division B when there is no excess capacity.
E. Calculate the contribution margin for the company if Division A is at capacity and sells 1,000 units to the external market and Division B purchases 1,000 units from an outside supplier.
F. Is it more profitable for the company to require Division A to transfer units to Division B? Explain.
G. If there are no outside suppliers and Division A is operating at capacity, is the company better off to have Division A sell externally or internally? Show your calculations.

14.32 Transfer Price, Sale to Outside Versus Inside Customer The Ajax division of Carlyle Corporation produces electric motors, 20% of which are sold to the Bradley division of Carlyle and the remainder to outside customers. Carlyle treats its divisions as profit centres and allows division managers to choose their sources of sale and supply. Corporate policy requires that all interdivisional sales and purchases be recorded at variable cost as transfer price. Ajax division's estimated sales and standard cost data for 2012, based on its full capacity of 100,000 units, are as follows:

	Bradley	Outsiders
Sales	$ 900,000	$8,000,000
Variable costs	(900,000)	(3,600,000)
Fixed costs	(300,000)	(1,200,000)
Gross margin	$(300,000)	$3,200,000
Unit sales	20,000	80,000

Ajax has an opportunity to sell the 20,000 units currently sold to the Bradley division to an outside customer at a

price of $75 per unit on a continuing basis. Bradley can purchase its requirements from an outside supplier for $85 per unit.

REQUIRED Assuming that the Ajax division desires to maximize its gross margin, should Ajax accept the new customer and drop its sales to Bradley for 2012? Why or why not?

PROBLEMS

14.33 Cost-Based and Market-Based Pricing, Elasticity, Uncertainties, Economy Effects John Fung has owned and operated Heritage Jewellery Store for a number of years. He uses the standard mark-up of 300% (known as a *triple key* in this industry) and uses an average cost that includes an allocation of overhead as the cost base. Lately, jewellery sales at the store have faltered as the country has faced a recession. John's son is taking a cost accounting course and suggests that his father should use a pricing formula based on the price elasticity of demand.

REQUIRED
A. In your own words, provide a plausible explanation for John's current use of cost-based pricing.
B. Explain elasticity to John in simple terms.
C. In your own words, explain how price changes affect demand for products that are highly elastic.

D. Explain why John's price elasticity of demand cannot be predicted with certainty.

E. List possible reasons why a product's price elasticity of demand would change. List as many reasons as you can.

F. Explain how changes in the economy affect prices. Give examples from the current business environment.

14.34 **Cost-Based Pricing, Death Spiral, Uncertainties, Customer Reaction** Suppose the owner of Haywood Ceramics

LO5

needs to raise prices to stay in business but is concerned that raising prices will result in a death spiral. To avoid a decline in sales, the owner is considering sending letters to her customers, explaining why the price increase is necessary. The letter would inform customers about the cost increases that necessitated the price increase, explain what the company is doing to keep costs as low as possible, and allow customers to place orders for a given time period at the current price.

REQUIRED **A.** Describe the death spiral in your own words.

B. Explain why the owner cannot be sure how customers will respond to a price increase.

C. Suppose the owner decides to send letters to her customers. From a customer's point of view, discuss possible pros and cons of this strategy.

D. Would you recommend that the owner send letters to her customers? Why or why not?

14.35 **Market-Based Pricing, Relevant Information** Java Alive, a small boutique coffee shop, has asked your

LO1, LO2, LO3

advice in setting pricing policies. Java has information about prices and sales during the past four years.

REQUIRED **A.** Explain how you would use the prices and sales information to suggest a possible pricing strategy.

B. What other information would you gather before you complete your recommendation? List as many types of information as you can.

14.36 **Market-Based Pricing, Customer Preferences** Transrapid is a new magnetically levitated train being developed to

LO1, LO2, LO3

run between major cities in Germany at a speed of 300 km per hour. Engineers developed a system with trains departing every 10 minutes. Suppose Transrapid asked you to research customer preferences and to recommend a pricing policy. It costs considerably more to have trains depart as frequently as 10 minutes apart, so a cost-based pricing schedule will result in ticket prices that are considerably higher than for alternative modes of transportation.

REQUIRED **A.** In addition to customer preferences, what information would you like to gather before recommending a pricing policy? Explain why each item you list is relevant.

B. Explain why it is important to understand customer preferences before building the system.

C. Is the need to consider customer preferences different for this organization than for other companies? Why or why not?

14.37 **Market-Based Price (Elasticity Formula), Uncertainties** Hanson & Daughters produces a premium label apple juice

LO4, LO5

to wholesalers at a current price of $7.00 per 4-litre container. Costs for a recent month, in which 100,000 4-litre containers were produced and sold were

	Variable	Fixed
Materials	$10,000	$ 0
Labour	20,000	40,000
Factory overhead	10,000	80,000
Selling and administration	10,000	100,000
Total	$50,000	$220,000

Hanson & Daughters' customers are loyal. Recently, a 10% increase in wholesale price resulted in only a 10% decrease in the number of litres sold.

REQUIRED **A.** Calculate the price elasticity of demand.

B. Calculate the profit-maximizing price.

C. Explain why the management of Hanson & Daughters cannot be certain that another 10% price increase would cause only another 10% decrease in number of litres sold.

D. Provide possible reasons why so many customers were willing to continue purchasing the apple juice when prices increased by 10%. List as many reasons as you can.

E. Describe the assumptions underlying the profit-maximizing price you calculated in Part B. How realistic are these assumptions for Hanson & Daughters? What might occur if these assumptions were not met for Hanson & Daughters?

F. What would you recommend to Hanson & Daughters concerning its price for apple juice? Explain your reasoning.

14.38 Cost Reduction and Market-Based Prices at a University Trudeau University offers an MBA degree that is widely respected around the world. The tuition for the program has always covered the costs of the program until a recent recession increased the sensitivity of students to the cost of tuition. The business school managers decided to freeze the tuition cost for the past few years. The director of the MBA program asked students in a cost accounting class to act as consultants for the program and to make recommendations on possible ways to reduce costs or increase tuition. You are part of a student team assigned to this project.

LO2, LO3

REQUIRED **A.** Is this problem open ended? Why or why not?

B. List relevant types of analyses that your team might perform.

C. Describe the steps you will take as you analyze the program, including the types of information you would like to use.

D. Explain how you would decide on an appropriate level for tuition.

14.39 Cost-Based Pricing in a Not-for-Profit Organization Mountain County Legal Services is part of a larger not-for-profit organization (Mountain County Resource Centre) that provides free legal and job placement services and houses a food bank for qualified clients. Last year's costs for 5,000 visits to legal services are presented here:

LO1, LO2, LO3

Lawyer's salary	$ 90,000
Part-time secretary	12,000
Miscellaneous supplies	6,000
Paralegals' salaries	70,000
Administrative costs[a]	34,000
Rent[b]	10,000
	$222,000

[a] A portion of the administrative costs of the Mountain County Services. These costs have been allocated to programs based upon the salary costs of the program.
[b] A portion of the rent for the Mountain County Resource Centre. Total rent is allocated on the basis of the space occupied by each program.

Expected grants for the next year from United Way and the province have been reduced due to an economic downturn. The organization's executive director is considering dropping legal services. Eliminating the legal services program will result in a savings of about $4,000 in administrative costs. The space vacated by legal services could be used by the food bank, which is presently renting quarters in another building for $8,000 a year.

The executive director decided that individuals receiving legal services from the resource centre are to pay for their services, with exceptions based upon need determined on a case-by-case basis. It is not clear what the director means when he says that clients are to pay for their services.

REQUIRED **A.** If the executive director means that each person using legal services should pay for his or her own avoidable costs, what minimum fee should be charged, on average, for a legal service visit?

B. If the executive director means that all of the people using legal services should collectively pay for the avoidable costs of the legal services program, what minimum fee should be charged, on average, for a visit?

C. If the executive director wants the fee to cover the total costs of Mountain County Legal Services, including avoidable and allocated costs, what minimum fee should be charged for a visit?

D. Suppose the centre begins charging the price you calculated in Part B. What problems might arise if these fees are implemented? Consider whether the price change would affect the clients' behaviour and then how that behaviour change might affect the legal services program.

E. Suppose the centre begins charging the price you calculated in Part C. Considering that the price is based on allocated costs, explain why this price might be viewed as arbitrary.

F. Discuss why a Mountain County executive might issue an edict about having clients pay for their services but not provide guidance about what the edict means.

14.40 Profit Effect of Price Change The accountants at French Perfumery have decided to increase the price of a scent
called Breezy by 10%, from $6.00 per bottle to $6.60. French's accountants expect the 10% price increase to
reduce unit sales by 20%. Current sales are 200,000 bottles, and total variable costs are $800,000.

LO1, LO3

REQUIRED   **A.** Estimate the pretax profit effect of the price change, assuming no effect on the variable cost rate, on total
fixed costs, or on sales of other products. (*Hint:* Calculate the contribution margin at the old and new prices
and volumes.)
B. How certain can the accountant be that volume will decline 20% if the selling price increases to $6.60? What
effect does this uncertainty have on the managers' decision to increase the selling price?

14.41 Transfer Price, Company Versus Division Profit, Idle Capacity The furniture division of International Woodworking purchases
lumber and makes tables, chairs, and other wood furniture. Most of the lumber is purchased from the Portneuf Mill,
also a division of International Woodworking. The furniture division and the Portneuf Mill are profit centres.

LO6

The furniture division manager proposed a new Danish-designed chair that will sell for $150. The manager wants
to purchase the lumber from the Portneuf Mill. Production of 800 chairs is planned, using capacity in the furniture
division that is currently idle.

The furniture division can purchase the lumber for each chair from an outside supplier for $60. International
Woodworkers has a policy that internal transfers are priced at variable cost plus allocated fixed costs.

Assume the following costs for the production of one chair:

Portneuf Mill		Furniture Division	
Variable cost	$40	Variable costs:	
Allocated fixed cost	30	Lumber: Portneuf Mill	$ 70
Fully absorbed cost	$70	Furniture division variable costs:	
		Manufacturing	75
		Selling	10
		Total variable cost	$155

REQUIRED   **A.** Assume that the Portneuf Mill has idle capacity and would incur no additional fixed costs to produce the
required lumber. Would the furniture division manager buy the lumber for the chair from the Portneuf Mill,
given the existing transfer price policy? Why or why not?
B. Calculate the contribution margin for the company as a whole if the manager decides to buy from the Portneuf
Mill and is able to sell 800 chairs.
C. What transfer price policy would you recommend if the Portneuf Mill always has idle (excess) capacity? Explain why
this transfer price policy provides incentives for the managers to act in the best interests of the company as a whole.
D. Explain how the idle capacity affects the recommendation in Part C.

14.42 Transfer Price, Incentives for Internal Services Avra Valley Services has two divisions: Computer Services and Management
Advisory Services. Both divisions work for external customers and, in addition, work for each other. Fees earned by
Computer Services from external customers were $400,000 in 2012. Fees earned by Management Advisory Services
from external customers were $700,000 in 2012. Computer Services worked 3,000 hours for Management Advisory
Services that year, and Management Advisory Services worked 1,200 hours for Computer Services. The total costs of
external services performed by Computer Services were $220,000, and for Management Advisory Services, costs were
$480,000.

LO6, LO7

REQUIRED   **A.** Determine the operating income for each division and for the company as a whole if the transfer price from
Computer Services to Management Advisory Services is $50 per hour and the transfer price from Management
Advisory Services to Computer Services is $60 per hour.
B. The manager of Computer Services has found another company willing to provide the same services as
Management Advisory Services at $50 per hour. All of the employees in both units are guaranteed 40-hour
work weeks. Currently, Management Advisory Services has idle capacity because of an economic downturn.
Calculate the change in operating income for the company as a whole if Computer Services uses outsourced
services instead of using Management Advisory Services.
C. Recommend a transfer price policy that would provide incentives to use the internal services. Explain your
recommendation.
D. Discuss possible qualitative factors that might affect the attractiveness of the outsourcing option.

14.43 **Transfer Prices, Setting the Range of a Transfer Price, Opportunity Cost, Taxes** Eutronics has two divisions – Division A

LO6, LO7, LO8 manufactures compressors and Division B uses compressors to make air conditioners. Each division operates as a profit centre and is free to buy and sell products internally and externally. The revenue and cost of a compressor is shown below:

Capacity	15,000
Selling price to external customers	$180
Direct Materials	20
Direct Labours	60
Variable Manufacturing Costs	10
Fixed Manufacturing Costs (based on capacity)	45

Division B currently purchases 6,000 compressors from Division A at full cost. A salesperson approached Division B and offered to sell the compressors at $120. The manager of Division B is negotiating the price with the manager of Division A.

REQUIRED   **A.** If Division A operates at 50% of its capacity and can produce 6,000 compressors for Division B, what is the range of the transfer price, if any? If you were the manager of Division A, what transfer price would you offer the manager of Division B?

B. If Division A operates at 90% of its capacity and needs to give up 4,500 units of its existing sales to transfer 6,000 compressors to Division B, what is the range of the transfer price, if any? If you were the manager of Division A, what transfer price would you offer the manager of Division B?

C. If Division A's tax rate is 30% and Division B's tax rate is 45%, and Division A operates at 50% of its capacity, what should the transfer price be to maximize Eutronics' profit and minimize its taxes? Will each manager prefer to use cost or market price as the transfer price? Explain.

14.44 **Transfer Price, Setting the Range of a Transfer Price, Opportunity Cost** Sonico Electronics operates as a decentralized

LO6, LO7 company. Sonico's Battery division manufactures batter chargers that are sold both externally to outside customers and internally to the Camera division. Battery division's annual capacity is 90,000 units. The revenue and costs associated with one battery charger are as follows:

Selling Price to external customers	$20
Variable Cost	12
Fixed Cost (based on capacity)	4

The Camera division would like to purchase 27,000 units of battery chargers; however, Cameron, the manager of the Camera division, is able to purchase the battery charger from an overseas supplier at $18.

REQUIRED   **A.** Assuming the Battery division operates at 60% capacity, what is the range of the transfer price, if any, for the battery charger? Cameron has learned that the Battery division operates below its capacity. He is willing to pay up to $17.50 for a battery charger. Should the Battery division accept the offer at $17.50?

B. Assuming the Battery division operates at 85% capacity, what is the range of the transfer price, if any, for the battery charger? Cameron has learned that the Battery division operates below its capacity. He is willing to pay up to $17.50 for a battery charger. Should the Battery division accept the offer at $17.50?

C. Assuming the Battery division operates at 100% capacity, what is the range of the transfer price, if any, for the battery charger? Cameron has learned that the Battery division operates at its capacity and understands that Sonico encourages internal transfer of products and services. He is willing to pay up to $18 for a battery charger. Should the Battery division accept the offer at $18?

14.45 **Transfer Price, Setting the Range of a Transfer Price, Special Order, Opportunity Cost** Atex Ltd., has two

LO6, LO7 divisions: a Parts Division and a Products Division. Each division operates as a profit centre. The Parts Division manufactures keyboards and is free to sell its product internally and externally. The Parts Division's annual capacity is 45,000 units and its fixed cost is $720,000. Currently, external sales represent 70% of the Parts Division's production capacity. The selling price for a keyboard is $60, and the variable cost is 60% of the sale.

The Products Division is developing a new specialty keyboards. Mr. Allain, the manager of the Products Division, has obtained three quotes from external suppliers, $70, $78, and $82. He also asked the Parts Division to provide a quote for 9,000 units.

To take the specialty keyboard order, the Parts Division needs to invest in a stamping machine, costing $36,000. In addition, the specialty keyboard will incur additional $15 of variable cost for new features; however, it will reduce the regular variable cost by $3 of commission cost due to internal transfer. It takes 2 regular keyboards to make 1 specialty keyboard.

REQUIRED
A. Calculate the minimum transfer price for the specialty keyboard order.
B. Establish the range for the transfer price, if any, between the two divisions.
C. If the two divisions agree to split the difference between the market price and the cost, what price should they agree on?
D. Should the Parts Division pursue this opportunity to sell the specialty keyboard internally?

14.46 International Transfer Price, Setting the Range of a Transfer Price, Opportunity Cost Eason Electronics manufactures
LO1, LO6, LO7, LO8 wheelchairs. It has two divisions—the Motors Division located in Canada and the Assembly Division located in Japan. The Motors Division was originally set up to supply its motors to Eason's Japanese plant to complete the wheelchairs. Over the years, the Motors Division experienced idle capacity and the senior management agreed that the Motors Division could sell its motors to external customers. As a result, each division operates as an independent profit centre. The Motors Division's revenue and cost information is as follows:

Capacity (in units)	12,000
Selling price per unit	$650.00
Direct Materials	95.00
Direct Labour	180.00
Variable Manufacturing Overhead	50.00
Fixed Cost (based on capacity)	162.50

The Assembly Division can purchase a similar quality of motors in Japan for $550 each. The Canadian tax rate is 40% and the Japanese tax rate is 30%.

The Motors Division currently sells 9,000 units to external customers and 3,000 units to the Assembly Division. The Motors Division uses the variable costing approach (i.e. variable cost + variable cost x 40% mark-up) as the transfer price. One of the Motors Division's local customers would like to increase their annual order by 1,000 units. As a result, the Motors Division would like to charge the Assembly Division $650 per unit for 3,000 units to compensate for its loss of 1,000 units of sale from the local customer. The Assembly Division manager was not pleased about the increase in price, and argued that he is willing pay up to his local price of $550 per unit.

REQUIRED
A. Calculate the minimum transfer price, based on Eason's transfer price policy.
B. Establish the range for the transfer price, if any, between the two divisions.
C. If you were the CEO of Eason Electronics, which transfer price—Motors Division's external selling price, Motors Division's minimum transfer price, or Assembly Division's purchasing price—should Eason Electronics use to maximize profit and minimize taxes?
D. If the Assembly Division can purchase any quantity from the Motors Division, what is the best course of action for Eason Electronics as a whole? Explain.

MINI-CASES

14.47 Cost-Based Pricing, Cost Allocation, Specialty Market Suppose Jackson Jets is a small company that customizes
 LO1, LO2, LO3 Learjets for wealthy clients. At present, the company's managers are negotiating with three potential customers for next year's sales. The company's accountants summarized cost information for each plane as follows:

	Potential Customer			
(In thousands)	Rock Star	CEO	Sports Figure	Total
Avoidable costs				
Basic jet plane	$ 800	$ 800	$ 800	$2,400
Production	200	1,200	600	2,000
Selling costs	100	200	100	400
Total avoidable costs	$1,100	$2,200	$1,500	$4,800

Unavoidable costs	
Production	$3,000
Administration	600
Total unavoidable costs	$3,600

The unavoidable costs are the overhead costs to customize the jets, such as facility costs (rent, amortization, etc.) and equipment-related costs. These costs are primarily fixed. The company has a policy of calculating price by applying a 50% mark-up on cost. Two potential cost-based pricing schemes follow.

REQUIRED   **A.** Calculate the selling price for each model under both alternatives, A and B.

> **Alternative A.** Under this alternative, unavoidable costs are allocated to the three contracts equally, and a mark-up of 50% is added to total costs.
>
> **Alternative B.** Under this alternative, unavoidable costs are allocated to each contract based on its proportion of avoidable costs, and then a mark-up of 50% is added to total costs.

B. Which alternative would you recommend? Would you want any additional information before making this decision?

C. The price differences under alternatives A and B are caused by arbitrary allocations for overhead costs that cannot be attributed directly to the product. Should such allocations influence prices?

D. Companies also face uncertainty in determining an appropriate mark-up percentage. Why is the mark-up 50% and not 20%, 30%, or some other amount? What should the mark-up be if only avoidable costs are included in the calculation? Most importantly, what are customers willing to pay?

14.48 **For-Profit Versus Not-for-Profit Pricing, Setting a Market Price** Suppose the Province of Alberta decided to preserve

some beautiful caves in the southwestern part of the province. To defray the cost of preservation, provincial managers decided to open the caves to guided tours. To prepare the caves for visitors, vapour locks were built so that the moisture content of the caves would remain stable. The province spent $10 million on the facilities. Now the managers need to decide on a price for the tours.

INFORMATION ANALYSIS

REQUIRED   The following questions will help you analyze the information for this problem. Do not turn in your answers to these questions unless your professor asks you to do so.

A. Describe how pricing policies in not-for-profit organizations are different from pricing policies in for-profit organizations.

B. Use the Internet or other sources to identify current prices for other similar attractions.

C. What additional information would you gather to evaluate the price?

D. Do you believe that the volume of tours is likely to be sensitive to the price charged for tours? Why or why not?

WRITTEN ASSIGNMENT

REQUIRED   The managers of the park department need your price recommendation. Turn in your answer to the following.

E. Use the information you learned from the preceding analyses to write a memo to the Parks Department, recommending a price for the tour. Provide appropriate information for department managers to understand your methodology and evaluate the risks associated with your price recommendation.

14.49 **Cost-Based and Market-Based Pricing, Collusion** Burton Turner and Short Whittum live in a small town in western

Manitoba. They both own gas stations and provide gasoline and engine repair services for the area. The town is somewhat isolated, and during the winter it is sometimes difficult to travel to other towns in the surrounding area. While having coffee one morning, Turner and Whittum discuss the prices they charge for gasoline and for repair services. They decide that it would be a good policy if they both set the same prices because then customers would choose between the two businesses based on the quality of service and the brand name of the gasoline.

REQUIRED   **A.** What pricing alternatives are available to Turner and Whittum for setting prices? List as many alternatives as you can.

B. Is this an open-ended problem? Why or why not?

C. Explore this problem from the perspectives of

   1. Turner and Whittum

   2. Customers

   3. Government officials

D. Compare and contrast the legal and ethical issues in this situation. How are they the same? How are they different?

E. Ignoring possible legal issues, is the proposed pricing policy of Turner and Whittum ethical? Why or why not?

F. Suppose you are a government official, and you receive an anonymous phone call, telling you that Turner and Whittum are charging the same prices for gasoline and repair services. How might you monitor the two businesses to determine whether their actions are illegal?

14.50 **Choice of Transfer Price, Fairness to Managers** [*Note:* This problem is based on transfer prices and incentives for a real company. However, the name of the company has been changed and the data are fictional.] Prem International has two large subsidiaries: Oil and Chemical. Oil is an oil-refining business, and its main product is gasoline. Chemical produces and sells a variety of chemical products.

LO6, LO7, LO8

Chemical owns a polystyrene processing plant next to Oil's refinery. The polystyrene plant was built at the same time that Oil built a benzene plant at the refinery. Benzene is the raw material needed by Chemical to produce polystyrene. Chemical's managers believe they can sell 50 million kg of polystyrene per year, which is less than full capacity. Following are Chemical's expected revenues and costs for the polystyrene plant (volume is measured using weight in kilograms rather than using a liquid measure such as litres, because weight is not affected by temperature):

	Per Kilogram
Selling price	$0.30
Costs: Benzene (to be purchased from Oil)	$?
Variable production costs	0.03
Fixed production costs	0.05

Oil can operate at full capacity and sell all of the gasoline it produces. Following are Oil's expected revenues and costs for the production of gasoline:

	Per Kilogram
Selling price	$0.16
Costs: Crude oil	$0.06
Variable production costs	0.02
Fixed production costs	0.07

For every kilogram of benzene that Oil produces, it will forgo selling a kilogram of gasoline. However, 50 million kilograms per year would be only a small portion of total volume at the refinery. Following are Oil's expected revenues and costs for the production of benzene (these costs include the costs of refining the crude oil):

	Per Kilogram
Selling price (to Chemical)	$?
Costs: Crude oil	$0.06
Variable production costs	0.04
Fixed production costs	0.09

REQUIRED

A. On a company-wide basis, should Prem International produce polystyrene this year? Why or why not?

B. Using the usual quantitative rules for short-term decisions (Chapter 4), what is the maximum price that Chemical's managers would be willing to pay for benzene?

C. Would Chemical's managers be willing to pay the maximum transfer price calculated in Part B? Why or why not?

D. Using the usual quantitative rules for short-term decisions (Chapter 4), what is the minimum price that Oil's managers would be willing to receive for benzene?

E. Would Oil's managers be willing to receive the minimum transfer price calculated in Part D? Why or why not?

F. What transfer price might be fair to the managers of both subsidiaries? Explain.

## CHAPTER 15

Strategic Management of Costs

After studying this chapter, you should be able to do the following:

LO1 Explain how value chain analysis, supply chain, and JIT are used to improve operations

LO2 Explain target costing and calculate target costs

LO3 Explain kaizen costing and compare it to target costing

LO4 Explain life cycle costing

LO5 Explain lean accounting and discuss how it is used

in brief Managers and accountants make decisions about long-term organizational strategies as well as short-term operating plans. These strategies and plans include mutually dependent decisions about how to control costs and price products to generate profits and achieve organizational goals. To be successful, managers must understand relationships with both internal and external suppliers and customers. Managers increasingly adopt practices such as target costing, kaizen costing, and just-in-time inventory management to help improve efficiency and achieve profitability goals. Understanding cost measurements and pricing methods, and their interrelationships, help managers make these types of decisions. ■

Value Chain Success at the Little Potato Company

© Fotomaton/Alamy Stock Photo

The Little Potato Company, located in Edmonton, Alberta, began as a one-acre experiment in 1996. From its humble father-daughter beginnings with personal door-to-door selling, The Little Potato Company (LPC) has grown into a multimillion dollar success story. As LPC began to grow, both father and daughter realized the importance of developing appropriate connections with growers, new product developers, and a variety of different customers.

The Little Potato Company produces small potatoes—on purpose. To be successful, LPC needed to develop high-quality, nutritious mini potatoes, provide fresh potatoes year round, and reach customers through multiple channels. As LPC grew and Angela Santiago took the helm, her father, Jacob van der Schaaf, focused on research and development of new varieties. Van der Schaaf travels around the world meeting with growers and developing personal relationships that help ensure a high-quality, consistent product year round. LPC partners with farmers in Alberta, Saskatchewan, PEI, the United States, Europe, and South America. Through rigorous trials, LPC now has proprietary rights to several mini-potato varieties ranging from 19 mm to 41 mm in diameter, including Baby Boomer, Piccolo, Blushing Belle, and Terrific Trio.

In the beginning, Santiago marketed the little potatoes at local farmers' markets and by personally calling on restaurant owners. Through persistence and the quality of the product, she gained the attention of a regional retailer who began carrying LPC products. LPC's success grew from there, and LPC now supplies national retailers across North America.

Santiago believes that LPC's success is closely tied to its strict quality control processes at its Edmonton plant, which processed more than 22 million kg of potatoes in 2013. Several times a year, LPC's retailers audit quality control procedures in receiving, washing, packaging, and shipping. One quality control procedure is to ensure that all potatoes in one package vary no more than 5 mm in size difference. This shared focus on quality control builds trust between LPC and its retailers.

Santiago's current goal is for the Edmonton-based LPC to become the biggest supplier of little potatoes in the United States—a tribute to the importance of the Albertan agriculture sector. Doing so will require continuing to make smart strategic business moves. Santiago states, "We're trying to make potatoes fun again…It's about giving a consumer a great experience with a potato." To achieve this goal, The Little Potato Company works with breeders from Holland to Central America to bring small, colourful potatoes to a growing consumer following.

SOURCE: "Taste Alberta: Edmonton Company Wants to Make Potatoes Fun Again," *Edmonton Journal*, June 10, 2013; Case Study: The Little Potato Company, Government of Alberta (http://www.productivity-alberta.ca/articles/13/case-study-the-little-potato-company); "The Little Potato Company: From Humble Beginnings To Great Success," September 18, 2009, *Food & Food Equipment News*; The Little Potato Company website at http://www.littlepotatoes.com.

Strategic Cost Analysis

Over the long term, profitable organizations continuously seek ways to become more efficient, reduce costs, and improve interactions with suppliers and customers. A variety of methods are available for analyzing and improving the systems used to produce and deliver goods and services.

Value Chain Analysis

As managers take a more strategic approach to decision making, understanding the relationships between internal and external suppliers and customers is critical. This knowledge helps managers identify and maintain the organization's competitive advantages and respond to competitive pressures with respect to costs and prices.

A **value chain** is the sequence of business processes in which value is added to a product or service. In 1985, Harvard professor Michael Porter introduced a generic value chain and suggested that the details of these models vary by industry.[1] Exhibit 15.1 is a diagram of a generic manufacturer's value chain that is similar to Porter's chain of primary activities. The value chain for a service organization is similar but focuses on the process for providing services rather than manufactured goods.

An organization's value chain encompasses not only customers and suppliers but even, in some cases, incorporates the customers' customers and the suppliers' suppliers. Analysis of the value chain leads to improved relationships between the organization and others in the value chain, creating an extended organization that can respond with flexibility to dynamic and competitive environments. In other words, value chains explicitly recognize that no organization operates in isolation from suppliers and customers.

▶EXHIBIT 15.1

Value Chain for a Manufacturer

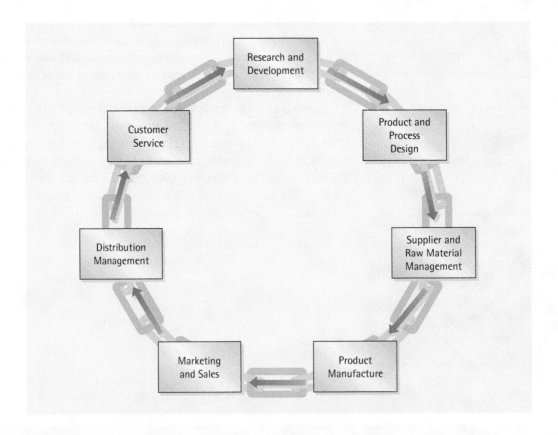

[1] M. Porter, *Competitive Advantage* (New York: The Free Press, 1985).

Value-Added and Non-Value-Added Activities

Value chain analysis involves studying each step in the business process to determine whether some activities can be eliminated because they do not add value. This analysis extends to suppliers and customers, and it includes shared planning, inventory, human resources, information technology systems, and even corporate cultures. Ultimately, the analysis leads to business decisions for improving value. Activity-based costing in combination with activity-based management is a useful approach for identifying non-value-added activities.

For example, Canada Post implemented an electronic package-tracking system and epost, an electronic bill payment system, to meet the changing needs of customers while reducing paperwork and improving package tracking. The managers believed that the traditional paper package-tracking system did not add value for Canada Post, and an increasing numbers of customers did not perceive paper bills as value added, even though the information was necessary. With these new systems, packages can be tracked directly by the customer, and bills are delivered to customers electronically. Both electronic systems eliminate paper-based processes and improve the flow of information, making it directly available to customers when they want it.[2] While the systems enable Canada Post to give customers updated information about their packages and bills, managers now have more planning information about capacity levels and future needs across locations. The new system allowed Canada Post to eliminate a non-value-added activity and also to add value by producing more timely information both for internal purposes and for customers.

Value-added activities are tasks or functions that increase the worth of an organization's products and services to customers. These activities include the manufacturing process and other operations that allow the organization to perform processes essential for attracting new and retaining old customers. **Non-value-added activities** do not directly affect customers. Some non-value-added activities, such as accounting, while essential and related to daily operations, are not usually related to customer value. When managing essential, non-value-added activities, the focus is on efficiency. Some non-value-added activities are unnecessary and can be eliminated directly or by changing processes. For example, some customer warranty work can be eliminated through better quality control during manufacturing or better inspection of completed units.

Before activities in the value chain can be improved or eliminated, they must be identified and then categorized as value-added or non-value-added activities. Some organizations use four categories, recognizing both that it may be possible to improve value-added activities and that time may be needed to eliminate non-value-added activities.[3] Exhibit 15.2 presents these

>CHAPTER REFERENCE

For more details about using activity-based costing (ABC) and activity-based management (ABM) to identify non-value-added activities, see Chapter 7.

Activity Classification	Action to Improve Value
A necessary activity that cannot be improved upon at this time	None
A necessary activity that could be changed to improve the process	Modify the process to improve value. *Example:* Plant layout could be changed so that materials handling activities are reduced.
An unnecessary activity that can eventually be eliminated by changing the process	Eventually eliminate the unnecessary activity. *Example:* Eliminate manual recording of employee hours using time cards. A new payroll system is eventually implemented. Plastic identity cards with magnetic strips are swiped through time clocks. The system electronically tracks hours worked and processes paycheques.
An unnecessary activity that can quickly be eliminated by changing the process	Immediately eliminate the unnecessary activity. *Example:* In team manufacturing, inspection of units completed can be eliminated if each team member inspects each unit before it passes to the next team member.

>EXHIBIT 15.2

Classification of Value-Added and Non-Value-Added Activities

---

[2] epost website, www.epost.ca.
[3] R. Kaplan and R. Cooper, *Cost and Effect* (Cambridge, MA: Harvard Business School Press, 1998).

four categories, with examples of actions that managers could take to improve value. The process of analyzing and categorizing activities also improves communication, as individuals in each part of the process begin to share their abilities, needs, and requirements with others in the value chain.

Value chain analysis encourages managers to consider whether they should outsource some of their value-added activities. Sometimes, outsourcing is less costly than performing an activity internally. Managers often choose to outsource an activity because it is not a core competency of the organization. For example, Canada Post management probably decided to outsource the IS/IT portion of its electronic tracking system and epost because technology development and implementation is not one of Canada Post's core competencies.[4] Ultimately, the decision of whether to outsource an activity depends on both quantitative and qualitative factors.

Supply Chain Analysis

As organizations work to increase profitability, improving their relationships with suppliers becomes a priority. Improvements can be identified through supply chain analysis. The **supply chain** is the flow of resources from the initial suppliers through the delivery of goods and services to customers and clients. The initial suppliers may be inside or outside the organization. Negotiating lower costs with suppliers is a straightforward way to reduce costs. Suppliers may be willing to reduce prices, particularly for organizations willing to sign long-term purchase commitments. Occasionally, organizations work with suppliers to help reduce their costs, so that the savings can be passed along. Suppose Mountain High Bikes, a mountain bike manufacturer, sends a team of employees to its handlebar supplier to help redesign the component to be lighter weight and sturdier and to require fewer parts and labour. If this effort were successful, both the cost of handlebars and their shipping costs would decrease.

Accountants analyze supply chains by determining inventory level requirements, starting with customer demand for products or services. Opportunities to reduce costs and improve quality are identified through tracking and analyzing usage patterns of raw materials, supplies, finished goods, and shipped goods. Vendors are included in inventory management decisions as part of this process. With close cooperation between the two parties, inventory levels can be managed to reduce both the quantitative costs of insurance and storage and the qualitative costs of quality changes and timeliness of delivery.

Using the Internet to Improve Inventory Supply

The Internet increasingly provides suppliers with access to information about their customers' inventory levels. Suppliers use this information to time deliveries so that their customers maintain desired inventory levels. Suppliers also use this information to improve their own production planning.

The cooperation between retailer Costco and its supplier Kimberly-Clark is a good example of supply chain efficiency. Kimberly-Clark uses an automated Internet system to monitor disposable diaper quantities in each Costco store. The system manages the reordering and delivery of goods as needed to maintain inventory levels.[6] This system reduces Costco's inventory costs while also enabling Kimberly-Clark to anticipate production needs and work with its own suppliers to receive raw materials in a timely manner.

Providing Internet access to product or service information can be risky, however. Organizations need adequate security measures such as firewalls to protect sensitive information that might have competitive value.

► CHAPTER REFERENCE
For more details about making non-routine decisions, such as whether to insource or outsource a service or product, see Chapter 4.

► BUSINESS PRACTICE
In one year, **Innovapost** reduced Canada Post's information technology infrastructure costs by 20% through improving the information technology component of its supply chain.[5]

► BUSINESS PRACTICE
Cisco Systems has a private information hub on the Internet that links manufacturers, distributors, and component suppliers. Cisco can use this hub to immediately notify its suppliers of any changes in requirements.[7]

---

[4] Canada Post has partnered with Innovapost to provide electronic solutions to package tracking and bill delivery update requirements. See http://innovapost.com/about/
[5] "About Innovapost," http://innovapost.com/about/
[6] E. Melson and A. Zimmerman, "Minding the Store: Kimberly-Clark Keeps Costco in Diapers...," *The Wall Street Journal*, September 7, 2000, p. A1.
[7] P. K. Tam, "Going Mobile," *Transportation and Distribution*, July 2003, p. 23.

EXHIBIT 15.3
Master Lock Company Uses Cellular Manufacturing

Jeffrey Phelps/AP Photo/The Canadian Press

Just-in-Time Production

With **just-in-time (JIT) production and inventory control systems**, materials are purchased and units are produced at the time customers demand them. JIT is considered a demand-pull system because products and their parts are manufactured just as they are needed for each step in the manufacturing process. In JIT inventory control systems, organizations work with suppliers so that goods or materials are delivered just as they are needed for production or for sale. Suppliers make frequent deliveries of small lots of goods directly to the production floor or to sales areas in merchandising organizations.

In JIT manufacturing systems, the production process is often broken into steps that are performed in manufacturing cells. A cell is an area where all of the equipment and labour is grouped for a particular part of the manufacturing process, as shown in Exhibit 15.3. Parts and supplies arrive "just in time" to be used for each specific manufacturing task. When one cell finishes its set of tasks, the product is either complete or moves to the next cell, where more work is performed. Production is continuous; as soon as team members finish their production tasks on one unit, another unit is begun. The product moves through all the cells until the manufacturing process is complete. The manufacturing sequence is organized not only to minimize handling and storage but also to minimize defect rates.

Successful implementation of JIT systems requires that organizations do the following:

- ► Find high-quality suppliers
- ► Choose a manageable number of suppliers
- ► Locate suppliers with short transit times for materials being delivered
- ► Develop efficient and reliable materials handling processes
- ► Develop management commitment to the JIT process

JIT systems reduce costs by maximizing the use of space, lowering defect rates, and increasing manufacturing flexibility. Each team member is responsible for product inspection so that defects are identified quickly and quality problems can be remedied immediately. When manufacturers produce a number of different product models under a JIT system, changeover to the next model occurs almost immediately. This approach enhances manufacturing flexibility. Experts in operations management believe that the JIT approach may be one of the most significant developments in management innovation in the past century.[8]

ALTERNATIVE TERMS

Some people use the term *lean production* or *kanban* to describe just-in-time production systems. The term *JIT* is also used more broadly, in conjunction with services such as "JIT education."

---

[8] R. J. Schonberger, *World Class Manufacturing: The Next Decade* (New York: The Free Press, 1996).

> **BUSINESS PRACTICE**
>
> One drawback of JIT systems is that production halts when suppliers are unable to deliver supplies as needed. Sometimes, unforeseen events interrupt the delivery schedule. For example, shortly after the terrorist attacks of September 11, 2001, increased security measures were implemented at all Canada–United States border crossings. Businesses reacted to these changes by altering trading behaviours, including shifting away from preferred, more efficient practices. Due to delays and unpredictability at the border, companies on both sides of the border began to stockpile inventory. Some companies with warehouses in Canada established redundant warehouses on the U.S. side of the border to hedge against unforeseen delays. This behaviour increases direct and indirect inventory costs.[9]

Other Benefits of Analyzing Production and Service Systems

Value chain analysis, supply chain analysis, and just-in-time systems provide benefits beyond reducing non-value-added activities and costs, such as inventory storage and insurance. These methods lead to further cost reductions by focusing management attention on minimizing rework, scrap, and waste. In addition, managers often identify opportunities to reduce production cycle times.

Sometimes, the use of one method leads to another method. For example, value chain analysis might encourage accountants to analyze their supply chain and adopt JIT to reduce non-value-added activities. Value chain analysis might also help accountants identify bottlenecks or other process constraints. Theory of Constraints analysis can be used to improve the system while balancing the flow of production with demand. Managers use a wide range of tools to analyze production and delivery systems, with the goal of improving cost and quality. Accountants help managers by bringing these tools to their attention and providing the analysis.

▶ **CHAPTER REFERENCE**

Chapter 17 introduces throughput accounting and further discusses production cycle times.

▶ **CHAPTER REFERENCE**

See Chapter 4 for more information about the Theory of Constraints.

Continuous Cost Improvement

Accountants use estimates of revenues and costs to provide information for a range of operating decisions. In the short term, the general rule is to sell goods or services as long as estimated revenues exceed estimated variable costs. However, in the long term, organizations need to earn a reasonable return on investment. Next, we discuss the following techniques used to plan for long-term profitability:

- ▶ Target costing
- ▶ Kaizen costing
- ▶ Life cycle costing

Although these methods alone do not result in increased profitability, they help accountants become more deliberate about profit planning. When costs appear to be too high, these methods also encourage accountants and managers to identify and implement cost management techniques.

▶ **CHAPTER REFERENCE**

For more information on short-term decisions, see chapters 3 and 4.

Target Costing

L02 Explain target costing and calculate target costs

When launching a new product, managers traditionally determined the cost of the product and then used the cost to help set a price that would achieve a desired profit margin. Given this information, the managers evaluated the feasibility of the new product. An alternative

---

[9] "Is Just-in-Case Replacing Just-in-Time? How Cross-Border Trading Behaviour Has Changed Since 9/11," *Trade, Investment Policy and International Cooperation National Security and Safety; Briefing,* The Conference Board of Canada; International Trade and Investment Centre, June 2007.

decision-making approach is **target costing**, which uses market-based prices to determine whether products and services can be delivered at costs low enough to make an acceptable profit. Competitors' products are *reverse engineered* (taken apart and put back together again) to better understand the manufacturing process and the product design. In turn, the product and manufacturing process are redesigned so that the product meets a pre-specified target cost. Organizations can then sell products at competitive prices and still earn profits.

In the late 1970s and early 1980s, Komatsu, a heavy equipment company, used target costing to develop products similar in quality and functionality to those of Caterpillar, but Komatsu was able to set its prices lower than Caterpillar's. Prior to the mid-1980s, Caterpillar was financially stable, but by the late 1980s, the company was struggling against a weak global economy and competition from Komatsu, losing $1 billion over a three-year period. Mark Thompson, a business analysis manager with Caterpillar's wheel-loader and excavator division, recalled, "We had to do something drastic. The viability of the company depended on it."[10] Caterpillar's managers turned to target costing, the same method that had enabled Komatsu to become so competitive. Caterpillar accountants and analysts studied publicly available financial statements to identify Komatsu's costs. They learned that Caterpillar's production costs were 30% higher than Komatsu's.

Next, Caterpillar's engineers purchased, tore apart, and reverse-engineered Komatsu's products to determine the processes and designs Komatsu used in manufacturing. Caterpillar managers then invested $1.8 billion in plant modernization. They eliminated non-value-added processes, examined their procedures for purchasing raw materials and supplies, moved to a just-in-time inventory system, and reduced the number of parts used in Caterpillar products. Using target costing techniques, Caterpillar produced record-setting profits.

©Taina Sohlman/iStockphoto

▷ **INTERNATIONAL**
Toyota, credited with inventing target costing, has been using this method since the 1960s.[11]

Target Costing Process

As highlighted in the Caterpillar example, target costing helps organizations improve production processes and profits. Target costing is the process of researching consumer markets to estimate an appropriate market price, and then subtracting the desired return to determine a maximum allowable cost. This target cost is the maximum cost at which the company can produce a good or service to generate the desired profit margin. The organization then determines whether the good or service can be designed and produced to meet the target cost. This step involves managing both the product design and manufacturing phases. If expected costs exceed the target, managers will choose not to provide a good or service. To date, target costing has been used primarily for products that have already been manufactured by other companies; however, it is increasingly being used for new goods and services.

The key value of target costing is that it focuses managers' attention on the design phase, where most cost savings potentially occur, because 70% to 80% of product costs are typically committed at this point. Costs that occur both when the manufacturing process is set up and during manufacturing are locked in during the design phase. For example, new equipment is chosen and direct materials are specified that will be used in production. Although the actual costs occur over a product's life cycle, the decisions made in the planning phase have the greatest influence over those costs. Under target costing, the decision to produce a good or service depends on expected costs developed in the design phase. The steps in a target costing design cycle are summarized in Exhibit 15.4. The description of each step follows.

Determine the Product Target Price, Quality, and Functionality. Accountants and managers use studies such as consumer surveys, focus groups, and market research of competitors' prices to determine a competitive price for a specific product. Researchers collect information about consumer preferences, including trade-offs customers are willing to make among price, quality, and functionality for a product or service. A competitive price *for a given level of product quality and functionality* can then be estimated. In industries where

---

[10] K. Kroll, "On Target," *IndustryWeek*, June 9, 1997, pp. 14–22.
[11] "On Target. . .Time After Time," *Journal of Product and Brand Management*, 5(5), 1996, pp. 8–10.

Steps in a Target Costing Design Cycle

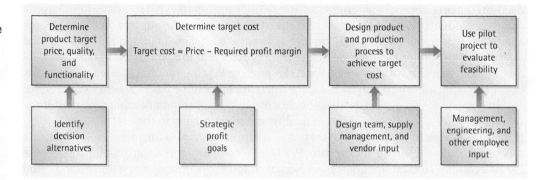

some customers are willing to pay higher prices for higher quality or more functionality, managers strategically differentiate their products and establish market positions. The same is true when there are customers willing to give up a certain amount of quality or functionality to obtain lower prices.

The automobile industry provides a good example of product differentiation. Some manufacturers emphasize a low price for lower levels of quality and functionality. Other manufacturers emphasize quality and are able to charge higher prices. Sometimes, functionality, such as four-wheel-drive capability or trucks with four-door cabs, is emphasized. Increases in functionality are usually accompanied by increases in product prices. When cars are being designed, the marketing department analyzes consumer preferences to determine the optimal levels of quality and functionality for a particular price.

Customers in some industries are unwilling to pay for higher quality or functionality. In Caterpillar's industry (heavy machinery), the products are used in construction. Purchasing decisions tend to revolve around price and only one quality factor—reliability. Extra functions such as air-conditioned cabs are unlikely to increase a product's marketability.

Determine Target Cost. After a competitive price is determined for specific levels of product quality and functionality, the required profit margin is subtracted from the price to arrive at the target cost:

$$\text{Target cost} = \text{Price} - \text{Required profit margin}$$

The required profit margin is usually a function of the organization's long-term strategic goals. Managers who use this method assume that producers cannot set the price but, instead, must take the market's price. Accordingly, the production decision focuses on the organization's ability to produce goods or services at the specified target cost.

Design Product and Production Process to Achieve the Target Cost. A product design team is assembled from personnel in product engineering, marketing, and accounting. This team designs the product at the specified levels of quality and functionality and then develops the manufacturing process. During the design phase, the team focuses on reducing the complexity of the product and manufacturing process to meet the target cost. If the team is unable to meet the target cost, the design process is reiterated with negotiations on possible trade-offs among price, quality, and functionality. If the product still cannot be manufactured at the target cost after several iterations, production plans are suspended. A similar process takes place in service industries; teams—including service-specific professional, marketing, and accounting personnel—design the type of service to be provided and the service delivery modes. The next step is taken only if the target cost is achieved in the design phase.

Use Pilot Project to Evaluate Feasibility. Once the production process has been designed so that the cost to manufacture a product is at or below the target cost, a pilot project replicates a small version of the production line to determine the feasibility of the product and process design and the cost. If the pilot project is successful, full production begins. If it is unsuccessful, the team returns to the design phase. Similar pilot projects are used in service organizations to evaluate feasibility.

Factors that Affect the Success of Target Costing

Target costing performs best under the following conditions:

► Product development and design phases are long and complex
► The production process is complex
► The market is willing to pay for differences in quality or function
► The manufacturer can push some cost reductions onto suppliers and subcontractors
► The manufacturer can influence the design of subparts

Target costing is inappropriate in industries with simple production processes, such as food products and beverages, which are typically unable to differentiate their products based on quality and functionality. In the food industry, advertising campaigns and brand name recognition influence price the most.

The following example describes the target costing process for a bike manufacturer.

mont-tremblant bikes, part 1
TARGET COSTING

example

©AlenaPaulus/iStockphoto

Mont-Tremblant Bikes (MTB) is a start-up company that manufactures high-quality mountain bikes that compete with products from companies such as **Trek Canada** and **Norco Performance Bikes**. One of MTB's employees has developed a new braking system that allows bikers to descend steep slopes using a consistent braking pattern that pumps both front and back brakes at regular, preset intervals, depending on the brake setting that the biker chooses. The marketing department surveyed current customers and found that they would be willing to pay more for this option. Because MTB's brand name is not yet well established, prices for its bikes need to be kept below those of its major competitors. MTB's owner, Lora Marks, wants the company to launch a line of bikes with the new braking system. Her accountant recommended that the company use target costing to develop the new product to ensure that the design is feasible.

Determine Product Target Price, Quality, and Functionality

After conducting customer surveys and a number of focus groups, MTB's marketing staff identified five features that are highly important to prospective customers: the weight of the bike, the bike's ability to withstand hard riding in difficult terrain for long periods of time, appearance, ease of handling, and riding comfort over rough terrain. Depending on the brand name of the bike and its components, the market price for competing models with these features ranges between $800 and $1,200. The model with the highest market share in that price range is priced at $949. From the survey and focus group information gathered, Lora believes that a bike with the new braking system and the same levels of quality and functionality as the competitors' models should be priced at $950 to achieve a 25% market share. She decides to call the new model the Mountain Braker.

Determine Target Cost

Lora sets a minimum profit margin of 10% on new products. Given this information, Lora's accountant sets the new product's target cost:

Price	$950
Less profit margin	95
Target cost	$855

Design Product and Production Process to Achieve Target Cost

Lora establishes a team to handle the product and manufacturing process design. The team consists of one person from each of the following areas: marketing, engineering, purchasing, accounting, and administration.

continued...

First, the team identifies an initial cost for the Mountain Braker. The engineer alters MTB's basic bike design to incorporate the new braking system. The cost estimate of $905 is higher than the target cost of $855, so the team considers ways to reduce the cost. The team assembles information about current costs and necessary cost reductions, assuming sales of 50,000 bikes. It identifies areas with the most potential for cost reduction and then establishes the following estimates for these reductions:

Cost Category	Current Cost per Bike	Target Cost	Cost Reduction Needed
New brake development	$ 50	$ 50	$ 0
Manufacturing	710	680	30
Total manufacturing costs	760	730	30
Selling and distribution	55	50	5
Warranty and support	35	30	5
Administration	55	45	10
Total cost	$905	$855	$50

Product Design Changes

The team decides to use value chain analysis (Exhibit 15.1) to seek opportunities for cost reduction. It focuses on the product design phase of the value chain. The engineer analyzes the current design, searching for steps in the manufacturing process and components that can be eliminated. The accountant provides cost information for prospective changes. The marketing person provides information about customer reactions to proposed changes.

Reflectors. The team suggests eliminating the reflectors mounted on the spokes. Because the Mountain Braker would be used primarily in very rough terrain, any reflectors are likely to break. Furthermore, the relatively few riders who use the bike on roads typically do not rely on reflectors but use battery-operated head and taillights instead. The accountant estimates that $15 per bike can be saved by eliminating both the reflectors and the process of mounting them. After sending emails to prospective customers, the marketing team member confirms that eliminating reflectors will not affect consumer demand for the product or expected price.

Bike Seats. When the engineer suggests a cheaper bike seat that is easier to mount, the marketing representative organizes a focus group with prospective customers to determine the effect on sales. Feedback from the focus group indicates that the price would have to be reduced if a lower-quality seat were installed, so this idea is dropped.

Supplier Negotiations

The team next focuses on the direct materials purchasing function in the value chain analysis, investigating cost reductions from current suppliers and searching for similar-quality components at reduced prices from new suppliers. Purchasing personnel meet with all the components suppliers to negotiate cost reductions.

Handlebars. The handlebar supplier suggests a new product with comparable quality to the current handlebars and at a cost reduction of $10 per bike. Marketing determines that the new handlebars would not affect customers' perceptions of quality.

Tires. Purchasing works with the company that supplies tires. Buying tires in larger lots can save the supplier delivery and storage costs, and MTB currently has storage space available. The new purchase agreement reduces costs by $5 per bike.

Tire Tubes. Purchasing finds a new tire tube vendor that can supply tubes at a cost reduction of $5 per bike.

Combined, the changes the team recommends are expected to reduce manufacturing costs by $35 ($15 + $10 + $5 + $5) rather than the needed $30. Thus, the target cost for manufacturing costs is met. The team now focuses on the remaining costs that need to be reduced.

Nonmanufacturing Costs

The target costing team meets with the marketing department and the director of finance to identify reductions in selling and distribution, warranty and support, and administration costs.

Selling and Distribution. Marketing is concerned that reducing commissions or advertising will affect total sales and potential market share gains for MTB, and wants no cost reduction on advertising or commissions for this new product. The successful introduction of the new braking system relies in part on individual sales representatives highlighting the feature and in part on an advertisement campaign featuring the braking system. However, the shipping company has agreed to a reduction in shipping costs of $5 per bike because MTB's volumes have been increasing rapidly; it is cheaper for the shipping company to ship large lots.

Warranty and Support. MTB's managers are concerned that reducing customer warranty and support costs—both areas in which MTB currently has a strong reputation—would be risky with a new product. If the company reduces these costs and then is unable to provide its current level of service, a loss of reputation could result. Fortunately, manufacturing costs were reduced by $5 more than originally planned. Therefore, the team decides not to reduce warranty and support costs at this time.

Administration. Some administrative functions, such as payroll, have recently been outsourced. It appears that the administrative cost reduction of $10 per bike will be easily met.

Total Planned Cost Reduction

The following summary shows the cost reduction estimates achieved by the design team:

Cost Category	Reduction Needed (Revised)	Reduction Achieved
New brake development	$ 0	$ 0
Manufacturing:	35	
Reflectors		15
Handlebars		10
Tires		5
Tubes		5
Selling and distribution (reduced shipping charges)	5	5
Warranty and support (no reduction necessary)	0	0
Administration (outsourcing services)	10	10
Total	$50	$50

Pilot Project to Evaluate Feasibility

After the team reconfigures the bike, a pilot manufacturing line is set up, and 100 bikes are produced. The first 50 bikes cost $780 to produce, but the manufacturing line employees learned how to install the new braking system more quickly, so the last 50 bikes cost $730, as projected.

The managers decide to begin full production of the new product. This decision turns out well for the company; the bike sells faster and in larger numbers than anticipated. ■

Kaizen Costing

Kaizen costing is continuous improvement in product cost, quality, and functionality. It is similar to target costing in that cost targets (goals) are set based on price predictions. However, kaizen costing occurs after a product is designed and the first production cycle is complete. Market prices tend to decrease over many products' life cycles. Under kaizen costing, accountants forecast declining prices and establish cost reduction goals to maintain

LO3 Explain kaizen costing and compare it to target costing

EXHIBIT 15.5

Kaizen Planning Process for Revenues and Costs

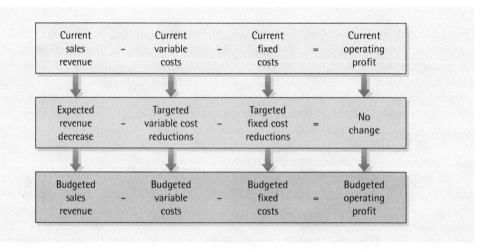

Current sales revenue	−	Current variable costs	−	Current fixed costs	=	Current operating profit
Expected revenue decrease	−	Targeted variable cost reductions	−	Targeted fixed cost reductions	=	No change
Budgeted sales revenue	−	Budgeted variable costs	−	Budgeted fixed costs	=	Budgeted operating profit

a desired level of profit margin. Therefore, the objectives of kaizen costing include not only continuous improvement but also continuous cost reduction.

Because kaizen costing relies on sales forecasts, the kaizen plan is similar to a budget, except that kaizen costing provides for explicit cost reductions. Exhibit 15.5 summarizes the kaizen planning process for revenues and costs.

INTERNATIONAL

To meet strategic objectives, **Daihatsu**, a Japanese manufacturer of compact cars, uses kaizen costing as part of its annual budgeting cycle, building in cost reduction and quality improvement goals.[12]

Planned Cost Reductions

In manufacturing organizations, estimated variable costs are the sum of estimates for direct material and direct labour costs as well as variable manufacturing overhead. Accountants and managers develop plans to estimate reductions for these variable costs. Estimated reductions in fixed costs are developed from human resource plans for fixed labour and service department personnel, combined with facility investment plans and fixed expense plans (design, maintenance, advertising, sales promotions, and general and administrative expenses). These estimated costs are based on the prior period's actual costs, adjusted for any anticipated price changes.

In service organizations, the estimated variable costs are developed from projections of supplies and direct labour that vary with the services provided, variable overhead, and any variable merchandising costs in retail industries. The estimated fixed costs are developed in the same manner used for manufacturing organizations.

Achieving Planned Cost Reductions

After the targeted cost reduction goals are set, each department is assigned responsibility for specific cost reduction amounts. These goals are met in several ways. One option is to use value chain analysis to redesign the production or service process to increase overall productivity and efficiency. Meetings may be held with manufacturing or service personnel to brainstorm ideas for cost reduction. To encourage idea generation, some companies even share any initial gains in cost reduction with the employees who suggested the cost-reducing changes. Another option is to use supply chain analysis, working with suppliers and issuing target cost reductions for intermediate manufacturing parts or service supplies. Some companies work with suppliers to develop new product and process designs needed to achieve cost reductions.

[12] Y. Monden and J. Lee, "How a Japanese Auto Maker Reduces Costs," *Management Accounting*, August 1993, pp. 22–27.

mont-tremblant bikes, part 2
KAIZEN COSTING

©AlenaPaulus/iStockphoto

Mont-Tremblant Bikes has now been producing Mountain Brakers for two years, and sales are beginning to drop because competitors are producing similar braking systems. MTB's marketing manager believes that if the company wants sales and market share to increase, prices will have to decrease. The accountant recommends that the company use kaizen costing to reduce the price and cost of the Mountain Braker.

Cost Reductions

The marketing manager estimates that the bike's price should be reduced by 10%, to be competitive with other manufacturers. Therefore, costs also need to be reduced by 10% to maintain the same percentage margin, although the dollar value of the margin will decrease. The bike's current price is $950, with a cost of $855. The new price will be $855, and the corresponding cost reduction needed is $85.50. The current margin is $95, and the new margin will be $85.50. The following summary assumes that reductions will be made proportionately across all cost categories:

Cost Category	Current Cost per Bike	Needed Cost Reduction (10% goal)
New brake development	$ 50	$ 5.00
Manufacturing	675	67.50
Selling and distribution	50	5.00
Warranty and support	35	3.50
Administration	45	4.50
Total	$855	$85.50

The same team that developed the Mountain Braker at target cost in the design phase meets again to suggest further cost reduction plans.

Product Design Changes

After careful analysis, the team finds no way to reduce costs for the new braking system at this time. Therefore, the $5 needed cost reduction for the brakes will have to come from another process or component.

Process Design Changes

Using value chain analysis, the team reviews both the manufacturing processes and the bike design, searching for non-value-added activities or components that can be eliminated.

Gears. A new gear system has been developed by one of the vendors, eliminating two steps in the manufacturing process. As a result, the engineer estimates that one labourer could be moved to another bike production line to replace a retiring worker, reducing total labour costs. This reduction amounts to $10 per bike.

Supply Chain Analysis

The MTB team meets with suppliers to determine whether cost reductions or product improvements are possible from the components used in manufacturing.

Wheels. The wheel and spoke vendor has improved the quality of its product and dropped the price, saving $13 per bike.

Frames. A new bike frame that is just as solid as the current frame has been developed from an innovative new alloy and will save MTB $35.

Tires. At the end of the last quarter, the supplier of tubes and tires asked for a small price increase. The purchasing department surveys vendor websites for tubes and tires. After contacting several different vendors, a price reduction is negotiated with a new supplier of tires. An additional vendor is added to supply tubes at a reduced price. These two cost savings amount to $10 per bike.

Overall, the team is able to achieve total cost reduction for manufacturing of $68 ($10 + $13 + $35 + $10). This amount is $0.50 more than is needed from manufacturing but leaves a $4.50 required reduction because the cost of brakes could not be reduced.

continued...

example

Nonmanufacturing Costs

The team now turns its attention to achieving the remaining cost reductions.

Marketing. The marketing representative points out that several top mountain bike race competitors currently using the new bike generate sales efficiently. Relying on their efforts costs less than the current advertising campaign. Therefore, the team decides to reduce advertising costs by $5 per bike, which meets the selling and distribution cost target.

Warranty and Support. Warranty and support costs are significantly lower than anticipated, primarily because the new braking system is so reliable. A reduction of $8 is easily attainable at this time. This amount is $4.50 ahead of target, making up for the lack of cost reduction from the brakes.

Administration. The team member from administration mentions that a new information system was installed last quarter. The department dropped some non-value-added activities, such as manual entry of production data. One staff member has resigned and will not be replaced. The savings will be at least the needed $4.50 per bike.

Total Planned Cost Reduction

The overall cost reduction targets and estimates are as follows:

Cost Category	Kaizen Cost Reduction	Actual Cost Reduction
New brake development	$ 5.00	$ 0.00
Manufacturing:	67.50	
Process change		10.00
Wheel and spoke system		13.00
Frame		35.00
Tires and tubes		10.00
Selling and distribution	5.00	5.00
Warranty and support	3.50	8.00
Administration	4.50	4.50
Total	$85.50	$85.50

Continuous Monitoring of Costs

The team reports back to the accounting department that the overall cost reduction targets can be met. After the changes have been made, the marketing department decides to cut costs even further. However, a problem arises with the braking system. To maintain the current quality, MTB will have to pay $4 more for components because several vendors have raised their prices. Even with these two changes, MTB is still below the kaizen cost reduction target. ■

Using Target and Kaizen Costing over Time

Target and kaizen costing are used together in organizations facing declining prices across time. Exhibit 15.6 provides a generic timeline showing the use of these two methods across

> **EXHIBIT 15.6**
> Target and Kaizen Costing over Time for a Product

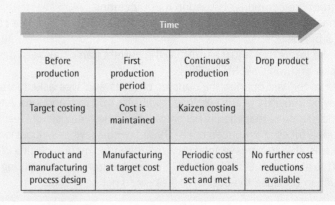

	Time		
Before production	First production period	Continuous production	Drop product
Target costing	Cost is maintained	Kaizen costing	
Product and manufacturing process design	Manufacturing at target cost	Periodic cost reduction goals set and met	No further cost reductions available

Similarities
- Rely on goal setting to achieve cost reduction.
- Focus on product design and the manufacturing process to find ways to reduce costs.
- Encourage organizations to work with suppliers to reduce costs.
- Use functional teams to determine where costs can be cut.
- Encourage employees to take an active part in the cost-cutting decision-making process.
- Take advantage of the trade-offs among price, functionality, and quality.
- Focus on continuous improvements in products and processes.

Differences
- Target costing occurs at beginning of the product life cycle, after which kaizen costing occurs after that.
- Target costing sets a single goal for cost; kaizen sets cost-reduction goals.

Common Advantage
- Use of goal setting encourages better performance.

Common Disadvantages
- Stress of cost reduction environment can impair employee well-being.
- Encourages organizations to forgo some products that have long-term profit potential.

EXHIBIT 15.7
Target Costing Compared to Kaizen Costing

a product's life cycle. Some organizations may lower margins before dropping the product, but at some point, the product is discontinued because cost is equal to price and no further cost reductions are possible.

Exhibit 15.7 compares target costing and kaizen costing, listing their similarities, differences, and common advantages and disadvantages.

15-1 self-study problem   Target and Kaizen Costing

LO2, LO3

You have recently been hired as an accountant for a start-up firm in the computer peripherals industry. The owners have developed and are manufacturing several wireless devices to enhance user mobility, such as a small electronic notebook. They want to become more competitive in this market and also develop several other products. They have asked you for ideas about ways to control costs and determine whether proposed new products will be profitable.

required

Write a memo to the owners, describing how they could use target costing and kaizen costing.

See the solution on page 687.

Life Cycle Costing

Life cycle costing is a decision-making method that considers changes in price and costs over the entire life cycle of a good or service—from the time the product is introduced, through a number of years. Some products have high up-front costs, such as research and development. Other products may incur large costs when the product is abandoned, such as environmental clean-up costs. Sometimes, products cannot achieve high revenues at the beginning of their life, but they generate increasing revenues over the product's life cycle. Under target costing, such products might be rejected even though they have good long-term potential. Under life cycle costing, managers consider the profitability of the product over a number of years. If forecasts predict that sales, over time, will cover all product costs and eventually add to profits, a life cycle budget is developed for both manufacturing and environmental costs, so that decision makers can evaluate their decision and identify possible areas for cost reductions across time.

LO4   Explain life cycle costing

BUSINESS PRACTICE
The Government of Canada used a Seven-Point Plan based on life cycle costing to analyze a proposed purchase of F-35 fighter jets.[13]

CHAPTER REFERENCE
Chapter 20 introduced sustainability life cycle costing, which incorporates costs external to the firm such as environmental and social costs. Chapter 13 described the net present value method of quantitative analysis.

Life cycle costing is used when the initial product is produced and sold at a loss, but accountants and managers anticipate that a combination of continued sales volumes and cost reductions over time will lead to profits in the long term. It is also used to identify products that may not be profitable when the costs of decommissioning the operation are included as part of total product costs (e.g., environmental clean-up costs when mines are shut down). In addition, life cycle costing is used to focus managers' attention on the high development or decommissioning costs during the product and manufacturing design phase, to encourage them to manage all these costs as they develop new products.

The video game market includes examples of product decisions that consider the product's life cycle. Video game manufacturers often sell consoles at a loss, but they expect continuing sales of games to eventually create profits for the entire product line. In addition, manufacturing cost reductions over time are anticipated. Another example of life cycle costing is the manufacture of printers and ink cartridges. Printers are often sold at a loss, but the revenue streams from ink cartridges more than make up for these initial losses. Because life cycle costing takes into account cash flows that occur over multiple time periods, the net present value method is usually used to analyze product profitability.

FOCUS ON ETHICAL DECISION MAKING: REVERSE ENGINEERING AND INFORMATION TECHNOLOGY

Reverse engineering is the "process of discovering technological principles of a device, object, or system" by taking it apart to "analyze its workings in detail." Reverse engineering is often used to understand or teach others how a device works, to maintain the device, or to "make a new device that does the same thing" for a lower cost. In the fast-paced world of information technology, the process of reverse engineering is being challenged. In 2005, Lexmark International Inc. tried to prevent Static Control Components Inc. from selling chips, in refurbished toner cartridges, for Lexmark laser prints. Lexmark claimed that the chips needed for the refurbished toner cartridge to communicate with the printer were proprietary. Many other cases where reverse engineering was used to develop a competing product, often at a lower cost are working their way through the court systems. Some software providers now include clauses in their licensing agreement that prohibit reverse engineering. These license agreements are shrink-wrapped or click-wrapped with products and their legitimacy is being questioned. Copyright legislation (including the Digital Millennium Copyright Act, Copyright Act of the US, Copyright Act of Canada) is all being scrutinized.

ETHICS AND INFORMATION TECHNOLOGY

Is it ethical for intellectual property (e.g., a software program) to be reverse engineered for the purpose of offering a similar product at a lower cost? Is it ethical for intellectual property (e.g., software) to be reverse engineered to allow for improved interoperability between the software and other IT products? Who are the various stakeholders in this situation? What factors would each stakeholder group consider most important?

Source: Reverse Engineering, NC State University, http://ethics.csc.ncsu.edu/intellectual/reverse/study/php; James Niccolai, "Court rules against Lexmark in printer case," Computerworld, February 22, 2005 www.computerworld.com/article/2569348/technology-law-regulation/court-rules-against-lexmark-in-printer-case.html.

[13] Next Generation Fighter Capability Annual Update, 2014, National Defence, Canada.

15-2 self-study problem   Life Cycle Costing With NPV

LO4

Zeelectronics plans to manufacture a revolutionary new cell phone called the HiPhone. Because the functions and interface of the phone are innovative, the product development and design phase will be extensive. The accountants have estimated five years of information for the product as follows:

	Year 1	Year 2	Year 3	Year 4	Year 5
Units manufactured and sold	1,000,000	1,325,000	1,625,000	1,900,000	2,000,000
Contribution margin per unit	$84	$84	$84	$84	$84
Fixed costs (including R&D)	$250,000,000	$100,000,000	$90,000,000	$80,000,000	$70,000,000

Zeelectronics will outsource production of the HiPhone, so no new investment in fixed assets is needed. The company pays an income tax rate of 25% and has income from other products to offset any losses from the HiPhone. The HiPhone project has a required rate of return of 12%.

required

A. Determine the net present value (NPV) of the cash flows of the HiPhone project over its life cycle. Ignore the effects of inflation.
B. In performing sensitivity analysis, which factors would you vary? Explain.
C. Would you recommend that Zeelectronics undertake the HiPhone project? Explain.

See the solution on page 688.

Lean Accounting

Lean accounting is a set of accounting principles and methods to support lean business practices and motivate continuous improvement. Lean accounting combines the methods and concepts of value chain analysis, cellular manufacturing, just-in-time inventory systems, operational performance measurements, activity-based management, and target and kaizen costing. Continuous improvement efforts are motivated and tracked using value stream analysis and visual control procedures.

LO5   Explain lean accounting and discuss how it is used

Value stream analysis is the process of analyzing business processes to identify the cost of individual value-added activities. This analysis is similar to value chain analysis, but with more specific activity categories grouped by functional roles. For example, costs for the "Product Manufacture" process in Exhibit 15.1 might be broken down into value stream costs for production labour, production materials, production support, machines and equipment, and facilities and maintenance.

Once value stream analysis is completed for a manufacturing process, production is reconfigured so that manufacturing is done within cellular systems. The total rate of production is set by customer demand, with production across cells managed by a kanban system. A **kanban** is a visual device—such as a card, floor space (kanban square), or production bin—that communicates to a cell that additional materials or products are demanded from the subsequent cell. This system is referred to as a **demand-pull system** because customer demand "pulls" production through the manufacturing process. This practice also allows inventory levels to be low, although a small, standard amount of inventory is planned to avoid delays in the production process. Kanban systems replenish inventory only as needed, avoiding large inventory buildup.

In a lean accounting system, performance measures such as the following are used to control operations:

▸ **Takt time**[14] = time available divided by units demanded from customers; represents the maximum time available to produce each unit; cells are designed to run at the takt time

▸ **Day-by-the-hour** (measured at the cell level) = number of units demanded per hour compared to number of units produced; a variance may be calculated as the number of units produced minus the number demanded; typically posted as a visual report in each cell and updated hourly

▸ **First time through (FTT)** (measured at the cell level) = total good units completed (total units produced minus reworked and rejected units) divided by total units completed; measured before any rework is performed

▸ **WIP to SWIP** (measured for a group of cells working on a single product) = current work-in-process inventory divided by standard work-in-process inventory (the amount of inventory the cells are designed to handle); typically measured at the end of a work shift to monitor the inventory pull system

▸ **Operational equipment effectiveness (OEE)** (measured at the individual machine level and usually only calculated for bottleneck equipment) = availability rate, times efficiency rate, times quality rate

availability rate = actual machine time available (planned machine time minus unplanned downtime) divided by planned machine time

efficiency rate = actual number of units produced divided by ideal number (planned number) of units produced

quality rate = number of good units transferred out (total units produced minus rejected units) divided by total units produced

Proponents of lean accounting argue that measures such as those shown above should not be used to evaluate manager or employee performance. Instead, lean accounting performance measures are typically used as diagnostic controls to identify and correct out-of-control situations, and as interactive controls to drive continuous improvement. Results are discussed collaboratively to solve problems and identify ways to improve production processes.

Similar lean accounting practices are used for both manufacturing and nonmanufacturing processes. Consider, for example, a shipping process. Because on-time shipping adds value to customers, the on-time shipment rate (percent of orders shipped on time) is a crucial performance measure. Accountants may also track the cost per shipment to monitor the success of continuous improvement initiatives. Similar to kaizen costing, cost and quality goals are set for each activity within a value stream, and progress toward the goals is monitored.

Accounting activities are also analyzed to identify and reduce non-value-added activities. For example, approvals and signoffs are reduced or eliminated. Accounts payable and accounts receivable processes are analyzed and computerized where possible. Because lean systems are combined with just-in-time inventory management, vendor payments can be based on the amount of inventory released to the production floor over a specified period. When customers have standing orders, invoices for production can be automatically triggered, on a weekly or monthly basis. Similar analysis is done for every accounting function, including general ledger, budgeting, and planning tasks.

---

[14] Takt time originates from the German word *taktzeit*, which translates as cycle time.

◢ **BUSINESS PRACTICE**

The **Productivity Alberta** website (http://goproductivity.ca) was developed by the Government of Alberta in partnership with other government agencies and industry organizations to help businesses improve productivity. One of Productivity Alberta's goals is to provide resources and services to businesses that will assist managers to improve their productivity. To partially achieve this goal, Productivity Alberta prepares and shares articles on current topics and company successes, hosts conferences, and provides online learning tools.

SUMMARY

LO1   Explain how value chain analysis, supply chain, and JIT are used to improve operations

GOAL

Continuously improve costs over the long term by the following:

- ▶ Enhancing efficiency
- ▶ Reducing costs
- ▶ Improving interactions with suppliers and customers
- ▶ Identifying and eliminating non-value-added activities
- ▶ Minimizing rework, scrap, and waste
- ▶ Reducing production cycle time
- ▶ Negotiating lower prices with suppliers

SUPPLY CHAIN ANALYSIS

JUST-IN-TIME PRODUCTION OR INVENTORY CONTROL SYSTEMS

Systems in which materials are purchased and units are produced as customers demand them

MANUFACTURER VALUE CHAIN

SUMMARY

LO2   Explain target costing and calculate target costs

TARGET COSTING

A decision-making method that considers prices as given and then determines whether products and services can be provided at costs low enough for an acceptable profit

TARGET COSTING DESIGN CYCLE

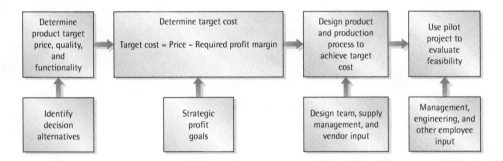

LO3   Explain kaizen costing and compare it to target costing

KAIZEN COSTING

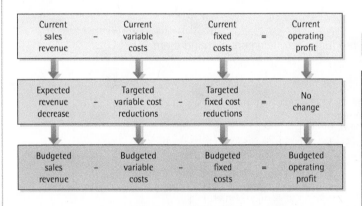

USE OF KAIZEN AND TARGET COSTING

| | | Time | | |

Before production	First production period	Continuous production	Drop product
Target costing	Cost is maintained	Kaizen costing	
Product and manufacturing process design	Manufacturing at target cost	Periodic cost reduction goals set and met	No further cost reductions available

LO4   Explain life cycle costing

LIFE CYCLE COSTING

Consider changes in price and costs over the entire life cycle of a good or service, from the time the product or service is introduced through a number of years:

► Allow initial losses or large decommissioning costs
► Expect a combination of sales volume increases and cost reductions over time

SUMMARY

L05 Explain lean accounting and discuss how it is used

LEAN ACCOUNTING

- Emphasizes cost reduction and continuous improvement in a manner similar to target costing and kaizen costing
- Production occurs in manufacturing cells with a demand-pull system
- Inventory is managed through a kanban just-in-time system

- Value stream analysis is used to examine and improve organizational processes from a customer value perspective
- A variety of value stream performance measures are used for manufacturing and support services

15-1 solution to self-study problem

Many possible approaches may be taken for writing a memo on these topics. The body of one possible memo follows—note that the memo is written to inform and help the managers of the company make a decision:

You asked for my recommendations about ways to control costs and to determine whether proposed new products will be profitable. In this memo, I briefly describe two techniques—target costing and kaizen costing—that could be implemented to achieve these goals.

Target Costing

Target costing helps determine whether a proposed new product will be profitable. This technique involves the following steps:

- Estimate the market price of the proposed product.
- Given the market price, determine what the cost must be to achieve our desired profitability.
- Estimate the costs of producing the product. If the estimated cost exceeds the target cost, search for ways to reduce costs. Drop the product idea if it is not feasible to achieve the target cost.
- For potentially feasible new products, conduct pilot production projects to further evaluate estimated costs.

The biggest advantage of target costing is that it would help us focus on ways to design both products and manufacturing processes to meet our profitability goals. If costs are too high, we will be forced to look for ways to reduce them, which might also lead us to make changes to the proposed features of a new product.

The target costing process would also help us involve everyone in the company in making product decisions and setting cost goals. This involvement would encourage employees to "buy in" to the target costs, which will help us achieve them.

Kaizen Costing

Kaizen costing helps control costs over the life of a product, taking into account the fact that selling prices decline over the lifespans of some products. The process for kaizen costing is similar to the process described for target costing. We would estimate the future selling prices of our existing products and determine the cost needed in order to achieve our desired profit.

Kaizen costing would help us make decisions about products we wish to continue. If we cannot find ways to reduce costs so that desired profitability for a product is achieved, then we should consider dropping the product.

solution to self-study problem

15-1

Risks

I believe that both of these methods would help us meet our goals. However, you should be aware of three major risks:

- Both methods involve a great deal of estimation of prices and costs. The rapid change in our industry presents a high risk of errors in our estimates, which might prevent us from achieving our profitability goals.
- Teams of personnel from marketing, engineering, production, and accounting would be needed for implementation. It will be critical for everyone to work toward common goals, rather than to focus only on their own work areas. Thus, the team members should be chosen carefully, and each person would need to understand that the teams have high priority.
- These techniques might discourage us from adopting new products or continuing existing products that have long-term value. The teams need to consider long-term as well as short-term factors in making final recommendations.

15-2 solution to self-study problem

A.

	A	B	C	D	E	F
6	Year	Sales Volume	Total CM less Fixed Costs	Income Tax (Cost) Savings	Net Cash Flows	Discounted
7	1	1,000,000	$(166,000,000)	$41,500,000	$(124,500,000)	$(111,160,714)
8	2	1,325,000	11,300,000	(2,825,000)	8,475,000	6,756,218
9	3	1,625,000	46,500,000	(11,625,000)	34,875,000	24,823,336
10	4	1,900,000	79,600,000	(19,900,000)	59,700,000	37,940,429
11	5	2,000,000	98,000,000	(24,500,000)	73,500,000	41,705,874
12					NPV	$ 65,143

The total contribution margin (CM) less fixed costs is calculated by multiplying the contribution margin per unit times the sales volume and subtracting the fixed costs. The loss in year 1 offsets income from other products, resulting in tax savings of $41,500,000. Expected income is positive in the other years, so taxes are deducted from cash flows.

B. The contribution margin, fixed costs, sales volumes, tax rate, and discount rate can all be varied to represent both a best and worst case scenario. In addition, managers may want to vary each input separately to determine how changes in estimates affect the NPV. For example, the NPV becomes ($5,628,828) using a discount rate of 14%.

C. Because the NPV is relatively small compared to cash flows, we would want to gather more information about the firm's ability to maintain or increase demand, the potential for cost reductions that would increase contribution margin, and competitor models and estimated market share.

QUESTIONS

15.1 What is a just-in-time manufacturing system? Why would organizations choose to adopt one?

15.2 Explain the similarities and differences among target costing, kaizen costing, and life cycle costing.

15.3 Identify three products for which target costing and kaizen costing could be used. Identify three products for which target costing and kaizen costing would be inappropriate.

15.4 Explain the value chain and list the ways that value chain analysis benefits organizations.

15.5 Explain the target costing cycle, and discuss the decision criteria used to determine whether a product will be manufactured using a target costing approach.

15.6 Supply chain analysis focuses particularly on one aspect of value chain analysis. Explain how supply chain analysis is performed, and how it relates to value chain analysis.

15.7 List some common advantages and disadvantages for target and kaizen costing.

15.8 List three ways that accounting functions can be improved under a lean accounting system.

15.9 What is value stream analysis and why do organizations use it?

15.10 Why is NPV used for life cycle costing but not for target or kaizen costing?

15.11 Describe the use of lean accounting applied to cellular manufacturing teams.

15.12 Explain life cycle costing. Why would this approach be useful for decision-making in the pharmaceutical industry? Why would this approach be useful in mining?

15.13 What is reverse engineering? When is it used? Is it ethical or unethical? Justify your answer.

15.14 Which two lean accounting performance measures focus on the cell level? Explain both measures.

15.15 What are the requirements of a successful JIT system? What are the expected benefits of a successful JIT system?

MULTIPLE-CHOICE QUESTIONS

15.16 How is Kaizen costing different from standard costing?
   a. Kaizen costing puts more emphasis on cost reduction than cost control.
   b. Kaizen costing puts more emphasis on cost control during the product design stage.
   c. Kaizen costing puts more emphasis on cost reduction during the product design stage.
   d. Kaizen costing puts more emphasis on the life cycle of the product.

15.17 Which of the following statements concerning target costing is correct?
   a. This approach is based on the observation that the firm should set its price so as to be able to cover its costs.
   b. The firm should devote resources to effectively market the product to improve profitability.
   c. The firm should not expect to significantly improve profitability through cost reductions after the product has entered production.
   d. The cost of the product cannot be calculated until it has been produced.

15.18 A company considers producing a new product and selling 20,000 units per year at a selling price of $60 per unit. It will cost $800,000 to design, develop, and produce the units. If the company desires a 16% return on investment, what is the target cost per unit?
   a. $ 6.40
   b. $ 9.60

   c. $40.20
   d. $53.60

15.19 Which of the following items is a limitation to total life cycle costing in a firm?
   a. Committed cost decisions are made by research and development people.
   b. Managers place enormous pressure on employees to reduce costs.
   c. Overhead costs are much higher than primary costs.
   d. It is difficult to attach some types of costs directly to a specific product line.

15.20 Which of the following statements concerning the approach of target costing is correct?
   a. This approach is based on the observation that the firm should set its price so as to be able to cover its costs.
   b. This approach is based on the principle that the firm should devote resources to effectively market the product to improve profitability.
   c. This approach is based on the principle that the firm should first determine the appropriate price for its product and then design and produce the product to achieve the cost that would lead to the desired profit.
   d. This approach is based on the observation that the cost of the product cannot be calculated until it has been produced.

EXERCISES

15.21 Value-Added and Non-Value-Added Activities Some activities add value to an organization, while others do not.
LO1 Determine whether each of the following activities is likely to be a value-added or non-value-added activity, and explain your choice.

REQUIRED **A.** Inspection activities
B. Moving materials to workstations
C. Manufacturing extra inventory to keep employees busy

15.22 JIT Production Big Bertram uses the just-in-time method to manufacture golf clubs. The manufacturing schedule
LO1 for the clubs is developed as customers place orders. Each club is made within a cell where five workers have production stations. The raw materials are delivered to the cell as needed. Each worker in the cell performs one step in the manufacturing process and then inspects the club before giving it to the next person. When a club is finished, it is set on a finished goods rack, which is sent to the packaging department at regular intervals.

REQUIRED **A.** What do we call a manufacturing system such as the one Big Bertram uses?
B. Describe general advantages of this type of system.
C. The supplier that manufactures the weights that are inserted in each club head would like to monitor Big Bertram's inventory levels through the Internet so that its new software program could release deliveries at appropriate times. List qualitative factors that might affect Big Bertram's decision about this proposal.

15.23 Target Costing A company plans to sell 20,000 units at a price of $60 per unit. The cost to bring the product to
LO2 market, including design and development, is $900,000. The desired return on investment (ROI) is 22.22222%.

REQUIRED Calculate the target cost per unit the company must achieve to ensure it attains its desired ROI.

15.24 Target Costing Suppose that Chevrolet used target costing to decide whether to produce a new vehicle, such as the
LO2 Chevrolet Spark.

REQUIRED **A.** Describe the steps Chevrolet's design team would have taken.
B. Explain why managers cannot easily predict demand for a new product such as the Chevrolet Spark.

15.25 Kaizen Costing Blade Runner produces regular scooters and motorized scooters, which are considered the
LO3 most reliable in the marketplace. Demand has been volatile, with huge increases in demand during Christmas and Hanukkah and just before university classes begin in the fall. In the past, the company filled demand by anticipating demand increases and manufacturing inventories ahead of time.

Recently, competition in the motorized scooter line has escalated, and Blade Runner needs to reduce prices and, therefore, cut costs. The motorized scooter's current cost is $150. To be competitive, the marketing department says the price should be 10% lower than the current price. Management currently achieves a pretax return of 10% on sales of the scooters and wants to continue this rate of return.

The following per-unit costs for motorized scooters are based on production of 700,000 per year:

Direct materials (variable)	$ 45
Direct labour (variable)	15
Machining costs (fixed amortization and maintenance)	10
Inspection costs (variable)	10
Engineering costs (fixed)	20
Marketing costs (fixed)	25
Administrative costs (fixed)	25
Total cost	$150

REQUIRED **A.** Calculate the price recommended by the marketing department.
B. Given the price you calculated in Part A, calculate the new contribution margin and the target cost.
C. Calculate the planned cost reduction for each cost category, assuming proportional cost reduction across categories.

15.26 Kaizen Costing, Proposed Cost Reductions, Uncertainties Refer to the information in Exercise 15.25. The kaizen
LO2, LO3 costing team made the following cost reduction suggestions:

Direct materials
   Suppliers agreed to cost reductions of $4.50 for direct materials.

Direct labour
   An engineer suggested that the scooters could be manufactured more quickly if production batches were cut
   in half. The engineer believes that a labour savings of $1.50 per scooter could be attained.

Machining costs
   The team has been unable to identify ways to reduce machining costs in the manufacturing process but suggests
   that some of the machining tasks could be outsourced to suppliers so that some parts are preassembled, thereby
   reducing the need for machine hours. This outsourcing would increase the cost of direct materials by $0.50 per
   unit but cut machining costs by $1.30 per unit. The supplier has been very reliable but does not currently have
   the machining expertise and would have to purchase equipment and hire several workers to fill these orders.

Marketing
   Marketing has agreed to combine ad campaigns for both products and believes the company will save $2.50
   per unit without losing sales.

Administration and Engineering
   No cost containment appears to be possible in administration because a new enterprise resource program was
   recently acquired. However, the head of engineering believes that his costs can be cut by $4.00 per unit. He
   believes that some employees are no longer needed because part of the new program was designed especially
   to provide information for product and manufacturing process design that had been hand collected in the past.

REQUIRED **A.** Calculate the new cost per category. Compare the total cost with the kaizen cost. Determine whether further
   cost containment efforts need to be made.
B. In your own words, describe the next step in the kaizen process.
C. List qualitative factors that might be relevant to Blade Runner's managers as they decide on any product or
   process changes. List as many factors as you can.
D. For each of the planned cost reductions, discuss uncertainties about whether the company will achieve the
   planned cost reduction.

15.27 Kaizen Costing, Design Change Effects Preeti Telang, the partner in charge of a small accounting firm, has launched
LO3 a kaizen costing program to reduce office support costs. She expects the program to reduce costs by at least 10%.
Information for the first six months of the program and estimated cost savings for the next six months follows.

	Actual Cost Last 6 Months	Estimated Cost Next 6 Months
Postage fees—deliver more reports and tax returns using fax; the company can make unlimited calls for a flat fee per month	$ 6,000	$ 5,500
Photocopy costs—outsource copy function to save labour cost	$ 2,500	$ 2,000
Labour costs—more efficient scheduling of support staff	$15,000	$14,500

REQUIRED **A.** Calculate the percent change in costs, and determine whether the kaizen cost goal is likely to be met.
B. Identify two possible quality problems that could arise from the planned changes to operations.

15.28 Value-Added and Non-Value-Added Costs A one-month summary of manufacturing costs for Rapid Routers
LO1 Company follows.

Direct materials	$40,000
Direct labour	20,000
Material handling costs	1,500
Product inspection and rework	2,000
Materials purchasing and inspection	500
Routine maintenance and equipment servicing	1,200
Repair of equipment	300

REQUIRED **A.** Classify each cost as value-added or non-value-added. Can each cost be classified in this manner? Explain.
B. Sum the non-value-added costs. What percentage of total costs is non-value-added?

C. Can any of the non-value-added activities be eliminated? Explain.

D. Can any of the costs for non-value-added activities be reduced? Provide an idea for reducing one non-value-added cost.

15.29 **Lean Accounting, Takt Time, Day-by-the-Hour, FTT** Sturdy Toy Company manufactures toy trucks. Orders for 9,400

LO5 trucks were received during March, with deliveries scheduled evenly throughout the month of April. Trucks are produced simultaneously in 10 manufacturing cells. Time available for production in each cell is 7 hours per day for 21 days during March.

REQUIRED A. Calculate the takt time.

B. At the end of the first hour of a day's production, one cell had completed five good trucks, including one truck that was reworked.

1. Calculate the day-by-the-hour results and the variance.
2. Calculate the first time through (FTT) rate.

15.30 **Lean Accounting, Takt Time, Day-by-the-Hour, FTT** School Dayz Binders manufactures 3-ring binders targeted at

LO5 the high school market. Orders for 47,000 binders were received during July, with deliveries scheduled evenly throughout the month of August. Binders are produced simultaneously in 5 manufacturing cells. Time available for production in each cell is 7.5 hours per day for 22 days during July.

REQUIRED A. Calculate the takt time.

B. At the end of the first hour of a day's production, one cell had completed 50 good binders, including 10 binders that were reworked.

1. Calculate the day-by-the-hour results and the variance.
2. Calculate the first time through (FTT) rate.

15.31 **Lean Accounting, WIP to SWIP** Wilderness Lights produces LED camping lanterns. The lanterns are produced in a

LO5 cellular system. Three cells perform the manufacturing tasks: Cell 1 assembles the LED light unit, Cell 2 adds the light unit to the lantern base, and Cell 3 attaches the handle. The standard work in process (SWIP) per shift is 120 lanterns. The following information is available for the last week of operations.

Day	Monday	Tuesday	Wednesday	Thursday	Friday
Actual WIP—Manufacturing Cells					
WIP	115	120	122	118	116

REQUIRED A. Calculate WIP to SWIP for the manufacturing cells for each day during the week.

B. Explain why the "ideal" WIP to SWIP value is one.

15.32 **Lean Accounting, OEE** (continuation of Exercise 15.31) Wilderness Lights produces LED camping lanterns. The LED

LO5 units are fabricated by robotic manufacturing equipment. The equipment has an ideal rate time of 10 LED units per hour, and work is performed in 7-hour shifts. Information for the first week of the month is as follows:

Day	Monday	Tuesday	Wednesday	Thursday	Friday
Production Results—Robotic Equipment					
Actual hours	7	7.5	7	6	6.5
Total units completed	70	78	68	60	65
Good units completed	65	70	64	45	65

REQUIRED A. Calculate each day's operational equipment effectiveness (OEE) for the robotic equipment.

B. Provide a possible reason why the OEE changes throughout the week.

15.33 **Target Costing** Frick N' Frack Company plans to sell 5,000 units of a new product at a price of $35 per unit. The

LO2 cost to bring the product to market, including design and development, is $155,000. The desired return on investment (ROI) is 15%.

REQUIRED Calculate the target cost per unit the company must achieve to ensure it attains its desired ROI. Given the above information, what are Frick N' Frack Company's choices?

15.34 **Target Costing** Linz Riding Apparel has identified a new market for half chaps for English-style riding. The half chaps

LO2, LO3 will be marketed to those riders with non-standard leg-calf dimensions (e.g., very short, very tall, muscular). The only market competition is from custom-made providers who regularly charge $350 per pair of half chaps. Linz would like to offer its half chaps to be competitive with the high quality off-the-shelf half chaps which sell for $125 (on average).

REQUIRED **A.** If Linz desires a 15% return on sales, what is the target cost?
B. The original cost estimate to design, produce, and sell the half chaps is $121.50. What are Linz Riding Apparel's options?
C. If Linz' management believes that this is a good business opportunity and the timing is right, what approach would you recommend to help them achieve their goals? Discuss how to implement your suggestion.

15.35 Life Cycle Costing EcoClean plans to introduce an environmentally friendly and pet-safe all-purpose cleaning solution.
LO4 Because the chemical nature of the product is innovative, the product development and design phase will be extensive. The accountants have estimated three years of information for the product as follows:

	Year 1	Year 2	Year 3
Units manufactured and sold	0	800,000	2,400,000
Contribution margin per unit		$ 5.00	$ 5.00
Fixed costs (including R&D)	$3,000,000	$2,500,000	$ 500,000

After the first three years, production and sales are expected to maintain a consistent level that meets EcoClean return on investment requirements. No end-of-life costs are predicted. EcoClean has income from other products to offset any initial losses from the new product; however, the project has a required rate of return of 8%.

REQUIRED **A.** Determine the net present value (NPV) of the cash flows of the project over its estimated first three years of its life cycle. Ignore the effects of inflation.
B. Would you recommend that EcoClean undertake the project? Explain.

PROBLEMS

15.36 Cost Reduction, JIT, Value Chain Analysis Budget Cupboards produces kitchen and bathroom cupboards that
LO1 incorporate unusual functions, such as specialty drawers for knives and kitchen tools, and kitchen appliance holders that pop up from under the countertop. Competition in this industry has recently increased. Budget's management wants to cut costs for its basic cupboard models, and then cut prices.

REQUIRED **A.** The following table lists potential areas for cost reduction. Two potential cost reductions are provided for the first area listed (design phase). For each of the remaining areas, identify two potential ways that Budget Cupboards' management could reduce costs.

Potential Area for Cost Reduction	Potential Cost Reductions	
	(1)	**(2)**
Example: Design phase	Work with suppliers to reduce direct materials costs	Redesign cupboards to use fewer parts
Manufacturing process		
Administration		
Changes in quality or functionality		

B. Budget does not currently use just-in-time production or value chain analysis. Describe several advantages of using these methods when price competition increases.

15.37 Target and Kaizen Costing, Uncertainties, Manager Incentives Suppose you are having a conversation with Sandy,
LO2, LO3 another student in this course. Sandy is confused about the differences and similarities between target costing and kaizen costing.

Another student, Kevin, overhears your conversation with Sandy and insists that neither of these methods is beneficial. Kevin argues that some companies have run into financial problems using these methods because their managers have manipulated the cost estimates to appear however they wanted. If the managers wanted to launch a new product or keep an old one, they made sure their cost estimates supported their decision.

REQUIRED **A.** In your own words, explain how target costing and kaizen costing are the same and how they are different.
B. Compare the information needed to apply the target costing and kaizen costing methods:

1. List the types of relevant information needed for each method.
2. List the uncertainties in the relevant information for each method.

C. Discuss ways in which managers might be able to create biased estimates under a target or kaizen costing system.

D. Kevin argues that the types of issues you described in Part C mean that target and kaizen costing are not beneficial. Discuss the validity of this argument.

15.38 Life Cycle Costing Fancy Fleece developed a new outdoor-wear fleece fabric that is both wind and water resistant but retains a soft and fuzzy feel. The research and development process was more expensive than Fancy's managers anticipated, and the materials in the fabric are also more expensive than anticipated. The managers believe that if Fancy prices the fleece to cover total costs, no one will buy it. The marketing department held several focus group meetings with manufacturers who produce and sell winter jackets and pants to determine an appropriate price. The marketing department also surveyed customers who recently purchased fleece jackets, to determine the premium they would be willing to pay for a jacket that is both wind and water resistant. The marketing department concluded that the new fleece fabric would sell at a price that covers variable costs but does not cover the total costs of production and development. You have been asked to help the managers decide whether to produce the fleece and how to price it if they do produce it.

LO1, LO2, LO3, LO4, LO5

REQUIRED
A. What kind(s) of analysis would you perform for this decision?
B. Explain whether it would generally be better for Fancy Fleece to use cost-based or market-based pricing.
C. Identify uncertainties about how much it will cost to produce the fleece. List as many uncertainties as you can.
D. Explain why the managers of Fancy Fleece cannot be certain that they would be able to sell the polar fleece to cover variable costs.

15.39 Lean Accounting, Takt Time, Day-by-the-Hour, FTT FasterLock Company manufactures padlocks. Orders for 4,704 padlocks were received during May, with deliveries scheduled evenly throughout the month of June. Locks are produced simultaneously in four manufacturing cells. Time available for production in each cell is 7 hours per day for 21 days during June.

LO5

REQUIRED
A. Calculate the takt time.
B. At the end of the first hour of a day's production, one cell had completed eight good locks, including one lock that was reworked.

1. Calculate the day-by-the-hour results and the variance.
2. Calculate the first time through (FTT) rate.
3. Assume the company expects an FTT rate of 90%. Was production in the cell out of control during the first hour of the day? Discuss.

C. Suppose the company had received orders for only 4,500 padlocks to be delivered during June. Would this mean that the workers in each cell could work more slowly than when 4,704 locks are ordered?

15.40 Lean Accounting, WIP to SWIP, OEE RollQuick Company produces lightweight wheelchairs for wheelchair athletes. The wheelchairs are produced in a cellular system. Three cells perform the manufacturing tasks: Cell 1 assembles the wheels on an axle, Cell 2 adds the footrest and frame for the seat, and Cell 3 attaches the seat to the frame. The standard work in process (SWIP) per shift is 21 chairs. The seats are fabricated by robotic manufacturing equipment. The equipment has an ideal rate time of nine seats per hour, and work is performed in 7-hour shifts. Information for the first week of the month is as follows:

LO5

Day	Monday	Tuesday	Wednesday	Thursday	Friday
Actual WIP—Manufacturing Cells					
WIP	21	18	19	22	21
Production Results—Robotic Equipment					
Actual hours	7	6	7	7	7
Total units completed	63	53	65	61	63
Good units completed	60	51	63	60	63

REQUIRED
A. Calculate WIP to SWIP for the manufacturing cells for each day during the week.
B. Explain why the "ideal" WIP to SWIP is one.
C. Calculate each day's operational equipment effectiveness (OEE) for the robotic equipment.
D. Provide a possible business reason why the OEE for Tuesday was significantly different than the OEE for the other days.

15.41 Lean Accounting, Takt Time, Day-by-the-Hour, FTT U-Go-Mugs Company manufactures souvenir travel mugs. Orders for
36,960 mugs were received during February, with deliveries scheduled evenly throughout the month of March. Mugs
are produced simultaneously in 8 manufacturing cells. Time available for production in each cell is 7 hours per day
for 22 days during March.

LO5

REQUIRED **A.** Calculate the takt time.
B. At the end of the first hour of a day's production, one cell had completed 30 good mugs, including 2 mugs that
were reworked.
  1. Calculate the day-by-the-hour results and the variance.
  2. Calculate the first time through (FTT) rate.
  3. Assume the company expects an FTT rate of 93.5%. Was production in the cell out of control during the
  first hour of the day (round to whole numbers)? Discuss.
C. At the end of the sixth hour of a day's production, one cell had completed 28 good mugs, including 4 mugs
that were reworked.
  1. Calculate the day-by-the-hour results and the variance.
  2. Calculate the first time through (FTT) rate.
  3. Assume the company expects an FTT rate of 93.5%. Was production in the cell out of control during the
  first hour of the day (round to whole numbers)? Discuss.
D. Suppose the company had received orders for only 32,340 mugs to be delivered during March. Would this
mean that the workers in each cell could work more slowly than when 36,960 mugs were ordered?
E. Evaluate the situation in part D from a strategic perspective.

15.42 Lean Accounting, WIP to SWIP, OEE Street Rider Company produces street quality long-boards. The long-boards
are produced in a cellular system. Three cells perform the manufacturing tasks: Cell 1 assembles the wheels on
an axle, Cell 2 adds the decorative decals to the long-board, and Cell 3 attaches the wheel assembly to the long-
board. The standard work in process (SWIP) per shift is 84 long-boards. The long-boards are fabricated by robotic
manufacturing equipment. The equipment has an ideal rate time of 14 boards per hour, and work is performed in
6-hour shifts. Information for the first week of the month is as follows:

LO5

Day	Monday	Tuesday	Wednesday	Thursday	Friday
Actual WIP—Manufacturing Cells					
WIP	84	76	72	88	84
Production Results—Robotic Equipment					
Actual hours	6	5.5	5	6	6.5
Total units completed	84	78	72	84	90
Good units completed	82	76	70	84	88

REQUIRED **A.** Calculate WIP to SWIP for the manufacturing cells for each day during the week.
B. Explain why the "ideal" WIP to SWIP is one.
C. Calculate each day's operational equipment effectiveness (OEE) for the robotic equipment.
D. Provide a possible business reason why the OEE changes throughout the week. Suggest a course of action for
Street Rider management.

15.43 Life Cycle Costing with NPV ELZ Ltd. manufactures electronic components. Recently, researchers have identified a
new process for manufacturing higher quality, more environmentally friendly components. Because the new process
is innovative, the product development and design phase will be extensive. However, the new components will not
require special handling at the end of their useful life. The accountants have estimated four years of information for
the product as follows:

LO4

	Year 1	Year 2	Year 3	Year 4
Units manufactured and sold	25,000	250,000	1,250,000	1,875,000
Selling price per unit	$ 6.00	$ 6.50	$7.00	$7.00
Variable costs per unit	$ 3.50	$ 3.50	$3.00	$3.00
Fixed costs	$ 750,000	$1,500,000	$ 500,000	$500,000
R&D costs	$2,000,000	$1,500,000	$ 50,000	$ 50,000

ELZ pays an income tax rate of 25% and has income from other products to offset any initial losses. The project has a required rate of return of 10%.

REQUIRED **A.** Determine the net present value (NPV) of the cash flows of the project over the estimated four years of its life cycle.

B. In performing sensitivity analysis, which factors would you vary? Explain.

C. Would you recommend that ELZ undertake the project? Explain.

15.44 **Life Cycle Costing with NPV** InstruChem manufactures chemical cleaning products. Due to recent environmental protection requirements, InstruChem must now improve the final disposition of its chemical by-products. These requirements will increase R&D costs, which are needed to develop the most efficient process to dispose of the by-product and will add new disposition costs when the regulations come into full effect in 2 years. The accountants have estimated five years of information for the product as follows:

LO4

	Year 1	Year 2	Year 3	Year 4	Year 5
Litres manufactured and sold	50,000	50,000	65,000	65,000	65,000
Selling price per litre	$ 15.00	$ 15.00	$ 16.50	$ 16.50	$ 16.50
Variable costs per litre	$ 5.00	$ 5.00	$ 5.50	$ 5.50	$5.50
Fixed costs	$150,000	$150,000	$150,000	$150,000	$150,000
R&D costs	$250,000	$250,000	$100,000	$ 10,000	$ 10,000
Disposition costs	$ 10,000	$ 10,000	$100,000	$ 50,000	$ 35,000

InstruChem pays an income tax rate of 20% and has income from other products to offset any initial losses. The project has a required rate of return of 7%.

REQUIRED **A.** Determine the net present value (NPV) of the cash flows of the project over the estimated five years of its life cycle.

B. In performing sensitivity analysis, which factors would you vary? Explain.

C. Would you recommend that InstruChem undertake the project? Explain.

D. What other qualitative factors would you consider when analyzing this project?

15.45 **JIT and Kaizen Costing, Design Change Effects** Cindi James, the manager in charge of a general store at a favourite summer holiday location, has launched a kaizen costing program to reduce operating costs by applying JIT concepts. She expects the program to reduce costs by at least 15% throughout the summer season. Information for the first two months of the program and estimated cost savings for the next two months follows.

LO1, LO3

	Actual Cost Last 2 Months	Estimated Cost Next 2 Months
Ordering costs—place more orders on-line; work with suppliers to have an integrated ordering system	$ 2,000	$ 1,500
Supplies costs—reassess approved vendor list; work with suppliers to have supplies delivered as needed	$ 5,000	$4,250
Labour costs—more efficient scheduling of sales staff	$32,000	$27,500

REQUIRED **A.** Calculate the percent change in costs, and determine whether the kaizen cost goal is likely to be met.

B. Identify two possible quality problems that could arise from the planned changes to operations.

C. To meet the labour savings estimate, sales staff will be scheduled on split-shifts (i.e., some sales people will work the busy morning rush, go home for a few hours, and then return to work the evening rush). Discuss the qualitative issues that should be considered for this cost savings measure. (Note: Split-shifts are legal.)

15.46 **Cumulative Exercise (Chapter 7) Target Costing, ABC** Fred's Auto Components manufactures seats for an automobile company. The automobile company wants a new seat designed to accommodate drivers and passengers who weigh 100 kilograms or more, and at a price that is 10% less than the current price. If Fred's cannot meet the requested cut in price, the manufacturer will ask other suppliers to bid for the contract. Fred's manufacturing team has redesigned the seats and the manufacturing process to reduce costs by 10%. Now a team is assembled to reconfigure some of the administrative support tasks. If these costs can also be reduced by 10%, Fred's will be able to meet the new price requirement. The company's accountant has developed monthly costs for each activity in the support process, as shown in the following table.

LO2

Activity	Cost Driver	Driver Quantity Per Month	Cost Per Driver
Ordering parts	Number of purchase orders	25	$ 50.00
Receiving and inspecting parts	Number of parts	7,500	$ 0.10
Materials handling	Number of parts	7,500	$ 0.20
Packaging seats for shipping	Number of seats shipped	1,500	$ 0.30
Shipping costs	Kilograms shipped	22,500	$ 0.50
Return of defective seats	Number of seats returned	15	$500.00

REQUIRED **A.** Calculate the total current cost of support activities per month.

B. As the manufacturing team redesigned the seats, the support team requested a 10% reduction in the number of parts. The manufacturing team was able to eliminate one part per seat. In addition, the support team negotiated a new rate with the shipping company to reduce the price per kilogram by $0.08. Calculate the new total cost per month to determine whether the 10% reduction goal has been met.

C. Discuss other factors that must be considered when designing and shipping the new seat.

15.47 **Life Cycle Costing, Auditing** Refer to the Next Generation Fighter Capability Annual Update and the Independent
LO4 Review: 2014 Department of National Defence Annual Update on Next Generation Fighter Capability Life Cycle Costs available at www.forces.gc.ca/en/about-reports-pubs/next-gen-fighter-independent-review-2014.page and answer the following questions.

REQUIRED **A.** Describe the Next Generation Fighter Capability: Life-Cycle Framework; include in your description the phases and an explanation of the phases (page 11/52 of the Annual Update is a good starting point). Explain why this approach is a life cycle approach.

B. Discuss the variance analysis between the years 2013 and 2014 that is presented in the Annual Update.

C. What are the risks and uncertainties in the proposed plan? Consider the risks in view of economic changes since the plan was proposed in 2012.

D. What was the conclusion of the independent review? What are the recommendations from the review team?

E. How is this review similar to an audit? How is it different from an audit?

MINI-CASES

15.48 **Cumulative Problem (Chapter 13) Life Cycle Costing, NPV with Sensitivity Analysis, Ethics** Larcker Logging Company is
LO4 preparing a bid for the right to clear-cut a large parcel of provincially-owned timberland. The bid will include a fixed

annual "stumpage fee" to be paid to the province, and company managers estimate that it will take five years to completely log the land. At the end of the contract, the company would be required to perform clean-up, including clearing the underbrush, removing logging waste, and replanting the area with Douglas fir, lodge pole pine, and tamarack trees. If the company fails to perform the clean-up, the province would impose a fine. In the past, the fine amounts have been much less than the clean-up costs. However, public concern has been growing about the failure of companies to replant timberland. Estimated revenue and costs and other relevant information follows:

Bid for annual stumpage fee	$ 300,000
Number of truckloads per year	1,300
Tonnes per truckload	20
Revenue per truckload	$ 1,750
Variable cost per truckload	$ 200
Annual fixed production costs	$ 150,000
Selling and delivery cost per tonne of logs	$ 50
Cost of clean-up (paid at the end of five years)	$1,700,000
Fine (paid if clean-up and replanting is not undertaken)	$1,000,000
Income tax rate	30%
Required rate of return	15%

ANALYZE INFORMATION

REQUIRED   The following questions will help you analyze the information for this problem. Do not turn in your answers to these questions unless your professor asks you to do so.

   A. Suppose you are working as an intern in the accounting department. The chief accountant has asked you to develop a net present value (NPV) analysis for this contract using a spreadsheet and ignoring inflation. You assume that the company will clean up the site at the end of the contract.

   B. When you present the spreadsheet to the accountant, he asks you to revise the NPV analysis to assume that the company will pay the fine instead of performing the clean-up.

   C. Identify as many business risks as you can for this contract.

   D. What factors would you vary in the NPV calculations as part of a sensitivity analysis? Explain.

   E. Analyze the potential ethical implications of paying the fine instead of performing the clean-up:

     1. Who would be affected by the company's decision?

     2. Would it be wrong for the managers to pay the fine instead of performing the clean-up? Identify the values you use when answering this question.

     3. Suppose the provincial government is considering a change to impose larger fines on companies that do not perform the clean-up. Should this business risk affect the managers' decision?

REQUIRED   Turn in your answers to the following.

   F. The accountant has asked you to draft a memo to the managers about whether the company should submit a stumpage fee bid of $300,000. Use the information you learned from the preceding analyses when drafting the memo.

   G. In your answer to Part F, how did you treat the costs of clean-up versus the fine? Explain the factors you weighed and the values you used to make your decision. Are these values consistent with your own personal values?

15.49 **Integrating Across the Curriculum: Ethics** Reread the Caterpillar case presented in this chapter. Komatsu reverse-engineered Caterpillar's products during the late 1970s and early 1980s. Komatsu's management used this information to design its products to compete effectively against Caterpillar. During the late 1980s, Caterpillar used this same method of reverse-engineering to redesign its products and manufacturing processes.

REQUIRED   **A.** Does reverse-engineering create an ethical problem? In other words, is reverse-engineering a form of business espionage?

   B. What are the social costs and benefits from reverse-engineering a competitor's product?

   C. When companies redesign their products and manufacturing processes for cost efficiency, they often reduce their reliance on manufacturing labour. What are the social costs and benefits of this practice?

15.50 **Professional Competencies** In today's business environment it is important to understand the global market place. Your knowledge should include an understanding of "global supplier demographics."

REQUIRED   Answer the following questions by integrating your knowledge from this chapter with your knowledge of the global market.

   A. What is meant by "global supplier demographics"?

   B. How might global supplier demographics affect the prices a company pays when it acquires resources (goods or services)? How can a company use this information when analyzing its cost of production?

   C. What is meant by "global customer demographics"?

   D. How might global customer demographics affect the market price for a product or service? How can a company use this information when analyzing its cost of production?

15.51 **Integrating Across the Curriculum: Information Technology**—*Inventory management system, data accuracy, internal controls, estimating benefits* During 2000, automobile parts company Mopar implemented a new inventory management system that cost $1.5 million. Mopar, a unit of Chrysler, distributed parts from three central and 11 regional warehouses to hundreds of parts dealers. The company filled orders for approximately one million line items per week from an inventory of 280,000 parts for Chrysler, Dodge, and Jeep brand vehicles.

   Mopar implemented the new system to improve its management of inventory levels. The company had previously maintained inventories based on forecasted demand but often ran out of some parts and carried inventory levels that were too high for other parts. When a customer ordered a part that was out of stock at a particular warehouse, the company incurred extra costs to search for the part at other warehouses. If the part was not found, Mopar placed a rush order to have it shipped directly to the customer from one of its 3,000 suppliers. When inventory of a part was too high, valuable warehouse space was wasted and the company incurred unnecessary inventory carrying costs. To reduce these types of problems, the company had manually tracked data for 100 of the highest-cost and best-selling parts. The managers used measures such as how often a part was out of stock to adjust inventory purchases.

The new inventory system included a database that would track parts at all warehouses as well as suppliers, customers, and forecast levels. The system helped managers identify $3.5 million in overstocked inventory. They expected an additional $10 million in annual savings from reduced backorders and rush orders.

Sources: Mopar's website, www.mopar.com; and J. Xenakis, "How to Slash Inventory Costs," *CFO.com*, December 13, 2000.

REQUIRED

A. Is Mopar's new inventory system likely to completely eliminate out-of-stock occurrences? Why or why not?

B. Discuss whether it would be beneficial for Mopar to institute a JIT inventory management system.

C. Benefits from Mopar's new system depend on the accuracy of data in its inventory database. Identify possible reasons the data may be inaccurate.

D. Describe possible internal controls that could prevent or detect and correct inaccuracies in Mopar's inventory database.

E. Mopar's managers expected to achieve $10 million in annual savings from reduced back orders and rush orders. Suppose you are asked to develop an estimate of these savings. How might you go about making the estimate? What types of data would you use? What types of assumptions would you need to make?

CHAPTER 16

Inventory Management

After studying this chapter, you should be able to:

LO1	Explain and calculate ordering and carrying costs
LO2	Calculate economic order quantity
LO3	Calculate the re-order point including safety stock
LO4	Analyze the impact of quantity discounts

in brief Managers and accountants are responsible for making short-term operating decisions that responsibly manage inventory costs. As part of these decisions, they must consider the trade-offs between divergent costs, the costs associated with the possibility of unexpected events, and special ordering opportunities offered by suppliers. Economic order quantity concepts help managers manage inventory costs. ■

Maximizing Inventory at Minimum Cost

Blend Images/Getty Images

SOURCES: G. Bensinger and K. Morris, "Amazon to Open First Brick-and-Mortar Site," Wall Street Journal, October 9, 2014; M. Periu, "Economic Order Quantity: The $545 Million Formula," American Express website, November 16, 2010; "Amazon.com to Acquire Diapers.com and Soap.com," Amazon.com news release, November 8, 2010; B. Urstadt, "What Amazon Fears Most: Diapers," Bloomberg Businessweek, October 7, 2010; E. Schonfeld, "Diapers.com on its Way to Selling Half a Billion Diapers, Raises $20 Million Debt Round," Techcrunch.com; Quidsi corporate website, www.quidsi.com.

When you sell more than 500 million diapers a year online with razor-thin profit margins, inventory management becomes a do-or-die situation. That's the case with Diapers.com, one of several e-commerce sites operated by **Quidsi**, an online retailer. Quidsi owns several massive warehouses, one of them large enough to fit 20 football fields. If it runs out of an item, it risks losing a customer, possibly forever. If it stocks too much of an item, it risks increasing inventory costs—the costs of ordering and holding (or carrying) inventory.

Quidsi's e-commerce sites carry hundreds of thousands of stock-keeping units—and the cost of keeping them in stock is considerable. Among other costs, Quidsi has an estimated 500 employees, plus expensive robots used to quickly retrieve any one of thousands of items from its warehouse shelves.

To help find the "sweet spot" of carrying just the right amount of inventory at minimum cost, Quidsi uses economic order quantity analysis before ordering products from manufacturers. The company developed an algorithm that combines the probability of an increase in sales of a particular item with the probability that a supplier will be late in delivering new stock. Quidsi then factors in another algorithm, which considers the size of an order it wants to place along with the cost of placing an order (such as verifying the order before it is placed and checking it when it is received), inventory carrying costs, and any bulk discounts that suppliers might offer for placing an even larger order. The result of this economic order quantity formula is an ideal order amount, which Quidsi says is accurate about 85 to 95% of the time.

Quidsi's revenues were approximately $300 million in 2010. Analysts estimate that such online businesses have operating margins between five and seven percent. But Quidsi's success attracted the attention of Internet giant Amazon.com, which bought Quidsi in late 2010 for approximately $500 million in cash plus the assumption of about $45 million in debt.

Quidsi (which is Latin for "what if") continues as its own company in the Amazon family, and operates additional e-commerce sites such as Soap.com (selling everyday consumer goods), Wag.com (pet supplies), YoYo.com (toys), and Casa.com (home décor). It delivers thousands of products to customers in more than 65 countries. No question, calculating economic order quantity is key to keeping Quidsi in business.

Inventory Costs

Quidsi's success depends in large part on managing hundreds of thousands different inventory items. Without proper consideration of the demand for each item, when items will be delivered, how much it costs to order items, and their huge warehousing costs, Quidsi would never have achieved its worldwide success. Managing inventory is important to both managers and accountants. Managers need to know that parts will be available when needed by production and that products will be available when customers are ready to purchase. Accountants monitor inventory costs to provide information about achieving strategic goals, especially those related to cost management. When evaluating the costs associated with inventory, accountants and managers must recognize the conflicting causes of costs. For example, holding minimum inventory may result in not having an item available when a customer wants it. Or, when assessing raw materials inventory, not having a part available when production needs it may result in a production shut-down or incurring an expensive rush order. On the other hand, carrying excess inventory increases storage or warehousing costs. Quidsi balances the costs of ordering huge numbers of inventory items against the costs of maintaining their massive warehouses. Ultimately, businesses need to manage inventory strategically to provide flexibility, to minimize inventory costs, and to avoid unnecessary costs associated with inventory. Without this delicate balance, companies like Quidsi will lose sales or sacrifice an already "razor-thin" profit margin.

Ordering and Carrying Costs

LO 1 Explain and calculate ordering and carrying costs

At a fundamental level, the total inventory costs include the purchase price of the inventory items, the costs of ordering inventory, and the cost of holding inventory in storage (e.g., warehouse). Of these three costs, the costs of ordering inventory and the cost of holding inventory increase and decrease in opposition to each other. When you think about these two types of costs you realize that the requirements to minimize each cost causes the other cost to increase. Let's look at ordering costs. Ordering costs are those costs associated with placing an order for parts or goods and include the cost of identifying an appropriate vendor, completing and checking an order requisition, preparing a purchase order, placing the order, handling any follow-up questions about the order, and receiving the order. To minimize ordering costs, a manager would place large, infrequent orders. The fewer the orders, the less time it takes for the manager to process the order resulting in a lower purchasing cost. However, when this large order arrives, there must be adequate space to store the items.

The costs of warehousing or storage space are the carrying costs of inventory. Warehousing costs may include all of the costs associated with maintaining a separate warehouse, including expenses like renting/mortgaging a building, climate control, lighting, water, repairs and maintenance, and personnel. Even when a separate warehouse is not maintained, the production facility or retail space must be large enough to hold the extra inventory. Then, the carrying costs are the marginal costs of operating a larger building.

Notice that ordering costs and carrying costs have an inverse relationship. If management decides not to have a separate warehouse or a larger facility, then smaller orders must be placed so as to store fewer inventory items. This will keep the carrying costs low but the increased number of orders will increase the ordering costs.

The total ordering and carrying costs is expressed in the following equation:

$$\text{Total cost} = \text{Ordering costs} + \text{Carrying costs}$$

We can then define the ordering costs as the cost to place a single order multiplied by the average number of orders placed in a year. This is expressed as:

$$\text{Ordering costs} = A/Q \times K$$

where:

A = the annual demand for parts or products

Q = the number of parts/products each time an order is placed

K = the cost of placing an order

The carrying costs are the cost of holding one unit in inventory multiplied by the average number of units in inventory. This is expressed as:

$$\text{Carrying costs} = Q/2 \times H$$

where:

Q = the number of parts/products each time an order is placed (Note: by dividing this quantity by 2, we have an average number of items held in inventory between placing orders)

H = the cost of carrying (or holding) one unit in inventory

Substituting into the total cost equation above, we have:

$$TC = (A/Q \times K) + (Q/2 \times H)$$

Exhibit 16.1 is the graphical presentation of this cost equation. Notice that ordering costs decline as the order quantity increases; carrying costs increase as the order quantity increases; and, total cost is the sum of the two curves. To manage inventory costs, the goal is to minimize the total costs. This is the lowest point on the total cost curve and can be calculated using the economic order quantity formula. This is Quidsi's "sweet spot"; the point just the right amount of inventory is on-hand in the warehouses at the least cost.

Assume that TimePiece Ltd. produces specialty grandfather clocks. They order high quality, unique gears from Unique Gears, Inc. The following information is available for TimePiece Ltd.

A = 20,000 gears

Q = 1,000 gears

K = $75 per order

H = $12 per gear

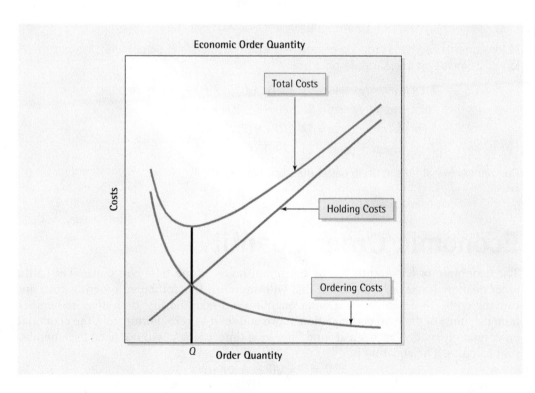

Economic Order Quantity

> EXHIBIT 16.1
Economic Order Quantity

Substituting into the total cost equation, we have:

$$TC = (A/Q \times K) + (Q/2 \times H)$$
$$TC = [(20{,}000 \text{ gears}/1{,}000 \text{ gears}) \times \$75] + [(1{,}000 \text{ gears}/2) \times \$12]$$
$$TC = \$1{,}500 + \$6{,}000$$
$$TC = \$7{,}500$$

This order quantity may not be the lowest cost option; therefore, management will want to explore other options. Calculating the economic order quantity is the next step.

example

aqua marine company—part 1

DmitrijsMihejevs/Shutterstock

The Aqua Marine Company is a regional distributor of aquarium products to local pet stores. One of the products that Aqua Marine offers to retailers is a small 1.5 gallon fish tank. Aqua Marine purchases these fish tanks from Aquariums Abundant, Inc. Aqua Marine purchases 140,625 fish tanks per year. Currently, their order size is 1,000 fish tanks. However, due to rising ordering costs, Gus Betts, the purchasing manager, is reassessing inventory management costs. He has determined that the most recent estimate for ordering costs is $20 per order; however, it costs only $2.50 per aquarium to hold fish tanks in inventory due to Aqua Marine's large warehouse space. As a first step in understanding inventory costs, Gus calculates the ordering costs and the carrying costs for 1.5-gallon fish tanks.

$$\text{Ordering costs} = A/Q \times K$$
$$\text{Ordering costs} = 140{,}625/1{,}000 \times \$20 \text{ per order}$$
$$\text{Ordering costs} = 140.625 \times \$20$$
$$\text{Ordering costs} = 141 \times \$20$$
$$\text{Ordering costs} = \$2{,}820$$

Gus rounded the 140.625 orders per year up to 141 orders per year because he cannot place a partial order.

$$\text{Carrying costs} = Q/2 \times H$$
$$\text{Carrying costs} = 1{,}000/2 \times \$2.50$$
$$\text{Carrying costs} = \$1{,}250$$

At the current usage and ordering pattern and a purchase price of $8 per tank, the total inventory costs including the purchase price are:

$$\text{Total inventory costs} = (A/Q \times K) + (Q/2 \times H) + \text{Purchase price}$$
$$\text{Total inventory costs} = \$2{,}820 + \$1{,}250 + \$1{,}125{,}000$$
$$\text{Total inventory costs} = \$4{,}070 + \$1{,}125{,}000$$
$$\text{Total inventory costs} = \$1{,}129{,}070$$

Gus wonders what he can do to better manage these costs. ■

Economic Order Quantity

The **economic order quantity** is the minimum point on the total cost curve. This is the order quantity (or re-order quantity) that will minimize the combined ordering costs and carrying costs. To determine this order quantity, you take the first derivative (remember, from calculus) of the total cost equation above and set it to zero. Fortunately, the economic order quantity model has been around for a long time and you will not need to remember your calculus. The equation is:

$$EOQ = Q = \sqrt{(2 \times A \times K)/H}$$

Applying this model to TimePiece Ltd. will show managers the most cost effective order quantity. Based on the information above:

$$EOQ = Q = \sqrt{\frac{2 \times A \times K}{H}}$$

$$EOQ = Q = \sqrt{\frac{2 \times 20,000 \text{ gears} \times \$75 \text{ per order}}{\$12 \text{ per gear}}}$$

$$EOQ = Q = \sqrt{\frac{\$3,000,000}{\$12}}$$

$$EOQ = Q = 500$$

This result tells managers that it would be more cost effective to place orders of 500 gears instead of 1,000 gears. Substituting 500 gears into the total cost equation, TimePiece Ltd. will now incur costs of $6,000; $1,500 less than the current situation.

The economic order quantity may be used to determine the quantity of products to order, the quantity of raw materials to order, the length of a production run, or the number of prototypes to make during product development and testing. This basic model does not consider special circumstances like quantity discounts or the timing of placing an order.

Assumptions

Similar to all equations used to support business decision-making, the economic order quantity has a number of underlying assumptions. This model assumes that managers know annual demand for inventory with certainty. It is unusual that managers know this demand with absolute certainty although some industries are more stable than others. When inventory fluctuates, managers may find that they have excess inventory on-hand for the time period or they may find that they are short inventory.

An additional assumption of the EOQ model is that demand for inventory or the usage rate of raw materials inventory is steady throughout the year. Similar to fluctuations in the known annual demand, variations in demand or usage rates will lead to inventory shortfalls or holding excess inventory.

Strengths and Weaknesses

When the EOQ model is a good fit for inventory usage and demand, it does provide a minimum cost re-order quantity. Quidsi estimates that the economic order quantity model that they use is accurate about 85 to 95% of the time. Further, these re-order quantities should provide sufficient inventory to meet customer needs. Without the use of technology, the calculation of EOQ is somewhat complicated. However, even most basic calculators can easily handle this calculation.

aqua marine company—part 2

After calculating the total cost of inventory for the 1.5-gallon fish tanks, Gus considers his options for decreasing inventory costs. He understands that ordering costs and carrying costs are inversely related and that the size of an order affects the total cost. Therefore, Gus calculates the economic order quantity.

$$EOQ = Q = \sqrt{\frac{2 \times A \times K}{H}}$$

$$EOQ = Q = \sqrt{\frac{2 \times 140,625 \text{ fish tanks} \times \$20 \text{ per order}}{\$2.50 \text{ per fish tank}}}$$

$$EOQ = Q = \sqrt{\frac{\$5,625,000}{\$2.50}}$$

$$EOQ = Q = 1,500 \text{ fish tanks per order}$$

Dmitrijs Mihejevs/Shutterstock

continued...

example

Total inventory costs = $(A/Q \times K) + (Q/2 \times H)$ + Purchase price

Total inventory costs = $[(140,625/1,500) \times \$20] + [(1,500/2) \times \$2.50]$
$+ (\$8 \text{ per tank} \times 140,625)$

Total inventory costs = $(93.75 \times \$20) + (750 \times \$2.50) + \$1,125,000$

Total inventory costs = $(94 \times \$20) + (750 \times \$2.50) + \$1,125,000$

Total inventory costs = $\$1,880 + \$1,875 + \$1,125,000$

Total inventory costs = $\$1,128,755$

Gus rounds the number of orders up from 93.75 to 94 because he cannot place 0.75 of an order. Depending on actual sales and any agreements that Gus negotiates with Aquariums Abundant, Inc. the 94th order may be for 1,500 fish tanks or fewer to match annual demand. Gus notes that the economic order quantity is greater than his current order size. This order quantity will reduce the number orders that he places in a year but increase the number of fish tanks in inventory. However, this new order quantity will decrease total inventory costs ($\$1,128,755 < \$1,129,070$).

Currently, Gus has a regular ordering schedule. With this new information, he wonders how he will need to adjust his ordering schedule. ▪

●● > STRATEGIC RISK MANAGEMENT: AQUA MARINE COMPANY PART 2

Gus recognizes that there is a trade-off between ordering costs and carrying costs. How did this trade-off affect his decisions? Organizations strategically manage trade-offs between costs; in this case, the cost of placing an order for inventory and the cost of providing storage space for the inventory when it is received. With advances in electronic communications and changing supply chain relationships, these opposing costs need to be re-evaluated and considered more integratively in negotiations.

Re-Order Point, Lead Time, and Safety Stock

LO3 Calculate the re-order point including safety stock

The economic order quantity model balances ordering costs and carrying costs of inventory to determine the size of an order or production run. The next step is to identify when to place the order (or start production) to manage inventory availability. The **re-order point** tells managers when to place an order (or start production). In establishing a re-order point, managers must consider usage (stated as average daily use of inventory), **lead time** and **safety stock**.

Lead time is the amount of time between placing an order and the receipt of the inventory. Managers must be aware of each vendor's lead time in order to have enough product on hand for use or sale until the next order arrives. In Exhibit 16.2, you can see that when TimePiece Ltd. has an economic order quantity of 500 gears, average usage of 100 gears per day, and a lead time of 2 days, the re-order point is when inventory is at 200 gears.

We can express this as the following equation:

Re-order point = Usage × Lead time

Re-order point = 100 gears/day × 2 days

Re-order point = 200 gears

This tells managers that an order of 500 gears (the economic order quantity) should be placed when inventory levels reach 200 gears and it will take 2 days for that order to arrive. The current

[1] Low, J., Rafai, S., and Taylor, A., "Using pEOQ to Help Save American Automakers," *Management Accounting Quarterly*, Fall 2009, Vol. 11, No. 1, pp. 1–13.

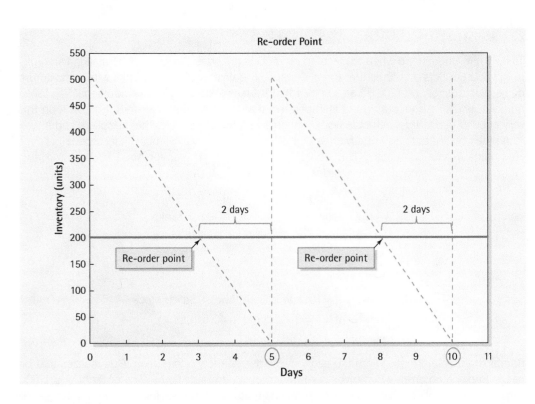

trend is to continually decrease lead times, which may help in decreasing carrying costs because managers no longer need to hold large quantities of inventory to wait for the next delivery.

Although lead times are decreasing and are usually identifiable with some certainty, managers must consider the impact of delays in receiving an order. The opposing considerations are the costs of carrying excess inventory versus the loss of sales or production time due to an unavailable item. To guard against this last possibility, managers carry **safety stock**. Safety stock is an extra quantity of goods above what is known to be needed to meet sales or production. Safety stock is calculated as the difference between the maximum daily usage and the average daily rate of usage multiplied by the number of days lead time. To consider safety stock, we modify the re-order point equation to the following:

$$\text{Re-order point} = (\text{Usage} \times \text{Lead time}) + \text{Safety stock}$$

During the holiday season, the managers of TimePiece, Ltd. are aware that demand for grandfather clocks tends to increase. This increase combined with the uncertainties associated with bad weather interfering with shipping makes the managers concerned about running out of gears, which would stop production of the grandfather clocks. They have decided to carry a safety stock of gears. To establish the new re-order point, the managers first must determine the amount of safety stock needed. They know that the average daily usage of gears is equal to 100 gears and that the historical maximum daily usage during peak seasons is 125 gears. With this information they calculate the safety stock as follows:

Maximum daily usage	125 gears
Average daily usage	100 gears
Difference	25 gears
Lead time	× 2 days
Safety stock	50 gears

This would result in adjusting the re-order point during peak seasons as follows:

$$\text{Re-order point} = (\text{Usage} \times \text{Lead time}) + \text{Safety stock}$$
$$\text{Re-order point} = (100 \text{ gears/day} \times 2 \text{ days}) + 50 \text{ gears}$$
$$\text{Re-order point} = 250 \text{ gears}$$

DmitrijsMihejevs/Shutterstock

example

aqua marine company—part 3

To help him understand when to place an order, Gus analyzes the sales of 1.5-gallon fish tanks to the retail outlets. He finds that the average daily sales are 400 fish tanks with a maximum daily sales quantity of 420. He also knows that it takes 2 days to receive additional fish tanks from Aquariums Abundant, Inc. It is imperative that Aqua Marine not run out of stock on this very popular fish tank. Stock-outs would encourage retailers to seek other suppliers and if they move their business to an Aqua Marine competitor, the retailers will most likely order all of their aquariums from a competitor. This would be a huge loss in sales for Aqua Marine. With this information, Gus calculates the re-order point.

Maximum daily sales	420 fish tanks
Average daily usage	400 fish tanks
Difference	20 fish tanks
Lead time	× 2 days
Safety stock	40 fish tanks

Re-order point = (Usage × Lead time) + Safety stock
Re-order point = (400 × 2 days) + 40 fish tanks
Re-order point = 840 fish tanks

Combining this information with the economic order quantity information, Gus realizes that he needs to place an order when inventory levels drop to 840 fish tanks. The order size is 1,500 fish tanks. Gus notices that this schedule means that he will be placing an order for 1.5-gallon fish tanks approximately every other day. He decides that it is time to talk with Aquariums Abundant Inc. to negotiate a preferred customer agreement with automatic re-orders. Gus hopes that this will decrease his ordering costs and save time. ◼

> STRATEGIC RISK MANAGEMENT: AQUA MARINE COMPANY—PART 3

Gus realizes that with his current cost structure he will be placing orders for a critical inventory item approximately every other day; however, his ordering costs are relatively high at $20 per order. How has the importance of the product and the ordering costs affected Gus' decisions and actions? As we become more aware of the various inventory-related activities that incur costs, managers strive to manage the trade-offs between these opposing costs. The trade-offs need to consider strategic positioning of the product. It is strategically important for Aqua Marine to not have an inventory outage on 1.5-gallon fish tanks. This product is a complementary good — when the sales of this product decline, the sales of other related products (e.g., gravel, filters, heaters) also decline. There is joint demand for these aquarium products.

Quantity Discounts

LO4 Analyze the impact of quantity discounts

Often, as order quantity increases quantity discounts become available. The standard economic order quantity and re-order point calculations do not consider quantity discounts. When the economic order quantity results in not taking quantity discounts, the foregone discount is an opportunity cost and needs to be considered in the decision-making process. The most straightforward way to do this is to evaluate the total cost equation above at the economic order quantity amount and then at each of the quantity discount points.

Consider the ordering decision if Unique Gears, Inc. has the following quantity discount policy.

Quantity	Price per Gear
1–499 gears	$5.00
500–999	$4.75
1,000–1,999	$4.50
2,000 +	$4.25

Order Size	Ordering Costs[a]	Carrying Costs[b]	Opportunity Cost[c]	Total Cost
500	$3,000	$ 3,000	$10,000	$16,000
1,000	$1,500	$ 6,000	$ 5,000	$12,500
2,000	$ 750	$12,000	$ 0	$12,750

[a] $A/Q \times K$ ($A = 20{,}000$ gears, $K = \$75$)
[b] $Q/2 \times H$ ($H = \$12$)
[c] $A \times (\text{price} - \$4.25)$

The economic order quantity is 500 gears. The total cost at this order quantity is $6,000 not including the purchase price of the gears ($2,375). Exhibit 16.3 demonstrates how to re-assess this decision considering the additional quantity discount points.

When considering the availability of quantity discounts, TimePiece, Ltd. should place orders of 1,000 gears to minimize their total costs of inventory (ordering costs + carrying costs + opportunity cost).

With advances in technology and greater awareness of supply chain concepts, businesses are continually working to minimize these inventory ordering costs by creatively working with their suppliers. The concept of just-in-time inventory was introduced in Chapter 6 and discussed further in Chapter 15. Value chain and supply chain concepts were also presented in Chapter 15.

aqua marine company—part 4

After a friendly negotiation, Aquariums Abundant Inc. has offered Aqua Marine Company the following quantity discount opportunities. Gus also negotiated an automatic re-order purchase plan that will decrease his ordering costs by 25%. Gus must now decide on the standard order quantity and re-order point for his agreement with Aquariums Abundant Inc.

Quantity	Price per Tank
1–1,000	$8.00
1,001–2,000	$7.60
2,001–3,000	$7.20
3,001–4,000	$6.80
4,001 +	$6.40

DmitrijsMihejevs/Shutterstock

Order Size	Ordering Costs	Carrying Costs	Price	Opportunity Cost	Total Cost
Q	K = $15.00	H = $2.50			
1	$2,109,375.00	$ 1.25	$8.00	$225,000.00	$2,334,376.25
1,500	$ 1,406.25	$1,875.00	$7.60	$168,750.00	$ 172,031.25
2,001	$ 1,054.16	$2,501.25	$7.20	$112,500.00	$ 116,055.41
3,001	$ 702.89	$3,751.25	$6.80	$ 56,250.00	$ 60,704.14
4,001	$ 527.21	$5,001.25	$6.40	—	$ 5,528.46

Ordering costs = $A/Q \times K$
Carrying costs = $Q/2 \times H$
Opportunity cost = $140{,}625 \times (\text{Price} - \$6.40)$

With the new agreement, Gus decides that his standard order must be 4,001 fish tanks. This order will be automatically placed every 7–8 days. The total inventory costs are $905,528.

Total inventory costs ($K = \$15$, $H = \$2.50$, $P = \$6.40$) $= \$5{,}528 + \$900{,}000 = \$905{,}528$

Gus is pleased with the new arrangement. When he presents his plan to upper management, he can show them that the new agreement will save Aqua Marine Company $223,221.54 ($1,128,750 from part 2 – $905,528 from part 4).

Total inventory costs ($K = \$20$, $H = \$2.50$, $P = \$8$) $= \$3{,}750 + \$1{,}125{,}000$
$= \$1{,}128{,}750$ (from part 2) ∎

► EXHIBIT 16.3
Quantity Discounts

example

16-1 self-study problem Calculating Economic Order Quantity with Quantity Discounts

Let's Go Fly A Kite, Inc. manufactures colourful box kite kits. Each kit includes a wooden frame, brightly coloured light-weight water repellent fabric to cover the ends of the frame, and kite string. The manufacturing process is not difficult; therefore, Jane and Michael have a relatively small facility. As a result, they must carefully monitor their inventory of wood and fabric. Jane is reviewing the ordering process for fabric and has the following information available:

Annual usage	?
Cost to place an order (K)	$9.00
Cost to carry one bolt (H)	$32.00
Price per bolt	$720.00

There are 90 metres of fabric on one bolt. Each kite uses 0.5 metres of fabric. Michael estimates sales to be 1,800,000 kites per year.

The supplier has offered a quantity discount option.

Quantity	Price per Bolt
1–99 bolts	$720
100–999 bolts	$702
1,000–4,999 bolts	$684
5,000–9,999 bolts	$666
10,000 + bolts	$648

required

A. Calculate the economic order quantity for Let's Go Fly A Kite's current level of production.
B. Evaluate the quantity discounts offered by the supplier.
C. Make a recommendation to Jane and Michael about the quantity to order.

See the solution on page 712.

●● > FOCUS ON ETHICAL DECISION MAKING: INVENTORY SHRINKAGE

The management of inventory is an important consideration in the success of a business. Inventory is a significant asset for both manufacturing and retail businesses and its management has an impact on costs and ultimately on profitability. Mismanaging inventories can result in significant costs for a business. An important component of inventory management is controlling shrinkage. Inventory shrinkage is the loss of inventory caused by employee theft, customer shoplifting, inventory counting errors, vendor fraud, accounting errors, and damaged or spoiled products.

To understand the magnitude of the problem, inventory shrinkage has been quantified by national organizations in Canada. A survey in 2012 by PriceWaterhouseCoopers (PWC) with the assistance of the Retail Council of Canada (RCC) reported that inventory shrinkage rates in Canada range from 0.4% to 2.19% with an average of 1.04% or a loss of $4 billion per year for retailers. The causes of inventory shrinkage vary. As reported in the 2012 PWC report, in Canada 35% of the inventory shrinkage is a result of employee theft, 32% is a result of shoplifting, and 9% is a result of gift card or merchandise return fraud.

To combat the effect of inventory shrinkage and the significance of the related costs, Canadian retailers have invested in technology, processes, and people. Retailers have instituted closed circuit televisions, security alarms and systems, armoured vehicle deliveries, and policies (for all stakeholders) that define the consequences of theft. A PWC survey (2012) on retail security reported that frequent inventory counts, hiring and training programs, and employee incentives are used by Canadian retailers to reduce inventory shrinkage. The Retail Council of Canada

(RCC) in cooperation with RBC (Royal Bank of Canada) issued a report entitled *Retail Business Security Self-Assessment Report* (2015), which provides independent businesses with best practices for inventory loss prevention; those practices range from orientation programs for employees to strategies for dealing with aggressive customers. Strategies to manage and reduce inventory shrinkage remain a priority for retailers in Canada.

Sources: PriceWaterhouseCoopers (PWC) Canadian Retail Security Survey (2012), www.pwc.com/ca/en/industries/retail-consumer/publications/security-survey.html; Retail Council of Canada Retail Business Security Self-Assessment Report (2015), http://www.retailcouncil.org/sites/default/files/documents/RCC_Security_Self_Assessment.pdf; Security Research Project, University of Florida, http://users.clas.ufl.edu/rhollin/srp/srp.html

ETHICS AND INVENTORY SHRINKAGE

Preventing the loss of inventory is one way to manage and reduce inventory costs. The front-line employees in retail businesses are a main factor in that prevention. How can managers incentivize employees to be vigilant about reducing inventory shrinkage caused by customer shoplifting? How can managers discourage inventory shrinkage related to employee theft?

SUMMARY

LO1 Explain and calculate ordering and carrying costs

A = the annual demand for parts or products
Q = the number of parts/products each time an order is placed
K = the cost of placing an order
H = the cost of carrying (or holding) one unit in inventory

$$\text{Ordering costs} = A/Q \times K$$
$$\text{Carrying costs} = Q/2 \times H$$
$$\text{TC} = \text{Ordering costs} + \text{Carrying costs}$$
$$\text{TC} = (A/Q \times K) + (Q/2 \times H)$$

LO2 Calculate economic order quantity

$$\text{EOQ} = Q = \sqrt{\frac{2 \times A \times K}{H}}$$

LO3 Calculate the re-order point including safety stock

Re-order point = (Usage × Lead time) + Safety stock
(Maximum daily usage − Average daily usage) × Lead time = Safety stock

LO4 Analyze the impact of quantity discounts

Compare total cost at economic order quantity to total cost at quantity discount break points.

16-1 solution to self-study problem

Required

A.

To calculate the economic order quantity, you must first determine the annual demand for bolts of fabric. Each kite uses 0.5 metres of fabric. Let's Go Fly A Kite produces 1,800,000 kites per year. At this production level, they will use 900,000 metres of fabric (1,800,000 × 0.5 m). Each bolt contains 90 metres of fabric; therefore, they will need 10,000 bolts of fabric (900,000 m ÷ 90 m per bolt). From here, substitute into the EOQ formula as follows:

$$EOQ = Q = \sqrt{\frac{2 \times A \times K}{H}}$$

$$EOQ = Q = \sqrt{\frac{2 \times 10,000 \times 9}{32}}$$

$$EOQ = Q = \sqrt{\frac{180,000}{32}}$$

$$EOQ = Q = \sqrt{5,625}$$

$$EOQ = Q = 75$$

B.

Order Size	Ordering Costs	Carrying Costs	Price	Opportunity Cost	Total Cost
Q	K	H			
10,000.00	$ 9.00	$ 32.00			
1	$90,000.00	$ 16.00	$720.00	$720,000.00	$810,016.00
100	$ 900.00	$ 1,600.00	$702.00	$540,000.00	$542,500.00
1,000	$ 90.00	$ 16,000.00	$684.00	$360,000.00	$376,090.00
5,000	$ 18.00	$ 80,000.00	$666.00	$180,000.00	$260,018.00
10,000	$ 9.00	$160,000.00	$648.00	—	$160,009.00

Ordering costs = $A/Q \times K$

Carrying costs = $Q/2 \times H$

Opportunity cost = $10,000 \times (\text{Price} - \$648)$

C.

Based on the economic order quantity calculation, Jane and Michael should place orders of 75 bolts of fabric. The analysis of the quantity discounts offered by their supplier indicates that Jane and Michael should order all 10,000 bolts of fabric in one order. Although this minimizes the costs, there are other factors to be considered before placing an order for a year's supply of fabric. Logistically, even if there is physical space to store the fabric, Jane and Michael need to consider ease of access to the stored fabric and they need to consider environmental factors (fabric may fade in uneven lighting conditions). Also, committing to a year's supply of fabric may limit the variety of colours and patterns. Are there seasonal trends that need to be considered either with respect to timing of the quantity of fabric needed or styles of fabric? The strategic goals of Let's Go Fly A Kite must be factored into this decision: Who are the target customers? What are their style preferences? Is cost more important than diverse pattern options?

QUESTIONS

16.1 Explain the opposing costs that are part of the economic order quantity calculation.

16.2 What are the assumptions of the economic order quantity equation?

16.3 What costs are included in carrying costs? Explain the relationship between these costs and inventory quantity.

16.4 What costs are included in ordering costs? Explain the relationship between these costs and inventory order quantity.

16.5 Discuss the contradictory factors that influence the safety stock decision.

16.6 Explain the components of the re-order point.

16.7 Explain how to adjust the re-order point to consider safety stock.

16.8 What risk is associated with mis-estimating the lead time?

16.9 How do quantity discounts affect the economic order quantity decision?

16.10 How is economic order quantity affected by just-in-time and supply chain concepts?

MULTIPLE-CHOICE QUESTIONS

Use the following information for the next two questions.

16.11 Smith and Jones, Inc. is evaluating its inventory costs. The following information is available:

Annual demand	4,500 units
Quantity ordered	100 units
Ordering costs (K)	$25 per order
Carrying costs (H)	$10 per unit

The total costs (ordering and carrying costs) are:
   a. $1,125
   b. $500
   c. $1,625
   d. $625

16.12 The economic order quantity for Smith and Jones, Inc. is:
   a. 100 units
   b. 150 units
   c. 450 units
   d. 625 units

16.13 West Inc. has provided the following information. Calculate the re-order point, taking safety stock into account.

Daily usage	110 units
Time to receive an order	5 days
Safety stock	220 units

   a. 550 units
   b. 220 units

   c. 770 units
   d. 1,650 units

16.14 An assumption of EOQ is that as carrying costs _____, ordering costs will _____.
   a. decrease, remain constant
   b. decrease, decrease
   c. increase, increase
   d. increase, decrease

16.15 Determine the least costly order quantity if:

EOQ	= 3,500 units
K	= $10 per unit
H	= $50 per unit
A	= 306,250 units

Quantity discounts:

0–250	$10 per unit
251–500	$9 per units
501–750	$8.10 per unit
751–1,000	$7.29 per unit
Above 1,000	$6.55 per unit

   a. 350 units
   b. 501 units
   c. 751 units
   d. 1,001 units

EXERCISES

16.16 Ordering and Carrying Costs Determine the inventory carrying costs, inventory ordering costs, and total inventory costs for Hickory Co. based on the following information:

LO1

Annual demand	7,000 units
Order quantity	70 units
Cost to place an order	$45
Cost of carrying inventory	$15
Purchase price	$11.50 per unit

16.17 Ordering and Carrying Costs The following information is available for Friendship Circle Co.:

LO1

Annual demand	400 cases
Order quantity	25 cases
Cost to place an order	$15
Cost of carrying inventory	$35
Purchase price	$125 per case

Determine the inventory carrying costs, inventory ordering costs, and total inventory cost for Friendship Circle Co.

16.18 Economic Order Quantity Arabica Ltd. uses 625 cartons of information pamphlets per year. The cost to place an order is $2.50 per order and the carrying costs for inventory are $5.00 per carton. Determine the economic order quantity.

LO2

16.19 Economic Order Quantity All Mint Co. uses 500 cases of material T per year. Ordering costs are $5.00 per case and carrying costs are $2.00 per case. Determine the economic order quantity.

LO2

16.20 Ordering Costs, Carrying Costs, and Economic Order Quantity Foxtrot Inc. uses 100 kilograms of material X per year. Material X costs $35.00 per kilogram. It costs $1.50 to place an order and $3.00 per kilogram to store material X. Currently, Foxtrot is ordering material X in 15-kilogram batches. Is this the most economical order size? If not, what is the economic order quantity? How much will Foxtrot save by using the EOQ?

LO1, LO2

16.21 Ordering Costs, Carrying Costs, and Economic Order Quantity Covey Ltd. uses 2,250 metres of fine gage brass each year. Brass wire costs $12 per metre, ordering costs are $50 per order, and carrying costs are $2.50 per metre. Currently, Covey orders 500 metres in each order. Is this the most economical order size? If not, what is the economic order quantity? How much will Covey save using the EOQ?

LO1, LO2

16.22 Re-order Point and Safety Stock Shirley's Home Made Cookies has an annual usage of 5,000 kg of chocolate chips, economic order quantity of 200 kg of chocolate chips, average usage of 25 kg per day, and a lead time of 3 days. Shirley's only bakes cookies 4 days per week and needs to keep a safety stock of one day's worth of chocolate chips. Determine the re-order point for chocolate chips.

LO3

16.23 Re-order Point and Safety Stock Lindsey's Equine Treats has an annual usage of 16,000 kg of oats, economic order quantity of 2,100 kg of oats, average usage of 120 kg per day including normal spillage, and a lead time of 5 days. Lindsey only bakes equine treats 3 days per week and needs to keep a safety stock of one week's worth of oats. Determine the re-order point for oats.

LO3

16.24 Quantity Discounts Glinda Co. has the following quantity discount policy with its supplier.

LO4

Quantity	Price per Unit
1–499 units	$15.00
500–999 units	$14.70
1,000–1,999 units	$14.15
2,000 units +	$13.30

The economic order quantity is 750 units and the annual usage is 21,094 units. The ordering cost (K) is $20 per order and the carrying cost of inventory (H) is $1.5 per unit. Determine the most cost effective order quantity.

16.25 Quantity Discounts Theodora Ltd. Has the following quantity discount policy with its supplier Evanora Inc.

LO4

Quantity	Price per Case
1–299 cases	$25.00
300–749 cases	$23.75
750–1,499 cases	$22.56
1,500 + cases	$21.43

The economic order quantity is 150 cases and the annual usage is 33,750 cases. The ordering cost (K) is $5 per order and the carrying cost of inventory (H) is $15 per unit. Determine the most cost-effective order quantity.

PROBLEMS

16.26 Economic Order Quantity, Re-order Point, Safety Stock Pioneer Aviation uses specialty gaskets in the production of a small aeroplane, X.224. During a year, Pioneer uses 15,625 gaskets with an average usage of 50 gaskets per day of production. The gaskets cost $45 each. Because the gaskets require some special handling, the carrying costs are $5 per gasket. The ordering costs are $10 per order. Currently, Pioneer Aviation is placing orders for 1,000 gaskets. However, some of these gaskets are being damaged due to limited availability of the needed special storage. Elastomers, Inc. is the supplier of the specialty gaskets and can usually fill an order in 2 days. Occasionally, Elastomers is backlogged, but they never take more than 3 days to fill an order. If Pioneer runs out of gaskets, production will stop.

LO1, LO2, LO3

REQUIRED **A.** Calculate the total ordering cost and carrying cost for the current order size.
B. Calculate the economic order quantity. Comment on whether this order quantity will help alleviate Pioneer Aviation's inventory storage concerns.
C. Calculate the appropriate re-order point. Discuss any potential problems with the timing of this re-order point.

16.27 Economic Order Quantity, Re-order Point, Safety Stock Fine Dining sells high-end stemware. During a year, Fine Dining sells 1,500 cases of stemware with average sales of 5 cases per day. The cases of stemware cost $245 each. Because the stemware is fragile and requires special handling, the carrying costs are $50 per case. The ordering costs are $15 per order. Currently, Fine Dining is placing orders every week (5 days lead time) for 25 cases. Although this usually met demand, Fine Dining has faced stock-outs and has had to disappoint customers. In reviewing historical sales records, managers learn that the maximum sales quantity is 7 cases per day.

LO1, LO2, LO3

REQUIRED **A.** Calculate the total ordering cost and carrying cost for the current order size.
B. Calculate the economic order quantity. Comment on how this order quantity will help impact Fine Dining's inventory handling concerns.
C. Calculate the appropriate re-order point, taking into account the occasional stock-out problems. Discuss any potential problems with the timing of this re-order point.

16.28 Economic Order Quantity, Safety Stock, Re-order Point, Set-ups Platters Plus wants to determine the most cost efficient production run for their dinner plates. This quantity should minimize the carrying costs of inventory and the setup costs of production. Management also wants to avoid stock-outs because this disrupts retail sales and creates rush orders which disrupt production of other dinnerware pieces. The following information is available:

LO2, LO3

Annual demand for dinner plates	240,000
Average daily demand for dinner plates	800
Maximum daily demand for dinner plates	896
Carrying cost per dinner plate	$0.26
Setup costs	$150
Lead time	5 days

REQUIRED   **A.** Calculate the economic production batch size.

B. Calculate the safety stock.

C. Calculate the re-order point (the inventory level when a new setup should be started). Discuss any potential problems with the timing of this re-order point.

16.29 **Re-order Point, Quantity Discounts** Nature's Scents uses specially designed and labelled bottles to package its line of natural shampoos and body washes. The following information is available to assist managers determine how many bottles to order and when to order.

LO2, LO3, LO4

Annual usage	562.5 cases
Cost to place an order (K)	$15.00
Cost to carry one unit (H)	$3.00
Daily usage	5 cases
Lead time	5 days
Price per case	$30.00

The supplier has offered a quantity discount option.

Quantity	Price per Case
1–100 cases	$30.00
101–250 cases	$28.50
251–1,000 cases	$27.00
1,001 + cases	$25.50

REQUIRED   **A.** Calculate the economic order quantity for Nature's Scents current level of production.

B. Evaluate the quantity discounts offered by the supplier.

C. Determine the re-order point.

D. Make a recommendation to Nature's Scents management about the quantity to order and the re-order point.

E. Would your recommendation change if the cost to carry a case of bottles in inventory increased to $45.00 per case? Would your recommendation change if the ordering cost decreased to $5.00 (keep the cost to carry inventory at $3.00)?

16.30 **Re-order Point, Quantity Discounts** Skip's Scooters builds motorized hobby scooters. Although they do most of the construction in-house, they purchase motors from a small engine manufacturer. Because the motor is specially made for Skip's, the ordering process is very detailed. The following information is available to assist managers determine how many motors to order and when to order.

LO2, LO3, LO4

Annual usage	900 motors
Cost to place an order (K)	$50.00
Cost to carry one unit (H)	$25.00
Daily usage	9 motors
Lead time	10 days
Price per case	$150.00

The supplier has offered a quantity discount option:

Quantity	Price per Motor
1–49 motors	$150
50–199 motors	$145.50
200–499 motors	$142.50
500–1,099 motors	$139.50
1,100 + motors	$135.00

REQUIRED **A.** Calculate the economic order quantity for Skip's Scooters, current level of production.

B. Evaluate the quantity discounts offered by the supplier.

C. Determine the re-order point.

D. Make a recommendation to Skip's Scooters' management about the quantity to order and the re-order point.

E. Would your recommendation change if the cost to place an order for a motor decreased to $40 per order? Would your recommendation change if the cost to place an order decreased to $35 per order but carrying costs increased to $35.00 per motor? What does this tell you about the order size?

Measuring and Assigning Costs for Income Statements

After studying this chapter, you should be able to do the following:

LO1	Prepare absorption and variable costing income statements and reconcile the resulting net incomes
LO2	Discuss the factors that affect the choice of production volume measures for allocating fixed overhead
LO3	Prepare absorption and variable costing income statements considering beginning inventory balances, and evaluate the impact of inventory on income
LO4	Prepare throughput costing income statements and evaluate absorption, variable, and throughput costing income

in brief Accountants use absorption costing for inventory and cost of goods sold when preparing financial statements according to IFRS OR Canadian ASPE. Under absorption costing, all production costs, including allocated overhead, are assigned to units manufactured. This accounting method provides useful information by matching production costs against revenues. However, managers often need information about incremental costs when making short-term operating decisions. Variable costing and throughput costing are two methods that accountants use to provide managers with incremental cost information. ■

Inventory Management: Scarcity or Abundance?

© Kristoffer Tripplaar/Alamy Stock Photo

Valeant Pharmaceuticals International, Inc., based in Laval, Quebec, joins **McAfee Inc., Coca-Cola, Bristol-Myers Squibb,** and others being questioned about managing inventory and earnings by "channel stuffing." *Channel stuffing* (also known as *trade loading* or *channel cramming*) is the process of pushing distributors to buy inventory that they do not need. In other words, the distributors end up purchasing and holding inventory in excess of market demand. Even under delayed payment options, the manufacturer recognizes revenue when the "sale" is made to the distributors and the distributors have larger-than-normal inventory balances on their balance sheets.

The signs leading up to allegations of channel stuffing have some similarities. There is early concern about not meeting sales and profit targets. Then, sales to distributors go up. Very often, there are deals with distributors for delayed payment options, rebates, or special financing. The distributors are not given many options about taking the excess inventory, because future "hot" product quantities or exclusive representative status are often tied to normal sales.

Under IFRS and U.S. GAAP, inventories and cost of goods sold must be accounted for using full absorption costing, in which both variable and fixed production costs are assigned to all units produced. When production increases, the cost per unit usually decreases because the fixed cost per unit generally decreases. Lower per-unit costs then result in a higher gross margin for each unit sold, leading to the appearance of higher profitability on the income statement. In addition, under absorption costing, when inventory levels increase during a time period, the cost of goods sold expense on the income statement is smaller than the production costs incurred, because some units (and their allocated fixed costs) are held in inventory.

These effects of full absorption accounting are not a problem, as long as sales levels do not decline. However, if sales slow and inventory from prior periods is sold, cost of goods sold expense will be higher than the production costs incurred during the period. In this case, declining sales have an especially negative effect on profits because of both declining revenue and higher cost of goods sold.

At the time of writing, Valeant was not under investigation by any North American authorities for channel stuffing. However, concerns from some investors that the company was inflating revenues by channel stuffing through a distributor pharmacy caused its share price to decline 25% over a two-day period. Valeant denied the allegations.

For companies convicted of channel stuffing, costs can be large. For example, in 2006, McAfee agreed to pay US$50 million to settle a suit that alleged that the company had inflated net revenue by US$622 million between 1998 and 2000. Bristol-Myers Squibb Co. agreed to pay US$150 million and perform numerous remedial undertakings. In July 2008, Coca-Cola settled its lawsuit for US$137.5 million.

SOURCES: D. Crow, "Valeant Troubles Cast Light on Specialty Pharmacies' Murky Side," *Financial Times*, October 22, 2015; B. Houk, "Coke: Channel-Stuffing and Channel Conflict," *TPMtoday*, February 15, 2006; U.S. Securities and Exchange Commission, "Bristol-Myers Squibb Company to Pay $150 Million to Settle Fraud Charges," www.sec.gov/news/press/2004-105.htm; "Coca-Cola Settles Stockholder Lawsuit with $137 Million," July 6, 2008, Agence France Press, http://afp.google.com/article/ALeqM5icIwE8QDkle8uVeQYi2ug_k3HCcA.

Absorption Costing and Variable Costing

Data and inferences about manufacturers' inventories and production costs are important to a company's managers and accountants, as well as to external users of the company's financial statements. Managers are interested in monitoring operations, whereas accountants are responsible for anticipating and providing the types of information that managers need. External users, such as investors, are interested in monitoring an organization's management and performance.

No single measure of inventory and cost of goods sold is best for all situations. Financial statement reporting requires average costs, but short-term, internal decision making requires only incremental costs. Managers use both variable and fixed cost information for monitoring operations. Meanwhile, Canadian accounting standards for private enterprises (ASPE) and international financial reporting standards (IFRS) determine how costs should be measured for reporting to external parties such as investors. With computerized accounting systems, accountants can easily calculate costs in a variety of ways; reports for outside distribution can be different from reports for inside management. In this section, we compare absorption costing, which is intended for outside distribution, with variable costing and throughput costing, which are often used for managerial decision making.

Absorption Costing

When accountants prepare financial statements according to Canadian ASPE and IFRS, they use absorption costing. Under **absorption costing**, all production costs are recorded on the balance sheet as part of the cost of inventory and are then expensed as part of the cost of goods sold when units are sold (Exhibit 17.1). Both fixed and variable production costs are assumed to have future value to the organization and are accordingly treated as **product costs**. They include direct materials, direct labour, and fixed and variable overhead.

Under absorption costing, direct costs are traced to products, and manufacturing overhead is allocated to products. Fixed overhead can be allocated to units using either an actual or budgeted allocation rate. If production volume is used as the allocation base, fixed

> **CHAPTER REFERENCE**
> In chapters 5 and 6, you learned two methods of product costing: job order costing and process costing.

> **EXHIBIT 17.1**
> Absorption Costing

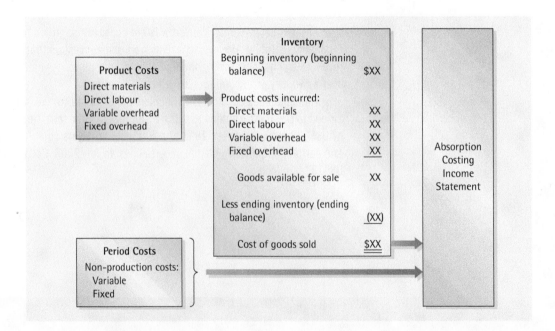

Inventory		
Beginning inventory (beginning balance)		$XX
Product costs incurred:		
Direct materials	XX	
Direct labour	XX	
Variable overhead	XX	
Fixed overhead	XX	
Goods available for sale	XX	
Less ending inventory (ending balance)	(XX)	
Cost of goods sold	$XX	

Product Costs
Direct materials
Direct labour
Variable overhead
Fixed overhead

Period Costs
Non-production costs:
Variable
Fixed

Absorption Costing Income Statement

EXHIBIT 17.2
Absorption Costing Income Statement

```
Revenue
  (Units sold × Price per unit)                              $XX

Cost of goods sold
  [Units sold × (Variable production cost per unit +
  Allocated fixed production cost per unit)]                 (XX)

       Gross margin                                           XX

Non-production costs
  (Selling, administrative, and other)                       (XX)

       Operating income                                      $XX
```

overhead cost can be allocated to units using either an actual or an estimated allocation rate, as follows:

$$\text{Actual fixed overhead allocation rate} = \frac{\text{Actual fixed overhead cost}}{\text{Actual production volume}}$$

$$\text{Estimated fixed overhead allocation rate} = \frac{\text{Estimated fixed overhead cost}}{\text{Estimated production volume}}$$

When using an estimated fixed overhead allocation rate, several choices are available for the estimated production volume; you'll learn about these later in the chapter.

Given the treatment of fixed overhead costs under absorption costing, both production and sales volumes affect the timing of the recognition of fixed overhead as an expense. If units are produced and sold this period, overhead costs incurred to produce these units are expensed this period. If units from last period are sold, some overhead costs from last period are expensed in this period. If units produced this period are not yet sold, the overhead allocated to those units will not be expensed until a future date, when the units are sold.[1] In the meantime, the overhead cost associated with those units is included in inventory on the balance sheet.

The absorption costing income statement (Exhibit 17.2) reflects the focus in Canadian ASPE and IFRS on distinguishing between production and non-production costs. All production costs are expensed as cost of goods sold to be matched against revenues when units are sold. Non-production costs—such as administration, marketing, and distribution costs—are treated as period costs. Canadian ASPE and IFRS requires that period costs be expensed when incurred because these costs are assumed to have no future benefit.

Variable Costing

Under **variable costing**, all variable costs are matched against revenues, and fixed costs are treated as period costs. Therefore, product costs consist of only variable production costs, such as direct materials, direct labour, and variable overhead costs (Exhibit 17.3). Then, inventory on the balance sheet includes only variable production costs under variable costing.

Expenses on a variable costing income statement are organized differently from those on an absorption costing income statement. In a variable costing income statement, all costs are separated into variable and fixed categories (Exhibit 17.4); variable production costs are reported separately from fixed production costs. Similarly, variable non-production costs, such as sales commissions, are reported separately from fixed non-production costs. All variable costs, both production and non-production, are subtracted from revenues to arrive at the contribution margin. Then, all fixed costs, both production and non-production, are

ALTERNATIVE TERMS

In financial accounting, *product costs* are the fixed and variable costs assigned to products. These costs remain in inventory until products sell and are also known as *inventoriable costs* or *capitalized costs*.

HELPFUL HINT

A cost is not the same as an expense. A *cost* is the value of resources given up to obtain an economic benefit. An *expense* is an income statement category that reduces net income.

INTERNATIONAL

International Accounting Standards (IAS) Number 2 requires inventory to include "all costs to bring the inventories to their present condition and location." Thus, all countries adopting IAS require absorption costing.[2]

---

[1] For simplicity, we ignore the income statement effects of possible inventory writedowns under financial accounting rules for the lower of cost or market.

[2] For more information about IAS, see the website of the International Accounting Standards Board, at http://www.ifrs.org/Pages/default.aspx.

▶EXHIBIT 17.3
Variable Costing

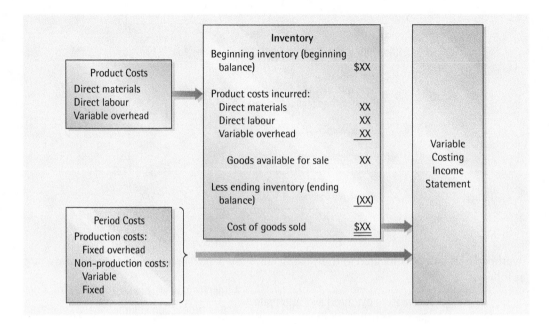

▶EXHIBIT 17.4
Variable Costing Income Statement

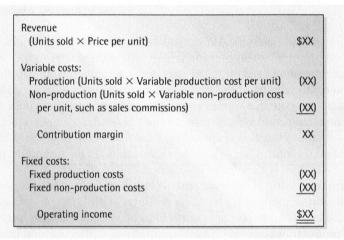

▣ ALTERNATIVE TERMS
Some people use the term *direct cost-ing* or *marginal costing* to describe the method also called *variable costing.*

▣ CHAPTER REFERENCE
You learned in Chapter 4 that managers often use the contribution margin when making non-routine operating decisions.

subtracted to determine operating income. This presentation makes it easier for managers to identify cash flows relevant to a product or service for internal decision making.[3]

Absorption Costing Compared to Variable Costing

Managers and other employees regularly make decisions about short-term resource alloca-tions within an organization. To do so, they estimate the effects of alternative decisions on cash flows (incremental revenues and costs). Because fixed costs are constant within a rel-evant range of activity, total fixed costs generally do not change under alternative short-term decisions. Thus, income statements based on absorption costing do not provide manag-ers or other users with the relevant information needed for short-term operating decisions, because they factor in costs that are not relevant to those decisions. Therefore, variable cost-ing income statements are often preferred for internal reporting.

---

[3] International Financial Reporting Standard IAS 2 "Inventories" requires the use of absorption costing. However, Section 10 of the Income Tax Act and Section 1801 of the Income Tax Regulations state that either direct (variable) costing or absorption costing is acceptable for income tax purposes. The method chosen should be the one that gives the true picture of income.

▷ INTERNATIONAL

Germany and many other European countries use *Grenzplankostenrechnung*, also known as GPK costing, as their cost accounting system. GPK costing roughly translates to "flexible standard costing" and is very similar to a variable costing system.[4]

●●● > RISK OF BIASED DECISIONS: WEASEL WORDS

WEASEL WORDS is a term used to describe phrases or claims so vague or ambiguous that they are essentially empty. For example, when advertisements claim that a retailer's products are "up to 75% off," the ads are misleading because they do not address whether all or only specific items are discounted at this rate, nor does the ad clearly identify the rate. The term *weasel words* is derived from weasels' behaviour of sucking the contents out of eggs and leaving empty shells that appear to be intact. While accounting terms have specific meanings in accounting, managers may be misled by their non-accounting assumptions about what the terms mean. For example, internal reports often refer to per-unit product costs. Managers often assume this per-unit cost is variable and use it inappropriately in decision making. Unfortunately, sometimes the reported per-unit cost includes an allocated amount of a fixed cost, as in absorption costing. These types of errors can be corrected by clearly noting (perhaps, a footnote notation) the type of cost reported and discussing the report with managers.

Although the use of variable costing for internal reports has many advantages, many organizations use absorption costing for both internal and external reporting. Often, managers traditionally used absorption costing because it was expensive and inconvenient to use two different reporting formats. Also, advocates of absorption costing for internal reporting believe that matching revenues and costs provides better information about opportunity costs for the organization. They believe that fixed costs are essentially capacity costs and, therefore, absorption costs reflect different products' use of capacity.

However, fixed costs do not vary with volume. Therefore, any cost projections made with absorption costing information will be inaccurate, unless the estimated volume in the projection is identical to the volume used to allocate the fixed costs. Larger projected volumes will overestimate costs, and smaller projected volumes underestimate costs. The following example compares income statements across time under absorption costing and variable costing.

boats afloat yacht company, part 1
ABSORPTION COSTING AND VARIABLE COSTING INCOME STATEMENTS

example

Boats Afloat Yacht Company recently organized to produce recreational yachts. The accountant, Joan Ardmore, prepared the second quarter income statements using absorption costing, as follows:

BOATS AFLOAT YACHT COMPANY
SECOND QUARTER INCOME STATEMENTS

	April	May	June	Quarter Total
Revenue @ $100,000 per unit	$100,000	$100,000	$300,000	$500,000
Cost of goods sold	100,000	70,000	210,000	380,000
Gross margin	0	30,000	90,000	120,000
Administrative and selling expenses	20,000	20,000	40,000	80,000
Operating income (loss)	$(20,000)	$ 10,000	$ 50,000	$ 40,000

© Rob Walls/Alamy

The sales manager, Stephanie Reynolds, analyzes these results and asks Joan to explain why a loss was posted in April but not in May, given that one boat was sold each month. The income statement was prepared using absorption costing, with fixed overhead allocated based on actual costs and actual production volumes. Joan decides to prepare variable costing

continued...

[4] C.S. Smith, "Going for GPK," *Strategic Finance*, April 2005, Volume 86, Issue 10; p. 36.

income statements for the same period so that she can more easily explain the absorption cost-ing income statement to Stephanie. Joan first reviews the information she gathered and her calculations for the absorption income statement. The selling price per yacht is $100,000, and the company incurred the following costs:

Variable Costs per Yacht	
Direct materials	$20,000
Direct labour	$15,000
Variable production overhead	$ 5,000
Variable selling	$10,000
Fixed Costs per Month	
Fixed production overhead	$60,000
Fixed administrative and selling	$10,000

Production and Sales Quantities	April	May	June
Production	1	2	2
Sales	1	1	3

Absorption Costing

When absorption costing is used, all production overhead (fixed as well as variable) is allocated to inventory. When the company produces only one product, fixed production overhead costs can be easily prorated among the actual units produced. The absorption cost per unit is the sum of the variable production cost per unit plus the actual fixed overhead allocation rate per unit:

ABSORPTION COST PER UNIT

	April	May	June
Fixed production overhead	$ 60,000	$60,000	$60,000
Divided by number of units produced	1	2	2
Actual fixed overhead per unit	60,000	30,000	30,000
Variable production costs per unit:			
Direct materials	20,000	20,000	20,000
Direct labour	15,000	15,000	15,000
Variable production overhead	5,000	5,000	5,000
Total variable cost per unit	40,000	40,000	40,000
Total absorption cost per unit	$100,000	$70,000	$70,000

ABSORPTION COST OF GOODS SOLD

	April	May	June
Number of units sold	1	1	3
Absorption cost of unit(s) sold:			
Produced during April	$100,000		
Produced during May		$70,000	$ 70,000
Produced during June			
(2 @ $70,000 each)			140,000
Total cost of goods sold	$100,000	$70,000	$210,000

During April, Boats Afloat produced and sold the same quantity of yachts, resulting in no ending inventory. In May, however, Boats Afloat produced two units and sold only one. Thus, one unit remained in inventory, at a cost of $70,000. Then in June, two units were produced and three were sold. June's cost of goods sold reflected sales of three units—two produced in June and one drawn from inventory. Inventory at the end of June was zero.

Joan now separates administrative and selling expenses into variable and fixed categories and prepares variable costing income statements. Notice that under variable costing, income for the months when one boat was sold (April and May) is the same:

ADMINISTRATIVE AND SELLING COSTS

	April	May	June
Variable selling cost per unit	$10,000	$10,000	$10,000
Times number of units sold	1	1	3
Total variable selling cost	10,000	10,000	30,000
Fixed administrative and selling expenses	10,000	10,000	10,000
Total administrative and selling expenses	$20,000	$20,000	$40,000

VARIABLE COSTING INCOME STATEMENTS

	April	May	June	Quarter Total
Revenue @ $100,000 per unit	$100,000	$100,000	$300,000	$500,000
Variable production expenses (for units sold)	40,000	40,000	120,000	200,000
Variable selling expenses	10,000	10,000	30,000	50,000
Contribution margin	50,000	50,000	150,000	250,000
Fixed production expenses	60,000	60,000	60,000	180,000
Fixed administrative and selling expenses	10,000	10,000	10,000	30,000
Operating income (loss)	$ (20,000)	$(20,000)	$ 80,000	$ 40,000

Reconciling Absorption and Variable Costing Incomes

Notice in the preceding example that when production levels are the same as sales levels, income is the same under absorption and variable costing. When production is greater than sales, absorption income is greater than variable income. In turn, when production is less than sales, absorption income is less than variable income. Reconciling the two incomes involves calculating the difference in overhead cost that is either added to or subtracted from inventory, because sales volumes do not equal production volumes. Exhibit 17.5 presents reconciliation calculations that are then illustrated in Boats Afloat Part 2.

> **EXHIBIT 17.5**
> Reconciling Absorption Costing and Variable Costing Income

	Absorption Versus Variable Costing[a]		
	Operating Income	**Inventory on the Balance Sheet**	**Reconciliation Calculations**
Production = Sales	Absorption costing income = Variable costing income	No change in inventory quantity on the balance sheet	No reconciliation needed because no difference in income
Production > Sales	Absorption costing income > Variable costing income	Inventory quantities on the balance sheet increase	Difference in income is equal to (1) Increase in absorption costing inventory, minus increase in variable costing inventory (2) Fixed overhead allocated during the current period to units added to inventory, minus fixed overhead allocated during the prior period to units removed from inventory
Production < Sales	Absorption costing income < Variable costing income	Inventory quantities on the balance sheet decrease	Difference in income is equal to (1) Decrease in absorption costing inventory, minus decrease in variable costing inventory (2) Fixed overhead allocated to units in prior period to units removed from inventory

[a]All comparisons assume either zero cost inflation/deflation or use of the FIFO cost flow assumption.

example

© Rob Walls/Alamy

boats afloat yacht company, part 2
RECONCILING ABSORPTION COSTING
AND VARIABLE COSTING INCOME STATEMENTS

Working from the two income statements, Joan prepares the following reconciliation report. Next, she shows Stephanie the two income statements and explains the preparation of each one. When Stephanie observes that the quarterly incomes under the two methods are the same, Joan points out that this occurred because the quarter had no beginning or ending inventories. Joan then shows Stephanie the reconciliation report and explains her calculations.

	April	May	June
Difference in income:			
Absorption costing income (loss)	$(20,000)	$10,000	$ 50,000
Variable costing income (loss)	(20,000)	(20,000)	80,000
Difference	$ 0	$30,000	$ (30,000)
Difference in change in inventory:			
Absorption costing:			
Ending inventory	$ 0	$70,000	$ 0
Beginning inventory	0	0	70,000
Increase (decrease)	0	70,000	(70,000)
Variable costing:			
Ending inventory	$ 0	$40,000	$ 0
Beginning inventory	0	0	40,000
Increase (decrease)	0	40,000	(40,000)
Difference	$ 0	$30,000	$ (30,000)

The only difference in inventory cost between absorption costing and variable costing is the amount of fixed overhead allocated to inventory under absorption costing. Therefore, the change in inventory difference can be presented by calculating the change in fixed costs included in absorption costing inventory. Ending inventory in May consists of one unit produced during May, when $30,000 in fixed overhead was allocated to each unit. This unit was then sold during June. The difference in operating income between absorption and variable costing is summarized as follows:

	April	May	June
Change in fixed costs included in absorption costing inventory:			
Fixed costs in ending inventory	$0	$30,000	$ 0
Fixed costs in beginning inventory	0	0	30,000
Increase (decrease)	$0	$30,000	$(30,000)

After examining the two different income statements and the reconciling report, Stephanie decides that she wants to receive monthly income statements using both methods. She wants the same financial statement information that is shared with banks and other external stakeholders, in case someone calls and has questions about the organization's financial performance measured under Canadian ASPE. But she also wants to use the variable costing income statement to analyze the operating performance of the organization and its managers.

Stephanie also wants to set up a profit-sharing plan for all employees, to reward them when the amounts received from sales cover the costs for the period. She realizes that the variable costing income statement provides this information by more accurately measuring substantive economic changes across time. ■

Absorption Costing Using Normal Costing

Under absorption costing in the Boats Afloat illustration, fixed production overhead was allocated to each yacht, based on the actual cost incurred and the actual number of yachts produced each month. An alternative method under absorption costing is to allocate fixed overhead costs using normal costing. Normal costing uses actual direct costs and actual production volumes, with an estimated fixed overhead allocation rate.

Suppose the accountant for Boats Afloat calculates an estimated fixed overhead allocation rate based on annual budget data. Assuming that budgeted fixed overhead is $720,000 and annual production is budgeted to be 24 units, the rate used for allocation would be estimated as follows:

$$\text{Estimated fixed overhead allocation rate} = \text{Estimated fixed overhead cost}$$
$$\div \text{Estimated production volume}$$
$$= \$720,000 \div 24 \text{ units}$$
$$= \$30,000 \text{ per units}$$

The fixed overhead allocation for the month of April would be as follows:

$$\text{Fixed overhead allocation} = \text{Actual units produced} \times \text{Estimated fixed overhead allocation rate}$$
$$= 1 \text{ unit} \times \$30,000 \text{ per unit}$$
$$= \$30,000$$

Motivation for Normal Costing

An estimated fixed overhead allocation rate is often preferred over using rates based on actual costs for three reasons: denominator, numerator, and information timeliness.

Actual Production Volumes Fluctuate (Denominator Reason). If overhead is allocated based on actual volume, then the fixed cost per unit could be artificially high or low in different time periods. In the Boats Afloat illustration, total cost per yacht varied from $70,000 to $100,000 because of differences in fixed production overhead per unit. These differences were caused by variations in production volume across individual months. If production volumes fluctuate randomly or seasonally, then an estimated fixed production overhead rate could be used to avoid distorting costs for individual units.

Fixed Production Overhead Costs Fluctuate (Numerator Reason). Fixed overhead costs often fluctuate throughout a time period. Suppose an organization is located in a region with cold winters. Utility costs for production facilities might be high during winter months and low during summer months. If fixed overhead is allocated based on actual costs incurred each month, units produced during the winter would be allocated higher overhead costs than units produced during summer months. When an estimated fixed production overhead rate is used, this type of per-unit cost distortion would be avoided.

Actual Volume and Fixed Overhead Costs Are Not Known Until After Accounting for the Period Is Completed (Information Timeliness Reason). Normal costing allows managers to assign costs to inventory before the accounting cycle has been completed. Managers often need to cost inventory during each month or shortly after a month's end. It might not be possible to gather and report complete cost and volume data quickly enough to use actual costs for fixed overhead allocation. As long as normal costs are reasonable estimates, they can be used for faster-paced valuations.

Allocation Rate Denominator Considerations

When calculating an estimated fixed overhead allocation rate, accountants choose the allocation base to use as the denominator. Allocation bases such as direct labour hours, direct

LO2 Discuss the factors that affect the choice of production volume measures for allocating fixed overhead

▶ **CHAPTER REFERENCE**
In Chapter 5, normal costing is described as a costing method that allocates overhead using an estimated overhead allocation rate and the actual quantity of the allocation base.

▶ **CHAPTER REFERENCE**
The methods used in this section with normal costing can also be used with standard costing. You learned about standard costing in chapters 6 and 11.

labour costs, machine hours, or number of units are often used. In this chapter, we focus on allocating fixed overhead based on production volumes or different measures of capacity to present the most general case. Capacity is a measure of the constraints within an organization. It can be measured in a number of ways.

Four different levels of capacity could be used as the estimated volume of production under absorption costing. Two of these measures are *supply-based capacity levels*; they measure the amount of capacity that is available for production:

> ▶ Theoretical capacity is the upper capacity limit; it assumes continuous—that is, uninterrupted—production, 365 days per year. Theoretical capacity is the maximum volume of goods or services that an organization could hypothetically produce.
> ▶ Practical capacity is the upper capacity limit that takes into account the organization's regularly scheduled times for production. Practical capacity excludes potential production that could take place during anticipated and scheduled maintenance downtimes, holidays, or other times in which production would normally be interrupted. In other words, practical capacity is theoretical capacity reduced for expected downtimes. Practical capacity is estimated using engineering studies and labour use patterns.

Two additional measures are *demand-based capacity levels*; they measure the amount of capacity needed to meet sales volumes:

> ▶ Normal capacity is an average use of capacity over time. Normal capacity is the typical volume of goods or services an organization produces to meet customer demand. IAS 2 requires the use of normal capacity for the allocation of fixed overhead to units of production for purposes of valuing inventory.
> ▶ Budgeted or expected capacity is the anticipated use of capacity over the next period. Budgeted or expected capacity is based on management's planned operations in which customer demand is forecast.

Volume Variance with Normal Costing

The volume variance is the difference between the amount of estimated fixed overhead costs used to calculate the allocation rate and the amount of fixed overhead costs actually allocated to inventory during the period. If allocated volume is greater than estimated volume, then too much fixed overhead is allocated to inventory, and the inventory amounts need to be reduced by the variance amount so that inventory is not stated at an amount higher than cost. If allocated volume is less than estimated volume, too little fixed overhead cost is allocated to inventory, and inventory values need to be increased by the variance amount. For example, suppose Boats Afloat estimates that fixed overhead costs will be $60,000 per month and fixed overhead is allocated to units using normal capacity of two units per month, or $30,000 per unit. In a month when only one yacht is produced, the volume variance would be as follows:

$$\text{Volume variance} = \text{Expected fixed overhead cost} - \text{Allocated fixed overhead cost}$$
$$= \$60,000 - \$30,000$$
$$= \$30,000$$

In this example, allocated overhead was less than estimated overhead, due to low production or idle facilities. In this case, Canadian ASPE (and IFRS) requires that unallocated fixed overhead be recognized as an expense in the period in which it is incurred. Fixed overhead allocated to each unit of production is not increased.

When preparing financial statements under IFRS and Canadian ASPE, this variance would be closed to cost of goods sold if it were immaterial. If the variance was material and there was an overallocation of fixed overhead, it would be prorated among cost of goods sold, finished goods, and work in process (if any). If the variance was material and there was an underallocation of fixed overhead, the variance would be recognized as an expense of the period and closed to cost of goods sold. In this example, the volume variance is the result of underallocated fixed overhead and would be considered material because it is large compared to estimated fixed overhead costs, so cost of goods sold would be increased.

✉ CHAPTER REFERENCE
IFRS and Canadian ASPE require adjustments for all variances, not just volume variances. Other variances that must be adjusted include the fixed overhead spending variance. Chapter 11 explains calculations for this and other variances.

Evaluating Denominator Choices

Because volume variances must be adjusted at the end of an accounting period, the inventory and cost of goods sold values on the financial statements are not affected by the choice of denominator when calculating the estimated fixed overhead allocation rate. Therefore, no income effects need to be considered when choosing the denominator value.

However, managers sometimes use information from the normal costing system for pricing and product emphasis decisions. In addition, the denominator choice often affects budgets. To provide the highest-quality cost information for planning and decision making, inventory values should reflect realistic estimates of the use of resources. The quality of information for decision making and planning decreases when absorption cost information is based on unrealistic capacity levels.

Another factor to consider in choosing the denominator is how the choice affects management of an organization's capacity. The largest costs in fixed overhead are often related to capacity; for example, building rent, amortization, utilities, and maintenance. Thus, we can think of the estimated fixed overhead allocation rate as an estimated cost of capacity per unit that could be used to motivate managers to use capacity efficiently. The best choice would allocate a cost to each unit produced, not only to emphasize the need to cover fixed costs, but also to provide information about the opportunity cost of unused capacity.

If theoretical capacity is used as the allocation base, the fixed overhead allocation rate is unrealistically small. Therefore, theoretical capacity is rarely used in practice. If normal or budgeted capacity is used, inventory values simply reflect the current use of capacity, which may not be the most efficient use. In contrast, practical capacity reflects an attainable target for production. When practical capacity is used in the denominator, the fixed overhead allocation rate reflects the cost of supplying capacity. Internal reports can be developed to highlight the capacity available versus the capacity used, and focus managers' attention on unused capacity. Thus, the use of practical capacity motivates managers to find new ways to use available capacity: increase demand, develop new products, or consider leasing out or eliminating unused capacity.

> **⊡ HELPFUL HINT**
>
> IFRS permits managers to defer closing variance accounts for interim financial statements if they expect any material variances to be absorbed by fiscal year end.

snowbirds
COMPARING RESULTS USING ACTUAL PRODUCTION VOLUMES AND NORMAL CAPACITY

Snowbirds is a small family-owned business that manufactures snowmobiles. Abel, the co-owner's son, has performed the company's accounting functions for several years. He always prepares variable costing income statements, because the family makes product-related decisions on a regular basis and prefers using incremental costs for those decisions. Recently, the family decided to apply for a loan to expand operations. The bank asked for this month's financial statements and wants them to conform to Canadian ASPE.

Variable Costing

The information for the current period reports along with Snowbirds' variable costing income statement follow. Snowbirds' prices and costs are as follows:

Price	$10,000 per snowmobile
Variable production costs:	
Raw materials	$ 2,000 per snowmobile
Direct labour and variable overhead	$ 2,000 per snowmobile
Fixed production costs	$60,000 per month
Selling and administrative costs:	
Variable	$ 500 per snowmobile
Fixed	$30,000 per month

© Tribune Content Agency LLC/Alamy Stock Photo

continued…

example

Beginning finished goods inventory for the year was zero. Average production is about 12 snowmobiles per month. Sales are seasonal, so in some months, no snowmobiles are produced or sold, while in other months, production and sales are high.

This month, beginning inventory was zero, 20 snowmobiles were manufactured, and 18 snowmobiles were sold.

VARIABLE COSTING INCOME STATEMENT

Revenue (18 × $10,000)		$180,000
Variable costs		
Production (18 × $4,000)	$72,000	
Selling (18 × $500)	9,000	81,000
Contribution margin		99,000
Fixed costs		
Production	$60,000	
Administrative and selling	30,000	90,000
Operating income		$ 9,000

Ending inventory is valued at $8,000 (2 units × $4,000 variable production cost per unit).

Absorption Costing with Actual Volume

When Abel develops the absorption costing income statement, he realizes that he needs to choose either actual volume or some estimate of volume to calculate the fixed overhead allocation rate. He decides to produce this month's statement both ways, to see how the two methods differ from each other and from the variable costing income statement information with which he is familiar.

First, Abel produces an absorption costing income statement using actual production levels. The actual fixed overhead allocation rate is $60,000 ÷ 20 units = $3,000 per unit. Accordingly, the absorption cost per unit is $7,000 ($4,000 variable cost plus $3,000 allocated fixed overhead), and cost of goods sold is $126,000 (18 units sold × $7,000 per unit):

ABSORPTION COSTING INCOME STATEMENT (ACTUAL VOLUME)

Revenue (18 × $10,000)	$180,000
Cost of goods sold (18 × $7,000)	126,000
Gross margin	54,000
Administrative and selling [$30,000 + (18 × $500)]	39,000
Operating income	$ 15,000

Ending inventory is valued at $14,000 [2 units × ($4,000 + $3,000)].

The difference in incomes between variable costing and absorption costing arises because allocated fixed overhead costs increase the value of the absorption costing inventory on the balance sheet. With no beginning inventory, the change in this illustration equals the fixed overhead costs that are included in ending inventory. The two units in ending inventory were each allocated $3,000 in fixed overhead. Therefore, total fixed overhead in ending inventory is $6,000. Abel prepares a formal reconciliation of the two incomes as follows:

Variable costing income	$ 9,000
Increase in fixed overhead costs in absorption inventory	
($6,000 ending – $0 beginning)	6,000
Absorption costing income	$15,000

Another way to reconcile the two incomes is to calculate the difference in the change in inventory cost between the two costing methods:

Increase in absorption costing inventory	
($14,000 ending − $0 beginning)	$14,000
Increase in variable costing inventory	
($8,000 ending − $0 beginning)	8,000
Difference	$ 6,000

Absorption Costing with Normal Capacity

Next, Abel allocates fixed overhead, using an estimated allocation rate based on a normal capacity level of 12 snowmobiles per month. In this case, the estimated fixed overhead allocation rate is $5,000 per unit ($60,000 ÷ 12 units). The cost of each unit produced under absorption costing is now $9,000 ($4,000 variable cost + $5,000 allocated fixed overhead).

ABSORPTION COSTING INCOME STATEMENT (NORMAL CAPACITY)	
Revenue (18 × $10,000)	$180,000
Cost of goods sold (18 × $9,000)	162,000
Gross margin	18,000
Administrative and selling [$30,000 + (18 × $500)]	39,000
Operating income (loss)	$(21,000)

Choice of Fixed Overhead Allocation Rate Denominator and Volume Variance Adjustment

After he completes the preceding calculations, Abel realizes that his choice of denominator level for the fixed overhead allocation rate affects the operating income, which, in turn, affects the bank's appraisal of Snowbirds' creditworthiness. Based on his analyses, he thinks the bank will view the company more favourably if fixed overhead is allocated using the actual production level. Income for the current period appears higher than when using normal capacity.

Although Abel does accounting for the family business, he is not formally trained as an accountant. Therefore, he is unsure whether his calculations and conclusions are accurate. He suspects that too much overhead has been allocated under the normal capacity version of the absorption costing income statement. He decides to meet with Matt Goodings, the company's CA.

Matt tells Abel, "I'm very impressed with what you've done here. I have only one comment about your calculations. When using an estimated volume to allocate fixed costs, there is always a volume variance—the difference between estimated and allocated fixed overhead cost. You estimated a normal capacity of 12 units per month but said that sales increased more than expected this year. You now expect that production will average more than 12 units per month. You estimated fixed overhead costs to be $60,000. However, under your estimated normal capacity, $100,000 (20 units × $5,000) of fixed overhead costs is allocated to units produced last month. Thus, you have a volume variance of $40,000—you allocated more overhead to snowmobiles than the estimated cost. Accounting standards require you to make an adjustment for this variance in your calculations to insure that only actual costs are recorded in inventory and cost of goods sold. I'll show you how." Matt shows Abel the following calculations:

Volume variance = Estimated fixed overhead − Allocated fixed overhead

= $60,000 − (20 units × $5,000 per unit)

= $40,000

> **HELPFUL HINT**
> As a rule of thumb in this textbook, we assume that a volume variance is material if it exceeds 10% of the estimated fixed overhead cost.

continued…

example

The volume variance of $40,000 is far more than 10% of the estimated fixed overhead cost of $60,000. Matt concludes that the variance is material and should be prorated among the 20 units produced that are in cost of goods sold and ending inventory. The adjustment is $2,000 per unit ($40,000 ÷ 20 units):

Adjustment for the volume variance:

Cost of goods sold ($2,000 × 18 units)	$36,000
Ending inventory ($2,000 × 2 units)	4,000
Total volume variance	$40,000

Because more fixed overhead was allocated than estimated, the absorption cost per unit should be reduced by $2,000 per unit. Abel recasts the income statement with the volume variance adjustment as follows:

ABSORPTION COSTING INCOME STATEMENT
(NORMAL CAPACITY WITH VOLUME VARIANCE ADJUSTMENT)

Revenue (18 × $10,000)		$180,000
Cost of goods sold:		
Normal costing (18 × $9,000)	$(162,000)	
Volume variance (18 × $2,000)	36,000	(126,000)
Gross margin		54,000
Administrative and selling [$30,000 + (18 × $500)]		(39,000)
Operating income (loss)		$ 15,000

Abel observes that the operating income using normal capacity with the volume variance adjustment is now identical to the operating income when actual volume was used to allocate fixed overhead. Therefore, the financial statements are not affected by the choice of denominator used for the estimated fixed overhead allocation rate. ■

The Effects of Beginning Inventory Balances on Income Reconciliation

LO3

Prepare absorption and variable costing income statements considering beginning inventory balances, and evaluate the impact of inventory on income

So far in this chapter, we have assumed no beginning inventories when we prepared the income statements. However, most organizations have units in inventory. To simplify our calculation, and in consideration of current IFRS. and Canadian ASPE reporting requirements, we assume either zero cost inflation/deflation or use of the first-in, first-out (FIFO) inventory cost flow assumption in this chapter. Under zero cost inflation/deflation, current period and prior period costs per unit are the same. Under FIFO, prior period inventory costs become part of cost of goods sold first. Any increase in inventory quantity on the balance sheet is valued using the current period costs.

To reconcile absorption costing and variable costing incomes under FIFO, we first need to determine whether inventory quantity increased or decreased during the period (i.e., whether production was higher or lower than sales). We then reconcile the incomes by using the general formulas shown in Exhibit 17.5. If inventory quantities increased during the period, the simplest way to reconcile incomes is to multiply the fixed overhead cost rate for the current period (adjusted for any volume variance) by the number of units added to inventory. If inventory quantities decreased, it is first necessary to determine the allocation rate that was originally used to allocate fixed overhead cost to each unit in beginning inventory. (For simplicity, we will assume that there is only one FIFO cost layer in beginning inventory.) Income is reconciled by multiplying this rate by the number of units that were removed from inventory during the current period.

golden hawks
ABSORPTION AND VARIABLE INCOME STATEMENTS WITH BEGINNING INVENTORIES

Your brother owns Golden Hawks, a company that produces kits for model airplanes that actually fly. Your brother has an MBA and has always prepared a simple spreadsheet showing the difference between the cash that comes in and cash that goes out during a period; he uses this information for planning and monitoring purposes. His tax accountant prepares tax reports. You have been asked to prepare financial statements for the business because your brother may want to ask others to invest in his company. You decide to prepare both variable and absorption income statements and explain to your brother the differences and uses of both.

During 2015, the company produced 10,000 kits and sold 9,000 of them. The kits sell for $200 each. Costs incurred in 2015 are listed here:

© age fotostock/Alamy Stock Photo

Materials purchased	$500,000
Materials used	$400,000
Other variable production costs	$800,000
Fixed overhead costs (estimated and actual)	$150,000
Variable selling costs	$135,000
Fixed selling and administrative costs	$200,000

In January 2015, 2,000 kits were in beginning inventory. Assume that the value of this inventory was $220,000 under variable costing and $250,000 under absorption costing. Ending inventory contains 3,000 kits because production exceeded sales by 1,000 kits during 2015.

Variable Costing

You first perform the calculations needed to prepare the variable costing income statement. These calculations include determining the production variable cost per unit:

$$\text{Total variable production cost} = \text{Materials used} + \text{Other variable production costs}$$
$$= \$400,000 + \$800,000 = \$1,200,000$$
$$\text{Variable cost per unit} = \$1,200,000 \div 10,000 \text{ units}$$
$$= \$120 \text{ per unit}$$

You also calculate the variable selling cost per unit:

$$\text{Variable selling cost per unit} = \text{Total variable selling cost} \div \text{Units sold}$$
$$= \$135,000 \div 9,000 \text{ units}$$
$$= \$15 \text{ per unit}$$

Using these calculations and other information provided, you create the following variable costing income statement:

VARIABLE COSTING INCOME STATEMENT

Revenue (9,000 units × $200)		$1,800,000
Less variable costs:		
Beginning inventory (2,000 units × $110)	$220,000	
Production (7,000 units × $120)	840,000	
Selling (9,000 units × $15)	135,000	1,195,000
Contribution margin		605,000
Fixed costs:		
Production overhead	$150,000	
Selling and administrative	200,000	350,000
Variable costing operating income		$ 255,000

continued...

You also determine the ending inventory:

Variable costing finished goods inventory:

Beginning inventory (2,000 units × $110)	$ 220,000
Add variable production costs (10,000 units × $120)	1,200,000
Goods available for sale	1,420,000
Less cost of goods sold [(2,000 units × $110) + (7,000 units × $120)]	1,060,000
Ending inventory (3,000 units × $120)	$ 360,000

You notice that variable cost per unit changed between last period and this period. Last period's inventory was valued at $110 each, and this period's production is valued at $120 each.

Absorption Costing Using Normal Capacity

You now perform the calculations needed to prepare the absorption costing income statement that would be used by bankers and other investors. You decide to use a normal capacity of 10,000 units per year to estimate a fixed allocation rate, because your brother indicates that this is the expected production, on average, under normal circumstances. (*Note:* This illustration has no work-in-process inventory.)

$$\text{Estimated fixed overhead allocation rate} = \text{Estimated fixed overhead cost} \div \text{Normal capacity}$$
$$= \$150,000 \div 10,000 \text{ units}$$
$$= \$15 \text{ per unit}$$

You then determine the volume variance:

$$\text{Volume variance} = \text{Estimated fixed overhead cost} - \text{Allocated fixed overhead cost}$$
$$= \$150,000 - (\$15 \text{ per unit} \times 10,000 \text{ units})$$
$$= \$0$$

Because there is no volume variance, no adjustments need to be made to inventory values or cost of goods sold. If there was an unfavourable (unallocated) volume variance as the result of low production or idle plant facilities, IFRS requires that the unallocated fixed overhead be expensed in the period in which it occurs (closed to cost of goods sold). If there is a favourable (over allocated) volume variance, due to abnormally high levels of production, IFRS requires that the amount of fixed overhead per unit of production be decreased so that inventories are not measured above cost (prorate the volume variance to inventories and cost of goods sold). You then prepare the absorption costing income statement. Note that the current period production costs include $120 of variable production costs, plus $15 of estimated fixed overhead per unit.

ABSORPTION COSTING INCOME STATEMENT

Revenue (9,000 units × $200)	$1,800,000
Cost of goods sold:	
Beginning inventory (2,000 units × $125)	
Current period production (7,000 units × $135)	1,195,000
Gross margin	605,000
Selling and administrative costs ($135,000 + $200,000)	335,000
Absorption costing operating income	$ 270,000

Finally, you calculate the ending absorption costing inventory amount:

Beginning inventory (2,000 units × $125)	$ 250,000
Add variable production costs (10,000 units × $120)	1,200,000
Add fixed overhead costs (10,000 units × $15)	150,000
Goods available for sale	1,600,000
Less cost of goods sold [(2,000 units sold × $125) + (7,000 units × $135)]	1,195,000
Ending inventory (3,000 units × $135)	$ 405,000

Reconciliation of Variable and Absorption Costing Income

You prepare a reconciliation to help your brother understand the difference between the variable costing and absorption costing income statements. Because inventory increased during the year, you calculate the increase in fixed overhead costs added to inventory this year to explain why absorption costing income was higher than variable costing income:

Variable costing income	$255,000
Increase in fixed overhead costs in absorption inventory	
(1,000 units added to inventory × $15 per unit fixed overhead cost)	15,000
Absorption costing income	$270,000

The reconciliation could also be calculated by determining the change during the year in the total amount of fixed overhead cost included in inventory. You notice that last period's inventory was $220,000 under variable costing and $250,000 under absorption costing. Because the only difference between the two methods is the allocation of fixed overhead cost, the $30,000 difference must consist only of fixed overhead cost allocated to units during one or more prior periods. Because beginning inventory held 2,000 units, the average fixed overhead cost in inventory was $15 per unit ($30,000 ÷ 2,000 units). This period, fixed production overhead is also $15 per unit. Therefore, the change in fixed costs included in inventory during 2012 is as follows:

Fixed cost in ending inventory (3,000 × $15)	$45,000
Fixed cost in beginning inventory (2,000 × $15)	30,000
Difference between absorption and variable costing income	$15,000

Absorption Costing Used for Internal Decision Making (Practical Capacity)

Because your brother would like to be able to use this information to examine his use of existing capacity, you perform the calculations needed to prepare the absorption costing income statement using practical capacity. You decide to use practical capacity of 15,000 units per year to estimate a fixed overhead allocation rate, because your brother may want to use this information to examine his use of existing capacity:

$$\text{Estimated fixed overhead allocation rate} = \text{Estimated fixed overhead cost} \div \text{Practical capacity}$$
$$= \$150,000 \div 15,000 \text{ units}$$
$$= \$10 \text{ per unit}$$

You then determine the volume variance:

$$\text{Volume variance} = \text{Estimated fixed overhead cost} - \text{Allocated fixed overhead cost}$$
$$= \$150,000 - (\$10 \text{ per unit} \times 10,000 \text{ units})$$
$$= \$50,000$$

You decide that the volume variance is the result of actual production being below the practical capacity of the business, and it is material because it amounts to one-third ($50,000 ÷ $150,000) of the estimated fixed overhead cost. This result means that Golden Hawks is underutilizing its production facilities. Underutilized facilities represent a potential opportunity to the business. If there is unmet demand for kits for model airplanes, Golden Hawks should consider increasing production. It may also be possible for Golden Hawks to expand or diversify its product offerings. If growth is not supported, then underutilized capacity indicates non-value-added costs of production, and an analysis should be undertaken to reduce these costs. (*Note:* This illustration has no work-in-process inventory.)

Now you prepare the absorption costing income statement. The absorption cost per unit sold is $135 ($120 variable cost + $10 fixed overhead allocation rate + $5 volume variance adjustment):

continued...

example

ABSORPTION COSTING INCOME STATEMENT

Revenue (9,000 units × $200)		$1,800,000
Cost of goods sold:		
Beginning inventory (2,000 × $125)	$250,000	
Current period production (7,000 × $130)	910,000	
Volume variance adjustment	50,000	1,210,000
Gross margin		590,000
Selling and administrative costs ($135,000 + $200,000)		335,000
Absorption costing operating income		$ 255,000

Finally, you calculate the ending absorption costing inventory amount:

Beginning inventory (2,000 units × $125)	$ 250,000	
Add variable production costs (10,000 units × $120)	1,200,000	
Add fixed overhead costs (10,000 units × $10)	100,000	
Add volume variance adjustment	50,000	
Goods available for sale		1,600,000
Less cost of goods sold		1,210,000
Ending inventory (3,000 units × $130)		$ 390,000

You also produce an alternative format for the absorption income statement with more detail, because it may be easier for your brother to understand:

ABSORPTION COSTING INCOME STATEMENT (WITH ADDITIONAL DETAIL)

Revenue		$1,800,000
Cost of goods sold:		
Beginning inventory	$ 250,000	
Variable production costs	1,200,000	
Fixed overhead costs allocated	100,000	
Adjustment for volume variance	50,000	
Cost of goods available for sale	1,600,000	
Ending inventory (3,000 × $130)	(390,000)	
Cost of goods sold		1,210,000
Gross margin		590,000
Operating costs:		
Variable selling	135,000	
Fixed selling and administrative expenses	200,000	335,000
Absorption costing operating income		$ 255,000

Notice that the variable costing and absorption costing net incomes are the same. This is because the amount of fixed overhead in beginning inventory (2,000 units × $15) is the same as the amount of fixed overhead in the ending inventory (3,000 units × $10). The result is that the same amount of fixed overhead is recognized as an expense on both the variable costing income statement ($150,000) and the absorption costing income statement [(2,000 units × $15) + (7,000 units × $10) + $50,000 volume variance)].

Using Variable and Absorption Costing Information

After you discuss these statements with your brother, he decides to prepare both statements on a monthly basis instead of using the spreadsheet that he previously developed. He wants the absorption costing income statement to be based on normal costing so he can monitor the information that people outside his company, such as bankers and any other creditors, will be using. However, he believes that the absorption costing income statement based on practical capacity will help him focus on the use of capacity. Each month, when he calculates the volume variance, he will know how close to practical capacity that month's operations were. He also wants variable costing income statements, because he believes this method represents a more accurate economic picture of his operations. ■

Incentives to Build Up Inventories

A key business risk for many managers is identification of appropriate levels of inventory. In this chapter's examples, absorption costing operating income is higher than variable costing operating income in periods when the inventory quantities increase. Under absorption costing, part of an organization's fixed overhead cost is recorded as inventory on the balance sheet. As inventory quantity increases, the amount of fixed cost included in inventory increases. Because that portion of fixed cost is not expensed until later, operating income also increases. As a result, managers using absorption costing have incentives to inappropriately build up inventory quantities, especially when sales during the current period decrease. Managers may be motivated by many factors:

- ► Managers' reputations often increase with reported operating income.
- ► Managers frequently receive bonus payments based on their ability to meet or exceed targeted operating income levels.
- ► Managers may be biased in their sales forecasts, preventing them from promptly recognizing a decline in sales.

Disincentives to Build Up Inventories

Managers might avoid inventory buildups for several reasons. If managers become aware of a sales decline, they could be unwilling to use an inventory buildup that, while strengthening short-term earnings, would negatively affect future earnings when those units are either sold or written off. If bonuses are based on variable costing income, managers will not be rewarded for inventory buildups. The channel stuffing examples that opened this chapter show another disincentive: analysts routinely monitor companies' inventory levels. Excessive inventory levels are often viewed as evidence of poor management or deteriorating sales. In addition, some organizations use just-in-time (JIT) inventory management. If all participants in the supply chain use JIT, the potential buildup of inventory is unlikely; therefore, income differences under absorption and variable costing are small. However, if a powerful member of the supply chain requires JIT deliveries but pushes excess production downstream (as in channel stuffing), the benefits to the supply chain are reduced.

Desirable Inventory Levels and Business Risk

In the channel stuffing examples, managers intentionally wanted dealers to carry higher inventories to better meet customer demand. Analysts felt that sales were in decline and that dealer inventory increases signalled a forthcoming decline in the company's financial health. It was not possible for outsiders such as investors to determine whether inventories were too high because of uncertainties about factors influencing future sales and production, such as the following:

- ► The extent to which long wait times would cause customers to buy from competitors
- ► The increase in sales as a result of inventory being readily available

▶ Whether an increase in inventories and corresponding decrease in customer wait times would reduce the mystique of a brand, causing a decrease in future product demand
▶ The most desirable production and inventory levels

To further complicate matters, outsiders could not know whether the managers were completely candid in explaining their production policies or whether their production decisions were biased.

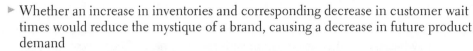

© iStockphoto/Simon Smith

●● > FOCUS ON ETHICAL DECISION MAKING:
CHANNEL STUFFING AT MCAFEE INC.

In January 2006, the SEC filed securities fraud charges against McAfee Inc. McAfee was charged with misleading investors by fraudulently overstating revenue and earnings by hundreds of millions of dollars from the second quarter of 1998 through 2000. Specifically, McAfee allegedly overstated cumulative net revenues by US$622 million during this time period.

McAfee, a leading maker of anti-virus software, used a variety of schemes to aggressively oversell products to distributors. Distributors were holding inventories that far exceeded expected consumer demand. McAfee incorrectly recorded these sales as revenue, while offering distributors a number of incentives—including deep price discounts, cash payments, and rebates—to continue to hold excess inventory. Through Net tools Inc., a wholly owned subsidiary, McAfee repurchased the excess inventories. These actions were concealed from the public by various methods. However, by December 2000, distributors were pushed to their limit and refused to buy additional inventory, which was the beginning of the unravelling of McAfee's channel-stuffing scheme.

In December 2000, McAfee announced that fourth-quarter sales would be 78% less than previously reported, and it also announced the unexplained resignations of the CEO, CFO, and president of the company. Before these announcements, McAfee stock was trading at US$11.75 per share. After the announcements, the stock hit a low of US$3.25, a US$1 billion loss in market capitalization.

McAfee restated its financial results five times during the period 1997 to 2004. In 2005, the external auditors again indicated that McAfee had material weaknesses in internal controls. In 2006, McAfee consented "without admitting or denying the allegations" to a court order requiring the company to pay a US$50 million civil penalty. Further, McAfee agreed to appoint an independent consultant to examine and recommend improvements to the system of internal controls. The court order required the distribution of the US$50 million to be in accordance with the Fair Funds provisions of the Sarbanes–Oxley Act.

Analysts had accused Harley-Davidson of channel stuffing. However, the excess inventories were sold in the next period. Had motorcycle sales decreased the next period, company officials might have been subject to the same regulatory actions as McAfee. A fine line separates managing inventories for valid business purposes and managing inventories for earnings manipulation.

Source: U.S. Securities and Exchange Commission Litigation Release No. 19520, January 4, 2006, *SEC v. McAfee, Inc., Civil Action No. 06-009 (PJH)(N.D.Cal.)(January 4, 2006), SEC Sues McAfee, Inc. for Accounting Fraud, McAfee Agrees to Settle and Pay a $50 Million Penalty,* www.sec.gov/litigation/litreleases/lr19520.htm; and *Securities and Exchange Commission v. McAfee, Inc. (f/k/a/ Network Associates, Inc.),* www.sec.gov/litigation/complaints/comp19520.pdf.

THINKING CRITICALLY ABOUT ETHICS AND CHANNEL STUFFING

Think about the following questions to explore the ethical issues surrounding channel stuffing. Why is channel stuffing both an ethical and a legal problem? Consider the viewpoint of investors who believe that the quality of information in financial statements is uniformly high in all firms. Why it is difficult to predict the amount of inventory that should be produced? How can managers and accountants avoid the appearance of channel stuffing, while ensuring that inventory stockouts do not occur?

---

[5] D. Boyd, L. Kronk, and R. Skinner, "The Effects of Just-in-Time Systems on Financial Accounting Metrics," *Industrial Management + Data Systems,* 102(3/4), 2002, pp. 153–165.

Throughput Costing

Throughput costing is a modified form of variable costing that treats direct labour and variable overhead as period expenses. Developed in the 1980s as part of the Theory of Constraints, throughput costing has become popular for internal reporting purposes. It was developed when some managers realized that product costs under both absorption and variable costing are excessive, because they include more than direct materials.

In many organizations, conversion costs such as direct labour and overhead do not vary proportionately with volume of production. Under throughput costing, inventory is valued using only direct material costs (Exhibit 17.6). All other costs are treated as period costs. The throughput contribution is defined as revenue less direct materials costs for the units sold. Accountants and managers in companies using Theory of Constraints methods believe that throughput costing helps them make better short-term decisions, because costs other than direct materials tend to be relatively fixed in the short run. For example, direct labour may be a fixed cost if workers are guaranteed a work schedule such as a 40-hour week. When direct labour is fixed and little or no variable overhead cost is involved, the variable income statement is similar to the throughput costing income statement. Exhibit 17.7 shows an income statement format for throughput costing.

Following is a throughput income statement, using data from the Golden Hawks illustration:

Revenue (9,000 units × $200 per unit)	$1,800,000
Direct materials (9,000 units × $40 per unit)	360,000
Throughput contribution	1,440,000
Other costs:	
Operating expenses	1,285,000
Throughput costing operating income	$ 155,000

Throughput contribution is revenue less the cost of direct materials for the units sold. The operating expenses of $1,285,000 include the costs of direct labour and variable overhead for the entire period (10,000 units × $80 per unit = $800,000), variable selling costs ($135,000), fixed production cost ($150,000), and fixed selling costs ($200,000). As an alternative format, totals for production- and non-production-related costs can also be presented separately. Ending inventory increased under throughput costing only by the amount of direct materials: 1,000 units × $40 per unit = $40,000.

CHAPTER REFERENCE
Operating decisions involving constrained resources, part of the Theory of Constraints, are discussed in more detail in Chapter 4.

L04 Prepare throughput costing income statements and evaluate absorption, variable, and throughput costing income

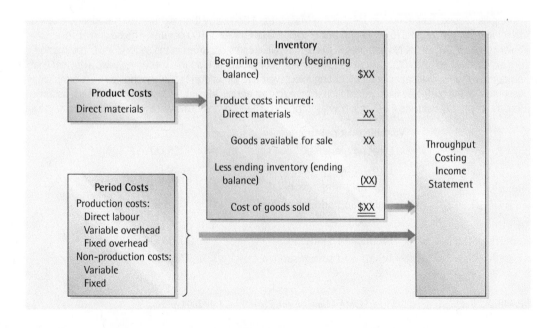

EXHIBIT 17.6
Throughput Costing

>EXHIBIT 17.7
Throughput Costing Income Statement

Revenue	
(Units sold × Price per unit)	$XX
Direct material costs:	
Production (Units sold × Direct materials unit cost)	(XX)
Throughput contribution	XX
Other costs:	
Production (Direct labour + Fixed and variable overhead)	(XX)
Non-production costs (Fixed and variable selling and administration)	(XX)
Operating income	$XX

>ALTERNATIVE TERMS

Some people refer to *throughput costing* as *super-variable costing*.

>BUSINESS PRACTICE

To improve **Embassy Food Specialties'** performance in the flavour industry, Martino Brambilla, owner and president, revamped the basis for staff bonuses. By basing the new measures on Theory of Constraints philosophy, Embassy Foods has improved delivery performance and reduced inventory levels needed to support operations.[6]

Variable costing income was $235,000. Throughput costing operating income is $80,000 less than operating income under variable costing. This difference arises because $80,000 (1,000 units × $80 per unit) of variable overhead and direct labour costs are included in inventory under variable costing, but expensed as a period cost under throughput costing.

Advantages of Throughput Costing

Throughput costing can be thought of as an extreme version of variable costing. Only direct material costs are assigned to inventory and cost of goods sold. When costs such as direct labour and overhead are categorized and treated as operating costs rather than product costs (inventory), managers' attitudes toward them tend to change. Managers are encouraged to reduce operating costs when needed, such as when sales decline, while under throughput costing, managers are more likely to consider reducing costs such as direct labour costs. Conversely, under absorption costing, many production costs are initially categorized as assets (inventory) until goods are sold. As a result, managers may perceive less need to reduce direct labour and overhead cost. Compared to absorption and variable costing, throughput costing also reduces the incentives for managers to build up inventory to inappropriate levels.

17-1 self-study problem   Absorption, Variable, and Throughput Costing

L01, L03, L04

During its second year of operations, Grilling Machines, a company that manufactures and sells electric tabletop grills, produced 275,000 units, and it sold 250,000 units at $60 per unit. The beginning inventory balance was 5,000 units. No changes in fixed or variable costs occurred in the second year. The managers expected to sell 220,000 units, the same volume of production as the preceding year. They set that amount as the normal capacity for allocating fixed overhead costs during the second year. For simplicity, assume that the budgeted fixed production overhead cost equals the actual cost this period. Also, assume that the company uses the FIFO cost flow assumption. The following costs were incurred during the year:

Variable cost per unit:		
Direct materials	$	15.00
Direct labour		10.00
Manufacturing overhead		12.50
Selling and administrative		2.50
Total fixed costs:		
Production overhead	$2,200,000	
Selling and administrative	1,375,000	

[6] P. Milroy, "Setting Your Sight Lines," *CMA Management*, 78(4), June/July 2004, p. 16.

required

A. Prepare income statements using absorption costing, variable costing, and throughput costing. Provide the details of your calculations in a schedule for each income statement.
B. Reconcile the difference between operating incomes based on absorption costing and variable costing. Create a schedule to show your work.
C. Reconcile the difference between operating incomes based on variable costing and throughput costing. Create a schedule to show your work.
D. Suppose the accountant for Grilling Machines used an actual fixed overhead allocation rate rather than an estimated rate. Using this method, calculate the cost of goods sold and ending inventory under absorption costing. Compare the results to those calculated in Part A.
E. If the volume variance is not material, how is it closed at the end of the period? Explain the reasoning behind this treatment.

See the solution on page 745.

Comparison of Absorption, Variable, and Throughput Costing

Exhibit 17.8 compares the assumptions used in absorption costing, variable costing, and throughput costing. These accounting methods differ, based on the costs that are considered product costs. Under absorption costing, all production costs are product costs. Under variable costing, only variable production costs are product costs. Under throughput costing, only direct materials costs are product costs. These methods affect how quickly production overhead and other costs are expensed on the income statement. Because managers monitor operating income, these methods affect how quickly they are motivated to consider changing production plans related to these costs.

Different Methods for Different Purposes

Before technology made it relatively easy to draw many different reports from one database, most organizations established an accounting system designed primarily to meet financial and tax accounting requirements. Because absorption costing is required by

> **EXHIBIT 17.8**
Comparison of Absorption, Variable, and Throughput Costing

Absorption Costing	Variable Costing	Throughput Costing
IFRS	Not IFRS	Not IFRS
Useful for external reporting purposes	Useful for performance evaluation and internal decision making	Useful for short-term capacity decision making; focuses managers' attention on reducing labour and overhead costs, because these are considered operating costs instead of product costs (inventory)
Direct material and direct labour are inventory costs	Direct material and direct labour are inventory costs	Only direct materials are inventory costs
Fixed and variable production overhead allocated to inventory	Fixed production overhead expensed as a period cost Variable production overhead allocated to inventory	Direct labour, fixed and variable overhead, and all other costs expensed as operational expense, a period cost
Administrative and selling costs (both fixed and variable) expensed as period costs	Administrative and selling costs separated into fixed and variable costs and expensed as period costs	Administrative and selling costs expensed as operational expense, a period cost
Inventory costs (including per-unit fixed and variable production costs) not expensed until the units are sold	Inventory costs (only production variable costs) not expensed until the units are sold	Inventory costs (only direct materials) not expensed until the units are sold

IFRS, Canadian ASPE, and income tax rules, it tended to be the only method used. With improved technology, organizations are now able to produce information reports for many different purposes.

Absorption costing income statements focus on matching production costs to revenues on the income statement. This information is important for external users, such as investors, who monitor the trends in product costs for an organization over time, and for comparison with competitors. Variable costing income statements are often used to evaluate the performance of a division or manager, or as a source for information for decision making. Throughput costing statements help managers determine the most efficient use of resources in the short term.

The income statements we learned about in this chapter develop cost information using production units as cost objects. To improve information for decision making and planning purposes, ABC, GPK, and RCA systems were developed to separate fixed and variable costs using cost objects that reflect activities or resource centres. These costing systems attempt to map costs more accurately to the use of resources. As demonstrated in Chapter 7, GPK and RCA are often used to develop income statements that are layered to provide contribution margins at the product, product group, business unit, and entire organization levels.

SUMMARY

LO1   Prepare absorption and variable costing income statements and reconcile the resulting net incomes

ABSORPTION COSTING

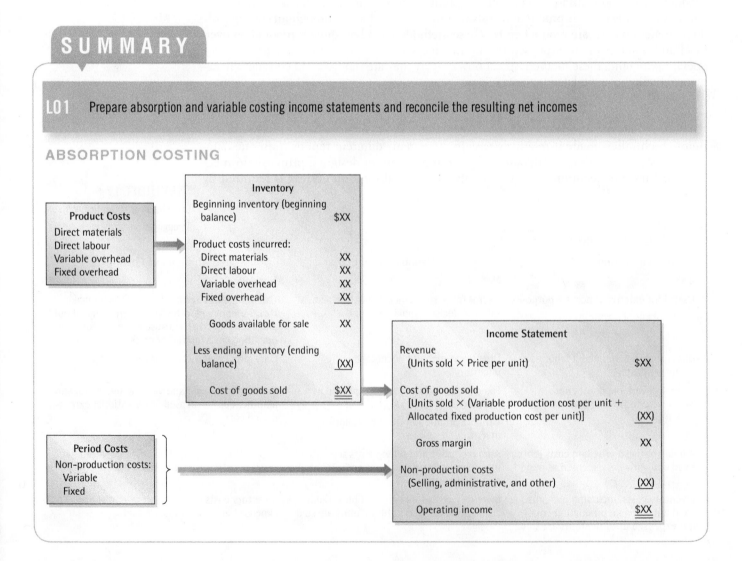

SUMMARY

VARIABLE COSTING

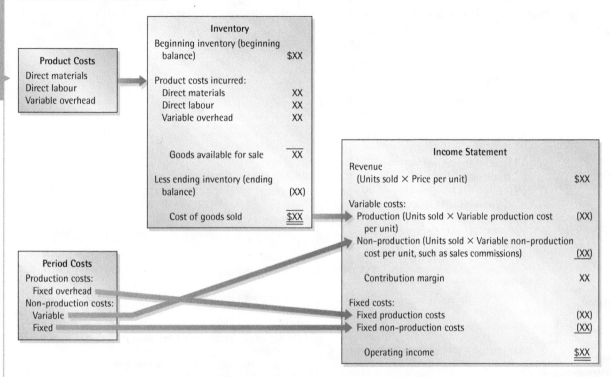

Discuss the factors that affect the choice of production volume measures for allocating fixed overhead

ACTUAL COSTING

$$\text{Actual fixed overhead allocation rate} = \frac{\text{Actual fixed overhead cost}}{\text{Actual production volume}}$$

NORMAL COSTING

$$\text{Estimated fixed overhead allocation-rate} = \frac{\text{Estimated fixed overhead cost}}{\text{Estimated production volume}}$$

ALTERNATIVE MEASURES OF PRODUCTION VOLUME FOR NORMAL COSTING

► Theoretical capacity
► Normal capacity
► Practical capacity
► Budgeted, or expected, capacity

VOLUME VARIANCE UNDER NORMAL COSTING

Volume variance = Expected fixed overhead cost
    − Allocated fixed overhead cost

► If material and overallocated: Prorate among all production during the period (units in work in process, finished goods, and cost of goods sold)
► If material and underallocated: Expense in the period by closing to cost of goods sold
► If immaterial: Allocate to cost of goods sold

Prepare absorption and variable costing income statements considering beginning inventory balances, and evaluate the impact of inventory on income

INCENTIVES TO BUILD UP INVENTORY

► Managers' reputations
► Bonus payments
► Biased sales forecasts

DISINCENTIVES TO BUILD UP INVENTORY

► Channel stuffing
► Poor inventory management
► JIT considerations

L04 Prepare throughput costing income statements and evaluate absorption, variable, and throughput costing income

THROUGHPUT COSTING INCOME STATEMENT

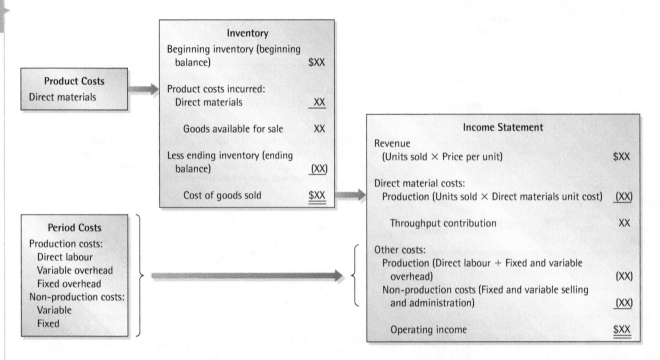

Absorption Costing	Variable Costing	Throughput Costing
IFRS	Not IFRS	Not IFRS
Useful for external reporting purposes	Useful for performance evaluation and internal decision making	Useful for short-term capacity decision making; focuses managers' attention on reducing labour and overhead costs because they are considered operating costs instead of product costs (inventory)
Direct material and direct labour are inventory costs	Direct material and direct labour are inventory costs	Only direct materials are inventory costs
Fixed and variable production overhead allocated to inventory	Fixed production overhead expensed as a period cost; Variable production overhead allocated to inventory	Direct labour, fixed and variable overhead, and all other costs expensed as operational expense, a period cost
Administrative and selling costs (both fixed and variable) expensed as period costs	Administrative and selling costs separated into fixed and variable costs and expensed as period costs	Administrative and selling costs expensed as operational expense, a period cost
Inventory costs (including per-unit fixed and variable production costs) not expensed until the units are sold	Inventory costs (only production variable costs) not expensed until the units are sold	Inventory costs (only direct materials) not expensed until the units are sold

17-1 solution to self-study problem

A. Calculations for the Absorption Costing Income Statement

Before calculating the product cost per unit, it is necessary to compute the fixed overhead cost allocation and the volume variance adjustment. The company's policy is to allocate fixed overhead using normal capacity, which was estimated at 220,000 units:

Estimated fixed overhead = $2,200,000 estimated fixed overhead
allocation rate   ÷ 220,000 normal volume of units
               = $10.00 per unit .

At the end of the year, the company must make an adjustment for its volume variance, which is the difference between total fixed overhead allocated to production and the original estimate of fixed overhead costs:

Estimated fixed overhead ($10 per unit × 220,000 units)	$2,200,000
Allocated overhead ($10 per unit × 275,000 units)	2,750,000
Volume variance	$ 550,000

The volume variance is considered material because it is greater than 10% of the estimated fixed overhead cost:

$$\$550,000 \div \$2,200,000 = 25\%$$

Material overapplied volume variances are adjusted to all units produced. For this problem, 250,000 of the units are in cost of goods sold, and 25,000 units are added to inventory. Because more fixed overhead cost was allocated than estimated, the absorption cost per unit must be reduced by the volume variance:

Volume variance per unit produced = $550,000 ÷ 275,000 units
                   = $2.00 per unit

Given the preceding calculations, the absorption product cost per unit is as follows:

Direct materials	$15.00
Direct labour	10.00
Variable overhead	12.50
Fixed overhead allocation rate	10.00
Subtotal before volume variance adjustment	47.50
Volume variance adjustment per unit	(2.00)
Total absorption cost per unit	$45.50

We can now calculate the value of ending inventory. This year, 275,000 units were produced and 250,000 were sold, causing inventory to increase by 25,000 units. Beginning inventory was 5,000 units, so ending inventory is 30,000 units. Also, recall that the costs in year 1 were the same as the costs in year 2. Because actual volume during year 1 was 220,000 units (rather than 275,000), no volume variance adjustment was needed in year 1. Therefore, beginning inventory was valued at an absorption cost of $47.50 per unit. Under the FIFO cost flow assumption, those costs are part of cost of goods sold, and the 30,000 units in ending inventory are valued at $45.50 per unit:

Ending inventory 30,000 units × $45.50 = $1,365,000

Because inventory increased during year 2, cost of goods sold under FIFO is calculated as the beginning inventory value, plus current year cost per unit times the additional number of units sold:

solution to self-study problem

17-1

Beginning inventory (5,000 units × $47.50)	$237,500
Current period production (245,000 units × $45.50)	11,147,500
Cost of goods sold	11,385,000

To prepare the reconciliation of total product costs in Exhibit 17.9, calculate the total amounts for each of the variable production costs, based on actual production of 275,000 units:

Direct materials (275,00 units produced × $15.00 per unit)	$ 4,125,000
Direct labour (275,000 units produced × $10.00 per unit)	2,750,000
Variable overhead (275,000 units produced × $12.50 per unit)	3,437,500
Total variable production costs	$10,312,500

The reconciliation of product costs shown in Exhibit 17.9 provides a double check on the accuracy of the cost of goods sold and inventory calculations.

Fixed and variable selling and administrative costs are combined on the absorption costing income statement:

Fixed selling and administrative	$1,375,000
Variable selling and administrative (250,000 units sold × $2.50)	625,000
Total selling and administrative	$2,000,000

▶ EXHIBIT 17.9

Absorption, Variable, and Throughput Costing Income Statements for Grilling Machines

Absorption Costing Income Statement		Variable Costing Income Statement		Throughput Costing Income Statement	
Revenue ($60 × 250,000)	$15,000,000	Revenue ($60 × 250,000)	$15,000,000	Revenue ($60 × 250,000)	$15,000,000
Cost of goods sold	(11,385,000)	Variable costs:		Cost of goods sold	(3,750,000)
Gross margin	3,615,000	Cost of goods sold	(9,375,000)	Throughput contribution	11,250,000
Selling and administrative	(2,000,000)	Selling and administrative	(625,000)	Other costs:	
Operating income	$1,615,000	Contribution margin	5,000,000	Production conversion costs	(8,387,500)
		Fixed costs:		Selling and administrative	(2,000,000)
		Fixed production overhead	(2,200,000)	Operating income	$ 862,500
		Fixed selling and administrative	(1,375,000)		
		Operating income	$ 1,425,000		

Reconciliation of Product Costs		Reconciliation of Product Costs		Reconciliation of Product Costs	
Beginning inventory	$ 237,500	Beginning inventory	$ 187,500	Beginning inventory	$ 75,000
Product costs incurred:		Product costs incurred:		Product costs incurred:	
Direct materials	4,125,000	Direct materials	4,125,000	Direct materials	4,125,000
Direct labour	2,750,000	Direct labour	2,750,000	Goods available for sale	4,200,000
Variable overhead	3,437,500	Variable overhead	3,437,500	Less ending inventory	(450,000)
Fixed overhead allocated	2,750,000	Goods available for sale	10,500,000	Cost of goods sold	$3,750,000
Volume variance	(550,000)	Less ending inventory	(1,125,000)		
Adjustment Goods available for sale	12,750,000	Cost of goods sold	$9,375,000		
Less ending inventory	(1,365,000)				
Cost of goods sold	$11,385,000				

Calculations for the Variable Costing Income Statement

The calculations for the variable costing income statement are similar to those for the absorption costing income statement, except fixed overhead is not allocated as a product cost. Therefore, the variable production cost per unit used in calculating cost of goods sold and inventory is as follows:

Direct materials	$15.00
Direct labour	10.00
Variable overhead	12.50
Total variable cost per unit	$37.50

Because last year's variable cost per unit is the same as this year's, the units in beginning inventory and the units added to inventory are each valued at $37.50 per unit:

Ending inventory 30,000 units × $37.50 = $1,125,000

Cost of goods sold is also valued at $37.50 per unit:

Beginning inventory (5,000 units × $37.50)	$ 187,500
Current period production (245,000 units × $37.50)	9,187,500
Cost of goods sold (250,000 units × $37.50 per unit)	$9,375,000

The reconciliation of product costs shown in Exhibit 17.9 provides a double check on the accuracy of the cost of goods sold and inventory calculations.

When preparing the income statement, variable selling and administrative costs are separated from fixed selling and administrative costs.

Calculations for the Throughput Costing Income Statement

The calculations for the throughput costing income statement are similar to those for the variable costing income statement, except that the only product cost is direct materials. Therefore, the cost per unit used in calculating cost of goods sold and inventory is

Direct materials	$15.00

Because last year's direct material cost per unit is the same as this year's direct material cost per unit, the units in beginning inventory and the units added to inventory are each valued at $15.00 per unit:

Beginning inventory (5,000 units × $15.00 per unit)	$ 75,000
Units added to inventory (25,000 units × $15.00 per unit)	375,000
Ending inventory	$450,000

Cost of goods sold is also valued at $15.00 per unit:

Cost of goods sold 250,000 units × $15.00 per unit = $3,750,000

The reconciliation of product costs shown in Exhibit 15.9 provides a double check on the accuracy of the cost of goods sold and inventory calculations.

All the production conversion costs are combined into a single line item on the throughput costing income statement:

Direct labour (275,000 units produced × $10.00 per unit)	$2,750,000
Variable overhead (275,000 units produced × $12.50 per unit)	3,437,500
Fixed overhead	2,200,000
Total conversion costs	$8,387,500

The fixed and variable selling and administrative costs are combined as previously calculated for the absorption costing income statement.

B. **Reconciliation of Absorption Costing and Variable Costing Income:**

Variable costing income		$1,425,000
Increase in fixed overhead costs in absorption inventory:		
Fixed overhead removed with beginning inventory (5,000 units × $10)		(50,000)
Fixed overhead in ending inventory [30,000 units × ($10 – $2)]		240,000
Absorption costing income		$1,615,000

Under absorption costing, $240,000 of this year's fixed overhead cost is held as ending inventory. In addition, $50,000 of last year's fixed overhead cost was removed from inventory; therefore, absorption costing income is $190,000 higher than variable costing income.

The difference in income also could be calculated using the difference between costing methods in the change in inventory during the year:

Change in absorption costing inventory:		
Ending inventory	$1,365,000	
Beginning inventory	237,500	
Change		$1,127,500
Change in variable costing inventory:		
Ending inventory	$1,125,000	
Beginning inventory	187,500	
Change		937,500
Difference between methods		$ 190,000

C. **Reconciliation of Variable and Throughput Costing Income**

Throughput costing income		$ 862,500
Increase in variable conversion costs in absorption inventory:		
Units added to inventory × Variable conversion cost per unit		
[25,000 units × ($10.00 + $12.50)]		562,500
Variable costing income		$1,425,000

Under variable costing, the direct labour of $10.00 per unit and the variable production costs of $12.50 per unit are held as ending inventory. Therefore, variable costing income is $562,500 higher than throughput costing income.

The difference in income also could be calculated using the difference between costing methods in the change in inventory during the year:

Change in variable costing inventory:		
Ending inventory	$1,125,000	
Beginning inventory	187,500	
Change		$937,500
Change in throughput costing inventory:		
Ending inventory	$ 450,000	
Beginning inventory	75,000	
Change		375,000
Difference between methods		$562,500

D. **Comparison of Actual Fixed Overhead Rate and Estimated Fixed Overhead Rate**

Using actual fixed overhead costs and actual production, the fixed overhead allocation rate is:

$2,200,000 ÷ 275,000 units produced = $8.00 per unit

This rate is equal to the net amount allocated in Part A under the normal costing method, after the adjustment for the volume variance:

Estimated fixed overhead allocation rate	$10.00
Volume variance adjustment per unit	(2.00)
Net fixed overhead allocation rate	$ 8.00

This calculation demonstrates that in periods of abnormally high production, it does not matter which volume measure is used to allocate fixed overhead during the year. Under absorption costing, any material, overapplied volume variance is adjusted to all units produced so that actual fixed overhead cost is reflected on the financial statements. Therefore, both cost of goods sold and the ending inventory balance will be the same as in part A.

E. **Explanation of How the Volume Variance Is Closed at the End of the Period**

When the volume variance is not material, accountants simplify the adjustment by allocating the entire amount to cost of goods sold. This simplification eliminates the need to revalue units in inventory. Although revaluing the inventory was not difficult for this self-study problem, the computations and accounting entries can become cumbersome when an organization has many products. By definition, an immaterial volume variance would not affect the decisions of people who rely on the financial statements. Therefore, it does not matter how the volume variance is adjusted. It is simplest to allocate the entire amount to cost of goods sold.

QUESTIONS

17.1 Explain the similarities and differences among absorption, variable, and throughput costing.

17.2 Explain how variable costing income statements can be reconciled to absorption costing income statements.

17.3 Explain why no volume variance occurs when variable costing is used.

17.4 The volume of production in a period has an effect on income calculated using absorption costing, but it has no effect on income calculated using variable costing. Explain.

17.5 The basic issue in variable and absorption costing could be said to be one of timing rather than amount. Explain.

17.6 What is the difference between a cost that is variable and variable costing?

17.7 What is the relationship between the quantity required to break even and the quantity used for denominator volume when determining the fixed overhead allocation rate?

17.8 If inventory physically increases during the period, income under absorption costing will be higher than income using variable costing. Explain.

17.9 Why does IFRS require absorption costing?

17.10 A firm uses variable costing for internal reports and updates these reports daily. It must convert the variable costing results to absorption costing results for external reports. How can this conversion be accomplished?

17.11 How are joint costs allocated under variable costing? (*Hint:* This question assumes knowledge of the information presented in Chapter 9.)

17.12 Explain how managers could use inventory levels to manage earnings under the absorption costing method.

17.13 Explain the differences between supply-based capacity levels and demand-based capacity levels.

17.14 What are the differences between theoretical, practical, normal, and budgeted capacities?

17.15 How are volume variances recorded in financial statements?

MULTIPLE-CHOICE QUESTIONS

The following information pertains to Questions 17.16 and 17.17:

Vintage Co. made 4,000 units of a product during its first year of operations and sold 3,000 units for $600,000. There was no ending work-in-process inventory. Total costs were $600,000:

Direct materials and direct labour	$250,000
Manufacturing overhead (50% fixed)	$200,000
Marketing and administrative costs (100% variable)	$150,000

17.16 What is the cost of the 1,000 units of finished goods ending inventory under variable costing?
  a. $150,000
  b. $125,000
  c. $112,500
  d. $ 87,500
  e. $ 62,500

17.17 What is the cost of the 1,000 units of finished goods ending inventory under absorption costing?
  a. $150,000
  b. $125,000
  c. $112,500
  d. $ 62,500
  e. $ 25,000

17.18 In Company LL, the fixed factory overhead per unit is $5 and the fixed selling administration charges are $11. This year, the company produced and sold 100,000 units of product. The company uses the LIFO method of accounting for its inventory. What would be the difference in income reported by the company if it used variable costing instead of absorption costing?
  a. $ 0
  b. $ 500,000
  c. $1,100,000
  d. $1,600,000

17.19 How does the accounting treatment of selling and administration costs differ between absorption and variable costing if more units are produced than are sold?
  a. The variable portion is added to the cost of ending inventory based on a *pro rata* portion of units produced to those sold.
  b. The fixed portion is added to the costs of ending inventory based on a *pro rata* portion of units produced to those sold.
  c. There is no difference in the treatment.
  d. Both fixed and variable portions are added to the cost of ending inventory based on a *pro rata* portion of units produced to those sold.

17.20 Which of the following statements is true about the variable cost method?
  a. It is always inappropriate for performing a profitability analysis.
  b. It is useful for determining the price of a product for a special order.
  c. It is always useful when fixing the price for a long period.
  d. It is helpful for performing target costing.

EXERCISES

17.21 **Absorption and Variable Income** Famous Desk Company manufactures desks for office use. The variable cost of
LO1 100 units in beginning inventory is $80 each. The absorption cost is $146.67 each. Following is information about this period's production:

Selling price	$300 per desk
Variable production cost	$80 per desk
Fixed production costs	$10,000 per month
Variable selling and administrative	$30 per desk
Fixed selling and administrative	$6,000 per month

REQUIRED **A.** Estimate operating income for a month in which 200 desks are manufactured and 220 are sold, if the company uses variable costing.
  B. Estimate operating income for a month in which 200 desks are manufactured and 220 are sold, if the company uses absorption costing and allocates fixed production costs to inventory using a rate based on normal capacity of 150 desks per month.

17.22 Absorption and Variable Income, Reconcile Incomes Rock Crusher Corp. produces two grades of sand, A100 and

LO1 A300, used in the manufacture of industrial abrasives. The results of operations last year were as follows:

	A100	A300	Total
Production	4,000 tonnes	6,000 tonnes	10,000 tonnes
Sales	3,000 tonnes	4,000 tonnes	7,000 tonnes
Revenue	$90,000	$150,000	$240,000
Variable production costs	$20,000	$ 15,000	$ 35,000
Variable selling costs	$15,000	$ 20,000	$ 35,000

Fixed production costs were $100,000, and fixed selling and administrative costs were $60,000. The company held no beginning inventories.

REQUIRED Prepare a spreadsheet that can be used to answer all of the following questions.
   A. If Rock Crusher uses a variable costing system, what was the operating income?
   B. If Rock Crusher uses absorption costing and allocates actual fixed production costs to inventory on the basis of actual tonnes produced, what was the operating income?
   C. Reconcile and explain the difference between your answers to Parts A and B.

17.23 Absorption and Variable Inventory and Income, Reconciliation Information for a start-up firm that is introducing a

LO1 new product follows.

Production costs:	
Variable	$40 per unit
Fixed	$10,000 per month
Selling and administration:	
Variable	$9 per unit
Fixed	$25,000 per month
Selling price	$89 per unit
Production volume	1,000 units
Sales volume	850 units

REQUIRED **A.** Using the variable costing method, (1) calculate the cost of ending inventory and (2) prepare an income statement.
   B. Using the absorption costing method, (1) calculate the cost of ending inventory and (2) prepare an income statement.
   C. Reconcile income under the two methods.

17.24 Absorption and Variable Inventory and Income, Reconciliation In the prior period, 5,000 units were produced and

LO1 sold; revenue was $200,000; and fixed costs were $60,000 for manufacturing and $50,000 for selling and administration. Variable costs were $40,000 for manufacturing and $30,000 for selling and administration. In the current period, 5,000 units were produced and 4,500 were sold. No changes occurred in prices or costs between the periods.

REQUIRED **A.** Using the variable costing method, (1) calculate the cost of ending inventory and (2) prepare an income statement for the current period.
   B. Using the absorption costing method, (1) calculate the cost of ending inventory and (2) prepare an income statement for the current period.
   C. Reconcile income under the two methods.

17.25 Absorption and Variable Income Vintage Co. made 4,000 units of a product during its first year of operations and

LO1 sold 3,000 units for $600,000. There was no ending work-in-process inventory. Total costs were $590,000, con sisting of the following:

Direct materials and direct labour	$250,000
Manufacturing overhead (45% fixed)	190,000
Selling and administrative	150,000

REQUIRED **A.** Calculate the cost of the 1,000 units of finished goods ending inventory under actual variable costing.

B. Calculate the amount that net income would change if Vintage Co. changed from actual variable costing to actual absorption costing.

17.26 Absorption and Variable Income (Relies on knowledge from Chapter 11) The Wye Co. Ltd. expects to produce 11,000 units of product RGW during its first year of operations. The following standard manufacturing costs per unit were established, based on this expected production volume:

Direct materials	$13
Direct labour	12
Variable overhead	11
Fixed overhead	6
Unit standard cost	$42

No variable selling and administrative costs were incurred during the year. At the end of the first year of operations, the accountant prepared income statements utilizing actual absorption costing, normal variable costing, normal absorption costing, standard variable costing, and standard absorption costing. These five income statements, randomly labelled A through E, are produced below:

	A	B	C	D	E
Sales	$540,000	$540,000	$540,000	$540,000	$540,000
Cost of sales	346,500	324,000	400,500	378,000	423,000
Variances:					
Direct materials		5,000		5,000	
Direct labour		20,000		20,000	
Variable overhead	15,000	15,000	15,000	15,000	
Fixed overhead			10,000	10,000	
Other costs	150,000	150,000	80,000	80,000	80,000
	511,500	514,000	505,500	508,000	503,000
Operating income	$ 28,500	$ 26,000	$ 34,500	$ 32,000	$ 37,000

REQUIRED **A.** Which income statement was prepared using actual absorption costing?

B. Which income statement was prepared using standard variable costing?

C. How many units of product RGW were actually produced during the year?

17.27 Absorption and Variable Costing Income The following information is summarized from the preliminary budget of Hamilton Limited for product EE01. Budgeted costs and revenues are based on a normal volume of 100,000 units for the year. Capacity is 120,000 units. There are no beginning inventories.

	Total	Per Unit
Budgeted revenue	$7,200,000	$72
Budgeted costs:		
Raw materials	900,000	9
Direct labour	1,200,000	12
Variable overhead	1,500,000	15
Fixed overhead	1,800,000	18
Variable selling and general	600,000	6
Fixed selling and general	600,000	6
Total budgeted costs	6,600,000	66
Budgeted income	$ 600,000	$ 6

During the year, 100,000 units were produced and 70,000 units were sold. There were no flexible budget variances for manufacturing, selling, and general expenses, and no sales price variance.

REQUIRED **A.** What amount of profit or loss for product EE01 would Hamilton Limited record for the year, assuming they use standard variable costing?

B. What amount of profit or loss for product EE01 would Hamilton Limited record for the year, assuming they use standard absorption costing?

17.28 **Throughput Inventory and Income, Reconciliation** Use the information from Exercise 17.24. The production variable cost ($40,000) includes $25,000 in direct materials and $15,000 in direct labour.

L04

REQUIRED **A.** Using the throughput costing method, (1) calculate the cost of ending inventory and (2) prepare an income statement for the current period.

B. Reconcile income under the throughput costing method with income under the variable costing method.

17.29 **Absorption and Variable Inventory and Income** Plains Irrigation uses absorption costing for its external reports and variable costing for its internal reports. Data concerning inventories appear here:

L01

Valuation Basis	September	October	November
Absorption cost	$1,346	$2,598	$2,136
Variable cost	$ 854	$1,647	$1,329

REQUIRED **A.** Why is the value of inventory for Plains Irrigation higher when absorption costing is used than when variable costing is used? Is this result always the case? Why or why not?

B. What is the relationship between absorption costing and variable costing operating income in October? (State which valuation basis will yield the higher operating income, and by how much the two operating incomes will differ.)

17.30 **Absorption, Variable, and Throughput Inventory and Income** Asian Iron began last year with no inventories. During the year, 10,500 units were produced, of which 9,400 were sold. Data concerning last year's operations appear here (in New Taiwanese dollars, NT$):

L01, L04

Revenue	NT$32,900
Variable direct materials costs	2,300
Variable direct labour costs	3,300
Variable manufacturing overhead	2,800
Variable selling	940
Fixed manufacturing overhead	8,250
Fixed selling and administrative costs	14,560

Variable manufacturing costs reflect the variable cost to produce the number of units manufactured. However, variable selling costs are not incurred until the units are sold, so they reflect the cost for the number of units sold. Asian Iron allocates actual manufacturing overhead costs to inventory, based on actual units produced.

REQUIRED **A.** Calculate the value of ending inventory on the balance sheet under the following:

1. Variable costing

2. Absorption costing

3. Throughput costing

B. Calculate operating income under each of the following methods:

1. Variable costing

2. Absorption costing

3. Throughput costing

C. Estimate the variable costing operating income if 12,110 units were produced and sold in a year.

17.31 **Calculations Using Balance Sheet Data** Inventory data for a manufacturing firm for the month of January follows. One set of figures is based on variable costing and the other set is based on absorption costing.

L01

	Balance Sheet 1	Balance Sheet 2
Inventory, January 1	$17,000	$38,000
Inventory, January 31	8,000	19,000

REQUIRED **A.** Which balance sheet is based on the absorption costing method? Explain.
B. During January, was production equal to, greater than, or less than sales for the month? Explain.
C. Calculate the dollar difference between variable costing income and absorption costing income for January.

17.32 Calculations Using Income Statement Data On your way to a meeting with the board of directors, your assistant provides you with last month's income statements—one based on the variable costing method and one based on the absorption costing method. Unfortunately, your assistant, who is new, has used absorption costing terminology for both income statements.

LO1

	Income Statement 1		Income Statement 2	
Sales		$8,672		$8,672
Cost of goods sold	$3,000		$4,032	
Other expenses	4,180	7,180	3,100	7,132
Net income		$1,492		$1,540

REQUIRED **A.** Which income statement is based on the variable costing method? Explain.
B. Was production equal to, greater than, or less than sales for the month? Explain.
C. Calculate the amount of fixed overhead for the month.

17.33 Absorption, Variable, and Throughput Income, Reconcile Incomes The following price and operating cost information applies to Happy Bikers Motorcycle Company:

LO1, LO4

Price	$10,000 per motorcycle
Variable production costs:	
Raw materials	$ 2,000 per motorcycle
Direct labour and variable overhead	$ 1,000 per motorcycle
Fixed production costs	$40,000 per month
Variable selling and administrative	$ 250 per motorcycle
Fixed selling and administrative	$40,000 per month

No beginning balance in finished goods is evident because the beginning inventory account on the balance sheet is zero. Average production is 10 motorcycles per month. Sales are seasonal, so in some months no motorcycles are produced, while in other months production is high. During the most recent month, the company produced 18 and sold 15 motorcycles.

REQUIRED **A.** Prepare an income statement for the most recent month, using the variable costing method.
B. Prepare an income statement for the most recent month, using the absorption costing method, and choose a denominator level that represents "normal" capacity.
C. Prepare an income statement for the most recent month, using the throughput costing method.
D. Prepare a schedule that reconciles the incomes among the three income statements.

17.34 Variable and Absorption Costing, Multiyear Analysis LeFiell Manufacturing produces specialized electronics components. The following information is for the past three years of operations. LeFiell Manufacturing uses FIFO costing.

LO1, LO3

	2015	2016	2017	Total
Units sold	14,000	15,000	16,000	45,000
Units produced	15,000	15,000	15,000	45,000
Fixed production costs	$500,000	$500,000	$500,000	
Variable production costs per unit	$ 75	$ 75	$ 75	
Selling price per unit	$ 200	$ 200	$ 200	
Fixed selling and administrative expenses	$100,000	$100,000	$100,000	

REQUIRED **A.** Calculate the value of ending inventory and net income before taxes for each year under absorption costing.
B. Calculate the value of ending inventory and net income before taxes for each year under variable costing.
C. Explain the difference in net income before taxes under the absorption costing and variable costing approaches for each year.

17.35 Throughput Costing, Multiyear Approach (Refer to Exercise 17.34) Assume that LeFiell Manufacturing management is considering using throughput costing for management decision making.

LO4

REQUIRED **A.** Calculate the value of ending inventory and net income before taxes for each year under throughput costing. Assume direct materials are $50 per unit.

B. Explain the difference in net income before taxes under the variable costing and throughput costing approaches for each year.

17.36 Variable and Absorption Costing, Multiyear Approach MacHine Company produces a part used in the manufacture of farm machinery. The following information pertains to the past three years of operations. MacHine Company uses FIFO costing.

LO1, LO3

	2015	2016	2017	Total
Units sold	5,000	5,500	6,000	16,500
Units produced	5,500	6,000	5,000	16,500
Fixed production costs	$200,000	$200,000	$200,000	
Variable production costs per unit	$ 55	$ 55	$ 55	
Selling price per unit	$ 175	$ 175	$ 175	
Fixed selling and administrative expenses	$ 50,000	$ 50,000	$ 50,000	

REQUIRED **A.** Calculate the value of ending inventory and net income before taxes for each year under absorption costing.

B. Calculate the value of ending inventory and net income before taxes for each year under variable costing.

C. Explain the difference in net income before taxes under the absorption costing and variable costing approaches for each year.

17.37 Throughput Costing, Multiyear Approach (Refer to Exercise 17.36) Assume that MacHine management is considering using throughput costing for management decision making.

LO4

REQUIRED **A.** Calculate the value of ending inventory and net income before taxes for each year under throughput costing. Assume direct materials are $20 per unit.

B. Explain the difference in net income before taxes under the variable costing and throughput costing approaches for each year.

17.38 Variable and Absorption Costing, Multiyear Approach WaterSafe Company produces a part used in the manufacture of aquarium filters. The following information pertains to the past three years of operations. WaterSafe Company uses FIFO costing.

LO1, LO3

	2015	2016	2017	Total
Units sold	15,000	16,500	18,000	35,500
Units produced	16,500	18,000	15,000	35,500
Fixed production costs	$600,000	$600,000	$600,000	
Variable production costs per unit	$165	$165	$165	
Selling price per unit	$275	$275	$275	
Fixed selling and administrative expenses	$150,000	$150,000	$150,000	
Variable selling and administrative expenses per unit	$15	$15	$15	

REQUIRED **A.** Calculate the value of ending inventory and net income before taxes for each year under absorption costing.

B. Calculate the value of ending inventory and net income before taxes for each year under variable costing.

C. Explain the difference in net income before taxes under the absorption costing and variable costing approaches for each year.

17.39 Throughput Costing, Multiyear Approach (Refer to Exercise 17.38) Assume that WaterSafe management is considering using throughput costing for management decision making.

LO4

REQUIRED   **A.** Calculate the value of ending inventory and net income before taxes for each year under throughput costing. Assume direct materials are $60 per unit.

B. Explain the difference in net income before taxes under the variable costing and throughput costing approaches for each year.

17.40 Absorption, Variable, and Throughput Inventory and Income, Reconciliation In the prior period, 10,000 units were produced and 9,000 were sold; revenue was $1,800,000; and fixed costs were $500,000 for manufacturing and $300,000 for selling and administration. Variable costs were $300,000 for manufacturing and $225,000 for selling and administration. In the current period, 10,000 units were produced and 10,500 were sold. No changes occurred in prices or costs between the periods.

LO1, LO3, LO4

REQUIRED   **A.** Using the variable costing method, (1) calculate the cost of ending inventory and (2) prepare an income statement for the current period.

B. Using the absorption costing method, (1) calculate the cost of ending inventory and (2) prepare an income statement for the current period.

C. Using the throughput costing method, (1) calculate the cost of ending inventory and (2) prepare an income statement for the current period. Assume direct materials are $15 per unit.

D. Reconcile income under the three methods.

PROBLEMS

17.41 Absorption and Variable Costing Income Statements, Reconciliation of Net Incomes The offices and factory of Okanagan Company were destroyed by a flood on July 31, 2016, the year-end date of the company. Almost all of the accounting records were lost in the flood and the company did not have a backup copy. Luckily, there was no loss of inventory because all of the units were sold by July 31, 2016. The company is a single product manufacturing company that was planning to use variable costing for internal management decisions. The company's accountant has found the following incomplete accounting records. His task is to reconstruct the 2016 income statement under both absorption and variable costing.

LO1, LO2, LO3

Sales	$900,000
Actual fixed manufacturing costs incurred	132,000
Actual variable manufacturing cost per unit for 2016 production	6
Net income, absorption costing	120,000
Contribution margin	360,000
Actual selling, general, and administrative expenses (all fixed)	42,000
Gross margin	162,000

The company had no work-in-process inventories. There was no under- or overapplied fixed or variable overhead. The full absorption cost per unit in finished goods inventory on August 1, 2015, was the same as the cost per unit for units produced during fiscal 2016. You have been asked by the accountant to assist him in preparing for a meeting with the company's board of directors.

REQUIRED   **A.** **1.** Calculate how many units were sold between August 1, 2015, and July 31, 2016.

   2. Calculate the unit production costs for the period August 1, 2015, to July 31, 2016.

   3. Calculate how many units were produced between August 1, 2015, and July 31, 2016.

B. Prepare an absorption costing income statement for the year ended July 31, 2016. Assume that 90,000 units were sold and 60,000 units were produced.

C. Prepare a variable costing income statement for the year ended July 31, 2016. Assume that 90,000 units were sold and 60,000 units were produced.

D. Prepare a reconciliation of the net income under absorption costing with net income under variable costing.

17.42 **Absorption and Variable Costing Income Statements, Reconciliation of Net Incomes** Hermione Corporation is a newly

LO1 formed manufacturing company expected to begin operations on January 2, 2016. The company has obtained 4,000 units of the product it intends to manufacture from a company that went out of business on December 31, 2015. These units were purchased at a cost of $5 per unit. The estimated production and nonmanufacturing costs are as follows:

Variable costs per unit	
Manufacturing	$7.50
Selling and administrative	$1.00
Fixed costs	
Manufacturing	$80,000
Selling and administrative	$55,000

Sales for the upcoming year (2016) are forecasted to total 96,000 units at a price of $12 per unit. The company plans to produce 100,000 units during 2016. Plant capacity is 100,000 units.

REQUIRED **A.** Prepare an absorption costing income statement and a variable costing income statement for the year ended December 31, 2016, assuming 100,000 units are produced and 96,000 units are sold. The company uses the FIFO method of inventory management. (*Note:* The units in beginning inventory are purchased and not manufactured.)

B. Prepare a reconciliation between the net incomes obtained from the two approaches.

17.43 **Absorption and Variable Costing Income Statements** The following is the cost data per unit for KopyKat Company's

LO1, LO2, single product, the "Kat":
LO3

Prime cost	$ 13
Variable manufacturing overhead	5
Variable selling and administrative	3
Fixed costs per month	
Manufacturing	$300,000
Selling and administrative	260,000
Total fixed cost	$560,000

The selling price per unit is $50. The production and sales data for October and November are as follows:

	Production	Sales
October	25,000	15,000
November	0	20,000

There were 10,000 units in finished goods inventory on October 1, with a value of $280,000. Total fixed costs have remained the same in September, October, and November. Similarly, the variable cost per unit has remained the same in September, October, and November. The company uses the FIFO inventory cost flow assumption.

REQUIRED **A.** Prepare an absorption costing income statement for October and November.

B. Adjust the absorption costing income to obtain the variable costing income. Do not prepare the variable costing income statements.

C. The CEO of KopyKat, who is provided with only the absorption costing income statement, is not pleased with the financial performance in November. "I thought we would do better in November since we were able to meet our sales target, which is higher than in the previous month. This does not make sense to me!" Indicate in which month the company performed better, in your opinion. Explain briefly to the CEO.

17.44 **Absorption and Variable Inventory and Income, Reconcile Incomes** Wild Bird Feeders produces deluxe bird feeders

LO1 for distribution to catalogue companies and wild bird stores. The company uses an absorption costing system for internal reporting purposes but is considering using variable costing. Data regarding Wild Bird's planned and actual operations for 2016 are presented here:

Beginning finished goods inventory in units		30,000

	Planned Activity	Actual Activity
Sales in units	140,000	125,000
Production in units	140,000	130,000

The planned per-unit cost figures shown in the following schedule were based on production and sale of 140,000 units in 2016. Wild Bird uses an estimated manufacturing overhead rate for allocating manufacturing overhead to its product; thus, a combined manufacturing overhead rate of $9 per unit was employed for absorption costing purposes in 2016. Any overapplied or underapplied manufacturing overhead is closed to cost of goods sold at the end of the reporting year:

	Planned Costs Per Unit	Total	Incurred Costs
Direct materials	$24.00	$ 3,360,000	$ 3,120,000
Direct labour	18.00	2,520,000	2,340,000
Variable manufacturing overhead	4.00	560,000	520,000
Fixed manufacturing overhead	5.00	700,000	710,000
Variable selling expenses	14.00	1,960,000	1,750,000
Fixed selling expenses	7.00	980,000	980,000
Variable administrative expenses	1.00	140,000	125,000
Fixed administrative expenses	6.00	840,000	850,000
Total	$79.00	$11,060,000	$10,395,000

The 2016 beginning finished goods inventory for absorption costing purposes was valued at the 2015 planned unit manufacturing cost, which was the same as the 2016 planned unit manufacturing cost. No work-in-process inventories were recorded at either the beginning or the end of the year. The planned and actual unit selling price was $99.00 per unit for 2016. You may want to use a spreadsheet to perform calculations.

REQUIRED
A. What was the value of Wild Bird's actual ending finished goods inventory on an absorption costing basis?
B. What was the 2016 actual ending finished goods inventory on an variable costing basis?
C. What were the manufacturing contribution margin and the total contribution margin under variable costing for Wild Bird's actual results for 2016?
D. Under absorption costing, determine the total fixed costs on the income statement:
 1. What were the fixed selling and administrative costs?
 2. What was the amount of overhead allocated to cost of goods sold at standard?
 3. Do we need to consider sales of units from last period?
 4. What was the amount of underapplied or overapplied overhead closed to cost of goods sold?
 5. Sum these amounts for the total fixed costs.
E. What was the total variable cost expensed in 2016 on the variable costing income statement?
F. Was absorption costing income higher or lower than variable costing income for 2016? Why?
G. What is the amount of difference in income using absorption costing versus variable costing? How did it arise?

17.45 Differences in Income, Choice of Absorption and Variable Costing Nova Scotia Lobsters Company is a privately held company that buys lobsters from local fishermen and then delivers them to restaurants in several of Nova Scotia's larger cities. The owners use variable costing income statements, but one owner's daughter, who has just started taking accounting classes at the local university, suggests that absorption income statements meet IFRS and should, therefore, be used.

LO1, LO2

REQUIRED
A. Explain the difference between absorption and variable income statements.
B. Provide possible reasons why the company uses variable costing income statements.
C. Provide possible benefits to the company from using an absorption costing income statement.
D. What type of statement would you recommend for Nova Scotia Lobsters Company? Why?
E. What additional information about Nova Scotia Lobsters Company would you like to have to improve your recommendation in Part D?

17.46 Absorption, Variable, and Throughput Income; Normal Capacity; Choice of Denominator Giant Jets is a French company that produces jet airplanes for commercial cargo companies. The selling price (in euros) per jet is €1,000,000. Currently the company uses actual volumes to allocate fixed overhead to units. However, Giant Jets'

LO1, LO2, LO4

accountant is considering the use of standard costs to produce the absorption income statements. The company anticipates the following:

Variable costs per jet:

Direct materials	€200,000
Direct labour	150,000
Variable production overhead	50,000
Variable selling	100,000

Fixed costs per year:

| Fixed production overhead | €600,000 |
| Fixed administrative and selling | 100,000 |

Sales and production quantities:

	2015	2016	2017
Production	10	6	8
Sales	10	4	10

REQUIRED
A. Prepare income statements using the variable costing method.
B. Prepare income statements using the throughput costing method.
C. Prepare income statements using the absorption costing method. Allocate fixed overhead using actual units produced in the denominator.
D. In your own words, define *normal capacity*.
E. Prepare an income statement using the absorption cost method and choose a denominator level that represents normal capacity. Explain your choice for normal capacity.
F. Prepare a brief summary that reconciles the incomes among the three income statements for each year.

17.47 Absorption, Variable, and Throughput Income and Inventory; Method for Manager Bonus Fighting Kites produces several different kite kits. Last year, the company produced 20,000 kits and sold all but 2,000 kits. The kits sell for $30 each. Costs incurred are listed here:

[LO1, LO2, LO3, LO4]

Materials purchased	$ 50,000
Materials used	40,000
Other variable production costs	60,000
Fixed production costs	100,000
Variable selling costs	18,000
Fixed selling and administrative costs	100,000

Beginning inventory last year held 2,000 kits. Assume that under variable costing the value of this inventory would have been $10,000. Assume that under absorption costing the value of this inventory would have been $15,000. Fighting Kites uses a FIFO cost flow assumption.

REQUIRED
A. If Fighting Kites uses variable costing, what was its operating income? What was the ending balance in finished goods inventory?
B. If Fighting Kites uses throughput costing, what was its operating income? What was the ending balance in finished goods inventory?
C. If Fighting Kites uses absorption costing and a denominator level of 25,000, what was its operating income?
D. If you were asked to make a recommendation for the absorption costing denominator level for next period's operations, what would you suggest? Explain your choice.
E. If the manager of Fighting Kites is given a bonus based on income, which type of income statement would you recommend for evaluating manager performance? Explain your choice.

17.48 Absorption and Variable Income and Uses, Reconcile Incomes Security Vehicles converts SUVs into luxury, high-security vehicles by adding a computerized alarm and radar system and various luxury components. The finished vehicles are sold for $100,000 each. Variable production costs (including the cost of the basic SUV) are about $60,000 per vehicle. Fixed production costs are $60,000 per month. The fixed costs for administrative and selling expenses are $20,000 per month plus $5,000 per vehicle sold.

[LO1, LO3]

At the beginning of last year, Security had no inventories of finished vehicles. In January, it produced four vehicles and sold three. In February, it produced five and sold six.

REQUIRED **A.** What is the operating income for January if Security uses a variable costing system?
B. What is the operating income for January if Security uses an absorption costing system?
C. Reconcile the difference between the absorption and variable costing operating incomes in February.
D. Explain why Security Vehicles might produce both variable and absorption income statements for the same time period.

17.49 **Throughput Costing, Reconciling Income** (Refer to Problem 17.48) Assume that Security uses throughput costing.

LO4

REQUIRED **A.** What is the operating income for January if Security uses throughput costing? Assume direct materials are $50,000 per vehicle.
B. Reconcile the difference between the variable and throughput costing incomes in February. (The variable costing income is calculated in Problem 17.48).
C. Explain why Security Vehicles might prefer the throughput costing income statement.

17.50 **Overapplied/Underapplied Overhead, Units Versus Machine Hours as Allocation Base** Northcoast Manufacturing Company, a small manufacturer of parts used in appliances, just completed its first year of operations. The company's controller, Vic Trainor, has been reviewing the actual results for the year and is concerned about the allocation of production overhead. Trainor uses the following information to assess operations:

LO1, LO2

- Northcoast's equipment consists of several machines with a combined cost of $2,200,000 and no residual value. Each machine has an output of five units of product per hour and a useful life of 20,000 hours.
- Selected actual data of Northcoast's operations for the year just ended is presented here:

Product manufactured	500,000 units
Machine utilization	130,000 hours
Direct labour usage	35,000 hours
Labour rate	$ 15 per hour
Total production overhead	$ 1,130,000
Cost of goods sold	$ 1,720,960
Finished goods inventory (at year end)	$ 430,240
Work-in-process inventory (at year end)	$ 0

- Total production overhead is allocated to each unit using an estimated, plant-wide rate.
- The budgeted activity for the year included 20 employees, each working 1,800 productive hours per year to produce 540,000 units of product. The machines are highly automated, and each employee can operate two to four machines simultaneously. Normal activity is for each employee to operate three machines. Machine operators are paid $15 per hour.
- Budgeted production overhead costs for the past year for various levels of activity are shown here:

Units of product	360,000	540,000	720,000
Labour hours	30,000	36,000	42,000
Machine hours	72,000	108,000	144,000
Production overhead costs:			
Plant supervision	$ 70,000	$ 70,000	$ 70,000
Plant rent	40,000	40,000	40,000
Equipment amortization	288,000	432,000	576,000
Maintenance	42,000	51,000	60,000
Utilities	144,600	216,600	288,600
Indirect material	90,000	135,000	180,000
Other costs	11,200	16,600	22,000
Total	$685,800	$961,200	$1,236,600

You might want to use a spreadsheet to perform calculations.

REQUIRED   **A.** Choose the budgeted level of activity (in units) closest to actual activity for the period, and determine the dollar amount of total overapplied/underapplied production overhead. Explain why this amount is material.

B. Vic Trainor believes that Northcoast Manufacturing Company should be using machine hours to allocate production overhead. Using the data given, determine the amount of total overapplied/underapplied production overhead if machine hours had been used as the allocation base.

C. Explain why machine hours might be a more appropriate allocation base than number of units.

D. Explain why using units as denominator volume might cause managers to build up inventories under absorption costing in periods when sales were slumping.

17.51 **Recommend Income Format** Your brother started a small business, GameZ, that produces a software game he developed. It is his first year in business, and he kept detailed records of the business. However, these records consist primarily of entries in his cheque book, plus information using a simple method of adding and subtracting cash on a spreadsheet.

LO1, LO2 LO3, LO4

Your brother has asked your advice about the kind of financial statements that would be helpful to his business. He would like you to prepare information for two different uses. First, he needs a small bank loan to provide cash during the low season at the end of summer. Most of his sales are made in December. He has a steady, low volume of sales most of the rest of the year, but sales drop to nearly zero in August, when school is beginning for many children. He wants to approach his bank about a line of credit that he could draw from in August and then pay off in January. In addition, he would like to be able to analyze information from his operations to make decisions about whether to develop a new game, what price to set, and how much he could devote to advertising. He also recently hired an assistant to whom he assigned a great deal of responsibility for general operations. He would like to be able to monitor and reward her performance in some way.

REQUIRED   Write a memo to your brother in response to his request. Include the following aspects in your memo.

A. Outline his possible choices for income statement formats.

B. List the advantages and disadvantages of each format.

C. Recommend and explain which type of statement should be used for each of his desired purposes.

17.52 **Absorption and Variable Income and Uses, Reconcile Incomes** Jungle Gyms Unlimited makes backyard playsets. The playsets are sold for $450 each. Variable production costs are about $150 per playset. Fixed production costs are $5,000 per month. The fixed costs for administrative and selling expenses are $2,000 per month plus $25 per playset sold.

LO1, LO3

At the beginning of April, Jungle Gym's had 10 playsets in inventory with a total production cost of $2,750. In April, it produced 50 playsets and sold 45. In May, it produced 50 playsets and sold 60.

REQUIRED   **A.** What is the operating income for April and May if Jungle Gym uses a variable costing system?

B. What is the operating income for April and May if Jungle Gym uses an absorption costing system?

C. Reconcile the difference between the absorption and variable costing operating incomes in April and May.

D. Explain why Jungle Gym might produce both variable and absorption income statements for the same time period.

17.53 **Throughput Costing, Reconciling Income** (Refer to Problem 17.52) Assume that Jungle Gym uses throughput costing.

LO4

REQUIRED   **A.** What is the operating income for April and May if Jungle Gym uses throughput costing? Assume direct materials are $80 per playset.

B. Reconcile the difference between the variable and throughput costing incomes in April and May. (The variable costing income is calculated in Problem 17.52).

C. Explain why Jungle Gym might prefer the throughput costing income statement.

17.54 **Overapplied/Underapplied Overhead, Units Versus Machine Hours as Allocation Base** Maui Manufacturing, a small manufacturer of electronic parts, has just completed its third year of operations. The company's controller, Leilani Sorter, has been reviewing the actual results for the year and is concerned about the allocation of production overhead. Sorter uses the following information to assess operations:

LO1, LO2

- Maui's equipment consists of several machines with a combined cost of $1,650,000 and no residual value. Each machine has an output of five units of product per hour and a useful life of 15,000 hours.
- Selected actual data of Maui's operations for the year just ended is presented here:

Product manufactured	375,000 units
Machine utilization	97,500 hours
Direct labour usage	26,250 hours

Labour rate	$ 11.25 per hour
Total production overhead	$ 847,500
Cost of goods sold	$ 1,290,720
Finished goods inventory (at year end)	$ 322,680
Work-in-process inventory (at year end)	$ 0

- Total production overhead is allocated to each unit using an estimated, plant-wide rate.
- The budgeted activity for the year included 20 employees, each working 1,800 productive hours per year to produce 405,000 units of product. The machines are highly automated, and each employee can operate two to four machines simultaneously. Normal activity is for each employee to operate three machines. Machine operators are paid $11.25 per hour.
- Budgeted production overhead costs for the past year for various levels of activity are shown here:

Units of product	270,000	405,000	540,000
Labour hours	30,000	36,000	42,000
Machine hours	54,000	81,000	108,000
Production Overhead Costs:			
Plant supervision	$ 52,500	$ 52,500	$ 52,500
Plant rent	30,000	30,000	30,000
Equipment amortization	216,000	324,000	432,000
Maintenance	31,500	38,250	45,000
Utilities	108,450	162,450	216,450
Indirect material	67,500	101,250	135,000
Other costs	8,400	12,450	16,500
Total	$ 514,350	$720,900	$927,450

REQUIRED **A.** Choose the budgeted level of activity (in units) closest to actual activity for the period, and determine the dollar amount of total overapplied/underapplied production overhead. Explain why this amount is material.

B. Leilani Sorter believes that Maui Manufacturing should be using machine hours to allocate production overhead. Using the data given, determine the amount of total overapplied/underapplied production overhead if machine hours had been used as the allocation base.

C. Explain why machine hours might be a more appropriate allocation base than number of units.

D. Explain why using units as denominator volume might cause managers to build up inventories under absorption costing in periods when sales were slumping.

17.55 Absorption, Variable, and Throughput Income and Inventory; Method for Manager Bonus Authentic Arts, Ltd. produces several different kits to make dreamweavers. Last year, the company produced 30,000 kits and sold all but 2,000 kits. The kits sell for $15 each. Costs incurred are listed here:

LO1, LO2, LO3, LO4

Materials purchased	$ 55,000
Materials used	45,000
Other variable production costs	30,000
Fixed production costs	50,000
Variable selling costs	6,000
Fixed selling and administrative costs	30,000

Beginning inventory last year held 2,000 kits. Assume that under variable costing the value of this inventory would have been $5,000. Assume that under absorption costing the value of this inventory would have been $9,000. Authentic Arts uses a FIFO cost flow assumption.

REQUIRED **A.** If Authentic Arts uses variable costing, what was its operating income? What was the ending balance in finished goods inventory?

B. If Authentic Arts uses throughput costing, what was its operating income? What was the ending balance in finished goods inventory?

C. If Authentic Arts uses absorption costing and a denominator level of 25,000, what was its operating income?

D. If you were asked to make a recommendation for the absorption costing denominator level for next period's operations, what would you suggest? Explain your choice.

E. If the manager of Authentic Arts is given a bonus based on income, which type of income statement would you recommend for evaluating manager performance? Explain your choice.

17.56 Absorption, Variable, and Throughput Income, Allocation Rates This year, Paintbrush, Inc., manufactured 55,000 units of part YS15, and it sold 50,000 units at $60 per unit. The beginning inventory balance was 1,000 units. No changes in fixed or variable costs occurred during the year. Previous sales had averaged 44,000 units, therefore, the management had set that amount as the normal capacity for allocating fixed overhead costs. For simplicity, assume that the budgeted fixed production overhead cost equals the actual cost this period. Also, assume that the company uses the FIFO cost flow assumption. The following costs were incurred during the year:

L01, L02, L03, L04

Variable Cost Per Unit:

Direct materials	$13.00
Direct labour	$ 2.00
Manufacturing overhead	$ 2.50
Selling and administrative	$ 0.50

Total Fixed Costs:

Production overhead	$440,000
Selling and administrative	$275,000

REQUIRED

A. Prepare income statements using absorption costing, variable costing, and throughput costing. Provide the details of your calculations in a schedule for each income statement.

B. Reconcile the difference between operating incomes based on absorption costing and variable costing. Create a schedule to show your work.

C. Reconcile the difference between operating incomes based on variable costing and throughput costing. Create a schedule to show your work.

D. Suppose the accountant for Paintbrush, Inc. used an actual fixed overhead allocation rate rather than an estimated rate. Using this method, calculate the cost of goods sold and ending inventory under absorption costing. Compare the results to those calculated in Part A.

E. If the volume variance is not material, how is it closed at the end of the period? Explain the reasoning behind this treatment.

17.57 Cumulative Exercise (Chapter 3): Breakeven, Absorption and Variable Income, Volume Alternatives Schatzberg Company's budget for its first year of operations follows.

L01, L02, L03

Fixed manufacturing cost	$150,000
Fixed selling and administrative costs	200,000
Variable manufacturing cost per unit	10
Variable selling and administrative cost per unit	5
Selling price per unit	25

The company's accountant estimated that normal capacity will be 50,000 units and used that volume to allocate overhead. During its first year, the company actually produced 40,000 units and sold 35,000.

REQUIRED

A. Calculate the breakeven point in units.

B. Develop an income statement using the absorption costing method, assigning the entire volume variance to cost of goods sold.

C. Develop an income statement using the absorption costing method, prorating the volume variance between inventory and cost of goods sold.

D. Assume the company needs to prepare financial statements that comply with U.S. GAAP. Which income statement (Part B or C) should the accountant prepare? Explain.

E. Develop an income statement using the variable costing method.

MINI-CASES

17.58 **Bonuses and Production Decisions, Profit Variances, Income Statement Format** Pine Producers (PP) is expect-

LO1, LO2, LO3

ing sales growth, and so it has built nearly identical automated plants in Grand Forks, British Columbia, and in Singapore to produce its new Pine Powerhouse.

Each plant manager is responsible for producing adequate inventories to meet sales orders and for maintaining quality, while producing the Pine Powerhouse at the lowest possible cost. Under PP's decentralized organization, each plant maintains its own accounting records. Quarterly reports are filed with the corporate controller's office and are then reviewed by corporate management. The following reports were filed for the third and fourth quarters by the two plants:

GRAND FORKS, BRITISH COLUMBIA, PLANT
INCOME STATEMENT FOR THIRD AND FOURTH QUARTERS
(IN THOUSANDS OF DOLLARS)

	Third Quarter	Fourth Quarter
Revenue	$97,452	$110,951
Cost of goods sold	77,165	74,613
Selling and administration expenses	12,378	12,632
Interest expense	4,312	4,251
Tax expense	1,259	6,809
Net income	$ 2,338	$ 12,646

GRAND FORKS, BRITISH COLUMBIA, PLANT
STATEMENT OF FINANCIAL POSITION FOR THIRD AND FOURTH QUARTERS
(IN THOUSANDS OF DOLLARS)

	Third Quarter	Fourth Quarter
Assets		
Cash	$ 2,346	$ 322
Inventory	12,872	30,972
Plant (net of amortization)	152,456	148,635
Total assets	$167,674	$179,929
Liabilities and Owners' Equities		
Accounts payable	$ 214	$ 1,782
Construction bond payable	140,385	138,426
Owners' equity	27,075	39,721
Total liabilities and OE	$167,674	$179,929

SINGAPORE PLANT
INCOME STATEMENT FOR THIRD AND FOURTH QUARTERS
(TRANSLATED TO CANADIAN CURRENCY, IN
THOUSANDS OF DOLLARS)

	Third Quarter	Fourth Quarter
Revenue	$101,832	$111,085
Cost of goods sold	82,127	87,990
Selling and administration expenses	10,943	10,453
Interest expense	3,854	3,733
Tax expense	1,718	3,118
Net income	$ 3,190	$ 5,791

SINGAPORE PLANT
STATEMENT OF FINANCIAL POSITION FOR THIRD AND FOURTH QUARTERS
(TRANSLATED TO CANADIAN CURRENCY, IN THOUSANDS OF DOLLARS)

	Third Quarter	Fourth Quarter
Assets		
Cash	$ 1,564	$ 3,642
Inventory	11,324	13,832
Plant (net of amortization)	142,342	138,580
Total assets	$155,230	$156,054
Liabilities and Owners' Equities		
Accounts payable	$ 347	$ 221
Bond payable	135,762	130,921
Owners' equity	19,121	24,912
Total liabilities and OE	$155,230	$156,054

The following questions will help you analyze the information for this problem. Do not turn in your answers to these questions unless your professor asks you to do so.

REQUIRED   INFORMATION ANALYSIS

A. Suppose each plant manager receives a bonus based on absorption costing operating income that is 5% of operating income. Calculate the bonus for each manager. Explain how this bonus plan might affect the managers' production decisions.

B. Examine changes in sales relative to cost of goods sold between the two quarters. What are two possible explanations for the Grand Forks plant's profit increase during the fourth quarter?

C. Assume that variable costs in this industry are an immaterial part of cost of goods sold. Recast the financial statements using the variable costing approach.

D. What would you conclude about the relative performances of the two plant managers in the fourth quarter?

Suppose you are the cost accountant for Pine Producers. Turn in your answers to the following.

REQUIRED   WRITTEN ASSIGNMENT

E. Write a memo to the CFO, recommending the type of income statement that would be best for monitoring divisional performance. Attach to the memo a schedule showing any computations that might be useful to the CFO. As appropriate, refer to the schedule in the memo.

17.59 Communication of Information All three professional accounting organizations recognize the importance of clear, con-cise communication. In this chapter, you learned three ways to present cost information in an income statement.

REQUIRED **A.** Discuss how each of these methods communicates different information about an organization's operations.

B. Why do uncertainties exist about the best way to communicate this information about an organization's operations?

C. Brainstorm with your classmates to create a list of strategies you could use to do a better job of adapting your communications for the setting and audience.

17.60 Integrating Across the Curriculum: Financial Accounting and Auditing—*Channel stuffing, uncertainties, error versus fraud, fraud incentives and costs* Auditors are responsible for verifying that public companies' financial statements are presented in accordance with generally accepted accounting principles (GAAP). This responsibility includes proper revenue recognition as well as proper absorption costing for inventories and cost of goods sold.

In this chapter, a number of real cases of channel stuffing were presented.

McAfee, Inc. tried a similar practice but was hit with several rounds of income restatements and inquiries from the SEC. In the McAfee case, sales did not increase in the next period. In fact, sales slowed down for a number of periods, but managers kept pushing inventory onto distributors. When the SEC investigates and asks companies to restate income, it alleges fraudulent behaviour on the part of managers. When companies restate income, they often explain that they were not behaving fraudulently, but they are restating income to appease the SEC. When auditors discover a misstatement (a situation in which the financial statements do not comply with GAAP), they must determine whether it is caused by an error or by fraud. An error is defined as an unintentional mistake, while fraud is intentional.

REQUIRED

A. In your own words, define *channel stuffing*.

B. Explain why the managers of companies such as McAfee or Valeant Pharmaceuticals cannot know for sure what their sales will be next period, or how much inventory to produce.

C. Explain why the customers of companies such as McAfee or Valeant Pharmaceuticals might be willing to purchase excess inventories.

D. Assume that you are a manager at Coca-Cola and are defending the decision to encourage dealers to stock up on inventory. Write a brief paragraph defending Coca-Cola's behaviour. (You might want to do some Internet research to support your position. Be sure to interpret the situation in your own words, as you believe a manager might respond. The SEC website, www.sec.gov, might be a good place to start.)

E. In the McAfee case, the company shipped merchandise to its customers and recognized the shipments as revenue. How could the SEC claim that McAfee had improperly recognized revenue? In other words, does channel stuffing violate revenue recognition under GAAP? In your answer, discuss and provide references to relevant financial accounting standards and concepts.

F. From an auditor's perspective, discuss the likelihood that McAfee's US$622 million overstatement of revenue resulted from error versus fraud.

G. Explain why it might be considered so important to continue showing sales and earnings growth that managers might behave in an allegedly fraudulent manner.

H. Describe the costs for the kind of behaviour described in Part G, in addition to negative reputation effects for the company.

18

Performance Evaluation and Compensation

in brief As organizations grow and diversify, additional accounting information is needed by owners to measure performance, monitor managers' actions, and motivate decisions that are in line with the company's vision, mission, and goals. Similarly, managers use accounting information to measure, monitor, and motivate the actions of employees. Before managers or other employees can be held accountable for the results of their decisions and actions, their rights and responsibilities should be defined. Then, return on investment, residual income, economic value added, and other measures can be used to gauge and reward performance.

LO1 Discuss how decision-making responsibility and authority are related to performance evaluation

LO2 Explain how responsibility centres are used to measure, monitor, and motivate performance

LO3 Calculate return on investment, residual income, and economic value added and explain how each is used to measure, monitor, and motivate performance

LO4 Discuss how compensation is used to motivate performance

Fast Tracking Employee Performance

Stephen C. Host/The Canadian Press

With the **Canadian National Railway Company** expecting a turnover rate of nearly half of its current employees over five years, hiring and retaining good people is a top priority. The company, a part of the Canadian landscape for nearly a century, hired 14,000 people from 2010 to 2014 to replace retiring or departed employees or to handle an increase in rail traffic. CN has a well-developed program to evaluate and motivate its more than 25,000 employees across Canada and the United States.

CN offers signing bonuses for some positions, and allows all employees to buy shares in the company at a discount. More than 75% of employees belong to the share ownership plan. At the end of 2014, CN had almost $13.5 billion in shareholders' equity and revenues of $12.1 billion.

Employees are given a performance review every four months; every 12 months, this includes a salary review. As part of performance reviews, feedback is sought from co-workers and other managers familiar with an employee's work. There are also variable performance incentives for non-unionized employees; about 20% of CN employees do not belong to a union.

To recognize employee contributions, CN managers can give employees a performance bonus or an on-the-spot reward. The company also has a President's Awards for Excellence program to recognize outstanding achievement in several categories, where the winners and their partners can spend a weekend at a resort in Florida.

The company participates in annual salary surveys conducted both in-house and by a third party, to ensure that its compensation packages are fair and competitive within the organization and competitive with other companies in the industry.

Another way the company motivates employees is by holding family activities, to recognize the importance of work-life balance. "We work in a demanding industry, and as a backbone of the economy, there's a lot riding on our rails and lot of pressure to perform. With a 24/7, 365 days a year operation, we couldn't function without family support. Our Family Days are a modest way of recognizing that," says CN CEO Claude Mongeau. "These events are also terrific for morale, because our employees feel tremendous pride about what we do when we show it to our friends and families."

CN has been recognized as an employer of choice multiple times, including making the list of Canada's Top 100 employers for 2016 and the 2015 Randstad Award list of top employers.

SOURCES: R. Yerema and K. Leung, "Canadian National Railway Company / CN: Recognized as One of Canada's Top 100 Employers (2016)," Mediacorp Canada Inc., November 8, 2015; "IBM Canada Ltd. Voted Canada's Most Attractive Employer," Randstad news release, April 23, 2015; CN 2014 annual report; CN corporate website, www.cn.ca.

Decision-Making Authority and Responsibility

LO1 Discuss how decision-making responsibility and authority are related to performance evaluation

One approach to measuring, monitoring, and motivating employee performance is to give specific decision-making authority to employees, holding them responsible and rewarding them for the results of their decisions. This idea lies behind the corporate form of business organization. Shareholders give managers authority to decide how corporations' resources are used. Then, shareholders hold the managers responsible for creating shareholder value. Similarly, the authority for decisions can be dispersed throughout an organization. Individual employees are held responsible for their decisions, and limits are placed on their decision-making authority. For example, the sales representatives are responsible for generating sales and attracting new customers. However, the sales representatives are not responsible for plant errors or safety in a plant.

Many different approaches can be taken in assigning decision-making authority. Managers can also periodically restructure authority within organizations. As the business environment becomes increasingly technical and competitive, the timeliness of decision making becomes increasingly important to economic success. The need for more timely decision making often encourages managers to reconsider how decision-making authority is assigned.

Centralized and Decentralized Organizations

When managers make choices about locating decision-making authority, they are also making choices about organizational structure. When decision making is *centralized*, the right to make or authorize decisions lies within top levels of management. When decision making is *decentralized*, the rights and responsibilities for decision making permeate all levels of the organization.

In the current dynamic business environment, many factors influence organizational structures, and changes in these structures are made over time. The type of knowledge needed for successful operations influences the location of authority and responsibility. When a company is a small organization, top managers are sufficiently knowledgeable about operations, but as the company grows, it becomes more difficult and costly to transfer knowledge about customer needs to top management and then back down to sales and production personnel. The owners may need to change the organizational structure to reflect the changing knowledge needs.

General Versus Specific Knowledge

Knowledge is an important source in organizations. The type of knowledge needed to make high-quality decisions affects the location of authority within organizations.

General knowledge, such as information about volume of sales or product prices when organizations sell few products, is usually easy to transfer from one person to another. Decisions based on general knowledge are likely to be centralized, made primarily by the chief executive officer (CEO) and other top managers. Transferring the general knowledge needed for decision making to an organization's headquarters is relatively easy and, therefore, not very costly. Examples of centralized organizations include small businesses, where the owner makes most of the operating decisions and relies on a few employees to carry out those decisions. Large businesses that produce few products, such as steel companies, are often centralized.

Some decisions require specific knowledge—that is, detailed information about particular processes, customers, or products—information that is costly to transfer within the organization. Examples of specific knowledge are the technical details of manufacturing or service delivery processes and information gained over time from working with individual customers. When decision makers need specific knowledge, they must either have the knowledge themselves or seek ways to obtain it. For many companies, specific knowledge of customer preferences is important to organizational success. When sales representatives in these companies work directly with customers and make decisions, customer service improves, as do timeliness and accuracy of decision making.

Technology and Globalization

Technology has enhanced global communications and reduced the costs of business transactions so that organizations can more easily locate units in other countries. Accordingly, organizations have become increasingly multinational. When organizations expand to other countries, managers within each country are likely to have specific knowledge of cultural and customer preferences. Decisions made at the unit level are likely to be more timely and of higher quality, because local decision makers best understand how to gather information relevant to operations in that country.

Choosing a Centralized Versus Decentralized Organizational Structure

Advantages and disadvantages of each type of organizational form are listed in Exhibit 18.1. Whether decision making within an organization should be centralized or decentralized is not always a straightforward decision. Organizations often begin with centralized decision making and then adopt a decentralized structure as they grow large. However, some large organizations find that a centralized approach is best, because it leads to greater alignment of decisions with the organizational vision and strategies.

For example, when Soichiro Honda founded Honda Motor Company in 1948, he personally made most of the product-related decisions, while his partner made the finance and marketing decisions. The firm was much larger in 1973, when Honda retired. A new decision-making process involving 30 senior executives was adopted. Research and design engineers were given more control over new model development. With this process, it was difficult for the company to respond to a more dynamic consumer market, and Honda began to lose market share. In the early 1990s, however, a new CEO re-established centralized decision making. Although employees resisted the change, decision making rested in the hands of a few powerful executives. This strategy produced the 1994 Accord, named one of the top 10 cars of 1994 by *Car and Driver* magazine.

> ◢ **BUSINESS PRACTICE**
> **Winnipeg Police Service** is using photo radar technology to monitor speeding violations at critical intersections. Photo radar technology is more vehicle specific than conventional radar.[1]

> ◢ **BUSINESS PRACTICE**
> Bob Grant, senior vice president of global transactions for Scotiabank, points out that even as multinational businesses expand into more countries, they are increasingly centralizing their treasury function.[2]

◢ **EXHIBIT 18.1**

Advantages and Disadvantages of Centralized and Decentralized Organizations

Centralized Organizations		Decentralized Organizations	
Advantages	**Disadvantages**	**Advantages**	**Disadvantages**
• Less monitoring of decisions	• More monitoring of employee effort because employees may be less motivated	• Timely decision making; appropriate for dynamic processes and unstable economic conditions	• Decisions may meet objectives of the decision maker's sub-unit but not meet organizational goals
• Decisions are intended to benefit the overall organization	• Decision makers may not have complete information, resulting in poorer-quality decisions	• Decisions are made by individuals who have the most knowledge and expertise	• Decisions may not be coordinated among sub-units, resulting in less effective decision making for the organization as a whole
• If decision makers have complete information, timely and efficient decisions are made	• When knowledge from sub-units is required, the decision-making process slows down	• Upper management has time to focus on organizational strategies	• Decision makers may not understand or agree with organizational strategies
• Good for stable operations and economic conditions	• Not appropriate for dynamic processes and volatile economic conditions	• Decision-making authority combined with reward systems provide more motivation to exert optimal effort at the sub-unit level	• Lack of coordination among sub-units may lead to duplication of products, services, and effort

[1] Winnipeg Police Service, Photo Radar Technology: How Do Mobile Photo Radar Vehicles Work?, at www.winnipeg.ca/police/safestreets/photoradar_tech.stm.
[2] L. Valentine, "Think Globally, Act Locally—Bob Grant, SVP, Global Transaction Banking, Scotiabank," *Bank Systems & Technology*, 45(2), February 2008, p. 22.

▶ EXHIBIT 18.2
Span of Control and Organizational Structure

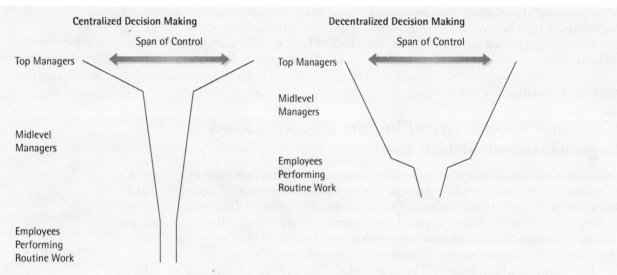

Adapted from R. Simons, *Levers of Organizational Design: How Managers Use Accountability Systems for Greater Performance and Commitment* (Boston: Harvard Business School Press, 2005), p. 92.

During the time period that Honda centralized decision making, many other organizations, such as Fiat, General Electric, and Motorola, decentralized theirs. With increased technology and access to information, timeliness of decision making becomes a competitive strategy. To increase the speed of decisions, organizations are increasingly giving decision-making authority to employees who have the most knowledge about the organization's production processes and customer characteristics. Leaner organizations with fewer middle managers more easily move decision authority up and down the hierarchy.

Organizational Structure and Span of Control

Once organizational structure and decision-making authority are established, responsibility for performance can be assigned to individuals within an organization. The **span of control** refers to the scope of people or other resources over which an individual is given decision-making authority, and for which he or she is held accountable. A span of control can range from narrow to wide. For example, a CEO with extensive authority has a *wide span of control*, while a retail store clerk with little authority has a *narrow span of control*.

In general, individuals toward the top of an organization's hierarchy have wide spans of control while individuals toward the bottom of the hierarchy have narrow spans of control. As shown in Exhibit 18.2, overall organizational structure also influences the span of control. When decision making is centralized, most employees have fairly narrow spans of control; the most flexibility in decision making is restricted to top managers. When decision making is decentralized, employees throughout the organization have greater authority. The overall hierarchical structure is shorter because fewer managers are needed; more employees report to a single manager (i.e., more employees and other resources are under the span of control for each manager).

Responsibility Accounting

▶ BUSINESS PRACTICE
The CEO of a health services organization restructured his business unit by pushing the decision making to lower levels to help develop his employees and to meet the goal of growing his organization by $37 million over 5 years.[3]

LO2 Explain how responsibility centres are used to measure, monitor, and motivate performance

Accounting information is used in both centralized and decentralized organizations to measure, monitor, and reward performance. In centralized organizations, information produced by the accounting system for decision making is used primarily by top managers who are

[3] G. Burns, "When the Structure Is Faulty," *Canadian HR Reporter*, 19(9), May 8, 2006, p. 16.

held responsible for both their effort and the quality of their decisions. Employees carry out tasks that result from these decisions and are held responsible for their effort and compliance with top-down decisions. Therefore, individual and team efforts require close monitoring to determine their contributions to success. Managers use variance and productivity reports to gauge employee (individual and team) efforts.

In decentralized organizations, decision making occurs throughout management levels and in the field. Employees in lower levels are held responsible for their efforts and the quality of their decisions. Therefore, accounting systems are used to provide decision-making information for all levels, from management to frontline employees. Broader accounting measures related to overall financial performance are then used to measure and monitor performance.

Responsibility accounting is the process of assigning authority and responsibility to managers of sub-units, and then measuring and evaluating their performance. Under responsibility accounting, managers are held responsible only for factors over which they have control. **Responsibility centres** are sub-units (e.g., segments, divisions, departments) in which managers are accountable for specific types of operating activities. Four common types of responsibility centres are cost centres, revenue centres, profit centres, and investment centres. Exhibit 18.3 provides specific examples of each responsibility centre and examples of performance measures that are likely to be used in these centres.

Cost Centres

In cost centres, managers are held responsible only for the costs under their control. Some cost centres provide support services that are relatively easy to monitor because their outputs are measurable. Cost centres are also used for sub-units that produce goods or services eventually sold by others. Managers in these cost centres are responsible for producing their goods or services efficiently. In **discretionary cost centres**, the output is not easily measurable in dollars or activities. Cost centres are found in for-profit, not-for-profit, and government organizations.

Cost centre managers are expected either to minimize costs for a certain level of output or to maximize output for a certain level of cost. Cost centre performance is measured and monitored several ways. Some organizations rely on cost budgets and variances. Measures of other factors, such as quality and timeliness of delivery, are also relevant.

▷ CHAPTER REFERENCE
Budgets are addressed in Chapter 10, and revenue and cost variances are addressed in chapters 11 and 12.

▷ EXHIBIT 18.3
Examples of Responsibility Centres and Performance Measures

Responsibility Centres	Examples	Performance Measures Used
Cost centres	Manufacturing departments	Cost budgets and variances
	Service production departments, such as road maintenance for a city	Comparisons to benchmark cost per unit or service
	Support departments, such as accounting and billing departments in a hospital	Efficiency measures (days to close, number of new products)
	Discretionary cost centres, such as marketing and research and development	Industry benchmarks (e.g., R&D as a percentage of sales)
Revenue centres	Travel agencies	Revenue budgets and variances
	Sales departments for manufacturers	Growth in revenues
		Customer satisfaction
Profit centres	Retail sales outlets for clothing, books, or restaurants	Revenue and cost budgets and variances
	Corporate divisions and departments responsible for revenues and costs	Accounting earnings such as operating income or earnings before or after taxes
Investment centres	Corporate divisions and business segments responsible for investment decisions	Return on investment (ROI)
		Residual income
		Economic value added (EVA)

Revenue Centres

In **revenue centres**, managers are held responsible for the revenues under their control. Revenue centres frequently sell products from manufacturing sub-units, and managers are expected to maximize sales. If the manager in a revenue centre is responsible for setting prices, gross revenues can be used as a performance measure. If corporate headquarters, rather than the manager, sets prices, then managers' performance can be evaluated using a combination of sales volumes measured in units and sales mix. Many organizations treat their sales departments as revenue centres and reward employees based on sales generated. In not-for-profit organizations, fundraising activities might be treated as a revenue centre.

Profit Centres

Managers in **profit centres** are held responsible for both revenues and costs under their control. Profit centres produce and sell goods or services and may include one or several cost centres, and profit centre managers are responsible for decisions about inputs, product mix, pricing, and volume of goods or services produced. Because profit centres include both revenues and costs, performance is typically measured using some combination of revenue and cost measures. Not-for-profit organizations tend to use revenue and cost budgets and variances as performance measures, although some focus managers' attention on operating margins when performance is poor. For-profit organizations use some measure of profits, such as accounting earnings.

> ▷ **CHAPTER REFERENCE**
> Chapter 19 describes the use of non-financial performance measures and the balanced scorecard approach to linking performance with a company's mission.

Investment Centres

Managers of **investment centres** are held responsible for the revenues, costs, and investments under their control. Investments include any assets related to the investment centre, such as fixed assets, inventory, intangible assets, and accounts receivable. Investment centres resemble profit centres, where profitability is related to the assets used to generate the profits.

Because investment centres include revenues, costs, and investment, performance measures need to address all of these factors. Later in this chapter, you will learn about three commonly used measures: return on investment (ROI), residual income, and economic value added (EVA).

©Fuse/Getty Images

example

computer wizards, part 1
RESPONSIBILITY CENTRES

Computer Wizards, headquartered in Happy Valley–Goose Bay (HVGB), Labrador, produces and sells computer monitors nationally and internationally. The HVGB facility is the original site for Computer Wizards and houses the administrative offices, as well as operations facilities. Jason Black is responsible for HVGB operations. The Red Deer (RD), Alberta operations are more recent and smaller in size. There are no administrative functions in RD. Cecilia Earnhart manages the RD operations. Due to growth and expansion opportunities, Computer Wizards' upper management has instituted a decentralized management structure with regular performance reviews for its two operating divisions. Although the two divisions differ in size, they are structurally similar, as depicted in the following organization chart.

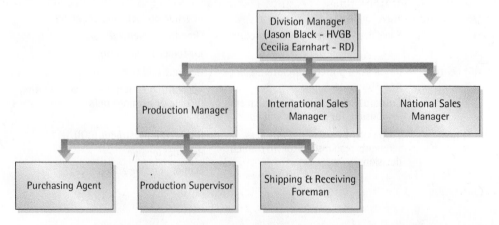

example

When evaluating performance, each division is assessed as an investment centre. Both Jason and Cecilia are responsible for cost and revenue management, profit achievement, and investment decisions. Variance analysis, profit achievement, and return on investment are all included in their performance evaluations. Within each division, personnel are evaluated depending upon individual responsibilities. The national and international sales managers are responsible for generating revenues through sales and managing sales-related costs. As such, these areas are considered revenue centres, with additional responsibility for sales-related cost management and performance evaluated based on sales volume, sales mix, and cost control. Variance from budget is a significant aspect of the performance review. The production manager is responsible for all aspects of the production process, including oversight of purchasing, production, and shipping and receiving. As such, this area is considered a cost centre, and performance is evaluated based on cost management, quality control, and on-time delivery. Variance analysis is a significant portion of the performance evaluation. The purchasing agent is predominantly responsible for materials price variances, and answers for quality issues associated with materials efficiency variances. The production supervisor is responsible for materials efficiency, labour efficiency, and variable overhead efficiency variances. The shipping and receiving foreman is responsible for on-time delivery variances. ■

Responsibility Centres, Managers' Incentives, and Diagnostic Controls

Top managers use judgment to decide the best types of responsibility centres for the organization. The choices depend on the size of the organization, the nature of operations, and the organizational structure. Ideally, responsibility centres should hold managers responsible only for decisions over which they have authority. For example, accounting departments are often viewed as cost centres, because their managers have authority primarily for the expenditure of resources. Similarly, business segments are generally treated as investment centres, because segment managers have authority over revenues, costs, and investment.

Responsibility centre accounting sometimes leads to suboptimal decision making. Too often, managers make decisions that are in the best interests of their own responsibility centres but suboptimal for the organization as a whole. Each type of responsibility centre has a specific set of potential problems. Managers in cost centres focus on minimizing costs and maximizing efficiency, which can lead to declines in quality and delivery timeliness. In turn, sales could drop, and the overall organization suffers. Similarly, revenue centre managers, who are typically rewarded for increasing revenues, may fail to consider product contribution margins and may inappropriately emphasize less-profitable products. These managers have incentives to offer discounts and generous payment terms that reduce overall profitability. In profit centres, managers are encouraged to stress short-run profits by cutting maintenance, research and development, and advertising costs that benefit long-term performance. Similarly, in investment centres, managers may reduce investment to increase short-term results, or they may invest in projects that are more or less risky than is appropriate for the organization. To address these problems, diagnostic control systems typically include appropriate performance measures, and incentive reward systems need to be implemented. Appropriate measures increase goal congruence: creating agreement between the interests of individual managers and the organization as a whole.

Investment Centre Performance Evaluation

Investment centres are common in large decentralized organizations. Because managers are responsible for costs and revenues, as well as for investments, the measures used for monitoring and motivating purposes typically include the return and the size of investment.

Performance evaluations can include financial and non-financial measures, and at the same time, companies may include internal and/or external measures. Exhibit 18.4 shows examples of financial measures.

LO3

Calculate return on investment, residual income, and economic value added and explain how each is used to measure, monitor, and motivate performance

	Financial Measures	Non-Financial Measures
External	• Stock prices	• Customer Satisfaction
Internal	Short-Term (1-year measure)	• Defect Rates
	• Return on Investment (ROI)	• Manufacturing lead time
	• Residual Income (RI)	• Employee Retention Rate
	• Economic Value Added (EVA)	

There are three short-term internal financial measures commonly used to evaluate investment centre performance:

▶ Return on investment
▶ Residual income
▶ Economic value added

Return on Investment

Return on investment (ROI) is the ratio of operating income to average operating assets. When ROI is used for internal control purposes to evaluate managers' performance, profit and investment should be under the control of the managers being evaluated. Thus, the operating income and the average operating assets are used. Operating income is calculated as earnings before interest and taxes (EBIT), while operating assets include all assets used in the production of goods or services, such as cash, accounts receivable, inventory, and plant and equipment. Non-operating assets, such as investments in other companies or property and equipment currently rented to other companies, are excluded from this calculation. When evaluating an entire company's performance, all assets would be included, because owners want to evaluate their return based on the entire investment. But when evaluating the performance of a sub-unit, judgment is used to determine which assets should be included. The average of beginning and ending operating assets is calculated for determining ROI for several reasons. First, ROI is intended to capture operations over a period of time, not just at the end of the time period. Second, operating assets could be manipulated by temporarily decreasing investment at the time performance is measured.

ROI is used to evaluate investment centre performance. It can be compared across sub-units within a single organization, among a group of firms within an industry, and within a single organization across time.[4] In addition, ROI can be decomposed into two components that provide additional information about performance. ROI is decomposed by multiplying both the numerator and denominator by revenue and then rearranging terms:

ROI = Operating income ÷ Average operating assets

= (Operating income ÷ Average operating assets) × (Operating income ÷ Revenue)

= (Revenue ÷ Average operating assets) × (Operating income ÷ Revenue)

Because revenue divided by average operating assets represents investment turnover, and operating income divided by revenue represents the return on sales, we can now rewrite the ROI formula:

ROI = Investment turnover × Return on sales

The decomposition of ROI into investment turnover and return on sales is often referred to as *DuPont analysis*. The method originated at the DuPont Company in the early 1900s so that results from a wider range of business activities could be compared. Investment turnover is a measure of the sales generated by each dollar invested in operating assets. Return on sales measures managers' abilities to control operating expenses related to sales during

---

[4] Another measure similar to ROI is return on total assets (ROA). This measure also shows how well assets are employed, and it is measured as follows:

$$\text{Return on total assets} = \frac{\text{Net income} + [\text{Interest expense} \times (1 - \text{Tax rate})]}{\text{Average total assets}}$$

Because after-tax interest expense is added back in the numerator, ROA is not influenced by how the assets were financed. This approach allows comparison across divisions or companies with differing amounts of debt, or for a single company that has changed its level of debt over time.

a period. This decomposition focuses attention on the role that assets play in generating revenues and the role that increased revenues and decreased costs play in generating profits. Improvement in ROI occurs when sales increase and costs do not increase proportionately (some cost is fixed), when costs are reduced for a given level of sales, or when investment decreases for a given level of income. In this manner, ROI provides managers guidance about factors that improve performance.

▶ **ALTERNATIVE TERMS**

The term *asset turnover* means the same as *investment turnover.* Similarly, the term *profit margin ratio* means the same as *return on sales.*

computer wizards, part 2
RETURN ON INVESTMENT

example

In preparation for the regular performance evaluation of its division, top managers of Computer Wizards have collected the following information about the HVGB and RD divisions.

	HVGB	RD
Average operating assets	$2,000,000	$200,000
Operating income	$ 500,000	$ 60,000

© Fuse/Getty Images

The top managers of Computer Wizards use ROI as one of the measures of performance of its divisions. Following are the calculations for each division:

HVGB's ROI = $500,000 ÷ $2,000,000 = 25%

RD's ROI = $60,000 ÷ $200,000 = 30%

Jason was recently hired from outside the company to improve operations in the HVGB division. One of his objectives is to achieve an ROI at least as high as that of the RD division. Jason calculates the ROI of the two divisions and performs a DuPont analysis as follows:

HVGB:

Return on sales = $500,000 ÷ $5,000,000 = 10%

Investment turnover = $5,000,000 ÷ $2,000,000 = 2.5 times

ROI = 10% × 2.5 = 25%

RD:

Return on sales = $60,000 ÷ $560,000 = 11%

Investment turnover = $560,000 ÷ $200,000 = 2.8 times

ROI = 11% × 2.8 = 30%

From this analysis, Jason learns that the HVGB division has lower performance in investment efficiency and operating efficiency, as well as overall ROI. He decides to investigate options for improving the division's profitability. There are three general strategies for increasing ROI: increase sales, decrease costs, or decrease investment in operating assets.

Increasing ROI

One alternative is to focus primarily on increasing sales. The HVGB division currently has idle capacity, and Jason would like to emphasize a new group of products. He believes that current capacity can support an increase in sales of $600,000, without requiring additional investment except for additional marketing costs. The increased sales would increase operating income by $60,000. The expected return on sales would then be

$560,000 ÷ $5,600,000 = 10%

and investment turnover would be

$5,600,000 ÷ $2,000,000 = 2.8 times

leading to an improved ROI, slightly lower than that of the RD division:

$560,000 ÷ $2,000,000 = 10% × 2.8 = 28%

Alternatively, Jason could focus on reducing expenses. He believes that manufacturing costs could be reduced by as much as $100,000. He would implement this plan using kaizen

continued...

costing—that is, by organizing a team with members from marketing, accounting, and engineering to analyze production activities and identify non-value-added activities that could be eliminated. Also, the products and manufacturing processes could be redesigned to reduce the number of parts or processes. If the team is successful and expenses are reduced by $100,000, operating income would be $600,000 instead of $500,000. This plan alone could increase return on sales to

$$\$600,000 \div \$5,000,000 = 12\%$$

and ROI would equal that of the RD division:

$$12\% \times 2.5 = 30\%$$

Jason considers one more approach to increase ROI. He can reduce the HVGB division's investment in operating assets. He knows that internal processes are inefficient; inventory and work in process are built up throughout different manufacturing areas. He would like to implement cellular production and just-in-time inventory practices. These modifications would allow the division to sell a small building currently in use. He estimates that these actions would reduce operating assets by $400,000. The investment turnover would then be

$$\$5,000,000 \div \$1,600,000 = 3.1 \text{ times}$$

and ROI would be

$$10\% \times 3.1 = 31\%$$

Jason knows that increasing sales, reducing costs, and changing production processes are all worthy long-term goals, but it will take a year or longer to see the results of any of these plans. He would prefer to increase ROI within a shorter time frame. Recently, a competitor made an offer to sell to the HVGB division a component that is currently manufactured in-house. If Jason purchases the component, operating earnings would decrease by $50,000, but he could easily sell the small building because most of it houses the production facility for the component. Investment turnover would still be 3.1 times (the same as the third option above), but return on sales would drop to 9% ($450,000 ÷ $5,000,000), and ROI would increase to 27%.

Choosing a Plan of Action

Jason decides to discuss his options with Renée LaPointe, the director of finance for Computer Wizards. All the plans he is considering require a great deal of time and effort. He believes that the strategies are sound but is uncertain whether his expectations can be met. An increase in sales depends in part on the continuing upswing of the economy. Cost reductions take time and concentrated effort on the part of employees. Changing the manufacturing process could take several years, because a new floor plan would have to be laid out, teams would have to be established, and work would be disrupted while the new lines were being implemented. Furthermore, the employees might need several months to learn how to work efficiently under the new system. The easiest choice is to outsource, and Jason knows that outsourcing would improve his ROI in the short run. However, he believes that focusing on in-house manufacturing cost reductions would be a better strategy for Computer Wizards in the long run. The company's use of ROI to measure performance discourages this type of strategy, so Jason wonders whether a different performance measure could be adopted that would better reward behaviour to benefit the overall organization. ■

ROI and Managers' Incentives. A division's ROI is easily compared with internal and external benchmarks and other divisions' returns on investment. Holding managers responsible for some level of ROI reduces their tendency to over invest in projects. Another advantage of ROI is that its components motivate managers to increase sales, decrease costs, and minimize asset investments.

However, ROI also discourages managers from investing in projects that reduce the division's ROI, even though they improve the ROI for the overall organization. Suppose Jason at Computer Wizards had an opportunity to invest $1,750,000 in a project that would generate sales of $2,500,000 and a return on sales of 10% (the same as the original assumptions) — $250,000 operating income per year. The division's ROI, including this investment, would be

$$\text{Investment turnover} = \$7,500,000 \div 3,750,000 = 2 \text{ times}$$
$$\text{ROI} = 10\% \times 2 = 20\%$$

Even though the investment reduces the division's ROI, Computer Wizards forgoes $250,000 if the project is not undertaken. If the level of risk and the return are comparable to those of projects from other divisions, Computer Wizards would prefer the benefits from this investment.

Another disadvantage of ROI is that it does not incorporate measures of risk. Managers can potentially increase ROI by investing in riskier projects, which often have higher returns than less risky projects. If they are rewarded solely for increasing ROI, managers may undertake risky projects, without considering the added risk to the organization. This problem arises more often when managers' time horizons are short, such as when they are planning to retire or move to another company. In such cases, managers often prefer immediate improvements in performance measures.

Furthermore, when managers with short time horizons evaluate projects based on ROI, they might inappropriately cut costs that provide long-term benefit for the organization. For example, they might cut research and development, maintenance, or employee training.

ROI is typically calculated using financial accounting assets and income. Under International Financial Reporting Standards (IFRS) and Canadian Accounting Standards for Private Enterprises (ASPE), assets are recorded at their original cost, and some intangible assets, such as brand name, are not recognized. These rules cause the investment in assets to be understated, particularly when the value of assets, such as property, has increased or when a company has significant intangible assets. Understatements in assets cause ROI and investment turnover to be overstated. In addition, IFRS and Canadian ASPE measures revenues and costs in ways that can distort ROI. For example, overhead or support department costs might be allocated to a division using a method that does not reflect the division's use of resources. If the division's costs are understated or overstated, ROI will be distorted.

Despite its drawbacks, ROI is widely used by businesses throughout the world. ROI is a common measure for any type of investment and may be used in nontraditional ways. Managers analyze ROI for a diverse set of business initiatives and activities, including marketing, information technology, and human resources.[6]

> **BUSINESS PRACTICE**
> Organizations often use nontraditional ways to measure ROI. The **Canadian Institutes of Health Research** funded a three-year project to investigate Canada's ROI from pharmaceutical care. The study aimed to analyze "the extent to which increased pharmaceutical spending improves population health—or saves money in other areas of the health care system."[5]

Residual Income

Because of the disadvantages of ROI just described, some organizations prefer to use residual income to measure performance of sub-units. **Residual income** measures the dollar amount of profits in excess of cost of capital, which is the required rate of return multiplied by average operating assets. It is calculated as follows:

$$\text{Residual income} = \text{Pre-tax operating income} - (\text{Required rate of return} \times \text{Average operating assets})$$

Many organizations set a minimum return expectation for operations and new investments. Residual income takes this expectation into consideration; it is the difference between actual operating income and the required income, given the organization's investment in operating assets and its required rate of return. The size of investment affects residual income less than ROI, because it is used only to value the dollar amount of expected return, not as a denominator. Compared to ROI, residual income is less influenced by changes in investment. Organizations use a variety of residual income measures, such as cash value added.[7] Below, we learn about economic value added, which is widely used.

> **CHAPTER REFERENCE**
> See Chapter 13 for a more complete discussion about determining the required rate of return.

---

[5] Centre for Health Services and Policy Research, Canada's Return on Investment from Pharmaceutical Care: A Population-Based Evaluation, at www.chspr.ubc.ca/research-area/project/canadas-return-investment-pharmaceutical-care-population-based-evaluation.

[6] See, for example, Booz & Company, "When Art Meets Science: The Challenge of ROI Marketing," strategy+business/Knowledge@Wharton, December 17, 2003; J. Edwards, "ROI Trumps Innovation for Software Users," CFO.com, June 26, 2006; and J. Hyatt, "The Metric System," CFO.com, July 15, 2009.

[7] See, for example, P. Erasmus, "The Relative and Incremental Content of the Value-Based Financial Performance Measure Cash Value Added (CVA)," *Management Dynamics* 17(1), 2008.

© Fuse/Getty Images

computer wizards, part 3
RESIDUAL INCOME

Jason consults with Renée, and they decide to investigate other performance measures. The first option they consider is residual income. The required rate of return for the company is 10%. Given the investment in operating assets, the required dollar amount of return for each division is as follows:

	HVGB	RD
Average operating assets	$200,000	$2,000,000
Times required rate of return	10%	10%
Required return	$200,000	$ 20,000

Residual income is calculated as follows:

	HVGB	RD
Operating income	$500,000	$60,000
Required return	200,000	20,000
Residual income	$300,000	$40,000

Renée explains that the HVGB division provides Computer Wizards with $300,000 in income above and beyond the required return. However, as they discuss the value of residual income as a performance measure, Jason suggests that it has some of the same problems as ROI, because it is still based on operating income. In addition, Renée cannot compare results in the HVGB division to RD's because of the size difference in the two divisions. Therefore, they decide to consider other alternatives. ∎

Residual Income and Managers' Incentives. The use of residual income does not penalize investment in projects with lower returns than current project returns. Suppose the HVGB division invests $1,750,000 in new assets that generate annual sales of $2,500,000 and operating income of 10% ($250,000). If this project is undertaken, the HVGB division residual income will be

Operating income ($500,000 + $250,000)	$750,000
Required return [($2,000,000 + $1,750,000) × 10%]	375,000
Residual income	$375,000

Because the project is expected to increase residual income by $75,000 ($375,000 – $300,000), managers would be motivated to invest in it. In general, when residual income is used as a performance measure, managers are willing to invest in any projects with returns equal to or greater than the required rate of return.

However, residual income has its own problems. Because it is an absolute dollar value, larger sub-units are more likely to have larger residual incomes. For Computer Wizards, the HVGB division's residual income is much greater than that of the RD division. As a result, managers find it difficult to compare performance across units.

A disadvantage it shares with ROI is that residual income increases as investment and costs decrease (holding sales constant). Therefore, managers may cut costs—such as research and development, maintenance, or employee training—that likely have long-term benefits for the organization.

Another problem with residual income occurs if senior managers from each sub-unit estimate their own required rate of return; they have incentives to set a required rate of return that is too low. In turn, a low required rate of return encourages managers to invest in less profitable projects. They may also invest in less risky projects and forgo riskier projects that would be profitable for the overall organization. Because operating income is measured using financial accounting information, residual income suffers from the same earnings-related problems as ROI.

Economic Value Added

Economic value added (EVA[8]) is a variation of residual income that incorporates a number of adjustments to reduce the disadvantages produced by residual income. Many different organizations have used EVA, including AT&T, Coca-Cola, Quaker Oats, and General Electric.[9] The basic EVA calculation follows:

$$\text{EVA} = \begin{array}{c}\text{Adjusted after-tax}\\ \text{operating income}\end{array} - \left[\begin{array}{c}\text{Weighted average}\\ \text{cost of capital}\end{array} \times \left(\begin{array}{c}\text{Adjusted total}\\ \text{assets}\end{array} - \begin{array}{c}\text{Current}\\ \text{liabilities}\end{array} \right) \right]$$

The *weighted average cost of capital* (WACC) is calculated by analyzing all sources of invested funds, including both debt and equity financing (valued as the opportunity cost to investors). It is the after-tax cost of all long-term financing for the company or division. The long-term financing includes long-term liabilities and shareholders' equity, or it can be calculated by subtracting current liabilities from the adjusted total assets. With EVA, each division can use its actual cost of capital, taking into consideration the industry and risk characteristics.

Weighted average cost of capital (WACC) is calculated by multiplying the cost of each source of financing by its weight and totalling the products. The formula for a company that uses both debt and equity financing is calculated as follows:

WACC = Weight of Debt × Cost of Debt × (1 − Tax Rate) + Weight of Equity × Cost of Equity

Suppose HVGB's total assets consist of $1,300,000 of debt, with a cost of 7.25% to borrow, and $700,000 of equity, with a required rate of return of 12.5%. HVGB's tax rate is 40%. The weight of its debt represents 65% of its total assets, and the weight of its equity represents 35% respectively. HVGB's WACC is 7.2%.

Source of Financing	Amount	Weight	Rate	After-tax	WACC
Debt	$1,300,000	65%	7.25%	(1 − 0.4)	2.83%
Equity	700,000	35%	12.50%	1	4.37%
Total	$2,000,000	100%			7.20%

$$\text{WACC} = 0.65 \times 0.0725 \times (1 - 0.4) + 0.35 \times 0.125 = 0.072$$

The adjustments made to develop the EVA calculation include substituting after-tax operating income for EBIT, which is consistent with using the (after-tax) WACC and also gives managers incentives to reduce taxes. Analysts and consultants recommend that organizations choose among 160 other adjustments to provide managers with incentives specific to the firm. One purpose of adjusting financial accounting income and assets is to minimize suboptimal decision making.

Measures used for internal purposes need not follow IFRS or Canadian ASPE but are created to reflect economic costs and benefits over time. For example, research and development costs, which must be recognized immediately as an expense under IFRS or Canadian ASPE, are often capitalized for EVA calculations. This adjustment encourages managers to invest in research and development projects that have long-term value for the organization. Similarly, long-term leases accounted for as operating leases under IFRS or Canadian ASPE are often treated as capital leases for EVA calculations. This adjustment reduces managers' incentives to use operating leases to artificially understate the organization's investment in assets. They are then encouraged to make long-term asset acquisition decisions based on the best alternative for the organization rather than based on their financial accounting treatment.

---

[8] EVA® is a registered trademark of Stern Stewart & Co.
[9] See D. McConville, "All About EVA," *Industry Week*, 243(8), April 18, 1994, pp. 55–57.

©Fuse/Getty Images

example

computer wizards, part 4
ECONOMIC VALUE ADDED

Jason and Renée next consider the use of EVA at Computer Wizards, and they calculate EVA for each division. Jason develops the following information:

	HVGB	RD
Total assets	$2,000,000	$200,000
Operating income	$ 500,000	$ 60,000
Weighted average cost of capital	7.2%	10%
Current liabilities	$ 20,000	$ 5,000
After-tax operating income	$ 300,000	$ 40,000
Tax rate	40%	33.33%

Jason and Renée first calculate EVA without any adjustments beyond income taxes:

$$\text{EVA} = \begin{array}{c}\text{Adjusted after-tax}\\\text{operating income}\end{array} - \left[\begin{array}{c}\text{Weighted average}\\\text{cost of capital}\end{array} \times \left(\begin{array}{c}\text{Total}\\\text{assets}\end{array} - \begin{array}{c}\text{Current}\\\text{liabilities}\end{array}\right)\right]$$

EVA HVGB:

After-tax operating income	$300,000
WACC × (Total assets – Current liabilities)	
[7.2% × ($2,000,000 – $20,000)]	142,560
	$157,440

EVA RD:

After-tax operating income	$40,000
WACC × (Total assets – Current liabilities)	
[10% × ($200,000 – $5,000)]	19,500
	$20,500

Because EVA incorporates income taxes, incentive is provided to minimize taxes paid. In addition, WACC is a more realistic capital charge than managers' subjective choices of required rates of return. The RD division operates in a riskier business environment than the HVGB division, which is reflected in its higher WACC.

Comparison of ROI, Residual Income, and EVA

After completing the EVA computations, Jason and Renée decide to examine the rankings of the two divisions using ROI, residual income, and EVA. Under ROI, the RD division (30%) appears to perform better than the HVGB division (25%). But under residual income and EVA, the HVGB division outperforms the RD division. They recognize that size has an effect on both residual income and EVA. Renée decides to use both ROI and EVA as performance measures. Jason suggests that Renée also consider the use of non-financial performance measures. He believes that increasing customer satisfaction should increase financial performance, because repeat and new customers will increase revenues. Renée agrees that by focusing on customer satisfaction, any potential customer-related problems are likely to be discovered sooner, and she agrees to give the measure further consideration. ■

EVA and Managers' Incentives. Generally, the advantages of EVA are the same as those for residual income. There are several specific advantages of EVA, which result from the various adjustments made to personalize the measure to each organization. These adjustments provide specific incentives that align the goals of managers with owners. However, some disadvantages need to be considered as well. For example, the appropriateness of the specific cost of capital for a division or an organization is a matter of judgment, as is the level of risk that has been incorporated. The adjustments are also a matter of judgment. We do not know how to perfectly measure economic revenues, costs, or assets, and a variety of acceptable ways provide different incentives. Because EVA is so complex, consulting firms must often be used to determine the appropriate adjustments. This process can be expensive and time consuming.

18-1 self-study problem   ROI, Residual Income, and EVA

LO3

Outdoor Express is a large manufacturer of recreational equipment. Performance of the camping division is measured as an investment centre, because the managers make all the decisions about investments in operating equipment and space. Following is financial information for the camping division:

Average operating assets	$2,000,000
Current liabilities	500,000
Operating income	300,000

The camping division's required rate of return is 12%, but Outdoor Express's weighted average cost of capital is 9%, and the tax rate is 30%.

required

A. Calculate return on investment for the camping division.
B. Calculate residual income for the camping division.
C. Calculate EVA for the camping division.
D. Briefly discuss the advantages and disadvantages of each method.

See the solution on page 789.

Issues Related to Investment

When using the financial measures, such as ROI, RI, and EVA, to evaluate employees' performance, the performance evaluation system should consider issues related to investment. As seen in the EVA calculation, the investments used are the total assets excluding current liabilities. In other words, the investment is the assets that are financed through long-term sources of funds, such as long-term liabilities and equity. The investments used in the calculations for ROI and RI are the average operating assets.

When a company invests in divisions at different times, it needs to determine what denominator should be used for the investment. For example, using historical cost for the investment is very different from using current cost, as well as using net book value and gross value. Older divisions may benefit from smaller historical costs and net book value as the denominator for the investment, while a newer division may show poorer performance using a bigger current cost as the denominator for the investment. Some adjustments may be required to ensure equity in evaluating divisional performances.

Motivating Performance with Compensation

Organizations use compensation contracts that provide incentives for employees to increase the value of the organization. These contracts include cash-based bonuses, stock options, and other types of bonuses based on stock prices. Earnings and growth targets are often set as goals in these compensation packages.

LO4   Discuss how compensation is used to motivate performance

Bonus System Incentives

As organizations increase in size, more sophisticated incentives packages are required to align the goals of employees and owners. Compensation contracts can be based on accounting earnings; other financial measures such as ROI, residual income, and EVA; and nonfinancial measures such as customer satisfaction or defects rates. Examples of financial performance measures are shown in Exhibit 18.7, along with examples of benchmarks or targets and the rewards that could be used to motivate behaviour.

> **BUSINESS PRACTICE**

In its seventh annual ranking of corporate governance in Canada, *Canadian
Business* ranked Montreal-based
SNC-Lavalin Group Inc. and Calgary-
based Nexen Inc. tied for the top spot.
Both organizations go well beyond
the required disclosure by providing
a complete breakdown of executive
compensation in an easy-to-read
presentation.[11]

> **CHAPTER REFERENCE**

Chapter 17 describes the relationship between inventories and income,
and it presents alternative income
calculations that reduce suboptimal
incentives.

> **CHAPTER REFERENCE**

Budgets are addressed more fully in
Chapter 10. Variance analysis and
behavioural implications are addressed
in Chapter 11.

Compensation contracts often include base salary and bonuses. The majority of Canadian employers offer performance-based incentives or bonuses. Bonuses may be a combination of cash, stock, stock options (options to buy stock in the future at a set price), and deferred compensation (salary or bonuses paid in the future, often after retirement). One study has reported that management incentive pay makes up approximately 17% of salary costs.[10]

A wide variation exists in compensation packages among executives, with an increasing demand for pay-for-performance packages. To protect shareholders, executive compensation is usually set by a committee of the board of directors. Ideally, the compensation committee consists of directors who are considered outsiders, with no formal connections to the management team. Bonuses are sometimes limited to some fraction of accounting earnings. In addition, shareholders may have the ability to vote periodically on compensation contracts. However, considerable evidence suggests that management compensation is not in fact independently determined, but rather that top managers influence the decisions made by the compensation committee.

There are ongoing concerns about the fairness of multimillion-dollar executive compensation packages. Some CEOs are receiving compensation packages that total 400 times the compensation of their average employee. These concerns and the visibility of large public scandals such as the one at Conrad Black's Hollinger International have contributed to the demand for greater transparency of corporate governance. In 2008, the Canadian Securities Administration released proposed amendments to the Statement of Executive Compensation, which will require greater transparency about executive compensation.[12]

Using Budgets to Monitor and Reward Performance

Budgets give managers authority over the use of an organization's resources. Accordingly, it seems reasonable to hold managers responsible for meeting budget benchmarks. However, when budget variances are used in performance evaluation, a number of challenges arise for managers being evaluated as well as for managers conducting the evaluation. Exhibit 18.5 provides examples of these challenges. Notice that most of these problems relate to holding managers responsible for results when they lack control over factors that affect the variances.

The investment centre performance measures we learned about in this chapter (ROI, residual income, and EVA) can also be tied to budgets and variances. Exhibit 18.6 illustrates a budget variance analysis for residual income. Individuals responsible for different aspects of performance can readily understand how their performance affects overall performance. When used as part of a performance evaluation system, this type of analysis is likely to increase goal congruence throughout an organization.

> **EXHIBIT 18.5**
Challenges in Appropriately Assigning Decision Rights

Challenges	Why They Arise	Specific Examples
Resentment	Department managers held responsible for costs over which they have no control	Allocated support department costs may be high because of poor management in support departments
Isolating the performance of individual managers	Interdependency among divisions and departments	Quality of customer services department affects ability of the sales department to meet future sales targets
Manager turnover	New manager is responsible for old manager's budget decisions	After the production manager is promoted to vice president, the new production manager faces unrealistic budget targets
Employee turnover	Employees are promoted, let go, or leave	Delays arise in hiring process, or a hiring freeze occurs
Uncontrollable external factors	Unanticipated changes in volumes, costs, or prices	Oil price and availability changes because of broken pipelines

[10] M. de Reus, "Bonuses Spreading, but Do They Work?" *Canadian HR Reporter*, 20(20), November 19, 2007, p. 19.
[11] J. Gray, "A Peek Inside," *Canadian Business*, 80(16/17), August 13–August 27, 2007, p. 57.
[12] M. Côté, "Are CEOs Overpaid?" *CA Magazine*, 140 (9), November 2007, p. 80; and E. Schiehll, "Canada: Improving the Transparency of Executive Compensation Practices," *Benefits & Compensation International*, 37(6), January/February 2008, p. 3.

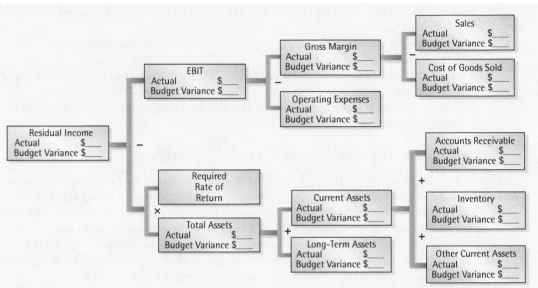

The analysis shown here could be extended further. For example, cost of goods sold could be broken down into raw materials, direct labour, variable overhead, and fixed overhead.

Performance Measure Targets

As organizations develop their operating plans and budgets, targets (i.e., *preset goals*) are often set for performance measures. These budgets and targets are often used to establish bonus payments. For example, stock bonuses granted to Paul Stebbins, CEO of World Fuel Services, depended on annual net income growth and three-year earnings-per-share growth. Targets for William Hickey, CEO of Sealed Air, included ten specific goals, including diluted earnings per share, net profit, return on assets, safety, and manufacturing quality. Blake Nordstrom, President of Nordstrom, receives a stock bonus if total shareholder return is positive and above average among retail peer companies.[13]

●●▷ RISK OF BIASED DECISIONS: REGRESSION TO THE MEAN

REGRESSION TO THE MEAN refers to the statistical tendency for observations in a series of data to move from the extremes toward the mean. In sports statistics, fans understand that players may perform exceedingly well in a particular game, but their performance in the next game may not attain the same high level. Because of this tendency, next year's baseball batting averages are better predicted by the performance average over the year than by the end-of-season performance. It is easy for individuals to overlook the regression to the mean effect in day-to-day decision making. For example, when an organization is performing exceedingly well in a particular year, managers tend to set high goals and standards for the next year. These goals may lead to false assumptions about the future period and inappropriate planning. An example of the regression to the mean phenomenon was the slowdown in housing prices after 2007. Although home values had increased at unprecedented rates in many locations, many homeowners, mortgage lenders, and other financial experts ignored the likelihood of a regression toward the mean. Managers need to incorporate knowledge of these statistical tendencies into their plans for the future through budgets and other forward-looking analyses.

Budget and Variance Adjustments

Because managers' budgets often include items not under their control, the following adjustments can be made when budgets are used to measure managers' performance.

---

[13] E. Lambert, "The Right Way to Pay," Forbes.com, May 11, 2009.

- ▶ Use a flexible budget to determine expected revenues based on budgeted prices and actual volumes.
- ▶ Use a flexible budget to determine expected variable costs based on budgeted variable cost rates and actual volumes.
- ▶ Remove allocated costs that are not controllable by managers in the departments receiving allocations.
- ▶ Update costs for any anticipated price changes in direct materials, direct labour, and overhead-related resources.

Long-Term Versus Short-Term Incentives

For many years, compensation practices were criticized because they were based on accounting earnings. In addition to the problems already described, managers could also reduce the level of investment in assets such as equipment, thereby reducing amortization expense and, in turn, increasing accounting earnings. However, the reduced investment negatively affects future earnings if sales are forgone because of either limited capacity or increases in maintenance and downtime costs for old equipment that should have been replaced. In addition, manufacturers sometimes increase revenues by forcing their customers to carry large inventories. These types of actions may increase short-term earnings but often have negative effects on long-term earnings potential.

To focus managers more on the long term, many companies increased the use of stock-based compensation. Stock options, in particular, became popular during the 1980s and 1990s. Tying compensation to the value of stock was viewed as a way to encourage managers and other employees to focus on increasing the long-term value of the company. However, company stock prices are sensitive to changes in earnings. Some managers engaged in unethical or illegal activities to boost reported income so that stock prices would remain stable or increase. Earnings manipulation was a significant problem during the early 2000s.

International Compensation

In the past, compensation practices outside North America often focused on factors other than stock price. In France and Germany, for example, CEO and top management rewards were sometimes tied to the average salary of all employees, because the board of directors included labour union representation. These types of contracts provide incentives to increase the wages of all employees. However, in the early 2000s, European companies, which were struggling to attract and retain highly skilled and talented people, began using stock options, or "free" shares, for top- and midlevel managers.

For example, a new law was passed in Germany in 1998, making it easier for companies to use stock options. About 50% of companies listed in Frankfurt's DAX 100 stock index now have stock option plans. European companies tend to link the options to specific performance hurdles, such as increases in share price relative to competitors. France, in a

▶ BUSINESS PRACTICE

Jim Balsillie stepped down as chairman of BlackBerry, then known as RIM, after it was announced that over 63% of stock options granted after February 2002 were improperly dated, giving executives a financial advantage. The company restated earnings through the end of its fiscal year 2006 by $250 million, and Balsillie and his co-CEO Mike Lazaridis had to pay $4.25 million each to help defray costs of investigating the errors and the restatement.[14]

▶ EXHIBIT 18.7

Financial Measures and Examples of Targets and Rewards

Financial Measures	Example of Benchmark or Target	Example of Rewards
ROI	20%	Cash bonus or stock-related reward
EVA	Dollar target or percentage change	Cash bonus or stock-related reward
Operating income or growth in income	Dollar target or percentage growth target	Cash bonus or profit sharing
Cost savings	Cost reduction of 5%	Gain sharing—employees receive a percentage of the savings
Revenue growth	10%	Cash bonus plus paid family vacation to award ceremony at resort destination

[14] J. E. Vascellaro, "RIM Sets Restatement, Shake-up on Board in Backdating Fallout; Profit Could Be Reduced By up to $250 Million; Balsillie Out as Chairman," *The Wall Street Journal*, March 6, 2007, p. A3.

previously unheard-of move, has also tied severance packages to performance. Recently, shareholders in Europe have begun to actively examine top executives' compensation packages. Shareholders in the United Kingdom have criticized several large companies, including telecommunications giant Vodafone Group and insurer Prudential, for paying excessive executive compensation or even for considering executive pay packages perceived as being too large.[15] In the Netherlands, Sweden, and Norway, shareholders have a binding vote on executive compensation packages. In Britain, they have a nonbinding vote, and some Spanish and Swiss companies are voluntarily giving shareholders a vote on the terms of executive compensation packages.[16]

Some countries still discourage stock options. In Belgium and Switzerland, managers are required to pay taxes on the potential gain at the time options are granted. If stock prices fall, managers are not allowed to receive a refund of taxes previously paid. In France, the capital gains tax rate is close to 50%, which greatly reduces the value of stock options.[17]

 > FOCUS ON ETHICAL DECISION MAKING:
LEVEL OF EXECUTIVE PAY: UNIVERSITY PRESIDENTS

In July 2008, *The Globe and Mail* revealed some of the details of the compensation packages received by the presidents of some of Ontario's universities. These packages include various perks, from modest car allowances to large payouts upon retirement, including the following:

- At McMaster University, President Peter George was offered a $1.4-million payout upon retirement, in $99,999 installments (an amount $1 below the required disclosure amount), in addition to a six-figure pension.
- At Queen's University, former principal Karen Hitchcock was offered an interest-free loan of up to $500,000 to take her job.
- At York University President Mamdouh Shoukri was offered a performance bonus of more than $81,000 for the first year and a $50,000 housing loan that would be forgiven for each year of service at York University.
- At the University of Western Ontario, President Paul Davenport was given a retirement allowance of two years' salary in monthly installments, totalling over $700,000.

All of the above contracts included a "no strings attached" paid leave policy. These university presidents were able to take paid leaves without having research requirements, medical reasons, or any other explanation attached as a condition of the leave.

Although other provinces disclose the details of university presidents' compensation packages, Ontario universities disclosed only salary and benefits information. After a two-year battle between the local media and the Information and Privacy Commissioner, McMaster led the way by disclosing the details of President George's compensation.

Some justify these large compensation packages based on the demands of the job. University presidents' responsibilities include external activities such as fundraising, government negotiations, attendance at public events, and internal leadership requirements. Others question some of these practices, based on problems in the private sector, with perks such as executive loans and paid leaves for administrators when the administrators are no longer active researchers and will not return to the academic ranks.

sources: E. Church, "University Presidents Receive Juicy Perks," *The Globe* and *Mail*, July 10, 2008; and McMaster University, Mandate and Qualifications, www.mcmaster.ca/avpira/accountability.html.

ETHICS OF COMPENSATION PACKAGES

Is the level of executive pay an ethical issue for boards of directors or university boards of governors? What should boards of directors or university boards of governors do to achieve better corporate governance over executive pay? How can a board of directors or advisory board re-evaluate and improve its approach to issues such as this one?

[15] D. Bilefsky, "Mad About Money," *The Wall Street Journal*, April 14, 2003, p. R3.
[16] "Business: Pay Attention; Executive Pay in Europe," *The Economist*, 387(8584), June 14, 2008, p. 82.
[17] D. Woodruff, "Europe, a Latecomer, Embraces Options," *The Wall Street Journal*, May 15, 2001, p. A18; D. Bilefsky, "Mad About Money," *The Wall Street Journal*, April 14, 2003, p. R3; and S. Mouthon, "France's new tax diminishes advantages of stock plans in employee compensation," Latham & Watkins LLP, 2013 http://www.lexology.com/library/detail.aspx?g=74ccb488-78c0-42d9-9f14-6c49cab12378.

SUMMARY

L01   Discuss how decision-making responsibility and authority are related to performance evaluation

CENTRALIZED AND DECENTRALIZED ORGANIZATIONS

Advantages and disadvantages: See Exhibit 18.1.

GENERAL VERSUS SPECIFIC KNOWLEDGE

Decision authority is related to the type of knowledge within an organization.

L02   Explain how responsibility centres are used to measure, monitor, and motivate performance

TYPES OF RESPONSIBILITY CENTRES

- Cost centres
  - Discretionary cost centres
- Revenue centres
- Profit centres
- Investment centres

ISSUES

Measuring performance at the responsibility-centre level can lead to suboptimal decisions.

L03   Calculate return on investment, residual income, and economic value added and explain how each is used to measure, monitor, and motivate performance

RETURN ON INVESTMENT (ROI)

$$\text{ROI} = \frac{\text{Operating income}}{\text{Average operating assets}}$$

DUPONT ANALYSIS

$$\text{ROI} = \left(\frac{\text{Sales}}{\text{Average operating asset}}\right) \times \left(\frac{\text{Operating income}}{\text{Sales}}\right)$$

ROI = Investment turnover × Return on sales

RESIDUAL INCOME

$$\text{Residual income} = \text{Operating income} - \left(\text{Required rate of return} \times \text{Average operating assets}\right)$$

ECONOMIC VALUE ADDED (EVA)

$$\text{EVA} = \text{Adjusted after-tax operating income} - \left[\text{Weighted average cost of capital} \times \left(\text{Adjusted total assets} - \text{Current liabilities}\right)\right]$$

WACC = Weight of Debt × Cost of Debt × (1 − Tax Tax Rate) + Weight of Equity × Cost of Equity

ADVANTAGES AND DISADVANTAGES

ROI is easier to compare across sub-units but motivates suboptimal decisions, both in long-term investment and short-term cost cutting.

Residual income provides more appropriate investment incentives than ROI but is not comparable across sub-units.

EVA minimizes suboptimal decision-making incentives but is complex to calculate and not comparable across sub-units.

L04   Discuss how compensation is used to motivate performance

BONUS SYSTEM INCENTIVES

Examples of performance measures

- ROI
- Residual income
- EVA
- Operating income or growth in income
- Cost savings
- Revenue growth

MOTIVATING LONG-TERM VERSUS SHORT-TERM PERFORMANCE

18-1 solution to self-study problem

A. ROI = Net operating income/Average operating assets = $300,000/$2,000,000 = 15%

B. Residual income = Net operating income – (Required rate of return × Investment)

$$= \$300,000 - (12\% \times \$2,000,000) = \$300,000 - \$240,000$$
$$= \$60,000$$

C.   EVA = After-tax operating income – [Weighted average cost of capital
      × (Total assets – Current liabilities)]

$$= [\$300,000 \times (1 - 0.30)] - [9\% \times (\$2,000,000 - \$500,000)]$$
$$= \$210,000 - \$135,000 = \$75,000$$

D. ROI and residual income motivate managers to reduce costs and investment, whereas EVA provides incentives to invest as long as the return is equal to or greater than the required rate of return. In addition, ROI and residual income do not include taxes, so no incentive is provided for managers to minimize taxes. EVA can be adjusted for intangibles such as leases and R&D spending. Therefore, it can be designed to minimize managers' abilities to artificially improve the performance measure.

QUESTIONS

18.1 Explain how return on investment (ROI) is calculated and how it can be decomposed into two financial measures.

18.2 Explain how and why the use of ROI for performance evaluation can cause managers to make decisions that could be harmful to an organization in the long run.

18.3 Explain how residual income is calculated, and define required rate of return in your own words.

18.4 Explain why the use of residual income for performance evaluation provides better incentives, in some ways, than ROI but still causes managers to make some decisions that could be harmful to an organization in the long run.

18.5 Explain the differences between general and specific knowledge. Give an example of an industry where knowledge is quite general and an example of an industry that requires specific knowledge.

18.6 Explain why organizational form may vary if specific knowledge versus general knowledge is needed for decision making.

18.7 Explain how EVA differs from residual income.

18.8 Identify the four different types of responsibility centres, and explain the general objectives of each.

18.9 A national corporation, Fast Print, decided to expand into several developing countries. The corporation has been managed under a centralized organizational form, but is considering changing to a decentralized form. List the advantages and disadvantages of making this change.

18.10 Explain how the span of control relates to responsibility accounting.

18.11 Discuss the use of budget variance analysis to understand residual income.

MULTIPLE-CHOICE QUESTIONS

18.12 Why is residual income a better measure for performance evaluation of an investment centre manager than return on investment?
   a. The problems associated with measuring the asset base are eliminated.
   b. Desirable investment decisions will not be neglected by high-return divisions.
   c. Only the gross book value of assets needs to be calculated.
   d. Returns do not increase as assets are depreciated.
   e. The arguments over the implicit cost of interest are eliminated.

18.13 Robert Motoz is the manager of Division B of a large manufacturing company. Division B purchases all of its direct materials from Division A at a negotiated transfer price. Division B manufactures a product and sells this product on the market. Robert Motoz makes all production efficiency decisions for the division, including replacing and upgrading manufacturing equipment. This represents which of the following types of responsibility centre?

a. Cost centre
b. Revenue centre
c. Profit centre
d. Investment centre
e. Discretionary centre

18.14 ZIL Inc. operates two divisions, which are treated as investment centres. Data for each division for Year 4 are as follows (in thousands):

	Division A	Division B
Net income	$ 50,000	$ 95,000
Total assets	$300,000	$650,000

The company's required rate of return is 12%. The president wishes to evaluate the performance of these divisions and is not sure whether to use return on investment (ROI) or residual income (RI) as the performance measure. Which division performed better, based on the ROI and RI performance measures?

a. Division A because its ROI and RI are higher than those of Division B

b. Division A because its RI is higher than that of Division B
c. Division B because its ROI is higher than that of Division A
d. Division B because its ROI and RI are higher than those of Division A
e. None of the above

18.15 A small company in Vancouver sold $788,000 worth of its products last year. Net income represents 24% of sales. Net operating profit after tax (NOPAT) and total capital are, respectively, $240,000 and $520,000. The weighted average cost of capital and the required cost of capital were, respectively, 15% and 12%. What is EVA?

a. $111,120
b. $126,720
c. $162,000
d. $177,600

18.16 Which of the following best describes the responsibility of an investment centre manager?

a. Evaluating alternative capital investments the organization must make.
b. Achieving a certain target revenue within the manager's organizational segment.
c. Achieving a certain target profit within the manager's organizational segment.
d. Maximizing segment revenues given a predetermined expenses limit.
e. Maximizing segment profit while making efficient use of the segment's investment in capital assets.

EXERCISES

18.17 Responsibility Centres, ROI, RI ZIL Inc. operates two divisions, which are treated as investment centres. Data for
LO3 each division for Year 4 are as follows (in '000s):

	Division A	Division B
Net income	$ 65,000	$140,000
Total assets	$400,000	$850,000

The company's required rate of return is 15%. The president wishes to evaluate the performance of these divisions and is not sure whether to use return on investment (ROI) or residual income (RI) as the performance measure.

REQUIRED Which division performed better based on the ROI and RI performance measures?

18.18 ROI, Required Rate of Return An investment of $900,000 is made to purchase assets to operate a business. After
LO3 one year of operations, the company reported sales of $1,200,000 on costs of $1,000,000. The company's residual income at the end of the year was $2,000.

REQUIRED What minimum required rate of return on investment has the company established?

18.19 Responsibility Centres, ROI, RI Spring Bulbs operates two divisions, which are treated as investment centres. Data for each division for the current year are as follows (in '000s):

LO2, LO3

	Division T	Division I
Net income	$ 85,000	$210,000
Total assets	$255,000	$840,000

The company's required rate of return is 12%. The president wishes to evaluate the performance of these divisions and is not sure whether to use ROI or RI as the performance measure.

REQUIRED Which division performed better based on the ROI and RI performance measures?

18.20 Responsibility Centres, Performance Measures Your brother recently bought a small business with several coffee carts located around the city. Two workers share responsibility for each cart. All beverages are prepared using identical recipes and ingredients, but the baked goods and other items sold by each cart are chosen by the employees who operate the carts each day. Your brother asked your advice in determining how best to compensate the employees. He thinks he should give them bonuses when costs are contained and pay them a flat salary otherwise.

LO1, LO2

REQUIRED
A. What type of responsibility centre is each cart?
B. List several financial performance measures that might be relevant for measuring employee performance.
C. List one non-financial measure that might be important to the success of this business.

18.21 RI, ROI, and EVA The following selected data pertain to Brannard Company's construction division for last year:

LO3

Sales	$2,000,000
Variable costs	$1,200,000
Traceable fixed costs	$ 200,000
Average invested capital (assets)	$3,000,000
Current liabilities	$ 200,000
Required rate of return	15%
Marginal tax rate	36%
Weighted average cost of capital	12%

REQUIRED
A. Calculate the residual income.
B. Calculate the return on investment.
C. Calculate the economic value added.

18.22 RI, ROI, and EVA The following selected data pertain to Coburg Company's furniture division for last year:

LO3

Sales	$5,000,000
Variable costs	$3,000,000
Traceable fixed costs	$ 500,000
Average invested capital (assets)	$7,500,000
Current liabilities	$ 500,000
Required rate of return	15%
Marginal tax rate	32%
Weighted average cost of capital	12%

REQUIRED
A. Calculate the residual income.
B. Calculate the return on investment.
C. Calculate the economic value added.

18.23 ROI, RI, Breakeven Point, Contribution Margin Oslo Company's industrial photo-finishing division, Rho, incurred the following costs and expenses in the last period:

LO3

	Variable	Fixed
Direct materials	$200,000	
Direct labour	150,000	
Factory overhead	70,000	$42,000
General, selling, and administrative	30,000	48,000
Totals	$450,000	$90,000

During the period, Rho produced 300,000 units of industrial photo prints, which were sold for $2.00 each. Oslo's investment in Rho was $500,000 and $700,000 at the beginning and ending of the year, respectively. Oslo's weighted average cost of capital is 15%.

REQUIRED **A.** Determine Rho's return on investment for the year.
B. Compute Rho's residual income (loss) for the year.
C. How many industrial photo print units did Rho have to sell during the year to break even?
D. What was Rho's contribution margin for the year?

18.24 EVA for Segments Following is information for the Fulcrum Company's three business segments located in Europe:

LO3

	Segment A	Segment B	Segment C
Pretax operating income	€ 8,000,000	€ 4,000,000	€ 6,000,000
Current assets	8,000,000	6,000,000	8,000,000
Long-term assets	32,000,000	26,000,000	16,000,000
Current liabilities	4,000,000	2,000,000	3,000,000

Fulcrum's applicable tax rate for the segments is 30%, and its weighted average cost of capital for each segment is 10%.

REQUIRED Which segment has the highest EVA?

18.25 EVA for Segments Following is information for the Pyramid Company's three business segments located in the United Kingdom:

LO3

	Segment Beta	Segment Alpha	Segment Psi
Pretax operating income	£2,000,000	£1,000,000	£3,000,000
Current assets	2,000,000	1,500,000	4,000,000
Long-term assets	8,000,000	6,500,000	8,000,000
Current liabilities	1,000,000	500,000	1,500,000

Pyramid's applicable tax rate for the segments is 25%, and its weighted average cost of capital for each segment is 8%.

REQUIRED Which segment has the highest EVA?

18.26 Residual Income, Solve for Unknown A business segment reports income of $50,000, residual income of $(10,000), and total assets of $400,000.

LO3

REQUIRED Calculate the minimum return required by management.

18.27 ROI, Solve for Unknowns Data for three business units are shown below.

LO3

	Unit 1	Unit 2	Unit 3
Income	$10,000	D	G
Investment	A	E	$300,000
Sales	B	$500,000	H
Return on investment	20%	F	25%
Return on sales	C	10%	15%
Investment turnover	3.0 times	2.0 times	I

REQUIRED Determine the unknowns indicated by letters (A) through (I).

18.28 ROI, Solve for Unknowns Data for three business units are shown below.

LO3

	Unit 1	Unit 2	Unit 3
Income	A	$10,000	$15,000
Investment	$60,000	D	G
Sales	$200,000	E	H
Return on investment	33.33%	20%	25%
Return on sales	B	F	I
Investment turnover	C	3.0 times	5.0 times

REQUIRED Determine the unknowns indicated by letters (A) through (I).

18.29 Span of Control, General and Specific Knowledge, Performance Measures Barnett's is a boutique clothing store serving high-income customers. The store has two departments: women's and men's. Each salesperson receives a base salary plus commissions on net sales (sales to customers less returns) and has the authority to resolve customer problems, including the following:

LO1, LO2

- Returning or exchanging merchandise
- Holding sale merchandise for individual customers

REQUIRED **A.** To be effective, do the salespeople require general knowledge, specific knowledge, or both?
  B. What are the pros and cons of giving salespeople the authority to resolve customer problems?
  C. Does each sales associate seem to have a wide, moderate, or narrow span of control? Discuss.
  D. Suppose the store owner is considering adopting a bonus plan. Discuss the advantages and disadvantages of each of the following measures as a basis for salesperson bonuses:
   1. Total store sales
   2. Department sales
   3. Store gross margin
   4. Department gross margin
   5. Store earnings before interest and taxes (EBIT)

PROBLEMS

18.30 ROI, Transfer Prices, Taxes, Employee Motivation Fowler Electronics produces colour plasma screens in its Windsor, Ontario, plant. The screens are then shipped to the company's plant in Detroit, Michigan, where they are incorporated into finished televisions. Although the Windsor plant never sells plasma screens to any other assembler, the market for them is competitive. The market price is $750 per screen.

LO2, LO3, LO4

   Variable costs to manufacture the screens are $350. Fixed costs at the Windsor plant are $2,000,000 per period. The plant typically manufactures and ships 10,000 screens per period to the Detroit plant. Taxes in Canada amount to 30% of pretax income. The Canadian plant has total assets of $20,000,000.

   The Detroit plant incurs variable costs to complete the televisions of $110 per set (in addition to the cost of the screens). The Detroit plant's fixed costs amount to $4,000,000 per period. The 10,000 sets produced each period are sold for an average of $2,500 each. The U.S. tax rate is 45% of pretax income. The U.S. plant has total assets of $30,000,000.

REQUIRED **A.** Determine the return on investment for each plant if the screens are transferred at variable cost.
  B. Determine the return on investment for each plant if the screens are transferred at market price.
  C. To reduce taxes, will Fowler prefer a transfer price based on cost or market price? Explain.
  D. Will the top managers in each plant prefer to use cost or market price as the transfer price? Explain.
  E. What method could be used to resolve potential conflict over the transfer price policy?

18.31 ROI, Residual Income, Explaining the Better Measure The following financial data are for the evaluation of performance for Prairie Mining:

LO3, LO4

Average operating assets	$500,000
Net operating income	$65,000
Minimum required rate of return	10%

Prairie Mining currently uses return on investment to evaluate investment centre managers. An accounting intern from the local university has suggested to the controller that residual income may be a better performance measure.

REQUIRED **A.** Calculate ROI for Prairie Mining.

B. Calculate residual income for Prairie Mining.

C. Write a brief memo to the controller, explaining why residual income is a better performance measure than ROI in this case.

18.32 **Lease Versus Buy Decision, ROI, Residual Income, EVA, Manager Incentives** Refer to the information in Problem

LO 2, LO3 18.31. The manager of Prairie Mining is considering a new project. She can buy or lease equipment that will reprocess tailings from old mines to remove any traces of gold left behind by the original separating processes. The purchase price of the equipment is $150,000. The cost to lease is $2,000 per month. The manager estimates the return (incremental revenues minus incremental expenses, including lease cost) to be $40,000 per year. She knows that purchasing the equipment will increase the value of average operating assets. If she leases the equipment, expenses will increase, but assets will not. (In other words, the lease will be accounted for as an operating lease.) Although it is more cost effective to purchase the equipment, the manager has decided to lease it.

REQUIRED **A.** Calculate the new ROI if the equipment is (1) purchased or (2) leased.

B. Calculate the new residual income if the equipment is (1) purchased or (2) leased.

C. One of the adjustments that can be made using EVA is to treat all operating lease costs as if they were purchases—in other words, to capitalize the lease. If Prairie Mining used EVA with this adjustment, how might the manager's incentives and behaviour change? Explain.

18.33 **ROI, Residual Income, Explaining the Better Measure** The following financial data are for the evaluation of perfor-

LO3 mance for Far North Logging:

Average operating assets	$800,000
Net operating income	$ 92,000
Minimum required rate of return	10%

Far North Logging currently uses ROI to evaluate investment centre managers. An accounting intern from the local university suggested to the controller that residual income may be a better performance measure.

REQUIRED **A.** Calculate ROI for Far North Logging.

B. Calculate residual income for Far North Logging.

C. Write a brief memo to the controller, explaining why residual income is a better performance measure than ROI in this case.

18.34 **ROI, Residual Income, EVA, Effect on Investment Decision, Performance Evaluation** Strong Welding Equipment

LO3, LO4 Company produces and sells welding equipment nationally and internationally. Following is information about two divisions after exchange rate corrections:

	Brazil	Canada
Invested capital (total assets)	$4,000,000	$400,000
Net operating income	$1,000,000	$120,000
Required rate of return	10%	10%
Weighted average cost of capital	9%	9%
Current liabilities	$ 80,000	$ 10,000
After-tax income	$ 600,000	$ 80,000

REQUIRED **A.** Calculate each division's ROI.

B. Calculate each division's residual income.

C. Calculate each division's EVA.

D. Suppose the Brazilian division had an opportunity to invest $3,500,000 in a project that would generate sales of $5,000,000 and return on sales of 10%, or $500,000. Would the division manager be likely to undertake this project if he or she is evaluated using ROI? Explain.

E. Recommend a performance evaluation measure that would increase the managers' incentives to make decisions that would be in the best interests of the owners.

18.35 **ROI, Residual Income, EVA, Effect on Investment Decision, Performance Evaluation** BackCountry Hiking Company
L03 produces and sells specialty camping equipment nationally and internationally. Following is information about two
divisions after exchange rate corrections:

	Germany	Canada
Invested capital (total assets)	$400,000	$2,000,000
Net operating income	$100,000	$ 750,000
Required rate of return	10%	10%
Weighted average cost of capital	9%	9%
Current liabilities	$ 8,000	$ 40,000
After-tax income	$ 60,000	$ 300,000

REQUIRED **A.** Calculate each division's ROI.
B. Calculate each division's residual income.
C. Calculate each division's EVA.
D. Evaluate the two divisions. Write a memo to the CEO explaining the performance of the two divisions.
E. Suppose the German division had an opportunity to invest $350,000 in a project that would generate sales
of $500,000 and return on sales of 10%, or $50,000. Would the division manager be likely to undertake this
project if he or she is evaluated using ROI? Explain.
F. Recommend a performance evaluation measure that would increase the managers' incentives to make
decisions that would be in the best interests of the owners.

18.36 **EVA, Performance Evaluation** You have been asked to make a presentation to your class on economic value added
L03 (EVA). You decide to use data from a company that produces vaccines to illustrate the concept. You have collected
the following information to prepare your example. You were not sure which information you would need, so you
 collected more data than necessary.

Total cost and expenses excluding interest	$630,000
Development costs expensed in 2016 under IFRS	53,825
Development costs capitalized in 2016 under IFRS	15,000
EVA-adjusted total capital, December 31, 2015	550,000
Impairment loss of goodwill included in the calculation of IFRS income	22,225
Net interest expense	25,000
Research costs expensed in 2016 under IFRS	75,700
Revenues for 2016	1,250,000

Additional information:
Marginal tax rate = 35%
Market yield on equivalent debt = 10%
Shareholders expect a return equal to market yield plus 5%
Capital structure: Debt represents 75%, equity 25%
Assume that R&D costs occurred on January 1, 2016
Capitalized development costs are amortized over a period of 5 years for the purpose of determining IFRS
    income.
Development costs are amortized over the same period in the EVA-adjusted net income.

REQUIRED **A.** Compute the net profit.
B. Compute the weighted average cost of capital.
C. Compute the EVA-adjusted net income before taxes.
D. Compute the EVA.
E. Interpret the EVA results.

18.37 **ROI, Residual Income, EVA, NPV, Manager Incentives** Dubois Garage Doors (DGD) Ltd., has two divisions—Doors
L02, L03, and Electronic Components, which operate in a decentralized manner. The financial information of each division
L04 is shown as follows:

	Doors	Electric Components
Sales	$1,200,000	$2,550,000
Variable Costs:		
Direct Materials	180,000	357,000
Direct Labour	420,000	816,000
Variable Overhead	120,000	204,000
Total Variable Costs:	720,000	1,377,000
Contribution Margin	480,000	1,173,000
Fixed Overhead (excluding interest expenses)	180,000	451,000
Operating Income (EBIT)	300,000	816,000
Total Assets	$960,000	$3,000,000
Current Liabilities	192,000	900,000
Debt: Equity	3:2	1:1
Cost of Debt	10%	10%
Cost of Equity	14%	12%
Tax Rate	30%	40%

The manager of the Electronic Components has an opportunity to invest in a new machine costing $550,000 with a useful life of 5 years. The new machine will have no residual value at the end of the 5th year. The new machine will be able to reduce the direct materials and direct labour by 10% and variable overhead by 5%. The existing machine was purchased 5 years ago for $450,000, and can last for another 5 years with no residual value in 5 years' time. If the new machine is purchased, the existing machine can be sold for $50,000. The new machine will be financed through debt and equity with the same current capital structure, and the same cost of debt and equity in the Electronic Components division.

REQUIRED   **A.** Calculate each division's ROI, RI, and EVA.
  B. Calculate the net present value for the new investment project for the Electronic Components division, using the WACC as the discount rate.
  C. Calculate the ROI, RI, and EVA for the new investment project, using the WACC for the investment.
  D. Based on the calculations from (B) and (D), should DGD proceed with the investment?
  E. If you were the manager of the Electronic Components division and your performance evaluation is based ROI, would you proceed with the investment?
  F. Recommend a performance evaluation measure that would increase the managers' incentives to make decisions that would be in the best interests of DGD.

18.38 **NPV, Payback Period, ROI, EVA, Manager Incentives** Nutex Company operates as a decentralized organization. Its chips division is an investment centre and the divisional manager, Ms. Chaudry, is free to invest in any project that adds value to Nutex. The chips division's total assets are $3,500,000 and current liabilities are $700,000. The chips division is one of the best performers in the company and its return on investment is 20%. The chips division's capital structure is 50% debt at a cost of 10%, and 50% equity with a cost of 14%.

LO2, LO3, LO4

Ms. Chaudry is considering purchasing new equipment for $860,000. Its anticipated seven-year life will generate additional revenue of $320,000 and operating expenses, excluding amortization, of $115,000 annually. The straight-line amortization method will be used. At the end of seven years it will have a salvage value of $20,000. Nutex's tax rate is 40%.

REQUIRED   **A.** What is the net present value of the investment, using the WACC as the discount rate?
  B. What is the point of indifference in terms of the incremental cash flow for the investment?
  C. What is the payback period?
  D. What is the EVA for the current financial state of the chips division without the new investment?

E. Assume the chips division will finance the investment with the same cost structure and the same costs. What are the chips division's ROI and EVA for the investment?

F. Comparing the chips division's ROI and EVA before and after the investment, should Ms. Chaudry proceed with the investment project, if her performance evaluation is based on these two financial measures?

18.39 ROI, RI, EVA CLOC, an international company, produces and sells children's watches in Canada and Taiwan. Each

LO2, LO3 division operates as an investment centre. The divisions' financial information is shown below:

	Canada	Taiwan
Total Assets	$2,500,000	$1,500,000
Current Liabilities	300,000	120,000
Net operating income	875,000	600,000
Required Rate of Return	7%	9%
Debt: Equity	1:1	2:3
Cost of Debt	6%	8%
Cost of Equity	10%	11%
Tax rate	30%	25%

CLOC evaluates its divisional managers' performance based on ROI and EVA. The divisional managers will receive a bonus equal to 10% of the division's ROI, as long as the division has a 30% ROI and a positive EVA.

REQUIRED
A. Calculate each division's ROI
B. Calculate each division's RI.
C. Calculate each division's EVA.
D. CLOC has an opportunity for the divisions to invest in a project costing $500,000 that would generate annual revenue of $700,000 and operating expenses of $520,000. Would the divisional manager be likely to proceed with this investment opportunity, if his/her bonus is equal to 10% of the division's ROI? Support your answer by calculating the new ROI and EVA, including the new investment.

MINI-CASES

18.40 Choosing Type of Responsibility Centre, Support Cost Allocation, ROI The ATCO Company purchased the Dexter

LO1, LO2, LO3 Company three years ago. Prior to the acquisition, Dexter manufactured and sold plastic products to a wide variety of customers. Since becoming a division of ATCO, Dexter only manufactures plastic components for products made by ATCO's Macon division. Macon sells its products to hardware wholesalers.

ATCO's corporate management gives the Dexter division management a considerable amount of authority in running the division's operation. However, corporate management retains the authority for decisions regarding capital investments, price setting of all products, and the quantity of each product to be produced by the Dexter division.

ATCO has a formal performance evaluation program for the management of all of its divisions. The performance evaluation program relies heavily on each division's return on investment. The accompanying income statement of Dexter division provides the basis for the evaluation of Dexter's divisional management.

The corporate accounting staff prepares all of the division's financial statements. The corporate general services costs are allocated on the basis of sales dollars, and the computer department's actual costs are apportioned among the divisions on the basis of use. The net division investment includes division fixed assets at net book value (cost less amortization [depreciation]), division inventory, and corporate working capital apportioned to the division on the basis of sales dollars.

DEXTER DIVISION OF ATCO COMPANY INCOME STATEMENT
FOR THE YEAR ENDED OCTOBER 31, 20XX (IN '000s)

Sales		$4,000
Costs and expenses:		
Direct materials	$ 500	
Direct labour	1,100	
Factory overhead	1,300	
Total	2,900	

Less: Increase in inventory	350	
Cost of goods sold		2,550
Engineering and research		120
Shipping and receiving		240
Division administration:		
Manager's office	210	
Cost accounting	40	
Personnel	82	
Total division administration		332
Corporate headquarters costs:		
Computer	48	
General services	230	
Total corporate headquarter costs		278
Total costs and expenses		3,520
Divisional operating income		$ 480
Net plant investment		$1,600
Return on investment		30%

REQUIRED   **A.** Discuss the financial reporting and performance evaluation program of ATCO Company as it relates to the responsibilities of Dexter division.

B. Based upon your response to Part A, recommend appropriate revisions of the financial information and reports used to evaluate the performance of Dexter's divisional management. If you conclude that revisions are not necessary, explain why they are not needed.

18.41 **Responsibility Centres, Performance Measures** Harry Klein, inventor, formed Peerless Load Levellers Company in 1955 to produce a simple three-piece device for automatically levelling loads on industrial conveyor belts. As the business grew and prospered, Klein expanded the factory and added employees, but he continued to control every aspect of the enterprise himself. Klein hired only individuals who would follow his orders unquestioningly. Over the years, the product mix was expanded to include several products, all variants of the original design.

Klein felt no need to develop a human resources function, accounting systems, or computerized business systems. He also felt that he did not need a budget process. "I know exactly how well we are doing," he would repeatedly assert. "Why do I need some new budgeting idea to tell me what I already know?"

In 1995, Peerless reached a level of 180 production employees, three managers (who reported directly to Klein), and 20 clerical people. The three managers were John Richards, shaping and forming department; Karl Willis, assembly department; and Susan Lyle, finishing department. Each manager was responsible for all aspects of his or her department's product manufacturing, including purchasing, production, inspection, and customer complaints.

In 2011, Klein passed away unexpectedly. The situation at Peerless turned to chaos because only Klein had the complete view of the company. Eileen Klein-Robb, Klein's daughter and the current president, had never been involved in the business and needed help quickly. She engaged Robert Snider, a consultant, to determine what Peerless needed to do to bring sense and structure to the operation.

Snider, after studying the operation, suggested that Peerless needed a method of evaluating, monitoring, and controlling performance, especially at the production level. Snider's recommendation would not change the reporting relationships of Richards, Willis, and Lyle. However, the functions of the three managers would change in the following ways:

- Richards would be the purchasing manager and handle all vendor relationships and raw materials inventories.
- Willis would be the production manager and oversee three newly promoted supervisors of the shaping and forming department, the assembly department, and the finishing department.
- Lyle would be the quality manager and oversee product quality, inspection, customer relations, and engineering changes.

Snider also suggested installing a responsibility accounting and budgeting system to control performance at the various levels of production and management. Klein-Robb, although interested in this system, was uncertain and wanted more information about responsibility accounting.

REQUIRED
A. List four characteristics and requirements for a responsibility accounting system.
B. Describe the following centres, and define the mission of each one when used with a responsibility accounting system:
  1. Cost centres
  2. Profit centres
  3. Investment centres
C. **1.** Identify at least three advantages that may be gained from a responsibility accounting system.
  2. Identify at least one major risk of using a responsibility accounting system.
D. If Eileen Klein-Robb were to incorporate Robert Snider's functional recommendations at Peerless Load Levellers, identify and explain at least two specific operational performance measures that Klein-Robb should implement for these roles:
  • John Richards, purchasing manager
  • Karl Willis, production manager

18.42 **Integrating Across the Curriculum—Business Law:** *Executive compensation for public companies, CSA disclosures*

The Canadian Securities Administrators (CSA) outlines specific disclosures about executive compensation for public companies. The following webpage contains information about CSA executive compensation disclosure regulations: www.securities-administrators.ca/aboutcsa.aspx?id=978.

REQUIRED
A. Discuss why the CSA requires special disclosures for executive compensation.
B. Conduct research to locate the annual CEO compensation report contained in a business publication such as *The Globe and Mail*. Pick a company in the report, and answer the following questions:
  1. What types of information does the report provide?
  2. What rating was given for the CEO compensation of your company? How was the rating determined?
C. For the company you selected in Part B, conduct research to identify the company's disclosures about executive compensation. Answer the following questions:
  1. Discuss the ease with which you located the executive compensation information.
  2. The CSA requires companies to "provide enough information and explanation to allow a reader to understand the disclosure elsewhere in this form." Discuss whether the information you found met this requirement.
  3. Summarize the major types of pay received by the company's CEO.
  4. Does the company appear to use performance-based pay in compensating its top executives? Explain.
D. Describe uncertainties about whether the CEO pay for your company was reasonable.
E. Draw your own conclusion about whether the CEO pay for your company was reasonable. Explain.

18.43 **Integrating Across the Curriculum—Finance:** *Calculation of weighted average cost of capital* The weighted average cost of capital (WACC) is the weighted average after-tax cost of an organization's various sources of financing, such as debt and stock. In this chapter, you learned that WACC is used when calculating economic value added. WACC is also used in capital budgeting (Chapter 13).

Calculations for the weighted average cost of capital are usually found in finance textbooks. The formula is simple: determine how much financing comes from various sources and then calculate the weighted average. For example, suppose a company has $600,000 financing from debt at a pretax interest rate of 7% and $400,000 financing from equity having a cost of 9%. The company's tax rate is 30%, and only the interest is tax deductible. WACC is 6.54%, calculated as follows:

Source	Market Value	After-Tax Proportion	Cost	Weighted Cost
Debt	$ 600,000	60%	4.9%	2.94%
Equity	400,000	40%	9.0%	3.60%
Total	$1,000,000	100%		6.54%

Although the computations are simple, it is not always easy to find the information needed for the computations. For example, consider the following balance sheet for Amazon.com as of December 31, 2007 (amounts in millions).[18]

EXCERPTS FROM BALANCE SHEET:

Current liabilities		$2,532
Long-term debt and other		$1,574
Common stock—$0.01 par value		
Authorized shares—5,000		
Issued and outstanding shares—847 shares	$ 4	
Additional paid-in capital	$ 3,063	
Treasury stock, at cost	($ 500)	
Accumulated other comprehensive income (loss)	$ 5	
Accumulated deficit	($1,375)	
Total stockholders' equity		$1,197
Total liabilities and stockholders' deficit		$6,485

EXCERPTS FROM NOTES 4 AND 5: LONG-TERM DEBT AND OTHER

The Company's long-term debt and other long-term liabilities are summarized as follows (in millions):

4.75% Convertible Subordinated Notes	$899
6.875% PEACS due February 2010	$350
Other long-term debt	$ 50
Less: Current portion of long-term debt	($ 17)
Tax contingencies	$ 98
Long-term capital lease obligations	$ 62
Construction liability	$ 15
Other long-term liabilities	$117

REQUIRED
A. Explain why book values might be poor estimates of market values for Amazon's debt and stock.
B. Which liabilities do you think should be included in the WACC computation? Explain your choices.
C. Identify possible sources of information for the following:
  1. Market value of common shares
  2. Cost of equity capital
  3. Market value for each type of debt
  4. Pretax interest rates
  5. Income tax rate

---

[18] Amazon.com financial statements are available at http://phx.corporate-ir.net/phoenix.zhtml?c=97664&p=irol-reportsAnnual.

19

Strategic Performance Measurement

After studying this chapter, you should be able to do the following:

L01	Discuss strategic decision making
L02	Describe how financial and nonfinancial measures are used to evaluate organizational performance
L03	Explain the balanced scorecard
L04	Explain how the balanced scorecard is implemented
L05	Discuss how the balanced scorecard affects strategic management and incentives

in brief Successful organizations adopt a strategic decision-making process to ensure that strategies and operating activities are aligned with the organization's vision and core competencies. They also engage in continuous improvement by monitoring and learning from the results of their strategies and operations. Accountants develop and track a variety of financial and non-financial measures to monitor results. The balanced scorecard is one formal method for identifying and measuring an organization's performance as it relates to the organization's vision. A strategy map identifies the interdependencies between key financial and non financial perfomance measures and how they link to achieve the organization's vision. Approaches such as the balanced score-card and strategy maps motivate individuals and units throughout an organization to work toward a common vision, and improve strategic and operating success. ■

The Balanced Scorecard: The Lifeblood of Decision-Making

Adrian Wyld/The Canadian Press

SOURCES: "Canadian Blood Services Performance Review: Final Report," Ernst & Young, April 2013; P. Crookall, "Building Trust Through Performance Management," *Canadian Government Executive*, Vol. 15, Issue 3, May 7, 2012; B. McDonald, "A Review of the Use of the Balanced Scorecard in Healthcare," BMcD Consulting, April 2012; "Palladium Group Honors Canadian Blood Services and the Republic of Korea's Ministry of Government Administration and Home Affairs with Prestigious BSC Hall of Fame Award," Palladium Group news release, October 10, 2007; "Canadian Blood Services Honoured for Excellence in Strategy Management," Canadian Blood Services news release, October 11, 2007; G. Sher, "Canada's Blood System: From Bust to Trust," *Globe and Mail*, November 26, 2007.

When Canadian Blood Services was created in 1998 to take over the management of the blood supply from the **Canadian Red Cross** everywhere except Quebec, the new non-profit organization was in a crisis management phase. Canadian Blood Services' first priority was to ensure the safety of blood and increase public confidence in the blood supply after tainted blood in the 1980s and 1990s resulted in thousands of Canadians becoming infected with HIV and hepatitis C. It was considered one of the worst public-health crises in Canada's history.

In 2003, Canadian Blood Services moved from crisis mode into strategic management. It adopted a strategy map and balanced scorecard approach to link their core values to their mission by evaluating key relationships. The strategy map links Leadership, Culture, and Resources to Saving and Improving Lives, Productively and Efficiently, by Leveraging Our Capabilities to improvements in Stewardship, which is directly linked to the organization's mission. Among the things it measures are volunteer satisfaction, safety indicators, and talent management.

Canadian Blood Services implemented balanced scorecards at all levels: its board of directors, Chief Executive Officer, corporate level, senior executives, and all divisions. Canadian Blood Services created an Office of Strategy Management headed by the Vice-President, Strategy Management, who reports directly to the CEO. This office is responsible for, among other things, monitoring balanced scorecard results and trying to improve them and align them with the organization's strategy.

The balanced scorecard approach achieved impressive results. The public's level of trust of the organization went from less than 50% to 85%. Key staff are expected to be competent in strategic management, just as they are in safety, security, and trust. In 2007, Canadian Blood Services became the first Canadian non-profit to be inducted into the Balanced Scorecard Hall of Fame for Executing Strategy from the professional services firm Palladium Group, Inc.

While many organizations use a balanced scorecard to merely measure their performance, Canadian Blood Services also uses it to manage its strategy. The organization says a balanced scorecard keeps it focused on making decisions based on data, not intuition, and allows it to manage changes such as reacting to the West Nile virus and being given a new mandate to manage tissue and organ donations.

"The balanced scorecard concept has improved our internal alignment, enhanced our metrics-based decision-making, and makes allocating resources against priorities easier," said Dr. Graham Sher, Canadian Blood Services' CEO. "In short, it has changed how we manage the blood system by crystallizing what's important to our organization and its mission." The balanced scorecard approach "has resulted in Canadian Blood Services moving forward with its change agenda and producing dramatic performance improvements."

Strategic Management and Decision Making

L01   Discuss strategic decision making

This textbook began with an overview of management decision making in Chapter 1. The process summary in Exhibit 19.1 assumes that managers make decisions in a strategic way. Periodically, managers clarify the organization's vision and core competencies. The vision is the core purpose and ideology of the organization, while the core competencies are the organization's strengths relative to its competitors. Strategies are ways in which managers can take advantage of core competencies while working toward the organization's vision. Strategies guide long-term decisions, such as the types of goods and services offered and the long-term methods of competition. Strategies also lead to operating plans, including an annual budget, and link these plans to long-term goals. In turn, operating plans guide short-term decisions such as decisions about launching advertising campaigns, hiring employees, or purchasing inventory. As organizations' operations unfold, results are measured and monitored against both short-term operating plans and long-term strategies. The feedback loops shown in Exhibit 19.1 lead to revisions at any of the levels of management decision making.

The nature of an organization's strategies and operating plans influences the types of strategic objectives that are used and tactical plans that are developed. **Strategic objectives**, the specific goals that managers choose to measure and monitor, help motivate employees to carry out strategies and plans.

▶EXHIBIT 19.1

Overview of Management Decision Making

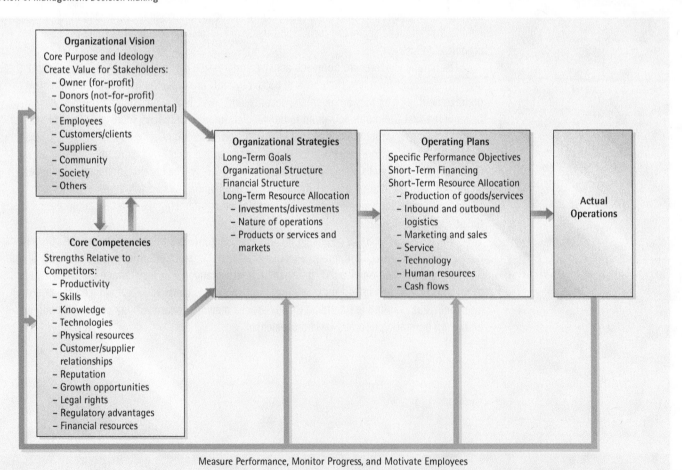

Organizational Vision

Core Purpose and Ideology
Create Value for Stakeholders:
- Owner (for-profit)
- Donors (not-for-profit)
- Constituents (governmental)
- Employees
- Customers/clients
- Suppliers
- Community
- Society
- Others

Core Competencies

Strengths Relative to Competitors:
- Productivity
- Skills
- Knowledge
- Technologies
- Physical resources
- Customer/supplier relationships
- Reputation
- Growth opportunities
- Legal rights
- Regulatory advantages
- Financial resources

Organizational Strategies

Long-Term Goals
Organizational Structure
Financial Structure
Long-Term Resource Allocation
- Investments/divestments
- Nature of operations
- Products or services and markets

Operating Plans

Specific Performance Objectives
Short-Term Financing
Short-Term Resource Allocation
- Production of goods/services
- Inbound and outbound logistics
- Marketing and sales
- Service
- Technology
- Human resources
- Cash flows

Actual Operations

Measure Performance, Monitor Progress, and Motivate Employees

For example, being the market leader for a specific product might be a long-term goal. This goal could be tied to the performance objective of achieving a 35% market share within a five-year time horizon. **Tactical plans**, or short-term plans and budgets, give employees specific guidance and responsibilities for progress toward strategic objectives. For example, the marketing department might develop plans and be given an annual budget to launch new promotional activities for increasing market share. The Canadian Blood Services used a balanced scorecard approach to help it increase public trust from less than 50% to 85%. This was a critical step in regaining public confidence in the Canadian blood supply.

A successful organization communicates to all employees its organizational vision, strategies, goals, and objectives. This communication helps align employee goals with organizational goals. Accountants develop and track financial and nonfinancial performance measures to evaluate the efforts of individual employees, teams, departments, divisions, and sub-units. When performance measures are monitored and communicated throughout the organization, progress toward the vision is more easily evaluated and rewarded.

Communicating the Organization's Vision

The concept of organizational vision—core purpose and ideology—is broad. Managers sometimes divide the vision into separate statements. The definitions of these statements vary from organization to organization. In general, a vision statement is a theoretical description of what the organization should become. Canadian Blood Services vision statement focuses on Canadians having confidence in the blood products provided by the organization. A mission statement is a high-level declaration of an organization's purpose. A core values statement is a summary of the beliefs that define the organization's culture. The core values of Canadian Blood Services are a "call to action" for how it works and include: safety, integrity, quality, respect, excelling, accountability, and openness.[2] Together, these statements convey the organization's overall direction and approaches toward its various stakeholder groups.

The vision and mission statements for Giant Tiger are shown in Exhibit 19.2. Giant Tiger's statements are closely aligned and highlight the importance of affordability and a family friendly environment. The mission statement for Giant Tiger is more specific than the vision statement about products and customers. The "What is Giant Tiger?" synopsis clearly points out the main goals of Giant Tiger for franchisees, managers, employees and interested external stakeholders to use in decision making.

▣ **ALTERNATIVE TERMS**

Strategic objectives are related to the term *preset goals*, introduced in Chapter 1, and are sometimes called *key performance indicators.*

▣ **BUSINESS PRACTICE**

Even as the world becomes increasingly complex, the common characteristic of great organizations in the past, present, and future is top leaders who carefully adapt cultures to future needs while "consistently adhering to well-understood values."[1]

Vision Statement:

To be Canada's favourite, affordable, and friendly family destination for fashion, food, and fun.

Mission Statement:

We endeavour to grow market share and profit by attracting customers and inspiring them to frequent visits with a compelling mix of current fashion, food, and family items arriving daily always at the best value and low everyday prices in a convenient, friendly, and highly entertaining shopping experience.

What is Giant Tiger?

• A truly Canadian franchised family discount store chain.

• A place of employment for over 6,500 people.

• An outlet for products of over 2,000 suppliers.

• A progressive, value-oriented, no-nonsense approach to retailing.

Source: Giant Tiger: www.gianttiger.com/. Used by permission.

▶ **EXHIBIT 19.2**
Vision and Mission of Giant Tiger

---

[1] G. M. C. Fisher, "Leading in an Increasingly Complex Society," *Technology in Society*, 26(2–3), April–August 2004, pp. 371–374.
[2] Canadian Blood Services, Our Values, accessed at www.blood.ca/en/about-us/mission_vision_values.

Managers do not always define and communicate their vision using vision, mission, and core values statements. For example, Giant Tiger is moving more toward a description of "Who we are" on its website. The description clearly communicates the mission, vision, and core values without using the business terms, to appeal to a wider reader audience.[3]

Clarifying Core Competencies and Developing Strategies

⊠ **CHAPTER REFERENCE**
Supply chain analysis, just-in-time production and purchasing, re-engineering, target costing, kaizen costing, and life cycle costing are discussed in detail in Chapter 15.

How an organization clarifies its core competencies and develops its strategies are closely related. Organizations are likely to be more successful when their core competencies and strategies are well aligned.

When identifying and choosing strategies, managers anticipate responses from customers, suppliers, competitors, and others. Managers must also continually visualize new ways to gain competitive advantage. Frequently, strategies that worked in the past must be modified or replaced. However, managers consider a few general types of strategies in their decision-making processes, as described next.

Cost Leadership. One way to compete effectively is to maintain lower costs than those of competitors. Company management continuously searches for cost reductions and then passes the savings on to its wholesalers, retailers, and then, the customers in the form of lower prices. Lower costs are achieved through techniques such as supply chain analysis, just-in-time production and purchasing, re-engineering, target costing, kaizen costing, and life cycle costing. Investments in new technologies and other long-term resources can also reduce costs.

⊠ **BUSINESS PRACTICE**
Giant Tiger's strategy is clear in its slogan, which proclaims that the company is the "all Canadian family discount store offering everyday low prices."[4]

Product Differentiation: Quality and Functionality. In industries with customers willing to pay higher prices for higher quality or more functionality, managers strategically differentiate their products and establish market positions. For example, Kodiak, a specialty footware company in Ontario, has achieved success by specializing in winter boots and working boots. Kodiak boots are specially designed to withstand the harsh Canadian winters.[5]

⊠ **CHAPTER REFERENCE**
Definitions for and examples of price skimming, penetration pricing, and peak load pricing are presented in Chapter 14.

Other Pricing Strategies. Sometimes managers engage in pricing strategies that take advantage of special circumstances through practices such as price skimming, penetration pricing, and peak load pricing. Some of these strategies work only for certain time periods, such as before competitors enter a market. Others, such as peak load pricing, can be used over long periods of time.

Developing Operating Plans

Once strategies are developed, they should lead to an organization's operating plans. Operating plans typically include tactical plans for achieving the strategic objectives. Budgets are often used to define performance objectives for revenues, costs, cash flows, and so on. Tactical plans describe specific operating activities. For example, Tim Horton's 2014 outlook included opening 140 to 160 new restaurants in Canada, 40 to 60 new full-serve restaurants in the United States, and additional capital expenditures between $180M and $220 M.[6]

[3] Giant Tiger website, www.gianttiger.com/category/about-us/who-we-are.do?nType=2.
[4] Giant Tiger website, www.gianttiger.com.
[5] J. Balakrishnan, J. B. Eliasson, and T. R. C. Sweet, "Factors Affecting the Evolution of Manufacturing in Canada: An Historical Perspective," *Journal of Operations Management*, 25(2), March 2007, pp. 260–283.
[6] Tim Hortons 2013 Annual Report, www.timhortons.com/ca/en/pdf/Tim_Hortons_2013_AR_full.pdf.

Strategic Decision Making Throughout an Organization

The strategic management process portrayed in Exhibit 19.1 applies to an organization as a whole. It also applies to subsets of an organization, such as business units, product lines, and functions (e.g., human resources, inventory management). Managers often develop strategic objectives as well as statements of vision, mission, and core values for individual divisions, product lines, and departments. These strategic objectives and related tactical plans help organizations assign decision authority and responsibilities to individual managers and other employees. When strategic objectives are well aligned throughout the organization, managers can more easily monitor the progress toward meeting overall goals within various parts of the organization.

> **CHAPTER REFERENCE**
> To learn more about assigning decision-making authority and responsibility centres, see Chapter 18.

Measuring Organizational Performance

Exhibit 19.3 illustrates a process that accountants and managers use to evaluate an organization's progress toward its vision. First, actual results are compared to plans. Then, any differences are analyzed. Finally, employees are rewarded, and improvements are identified for future planning. Re-evaluation of the vision is also often undertaken at this time. Both financial and nonfinancial measures are used to monitor performance and to provide information for this process.

> **LO2** Describe how financial and nonfinancial measures are used to evaluate organizational performance

Financial Measures

Managers traditionally relied on **financial measures** that provide information measured in dollars or ratios of dollars. Sales, costs, and operating income are among those measures usually obtained from the financial accounting system, which is designed to report financial measures for the overall organization, divisions, product lines, and departments. Financial measures are also used to compare budget numbers to actual results. Traditional financial measures are lagging measures, which are indications of what has already happened. They are often highly aggregated, which limits their usefulness in decision making about future planning. Lagging measures are also easily manipulated to indicate favourable short-term performance.

In its 2013 annual report, Tim Hortons' management reported several financial measures, including company-wide revenues, operating income, diluted EPS, the current ratio, the quick ratio, and the debt-to-equity ratio. It also reported same-store sales growth.[8] In all likelihood, more detailed information was used to evaluate performance for each franchise, but that information is not publicly available.

> **BUSINESS PRACTICE**
> CCM, known as Canada's source for skates, began operations in 1899 as Canada Cycle and Motor Co. Ltd., a producer of bicycles and the first truly Canadian car. Due to the economics of the auto business, CCM sold off the auto manufacturing part of the business and then the bicycle business to focus on skates.[7]

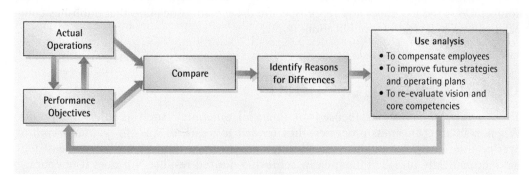

> **EXHIBIT 19.3**
> Monitoring Measurable Performance Objectives

---

[7] J. Balakrishnan, J. B. Eliasson, and T. R. C. Sweet, "Factors Affecting the Evolution of Manufacturing in Canada: An Historical Perspective," *Journal of Operations Management*, 25(2), March 2007, pp. 260–283.
[8] Tim Hortons 2013 Annual Report, www.timhortons.com/ca/en/pdf/Tim_Hortons_2013_AR_full.pdf.

Nonfinancial Measures

Nonfinancial measures provide performance information that cannot be measured in dollars. Defect rates, customer satisfaction, throughput time, and employee retention are among the nonfinancial measures used frequently in recent years to reflect performance that promotes long-term financial success. Nonfinancial measures are often **leading measures**, which are indicators of performance drivers. These measures capture information about processes, markets, customers, and employees. Leading measures are often stated in non-monetary terms and are forward looking.

Tim Hortons' sustainability report includes many nonfinancial measures. For example, under the "Individuals" factor, Tim Hortons measures sodium content, scholarships awarded, and guest comments. To assess their commitment to the community, Tim Hortons measures the number of disadvantaged children participating in their various sponsored programs and the number of farmers participating in partnership projects with the company.[9]

Using a Combination of Measures

A combination of measures is often used to monitor and motivate performance within an organization, as no single measure provides a complete picture of performance. Managers in different areas and at different levels within an organization need different types of information. These managers are responsible for different decisions and control different organizational resources, and no single measure will capture all these dimensions of responsibility. In addition, a combination of financial and nonfinancial measures is usually more consistent with an organization's long-term goals than financial measures alone, because visions and strategies are multifaceted.

One of Tim Hortons' main strategies is to provide customers with quick, friendly service. If managers were to use only a measure of how fast a customer is served to monitor and motivate performance, employees might be encouraged to prepare food in advance so that it could be delivered more quickly to customers or to minimize customer interaction. However, this practice would conflict with Tim Hortons' "always fresh" strategy that requires food to be freshly prepared—a fresh pot of coffee is made every 20 minutes. Customer sales might, ultimately, decline if the quality were lowered. In addition, advance preparation would probably increase waste, thereby increasing costs and lowering profits. To address all these goals simultaneously, Tim Hortons' managers monitor multiple performance measures, like customer delivery time, customer satisfaction, sales trends, and the cost of food products sold. These performance measures are presented in a strategy map, which shows the linkages between the measures and the ultimate impact on the organization's goal.

Once a set of performance measures is chosen, the information system is designed to collect data and produce periodic reports for these measures and their trends. For example, Wendy's service delivery time and customer preference measures might be obtained from data reported by outsiders, such as industry analysts, or from internal research. Sometimes, competitors agree to collect and report specific data to an association that publishes comparative data in an industry publication.

Balanced Scorecard

LO3   Explain the balanced scorecard

Traditionally, organizations focused on financial outcomes, such as sales and profits. When evaluating business processes, they tended to focus on ways to maintain control over product costs. Although financial outcomes are important, this limited focus does not automatically provide guidance in achieving desired results. Nor does it encourage

---

[9] Tim Hortons, *Making a True Difference: Sustainability and Responsibility* : 2014 Performance Highlights, http://sustainabilityreport.timhortons.com/2014-performance-report.pdf

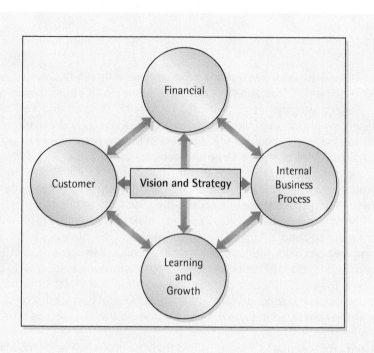

improvements when current financial results are satisfactory. Some organizations focused on long-term strategies, but their approaches were often informal and piecemeal. For example, organizations would collect data about customer satisfaction, but then only use the data to find areas that need immediate improvement, not as part of an overall strategic approach.

In the early 1990s, Harvard University professor Robert Kaplan and consultant David Norton developed the balanced scorecard, a formal method to incorporate both financial and nonfinancial performance measures into organizational management systems. The aim of the balanced scorecard is to translate organizational visions and strategies into performance objectives and related measures that can be monitored over time. The balanced scorecard approach helps managers more fully integrate strategies throughout the organization, anticipate and prevent possible future problems, and identify and take advantage of opportunities.

At the heart of the balanced scorecard is a continuous strategic analysis of the organization from multiple perspectives. The most common approach is to use the four perspectives shown in Exhibit 19.4: financial, customer, internal business process, and learning and growth. Within each perspective, managers and other employees study the organization and identify linkages with other perspectives to create a strategy map. For example, if employees are better trained (under learning and growth), they are more likely to make suggestions that improve customer-related business processes, such as reducing the time between receipt of a customer order and product delivery. As customer satisfaction increases, financial performance is also more likely to increase. These analyses help accountants and managers identify the most important performance objectives—the aspects of operations that must be successful for the organization to achieve its vision. Measures are then developed for the performance objectives within each perspective to help managers and employees monitor and work toward long-term goals.

▶ BUSINESS PRACTICE
Ultra Electronics Maritime Systems, Nova Scotia, has rolled out balanced scorecard objectives so that even objectives for office employees are tied to strategic initiatives. Donna Rice, CMA, FCMA—the company's vice president of finance and administration—stated, "The balanced scorecard has given everyone a closer connection to our results and to business process in general."[10]

---

[10] R. Colman, "Navigating Strategic Change," CMA *Management*, 80(6), October 2006, p. 40.

example

royal philips electronics
ADOPTING THE BALANCED SCORECARD

Ihar Ulashchyk/Getty Images

By 2011, **Royal Philips Electronics** was a global conglomerate with 116,000 employees and sales outlets in 150 countries. Philips Canada, located in Markham, Ontario, began operations in 1934. Philips Canada employs more than 500 Canadians in sales and service of medical systems for diagnosis and therapy, lighting technologies, shavers, and consumer electronics. In the early 2000s, the Philips board of management in Europe responded to a perceived need to streamline management of such a large and complex organization with a diverse group of product lines and divisions. They decided that the balanced scorecard could be used both to align the organization around the company's vision and to help employees better understand the business and their respective contributions to the overall organization.

In 2002, Philips' organizational vision was "Let's make things better." This vision included making better products, better systems, and better services. The strategy at Philips was to find new ways to improve products and to offer innovative products to consumers. The company's quality program encompassed all employees. The overall strategy was to strive to be one of the best companies in the world: the best to trade with, work for, and invest in. To help achieve its goals, Philips underwent a balanced scorecard analysis. Several balanced scorecard measures developed for Philips are listed in Exhibit 19.5. We discuss these measures next, as we learn about each perspective.

By 2004 and probably due to insights gained from the analysis, Philips modified its organizational vision to be to bring "sense and simplicity" to people. The updated strategy was to strive to be a "truly market driven and people centric company." In September 2006, Philips sold 80.1% of its semiconductor business. Building on its previous analysis, Philips' "Vision 2010" was unveiled in the 2007 annual report. In line with Vision 2010, in January 2008, the organizational structure was simplified. After successfully repositioning Philips through the guidelines of Vision 2010, top management released Vision 2015 in September 2010. This new strategic plan builds on the successes of its predecessor and charts a course for growth and a stronger commitment to "sense and simplicity."

Source: Royal Philips Electronics website, www.philips.com; and A. Gumbus and B. Lyons, "The Balanced Scorecard at Philips Electronics," *Strategic Finance*, November 2002, pp. 45–49. See also "About Philips," www.philips.ca/about/index.page; http://www.annualreport2010.philips.com/content_ar-2010/presidents_message.asp?global_en_ar2010_relatedlinks#section5&origin=search. ■

Financial Perspective and Related Measures

When accountants and managers analyze their organizations from a **financial perspective**, they identify desired financial results, given the organization's vision. For-profit organizations usually have goals of providing owners with some level of return on investment. Not-for-profit organizations typically have financial goals of maintaining a certain level of financial liquidity and stability, accumulating sufficient resources for some long-term purpose, or gaining maximum efficiency from resources. Financial goals and objectives encourage managers to evaluate the effectiveness of their strategies and operating plans, based on the economic well-being of the organization. They also help employees relate the activities they perform to the organization's financial outcomes.

> **CHAPTER REFERENCE**
>
> For more information about return on investment, residual income, and economic value added, see Chapter 18. For budgets and their variances, see chapters 10 and 11.

Financial perspective measures are designed to determine an organization's progress toward desired financial results. In for-profit organizations, these measures are usually related to profitability, growth, and owner value. Common measures include operating income, return on investment, residual income, and economic value added. In not-for-profit organizations, financial measures often include operating income, cost per service provided, and variances from budgets.

Some of the financial perspective measures adopted by Philips are shown in Exhibit 19.5. Similar measures are used by other large conglomerate for-profit organizations. Economic profit implies measuring long-term profitability, whereas income from operations measures

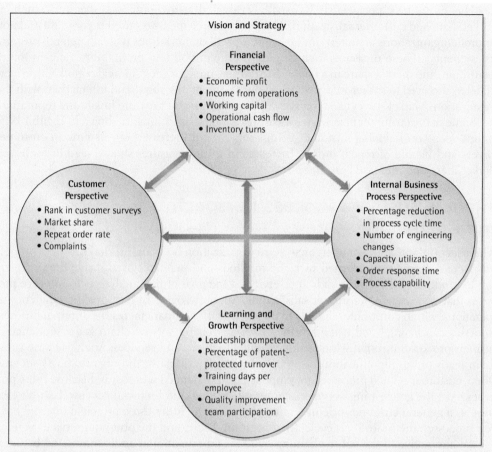

Source: *Strategic Finance* by Institute of Management Accountants Copyright 2002 Reproduced with permission of INSTITUTE OF MANAGEMENT ACCOUNTANTS in the format Textbook via Copyright Clearance Center.

EXHIBIT 19.5
Balanced Scorecard Measures at Royal Philips Electronics

short-term results. Focusing managers' attention on inventory turns, working capital, and operational cash flows should increase operating income and add to long-term economic profits.

Customer Perspective and Related Measures

When accountants and managers analyze an organization from a customer perspective, they are concerned with identifying the customers they want and developing strategies to get and keep them. The analysis includes identifying the targeted customers, markets, and products that are most consistent with the organization's vision and core competencies. Organizations that better meet customer needs—creating value for customers—are also more likely to generate desired financial results. Thus, this link connects the financial and customer perspectives. In assessing customer needs, managers consider their organizational strategies and examine the nature of products or services compared to consumer views about trade-offs among price, quality, and functionality.

In evaluating an organization's relationship with customers, managers consider processes such as delivery time and accuracy. Ordering and payment processes are also important. For example, customers increasingly demand sophisticated e-business capabilities. In addition, future changes in customer preferences and competition must be considered. Philips has recognized the needs of its customers by introducing EcoVision5, which specifies three sustainability performance indicators: care, energy efficiency, and materials. EcoVision5 includes targets for all of the key performance indicators and assigns a specific business segment to take a leadership role in achieving the targets.[11]

---

[11] Philips, "EcoVision5," www.philips.com/sites/philipsglobal/about/sustainability/ourfocus/ecovision5.page.

The customer's perspective is usually evaluated using outcome measures such as market share and customer satisfaction. The performance measures used in for-profit and not-for-profit organizations are often similar (not-for-profit organizations typically refer to customers as clients). These measures include customer retention and profitability, new customer acquisition, and market share in a targeted market segment or geographical region. Customers are often surveyed to gather information on their perceptions about and interactions with the organization. Market surveys and focus groups are also used to measure image and reputation.

Some of the customer perspective measures adopted by Philips are shown in Exhibit 19.5. Philips' focus on reducing customer complaints should increase both its rank in customer surveys and its rate of repeat orders. Increases in these measures should lead to increased market share and increased profitability.

Internal Business Process Perspective and Related Measures

When accountants and managers analyze an organization from an **internal business process perspective**, they are concerned with the methods and practices used inside the organization to produce and deliver goods and services. One goal of this analysis is to improve processes that will increase customer satisfaction. Another goal is to improve the efficiency of operations, which contributes directly to the organization's financial results. Internal business processes can be analyzed using a value chain approach. A value chain is the sequence of business processes through which value is added to goods and services. Analysis of the value chain leads to the identification of processes that are critical to the organization's success. Often, customer-related processes are emphasized in balanced scorecards, because these processes have the greatest impact on customer satisfaction and financial success. Exhibit 19.6 presents a generic customer-oriented value chain that includes three principal internal business processes: the innovation cycle, the operations cycle, and the post-sales service cycle.

An alternative to the value chain approach is an operational audit conducted by internal auditors. An operational audit is an objective and systematic examination of evidence to provide an independent assessment of the performance of an organization, program, activity, or function. Operational audits provide information to improve accountability and facilitate decision making.

Innovation Cycle and Related Measures. The first step in the value chain, the **innovation cycle**, is concerned with processes to identify customer needs and to design goods and services that meet those needs. Many organizations mistakenly focus their efforts primarily on more efficient production of existing products. Yet goods and services must meet customer needs. The balanced scorecard encourages managers to establish internal processes that identify customer preferences for quality, functionality, and price and also predict the potential market size. Organizations often use market and customer research to identify and nurture new markets, new customers, and new needs of current customers. Managers

► EXHIBIT 19.6
Customer-Oriented Value Chain Analysis

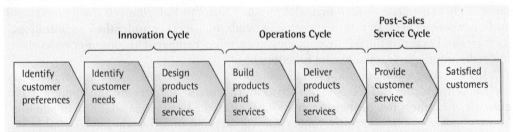

Source: Robert S. Kaplan and David P. Norton, "Linking the Balanced Scorecard to Strategy," in California Management Review. Vol. 39, no. 1 (Fall 1996), pp. 53–79. © 1996 by the Regents of the University of California. Reprinted by permission of the University of California Press.

---

[12] M. Semansky, "Small Is Beautiful," *Marketing*, 113(7), April 28, 2008, p. 26.

brainstorm completely new products and also develop new opportunities and markets for existing products. An example of innovative change to an existing product is repackaging soup so that consumers can heat a single serving in the microwave without pouring the soup from a can into a different container.

The innovation process also ensures that proposed goods and services are produced efficiently, given an organization's core competencies. For example, organizations use target costing and kaizen costing to reduce product prices and improve quality.

Operations Cycle and Related Measures. The second step in the value chain, the opera-tions cycle, is concerned with production and delivery of goods or services that are identified and designed in the innovation cycle. The operations cycle addresses the short-term well-being of the organization. It begins with the systems used to accept and process customer orders and is complete with delivery of the good or service. Quality, efficiency, consistency, and on-time delivery are emphasized in this part of the value chain.

Historically, many organizations focused on the operations process. Cost containment goals and cost monitoring methods were often in place at the commencement of operations. Traditional financial measures such as standard costs, budgets, and variances were often used to monitor operational performance. This focus sometimes led to suboptimal behav-iour. For example, efficiency measures create incentives to build inventories so that labour and machines are kept busy. Quality is sacrificed to increase efficiency. Excessive inventory levels and poor quality are costly to organizations over time. As a result, traditional measures of operations may be only a small part of the balanced scorecard approach.

Over the past several decades, organizations have increasingly competed on quality and timely delivery, in addition to price. Measurements of quality, cycle time, and cost are developed to monitor and enhance performance in these areas. With the growth of Internet sales, competition on price and product customization has intensified. For example, price information about computers and peripherals is widely available on the Internet, both by manufacturers such as Dell and Apple Computer and by retail sellers such as Best Buy (www.bestbuy.ca). To be competitive, organizations must improve their operations processes to meet or beat their competitors' prices, quality, and reliability.

Organizations that specialize in custom products often measure the accuracy with which orders are completed and the speed of delivery. The specific operating characteristics identified and monitored as performance objectives depend on the organization's vision, core competencies, and strategies. Managers choose performance measures to monitor orga-nizational progress, rewarding positive trends in areas that lead to customer satisfaction and financial success.

Post-Sales Service Cycle and Related Measures. The final step in the value chain, the post-sales service cycle, considers the service provided to customers after product delivery. Post-sales services include providing warranty work, handling returns, correcting defects, and collecting and processing payments. In addition, when products are highly sophisticated, organizations often train the employees who will be using them. Another aspect of the post-sales service cycle is the safe disposal of hazardous wastes and by-products.

For some organizations, post-sales service is part of a product differentiation strategy. Hospitals have recently focused on the billing and collection processes of post-sales service. By emphasizing accurate coding on patient bills, hospitals have fewer claims denied by insurers and increase their operating revenues. To achieve greater accuracy in coding, many hospitals provide in-depth employee training and hire better-educated employees in their billing and collections departments.

Performance measures for customer-related post-sales service could include aspects of the billing and collections cycle, such as the dollar amount of bad debts and days in accounts receivable. In addition, costs for warranty work and rework can be measured, or the number of defective products returned or reworked can be tracked. Measures for waste and by-product disposal could include number of kilograms of waste and clean-up costs.

---

[13] G. H. Anthes, "ROI Guide: Balanced Scorecard," *Computer World*, February 17, 2003.

Traditional Versus Balanced Scorecard Approaches to Internal Business Processes. Traditionally, internal operations were monitored to improve existing operations. With the balanced scorecard approach, the emphasis is on identifying *new* processes and eliminating non-value-added processes. In addition, the balanced scorecard approach strives to incorporate innovative processes into operations, whereas traditional measurement systems emphasize delivery of today's products to current customers.

Some of the internal business process perspective measures adopted by Philips are shown in Exhibit 19.5. Reductions in cycle time free resources for alternative uses. Philips continually improves current products and develops new products and, therefore, benefits from reduced cycle times for current products. As the number of engineering changes increases, disruption of the manufacturing cycle increases, because new designs are implemented or different components are required in the manufacturing processes. Optimal response time keeps inventory levels low but also reduces potential stock-outs.

Learning and Growth Perspective and Related Measures

When accountants and managers analyze an organization from a learning and growth perspective, they are concerned with achieving future success by discovering new and better strategies. They also want to improve customer satisfaction and internal business processes, ensure that employees have sufficient knowledge and expertise, and check that internal processes support existing strategies. The learning and growth perspective is naturally linked to the internal business process perspective. As managers focus on improving internal business processes, they also identify opportunities for enhancing the capabilities of employees, information systems, and operating procedures. To take advantage of these opportunities, employee training and education are emphasized, as is the development of information technology and systems. For example, Walmart developed innovative uses of technology to identify potentially profitable products and improve efficiency of its supply chain. By analyzing and improving procedures, organizations also work toward aligning the goals and objectives of all stakeholders, including employees, suppliers, customers, and shareholders. Implementation of a balanced scorecard system is an example of this type of process; it is a formal method for engaging in learning and growth throughout an organization.

Employee learning and growth measures include satisfaction, retention, training, and skill development. These measures are tailored for the type of organization and industry. To assist in decision making, information systems must produce timely, reliable, and accurate information about customers, competitors, and operations. Measures of information timeliness and accuracy include number of days to close (the amount of time that elapses before financial statements are available to managers) and errors per report. Over time, company policies become outdated. These policies need to be analyzed periodically to determine whether they are current or should be changed in response to new knowledge or technologies. A performance measure could be the number of times that policies and procedures are reviewed over a five-year period. To monitor learning and growth measures, current performance of operations is usually used as a baseline, and improvements are evaluated over time.

Some of the learning and growth perspective measures adopted by Philips are shown in Exhibit 19.5. Because research and development is such a large part of Philips' strategy, the percentage of patent-protected turnover (sales to value of patent assets) is measured and monitored to determine returns on investments in research and development. In addition, employee training needs to be current and appropriate. Setting benchmarks for an optimal amount of employee training helps managers provide funds and time for employee training.

---

[14] C. A. Boivie, "Red Light, Green Light: How One CIO Used Project Management Discipline and the Traffic Light Report to Align Her IT Department with Her Company's Business Goals," *CIO*, 19(17), June 15, 2006, p. 1.

Balanced Scorecard Performance Measures and Concepts Introduced in Prior Chapters

Many performance measures or concepts related to the four perspectives in balanced score-cards were introduced earlier in the textbook. The cost function and cost-volume-profit techniques introduced in chapters 2 and 3 can be used during balanced scorecard imple-mentation to anticipate the financial effects of operating changes in the internal business process and customer perspectives. Chapter 4 explored decisions that affect internal busi-ness processes, such as make or buy decisions, optimal use of constrained resources, and the effects of bottlenecks on production. Chapters 5 and 6 addressed the customer and internal business perspectives by introducing quality issues and explaining how quality costs are cal-culated and recorded. Chapter 7 presented information related to the customer and internal business perspectives, including customer profitability calculations, costs and benefits of reducing defect rates and investing in quality improvements, and alternative ways to mea-sure capacity. Chapters 10, 11, 13, 14, 15, and 18 introduced a variety of measures related to financial performance.

●●⊘ RISK OF BIASED DECISIONS: INFORMATION OVERLOAD

INFORMATION OVERLOAD refers to an excess amount of information, making it difficult for individuals to absorb and use information effectively. Information overload makes it difficult for managers to identify informa-tion that is crucial to maintaining efficient operations or that may signal the need for change, thus increasing the likelihood of poor decisions. This problem intensifies as operations become more complex and managers attempt to monitor ever-increasing numbers of performance measures. Strategic management systems such as balanced scorecards can either increase or decrease information overload. Some organizations develop overly complicated balanced scorecards, making it difficult for managers to maintain their strategic focus. Accordingly, most experts recommend keeping the number of strategic objectives and individual measures at reasonably low levels. However, reducing the numbers of objectives and measures can lead to biased decision making if key business risks or link-ages are not addressed in the scorecard design.

Implementing the Balanced Scorecard

The process of implementing the balanced scorecard is summarized in Exhibit 19.7. These general steps are customized for each organization.

LO4 Explain how the balanced scorecard is implemented

Clarifying Vision, Core Competencies, and Strategies

Clarifying an organization's vision, core competencies, and strategies is central to the bal-anced scorecard approach. The vision provides an overall direction for the organization. The core competencies and strategies provide guidance for achieving the organizational vision over the long term. To clarify the vision, statements are developed at the organiza-tional level and for divisions, product lines, or departments. This process leads to discus-sion and consensus, which further clarify an organization's purpose. Similarly, the process of clarifying core competencies and strategies helps others understand how to achieve the organization's vision.

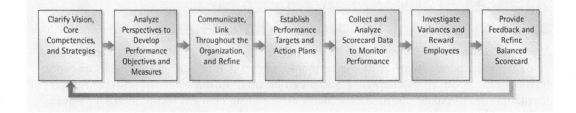

≥ **EXHIBIT 19.7**

Steps in Implementing the
Balanced Scorecard

Analyzing Perspectives to Develop Performance Objectives and Measures

The next step after clarifying is to analyze the organization from the four perspectives. This step translates the organization's vision and strategies into a set of performance objectives within each perspective. The analyses identify what the organization must do well to attain its vision, focusing on the linkages between perspectives. The strategic objectives should be limited to factors that achieve the organization's vision and strategies and are measurable.

The **strategy map** presents a visual summary of the strategic objectives for the four perspectives of the balanced scorecard. The map is often presented as a set of hypothesized cause-and-effect relationships. Consider the information for Philips' balanced scorecard shown in Exhibit 19.5. Specific types of employee training (learning and growth perspective) could lead to improved order response time (internal business process perspective), in turn leading to greater market share (customer perspective), and finally, to higher income from operations (financial perspective). The process of creating a strategy map requires managers to clarify strategic priorities and to explain how high-level strategies link to the work done by employees throughout the organization. Thus, the strategy map becomes both a strategic planning tool and a communication device. The Community Hospital illustration in Appendix 19A includes a strategy map example.

Strategy maps were originally adopted as a tool to help managers construct the balanced scorecard. However, because these maps create a one-page picture of the most important aspects of organizational strategy, many managers realized their value as a strategic tool. Strategy maps provide an easy way to communicate what the organization plans to accomplish. In addition, the process of developing the strategy map at the organizational and sub-unit levels requires discussion and consensus among teams of managers, and thus improves the alignment of efforts.

Communicating, Linking Throughout the Organization, and Refining

The balanced scorecard is usually presented as a top-down plan. High-level executives define the vision, core competencies, and strategies of the organization and then communicate them to divisions and departments. Yet success of the balanced scorecard approach depends on the efforts of individuals throughout an organization. To succeed, the balanced scorecard must be communicated both up and down the organization. Links must be developed between organizational, divisional, departmental, and individual objectives. Aligning goals increases the likelihood that all employees work together.

To strengthen the alignment of strategic goals, the organization level balanced scorecard is "rolled-out" to all segments (e.g., divisions, departments, product lines, etc.) of the organization. This is best accomplished by preparing balanced scorecards for each segment that are directly linked through the vision statement to the organization's balanced scorecard. In this way, it is clear that achieving the segment vision also supports achieving the organization vision. Then, segment perspectives are identified and linked through a

[15] Chen, Y., Yu, Z., and Lin, T. W., "How ZYSCO uses the Balanced Scorecard," *Strategic Finance*, January 2015, pages 27–36.

strategy map. Objectives, measures, and targets are developed for each segment perspective. Collectively, the segment balanced scorecards represent the whole organization. From the segment balanced scorecards, each individual can understand how his/her work contributes to achieving the organization's goals.

Sometimes the results of multiple units are formally combined into the results of another unit. For example, the results of individual departments might be combined into the results of a division. Exhibit 19.8 shows an abbreviated version of the balanced scorecard from the Finance and Administration Division at Carleton University. It provides a sampling of the initiatives that make up the university's strategic plan.[16] Data for the Athletics, Computing and Communications Services, Finance, Human Resources, Institutional Research and Planning, Internal Audit and Advisory Services, Pension Fund Management, Physical Plant, University Safety, and University Services departments are combined

▶EXHIBIT 19.8

Balanced Scorecard at Carleton University

Finance and Administration Division

Strategic Planning

Strategic Measures and Initiatives: 2014–2015

Quadrant	Objective	Measures	Initiatives	Accountability
Our Customers	C.1: Provide quality, responsive and helpful service.	Employee and customer satisfaction rating	C.1.1. Share and discuss with dept./unit feedback received from the customer groups.	F & A Leaders
			C.1.2. Revisit Service Excellence standards and their impact.	F & A Leaders
	C.2 Foster a culture of service excellence.	Each dept./unit has a clear understanding of the needs and values of their key customer groups.	C.2.1 Focus on the Voice of the Customer: a) Understand the needs and values of Key Customer Groups.	F & A Leaders
Stewardship of Resources	F.2: Manage risks that affect the university.	Key Risk indicators developed.	F.2.1. Develop Key Risk indicators.	AVP Financial Services
The Way We Work	I.1: Deliver a consistent methodology to document key processes and procedures.	Methodology selected.	I.1.1. Select methodology and tools to document key processes.	Director, OQI–Lead, AVP (University Services), CIO and Excellence Working Group
		Pilot project implemented.	I.1.2. Pilot methodology and tools to document key processes.	Director, OQI–Lead, AVP (University Services), CIO and Excellence Working Group
Our Employees	L.1: Provide a healthy workplace and supportive environment.	Evaluation of health promotions.	L.1.1. Provide Health Promotion workshops/information sessions/ resource areas that further engage our employees.	AVP (University Services), Director, OQI
		Increase in participation.	L.1.1. a) Provide flexibility for staff to participate in Health Promotion.	F & A Leaders
		There is an increased awareness of work–life balance options.	L.1.2. Enhance work-life balance by raising awareness of available options.	AVP Human Resources
		Successfully implemented Healthy Workplace Plan.	L.1.3. Implement Healthy Workplace Plan–Year One.	F & A Leaders

Source: Carleton University's Finance and Administration Division Balanced Scorecard, Strategic Measures and Initiatives, 2014–2015, http://carleton.ca/finance-admin/ strategic-initiatives; 2014–2015 balanced scorecard, http://carleton.ca/finance-admin/wp-content/uploads/Copy-of-Balanced-ScorecardFAdivision2014-2015.pdf

---

[16] Carleton University Finance and Administration website, http://carleton.ca/finance-admin/strategic-initiatives; 2014–2015 balanced scorecard, http://carleton.ca/finance-admin/wp-content/uploads/Copy-of-Balanced-Scorecard FAdivision2014-2015.pdf

into a single balanced scorecard within the Finance and Administration division. For instance, the Athletics department provides a broad spectrum of athletic opportunities to the Carleton community. The University Safety department's goal is to provide excellent customer service with respect to safety to the Carleton community. However, all departments share the same mission: to "contribute to Carleton's academic mission of teaching, research, and community service by providing professional services that are effective, efficient, and timely."

Sometimes, a common set of balanced scorecard measures is used across departments. For example, the student customer satisfaction rating and the employee customer satisfaction rating in Exhibit 19.8 are identical for the University Services, Computing and Communications Services (CIO), Physical Plant, Human Resources, Finance, and Pension Fund Management departments. These measures are common because some of the performance objectives are the same. Common measures help ensure consensus throughout the organization, minimizing the need to develop separate systems for data collection. Measures that differ across offices relate to operating activities that are unique to individual offices.

Organization-wide implementation of the balanced scorecard, such as occurred at Carleton University, requires significant amounts of communication and time. The process often begins with pilot projects and then expands across the organization as experience is gained and additional buy-in takes place. Refinements are often made to the original balanced scorecard after organizations have implemented it at the lowest levels.

Establishing Measures, Tactical Plans, and Performance Targets

It is not sufficient for an organization to create the balanced scorecard to measure progress toward its long-term vision and strategies. The organization must also establish specific performance measures, tactical plans, and performance targets, all of which are usually tied directly to each strategic objective in the balanced scorecard.

For each strategic objective, one or more measures are identified to monitor the organization's progress. The measures are a combination of financial and nonfinancial, covering both quantitative and qualitative data. Accountants are often more comfortable with quantitative measures, such as the average time to complete a customer's order or the number of new customers obtained. However, qualitative data, such as the results of customer and employee satisfaction surveys, are useful for some strategic objectives. Companies are increasingly using *voice of the customer* marketing research techniques such as Philips' customer satisfaction survey. Input measures capture activity or effort, whereas outcome measures capture results. For example, the measures for Philips' balanced scorecard in Exhibit 19.5 include both order response time (an input measure) and market share (an outcome measure). Overall, balanced scorecards usually contain a range of measures.

Tactical plans, sometimes called *strategic initiatives*, are the short-term plans and budgets that enable employees to work specifically toward each strategic objective. **Performance targets** are the goals set for individual measures, typically over three- to five-year periods with interim milestones. Targets increase the organization's focus on long-term results and assist managers in monitoring results.

For example, Rob Scullion, CGA, reports the success story of Thomas Press's use of the balanced scorecard to get employees to work toward common goals. The Thomas Press scorecard includes objectives, goals, measures, and key performance factors for each of the four perspectives. For example, the financial perspective objective is to "maximize customer alteration revenue." The goal for this objective is to "eliminate occurrences of alterations/changes not being invoiced." To measure achievement of this goal, Thomas Press calculates the "percentage of total sales attributable to client changes." The key performance factor or action plan is to "ensure that client changes are quoted and pre-approved by the client." Although these financial targets were not met in the first year of implementation of the balanced scorecard, many of the other objectives were met. As a result, the employees received a bonus for the objectives that were achieved, although it was not the maximum bonus available as the financial objectives were missed.[17]

When the balanced scorecard is used to compensate employees, different weights are placed on various measures in employee bonus packages. For example, if customer satisfaction ratings are inadequate, bonuses are made more dependent on improved satisfaction ratings. However, finding the optimal weighting among measures is difficult. If too much weight is put on customer satisfaction and not enough is put on financial measures, employees may spend a great deal of time in activities that increase satisfaction but do not improve profits.

Collecting and Analyzing Scorecard Data

Balanced scorecard measures are captured periodically, which might mean monthly, quarterly, annually, or for other time frames. Scorecard data are collected and analyzed for different measures using different time frames. For example, some of the measures for "The Way We Work" perspective in Exhibit 19.8 are collected and monitored annually while others are updated throughout the year or as projects are completed.

Before calculations and comparisons to targets can be performed, systems for data collection must be established. In some cases, accounting systems are developed to capture relevant data. Nonfinancial measurement instruments may need to be developed. Survey instruments are either acquired or developed. Methods then need to be established for collecting samples and summarizing results. Balanced scorecard measures are compared to targets and ongoing trends are analyzed.

Investigating Variances and Rewarding Employees

Actual results are compared to performance targets to determine whether the results are better or worse than desired. Then significant variances are analyzed to identify their causes, leading to modifications in future plans. Throughout time, trends in balanced scorecard measures are monitored and analyzed. Once targets are achieved, new targets may be set or new measures may be introduced. If the balanced scorecard is also used for employee compensation, rewards are computed and distributed in accordance with previously determined agreements.

Providing Feedback and Refining the Balanced Scorecard

An important part of the balanced scorecard method is the feedback loop that uses results and experience to refine the process. Managers use their analysis of balanced scorecard results to evaluate the success of their strategies and operating plans. This evaluation leads to revisions in organizations' visions, core competencies, strategies, and operating plans.

The effectiveness of the balanced scorecard is also gauged at this stage. Accountants and managers modify the set of measures to adapt to changes in the organization and to provide better information over time. Some measures may be dropped or changed, and new measures may be added. An example of the implementation of the balanced scorecard in a healthcare setting is presented in the appendix to this chapter.

[17] R. Scullion, "The Scorecard Part II," *Canadian Printer*, Vol. 113(4), June 2005, p. 56.
[18] R. Angel and D. L. Carlson, "Just DO IT," *CA Magazine*, 140(6), August 2007, p. 28.
[19] Y. C. L. Chan, "Cascading a Clear Focus," *CMA Management*, 81(6), October 2007, p. 28.

Balanced Scorecard, Strategic Management, and Incentives

The balanced scorecard (and similar types of scorecard systems) can be a useful part of the feedback loop shown in Exhibit 19.1; they contribute to an organization's management control systems by measuring and monitoring organizational performance and motivating employees to take actions consistent with organizational strategies. In this section we summarize the strengths of balanced scorecards and identify a number of weaknesses.

Strengths

Organizations are under increasing pressure to meet customer needs, use resources efficiently, compete effectively under changing conditions, employ new technologies and operating methods, and provide a good return to shareholders. These demands require more effective implementation of vision and strategies. The proponents of the balanced scorecard method argue that it improves performance by helping organizations integrate their visions and strategies into operations more completely. Many of the advantages of this approach, already described, are summarized in Exhibit 19.9.

Weaknesses

> **BUSINESS PRACTICE**
>
> While president and CEO of **GE Canada Commercial Finance**, Equipment Financing, Canada, Patrick Palermer stressed the importance of senior management buy-in for the successful use of the balanced scorecard to manage business.[20]

Any method designed to help organizations improve management decision making involves weaknesses, because the process of management decision making is inherently uncertain. No perfect solutions have yet been discovered. Major weaknesses of the balanced scorecard approach are summarized in Exhibit 19.9. First, the balanced scorecard faces questions about its costs and benefits. Considerable time and effort are needed to develop and use the balanced scorecard. Outside consultants are often employed, and the time involved for key managers can be considerable.

> **EXHIBIT 19.9**
>
> Strengths and Weaknesses of Balanced Scorecard

Strengths	Weaknesses
Communication and linkages: • Encourages clarification and updating of vision and strategies • Improves communication and consensus throughout the organization • Links short-term and long-term performance objectives to the vision and strategies	Implementation is expensive and time consuming Uncertainties: • Appropriateness of vision and strategies • Accuracy of identified core competencies • Best set of performance objectives and measures • Reliability of scorecard data • Reasonableness of targets • Doubt about links among perspectives
Guidance for improvements: • Enables periodic performance reviews of progress toward vision and strategies • Leads to improved financial performance • Helps managers use operational data for decision making	Mistakes in implementation: • Ambiguous or generally defined objectives • Information systems not integrated • Insufficient resources • Lack of senior management support • Focusing on inappropriate objectives
Motivation: • Aligns unit and individual goals with the organizational vision and strategies • Motivates employee effort • Reduces optimization of sub-units at the expense of the organization as a whole • Promotes action toward achieving strategies	Biases: • Manager selection of familiar or easily attainable objectives and measures • Resistance from units and individuals • Process viewed as a temporary fad May be inappropriate for compensation. Vision may not adequately capture core values, including relations with regulators, approach toward the environment, etc.

[20] D. Rivest, "Creating the Digital Cockpit," *CMA Management*, 80(1), March 2006, p. 36.

Business Risks and Uncertainties. Business risk and uncertainty are part of any balanced scorecard. The underlying assumptions are that the vision and core competencies have been properly identified, and that implementation of the organization's strategies leads to success. However, the best choices for a vision and set of strategies are ambiguous; managers might incorrectly identify the organization's strengths relative to competitors.

Furthermore, the process of identifying appropriate performance objectives and measures is not straightforward. The balanced scorecard methodology requires managers to identify the most important aspects of operations, yet these cannot be known with certainty. Once performance objectives are selected, additional uncertainty about the best set of measures arises. Some measures are more reliable than others, although less reliable measures can at times address a more relevant aspect of operations.

Uncertainties about choices of information for the balanced scorecard challenge managers and accountants. For example, potential customer satisfaction measures include market share, number of return customers, number of new customers, and ratings on satisfaction surveys. Although the number of return customers and number of new customers can be measured with a high degree of accuracy, this information may not be as relevant for gauging customer satisfaction as other measures. Market share may or may not be reliable, depending on the accuracy of information about total industry sales. Many factors influence the reliability of survey ratings, including the survey design, methods for collecting samples, and the types of customers surveyed. To decide on the best measure, managers and accountants need to weigh the quality and relevance of information across potential measures.

Another uncertainty is the best choice for performance targets, including how quickly an organization should be able to achieve its strategic objectives. Low targets may fail to motivate sufficient effort. High targets discourage performance when employees perceive them as being unrealistic.

The balanced scorecard assumes specific linkages among the four perspectives. In particular, it assumes that improved performance in internal business processes and in learning and growth lead to improved customer-related measures. In turn, improved customer-related measures are assumed to lead to improved financial performance. These assumptions, however, might not hold because of uncertainties about the measures and about the interrelationships among aspects of an organization's activities. Each organization must commit to the effort and time it takes to identify the perspectives and linkages that describe its strategic objectives.

Mistakes in Implementation. Analysts and consultants point out a number of areas where mistakes are often made in balanced scorecard implementations, leading to poor results. Sometimes performance objectives are ambiguous or defined too generally, reducing the effectiveness of a balanced scorecard in communicating the actions needed to achieve the organization's vision and strategies. Sometimes, the organization's information systems are not designed to adequately capture information needed. The balanced scorecard can be expensive to implement and may face inadequate resources for designing, implementing, communicating, following through on results, and refining the methodology over time. Although senior managers are generally involved in the initial adoption of the balanced scorecard, they may give the process inadequate support.

Another mistake relates to the selection of inappropriate objectives. Author Jim Collins argues that many companies focus on the wrong financial measures. His research suggests that managers of the best-performing companies often succeed because they adopt more insightful measures to monitor their businesses. For example, Gillette shifted its focus from profit per division to profit per customer. This shift helped the company recognize the importance of repeatable purchases of high-margin products such as Mach3 razor cartridges. Companies where managers failed to adopt similarly insightful measures were not as successful.[21]

---

[21] J. Collins, *Good to Great: Why Some Companies Make the Leap . . . and Others Don't* (New York: Harper Business, 2001), pp. 106–107.

Barriers to Implementing Strategies

Balanced scorecard proponents argue that strategies often fail in organizations because strategies and operations are disconnected. Kaplan and Norton argue that four barriers prevent strategic implementation:[22]

Vision Barrier	Few people in an organization understand its strategies.
People Barrier	Most employees' incentives are not linked to organizational strategy.
Resource Barrier	Resources, including time, energy, and money, are allocated without explicit links to organizational strategy.
Management Barrier	Top managers spend too little time discussing strategy.

Theoretically, the balanced scorecard should help companies overcome (or reduce) these barriers, align operations more closely with strategy, and lead to greater strategic success.

Biases. Several types of biases reduce the effectiveness of the balanced scorecard. Recent research suggests that managers select performance measures with which they are most familiar—measures that may not induce behaviour that leads to financial success.[23] In addition, managers have incentives to choose performance objectives and measures that highlight areas that are strengths instead of areas that need improvement. Further, technology allows for the collection of a great deal of data and the use of sophisticated analysis tools. Management biases may result in choosing data or analytical tools that support desired outcomes. Any organizational change is likely to encounter resistance. For example, employees may view the balanced scorecard as a temporary management whim that does not deserve their attention. These types of resistance can prevent the organization-wide commitment and effort required for balanced scorecard success.

Other Factors. Some questions surround whether or how the balanced scorecard should be used to compensate employees. Because of the uncertainties already discussed, many employees perceive balanced scorecard measures to be unfair for use in compensation calculations. In addition, weights or other formulaic approaches for using balanced scorecard results lead to game-playing and suboptimization, which are contrary to the purpose of the balanced scorecard.

Another criticism of the balanced scorecard approach is that it does not adequately capture core values, including relations with regulators or approaches toward the environment. An organization's core values are theoretically embedded in its vision and strategies. However, current literature on the balanced scorecard places little emphasis on values.

How Valuable Is the Balanced Scorecard?

Given the perceived weaknesses in the balanced scorecard, some people are inclined to dismiss this methodology; they want greater certainty about benefits. However, any method that managers use to help develop and implement business strategies is subject to significant

---

[22] P. R. Niven, *Balanced Scorecard Step-by-Step: Maximizing Performance and Maintaining Results*, 2e (John Wiley & Sons, 2006), pp. 10–11.
[23] M. Lipe and S. Salterio, "The Balanced Scorecard: Judgmental Effects of Common and Unique Performance Measures," *The Accounting Review*, 75(3), July 2000, pp. 283–296.

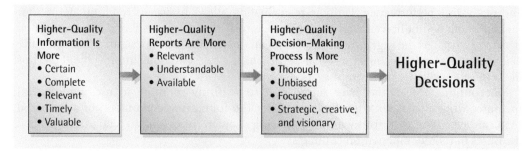

uncertainty. You learned in Chapter 1 about the path to higher-quality management decisions, presented again in Exhibit 19.10. Higher-quality decisions occur from use of the
following:

► Higher-quality information
► Higher-quality reports
► Higher-quality decision-making processes

The best questions to ask about the balanced scorecard methodology are whether it
helps managers and employees throughout an organization make higher-quality decisions
and whether the benefits from improved decision making exceed the costs of implementing and
maintaining the balanced scorecard. Is the information in the balanced scorecard of higher
quality than the information managers previously used? Are balanced scorecard reports
more relevant, understandable, and available on a timely basis? Does use of the balanced
scorecard encourage managers and other employees to be more thorough, less biased, more
focused, and more strategic, creative, and visionary? Proponents of the balanced scorecard
methodology argue that the answer to each of these questions is "Yes." They also point out
that the balanced scorecard should not be viewed as a static formulaic approach. Instead, it
must be re-evaluated and refined periodically to provide better information for monitoring

19-1 self-study problem   Balanced Scorecard Implementation, Pros and Cons

LO3, LO4,
LO5

Mountain High Bikes (MHB) wants to implement the balanced scorecard. Its mission statement
reads, "We build high-quality, reliable bikes at competitive prices." The company's competitive strategy is to continuously improve the functionality, reliability, and quality of its bikes, while holding prices
at levels similar to competitors. The company operates three sub-units organized around the product
lines for the three types of mountain bikes it currently produces. A fourth bike line in development
includes a finished design, with engineers currently working on the plans for the manufacturing process. MHB sells directly to bike shops and operates an Internet site that allows bike shops to place
orders for customized products.

required

A. Describe the implementation cycle for the balanced scorecard at MHB.
B. Describe the four perspectives of the balanced scorecard and list one or more performance
   objectives for each perspective that are likely to be important for MHB.
C. Pick one performance objective for each perspective in Part B and identify two or more potential
   measures. Explain how each measure would link to improve financial performance.
D. Describe the pros and cons of implementing the balanced scorecard for MHB.

See the solution on page 835.

and motivating performance. Periodic re-evaluation allows managers to eliminate or alter measures that do not fit well, and to identify potential new measures that offset unintended negative effects. As the organization learns, it can do a better job of designing and using the balanced scorecard. Organizations that fail to engage in continuous improvement are less likely to achieve high-quality results.

Accounting researchers have found that some firms continue to use nonfinancial measures while others abandon their use, after the initial implementation of a balanced scorecard type model.[24] Firms with the following characteristics tend to retain nonfinancial measures in their compensation contracts:

▶ Prospector firms with strategies that emphasize new product development and sales
▶ Firms with quality initiatives
▶ Firms in regulated industries
▶ Firms in industries with longer product development cycles

Distressed firms tend to abandon their use of nonfinancial measures. These firms may not have experienced benefits from nonfinancial measures and decide to focus primarily on financial results.

Balanced Scorecard and Levers of Control

The balanced scorecard can also be a key part of an organization's management control system. It is closely related to three of Simons' levers of control: beliefs systems, diagnostic control systems, and interactive control systems.

Beliefs Systems. Balanced scorecards can reduce the vision barrier by engaging people throughout the organization in discussions about organizational vision, strategies, and links

© NetPhotos/Alamy Stock Photo

●● > FOCUS ON ETHICAL DECISION MAKING: ACCOUNTABLE VOLUNTEER ORGANIZATIONS

Certified management accountants (CMAs) in Canada have helped volunteer-sector organizations develop accountability frameworks that measure progress in achieving their missions. The number and size of volunteer organizations is significant. Canada has 177,000 volunteer organizations with revenues of $90.5 billion, amounting to 12% of the Canadian gross domestic product. These organizations provide community and social services; organize cultural, educational, and recreational activities; and lobby for social, political, and economic change.

Some of these volunteer organizations have had serious problems, eroding public faith. For example, the Multiple Sclerosis Society of Canada fired members of its Calgary board because they had allegedly exceeded their power. The Canadian Society of Association Executives invested in technology projects that failed to meet their original financial projections, resulting in a $550,000 deficit for fiscal year 2001–2002. In 1996, 71% of survey respondents saw a need for greater accountability in this sector. Similar problems have arisen in the United States. For example, the American Red Cross has been criticized by some for its management of donations to the Liberty Disaster Relief Fund for the victims of the attacks on September 11, 2001.

Problems such as these prompted federal, provincial, and municipal governments to review existing volunteer sector codes, laws, and regulations. In addition, some volunteer organizations enlisted the help of CMAs to develop comprehensive performance measurement systems to gauge progress in achieving their missions. The organizations themselves are concerned that failing to meet public expectations in terms of quality and value will increase the opportunities of for-profit organizations to perform the same services.

---

[24] H. Hasab Elnaby, A. Said, and B. Weir, "The Retention of Nonfinancial Performance Measures in Compensation Contract," *Journal of Management Accounting Research* 17, 2005, pp. 23–42.

The CMAs encouraged the balanced scorecard approach for volunteer organizations. One organization adopting this approach is the **Ontario Physical and Health Education Association**, which helps children and youth live active, healthy lives. The organization set the following goals for measurement in its balanced scorecard:

- Improvement of performance, coordination, and productivity

- Greater focus on business objectives and clients' expectations

- Achievement and maintenance of high-quality goods and services to meet clients' stated and implied needs

An advantage of the balanced scorecard approach for volunteer organizations is the documentation it requires of financial and nonfinancial performance. When these organizations seek donations and grants from the local community and from provincial and federal governments, they produce evidence of their progress toward achieving their goals. Balanced scorecard reports reassure donors and grant selection committees that resources are used effectively and efficiently. A disadvantage is that the costs to the organization may exceed the benefits, particularly because resources allocated to the implementation process are no longer available for an organization's program.

Source: C. Markham, "Charity's Changed Environment," *CMA Management*, December 2002/January 2003, pp. 24–28; A. M. Chaker, "Red Cross Gives Disaster Relief to Tony Enclave," *The Wall Street Journal*, February 7, 2002, p. B1; and S. Brill, "An Excess of Riches," *Newsweek*, February 11, 2002, p. 40.

ETHICS OF RESOURCE USE

Is the efficient and effective use of resources an ethical issue for the managers of not-for-profit organizations? How is the well-being of society affected when not-for-profit organizations fail to use resources in an efficient and effective way? What ethical values would be present in the strengths and weaknesses of using a balanced scorecard in a not-for-profit organization?

to operating plans. Well-designed strategy maps visually communicate the links between what employees do and overall organizational goals. The process of designing and implementing a balanced scorecard motivates managers to explicitly clarify and prioritize strategic objectives and communicate them throughout the organization.

Diagnostic Control Systems. Balanced scorecards can reduce the people and resource barriers if they are integrated with budgeting and employee performance evaluation. Strategic objectives can be tied to specific tactical plans and measures, with results monitored regularly. Responsibility for achieving short-term and long-term targets can be assigned and rewarded. Resources are less likely to be wasted on non-strategic projects.

Interactive Control Systems. Balanced scorecards can reduce the management barrier by engaging managers in regular discussions about strategy. Organizational learning occurs as managers discuss evidence about the cause-and-effect links among the four perspectives and consider reasons for differences between planned and actual performance. The balanced scorecard is also intended to be flexible; managers are encouraged to re-evaluate and revise strategies, strategic objectives, and tactical plans as conditions change over time.

> **BUSINESS PRACTICE**
> In 2008, **The Hackett Group** found that 37% of world-class organizations use a mature balanced scorecard that combines financial and operational measures, compared to only 14% of peer-group companies.[25]

[25] The Hackett Group, "Business Performance Reports per Billion Dollars of Revenue," *Finance Metric of the Month*, July 2008.

APPENDIX 19A

An Example of Implementing the Balanced Scorecard: Community Hospital

Two hospitals in a U.S. city near the Mexican border have trauma centres, but neither trauma centre is financially successful. Because the town needs at least one trauma centre, the state and local governments meet with hospital officials to determine the best course of action. Both hospitals have spent considerable time reviewing their visions, core competencies, and current business strategies. They agree that only the teaching hospital should continue operating a trauma centre. The teaching hospital's mission is to provide both high-quality patient care and a learning centre for medical students. The teaching hospital needs a trauma centre so that medical students can prepare more thoroughly for careers as physicians and specialists. Teaching hospitals also have a mission to provide care to patients who are unable to pay,[26] and the trauma centre provides treatment for a large number of uninsured patients every year. Therefore, the decision to continue treating patients at the trauma centre fits well with the teaching hospital's mission.

> **▶ BUSINESS PRACTICE**
>
> As part of the quality improvement initiative in the health care system in Ontario, balanced scorecards were developed for specific medical services by the **Ontario Hospital Association (OHA)** and the Ontario government. These balanced scorecards are used by hospital administrators for strategic planning and evaluation purposes and by the general public for performance evaluation and comparison of service providers. Sunnybrook Health Sciences Centre shares its performance on its eight strategic goals, which are grouped into three dimensions on their interactive website.[27]

Top managers at the teaching hospital decide to institute the balanced scorecard. They focus first on service in the trauma centre, because many more patients will be admitted when the other hospital closes its trauma centre. These managers believe that new measures of efficiency could help ease the transition.

The managers are also concerned about the current losses incurred by the trauma centre. Care is provided for a number of patients who are unable to pay, including undocumented immigrants who, in attempting to cross the border desert in the heat of summer, suffer from dehydration and heat exhaustion. Uninsured car accident and gunshot wound victims also require care. Clinical processes in the trauma centre need to be both cost effective and high quality to maintain the hospital's reputation.

Clarifying Vision, Core Competencies, and Strategies

A team of hospital administrators and trauma centre employees meet to discuss the balanced scorecard implementation. The team decides that the hospital's vision, core competencies, and strategies also apply to the trauma centre. The hospital and trauma centre's patient care goals are to provide high-quality care in a timely manner and at a low cost for all patients, and also to provide care for patients who are unable to pay. The hospital and trauma centre's teaching goals are to provide a high-quality education for medical students, focusing on technological developments and innovative patient care treatment.

---

[26] The Commonwealth Fund Task Force on Academic Health Centers, "A Shared Responsibility: Academic Health Centers and the Provision of Care to the Poor and Uninsured," April 2001, www.commonwealthfund.org/publications/fund-reports/2001/apr/a-shared-responsibility--academic-health-centers-and-the-provision-of-care-to-the-poor-and-uninsured.

[27] Sunnybrook's Strategic Balanced Scorecard, December 2014, http://sunnybrook.ca/uploads/1/welcome/strategy/final_balanced_scorecard_board_december_2014.pdf.

Analyzing Perspectives, Developing Strategic Objectives, and Creating a Strategy Map

The team decides that the standard four perspectives (financial, customer, internal business process, and learning and growth) are appropriate for analyzing the trauma centre strategies and operations.

Financial Perspective. From a financial perspective, the hospital needs to at least break even to guarantee ongoing operations. The controller analyzes historical records for the trauma centre and finds that it has always operated at a loss. Until last year, research grants and government subsidies were usually enough so that the centre broke even. The financial perspective is important, because the centre needs financial resources to continuously update the equipment and technology needed to provide high-quality patient care. The team concludes that the most important strategic objectives for the financial perspective are to increase revenues and provide cost-efficient care.

Customer Perspective. Next, the team analyzes the customer perspective, focusing on two major customer groups: patients and the general public. The general public is concerned primarily with the overall reputation of the trauma centre, which depends on its ability to provide high-quality care in a timely manner. Maintaining a strong reputation increases the likelihood of future funding from research grants and government subsidies, and it increases the volume of patients who use the centre's services.

Patients are concerned with overall reputation and also the care they personally receive. After discussing the various factors that influence patient satisfaction, the team concludes that trauma centre patients are most concerned about the quality of care they receive and the amount of time they need to wait for service. The team believes that improving these two factors will lead to higher volumes of patients, which will increase revenues and reduce average cost per patient.

The team realizes that the two customer groups are interested in the same factors. Therefore, the team combines the two groups on the balanced scorecard and identifies only two customer-related strategic objectives—one for quality of care and one for timeliness.

Internal Business Process Perspective. The team next analyzes the internal business process perspective. To achieve the customer-perspective strategic objectives, internal processes need to focus on both the quality of medical treatment and timeliness. To achieve financial objectives, internal processes must also contain costs. The team identifies strategic objectives for three aspects of internal processes that are essential for the customer and financial strategic objectives, as described below.

The first strategic objective is to improve the centre's processes for admission, treatment, and discharge. Delays in service often occur when patients are transferred from one activity to another. The team believes that improved processes could reduce patient waiting time. The team would also like to motivate improvements in routine care, such as delivering medications, changing wound dressings, and answering call buttons. Process improvements include innovative ways to streamline daily routines, increase patient comfort, and deliver positive medical outcomes. In addition, the team would like to see greater focus on processes for discharging patients. Sometimes, patients are readmitted because complications arise at home. For example, patients may be readmitted when they become dehydrated at home. Some medications require patients to drink extra amounts of water, a requirement that must be carefully explained during the discharge instruction process so that patients can recover quickly and not require readmission. Some insurance companies will not pay for readmissions, and patients are unhappy when they have to return to the hospital.

The second strategic objective is to optimize staff scheduling. Sometimes patients must wait for long periods of time, a problem that cannot be fully resolved because of the random patterns in which patients come to the trauma centre. However, the team believes that

> **BUSINESS PRACTICE**
>
> The three dimensions chosen by Sunnybrook Health Sciences Centre are quality of patient care, research and education, and sustainability and accountability. These dimensions were considered critical to the success of the Sunnybrook health care organization. The strategic goals were identified in reference to these three dimensions.[28]

---

[28] Sunnybrook's Strategic Balanced Scorecard, December 2014, http://sunnybrook.ca/uploads/1/welcome/strategy/final_balanced_scorecard_board_december_2014.pdf.

> **EXHIBIT 19.11**
Strategy Map for Community Hospital
Trauma Centre

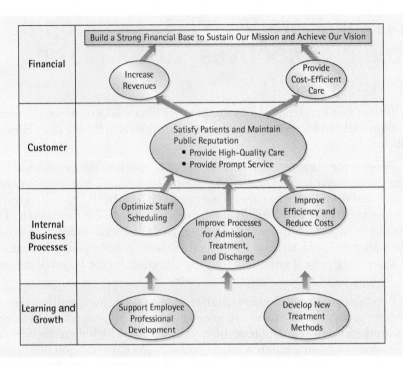

improvements can be made to staff scheduling, while simultaneously improving patient service and maintaining control over costs.

The third strategic objective is to improve efficiency and reduce costs. The team believes that staff members can identify a variety of ways to reduce costs and would like to encourage a greater focus on efficiency. For example, a number of uninsured patients do not realize that they are eligible for Medicaid insurance. Appropriately trained admissions personnel can assist patients in identifying insurance sources to help cover their hospital charges. By increasing the number of insured patients, the hospital is highly likely to decrease bad debts and charity care.

Learning and Growth Perspective. Finally, the team focuses on the learning and growth perspective and identifies two strategic objectives. First, the centre needs to continuously develop new treatment methods, which improve patient care and contribute to the centre's reputation. Second, the centre needs to support employee professional development. Because new technologies and care-giving practices are developed continually, the hospital and trauma centre provides a variety of medical education classes for nurses and other department staff.

Strategy Map. The strategy map shown in Exhibit 19.11 summarizes the team's work so far. The ovals represent the strategic objectives, and arrows show the cause-and-effect linkages between objectives. Because the learning and growth objectives relate to the centre's activities, arrows from that perspective are not linked to specific strategic objectives. All linkages ultimately lead to the centre's ability to build a strong financial base to sustain its mission and achieve its vision.

Many not-for-profit organizations place the highest strategic priority on the customer perspective, which is most closely related to organizational purpose. However, the team decided that the trauma centre should place highest priority on the financial perspective, to ensure that adequate attention is paid to financial stability.

Communicating, Linking Throughout the Organization, and Refining

After the team develops a tentative balanced scorecard for the trauma centre, the plan is presented to top hospital administrators and to employees in the centre. The administrators

> **BUSINESS PRACTICE**
To improve information transparency, Sunnybrook presents its strategic balanced scorecard on its website. Users may access increasing detail about each of the goals through the interactive features online or download a complete copy of the balanced scorecard.[29]

[29] Sunnybrook's Strategic Balanced Scorecard, December 2014, http://sunnybrook.ca/uploads/1/welcome/strategy/final_balanced_scorecard_board_december_2014.pdf.

consider whether the trauma centre objectives align with the overall hospital mission, strategies, and objectives. They believe that this scorecard appropriately addresses the hospital mission and praises the team. Employees and medical students also feel that the scorecard helps them understand how the trauma centre's objectives should be carried out. The team also gathers ideas from employees about possible measures.

Establishing Performance Targets and Action Plans

The team is now ready to finish designing the balanced scorecard. The first step is to identify one or more measures for each strategic objective shown in Exhibit 19.12. As the team identifies relevant measures, it also considers the availability of data and the quality of each measure.

Financial Measures. For the strategic objective "increase revenues," the team chooses two measures: total revenue and ratio of reimbursement to cost. Total revenue directly measures the amount of revenue. However, the team is concerned that revenue is measured with error, and the information may not be of quality high enough for a performance measure. The hospital's accounting system tracks patient charges for supplies and services by department; however, reimbursement (i.e., patient revenue) is tracked at the hospital level, because different payers pay different portions of charges, and some patients do not pay. Therefore, the patient revenue is allocated to the trauma centre based on its average mix of care for nonpaying, Medicare, insurance, and other patients. Nevertheless, the team decides to use total revenues for now, and to consider alternative measures after more experience with the balanced scorecard is gained. The ratio of reimbursement to cost, calculated as patent revenue divided by operating costs, addresses the trauma centre's ability to receive payment for its services.

BUSINESS PRACTICE

Each of Sunnybrook's eight strategic goals is elucidated in specific objectives. Specific indicators are identified and baseline, target, and current achievement levels are provided for each objective.[30]

EXHIBIT 19.12
Balanced Scorecard for Community Hospital Trauma Centre (Monthly Targets)

Perspective	Strategic Objectives	Measures	Targets
Financial	Increase revenues	• Total revenue	$5,650,000
		• Ratio of reimbursement to cost	65%
	Provide cost-efficient care	• Operating margin ratio	1%
		• Excess income margin ratio	3%
Customer	Provide high-quality care	• Average patient satisfaction rating (1–5, with 5 being highest)	4
		• Number of medication errors	1 error
	Provide prompt service	• Average nurse response time	2 min.
Internal Business Process	Improve processes for admission treatment, and discharge	• Number of process improvements in routine care	2
		• Readmission rate	1 readmit
		• Time spent on discharge instructions	20 min.
	Optimize staff scheduling, improve efficiency, and reduce costs	• Medical staff costs to patient revenues	30%
		• Average cost per patient	$31,400
Learning and Growth	Develop new treatment methods	• Number of new treatment methods developed	1 new method
	Support employee professional development	• Average training hours per employee	5 hours

[30] Sunnybrook's Strategic Balanced Scorecard, December 2014, http://sunnybrook.ca/uploads/1/welcome/strategy/final_balanced_scorecard_board_december_2014.pdf.

For the strategic objective "provide cost-efficient care," the team chooses two profit margin measures that are used by the hospital as a whole. Both ratios address the trauma centre's ability to control costs relative to revenues. The operating margin ratio, calculated as operating margin divided by patient revenue, measures profitability, considering only operating costs and revenues. The excess income margin ratio, calculated as operating plus non-operating income divided by operating plus non-operating revenue, takes into account non-operating revenue in the form of donations and grants, which typically supply the needed funds for expansion or new technology.

Customer Measures. For "provide high-quality care," the team identifies two measures: average satisfaction rating for quality of nursing and treatment care, and number of medication errors. The hospital outsources patient satisfaction surveying, and it monitors average satisfaction by department to focus on patients' perceived quality of care. However, the survey results are only available quarterly. The department wants measures that predict patient satisfaction and that can be monitored daily. With timely feedback, problems will be identified and corrected quickly, before too many patients are unhappy with some aspect of service. Therefore, the team would like to identify several quality-of-care measures. Currently, data are available for the number of medication errors, so that measure is chosen for the initial balanced scorecard. Additional measures will be identified in the future.

For "provide prompt service," the team identifies two measures: average nurse response time and average non-treatment time. The team believes that most patients would care about the average time they wait for a nurse to respond to their call buttons. Patient survey information is gathered by the Quality and Utilization Department. Although the team would like daily information, surveys about nurse response time to call buttons are given randomly to 20% of the trauma centre patients during the first three days of each month. The accounting department does not have time to track this measure more frequently. However, the team believes that data are available for calculating the average non-treatment time for trauma patients. The centre already records the time that each patient arrives and is discharged, and estimates of treatment times can be calculated from billing records. The team is not sure about the quality of this measure, so it will be used initially on an experimental basis.

Internal Business Process Measures. For "improve processes for admission, treatment, and discharge," the team identifies three measures: number of process improvements in routine care, readmission rate, and time spent on discharge instructions. Using the number of process improvements as a performance measure will encourage employees to generate new ideas. Once a month, accountants will meet with physicians and nurses to determine the number and type of improvements in routine care-giving processes. The readmission rate, calculated as the number of readmissions for the same medical condition divided by the total number of admissions, measures the quality of initial care and is likely to influence patient satisfaction. The trauma centre's managers consider post-treatment service to be very important. Service after a patient leaves the centre contributes to the quality of the patient's care. The team decides to measure this aspect using the time spent on discharge instructions per patient, which will be reported by discharge nurses using a new form developed by the accounting department. With more time spent on discharge instructions, patients should experience better home care, reducing the probability that they will be readmitted. The team considers measuring the number of phone calls made and e-mails sent with follow-up questions about patient home care, but decides that it is more important to focus on instructions before the patient goes home.

For "optimize staff scheduling," the team identifies one measure: the ratio of medical staff costs to patient revenues. The ratio should decrease if medical staff is used more efficiently. However, one of the customer perspective strategic objectives is to provide prompt service. Therefore, the team believes it may be difficult to evaluate results for this measure. Unfortunately, the team is unable to identify an alternative.

For "improve efficiency and reduce costs," the team considers several alternative ways to measure cost containment, but decides to focus initially on a general measure of cost. They

---

[31] Sunnybrook's Strategic Balanced Scorecard, December 2014, http://sunnybrook.ca/uploads/1/welcome/strategy/final_balanced_scorecard_board_december_2014.pdf.

choose the average cost per patient, calculated as total operating costs divided by the number of patient admissions. This measure can be monitored as frequently as desired, allowing trauma centre managers to quickly identify any adverse trends in cost. It also provides a way for managers to monitor cost effects when new procedures are implemented. Patient-care cost data in the trauma centre is quite accurate, although patient costs include fixed cost allocations. Any change in the allocation bases or methods reduces comparability of patient cost information over time.

> **⊠ BUSINESS PRACTICE**
>
> A number of Sunnybrook's objectives have multiple indicators. For example, Objective 2.5.1 (to enhance collaboration and our educational leadership profile with the University of Toronto, our partners and within the broader health system) includes four indicators: Student Experience (% Placement Met/Exceeded Expectations), Student Experience (% Would Recommend Sunnybrook), Non-Physician Staff with Academic Appointment to Professional School, and Ranking within TAHSN Hospitals for Number of Structured IPE Placements. Each indicator is assessed against a baseline and a specific target.[32]

Learning and Growth Measures. For "develop new treatment methods," the team decides to track the number of new treatment methods developed. Once a month, accountants will meet with physicians and nurses to determine the number and type of new treatment methods developed.

For "support employee professional development," the team decides to track the average number of training hours per employee. Employees estimate their time in training each month. Because they do not always fill out the reports, they are contacted by accounting each month to update any missing estimates. The team believes that this measure will encourage employees to take advantage of courses offered.

Establishing Performance Targets. The team meets with various employee groups before setting performance targets. Initially, performance is likely to be benchmarked against last year's performance, if data are available. The team also needs to meet with personnel at the other hospital to collect information about its trauma centre. Because measures for the combined trauma centres are likely to be different from the current centre, a transition period will be needed to determine appropriate benchmarks. During the transition time, trauma centre staff hired from the other hospital will be introduced to the scorecard. Within several months, targets can be refined for every performance measure, and monitoring will begin. The complete set of performance measures with initial targets is shown in Exhibit 19.12.

Developing Tactical Plans. In conjunction with setting performance targets, managers and other personnel will establish tactical plans for each strategic objective. The tactical plans will include budgets, when needed, and assign responsibility for results. For example, the strategic objective to optimize staff scheduling might be achieved by purchasing and implementing new optimization software. This plan would require a budget for software and personnel time.

> **⊠ BUSINESS PRACTICE**
>
> At Sunnybrook, current results for each indicator are compared to the immediately previous reporting period and a target level of achievement and the baseline comparator. Further, a colour coding system was developed so that the reader can readily identify which indicators are worse than the baseline and target (red) through a progression up to equal to or better than target (green).[33]

Completing the Balanced Scorecard Implementation Process

Once the balanced scorecard for the current period is completed, the trauma centre will advance through the remaining implementation steps (Exhibit 19.7). Data will be collected and analyzed to monitor performance. Information from the scorecard, including variances between actual and targeted performance, will be evaluated to determine areas in need of improvement. In addition, the current balanced scorecard will be re-evaluated and changed as appropriate. Employees responsible for performance will be rewarded. Periodically, the balanced scorecard design will be reconsidered.

---

[32] Sunnybrook's Strategic Balanced Scorecard, December 2014, http://sunnybrook.ca/uploads/1/welcome/strategy/final_balanced_scorecard_board_december_2014.pdf.
[33] Ibid.

●● > STRATEGIC RISK MANAGEMENT: **COMMUNITY HOSPITAL**

STRATEGY MAP LINKAGES When creating the strategy map (Exhibit 19.11), the trauma centre balanced scorecard team did not link the internal business process objective "improve efficiency and reduce costs" directly to the financial objective "provide cost-efficient care." Instead, the team linked the internal business process objective first to the customer perspective, which, in turn, linked to the financial objective. This practice reduces the risk that cost-cutting measures that reduce customer service to inappropriately low levels will be taken.

SUMMARY

LO1   Discuss strategic decision making

OVERVIEW OF MANAGEMENT DECISION MAKING

Vision, Mission, Core Values Statements, Strategic Objectives, and Tactical Plans

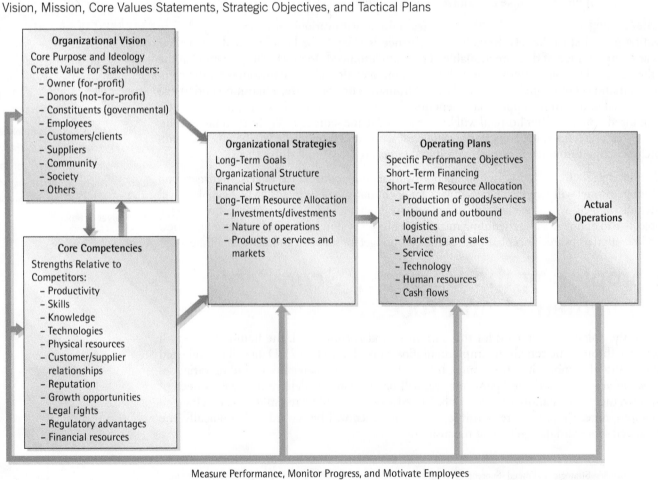

Organizational Vision
Core Purpose and Ideology
Create Value for Stakeholders:
 – Owner (for-profit)
 – Donors (not-for-profit)
 – Constituents (governmental)
 – Employees
 – Customers/clients
 – Suppliers
 – Community
 – Society
 – Others

Core Competencies
Strengths Relative to Competitors:
 – Productivity
 – Skills
 – Knowledge
 – Technologies
 – Physical resources
 – Customer/supplier relationships
 – Reputation
 – Growth opportunities
 – Legal rights
 – Regulatory advantages
 – Financial resources

Organizational Strategies
Long-Term Goals
Organizational Structure
Financial Structure
Long-Term Resource Allocation
 – Investments/divestments
 – Nature of operations
 – Products or services and markets

Operating Plans
Specific Performance Objectives
Short-Term Financing
Short-Term Resource Allocation
 – Production of goods/services
 – Inbound and outbound logistics
 – Marketing and sales
 – Service
 – Technology
 – Human resources
 – Cash flows

Actual Operations

Measure Performance, Monitor Progress, and Motivate Employees

SUMMARY

LO2   Describe how financial and nonfinancial measures are used to evaluate organizational performance

FINANCIAL MEASURES

Information measured in dollars or ratios of dollars

NONFINANCIAL MEASURES

Information that cannot be measured in dollars

MONITORING MEASURABLE PERFORMANCE OBJECTIVES

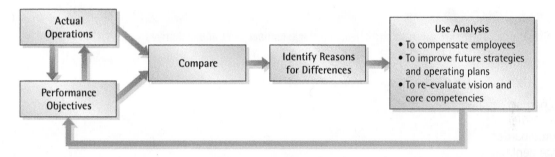

LO3   Explain the balanced scorecard

BALANCED SCORECARD

Formal method to incorporate both financial and nonfinancial performance measures into organizational management systems

Translates organizational vision and strategies into performance objectives and related performance measures that can be monitored over time

FOUR PERSPECTIVES

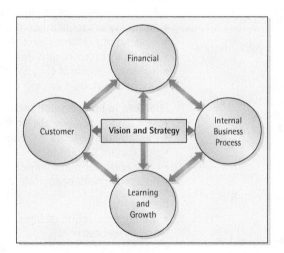

IDENTIFYING INTERNAL PROCESSES CRITICAL FOR SUCCESS

▶ Innovation cycle
▶ Post-sales service cycle
▶ Operations cycle

SUMMARY

LO4   Explain how the balanced scorecard is implemented

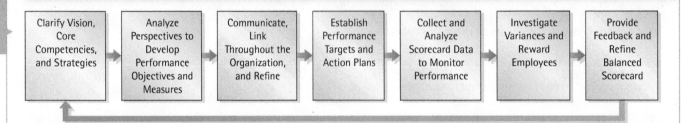

Clarify Vision, Core Competencies, and Strategies → Analyze Perspectives to Develop Performance Objectives and Measures → Communicate, Link Throughout the Organization, and Refine → Establish Performance Targets and Action Plans → Collect and Analyze Scorecard Data to Monitor Performance → Investigate Variances and Reward Employees → Provide Feedback and Refine Balanced Scorecard

LO5   Discuss how the balanced scorecard affects strategic management and incentives

BARRIERS TO IMPLEMENTING STRATEGIES

▶ Vision barrier
▶ People barrier
▶ Resource barrier
▶ Management barrier

BALANCED SCORECARD AND LEVERS OF CONTROL

▶ Beliefs systems
▶ Diagnostic control systems
▶ Interactive control systems

BALANCED SCORECARD STRENGTHS AND WEAKNESSES

Strengths	Weaknesses
Communication and linkages: • Encourages clarification and updating of vision and strategies • Improves communication and consensus throughout the organization • Links short-term and long-term performance objectives to the vision and strategies	Implementation is expensive and time-consuming **Uncertainties:** • Appropriateness of vision and strategies • Accuracy of identified core competencies • Best set of performance objectives and measures • Reliability of scorecard data • Reasonableness of targets • Doubt about links among perspectives
Guidance for improvements: • Enables periodic performance reviews of progress toward vision and strategies • Leads to improved financial performance • Helps managers use operational data for decision making	**Mistakes in implementation:** • Ambiguous or generally defined objectives • Information systems not integrated • Insufficient resources • Lack of senior management support • Focusing on inappropriate objectives
Motivation: • Aligns unit and individual goals with the organizational vision and strategies • Motivates employee effort • Reduces optimization of sub-units at the expense of the organization as a whole • Promotes action toward achieving strategies	**Biases:** • Manager selection of familiar or easily attainable objectives and measures • Resistance from units and individuals • Process viewed as a temporary fad May be inappropriate for compensation. Vision may not adequately capture core values including relations with regulators, approach toward the environment, etc.

19-1 solution to self-study problem

A. Steps for implementing the balanced scorecard for MHB (see Exhibit 19.7):

1. *Clarify Vision, Core Competencies, and Strategies* MHB has already developed its mission statement. The company's managers should also consider writing a vision statement and core values statement. In addition, the managers need to clarify the company's core competencies. Even though the company has already specified its strategies, the managers should review them and revise them as necessary.

2. *Analyze Perspectives to Develop Performance Objectives and Measures* Managers need to analyze the company's vision and strategies from each of the four perspectives for the balanced scorecard: financial, customer, internal business process, and learning and growth. Within each perspective, they need to identify performance objectives and related measures. To identify performance objectives, the managers must determine the critical actions that the organization must take to achieve its strategies. They need to define what they mean by high quality from a customer's perspective. They also need to analyze competitors' prices and quality to determine the amount of cost containment and levels of quality needed.

3. *Communicate, Link Throughout the Organization, and Refine* The managers need to develop a communication plan and obtain assistance from personnel throughout the organization in clarifying and refining the decisions made in Steps 1 and 2. The managers should then decide whether the different sub-units should develop their own balanced scorecards. The final set of performance objectives and measures must be communicated effectively to align employee efforts with the company's objectives.

4. *Establish Performance Targets and Action Plans* Through discussions among management and employees at different levels in the company and analysis of previous results, performance targets and action plans are developed for each performance objective. The managers must also decide whether to use the balanced scorecard data for employee compensation. For employees whose compensation depends on the results, managers need to prioritize the objectives that relate to that employee's performance and establish a weighting scheme for linking rewards to performance. For example, production line employees could receive bonuses when production quantity and quality reach target levels.

5. *Collect and Analyze Scorecard Data to Monitor Performance* The managers need to ensure that information systems are in place to collect and report scorecard data. Trends can be noted. As data are collected, actual results can be compared to targets.

6. *Investigate Variances and Reward Employees* The managers need to analyze reasons for variance from targets. They also need to consider what the results mean for future strategies, operating plans, and performance objectives.

7. *Provide Feedback and Refine Balanced Scorecard* The managers need to establish a feedback loop so that the information they learn is used to make adjustments as they go through the balanced scorecard process in the future. It means a re-evaluation of the process, beginning at Step 1, as necessary.

B. Four perspectives and possible performance objectives:

The *financial perspective* analyzes the economic consequences of MHB's operations and decisions. A possible performance objective is a profitability level that is in the top quartile in the industry.

The *customer perspective* analyzes the role of customers in MHB's success. Possible performance objectives:

• Provision of goods and services that satisfy customers so that they remain loyal.

• An increase in the size of the loyal customer base.

The *internal business process perspective* analyzes the role of the company's internal methods and practices in MHB's success. Possible performance objectives:

- Continuous improvements in functionality and quality that are important to customers (innovation cycle).
- Production of each bike as cost effectively as possible, in a timely manner (operations cycle).
- Reliable products, with few returns and little warranty work (operations and post-sales service cycle).
- Customer satisfaction with interactions that occur after purchase (post-sales service cycle).

The *learning and growth perspective* analyzes the role of continuous improvement efforts in MHB's success. Possible performance objectives:

- Productive and well-trained employees.
- Systems that support operations in a cost-effective manner.

C. Performance Objective	Measures and Links to Financial Performance
Financial Perspective A profitability level in top quartile in the industry	• Operating margin: A higher operating margin leads to higher profits, which is a common indicator of financial success. • Economic value added: EVA takes into account the level of profits as well as the cost of capital. • Average price per bike: The average price feeds into both operating margin and EVA. As prices go up, if costs and volumes are held constant, operating margins and EVA should increase.
Customer Perspective Provision of goods and services that satisfy customers so that they remain loyal	• Customer satisfaction ratings (with emphasis on quality and price satisfaction): If customer satisfaction ratings are high, MHB is likely to keep its current customers and add new ones, which would lead to higher market share, higher sales volumes, better operating margins, and higher EVA. • Market share: Higher market share would lead to higher sales volumes, better operating margins, and higher EVA. • Number of return customers and number of new customers: If the number of return and new customers increases, then sales volumes should also increase, leading to better operating margins and higher EVA.
Internal Business Process Perspective Reliable products with few returns and little warranty work	• Number of bikes returned: If return rates and warranty work are low, customers are more satisfied and sales increase, leading to higher profits. In addition, MHB spends less on post-sales service, which also increases profits. • Dollar value of warranty work: Same as above.
Learning and Growth Perspective Productive and well-trained employees	• Employee retention: Satisfied and well-trained employees are less likely to leave the company. They also will monitor quality and efficiency of the production lines and make suggestions for improvements, leading to better cost efficiency and higher-quality products, in turn leading to higher profits. More satisfied employees are also more likely to have positive interactions with customers, leading to improved sales and higher profitability. • Employee hours of training: Better training improves performance of work and interactions with customers, leading to higher sales and lower costs, increasing profits.

D. **Pros:** MHB begins the process of clarifying and updating its vision. Communication improves throughout the organization as the vision and strategies are refined. Long-term and short-term performance objectives are linked to the vision and strategies. This linkage enables employees to understand their contribution to the overall organization and aligns employee goals with those of MHB. Individual employees use their scorecards to guide their efforts toward reaching MHB's goals and objectives. MHB managers will periodically review their vision and core competencies and their progress toward achieving them. Managers also have better information for decision making. These actions should lead to improved financial performance.

Cons: Implementing the balanced scorecard is expensive and time consuming. If MHB is already operating efficiently, the benefits from implementing the scoreboard may not be as large as the costs. If the vision or understanding of core competencies is inappropriate or inadequate, goals and objectives in the balanced scorecard may not relate to improved financial performance. If targets are unreasonably high or low, employees have no motivation to meet them. If the objectives are not well thought out and communicated clearly, employees may not understand the objectives or how they relate to overall organizational performance. Measures could be chosen for which no data are available, or the data available could be measured incorrectly or with error. Managers may choose performance measures that represent their strengths rather than making unbiased choices.

QUESTIONS

19.1 Explain the differences between financial and nonfinancial performance measures and give two examples of each.

19.2 Identify four potential perspectives for the balanced scorecard and explain how they are related.

19.3 Allied Trucking moves produce from farms to markets. Its managers decided to implement the balanced scorecard around the company's vision statement: "We aim to be the industry leader in cost-effective and timely delivery of produce." Provide two potential performance measures for each of the four perspectives for the balanced scorecard for Allied Trucking.

19.4 Explain what core competencies are. How do they relate to organizational strategies?

19.5 Suppose that a car dealership decided it would no longer compensate employees with sales commissions but instead pay a salary with a bonus for high customer satisfaction ratings. What problems would you foresee from the dealership's financial perspective?

19.6 Describe the implementation process for the balanced scorecard.

19.7 What is strategic decision making? What role does it play in the balanced scorecard?

19.8 Search online to locate current information about the vision, mission, core values, or similar attributes of **McDonald's** and **Wendy's**. List the similarities and differences between McDonald's and Wendy's vision, mission, and core values.

19.9 Pick two public companies, go to their websites, and identify their major strategies. Pick one of these companies and go to the website of a competitor in the same industry. For example, if you chose **Home Depot** (www.homedepot.ca/en/home/corporate-information.html), you might go to the website of **RONA** (www.rona.ca/corporate/about-us). Compare the strategies of the two companies, listing any similarities and differences.

19.10 Explain why demand for relevant and useful information may increase in the future. What professional skills will help you meet that need?

19.11 Explain why you will need to continuously learn new accounting techniques, as well as develop in-depth knowledge about industries in which you work.

19.12 If managers choose the nonfinancial measures upon which they will be evaluated, they may be biased in their choices. Explain and give an example of such a bias.

19.13 If it is difficult to accurately measure customer satisfaction because only customers who purchase items are surveyed, should the measure be assigned more or less weight than a more accurate customer-related statistic such as market share? Explain.

19.14 What is a performance target and why is it important to use them with a balanced scorecard?

19.15 What is a strategy map and how does it relate to the balanced scorecard?

MULTIPLE-CHOICE QUESTIONS

19.16 Which of the following is considered an adequate performance measure in the internal process perspective of the balanced scorecard?
   a. Customer complaints
   b. Number of repeat orders
   c. Revenue per employee
   d. Revenue per product

19.17 A well-designed performance measurement system will include which measures?
   a. Measures related to the goals of the organization.
   b. Measures primarily focusing attention on immediate short-term concerns.
   c. Reasonably objective and easily quantified measures.
   d. Both a and c.
   e. All of a, b, and c.

19.18 Which of the following is an advantage of the balanced scorecard for evaluating manager's performance?
   a. It covers a range of activities over the short term.
   b. It covers a range of activities over the long term.

   c. It forces a company to consider the range of activities that lead to success, not just short-term financial criteria.
   d. It is subject to manipulation.

19.19 Which of the following is considered an adequate performance measure in the learning and innovation perspective of the balanced scorecard?
   a. Cycle time
   b. Employee turnover
   c. Number of new customers
   d. Revenue growth

19.20 Which of the following is a *disadvantage* of the balanced scorecard for evaluating a manager's performance?
   a. It forces a company to consider the range of activities and results that lead to success, not just short-term financial criteria.
   b. It suggests to management that customers, learning and innovation, internal processes, and income are all important.
   c. It is subject to manipulation.
   d. It covers a range of activities over both the long and short terms.

EXERCISES

19.21 **Management Decision Making Process** Erika is trying to explain the management decision-making process to a group of her friends who are not business majors. She decides to use her friend Kelli as an example. Kelli's goal is to become a sign language teacher and interpreter. She will need to complete a university degree in Deaf Studies and pass exams for both her teaching credential and her sign language interpreter's credential. Kelli is in her third year of university and her average is an 82 with higher marks in more applied courses. Kelli is considered a "hard worker" but she struggles with extreme test anxiety brought on by a learning disability. She has been signing for five years and occasionally has jobs that require her signing skills. She has a part-time job at a local Staples where she has steadily moved into a management position. Her parents provide financial assistance for 50% of her schooling. She has student loans for any amount that she cannot fund. Kelli pays for the operating costs of her car, which her parents gave her to attend university. Kelli lives at home, which helps with the finances and her mom is always there to provide encouragement.

REQUIRED Use Kelli's situation to explain the management decision-making process to Erika's non-business friends.

19.22 Balanced Scorecard Measures for Financial Perspective Following is financial information for the last period for
China Express, a regional company with a number of fast-food stores:

LO2, LO3

Revenue from operations	$10,450,200
Operating costs	9,927,690
After-tax profits	391,883
Cost of capital	12%
Required rate of return	15%
Average assets	$ 4,180,080

REQUIRED   Describe and calculate several measures that could be used for the financial perspective.

19.23 Financial and Nonfinancial Measures Managers increasingly use a mixture of financial and nonfinancial measures
for organizational performance.

LO2

REQUIRED   In the following list of performance measures, identify those that are financial (F) and those that are nonfinancial (N).
_____ **A.** Customer satisfaction ratings
_____ **B.** Market share
_____ **C.** Operating margin
_____ **D.** Return on sales
_____ **E.** Annual average purchase amount per customer
_____ **F.** Defect rate
_____ **G.** Normal spoilage
_____ **H.** Labour efficiency variance
_____ **I.** Number of new products developed annually
_____ **J.** Revenues from new products introduced this year

19.24 Balanced Scorecard Measures for Customer Perspective Flowing Wells High School is in the process of developing
its balanced scorecard. The administrators have decided that their customers are parents and future employers of
their students. They believe the students are their products.

LO2, LO3,
LO4

REQUIRED   Discuss whether each of the following potential measures would be useful for the customer perspective in the balanced scorecard:
A. Parent ratings of satisfaction with the high school curriculum
B. Graduation rate
C. Percentage of students employed during the summer after graduation
D. Employer satisfaction ratings for Flowing Wells High School graduates
E. Monthly earnings of graduates
F. Number of graduates attending classes beyond high school
G. Cost per student per year
H. Number of classes per student per semester
I. Average number of college credit hours completed per teacher

19.25 Learning and Growth Perspective Suppose Sparkman Corporation, a large pharmaceutical company, is concerned
about the ability of its research and development department to develop profitable new prescription drugs.
Approval for a new drug must go through a pre-clinical stage, three clinical trial stages, and then an approval
process with Health Canada. It takes 6 to 15 years to meet all these requirements. Because the life of a patent
is 20 years, and patents are applied for before the start of the pre-clinical stage, the company can then market
the drug for a period from 5 to 14 years before the patent expires.[34] Once a patent expires, competitors can
produce generic versions of the drug. Employees currently participate in profit-sharing plans, but the company
wants to give additional bonuses to improve performance. Sparkman management decided to implement the
balanced scorecard approach.

LO2, LO3

REQUIRED   **A.** Explain why monitoring and rewarding nonfinancial performance might be particularly important for Sparkman.
B. List one objective for Sparkman's learning and growth perspective.
C. List two performance measures for the objective you chose in Part B.

[34] Health Canada website, http://hc-sc.gc.ca/dhp-mps/homologation-licensing/index-eng.php; and Canadian Pharmacists Association, *Drugs: From Research Lab to Pharmacy Shelf*, January 2007 at http://people.stfx.ca/ksaulnie/DrugApprovalProcess_Mar2007.pdf.

19.26 **Balanced Scorecard Measures for Four Perspectives** Part of the process for developing the balanced scorecard is to identify one or more measures for each perspective.

LO2, LO3, LO4

REQUIRED Categorize each of the following potential balanced scorecard measures according to the following perspectives:

F   Financial
C   Customer
I   Internal business process
L   Learning and growth

_____ **A.** Percentage of customer orders delivered on time
_____ **B.** Ratio of research and development cost to number of new products developed
_____ **C.** Economic value added (EVA)
_____ **D.** Number of hours of employee training
_____ **E.** Direct labour price variance
_____ **F.** Market share
_____ **G.** Percentage of customer orders delivered without error
_____ **H.** Days in accounts receivable
_____ **I.** Throughput time
_____ **J.** Direct materials efficiency variance
_____ **K.** Asset turnover
_____ **L.** Employee retention rate
_____ **M.** Percentage of bad debts collected
_____ **N.** Customer satisfaction ratings
_____ **O.** Number of degrees and certificates held per employee or department
_____ **P.** Percentage of purchase orders that are error free

19.27 **Strategic Plans, Balanced Scorecard Measures for Not-for-Profit Organization** Suppose you have been invited by a classmate to help found a new not-for-profit organization named Students Care. The organization's purpose is to provide scholarship money for children in Africa who have become orphans because of the AIDS epidemic. The organization will operate only on campus, and the target donors are students. Suppose a prominent business executive has offered to coordinate distribution of the scholarship funds to needy students, but he wants to see a business plan for the organization that describes the organizational vision and lists the core competencies, strategies, and operating plans.

LO1, LO2, LO3, LO4

REQUIRED **A.** Explain what each item on the executive's list means. For each item, provide a possible example for "Students Care."
B. Consider the perspective of internal business processes. Your classmate wants to measure the number of hours per week that volunteers spend collecting donations, but you believe it should be dollars collected per volunteer hour spent in collection, measured on a weekly basis. Give one advantage and one disadvantage for each measure.
C. You have had difficulty determining a measure of learning and growth, but a campus association recently organized a series of short workshops on improving student fundraising activities, as well as other aspects of governing student organizations. Discuss the advantages and disadvantages of using the number of Students Care volunteers attending workshops as a measure for this perspective.

19.28 **Balanced Scorecard Measures the Customer Service Quadrant** Refer to the Carleton University balanced scorecard in Exhibit 19.8. The full version of the scorecard is available on the Carleton University website: http://carleton.ca/finance-admin/wp-content/uploads/Copy-of-Balanced-ScorecardFAdivision2014-2015.pdf.

LO2, LO3, LO4

REQUIRED **A.** Describe how each of the following measures might be calculated (be specific about the data used):
   1. Student customer satisfaction rating
   2. Employee customer satisfaction
   3. Customer satisfaction rating
B. Assuming the type of data and calculation you described in Part A, provide one advantage and one disadvantage for each measure.

19.29 **Balanced Scorecard Measures for the Stewardship of Financial Resources** Refer to the Carleton University balanced scorecard in Exhibit 19.8. The full version of the scorecard is available on the Carleton University website:

LO2, LO3, LO4

http://carleton.ca/finance-admin/wp-content/uploads/Copy-of-Balanced-ScorecardFAdivision2014-2015.pdf.

REQUIRED **A.** Describe how each of the following measures might be calculated (be specific about the data used):
1. Annual, actual financial operating results for university compared to budgeted operating result
2. Successful delivery of Capital Programs
3. Assign tasks and track accomplishments
4. Employee satisfaction rating (I'm encouraged to make suggestions)
5. Emergency response strategy refined

B. Assuming the type of data and calculation you described in Part A, discuss how well each measure relates to the stated objective.

19.30 **Balanced Scorecard Perspectives, Performance Objectives, and Measures** Perspectives, performance objectives, and

LO2, LO3

potential performance measures for the balanced scorecard at Holiday Resorts are as follows:

PERSPECTIVES:
I.   Financial
II. Customer
III. Internal business
IV. Learning and growth

Performance objectives:
a. Reduce housekeeping costs
b. Improve the quality of and results from advertising campaigns
c. Decrease vacancy rate during the off-season
d. Increase number of return customers
e. Increase overall profits
f. Increase the use of web-based reservations
g. Retain high-quality employees
h. Increase the number of activities available to customer
i. Improve the quality of stay for vacationers
j. Provide employee training in quality customer service
k. Reduce error rate in reservations

Potential performance measures:
1. Operating margin
2. Customer complaint rate
3. Survey customers at check-in about how they first heard about the resorts
4. Housekeeping cost per room
5. Number of employee hours spent in training
6. Error rate in reservation process
7. Percentage of reservations made using the website
8. Customer surveys about satisfaction and quality
9. Employee turnover rates
10. Number of activities per resort that are available to customers
11. Percentage and number of return customers
12. Number of hours of employee training offered
13. Vacancy rates
14. Customer focus groups inquiring about quality and potential success of advertising
15. Number of suggestions that improve quality of service

REQUIRED **A.** For each perspective (I–IV), identify at least one appropriate performance objective (a–k).
B. For each performance objective (a–k), identify at least one appropriate performance measure (1–15).

19.31 **Barriers to Implementing Strategies** A properly designed balanced scorecard should help eliminate barriers to imple-

LO5

menting organization strategies. This chapter has identified four barriers: vision barrier, people barrier, resource barrier, and management barrier.

REQUIRED Describe each barrier and explain how the balanced scorecard would help minimize the barrier. Identify a measure that could be used to monitor improvement related to each barrier.

PROBLEMS

19.32 Balanced Scorecard and Implementation Candi Canyon works in a resort location. During peak seasons the resort
L03, L04 hires a large number of university students who live in dormitory-style housing at the resort. The dorms are
approximately 2 km from the students' job locations. In addition, on their off days, students enjoy participating
in activities available at the resort or going into the local town about 5 km away. Most of the students do not own
cars. A group of entrepreneurial students are developing a plan to propose a "bike share" program. These programs operate successfully in large cities like Toronto and are similar to the "car share" programs.

REQUIRED **A.** Draft a mission statement for the proposed business opportunity.
B. Identify two performance objectives for each of the four balanced scorecard perspectives.
C. Select one performance objective for each of the four perspectives and identify a potential performance
measure for each. Explain your choices.
D. Draw a strategy map using your performance measures. Explain the relationships between your measures.

19.33 Balanced Scorecard and Implementation Dr. Mark Moreland, a dentist, has decided to join a small group of dentists
L03, L04 so that he no longer has to be on call every night. Practice members share the responsibility for emergencies
with other members of the group. In the past, Mark differentiated his practice by specializing in the treatment of
families with children. None of the other dentists specialize in families, but all of them treat some children. Mark's
son has just finished an accounting degree and recommends that the dental group consider implementing the
balanced scorecard as they develop the policies and practices for the new group.

REQUIRED **A.** Explain what each of the four perspectives of the balanced scorecard means in the context of a dental group.
B. Recommend several methods the group could use to assess a performance objective of patient satisfaction.
C. Recommend two measures for each of the four perspectives for the dental group. Explain your
recommendations.

19.34 Balanced Scorecard, Financial and Nonfinancial Measures Dyggur Equipment manufactures and sells heavy equip-
L02, L03, ment used in construction and mining. Customers are contractors who want reliable equipment at a low cost. The
L04 firm's strategy is to provide reliable products at prices lower than its competitors. Management wants to emphasize quick delivery and quick turnaround when equipment needs repair or service, so that contractors are not
without their equipment often or for long. Dyggur is considering the following performance measures for use in its
balanced scorecard.

REQUIRED Categorize each of the following potential balanced scorecard measures as follows (some measures may fall into
multiple categories):
F   Financial
C   Customer
I   Internal business process
L   Learning and growth
_____ **A.** Manufacturing cycle time per product
_____ **B.** Market share
_____ **C.** Average ratings on customer satisfaction surveys
_____ **D.** Average cost per unit
_____ **E.** Economic value added
_____ **F.** Percentage of receivables collected
_____ **G.** Dollar value of warranty work
_____ **H.** Time between order and delivery
_____ **I.** Time it takes to repair returned equipment
_____ **J.** Number of focus groups for new products
_____ **K.** Number of new uses for current products
_____ **L.** Number of times new technology is applied to current products
_____ **M.** Number of product change suggestions from sales
_____ **N.** Number of engineering change orders to improve manufacturing cycle
_____ **O.** Revenue growth
_____ **P.** Employee training hours
_____ **Q.** Number of quality improvement suggestions from employees

_____ **R.** Number of new customers
_____ **S.** Number of repeat customers
_____ **T.** Employee turnover rate
_____ **U.** Defect rates for manufacturing production
_____ **V.** Percentage of error-free rates in:
    _____**1.** Purchasing
    _____**2.** Billing
    _____**3.** Customer record keeping

19.35 Strategy, Balanced Scorecard Measures and Process Refer to the information in Problem 19.34. Dyggur Equipment wants to offer weekend servicing of heavy equipment. None of its competitors offer this service, and management believes this service will bring in new business and help retain current customers.

LO1, LO2, LO4

REQUIRED
A. List several advantages and disadvantages of this strategy.
B. List one financial and two nonfinancial performance measures that could be used to monitor the success of this plan.
C. Suppose the managers decide to launch this new service. At the end of the first year of operating weekend service, performance is evaluated by gathering and analyzing measures such as those identified in Part B. How can this information be used to improve performance for the next period?

19.36 Balanced Scorecard in Not-for-Profit In the October 2014 issue of *Strategic Finance*, authors Thomas Albright, Chad Gerber, and Paul Juras present a balanced scorecard for a not-for-profit governmental agency—the US Navy ("How Naval Aviation Uses the Balanced Scorecard," pp. 21–28; available at www.imanet.org/docs/default-source/sf/10_2014_juras-pdf). After reading this article, answer the following questions.

LO2, LO3, LO4

REQUIRED
A. The authors propose eliminating the financial and customer perspectives. Explain why they did this, what perspectives they did use, and why they chose these perspectives.
B. The authors provide a strategy map (Figure 2) that shows the linkages between the perspectives. Describe these linkages.
C. Choose an objective in any of the perspectives and explain how one of the measures impact the objective and what initiatives the Navy has undertaken to achieve the target for your chosen measure.
D. In the "Lessons Learned" section, the authors speculate that the approach presented could also apply to police or firefighters. Do some research online to learn more about one of these two services, and:
  i. identify the mission of the service
  ii. identify the perspectives that you would suggest for a balanced scorecard
  iii. identify one measure for each perspective
  iv. draw a strategy map

19.37 Balanced Scorecard in Service Organization, Rollout of Balanced Scorecard Large international and regional accounting firms typically include an Audit/Assurance Group, a Tax Group, and support staff (e.g., human resources, secretarial staff, internal accounting). Research one of the large international accounting firms (e.g., Delloitte, PwC, KPMG, E&Y, Grant Thornton, BDO) to identify the mission of the firm and the missions of the assurance, tax, and support groups.

LO3, LO4

REQUIRED
A. Develop a balanced scorecard for the accounting firm that includes one objective for each perspective and one measure for each objective. Present your balanced scorecard as a strategy map that shows the linkages between your measures.
B. Develop balanced scorecards for the Assurance, Tax, and Support groups. Identify one objective for each perspective. Explain how the group balanced scorecard supports the achievement of the overall firm goals.

19.38 Cumulative Exercise (Chapter 3): Wait Tme, Strategy Map, Breakeven Point, Business Risks The local urgent care clinic employs two physicians and a physician's assistant who treat patients. On average, each patient requires about 15 minutes per visit. The clinic is open for 8 hours per day and closed on weekends. The average revenue

LO2, LO4

per patient is $55. Supplies per patient visit are about $2. The clinic operates at full capacity on Mondays, Tuesdays, and Fridays, and about 10 patients per day leave when they see the long wait lines. On Wednesdays and Thursdays, wait times are short. The clinic tracks its wait time, which has been increasing over the last six months. Because of customer dissatisfaction with the wait times, the clinic is considering a change. The physicians would like to hire a nurse practitioner to treat patients that appear to have simple medical problems such as colds or flu. The nurse practitioner would be hired to work part-time on Mondays, Tuesdays, and Fridays. The cost of the nurse is $65 per hour including benefits.

REQUIRED   **A.** Draw a strategy map showing possible cause-and-effect relationships between improvements in wait time and the internal process, customer, and financial perspectives. (*Hint*: First identify a possible strategic objective related to wait time for each perspective.)

B. Calculate the breakeven point in number of patient visits per day (on Mondays, Tuesdays, and Fridays) for hiring a nurse practitioner.

C. List at least three business risks that could be considered as part of the decision-making process.

D. What is your recommendation to the physicians about hiring a nurse practitioner? Explain.

19.39 **Mission Statement, Strategy, Balanced Scorecard Implementation** Squeezers Juice and Tea Company manufactures organic juices and chai teas that are sold at whole foods stores. Several of its products have been featured in movies because the company's products are popular with celebrities. The owners and employees value organic products and innovative combinations of juices and teas with outstanding taste. Several employees have found sources of unusual ingredients from organic farmers around the world. The ingredients are more expensive than those used by other juice manufacturers. Although Squeezers cannot set unrealistically high prices, it focuses on high quality. Demand for the company's products is stable, even though it sets the highest prices for juices in its market.

LO1, LO2, LO3, LO4

Recently, the costs of several unusual ingredients increased because of weather conditions. The owner is concerned that increasing prices any further could reduce demand. She has attended a business workshop and learned about the balanced scorecard. She wants to incorporate the balanced scorecard at Squeezers.

REQUIRED   **A.** Draft a potential mission statement for Squeezers. Explain how you decided what should be included in the statement and how it should be worded.

B. Explain the company's business strategy and core competencies.

C. Identify several performance objectives for each of the four perspectives.

D. Select two performance objectives for each of the four perspectives and identify a potential performance measure for each. Explain your choices.

E. Describe possible methods for collecting the data needed for each of the performance measures in Part D. For example, what existing information might be available? What new record keeping might be required? Would the company need to develop surveys?

19.40 **Balanced Scorecard Measures** Dave's BBQ owns a number of stores that sell fast food. As part of its compensation packages, Dave's BBQ provides employees with bonuses based on customer satisfaction surveys. Recent analysis of the data shows a positive correlation between survey ratings and sales; that is, as customer satisfaction increases, sales increase. However, at a certain point in this trend, sales plateau even though the ratings continue to increase. In addition, increasing customer satisfaction causes costs to increase also, because more time is spent with each customer and more employees are on hand to help with food preparation and cashiering to reduce the time that customers wait for their food to be prepared. Other factors that appear to affect customer satisfaction are the general cleanliness of the store and the attitudes of the cashiers as they provide customer service. A factor that strongly affects sales at each store is its health department rating. These ratings are published in the local daily newspaper. When a store has a low rating, sales at that outlet drop off until publication of an improved rating occurs. The owner wants to add one or more financial performance measures to the bonus package so that employees will earn more money when customer satisfaction increases at the same time that financial performance is also increasing.

LO2, LO3, LO4

REQUIRED   **A.** Describe advantages and disadvantages of using a combination of performance measures reflecting the customer and financial perspectives.

B. Management would like to add other customer-related measures and is considering replacing survey satisfaction with some other measure. List one potential measure and list at least one advantage and one disadvantage for it.

C. List one additional performance measure that could be included in the compensation package. Explain what it is and what it would contribute.

19.41 Participative Strategic Planning Process and Benefits, Manager Behaviour (Assumes knowledge from management classes) Quantum Computers produces and sells laptop computers. The company is currently deciding whether to continue concentrating on the laptop computer market or to expand by entering the highly competitive com puter desktop workstation market.

LO1, LO4, LO5

Most of the management staff has been with Quantum for a long time. Michael Mitchem, Quantum's president, wants his management staff to assist him in Quantum's strategic planning process. Mitchem has scheduled a three-day offsite meeting for the management staff to join together for the company's strategic planning process.

REQUIRED **A.** What functional areas should be discussed during the strategic planning process?
B. Identify at least six factors to be considered in a thorough strategic planning process that will move a company such as Quantum to another level of product development.
C. Identify at least three benefits that Quantum can derive from a participatory strategic planning process.
D. Discuss the expected behaviour of the managers at Quantum who participate in the three-day offsite strategic planning meeting.

19.42 Balanced Scorecard, Strengths and Weaknesses Brewster House is a not-for-profit shelter for the homeless. Lately, funding has decreased but the demand for overnight shelter has increased. In cold weather, clients are turned away because the shelter is full. The director believes that the current capacity could be used more efficiently. No one has taken time to analyze the physical layout of the shelter and current use of space. Several rooms are used for storage that could probably be used for temporary housing. The stored boxes need to be sorted and moved. Volunteers currently assign beds and manage overnight housing because the director is busy with fund-raising. Volunteers work just a few shifts each week, so no one has taken responsibility for coordinating improvements in the services offered. The director is considering whether to implement the balanced scorecard to focus the attention of all volunteers on areas that need improvement.

LO3, LO4, LO5

Brewster receives funds from several sources, including a set annual budget from the province and direct donations from supporters. The director develops a budget each year based on expected funding, but she cannot precisely predict donations. The budget is used primarily to justify funding requests submitted to the county.

The director has asked a group of accounting students from the local university to evaluate operations and recommend whether the organization should develop the balanced scorecard. She cannot give bonuses based on the measures, but she wonders whether developing and monitoring performance measures would encourage the volunteers to increase the use of capacity. She also wonders whether some information from the balanced scorecard could be used to show donors the effectiveness of operations.

REQUIRED **A.** Describe several potential costs and benefits of the balanced scorecard for this organization.
B. Describe one potential measure for each scorecard perspective appropriate for Brewster House. Explain how information for each measure will be collected.
C. Prepare a memo to the director that recommends whether Brewster House should adopt the balanced scorecard. In writing the memo, consider what information the director needs from you to help her make a decision.

19.43 Cumulative Exercise (Chapters 4 and 7): ABC, ABM, Customer Profitability, Keep or Drop The sales manager of a children's clothing manufacturer and wholesaler is analyzing the profitability of two groups of customers. One group consists of small, family-owned stores that purchase frequent small orders with very specific types of clothing that may require special handling during the manufacturing process. The other group consists of discount retailers that buy large lots of standard clothing at a standard mix but at lower prices. Recently, the firm has implemented a balanced scorecard and has begun to collect financial and nonfinancial data for each type of customer. The firm is considering whether it would be worthwhile to concentrate on one type of customer as a differentiation strategy. The accountant has gathered the following relevant information for the past month.

LO3, LO4

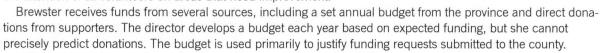

	Family Stores	Discount Retailers
Number of customers	150	25
Revenues	$750,000	$1,350,000
Direct costs (DM and DL)	$375,000	$ 625,000
Delivery costs	$ 41,400	$ 21,000
Number of returns	510	250
Number of change orders	136	2
Number of deliveries	345	35

Following are the performance measures used to analyze customer benefit by group.
Revenue per customer
Revenue less direct costs per customer
Distribution costs per customer
Number of returns per customer
Change orders per customer
Number of deliveries per customer

REQUIRED   **A.** Calculate the performance measures for each customer type.

B. What amount of savings in customer costs would be required for the clothing manufacturer to be indifferent to keeping or dropping each one of these customers?

C. Based on the information in Part B, would you recommend a differentiated strategy?

D. Suppose that the estimated incremental set-up costs for each change order are about $200. What type of customer strategy might be helpful to reduce these costs?

19.44 **Strategies and Balanced Scorecard Measures for a Country** Brian Henshall, foundation emeritus professor of management at The University of Auckland, suggests a number of potential performance measures that could be used to monitor performance for the country of New Zealand. Henshall recommends that the country publish measures monthly to gauge progress. He also argues that a discussion of potential performance measures would help citizens define what they want. Ultimately, the measures could be used to monitor the performance of elected officials. Following are some of Henshall's suggestions.

LO1, LO2, LO3, LO4

www.wiley.com/
go/eldenburgcanada

Tangible wealth:
- Gross domestic product (GDP) percentage change as a measure of growth
- The ratio of government wealth creation to business wealth creation as a measure of government economic performance
- GDP per person employed and per total number of people in New Zealand as efficiency measures
- New Zealand dollar exchange rate (percentage change for last quarter or last year) as a measure of economic stability
- Number of bankrupt firms to all trading entities as a measure of business stability

Environmental intangible wealth:
- A pollution index that measures degradation of the environment from pollution
- A ratio of protected land relative to total government-owned land
- A ratio of alternative energy resources relative to total energy produced

Physical and social infrastructure:
- Educational expense as a percentage of GDP
- Health care expense as a percentage of GDP
- Accidents index
- Serious crimes index

Demographics:
- Changes in population growth, year to year
- Growth in education levels
- A demographic index that monitors innovations by diversity of peoples
- Unemployment rates

Source: B. D. Henshall, "Kiwi Scorecard," *New Zealand Management*, 49(6), July 2002, pp. 15ff.

REQUIRED   **A.** Suppose government officials developed an objective to increase the number of college graduates because they believe increased education will lead to increased GDP. Brainstorm and identify several ideas for action plans to carry out this strategy.

B. Pick one of your ideas from Part A and discuss its pros and cons.

C. Brainstorm ideas for action plans to increase the number of high school graduates.

D. Pick one of your ideas from Part C and discuss its pros and cons.

E. Research information on the Internet to determine appropriate target graduation rates for high school and university levels. Use your research findings to recommend targets for New Zealand. Explain.

19.45 Strategy, Balanced Scorecard for Organization and Employee Mark Hopper owns Dane Champions, a dog kennel

LO2, LO3, LO5

that raises champion Great Danes for showing and breeding. His vision is to be the best-known breeder of Great Danes, globally. His strategy is to breed and sell dogs of outstanding lineage from the standpoint of both physical health and good-natured temperaments. Following is information about operations over the past year:

Number of breedings	10
Number of puppies	45
Number of puppies sold	40
Number of puppies returned	2
Revenue from puppies	$ 24,000
Kennel operating costs (not including Mark's salary)	$ 35,000
Travel expenditures	$ 55,000
Number of trips to dog shows	20
Winnings from dog shows	$110,000
Number of championships	17
Number of dogs shown	4
Puppy owners' average satisfaction rating on a scale of 1 to 5, with 5 as most satisfied	4.5
Training time to prepare puppies for new homes (total hours)	14
Training time to prepare dogs for shows (hours per week, per dog)	2

REQUIRED
A. Is the company's strategy one of cost leadership or product differentiation? Explain.
B. Prepare a simple balanced scorecard with one performance measure for each of the four perspectives for Dane Champions, using only the data presented. Explain your choices.
C. Draw a strategy map that includes your performance measures. Explain the linkages between your measures.
D. Kennel operating costs include the cost of a local high school student who cleans out the kennels every afternoon after school. Mark is considering whether to set up an individual scorecard for the student. He pays only minimum wage, and although the student is fairly slow, the kennels are kept reasonably clean. Mark wonders whether the student would resent being monitored more closely. Describe one reason for using a scorecard with the student and one reason against using it.

19.46 Performance Measures, Variances, Evaluation Refer to Problem 19.45 (Dane Champions). Mark Hopper has chosen

LO2, LO3, LO4, LO5

to monitor the following measures:
Financial perspective: Operating margin.
Customer perspective: Puppy owners' average satisfaction and number of puppies returned.
Internal processes: Training time spent to prepare dogs for both homes and shows.
Learning and growth perspective: Number of champions compared to number of dogs shown.

		Last year's results	Targets
Revenues ($24,000 + $110,000)	$134,000	$134,000	+5%
Expenses ($35,000 + $55,000)	90,000	$90,000	+3%
Owners' average satisfaction (on a scale of 1 to 5)		4.5	4.75
Number of puppies returned		2 out of 40	2.5%
Training time to prepare dogs for new home		14 hours in total	15 hours
Training time to prepare dogs to show		2 hours per week	4 hours per week
Number of championships		17	25
Number of dogs shown		4 dogs shown	5 dogs

REQUIRED   **A.** Analyze Dane Champions, most recent results against the balanced scorecard targets presented above.

		Current results
Revenues ($24,000 + $110,000)	$134,000	$144,050
Expenses ($35,000 + $55,000)	90,000	$93,150
Owners' average satisfaction (on a scale of 1 to 5)		4.8
Number of puppies returned		2 out of 60
Training time to prepare dogs for new home		12 hours in total
Training time to prepare dogs to show		5 hours per week
Number of championships		32
Number of dogs shown		6 dogs shown

B. Discuss whether Mark Hopper has achieved his strategic objectives. Make suggestions for the upcoming year.

19.47 **Performance Measures, Variances, Evaluation** Lodgepole Theatre's mission is to provide affordable family movies for the local community. Lodgepole management has developed the following balanced scorecard objectives, measures, and targets.

LO 2, LO 3, LO 4, LO 5

Financial Perspective: To earn sufficient funds to sustain the theatre and give something back to the community.

Measure	Target	Baseline results
Profit	+3%	$150,000
Cash Balance	+3%	$ 35,000

Customer Perspective: To have satisfied, repeat customers.

Measure	Target	Baseline results
# Repeat Customers	+5%	5,000 repeat customers

Internal Business Processes Perspective: To use technology to support business growth.

Measure	Target	Baseline results
# e-tickets presented	+2%	500

Learning and Growth Perspective: To have technology aware employees.

Measure	Target	Baseline results
# training classes/employee	+1	0.5

REQUIRED   **A.** Based on the following current results, comment on Lodgepole Theatre's performance.

Profit	$153,750
Cash Balance	$ 36,050
# Repeat Customers	5,500
# e-tickets presented	490
# training classes/employee	1.75

B. Considering Lodgepole Theatre's mission and objectives, make recommendations for one additional measure for each perspective. Justify your choices by explaining the linkages between the existing measures, your measures and the mission of Lodgepole Theatre.

C. Lodgepole Theatre consists of two divisions: Movies and Food Service. The Movie division is responsible for identifying and acquiring appropriate movies. The theatre has three screens and operates from noon until midnight. The manager of this division is also responsible for scheduling the movies and managing ticketing. The Food Service division is responsible for providing typical movie treats, such as popcorn, candy, and beverages. Based on the Lodgepole Theatre's balanced scorecard, develop a balanced scorecard and strategy map for each of these divisions. Make sure that each division's balanced scorecard supports the theatre's balanced scorecard.

19.48 **Balanced Scorecard Variances** A large hardware store has used the balanced scorecard approach for several
years. The store's vision is to provide customers with low-cost goods and a high-quality shopping experience. The
company's strategy has been to focus on reducing wait time for help on the floor and at the check-out counter.
Information for the past two years follows:

LO2, LO3, LO4

	2015	2016
Average sale (total revenue÷total invoices)	$ 15	$ 12
Average variable cost per sale	$ 7	$ 7
Average customer wait time at counter	1.5 minutes	1.5 minutes
Average customer wait time for help on the sales floor	3 minutes	2 minutes
Shipping cost per order	$ 18	$ 15
Total returns	$ 57,000	$ 60,000
Total revenue	$800,000	$748,000
Total labour cost	$200,000	$220,000
Utilities cost (electricity and phone)	$ 2,100	$ 2,400
Number of items out of stock	120	180
Employee turnover	2	3

REQUIRED **A.** Classify each performance measure according to one of the four balanced scorecard perspectives.
B. Analyze the change in each performance measure from 2015 to 2016. Give one possible reason for the change.
C. Which performance measures need further investigation? Explain.
D. What do the balanced scorecard results suggest about the success of the company's strategy to reduce wait
time? Explain.
E. When an organization focuses on one strategy, problems sometimes arise in other areas. Do the balanced
scorecard results provide evidence of possible deterioration in any operational areas? Explain.

19.49 **Performance Measures, Variances** A new fast food store is using a balanced scorecard to monitor its operations. The
store's vision is to provide customers with low-cost meals and a high-quality eating experience. The company's
strategies have been to focus on keeping prices low by minimizing food waste and keeping customer wait times
at the counter and drive-through window as low as possible. Information for the last two months follows. The store
currently operates 12 hours per day, from 11:00 a.m. to 11:00 p.m.

LO2, LO3, LO4

	July	August
Average sale (total revenue÷total invoices)	$ 14	$ 18
Average variable cost per sale	$ 6	$ 7
Average kilograms of food waste per day	70	68
Average customer wait time at counter	3 minutes	3.2 minutes
Average customer wait time at window	1.5 minutes	2 minutes
Average number of cars in wait line	3 cars	4 cars
Average customers per hour	45	43
Total revenue	$226,800	$278,640
Total labour cost	$ 44,550	$ 45,000
Utilities cost (electricity and phone)	$ 2,100	$ 2,400
Employee turnover	2	1

REQUIRED **A.** Classify each performance measure according to one of the four balanced scorecard perspectives.
B. Analyze the change in each performance measure. Give one possible reason for any changes.
C. Which performance measures need further investigation? Explain.
D. When an organization focuses on one strategy, problems sometimes arise in other areas. Do the balanced
scorecard results provide evidence of possible deterioration in any operational areas? Explain.

MINI-CASES

19.50 Evaluate Balanced Scorecard Design Frieda's Fizz brews specialty soft drinks, including root beer and other flavours. Its vision is "To proudly produce and sell extraordinarily smooth, rich, and delicious soft drinks to satisfy kids of all ages." The company has a reputation for high quality and unique flavour, enabling it to sell soft drinks at a premium price to gourmet grocery stores in the Toronto area. The company's managers plan to expand the business to other geographic regions, but they want to ensure that they maintain high quality as the company grows. They have decided to implement the balanced scorecard, and they have chosen the following balanced scorecard measures:

L02, L03, L04, L05

Financial Perspective:
1. Breakdown of manufacturing cost per case: ingredients, direct labour, packaging materials, and overhead
2. Operating profit per case
3. Return on investment

Customer Perspective:
4. Number of customer complaints related to taste, freshness, package integrity, appearance, and foreign objects
5. Quality index (an internal measure of manufacturing quality, including microbiology and chemistry)
6. Percentage sales growth

Internal Business Process Perspective:
7. Ratio of plant production hours to total available time
8. Throughput (number of cases packaged)
9. Waste and scrap as a percentage of total production cost

Learning and Growth Perspective:
10. Number of work-related injuries
11. Number of training hours per employee
12. Number of community volunteer hours per employee

REQUIRED   INFORMATION ANALYSIS

The following questions will help you analyze the information for this problem. Do not turn in your answers to these questions unless your professor asks you to do so.
A. Explain why uncertainties exist about the best balanced scorecard measures for Frieda's Fizz. (Do *not* discuss any of the measures already listed. Instead, focus on why any set of measures might not provide ideal information and on why the managers cannot know with certainty which set of measures is best.)
B. For each balanced scorecard perspective:
1. Describe the strengths and weaknesses of the measures chosen for that category.
2. Reach a conclusion about the reasonableness of the set of balanced scorecard measures for that category.
C. What are the pros and cons of implementing the balanced scorecard?
D. How valuable do you think the balanced scorecard will be in helping the managers of Frieda's Fizz meet its vision? Explain.

REQUIRED   WRITTEN ASSIGNMENT

The managers of Frieda's Fizz want your evaluation of their proposed balanced scorecard. Turn in your answer to the following.
E. Use the information you learned from the preceding analyses to write a memo to the managers, presenting your evaluation of (1) whether they should adopt the balanced scorecard and (2) the proposed balanced scorecard design. As you write the memo, consider what information the managers will need from you to help make a final decision.

19.51 Corporate Social Responsibility, Monitoring Measures As of 2007, coffee-drinking Canadians drank an average of approximately 2.6 cups a day, which adds up to over 40 million cups of coffee *each day*. A growing debate surrounding the coffee Canadians drink is brewing—the issue of fair trade coffee.

L01, L02

Fair trade is not just about coffee. The concept began in the mid-1940s, with craft items made by artisans in developing countries, and has spread to include coffee, tea, chocolate, bananas, and other products. The basic idea of fair trade is to pay primary producers a "fair price" for their products. Fair trade products must meet a specific set of criteria, and compliance is independently verified.

Most of the coffee sold in Canada and world-wide is not labelled "fair trade." Most coffee is produced in developing, low-income countries. Coffee farmers typically live in what Canadians would classify as poverty conditions. Coffee producers are paid approximately $0.54 to $0.60 per pound of coffee beans. Producers' costs are estimated to be $0.60 to $0.90 per pound of coffee beans. Under fair trade agreements, producers are paid a minimum of $1.26 per pound. Fair trade status requires that producers conform to specific conditions pertaining to environmental conditions, labour practices, education, and income distribution. Fair trade farms must be democratically run cooperatives of small to medium size. The intention is that the role of the "middleman" be eliminated or greatly reduced. Under fair trade agreements, the communities of the producers also receive benefits such as medical and education facilities, educational materials, and support for other community projects. Coffee bearing the "fair trade" label sells for $1 or more extra per pound retail.

If more money goes to the producers, how can fair trade be controversial? Jose Felix Centeno Castillo represents a farming cooperative in Nicaragua. His coffee beans do not bear the "fair trade" label. Yet, his cooperative is paid $1.61 per pound for their beans. He points out that the "fair trade" label comes at a cost—a cost that would erode his cooperative's earnings by hundreds of dollars per year. That is money the farmers need to feed and educate their families. Castillo's group is not alone. Other producers meet or exceed the environmental sustainability, fair labour practices, and education requirements of fair trade but do not apply for or cannot afford the approximate $0.10 per pound for fair trade status. Large company-owned coffee farms are excluded from fair trade status even if they adhere to the standards of fair trade simply because they are not democratically run cooperatives. A number of small, Canadian coffee roasters and retailers, such as Just Us! Coffee Roaster Co-Op, carry exclusively fair trade products. The largest Canadian-based coffee roast-retailer, Timothy's World Coffee, now carries a number of "fair trade" labelled coffees. Even the large canned coffee producer Procter & Gamble has a line of fair trade coffee that it sells under the Millstone label. After a number of rallies and protests across Canada and the United States, Starbucks has started to offer fair trade coffees. Other roasters and retailers, such as JBR Gourmet Foods and Seattle's Best Coffee, have developed incentive systems that pay higher prices to farmers for higher-quality coffee beans, while providing additional support for community service projects in the growers' local communities. Many of these brands do not carry the "fair trade" label, and not all of these farmers' co-ops pay for a "fair trade" label.

Sources: CBC News, *In Depth: Fair Trade: An Alternative Economic Model*, April 23, 2007; A. Markey, "Coffee—Fair Trade Tea and Coffee Links Canadians to Post-tsunami Recovery," *Straight Goods in the Straight Goods Cyber*, February 12, 2005; J. Batsell, "Coffee—Fair Trade Coffee Demand Sparks Debate on Workers' Wages, Lives," *The Seattle Times*, October 7, 2004; S. Laidlaw, "Coffee—Prof Wonders What's Fair About Fair Trade?" *The Toronto Star*, March 21, 2007; C. Havard, "Coffee—Timothy's World Coffee Launches Fair Trade Certified Coffees," *TransFair Canada*, May 13, 2004; and "Coffee—Starbucks Campaign—Protesters Demand Starbucks Pay Fair Prices for Beans," *Associated Press Canada*, February 23, 2002.

REQUIRED
A. Describe whether and how corporate social responsibility (i.e., business practices related to human rights, labour standards, and the environment) affects your decisions as a consumer.
B. Is it possible for you to know the conditions under which the products you purchase are produced? Why or why not?
C. Is it possible for managers of companies such as Timothy's, Starbucks, or Procter & Gamble to know with certainty that their outsource partners comply with agreed-upon working conditions? Why or why not?
D. What does it mean for coffee roasters and retailers to include compliance monitoring costs in their purchasing decision processes?
E. Identify and explain four measures that a coffee roaster or retailer could use to monitor worker conditions at suppliers' farms. For each measure, describe how the company might collect reliable data.
F. How should coffee roasters and retailers weigh corporate social responsibility and profits when deciding whether or how to outsource manufacturing? Describe the values you use in drawing your conclusions.

19.52 Strategic Planning, SWOT Analysis, Continuous Improvement

LO1, LO2, LO3, LO4, LO5

Accountants are required to understand the process of strategic planning including analyzing an organization's strengths, weaknesses, opportunities, and threats.

REQUIRED
A. Explain why uncertainties about an organization's strengths, weaknesses, opportunities, and threats lead to uncertainties about the organization's core competencies and strategies.

B. Explain the role of strategic information in the following:
  1. Identifying an organization's core competencies
  2. Choosing strategies
  3. Choosing measures for the balanced scorecard
C. Explain why the use of both financial and nonfinancial measures is important for evaluating an organization's performance.
D. Explain the purpose and importance of the feedback loops in Exhibit 19.1, Exhibit 19.3, and Exhibit 19.7.
E. Explain why the process of developing the balanced scorecard is never complete.

19.53 **Integrating Across the Curriculum—Management and Marketing:** *SWOT analysis* A common business analysis technique is a SWOT analysis, or analysis of an organization's strengths, weaknesses, opportunities, and threats. In marketing, a SWOT analysis is often used to decide whether to launch a new product or to identify ways to improve an existing product. In management, SWOT analyses might be used to assist managers in identifying viable strategies.

[LO1, LO3, LO5]

While multinational giants such as Loblaw have dominated the grocery store industry, **Triple 4 Advertising** has been successfully defending business for independent grocers. Triple 4 Advertising is a Moose Jaw, Saskatchewan-based merchandising group that includes more than 520 grocery and convenience stores in Alberta, Manitoba, Saskatchewan, and northwestern Ontario. Established in 1994 by Harry Watson and David Klatt, Triple 4 is the fastest-growing association of independents in the country.

Triple 4 was created from Watson's expertise in the grocery business. He knew that offering customers reasonably competitive prices was critical for independent grocers' survival. In the prairies, residents do not hesitate to drive for many hours to the larger communities just to benefit from the lower-priced goods at one of the large chain stores. Triple 4 knew it could not possibly sell at large chain store prices, but developing an alliance of small, independent stores to create a larger buying group would allow the independents to come closer to competing with large store prices. Small stores could then retain customers who might otherwise be willing to commute longer distances. The company developed a long-term strategy that involved receiving the best possible discounts and rebates from wholesalers by purchasing large quantities of goods as a group. In 1997, the company strengthened its reputation by joining Distribution Canada Inc., a national alliance of independent grocers. That year also saw Triple 4 strike a deal with Pratt's Wholesale that included a fixed freight charge for all Triple 4 member stores. As a result, membership increased to 74 independent grocers that year. Membership continued to grow, and by the summer of 2007, the group had further increased to 519 members.

An important success factor for Triple 4 is how it treats its members. What started out as getting the best wholesaler prices and lowering expenses has expanded to assistance in areas such as developing store blueprints and decor; acquiring deals on debit/credit card services; managing long-term liabilities; providing life insurance, property insurance, and dental care; providing educational resources; and hosting trade shows. The store-specific support improves the trust and confidence that the member stores have in the Triple 4 organization. Because the focal point of Triple 4's long-term strategy is increasing the number of members to optimize the group advantage, the owners must consider the risk of not being able to provide its member retailers with individual attention as the number of members grows.

In 2010, Triple 4 Advertising's Harry Watson was recognized for his accomplishments in the small, independent grocer industry when he received the ABEX Business Leader of the Year Award.

Sources: J. Tutunjian, "Big Ideas in the Big Sky Country, "Canadian Grocer, 121(8), October 2007, pp. 20 -26; Triple 4 Advertising Ltd. website, www.finefoods.ca; and The ABEX Awards media release, http://www.finefoods.ca/Images/News/Abex/Abex%20Awards%20Winner%20 2010.pdf.

REQUIRED
A. What appear to be Triple 4's strengths relative to competitors (i.e., its core competencies)?
B. What appear to be Triple 4's weaknesses relative to competitors (e.g., Walmart)?
C. An organization's opportunities are identified by looking at the external environment and discovering potential new markets, technologies, or other prospects. What types of opportunities does Triple 4 currently appear to be taking advantage of?
D. What appear to be major threats to Triple 4's future success?
E. Discuss how the balanced scorecard can assist an organization in addressing its strengths, weaknesses, opportunities, and threats.

19.54 Balanced Scorecard, Strategy, Performance Measures

LO2, LO3 A large discount store has used a balanced scorecard for several years. The store's vision is to provide customers with affordable products in a family-friendly shopping environment. The company's strategy has been to focus on reducing the wait times for customers when checking out and when asking questions on the sales floor. Performance measures for the last two years follows.

	Year 1	Year 2
Average sale (total revenue/total invoices)	$ 37.5	$ 30
Average variable cost per sale	$ 15.75	$ 12
Average customer wait time at counter	2.5 minutes	2 minutes
Average wait time for sales floor help	3 minutes	2 minutes
Total returns	$ 142,500	$ 135,000
Total revenue	$2,000,000	$1,683,000
Total labour cost	$ 500,000	$ 495,000
Utilities cost (electricity and phone)	$ 5,250	$ 5,500
Number of items out of stock	120	180
Employee turnover	3	5

REQUIRED
A. Classify each performance measure according to one of the four balanced scorecard perspectives.
B. Analyze the change in each performance measure from Year 1 to Year 2. Give one possible reason for any changes. Identify the employee most likely to be able to explain the change in performance.
C. Which performance measures need further investigation? Explain.
D. What do the balanced scorecard results suggest about the success of the company's strategy to reduce wait time? Explain.
E. When an organization focuses on one strategy, problems sometimes arise in other areas. Do the balanced scorecard results provide evidence of possible deterioration in any operational areas? Explain. What additional measures would you recommend for each perspective?
F. Identify future targets for each measure currently being used and those you recommend in Part E. that would move the company closer toward its joint goals of affordable products in a family-friendly environment.

CHAPTER 20

Sustainability Accounting

After studying this chapter, you should be able to do the following:

LO1 Explain sustainability and sustainable management

LO2 Discuss sustainability accounting, sustainability management accounting, and sustainability reporting

LO3 Identify and explain the motivations and frameworks for external sustainability reporting

LO4 Explain the use of management accounting tools for sustainability management and reporting

LO5 Discuss the future direction of cost accounting

in brief

In the last decade, more emphasis has been placed on the role of environmental and social issues in business operations. Organizations are increasingly incorporating these issues in strategic management and reporting on environmental and social performance. Many of the management and cost accounting practices learned in earlier chapters of the textbook can be adapted to provide information that managers need to measure, monitor, and motivate organization decisions affecting the environment and society. These methods include identifying relevant quantitative and qualitative information for short-term and long-term decisions, process costing, activity-based costing, Grenzplankosten-rechnung (GPK), resource consumption accounting (RCA), life cycle costing, variance analysis, net present value and other capital budgeting techniques, value chain analysis, performance measurement, and balanced scorecards. In addition, new management and cost accounting practices are being developed, such as tracking the inputs, uses, and outputs of materials and energy through an organization's operations to help managers identify opportunities for reducing waste and emissions. ■

The Peak of Social and Environmental Reporting at Mountain Equipment Co-op

Keith Beaty/Toronto Star via Getty Images

Mountain Equipment Co-op (MEC), a retailing cooperative that sells outdoor gear, clothing, and services, was incorporated on August 2, 1971, with six members. As an outdoor equipment retailer, the environment has always been part of the MEC business. MEC has been publicly recognized for its sustainability efforts, and has consistently ranked at or near the top of the list of Corporate Knights' Best 50 Corporate Citizens in Canada.

Throughout MEC's history, the co-op has supported sustainable environmental initiatives. Through partnerships with a number of national organizations, including the Canadian Avalanche Centre, Parks Canada, the Canadian Parks and Wilderness Society, and Leave No Trace, among others, MEC provides financial support and leadership for environmental protection efforts. In 2007, MEC became the first major retailer in Canada to join 1% For the Planet, a group of businesses that have pledged to donate 1% of gross sales to environmental projects. To date, MEC has contributed over $29 million to Canadian conservation projects. In 2014, MEC launched a Wholesale Brand Partner Sustainability Program to encourage its suppliers to adopt environmentally friendly production practices, such as using organic and recycled materials.

MEC also internalizes its commitment to social and environmental responsibility when building or renovating stores. In 2002, the Winnipeg store was voted the most energy efficient retail building in Canada. The Burlington store, built in 2008, was the first of the new generation stores built to meet LEED gold certificate standards. All new stores, and its new Vancouver head office built in 2014, incorporate green initiatives, including geothermal energy generation, wind-generated power, solar panels, storm water retention systems, recycled and reusable building materials, and bike racks in the parking lot.

In 2011, MEC made its accountability report available on its website. The online dashboard reports on eight key areas of sustainability and allows for regular, automatic updates to the information. For each of the key areas, both summary information and the detailed underlying data are available for any interested reader. In 2014, MEC combined its accountability report with its financial report, seeing the two as inseparable. "For me, the thing I'm most proud of is the fact that our year-end report this year will be an integrated business and sustainability report," said David Labistour, MEC's chief executive officer. Making this information publicly available supports MEC's goal of being environmentally, socially, and economically responsible.

In this chapter, we will explore MEC's sustainability initiatives as we learn about practices used by organizations to measure, monitor, and motivate improved social and environmental performance. Management accountants contribute to these efforts by establishing internal and external measurement and reporting processes, and by applying the management accounting tools we have learned throughout this textbook to social and environmental activities.

SOURCES: "2015 Best 50 Results," *Corporate Knights* magazine, Summer 2015; Tara Perkins, "Top Company Profile: Mountain Equipment Co-op," *Corporate Knights* magazine, Summer 2014; Mountain Equipment Co-op 2014 annual report; Mountain Equipment Co-op corporate website, www.mec.ca.

Sustainable Management

Over the last several decades, entities around the world such as MEC have begun to account for their environmental and social practices. Because this is a rapidly evolving area, new terms are being introduced and the meaning of terms may change in the future. Currently, the term *sustainability* has been increasingly used as a business-related term.

Sustainability and Sustainable Management

The International Federation of Accountants (IFAC) defines sustainability and sustainable development as presented in the Brundtland Report: "Sustainable development is development that meets the needs of current generations without compromising the ability of future generations to meet their own needs."[1] Implementation of this definition requires consideration of the "three pillars" of economics, environment/ecology, and society.[2] The *Dictionary of Sustainable Management* defines sustainable management as "the ability to direct the course of a company, community, organization, or country in ways that restore and enhance all forms of capital (human, natural, manufactured, and financial) to generate stake-holder value and contribute to the well-being of current and future generations."[3] These definitions are broad; they encompass a wide range of future as well as current and past organizational activities. Also, the notion of sustainability is highly complex, and as a worldwide concept it is open to different interpretations, mainly because of multiple cultures, legal systems, and interest groups.

> **ALTERNATIVE TERMS**
>
> Other terms addressing sustainability issues in a business context include *corporate social responsibility (CSR); social accounting; social audit; triple bottom line; corporate responsibility; corporate citizenship; business ethics; corporate environmental responsibility; environmental ethics; green business; ecological footprinting; values-led business; risk management;* and *health, safety, and environment (HSE).*

Strategic Process for Sustainable Management

As discussed more fully in chapters 1 and 19, the strategic management process shown in Exhibit 20.1 assumes that managers make decisions in a strategic way. Accordingly, sustainable management involves addressing sustainability issues in each aspect of the strategic management process. To better understand the implications, we consider how each part of Exhibit 20.1 relates to sustainable management at MEC.

Organizational Vision. Traditionally, the vision of for-profit companies has focused primarily on economic success. Under sustainable management, organizations focus simultaneously on three value systems, often referred to as the **triple bottom line**: economic, environmental, and social value systems. However, no agreement exists about how the three dimensions should be prioritized. MEC's managers believe that all three parts are pervasive to the co-op's existence and have highlighted the importance in the co-op's mission, values, vision, and sustainability goals. MEC defines its sustainability position:

"We strive to make great products that lessen our impact on the environment and improve the lives of people we touch."[4]

> **EXHIBIT 20.1**
> Overview of Strategic Management Process

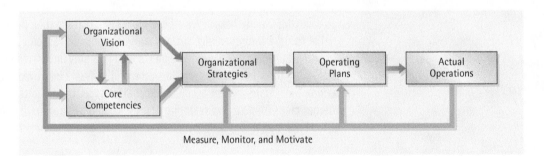

Measure, Monitor, and Motivate

---

[1] Report of the Brundtland Commission, "Part I, Section 2: Towards Sustainable Development," in *Report of the World Commission on Environment and Development: Our Common Future* (Oxford University Press, 1987), www.un-documents.net/wced-ocf.htm.
[2] IFAC, Sustainability Framework 2.0: Professional Accountants as Integrators, March 2011. Available at www.ifac.org.
[3] Available from www.sustainabilitydictionary.com/sustainable-management.
[4] From MEC charter, www.mec.ca/AST/ContentPrimary/AboutMEC/AboutOurCoOp/MecCharter.jsp and www.mec.ca/AST/ContentPrimary/AboutMEC/Sustainability.jsp.

MEC presents a detailed Sustainability Report in which it reports the achievement of people, planet, and product sustainability targets based on their goals:

People: We're committed to understanding and improving social and environmental conditions in our supply chain.

Planet: Through efficiency and innovation we use fewer natural resources and reduce our overall impact.

Product: We make products that function well, are durable and leave a lighter footprint on the environment.

Most companies continue to focus primarily on creating economic value, and they typically address environmental and social ideologies in separate reports. For example, the mission of Airbus S.A.S., one of the world's largest aircraft manufacturers, is "to meet the needs of airlines and operators by producing the most modern and comprehensive aircraft family on the market, complemented by the highest standard of product support."[5] An "Ethics and Compliance" section of the company's website describes its values related to diversity, integrity, quality, and safety and an "Eco-efficiency" section describes its commitment to environmental concerns.[6]

In deciding whether or how sustainability issues should affect organizational vision, many managers differentiate between internal and external impacts. **Internal impacts** are costs and benefits inside the organization that are recognized in the entity's conventional accounting system. For example, the cost and availability of raw materials are internal impacts for a manufacturer. **External impacts** are costs and benefits that are not generally accounted for in an entity's conventional accounting system. External impacts are also called **externalities**, or spillover effects of transactions on stakeholders who are not directly involved. For example, pollution by a raw material supplier that adversely affects the health of surrounding residents is a negative externality. The costs of the pollution are not accounted for in the material supplier's accounting system and the health problems are a spillover effect on the local residents of having the raw material producer in the community. Over time, some external impacts become internal impacts due to new laws and regulations or stakeholder pressure. For example, a 2001 Japanese law retroactively applies nitrogen oxide emissions standards to old vehicles in Tokyo. Proponents of sustainable management argue that organizations should avoid negative externalities by incorporating both internal and external impacts in their organizational vision and the entire strategic management process.

Enterprise risk management considerations also influence how managers envision their approach to sustainable management. Sustainability encourages managers to become more aware of long-term economic, environmental, and social risks. As managers establish organizational vision, they take into account the organization's risk appetite, or willingness to take on risk.

Core Competencies. It is unclear whether sustainability management practices could be a competitive advantage. Clearly, the founding members of MEC were not profit oriented, as is evidenced by their form of business—a cooperative—and their emphasis on bringing quality outdoor gear to Canadian outdoor enthusiasts. Today, they specifically recognize the "increased demands for sustainability leadership and transparency" and have responded by making their Accountability Report publicly available on the MEC website. Unfortunately, many managers are unwilling to engage in sustainable management practices unless they believe the organization will benefit economically or avoid economic disadvantages. In recent years, managers and accountants have been increasingly concerned with building a "business case" for sustainable management by identifying and measuring the costs and benefits.

Organizational Strategies. Strategies are plans that managers develop to take advantage of core competencies while working toward the organization's vision. Thus, strategies for sustainable management are unlikely to be developed unless managers have first identified sustainability as part of the organizational vision and core competencies. By integrating

> **ALTERNATIVE TERMS**
>
> *Internal impacts* are also called *direct* or *private impacts* or *internal costs and benefits*. *External impacts* are also called *indirect* or *social impacts* or *external costs and benefits*.

---

[5] Airbus S.A.S., www.airbus.com/company/aircraft-manufacture.
[6] Airbus S.A.S., www.airbus.com/company/corporate-social-responsibility/ethics/; www.airbus.com/company/eco-efficiency.

sustainability in all aspects of the organization (i.e., products, buildings, partnerships), MEC has committed to developing organizational strategies to specifically achieve sustainability goals.

Operating Plans. Strategies lead to operating plans, including budgets and short-term tactical decisions. Specific operating plans are needed to carry out strategies related to sustainable management. For example, MEC committed to diverting 92% of waste at all stores and facilities in 2014. To achieve this target, MEC's 2014 operating plans most likely included specific tactics for recycling, reusing, and composting waste materials.

Actual Operations. Companies traditionally measured and tracked primarily financial results. In recent years, companies increasingly measure and monitor their environmental and social performance. MEC publicly discloses its sustainability performance in its annual Accountability Report. These reports will continue to evolve over time and currently include qualitative and quantitative assessments of environmental and social performance compared to goals.

Feedback Loop. The feedback loops in Exhibit 20.1 help managers monitor their organizations' progress toward long-term and short-term goals. For example, MEC annually compares its actual achievement for each sustainability indicator to its target and explains how targets were met, why some were not achieved, and future plans. In general, three methods are used to evaluate organizational sustainability performance: internal measurement for specific goals, benchmarking against the activities of other organizations, and feedback from stakeholders.

The feedback loop is not intended to involve only an organization's managers. A key principle of sustainable management is incorporation of feedback from many stakeholder groups, to reflect upon and guide business conduct. Feedback might be obtained from groups such as the business community, investors, labour, and civil society. Information about sustainability strategies, operating plans, and actual outcomes serves as the basis for stakeholder input into the sustainable management process.

The feedback loops can also lead to revisions at any level of sustainable management. Achieving sustainability outcomes is a complex process that often requires substantive change. The focus of organizational vision, strategies, and operating plans often evolves as managers learn more about environmental and social issues and gain greater experience.

© Thomas Imo/Alamy

●● > FOCUS ON ETHICAL DECISION MAKING: ROOTING OUT BRIBERY

During 2009, Siemens AG, a German-based electronics and engineering conglomerate, agreed to pay 1.2 billion euros to settle German and U.S. government bribery charges. In the course of the legal proceedings, the company had incurred an additional 1 billion euros in legal expenses.

U.S. and German investigators began looking into charges of bribery at Siemens during 2004. The investigations ultimately revealed that Siemens paid bribes and kickbacks to obtain contracts for projects, including national identity cards in Argentina, mass transit in Venezuela, a cell phone network in Bangladesh, and United Nations oil-for-food in Iraq. The U.S. Securities and Exchange Commission estimated that bribes to officials in Asia, Africa, Europe, the Middle East, and Latin America had totalled U.S. $1.4 billion.

In spite of company guidelines, the Federal Bureau of Investigation Washington office head, Joseph Persichini Jr., concluded that bribery had become a business strategy and part of standard operating procedures at Siemens. Following a company offer of amnesty, 110 managers came forward with reports of wrongdoing and Siemens revamped its compliance program.

In May 2011, the new compliance program was put to the test when three sales employees agreed to pay bribes in exchange for an energy contract. After officials received a tip-off through the company hotline, an investigation was launched, authorities were notified, and appropriate actions were taken. The event was hailed as proof that Siemens had righted previous faulty control procedures.

Bribery is closely associated with *corruption*, which is defined by Transparency International as "the abuse of entrusted power for private gain. It hurts everyone whose life, livelihood or happiness depends on the integrity of people in a position of authority." The table below summarizes the costs of corruption (adapted from Transparency International, 2010):

Political	Social
• Hinders democracy and rule of law • Prevents development of accountable political leadership Economic • Depletes national wealth • Diverts scarce public resources to large expensive projects • Discourages investments in rural area infrastructure such as schools, hospitals, roads, or the supply of power and water • Distorts competition and deters business investment	• Undermines trust in the political system, institutions, and leadership • Encourages apathy • Enables leaders to turn national assets into personal wealth • Encourages emigration of able and honest citizens Environmental • Enables investment in polluting industries • Exploits natural resources • Gives preference to large, environmentally devastating projects

Source: M. Karpstein and A. Preuschat, "UPDATE: Siemens Sues Former Executives Linked to Bribery Case," *Dow Jones Newswires*, January 25, 2010, online at wsj.com; "Ungreasing the Wheels," *The Economist*, November 19, 2009, www.economist.com; C.C. Verschoor, "Siemens AG Is the Latest Fallen Ethics Idol," *Strategic Finance*, November 2007; E. Lichtblau and C. Dougherty, "Siemens to Pay $1.34 Billion in Fines," *The New York Times*, December 16, 2008, nytimes.com; investor relations section of Siemens AG website, w1.siemens.com; "Stopping the Rot," *The Economist*, March 6, 2008, www.economist.com; Transparency International, "What Is Corruption?", available at www.transparency.org/about and Transparency International, "What Are the Costs of Corruption?", available at www.transparency.org/whoweare/organisation/faqs_on_corruption#costsOfCorruption; "Siemens Compliance Program Made The Catch, Company Says," *The Wall Street Journal*, June 10, 2011, http://blogs.wsj.com/corruption-currents/2011/06/10/siemens-compliance-program-made-the-catch-company-says/tab/print/.

ETHICS AND SIMILAR CODES OF CONDUCT IN PRACTICE

The Siemens bribery scandal highlights the fact that formal guidelines do not prevent unethical or illegal behaviour. This scandal also illustrates the broader sustainability impacts of bribery. Consider the following questions. How can illegal behaviours such as bribery occur even when an organization's ethics or a similar code of conduct explicitly prohibits the behaviour? What values and priorities might encourage an employee to pay a bribe to a foreign official? Why is bribery difficult to monitor and control? How can organizations increase the likelihood that employees will comply with a code of ethics? In what ways is corruption an impediment to sustainable management?

Sustainability and Levers of Control

Exhibit 20.2 summarizes several ways in which control systems can be used to support sustainable management. Strategies and operating plans for improved sustainability are unlikely to be achieved without adequate communication via beliefs systems, and boundary systems help to clarify which types of practices should be avoided. Measurement systems can be established to help managers monitor progress toward preset goals and to create incentives to achieve them. Interactive systems can lead to new insights about sustainability challenges and opportunities.

Sustainability Accounting and Reporting

No authoritative definitions currently exist for sustainability accounting, and no common agreement has been reached on sustainable reporting practices. Nevertheless, these terms

Beliefs Systems

- Communicate organizational vision for sustainable management
- Motivate managers to prioritize and coordinate financial, environmental, and social value systems

Interactive Control Systems

- Engage in organizational learning by investigating the strategic opportunities and threats revealed by differences between planned and actual sustainability performance
- Reevaluate and revise sustainable management strategies and operating plans as conditions change

Boundary Systems

- Prohibit specific activities, such as purchasing raw materials from suppliers that fail to meet organizational social or environmental standards
- Establish codes of conduct for financial, environmental, and social practices

Diagnostic Control Systems

- Monitor planned versus actual sustainability performance to maintain control over preset goals
- Motivate managers to improve financial, environmental, and social performance
- Assign responsibility and reward employees for achieving

L02 Discuss sustainability accounting, sustainability management accounting, and sustainability reporting

are used widely in business, and significant efforts are underway to develop globally accepted definitions and practices. In this section of the chapter, we will learn tentative definitions, gain an understanding of general principles, and explore recent developments.

Sustainability Accounting and Sustainability Management Accounting

Sustainability accounting is the systematic recording, reporting, and analysis of quantitative and qualitative information about sustainable management practices and performance. Sustainable accounting may incorporate activities traditionally related to management and cost accounting, financial accounting, or auditing and other assurance services. Sustainable accounting may also incorporate new and creative activities, as accountants work with individuals from other disciplines such as the natural and social sciences and engineering.

In this chapter, we are primarily concerned with **sustainability management accounting**, which involves accounting activities to assist in the sustainable management process, such as designing and evaluating business processes, budgeting and forecasting, implementing and monitoring internal controls, and analyzing, synthesizing, and aggregating information.[7] Sustainability management accounting applies a sustainability lens to the management accounting techniques discussed in the earlier chapters of this textbook.

Internal and External Sustainability Reporting

Wide variations exist in organizational strategies for communicating information about sustainability efforts and performance, called **sustainability reporting**. Exhibit 20.3 highlights the role of information systems and provides examples of internal and external sustainability reporting.

Internal sustainability reports are designed to provide information for sustainability management decisions, as introduced in Exhibit 20.1, and to support the control systems shown in Exhibit 20.2. Some internal reports, such as monthly worker injury rates or volumes of waste, are issued regularly. Other internal reports, such as an environmental and social analysis of a potential business acquisition, are generated for onetime use. Later in the chapter, we will learn specific management accounting methods that can be used to develop a wide range of internal reports.

---

[7] We use the terms *sustainability accounting* and *sustainability management accounting* to refer to accounting processes that address financial, environmental, and social value systems, consistent with the definition for sustainability provided earlier in the chapter. In addition, our definitions include both internal and external impacts. Earlier textbooks tend to refer only to *environmental accounting* and focus primarily on the internal impacts that would be included in financial statements.

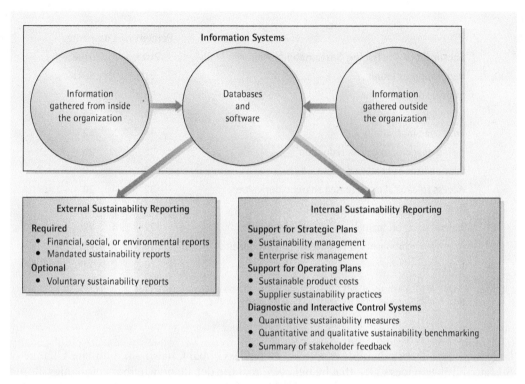

External sustainability reports can be distributed to different constituencies for many purposes. Some of these reports are required, while others are optional. Regulators may require compliance reports for laws such as minimum wages or maximum pollution levels. Financial statements issued to shareholders and financial institutions may require accruals for environmental liability costs. In Canada, most aspects of sustainability reporting are voluntary and unregulated. However, legislation in countries such as France, Germany, and Norway is driving an increase in sustainability reporting.

External Sustainability Reporting

Companies increasingly issue external sustainability reports, as is evident in KPMG International's 2011 survey of "corporate responsibility" reports issued by the 250 largest companies worldwide and the largest 100 companies within each of 22 countries. Worldwide, approximately 95% of these companies issued some type of sustainability report in 2011, compared with approximately 80% in 2008. The biggest proportion of large companies issuing a report was in the United Kingdom (100%), followed by Japan (99%) and South Africa (97%), with 79% of Canadian companies reporting on social and environmental issues.[8]

LO3 Identify and explain the motivations and frameworks for external sustainability reporting

Motivations for External Sustainability Reporting

Why do so many large companies choose to issue sustainability reports, especially in countries where the reports are voluntary?[9] Exhibit 20.4 lists the most common factors cited by the 250 largest companies in KPMG's 2011 and 2008 surveys. Overall, the most common factors in 2011 were reputation or brand and ethical considerations. Regardless of the reason for reporting corporate responsibility, the 2013 report indicates that the reporting rate in the world's largest 250 companies had stabilized at approximately 93%. As a result of continued,

[8] Country data are based on the percent issuing stand-alone reports plus the percent issuing a report integrated with the annual report. Source: KPMG International, *KPMG International Survey of Corporate Responsibility Reporting 2011*, November 2011, Amstelveen, The Netherlands: KPMG International, p. 10.

[9] Some aspects of sustainability reports are required in the United States for public companies under SEC regulations. For example, companies must report information about material litigation, liabilities, and other types of risks. However, most large companies' sustainability reports include significant amounts of information that is not required.

Factor Cited for Issuing Sustainability Report	Percent of Companies	
	2011	2008
Reputation or brand	67%	55%
Ethical considerations	58	69
Innovation and learning	44	55
Employee motivation	44	52
Risk management or risk reduction	35	35
Economic considerations	32	68
Access to capital or increased shareholder value	32	29
Strengthened supplier relationships	22	32
Market position (market share) improvement	22	22
Improved relationship with government authorities	18	21
Cost savings	10	17

Source: KPMG International, *KPMG International Survey of Corporate Responsibility Reporting 2011*, November 2011, Amstelveen, The Netherlands: KPMG International, p. 19.

large increases in sustainability reporting, KPMG's Global Chairmain, Climate Change & Sustainability Services stated that he believes "that the debate on whether companies should report on CR or not is dead and buried."[10] The questions that need to be addressed are what to report, how to report, and how to maximize the value of reporting for stakeholders.

Large companies are more likely than smaller companies to issue a sustainability report. However, two main factors are likely to encourage increased sustainability reporting by smaller companies. First, many smaller companies are developing "green" products and are likely to use sustainability reporting as a means of marketing to consumers. Second, smaller businesses often supply goods and services to large companies, which are increasingly demanding that their supply partners satisfy a range of environmental and social standards.

●●● ▷ RISK OF BIASED DECISIONS: GREENWASHING

Companies are increasingly labelling their products and services as "green." Some companies appear to spend significant resources on publicity about being environmentally friendly without making substantive changes in their environmental impact, a practice referred to as greenwashing. For example, hotels have been accused of with greenwashing for publicizing water and energy savings from giving guests the option to reuse towels and bed sheets, while they continue to waste large amounts of water and energy on lighting, kitchen operations, grounds keeping, and vehicle fleets. Consumer product companies may label their products with "green" certifications that are created by the companies themselves. Even government-sponsored certifications for products such as organic foods may be unreliable. Some companies have lied about environmental claims, such as the percentage of recycled content in paper.

The concern is that consumer decisions may be biased because people are misled by greenwashing. Greenwashing Index, a collaboration between EnviroMedia Social Marketing and University of Oregon, recommends that consumers use the following criteria to evaluate companies' green claims:

- Look for misleading words, visuals, and graphics (e.g., natural images) that imply products or companies are more environmentally friendly than they actually are
- Consider whether green claims are vague or unproven

---

[10] Yvo de Boer, KPMG's Global Chairman, Climate Change & Sustainability Services, The KPMG Survey of Corporate Responsibility Reporting 2013, December 2013, pp. 10.

- Assess environmental claims for possible overstatement or exaggeration
- Identify situations where information is omitted or masked to divert attention from environmentally damaging aspects of a company's operations

  Companies can reduce accusations of greenwashing by:
- Providing independent and unbiased evidence of environmental benefits or improvements
- Publishing an environmental strategy with defined objectives that are integrated into strategic management
- Implementing a system for measuring and monitoring environmental strategic objectives
- Including environmental dimensions in performance measurement systems
- Assessing and addressing enterprise risks, including long-term environmental issues

Sources: Greenwashing Index, "Greenwashing Index Scoring Criteria" and "What Is Greenwashing? It's Whitewashing, But With a Green Brush," www.greenwashingindex.com; KPMG International, *KPMG International Survey of Corporate Responsibility Reporting 2008*, October 2008, Amstelveen, The Netherlands: KPMG International, pp. 2, 20, and 72; and R. Lamb, "How Greenwashing Works," January 25, 2008, HowStuffWorks.com.

Frameworks and Guidelines for External Sustainability Reporting

As discussed earlier, wide variation exists in organizational strategies for sustainability reporting. This variation makes it difficult for stakeholders to interpret and compare sustainability information and leads to scepticism about whether managers are providing sustainability information in a transparent way versus engaging in "impression management." In addition, the fact that most sustainability disclosures are voluntary leads to concerns that the reports are biased. To alleviate these concerns, initiatives are emerging to develop standards for sustainability reporting.

Global Reporting Initiative (GRI). Global Reporting Initiative (GRI) is a network organization based in Amsterdam that has developed a freely available framework for disclosure on economic, environmental, and social performance. GRI's *Sustainability Reporting Guidelines*™ include reporting principles and recommendations for specific types of disclosures and performance measures, referred to as *GRI indicators*. KPMG's 2013 survey found that 82% of the world's 250 largest companies used GRI sustainability reporting guidelines.[12] Exhibit 20.5 provides examples of GRI indicators in economic, environment, and four social performance categories.

The GRI indicators are designed to provide information to stakeholders and also to encourage improved sustainability. For example, environment indicator G4-EN27 requires the organization to report the products and packaging materials that are recycled on behalf of the organization as a percent of total products sold during the period, by product category. Companies reporting these data are more likely to establish programs to collect products at the end of their lives, identify opportunities for reusing materials and components, and design products and packages that can be recycled.

Some of the GRI indicators also encourage greater international conformity of laws. For example, social performance indicator G4-LA6 requires the organization to report rates of injury, occupational diseases, lost days, and absenteeism, and total number of work-related fatalities by region. Reports must indicate whether national law complies with reporting standards issued by the International Labour Organization (ILO), a United Nations agency that promotes decent working conditions around the world through cooperation of governments, employers, and workers.[13]

> **INTERNATIONAL**
>
> Years after the oil spill in the Gulf of Mexico, **BP** continues to work to rebuild public trust and improve awareness of their approach to sustainability, including providing an online sustainability report in multiple languages.[11]

---

[11] See www.bp.com/en/global/corporate/sustainability/about-our-reporting/Sustainability-report.html.
[12] Information about GRI is available at www.globalreporting.org.
[13] Information about ILO is available at www.ilo.org.

▶EXHIBIT 20.5

Examples of Global Reporting Initiative (GRI) Core Indicators

ECONOMIC

G4-EC1 – Economic value generated and distributed	Economic value generated = Net sales plus revenues from financial investments and sales of assets
	Economic value distributed includes these:
	• Operating costs = Payments to suppliers, non-strategic investments, royalties, and facilitation payments
	• Employee wages and benefits = Total monetary outflows for employees (current payments, not future commitments)
	• Payments to providers of capital = All financial payments made to the providers of the organization's capital
	• Payments to government (by country) = Gross taxes
	• Community investments = Voluntary contributions and investment of funds in the broader community (includes donations)

ENVIRONMENT

G4-EN2 – Percentage of materials used that are recycled input materials	Recycled input materials used = Weight or volume of input materials that replace virgin materials, excluding by-products and non-product outputs.
	Total input materials used = Weight or volume of direct materials used that are present in a final product including raw materials, semi-manufactured goods or parts, and packaging materials.
	Any estimation methods used must be disclosed.
G4-EN28 – Percentage of products sold and their packaging materials that are reclaimed by category	Calculated as a percent of products sold within the reporting period. Products and their packaging materials reclaimed within the reporting period = Products and packaging materials at the end of their useful life that are collected and treated on behalf of the reporting organization; requires separation into raw materials or components and use by the organization or others; excludes rejects and product recalls.
	Data may be collected internally or obtained from external contractors.

SOCIAL PERFORMANCE: LABOUR PRACTICES AND DECENT WORK

G4-LA6 – Type of injury, occupational diseases, lost days, and absenteeism, and total number of work-related fatalities, by region and by gender	Workforce includes total employees and independent contractors working on-site.
	When reporting accident statistics, the organization must disclose whether data are based on International Labour Organization (ILO) standards for recording and notification of occupational accidents and diseases.
	Data must comply with specific definitions for each health and safety category.

SOCIAL PERFORMANCE: HUMAN RIGHTS

G4-HR5 – Operations and suppliers identified as having significant risk for incidents of child labor, and measures taken to contribute to the effective abolition of child labor	Significant risks of child labour may arise from the type of operations (e.g., manufacturing plants) or specific countries or geographic areas.
	Reporting of measures taken must follow ILO 'Tripartite Declaration of Principles Concerning Multinational Enterprises and Social Policy and OECD Guidelines for Multinational Enterprises.

SOCIAL PERFORMANCE: SOCIETY

G4-SO5 – Confirmed incidents of corruption and actions taken	Required disclosures include the following:
	• Total number and nature of confirmed incidents of corruption.
	• Number of incidents in which employees were dismissed or disciplined for corruption
	• Number of incidents in which business partner contracts were not renewed due to violations related to corruption
	• Existence of and outcomes from any concluded legal cases regarding corrupt practices brought against the reporting organization or its employees during the reporting period

EXHIBIT 20.5
(Continued)

SOCIAL PERFORMANCE: PRODUCT RESPONSIBILITY

G4-PR2 – Total number of incidents of non-compliance with regulations and voluntary codes concerning the health and safety impacts of products and services during their life cycle, by type of outcomes	Must report the total number of incidents for: • non-compliance with regulations resulting in a fine or penalty • non-compliance with regulations resulting in a warning • non-compliance with voluntary codes

Indicators and protocols were adapted from the following Global Reporting Initiative™ publications:

Global Reporting Initiative: G4 Sustainability Reporting Guidelines, Implementation Manual, 2013, Global Reporting Initiative, Amsterdam, The Netherlands, https://www.globalreporting.org/resourcelibrary/GRIG4-Part2-Implementation-Manual.pdf

International Organization for Standardization (ISO). International Organization for Standardization (ISO), the world's largest developer of international standards, released ISO 26000 – *Guidance for Social Responsibility* during 2010.[14] ISO 26000, among other benefits, provides principles for sustainability reporting, guidance for several major reporting areas, and recommendations for implementation. An overview of the proposed guidelines for sustainability reporting is shown in Exhibit 20.6.

Recognition for High-Quality Sustainability Management and Reporting

As the criteria for sustainability reporting becomes more well-defined and standardized, the comparability and quality of organizations' reports should increase. In addition, investors and other stakeholders are increasingly seeking information to help them identify organizations with higher-quality sustainable management practices. This demand has led to markets for analyst and benchmarking reports. One example is described below.

Corporate Knights Magazine publishes an annual list called the "Global 100 Most Sustainable Corporations." Companies are chosen based on analyses of 10 sustainability indicators, including CEO-to-average worker pay, the ratio of sales to carbon dioxide emissions, ratio of sales to waste, and whether at least one senior officer's pay is linked to sustainability.[15] In the 2015 list, Biogen Idec (United States) was ranked first, with Canadian-based Tim Hortons ranked eleventh.[16]

BUSINESS PRACTICE

Gordon Hicks, CEO of Brookfield Global Integrated Solutions, was named the "Greenest chief executive in Canada 2015" by Corporate Knights for "doing the best job of earning profits while preserving the planet."[17]

---

[14] Information about ISO is available at www.iso.org. Although the proposed ISO guidelines use the term *social responsibility* instead of *sustainability*, the concepts are consistent with those discussed in this chapter.

[15] Corporate Knights, Key performance indicators, January 22, 2014, 2014 Global 100, www.corporateknights.com/reports/2015-global-100/key-performance-indicators.

[16] Global 100 Most Sustainable Corporations in the World www.corporateknights.com/reports/2015-global-100/2015-global-100-results-14218559.

[17] Corporate Knights, Greenest chief executive in Canada 2015, Brenda Bouw, Summer 2015, www.corporateknights.com/magazines/2015-best-50-issue/greenest-chief-executive-canada-2015-14332248.

▶EXHIBIT 20.6
Overview of ISO 26000 Guidelines for
Sustainability Reporting

Reporting on Social Responsibility

An organization should, at appropriate intervals, report about its performance on social responsibility to stakeholders affected, and a growing number do. Reporting to stakeholders can be done in many different ways, including stakeholder-group meetings, letters describing the organization's activities related to social responsibility for a defined period, website information, and periodic social responsibility reports.

In reporting to its stakeholders, an organization should include information about its objectives and performance on the core subjects and relevant issues of social responsibility. It should describe how and when stakeholders have been involved in the organization's reporting on social responsibility.

The organization should provide a fair and complete picture of its social responsibility performance, including achievements and shortfalls and the ways in which the shortfalls will be addressed.

An organization may choose to cover its activities as a whole at one time, or report separately on activities at a particular location or site. Community groups often consider smaller, location-specific reporting more useful than organization-wide reporting.

Publication of a social responsibility report can be a valuable aspect of an organization's activities on social responsibility. In preparing a social responsibility report, an organization should take account of the following considerations:

- the scope and scale of an organization's report should be appropriate for the size and nature of the organization;

- the level of detail may reflect the extent of the organization's experience with such reporting; in some cases, organizations initiate their efforts with limited reports covering only a few key subjects, and in subsequent years, expand coverage as they gain experience and have sufficient data on which to base a broader report;

- the report should describe how the organization decided upon the issues to be covered and the way those issues would be addressed;

- the report should present the organization's operational performance, products and services in a broader sustainability context;

- a report can be produced in a variety of forms, depending on the nature of the organization and on the needs of its stakeholders; these may include electronic posting of the report, web-based interactive versions or hard copies, or as a stand-alone document or part of an organization's annual report.

Source: International Organization for Standardization (ISO), *Guidance on Social Responsibility*, Draft International Standard ISO/DIS 26000, 2009, Geneva: ISO, p. 75. Permission to use extracts from ISO/DIS 26000:2009 was provided by Standards Council of Canada. No further reproduction is permitted without prior written approval from Standards Council of Canada.

To remain on the Global 100 (or any other sustainability-benchmarking list), organizations must continually meet the stringent sustainable management and reporting requirements of that list. The requirements ensure that sustainable management is an integral part of the entity's culture, and that management control systems provide support for high-quality sustainable management (as highlighted in exhibits 20.1, 20.2, and 20.3). Organizations that excel in applying the GRI reporting framework, ISO guidelines, or similar standards are more likely to have the type of sustainability management accounting system that will satisfy these requirements.

Sustainability Management Accounting Tools

L04 Explain the use of management accounting tools for sustainability management and reporting

When fully integrated into an organization, sustainable management affects everything the organization does. Accordingly, sustainability principles can affect almost any area of management accounting. Exhibit 20.7 lists key management accounting questions that have been addressed throughout this textbook and summarizes the general effects of adopting sustainable management practices.

Identifying and incorporating sustainability factors into information systems and decision analyses is often a difficult task. In this section, we learn several commonly used methods.

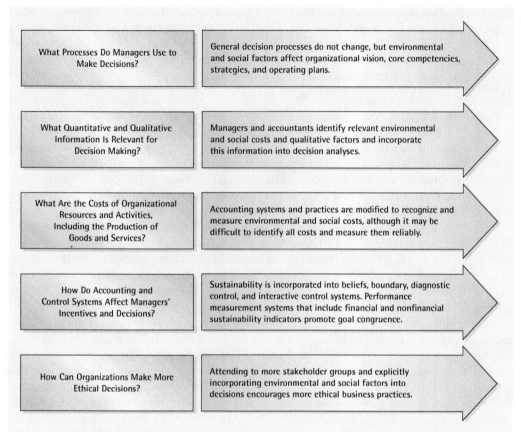

Key Management Accounting Questions
and Effects of Sustainable Management

Relevant Sustainability Costs and Benefits for Decision Making

Throughout this textbook, we have identified relevant information for a wide range of decisions, including the following:

- Insource or outsource a product or service
- Keep or drop a product, service, or customer
- Accept or reject a special order
- Emphasize products that optimize the contribution margin
- Process a joint product beyond the split-off point
- Accept or reject a strategic investment
- Choose among alternative strategic investments

Traditional management accounting practices tend to overlook potentially significant sustainability costs and benefits within these decisions, because (1) accounting recognition is delayed when costs are contingent on future events (e.g., lawsuits), (2) relevant revenues and costs are not isolated in the accounting system (e.g., recycling revenues and normal waste costs included in product costs), (3) relevant costs are not measured (e.g., externalities or image and relationship costs), or (4) opportunity costs are not measured (e.g., forgone revenues and costs from alternative product design or production methods).

Timing of Costs and Benefits. The consequences of environmental and social responsibility activities often occur years after the related management decisions and operations. Examples include lawsuits over environmental contamination or decommissioning costs for closure of a manufacturing facility. Accounting systems do not typically recognize these types of costs at the time of the initial investment or operating decisions. Accordingly, the current-period accounting system may include costs and benefits from prior years' operations, and some costs and benefits related to the current period are missing; they will be realized in the future.

To calculate relevant cash flows for current-period decisions, these types of timing issues must be addressed. Costs and benefits arising from prior year operations are irrelevant for current-period decisions, so they should be ignored when estimating the effects of current decisions. Estimation techniques must be used to determine future cash flows that are expected to arise from current decisions.

Measuring Internal and External Costs and Benefits. When learning about the influence of sustainable management on organizational vision, we differentiated between internal impacts—costs and benefits that directly affect an organization—and external impacts or externalities—costs and benefits that are not generally accounted for in an entity's conventional accounting system. Although classifying costs and benefits into these two categories is helpful in thinking about environmental and social responsibilities, in practice it is useful to separate internal costs into additional categories, in part because managers and accountants must choose how deep they want to delve when identifying relevant sustainability costs and benefits.

Exhibit 20.8 outlines five levels of costs for sustainability management accounting practices. The categories range from 1 (easiest to measure) to 5 (most difficult to measure). The sum of levels 1 to 4 is generally referred to as internal cost, while external costs are classified as level 5. Level 5 externalities might previously have been ignored by organizations, but sustainability management is optimized when sustainability management accounting control systems identify and internalize all current (and potential future) externalities.

Sometimes, markets are developed that make it easier to measure sustainability costs. For example, carbon markets can be used measure the value of greenhouse gas emissions (e.g., the European Union Greenhouse Gas Emission Trading System). These markets can dramatically alter decision-making processes related to resource allocation. Organizations that account for carbon emissions, as suggested by the Global Reporting Initiative, need to track and report monthly and/or annual emission targets as if they were potential revenue or liabilities within the organization. Carbon accounting will therefore affect processes along the entire value chain—from the choice of raw materials and suppliers, design or re-engineering requirements, type of energy used in production processes, methods of waste management adopted, insourced or outsourced production, packaging and transportation options, and the firm's reputation among suppliers, staff, and potential and existing customers.

> **EXHIBIT 20.8**
Categories for Sustainability Costs

Internal Costs	
Level 1	**Conventional Costs** – Includes the costs of direct raw materials, utilities, labour, supplies, structures, capital equipment, and related depreciation.
Level 2	**Hidden Costs** – Includes up-front environmental and social costs, such as search costs relating to finding sustainability-conscious suppliers, initial design costs of preferable sustainable products, regulatory costs that are often obscured in overhead costs, and future decommissioning or remediation costs.
Level 3	**Contingent Costs** – Defined in probabilistic terms and includes fines for breaching environmental or social requirements, clean-up costs, lawsuits relating to unsound environmental, employment, or other practices.
Level 4	**Image and Relationship Costs** – Are difficult to determine and would seldom be separately identified within an accounting system. However, they could be expected to exert influence on the value of some intangible assets such as goodwill, brand names, and so forth.
External Costs	
Level 5	**Externalities** – Costs that an entity imposes on others as a result of its operations but which the entity typically ignores. These costs include environmental or social damage that the organization caused but is not held accountable for, such as adverse health effects resulting from water pollution that does not violate laws and regulations. It is difficult and sometimes controversial to put a cost on these effects and, with the exception of a few organizations worldwide, most entities ignore them when calculating profits. However, physical measures can be developed, and indicators can be used to assess performance.

Adapted from United States Environmental Protection Agency (EPA), *An Introduction to Environmental Accounting As a Business Management Tool: Key Concepts and Terms*, June 1995, Washington, D.C.: EPA.

More Accurate Assignment of Sustainability Costs

In many organizations, sustainability costs are not recorded separately through the accounting system. Depending on the nature of the costs, they may be included in a variety of accounts, such as direct materials assigned to units of product (e.g., scrap), manufacturing overhead (e.g., waste disposal), or general and administration overhead (e.g., public relations and legal costs). The identification and classification of sustainability cost objects and their related costs require entity-wide involvement. Tracking and tracing sustainability costs, and identifying cost pools and related cost drivers, are crucial for sustainability management accounting purposes. Before sustainability costs can be allocated to cost objects, consensus among the key managers is vital. The cost object might be individual business units, production departments, costs centres, production lines, specific equipment, or even individual jobs, products, or services. Input from department managers is important, particularly where the performance of that unit or manager is affected by sustainability cost consumptions.

The following illustration demonstrates a problem that arises when environmental costs are aggregated and allocated using a traditional allocation base such as direct labour hours. Products A and B appear equally profitable when sustainability costs are included in manufacturing overhead and allocated on the basis of direct labour hours at an overhead allocation rate of $50 per hour for two direct labour hours for each product. The per-unit revenues, costs, and profit are shown here.

	Product A	Product B
Revenues	$300	$400
Direct labour	50	40
Direct materials	50	160
Manufacturing overhead	100	100
Profit	$100	$100

To improve managers' understanding of each product's costs and profitability, activity-based costing (ABC) could be used to analyze the manufacturing overhead costs. Assume that three activity pools and cost drivers are identified. The first cost pool consists mostly of indirect labour costs, and the cost driver for this pool is direct labour cost. The allocation rate for the indirect labour pool is 10% of direct labour cost. The second cost pool is related to material handling, and this cost is allocated based on number of parts per product. Product A has nine parts and Product B has seven parts. Material handling costs are allocated at $5 per part. The third cost pool is related to hazardous waste clean-up costs, and these costs are traced directly to each manufacturing process. The environmental cost traced to each unit of Product A amounts to $10, while $89 is traced to each unit of Product B. Using these ABC costs, the profitability of each product is recalculated as follows.

	Product A	Product B
Revenues	$300	$400
Direct labour	50	40
Direct materials	50	160
Indirect labour pool	5	16
Material handling pool	45	35
Environmental cost pool	10	89
Profit	$140	$ 60

When costs are mapped more accurately to the use of resources, less cross-product cost subsidization occurs (discussed more thoroughly in Chapter 7). Products with greater environmental or social costs may appear to be more profitable when these costs are allocated to all products based on traditional allocation bases, such as direct labour hours. Once costs are traced more accurately, managers can make better decisions, such as product emphasis and whether to keep or drop a product. Accounting for sustainability might require isolating and tracking sustainability costs to the cost object, in this case each product.

We learned in Chapter 7 that ABC, Grenzplankostenrechnung (GPK), and resource consumption accounting (RCA) enhance the understanding of business processes associated with each product by allocating costs on the basis of the activities and resources that trigger costs. ABC, GPK, and RCA map costs more accurately to cost objects and, therefore, may better identify internal and external sustainability costs and benefits.

Material Flow Accounting

Because of worldwide concerns about the environment, considerable efforts have been made to integrate environmental management practices into the accounting systems of individual organizations. Material flow accounting, also called *input-output analysis*, is the process of analyzing the movement of all physical materials through an organization's operations.[18] This accounting method assumes that all physical inputs must eventually become outputs, so total inputs must equal total outputs.

Inputs include all direct and indirect manufacturing materials, regardless of how obtained: product packaging materials; merchandise acquired; operating materials such as office supplies, cleaning supplies, and lighting fixtures; and water. Inputs also include all forms of energy, including electricity, gas, coal, solar power, and wind. Materials and energy inputs are usually tracked separately.

Outputs are divided into three major categories: products, waste, and emissions. Product outputs include physical products that will be sold—including related packaging materials—plus by-products. Waste may be hazardous or nonhazardous and includes any physical inputs that are not present in product outputs. Accordingly, some inputs, such as office supplies and cleaning supplies and manufacturing scrap, are always categorized as waste outputs. Emissions include air streams that are contaminated with pollutants such as carbon monoxide or particulate matter, plus radiation, noise, and heat.

Material flow accounting may be used to (1) demonstrate compliance with laws and regulations, (2) generate data for sustainability reporting, or (3) help managers monitor and control levels of waste and emissions. Managers are encouraged to reduce material waste and energy emissions, making operations more environmentally friendly and potentially reducing costs. Sometimes, the process of developing a material flow accounting system encourages waste reduction. For example, employees who learn that all office supplies are classified as waste may seek ways to reduce office supply use.

Material Flow Cost Accounting

Material flow cost accounting is the process of analyzing and tracking the physical units and costs of materials and energies through a manufacturing process. Similar to material flow accounting, all inputs and outputs of materials and energy are tracked. However, material flow cost accounting is concerned only with inputs and outputs of a manufacturing process. Waste of materials (including all scrap and defective units) and energy emissions are often referred to as *negative product* because they use resources but are not value-added. Final product that is produced and transferred out is often referred to as *positive product* to emphasize that all inputs should be oriented toward its production.

Material flow cost accounting is similar to process costing (Chapter 6), in that both physical units and costs are tracked. However, costs are assigned separately to waste and emissions, similar to the method we learned for abnormal spoilage in Chapter 6. This practice avoids "burying" the costs of waste—even unavoidable scrap and heat loss—in the costs

---

[18] Material flow accounting is also used in the context of nations or regions. In this chapter we discuss only its application to business organizations, as described in International Federation of Accountants (IFAC), *Environmental Management Accounting, International Guidance Document*, August 2005, New York: IFAC.

of products transferred out of a production process. A similar approach can be used to track the cost of waste in job costing and other accounting systems.

The uses of material flow cost accounting are similar to those described above for material flow accounting. However, material flow cost accounting provides even greater incentives to reduce waste rather than rely on recycling.[19]

Following is a numerical illustration of material flow cost accounting using process costing data for Premier Plastics. Parts 1–3 of this illustration can be found in Chapter 6.

example

premier plastics (part 4)
MATERIAL FLOW FIFO COST REPORT

Premier Plastics manufactures attractive CD/DVD racks and is faced with increasing pressure from consumer groups and government regulators to begin issuing sustainability reports. Nancy Redhouse, the company's cost accountant, has decided to conduct a pilot study by modifying the plastic molding department cost report to incorporate ideas from material flow cost accounting.

Under material flow cost accounting, all wasted materials are treated as "negative product"; they are assigned both raw material and conversion costs and are shown separately from the cost of "positive product," which is accounted for as inventory. Nancy learns from the molding department manager that 5% of the raw materials used in the department become scrap as a normal part of the production process. This means that only 95% of the raw material and conversion costs incurred each month are assigned to units produced. In addition, the department experiences both normal and abnormal spoilage. Nancy modifies the July FIFO cost report with spoilage (Exhibit 6.12) to separate all waste and spoilage costs from the cost of work in process and good units transferred out. The revised July cost report is shown in Exhibit 20.9.

Nancy notices that removing the costs associated with waste causes the cost of units transferred out of the department to decrease from $10.40 per unit (Chapter 6) to $9.88 per unit. In addition, the report clearly shows $15,617 as the total monthly cost of wasted materials. However, Nancy knows that the revised report does not yet fully reflect all material flows. In particular, it does not include energy flows. She would also like the report to reflect more accurate measures of materials wasted rather than relying on an estimate from the department manager. Nancy plans to discuss with the molding department manager ways to begin measuring and capturing the flow of all materials and energy. ■

michaklootwijk/Getty Images

Sustainability Life Cycle Costing

Life cycle assessment evaluates all the activities involved in the design, development, production, sale, transportation, and disposal of a product or service, as shown in Exhibit 20.10. The life cycle of a product or a service is often referred to as *cradle to grave* or *cradle to cradle*.

●● ＞ STRATEGIC RISK MANAGEMENT: PREMIER PLASTICS (PART 4)

ACCOUNTING FOR MANUFACTURING MATERIAL FLOW In Premier Plastics (Part 4), Nancy planned to pursue ways to track all material and energy flows in the molding department. Once new tracking systems are in place, only the costs for materials used to create good units would be transferred out. The costs of all spoilage, scrap, and other forms of waste would remain in the department. How might this information affect manufacturing operations? The manager would be more motivated to reduce levels of "normal" waste and to seek more energy-efficient manufacturing processes. In addition, the material flow data could be used by Premier Plastics in a sustainability report. Public reporting of material flow information would put greater pressure on all managers to reduce waste.

---

[19] Environmental Industries Office, Environmental Policy Division, *Guide for Material Flow Cost Accounting* (Ver.1), March 2007, Tokyo: Japanese Ministry of Economy, Trade and Industry.

▶EXHIBIT 20.9
Premier Plastics Molding Department
Tentative Material Flow Cost Accounting
Report

Premier Plastics For the Month Ended July 31

FIFO Method

Cost Summary	Beginning WIP	Current Cost	Total Cost
Direct materials	$ 8,400[a]	$ 28,560	$ 36,960
Conversion costs	10,125[a]	86,184	96,309
Total costs	$18,525	$114,744	$133,269

[a]Under cost flow accounting, the costs in beginning WIP should be reduced for material wasted during the previous month. For simplicity, beginning WIP is not modified in this illustration.

Unit Summary	Physical Units	Equivalent Units DM	Equivalent Units CC
Beginning WIP	3,000	3,000 (100%)	1,500 (50%)
This period's work and costs:			
Complete beginning WIP	3,000	0 (0%)	1,500 (50%)
Good units started and completed	8,000	8,000 (100%)	8,000 (100%)
Ending WIP	1,200	1,200 (100%)	840 (70%)
Spoiled units	1,000	1,000 (100%)	1,000 (100%)
Units to account for	13,200	10,200	11,340
Less: spoilage	1,000		
Total good units	12,200		

Equivalent Unit Cost

Direct materials	$2.66 [($28,560/10,200) × 95%]
Conversion costs	7.22 [($86,184/11,340) × 95%]
Cost per equivalent unit	$ 9.88 ($10.40 × 95%)

Cost Assignment	Units	Costs
Beginning WIP	3,000	$18,525
Direct materials		0 (0 × $2.80)
Conversion costs		10,830 (1,500 × $7.22)
Units completed		29,355
Good units started and completed	8,000	79,040 (8,000 × $9.88)
Total transferred out	11,000	108,395
Waste:		
Spoilage		9,880 (1,000 × $9.88)
Scrap		5,737 [($28,560 + $86,184) × 5%]
Total costs of waste		15,617
Ending WIP:	1,200	
Direct materials		3,192 (1,200 × $2.66)
Conversion costs		6,065 (840 × $7.22)
Total ending WIP cost		9,257
Total good units and costs accounted for	12,200	$133,269 ($108,395 + $15,617 + $9,257)

In sustainability management accounting, life cycle costing involves summing the costs of these activities throughout both internal and external value chains.

Life cycle assessments can be quite detailed and time consuming. Consider a life cycle assessment for a cell phone. The various components of the cell phone might have different life cycles and environmental impacts. Therefore, a more complete life cycle assessment would include analyses for each of the cell phone components, including the circuit board, microprocessor, memory chip, liquid crystal display (LCD), battery, antenna, keypad, speaker, microphone, and casing.

▶ CHAPTER REFERENCE
Traditional life cycle costing, introduced in Chapter 15, is concerned with changes in price and costs over time and usually does not consider external costs.

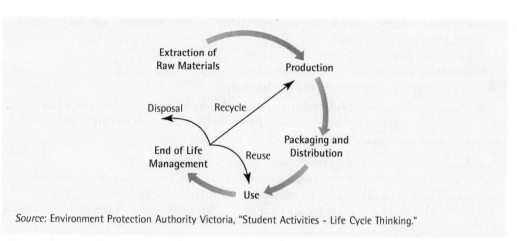

▶ EXHIBIT 20.10
Life Cycle of a Product

Source: Environment Protection Authority Victoria, "Student Activities - Life Cycle Thinking."

Life cycle assessment is integral to sustainability management and is about making more informed decisions related to the inputs and outputs of the organization's value chain. This type of analysis can provide relevant information and motivate decisions such as those listed below:

- Products manufactured (decisions may be made to drop or outsource)
- Preferred sustainability suppliers
- Re-engineering the design of a product or service
- Re-engineering operating processes to accommodate changes in energy sources, waste disposal, packaging, and recycling
- Post-sales customer service (such as product buy-back or recycling programs)

Life cycle assessment is used frequently in the context of environmental accounting, because it encourages organizations to identify and reduce environmental impacts. However, this type of assessment is also useful for non-environmental social issues. For example, at the time a manufacturing facility is built, managers rarely consider the community effects that will occur if the plant is closed at a future time. Life cycle assessments and costing encourage managers to take these factors into account throughout the life of an investment project.

Sustainability and Capital Budgeting

We learned in Chapter 13 that strategic investment decisions require analysis of quantitative as well as qualitative information. However, sustainability quantitative and qualitative information for capital budgeting decisions can be particularly difficult to identify and assess.

Quantitative cash flows for capital budgeting decisions include the following general categories:

- Initial investment
- Incremental operating cash flows
- Terminal cash flows

These same cash flow categories apply under sustainable management. However, incremental operating cash flows are often affected by sustainable management initiatives. Benefits such as the following may be built into operating or terminal cash flow projections:[20]

- Reduction of internal and external waste disposal costs (including related equipment and transport), insurance, and liability
- Reduction in worker health costs, and reduced risk of accidents and worker absenteeism through less use of dangerous materials
- Reduction in external stakeholder liabilities and contingencies
- Savings in energy, water, materials, packaging, and scrap
- Earnings from emerging or new products and by-products
- Earnings from carbon credit trading

---

[20] Adapted from information contained in: United Nations Division for Sustainable Development, *Environmental Management Accounting Procedures and Principles*, prepared for the Expert Working Group on Improving the Role of Government in the Promotion of Environmental Management Accounting, 2001, New York: United Nations.

- ► Improved relations with authorities, which may shorten waiting times for permits and regulated procedures
- ► Reduction of end-of-life remediation costs
- ► Increased access to customers and markets
- ► Improved employee morale and productivity

Managers also need to consider external costs and some internal costs that are not traditionally included in capital budgeting decisions. Based on the categories shown in Exhibit 20.8, additional sustainability cash flows may include the following:

- ► Administration costs (e.g., monitoring, reporting, and training)
- ► Contingency costs (e.g., potential cleanup, accidents, compensations, fines)
- ► Image benefits and costs (often referred to as "intangible" costs and benefits)
- ► External costs (e.g., effects on the community during the project life and after operations are closed)

One way to identify relevant sustainability information is to consider the criteria in various sustainability publications. For example, relevant cash flows or qualitative factors are addressed in the Global Reporting Initiative's core indicators (see Exhibit 20.5). The United Nations Division for Sustainable Development calculation sheet shown in Exhibit 20.11 lists a range of costs and benefits for environmental investments and projects.

When estimating future cash flows involving sustainability, data for years further into the future are often more difficult to quantify and are, therefore, less accurate. Consideration of the quality of information is crucial, and sensitivity analysis must be performed around critical variables. Specialists can be hired to ensure that all relevant factors are considered and to develop reasonable cash flow estimates.

Although many sustainability costs and benefits can be estimated only roughly, organizations benefit from the process of recognizing and quantifying them. For example, these types of analyses identify the post-investment profitability of sustainability projects. Managers may also uncover potential hidden or contingent costs relating to existing operations and future projections.

Sustainability Balanced Scorecard

The balanced scorecard introduced in Chapter 19 is a performance measurement system that links key financial and nonfinancial performance measures with business strategy. Balanced scorecards are typically organized around four perspectives: financial, customer, internal business process, and learning and growth. Assuming that sustainable management is integrated into an organization's strategic management process, then sustainability should be incorporated into management control systems such as the balanced scorecard.

Sustainable management strategic objectives can be incorporated into a balanced scorecard system in three ways:[21]

1. Environmental and social strategic objectives can be integrated within the traditional four perspectives.
2. An additional "sustainability" perspective can be added to the scorecard.
3. A separate sustainability balanced scorecard can be developed.

Integrating Sustainability into Existing Scorecard. If the sustainability strategic objectives are integrated within the existing scorecard, these objectives will be monitored in conjunction with other key strategic objectives. Sustainability objectives tend to fit most readily into the internal business process and learning and growth perspectives. To illustrate, Exhibit 20.12 demonstrates how sustainability objectives and performance measures can be integrated into these two perspectives of the balanced scorecard of the Community Hospital Trauma Centre from Chapter 19. Compare Exhibit 20.12 with Exhibit 19.12 to identify the additional sustainability objectives and measures. The customer perspective may also be relevant if successful sustainability practices are rewarded by increased demand for products and services. In turn, sustainability benefits and costs would likely be reflected in the financial perspective.

---

[21] F. Figge, T. Hahn, S. Schaltegger, and M. Wagner, "The Sustainability Balanced Scorecard—Linking Sustainability Management to Business Strategy," *Business Strategy and the Environment* 11, 2002, pp. 11, 269–284.

> EXHIBIT 20.11

Calculation Sheet for Environmental Investments and Projects

Environmental Cost/Expenditure Categories	Initial Investment	Year 1	Year 2	Year 3	...Year X	Future Liability	Soft Factors
1. Waste and Emission Treatment							
1.1 Depreciation for related equipment							
1.2 Maintenance, operating materials, services							
1.3 Personnel							
1.4 Fees, taxes, charges							
1.5 Fines and penalties							
1.6 Insurance and environmental liabilities							
1.7 Provisions for clean-up costs, remediation							
2. Prevention and Environmental Management							
2.1 External services for environmental management							
2.2 Personnel for general environmental management activities							
2.3 Research and development							
2.4 Extra expenditure for integrated technologies							
2.5 Other environmental management costs							
3. Material Purchase Value of Non-Product Output							
3.1 Raw materials							
3.2 Packaging							
3.3 Auxiliary materials							
3.4 Operating materials							
3.5 Energy							
3.6 Water							
4. Processing Costs of Non-Product Output							
Total Environmental Expenditure							
5. Environmental Revenues							
5.1 Subsidies, awards							
5.2 Other earnings							
Total Environmental Revenues							
6. Soft Factors							
6.1 Increased sales, customer satisfaction, new markets, differentiation from competitors, improved customer relationships							
6.2 Improved corporate image							
6.3 Improved contacts with authorities and agencies, reduced legal compliance costs							
6.4 Reduced risks for accidents, liabilities, contaminated land							
6.5 Increased creditworthiness, better ratings by investment companies							
6.6 Better community relations							
6.7 Increased employee motivation and morale, less worker illness and absenteeism							
Total Benefit							

Adapted from: United Nations Division for Sustainable Development, *Environmental Management Accounting Procedures and Principles*, prepared for the Expert Working Group on Improving the Role of Government in the Promotion of Environmental Management Accounting, 2001, New York: United Nations, pp. 107–108.

▶ EXHIBIT 20.12
Integration of Sustainability Into Internal Business and Learning and Growth Perspectives of the Balanced Scorecard for Community Hospital Trauma Centre

Perspective	Strategic Objectives	Measures
Internal Business Process	Improve Processes for Admission, Treatment, and Discharge	• Number of process improvements in routine care • Readmission rate
	Optimize Staff Scheduling	• Time spent on discharge instructions
	Improve Efficiency and Reduce Costs	• Medical staff costs to patient revenues • Average cost per patient
	Reduce Negative Environmental Impact	• Total direct and indirect greenhouse gas emissions • Percent of supplies purchased that contain recycled content • Percent of non-medical waste that is recycled
Learning & Growth	Develop New Treatment Methods	• Number of new treatment methods developed
	Support Employee Professional Development	• Average training hours per employee
	Promote Health in the Community	• Number of healthy living courses offered free of charge
	Provide a Positive Working Environment	• Number of volunteer hours contributed by staff members to public health initiatives • Rates of injury, lost days, and absenteeism • Employee satisfaction survey

One concern with the integrated scorecard is that firms could focus primarily on financial results and de-emphasize environmental and social objectives—especially if sustainability objectives are not linked to financial objectives using a *strategy map* (Chapter 19). Depending on how measures are integrated into the balanced scorecard, there is a risk that the organization might ignore externalities to focus on only one bottom line instead of a triple bottom line.

Adding a Sustainability Perspective. An alternative is to add a sustainability perspective to the other four perspectives, which reinforces sustainability as central to the organization's mission and strategies. Under this approach, four to six sustainability strategic objectives and measures would probably be added to the balanced scorecard. The importance placed on achieving these objectives would depend on their weight relative to the weights of other objectives. A problem that has been previously identified with balanced scorecard use is that too much emphasis tends to be placed on the financial perspective.[22] The risk is that sustainability objectives may receive a relatively lesser weighting and, therefore, receive less attention by managers.

A Separate Sustainability Scorecard. A separate sustainability balanced scorecard would enable sustainability teams or departments to more closely monitor the social, environmental, and financial dimensions. In addition, a sustainability balanced scorecard could be developed to generate a business case for adopting sustainable management practices. Use of a separate scorecard would reduce the likelihood that managers would perceive sustainability objectives and measures as an unimportant add-on. Conversely, a separate sustainability balanced scorecard might contribute to the idea that sustainability is not central to an organization's mission and vision.

Sustainability Scorecard Measures. As with any balanced scorecard design, sustainability measures should be tailored to the organization's strategic objectives. Ideas for measures may be obtained from Global Reporting Initiative core indicators (Exhibit 20.5) or other resources. Typical measures for environmental objectives address energy and water consumption and efficiency, greenhouse gas emissions, and waste. Social measures might relate to labour practices, human rights, product responsibility, compliance with laws and regulations, or other factors.

---

[22] M. Lipe and S. Salterio, "The Balanced Scorecard: Judgmental Effects of Common and Unique Performance Measures," *The Accounting Review*, vol. 75, no. 3, 2000, pp. 283–98.

Role of Management Accounting in Sustainability

In Chapter 1, we learned that strategic cost management refers to a simultaneous focus on reducing costs and strengthening an organization's strategic position. In no other area is strategic cost management more useful than in sustainability. In its statement of management accounting, titled, "The Evolution of Accountability—Sustainability Reporting for Accountants," the IMA identified the following opportunities for management accounting to assist organizations as they pursue sustainability initiatives:[23]

Management of Environmental Systems:

- Limiting loss of reputation and brand value from non-compliance with environmental standards
- Avoiding unnecessary internal costs of handling and managing toxic materials, hazardous waste, and other supplies
- Reducing employee health care costs associated with environmental conditions
- Implementing quality initiatives to reduce waste levels (e.g., scrap, excessive by-products, and printing)
- Increasing use of by-products and recycling to reduce internal and external disposal costs
- Reducing product liability risks
- Investing in capital projects to reduce externalities from wastewater and power consumption
- Improving site management to reduce remediation liabilities
- Modifying work practices such as using technology instead of travel, using electronic instead of paper documents, and allowing employees to work from home
- Reducing environmental impact through better facility management, such as passive heating and better space utilization

Management of Social Systems:

- Complying with labour laws, regulations, and accepted standards
- Providing education and training for employees, including safety
- Meeting and exceeding regulations and recommendations for equal employment opportunities
- Monitoring purchases from and investments in the local community
- Developing approaches for nondiscrimination, freedom of association, right to work, treatment of employee grievances and complaints, and respect for community rights
- Ensuring compliance with anti-corruption practices and balancing power within the community
- Monitoring the impact of operations, products, and services on the community

Envisioning the Future of Cost Accounting

Throughout this textbook, you have learned that cost accounting information is increasingly defined to include both financial and nonfinancial information and also to include things that do not relate strictly to the allocation of costs. The demand for new and expanded information results from increased pressure for accountants to provide more relevant and useful information for internal decision making. Accountants promote better decision making in their organizations by providing better information, and also by recommending and helping their organizations adopt appropriate management techniques. For example, you learned about the balanced scorecard in this chapter. As experts on measurement, accountants play critical roles in helping their organizations successfully implement balanced scorecards.

A huge array of new management tools and techniques has been introduced in recent years, and this trend will likely continue. In addition to the balanced scorecard, several other prominent techniques are introduced throughout this textbook, including strategic planning (chapters 1 and 19), core competencies (chapters 1 and 19), mission and vision statements

LO5 Discuss the future direction of cost accounting

---

[23] Institute of Management Accountants, *The Evolution of Accountability—Sustainability Reporting for Accountants*, Statement of Management Accounting 67, 2008, Montvale, NJ: IMA, pp. 20 and 22.

(chapters 1 and 19), corporate code of ethics (chapters 1 and 19), enterprise risk management (Chapter 1), activity-based management (Chapter 7), customer profitability analysis (Chapter 7), outsourcing (Chapter 4), business process re-engineering (Chapter 14), sensitivity analysis (part of scenario and contingency planning, chapters 3, 4, and 12), quality concepts (chapters 5, 6, and 7), shared service centres (Chapter 8), supply chain management (Chapter 15), lean accounting (Chapter 15), price optimization models (Chapter 14), decision rights (Chapter 18), economic value added (Chapter 18), and sustainability management (Chapter 20). As new tools and techniques are introduced, accountants add value by learning about them and evaluating whether they are appropriate for their organizations. Sometimes, it is difficult to know whether a given technique is useful until a significant number of organizations have implemented and gained experience in its use. Over time, the best techniques are increasingly used, while the less useful techniques become less prevalent. One way to gauge the potential usefulness of a management technique is to gather data about its implementation among other organizations. For example, Exhibit 20.13 presents data about the use of and satisfaction with 25 top management tools during the year 2011.

Although the approaches in Exhibit 20.13 are widely used, they are likely to work best for specific types of organizations. For example, activity-based management is less useful for companies with simple processes and few overhead activities than it is for organizations with multiple and complex products that use advanced manufacturing systems. Accountants add value by understanding the strengths and weaknesses of each approach and determining whether an approach would be a good fit for their organizations.

In the past, accountants spent most of their time recording events and preparing reports based on prior-period results. Over the past several decades, technology has created less need for accountants to spend time on bookkeeping activities. Instead, they spend more time helping their organizations respond to current conditions in the business environment and preparing for anticipated and unanticipated changes over time.

Organizations expect their accountants to continuously learn. As new tools and techniques are developed, accountants need to evaluate the appropriateness of these techniques for their respective organizations. Cost-benefit analyses should be prepared to help managers make high-quality decisions. Mathematical modelling may become a more important part of accountants' skill sets. Creative, innovative, and thoughtful analyses will be crucial to the success of individual accountants and their organizations.

> EXHIBIT 20.13

Use of Management Tools and Techniques

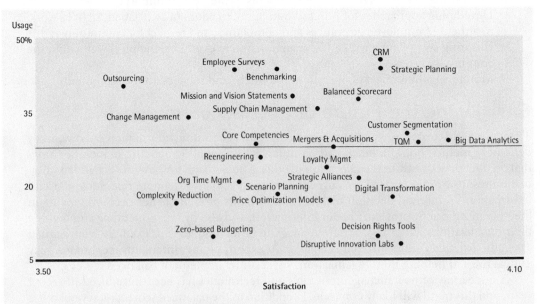

Source: Darrell Rigby and Barbara Bilodeau; Management Tools and Trends 2015, Bain & Company, Figure 8, p. 14, www.bain.com/Images/BAIN_BRIEF_Management_Tools_2015.pdf.

[24] "CMA Canada Partnership Balanced Scorecard," *CMA Management*, 81(7), November 2007, p. 14

20-1 self-study problem   Life Cycle Assessment

The managers of Dig Deep Mining identified a mineral deposit and determined that the investment meets the company's strategic and financial objectives. Just before investing in the mineral deposit, the managers became aware of proposed new regulations that would require site clean-up after the mine closes. The regulations would require returning the land as closely as possible to its original condition by filling the open pit with mine tailings (dirt removed from the pit) and planting native vegetation. If the clean-up work is not done, the government would probably levy a large fine, estimated to be 10% of the net present value of the earnings from the mine. Information about the mining operation follows.

Initial investment	$2,000,000
Expected annual cash flows	$ 447,700
Clean-up costs	???
Project life	10 years
Required rate of return	15%

required

A. Calculate the maximum amount that the company could pay for clean-up costs and still earn the required rate of return on the mine operation, ignoring taxes and inflation. *Hint*: Set up the net present value (NPV) formula using cash flows and present value factors, and solve for the clean-up value that would achieve NPV of zero.
B. Calculate the estimated penalty if the clean-up is not performed.
C. List the pros and cons of cleaning up the site versus paying the penalty.

See the solution on page 881.

20-2 self-study problem   Material Flow Accounting, Life Cycle Assessment, and Sustainable Management

Samantha Deleau and Becky Honeychurch sell folk art wood carvings at a Saturday market and have adopted a policy of being as environmentally friendly as possible. They purchase driftwood from a local collector, and they use only non-toxic paints made from milk protein, lime, clay, and natural pigments. They purchase and use only manual carving tools that last for many years, and they apply paint with purchased brushes and sponges that they clean using water. They wrap finished carvings in used newspaper collected from neighbours, and store them in used cardboard boxes collected from local retail stores. Periodically, Becky uses the company-owned van to pick up wood, newspaper, and boxes from their various suppliers. Paint and other supplies are ordered online and delivered. On Saturdays, Samantha and Becky drive the van 50 kilometres each way to the Saturday market, where they sell carvings to customers. Paper and boxes that cannot be reused are placed in recycling bins provided by the market. During the week, Samantha and Becky create the wood carvings and perform administrative duties in a rented space, which they furnished with used office and work furniture. They pay for water and electricity based on usage, plus a flat monthly fee for garbage pickup. They hire a janitorial company for a flat fee and provide their own environmentally friendly cleaning supplies.

required

A. List as many materials inputs as you can that would be included in Samantha and Becky's traditional accounting system.
B. For each materials input listed in Part A, determine whether the related output would most likely be classified as positive product or as waste and emissions (i.e., negative product). *Hint*: Some inputs might create more than one type of output.
C. Describe how the material flow analysis performed in Parts A and B might encourage managers to reduce waste and emissions.
D. List several examples of inputs external to Samantha and Becky's traditional accounting system that they should take into account in a life cycle assessment of their product.
E. Do Samantha and Becky seem to practise sustainable management? Explain.

See the solution on page 882.

SUMMARY

L01   Explain sustainability and sustainable management

SUSTAINABILITY

INTERNAL IMPACTS

EXTERNAL IMPACTS (EXTERNALITIES)

SUSTAINABLE MANAGEMENT

TRIPLE BOTTOM LINE
- ► Economic
- ► Environmental
- ► Social

OVERVIEW OF STRATEGIC MANAGEMENT PROCESS

Measure, Monitor, and Motivate

RISK APPETITE

SUSTAINABILITY AND LEVERS OF CONTROL
See Exhibit 20.2

L02   Discuss sustainability accounting, sustainability management accounting, and sustainability reporting

SUSTAINABILITY ACCOUNTING

SUSTAINABILITY MANAGEMENT ACCOUNTING

SUSTAINABILITY REPORTING
- ► Internal
- ► External

L03   Identify and explain the motivations and frameworks for external sustainability reporting

MOTIVATIONS
See Exhibit 20.4

FRAMEWORKS
- ► GRI Sustainability Reporting Guidelines
- ► ISO 26000
- ► Other

RECOGNITION FOR HIGH-QUALITY SUSTAINABILITY MANAGEMENT AND REPORTING

GRI CORE INDICATORS
- ► Economic
- ► Environment
- ► Social Performance
  - – Labour Practices and Decent Work
  - – Human Rights
  - – Society
  - – Product Responsibility

SUMMARY

LO4 Explain the use of management accounting tools for sustainability management and reporting

KEY MANAGEMENT ACCOUNTING QUESTIONS AND EFFECTS OF SUSTAINABLE MANAGEMENT

See Exhibit 20.7

CATEGORIES FOR SUSTAINABILITY COSTS

Internal costs

▶ Conventional costs
▶ Hidden costs
▶ Contingent costs
▶ Image and relationship costs

External costs

▶ Externalities

MATERIAL FLOW ACCOUNTING

RELEVANT SUSTAINABILITY COSTS AND BENEFITS

MORE ACCURATE ASSIGNMENT OF SUSTAINABILITY

MATERIAL FLOW COST ACCOUNTING

SUSTAINABILITY LIFE CYCLE COSTING

SUSTAINABILITY AND CAPITAL BUDGETING

SUSTAINABILITY BALANCED SCORECARD

LO5 Discuss the future direction of cost accounting

INCREASING FOCUS

▶ Information to predict future operations
▶ Both financial and nonfinancial information

▶ Continuous learning of new techniques
▶ More relevant and useful information
▶ Creativity, innovation, and thoughtful analysis

20-1 solution to self-study problem

A. The maximum amount of clean-up cost to achieve NPV of zero is calculated as follows:

- Initial investment + Annual CF × (PVFA 10 years, 15%) – Clean-up × (PVF 10 years, 15%) = 0
- $2,000,000 + $447,700 × 5.019 – Clean-up × 0.247 = 0
- Clean-up × 0.247 = $2,000,000 – $2,247,006

Clean-up = $247,006 ÷ 0.247 = $1,000,024

B. Estimated penalty if clean-up is not performed: 10% of $2,247,006 = $224,701

C. Pros of clean-up:

- Enhance reputation as a good corporate citizen (from an environmental perspective)
- Help achieve sustainability strategic objectives (if they exist)
- If clean-up costs are $1,000,024 or less, expect to achieve required rate of return on the mine
- Avoid estimated penalty of $224,701

Cons of clean-up:

- Forgo approximately $775,323 ($1,000,024 – $224,701) of profit in the future

20-2 solution to self-study problem

A and B. A list of potential inputs and related outputs is shown below.

Inputs in Accounting System	Type of Output(s)
Driftwood	Wood in finished carving: Positive product
	Wood shavings: Waste and emissions
Paint	Paint: Positive product
	Paint containers and extra paint washed off of brushes and sponges: Waste and emissions
Carving tools	Waste and emissions
Brushes and sponges	Waste and emissions
Van	Waste and emissions
Gasoline for van	Waste and emissions
Supplies and parts for van (tires, oil, etc.)	Waste and emissions
Rental space	Waste and emissions (assuming that the space deteriorates with use)
Electricity	Waste and emissions
Water	Waste and emissions
Office and work furnishings	Waste and emissions
Office supplies	Waste and emissions
Cleaning supplies	Waste and emissions

Note: Garbage pickup is not listed as an input because it is a service—not acquisition of materials. Similarly, labour costs (for businesses that have them) would not be classified as materials inputs.

C. In traditional accounting systems, all product costs are recorded as part of the cost of the product—regardless of whether resources are used efficiently or are converted to emissions. The material flow analysis performed in Parts A and B highlights how few of the physical materials used by a company become part of the final product, which, in turn, encourages managers to seek ways to reduce waste and emissions.

D. A life cycle assessment would incorporate materials inputs used by external parties when generating materials used by Sandra and Becky. Examples include the materials used to create the paint (such as raw materials, indirect materials, equipment, energy, and administrative supplies) and materials used to create the electricity (such as power plant equipment, energy, and janitorial supplies). A life cycle assessment would also include materials consumed by external parties when using an organization's product (e.g., paper consumed when using a printer). However, Sandra and Becky's product does not require external parties to consume any additional materials.

E. This question can mean many different things. One way to approach it is to consider whether Sandra and Becky have attempted to address each of the three sustainability value systems: economic, environment, and social. This problem provides information primarily about environmental aspects of the business; we know little about economic and social system practices. Therefore, we cannot draw conclusions about whether Sandra and Becky seem to practise all major aspects of sustainable management.

With respect to environmental systems, Sandra and Becky have adopted a number of practices that maintain or increase added value without creating long-term threats. For example, they use recycled office and work furniture, driftwood, newspaper, and boxes rather than acquiring newly produced materials. They also purchase non-toxic paints and environmentally friendly cleaning supplies, and they reuse materials such as brushes and sponges. At the same time, Sandra and Becky can probably improve other aspects, such as the environmental effects associated with van and electricity usage.

QUESTIONS

20.1 In your own words, define the terms sustainability, sustainable management, and sustainability management accounting.

20.2 Should every organization integrate sustainable management into their operations and processes regardless of the complexity and impact of their operating activities?

20.3 Define the term externalities in your own words and provide an example.

20.4 Will organizational efforts toward sustainability result in reduced organizational profits?

20.5 Describe the relationship between sustainability reporting and sustainability management accounting.

20.6 What types of management decisions would benefit from an analysis of sustainability costs and benefits?

20.7 Why would ethical decision making be part of a sustainability management framework?

20.8 What are the potential internal and external benefits from analyzing the flow of materials and energy in an organization?

20.9 Identify several measures that might be included in a sustainability balanced scorecard.

20.10 What are some of the factors that managers should consider when implementing sustainability practices in their organizations?

20.11 List two benefits that result from developing a separate sustainability scorecard.

20.12 List one pro and one con for incorporating sustainability activities into the four perspectives in a typical balanced scorecard.

20.13 List one pro and one con for adding a fifth perspective, a sustainability perspective, to a balanced scorecard.

20.14 Why should a sustainability report "describe how and when stakeholders have been involved" (ISO 26000, Exhibit 20.6)?

20.15 In your own words, describe how sustainability issues can be incorporated into an organization's beliefs, boundary, diagnostic control, and interactive control systems.

MULTIPLE-CHOICE QUESTIONS

20.16 Which of the following terms is not used when discussing sustainability in a business context?
  a. Corporate social responsibility
  b. Social accounting
  c. Triple bottom line
  d. Throughput accounting

20.17 Interactive control systems are integral for which of the following?
  a. Engaging in organizational learning by investigating the strategic opportunities and threats revealed by differences between planned and actual sustainability performance.
  b. Assigning responsibility and rewarding employees for achieving sustainability goals.
  c. Establishing codes of conduct for financial, environmental, and social practices.
  d. Communicating organizational vision for sustainable management.

20.18 Which of the following describes the Global Reporting Initiative (GRI)?
  a. A network organization that has developed a freely available framework for disclosure on economic, environmental, and social performance.
  b. A United Nations agency that promotes decent working conditions around the world.
  c. The world's largest developer of international standards.

  d. A magazine that publishes an annual list of sustainable corporations.

20.19 The five levels of costs for sustainability management accounting practices include which of the following?
  a. Conventional costs, hidden costs, contingent costs, internalities, externalities
  b. Variable costs, controllable costs, sustaining costs, internalities, externalities
  c. Conventional costs, hidden costs, contingent costs, image and relationship costs, externalities
  d. Unit costs, conventional costs, hidden costs, contingent costs, image and relationship costs

20.20 Which of the following describes externalities?
  a. Costs that an entity imposes on others as a result of its operations but which the entity itself typically ignores.
  b. Exert influence on the value of some intangible assets such as goodwill, brand names, and so forth.
  c. Defined in probabilistic terms and include fines for breaching environmental or social requirements, clean-up costs, and lawsuits.
  d. Up-front environmental and social costs, such as search costs relating to finding sustainability-preferable products, regulatory costs that are often obscured in overhead costs, and future decommissioning or remediation costs.

EXERCISES

20.21 Sustainability Values, Strategies, Operating Plans Go to the website of one of your favourite companies and identify statements and policies regarding the company's sustainability values:

LO1

www.wiley.com/
go/eldenburgcanada

- Economic
- Environmental
- Social

REQUIRED **A.** Are you able to determine whether one or more of these three value systems is more important to the company's vision? Explain.

B. If possible, identify examples of the company's strategies or operating plans related to environmental or social values.

20.22 Continuous Improvement of Sustainable Management, Feedback Go to the "History" and/or "Social & Environmental Assessment Reports" section of Ben & Jerry's website (www.benjerry.com/about-us or www.benjerry.com/about-us/sear-reports).

LO1

www.wiley.com/
go/eldenburgcanada

REQUIRED **A.** Identify at least two changes that Ben & Jerry's made after 1987 in its sustainability practices.

B. Describe how the feedback loop in Exhibit 20.1 might have helped the company's managers make the changes you identified in Part A.

20.23 Internal and External Impacts The All Bamboo company manufactures clothing made from renewable bamboo fibre. The company purchases fabric from Malaysian suppliers and manufactures clothing in Canada. All Bamboo's managers are analyzing the impact of their business operations on internal and external stakeholders.

LO1

REQUIRED **A.** Classify each impact, 1–12, as internal (I), external (E), or both (B).

1. Health and safety of All Bamboo employees
2. Health and safety of fabric supplier employees
3. Wastewater generated by fabric suppliers
4. Fabric scraps from clothing manufacturing
5. Use of harsh chemicals to turn bamboo into fibre
6. Conversion of land from food crops to bamboo
7. Shipping of bamboo fabric to All Bamboo's manufacturing plant
8. End-of-life transfer of bamboo clothing to landfills
9. Energy used in clothing manufacturing
10. Clothing customer satisfaction
11. All Bamboo employee satisfaction
12. Sales of All Bamboo clothing

B. Due to limited resources, All Bamboo's managers need to prioritize which of the impacts they should attempt to reduce during the next five years. Which three impacts do you believe are most important? Explain how you decided.

20.24 Cumulative Exercise (Chapter 13): Equipment Replacement, Environmental Improvement Axel Corporation is planning to buy a new machine that will reduce the amount of water used in its manufacturing process by filtering and recycling the water. The company's required rate of return for equipment investment is 16%. The machine costs $150,000 and should save about $30,000 per year in water costs. The vendor stated that the equipment should last 10 years. Ignore taxes and inflation.

LO1, LO4

REQUIRED **A.** What is the NPV for this project? Based on the NPV, should Axel make the purchase?

B. What is the internal rate of return (IRR) for this project?

C. What is the payback period?

D. What qualitative factors, including strategic risks, might affect this decision?

20.25 GRI Indicators, Measurement Bias A large university requires each faculty to submit an annual report that includes the average salary of teaching staff by rank; by rank and gender; and by rank, gender, and racial diversity.

LO3

REQUIRED **A.** Identify the GRI Indicator addressed by the university's required report.

B. Faculty members are paid salaries, although some programs pay supplemental compensation for teaching courses in addition to the regular load. Would the supplemental compensation be included in the GRI Core Indicator measure?

C. This measure may be misleading in the accounting department because salaries for new hires have been inflating rapidly, whereas salaries for those who have been at the university for a number of years have not inflated much because of budget constraints. Explain how this factor might distort measurements in the annual report submitted to the university.

20.26 **Sustainability Cost Classification** Below is a list of categories for sustainability costs (Exhibit 20.8).

L04

Level 1 – Conventional costs
Level 2 – Hidden costs
Level 3 – Contingent costs
Level 4 – Image and relationship costs
Level 5 – Externalities

REQUIRED Classify each sustainability cost, A–Q, according to its appropriate category (Level 1, 2, 3, 4, or 5). Assume that each cost was incurred during the current year unless stated otherwise.

A. Clean-up costs from a chemical accident
B. Costs of a community relations program
C. Fees to obtain licensing permits for a new production process
D. Dismantling and disposal of equipment to close a facility
E. Disposal of production waste
F. Design of environmental product labelling
G. Feasibility studies regarding a new process that will reduce hazardous waste
H. Future compliance costs related to new government regulations
I. Habitat and wetland protection
J. Landscaping around factory site
K. New manufacturing equipment costs
L. Employee injury medical costs
M. Raw materials for manufacturing
N. Clean up long-term environmental damage at a mining location
O. Site studies to develop more rigorous pollution control
P. Legal expenses for a lawsuit claiming workplace gender bias
Q. Development of sustainability reports

20.27 **Material Flow Accounting, Sustainable Management** The managers of Green Springs Bottled Water have launched a

L01, L04 new environmental assessment program. The first step in the program is to conduct a pilot study of the material flow in one of the company's bottling plants. The plant produces bottled water that is delivered to retail stores in cases of plastic bottles. Plant operations include the following activities:

1. Filtering the water
2. Making pre-forms (small test tube–like plastic containers) from plastic pellets
3. Producing bottles by inserting the pre-forms into molds and filling them with very hot air
4. Filling the bottles with filtered water
5. Installing bottle caps
6. Labelling the bottles
7. Testing the product
8. Assembling cardboard bases
9. Placing bottles on the cardboard and wrapping them with plastic film
10. Putting the packaged bottles on pallets
11. Delivering pallets on trucks to retail stores
12. Cleaning the plant and equipment
13. Maintaining and repairing the production equipment
14. Putting plastic waste materials in a bin
15. Voluntarily collecting used bottles from retail stores

16. Delivering plastic waste materials and used bottles to a plastic recycling company
17. Performing administrative functions, such as plant management, logistics, purchasing, accounting, and human resources

REQUIRED **A.** For each activity (1–17):

1. Provide an example of an input material that is likely to be used during the activity.
2. Determine whether at least some of the input materials for the activity would be classified as positive product (as opposed to waste and emissions). Explain briefly.

B. How might activity 15 (voluntarily collecting used bottles from retail stores) contribute to sustainable management?

20.28 **Cumulative Exercise (Chapter 6): Material Flow FIFO Cost Report, Spoilage, Scrap** Victoria's Closet mass-produces luxurious sleepwear for women. Consider the following data for the flannel nightgown department for the month of January. All direct materials are added at the beginning of production in the department, and conversion costs are incurred evenly throughout production. Inspection occurs when production is 100% completed. Normal spoilage is 6,600 units for the month.

LO4

	Physical Units
Beginning WIP (25% complete)	11,000
Started during January	74,000
Total to account for	85,000
Good units completed and transferred out during current period:	
From beginning work in process	11,000
Started and completed	50,000
Spoiled units	8,000
Ending WIP (75% complete)	16,000
Total accounted for	85,000
Costs	
Beginning WIP:	
Direct materials	$220,000
Conversion costs	30,000
Total beginning WIP	250,000
Costs added during current period:	
Direct materials	1,480,000
Conversion costs	942,000
Costs to account for	$2,672,000

REQUIRED Prepare a material flow cost report using the FIFO method. Assume that the production process wastes 10% of all raw materials before taking into account spoilage. For simplicity, do not adjust the costs for beginning work in process.

20.29 **Cumulative Exercise (Chapter 13): Life Cycle Assessment, NPV** The city needs a new site for a garbage landfill. When the landfill is closed, the city wants to minimize future environmental problems by ensuring that at least 3 metres of dirt cover the garbage. Then, the area would need to be planted with meadow grasses and a variety of trees. Information about a potential landfill follows.

LO4

Initial investment	$3,000,000
Expected annual cash flows	$ 378,092
Clean-up costs	???
Project life	10 years
Required rate of return	8%

REQUIRED Calculate the maximum amount that the city could pay for clean-up costs and still earn the required rate of return on the landfill, ignoring taxes and inflation.

20.30 **Cumulative Exercise (Chapter 7): ABC Allocation** Variable costs per unit for two products made by the Flibberty Gibbet Company are shown below.

L04

	Wackers	Wonkers
Direct labour	$100	$ 80
Direct materials	150	60
Variable overhead	50	20
Total variable costs	$300	$160

Flibberty Gibbet managers have not kept up with more recent costing methods, and they allocate fixed manufacturing overhead based on direct labour hours. Each product requires two direct labour hours, and the cost pool for fixed manufacturing overhead is $400,000 during a period when about 8,000 direct labour hours are used. Wackers sell for $600 each and Wonkers sell for $400 each.

The company recently hired a new accountant who decided to develop a more current method to allocate fixed manufacturing overhead costs, especially the costs related to disposal of hazardous waste chemicals used in the manufacturing process for Wackers. The accountant developed a simple ABC costing system by separating fixed manufacturing overhead costs into the following three new cost pools. Current-year information for each cost pool follows.

Pool	Costs	Allocation Base	Volume
Indirect labour	$ 80,000	Direct labour hours	8,000
Material handling	200,000	Number of parts	50,000
Environmental	120,000	Units of Wackers	1,000
Total	$400,000		

Wackers has 11 parts, and Wonkers has 8 parts.

REQUIRED **A.** Use the current allocation system (direct labour hours) to allocate fixed manufacturing overhead costs, and calculate the net profit for each unit of Wackers and Wonkers.
B. Use the new ABC system to allocate fixed manufacturing overhead costs, and calculate the net profit for each unit of Wackers and Wonkers.
C. Explain why the results from Part A are different from the results in Part B.

20.31 **Interpreting Sustainability Report Information** Unilever sells products such as Ben & Jerry's and Breyer's ice cream, Hellman's mayonnaise, and Lipton tea. The company published a report showing comparisons of sustainability indicators for 2008 and 2007.

L03

Source: Unilever, *Sustainable Development 2008: An Overview*, Rotterdam, The Netherlands: Unilever N.V., p. 31.

REQUIRED For each of the sustainability indicators A–I, explain whether the change from 2007 to 2008 suggests an improvement or deterioration in Unilever's sustainable management.

	2008	2007
A. Investment in research and development (€ millions)	927	868
B. Water use (cubic metres per tonne of production)	2.96	3.05
C. Total waste (kg per tonne of production)	7.89	7.56
D. Operating profit (€ millions)	7,167	5,245
E. Total taxes paid (€ millions)	1,455	1,312
F. Number of manufacturing sites	273	284
G. Number of consumer recalls	5	10
H. Total recordable accident frequency rate (per 100,000 hours)	0.21	0.26
I. Carbon dioxide (CO_2) from energy (kg per tonne of production)	146.77	149.18

20.32 Future Direction of Accounting Information Think about the type of work you will perform in your future career.

LO6

REQUIRED
A. Give examples of the types of financial and nonfinancial information you will probably use in your work.
B. List several methods you could use to produce information that will help predict future operations for your employer or for clients.
C. What types of continuous learning do you foresee in your career?
D. Explain why you may need to use creative or innovative ideas in your career.

PROBLEMS

20.33 Sustainability Reporting, Performance Measures Bombardier's goal is "to continuously find better ways to bridge distances and bring people together." In working towards this goal, Bombardier uses a product innovation lifecycle (www.bombardier.com/en/sustainability/sustainability-approach/our-product-innovation-lifecycle.html). The goal of this approach is "to innovate at every stage to meet and exceed customer expectations" with sustainable, high-performing solutions.

LO3, LO4

REQUIRED
A. Describe Bombardier's Product Innovation Lifecycle.
B. Suggest a performance indicator for each step in the Product Innovation Lifecycle.

20.34 Sustainability Reporting, GRI Framework Toronto-Dominion Bank (TD) prepares a Corporate Responsibility Report in accordance with G4 guidelines. See the report at www.td.com/document/PDF/corporateresponsibility/2014-Final-CRR_EN.pdf. See the G4 GRI Index at www.td.com/corporate-responsibility/report-centre/gri-2014/index.jsp.

LO3, LO4

REQUIRED On the G4 GRI Index website, explore the Standard Disclosures: Economic, Environment, Labour Practices, Product Responsibility, Society, and Product and Service Impact.

A. Under Product Responsibility:
   i. Which G4 Indicators is TD reporting?
   ii. Summarize TD's Disclosure on Management Approach (DMA) for Customer Privacy.
B. Under the Environment:
   i. Which G4 indicators is TD reporting for Energy?
   ii. Analyze the Appendix: Performance Data: Detailed Environmental Performance.
      a. What does the √ (check mark) in this report mean? Why is this significant?
      b. Discuss TD's performance for Total greenhouse gas emissions.

20.35 Sustainability and Balanced Scorecard You have been appointed the assistant-controller of a major manufacturer of newsprint, fine paper, and different types of specialty papers. Michaela, the controller, has been asked by the board of directors to prepare a project for a sustainable balanced scorecard. All Michaela knows is that such a scorecard uses different measures in three different dimensions: economic, environmental, and social. Michaela would like you to help with this project by providing some examples of measures that could be included in each dimension.

REQUIRED Briefly describe corporate sustainability and provide Michaela with at least *two* examples of measures for each dimension that should be used in a sustainable balanced scorecard. Explain the relevance of your examples.

20.36 Cumulative Problem (Chapter 6): Material Flow FIFO Cost Accounting, Spoilage, Waste The Rally Company operates under a process cost system and uses the weighted average method. All direct materials are added at the beginning of production in the department, and conversion costs are incurred evenly throughout production. Inspection occurs when production is 100% completed.

Following are data for July. All unfinished work at the end of July is 25% completed. The beginning inventory is 80% completed.

Beginning inventories	
Direct materials	$ 4,000
Conversion costs	3,200
Costs added during current period	
Direct materials	$36,000
Conversion costs	32,000

Physical units

Units in beginning inventory	2,000
Units started this month	18,000
Total units completed and transferred out	14,800
Normal spoilage	1,000
Abnormal spoilage	1,000

REQUIRED **A.** Following a material flow analysis, the company's accountant estimates that 15% of the direct materials and 80% of conversion costs are classified as "waste and emissions." Assume these percentages apply to both beginning inventories and current period costs. Prepare a material flow cost report using the FIFO method.
B. Provide a possible explanation for the higher proportion of waste in conversion costs compared to direct materials.
C. Should the managers of Rally Company establish a goal of eliminating all waste and emissions? Explain your reasoning.
D. Suppose the managers are interested in presenting Rally as a company that is concerned about the environment. What are the pros and cons of publicly reporting data about the amount of waste in the company's manufacturing operations?

20.37 Cumulative Problem (Chapter 5): Material Flow Job Cost Accounting, Spoilage, Scrap Bayer Company manufactures wooden bed frames, consisting of headboards, footboards, and rails. The company's accountant is preparing a pilot study of one job to determine how costs for the job would be handled in a material flow cost accounting system. For now, the accountant is focusing only on the flow of physical materials, excluding energy.

LO 2, LO 4

Variable costs traced and allocated to job 483, a batch of 10 frames, consist of the following:

Wood	$2,350
Other direct materials (stain, fittings, etc.)	180
Direct labour	1,500
Variable manufacturing overhead (10% × direct labour cost)	150

The preceding costs include both normal and abnormal spoilage. Normal spoilage occurred when one of the wood panels split during planing. Direct costs for the panel to the point of spoilage consisted of $50 for wood and $40 for direct labour. The broken panel was scrapped. Abnormal spoilage occurred when a forklift malfunctioned and damaged wood costing $400 that was purchased specially for the job. The spoilage occurred before any processing. The damaged wood was sold for $25.

The company's manufacturing process includes planing and cutting the wood, which produces scrap. For job 483, approximately 15% of the total volume of the wood processed became scrap. This amount of scrap is considered normal. The proceeds from sale of scrap are insignificant.

Other direct materials and variable manufacturing overhead include both positive product and waste (i.e., negative product). The accountant estimates that 50% of other direct materials and 100% of variable overhead costs are waste.

REQUIRED **A.** Calculate the total variable cost that should be assigned to job 483, assuming the company uses a traditional job costing system (see Chapter 5).
B. Calculate the total variable cost that should be classified as product costs for job 483 in the company's material flow cost accounting system.
C. Provide a possible explanation for the higher proportion of waste in variable manufacturing overhead costs compared to other direct materials.
D. Suppose the managers of Bayer Company are evaluating the profitability of the customer for job 483. Should the managers use total variable costs from Part A or Part B for this analysis? Explain your reasoning.
E. In what ways might the use of material flow job cost accounting lead to changes in behaviour at Bayer Company?

20.38 Carbon Offsets for Business Air Travel Many airline companies offer a carbon offset program, in which customers can contribute a small fee to plant trees, develop wind or solar power, or other projects to make up for the environmental damage caused by air travel. These programs provide air travellers with a calculator to determine the amount of offset needed, typically based on distance flown. However, controversy exists about whether air travel carbon offset programs are appropriate. Responsible Travel was one of the first companies to offer this type of program in 2002, but it cancelled its program during 2009. In an interview, managing director Justin Francis stated, "The carbon offset has become this magic pill, a kind of get-out-of-jail-free card."

LO1

Suppose the managers of an accounting firm are considering whether to purchase carbon offsets for the business air travel of personnel. Conduct research on the Internet or access the articles under the sources listed below to learn more about these programs.

Sources: P. Gogoi, "Carbon Offsets Take Flight," *BusinessWeek.com*, March 24, 2008; and E. Rosenthal, "Paying More for Flights Eases Guilt, Not Emissions," *The New York Times*, November 18, 2009.

REQUIRED   **A.** In your own words, explain the term *carbon offset*.

B. Describe at least three arguments for and three arguments against the firm's purchase of carbon offsets for business air travel.

C. Would you recommend that the firm purchase carbon offsets for business air travel? Explain how you weighed the pros and cons to reach your conclusion.

20.39 Sustainable Management, Standards, Life Cycle Assessment, Material Flow Accounting Unilever sells products such as Ben & Jerry's and Breyer's ice cream, Hellman's mayonnaise, and Lipton tea. The company published a 33-page, printed version of its 2008 sustainability report overview. The back cover included the following statements:

LO2, LO3, LO4

Printing
Scanplus (ISO 14001: 2008)

www.wiley.com/
go/eldenburgcanada

Paper
Greencoat Plus Velvet contains 80% recycled fibre and has been independently certified according to the rules of the Forest Stewardship Council (FSC).

If you have finished with this report and no longer wish to retain it, please pass it on to other interested readers or dispose of it in your recycled paper waste.

Source: Unilever, *Sustainable Development 2008: An Overview*, Rotterdam, The Netherlands: Unilever N.V.

REQUIRED   **A.** Unilever used a printing process (Scanplus) that followed ISO 14001 standards. Perform research on the Internet to identify in general what it means to follow ISO 14001 standards.

B. Unilever used paper with recycled fibre content that was certified based on Forest Stewardship Council (FSC) rules. Perform research on the Internet to identify in general what it means to follow FSC rules.

C. What does it mean for compliance with FSC rules to be "independently certified"?

D. In general, how do the printing standards and paper certification contribute to Unilever's sustainable management?

E. Create a life cycle assessment of Unilever's printed sustainability report. Assume that Unilever outsources the printing but handles its own distribution by mailing the reports.

F. Would the inputs for the printed report be classified as waste outputs? Explain.

20.40 Cumulative Problem (chapters 4 and 12): Relevant Costs, NPV, Business Risk, Sustainability Arguments Many citizens of Grayville Township travel each work day between Grayville and a nearby city, Megametropolis. To reduce the need for building more lanes on the freeway and to comply with local sustainability policies, the township has decided to establish an express bus service that uses environmentally friendly fuel. Grayville plans to charge $2.00 for a one-way fare. Township managers want to purchase either a 32- or 52-passenger bus. Following are data for the buses.

LO4

	32	52
Number of passengers	32	52
Number of buses	6	4
Useful life	8 years	8 years
Purchase price per bus	$180,000	$210,000
Average litres per 100 km	25	33
Salvage value per bus	$ 6,000	$ 7,000
Drivers' hourly wage	$20	$25
Fuel price per litre	$ 1.20	$ 1.20
Other annual cash expenses	$ 4,000	$ 3,000

During the four hours of "rush hour" traffic each day, all buses would be in service and expected to operate at full capacity (township regulations prohibit bus passengers from standing). The buses would make six round trips during these periods. For the other 16 hours of operation, about 500 passengers are expected to ride the buses, and only four buses would cover the route. Part-time drivers would be used for the extra time during rush hours. A bus travelling the route all day would go 480 km, and one travelling only during rush hours would go 120 km per day during the 260 work days each year.

REQUIRED **A.** Prepare a schedule for the estimated annual revenues for each alternative.

B. Prepare a schedule for the estimated annual drivers' wages for each alternative.

C. Prepare a schedule for the annual cost of fuel for each alternative.

D. Assuming that Grayville requires a minimum rate of return of 12%, calculate the net present value of each bus option. Ignore inflation and taxes.

E. List two business risks that could affect this decision.

F. Based on your preceding analyses, which type of bus should the city purchase? Explain your reasoning.

G. Suppose an editorial in the Grayville newspaper argued that the township should not launch the bus service because it would harm the environment by encouraging more people to move into Grayville and then commute to Megametropolis. Furthermore, the editorial claimed that there are no environmentally friendly fuels; any fuel used would cause environmental damage. Evaluate the reasonableness of these arguments.

MINI-CASES

20.41 **Cumulative Mini-Case (Chapter 7): Traditional Costing, ABC, Sustainability Costs** Keystone Company produces two products: Regular and Premium. Regular is produced in high volumes through a robotic process with no hazardous waste. Premium's production process generates large quantities of hazardous wastes. A competitor produces only one product very similar to Regular. Keystone Company sells Regular at its competitor's price to maintain current volumes. Regular does not appear to be profitable, but Keystone Company has not dropped Regular because of its commitment to increase its sustainable management activities. Although another competitor produces Premium, Keystone sells Premium at a profit and its managers believe they can increase market share considerably.

L04

Keystone uses a traditional costing system and allocates overhead costs based on direct labour hours. Annual production of Regular is 10,000 units and Premium is 1,500 units. Each product requires four direct labour hours per unit. However, Premium requires more machine setups and quality inspections than Regular. Premium is produced in small batches that are ordered and run much more frequently than Regular. Regular requires 10 components and Premium requires 5. Only 20% of the facility is devoted to Premium production, with the remainder used for Regular. Keystone's manufacturing overhead costs total $2,070,000. Direct material and labour costs for each product are as follows:

	Regular	Premium
Direct materials	$300	$200
Direct labour (4 hours @ $25 per hour)	100	100

The managers of Keystone are considering adopting an activity-based costing system with the following activities and cost drivers for manufacturing overhead costs:

Activity	Cost Driver	Cost	Product Regular	Premium
Unit Level:				
Machine costs	Machine hours	$ 250,000	2,000	3,000
Batch Level:				
Quality control	Quality inspections	700,000	2,500	7,500
Preparing for new batch	Machine setups	202,500	3,375	6,750
Product Level:				
Product research and development, maintenance, and waste control	Number of components	517,500	3	3
Facility Level:				
Plant depreciation, property insurance, property taxes, and maintenance	Not applicable	400,000		
Total manufacturing overhead cost		$2,070,000		

Based on a special study, Keystone's accountants determined that product-level costs of $517,500 could be broken down even further, as follows:

Research and development and maintenance	$207,000
Environmental reporting requirements	500
Environmental inspections	60,000
Waste treatment costs on site	100,000
Landfill disposal costs	150,000
Total product-level costs	$517,500

The special study also determined that the product research and development and maintenance costs can be properly allocated to products based on the number of components in the product. All of the environmental costs are associated with Premium.

Note: This case was adapted from Management Institute for Environment and Business (1991).

REQUIRED **A.** Assume that Keystone uses the traditional cost accounting system:
  1. Calculate the manufacturing overhead cost allocation rate.
  2. Allocate manufacturing overhead to both products, and calculate the cost per unit of Regular and Premium.
B. Assume that Keystone uses the activity-based costing system without the special study:
  1. Calculate the manufacturing overhead cost allocation rate for each activity cost pool.
  2. Allocate manufacturing overhead costs to each type of product and calculate the cost per unit of Regular and Premium.
  3. Compare the results of this allocation to the traditional allocation in Part A. Explain any differences.
C. Assume that Keystone uses the special study to modify the activity-based costing system:
  1. Reallocate the product-level costs and calculate the cost per unit of Regular and Premium.
  2. Compare the results of this allocation to the ABC allocation in Part B. Explain any differences.
D. How might a traditional versus an ABC costing system affect Keystone Company's managers' perceptions of the company's competitive position?
E. Before making a decision about keeping or dropping one of these products, what additional information do you need? Would GPK or RCA information add value for this type of decision? Explain.

GLOSSARY

Note: Numbers in parentheses refer to the page(s) on which the term is found.

Abnormal spoilage. Spoilage that is not part of normal operations. (224, 273)

Absorption costing. All production costs, including direct materials, direct labour, and manufacturing overhead, are assigned to inventory as product costs. (203, 720)

Accounting system. Computerized or manual structure of procedures and records that document organizational performance.

Accrual accounting rate of return (AARR). Capital budgeting method that measures the expected increase in average annual operating income as a percent of the initial increase in investment. (590)

Activity. A type of task or function performed in an organization. (295)

Activity-based budgeting. Uses activity cost pools and their related cost drivers to anticipate the costs for individual activities. (466)

Activity-based costing (ABC). Process of assigning overhead costs to specific activities in a manufacturing or service delivery process. (295)

Activity-based management. Process of using ABC information to evaluate the costs and benefits of production and internal support activities and to identify and implement opportunities for improvements in profitability, efficiency, and quality within an organization. (313)

Activity-based transfer prices. Cost-based transfer price based on unit-level, batch-level, and possibly some product-level costs for products transferred, plus an annual fixed fee that is a portion of the facility-level costs. (640)

Actual allocation rate. Allocation rate calculated by dividing actual overhead cost by the actual quantity of the allocation base. (208)

Actual costing. Method for allocating overhead costs using the actual allocation rate and actual quantity of the allocation base. (211)

Actual operations. The various actions taken and results achieved over a period of time, including customer orders received, revenues earned, number of employees hired, costs incurred, units of goods or services produced, cash received and paid, etc. Data about actual operations are collected and measured by the organization's information system and then used to monitor and motivate performance. (6)

Actual overhead allocation rate. Calculated by dividing actual overhead cost by the actual quantity of the allocation base. (210)

Adjusted R-square. Reflects an estimate of the percent of variation in the dependent variable that is explained by the independent variable(s) in regression analysis. When estimating a cost function, the percent of cost that is explained by the cost driver(s). (59)

After-tax profit (loss). In general, revenues minus expenses and income taxes. Under GAAP, all revenues and gains minus all expenses, losses, and income taxes. (99)

Algebraic method. See *reciprocal method*.

Allocated overhead. Amount of overhead cost allocated to a cost object. May be based on an actual or estimated allocation rate times an actual or estimated volume of the allocation base. Also see *normal costing* and *actual costing*. (218)

Allocating costs. Assigning indirect costs to a cost object. Costs are allocated if they cannot be traced to a cost object. (315, 346)

Allocation base. Measure of activity, preferably a cost driver, used to allocate costs to a cost object. Examples include number of units, labour hours, labour costs, machine hours, number of parts, and sales. (209)

Allocation rate. Dollar amount per unit of allocation base used to allocate overhead to each cost object. (210)

Allocative efficiency. This considers the costs of the input mix and the price paid by the consumer for the output. (561)

Alpha coefficient. See *intercept*.

American Institute of Certified Public Accountants (AICPA). Professional organization for CPAs in the United States.

Analysis at the account level. Method for estimating a cost function by reviewing the pattern of past costs in the accounting system and using knowledge of operations to classify the cost as variable, fixed, or mixed. (52)

Anchoring trap. A bias in which estimates are developed by focusing on an initial piece of information called an anchor. This anchor may be based on irrelevant or only partially relevant information. (492)

Application base. See *allocation base*.

Applied overhead. See *allocated overhead*.

Applying costs. See *allocating costs*.

Appraisal activities. Quality-related tasks or functions undertaken to identify defective units of goods or services. (311)

Appraisal costs. Costs of quality for *appraisal activities*.

Asset turnover. See *investment turnover*.

Assigning costs. Practice of measuring costs for a cost object; includes tracing direct costs and allocating indirect costs. (248)

Assumption. Hypothesis, belief, or conjecture made when something is not known with certainty. In cost accounting, assumptions exist for the various quantitative analysis techniques (e.g., CVP or regression analysis) and general decision rules (e.g., for product emphasis decisions). People also make assumptions to create cost accounting information (e.g., linear cost function). Poor-quality assumptions lead to poor-quality information and decisions. Failure to objectively analyze assumptions can lead to biases. (25, 51)

Attainable standards. Standards that are set at achievable levels, but without much slack. Contrast with *ideal standards*. (490)

Average cost. Arithmetic mean cost, computed as total costs (TC) divided by the quantity (Q) of activity or production. (65)

Average rate of return. See *accrual accounting rate of return*.

Avoidable cash flows. See *relevant cash flows.*

Balanced scorecard. A formal approach used to help organizations translate their vision into objectives that can be measured and monitored using both financial and nonfinancial performance measures. (11)

Batch-level activities. Tasks or functions undertaken for a collection of goods or services that are processed as a group. Batch-level costs do not relate to the number of units in the batch but, instead, relate to the number of batches processed. (305)

Belief systems. An organization's core values that inspire and direct employees to take actions that are consistent with the organization's vision. (8)

Benchmark. A measurement or standard that serves as a reference for evaluating performance. (449–452)

Beta coefficient. See *slope coefficient.*

Beyond budgeting. An approach calling for separation of budgeting from performance evaluation; manager or employee performance is evaluated relative to internal or external benchmarks. (468)

Biased information. Unfair or distorted data that inhibit high-quality decision making.

Biases. Preconceived notions that are adopted without careful thought; cause decision makers to ignore weaknesses in their preferred course of action and prevent them from adequately exploring alternatives. (18)

Bid rigging. An agreement with another person that interferes with the bidding process. (638)

Binding constraint. A resource, such as the number of hours available for inspection, which limits production at the optimal solution of a linear programming problem. (163)

Bottleneck. Any process, part, or machine that limits overall capacity. (160)

Bottom-up budgeting. See *participative budgeting.*

Boundary systems. Establish limits on individual behaviour. (8)

Breakeven point. Level of operating activity at which revenues cover all fixed and variable costs and there is no profit. (98)

Budget. A formalized financial plan for operations of an organization for a specified future period. Used to assign decision rights to individual managers within an organization. (440)

Budget adjustments for performance evaluation. Modifications made when budgets are used to measure managers' performance. (452)

Budget assumptions. Plans and predictions about next period's operating activities; used to develop a master budget. (442)

Budget cycle. Series of steps used to develop and use budgets. (441)

Budget ratcheting. The practice of raising manager and employee performance targets to induce greater productivity. (462)

Budget variance. Difference between budgeted and actual results (e.g., revenues, expenses, or cash flows). (459)

Budgetary slack. Practice of intentionally setting revenue budgets too low and cost budgets too high. (462)

Budgeted application rate. See *estimated allocation rate.*

Budgeted capacity. Anticipated use of capacity over the next period, based on management's planned operations. (728)

Budgeted financial statements. Forecasts of the future income statement, balance sheet, and cash flows, given an organization's master budget. (442)

Budgeted indirect cost rate. See *estimated allocation rate.*

Business intelligence (BI). An information system that supports management efforts to save costs and improve profitability through the use and communication of information within an organization and with external parties such as customers and suppliers. (12)

Business Process Management (BPM). Software that supports the design, execution, and monitoring of repetitive, day-to-day business processes. (12)

Business risk. The possibility that an event could occur and interfere with an organization's ability to meet strategic goals or operating plans. (16)

Business segment decision. *See keep or drop decision.*

By-product. Joint product that has low sales value compared to other joint products. Contrast with *main product.* (402)

Capacity. In cost accounting, usually refers to the volume of goods or services possible, given existing investments in production assets. (318)

Capacity utilization. Relative amount of productive capacity used. (507)

Capital budget. Budget for long-term investment. (540, 800–801)

Capital budgeting. Process for choosing among investment opportunities that have cash flows occurring over a number of years. (578)

Carrying costs. Costs of warehousing or storage space. (702)

Cash budget. Budget for cash receipts, cash disbursements, and short-term financing, including the expected amounts and timing of cash flows. (439–444, 462)

Cause-and-effect relationship. The influence of an activity on cost; considered when classifying a cost as direct or indirect and when evaluating potential cost drivers. (45)

Centralized decision making. Decision-making authority lies within the top levels of management. Contrast with *decentralized decision making.* (700, 701)

Chartered Accountant (CA). A professional designation granted to individuals who successfully earn a university degree, complete 30 months of approved practical employment experience, complete the professional program, and pass the Uniform Evaluation (UFE). The Canadian Institute of Chartered Accountants (CICA) represents over 74,000 CAs and 10,000 students in Canada and Bermuda.

Certified General Accountant (CGA). A professional designation granted to individuals who successfully complete a program of professional education, comprehensive examinations, and approved practical experience. CGA Canada represents over 71,000 students and CGAs in Canada and around the world.

Certified Management Accountant (CMA). A professional designation granted to individuals who successfully complete a university degree, pass an entrance exam, and complete a two-year Strategic Leadership Program while gaining professional experience. CMA Canada represents over 40,000 CMAs and 10,000 students in Canada and around the world.

Cognitive bias. Errors in judgment caused by the way people's minds process information. (18)

Committed cost. Cost that remains fixed regardless of activity levels. (322)

Common cost. Cost for a resource that is shared among two or more departments, activities, products, or other cost objects. Also called *indirect cost, overhead cost,* or *joint cost.* (346)

Competitive advantage. See *organizational core competencies.*

Constant (in dollar amount) cost. See *fixed cost.*

Constant gross margin NRV method. Allocates joint costs so that the gross margin percentage for each main product is identical. (405)

Constrained resource. See *constraint.*

Constraint. Limit that restricts an organization's ability to provide enough products (goods or services) to satisfy demand. Also called *constrained* or *scarce resource.* (160)

Continuous budgets. See *rolling budget.*

Contribution margin. Total revenues minus total variable costs. (96)

Contribution margin budget variance. Difference between standard contribution margin based on static budget and actual contribution margin. (548)

Contribution margin per unit (CMu). Selling price per unit minus variable cost per unit. (96)

Contribution margin percentage. See *contribution margin ratio.*

Contribution margin ratio (CMR). Percent by which the selling price (or revenue) per unit exceeds the variable cost per unit or contribution margin as a percent of revenue. (97)

Contribution margin sales mix variance. Difference in contribution margin caused by a difference between standard and actual sales mix, given the standard contribution margin and actual quantity of units sold. (551)

Contribution margin sales quantity variance. Difference in contribution margin caused by a difference between standard and actual quantities sold, given the standard contribution margins and standard sales mix. (552)

Contribution margin sales volume variance. Difference in contribution margin caused by differences between standard and actual sales volumes, times the standard contribution margins. (549)

Contribution margin variance. Difference in contribution margin caused by differences in contribution margin per unit, given the actual volume of sales. (548)

Conversion costs. Direct labour and production overhead costs. (252)

Core competencies. See *organizational core competencies.*

Core values statement. Summary of the beliefs that define the organization's culture. (8)

Cost accounting. According to IMA Statement on Management Accounting No. 2, "a technique or method for determining the cost of a project, process, or thing," with costs determined through "direct measurement, arbitrary assignment, or systematic and rational allocation." (10)

Cost allocation. Assigning indirect costs to a cost object. Costs are allocated if they cannot be traced to a cost object. (315, 346)

Cost allocation base. See *allocation base.*

Cost application base. See *allocation base.*

Cost assignment. See *assigning costs.*

Cost-based contract. Contract in which the vendor is reimbursed based on the costs incurred to produce the good or service. Contrast with *fixed-price contract.* (373)

Cost-based price. Product selling price determined by adding a mark-up to some calculation of the product's cost. Requires selection of a cost base and a mark-up rate. (628)

Cost-based transfer pricing. Transfer price based on the cost of the goods or services transferred. (640)

Cost behaviour. The variation in costs relative to the variation in an organization's activities. (46)

Cost-benefit analysis or cost-benefit trade-offs. Investigation to determine whether the benefits exceed the costs for a proposed course of action. Often used to evaluate whether to add features or complexity to a cost accounting system. (65)

Cost centre. Responsibility centre in which managers are accountable for producing goods or services efficiently (minimizing costs for a certain level of output, or maximizing output for a certain level of cost). (324)

Cost driver. Some input or activity that causes changes in total cost for a cost object. (48)

Cost function. Algebraic representation of the total cost of a cost object over a relevant range of activity, represented as $TC = F + V \times Q$. (48)

Cost hierarchy. General categories of activities based on different levels of operations. Used to identify activities and assign costs in an ABC system. (297–299)

Cost leadership. Strategy to gain competitive advantage by maintaining lower costs than competitors. (734)

Cost management. See *strategic cost management.*

Cost object. A thing or activity for which we measure costs, such as a particular production activity, an individual product, a product line, a project, an individual or group of customers, a department, or even the entire company. (42)

Cost of capital. See *weighted average cost of capital.*

Cost of quality. Costs incurred to insure high quality and/ or the actual and opportunity costs from problems with poor quality. Also see *quality-related activities.* (273)

Cost pool. Group of individual costs that are accumulated in the accounting system for a particular purpose. Examples include overhead costs or department-level process costs. (209)

Cost tracing. See *tracing costs.*

Cost-volume-profit (CVP) analysis. Technique that examines changes in profits in response to changes in sales volumes, costs, and prices. Used to identify the levels of operating activity needed to avoid losses, achieve targeted profits, plan future operations, and monitor organizational performance. (96)

Cost-volume-profit (CVP) graph. Diagram of the relationship between total revenues and total costs; illustrates expected changes in an organization's profits under different volumes of activity. (98)

Costs of goods sold. Name given on the income statement for product costs, or total manufacturing costs of units that are sold during the period. (13)

Cumulative average-time learning curve. Learning curve approach in which the cumulative average time to produce a unit declines by a constant percentage each time the cumulative quantity of units produced doubles.

Custom (or customized) product or service. One-of-a-kind product or service that is produced according to the needs of an individual customer. (203)

Customer-level activities. See *customer-sustaining activities.*

Customer perspective. Translation of organizational vision and strategies in terms of creating value for customers; part of a balanced scorecard. (811)

Customer profitability analysis. Evaluation of customer service costs and profitability, often using activity-based management. (308)

Customer-sustaining activities. Tasks or functions undertaken to service past, current, and future customers. These costs tend to vary with the needs of individual customers or groups of customers. (298)

CVP analysis. See *cost-volume-profit analysis.*

Death spiral. Deterioration in profitability caused by the use of cost-based pricing for a product with elastic demand. When sales volumes drop, fixed costs are spread over fewer units, leading to higher cost-based prices and further decline in sales. (633)

Decentralized decision making. Decision-making authority permeates all levels of the organization. Contrast with *centralized decision making.* (700, 701)

Decision-making authority. The decisions that *agents* are authorized to make on behalf of *principals.* (700, 702)

Decision model. Systematic method using quantitative and/or qualitative information to choose between alternatives.

Decision quality. The characteristics of a decision that affect the likelihood of achieving a positive outcome. Also see *higher-quality management decisions.* (19)

Decision rights. Responsibilities and financial decision-making authority of individual managers. (441)

Declining balance method. Accelerated method of calculating depreciation, in which depreciation is higher in the early years of the estimated useful life than in the later years. (558)

Deflation. Increase in the general purchasing power of the monetary unit, meaning that fewer monetary units, such as dollars, are needed to purchase goods or services. Opposite of *inflation.* (598)

Degree of operating leverage. Index of the extent to which the cost function consists of fixed costs. (114)

Demand-based capacity levels. Measure the amount of capacity needed to meet sales volumes. Include *normal capacity* and *budgeted* or *expected capacity.* (662)

Demand-pull system. See *just-in-time production and inventory control systems.*

Dependent variable. In regression analysis, the variable whose values are explained by changes in one or more independent variables. When estimating a cost function, the dependent variable is the cost. (58)

Diagnostic control systems. Measure, monitor, and motivate employees to achieve preset goals. (9)

Differential cost. See *marginal cost.*

Direct cost. Cost that is easily traced to a cost object; a clear cause-and-effect relationship generally exists between the cost object and the cost. (45)

Direct costing. Another term for *variable costing.*

Direct labour efficiency variance. Difference between standard and actual quantity of direct labour used for the actual amount of goods or services produced, valued at the standard labour price. (509)

Direct labour price variance. Difference between standard and actual price, times the actual amount of direct labour hours worked. (508)

Direct materials efficiency variance. Difference between standard and actual quantity of direct materials used for the actual amount of goods or services produced, valued at the standard materials price. (509)

Direct materials price variance. Difference between standard and actual price, times the actual amount of direct materials purchased or used. (508)

Direct method. Allocates support department costs only to the operating departments. Reflects none of the interactions among support departments. (352)

Discount rate. Interest rate that is used across time to reduce the value of future dollars to today's dollars. (583)

Discounted cash flow. See *present value.*

Discretionary cost. Reflects periodic (usually annual) decisions about the maximum amount that will be spent on costs for activities such as advertising, executive travel, or research and development. Amount spent can easily be altered during the period. (49)

Discretionary cost centre. Cost centre for which output is not easily measurable in dollars or activities. (773)

Disposal value. See *terminal value.*

Downward demand spiral. See *death spiral.*

Driver. See *cost driver.*

Dual-rate allocation. Practice of allocating fixed and variable support department costs separately, using different allocation bases to reflect the flow of resources more accurately. Contrast with *single-rate allocation.* (365)

Dual-rate transfer pricing. Transfer price in which the selling department is credited for the market price and the purchasing department is charged the variable cost. (641)

Dumping. Illegal practice in which a company sells products in a different country at prices below the market value in its own country. (638)

DuPont analysis. Decomposition of return on investment (ROI) into investment turnover and return on sales. (707)

Dysfunctional decision. See *suboptimal decision.*

Economic order quantity. The minimum point on the total cost curve. This is the order quantity (or re-order quantity) that will minimize the combined ordering costs and carrying costs. (704)

Economic plausibility. When estimating a cost function, refers to the likelihood that a potential cost driver causes changes in the cost being estimated. (67)

Economic value added (EVA). Type of residual income that incorporates a number of adjustments to operating income and operating assets. (781)

Economies of scale. A reduction in cost per unit due to operational efficiencies as the volume of activity increases. (50)

Efficiency variance. Difference between standard and actual quantity of resources used in the production of goods or services, valued at the standard price. (508)

Elastic demand. Price changes have a substantial effect on the quantity demanded. Contrast with *inelastic demand*. (594)

Engineered estimate of cost. Method for estimating a cost function by analyzing and assigning costs to the labour time, materials, and other resources used in each activity. (52)

Enterprise resource planning (ERP). Software program system that supports databases and automates business processes, such as production, distribution, human resources, and financial accounting; often includes both financial and nonfinancial information. (49)

Enterprise risk management (ERM). Continual process of identifying, assessing, mitigating, and monitoring relevant business risks in a comprehensive and integrated way. (16)

Environmental cost analysis. Evaluation of the costs and benefits associated with environmental performance, often using activity-based management. (310)

Envisioning. Step 4 in *Steps for Better Thinking*; acting strategically to recognize change and new threats and also to visualize new opportunities. (25)

Epsilon. See *error term*.

Equivalent units. Resources used in partially completed units relative to the resources needed to complete the units. (254)

Error term. In simple regression analysis, the distance between each observation and the regression line. When estimating a cost function, the difference between the actual and estimated cost for a data point. Also called *epsilon* or *residual*.

Estimated allocation rate. Allocation rate calculated by dividing estimated overhead cost by the estimated quantity of the allocation base. (210)

Estimated application rate. See *estimated allocation rate*. (210)

Ethical decision making. Process for making ethical decisions that involves identifying ethical problems as they arise, objectively considering the well-being of others and society when exploring alternatives, clarifying and applying ethical values when choosing a course of action, and working toward ongoing improvement of personal and organizational ethics. (20)

Expected capacity. See *budgeted capacity*.

Exploring. Step 2 in *Steps for Better Thinking*; involves thorough analysis of the strengths and weaknesses of different alternatives by acknowledging and controlling biases, considering uncertainties, interpreting information from different viewpoints, recognizing and evaluating assumptions, and gauging the quality of information. (25)

External impacts. Costs and benefits that are not generally accounted for in an entity's conventional accounting system. Externalities have an impact on stakeholders who are not directly involved in the business transaction, which is considered a "spillover effect." Also called *externalities*. (857)

External report. Document that presents information for use outside an organization, such as financial statements, news releases, inventory reports for suppliers, tax returns, and regulatory reports. (11)

Externalities. Costs and benefits that are not generally accounted for in an entity's conventional accounting system. Externalities have an impact on stakeholders who are not directly involved in the business transaction, which is considered a "spillover effect." Also called *external impacts*. (857)

Facility-level activities. See *facility-sustaining activities*.

Facility-sustaining activities. Tasks or functions undertaken to provide and manage an area, location, or property. These activities occur no matter how many customers are served, products are sold, batches are processed, or units are produced. (298)

Factory burden or factory overhead cost. See *overhead cost*.

Fairness bias. A tendency to reject benefits for offers that are perceived as unfair. (366–367, 373)

Favourable variance. Budget variance in which actual results are better than budgeted results (e.g., actual revenues are larger than the budget, or actual costs are lower than the budget). (459)

Financial accounting. The process of preparing and reporting financial information that is used most frequently by decision makers outside the organization, such as shareholders and creditors. (10)

Financial budget. Budget for capital expenditures, long-term financing, and cash flows. (442)

Financial information. Knowledge, facts, data, or factors that can be measured in dollars or ratios of dollars. (10)

Financial measure. Performance measure that provides information in dollars or ratios of dollars. (807)

Financial perspective. Translation of organizational vision and strategies in terms of desired financial results; part of a balanced scorecard. (810)

Finished goods. Usually refers to the general ledger account used to account for the cost of inventory that is available for delivery or sale to customers.

First-in, first-out (FIFO) method. In process costing, a method in which the current period's costs are used to allocate cost to work performed this period. (254)

Fixed cost. Cost that does not change with small changes in activity levels of a cost object. (47)

Fixed overhead budget variance. Difference between allocated fixed overhead cost and actual fixed overhead cost. (515)

Fixed overhead cost pool. Cost pool used to accumulate only fixed overhead costs. (294)

Fixed overhead spending variance. Difference between estimated fixed overhead costs (i.e., static budget) and actual fixed overhead costs. (516)

Fixed overhead volume variance. See *production volume variance*.

Fixed-price contract. Contract in which the vendor provides products or services at a specific price. Contrast with *cost-based contract*. (373)

Flexible budget. Budget that reflects a range of operations. When evaluating actual results at the end of a period, the flexible budget is set at the actual sales or production volume and used as a benchmark for analyzing variances. (455)

Flexible budget variance. Budget variance (difference between budgeted and actual results) calculated using a flexible budget. (449)

Flexible cost. Cost that varies proportionately with activity levels; a variable cost of an activity. (322)

Forecasted financial statements. See *budgeted financial statements.*

Full costing. See *absorption costing.*

Future value. Amount to be received in the future, calculated for a given number of years at a given interest. (581)

General decision rule. See *general rule.*

General knowledge. Information that is easy to transfer from one person to another within an organization. Contrast with *specific knowledge.* (770)

Generally Accepted Accounting Principles (GAAP). The set of accounting methods and disclosures typically used to prepare financial statements for distribution to external parties; not always ideal for management decision making. (489, 652)

General rule. Guideline for making a decision, often based only on quantitative information. (146, 155)

Goals. See *long-term goals* and *performance target.*

Goodness of fit statistic. See *adjusted R-square.*

Half-year convention. Convention for calculating depreciation under the modified asset cost recovery system (MACRS), in which assets are assumed to be purchased halfway through the year of acquisition. (558)

Higher-quality management decisions. The use of higher-quality information, higher-quality reports, and a higher-quality decision-making process to increase the likelihood of achieving positive outcomes; involve fewer deficiencies such as uncertainties and biases. (10)

High-low method. Specific application of the two-point method for estimating cost functions using the highest and lowest data points of the cost driver. (54)

Homogeneous activities. Tasks or functions that are related in a logical manner and consume similar resources. (306)

Hurdle rate. See *required rate of return.*

Hybrid costing. Accounting approach for assigning product costs using a combination of both job and process costing. (272)

Hybrid product or service. Mostly uniform product or service that is partially customized according to the needs of an individual customer. (204)

Ideal standards. Standards that are achievable under ideal operating conditions. Contrast with *attainable standards.*

Identifying. Step 1 in *Steps for Better Thinking*; involves recognizing an open-ended problem, obtaining relevant information, and acknowledging uncertainties. (25)

Idle capacity. See *slack resource.*

Incentives. Factors that motivate and influence behaviour. In agency theory, compensation incentives such as bonuses or stock options may be used to encourage desired actions or behaviour. (747)

Incongruent goals. In agency theory, conflicts of interest that encourage *agents* to take actions that are not in the best interests of *principals.*

Incremental cash flows. See *relevant cash flows.*

Incremental cost. See *marginal cost.*

Incremental cost allocation method. Allocates common costs to the most responsible user based on the cost that would have been incurred had the services not been shared. Then the next most responsible user is allocated the incremental cost to use the shared resource. (373)

Independent variable. In regression analysis, a variable used to explain changes in the dependent variable. When estimating a cost function, an independent variable is a potential cost driver. (58)

Indifference point. The level of activity where costs or profits are equal across multiple alternatives. (116)

Indirect cost. Cost that is not easily traced to a cost object; no clear cause-and-effect relationship exists between the cost object and the cost, or the cost of tracing the cost to the cost object exceeds the benefit. Also called *common cost.* (45)

Indirect cost rate. See *allocation rate.*

Industrial engineering method. See *engineered estimate of cost.*

Inelastic demand. Price changes have little effect on the quantity demanded, and factors such as quality and the ability to customize are more important, within limits, than price. Contrast with *elastic demand.* (594)

Inflation. Decline in the general purchasing power of the monetary unit, meaning that more monetary units, such as dollars, are needed to purchase goods or services. (598)

Information. See *relevant information.*

Information bias. Errors in judgment caused by data that are consistently overestimated, underestimated, or mis-represented. (18)

Information system. Computerized or manual structure of procedures and records. (11)

Innovation cycle. Internal business processes concerned with identifying customer needs and designing goods and services to meet those needs. (812)

Input measures. Performance measures that capture activity or effort. (746)

Insourcing. The practice of providing goods or services from internal resources. The opposite of outsourcing. (151)

Institute of Management Accountants (IMA). International organization of financial management executives and accountants that provides a wide variety of information and activities for its members, including local meetings with informative speakers, continuing professional education, and web-based and printed information about current management and cost accounting practices.

Intellectual capital. Information held in the minds of employees; generally not formally captured by the information system, preventing it from being readily accessible by managers. (11)

Interactive control systems. Recurring sets of information that demand attention from managers at many levels. (9)

Intercept. Fixed cost when estimating a cost function using regression analysis. Also called *alpha coefficient* or intercept parameter. (53)

Intermediate product. Product transferred from one department to another, where further assembly takes place before final sale to an external customer. Product transfers are recorded using a *transfer price.*

Internal business process perspective. Translation of organizational vision and strategies in terms of the efficiency and effectiveness of practices used inside organizations to produce and deliver goods and services; part of a balanced scorecard. (812)

Internal consistency. In net present value calculations involving inflation, refers to the consistent use of either the real method or the nominal method. (561)

Internal impacts. Costs and benefits inside the organization that are recognized in the entity's conventional accounting system. (857)

Internal rate of return (IRR). Capital budgeting method that determines the discount rate necessary for the present value of the discounted cash flows to be equal to the investment (i.e., the discount rate at which the project's net present value equals zero). (587)

Internal report. Document that presents information for use only inside an organization, such as a capital budget, analysis of a potential acquisition, operating and other budgets, bonus computations, and analysis of supplier quality. (11)

Internal service department. See *support department*

Inventoriable costs. See *product costs.*

Investment centre. Responsibility centre in which managers are accountable for revenues, costs, and investments. (774)

Investment turnover. Revenue divided by average operating assets; measures sales generated by each dollar invested in operating assets. (707)

Irrelevant cash flows. Cash flows that occur regardless of which course of action or decision alternative is chosen. Also called *unavoidable cash flows.* (13)

Irrelevant information. Knowledge, facts, data, factors, or issues that do not help the decision maker evaluate and choose among alternative courses of action; does not vary with the action taken. (13)

ISO 9000. Standards designed to improve quality management and facilitate business-to-business transactions. (225)

Job. Customized production of one unit or multiple units in a group for an individual customer. (204)

Job cost record. Manual or electronic record that contains all of the costs traced and allocated to a specific job. (207)

Job costing. Process of assigning costs to custom products or services. (206)

Job order costing. See *job costing.*

Job record. See *job cost record.*

Job sheet. See *job cost record.*

Joint costs. Common costs to produce a group of goods or services, and incurred prior to the split-off point; cannot be traced to individual joint products. (402)

Joint products. Goods or services that are created simultaneously with other goods or services, using common resources. (402)

Joint-versus-separate preference reversal. A tendency to react emotionally to a decision when only one option exists but to use a more objective decision rule when multiple options exist. (402)

Just-in-time (JIT) production and inventory control systems. Systems in which materials are purchased and units are produced at the time customers demand them. In JIT inventory control systems, organizations work with suppliers so that goods or materials are delivered just as they are needed for production or for sale. In JIT manufacturing systems, the production process is often broken into steps that are performed in manufacturing cells. (671)

Kaizen budget. Sets targeted cost reductions across time, anticipating market price reductions across the life of a product. (468)

Kaizen costing. Planning process for achieving continuous improvement in product cost, quality, and functionality. Similar to target costing, but occurs after the product has been designed and the first production cycle is complete. (677)

Kanban. A visual device that communicates to a cell that additional materials or products are demanded from the subsequent cell. Also see *manufacturing cell.* (639)

Kanban cellular manufacturing. See *just-in-time production and inventory control systems.*

Keep or drop decision. Non-routine decision to continue or to stop operations for a product, group of products (product line), or business segment. Also called *product line decision* or *business segment decision.* (146–150)

Knowing. Knowledge and basic skills needed to deal with a problem. The foundation of *Steps for Better Thinking.* (25)

Lagging measures. Indicators of what has already happened. They are often highly aggregated and of limited usefulness in decision making about future planning.

Lead time. The amount of time between placing an order and the receipt of the inventory. (706)

Leading measures. Indicators of performance drivers that capture information about processes, markets, customers, and employees. They are often stated in non-monetary terms and are forward looking. (808)

Lean accounting. A set of accounting principles and methods to support lean business practices and motivate continuous improvement. (683)

Lean production. See *just-in-time production* and *inventory control systems.*

Learning and growth perspective. Translation of organizational vision and strategies in terms of discovery and human capital; part of a balanced scorecard. (814)

Learning curve. Rate at which labour hours decrease as the volume of production or services increases. Also see *cumulative average-time learning curve.* (72)

Least-squares regression. See *simple regression analysis* and *multiple regression analysis.*

Life cycle assessment. Evaluates all the activities involved in the design, development, production, sale, transportation, and disposal of a product or service. (799)

Life cycle costing. Decision-making method that considers changes in price and costs over the entire life cycle of a good or service, from the time the product is introduced through a number of years. (681)

Linear programming. A mathematical technique that maximizes a linear objective function (such as the sum of contribution margins from multiple products) subject to linear constraints (such as the number of hours available for different manufacturing or services processes). (163)

Linear regression. See *simple regression analysis* and *multiple regression analysis.*

Long-term goals. Strategic targets that managers plan to achieve over a long time period (longer than one year); used to monitor long-term organizational performance. Sometimes called objectives. (4)

Main product. Joint product that has high sales value compared to other joint products. Contrast with *by-product*. (402)

Make or buy decision. See *outsourcing*.

Management accounting. Process of gathering, summarizing, and reporting information used internally by managers to make decisions; includes measurement of costs as well as other financial and nonfinancial information. (10)

Management by exception. Management emphasis on variances to control operations.

Management control systems. The feedback loop encompassing the systems and routines that managers use to increase the likelihood of organizational success. (7)

Management decision making. Methodical process for making decisions that begins with organizational vision and organizational core competencies, which lead to organizational strategies, then to operating plans, and finally to actual operations. Actual operations are measured and monitored against strategies and plans to motivate performance throughout the organization and to guide revisions to the entire process. (4–7)

Manufacturing cell. Area where all of the equipment and labour is grouped for a particular part of the manufacturing process. See *kanban*. (627)

Manufacturing overhead cost. Overhead cost related to manufacturing activities. (200–202)

Margin of safety. Excess of an organization's expected future sales (in either revenue or units) above the break-even point. (113)

Margin of safety percentage. Margin of safety as a percentage of actual or estimated sales (units or revenues). (113)

Marginal cost. Incremental cost of an activity, such as producing the next unit of goods or services. (43)

Marginal costing. See *variable costing*.

Market-based price. Product selling price determined using some measure of customer demand. (632)

Market-based transfer price. Transfer price based on competitors' prices or on the supply and demand relationship. (641)

Market share variance. The difference between the budgeted market share percentage and the actual market share percentage achieved for the standard contribution margin. (555)

Market size variance. A market related variance; this variance is favourable when the actual market volume is greater than the budgeted market volume. (555)

Mark-up. Increase in cost to arrive at a product's selling price, expressed in dollars or as a percentage of cost or selling price. (588)

Master budget. Comprehensive plan for an upcoming financial period, usually a year. (442)

Material flow accounting. The process of analyzing the movement of all physical materials through an organization's operations. (870)

Material flow cost accounting. The process of analyzing and tracking the physical units and costs of materials and energies through a manufacturing process. (870)

Materiality. Significance of an amount (e.g., cost, variance, or adjustment). Amounts are generally viewed as material if their treatment would affect the decisions of people who rely on reported values. (213)

Measure. Value assigned (noun) or the process of assigning a value (verb) to an object through calculation, appraisal, estimation, or some other method. See also *financial measure* and *nonfinancial measure*. (7)

Measuring performance. In cost management, a process of capturing and assigning values to financial or nonfinancial information about actual operations; used to monitor and motivate organizational performance. (7, 730–779)

Method of least squares. See *multiple regression analysis* and *simple regression analysis*.

Mission statement. High-level declaration of the organization's purpose. (8)

Mixed cost. Cost that is partly fixed and partly variable. (47)

Mix variance This explains trade-offs between the quantity used of the different inputs by comparing the actual mix of the inputs used to the standard mix for the inputs. (558)

Monitoring progress. In cost management, a process of measuring and comparing actual operations to plans such as budgets and long-term goals to evaluate the success of decisions and motivate employees. (7)

Motivating employees. In cost management, a process of measuring organizational performance and monitoring the results to encourage employees to work toward the organizational vision; often involves the use of incentives tied to pay or other employee benefits. (7)

Multicollinearity. High correlation among independent variables in a regression analysis, causing coefficients to be inaccurate. (69)

Multiple regression analysis. Statistical technique that measures the average change in a dependent variable for every unit change in two or more independent variables. When used to estimate a mixed cost function, the independent variables are potential cost drivers. (58)

Negotiated transfer price. Transfer price based on an agreement reached between the managers of the selling and purchasing departments. (641)

Net income (loss). See *after-tax profit (loss)*.

Net present value (NPV) method. Capital budgeting method that determines whether an organization would be better off investing in a project based on the net amount of discounted cash flows for the project. (581)

Net realizable value (NRV) method. Allocates joint costs using the relative value of main products, taking into account both the additional sales value that is created and costs that are incurred after joint production ends. (405)

Nominal discount rate. See *nominal rate of interest*.

Nominal method. Approach for calculating discounted cash flows in which cash inflows and outflows are forecast in nominal dollars (inflated) and discounted using a nominal discount rate. (599)

Nominal rate of interest. Rate of return required on investments when inflation is present. Calculated by increasing the real rate of interest by the expected rate of inflation. (598)

Nonfinancial information. Knowledge, facts, data, or factors that cannot be measured in dollars or ratios of dollars.

Nonfinancial measure. Performance measure of information that cannot be quantified in dollars. (808)

Noninventoriable costs. See *period costs.*

Nonrational escalation of commitment. Committing more resources to a project that was originally based on a poor decision. (19)

Non-value-added activities. Tasks or functions that are unnecessary and waste resources because they do not increase the worth of an organization's goods or services to customers. (314, 669)

Normal capacity. Average use of capacity over time; typical volume of goods or services produced. (728)

Normal costing. Method for allocating overhead costs using an estimated allocation rate and actual quantity of the allocation base. (210)

Normal spoilage. Spoilage that arises as part of regular operations. (224, 273)

Objective function. In linear programming, the mathematical function to be optimized. Also called *target function.* (163, 171–172)

One-time-only special order. See *special order.*

Open-ended problems. A problem with no single "correct" solution, often due to significant uncertainties. The decision maker's task is to find the best—not the only— possible solution. (24)

Operating budget. Budget for revenues, production, and operating costs. (442)

Operating department. Department or division within an organization that manufactures goods or produces services for external customers or clients. (346)

Operating income (loss). Operating revenues minus operating expenses. (98, 99)

Operating plans. Specific short-term decisions that shape the organization's day-to-day activities, such as drawing cash from a bank line of credit, hiring an employee, or ordering materials; often include specific performance objectives, such as budgeted revenues and costs. (6)

Operation costing. Type of hybrid costing used when similar batches of identical products are manufactured; units in each batch are identical, but the processing varies across batches. (272)

Operational audit. Objective and systematic examination of evidence to provide an independent assessment of the performance of an organization, program, activity, or function. (740)

Operations cycle. Internal business processes concerned with the production and delivery of goods or services. (813)

Opportunity cost. Benefit forgone when one alternative is chosen over the next best alternative. (45)

Opportunity costs of spoilage. Benefit forgone from the production of spoiled units. (224–225, 228)

Optimal solution. In linear programming, a solution that maximizes the objective function. (163)

Ordering costs. Costs associated with placing an order for parts or goods, including the costs of identifying an appropriate vendor, completing and checking an order requisition, preparing a purchase order, placing the order, handling any follow-up questions about the order, and receiving the order. (702)

Organization-level activities. See *organization-sustaining activities.*

Organization-sustaining activities. Tasks or functions undertaken to oversee the entire entity; activities that occur no matter how many facilities are operated, customers are served, products are sold, batches are processed, or units are produced. (298)

Organizational core competencies. The organization's strengths relative to competitors; closely related to *organizational vision.* (4)

Organizational strategies. Approaches that managers use to take advantage of core competencies while working toward the organizational vision; guide long-term decisions, such as the proportion of financing through debt and equity, types of goods and services offered, and investments in property, plant, and equipment. (5)

Organizational vision. Core purpose and ideology of an organization, which guides the organization's overall direction and approaches toward various stakeholder groups. (4)

Outcome measures. Performance measures that capture results. (740, 746)

Outlier. In regression analysis, a data observation that is much larger or much smaller than usual, unduly influencing the results. (71)

Output measure. A calculation, recording, or measure of the number of units produced or services provided. (324)

Outsourcing. The practice of hiring outside vendors to supply products and services. Outsourcing decisions are also called *make or buy decisions.* (151)

Overabsorbed overhead or indirect costs. See *overapplied overhead.*

Overallocated overhead or indirect costs. See *overapplied overhead.*

Overapplied overhead. Occurs when actual costs are less than the total amount of overhead allocated to inventory accounts. (214)

Overhead allocation rate. See *allocation rate.*

Overhead cost. Often refers to a pool of production costs other than direct materials and direct labour. May also refer to other types of *common costs,* such as general and administrative costs. (45)

Overhead cost pool. Cost pool used to accumulate overhead costs. (207, 227)

Overhead variance adjustment. General ledger entry to eliminate overapplied or underapplied overhead at the end of an accounting period. (515)

Partial productivity measure. An assessment of the output achieved for each individual input, one input at a time. (562)

Participative budgeting. Budget requests that are communicated "bottom up" from departments to members in top management who are responsible for final budget approval. (462)

Payback method. Capital budgeting method that measures the amount of time required to recover the initial investment. (589)

Peak load pricing. Practice of charging different prices at different times to reduce capacity constraints. (637)

Peanut butter costing. Practice of spreading overhead costs to products without regard to their use of resources. (314, 323)

Penetration pricing. Practice of setting low prices when new products are introduced to increase market share. (637)

Performance measure. An indicator, usually calculated quantitatively, that is used to monitor performance of an organization, sub-unit, process, manager, or other object. (703, 704)

Performance targets. Goals set for individual measures; typically over a three- to five-year period with interim milestones. (818)

Period costs. All costs other than production costs that are assigned to the cost of inventory, including non-production costs such as administration, marketing, and distribution. (13)

Physical output method. Allocates joint costs using the relative proportion of physical output for each main product. (404)

Piecewise linear cost function. Cost function in which the variable cost per unit changes across relevant ranges of activity. (48)

Positive illusions. Beliefs that one is superior to others across a variety of traits and social contexts. (639)

Post-investment audit. Provides feedback about whether operations are meeting expectations for a capital budgeting project. (593)

Post-sales service cycle. Internal business processes concerned with the service provided to customers after product delivery. (813)

Practical capacity. Upper capacity limit under typical operating conditions, assuming that some downtime is unavoidable for maintenance and holidays. *Theoretical capacity* reduced for expected downtimes. (308, 728)

Predatory pricing. Illegal practice of setting prices low to drive competitors out of the market and then raising prices. (638)

Predetermined application or overhead rate. See *estimated allocation rate.*

Predicted financial statements. See *budgeted financial statements.*

Predisposition bias. Errors in judgment caused by preferences, attitudes, or emotions that prevent objective analysis. (18)

Present value. Value in today's dollars of an amount to be received in the future, calculated for a given number of years at a given interest. (581)

Preset goals. Goals set by management for variables—such as income, market share, and manufacturing output—that are critical to organizational success. (9)

Prevention activities. Quality-related tasks or functions undertaken to produce defect-free units of goods or services. (311)

Price discrimination. Illegal practice of setting different prices for different customers if the intent is to lessen or prevent competition. (638)

Price elasticity of demand. Sensitivity of sales to price increases. (634)

Price fixing. An agreement between competitors to sell a common product at the same price, resulting in a mutual benefit to the sellers at the expense of the buyers. (638)

Price gouging. Practice of charging a price viewed by consumers as too high. (637)

Price maintenance. Use of business influence to encourage an increase or discourage a decrease in the price of a product in Canada. (638)

Price skimming. Practice of setting a higher price for a product or service when it is first introduced. (637)

Price variance. Difference between standard and actual prices paid for resources purchased and used in the production of goods or services. (507)

Primary costs. A cost-relevant item in the chart of accounts, for which a corresponding general ledger account exists in financial accounting; for example, material costs. (325)

Prime costs. Direct material and direct labour costs. (42, 200)

Prioritizing. Step 3 in *Steps for Better Thinking;* making trade-offs and choosing the best possible alternative for an open-ended problem, and then efficiently implementing it. For managers, includes ensuring that the organization's values, core competencies, and strategies are adequately considered; and motivating performance within the organization. (25)

Process costing. Method for allocating both direct and overhead costs to continuous-flow processing lines; it is the approach generally used for mass-produced products. Direct and indirect costs are traced and allocated to production departments, and then allocated to units. (205, 252)

Product cost cross-subsidization. Cost allocations that do not represent the use of resources, resulting in the over allocation of costs to some products and the underallocation of costs to others. (314, 323)

Product costs. Direct and indirect production costs that are assigned to the cost of inventory on the balance sheet and then expensed as part of cost of goods sold when units are sold. (202, 205, 720)

Product differentiation. Practice of strategically positioning a product based on its quality or functionality. (734)

Product emphasis decision. Deciding which products to emphasize.(159)

Product-level activities. See *product-sustaining activities.*

Product line decision. See *keep or drop decision.*

Product-mix decision. See *product emphasis decision.*

Product-sustaining activities. Tasks or functions undertaken to support the production and distribution of a single product or line of products. These activities are not related to units or batches, but to individual products or product lines. (298)

Production department. See *operating department.*

Production volume variance. Difference between the standard amount of fixed overhead costs for the actual amount of goods or services produced and the estimated fixed overhead costs (i.e., static budget). (516)

Productivity The ratio of outputs achieved for the inputs used. (561)

Profit centre. Responsibility centre in which managers are accountable for both revenues and cost (i.e., profits). (774)

Profit margin ratio. See *return on sales.*

Profit-maximizing price. Product selling price calculated using variable costs and an estimate of the product's price elasticity of demand. (594–595)

Profitability index. Ratio of the present value of the benefits to the present value of the costs of a capital budgeting opportunity. (583)

Pro forma financial statements. See *budgeted financial statements.*

Proportional costs. Costs that are attributable to changes in volumes of resource use. (324)

P-value. Statistical probability that an alpha or beta coefficient is significantly different from zero in a regression analysis. Used to assess whether fixed and variable costs are greater than zero when estimating a cost function. (58–59)

Qualitative information. Factors that are not valued in numerical terms. (145)

Quality cost. See *cost of quality*.

Quality-related activities. Tasks or functions undertaken to minimize the opportunity costs that arise when customers have problems with defective units or low-quality services. Include four types of activities: prevention, appraisal, quality-related production, and quality-related post-sales. (311, 312)

Quantitative analysis. Computation and interpretation of numerical information when addressing a problem. (144, 145)

Quantitative information. Numerical information that is available for addressing a problem. (145)

Quantity variance. See *efficiency variance*.

Radio frequency identification (RFID) tags. Attached to inventory to allow tracking via active or passive radio signals. (39)

Rate variance. See *price variance*.

Real discount rate. See *real rate of interest*.

Real method. Approach for calculating discounted cash flows in which cash inflows and outflows are forecast in real dollars (no inflation) and discounted using a real rate. (599)

Real rate of interest. Rate of return required on investments when no inflation is a factor; sum of the risk-free rate and a risk premium. (598)

Recency effect. A bias in which people rely too heavily on recent experiences or information. (434)

Reciprocal method. Simultaneously allocates costs among support departments and then from support departments to operating departments; allows for all of the interactions among departments. (362)

Regression analysis. See *simple regression analysis* and *multiple regression analysis*.

Relax a constraint. Making one or more changes in operations to reduce or eliminate a constraint. (167)

Relevant cash flows. Cash flows that occur under one course of action or decision alternative, but not under another. Also called *incremental* or *avoidable cash flows*. (13)

Relevant costs. Costs that occur under one course of action or decision alternative, but not under another. See also *relevant cash flows*. (14–15)

Relevant information. Knowledge, facts, data, or factors that help the decision maker evaluate and choose among alternative courses of action; concerns the future and varies with the action taken. (13)

Relevant range. Span of activity for a given cost object, where total fixed costs remain constant and the variable cost per unit of activity remains constant. (43)

Re-order point. An inventory level that tells managers when to place an order (or start production). (706)

Required rate of return. Minimum acceptable discount rate established by management for a capital budgeting project. (545)

Residual. See *error term*.

Residual income. Performance measure calculated as the dollar amount of actual profits in excess of a required rate of return on average operating assets. (779)

Residual value. See *terminal value or terminal cash flow*.

Resource consumption accounting (RCA). A principle-based approach to management accounting that enhances management decision making for the purposes of achieving enterprise optimization. (325)

Resource cost pool. A grouping of homogeneous resources. (325)

Responsibility accounting. Process of assigning decision-making authority and responsibility to managers of subunits and then monitoring their performance. (773)

Responsibility centre. Sub-unit (e.g., segment, division, or department) over which managers are accountable for specific types of operating activities. (773)

Return on investment (ROI). Performance measure calculated as the ratio of operating income to average operating assets; measures profitability relative to asset investment. (776)

Return on sales. Operating income divided by revenues; measures managers' abilities to control operating expenses relative to sales. (707)

Revenue budget variance. Difference between actual and standard (or budgeted) revenues. (546)

Revenue centre. Responsibility centre in which managers are accountable for revenues. (774)

Revenue-generating department. See *operating department*.

Revenue sales quantity variance. Difference between standard and actual quantity of units sold, multiplied by the standard selling price. (546)

Reverse engineering. The process of taking a competitor's product apart and putting it back together again to better understand the manufacturing process and the product design. (629)

Rework. Spoiled units that are repaired and sold as if they were originally produced correctly. (225)

Risk-free rate. "Pure" rate of interest paid on short-term government bonds (without considering inflation). (598)

Risk premium. Rate of return above the risk-free rate that businesses demand for undertaking risks. (598)

Rolling budget. Budget prepared monthly or quarterly that reflects planning changes going forward, often through the next 12 to 16 months. Planning changes include the most recent results as well as changes in business strategy, operating plans, and the economy. (466)

Safety stock. An extra quantity of goods above what is known to be needed to meet sales or production. (706, 707)

Sales mix. Proportion of different products or services that an organization sells. (102)

Sales price variance. Difference between standard and actual selling price, multiplied by the actual volume of goods or services sold. (546)

Sales value at split-off point method. Allocates joint costs based on the relative sales value of main products at the point where joint production ends. (405)

Salvage value. See *terminal value or terminal cash flow*.

Sarbanes–Oxley Act. Requires U.S. public company managers and boards of directors to assume greater legal responsibility, such as self-assessing internal controls and financial reporting risk, and increasing the oversight of managers and auditors by the board of directors and its audit committee. (22, 348, 672)

Scarce resource. See *constraint*.

Scatter plot. Graphical technique in which data points for past costs are plotted against a potential cost driver. Visual analysis of a scatter plot is used to study the relationship between a cost and a potential cost driver and to decide whether the cost might be completely fixed, completely variable, or mixed. (52)

Scattergraph technique. See *two-point method*.

Scrap. Bits of direct material left over from normal manufacturing processes. Scrap sometimes has value and can be sold, and sometimes it is discarded. (225)

Secondary costs. Portrays internal value flows, such as those found in internal activity allocation and overhead calculations; for example, production costs, material overheads, and production overheads. (326)

Semifixed. See *stepwise linear cost function*.

Semivariable cost. See *mixed cost*.

Sensitivity analysis. Use of quantitative and qualitative information to study changes in results with changes in various assumptions. (106, 165)

Separable costs. Incremental production costs for a joint product incurred after the *split-off point*. (402)

Sequential method. See *step-down method*.

Service department. See *support department*.

Simple regression analysis. Statistical technique that measures the average change in a dependent variable for every unit change in one independent variable. When used to estimate a mixed cost function, the independent variable is a potential cost driver. (58)

Single-rate allocation. Practice of using only one base to allocate both fixed and variable costs. Contrast with *dual-rate allocation*. (365)

Six Sigma. Quality program developed by Motorola that focuses on achieving a defect rate of fewer than 3.4 defects per million items. (225)

Slack resource. A resource such as capacity or direct materials that is not binding and could be used if there were no other binding constraints. (163)

Slope coefficient. Variable cost per unit of a cost driver when estimating a cost function using regression analysis. Also called *beta coefficient* or slope parameter. (58)

Source documents. Manual or electronic records created to capture and provide information about transactions or events. Examples include employee time records and raw material requisitions. (207)

Span of control. The scope of people or other resources over which an individual is given decision-making authority and is, therefore, held accountable. (772)

Special order. Customer order that is not part of the organization's normal operations. (146, 155–159)

Special order decision. Decision about whether to accept or reject a customer order that is not part of the organization's normal operations. (155)

Specific knowledge. Detailed information about particular processes, customers, or products; information that is costly to transfer within the organization. Contrast with *general knowledge*. (770)

Split-off point. Point during production at which individual joint products can be identified. (402)

Spoilage. Units of product that are unacceptable and are discarded, reworked, or sold at a reduced price. (223, 273)

Squared error. In simple regression analysis, the square of the distance from each observation to the regression line. When estimating a cost function, the squared difference between the actual and estimated cost for a data point. (58)

Stand-alone method. Allocates common costs using weights based on information about the individual users of a cost object. (373)

Standard cost. Cost that managers expect to incur for production of goods or services under operating plan assumptions. (270, 502)

Standard cost variance. Difference between a standard cost and an actual cost. (503)

Standard cost variance adjustment. General ledger entry to close standard cost variance accounts at the end of an accounting period. (489)

Standard costing system. Accounting system that initially assigns costs to products based on standards. (503)

Standard error. In regression analysis, provides an estimate of the expected amount of variation in a coefficient. (58)

Standard fixed overhead allocation rate. Standard dollar amount per unit of allocation base used to allocate fixed overhead to products. (515)

Standard overhead allocation rate. Standard dollar amount per unit of allocation base used to allocate overhead to products. Also see *estimated allocation rate*. (514)

Standard variable overhead allocation rate. Standard dollar amount per unit of allocation base used to allocate variable overhead to products. (514)

Static budget. Budget based on forecasts of specific volumes of production or services. (455)

Static budget variance. Budget variance (difference between budgeted and actual results) calculated using a static budget. (447)

Status quo bias. The tendency for people to preserve the status quo rather than to risk trying something new. (323)

Step-down method. Allocates support department costs one department at a time to the remaining support and operating departments in a cascading manner until all support department costs have been allocated. Recognizes that support departments provide support for operating departments as well as other support departments, but addresses only part of the interactions. (360)

Steps for Better Thinking. Decision-making process that leads to higher quality decisions. Also a cognitive development model that was used to define levels of complexity within the *AICPA Core Competency Framework*. (24–25)

Steps in ethical decision making. See *ethical decision making*.

Stepwise linear cost function. Cost function in which fixed cost changes across relevant ranges of activity. (48)

Straight-line depreciation. Method of calculating depreciation, in which the asset cost is spread uniformly over the estimated useful life of the asset. (556)

Strategic cost management. Expansion of *management accounting* to simultaneous focus on reducing costs and strengthening an organization's strategic position. (11)

Strategic decision making. See *management decision making*.

Strategic objectives. The specific goals that managers choose to measure and monitor; help motivate employees to carry out strategies and plans. (804)

Strategies. See *organizational strategies*.

Strategy map. A visual summary of the strategic objectives for the four perspectives of the balanced scorecard. (816)

Suboptimal decision. Decision that is not in the best interests of the organization as a whole. (9)

Sunk cost. Expenditures made in the past, which cannot be changed by any future decisions; unavoidable and therefore not relevant to decision making. (46)

Super-variable costing. See *throughput costing*.

Supply-based allocation rate. Overhead cost allocation rate based on estimated costs and practical capacity. Allows measurement of the cost of capacity used, as well as the cost of unused capacity.

Supply-based capacity levels. Measures of the amount of capacity that is available for production, including *theoretical capacity* and *practical capacity*. (662)

Supply chain. Flow of resources from the initial suppliers (internal or external) through the delivery of goods and services to customers and clients. (670)

Support department. Department or division within an organization that provides services used internally and that supports the operating departments. (346)

Sustainability accounting. The systematic recording, reporting, and analysis of quantitative and qualitative information about sustainable management practices and performance. (860)

Sustainability management accounting. Accounting activities to assist in the sustainable management process, such as designing and evaluating business processes, budgeting and forecasting, implementing and monitoring internal controls, and analyzing, synthesizing, and aggregating information. (860)

Sustainability reporting. Strategies for communicating information about sustainability efforts and performance. (860)

Sustainable management. Consideration of the environment, economics, and people of today and future generations when leading an organization or social/political community. (856)

SWOT analysis. Identification of an organization's core competencies through studying its strengths, weaknesses, opportunities, and threats. (4)

Tactical plans. Short-term plans and budgets that provide specific guidance and responsibilities for progress toward strategic objectives. (805)

Target cost. Target price less required profit margin. (628)

Target costing. Product decision-making approach that uses market-based prices to determine whether products and services can be delivered at low enough costs for an acceptable profit. Product and manufacturing processes are redesigned so that the product meets a pre-specified target cost. (673)

Target function. See *objective function*.

Target price. Competitive product selling price for a given level of product quality and functionality. (629)

Tax shield. Depreciation deduction for the initial investment cost of a capital budgeting project, taken on future years' income tax returns. (557)

Technical efficiency Occurs when a business produces the maximum quantity of outputs for the minimum quantity of inputs. (561)

Terminal value or terminal cash flow. Cash flows that occur at the end of a project's life. (540)

Theoretical capacity. Upper capacity limit, assuming continuous, uninterrupted production 365 days per year. Maximum volume of goods or services that an organization could hypothetically produce. (728)

Theory of Constraints. Formal method used to analyze organizational constraints and improve operations. (160)

Throughput. Rate at which products are manufactured and sold. (521)

Throughput costing. Extreme version of variable costing, in which only direct material costs are assigned to inventory as product costs. Assumes that direct labour and overhead do not vary proportionately with volume of production. (739)

Time-adjusted rate of return. See *internal rate of return*.

Time value of money. Concept that a dollar received today is worth more than a dollar received in the future. (578)

Top-down budgeting. Strategies and targets that are communicated from top management to division and department managers who incorporate them into the budgeted operating plans. (456)

Total productivity measure The output achieved for all of the combined inputs. (562)

Total quality management. Procedures and policies aimed at organization-wide continuous improvement. (225)

Tracing costs. Assigning direct costs to a cost object. To be traced, a cost must be easily linked or attached to the cost object. (203, 205)

Traditional costing systems. The practice of accumulating overhead costs in a small number of cost pools and allocating costs using bases that do not necessarily drive costs, such as labour hours, labour costs, and machine hours. (257)

Transfer price. Price used to record revenue and cost when goods or services are transferred between responsibility centres in an organization. (638)

Transferred-in costs. In process costing, costs transferred from one processing department to the next. (261)

Triple bottom line. See *sustainable management*.

T-statistic. Alpha or beta coefficient relative to its standard error in a regression analysis. Used to assess whether fixed or variable costs are greater than zero when estimating a cost function. (58–59)

Two-point method. Algebraic method for estimating a mixed cost function using any two data points of the cost and cost driver, preferably two representative points. (53)

Unadjusted rate of return. See *accrual accounting rate of return*.

Unavoidable cash flows. See *irrelevant cash flows*.

Underabsorbed overhead or indirect costs. See *underapplied overhead*.

Underallocated overhead or indirect costs. See *underapplied overhead*.

Underapplied overhead. Occurs when actual costs are greater than the total amount of overhead allocated to inventory accounts. (214)

Unfavourable variance. Budget variance in which actual results are worse than budgeted results (e.g., actual costs are greater than budgeted or actual revenues are less than budgeted). (459)

Uniform product or service. Product or service that is produced identically for all customers. (203, 204)

Unit-level activities. Tasks or functions undertaken to produce individual units manufactured or services produced. Unit-level activities need to be performed for every unit of good or service, and therefore the cost should be proportional to the number of units produced. (305)

Usage variance. See *efficiency variance.*

Value-added activities. Tasks or functions that increase the worth of an organization's goods or services to customers. (314, 669)

Value chain. Sequence of business processes in which value is added to a product or service. Encompasses customers and suppliers as well as, in some cases, the customers' customers and the suppliers' suppliers. (668)

Value chain analysis. Process of studying each step in the business process to determine whether some activities can be eliminated because they do not add value. (624–626)

Value stream analysis. The process of analyzing business processes to identify the cost of individual value-added activities. (683)

Variable cost. Cost that changes proportionately with changes in volumes or activity levels. (47)

Variable cost ratio. Total variable costs divided by total revenue.

Variable costing. Only variable production costs, such as direct materials, direct labour, and variable manufacturing overhead, are assigned to inventory as product costs. (721)

Variable overhead budget variance. Difference between allocated variable overhead cost and actual variable overhead cost. (515)

Variable overhead cost pool. Cost pool used to accumulate only variable overhead costs. (207)

Variable overhead efficiency variance. Difference between the total expected variable overhead costs for the actual amount of goods or services produced (i.e., the flexible budget) and the standard amount of variable overhead for the actual volume of the allocation base. (516)

Variable overhead spending variance. Difference between the total expected variable overhead costs for the actual amount of goods or services produced (i.e., the flexible budget) and actual variable overhead costs. (515)

Variance analysis. The process of calculating variances and then investigating the reasons they occurred. (500)

Vision statement. Theoretical description of what the organization should become. (8)

Volume discount. Price reduction or refund received from suppliers of goods or services based on exceeding a specified volume of activity. (50)

Volume of activity. The quantity of a task or function (such as number of product units produced, facilities operated, or customer sales calls made) performed in an organization over a period of time. Also called level of activity or volume of cost driver; Q in the cost function. (48)

Volume variance. Difference between the estimated fixed overhead costs used to calculate the estimated allocation rate and the amount of fixed overhead costs actually allocated to inventory during the period. Also see *production volume variance.* (728)

Weasel words. Phrases or claims so vague or ambiguous that they are essentially empty. (657)

Weighted average contribution margin per unit. Average contribution margin per unit for multiple products, weighted by the sales mix. (105)

Weighted average contribution margin ratio. Average contribution margin ratio for multiple products, weighted by the sales mix. (105)

Weighted average cost of capital (WACC). Weighted average after-tax rate for the costs of the various sources of long-term financing such as debt and stock. Sometimes used as the *discount rate* in capital budgeting. (583)

Weighted average method. In process costing, a method in which costs from beginning WIP (performed last period) are averaged with costs incurred during the current period and then allocated to all units completed and ending WIP. (254)

What-if analysis. See *sensitivity analysis.*

Work in process (WIP). Usually refers to the general ledger inventory account used to accumulate costs for partially complete manufactured goods. Also used generically to refer to any good or service that is partially complete. (262–272)

Work in progress. See *work in process.*

Work-measurement method. See *engineered estimate of cost.*

Yield variance. See *efficiency variance.*

Zero-based budgeting. Budgets developed as if there were no information about budgets or costs from prior budget cycles available. (465)

Zero defect policy. Operating practice that does not allow for any normal spoilage. (226)

NAMES AND ORGANIZATIONS INDEX

SUBJECT INDEX

 ETHICS HOMEWORK PROBLEMS

Each chapter includes at least one homework problem that asks students to apply *ethical decision making*. Each problem contains ambiguities, conflicts of interest, and value judgements.

Problem	Organization and Topic
1.26	Effects of fraudulent financial statements or unethical behaviour
1.28	Communication of ethical values to employees
1.43	Student collaboration on homework and professor policy in a university course
1.47	Workplace pressure to falsify time report in city government
1.50	WalMart and Proctor & Gamble consumer research on RFID technology
2.52	Timeliness and quality of budget information for a family-owned business
3.50	Biases in business plan for travel agency
4.45	Foreign versus domestic product
4.46	Conflict of interest in outsourcing decision
4.50	Texas Society of CPAs and AICPA; CPA responsibilities for quality of work and confidentiality for outsourcing of income tax return preparation
5.45	Accounting for sale of scrap by construction contractor
6.61	Britain's Health and Safety Commission targets and risks; responsibilities and company goals for workplace health and safety
7.52	Corporate and governmental responsibilities for environmental accounting reports; compare Canadian and Japanese companies
8.49	Allocation of costs for supporting departments and operating departments
8.53	Allocation of administration and public relations costs under professional basketball player contract
9.48	Joint cost decision and company-wide versus division manager interests
9.50	Mad cow disease and the use of animal by-products in livestock feed
10.58	Responsibility of new staff accountant in CA firm to seek help from supervisor
11.48	Student behaviour within college course grade system
13.53	Use of cost-benefit analysis by Ford Motor Company for the Pinto
14.49	Price collusion between two owners of gasoline stations in a small town
15.48	Use of NPV with sensitivity analysis to determine the actions of a logging company
17.60	Manager incentives for channel stuffing
19.51	Corporate responsibility regarding fair trade coffee

INTEGRATING ACROSS THE CURRICULUM HOMEWORK PROBLEMS

One or two *Integrating Across the Curriculum* problems in each chapter ask students to integrate cost accounting material with the content of other accounting and business core courses.

Problem	Subjects	Topics
1.49	Auditing	Measuring and interpreting product defect information
1.50	Technology and Information Systems	RFID technology information and internal reports
2.58	Statistics	Improve cost function estimate using multiple regression with cost inflation and lagged cost driver
3.60	Economics Marketing	Create demand and cost functions and perform CVP analysis with nonlinear revenue
4.59	Finance	Currency, exchange rate uncertainty, and special order decision
4.60	Operations Management	Shifting product emphasis to create a new sales mix; risk appetite
5.60	Financial Accounting and Auditing	Research financial accounting rules; audit overhead allocation policy
6.63	Production Management	Batch versus continuous processing, usefulness of process costing
7.52	Corporate Social Responsibility	Corporate responsibilities and use of ABC for environmental accounting reports
8.58	Not-for-Profit Accounting	Allocating common costs, restricted fund method
9.50	Economics and Governmental Regulation	Beef by-products in animal feed, by-product economics, regulator responsibilities
10.61	Financial Accounting and Attestation	Prospective financial statements, types of attestation, assumptions
11.53	Auditing	Auditor evaluation of variances for error and fraud; accounting principles for variances
13.55	Finance	Weighted average cost of capital, estimation problems
15.49	Ethics	Reverse engineering of a competitor's product
15.51	Information Technology	Inventory management system adopted by Mopar, data accuracy, internal controls, estimating benefits
17.60	Financial Accounting Auditing	Channel stuffing, uncertainties, error versus fraud, fraud incentives and cost
18.42	Business Law	Executive compensation for public companies, CSA disclosures
18.43	Finance	Calculation of weighted average cost of capital
19.53	Management and Marketing	SWOT analysis for **Triple 4 Advertising**